CANADA

MAINE

MINNESOTA

Lake Superior

VERMONT

NEW HAMPSHIRE

Lawrence *Lexington*

MICHIGAN

Lake Huron

Seneca Falls *Saratoga*

Lowell ■*Salem*

Brook Farm ■Boston

MASSACHUSETTS *Plymouth*

• St. Paul

Lake Ontario

Rochester

Albany

WISCONSIN

MICHIGAN

Flint

Buffalo • NEW YORK

Woodstock

Pawtucket

Hyde Park Hartford

RHODE ISLAND

Lansing ✪

Lake Michigan

Detroit

Newburgh

CONNECTICUT

• Madison

Dearborn

Lake Erie

PENNSYLVANIA

Oyster Bay

New York • *Levittown*

IOWA

Des Plaines

Cleveland •

Kent State University

Bethlehem

Statue of Liberty

Princeton

✪ Des Moines

Chicago •

Haymarket Square

■*Tippecanoe*

Canton ■

Harrisburg ✪ Trenton

Grovers Mill

ILLINOIS

Gnadenhutten

Homestead

Pittsburgh •

NEW JERSEY

Philadelphia

Springfield ✪

Greenville ■

✪ Columbus

Gettysburg

Dover

Indianapolis ✪

Dayton ■

OHIO

MARYLAND

DELAWARE

Harpers Ferry

Three-Mile Island

INDIANA

WEST VIRGINIA

Washington, D.C. ☸

Annapolis

Westminster College

Alton ■

St. Louis •

VIRGINIA

Charleston •

Richmond •

✪ Frankfort

Appomattox ■

Norfolk •

Jamestown ■

Jefferson City

East St. Louis ■

KENTUCKY

MISSOURI

White River

ATLANTIC OCEAN

Roanoke Island ■

✪ Raleigh

✪ Nashville

NORTH CAROLINA

TENNESSEE

Dayton ■

Shiloh ■

Memphis •

Scottsboro ■

SOUTH CAROLINA

ARKANSAS

Little Rock ✪

Hope ■

MISSISSIPPI

ALABAMA

✪ Columbia

Charleston •

Stono ■

Jackson State University

Selma ■

✪ Montgomery

GEORGIA

Port Royal ■

LOUISIANA

✪ Jackson

Baton Rouge ✪

Mobile •

✪ Tallahassee

St. Augustine ■

Pensacola

New Orleans •

Cape Canaveral

FLORIDA

Gulf of Mexico

BAHAMAS

0		150		300 miles
0	150		300 kilometers	

■ *Important places in American Passages*

D0164332

AMERICAN PASSAGES

A HISTORY OF THE UNITED STATES

HARCOURT BRACE

soon to become

Harcourt College Publishers

A Harcourt Higher Learning Company

Soon you will find Harcourt Brace's distinguished innovation, leadership, and support under a different name . . . a new brand that continues our unsurpassed quality, service, and commitment to education.

We are combining the strengths of our college imprints into one worldwide brand: Harcourt Our mission is to make learning accessible to anyone, anywhere, anytime—reinforcing our commitment to lifelong learning.

We'll soon be Harcourt College Publishers. Ask for us by name.

One Company
"Where Learning Comes to Life."

AMERICAN
PASSAGES

A HISTORY OF THE UNITED STATES

EDWARD L. AYERS

University of Virginia

LEWIS L. GOULD

University of Texas at Austin

DAVID M. OSHINSKY

Rutgers University

JEAN R. SODERLUND

Lehigh University

HARCOURT COLLEGE PUBLISHERS

Fort Worth Philadelphia San Diego New York Orlando Austin San Antonio
Toronto Montreal London Sydney Tokyo

Publisher	Earl McPeek
Executive Editor	David Tatom
Market Strategist	Steve Drummond
Project Editor	Laura J. Hanna
Art Director	Linda Beaupré
Production Manager	Diane Gray

Cover image: Thomas Kensett, *Eaton's Neck, Long Island.* The Metropolitan Museum of Art, Gift of Thomas Kensett, 1874. (74.29) Photograph © 1984 The Metropolitan Museum of Art.

ISBN: 0-03-072479-1

Library of Congress Catalog Card Number: 99-64475

Address for Domestic Orders
Harcourt College Publishers, 6277 Sea Harbor Drive, Orlando, FL 32887-6777
800-782-4479

Address for International Orders
International Customer Service
Harcourt, Inc., 6277 Sea Harbor Drive, Orlando, FL 32887-6777
407-345-3800
(fax) 407-345-4060
(e-mail) hbintl@harcourtcollege.com

Address for Editorial Correspondence
Harcourt College Publishers, 301 Commerce Street, Suite 3700, Fort Worth, TX 76102

Web Site Address
http://www.hbcollege.com

Harcourt College Publishers will provide complimentary supplements or supplement packages to those adopters qualified under our adoption policy. Please contact your sales representative to learn how you qualify. If as an adopter or potential user you receive supplements you do not need, please return them to your sales representative or send them to: Attn: Returns Department, Troy Warehouse, 465 South Lincoln Drive, Troy, MO 63379.

Printed in the United States of America

0 1 2 3 4 5 6 7 8 048   9 8 7 6 5 4 3 2

Harcourt College Publishers

ABOUT THE AUTHORS

EDWARD L. AYERS   Edward Ayers is the Hugh P. Kelly Professor of History at the University of Virginia. He was educated at the University of Tennessee and Yale University, where he received his Ph.D. in American Studies. He has written and edited five books. *The Promise of the New South: Life After Reconstruction* (1992) won prizes for the best book on the history of American race relations and on the history of the American South. It was a finalist for both the National Book Award and the Pulitzer Prize. He is the co-editor of *The Oxford Book of the American South* (1997) and *All Over the Map: Rethinking American Regions* (1996). Ayers has won a number of teaching awards, including the Outstanding Faculty Award from the State Council of Higher Education and the Distinguished Young Teacher Award from the Alumni Board of Trustees.

Ayers' current work is "The Valley of the Shadow: Two Communities in the American Civil War." The World Wide Web version of the project has been ranked as one of the top forty education sites in the world by the *Encyclopedia Britannica* and named as the best Civil War site by Yahoo! Ayers is Executive Director of the Center for Digital History, an institute at the University of Virginia dedicated to crafting and teaching history in new media. Ayers is the author of Chapters 9–15.

LEWIS L. GOULD   Lewis Gould is the Eugene C. Barker Centennial Professor Emeritus at the University of Texas at Austin. After receiving his Ph.D. from Yale University, he began a teaching career in which he had more than ten thousand students. He was recognized for outstanding undergraduate teaching in large lecture sections of the American History survey and for his excellent graduate teaching. He remains active in teaching correspondence and distance learning courses at The University of Texas at Austin in Texas History, Women's History, and American Diplomatic History.

Gould is a nationally recognized authority on First Ladies and the presidency. His comments have appeared in numerous press accounts about presidential wives, including *The New York Times, The Washington Post,* and *The Los Angeles Times.* He has appeared on C-Span, The CBS Morning News, Nightline, the ABC Evening News, and a large number of nationally syndicated radio programs. He also participated in the PBS program on Lyndon Johnson and the A&E biography of Lady Bird Johnson. Among his important publications are *American First Ladies: Their Lives and Their Legacy* (1996); *1968: The Election That Changed America* (1993); *The Presidency of Theodore Roosevelt* (1991); *Lady Bird Johnson and the Environment* (1988); and *The Presidency of William McKinley* (1980). Gould is the author of Chapters 16–24, 31, and 32.

DAVID M. OSHINSKY   David Oshinsky received his undergraduate degree from Cornell University and his doctorate from Brandeis. He has taught history for the past 26 years at Rutgers University, where he holds the Board of Governors Chair and is presently chairman of the History Department. Oshinsky is the author of four books, including *A Conspiracy So Immense: The World of Joe McCarthy* (1983), which was voted one of the year's "best books" by the "New York Sunday Times Book Review," and won the Hardeman Prize for the best work about the U.S. Congress. His latest book, *"Worse than Slavery": Parchman Farm and the Ordeal of Jim Crow Justice* (1996), won both the Robert Kennedy Book Award for the year's most distinguished contribution to the field of human rights, and the American Bar Association's Scribes Award for distinguished legal writing.

Oshinsky is a regular contributor to scholarly journals, to the "Washington Post Book World," "New York Sunday Times Book Review," "New York Times Op-Ed Page," and "New York Times Sunday Magazine." He has been awarded a senior fellowship by the National Endowment for the Humanities and will spend 1999–2000 as a Phi Beta Kappa Visiting Scholar. Oshinsky is the author of Chapters 25–30.

JEAN R. SODERLUND   Jean Soderlund is Professor and Chair of the Department of History at Lehigh University and Co-Director of the Lawrence Henry Gipson Institute for Eighteenth-Century Studies. She received her Ph.D. from Temple University and was a post-doctoral fellow at the Philadelphia Center for Early American Studies at the University of Pennsylvania. Her book, *Quakers and Slavery: A Divided Spirit,* won the Alfred E. Driscoll Publication Prize of the New Jersey Historical Commission. Soderlund was an editor of three volumes of the Papers of William Penn (1981–1983) and co-authored *Freedom by Degrees: Emancipation in Pennsylvania and Its Aftermath* (1991).

She has written articles and chapters in books on the history of women, African Americans, Native Americans, Quakers, and the development of abolition in the British North American colonies and early United States. She is currently working on a study of race and cultural identity in early New Jersey and Pennsylvania. She is a council member of the Philadelphia Center for Early American Studies, the Pennsylvania Historical Association, and the David Library of the American Revolution, and served as a committee chair for the American Historical Association. Soderlund is the author of Chapters 1–8.

IT'S ABOUT TIME

Everyone who writes about history faces the same problem: how do we get the past to stay still long enough to see it clearly? Textbooks on the history of the United States typically pursue one topic at a time. They devote chapters to a particular part of the country, such as the slave South or the Old West, or focus on broad topics such as immigration, urbanization, or industrialization. They place certain groups or individuals in special boxes or on specially colored pages. They set aside politics or diplomacy for long periods while they describe social or cultural life. Such ways of organizing textbooks have obvious costs—loss of continuity, context, and narrative force—but these strategies have seemed necessary bargains with the complexity of the past.

This book follows a different strategy. Rather than isolating people and topics it integrates them into the flow of time. Rather than sorting topics into tidily organized chapters, we show the complicated and subtle ways that strands of history interact. Each chapter is devoted to a particular sequence of years, carefully following the contours of events, weaving politics, economics, and culture into an interrelated pattern. As a result, foreign policy and domestic life connect and influence one another. The history of blacks and whites, men and women, emerge as parts of the same stories. Authors and artists speak of their particular times. Political battles continually punctuate the story. Depressions and panics disrupt the lives of people in every class. Technological innovations do not merely happen but emerge as solutions to felt problems.

Students who read *American Passages* come to understand that history is often about the unexpected. No one, after all, could have predicted figures such as Thomas Paine, Harriet Beecher Stowe, Henry Ford, or Martin Luther King, Jr. Nor could Americans have foreseen events such as Bacon's Rebellion, John Brown's Raid, the Haymarket Riot, or the Watergate break-in. While long-term processes are fully treated in this book, it also strives to show that history often turns around unique events, unintended outcomes, and singular individuals. *American Passages* calls our attention to the twists and turns of history, to the way various facets of history are connected.

Not only does the thoroughly chronological organization of this book make for a good story, we believe, but it helps history make sense. In our own lives, after all, things happen simultaneously. Every newspaper and news show reminds us of the way that events abroad touch on events at home, the way that politics and economics entangle, the pervasiveness of a particular book or film in a certain season. We are used to the idea that our lives are defined by a mixture of major and minor events, by the interplay between the momentary and the momentous. The past was like that as well.

American Passages offers several tools to help us see the past as a whole. Its timelines and "Passages" sections provide broad overviews that connect across chapters. Its illustrations and graphs are tightly woven into the narrative. Its rich Web site amplifies the themes and materials of the book, offering hundreds of documents, maps, illustrations, and multimedia selections carefully attuned to the time in which they were produced. We hope that such a story will help convey the excitement, drama, and importance of this nation's past.

ANCILLARY ITEMS

Test Manual, Volume I: To 1877;
Volume II: From 1863
Marlette Rebhorn, Austin Community College
This test manual provides the instructor with a variety of question styles which emphasize critical thinking skills for the student. In addition to multiple choice questions, there are identification questions, essay questions, and book report questions. This item is free to instructors.

Computerized Test Banks
The EXAMaster+ system simplifies test generation and allows instructors the flexibility to add or edit questions. It includes all test items from both volumes of the printed Test Bank and is free to instructors. Available in the following formats: CD-ROM for MS Windows™ and Macintosh®, 3.5″ disks in both MS Windows™ and Macintosh®.

Instructor's Manual, Volume I: To 1877;
Volume II: From 1863
Barbara Stites, Los Angeles City College
This guide is designed to support the instructor in preparing lectures and developing discussion questions and assignments. This manual contains objectives for each chapter; a "Making it Real" section which provides recommendations for assignments, lecture topic suggestions, and a "Further Resources" part which lists additional readings and audio and visual resources.

Overhead Transparency Acetates
Burt Rieff, University of North Alabama
This full color OHT package contains over 180 transparencies comprising most of the outstanding maps, charts, and graphs from *American Passages.* Also included are a number of carefully selected images from the text. Provided for each acetate are teaching notes which provide the instructor with a brief explanation of each acetate, features to note, and questions to facilitate classroom discussion.

American Passages: A History of the United States Online Resources
This innovative *American Passages* Web site provides access to many online resources for both instructors and students. On this site can be found the following:

- Chapters: All items are organized according to the same thirty-two chapters contained in the *American Passages* text. Within each chapter, the primary source materials are presented in modules organized around a particular event, place, time, or theme within the chapter's chronological structure.
- Exercises: Study questions, with answers, encourage students to think more deeply about the primary source materials, the issues and themes to which they connect, and the relevant parts of *American Passages* to which they relate. The exercises follow a variety of strategies: some focus on a particular document; others concentrate on several documents within one chapter, still others address themes and issues which connect items in different chapters and across time periods.
- Links: An annotated list of links directs students outside the *American Passages* Web site to especially useful and relevant content-rich sites on the Internet. The list is organized by chapter and is designed to complement material presented both in the Web site and in the text.
- Maps: Dynamic and animated interactive maps dramatically illustrate major developments and changes occurring over a period of time.
- Index: Several indices provide an archive of all primary source materials in the site. The indices point to summaries of the documents and to the documents themselves. Students may browse by subject, chapter, date, and type of item.

American Passages Web site Manual
It's about time . . . for an American history textbook and its Web site to be fully integrated; for the narrative of the text and the primary materials of the Web site to work together to heighten students' understanding of the past; and for both components to be organized chronologically so as to remain true to the flow of history.

Study Guide, Volume I: To 1877;
Volume II: From 1863
Richard McMillan, Los Angeles Pierce College
This Student Resource Guide is organized to assist the student in his or her comprehension of the material found in each chapter. It contains not only a thorough chapter outline, but also includes essay questions, identification questions, and objective questions which provide

aid in the student's understanding of the text. At the end of each chapter are map exercises, which reinforce the student's geographical knowledge as well.

Computerized Student Tutorial

Available to students, at an affordable price, are a variety of interactive exercises taken directly from the Student Manual.

American Passages Historical Geography Guide, Volume I: To 1877; Volume II: From 1863

Marlette Rebhorn, Austin Community College
This mapping workbook provides students with challenging and engaging exercises designed to test their geographical knowledge. In addition to labeling exercises there are also fill-in questions to reinforce the student's comprehension.

United States History Documents Collection, Volume I: To 1877; Volume II: From 1863

Robert Weise, Eastern Kentucky University
This outstanding collection of documents includes over 100 primary source readings with introductory notes for each selection. This is available free to instructors and may be purchased by the student.

PowerPoint Slide Archive for U.S. History Presentation CD-ROM

Prepared by Raymond M. Hyser and J. Christopher Arndt, James Madison University
This electronic archive is intended to enhance lectures by providing historical photos, cartoons, posters, maps, charts and graphs as well as lecture outlines, which can be used as framework for the material. The 1642 slides (including 669 photos and 143 maps) are organized in chronological units. The professor has flexibility to edit, add, delete, and rearrange slides into customized presentations. The CD-ROM includes separate indexes of the images, maps, and charts/graphs for ease in locating specific illustrations, as well as PowerPoint viewers for both Mac and PC platforms.

The American History CD-ROM

The American History CD-ROM is an interactive learning tool that provides a vast library of pictures, film clips, sound recordings, and maps. It is indexed and organized in a unique, flexible format that makes it easy to explore U.S. history from ancient times through the 1990s. Features include: Overviews, narrated by Charles Kuralt; thousands of captioned illustrations; 68 motion pictures; dozens of brief sound bites; a quiz that offers students several levels and options for self-assessment; and *The Histriopix Game,* a challenging test of students' recall for key concepts and information that is conveyed through the images. In addition to independent study, students and professors can create lessons, lesson plans, and presentations. Adoption requirements apply.

Second World War Photo CD-ROM

The Second World War CD-ROM is a three-disc set that features selections from the National Archives. It includes more than 900 black and white images taken during the war that are accompanied by historically accurate captions. Adoption requirements apply.

Zane Publishing's Home Library CD-ROM Package for U.S. History

The home library includes a 10-disc CD-ROM package that covers major subject areas in U.S. history, ranging from the 1700s to the present. Topics include Jacksonian Democracy, the Civil War, Reconstruction, the American West, the Great Depression, U.S. Government, U.S. Foreign Policy from 1788 to 1933 and 1933 to 1963, and the Social Reform movement. Adoption requirements apply.

U.S. History Videos/*Films for the Humanities*

Contact your local Harcourt sales representative for a complete listing of the many videos that are available from the extensive *Films for the Humanities* catalog. Adoption requirements apply.

U.S. History Videos/*Arts and Entertainment*

Many outstanding U.S. history selections are available from the *Arts and Entertainment* video library. Choose from "American Revolution," "Civil War Journal," "The Real West," "Mike Wallace's Twentieth Century," and selections from *A & E*'s extensive *Biography* series collection. Adoption requirements apply.

Twentieth-Century American History Video Disk

The history of the American 20th century comes alive in a one-hour videodisk produced expressly for Harcourt by Fountain Communications. It addresses the pressing issues that Americans have faced in this century: immigration, the Great Depression, the Second World War, the Cold War, the United States in the 1950s, the civil rights movement, the Vietnam War, and the women's movement. Adoption requirements apply.

ACKNOWLEDGMENTS

I would like to thank my students and colleagues at the University of Virginia, who have helped me struggle with the tough questions of American history. I am grateful, too, to the diligent Harcourt editors David Tatom, Kristie Kelly, and Laura Hanna for their patience, good will, and good advice in the creation of this book. Thanks also go to Linda Beaupré, designer; Diane Gray, production manager; and Lili Weiner, photo researcher. Finally, I am very appreciative of my co-authors, who have been engaged scholars, thoughtful critics, devoted teachers, and good friends throughout the years it took us to write *American Passages*.

EDWARD L. AYERS

I would like to acknowledge the help of the following former students who contributed in constructive ways to the completion of the textbook: Martin Ansell, Christie Bourgeois, Thomas Clarkin, Stacy Cordery, Debbie Cottrell, Patrick Cox, Scott Harris, Byron Hulsey, Jonathan Lee, John Leffler, Mark Young, and Nancy Beck Young. Karen Gould gave indispensable support and encouragement throughout the process of writing the text. I am grateful as well to the readers of my chapters who made so many useful and timely criticisms.

LEWIS L. GOULD

I would like to thank my colleagues and students at Rutgers for allowing me to test out an endless stream of ideas and issues relating to modern American history, and also for their thoughts on how a good college textbook should "read" and what it should contain. As always, the support and love of my family—Matt, Efrem, Ari, and Jane—was unshakable. Above all, I must commend my co-authors and my editors at Harcourt for their remarkable patience and professionalism during this long collaborative process.

DAVID M. OSHINSKY

I am grateful to my husband, Rudolf Soderlund, and my family for their support throughout this project. My mother, Joyce Ruth, went well beyond the limits of parental duty by reading and critiquing each chapter. Many scholars in the colonial and early national periods shared their ideas verbally and through publications. I received very helpful comments from James S. Saeger, Roger D. Simon, Marianne S. Wokeck, my co-authors of this text, and the anonymous readers for the press.

JEAN R. SODERLUND

LIST OF REVIEWERS

Joseph Adams	St. Louis Community College, Meramec Campus
Charles Allbee	Burlington Community College
Julius Amin	University of Dayton
Melodie Andrews	Mankato State
Robert Becker	Louisiana State University
Peter Bergstrom	Illinois State
John Brooke	Tufts University
Neil Brooks	Essex Community College
Colin Calloway	Dartmouth
Milton Cantor	University of Massachusetts
Kay Carr	Southern Illinois University
Paul Chardoul	Grand Rapids Junior College
Myles Clowers	San Diego City College
William Cobb	Utah Valley State College
David Coon	Washington State University
Stacey Cordery	Monmouth College
Debbie Cottrell	Smith College
David Cullen	Collin County Community College
Christine Daniels	Michigan State University
Ronnie Day	East Tennessee State University
Matthew Dennis	University of Oregon
Robert Downtain	Tarrant County Junior College—Northeast Campus
Robert Elam	Modesto Junior College
Linda Foutch	Walter State Community College
Robert G. Fricke	West Valley College
David Hamilton	University of Kentucky
Beatriz Hardy	Coastal Carolina University
Peter M. G. Harris	Temple University
Thomas Hartshorne	Cleveland State University
Ron Hatzenbuehler	Idaho State
Robert Hawkes	George Mason University
James Houston	Oklahoma State University
Raymond Hyser	James Madison University
Lillian Jones	Santa Monica College
Jim Kluger	Pima Community College
James Lacy	Contra Costa College
Alton Lee	University of South Dakota
Liston Leyendecker	Colorado State University
Robert Marcom	San Antonio College
Greg Massey	Freed-Hardeman
Michael Mayer	University of Montana
Elsa Nystrom	Kennesaw State
David O'Neill	Rutgers University
Betty Owens	Greenville Technical College
Mark Parillo	Kansas State University
J'Nell Pate	Tarrant County Junior College, Northeast Campus
Louis Potts	University of Missouri at Kansas City
Noel Pugach	University of New Mexico
Alice Reagan	Northern Virginia Community College
Marlette Rebhorn	Austin Community College, Rio Grande Campus
David Reimers	New York University
Hal Rothman	Wichita State University
Ralph Shaffer	California Polytechnic University
Kenneth Smemo	Moorhead State University
Jack Smith	Great Basin College
Thaddeus Smith	Middle Tennessee State University
Phillip E. Stebbins	Pennsylvania State University
Marshall Stevenson	Ohio State University
William Stockton	Johnson County Community College
Frank Towers	Clarion University
Daniel Usner	Cornell University
Daniel Vogt	Jackson State University
Stephen Webre	Louisiana Technical College
John C. Willis	University of the South
Harold Wilson	Old Dominion University
Nan Woodruff	Pennsylvania State University
Bertram Wyatt-Brown	University of Florida
Sherri Yeager	Chabot College
Robert Zeidel	University of Wisconsin

LIST OF DOCUMENTS

LIST OF MAPS

LIST OF TABLES

LIST OF CHARTS AND GRAPHS

BRIEF TABLE OF CONTENTS

Detailed Table of Contents

PASSAGES
1877–1909   568

CHAPTER 19   DOMESTIC TURMOIL AND OVERSEAS EXPANSION, 1893–1901   644

CHAPTER 20   THEODORE ROOSEVELT AND PROGRESSIVE REFORM, 1901–1909   678

PASSAGES
1909 – 1933   708

CHAPTER 21   PROGRESSIVISM AT ITS HEIGHT, 1909 – 1914   714

CHAPTER 22   OVER THERE AND OVER HERE: THE IMPACT OF WORLD WAR I, 1914–1921   748

PASSAGES
1933–1960   854

CHAPTER 25   THE NEW DEAL, 1933–1939   860

CHAPTER 26   THE SECOND WORLD WAR, 1940–1945   896

PREHISTORY TO
—1763—

And so we journeyed for seventeen days, at the end of which we crossed the river [Rio Grande] and traveled for seventeen more. At sunset, on plains between some very tall mountains, we found some people who eat nothing but powdered straw for a third of the year. Since it was that season of the year, we had to eat it too. At the end of our journey we found a permanent settlement where there was abundant corn. The people gave us a large quantity of it and of cornmeal, squash, beans and cotton blankets. . . . From here we traveled [to where people] gave me five emeralds made into arrowheads. . . . Since they seemed very fine to me, I asked them where they had gotten them. They told me that they brought them from some very high mountains to the North.

—CABEZA DE VACA, 1542[*]

F ROM 1534 TO 1536, the Spanish explorer, Álvar Núñez Cabeza de Vaca, and three others, including a black man, Esteban, traveled through Texas and northern Mexico, trying to reach Mexico City. They had been part of an expedition to Florida that ran afoul of Apalachee Indians, escaped across the Gulf of Mexico in makeshift boats, then were enslaved in Texas by Karankawa Indians. In his *Relación,* Cabeza de Vaca described their adventures, including the harrowing passage across the gulf, long journeys without food, and sojourns among Texas Indians.

Warpaths, ocean voyages, hunting trails, trade routes, death, communication and exchange among people—creating societies in America embodied passages of every kind. Asians moved across the Bering land bridge more than 14,000 years ago, settling throughout North and South America. Over time, they created distinct cultures in every part of the hemisphere, from the empire-building Aztecs of Mexico to the peaceful Lenape, whom the English called Delawares, of eastern North America. Over thousands of years, American civilizations rose and fell, as empires built pyramids and temple mounds, developed cities and cultures, and competed for territory and trade.

Map

Hudson Bay

BLACKFEET
ATSINA
SALISH
NEZ PERCE
CROW
MANDAN
TETON SIOUX
CHEYENNE
SANTEE SIOUX
OGLALA SIOUX
PAWNEE
OTO
IOWA
KANSA
UTE
ARAPAHO
MISSOURI
ILLINOIS
MIAMI

CREE
OJIBWA
MENOMINEE
SAUK
FOX
KICKAPOO
HURON
IROQUOIS
SUSQUEHANNA
DELAWARE
OTTAWA
ALGONQUIN

MONTAGNAIS NASKAPI
MICMAC
ABENAKI
SOKOKI

Quebec (1608) France

MASSACHUSETTS
Plymouth (1620) England
WAMPANOAG
NARRAGANSETT
PEQUOT
New Netherland (1624) United Provinces

POWHATAN
TUSCARORA
Jamestown (1607) England
Roanoke Island (1585–87) England

KLAMATH
MODOC
NORTHERN PAIUTE
MAIDU
WASHO
POMO
SHOSHONE
COSTANOAN
SALINAN
CHUMASH
MOHAVE
SERRANO
PAPAGO
PIMA
OPATA
COCHIMI
APACHE
MESCALERO
COMANCHE
LIPAN
CONCHO
COAHUILTEC

HOPI
NAVAJO
ZUNI
PUEBLO
New Mexico (1598) Spain
KIOWA
OSAGE
WICHITA
CADDO
NATCHEZ
ATAKAPA

QUAPAW
CHICKASAW
SHAWNEE
YUCHI
CHEROKEE
CATAWBA
CREEK
CHOCTAW
APPALACHEE
TIMUCUA
CALUSA

St. Augustine (1565) Spain

ATLANTIC OCEAN
PACIFIC OCEAN
Gulf of Mexico
Great Lakes

Hunting and gathering
Mostly agricultural

Body

In the fifteenth century A.D., Western Europeans came to America to fish, trade, and establish colonies, bringing new technology, lust for wealth, and destructive microbes that spelled death for millions of Native Americans. The Europeans adapted their traditions and goals to exploit the abundant, yet often unfamiliar, resources of the New World. The Spanish struck it rich with the Potosí and Zacatecas silver mines that financed their religious wars in Europe and became the envy of other nations. Privateers from France, England, and the Netherlands attacked the Spanish silver fleets, while explorers searched unsuccessfully for mines in North America. Instead, they found treasures in furs, sugar, tobacco, and rice.

To reap fortunes from the earth, the colonizers first exploited Native Americans, who died in such numbers from disease and harsh treatment that Europeans turned to another continent, Africa, for laborers. Portugal had developed the Atlantic slave trade during the fifteenth century, initially buying slaves to toil on sugar islands near Africa. With the development of sugar, and later tobacco and rice, in America, the Portuguese and other Europeans purchased millions of people from African merchants for transport across the Atlantic. For more than 350 years, the cultures, sweat, and blood of enslaved Africans enriched the New World societies.

From the sixteenth century on, Europeans battled for North America with Native Americans and among themselves. The French settled Canada and the Mississippi Valley, primarily for furs. Spain held Florida, Texas, and New Mexico as outposts to protect its silver mines and fleets. The English founded colonies in New England, the Chesapeake,

and Carolinas for economic opportunity and religious freedom. In 1664, they pushed the Dutch out of New Netherland, thus connecting their chain of colonies along the Atlantic. Throughout America, Europeans hoped for a new chance in the New World.

The thirteen mainland British colonies had various beginnings, charters, provincial governments, economic bases, peoples, and religions. Yet they all had ties with England, in language, imperial government and laws, culture, and commerce. During the eighteenth century, the colonies forged closer bonds with the English—with greater participation in imperial wars, increased trade, and better communication. At the same time, the British provinces also became more distinctly American, as people from Africa,

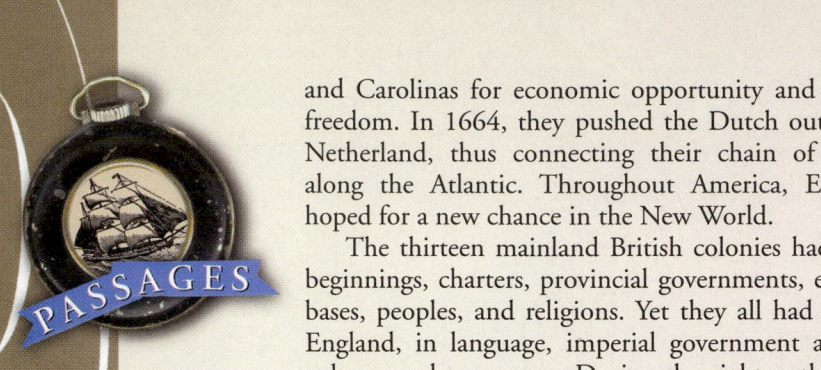

PASSAGES

POPULATION GROWTH OF THE THIRTEEN BRITISH MAINLAND COLONIES, 1630–1760

1630	1640	1650	1660	1670	1680	1690
4,646	26,634	50,368	75,058	111,935	151,507	210,372

Map labels

PACIFIC OCEAN

ATLANTIC OCEAN

Gulf of Mexico

Hudson Bay

Tribes and places (west to east):
BLACKFEET, ATSINA, SALISH, NEZ PERCE, CROW, MANDAN, TETON SIOUX, CHEYENNE, KLAMATH, MODOC, NORTHERN PAIUTE, SHOSHONE, SANTEE SIOUX, SAUK, FOX, KICKAPOO, IOWA, OTO, PAWNEE, MAIDU, WASHO, POMO, COSTANOAN, SALINAN, UTE, OGLALA SIOUX, KANSA, MISSOURI, CREE, OJIBWA, OTTAWA, ALGONQUIN, MENOMINEE, MONTAGNAIS NASKAPI, MICMAC, ABENAKI, IROQUOIS, SUSQUEHANNA, DELAWARE, POWHATAN, TUSCARORA, CHUMASH, MOHAVE, HOPI, NAVAJO, ZUNI, PUEBLO, KIOWA, OSAGE, ILLINOIS, MIAMI, SHAWNEE, YUCHI, CHEROKEE, CATAWBA, SERRANO, APACHE, COMANCHE, WICHITA, CADDO, CHICKASAW, CREEK, CHOCTAW, NATCHEZ, PAPAGO, PIMA, OPATA, MESCALERO, LIPAN, CONCHO, ATAKAPA, APPALACHEE, TIMUCUA, CALUSA, COAHUILTEC, COCHIMI

Places: Fort Tadoussac, Quebec, Trois Rivières, Montreal, Penobscot, Portsmouth, Boston, Plymouth, Providence, Hartford, New Haven, New York, Philadelphia, Wilmington, Annapolis, St. Mary's, Jamestown, Edenton, Wilmington, Charles Town (Charleston), Port Royal, Fort San Mateo, St. Augustine, St. Lucia, Pensacola, Fort Maurepas, Fort Arkansas, Fort Prudhomme (Memphis), Cahokia, Kaskaskia, Fort St. Louis, Fort Crevecoeur, Fort St. Joseph, Fort Mackinac, Sault Ste. Marie, Fort Frontenac, Green Bay, LaPoint du St. Esprit, Santa Fe, El Paso del Norte, Saltillo, Fort St. Louis, Lake Superior, Lake Michigan, Lake Huron, Lake Ontario, L. Erie, Ohio R., Rio Grande

FRENCH, ENGLISH, SPANISH

Legend: Settled areas (non-Indian) | Forests | Non-forested open land

Map labels:

UNEXPLORED

BLACKFEET
SALISH
NEZ PERCÉ
ATSINA
CREE
CROW
MANDAN
TETON SIOUX
CHEYENNE
SANTEE SIOUX
KLAMATH
MODOC
NORTHERN PAIUTE
SHOSHONE
MAIDU
WASHO
POMO
COSTANOAN
SALINAN
CHUMASH
UTE
ARAPAHO
OGLALA SIOUX
PAWNEE
IOWA
OTO
KANSA
MISSOURI
MOHAVE
SERRANO
HOPI
ZUNI
NAVAJO
PUEBLO
APACHE
PAPAGO
PIMA
OPATA
COCHIMÍ
CONCHO
MESCALERO
LIPAN
COAHUILTEC
KIOWA
OSAGE
COMANCHE
WICHITA
CHICKASAW
CREEK
CHOCTAW
NATCHEZ
ATAKAPA
CALUSA
APPALACHEE
CATAWBA
CHEROKEE
DELAWARE
SHAWNEE
MIAMI
ILLINOIS
IROQUOIS
ALGONQUIN
OTTAWA
MENOMINEE
SAUK
FOX
KICKAPOO

Hudson Bay
OJIBWA
Lake Superior
Lake Michigan
Lake Huron
L. Erie
L. Ontario
St. Lawrence R.
Ohio R.
Mississippi R.
Rio Grande

Quebec
Montreal
Fort Frontenac
Fort Michilimackinac
Fort Niagara
Fort Detroit
St. Joseph
LeBaye
St. Louis
Ste. Genevieve
Kaskaskia
Vincennes
Arkansas Post
Natchitoches
Natchez
Nacogdoches
Mobile
Pensacola
New Orleans
St. Augustine

Taos
Santa Cruz de la Cañada
Santa Fe
Albuquerque
El Paso
Chihuahua
Saltillo

Falmouth
Portsmouth
Boston
Plymouth
Providence
Hartford
New Haven
New York
Philadelphia
Wilmington
Baltimore
Annapolis
Richmond
Williamsburg
Norfolk
Edenton
New Bern
Wilmington
Columbia
Charleston
Savannah
Fort Toulouse

PACIFIC OCEAN
ATLANTIC OCEAN
Gulf of Mexico

Legend: Spanish | English | French

Ireland, and the European continent diversified the population and its culture. With natural population growth and swelling immigration, the British colonies expanded across the continent.

Native Americans responded to depopulation, defeat, and white expansion by creating new worlds of their own. Despite some military successes, they ultimately reshaped their communities and cultures, as disease worked its tragic course and European-American societies grew. The surviving members of Indian nations often merged to forge new ethnic identities, or lived together in multi-ethnic communities, often with whites and escaped slaves. Some retained remnants of their land within white settlements, while the majority moved to the frontier for political autonomy.

Three centuries passed from the time Western European fishermen first camped on North American shores until Great Britain and its colonies expelled France from the continent with the French and Indian War. By 1763, the land and people of America had permanently changed.

* Martin A. Favata and José B. Fernandez, *The Account: Álvar Núñez Cabeza de Vaca's Relación* (1993), p.103.

1700	1710	1720	1730	1740	1750	1760
50,888	331,711	466,185	629,445	905,563	1,170,760	1,593,625

	38,000 BC	1000 AD	1300	1400	1500

POLITICS & DIPLOMACY

38,000-12,000 BC: Ancient hunters migrate to America
300-1600 AD: Ghana, Mali, and Songhay empires in West Africa
700-1450 AD: Cahokia and other Mississippian centers in North America

c. 1000 AD: Leif Eriksson's colony on Newfoundland
c. 1300 AD: Aztecs settle in Valley of Mexico

1420: Prince Henry of Portugal begins exploration
1492: Christopher Columbus crosses Atlantic Ocean
1513: Juan Ponce de León explores Florida for Spain
1519: Magellan's expedition to circumnavigate world
1521: Hernán Cortés conquers Aztecs
1528: Cabeza de Vaca to Florida and Texas
1540: Coronado explores American Southwest

SOCIAL & CULTURAL EVENTS

1324: Gonga-Mussa's pilgrimage to Mecca

1507: Martin Waldseemüller names New World after Amerigo Vespucci
1517: Martin Luther challenges the Church of Rome
1534: English Act of Supremacy
1536: John Calvin's *Institutes of the Christian Religion*
1542: Bartolomé de las Casas's *A Short Account of the Destruction of the Indies*

ECONOMICS & TECHNOLOGY

Pre-2500 BC: Corn developed as staple crop in central Mexico
c. 1200 BC: Corn produced in American southwest

1440s: Portuguese mariners take Africans as slaves
c. 1450: European fishermen at Grand Banks off Newfoundland
c. 1452: Portugal begins sugar production on Madeira
c. 1460: European improvements in navigation and ships
1478: Abraham Zacuto calculates latitude using sun
1502: Enslaved Africans imported in Spanish America
1503: Spanish Casa de Contratación to supervise trade
1540s: Silver mines at Zacatecas and Potosí

c. 1550: Iroquois form confederacy

1565: Spanish found St. Augustine, Florida

1585: English colony at Roanoke Island

1599: Spanish destroy Ácoma

1607: English colony at Jamestown

1608: French establish Quebec

1620: Separatists found Plymouth

1630: Puritans establish Massachusetts Bay Colony

1634: The *Ark* and the *Dove* arrive in Maryland

1642: English Civil War begins

1643: New England Confederation

1663: Carolina proprietors receive charter

1664: English forces conquer New Netherland

1675: Metacom's War
Bacon's Rebellion

1680: Popé's Rebellion

1681: William Penn receives Pennsylvania charter

1688: Glorious Revolution in England

1689: Massachusetts, New York, and Maryland revolutions

1691: Salem witchcraft hysteria

1699: French establish Louisiana

1712: Slave revolt in New York City

1732: Founding of Georgia

1739: Stono Uprising in South Carolina

1754: Albany Congress

1754-1763: French and Indian War

1763: Pan-Indian war in Ohio Valley and Great Lakes

1585: John White's drawings of Roanoke

1590: Theodor de Bry's *America*

1636: Harvard College established
Roger Williams's exile to Rhode Island

1637: Anne Hutchinson tried for heresy

1638: First printing press in the English colonies

1639: French establish first hospital in North America

1647: Massachusetts requires town schools

1649: Maryland's act for religious toleration

1650: Anne Bradstreet's *The Tenth Muse Lately Sprung Up in America*

c.1661: Henri Couturier's portrait of Peter Stuyvesant

1662: Halfway Covenant

1663: John Eliot's Bible in Massachusetts Indian language

c.1674: *Mrs. Freake with Baby Mary* by unknown artist

1682: Publication of *The Narrative of the Captivity and Restoration of Mrs. Mary Rowlandson*

1687: *Isaac Newton's Principia Mathematica*

1688: Germantown, PA, Quakers issue antislavery protest

1690: John Locke's *Essay concerning Human Understanding*

1693: College of William and Mary founded

1695: Jews worship openly in New York

1704: First regular newspaper in Anglo-America, *The Boston News-Letter*

1716: Theater built in Wiliamsburg, Virginia

1720: Theodore Jacob Frelinghuysen's revivals in New Jersey

1721: Smallpox inoculation in Boston

1731: Benjamin Franklin's circulating library in Philadelphia

1739: George Whitefield tours northern colonies

1751: Benjamin Franklin's reports on electricity

1752: Adoption of Gregorian Calendar in Anglo-America

1761: John Winthrop observes the transit of Venus

1763: Rise of Delaware prophet Neolin

1562: John Hawkins interlopes in slave trade

c. 1585: Growth of Amsterdam as mercantile center

1602: Dutch East India Company

1617: Tobacco successful staple crop in Virginia

c. 1619: Africans arrive in Virginia

1621: Dutch West India Company

1640s: Sugar production in English West Indies

1642: French found Montreal for fur trade

1651: First English Navigation Act

1672: Royal African Company

1673: Regular postal route between Boston and New York

1670s: Shift to slaves in Chesapeake

1698: Royal African Company loses slave trade monopoly

1699: Woolen Act

1700s: Adoption of rice in South Carolina

1720s: Expansion of German and Scots-Irish immigration

1732: Hat Act

1733: Molasses Act

1740s: Eliza Pinckney cultivates indigo in South Carolina

1750: Iron Act
Georgia legalizes slavery

1750s: British colonial trade expands with Southern Europe
"Consumer revolution" in British colonies

early 1760s: Economic slump in British colonies

CHRISTOPHER COLUMBUS

Christopher Columbus, an Italian mariner, was convinced he could find a direct route to Asia by sailing west. He was wrong, and instead opened the Western Hemisphere to European conquest and settlement.

Chapter 1

CONTACT, CONFLICT, AND EXCHANGE IN THE ATLANTIC WORLD TO 1590

ON OCTOBER 12, 1492, the *Santa Maria, Pinta,* and *Niña,* under command of the Italian navigator Christopher Columbus, sighted an island in the Caribbean Sea he called San Salvador. The expedition took much preparation and bravery, for no one had followed this route before. A seasoned sailor, Columbus had gained a taste for exploration on an earlier trip to Iceland. He spent years trying to obtain support from the rulers of England, France, Portugal, and Spain for a voyage westward across the Atlantic Ocean to find Asia. Finally he convinced Isabella and Ferdinand of Spain to provide funds. If he found a transatlantic route to Asia, Columbus argued, Spain would have the competitive edge in eastern markets over Portugal, which had not yet reached India.

Sailing from one Caribbean island to another, Columbus met many Native Americans, whom he described as "very well formed, with handsome bodies and good faces." He called them *"Indios,"* or Indians, because he thought he had reached islands in the Far East. For the rest of his life, until his death in 1506, Columbus believed he had found Asia. What he actually had done was initiate the conquest and settlement of two continents—the Americas—whose vast extent and riches were previously unknown to Europeans.

Columbus's arrival had momentous consequences for the peoples of America, Europe, and Africa. For Native Americans, whose ancestors had arrived from Asia thousands of years earlier, white men and sailing ships spelled demographic catastrophe. Within 150 years, the pre-contact Indian population was reduced by 90 percent, their cities conquered and destroyed, and, for many, their lands appropriated for farming and grazing livestock. For Europeans, Columbus's unexpected "discovery" represented new challenges and opportunities, some of many they experienced as they explored the far reaches of the globe. For sub-Saharan Africans, the navigator's landfall half a world away signaled the burgeoning slave trade, which over the next four centuries transported at least 10 million Africans across the Atlantic to work and die on plantations and in mines. To exploit the riches of America, Europeans used the labor of both Native Americans and Africans.

Yet contact among Native Americans, Europeans, and Africans involved more than conquest, enslavement, and death. Together the three major cultural groups created new traditions and societies in the New World. While the Europeans must be declared winners in the contest for power, the American colonies were shaped by exchange of knowledge, culture, and work among all participants. Contact introduced new crops and technology to inhabitants of both the Old and New Worlds. Three major cultural traditions came together in the Western Hemisphere. The patterns of

CHRONOLOGY

38,000–12,000 B.C.   Migration of ancient hunters to the Americas

300–900 A.D.   Height of Mayan civilization in Yucatan

300–1600 A.D.   Succession of empires, Ghana, Mali, and Songhay, in West Africa

700–1450 A.D.   Mississippian people build Cahokia and other urban centers in North America

c. 1000 A.D.   Leif Eriksson establishes Viking colony on Newfoundland

c. 1300 A.D.   Aztecs settle in Valley of Mexico

1420   Prince Henry of Portugal initiates search for ocean route to Asia

1440s   Portuguese mariners take Africans as slaves

c. 1452   Portugal begins sugar production on Madeira

c. 1460–1500   European improvements in navigation and ships

1487   Bartholomeu Dias of Portugal rounds Cape of Good Hope

1492   Christopher Columbus crosses Atlantic Ocean

1494   Treaty of Tordesillas establishes Line of Demarcation

1497–1498   Vasco da Gama reaches India for Portugal

1517   Martin Luther challenges the Church of Rome

1519–1521   Hernán Cortés conquers the Aztecs

1519–1522   Magellan's expedition circumnavigates the world

1528–1536   Cabeza de Vaca's adventures in Florida and Texas

1534   Act of Supremacy separates England from the Church of Rome

1539–1542   Hernando de Soto explores the region from Florida to the Mississippi River

1540–1542   Coronado explores the American Southwest

1541   Cartier establishes Charlesbourg-Royal in Canada

1556   Philip II of Spain takes the throne

1558   Elizabeth I becomes queen of England

1564   French Huguenots build Fort Caroline in northern Florida

1577–1580   Francis Drake circumnavigates the globe

1585   English attempt colonization at Roanoke Island

1588   English defeat the Spanish Armada

annihilation, exploitation, resistance, accommodation, and trade created new cultures and social systems throughout the hemisphere.

THE FIRST AMERICANS

In 1492, an estimated 70 million Native Americans lived in North and South America. They possessed widely divergent cultures, ranging from the Inuit who hunted seal and walrus along the shores of the Arctic Ocean, to the Aztecs of central Mexico and Incas of the Peruvian Andes who lived in state-level agricultural societies. In the geographic area that now encompasses the United States, they included mound-building farmers of the Mississippi valley, the pueblo-dwelling Hopi and Zuñi Indians and nomadic Apaches of the southwest, and the Iroquois and Algonquians of the eastern woodlands.

Native American Societies Before Contact

These diverse peoples were descendants of small bands of hunters who crossed the Bering land bridge from Siberia to Alaska some time between 40,000 and 14,000 years ago. When the glacier covering much of Canada receded, they followed big game south from Alaska, through western Canada, to the Great Plains. Among the earliest evidence of their arrival, dating from about 12,000 B.C., are sites containing human remains and the skeletons of animals with the stone spearheads used to slay them. As the climate of North America became warmer with the end of the Ice Age,

BERINGIA

ARCTIC
OCEAN

NORTH

AMERICA

ATLANTIC
OCEAN

• Hopewell
Great
Serpent
Mound

• Cahokia

ANASAZI
• Mesa Verde
• Chaco Canyon

HOHOKAM
Snaketown

PACIFIC

OCEAN

Gulf of
Mexico

AZTECS
• Teotihuacán
• Tenochtitlán

Yucatán
Peninsula

MAYA

Caribbean Sea

Migration patterns

SOUTH
AMERICA

MAP 1.1 | **AMERICA BEFORE COLUMBUS**

and perhaps as a result of overhunting, several species of large animals disappeared, including mammoths, horses, steppe bison, camels, and mastodons. Buffalo remained plentiful on the Great Plains, but elsewhere Indians hunted smaller game, fished, and collected berries, seeds, and nuts. As groups migrated throughout North and South America and adapted to their environments, their cultures and languages diverged.

When ancient Americans began cultivating crops, they laid the foundation for more densely populated

societies. Agriculture evolved first in Central America and somewhat later in Peru. Of greatest importance to Indians of North America was the development of maize, or Indian corn, probably from the grass *teosinte,* which grew in dry areas of Mexico and Guatemala. Through a process of selective planting, over hundreds of years, farmers enlarged the size of the cob and seeds, thus increasing the amount of food per cob. Even so, the earliest known corncobs are only slightly longer than one inch. In addition to maize, early Mexicans domesticated beans, squash, chili peppers, and avocado. Agriculture proved revolutionary for some ancient American societies, as higher yields spurred population growth and a greater division of labor.

Between 1500 B.C. and Columbus's arrival, civilizations rose and declined throughout the Americas—just as the ancestral cultures of the Europeans developed in ancient Egypt, Greece, and Rome. Ancient Americans built empires, much like their counterparts in the Mediterranean, with cities, extensive trade networks, systems of religion and knowledge, art, architecture, and hierarchical social classes. Two of the best-known civilizations of pre-contact America were the Mayan, located on the Yucatan peninsula, and the Mexican. The Maya, at their height from 300 to 900 A.D., built cities of stone pyramids, temples, and palaces, with populations ranging to more than 60,000. Mayan kings, considered divine, extended their empire to over fifty different states and maintained trade with distant peoples. Stone and wood carving, jade jewelry, wall painting, and pottery revealed Mayan artistry. They had a numeral system based on units of twenty, hieroglyphics, a knowledge of astronomy, and several calendars—one of 365 days and another of 260 days, which correlated approximately with human fertility (an average pregnancy lasts 266 days) and the agricultural growing season.

The Mexicans, who lived in the Valley of Mexico, built the city of Teotihuacán east of Lake Texcoco. Its population of about 200,000 depended on intensive farming of nearby irrigated lands. The grid-patterned Teotihuacán, which Mexicans considered the place where time began, held at its core the Pyramid of the Sun and the Pyramid of the Moon. Even after the city's decline it retained religious significance for later Mexicans and became a place of pilgrimage.

The Aztecs settled in the Valley of Mexico in the fourteenth century, building their capital, Tenochtitlán, on the only vacant land available, an island in

A Mayan jade death mask, c. 700 AD.

Lake Texcoco which they connected to the shore by causeways. They cultivated intensively the marshlands surrounding their island and built a militaristic state. By the time the Spanish *conquistadores* arrived in 1519, the Aztecs controlled territory from the Pacific to the Gulf Coast. One Spaniard described Tenochtitlán as they approached: "And when we saw all those towns and villages built in the water, and other great towns on dry land, and that straight and narrow causeway leading to Mexico, we were astounded. These great towns . . . and buildings rising from the water, all made of stone, seemed like an enchanted vision." The Aztecs required tribute from the people they conquered—gold, feathers, turquoise, food, cotton, and human beings for sacrifice. The Aztecs believed that every day they had to feed human hearts to the sun god, Huitzilpochtli, to prevent the world from coming to an end.

To the north of the Valley of Mexico, Indians also developed distinctive cultures. The Hohokam occupied desert lands in Arizona and northern Sonora, where, with irrigation, they cultivated Indian corn,

The Pyramid of the Sun, located in the center of Teotihuacán, the ancient Mexican capital.

cotton, squash, and beans. Their canals, up to ten miles long, diverted water from nearby rivers. When Athabaskan raiders from the north attacked Hohokam towns, they tried to protect themselves by building high adobe walls, then after 1400 A.D. simply abandoned many of their villages.

Enemy attacks and crop failures from lack of rain forced other Indians of the southwest to leave their towns. The Anasazi farmers of northern Arizona and New Mexico, Colorado, and Utah relied on rain and floods to water their crops. One of their settlements was Pueblo Bonito in Chaco Canyon, which housed perhaps 1,000 people in 800 rooms surrounded by high walls; another was the complex of rock dwellings built high in the canyon cliffs at Mesa Verde. While both were deserted during the fourteenth century, descendants of the Anasazi—the Hopi and Zuñi Indians—witnessed Spanish exploration. The Spanish called them "Pueblo" Indians for the adobe villages with large apartment dwellings in which they lived.

Farther east, in a large area drained by the Mississippi River, by 1000 B.C. early Americans developed civilizations characterized by large earthen burial mounds, some sixty feet high. These mounds entombed corpses and such grave goods as tobacco pipes, copper beads and spoons, bracelets, and beads made from seashells. The Great Serpent Mound, located near Cincinnati, Ohio, is the most famous of their earthworks. These Mississippian people lived in small villages along rivers, hunted game, fished, and raised squash, Indian corn, sunflowers, and gourds. As evidenced by the grave goods, their trading network extended from the Gulf Coast (shells) to Lake Superior (copper). By 700 A.D., the Mississippian people constructed large towns, such as Cahokia, which was located near the confluence of the Mississippi, Illinois, and Missouri rivers. At the center of these towns were large rectangular mounds topped by temples and mortuaries in which members of the upper class were buried. Around 1200 A.D., Cahokia and its environs

Hohokam pottery decorated with bird motif, c. 700–900 AD, found at Snaketown, Arizona.

Secotan village, 1585, by the Englishman John White, who journeyed to North America with the Roanoke expedition. His watercolor drawings depict Algonquians of the North Carolina coast.

had about 40,000 residents but by 1450, the region's population declined, perhaps as a result of illness spread by urban crowding.

People of the Eastern Woodlands

Along the Atlantic seaboard extending inland to the Appalachian Mountains, where the English, French, and Dutch later colonized, lived Native Americans of two major language groups, the Algonquian and the Iroquois. The eastern woodlands incorporated a wide variety of habitats, from beach to highlands. In most parts, decent soil and moderate rainfall and temperatures supported agriculture and many kinds of game, fish, and wild plants. Algonquian-speaking people dominated the Atlantic coast from Canada to Florida; they included the Pokanokets, Narragansetts, and Pequots in New England; the Delawares of the middle Atlantic region; and members of the Powhatan confederacy in what became Virginia. Many of the Iroquois lived in the Finger Lakes area of central New York. They belonged to five tribes: the Mohawks, Oneidas, Onondagas, Cayugas, and Senecas, from east to west, who banded together in the Iroquois confed-

eracy to unite against their enemies and stop feuding among themselves. Iroquoian people who were not part of the confederacy included the Hurons of the eastern Great Lakes and the Susquehannocks of central Pennsylvania and Maryland.

While important cultural differences existed between the two language groups and even among bands within each group, Indians of the eastern woodlands had much in common. They held land cooperatively, without private ownership. The tribe as a whole claimed ownership rights, not individual members or families. Except in far northern New England, where the growing season was too short to plant corn, Indians had a mixed economy of agriculture, gathering,

Woman and girl of Pomeioc, another watercolor by John White, 1585. Algonquian women cared for children and raised crops, including corn and tobacco.

fish, etc." The combination of corn, squash, and beans enriched the soil, providing high yields from small plots of land; eaten together these foods were high in protein. The Native Americans cleared land by girdling the large trees (removing a strip of bark around the trees about three feet from the ground), thus killing them. When the trees died, the Indians removed them, burned the underbrush, and sowed crops among the stumps. Eastern woodlands people used nets and weirs to catch fish and, to assure good hunting, they periodically burned underbrush from sections of forest, thus giving ecological advantages to species of trees such as pines and oaks, which were resistant to fire. The burning stimulated the growth of lush grass, providing fodder for deer and other game. The fires allowed some sunlight to penetrate the forest, promoting the growth of strawberries, raspberries, and blackberries, and creating an environment very much like a park.

Indian religions, though widely diverse in many ways, incorporated a common worldview. The people of the eastern woodlands believed that the earth and sky formed a spiritual realm of which they were a part, not the masters. They made no distinction between the secular, or nonreligious, and the sacred. They feared the power of nature, recognizing its control over crops, the availability of game, and the weather. Spirits inhabited the earth and could be found in plants, animals, rocks, or clouds. Each spirit, or *manitou,* could become the guardian of a young Indian man (less often a young woman), who, in search of a manitou, went into the woods alone, without eating or sleeping perhaps for days. If the spirit made itself known, it would provide help and counsel to the individual for the rest of his life. These Native Americans also believed in a Master Spirit or Creator, who was all-powerful and all-knowing, but whose presence was rarely felt. Religious leaders were *shamans,* who performed rituals, such as making sacrifices of food, tobacco, furs, or weapons, to influence weather conditions or ward off danger. They were usually men, but in some communities were women. Indians believed that shamans, through religious ritual, could cure illness, interpret dreams, bring good weather, and predict the future.

The kinship group, or extended family, formed the basis of Native American society and government. The heads of kinship groups chose the band's chief leaders, called *sachems,* who with advice assigned fields for planting, decided where and when to hunt, managed trade and diplomacy with other Indians and

fishing, and hunting. Women were responsible for raising corn, squash, beans, and (where possible) tobacco. They also gathered nuts and fruit, built houses, made clothing, took care of the children, and prepared meals, while men cleared land, hunted, fished, and protected the village from enemies. Because this division of labor between the sexes was quite different from that of England and the Continent, Europeans believed that Indian women worked too hard. One Englishman said, "Their wives are their slaves, and do all the work; the men will do nothing but kill beasts,

Man with Body Paint *by John White, 1585. Men were the political leaders, warriors, and hunters in Algonquian society.*

Europeans, and judged whether or not to go to war. Among Algonquian-speaking natives, the heads of extended families were men, as were the sachems they chose. But in Iroquois culture women served as clan leaders, taking a share of political power. Iroquois society was matrilineal, with family membership passing from mother to children; and matrilocal, as the husband left his family to live with his wife's. A woman divorced her husband by setting his possessions outside the door; a man could divorce his wife by removing his belongings from her family's longhouse. Women elders could not speak publicly at tribal coun-

cils or serve as sachems, but they chose these political leaders and advised them on such matters as waging war.

Thus, in 1492, at the time Columbus crossed the Atlantic, highly complex and differentiated societies existed in North and South America. The Americas were not a vacant land, a wilderness waiting to be tapped. Dense populations inhabited parts of South, Central, and North America, sustaining elaborate networks of empire and trade. Throughout the hemisphere, Indian people had distinctive cultures tied to the resources of their environment. Despite this wide variety of languages and cultures, as different from one another as those of European countries, most Europeans adopted the single name that Columbus mistakenly employed — Indians. An alternative the colonists used was "savages," the term the French preferred. The view of many Europeans, that Native Americans had undifferentiated, uncivilized societies, justified conquest and expropriation of their lands.

BEGINNING OF EUROPEAN OVERSEAS EXPANSION

The Europeans who invaded the Americas after 1492 had more in common with Native Americans than they liked to admit; nevertheless, in important ways, their cultures were distinct. Europeans spent most of their energy producing or gathering food: They farmed, raised livestock, and gathered nuts and berries. In the south and west of England, for example, where the land was fertile, farmers engaged in intensive cultivation of wheat, rye, and other crops. In most of England and Wales, however, where the land was hilly and less fertile, farmers planted just an acre or two and spent more time gathering. In contrast to Native Americans, Europeans believed in private property, that individuals could own land and thus had the right to sell, fence, plant, erect buildings, hunt, cut lumber, and exclude others from use.

The societies from which most colonizers came, particularly Spain, France, and England, were patriarchal, meaning that descent followed the father's line and political power was nearly always in the hands of men. Men dominated their wives and children, and by extension dominated society. Though women occasionally took the throne, for instance, Isabella of Spain

MAP 1.2 | EUROPE AND WEST AFRICA IN THE 15TH CENTURY

and Elizabeth I of England, men controlled government, the church, and the military. Married women were considered subordinate to their husbands and under most circumstances could hold no personal property or real estate, a significant handicap in a society based on private property. For example, under English common law—the legal system that had evolved by custom and court precedent over centuries—a married woman was a *feme covert,* or covered woman, who could not own or manage property, make a contract, write a will, take custody of her children, own a business, or sue in court, without her husband's permission. An unmarried woman or widow, in legal terms a *feme sole,* was not subject to these restrictions.

In the fifteenth century, as Europeans began exploring the reaches of the "Ocean Sea," as they called the Atlantic, the pope headed a united Christian church in western and central Europe. At the same time, monarchs consolidated power in Portugal, Spain, France, and England, providing financial support and a greater sense of national identity to fuel European expansion. In turn, wealth from distant empires and trade funded wars among these emerging nations.

Trade with the East

When Columbus sailed out into the Atlantic Ocean in 1492, he expected to establish a new trade route with Asia, not discover and colonize a New World. He was unaware of the voyages of the Viking Leif Eriksson and his family, who established a short-lived colony in Newfoundland around 1000 A.D. In the fifteenth century, eastern trade was a chief source of riches, for affluent Europeans wanted black pepper, cinnamon, cloves, mace, nutmeg, and ginger for preserving and flavoring their food. The spices would not grow in Europe, so merchants commanded high prices for transporting them from India, the East Indies, and other parts of East Asia. Imports also included silk, cotton cloth, rugs, perfumes, rubies, sapphires, and emeralds.

Before 1500, Arab and Italian merchants dominated the eastern trade. Arabs controlled eastern trading centers and carried goods across the Arabian Sea in *dhows*—boats with lateen, or triangular, sails—to the Red Sea and Persian Gulf. From there caravans took cargoes to Mediterranean ports for purchase by Italian merchants, particularly traders from Venice and Genoa. The Italians then distributed the spices

and luxuries throughout Europe by way of pack train and coastal shipping. European cities developed to handle the exchange of valued eastern products in return for silver, gold, woolen and linen cloth, furs, and leather. Centers of trade and banking included Paris, Lyons, Amsterdam, London, Hamburg, Danzig, Barcelona, Cadiz, and Lisbon, in addition to Venice and Genoa. The rise of great cities accompanied the growth of unified political states. Merchants provided funding for kings to consolidate small feudal states into nations. In Portugal, Spain, France, and England, commercial interests supported unification to obtain social order, monopolistic privileges, and standardized codes of law.

Portugal Explores the West African Coast

Early in the fifteenth century, Prince Henry of Portugal, called "the Navigator," decided to challenge the Arab and Italian hold on eastern commerce. The son of King John I, Henry brought together men interested in overseas trade and exploration at his court on Cape St. Vincent, overlooking the Atlantic Ocean. Many were Italian navigators, whose experience came from the Mediterranean trade. Beginning in 1420, Prince Henry sent ships down the western coast of Africa into parts unknown. He had four goals: to increase the power of Portugal by adding territorial possessions; to benefit economically from commerce with the African coast; to reach Asia and take a share of that trade; and to spread Christianity, and thereby combat the expansion of Islam in Africa. The Portuguese knew West Africans through the centuries-long exchange across the Sahara of African rubber, ivory, slaves, and gold, for European fruit, wheat, and sugar.

Headway down the African coast was slow, despite the lure of trade, because European sailors knew nothing of the ocean beyond Cape Bojador. Their sea charts were guesses, and their navigational instruments rudimentary. In 1420, cartographers knew a great deal about the Mediterranean Sea and constructed highly accurate charts, called *portolano,* of its shorelines and harbors. Such maps did not exist for the West African coast, so one task of Prince Henry's explorers was to chart their progress. Seamen had heard that monsters, and perhaps even Satan, dwelled in the waters beyond Cape Bojador, while other stories told that the ocean boiled at the equator. In fact, strong south-

Prince Henry the Navigator, of Portugal, who sponsored exploration down the west coast of Africa to find a sea route to Asia. From a painting by Nuno Gonçalves.

ward ocean currents facilitated outbound progress, but made return to the Mediterranean difficult. From ancient mathematicians and geographers, most notably Ptolemy, mapmakers knew that the world was round, but they also adopted Ptolemy's belief that a southern continent joined Africa to China, thus eliminating the possibility of a sea route from the Atlantic to the Indian Ocean. Prince Henry challenged current wisdom by sending ships down Africa's coast to find a route to the east.

New Technology

In the early and mid-fifteenth century, the lack of adequate instruments hampered navigation. The first Por-

tuguese navigators tried not to lose sight of land. Compasses had been in use since at least the thirteenth century, but not until about 1460 did Europeans develop the means of determining latitude (distance north or south from the equator). In the Northern Hemisphere, sea captains calculated the height of the Pole Star from the horizon to determine their latitude. The Pole Star cannot be seen south of the equator, however, so navigators there measured the altitude of the sun at midday. In making these calculations, they used the astrolabe or the quadrant to determine the angle of the sun from the horizon, then consulted astronomical tables that Abraham Zacuto, a Jewish astronomer, compiled in 1478. A method for determining longitude remained unknown until the eighteenth century.

Improvements in ships and gunnery during the fifteenth century also aided exploration and conquest. By 1400 it had become clear that Mediterranean galleys, powered by oarsmen, were impractical in the high waves of the Atlantic. The first European ocean-going ships were square-rigged. Their broad sails could power large vessels, but they required a favorable tailwind to proceed from one point to another. The square-rigged ships could not explore ragged coastlines. To increase maneuverability, Portuguese seafarers designed the caravel with lateen rigging, which the Arabs originated on their dhows. The most successful Portuguese ship for long voyages was the *caravela redondo,* the square-rigged caravel, developed late in the fifteenth century and adopted by other European nations. This ship combined the speed of square rigging with the more responsive handling of lateen sails. For protection from privateers and in time of war, the Portuguese mounted artillery on the caravels and by 1500 introduced the practice of broadside fire. They changed nautical warfare by sinking enemy vessels with gunfire instead of boarding them with foot soldiers.

Despite these improvements in the design of ships, they remained uncomfortable places in which to live on voyages of months and years. Except for senior officers, none of the seamen had regular sleeping quarters—they slept on deck, or below in bad weather. Their shipmates included rats and cockroaches. When it rained, everything got wet, including the cooking fire built in a sandbox on deck. The mariners ate ship's hardtack, beans, and salt pork and beef, and drank mostly wine, since their casked water quickly became foul.

Engraving by Stradunuse of an early sixteenth-century cosmographer working in his study with contemporary instruments, including dividers, rule, compass, quadrant, and sand glass.

AFRICA AND THE ATLANTIC SLAVE TRADE

Despite their fears and limited technology, the Portuguese explorers ventured farther and farther down the West African coast. In 1434, Gil Eannes sailed past Cape Bojador. Subsequent voyages established a lucrative coastal trade in slaves, gold, and malaguetta pepper in the Senegal region and farther south and east to the Gold Coast and Benin. Merchants now began investing in expeditions, seeing the profits to be made. Up to that point, Prince Henry had financed the voyages himself. Between the 1440s and 1505, Portuguese traders transported 40,000 Africans to perform domestic labor in Portugal and Spain, and to work on the sugar plantations of the Azores, Madeira, and Canary Islands in the Atlantic.

West African Cultures

Several great empires had risen and fallen in the area bounded by the Mediterranean Sea, the Gulf of Guinea, and the Atlantic Ocean. From before 300 A.D. to 1600, a succession of empires—Ghana, Mali, and Songhay—dominated the area. They had large armies, collected tribute over vast distances, and traded with Europeans and Arabs. Like Native Americans and Europeans, West Africans were predominantly agricultural people. Ghana declined by 1100 as a result of droughts that dried up several rivers. Mali then took control, as its monarchs, with access to the rich gold mines of Bure, regulated the gold trade. The Mali kings were followers of Islam: One of the most famous, Gonga-Mussa, made a pilgrimage to Mecca in 1324 to fulfill his religious duty as a Muslim. His caravan is said to have included 60,000 people and 80 camels carrying over 24,000 pounds of gold.

This 1375 European map of northwest Africa shows an Arab trader approaching Mansa Musa of Mali, who is holding a large nugget of gold.

A bronze relief of Benin, a powerful kingdom when the Portuguese began trading along the African coast in the late fifteenth century.

Mali provided stable government over a wide area until the fifteenth century, when Songhay successfully challenged its dominance. Songhay was centered at Gao and had been subordinate to Mali in the time of Gonga-Mussa. Under Sonni Ali, who ruled from 1468 to 1492—as the Atlantic slave trade developed—Songhay captured Timbuktu, an important trading and cultural center of Mali, consolidating power over a large part of West Africa. Askia Mohammed, who ruled from 1493 to 1528, expanded the empire even farther. In waging wars, the Songhay armies, like those of other African states, captured and enslaved their enemies. Askia Mohammed strengthened ties with other Muslims and reformed government, banking, and education. He introduced a uniform system of weights and measures, adopted Islamic law, and encouraged intellectual growth at Timbuktu and Gao, drawing scholars from throughout West Africa, Asia, and Europe. After Askia Mohammed's reign, Songhay declined; Moroccans conquered Timbuktu in 1593.

Beyond these empires, along the West African coast lay smaller states with highly developed cultures. While influenced by Islam, they retained much of their traditional religions, including some belief in witchcraft and the power of charms. Divine kings governed many of the coastal states as the sacred, physical symbols of their realms. Like Native Americans and Europeans, the people of Africa kept religion central to their lives and endowed their leaders with both political and religious authority.

Most important in traditional African religions was a single all-powerful God, the Creator. Africans generally believed, however, that God was "too high exalted above us, and too great to condescend so much as to trouble himself or think of Mankind." Thus, the Creator provided lesser gods, including gods of rain, thunder, and lightning; of rivers and lakes; of animals, trees, and hills. These gods could be benevolent or harmful, so people had to seek positive relationships through rituals, sacrifice, and prayer. Africans also believed that their ancestors watched over the extended family, with power over fertility, health, even life. When the eldest father, or patriarch, of a kinship group died, his spirit became a god. Elaborate funeral rites demonstrated the importance of the dead to the living. All family members paid respect to the deceased, whose internments were delayed until distant relatives could arrive. Before his death, the patriarch had been the extended family's priest; he communicated with its ancestors through prayer and the sacrifice of animals such as chickens and sheep. The patriarch also served as political leader. Thus in many African societies, the state, religion, and family united under a single hierarchical structure.

Kinship in West Africa varied from one culture to another, as extended families could be either patrilineal or matrilineal. In all cases, however, a child belonged to only one kin group, that of the father or the mother. If the system was patrilineal, then descent and paternal responsibility flowed from father to child. If it was matrilineal, descent proceeded from mother to child, but the mother's brother, not the mother, assumed responsibility and control. When a woman married, she remained a member of her own kin group, but usually went to live with her husband's family. The intended husband compensated her family for the loss of her services with a payment called bridewealth, which did not represent purchase of the woman herself. *Polygyny,* or having more than one wife, was legal in African societies, but generally reserved to men of high status. Kinship groups paid the bridewealth for the services of the first wife, not a second, and few men could meet the expenses for marrying another. When men had more than one wife, each woman lived with her children in a separate house.

The extended family formed the basis of economic organization, holding land in common and assigning plots to individual families. Women and men worked in fields growing crops such as rice, cassava, wheat, millet, cotton, fruits, and vegetables. They had live-stock, including cattle, sheep, goats, and chickens. Families produced food for their own use and for the market, where women were the primary traders. Artisans were skilled in textile weaving, pottery, basketry, and woodwork. They also made tools and art objects of copper, bronze, iron, silver, and gold. As in the case of Native Americans, West Africans had experienced the rise and fall of empires and possessed diverse, complex cultures at the time Europeans arrived on their shores in the mid-fifteenth century.

The Atlantic Slave Trade Begins

Over the course of four centuries, West Africa lost to the Atlantic slave trade at least 20 million people, of whom 10 million actually survived to toil in American fields. Slavery had existed in Africa and throughout the Mediterranean for centuries before the Portuguese arrived on the West African coast. African slavery was different, however, from the institution that developed in America. In comparison with plantation areas of the New World, a small percentage of African people were in bonds. Most African slaves were prisoners of war; others had committed some offense that caused their kinfolk to banish them. All were considered "outsiders." While most bond-

A Fula town in West Africa, drawn by a European. West Africans, like Europeans but not Native Americans, kept domestic livestock. Note that this village is raising Indian corn, a Native American crop.

men and women did menial work, the primary function of slavery in West Africa was social rather than economic—to provide a place in society for people cut off from their families. Trans-Saharan traders transported some African slaves for sale to wealthy European households where they served as domestic workers and artisans. Because this trade was limited, most slaves remained in West Africa, where they lived under the protection of law, achieved status as a member of a household, married, and had children. Enslaved Africans could be transferred from one owner to another at will, but their children could not be sold and were frequently emancipated. Traditionally, slavery had a quite different meaning in Africa than what developed in the New World.

The plantation slave system that became dominant in America began near Africa, however, before Columbus crossed the Ocean Sea. Portugal began growing sugar as early as 1452 on the island of Madeira, off West Africa. Sugar cane, which originated in South Asia, required large amounts of menial, unpleasant labor in a hot climate; thus workers were generally coerced. To supply Madeira, Portuguese merchants purchased black slaves from Muslim trans-Saharan traders and from Africans along the coast. When sugar production could expand no farther in Madeira for lack of land, the Portuguese colonized the small islands in the Gulf of Guinea: São Tomé, Príncipe, and Fernando Po. Sugar production was successful, but mortality was high and the demand for laborers great, spurring growth of the slave trade on the Gold Coast. By the end of the fifteenth century, before European settlement in America, Portugal developed both the plantation system that consumed large numbers of African slaves and the commercial mechanism for purchasing human beings from African traders. The growth of slavery and the slave trade in America after 1500 represented an expansion of these earlier developments, not innovations.

SPAIN AND PORTUGAL DIVIDE THE GLOBE

Once Portugal had established trade on the West African coast, Spanish merchants tried to participate. Prince Henry appealed to the pope, who in 1455 gave Portugal sole possession of lands to the south and east toward India. Mariners and merchants from other nations who attempted to trade in Africa were to be thrown into the ocean. In an age when the line between religious and secular authority was blurred, the pope's decision gave Portugal a monopoly on the Atlantic slave trade, and in effect sanctioned that commerce in return for efforts to Christianize the "heathen." Spain and Portugal affirmed the decision with the Treaty of Alcaçovas (1479), in which Spain recognized Portugal's sphere of interest in Africa, and Portugal acknowledged Spain's claim to the Canary Islands.

As the Portuguese sailed south, they came to recognize the vastness of the African continent. They made rapid progress only after 1482, when King John II of Portugal, a geographer himself, stepped up the program of discovery. In 1483, Diogo Cão reached the Congo River and in 1487 Bartholomeu Dias rounded the Cape of Good Hope. The Portuguese now knew that a sea route to India existed, yet the enormity of the enterprise discouraged them from immediately sending out ships.

Columbus Sails West

Because the Spanish recognized Portugal's claim to Africa and the eastern sea route, they had to find

Columbus's arrival in America, by Theodor de Bry.

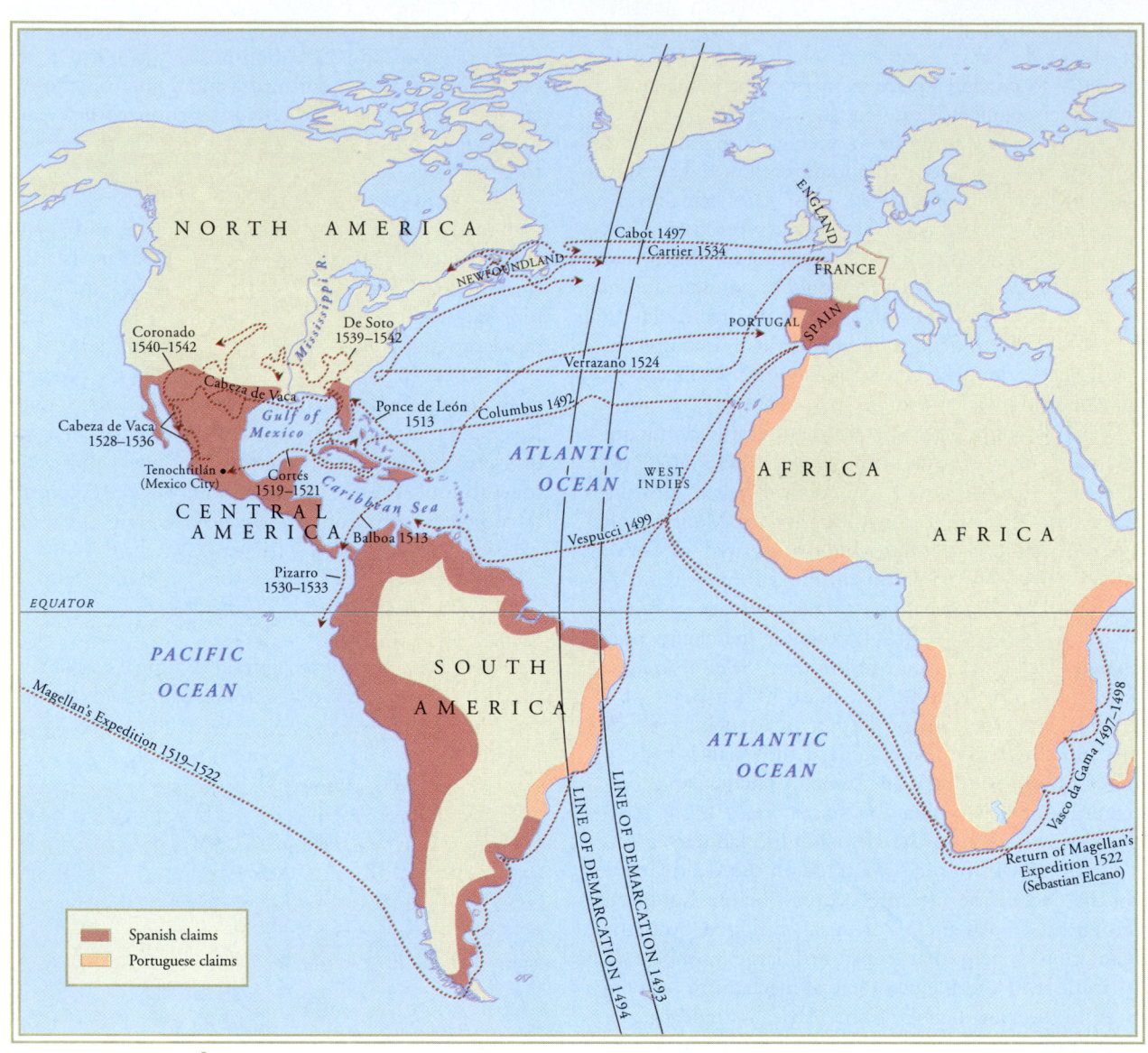

MAP 1.3 | EUROPEAN EXPLORATIONS, 1492–1542

another course if they were going to trade with the Far East. Thus, Isabella and Ferdinand funded Columbus, despite their skepticism of his calculation of the distance to Asia, which turned out to be a serious underestimate. In August 1492, Columbus sailed west from the Canaries, taking advantage of the favorable current and trade winds that flow westward north of the equator then circle clockwise in the Gulf of Mexico to

emerge as the Gulf Stream. The ships reached San Salvador in October, but Columbus thought they had located the East Indies. Hoping to establish trade, Columbus sailed southward to Cuba, then touched Hispaniola, where Native Americans offered gold in return for the trade goods he brought. When the Spanish lost their flagship *Santa Maria* on a coral reef, they built a small fort with its timbers.

Leaving behind a small contingent of men, Columbus set out for home in January 1493, again found favorable winds, but encountered a violent storm and sought shelter in Portugal. King John II, whose explorers had not yet reached India by sailing around Africa, refused to believe that Columbus located Asia. The lands he had found, the king claimed, lay within Portugal's sphere.

Spanish and Portuguese "Spheres"

Isabella and Ferdinand rejected Portugal's argument, petitioning Pope Alexander VI, who was Spanish, to grant them dominion over the newly discovered lands. After negotiations with John II, the pope established a Line of Demarcation, giving all lands "discovered or to be discovered" west of the line to Spain and all lands east of the line to Portugal. The Treaty of Tordesillas, which finalized the negotiations in 1494 and located the line 370 leagues (about 1,000 miles) west of the Azores, expanded the principle of "spheres of influence" by which European nations sought to dominate most of the world. Portugal retained its rights to the Atlantic slave trade and the sea route around Africa to India. Spain received permission to explore, conquer, and Christianize all lands and people to the west. The question of where Portuguese and Spanish spheres should be divided in the Far East was left unresolved until 1529, when the Treaty of Saragossa established a line seventeen degrees to the east of the Moluccas (Spice Islands), thus placing most of Asia within Portugal's sphere.

Between 1494 and 1529, Portugal and Spain sent out expeditions to explore the reaches of their spheres and to find the sea routes to the East. Columbus made three more voyages to the west: In November 1493 he sailed with seventeen ships to the Lesser Antilles, Puerto Rico, and Hispaniola, where he reestablished the colony, which Native Americans had destroyed in the interim. Later he explored the shores of South and Central America. Meanwhile, Columbus's claim that he had found a passage to the East by sailing west prodded the Portuguese to complete their efforts to reach India. In 1497–1498, Vasco da Gama rounded the Cape of Good Hope, sailed across the Indian Ocean, returning to Portugal with a cargo of pepper and cinnamon. The voyage to India was much more difficult than Columbus's Atlantic crossing. During the two-year journey that included at least 300 days at sea, more than one-third of the sailors died. In 1500, Portugal instructed Pedro Álvares Cabral to find the Cape of Good Hope by sailing west. Instead, he touched the coast of Brazil, further convincing the Portuguese that this was not Asia, but lands previously unknown. On the basis of Cabral's expedition and because a section of Brazil lay east of the Line of Demarcation, Portugal claimed that part of South America. Amerigo Vespucci, a native of Florence, made two separate voyages, in 1499 and 1501, for Spain and Portugal respectively. He explored much of the Atlantic coast of South America, demonstrating that it was a huge land mass that had to be circumnavigated to reach Asia. In reward for his insights, many Europeans associated his name—not that of Columbus—with the newly "discovered" continents.

An Expanding World

Despite the promise of riches in America, Europeans continued to search for a western sea route to Asia. Ferdinand Magellan convinced King Charles I of Spain that he could sail around the cape of South America and claim the Molucca Islands, which he believed lay within Spain's sphere. Magellan was Portuguese but his country gave him no support for his plan since they already had a profitable sea route to the East. With five ships, in 1519 Magellan set out on an expedition that would take three years. The voyagers experienced shipwreck, a harrowing passage through the straits subsequently named for Magellan, and starvation: The Pacific was so much wider than anticipated that the mariners had to eat ship rats and leather to survive. When inhabitants of the Philippines killed Magellan, Sebastian del Cano took command, returning to Spain with one surviving ship, laden with cloves. Together, Magellan and del Cano commanded the first circumnavigation of the globe. In doing so, however, they demonstrated that the southwest passage through the Straits of Magellan and across the Pacific Ocean was much more difficult than envisioned.

England and France also wanted a part of the eastern trade, so they ignored the pope's division of the world between Spain and Portugal. With their more northerly location and some knowledge of the coast of North America, they sought a northwest passage to the East. During the fifteenth century (before Columbus's landfall), seafarers from England and France had

Admiral Christopher Columbus's Diary Account of Reaching America, October 12, 1492

This document is from an abstract of Columbus's diary made by the Spanish missionary Bartolomé de las Casas. The Admiral's original diary no longer exists. This selection begins as the Europeans sight land and describes their first contact with the Native Americans. Because Columbus thought his expedition had reached the East Indies, he called the people Indians.

At two hours after midnight the land appeared, from which they were about two leagues distant. They hauled down all the sails . . . passing time until daylight Friday, when they reached an islet of the Lucayas, which was called Guanahani in the language of the Indians. Soon they saw naked people; and the Admiral [Columbus] went ashore in the armed launch, and Martín Alonso Pinzón and his brother Vicente Anes, who was captain of the *Niña*. The Admiral brought out the royal banner and the captains' two flags with the green cross, which the Admiral carried on all the ships as a standard, with an F and a Y, and over each letter a crown, one on one side of the ✝ and the other on the other. Thus put ashore they saw very green trees and many ponds and fruits of various kinds. The Admiral called to the two captains and to the others who had jumped ashore and to Rodrigo Descobedo, the recorder of the whole fleet, and to Rodrigo Sánchez de Segovia; and he said that they should be witnesses that, in the presence of all, he would take, as in fact he did take, possession of the said island for the king and for the queen his lords, making the declarations that were required, and which at more length are contained in the testimonials made there in writing. Soon many people of the island gathered there. What follows are the very words of the Admiral in his book about his first voyage to, and discovery of, these Indies. I, he says, in order that they would be friendly to us—because I recognized that they were people who would be better freed [from error] and converted to our Holy Faith by love than by force—to some of them I gave red caps, and glass beads which they put on their chests, and many other things of small value, in which they took so

caught tuna, cod, mackerel, and other fish that teemed in the Newfoundland Banks. Some sailors had camped ashore, where they dried their catch and traded with Native Americans. When King Henry VII of England sent John Cabot, an Italian whose name was really Giovanni Caboto, in search of a northwest passage in 1497, the expedition reached Newfoundland. Cabot sailed again the next year, but most of his ships were lost and he died at sea. While the English were discouraged by Cabot's failure to find a passage or bring back valuable goods, nevertheless, his efforts supported England's later claim to land in North America.

A generation after Cabot, the French entered the search for a route to Asia. In 1524, King Francis I sent another Italian, Giovanni da Verrazano, to look for the elusive passage. Landing at Cape Fear (now North Carolina), Verrazano sailed north along the Atlantic seaboard to Newfoundland, finding no evidence of a waterway through the continent. In expeditions dating 1534 and 1535, Jacques Cartier hoped to find the route by way of the gulf and river of St. Lawrence. He mapped the river and in 1541 established a short-lived colony named Charlesbourg-Royal near the future site of Quebec. While neither Verrazano nor Cartier found

much pleasure and became so much our friends that it was a marvel. Later they came swimming to the ships' launches where we were and brought us parrots and cotton thread in balls and javelins and many other things, and they traded them to us for other things which we gave them, such as small glass beads and bells. In sum, they took everything and gave of what they had very willingly. But it seemed to me that they were a people very poor in everything. All of them go around as naked as their mothers bore them; and the women also, although I did not see more than one quite young girl. And all those that I saw were young people, for none did I see of more than 30 years of age. They are very well formed, with handsome bodies and good faces. Their hair [is] coarse—almost like the tail of a horse—and short. They wear their hair down over their eyebrows except for a little in the back which they wear long and never cut. Some of them paint themselves with black, and they are of the color of the Canarians, neither black nor white; and some of them paint themselves with white, and some of them with red, and some of them with whatever they find. And some of them paint their faces, and some of them the whole body, and some of them only the eyes, and some of them only the nose. They do not carry arms nor are they acquainted with them, because I showed them swords and they took them by the edge and through ignorance cut themselves. They have no iron. Their javelins are shafts without iron and some of them have at the end a fish tooth and others of other things. All of them alike are of good-sized stature and carry themselves well. I saw some who had marks of wounds on their bodies and I made signs to them asking what they were; and they showed me how people from other islands nearby came there and tried to take them, and how they defended themselves; and I believed and believe that they come here from *tierra firme* to take them captive. They should be good and intelligent servants, for I see that they say very quickly everything that is said to them; and I believe that they would become Christians very easily, for it seemed to me that they had no religion. Our Lord pleasing, at the time of my departure I will take six of them from here to Your Highnesses in order that they may learn to speak. No animal of any kind did I see on this island except parrots. All are the Admiral's words.

a northwest passage, they supplemented European knowledge of North America and supported France's claim to part of the continent.

THE SPANISH EMPIRE IN AMERICA

Because England and France showed only occasional interest in America before 1560, and Portugal focused on the eastern trade and Brazil, the Spanish had little interference from other Europeans in exploring and settling the rest of the New World. By 1543, their colonies extended south to Chile and north through Mexico; they had explored from Florida to California in what is now the United States. From Columbus's first colony, on the island of Hispaniola, Spanish conquistadores advanced from island to island in the West Indies, then moved to conquer the people of Mexico and Central America. Lured by stories of cities of gold, they ascended the Andes and crossed deserts. The conquistadores expected to make their fortune in America

and retire to Spain. Their chief objective was to get rich. In contrast, the Spanish Crown had a more complicated set of goals in colonizing America: to enhance its power among European nations by dominating huge territories in the west; to exploit the wealth of these lands, especially gold and silver; and to convert the conquered Americans to Christianity. While in many ways the goals of the Spanish monarchy and its settlers overlapped, sometimes their interests diverged, especially when it came to the welfare of Native Americans. Often, when they wished, the colonists could subvert the will of the government because its gears worked so slowly and its center of power rested in far-off Spain.

Spanish Conquest

From Hispaniola, the Spanish conquered nearby islands and then wealthier and more powerful peoples on the mainland. When they found little gold on Hispaniola, the conquerors exploited the remaining resources of the island: the labor of its inhabitants and the land. The natives died when the Spanish enslaved them to work on plantations and tend livestock. European diseases took their toll, as did cruel treatment and the psychological effects of bondage. As a result, the colonists sent slave-raiding parties to other islands and to the mainland. The conquistadores who first explored Cuba in 1508 were seeking slaves and gold. For the same reasons they colonized Puerto Rico in 1509. Juan Ponce de León, known for his search in 1513 for the legendary "fountain of youth" in Florida and Yucatan, sought Indian slaves. The same year Vasco Núñez de Balboa led explorers across the Isthmus of Panama, becoming the first Europeans to see the Pacific Ocean.

As the Spanish explorers became aware of the vastness of the Americas and the potential for riches, they organized militarily to subdue the Americans. Despite the small size of their armies, the Spanish prevailed over large empires, in part because of superior technology, including metal weaponry and the use of horses and ships, and in part because they made alliances with the enemies of the Indian emperors. They also had help from disease. The conquistadores, in their quest for wealth and glory, competed with one another to conquer the Native Americans. The most famous of these conquerors is Hernán Cortés who, in 1519, launched an expedition against the Aztecs, who them-

Portrait medal of Hernán Cortés, who conquered the Aztecs, produced when he visited Spain in 1529.

selves had recently consolidated their Mexican empire. With an army of only 500 troops, Cortés persuaded the Totonacs of Cempoala, who were dominated by the Aztecs, to join him. Then defeating the Tlaxcalans and gaining their support as well, he marched to Tenochtitlán, the Aztec capital. The Spanish and their Indian allies entered the city without opposition and seized Moctezuma, the emperor. When Cortés outlawed human sacrifice, denied the primacy of Aztec gods, and made incessant demands for gold, Aztec priests and people rebelled. In the heat of battle, they killed Moctezuma and forced the Spanish and their allies to retreat, slaying many as they tried to escape across the causeways linking Tenochtitlán with the shore of Lake Texcoco. Cortés was not finished, however, and in 1521 with reinforcements advanced methodically on the Aztec capital. This time the Spanish built small ships to cross Lake Texcoco, took control of all causeways, and destroyed Tenochtitlán building by building. A smallpox epidemic killed many Aztecs. The conquerors rebuilt the city as Mexico City, the Spanish capital of Mexico, which they called New Spain.

After 1521, the Spanish extended their conquest through Mexico, Central and South America. Having defeated the Aztecs, Cortés sent troops to take

Guatemala; in 1524 rival conquistadores took control of Honduras. Then they advanced to the south, as Francisco Pizarro vanquished the Incas of Peru in 1531–1534, and others expanded into Argentina and Chile. The Spanish also explored the lands north of Mexico, in the area that is now the United States. Alonso Álvarez de Pineda in 1519–1520 sailed the coastline of the Gulf of Mexico from Florida to Mexico, demonstrating the existence of a continent of North America, not just islands.

Exploration of Florida and the American Southwest

In 1528, the Spanish conquistador Pánfilo de Narváez led an expedition to Florida in quest of cities of gold. Though his venture failed, it led to later exploration of territories that became the southern United States. Narváez and his men landed at Tampa Bay where they met Native Americans who immediately warned them to return to the sea. When the Europeans refused, and spoke of their search for silver and gold, the Indians directed them to the north, to a place called "Apalachen," near the present site of Tallahassee. The Spanish left their ships and most of their supplies, marching northward through insect- and snake-infested terrain. Soon discouraged, they made the mistake of kidnapping a chief of the Apalachees, who had initially been friendly. Highly skilled archers, the Indians attacked, convincing the Spanish to return to New Spain immediately. The soldiers constructed barges, with sails made from their shirts, to carry them across the Gulf of Mexico. When storms separated the craft, most of the explorers, including Narváez, were lost at sea.

Two barges crossed the gulf intact, beaching their occupants on the Texas coast, probably at Galveston Island. The native Karankawas enslaved the survivors, who were nearly starved and lacked weapons or horses. After several years, one of the Spaniards, Álvar Núñez Cabeza de Vaca, who had become an Indian priest and healer, escaped with three others, Alonso del Castillo, Andrés Dorantes, and Esteban, a black slave. They hoped to reach New Spain, but lacked maps or instruments to find their way. For several years they sojourned with a series of Native American peoples, learning their languages and customs. The Spanish earned the Indians' friendship and respect with seemingly miraculous cures. When they finally reached Mexico City in 1536, Cabeza de Vaca told the Spanish viceroy about their journey and tales that they had heard of treasures in the north.

Cabeza de Vaca's report, which he later published, excited interest in exploring lands north of Mexico. When Cabeza de Vaca refused to head an expedition, the viceroy sent the enslaved man, Esteban, with a Franciscan monk, Fray Marcos de Niza, along with several Indians, to scout for the "Seven Cities of Cibola." When Esteban was killed by Zuñis, Fray Marcos returned to Mexico City with extravagant claims that the seven cities existed, that the land flowed with riches.

In 1540, an army of 336 Spanish and about 1,000 Indians marched north under command of Francisco Vásquez de Coronado, with Fray Marcos as their guide. The explorers intended to conquer the cities of gold, claiming the wealth for themselves and the king of Spain. Like Narváez in Florida, they were disappointed. The "golden" city that Fray Marcos had spotted was actually a Zuñi Indian pueblo, Hawikúh, made of adobe, not gold. Coronado sent the monk back to Mexico City with the complaint, "He has not told the truth in a single thing that he said, but everything is the opposite of what he related, except the name of the cities and the large stone houses." The Zuñis resisted the intruders, but were conquered, then informed the Spanish that the Seven Cities lay to the west. Another Indian, whom the Spanish named "El Turco" (the Turk), told stories about great wealth in the country to the east. Over the next year, Coronado's troops explored in both directions. They encountered the Hopi of northeastern Arizona and buffalo-hunting Indians of the Great Plains, saw the Grand Canyon, and traveled as far east as Kansas. They found no gold or silver but left descriptions of a substantial part of the American Southwest.

To reinforce Coronado's army, the viceroy in 1540 sent Hernando de Alarcón by ship up the western coast of Mexico. Though the two explorers failed to make contact, Alarcón sailed into the Colorado River, investigating its banks for several weeks. Two years later, Juan Rodríguez Cabrillo sailed with two ships up the coast of Baja California, past San Diego Bay. They were the first Europeans to visit what is now California. After Cabrillo died in January 1543, his deputy Bartolomé Ferrelo sailed almost as far north as Oregon, passing San Francisco Bay without actually seeing it because of fog.

Unknown to Coronado, an expedition led by Hernando de Soto, governor of Cuba, came within a few

AN AZTEC REPORT OF THE FALL OF TENOCHTITLÁN
1521

The Aztecs fought the Spanish and their Indian allies for months before the invaders, led by Hernán Cortés, prevailed. This document gives an Aztec view of the surrender and shows the immediate impact of the conquest on ordinary men, women, and children.

And when night had fallen, then it rained and sprinkled at intervals. Late at night the flame became visible; just so was it seen, just so it emerged as if it came from the heavens. Like a whirlwind it went spinning around and revolving; it was as if embers burst out of it—some very large, some very small, some like sparks. Like a coppery wind it arose, crackling, snapping, and exploding loudly. Then it circled the dike and traveled toward Coyonacazco; then it went into the middle of the lake there to be lost.

None shouted; none spoke aloud.

And on the next day, nothing more happened. All remained quiet, and also our foes [so] remained.

But the Captain [Cortés] was watching from a roof-top at Amaxac—from the roof-top of [the house of] Aztauatzin—under a canopy. It was a many-colored canopy. He looked toward [us] common folk; the Spaniards crowded about him and took counsel among themselves.

And [on our side] were Quauhtemoc and the other noblemen—the vice ruler Tlacotzin, the lords' judge Petlauhtzin, the captain of the armies Motelchiuhtzin; the constable of Mexico; and the lord priest; and also the noblemen of Tlatilulco—the general Coyoueuetzin; the commanding general Temilotzin; the army commander Topantemoctzin; the chief justice Auelitoctzin; the captain of the armies Uitziliuitzin; and the courier Uitzitzin. All of these noblemen were assembled at Tolmayecan; they appeared to consult among themselves how to do that which we were to undertake and how we should yield to [the Spaniards].

Thereafter only two [men] took Quauhtemoc in a boat. The two who took him and went with him were the seasoned warrior Teputzitoloc, and Yaztachimal, Quauhtemoc's page. And the one who poled [the boat] was named Cenyaotl.

And when they carried Quauhtemoc off, then there was weeping among all the common folk. They said: "Now goeth the young lord Quauhtemoc; now he goeth to deliver himself to the gods, the Spaniards!"

And when they had betaken themselves to bring and disembark him thereupon all the Spaniards came to see. They drew him along; the Spaniards took him by the hand. After

hundred miles of his own company at about the same time. In 1539, De Soto and about 600 troops landed in Tampa Bay. Over the next three years, with aid in translating from a survivor of the Narváez disaster who was living with the Indians, they trekked through the southeast, exploring lands hitherto unknown to the Spanish but finding no gold. The Spanish plundered the populous, thriving towns of the Apalachees and other Florida Indians who were part of the Mississippian cultures, with temple mounds and long-range trading networks. Stealing food, taking Indians as slaves, cutting off limbs, and killing those who re-

that they took him up to the roof-top, where they went to stand him before the Captain, the war leader. And when they had proceeded to stand him before [Cortés], they looked at Quauhtemoc, made much of him, and stroked his hair. Then they seated him with [Cortés] and fired the guns. They hit no one with them, but only made them go off above, [so that] they passed over the heads of the common folk. Then [some Mexicans] only fled. With this the war reached its end.

Then there was shouting; they said: "Enough! Let it end! Eat greens!" When they heard this, the common folk thereupon issued forth. On this, they went, even into the lagoon.

And as they departed, leaving by the great road, once more they there slew some, wherefore the Spaniards were wroth that still some again had taken up their obsidian-bladed swords and their shields. Those who dwelt in house clusters went straightway to Amaxac; they went direct to where the ways divide. There the common folk separated. So many went toward Tepeyacac, so many toward Xoxouiltitlan, so many toward Nonoalco. But toward Xolloco and toward Macatzintamal no one went.

And all who lived in boats and [in houses] on poles, and those at Tolmayecan, went into the water. On some, the water reached to the stomach; some, to the chest; and on some it reached to the neck. And some were all submerged, there in the deeps. Little children were carried on the backs [of their elders]; cries of weeping arose. Some went on happy and rejoicing as they traveled crowding on the road. And those who owned boats, all the boatmen, left by night, and even [continued to] leave all day. It was as if they pushed and crowded one another as they set out.

And everywhere the Spaniards were seizing and robbing the people. They sought gold; as nothing did they value the green stone, quetzal feathers and turquoise [which] was everywhere in the bosoms or in the skirts of the women. And as for us men, it was everywhere in [our] breech clouts and in [our] mouths.

And [the Spaniards] seized and set apart the pretty women—those of light bodies, the fair[-skinned] ones. And some women, when they were robbed, covered their face with mud and put on old, mended shirts and rags for their shifts. They put all rags on themselves.

And also some of us men were singled out—those who were strong, grown to manhood, and next the young boys, of whom they would make messengers, who would be their runners, and who were known as their servers. And on some they burned [brand marks] on their cheeks; on some they put paint on their cheeks; on some they put paint on their lips.

And when the shield was laid down, when we gave way, it was the year count Three House and the day count was One Serpent.

sisted, De Soto's men marched north from the Florida peninsula, through central Georgia to the Carolinas, then west across the Appalachians into the Tennessee River valley. They followed the river south into Alabama, then traveled west toward the Mississippi, which the Native Americans called the "Father of Waters." Still intent on finding the Seven Cities of Cibola, despite heavy losses when Chickasaws burned their camp and supplies, De Soto crossed into Arkansas. After he died of a fever in 1542 and was buried in the Mississippi, the 300 survivors of his expedition safely reached New Spain by boat.

The failure of Coronado and De Soto to find the Seven Cities ended exploration of the region north of Mexico for forty years. Indeed, in 1542, the initial period of Spanish expansion came to a close throughout America. They had sufficient land for agriculture, so, without discovery of precious metals, they had little immediate reason to push farther into North America. During the half century since Columbus sailed west, monumental changes had taken place in the New World. Contact and exchange among Native Americans, Europeans, and Africans created new political and social systems. While the Spanish expected to conquer the people of America and create a society much like the one at home, the results of colonization proved different than planned.

Spanish Patterns of Colonization

As conquest of the Americas progressed, Spain established a colonial government that, in theory, was supposed to be uniform throughout the empire. Its purposes were to convert Native Americans and bring them under control of the Spanish monarchy, and to exploit their labor and the wealth of the New World. In reality, the Spanish were only partly successful in imposing their rule over the Indians. The colonial government was most effective in central Mexico and the Andes, where the Europeans substituted their own imperial rule for that of the Aztecs and Incas. Ordinary families now paid tribute to the Spanish instead of Indian emperors. Native Americans in northern Mexico, Florida, Arizona, New Mexico, and central Chile, who had never been subject to empires, evaded Spanish rule, in some cases for centuries. Many in the fringe areas, such as Apaches, avoided Spanish domination altogether because their bands were highly mobile and autonomous.

The Spanish colonial administration was hierarchical and tied closely to Spain. Sovereignty, or supreme political power, rested in the monarch who had the last word in all decisions. The Spanish, like other Europeans at the time, believed that God vested such power in the Crown. Neither Spanish colonists nor Indians had much say in making and enforcing laws. The right of subjects to appeal official decisions to the king, however, along with delays in decision making caused by distance, corruption, and bureaucratic inefficiency, introduced flexibility into the rigid governmental structure.

Directly below the monarch in colonial matters was the Council of the Indies, located in Spain and composed of men who knew little about conditions in the New World. The council's power over the settlements was all-encompassing: It regulated trade, appointed officials, made laws, and determined who should be allowed to emigrate. The highest officials residing in America were the viceroys, who ruled "in the place of the king." They held court in their palaces with ceremonies and etiquette similar to the king's. In the sixteenth and seventeenth centuries the Spanish empire consisted of two viceroyalties: New Spain, with its capital in Mexico City, and Peru, with its capital in Lima. The viceroyalties were divided into provinces, ruled by governors and *audiencias,* which advised the governors and functioned as courts to settle disputes and judge criminal cases. The audiencias could appeal all decisions to the king, thus limiting the wide powers of the viceroys and governors. So did, at least in theory, the *residencia,* which investigated these officials at the end of their terms and reported any corruption to Spain.

In central Mexico and Peru, the Spanish viceroys, governors, and audiencias took the place of the ruling native elite. At the local level, native leaders often retained their positions or were replaced by Indian rivals to act as intermediaries between the Native Americans and Spanish officials. These native leaders, called *caciques,* headed the Indian towns, collected tribute from every household, and recruited forced laborers upon the demand of the colonial authorities. The caciques received a portion of the tribute they collected.

Spanish Mercantilism

The Crown regulated commerce in the colonial empire through the *Casa de la Contratación,* a trading house founded in 1503 in Seville. Thus Spain elaborated its economic policy of mercantilism, which held that nations had monopolistic rights to trade with their colonies. With tight governmental control, the primary goal of economic activity under mercantilism was to achieve a favorable balance of trade. Colonies were expected to serve as markets for goods from the home country and provide raw materials, gold, and silver to increase its wealth. All merchants desiring to send ships to Spanish America needed permission from the Casa, as did anyone wishing to emigrate. The Casa denied leave to persons of Jewish ancestry, for ex-

ample, though in fact many found passage to America without official permission. To the monarch, a crucial function of the Casa was registration of precious metals, because the king received one-fifth, called the "royal fifth," of all silver and gold. The Spanish monarch claimed sovereignty over all the land and people of his empire. Colonists had to obtain permission to build plantations and mines. In return they paid taxes to the king and, if they found precious metals, the royal fifth.

When Columbus, on his first voyage, obtained gold from the inhabitants of Hispaniola, he raised expectations of great wealth. Beyond the pearl fisheries off the coast of Venezuela and some gold ornaments, however, the explorers at first met disappointment. Even the Aztecs failed to satisfy the Spanish thirst for gold, so most colonists turned to agriculture, especially sugar and livestock production, to make their fortunes. Then, in the 1540s, the Europeans located two immensely rich silver mines, one at Potosí in present-day Bolivia and the other at Zacatecas in Mexico. These mines yielded huge amounts of silver. Between 1500 and 1650 about 181 tons of gold and 16,000 tons of silver officially reached Europe from America; probably much more was smuggled. The gold was more important before the 1540s and the silver after. Production of silver expanded greatly in the 1570s with the introduction of mercury to the refining process.

The Spanish organized their silver trade to outwit privateers of other nations, especially France and England. In 1565, the Spanish founded St. Augustine in Florida as a base to fight the buccaneers and to rescue crews and cargo from ships wrecked in hurricanes and on shoals. Sea captains hugged the Florida coast to help navigate as they caught the Gulf Stream home. St. Augustine, the first permanent European settlement in what is now the United States, also reinforced Spain's claim to North America (as discussed later in this chapter). The Spanish devised a convoy system to protect their fleets. Two convoys left Seville each year carrying goods such as wine, swords, books, oil, grain, clothing, and other luxuries: One left in May headed for Mexico, and the other departed in August for the Isthmus of Panama, from which mules carried the goods to Peru. Both convoys stayed the winter with the intention of meeting in Cuba by early summer so they could return to Spain before the onset of hurricanes. The Panama fleet sometimes ran into trouble when the mule train carrying Potosí silver arrived late. The silver could be delayed by as much as two months in Bolivia because of lack of rain, which was needed to refine the ore.

For the Spanish monarchy, the discovery of rich mines fulfilled their dreams in the New World. The king used the bullion to pay for his European wars—60 percent of the precious metals left Spain immediately. American silver and gold helped to create what has been called a "price revolution," or inflation, throughout Europe. With the immense supply of the metals their value declined and the prices of other goods increased. Merchants depended on the bullion to pay for luxuries from the East. Goods worth about one-half the value of the metals were returned to the colonies in subsequent fleets.

New World Societies

While the Spanish colonists changed America significantly, the new societies were not exactly what they had planned. If some European settlers hoped to duplicate Spanish society and culture, and have millions of Christianized Indian workers do their bidding, they were disappointed. For a number of reasons, including the lack of women among Spanish immigrants, the catastrophic level of native deaths, and the resistance of Indians to conversion, the developing New World societies diverged from what both the Spanish and Native Americans had previously known.

Despite continuing emigration from Spain and rapid demographic decline among the Native Americans, the Spanish colonists remained a small percentage of the population. In 1550 about 100,000 whites lived in the Spanish colonies. By comparison, the population of the Aztec empire before the conquest had been an estimated 25 million; of Peru, 9 million. With the devastating effects of diseases that Europeans brought to the Western Hemisphere, by 1570 the number of natives in central Mexico was only 2.6 million and in Peru 1.3 million.

In conquering the Native Americans, the chief ally of the Spanish was disease, of which smallpox was most lethal. Other Old World killers included measles, chicken pox, influenza, whooping cough, diphtheria, malaria, amoebic dysentery, and bubonic plague. The Indians had no immunity to these diseases because the microbes were new to the Western Hemisphere. Disease spread from one native population to another, infecting the people of North

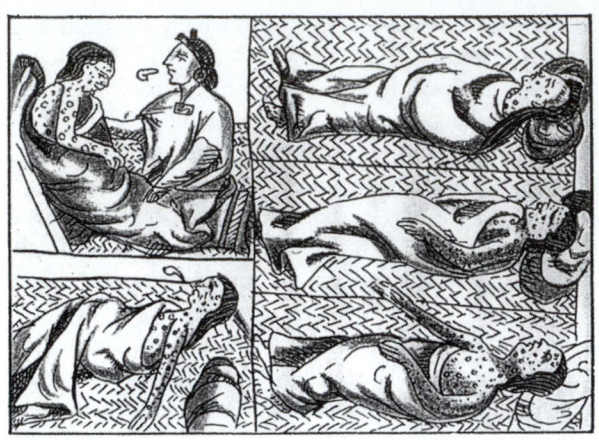

Sixteenth-century drawings of Aztecs suffering from smallpox when the Spanish invaded.

America even before the English and French established colonies along the Atlantic coast. Some regions of the continent seemed uninhabited to European latecomers because of prior contact with disease. As the native population of the Americas declined by an estimated 90 percent, whole tribes were eliminated and others weakened severely.

Nevertheless, most surviving Native Americans resisted assimilation to Spanish culture: They retained their languages, clothing, housing, agricultural methods, and, to a considerable extent, religion. The degree to which they blocked acculturation depended largely on class. The Spanish focused much attention on the caciques and their sons, with whom they interacted more frequently than with ordinary Indians. Many caciques learned to speak Spanish, converted to Christianity, and adopted Hispanic clothing, housing, and furniture. Their sons attended schools where they learned Latin and other advanced subjects. The common Indians avoided some Spanish ways of living and accepted others. They raised and ate chickens, but grew wheat primarily to pay as tribute. They abhorred cattle, which trampled their crops, but groups like the Apache quickly accepted the horse. Natives favored their digging-sticks over the European plow, which would have required the use of draft animals and alteration in the assignment of fields.

The "Columbian exchange," as the transfer of culture among Americans, Europeans, and Africans has been called, did not proceed in just one direction.

While the Europeans introduced deadly diseases, livestock, European wheat, the wheel, firearms, and Christianity to the Indians, the Native Americans in turn provided crops that had a major impact on the growth of world populations. The white potato of South America became a major staple in northern Europe; the sweet potato, cassava, and Indian corn are important throughout the world. Native Americans also helped Europeans adapt to the New World environment, for example, by showing them how to raise Indian corn, catch fish using weirs, and build canoes.

The complexity of interaction between the Spanish and Native Americans can be seen most vividly in religion. The Europeans had a mandate from the pope to convert the "pagans" of America to Christianity. The missionaries believed their goal was just, that it was an act of humanity to introduce the Indians to Catholicism, which they understood to be the only true religion. The Spanish eliminated human sacrifice and destroyed temples and relics, but for the most part avoided forced conversion. At first, the missionaries expected most Native Americans to accept Spanish religious practice without change, as many Indians consented to baptism and voluntarily built churches in every town. But most Indians merged the European faith with rituals and beliefs of their traditional religions, resulting in *syncretism,* the blending of two faiths. For example, some natives added the Christian God to their polytheistic system; others focused on the saints or the Trinity rather than the supreme God. In some churches, idols stood behind Catholic altars. Indians organized *cofradías,* which were societies to raise money for church functions and festivals. The natives controlled the cofradías and at times asserted independence from the Spanish church authority.

The retention of native beliefs and practices disappointed many Spanish priests, who would accept nothing less than complete submission to their form of Catholicism. Nevertheless, missionaries worked for humane treatment of Indians, challenging other Spaniards who denied that natives were human. Colonists often justified enslaving Indians because they had "inferior" cultures and religion. A number of priests, of whom Bartolomé de las Casas is best known, condemned the cruelty and enslavement. In his *Short Account of the Destruction of the Indies,* written in 1542 for the Crown, Las Casas argued for more enlightened policies. Describing atrocities and slaughter in one colony after another, he informed the king of "the excesses which this New World has witnessed,

all of them surpassing anything that men hitherto have imagined even in their wildest dreams."

Forced Labor Systems

Because the Spanish colonists were few in number and had no intention of working in mines or fields, they adopted ways to compel Native Americans to work. When the first explorers on Hispaniola tried to consign the native Arawaks to slavery, most of the Indians died. In 1500, the Spanish Crown ruled that only Indians captured in a "just war" could be forced into perpetual bondage. This judgment had little impact because conquistadores could define as hostile any natives who resisted capture, thus rationalizing slavery. In 1513, the government drew up a document called the *Requerimiento* (or Requirement), which explorers read when they entered an Indian town for the first time. The requerimiento informed the natives that they must accept the sovereignty of the Catholic church and the Spanish monarchy. If they did, they would become Spanish subjects in peace; if they did not, the soldiers would "make war against you . . . take you and your wives and your children and . . . make slaves of them . . . and shall do to you all the harm and damage that we can." By the time the king outlawed most Native American slavery in 1542, the Arawaks of the West Indies had been destroyed. The Spanish had expropriated their lands for sugar plantations, replacing the Indians with enslaved Africans. On the mainland, the Spanish government established two forms of forced Indian labor. In neither type were the natives actually enslaved, but they could be required to perform service. With the *encomienda*, Indians living on specified lands had to pay tribute to individual colonists and sometimes provide labor for which they received minimal wages. At first, the encomienda system included no transfer of land to the colonists, but as the numbers of Native Americans declined and Spanish increased, the colonists took Indian property for farms and ranches. By the seventeenth century, grazing livestock—sheep, horses, mules, goats—replaced Indian farms on vast stretches of Spanish America.

An exterior view of Potosí, the Spanish silver mine in what is now Bolivia. The mine yielded immense wealth, but with a dreadful toll as laborers worked in harsh conditions deep underground.

In 1600, about 1 million Indians survived in central Mexico, down from 25 million a century before. This severe decline was obviously catastrophic for the natives, but also caused problems for the Spanish who depended upon them for food and labor. Thus, the government devised the *repartimiento* system, which rationed labor for both public and private projects. Indians could be forced to work in mines, agriculture, or public works for several weeks, months, or even a year. For example, natives labored for yearlong stints at the Potosí silver mines in Bolivia, where they were paid and provided subsistence, but had to travel long distances from their homes (often for several weeks) to reach the mines. They experienced harsh conditions and, as a result, many died. At Potosí, workers assigned as carriers climbed some 600 feet through tunnels about as wide as a man's body with heavy loads of silver ore on their backs. Those who worked in refining were exposed to mercury poisoning because part of the process involved walking with bare legs through the slurry of mercury, water, and ore. As the Indian population declined, in consequence of disease and these conditions, the Spanish had difficulty in finding enough workers. When they attempted to increase the length and frequency of work periods, Indians resisted the changes, sometimes successfully.

As early as 1502, on West Indies plantations, the Spanish turned to the people of Africa because they knew that Native Americans could not meet their insatiable labor demands. The Spanish took this step easily because they had already purchased Africans from Portuguese traders to work in Spain and on the sugar plantations of the Canary Islands. The government set up a system of licenses, or *asientos,* for merchants to supply certain numbers of slaves. During the sixteenth century, ships transported approximately 75,000 Africans to Spanish America, with perhaps an equal number dying en route, either in Africa or at sea. Compare this number of enslaved Africans with the estimate of 100,000 Spanish colonists in America in 1550. The Spanish imported Africans to work on sugar plantations in the West Indies and coastal areas of the mainland where most Native Americans had died. Severe work regimes and rampant disease also resulted in high death rates among imported blacks. Slavery in New Spain—and indeed in all of the New World colonies—was harsher than what bondpeople had experienced in Africa.

PROTESTANT NORTHERN EUROPEANS CHALLENGE CATHOLIC SPAIN

Until 1560, French and English activity in America remained much more tentative and sporadic than Spain's. While fishing expeditions regularly visited the North American coast, setting up summer camps, trading with Native Americans, and undoubtedly spreading disease, initiatives for permanent colonies gained little support. But significantly, religious and political change in Northern Europe in the sixteenth century provided the impetus to test Spain's domination of the New World. In the age of Reformation and religious wars, America became both a refuge for religious dissidents and a battlefield on which European nations fought for wealth, glory, and national sovereignty.

The Protestant Reformation

When the German priest Martin Luther in 1517 circulated his ninety-five theses against the sale of indulgences, the Church of Rome was the sovereign faith of western and central Europe. Luther challenged the unity of western Christianity because he believed the church was corrupt. The sale of indulgences, which were supposed to reduce the amount of time a deceased person spent in purgatory, was an example of its waywardness. Luther believed that people received salvation as a gift from God in return for faith ("justification by faith") rather than for good works. They could not earn salvation from eternal hellfire by taking pilgrimages, giving money to the church, hearing masses, or going on crusades against the Muslims. Luther also challenged the authority of priests, arguing for a "priesthood of all believers." Christians should seek the word of God in the Bible, which he translated into German to make more available to laypeople. He believed that he had found the way to salvation by reading scripture and suggested that others do the same. Luther contended that the Bible recognized only two sacraments, baptism and communion, not the seven authorized by the Catholic church. He opposed the requirement of celibacy for priests, marrying Katharina von Bora, a former nun.

Luther's teachings led to many divisions in western Christianity, as common people and princes alike adopted his beliefs. In Germany, which was composed of many individual states, some princes accepted Lutheranism and others remained Catholic. They expected their subjects to follow their example. Lutheranism spread through northern Germany and into Scandinavia. Luther inspired other critics of Catholicism to offer variant Protestant doctrines, including the Mennonites, Hutterites, and Swiss Brethren, all called Anabaptists because they required adult baptism as the sign of membership in their community of believers.

The most influential of the systems of belief that Lutheranism spawned was that of John Calvin, a native of France, who attempted to create a model society at Geneva, Switzerland. Followers of Calvin established churches in the Reformed tradition: They were known variously as French Huguenots, English Puritans, Scottish Presbyterians, and Dutch and German Reformed. Calvin agreed with Luther in challenging many Catholic teachings, but went further, arguing that humans were totally depraved and could do nothing to save themselves. This concept of predestination meant that God alone determined who would be saved (the "elect") and who would go to hell. Through communion with God, the elect learned that they were saved; they strove to live blamelessly to reflect their status.

Calvin and his followers convinced the city council and churches of Geneva to adopt many Reformed doctrines, stripping the churches of decoration, images, and colorful rituals. The Bible, as interpreted by Calvin, became the basis for law. The civil government punished moral offenders and nonbelievers identified by the church elders. The Calvinists disciplined individuals for dancing, charging high medical fees, wearing fancy clothes, and insubordination. They forced one man to walk through the city wearing only a shirt because he criticized Calvin, and burned another at the stake for heresy. While Calvin failed to obtain all of his demands from the Geneva council, he came close to establishing a theocracy, in which the church fathers ruled in the name of God. His Puritan successors in New England in the next century found much to emulate in Calvin's Geneva.

Protestant ideas spread to France and England quickly. In France, Calvin attracted many adherents, called Huguenots, among the nobles and prosperous commoners, though relatively few peasants adopted the faith. The French monarchy considered Protestants a threat to its monopoly of power and the established Catholic church. Even after the Edict of Nantes of 1598, which offered freedom to worship, Huguenots faced serious discrimination.

In England, years before Luther, opposition had existed to the Catholic hierarchy, its taxes, monasteries, and the use of images in church. Thus Henry VIII found sympathy for his break with Rome when the pope refused to allow an annulment of his marriage to Catherine of Aragon. Henry wanted to marry Anne Boleyn, who he hoped would provide a male heir. Parliament passed the Act of Supremacy (1534), mandating that the king be "taken, accepted, and reputed the only supreme head on earth of the Church of England." The Crown dissolved the monasteries and confiscated their property. Henry was no Lutheran, however, for the Six Articles (1539) that formed the theological basis of Anglicanism confirmed Catholic beliefs on priestly celibacy, the mass, confession, and sacraments. But because the Six Articles were ambiguous on many points, the Church of England from its inception allowed a fairly wide range of doctrine. In 1552, the revised Anglican prayer book incorporated many Protestant beliefs. Soon after, Henry's daughter Mary I attempted to force England back to the Church of Rome. Her persecution of Protestants earned her the name "Bloody Mary"; her marriage to the staunch Catholic Philip II of Spain inspired an English nationalism that fused loyalty to church and state. When Mary died in 1558, her half-sister, Elizabeth I, became queen, ending the immediate threat that England would return to Catholicism. The new English monarch and a large proportion of her subjects identified Spain as a threat to their national church, now Protestant, and their independence as a nation.

Under Elizabeth, the English confronted Spain on a number of fronts, leading to a showdown against invasion in 1588. In the religious struggles of the late sixteenth century, England became a dominant Protestant power, supported the Dutch revolt against Philip II, and challenged Spain's monopolistic claims to the New World. Though pragmatic and more interested in power than theology, Elizabeth confirmed England's break with the pope and approved earlier moderate Protestant reforms. The Act of Uniformity (1559) required adherence to the Anglican Book of Prayer. The queen suppressed resistance from both Calvinists, who

Queen Elizabeth I at the time of England's defeat of the Spanish Armada. With the globe, the artist suggests Elizabeth's interest in exploration, resting her hand on North America.

The Dutch rebelled against this persecution, foreign control, and high taxes. In 1581, the northern part of the Netherlands, composed of seven provinces, including Holland, declared its independence as the United Provinces. The southern region, called the Spanish Netherlands (now Belgium), remained under Philip's control. When Elizabeth sent aid to the United Provinces in 1585, she in effect declared a war on Spain that lasted until her death in 1603. The most important battle occurred in 1588, when Philip sent his mighty Armada of 130 ships and 30,000 men to invade England. The English defeated the Armada, despite the heavy odds against them, thus preserving their national sovereignty and religion.

French Huguenots and English Sea Dogs

In France, in the mid-sixteenth century, persecution led some Protestant Huguenots to look to America as a refuge, as well as a source of wealth. Though the French monarchy had not followed up Jacques Cartier's unsuccessful effort to colonize Canada, in 1555, a group of wealthy Frenchmen sent Huguenot settlers to Brazil. When disputes occurred among the colonists, some returned to France; the Portuguese, who claimed Brazil, killed or enslaved the majority who remained. In 1562, Huguenots tried again, establishing Charlesfort on the South Carolina coast, in part to attack the Spanish silver fleet as it headed home. When the Spaniards moved against the small French colony in 1564, they found it already abandoned. But the Huguenots attempted another settlement that year, this one at Fort Caroline on the St. Johns River in northern Florida. The Spanish quickly destroyed it, murdering most of the settlers and establishing their own outpost at St. Augustine. They sent missionaries as far north as the Chesapeake Bay, but withdrew to Florida in the face of strong resistance from Native Americans.

The English "sea dogs," the adventurers who propelled their nation into competition for America and preyed on Spanish treasure ships, learned a great deal about the New World from the Huguenots. With Elizabeth I's ascension to the throne in 1558, seafarers and colonizers like John Hawkins, Francis Drake, Humphrey Gilbert, and Walter Raleigh gained favor and support. Hawkins visited Fort Caroline in 1565, before the Spanish destroyed it; other Englishmen gained knowledge of the North American coast from

wanted further reforms, and the supporters of Rome. She withstood opposition from Catholics most firmly. Some Catholics turned to Elizabeth's cousin, Mary, Queen of Scots, a Roman Catholic and heir to the English throne. In 1587, after several unsuccessful plots on Elizabeth's life, Mary was tried as a conspirator and beheaded.

One of Mary, Queen of Scot's most fervent supporters was Spain's Philip II, who considered himself the champion of Catholicism. Throughout Europe he strove to wipe out the Protestant heresy. He considered Elizabeth a dangerous foe, not least for her support of the revolt in the Netherlands, a part of his vast domains. When many Dutch adopted Calvinism, Philip retaliated with his Inquisition, executing thousands.

the French. The English also acquired a taste for conquest in Ireland, where their brutal subjugation of the native Irish presaged later actions against the Indians.

The English took their time before attempting an American colony. As the slaughter of Fort Caroline Huguenots made clear, the Spanish remained a serious threat. Thus for two decades, until the 1580s, English adventurers sought wealth by sea—by interloping in the slave trade and as privateers. In 1562, the sea captain John Hawkins violated Spanish mercantilist regulations by taking 300 Africans to Hispaniola without a license. The local Spanish officials, contrary to government policy, allowed him to exchange the slaves for sugar and hides because the colony needed labor. Hawkins made a second voyage, earning another handsome profit, this time mostly in silver. When the Spanish authorities protested, Elizabeth forbade further expeditions, but reversed her decision in 1567, with dire results. On his third voyage, Hawkins was conducting business in the harbor of San Juan de Ulúa, Mexico, when the annual fleet arrived from Spain several weeks early, destroying three of his ships. Hawkins and his cousin Francis Drake escaped with two badly damaged vessels; they returned to England, their crews nearly starved.

Hawkins stopped interloping in Spanish trade, but other English privateers followed, preying on Spanish ships and settlements. The most famous was Francis Drake, who in 1572, with the help of Native Americans and runaway African slaves, intercepted the mule train carrying Potosí silver across Panama. Five years later he set out to circumnavigate the globe. Following Magellan's route through the straits, he attacked Spanish towns along the Pacific coast, captured Peruvian silver, explored the North American coast for evidence of a northwest passage, and returned to England in 1580 by way of Asia and the Cape of Good Hope. Six years later, when England and Spain were formally at war, Drake attacked Spanish ports in America, including St. Augustine in Florida, which he looted and burned.

While Drake was making his fortune, and that of his queen, through piracy, other Elizabethan sea dogs hoped to make their mark by starting colonies. With experience in Ireland, they decided to ignore Spain's claim to North America. On the basis of Cabot's voyage of 1497, Elizabeth granted a charter to Humphrey Gilbert, who sailed to Newfoundland in 1583. He assumed ownership for the English Crown, collecting dues from fishermen. Nothing came of Gilbert's colony, however, as he was lost at sea on his return to England.

Walter Raleigh then attempted a settlement farther south, in the land named for the "virgin" Queen Elizabeth. This effort ended tragically. In 1585, after looting in the Spanish West Indies along the way, the first group of settlers arrived at Roanoke Island in a part of Virginia that later became North Carolina. Their goals were to solidify England's claims in North America and search for silver and gold. After their ships returned home leaving them with short supplies, the colonists tried to force neighboring Indians to provide food. Quickly a pattern of hostility emerged between the English and Native Americans. Francis Drake saved the Roanoke colonists from starvation, carrying them home in 1586. A year later, Raleigh sent out another expedition which also suffered from lack of provisions. This time the war with Spain prevented ships from returning to Roanoke until 1590, when all that was left of the colony was the word "Croatoan" carved on a tree. The colonists may have moved to nearby Croatoan Island, or farther inland to live with Native Americans, but the fate of the "Lost Colony" has never been determined. The most enduring legacy of Roanoke was the introduction of tobacco and the potato in Ireland and England. The English did not colonize successfully in North America until the founding of Jamestown in 1607.

CONCLUSION

By 1590, the Spanish had created an empire that extended from South America through the West Indies and Mexico. They funded their European wars to extinguish Protestantism with American silver and gold. The Portuguese, united under the Spanish Crown in 1580, had developed the Atlantic slave trading system that sent enslaved Africans to Brazil and New Spain.

The irony of colonization in America was that European nations at war over religion and national influence in the Old World emulated one another in the New. The Spanish and Portuguese provided the model for later colonizers in expropriating land and labor from Indians and Africans. With superior weaponry and the will to conquer, Europeans justified their behavior toward the people of America and Africa by emphasizing religious and cultural differences,

ignoring much that they had in common. While European nations organized colonization in various ways, all sought mercantilistic ends. In the early seventeenth century, when the English, French, and Dutch settled in North America, their goals were very similar to those of Spain. They hoped to locate precious metals, find the elusive northwest passage, exploit Indian labor, extend Christianity to America, and expand the power of the state.

RECOMMENDED READINGS

Bethell, Leslie, ed. *Colonial Spanish America* (1987). Essays provide useful syntheses on the development of the Spanish colonies.

Casas, Bartolomé de las. *A Short Account of the Destruction of the Indies.* Ed. and trans., Nigel Griffin (1992). A priest's sharp denunciation of Spanish colonization, written in 1542.

Davidson, Basil. *The Search for Africa: History, Culture, Politics* (1994). A recent, readable history by a veteran historian of the continent.

Kupperman, Karen Ordahl. *Roanoke: The Abandoned Colony* (1984). A lively account of the early English attempt to settle in North America.

Meinig, D. W. *The Shaping of America: A Geographical Perspective on 500 Years of History, Vol. 1: Atlantic America, 1492–1800* (1986). Provides a broad cultural view of European expansion.

Nash, Gary B. *Red, White, and Black: The Peoples of Early North America,* 3d ed. (1992). An excellent introduction to the meeting of cultures in the New World.

Parry, J. H. *The Establishment of the European Hegemony, 1415–1715: Trade and Exploration in the Age of the Renaissance,* 3d ed. (1966). A short, interesting introduction to the European explorations.

Quinn, David B. *North America from Earliest Discovery to First Settlements: The Norse Voyages to 1612* (1977). A comprehensive source on early European explorations.

Weber, David J. *The Spanish Frontier in North America* (1992). The best synthesis on Spanish exploration and colonization north of Mexico.

Native American Cultures Before 1492
Dowd, Gregory Evans. *A Spirited Resistance: The North American Indian Struggle for Unity, 1745–1815* (1992).

Driver, Harold E. *Indians of North America,* 2d ed. (1969).

Fagan, Brian M. *Kingdoms of Gold, Kingdoms of Jade: The Americas Before Columbus* (1991).

Josephy, Alvin M., Jr. *America in 1492: The World of the Indian Peoples Before the Arrival of Columbus* (1991).

Josephy, Alvin M., Jr. *500 Nations: An Illustrated History of North American Indians* (1994).

Kehoe, Alice B. *North American Indians: A Comprehensive Account* (1981).

Ortiz, Alfonso, ed. *Handbook of North American Indians,* vols. 9, 10: *The Southwest* (1979, 1983).

Early Contact Between Native Americans and Europeans
Crosby, Alfred W., Jr. *The Columbian Exchange: Biological and Cultural Consequences of 1492* (1972).

Kupperman, Karen Ordahl. *Settling with the Indians: The Meeting of English and Indian Cultures in America, 1580–1640* (1980).

Salisbury, Neal. *Manitou and Providence: Indians, Europeans, and the Making of New England, 1500–1643* (1982).

Seed, Patricia. *Ceremonies of Possession in Europe's Conquest of the New World, 1492–1640* (1995).

Thornton, Russell. *American Indian Holocaust and Survival: A Population History Since 1492* (1987).

Africa and the Atlantic Slave Trade
Curtin, Philip D. *The Atlantic Slave Trade: A Census* (1969).

Curtin, Philip D. *The Rise and Fall of the Plantation Complex: Essays in Atlantic History* (1990).

Davidson, Basil. *The African Slave Trade: Precolonial History, 1450–1850,* rev. ed. (1980).

Fage, J. D. *A History of West Africa: An Introductory Survey,* 4th ed. (1969).

Lovejoy, Paul E., "The Volume of the Atlantic Slave Trade: A Synthesis." *Journal of African History* 23 (1982): 473–501.

Miller, Joseph C. *The Way of Death: Merchant Capitalism and the Angolan Slave Trade, 1730–1830* (1988).

Oliver, Roland, ed. *The Cambridge History of Africa, Vol. 3: From c. 1050 to c. 1600* (1977).

Raboteau, Albert J. *Slave Religion: The "Invisible Institution" in the Antebellum South* (1978).

Solow, Barbara L., ed. *Slavery and the Rise of the Atlantic System* (1991).

Thornton, John. *Africa and Africans in the Making of the Atlantic World, 1400–1680* (1992).

European Explorations
Cipolla, Carlo M. *Guns, Sails, and Empires: Technological Innovation and the Early Phases of European Expansion, 1400–1700* (1965).

Dunn, Oliver, and Kelley, James E., Jr., eds. *The Diario of Christopher Columbus's First Voyage to America, 1492–1493* (1989).

Favata, Martin A., and Fernández, José B., trans. *The Account: Álvar Núñez Cabeza de Vaca's Relación* (1993).

Parry, J. H. *The Age of Reconnaissance* (1963).

Phillips, William D., Jr., and Phillips, Carla Rahn. *The Worlds of Christopher Columbus* (1992).

Scammell, G. V. *The First Imperial Age: European Overseas Expansion, c. 1400–1715* (1989).

Spanish Empire

Bethell, Leslie, ed., *The Cambridge History of Latin America,* vols. 1 and 2 (1984).

Burkholder, Mark A., and Johnson, Lyman L. *Colonial Latin America* (1990).

Elliott, J. H. *Imperial Spain, 1469–1716* (1963).

Gibson, Charles. *Spain in America* (1966).

Lockhart, James, and Schwartz, Stuart B. *Early Latin America: A Short History of Colonial Spanish America and Brazil* (1983).

Lynch, John. *Spain Under the Hapsburgs,* 2 vols. (1964, 1969).

McAlister, Lyle N. *Spain and Portugal in the New World, 1492–1700* (1984).

Pagden, Anthony. *Lords of All the World: Ideologies of Empire in Spain, Britain and France c. 1500–c. 1800* (1995).

Parry, J. H. *The Spanish Seaborne Empire* (1966).

Super, John C. *Food, Conquest, and Colonization in Sixteenth-Century Spanish America* (1988).

ARRIVAL OF A SPANISH MISSIONARY

Navajo wall art in the Canyon del Muerto, Arizona, showing the arrival of a Spanish missionary and soldiers in the late sixteenth or early seventeenth century.

Chapter 2

COLONIZATION OF NORTH AMERICA, 1590–1675

In 1590, THE only permanent European settlement in what is now the United States was St. Augustine, the struggling Spanish town in Florida that the English privateer Francis Drake had burned four years earlier. Spain was much more concerned with its silver mines and West Indies plantations than in colonizing along the Atlantic coast, yet wanted to prevent intrusion by other nations, for good reason. In the late sixteenth century, buccaneers from France and England thought the best way to get rich was by looting the Spanish silver fleet and ports. Their countrymen had tried to settle in North America and find a northwest route to Asia without success.

By 1675, however, the major European nations had planted colonies in America. The West Indies became a magnet, with colonizers vying for tiny islands as sugar boomed. In North America, the Spanish held Florida and New Mexico, the French occupied Canada, and the English had a string of settlements along the Atlantic coast. Unlike the highly centralized Spanish empire, English colonization proceeded with little regulation from the Crown, resulting in a variety of social, economic, and political structures. The English government even helped to create the diversity by granting different kinds of charters to individuals and groups.

The expansion of European settlement, particularly in the Chesapeake Bay area and New England,

changed the countryside forever. Cheap, even free land and developing commerce offered opportunity to men and women of all economic classes who were willing to risk their lives by crossing the Atlantic. Their farms eliminated Indian hunting lands, altering the ecological balance of plants and animals. Though many Native Americans resisted the European invasions, disease seriously undermined their power, modifying and sometimes destroying their cultures. The fur trade also changed the cultural values of many Indians, drawing them into Atlantic commerce and tempting them to overhunt. For Native Americans from New Mexico to Canada, European colonization was a disaster.

THE SPANISH IN NORTH AMERICA

After Coronado and De Soto in the early 1540s failed to locate cities of gold, Spain abandoned further exploration in North America. Then, Francis Drake's voyage along the Pacific coast during his circumnavigation of the earth in 1577–1580 raised alarms of foreign interest in the region north of Mexico. In 1581, the viceroy of New Spain gave Franciscan priests permission to establish missions among the Pueblo

CHRONOLOGY

1598 Spanish expedition into New Mexico	**1625** Charles I becomes king of England
1599 Destruction of Ácoma by the Spanish	**1630** Massachusetts Bay Colony founded by Puritans
1603 James I takes the English throne	**1634** The *Ark* and the *Dove* arrive in Maryland
1605 French establish Port Royal	**1636** Founding of Connecticut and Rhode Island
1607 English found colony at Jamestown	**1637** Massachusetts and Connecticut troops destroy the Pequots
1608 French establish Quebec	Anne Hutchinson is tried for heresy
1609 Henry Hudson explores for the Dutch East India Company	**1642–1648** English Civil War
1609–1614 Anglo-Powhatan War in Virginia	**1649** Charles I of England is beheaded
1616–1618 Plague epidemic decimates eastern New England natives	**1651** English Parliament passes first Navigation Act
1619 Africans arrive in Virginia	**1660** Charles II of England becomes king
Virginia Company establishes a representative assembly	**1663** Carolina proprietors receive charter
1620 Separatists found the Plymouth colony	**1664** English forces conquer New Netherland; New York and New Jersey are founded
1622 Native Americans attack the Virginia colony	**1673** Dutch recapture New York, then return the colony to England with the Treaty of Westminster (1674)
1624 Virginia Company loses charter; Virginia becomes a royal colony	
Dutch West India Company establishes New Netherland	

Indians of the Rio Grande Valley. The friars named the area San Felipe del Nuevo México, sending reports to the viceroy of legendary riches. The missionaries described the Pueblos, who raised corn and lived in towns with apartment-style houses, as friendly and numerous: Thousands could be made Christian and forced to labor for Hispanic colonists. But by the time a party arrived in 1582 to escort the Franciscans back to Mexico, the missionaries had been killed by the Native Americans they sought to convert and control.

Settlement of New Mexico

Despite this setback, Spaniards remained interested in the region. Conquistadores needed permission from

the Crown to invade new lands, however, for the king had issued Orders for New Discoveries (1573), which more strictly regulated colonization, in part to protect Native Americans from the atrocities Bartolomé de las Casas had described decades earlier. When one would-be conqueror led an illegal expedition into New Mexico in 1590, he was arrested and returned to Mexico City in chains.

The Spanish government delayed appointing a governor of New Mexico until 1595, when the viceroy authorized Juan de Oñate to undertake settlement with his own funds. Oñate, a native of Mexico whose father had helped discover the Zacatecas silver mines, inherited great wealth and obtained even more by marrying Isabel Tolosa Cortés Moctezuma, a descendant of both Cortés and the Aztec emperor. The expedition proved

expensive as delays increased costs. Finally, in 1598, 129 soldiers, their families, servants, and slaves, eighty-three baggage wagons, and 7,000 head of livestock headed north, all subsidized by Governor Oñate. Ten Franciscan missionaries accompanied the colonists. Oñate expected his investment to yield an empire. As he wrote King Philip II, "I shall give your majesty a new world, greater than New Spain." The governor envisioned mines of silver and gold and a water passage through the continent. He believed his province would extend from the Atlantic to the Pacific.

Upon arrival in New Mexico, Oñate declared Spanish sovereignty over Pueblo lands. In a ritual complete with trumpets and High Mass, he promised peace and prosperity to those who cooperated. According to the Spanish, the Pueblos acquiesced "of their own accord": Previous experience with Coronado and more recent explorers probably convinced them they had little choice. The Franciscans founded missions in the largest pueblos and supervised construction of a church in the Tewa pueblo, Yungé, which the Spanish designated as their capital, San Gabriel.

For some months, the Spanish and the Indians coexisted without serious incident. The colonists moved into the Pueblos' apartments in Yungé, now San Gabriel, forcing the inhabitants to depart. Soon the Indians tired of providing food, which they had intended as gifts but the Spanish considered tribute. The soldiers resorted to murder and rape to obtain supplies. The crisis came in December 1598, when a Spanish troop demanded provisions from the people of Ácoma, a pueblo high atop a mesa west of the Rio Grande. One of Coronado's party had described Ácoma as "the greatest stronghold ever seen in the world." The Pueblos refused to give flour to the soldiers and killed eleven men, including Oñate's nephew, when they attempted to take the food by force. Oñate swiftly punished the village so others would not join in revolt. His small army laid siege to Ácoma with several cannon; men and women defended the town with arrows and stones. The Spanish killed approximately 500 men and 300 women and children; they captured the survivors, including eighty men and 500 women and children. The town was leveled. Everyone was sentenced to servitude, and each man over age twenty-five had one foot cut off. The Ácomas would not rebuild their town until the late 1640s.

With this harsh action, Oñate only temporarily prevented further resistance among the Pueblos, for another town rebelled the following year. The colonists also complained of food shortages and the governor's mismanagement; many returned to Mexico.

The Pueblo stronghold at Ácoma, which revolted against the Spanish in 1598.

Oñate's long absences from the capital to explore for gold and silver—unsuccessfully—added to this discontent. The Franciscans charged that his cruelty to the Indians made conversion difficult. Bankrupt, Oñate was removed as governor, tried, and found guilty of mistreating the Native Americans and some of his settlers. He was banished from New Mexico, but renewed his wealth at the Zacatecas mines, sailed to Spain, where he received a knighthood and position as the Crown's chief inspector of mines.

After Juan de Oñate's departure, New Mexico became a royal province, but developed slowly. Pedro de Peralta, the next governor, established a new capital at Santa Fe in 1610. While the Franciscans maintained their missions among the Pueblos, as late as 1670 only 2,800 Spanish colonists lived in the Rio Grande valley. The Hispanics lived on farms and ranches along the river, exploiting the Pueblos' labor through the encomienda system (see Chapter 1) to produce hides, blankets, sheep, wool, and pinenuts for sale in Mexico.

Spanish Missions in New Mexico and Florida

The Franciscan missionaries, who assumed a major role in colonizing the Spanish borderlands during the seventeenth century, were members of the Catholic religious order that Francis Bernardone of Assisi had founded (in Italy) in 1209. The friars vowed not to engage in sexual relations or acquire property, living on the gifts of others. Unlike other religious brotherhoods, which remained in seclusion, the Franciscans operated in the world among ordinary Christians; with exploration of the Americas, they sought to convert a hemisphere, even if that meant martyrdom by hostile Indians. The Orders for New Discoveries of 1573 gave primary responsibility to the monks for "pacifying" the Indians of New Mexico and Florida.

During the first part of the seventeenth century, many Pueblos of New Mexico seemed to accept the Franciscans' message. The friars arrived in villages offering gifts of food, metal tools, beads, and clothing. Placing some confidence in the priests, the natives agreed to build convents and churches, using their traditional methods of construction. Women built the walls, while men did carpentry. The priests decorated the sanctuaries with paintings, statues, and silver chalices, attempting to capture the Indians' devotion through sacred rituals and music. The Franciscans created missions by imposing their influence over existing Indian towns, backed by threat of military force. In both New Mexico and Florida, the missionaries were most successful among Native Americans who lived in villages before contact. In New Mexico, the Spanish started more than fifty churches by 1629; in Florida, missions extended west from St. Augustine to the Gulf Coast and north into Georgia (or Guale, as the region was called).

The Native Americans who came under Spanish control could, in theory, choose whether or not to accept Christian baptism, but all recognized that soldiers supported the priests. The Franciscans expected the natives to learn the catechism and enough of the Castilian (Spanish) language to communicate, and to adopt European dress, food, and farming methods. The friars understood conversion to mean acceptance of Spanish customs as well as Christianity. Many Indians embraced Catholicism—the Franciscans claimed that 35,000 Pueblos had accepted baptism by 1626—but in doing so, modified the religion. The Indians held on to ancient rituals and beliefs despite the friars' efforts to eradicate them. Even in the twentieth century, the Pueblos preserved both native and Catholic religious practices. Christian Indians in Florida continued to play a ball game during the 1600s until the missionaries realized it had religious significance and abolished the game, calling the pole used as a target, the "ballpost of the devil."

In merging Indian gods with the Christian trinity and adding Catholic holidays to native celebrations, Native Americans altered Spanish Catholicism. With the "Lady in Blue," they created a religious tradition that both the Indians and Spaniards accepted. In the 1620s, Plains Indians reported that a nun appeared to them, telling them in their language to become Christians. Though the woman remained invisible to the missionaries, they believed the stories, which persisted for generations. On a trip to Spain, one priest discovered that a Franciscan nun, María de Jesús de Agreda, claimed to have made flights to America with the help of angels, though she later denied most of her tale. Despite this denial, María de Agreda's initial claims and the Indians' visions together created the resilient legend of the Lady in Blue.

THE ENGLISH INVADE VIRGINIA

New Mexico and Florida remained marginal outposts in the Spanish empire, places where small Hispanic populations dominated some Indians through forced labor and missions. Spanish control was tenuous because their military forces were small and cultural influence weak. In the aftermath of the Spanish Armada's failure to conquer England, Philip II's government proved incapable of preventing other European nations from settling in North America, albeit well north of St. Augustine. During the first decade of the seventeenth century, the English, French, and Dutch stepped up activity; they sent expeditions to fish, search for a northern passage to the East, trade for furs, and establish colonies.

English Context of Colonization

Seventeenth-century England was an intensely hierarchical society, in which the king claimed divine right, or God-given authority, and the nobility and gentry dominated Parliament. But it was a society undergoing turmoil and change. Elizabeth I's successor was her cousin, James I, who governed from 1603 until 1625, when he died and his son, Charles I, took the throne. Both James and Charles had strife-torn reigns marked by power struggles with Parliament, culminating in Charles's loss of the English Civil War and his beheading in 1649. Parliament was composed of two houses: the House of Lords, made up of nobles and high church officials; and the House of Commons, who were elected representatives from the counties and boroughs. The Commons normally comprised country gentry, government officials, and lawyers; the electorate included male landowners, or an estimated 15 to 30 percent of all Englishmen. By imposing levies without Parliament's consent, James I and Charles I challenged its prerogative to approve or reject new taxes. For their part, the legislators tried to whittle away at royal powers, claiming the right to initiate legislation rather than wait for the king and his councilors to submit bills for consideration. The fundamental issue concerning how the powers of the king versus property holders, as represented in Parliament, should

James I of England, who chartered the Virginia and Plymouth companies to colonize North America. Portrait by Daniel Mytens, 1621.

be balanced remained unsettled until the Glorious Revolution of 1688.

Economic developments loosened English society, giving individuals greater opportunity to change from one social class or occupation to another, though traditional class distinctions remained in place. Many found it necessary to move geographically, as the woolen industry expanded in England, causing landowners to raise more sheep to meet the demand for wool. In what has been called the "enclosure movement," landlords ended leases for tenant farmers living on their lands, confiscating common fields that peasant communities had shared for grazing their livestock and raising crops. The landowners enclosed the commons with fences and hedges. In 1500, peasants had

farmed 70 percent of arable land in England, but by 1650, they farmed only 50 percent. Thus many tenants were forced from the land. Some went to London, where the population expanded from 55,000 in 1520 to 475,000 in 1670. Others were among the colonists who signed for America.

A developing economy meant dislocation and uncertainty for poor English tenants; it spelled opportunity for merchants. They found it first in the woolen trade with Antwerp, in what is now Belgium. When this trade declined after 1550, English merchants looked for alternative investments, which they found as war with Spain brought demand for coal, lead, glass, ships, salt, iron, and steel. Investors formed joint-stock companies to explore trade routes, establish new markets, and attract settlers to Ireland. The companies obtained capital by selling stocks, which were expected to earn a profit within a few years. These investments were risky, for shareholders were liable for all company debts. The stocks could also be im-

mensely profitable, as in the case of Francis Drake's circumnavigation of the globe, which brought a 4,600 percent profit. Other joint-stock ventures included the Guinea, Muscovy, and East India companies, created respectively to trade with Africa, Russia, and Asia.

Joint-stock companies also provided capital for the first permanent English colonies in America, at Jamestown, Plymouth, and Massachusetts Bay. Unlike the Spanish monarchy, the English Crown had little role in funding, or even governing, its first New World settlements. In 1606, James I granted a charter to the Virginia Company with rights to settle colonies in North America. The Virginia Company included two groups, one in London and the other in Plymouth, in the west of England. The groups received overlapping claims, with the Plymouth group obtaining lands from what is now Maine to Virginia and the London group receiving Connecticut to the Carolinas. Either could settle in the overlapping area, but initial colonies had to be at least one hundred miles apart.

London in 1616, a magnet for people from rural England. London Bridge, in the center right, crosses the Thames River.

In this conjectural view of Jamestown c. 1614, the fortified wall shows concerns for defense against the Spanish and the Powhatan confederacy.

Jamestown

In 1607, the Virginia Company of London funded the first permanent English colony at Jamestown, retaining control until the Crown revoked its charter in 1624. When the first 104 settlers arrived in Virginia in May 1607, they had endured a long winter crossing. The native inhabitants watched the invaders select a site on the James River, chosen for safety from Spanish attack, but—unknown to the English—next to malarial swamps. The Native Americans called their territory Tsenacommacah, or "densely inhabited land." They were Algonquian-speaking Indians; most belonged to a confederacy that Powhatan, head sachem of the Pamunkey tribe, had forged in eastern Virginia. Before the arrival of the English, the chief unifying force among the bands of the Powhatan confederacy was the threat from powerful enemies, the Manahoacs and the Monacans, who controlled lands to the west,

in the Virginia piedmont. The leaders of tribes subject to Powhatan were supposed to follow his direction, pay tribute, and provide military assistance, but they sometimes refused.

One of Powhatan's brothers, in line for the head sachem's position, was Opechancanough, described as having "large Stature, noble Presence, and extraordinary Parts" and "perfectly skill'd in the Art of Governing." Historical evidence suggests that Opechancanough was born around 1544 and, at about age sixteen, was taken by a Spanish ship to Spain, where he received instruction in the Castilian language and Christianity. He adopted the name Don Luis de Velasco, after the viceroy of New Spain. The new Don Luis stayed with the Spanish, in Spain and America, until 1570, when he accompanied several missionaries to his homeland on Chesapeake Bay. He broke with the priests when they criticized him for taking several wives, and murdered them the next year. If

Opechancanough and Don Luis were the same man, as seems likely, he was well prepared with knowledge of the Europeans when the Jamestown settlers arrived.

The English colony's first decade was a struggle, as the Virginia Company and the settlers made one mistake after another. From the outset, the company ran Virginia as a business enterprise, keeping control of government, land, and trade. Settlers were company employees, not landholders. To satisfy investors, the company instructed the colonists to search for gold and silver mines, find a passage to Asia, and establish industries and trade that would offer handsome returns. The company had chosen individuals for these purposes, not people who were willing to grow crops. Among the first Jamestown settlers were many gentlemen, who by definition avoided manual labor. They were adventurers who expected to strike it rich and return to England. The rest of the first colonists, who were nearly all men, included the gentlemen's personal servants, a jeweler, goldsmith, perfumer, carpenters, blacksmiths, and some laborers. No one described himself as a farmer.

When the colonists failed to locate mines or a passage to the East, their lives became aimless. Rather than plant crops or even hunt and fish in their bountiful environment, they expected the Virginia Company and neighboring Indians to provide food. When sufficient provisions failed to arrive, the settlers starved. One of the leaders, a young officer named John Smith, took control in 1608, stabilizing the colony briefly by making everyone work. When criticism of his strict discipline reached company officials the next year, they removed him from command. During the particularly bitter winter of 1609–1610, one man killed his pregnant wife and chopped her up, planning to eat her body. Others dug up graves to eat the corpses. By spring 1610, only sixty colonists remained of at least 600 who had come to Jamestown in three years. Though some had returned to England or escaped to live with the Indians, the majority died of starvation and disease, most likely dysentery and malaria. The death rate during these early years is estimated at about 50 percent.

The Virginia Company took several steps to make its venture profitable. It continued to send settlers and supplies, though the former died at a high rate and the latter were insufficient. In 1609, without gold mines or a trade route to Asia, the Virginia Company hoped to salvage its investment by exploiting the land. It recognized that profits had to come from a staple crop. To recruit farmers, the company offered each emigrant one share of stock and a parcel of land after seven years of service. The settlers remained employees of the company in the meantime, with assigned tasks and the obligation to buy all supplies and ship all products through the company store.

Still, the Jamestown settlers lacked discipline and refused to work. When Sir Thomas Dale arrived as governor in May 1611, he found nothing but a few gardens planted and the inhabitants at "their daily and usual work, bowling in the streets." Thus, he established his *Laws Divine, Morall and Martiall*, which were mostly martial. The men received military ranks, were divided into work gangs, and proceeded from home to work—and to church twice daily—at the beat of a drum. Laws prescribed death for a variety of crimes, including rape, adultery, theft, lying, slander against the company, blasphemy, killing any domestic animal including a chicken without permission, and stealing an ear of corn. For taking two or three pints of oatmeal, one man had a large needle thrust through his tongue, then was chained to a tree until he starved. For the first offense of failing to work regular hours, an idler was tied neck to heels all night. The punishment for a second offense was whipping and for a third offense, death. Though the required hours of work were reasonable—five to eight hours per day in the summer and three to six in the winter—the punishments specified in "Dale's Laws" became a scandal in England, discouraging prospective emigrants. In the words of John Smith, "no man will go from [England] to have less liberty there."

The Struggle for Virginia

In searching for gold and silver, the Jamestown adventurers had imitated Spain. They expected to put the Indians to work in mines and fields, as in Mexico, but the inhabitants proved too few in number for an adequate workforce, yet too powerful for the wretched gang of English settlers to conquer. During the early years at Jamestown, the English seemed irrational in their dealings with the Native Americans. To many colonists, despite their desperate need for provisions, the natives were barbarians with savage customs and a heathen religion. While some settlers attempted to trade for food, others burned Indian villages and crops. They stole corn and killed.

In 1608–1609, Captain John Smith tried to force the sachems to provide food. His life had been spared by the Indians several times, including one occasion

C. Smith taketh the King, of Pamavnkee prisoner. -1608.

John Smith threatening Opechancanough in 1608, with images in the background of skirmishes between colonists and Indians that took place at other times, not on this occasion. From Smith's Generall Historie of Virginia.

when Powhatan's daughter Pocahontas intervened on his behalf. Nevertheless, he kidnapped two men, obligating Opechancanough to beg for their release. Next, he entered the Pamunkey village with soldiers demanding food, which the Indians refused to give, and again humiliated the tall sachem: In Smith's words, he did "take this murdering Opechancanough . . . by the long lock of his head; and with my pistol at his breast, I led him [out of his house] amongst his greatest forces, and before we parted made him [agree to] fill our bark with twenty tuns of corn." Otherwise, Smith warned, he would load the ship with their "dead carkases."

Opechancanough probably never forgot this scene. Between 1609 and 1614, full-scale war existed between the Virginia colonists and the Powhatan confederacy. The English, who received reinforcements of experienced soldiers and arms from the Virginia Company, defeated Powhatan, taking control of the

James River. Powhatan faced another disappointment when Pocahontas married John Rolfe, accompanying him to England, where she died. The colonists had less success against Opechancanough, who began consolidating his power among the Virginia natives.

In contrast to Spain, the English Crown failed to take responsibility for protecting any rights of Native Americans and, over the entire colonial period, English churches showed little interest in converting them. When colonists had sufficient power, they enslaved Indians, sending them away from their homelands to prevent escape. The English justified expropriation of native lands with several doctrines. One was the belief that the king of England, as the Christian monarch, received sovereignty over North America from God. Thus, the Virginia Company, and later other groups and individuals, obtained rights to land from the Crown, not the Indians. The other basis for taking native territory was the legal concept, *vacuum domicilium*, which meant that lands not occupied could be taken. To the English, "occupation" meant improving the land with buildings, fences, and crops; they did not recognize Indian sovereignty over the vast stretches of hunting lands that extended beyond small villages and fields. Even when the English purchased land from the Indians, their contrasting concepts of ownership caused grave misunderstanding. While the colonists believed in private property, the natives had no such concept of exclusive ownership, but rather thought they were selling the rights to use lands for hunting, fishing, and communal farming. They expected to continue using the territory they had "sold" for these purposes. Conflicts resulted when, for example, a settler's cattle trampled Indian crops, or when a native killed a colonist's cow, mistaking it for a deer. Ultimately, as disease ravaged the Native American population, white settlers dispossessed the Indian survivors of their lands.

Tobacco Boom

Demand for land became paramount in Virginia after 1617, when the colonists discovered tobacco as a staple crop. Though James I called smoking "a custom loathsome to the eye, hateful to the nose, harmful to the brain, dangerous to the lungs, and in the black stinking fumes thereof, nearest resembling the horrible stygian smoke of the pit that is bottomless," the habit consumed England. The mercantilist advantages were clear. With production in Virginia, the English could

Earliest known illustration of an American tobacco factory, c. 1670.

MENAGERIE

acquire tobacco from its own colony, rather than pay premium prices to foreign countries, and could generate an industry to process the leaves for domestic use and export. For Virginians, the tobacco trade meant capital to develop the colony, attract settlers, and purchase manufactures from home. Tobacco became the first staple crop in England's colonial mercantilist system, followed by sugar, after 1640, in the West Indies.

In 1619, the Virginia Company made several changes to encourage the colony's growth. It updated the land policy, granting "headrights" of one hundred acres of land to those who came before 1616 and fifty acres to those who came after. Settlers who paid their own way received land immediately; those who immigrated at the company's expense received land after seven years of service. Virginia settlers thus fell into two categories: freeholders who paid for their own transportation; and servants, whose way the Virginia Company or someone else financed, and who received a headright only after their time expired. Recipients of headrights did not pay for the land, but owed quitrents, annual payments to the company, of one shilling per year for each fifty acres. The company hoped these charges would ensure a steady income. Also in 1619, the Virginia Company relaxed its hold on the government of Virginia by establishing an assembly of elected delegates. The governor, who was appointed by the company, retained the right to veto all laws; the company's General Court in London could also disallow any decision. The Virginia Company also adopted English common law to replace the martial law under which the colony had operated.

While the revised land policy and the assembly gave settlers a greater stake in society, the adoption of tobacco assured Virginia's ultimate success. Finally, the colonists had found a way to wealth: During the 1620s, tobacco drew high prices, as much as three shillings per pound. Virginia became the first North American "boom town," as settlers threw all of their energies into growing tobacco. Between 1617 and 1623, approximately 5,000 new immigrants arrived. Because the amount of the crop a planter could grow depended largely on the number of workers, those with capital eagerly paid for transporting servants. The Virginia Company imported workers too, but still failed to show a profit, partly because company officials diverted many servants to their own plantations.

Africans in Early Virginia

To strike it rich from tobacco, Virginia planters also purchased Africans, probably even before 1619 when a Dutch ship brought about twenty blacks. Though

some of these Africans became servants, with terms shorter than lifetime bondage, others probably were slaves. Little is known of their status during the early decades. While, over the years, slave traders brought more Africans to Virginia, English servants provided most of the labor in the colony until late in the seventeenth century. In 1625, Africans numbered twenty-three of 1,200 Virginia colonists. Fifteen were the property of two men: Abraham Peirsey, the wealthiest man in the colony, and George Yeardley, who had served as governor. In 1660, about 900 blacks and 24,000 Europeans lived in the Chesapeake Bay area.

In contrast, by that same year, Africans outnumbered whites in Barbados, the richest of the English West Indies. Founded in 1627, Barbados quickly turned to sugar production, importing Africans to raise and process the crop. The white islanders created a harsh slave regime to prevent organized rebellion and force the rapidly growing black population to perform hard, repetitive labor.

Until the 1660s, conditions for Africans remained less rigid in Virginia than in the West Indies, for no law codifying slavery existed. Some Virginia blacks achieved freedom, married, and a few acquired land. For example, by the 1650s, free blacks Anthony and Mary Johnson owned a 250-acre plantation on Virginia's eastern shore and, like neighboring whites, protected their property by going to court. Even so, other Africans remained in bondage, as Virginians adopted the practice by example from the Portuguese, Spanish, and Dutch. In purchasing people from slave traders, the white colonists bought into the Atlantic slave system.

Early Virginia documents distinguished consistently between white servants and blacks, always with the suggestion that Africans were subordinate. In a 1627 will, Governor Yeardley bequeathed his "goode debts, chattels, servants, negars, cattle or any other thing" to his heirs. Censuses of the 1620s also point to the lower regard for Africans: English settlers were listed with full names while most Africans were enumerated simply with a first name or designated as "negar" or "Negro." For example, Anthony and Mary Johnson were called "Antonio a Negro" and "Mary a Negro Woman" in early records. The Virginia tax law of 1643 further demonstrated that the colonists viewed Africans as different from themselves. Everyone who worked in the field was to be taxed—all men and black women. White women apparently were not expected to tend tobacco. Virginia also excepted blacks, but not white servants, from the obligation to bear arms.

The Colony Expands

The colonists had found the way to success—by growing tobacco—but Virginia experienced difficulty for many years. Because mortality remained high and settlers had few children, the population grew slowly despite immigration that averaged about 1,000 people per year. From 1619 to 1640, the population rose from 700 to about 8,000, though approximately 20,000 immigrants had arrived during that time. Dysentery, typhoid fever, and malaria took their toll on new settlers who suffered a period of "seasoning" after their arrival in Virginia. A 1625 census indicated that more than three-quarters of the Virginia colonists were male and less than one-fifth were children, statistics that reflected high immigration in these early years. Men were much more likely to migrate to the colonies than women. Many people came as servants, which meant that they could not legally marry and have children for years, until their terms expired. The census also provided ample evidence of mortality and disrupted families, as many of the married couples were childless, in part because of high infant and childhood mortality. And with short life expectancy for adults, more than one-half of the colony's children had lost one parent, and one-fifth apparently had no relatives in Virginia at all. The census revealed the misery of living in early Virginia despite the prospect of getting rich. Young men and women who left England to become servants in Virginia gambled with their lives to obtain land, which they could not gain at home. Many thought the risk worth taking: Between 1607 and 1680, about 65,000 Europeans immigrated to Virginia.

By 1621, Opechancanough and a prophet Nemattanew, whom the colonists called "Jack of the Feathers" because he wore clothes covered with plumes, recognized the threat of increased immigration. Now that the English had tobacco, they were not going to leave. Nemattanew inspired a nativist religious revival among the Powhatans, rejecting Christianity and European customs. Opechancanough organized a military offensive to push the English back into the sea. At the same time, he used diplomacy to convince the settlers to lower their guard. He even told them that they were welcome to take unoccupied lands. When several whites killed Nemattanew in 1622, Opechancanough rallied his troops, slaying one-fourth of the settlers before the colony could react. A ten-year war followed, in which each side tried to annihilate the other, but failed, and in 1632 agreed to peace.

Though the bankrupt Virginia Company lost its charter in 1624, in the wake of the 1622 massacre,

RICHARD FRETHORNE,
A VIRGINIA COLONIST,
WRITES HOME, 1623

Conditions in Virginia remained terrible for immigrants in the 1620s, as Richard Frethorne tells his parents at home in England. A year after the 1622 massacre by the Powhatan confederacy, the Englishman reports ongoing hostilities and the settlers' constant fear of "the enemy."

Loving and kind father and mother:

My most humble duty remembered to you, hoping in God of your good health, as I myself am at the making hereof. This is to let you understand that I your child am in a most heavy case by reason of the nature of the country, [which] is such that it causeth much sickness, [such] as the scurvy and the bloody flux and diverse other diseases, which maketh the body very poor and weak. And when we are sick there is nothing to comfort us, for since I came out of the ship I never ate anything but peas, and loblollie (that is, water gruel). As for deer or venison I never saw any since I came into this land. There is indeed some fowl, but we are not allowed to go and get it, but must work hard both early and late for a mess of water gruel and a mouthful of bread and beef. A mouthful of bread, for a penny loaf must serve for four men which is most pitiful. [You would be grieved] if you did know as much as I [do], when people cry out day and night—Oh! that they were in England without their limbs—and would not care to lose any limb to be in England again, yea, though they beg from door to door. For we live in fear of the enemy every hour, yet we have had a combat with them on the Sunday before Shrovetide, and we took two alive and made slaves of them. But it was by policy, for we are in great danger, for our plantation is very weak by reason of the death and sickness of our company. For we came but twenty for the merchants, and they are half dead just; and we look every hour when two more should go. Yet there came some four other men yet to live with us, of which there is but one alive; and our Lieutenant is dead, and [also] his father and his brother. And there was some five or six of the last year's twenty, of which there is but three left, so that we are fain to get other men to plant with us; and yet we

immigration to the colony continued. Its economic promise helped convince the English Crown to claim it as a royal colony. Desire for new tobacco lands placed constant pressure on the Powhatans, so in 1644, Opechancanough launched another attack. This time the Indians killed 500 settlers, a much smaller proportion than in 1622. After two years of war, the Powhatans submitted and Opechancanough, now "so decrepit that he was not able to walk alone," was captured and murdered by a guard. The 1646 treaty required the Native Americans to live on lands north of the York River and, to symbolize their subordination, pay an annual tribute of twenty beaver skins.

Colonists expanded rapidly north and south of the James River and to the eastern shore, having defeated their most dangerous opponents.

FISHING, FURS, AND SETTLEMENTS IN THE NORTH

While settlers and Native Americans struggled for Virginia during the first decades of the seventeenth

are but 32 to fight against 3000 if they should come. And the nighest help that we have is ten miles of us, and when the rogues overcame this place [the] last [time] they slew 80 persons. How then shall we do, for we lie even in their teeth? They may easily take us, but [for the fact] that God is merciful and can save with few as well as with many, as he showed to Gilead. And like Gilead's soldiers, if they lapped water, we drink water which is but weak.

And I have nothing to comfort me, nor there is nothing to be gotten here but sickness and death, except [in the event] that one had money to lay out in some things for profit. But I have nothing at all—no, not a shirt to my back but two rags (2), nor no clothes but one poor suit, nor but one pair of shoes, but one pair of stockings, but one cap, [and] but two bands. My cloak is stolen by one of my own fellows, and to his dying hour [he] would not tell me what he did with it; but some of my fellows saw him have butter and beef out of a ship, which my cloak, I doubt [not], paid for. So that I have not a penny, nor a penny worth, to help me to either spice or sugar or strong waters, without the which one cannot live here. For as strong beer in England doth fatten and strengthen them, so water here doth wash and weaken these here [and] only keeps [their] life and soul together. But I am not half [of] a quarter so strong as I was in England, and all is for want of victuals; for I do protest unto you that I have eaten more in [one] day at home than I have allowed me here for a week. . . .

Good father, do not forget me, but have mercy and pity my miserable case. I know if you did but see me, you would weep to see me; for I have but one suit. (But [though] it is a strange one, it is very well guarded.) Wherefore, for God's sake, pity me. I pray you to remember my love to all my friends and kindred. I hope all my brothers and sisters are in good health, and as for my part I have set down my resolution that certainly will be; that is, that the answer of this letter will be life or death to me. Therefore, good father, send as soon as you can; and if you send me any thing let this be the mark. ROT

Richard Frethorne,
Martin's Hundred

century, French, Dutch, and English adventurers explored and colonized the region to the north. French and English sailors had fished the Newfoundland Banks since the fifteenth century. By 1600, groups monopolized specific waters, such as the French who caught walrus in the Gulf of St. Lawrence. The beaver furs that Europeans obtained in petty trade with Native Americans became popular in Europe for making felt hats, exciting merchants in France, the Netherlands, and England to seek more permanent arrangements. All three nations claimed the northern territories as their own, ignoring, of course, the prior ownership of the Indians.

New France

In North America, French traders focused on furs, for Europeans prized the thick animal pelts of frigid Canada. When a ship sent to North America in 1582 returned to France with a cargo of furs earning a 1,500 percent profit, merchants enthusiastically organized more voyages and considered colonies to facilitate trade. Samuel de Champlain established the first successful French colony in the New World. Working for Pierre du Gua de Monts, who had received a charter from the French king, in 1605 Champlain planted a temporary base at Port Royal on the Bay of Fundy in

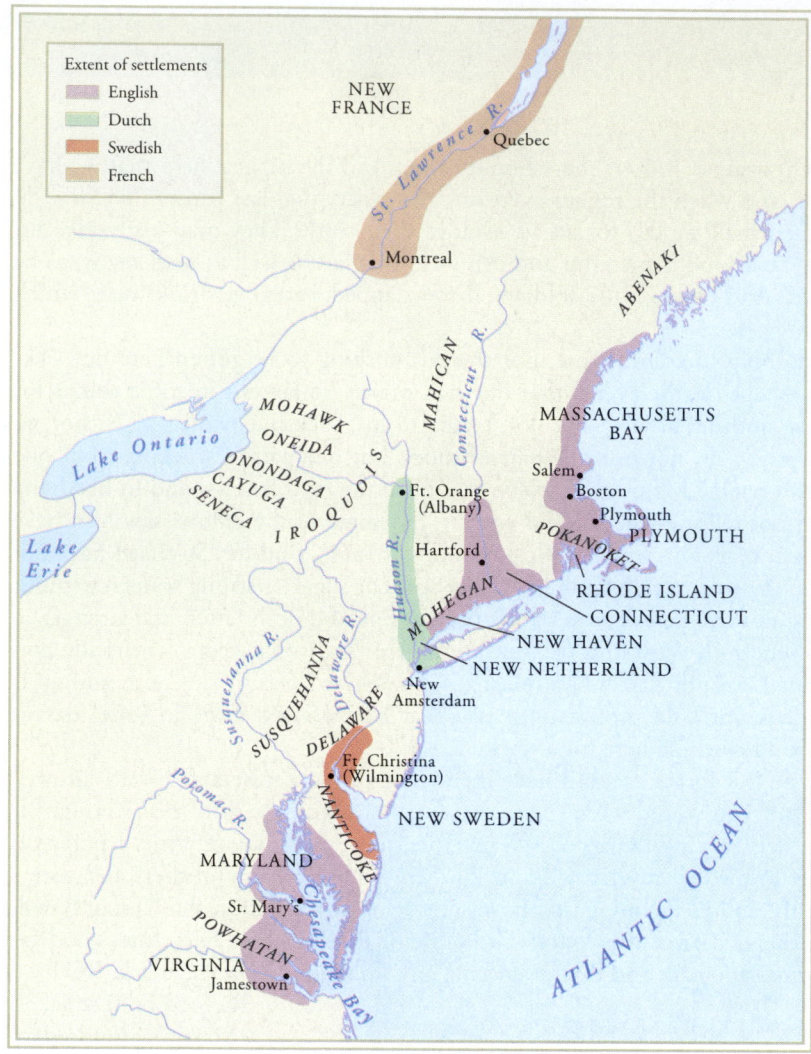

MAP 2.1   FRENCH, ENGLISH, DUTCH, AND SWEDISH COLONIES IN EASTERN NORTH AMERICA, 1650

alliances with several groups: the Montagnais, who lived in the region north of the St. Lawrence River and like the Algonquins and Micmacs spoke Algonquian languages; and the Hurons, who were Iroquoian and lived north of Lake Ontario, a location that enabled them to link the French outposts with the interior, the source of the most valuable furs. In 1609, to demonstrate allegiance to his allies, Champlain helped them fight a group of Iroquois from what is now New York, thus making the Five Nations enemies of New France. He also explored the watershed of the St. Lawrence River and lands as far west as Lake Huron, thereby establishing France's claim to the interior of North America.

In 1627, Quebec was still essentially a trading post with about 100 French inhabitants, including few women. Cardinal Richelieu, who for all practical purposes ruled France, organized the Company of One Hundred Associates to spur colonization. The company received a charter for territory from the Arctic Circle to Florida and from the Atlantic to the Pacific, with a monopoly on the fur trade and power to establish a feudal system of land tenure. The company also pledged to send missionaries to the Indians, to bring them "to the knowledge of the true God" and grant them the status

Canada. He sailed south to Cape Cod looking for a permanent site, but decided in 1608 to retain Port Royal and establish a main settlement on the St. Lawrence River. The French chose Quebec, which meant "the place where the river narrows" in Algonquian, an ideal location for controlling the Canadian interior.

For two decades, both Port Royal and Quebec remained little more than trading posts. The French had already traded with the Micmacs of the coastal region and Algonquins of the St. Lawrence Valley. Champlain strengthened these ties, and made new

of "natural French" when they were baptized. In fact, the French missionaries, like the Spanish, took seriously their mandate to convert Native Americans. They established missions in Indian villages and learned their languages, looking for similarities between the two cultures in an effort to make the Indians part of French society.

Because the company focused on the fur trade and considered transporting settlers too expensive, in 1663 just 3,000 French settlers lived in the colony. The Crown revoked the company's charter, making New France a royal province. Nevertheless, population

growth remained slow. From the beginning, the government refused to allow Protestants, who were the most likely immigrants, to settle there; it wanted to maintain control of the society through the Catholic church. Further, New France developed under feudal land tenure, in which wealthy lords received large manors, or *seigniories*, along the St. Lawrence River. Ordinary settlers on these manors became tenants rather than independent farmers. Lacking the opportunity to improve their status in the New World, French peasants were reluctant to make the dangerous transatlantic voyage.

The fur trade and small population made French relations with the Native Americans different from those of New Spain and Virginia, where labor demands and white expansion put greater pressure on the Indians. The most efficient way to obtain furs was to offer desirable products from Europe, including textiles, metal tools, guns, pots, and alcohol, not drive trading partners from the land or exploit their labor. One French priest reported that, at least for a while, the Montagnais thought they were getting the better deal: "I heard my [Indian] host say one day, jokingly, *Missi picoutau amiscou,* 'The Beaver does everything perfectly well, it makes kettles, hatchets, swords, knives, bread; and in short, it makes everything.' He was making sport of us Europeans . . . [and said], showing me a beautiful knife, 'The English have no sense; they give us twenty knives like this for one Beaver skin'."

Nevertheless, the French arrival had tragic effects for the Indians of Canada, who succumbed to disease in large numbers. The demand for furs altered cultural attitudes and intensified hostility among nations, as with the Hurons and the Iroquois of New York. In keeping with their religion, Indians had taken only what they needed from nature and little more; they generally used entire animals, the meat as well as the skins. With the fur trade, natives killed animals just for their furs and in numbers far greater than before. As a result, the balance of nature that the Native Americans had maintained was broken. They had to reach farther and farther back into the continent as they exterminated the deer, beaver, and other fur-bearing animals.

New Netherland

In the first decade of the seventeenth century, the Dutch, too, challenged the dominance of Spain in the New World. The seven northern United Provinces had declared independence from Spain in 1581 and remained at war until 1609, when they signed a twelve-year truce. With its expiration, the war resumed and continued as part of the Thirty Years' War, which ended in 1648 with the Treaty of Münster, recognizing Dutch independence. The revolt failed in the southern Netherlands, forcing Calvinists to flee north.

Despite this ongoing struggle, Dutch commerce flourished. The migration of Protestants from Antwerp, which had been the thriving business center of the southern provinces, to Amsterdam transferred capital and commercial know-how to the north. As Antwerp foundered, Amsterdam tripled in size between 1585 and 1622, with a mercantile community eager to start new ventures. Because land was scarce and high priced in the Netherlands, and agriculture insufficient, affluent individuals put their capital into trade. They formed joint-stock companies to challenge the dominance of Portugal and Spain (which Philip II united in 1580) in Asia, Africa, and the West Indies. In 1602, merchants formed the United East India Company, which six years later had 160 ships around the globe. In 1609, the company sent out Henry Hudson, an Englishman, to search for the long-sought northwest passage through North America. He sailed up the river that later bore his name, trading for furs with the Native Americans. The pelts brought a good return in Holland, so the company dispatched traders who set up a post near the present site of Albany and explored Long Island Sound and the Connecticut River. In 1621, the Dutch government chartered another group, the West India Company, to establish commerce and colonies in America. Like the East India Company, it received broad powers, including the rights to make war and sign treaties. During the seventeenth century, the Dutch muscled their way to control a large part of international commerce, including the Atlantic slave trade and routes to Asia. They wrested the African slave trading fort of El Mina and Brazil sugar plantations from the Portuguese, changed the fishing industry off Newfoundland by sending "sack" ships to purchase fish rather than catch them, and captured the Spanish silver fleet off Cuba in 1628.

To provide a base for trade in the Hudson River region, in 1624 the Dutch West India Company appointed Cornelius Jacobsen May to found New Netherland; the first colonists were mostly Protestant refugees from the Spanish Netherlands. They

The Seal of the Province of New Netherland, 1623, with an image of a beaver in center, evokes the Dutch focus on trade.

established their primary settlement, called New Amsterdam, on Manhattan Island, and maintained trading posts at Fort Orange (near Albany), and on the Delaware and Connecticut rivers. As in Jamestown, the first settlers were employees of the company who received no land of their own. The company paid for their transportation, tools, livestock, and two years' worth of supplies, assigning them company land on which to plant. The colonists were expected to trade only with the company. The government consisted of appointed company officers headed by a director-general, or governor, with wide powers. The colonists could not elect an assembly or any of their officials.

With good soil on Manhattan Island and in the upper Hudson Valley, the lucrative fur trade, and lumbering, the colony prospered economically, though its population grew slowly. Brewing became the second most important industry; in 1638, New Amsterdam residents complained that they were losing sleep from the singing of drunken sailors. People of many nationalities and religions arrived to take advantage of the Dutch policy of religious freedom, but few Dutch could be convinced to emigrate. In 1629, the company attempted to spur population growth by offering huge manors, called patroonships, to any member of the company who transported fifty persons to work his land. On the Hudson River, each patroonship extended for miles along one bank or both banks, as far back into the countryside as the lord, or patroon, wanted—or the Native Americans allowed. Similar to New France, the settlers were tenants of the manor, owing feudal dues to the lord. This arrangement attracted few settlers: In fact it discouraged immigration because the manors tied up large tracts that might otherwise go to small farmers. The only patroonship to succeed was Rensselaerswyck, on the upper Hudson River, which had Fort Orange at its center.

At first, New Netherland had good relations with the Indians because the colony grew slowly and depended on the fur trade. In the famous 1626 purchase, Director-general Peter Minuit exchanged goods worth about 60 guilders for Manhattan Island. Upriver, the Dutch bought furs from the Iroquois, the enemies of the Algonquians and Hurons who supplied the French, thus contributing to the devastating warfare among tribes. When game near the Hudson River quickly gave out, Dutch merchants encouraged the Mohawks, the easternmost of the Five Nations, to take control of the Huron supply routes from the interior of Canada. By the late 1640s, the Iroquois, with help from epidemics, destroyed the Hurons, a nation of about 20,000 people. At the same time, constant warfare and disease seriously debilitated the Iroquois as well.

In the region surrounding New Amsterdam, relations deteriorated between the whites and the Indians after 1638. As with the English, the Dutch and natives had different conceptions of land ownership. While the Indians understood that they had sold rights to share the land and intended to continue using it themselves, the Dutch believed they had bought exclusive rights. Violence erupted as the settlers' cattle trampled the Indians' corn, and dogs belonging to Native Americans attacked Dutch livestock. The Dutch also had trouble distinguishing among friendly and hostile Indians: for example, after some Hackensacks killed two settlers in 1642, eighty Dutch soldiers attacked two villages of Wecquaesgeeks, allies of the New Netherland government. Beginning in 1640, the Dutch and Indians of the lower Hudson Valley fought a series of damaging wars that ended only in 1664, when the English took control of New Netherland and made peace with the Native Americans.

New England Before the Pilgrims

Along the coast of New England, relations between the Indians and English were rocky from the start. Before the Pilgrims established Plymouth in 1620, a number of expeditions explored the region, traded,

Theodor de Bry's illustration emphasizes friendly exchange rather than hostility between Bartholomew Gosnold and the Indians of Martha's Vineyard. De Bry also suggests a larger fleet than Gosnold's single ship, the Concord.

and tried to colonize. In 1602, Bartholomew Gosnold and thirty-two men sailed the *Concord* to Maine, expecting to establish a colony. They continued south to Martha's Vineyard, where they stayed five weeks, trading for furs. When they alienated the natives and one of their men was wounded, Gosnold and his crew returned to England. In 1607, the Plymouth group of the Virginia Company sent an expedition to the Kennebec River in Maine, but the colony lasted only one year. The company abandoned efforts to establish a permanent base, instead funding voyages for fish and furs. The English immediately came up against the French at Port Royal and Quebec, and traded with their enemies among the Indians. Like the Dutch and French, the English set up commercial networks with tribes who had contested land and resources before the Europeans arrived, thereby intensifying these rivalries with competition for furs and European goods.

Even before the founding of Plymouth, then, the natives of New England had considerable experience with the English. Sadly, this contact had catastrophic effects on the Indian population and foretold future relations. A plague epidemic brought by Europeans swept eastern New England during 1616–1618, killing thousands. Large areas along the coast were depopulated, opening them for English settlement in the 1620s and 1630s. The Massachusetts natives were initially friendly and interested in trade, but good relations proved elusive. The English shot some Native Americans and set dogs on others. A few they kidnapped, then expected them to serve as diplomats to their people. The English also made trade agreements, then failed to honor them. By the time the Pilgrims arrived in 1620, the surviving Indians along the coast had been severely weakened by disease and were understandably wary of the newcomers.

RELIGIOUS EXILES FROM ENGLAND

While the colonizers of Virginia, New France, and New Netherland had primarily economic motives, the English founders of Plymouth, Massachusetts Bay, and

Maryland sought a place where they could practice their religion free from persecution and at the same time earn a decent living. Like other European nations, seventeenth-century England was rife with religious controversy, as Protestant and Catholic dissidents challenged the monopoly of the Church of England. The government required attendance at Anglican worship and financial support of ministers. When dissenters refused to obey, holding separate services, they could be imprisoned and fined. Roman Catholics could also be stripped of their property and jailed for life if they refused to take the oath of supremacy to the king, which denied the authority of the pope. The search for freedom of worship, which the king permitted in America but not at home, became a major impetus for crossing the Atlantic.

English Calvinists

By 1603, when James I took the throne, two strains of English Calvinism, or Puritanism, had developed. One group included the Separatists, or Pilgrims, who founded Plymouth in 1620; the others, known as Puritans, established the Massachusetts Bay colony ten years later. Both groups charged that the Anglican church retained too much Catholicism, that it needed to be "purified" of its rituals, vestments, statues, and bishops. They rejected the church hierarchy, believing each congregation should govern itself. The Separatists started their own congregations, abandoning all hope that the church could be reformed. The Pilgrims' decision to begin a colony in America, away from European corruption, was the ultimate expression of this separatism. The Puritans, on the other hand, were non-separating congregationalists who hoped to reform the Church of England from within. Their purpose in founding Massachusetts Bay was to build a society to serve as a model for corrupt England and other English colonies. In coming to America, the Puritans were separating themselves geographically, but would use their isolation to develop a moral government which they hoped the people of England would someday make their own.

The Plymouth Colony

The Pilgrims were a small band who had originated in Scrooby, England, where they established a separate congregation. In 1607, when some were jailed as nonconformists, they decided to leave England for the Netherlands, which offered freedom of worship. The Pilgrims settled in Leyden, but were unhappy there, too. They found Dutch society corrupt and feared for their children's souls. With difficulty locating work and a preference for English government, the Pilgrims made an agreement with a group of London merchants who obtained a patent for land from the Virginia Company. In exchange for funding to go to America, the Pilgrims promised to send back fish, furs, and lumber for seven years. James I offered the Pilgrims freedom to worship in their colony.

Thirty-five of the Leyden congregation, a minority, chose to emigrate. Sailing first to England, they joined sixty-seven others, of whom many were not Separatists. In September 1620, the *Mayflower* departed Plymouth, England, crowded with 102 passengers, about twenty crew members, and assorted pigs, chickens, and goats. Headed for Virginia, the ship reached Cape Cod on November 9th. In shallow waters, fearing shipwreck, the exhausted travelers built their colony at Plymouth, even though they were outside the jurisdiction of the Virginia Company. Their decision entailed risks because they now lacked a legal basis for governing themselves or for claiming land. The first problem was most urgent because some of the colonists questioned the authority of the Pilgrim leaders. The group avoided a revolt by drafting and signing the "Mayflower Compact," a social compact by which they agreed to form a government and obey its laws. The London merchants eventually solved the second problem by obtaining title to the land.

Plymouth's first years were difficult, though the settlers found unused supplies of corn left by Indians struck recently by an epidemic, and chose the site of a deserted Patuxet village with relatively clear fields. Over the first winter they built houses, but one-half of the colonists died of disease and exposure to the cold. In the spring of 1621, they planted corn with the help of Squanto, perhaps the lone surviving Patuxet, and other crops.

The natives helped the Plymouth Colony, despite earlier problems with Englishmen. In 1614, Squanto and about twenty other Patuxets had been kidnapped by an English sea captain, who intended to sell them as slaves in Spain. Saved from bondage by Spanish priests, Squanto made his way to England, where he learned the language, then to Newfoundland, and finally back to Patuxet in 1619. There he found

THE MAYFLOWER COMPACT, 1620

When the *Mayflower* reached land at Cape Cod (in what is now Massachusetts) and the colonists decided to settle there instead of prolonging their difficult journey, they lacked the legal basis (a charter) to establish a government. Thus, the adult males of the colony signed a mutual agreement for ordering their society, what John Locke called, decades later, a "social compact."

In the name of God Amen. We whose names are underwriten, the loyall subjects of our dread soveraigne Lord King James by the grace of God, of great Britaine, Franc, & Ireland king, defender of the faith, &c.

Haveing undertaken, for the glorie of God, and advancements of the Christian faith and honour of our king & countrie, a voyage to plant the first colonie in the Northerne parts of Virginia, doe by these presents solemnly & mutualy in the presence of God, and one of another, covenant & combine our selves togeather into a civill body politick; for our better ordering, & preservation & furtherance of the ends aforesaid; and by vertue hearof to enacte, constitute, and frame shuch just & equall lawes, ordinances, Acts, constitutions, & offices, from time to time, as shall be thought most meete & convenient for the generall good of the Colonie: unto which we promise all due submission and obedience.

In witnes whereof we have hereunder subscribed our names at Cap-Codd the · 11 · of November, in the year the raigne of our soveraigne Lord King James of England, France, & Ireland the eighteenth and of Scotland the fiftie fourth. An°: Dom. 1620.

John Carver	John Turner
William Bradford	Francis Eaton
Edward Winslow	James Chilton
William Brewster	John Crakston
Isaac Allerton	John Billington
Myles Standish	Moses Fletcher
John Alden	John Goodman
Samuel Fuller	Degory Priest
Christopher Martin	Thomas Williams
William Mullins	Gilbert Winslow
William White	Edmund Margeson
Richard Warren	Peter Brown
John Howland	Richard Britterige
Stephen Hopkins	George Soule
Edward Tilley	Richard Clarke
John Tilley	Richard Gardiner
Francis Cooke	John Allerton
Thomas Rogers	Thomas English
Thomas Tinker	Edward Doty
John Rigdale	Edward Leister
Edward Fuller	

unburied bodies of many of his people who had perished in the epidemic. One Englishman described the scene: "[T]heir bones and skulls made such a spectacle. . . . it seemed to me a new found Golgotha."

At harvest in 1621, the Indians and colonists celebrated together for three days. The future seemed bright for the fifty-one surviving colonists, but soon after their feast, the ship *Fortune* arrived with thirty-five new settlers, for whom no food was available until the next year's crop. When the colonists filled the *Fortune* with furs and lumber in hopes of starting to repay their debt to the London merchants, the French captured the ship.

By 1623, though, the Plymouth Colony was well established and growing, as new immigrants arrived. The community solved the problem of food supply by assigning individual plots to families, making them responsible for their own food. Still, the hard-working colonists had trouble fulfilling their bargain with the merchants, as all of their efforts came to naught. During a trading voyage, the crew mutinied. On one fishing trip, the ship sank; when it was raised and sent out again, the Spanish captured it. The London merchants gave up, ended the partnership, and in 1626 agreed to sell the land to the colonists for a large sum, which they paid by 1645, receiving a patent of ownership. While Plymouth's economic fortunes improved, the colony remained small and self-consciously separate from the larger group of English dissenters who streamed into New England.

Reconstructed village at Plymouth, with fences to protect gardens from roaming livestock.

The seal of the Massachusetts Bay Company, 1629, shows an Indian calling to the English, "Come over and help us."

The Great Puritan Migration

The Puritan migration to Massachusetts Bay was much larger and more tightly organized than Plymouth. During 1630, the first year, 700 women, men, and children arrived in eleven ships. Though at least 200 died during the first winter because of lack of food and bitter weather, the colony grew quickly. The Massachusetts Bay Company, made up primarily of Puritans, organized the "great migration" of about 12,000 people who came to Massachusetts during the 1630s. From King Charles I, the company obtained a charter specifying its government and the colony's boundaries. When most of the company officials emigrated, taking the charter with them, they greatly enhanced the colony's independence from the Crown and the Anglican church.

Thus the Massachusetts Bay colonists, unlike the first settlers of Jamestown and Plymouth, had their own charter and did not answer to London merchants who expected handsome profits. The Puritans themselves financed colonization; they included wealthy investors as well as many middling families who could pay their own way. As a result, the founders devoted much of their energy to creating a model society, a godly commonwealth. In the words of leader John Winthrop, the colony would be "as a Citty upon a Hill, the Eyes of all people are upon us; soe that if

Unlike most English colonists, John Winthrop came from a well-to-do background. He helped finance the Massachusetts Bay colony and served as governor.

wee shall deale falsely with our god in this worke wee have undertaken and soe cause him to withdrawe this present help from us, wee shall be made a story and a by-word through the world." The Puritans believed that in addition to their charter from the king, which set up their secular government, they had a covenant with God that bound them to create a moral community. The Puritans, as Calvinists, held that individuals were saved from eternal damnation by faith, rather than by good works. Men and women could seek to avoid sin, work hard, and help their neighbors throughout their lives, but unless they were among God's chosen, or the "elect," they would go to hell. Under the covenant, the elect were responsible for the behavior of unsaved members of their households and the community at large. The Puritan leaders were responsible to God. They thought that if they maintained a moral society, the Lord would help it prosper.

In Massachusetts, the Puritans restructured the company government to create their version of a godly commonwealth. According to the Massachusetts Bay charter, the company officials included a governor, deputy governor, and executive board of eighteen "assistants," to be elected by "freemen" (stockholders) who would meet in a general assembly, called the General Court. These officers, as long as they did nothing in violation of the laws of England, could make laws and regulations, appoint lower officials, grant lands, and punish lawbreakers. The colony's leaders changed the rules to allow all male church members (the male elect), not just stockholders in the company, to become freemen. In theory, every freeman would be a member of the General Court, or colonial legislature. But as the population grew and towns formed quickly, freemen voted in town meetings for representatives to the assembly.

With the governor and assistants, the General Court drew up a law code for the colony, which after several revisions was published as the *Laws and Liberties of Massachusetts* (1648). The code was a combination of biblical law, English common law, and statutes tailored specifically to colonial needs. It protected the liberties of individuals by upholding trial by jury and due process of law, including the rights of the accused to a prompt, public trial and to call witnesses. It also prohibited feudal tenure of lands and outlawed slavery, "unless it be lawfull captives, taken in just warrs, and such strangers as willingly sell themselves or are solde to us." This provision limited the possibility that whites would be enslaved, but had little effect on black bondage. The *Laws and Liberties* prescribed the death penalty for many fewer crimes than in England, but included as capital offenses blasphemy and adultery (in cases where the woman was married), which under the English common law were lesser crimes. Children could be put to death for failing to respect their parents, while fornicators were required to marry and be whipped or fined. The code enabled judges to extend the terms of negligent servants and send back to England any married persons who arrived in Massachusetts without their spouses. While these terms may seem harsh, the colony did not actually impose the death penalty for blasphemy or abuse of parents by children, and executed only two people for adultery. The magistrates evidently wanted to instill fear in the hearts of potential offenders rather than exact harsh punishments. With trial by jury and due process, Massachusetts preserved important civil liberties.

The Puritans attempted to create a theocracy, a government operated according to God's will, as determined by the colony's patriarchs. They were sure that their religion was the only one God ordained. The Puritan government was composed of members of the elect; ministers advised the magistrates but could not serve officially. The government required all inhabitants to attend Puritan churches whether or not they accepted the faith. Persons who disagreed with orthodox doctrines, and made their position known, could be expelled, whipped, fined, and even executed. The church was the center of each town, with all property owners paying taxes for its support. Though the Puritans had suffered persecution for their beliefs in England, they refused to allow freedom of worship in Massachusetts. Instead, they replaced one established church for another.

The Fairbanks House in Dedham, Massachusetts, was originally built c. 1637 and later expanded, as shown in this 1880 photograph.

Massachusetts Society

Unlike the Jamestown settlers, a large proportion of Puritan immigrants came in families. Many originated from Norfolk, Suffolk, and Essex (together called East Anglia), Kent, London, and the West Country. Fewer came from the north of England. East Anglia, located directly across the North Sea from the Netherlands, was the center of both the wool trade and Puritanism. By 1630, its residents had kept contact with European Calvinists for almost a century. Entire congregations and their ministers, ostensibly part of the Church of England, adopted Puritan ways. They conducted services without the Book of Common Prayer and tore down communion rails. For decades they had worshipped freely, protected by the local Puritan gentry. Then during the 1620s and 1630s, the Puritans faced a series of hardships, including a depressed market for woolen cloth, poor harvests, and bubonic plague. Charles I and the Anglican church hierarchy, most notably Archbishop William Laud, enforced laws against nonconformists, removing Puritan ministers from their pulpits. Many families—grandparents, parents, children, and servants—migrated to Massachusetts, where they could make a new start under a congenial government. Some entire communities accompanied their ministers.

In Massachusetts, the migrants created towns that often resembled the ones they had left. When a group arrived, its leaders petitioned the General Court for a place to settle and permission to establish a church and town government. The town meeting, composed in some places of male church members only and in others of all male landowners, elected a board of selectmen who administered town business, including road building, maintenance of schools, and law enforcement. The town meeting also divided the town lands. The amount of land a family received depended upon its wealth and social status. Typically, a town followed one of two patterns of land distribution, according to the kind of land tenure its founders knew in England. Emigrants from East Anglia generally chose the *closed field* system, in which families received individual farms, with house lot and land for planting, grazing livestock, and cutting lumber. These settlers also created commercial towns, such as Ipswich, that quickly entered the West Indies trade. In contrast, emigrants from Yorkshire, in northern England, chose the *open field* system, designating town lands for different purposes—house lots lined up in compact rows, fields, meadows, and wood lots. In Rowley, Massachusetts, for example, families received strips in the fields, where they grew crops in cooperation with their neighbors. Together they made many decisions, including which fields to plant and which to leave fallow. Families also received "stinting rights," or permis-

sion to pasture animals on common lands. The number of cattle and sheep a family could pasture depended upon the size of their lands.

The Puritan notion of an ideal community defined the ways in which they acted toward one another and toward outsiders. If the model society were to succeed, everyone had to have a place, in the family, church, and commonwealth. Like other English, the Puritans kept a hierarchical social order. In the family, the husband was superior to the wife, but together they ruled the children and servants. In the church, the minister and elders dominated the congregation. In the commonwealth, the officials led the people. Ideally, this hierarchy required little coercion, when people saw themselves as part of the community and worked for the common good, or "weal" (hence "commonwealth"), rather than for their own benefit. They understood that all humans were equal spiritually—because everyone had the possibility of being saved—but accepted social inequality as the will of God.

Most Puritan women accepted a subordinate place in their society without complaint. They viewed themselves as part of a community and a family, with duties determined by their sex and age, not as individuals with equal rights. Official records often listed wives without their given names, as in the case of "John Brown his wife." Women raised children; kept the house and garden; preserved fruits and vegetables; made beer, cider, cheese, and butter; tended livestock and poultry; spun and wove cloth; sewed clothing, cared for the sick, and supervised the training of daughters and servants. Women often specialized in certain trades, such as spinning, weaving, poultry-raising, or medicine; they conducted trade among themselves, separate from the commercial networks of their husbands. Men had responsibility for raising grain such as wheat, Indian corn, and rye; cutting firewood; and maintaining the fences, buildings, and fields. In addition to farming, many followed a trade or profession such as fishing, carpentry, shopkeeping, overseas trade, medicine, or the ministry. Only men could vote in church and town meetings, serve as government officials, or become ministers. They were the heads of household, representing their wives and children in public affairs. Only when a man became incapacitated, or was away from home, was his wife expected to take his place at work or to represent the family in legal matters or disputes. She temporarily as-

Mrs. Elizabeth Freake and Baby Mary, *painted c. 1674 by an unknown artist, illustrates one of the many roles of seventeenth-century women, that of mother. The wife and child of a successful merchant, their clothing depicts the family's wealth.*

sumed the role of "deputy husband," then yielded it when he became well or returned. Puritans recognized women's ability in public matters, but expected them normally to confine themselves to accepted women's tasks.

The role of Puritan women in the church was indicative of their place in society. On the one hand, women were the spiritual equals of men, held responsibility for the religious education of their children, and formed one-half (and as time went on a greater proportion) of church members. On the other hand, the Puritans emphasized the inheritance of Eve, who they believed led Adam to sin in the Garden of Eden. Women were expected to keep quiet in the church. They could not preach or vote on church business, though they could exert informal influence on their husbands. The Puritans, like other Christians of the time, embraced Saint Paul's instruction to the Corinthians: "Let your women keep silence in the

Churches. . . . And if they will learn anything, let them ask their husbands at home." The Puritans believed that by nature women, as daughters of Eve, were morally and intellectually weak. They had to submit to their husbands for guidance. The pain of childbirth was God's punishment of all women for Eve's seduction of Adam. Although a few rebelled against the injunction to keep quiet, and some were consequently tried as heretics or witches, most Puritan women and girls accepted their subordination to men.

In this patriarchal society, children deferred to their fathers, assuming a subservient role until they were able to establish households of their own. Though some New England colonists held servants and a few owned enslaved Africans, sons and daughters comprised the majority of the workforce. Families on average had five children who reached adulthood. They worked for their parents until marriage—longer in the case of sons who inherited the family farm. Unlike seventeenth-century Virginia, living conditions in Massachusetts promoted patriarchy, for life expectancy was long. Persons who survived childhood diseases often lived past age sixty or even seventy. Thus, eldest sons could be middle-aged before their fathers died and willed them control of the family homestead. On the other hand, younger sons who had little hope of receiving the farm often moved away from their parents, settling in the new towns that developed throughout New England. Parents usually attempted to give all of their children a start in life, with a farm, apprenticeship, money, or college tuition to sons, and personal property or cash to daughters.

Connecticut and New Haven

An early destination for emigrants looking for good land was Connecticut. The first Puritans went there to trade with Native Americans, but when news of attractive land in the Connecticut Valley arrived in Massachusetts, many settlers decided to move. The Earl of Warwick owned the rights to the land at the mouth of the Connecticut River, which he ceded to a group of Puritan noblemen. To build a trading post and settlement they sent John Winthrop, Jr., who convinced Thomas Hooker, the minister of Newtown, Massachu-

setts, to lead some of his congregation there. Another group left from Dorchester. They founded Connecticut in 1636, followed by families who could not obtain suitable land in the old settlements and established towns up the Connecticut River and on Long Island. Though they had no charter from the king, the founders agreed upon the *Fundamental Orders of Connecticut,* which created a General Assembly of representatives from each town. In most respects, the Connecticut government resembled that of Massachusetts, with the exception that freemen, or voters, did not have to be church members. The assembly elected a governor, who could serve only one year at a time, and a group of magistrates who functioned as the upper house of the assembly. As in Massachusetts, Puritanism was the only recognized religion and received tax support.

As white settlement expanded, relations between the Puritans and Native Americans deteriorated. Like other English, the Puritans believed that the Indians worshipped the devil and had barbarous customs. The settlers justified expropriation of native lands on the basis of *vacuum domicilium.* Even more, the Puritans considered the Indians "strangers," who could have no role in building the model society. They were dispensable and dangerous, presenting a dual threat because their customs could corrupt the holy commonwealth and they resented their loss of lands.

The 1637 war against the Pequots of eastern Connecticut showed the lengths to which the New England settlers could go. The Pequots, a powerful tribe, attempted to unite New England Indians against the English. They traded with the Dutch, thus encouraging Dutch claims to Connecticut. In May 1637, troops from Massachusetts and Connecticut, with their Indian allies, the Narragansetts, attacked a Pequot village on the Mystic River before dawn, killing hundreds of sleeping women, children, and old men. The Pequots who escaped this massacre, mostly young men absent from the town, were later executed or enslaved. The Treaty of Hartford (1638) declared their nation dissolved.

Shortly after the Pequot War, in 1638, a group of staunch Puritans established New Haven, on the Long Island Sound west of the Connecticut colony. Persecuted in England, Reverend John Davenport took his flock first to Boston, but decided to move on. They had no charter for New Haven, so the freemen made

the Bible their law, eliminating trial by jury, for example, because it had no scriptural basis. Only male church members could vote. The colony grew, despite its lack of legal authority, as the settlers built towns farther west along the sound and on Long Island. Together, the towns agreed upon a government comprised of a governor, magistrates, and a representative assembly.

Exiles to Rhode Island

The founding of Rhode Island resulted from another kind of emigration from Massachusetts, that of persons who refused to subordinate their own beliefs to those of the Puritan magistrates. The first was Roger Williams, a likeable but stubborn, independent-minded minister, who challenged Massachusetts Bay's policy toward the Indians and its theocratic laws. Williams had studied divinity at Cambridge University, where he became a vocal Separatist, rejecting the Anglican church altogether. He immigrated to Massachusetts Bay in 1631, arousing the colony when he refused the pulpit in Boston church because its members had not renounced the Church of England. He explained, "I durst not officiate to an unseparated people, as upon examination and conference I found them to be."

Williams then accused Massachusetts of holding fraudulent title to its territory because the king had no authority to give away Indian lands. The king's grant depended upon "a solemn public lie." The colony should send the charter back to the king for correction; the settlers should return to England if they could not obtain rights from the true owners of the land. Williams raised a troublesome issue that the Puritan officials refused to recognize, so they ordered him to be still. He would not be quiet, soon broaching the issues of religious freedom and separation of church and state. "Forced worship stinks in God's nostrils," he proclaimed. "There is no other prudent, Christian way of preserving peace in the world, but by permission of differing consciences." He attacked the laws requiring church attendance and tax support of Puritan churches. Williams feared that government would pollute the church, not that giving legal preference to one religion was unfair. He opposed laws regulating religion to protect the church from state interference.

The General Court banished Williams from Massachusetts for challenging the government; in 1636 he went to Narragansett Bay. There he purchased land from the Narragansett Indians, establishing Providence Plantation at the Great Salt River. With the sympathizers who joined him, he created a society based on religious toleration, separation of church and state, and participation in government by all male property owners. Church membership was not a requirement to vote. In fact, Williams welcomed people of all religions to Providence Plantation, as long as they accepted the right of others to worship freely. Williams himself became wealthy through trade with the Native Americans and the Dutch. In 1638, he transferred ownership of Providence to a group of thirteen associates, of whom he was one. This board had responsibilities much like the selectmen of Massachusetts towns.

Another exile from Massachusetts was Anne Hutchinson, a midwife and nurse, who in 1634 arrived in Boston with her husband, merchant William Hutchinson, and children. She had given birth to fourteen sons and daughters, of whom three died before the family left England; she had one more child in 1636. As Hutchinson assisted women in childbirth and sickness, she became convinced that Bostonians placed too much emphasis on good works and not enough on faith. She was a follower of one of Boston's ministers, the influential John Cotton, who stressed the importance of the individual's relationship with God over the obligation to obey laws. Hutchinson went further than Cotton, nearly saying that if a person were saved it did not matter how she or he behaved, a belief known as the Antinomian heresy.

To the orthodox Puritan faction led by Governor John Winthrop, Hutchinson was a threat for several reasons. She emphasized individual judgment over the community's, thus questioning the authority of the colony's leaders. She told the Puritan patriarchs that God spoke to her directly, that she did not need the assistance of magistrates and ministers in interpreting God's will. They feared that the community would disintegrate if everyone heeded her words. Further, Hutchinson went outside the accepted role of women by taking a public stand on religion. But most seriously, she became the standard bearer for a group who contested power with the Winthrop faction. In 1637, Winthrop's government put Hutchinson on trial for

defaming ministers and exiled her from the colony. With her family and supporters she founded a colony at Portsmouth on Narragansett Bay. When she later had a miscarriage, Winthrop pronounced the "monstrous birth" God's judgment upon her. Even more fitting, the Puritans thought, was her death in 1643 at the hands of Native Americans, after she moved to New Netherland.

Following the settlement of Williams and Hutchinson on Narragansett Bay, several other dissenters established colonies there. William Coddington, a supporter of Hutchinson, started the town of Newport; and Samuel Gorton, who had first migrated to Massachusetts because he thought they practiced religious freedom, founded Warwick. The four leaders had trouble cooperating, but knew they needed a charter from the English government to avoid annexation by Massachusetts. Roger Williams went to England for that purpose, in the midst of the Civil War. The 1644 Rhode Island charter, which Parliament granted, united the four settlements under one representative assembly, which could pass statutes consistent with the laws of England. The Rhode Island colonists based their government on Williams's principles of freedom of worship, separation of church and state, and wide participation in government.

The Proprietary Colony of Maryland

In 1632, Charles I granted a charter for Maryland, the first successful proprietary colony in his domains. George Calvert, the first Lord Baltimore, had served in high office until he converted to Catholicism. Forced to resign, but still a royal favorite, Calvert requested a grant in America to build a haven for Catholics. He also expected to support his family by selling the land. He died before obtaining the charter, so his son, Cecilius Calvert, the second Lord Baltimore, became lord proprietor of Maryland. The colony was carved out of the northern part of Virginia, much to the dismay of its residents. Calvert received ownership of the soil and was sovereign in government, subject only to the king. His dues to the Crown were a token tribute of two Indian arrowheads each year.

Calvert soon discovered that the cost of colonization was great. He spent £40,000 for two ships, the

Cecilius Calvert, the second Lord Baltimore, with his grandson and an enslaved African. Calvert was proprietor of Maryland until 1675 when he died and the boy's father, Charles, succeeded him.

Ark and the Dove, with supplies to send the first 150 settlers, who arrived in Maryland in 1634. The proprietor planned a feudal system in which manorial lords held large tracts, which they rented to tenants. For example, a person who transported five laborers at a total cost of £20 received a manor of 2,000 acres. Among his manorial rights, the lord could establish a court for trying cases among his tenants.

Though Maryland settlers suffered no "starving time" as in Virginia and had a cash crop in tobacco, the colony grew slowly. Mortality was high and immigration sluggish. By 1642, Calvert had granted rights

for only sixteen manors, mostly to wealthy Catholic friends. These manors comprised 31,000 acres, or more than 80 percent of the patented land. To improve his income, Calvert distributed farms to more ordinary immigrants, who had to pay annual quitrents. Over the seventeenth century, rich investors acquired sixty manors but by far most settlers were small landowners.

The extension of land ownership beyond Calvert's circle of loyal supporters created problems for the lord proprietor. Under the charter, he was obligated to call together an assembly of freemen, or landowners, to enact laws. Calvert interpreted this to mean that they should approve legislation he prepared, while the freemen, meeting first in 1635, claimed the right to draft the code of laws. Calvert refused to accept their draft, so for three years the colony operated without a code. In 1638, they reached a compromise, with the proprietor and assembly each drafting some of the bills. The colony finally had a legal basis for governing and punishing crime.

But the struggle for power between the proprietor and freemen continued, intensifying on account of religion. The ordinary planters, who formed the majority of freemen and were mostly Protestant, resented the power of the Catholic elite. They were strongly prejudiced against Catholics and had little sympathy for Calvert's vision of a society in which all Christians could worship freely. Religious and political strife became most acute in Maryland during the English Civil War and the Puritan Commonwealth, from 1642 to 1660.

Impact of the English Civil War

For two decades, the English Civil War altered the political situation in England, with unsettling effects on the colonies. The war—or more accurately, the revolution—resulted from a contest for power between Parliament and Charles I, who claimed absolute power and attempted to raise taxes without approval of the legislature. Charles imprisoned opponents without due process, and launched a crusade, carried out by Archbishop Laud, to force all his subjects, even those in Presbyterian Scotland and Catholic Ireland, to conform to the Anglican church. In 1642, war broke out between the "Cavaliers," or royalists, and the "Roundheads," or parliamentary forces, of whom many were Puritans. Oliver Cromwell led the Roundheads to victory in 1648; the following year they beheaded the king.

The revolutionaries attempted to rule through an elected Parliament, but conflicting factions of Puritans and radical sects undermined their plans. Some radical theorists wanted an entire restructuring of society—in the words of one contemporary, "a world turned upside down." They called for extension of the vote to all men and redistribution of land. The gentry and wealthy merchants who had led Parliament to victory considered these ideas anathema. In 1653, to reestablish control, they named Cromwell the Lord Protector of the Commonwealth of England, Scotland, and Ireland. Cromwell ruled alone, backed by the army, until his death in 1658. An attempt failed to make his son Richard the successor, and two years later, the monarchy was restored. The accession of Charles II did not mean a complete reversal to the time of his father. Most important, the king confirmed Parliament's right to approve taxes and abolished the royal courts that had punished opponents of the Crown. But the Restoration brought the Cavaliers back into power, making the Anglican church the state religion once again.

The struggle for power during the Civil War and its aftermath had repercussions in the colonies. Initially, the rebellion of English Puritans against the king raised hopes among New Englanders that English society would be reformed. Some colonists returned to join the battle. Most stayed in America, however, convinced that English society would not be purified. Of more practical importance to the New England colonies was the lack of military protection from England. Plymouth, Massachusetts, Connecticut, and New Haven counted among their enemies the French, Dutch, Native Americans, and Rhode Island. In 1643, they joined together to form the New England Confederation. Rhode Island also requested membership but was refused. The confederation agreed to share the cost of war, provide soldiers in proportion to population, and make no treaties without each colony's consent. They also mutually promised to return fugitives and arbitrate disputes among themselves. The New England Confederation was the first league of colonies in English North America and the only successful one before the Revolutionary War. In assuming power to conduct war and make treaties, it went beyond colonial rights. The English government, in

Charles II, who became king upon the restoration of the English monarchy in 1660, fostered colonization in North America, in part, to pay his debts.

stricted the right of Catholics to worship, and created a Puritan code of behavior, including laws against swearing, drunkenness, and breaking the sabbath. Calvert appealed to Oliver Cromwell, who confirmed his proprietorship, but Lord Baltimore regained control of the colony only in 1657, after a period of local civil war.

ENGLISH COLONIZATION AFTER 1660

The accession of Charles II in 1660 initiated a new phase of colonization, in which the English government, at least in fits and starts, paid more attention to its colonies than it had before the Civil War. In 1662, the Crown granted Connecticut a charter that included New Haven, and the following year confirmed the charter Rhode Island had received from Parliament. To end the Dutch trade that had flourished with the English colonies during the 1640s and 1650s and to tighten colonial administration, the king and Parliament approved a series of navigation acts that formed the basis of a mercantilist colonial policy.

Navigation Acts

The English Commonwealth, recognizing the growing economic value of the colonies, had passed the Navigation Act of 1651. The law required that goods brought to England or its colonies from Asia, Africa, or America be carried on English ships (including those of its colonies). Goods from European nations had to be transported on either English ships or those of the country of origin. The chief purposes of the act were to encourage growth of England's merchant marine and to challenge Dutch ascendancy on the seas and in colonial ports. The Commonwealth went further in 1652–1654, with the first Anglo-Dutch War, by attacking Dutch vessels in the English Channel and North Sea. The English took more than one thousand Dutch ships, greatly expanding their merchant fleet.

the midst of Civil War, was too preoccupied to react.

In the Chesapeake colonies, whose governments had close ties to the king, the Civil War and its aftermath were more disruptive. In 1652, after some delay, the English Commonwealth removed the royalist Virginia governor, William Berkeley, because he had proclaimed Charles II the king upon his father's execution. In Maryland, the parliamentary revolt weakened the position of Lord Baltimore, whose authority came directly from the king. Protestants, especially Puritans, constituted an antiproprietary force. Ironically, the proprietor had encouraged Puritans to migrate from Virginia, where they had suffered Governor Berkeley's persecution. Calvert approved the "Act Concerning Religion" (1649), which guaranteed freedom of religion to all Christians. Nevertheless, in 1654, the Maryland Puritans established a commonwealth. Their assembly deposed the proprietor's government, re-

The Navigation Acts of 1660, 1663, and 1673 confirmed the 1651 restrictions on transport and created a list of "enumerated articles"—major colonial products including tobacco, sugar, indigo, cotton, ginger, and dyewoods—which could be shipped only to England or another English colony. The colonists could not sell these goods directly to other nations. The "articles" first went to England, where they were taxed and reexported by English merchants, who benefited from the business. Conversely, with some exceptions including salt, horses, and wines, all goods shipped from other nations to the English colonies had to go to England first. The colonists considered these laws detrimental because English middlemen added charges to products going in both directions. The English government created a colonial administration to enforce the acts, but the results were complicated and inefficient. Colonial governors, required to ban foreign ships from their ports, lacked the resources (and in many cases the will) to eliminate smuggling.

Carolina

Charles II was penniless when he ascended the throne and owed substantial debts to his supporters. Expansion of the colonial empire permitted him to repay these creditors with land and offices, and at the same time advance England's commerce and national power. Carolina, named for the king, was the first post-Restoration colony on the North American mainland. In 1663, the area between Virginia and Spanish Florida was unoccupied by Europeans, but Spain had better title to the land than England. Nevertheless, the English proceeded with plans to establish a colony and, with the Treaty of Madrid (1670), obtained Spain's concession of lands north of present-day Charleston. The chief promoters of Carolina were Anthony Ashley Cooper, Governor William Berkeley of Virginia, and John Colleton, a West Indies planter. They obtained help from five men who were close to the king; together the eight associates became proprietors of Carolina. They obtained a charter like Maryland's, permitting them to make laws with the consent of the freemen. The proprietors received wide latitude in matters of religion, with the power to build churches and offer freedom of worship. They drew up the "Fundamental Constitutions of Carolina," creating a complicated feudal society with nobles and lords, a scheme the ordinary settlers of Carolina refused to accept. As in Maryland and elsewhere, immigrants wanted land ownership, not tenancy. And freemen who owned property demanded a voice in government.

Two colonies developed in Carolina. Small planters from Virginia built the first, which later became North Carolina. As early as 1653, people had settled on the shores of Albemarle Sound, where they raised tobacco, corn, and livestock. In 1664, William Berkeley, governor of Virginia and one of the Carolina proprietors, sent William Drummond to organize a council and assembly. The Albemarle settlement remained poor, a haven for pirates, and difficult to govern. In 1691, the Carolina proprietors effectively established North Carolina by appointing a separate governor.

The second Carolina colony, which the proprietors actually planned, was located at Charles Town, in the future South Carolina. After two unsuccessful attempts, Anthony Ashley Cooper in 1670 organized a permanent settlement. South Carolina has been called "the colony of a colony" because so many of its early settlers came from the West Indies island of Barbados, which had run out of vacant land. The Barbadian planters had money to develop plantations in Carolina and owned African slaves to do the work. The proprietors partially abandoned their feudal land scheme, offering generous acreages to household heads for each person brought to the colony. A planter, with his own family and several enslaved blacks, could qualify for hundreds of acres. From the colony's founding, a large proportion of South Carolinians were African slaves, comprising between one-fourth and one-third of the settlers during the earliest years. They produced food, livestock, firewood, and barrel staves for Barbados, where sugar was the dominant crop.

New York and New Jersey

To control North America, the English next had to seize New Netherland. With a series of outposts, the Dutch held the region between Connecticut and Maryland, including lands on the Delaware River that Sweden settled in 1638 and the Dutch took in 1655. The English justified their attack in 1664 against New

Netherland on several grounds, including John Cabot's 1497 voyage to the region and Dutch illegal trade with English colonies. Settlers from New England living under Dutch jurisdiction complained that Governor Peter Stuyvesant ruled as a dictator. They reported to the English that Dutch military defenses could not withstand attack. James, the duke of York, Lord High Admiral of the Navy, urged his brother, Charles II, to send a fleet. The king granted James a proprietary charter for lands between the Connecticut and Delaware rivers, as well as Long Island, Nantucket, Martha's Vineyard, and part of present-day Maine. The charter gave the duke wide governmental powers, even dispensing with an assembly, which the Maryland and Carolina charters required. The duke could write his own legal code as long as it conformed to the laws of England; inhabitants had no role in making laws, but could appeal court judgments to the king.

With charter in hand, James forced out the Dutch. In 1664, his deputy governor, Richard Nicolls, with

Governor Peter Stuyvesant in 1664 surrendered New Amsterdam to the English without a fight. This portrait, painted c. 1661, is attributed to Henri Couturier.

four ships and 400 soldiers, took New Amsterdam without a fight—the Dutch defenses were indeed inadequate. The second Anglo-Dutch War (1665–1667) in part resulted from this action. Assuming ownership, James called his colony New York, but granted the land between the Delaware and lower Hudson rivers to John Lord Berkeley and Sir George Carteret, who named the area New Jersey. Though not mentioned in his charter, James also claimed the region west of the Delaware River, later Pennsylvania and Delaware, which he administered though New York.

Despite his extensive powers, as granted in the charter, James realized that he had to make New York attractive to inhabitants and future settlers if his colony was to prosper. He gave residents the choice of keeping their Dutch citizenship or becoming naturalized as English subjects. In 1665, he issued a legal code, called the "Duke's Laws," which guaranteed freedom of religion, recognized preexisting titles to land, and allowed New Englanders living in towns on Long Island to choose selectmen. The New York government consisted of a governor and council appointed by the duke, but no legislature.

When England and the Netherlands continued their rivalry in the third Anglo-Dutch War (1672–1674), the Dutch easily recaptured New York. After sixteen months they returned the colony to England as part of the Treaty of Westminster (1674). Receiving a new charter, James resumed possession of New York and reconfirmed his grants to New Jersey. Since 1664, that proprietorship had undergone several changes. A line drawn diagonally from the Delaware River to the Atlantic Ocean divided the territory into two colonies, West New Jersey and East New Jersey. Berkeley had sold West Jersey to a Quaker, Edward Byllinge, who then transferred title to a group of coreligionists, including William Penn. The duke confirmed Carteret's right to East Jersey immediately, but waited until 1680 to approve the Quaker proprietorship of West Jersey.

CONCLUSION

During the first three-quarters of the seventeenth century, the English, French, and Dutch ended Spain's

mastery of the New World. By 1675, in North America, the English held colonies along the Atlantic coast from New England to the Carolinas. The French controlled Canada, where its settlements grew slowly, and had explored the Great Lakes and the upper Mississippi Valley. The Dutch established, but lost, New Netherland, just as their commercial empire expanded, then faced serious threats. The Spanish, though more vulnerable than a century earlier, retained its borderland outposts in New Mexico and Florida. Everywhere the Europeans colonized, the Indians died from epidemic disease. Their relations with the white invaders depended a great deal on the numbers of Europeans who arrived, their attitudes, and goals of settlement.

From the beginning, the English colonies were diverse—in their form of government, degree of stability, relations with Native Americans, and economic base. The Crown fostered this variety by granting charters to an assortment of companies and individuals, including Puritan and Catholic opponents of the established church. Virginia and Maryland prospered from tobacco, but battled persistent high mortality. Still, in the mid-seventeenth century, the Chesapeake was "the best poor man's country" for English people willing to take risks. Most New Englanders came primarily to start a model society based on their Calvinist beliefs. They enjoyed a healthier climate than the people of the Chesapeake, but inferior soil. They supported themselves modestly by fishing and mixed farming, developing trade with the West Indies to pay for English imports. In New Mexico, Hispanic colonists exploited the Pueblos' labor to support their trade with Mexico, while Catholic missionaries tried to claim the Indians' souls. In all three areas—New England, the Chesapeake, and New Mexico—pressures between Europeans and Native Americans, and within the colonial societies, would soon erupt in war.

RECOMMENDED READINGS

Anderson, Virginia D. *New England's Generation: The Great Migration and the Formation of Society and Culture in the Seventeenth Century* (1991). Compares the motivations and experiences of Puritan settlers with succeeding generations.

Berkin, Carol. *First Generations: Women in Colonial America* (1996). A balanced survey of women of different backgrounds.

Breen, T. H., and Innes, Stephen. *"Myne Owne Ground": Race and Freedom on Virginia's Eastern Shore, 1640–1676* (1980). Focuses on opportunities of free blacks before the onslaught of rigid racial slavery.

Cronon, William. *Changes in the Land: Indians, Colonists, and the Ecology of New England* (1983). Contrasts Native American and settler use of the environment.

Dunn, Richard S. *Sugar and Slaves: The Rise of the Planter Class in the English West Indies, 1624–1713* (1972). An insightful history of the creation of slave regimes in the English Caribbean.

Greene, Jack P. *Pursuits of Happiness: The Social Development of Early Modern British Colonies and the Formation of American Culture* (1988). Provides a useful framework for understanding the various ways in which British settlements evolved.

Gutiérrez, Ramón A. *When Jesus Came, the Corn Mothers Went Away: Marriage, Sexuality, and Power in New Mexico, 1500–1846* (1991). Provocative evaluation of Spanish settlement, focusing particularly on women's status.

Morgan, Edmund S. *American Slavery, American Freedom: The Ordeal of Colonial Virginia* (1975). A detailed, stimulating account of English settlement and the transition to slavery.

Ulrich, Laurel Thatcher. *Good Wives: Image and Reality in the Lives of Women in Northern New England, 1650–1750* (1982). Considers the various roles of colonial women.

Wood, Peter H. *Black Majority: Negroes in Colonial South Carolina from 1670 Through the Stono Rebellion* (1974). Demonstrates the impact of rice culture on blacks in the Lower South.

Native Americans and Indian-European Relations

Axtell, James. *The Invasion Within: The Contest of Cultures in Colonial North America* (1985).

Bridenbaugh, Carl. *Early Americans* (1981).

Delage, Denys. *Bitter Feast: Amerindians and Europeans in Northeastern North America, 1600–64* (1993).

Lurie, Nancy O. "Indian Cultural Adjustment to European Civilization," in James M. Smith, ed., *Seventeenth-Century America: Essays in Colonial History* (1959).

Merrell, James H. *The Indians' New World: Catawbas and Their Neighbors from European Contact Through the Era of Removal* (1989).

Nash, Gary B. *Red, White, and Black: The Peoples of Early North America*, 3d ed. (1992).

Richter, Daniel K. *The Ordeal of the Longhouse: The Peoples of the Iroquois League in the Era of European Colonization* (1992).

Richter, Daniel K. and Merrell, James H., eds. *Beyond the Covenant Chain: The Iroquois and Their Neighbors in Indian North America, 1600–1800* (1987).

Salisbury, Neal. *Manitou and Providence: Indians, Europeans, and the Making of New England, 1500–1643* (1982).

Sweet, David G., and Nash, Gary B., eds. *Struggle and Survival in Colonial America* (1981).

Trigger, Bruce G. *Handbook of North American Indians, Vol. 15: The Northeast* (1978).

Wood, Peter H., Waselkov, Gregory A., and Hatley, M. Thomas., eds. *Powhatan's Mantle: Indians in the Colonial Southeast* (1989).

New France

Eccles, W. J. *The Canadian Frontier, 1534–1760,* rev. ed. (1983).

Eccles, W. J. *France in America* (1972).

Harris, R. Cole, ed. *Historical Atlas of Canada, Vol. 1: Origins to 1800* (1987).

Jaenen, Cornelius J. *Friend and Foe: Aspects of French-Amerindian Cultural Contact in the Sixteenth and Seventeenth Centuries* (1976).

Trigger, Bruce G. *Natives and Newcomers: Canada's "Heroic Age" Reconsidered* (1985).

New Netherland and the English Conquest

Condon, Thomas J. *New York Beginnings: The Commercial Origins of New Netherland* (1968).

Goodfriend, Joyce D. *Before the Melting Pot: Society and Culture in Colonial New York City, 1664–1730* (1992).

Kammen, Michael. *Colonial New York: A History* (1975).

Merwick, Donna. *Possessing Albany, 1630–1710: The Dutch and English Experiences* (1990).

Rink, Oliver A. *Holland on the Hudson: An Economic and Social History of Dutch New York* (1986).

Ritchie, Robert C. *The Duke's Province: A Study of New York's Politics and Society, 1664–1691* (1977).

Seventeenth-Century England

Campbell, Mildred. *The English Yeoman Under Elizabeth and the Early Stuarts* (1942).

Clark, Peter, and Slack, Paul, eds. *Crisis and Order in English Towns, 1500–1700: Essays in Urban History* (1972).

Hill, Christopher. *The World Turned Upside Down: Radical Ideas During the English Revolution* (1972).

Notestein, Wallace. *The English People on the Eve of Colonization, 1603–1630* (1954).

Wrightson, Keith. *English Society, 1580–1680* (1982).

Chesapeake and South Carolina

Billings, Warren M., Selby, John E., and Tate, Thad W. *Colonial Virginia* (1986).

Carr, Lois Green, Menard, Russell R., and Walsh, Lorena S. *Robert Cole's World: Agriculture and Society in Early Maryland* (1991).

Carr, Lois Green, Morgan, Philip D., and Russo, Jean B., eds. *Colonial Chesapeake Society* (1988).

Craven, Wesley Frank. *White, Red, and Black: The Seventeenth-Century Virginian* (1971).

Land, Aubrey C. *Colonial Maryland: A History* (1981).

Main, Gloria L. *Tobacco Colony: Life in Early Maryland, 1650–1720* (1982).

Norton, Mary Beth. *Founding Mothers and Fathers: Gendered Power and the Forming of American Society* (1996).

Salmon, Marylynn. *Women and the Law of Property in Early America* (1986).

Silver, Timothy. *A New Face on the Countryside: Indians, Colonists, and Slaves in South Atlantic Forests, 1500–1800* (1990).

Sirmans, M. Eugene. *Colonial South Carolina: A Political History, 1663–1763* (1966).

Tate, Thad W., and Ammerman, David L., eds. *The Chesapeake in the Seventeenth Century: Essays on Anglo-American Society and Politics* (1979).

Weir, Robert M. *Colonial South Carolina: A History* (1983).

New England

Allen, David Grayson. *In English Ways: The Movement of Societies and the Transferal of English Local Law and Custom to Massachusetts Bay in the Seventeenth Century* (1981).

Bailyn, Bernard. *The New England Merchants in the Seventeenth Century* (1955).

Dayton, Cornelia Hughes. *Women Before the Bar: Gender, Law, and Society in Connecticut, 1639–1789* (1995).

Demos, John. *A Little Commonwealth: Family Life in Plymouth Colony* (1970).

Foster, Stephen. *The Long Argument: English Puritanism and the Shaping of New England Culture, 1570–1700* (1991).

Greven, Philip J., Jr. *Four Generations: Population, Land, and Family in Colonial Andover, Massachusetts* (1970).

Hall, David D. *Worlds of Wonder, Days of Judgment: Popular Religious Belief in Early New England* (1989).

Hall, David D., Murrin, John M., and Tate, Thad W., eds. *Saints and Revolutionaries: Essays on Early American History* (1984).

James, Sydney V. *Colonial Rhode Island: A History* (1975).

Martin, John Frederick. *Profits in the Wilderness: Entrepreneurship and the Founding of New England Towns in the Seventeenth Century* (1991).

Morgan, Edmund S. *The Puritan Family: Religion and Domestic Relations in Seventeenth-Century New England,* rev. ed. (1966).

Morgan, Edmund S. *The Puritan Dilemma: The Story of John Winthrop* (1958).

Morgan, Edmund S. *Visible Saints: The History of a Puritan Idea* (1963).

Vickers, Daniel. *Farmers and Fishermen: Two Centuries of Work in Essex County, Massachusetts, 1630–1850* (1994).

METACOM

Metacom, the Wampanoag leader, who in 1676 tried to drive the New England settlers back "into the Sea."

Chapter 3

CRISIS AND CHANGE,

1675–1720

IN FEBRUARY 1676, Narragansett Indians burned Lancaster, Massachusetts, killing many of the English settlers and taking others prisoner, including Mary White Rowlandson, a minister's wife, and her three children. The Narragansetts had joined the Wampanoags and other New England Algonquians the preceding June, under leadership of the Wampanoag sachem, Metacom, to destroy the European settlements. In the Indians' words, according to Rowlandson, "they would knock all the Rogues in the head, or drive them into the Sea, or make them flie the Country."

In a published narrative of her captivity, Rowlandson described her eleven-week ordeal, during which she traveled more than 150 miles, mostly on foot, as the Narragansetts attacked towns and fought the colonial forces. Though Rowlandson began her captivity with hatred toward the Indians, whom she called "Barbarous Creatures," she came to respect some as individuals and to appreciate aspects of their culture. She was most impressed, she said, that while the Algonquians had little corn, "I did not see (all the time I was among them) one Man, or Woman, or Child, die with Hunger." They ate "Ground-nuts . . . also Nuts and Acorns, Hartychoaks, Lilly-roots, Ground-beans, and several other weeds and roots that I know

not." Desperately hungry, Rowlandson ate unfamiliar foods too, surviving to rejoin her husband in Boston. Though she credited God for keeping her alive, clearly her adaptability helped pull her through.

Metacom's War was just one of the crises that afflicted colonial America in the years 1675 to 1680. In fact, the last quarter of the seventeenth century was generally a period of turmoil and change. In the Chesapeake, at the time of Metacom's War, a comparatively minor skirmish between Indians and whites escalated into serious warfare, resulting in Bacon's Rebellion, a civil war among the English settlers of Virginia. In 1680, the Pueblos expelled their Spanish taskmasters from New Mexico for thirteen years. During the 1680s, an unstable English government disrupted politics in the colonies. Charles II died just a few years after granting a charter for Pennsylvania. His brother, James II, a Roman Catholic, succeeded him and attempted to make sweeping changes in both the home and colonial governments, including consolidation of many colonies under the Dominion of New England. James's efforts met strong resistance: The Glorious Revolution of 1688 in England quickly ended his reign. The following year, settlers in Massachusetts, New York, and Maryland overthrew his provincial governments, declaring allegiance to the new king and

CHRONOLOGY

1675	Appointment of English Lords of Trade
1675–1676	Metacom's War
	Bacon's Rebellion
1678	Charles II demands renegotiation of Massachusetts charter
1680	Popé's Rebellion
1681	William Penn receives Pennsylvania charter
1682	La Salle claims the Mississippi Valley for France
1683	Iroquois of New York defeat New France
1684	Revocation of Massachusetts charter
1685	James II becomes king of England
	Dominion of New England created
1688–1689	Glorious Revolution in England
	William and Mary ascend throne
1689	Revolutions in Massachusetts, New York, and Maryland
1689–1697	King William's War
1690	Spanish settlements in Texas
1691	Massachusetts receives its new charter
1691–1692	Salem witchcraft hysteria
1693	Spanish regain control of New Mexico
1696	Board of Trade and Plantations replaces Lords of Trade
1698	Royal African Company loses slave trade monopoly
1699	French establish Louisiana
1701	Iroquois treaty of neutrality
1702–1713	Queen Anne's War
1704	South Carolina defeats Spanish Florida
1712	Slave revolt in New York City
1715	Calverts regain Maryland government
	Yamassee War in South Carolina

queen, William and Mary. In Massachusetts, the impact of years of political uncertainty helped spread witchcraft hysteria from Salem to other towns.

From 1689 to 1713, European wars spilled into North America, fueling conflicts in Florida and Canada among Native Americans, English, French, and Spanish. The French moved south through the Mississippi Valley and founded Louisiana, while the English pushed south into Florida, west across the Appalachian Mountains, and north into Maine. As the English colonies expanded and matured, their economies and labor systems diverged, particularly with the entrenchment of slavery in the south. While slave traders imported Africans into all of the English provinces by 1700, by far the largest proportion worked in fields of tobacco and rice. Even with so much conflict during the late seventeenth century, planters built successful staple crop economies in the southern colonies, while northerners profited from networks of trade with England, Europe, and the slave regimes of the Caribbean, Carolina, and the Chesapeake.

REBELLIONS AND WAR

The wars of 1675 to 1680 in New England, Virginia, and New Mexico resulted from pressures that had been building for decades. In Massachusetts, the spread of settlement as second and third generations of colonists came of age forced Native Americans to defend their homes. In Virginia, demands of ex-servants for good land precipitated a civil war, while in New Mexico, severe droughts deepened opposition to forced labor and religious persecution, impelling the Pueblos to rid themselves of Spanish overlords. After the upheavals, elites in each settlement made changes that avoided further serious revolt.

Decline of New England Orthodoxy

In 1675, with the prospect of a major Indian war, Massachusetts seemed to have lost sight of the goals of

The Hingham, Massachusetts, church was originally built in 1681, when ship carpenters framed the interior of the roof as a ship's keel in reverse (left). The exterior view (right) reflects renovations completed in the eighteenth century.

its first settlers. When the Indians attacked, Puritan ministers warned the sons and daughters of the founding generation that God was punishing them for their faithlessness and sin, for their departure from the godly commonwealth.

In fact, Puritan church membership had declined since 1650, especially among men, who were less successful than women in reaching God, of being saved. After mid-century, women became a large proportion of the "elect," comprising 60 percent, and in some congregations 75 percent, of newly admitted members. The ministers believed that men were becoming more worldly, thus undermining the church's social and political authority. A related problem was that the children of nonchurch members could not be baptized. In 1662, the clergy devised an alternative to full church membership, the Half-Way Covenant, to keep influential citizens within the religious community. The covenant permitted adults who had been baptized but who were not yet saved to be "half-way" members. In congregations that accepted this innovation (not all churches did), people could assume partial status by showing that they understood Christian principles and would strive to obey God. As unconverted members, they were not entitled to take communion, but could have their children baptized.

The growth of competing religions in New England also proved to Puritan ministers that the model society had failed. Believing theirs to be the only true religion, Puritans rooted out dissent, as with Roger Williams and Anne Hutchinson in the 1630s. After 1650, though, the Quakers and Baptists threatened religious unity. The Society of Friends, or Quakers, was a radical Protestant sect born in the turmoil of the English Civil War. Like the Puritans, they were reformers who believed that the Church of England was corrupt and should be purified of its rituals, decorations, and hierarchy. But the Quakers went even further. They claimed that the Puritans also practiced false doctrine by paying ministers to preach, relying too much on the Bible as the word of God, and retaining the sacraments of baptism and communion. The Friends believed that God communicated directly with individuals, through the "Spirit" or "Light." They worshipped by gathering in plain meetinghouses (or in the early years, in fields and private houses) to "wait upon the Lord." In worship services, they had no Bible reading, prepared sermon, music, or ritual.

Statue of Mary Dyer, the Quaker missionary hanged in Massachusetts in 1660.

Rather, they waited in silence for the Spirit to inspire one or several of the congregation to communicate God's message. Those to whom the Spirit manifested itself regularly were ministers, including women as well as men. They required no advanced learning because their words were supposed to come straight from God, not a prepared text.

Appalled by these Quaker teachings, Puritan leaders tried to prevent their spread by deporting the traveling English missionaries who arrived on their shores. The ministers were stubborn, however, repeatedly returning to Massachusetts. They interrupted Puritan church services, preached in the streets, and made some converts among the people. The Puritan magistrates arrested and whipped them, even cropping their ears. In 1658, the General Court prescribed the death penalty for Quakers who returned after banishment. Several missionaries were hanged, including Mary Dyer in 1660, who had determined to "look their bloody laws in the face."

The hangings proved a turning point in the history of New England, for they caused consternation on both sides of the Atlantic. When Charles II demanded an explanation, the Puritans—fearing the loss of their charter—ended the executions. The magistrates continued to persecute nonconformers, but over the decades following 1660 realized that their policy of intolerance had failed. Rhode Island, a haven for people of all religions, served as a base for Quaker missionaries to evangelize in the Puritan colonies, further supporting its reputation among Puritans as "the sewer of New England." The Baptists, whose objection to infant baptism was their chief disagreement with orthodox Puritans, increased in numbers after approval of the Half-Way Covenant, which they vehemently opposed. They believed that a church should include only the saved, indeed that only the saved should be baptized. Despite persecution, dissenters successfully formed congregations throughout New England.

Metacom's War

Despite the Puritan ministers' plaintive cries, increasing worldliness and religious diversity did not cause Metacom's War. Rather, the unceasing expansion of white settlers into the frontier destroyed the relative peace between the Algonquians and the settlers of New England. By 1675, more than 50,000 whites inhabited the region. With a healthful environment, the colonists had successfully heeded the biblical injunction "to be fruitful and multiply." They had large families of sons and daughters who desired farms of their own. These settlers occupied more and more of the hunting, fishing, and agricultural lands of the Indians who, decimated by European diseases and outnumbered by the whites, recognized the threat to their ways of life.

Since the massacre of the Pequots in 1637, the Puritans and Native Americans of New England had managed an uneasy peace. The colonists traded for furs with local nations and with the Mohawks, the closest nation of Iroquois in New York. Some Puritan ministers, of whom John Eliot is best known, convinced several local tribes who were greatly diminished by disease and loss of lands to dwell in "praying towns." In these villages, adjacent to but separate from the towns of white settlers, the Indians were supposed to adopt English customs and learn the fundamentals of Puritan religion. By 1674, Eliot had organized four-

Map 3.1   New England at the Time of Metacom's War, 1675–1676

teen praying towns of Native Americans who took the first steps toward giving up their traditional ways.

Many New England Indians kept their autonomy, however, including the Wampanoags of Plymouth and Mohegans of Connecticut. Even so, they remained allies of the Puritan governments for many years. Trouble began in 1671, when the Plymouth government attempted to subordinate the Wampanoags by forcing them to surrender their firearms and obtain permission to sell land. Metacom, whom the colonists called King Philip as an insult, built a league with neighboring

tribes. When John Sassamon, an Indian educated at Harvard College, informed the Plymouth government of impending attack and was murdered, the white authorities hanged three Wampanoags for the deed.

Metacom mobilized Algonquians throughout New England, attacking fifty-two of ninety English towns within the region, including some within twenty miles of the coast. White refugees fled to Boston. But by the end of summer 1676, with the help of the Mohawks, the colonial governments turned back the attack, as disease, hunger, and a weapons shortage weakened

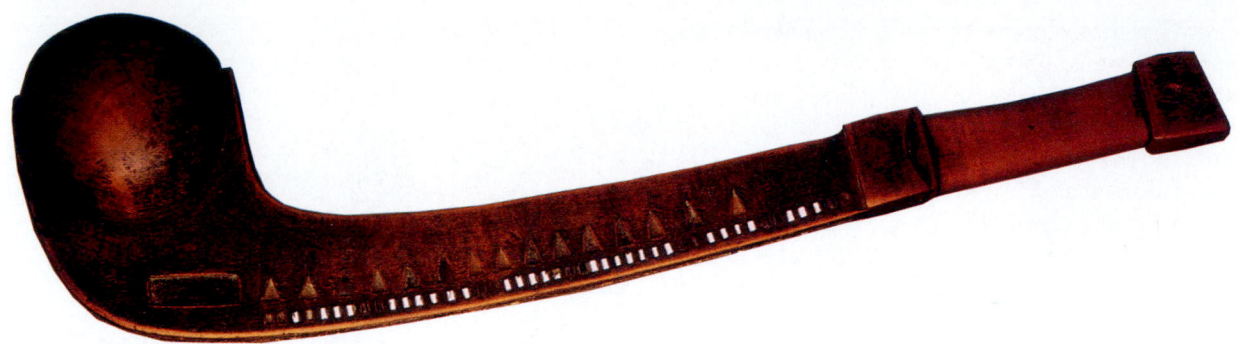

Metacom's war club, inlaid with wampum beads. This club was stolen in 1970 from the Fruitlands Museum in Harvard, Massachusetts.

Metacom's troops. The war took a heavy toll on both sides, for the Algonquians destroyed twelve towns and killed many colonists. White frontier settlement would not reach its 1675 limits for another forty years.

For the Indians of southern New England, the war was calamitous. Thousands died and many others were enslaved. Even bands who supported the English lost autonomy. At the outbreak of war, the colonists had forced residents of the praying towns, who were allies of the white governments, to live on desolate Deer Island in Boston Harbor, where they suffered from lack of food and shelter. Some of the Indian men later fought in the colonial militia against Metacom, but when the war was over, all Native Americans in southern New England had to live in praying towns, now essentially reservations, where they worked as servants or tenant farmers for neighboring whites. Metacom was killed, his head paraded before the white settlements, and kept on a pole in Plymouth for twenty years; his wife and son were sold as slaves.

War in the Chesapeake

Just as New England struggled over land in Metacom's War, Virginia faced a similar crisis in Bacon's Rebellion. The Chesapeake uprising was more complicated, for it involved civil war among the English as well as Indian-white conflict. But at its root, the chief issue was land: How could the competing interests of landless immigrants and dispossessed natives be resolved? Since the 1640s, the white population of Virginia and

Maryland had grown quickly with the arrival of immigrants—both wealthy and poor—who sought to increase their fortunes in America. By 1670, approximately 40,000 colonists lived in the Chesapeake, including native-born sons and daughters of early settlers as well as the more recent arrivals. Among the new immigrants were servants who expected to obtain land upon completing their terms.

In the 1670s, however, many Virginians discovered that the combination of low tobacco prices and high land prices blocked their dream of obtaining plantations. They received headrights, but could find no good vacant tobacco land to claim. Part of the problem, these landless freemen believed, was that the Indians held too much territory. Specifically, the 1646 treaty between the Virginia government and the Powhatans designated the area north of the York River for Native Americans. This agreement had been acceptable to whites in the 1640s when space south of the York seemed ample, but was unsatisfactory thirty years later, when white settlement was pushing north. It was also true, many freemen recognized, that wealthy planters, powerful in government, speculated in large acreages that they left empty while others starved for land.

The first flames of war occurred in July 1675, when some Doeg Indians attempted to take hogs as payment for a settler's unpaid debt. After people on both sides were killed, the Susquehannocks, who were allies of both the Doegs and the Virginia government, got involved. When the Susquehannocks attacked frontier settlements, a thousand-man army of Virginia

and Maryland colonists marched against their village on the Potomac River. Vastly outnumbered, several sachems agreed to negotiate, but when they left their stockade, the colonists murdered them. During the winter of 1675–1676, the Susquehannocks retaliated, raising fears that Metacom's War had spread south. Discontented and vengeful colonists responded indiscriminately, killing friendly neighboring Indians rather than those who were actually attacking the frontier.

The landless freemen found a leader in Nathaniel Bacon, also a newcomer but of a different class. Only twenty-nine years old, Bacon belonged to a wealthy family and had come to Virginia with enough money to purchase a large plantation. Governor Berkeley nominated him to the Virginia council, despite his youth, giving him other privileges as well. Nevertheless, Bacon evidently saw his opportunity to challenge Berkeley for leadership of the colony by mobilizing freemen and small planters against the Indians. While Berkeley wanted peace with the Susquehannocks, Bacon's forces intended to annihilate all of the natives, whether friends or foes, because they viewed all Indians as obstacles to white control of the land. The settlers knew that the natives were weak, with just a fraction of their pre-1607 population. Bacon's supporters

Sir William Berkeley was governor of Virginia for more than a quarter century. He alienated landless Virginians by ignoring their grievances and attempting to keep peace with the Indians.

also demanded a greater voice in the Virginia government, for they believed that the large planters who dominated the Assembly were out for their own profit, while ignoring the needs of ordinary settlers.

Governor Berkeley declared Bacon a traitor, sent troops to end his forays against the Indians, and requested reinforcements from England. The governor also called new elections that brought many Bacon supporters into the House of Burgesses. The delegates passed measures to stop the political abuses of the elite: They extended suffrage to landless freemen, taxed provincial councilors, required the election of local representatives for assessing taxes, and placed limits on the terms and fees of local officials. These efforts failed to end the rebellion, as Bacon's army burned Jamestown. For months, Virginians plundered the plantations of neighbors who took the other side. Few

A reconstruction of a typical Chesapeake colonist's house at the Godiah Spray tobacco plantation at historic St. Mary's City, Maryland.

MARY ROWLANDSON'S NARRATIVE OF HER CAPTURE BY NARRAGANSETT INDIANS, 1676

Mary Rowlandson was the wife of the minister of Lancaster, Massachusetts, which the Narragansetts assaulted in 1676 during Metacom's War. The following account of the attack, taken from the published narrative of her captivity, illustrates the religious framework in which she cast her experiences.

At length they came and beset our own House, and quickly it was the dolefullest day that ever mine eyes saw. The House stood upon the edge of a Hill; some of the *Indians* got behind the Hill, others into the Barn, and others behind any thing that would shelter them; from all which Places they shot against the House, so that the Bullets seemed to fly like Hail; and quickly they wounded one Man among us, then another, and then a third. About two Hours (according to my observation in that amazing time) they had been about the House before they could prevail to fire it. . . . They fired it once, and one ventured out and quenched it; but they quickly fired it again, and that took. Now is that dreadful Hour come that I have often heard of, (in the time of the War, as it was the Case of others,) but now mine Eyes see it. Some in our House were fighting for their Lives, others wallowing in their Blood; the House on fire over our Heads, and the bloody Heathen ready to knock us on the Head if we stirred out. Now might we hear Mothers and Children crying out for themselves and one another, *Lord, what shall we do?* Then I took my Children (and one of my Sisters, hers) to go forth and leave the House; but as soon as we came to the Door and appeared, the *Indians* shot so thick that the Bullets rattled against the House as if one had taken an handful of Stones and threw them; so that we were fain to give back. We had six stout Dogs belonging to our Garrison, but none of them would stir, though another time, if an *Indian* had come to the Door, they were ready to fly upon him, and tear him down. The Lord hereby would make us the more to acknowledge his Hand, and to see that our Help is always in him. But out we must go, the Fire increasing and coming along behind us roaring, and the *Indians* gaping before us with their Guns, Spears, and Hatchets to devour us. No sooner were we out of the House but my Brother-in-Law (being before wounded, in defending the House, in or near the Throat) fell down dead, whereat the *Indians* scornfully shouted

white fatalities resulted from this depredation, however, as rebels vented most of their frustration by killing Indians, not fellow colonists. The rebellion finally ceased with Bacon's death, probably of dysentery, in October 1676. The war marked a serious defeat for the Indians of the Chesapeake, who lost the protection of the 1646 treaty and gradually surrendered their lands.

Bacon's Rebellion awakened the Virginia elites to the dangers of a large class of landless freemen, but re-

sulted in no substantive political change. A new assembly in 1677 reversed the reform acts of the 1676 House of Burgesses, including the law extending the vote to landless freemen. A commission appointed by the Crown to end the rebellion also opposed expanding popular power, stating that to grant suffrage to unpropertied men was "repugnant to the Lawes of England and to the Lawes and Peace of the Colony." The commission did call for taxing "the great Ingrossers of Lands" who caused "misery and mischiefs" by "occa-

and hallowed, and were presently upon him, stripping off his Clothes. The Bullets flying thick, one went thorow my side, and the same (as would seem) thorow the Bowels and Hand of my dear Child in my Arms. One of my eldest Sister's Children (named William) had then his Leg broken, which the *Indians* perceiving, they knock'd him on the head. Thus were we butchered by those merciless Heathen, standing amazed, with the Blood running down to our Heels. My elder sister, being yet in the House, and seeing those woful Sights, the Infidels hauling Mothers one way and Children another, and some wallowing in their Blood, and her elder son telling her that (her Son) William was dead, and myself was wounded; she said, *And, Lord, let me die with them!* which was no sooner said but she was struck with a Bullet, and fell down dead over the Threshold. I hope she is reaping the Fruit of her good Labours, being faithful to the Service of God in her Place. In her younger years she lay under much trouble upon Spiritual accounts, till it pleased God to make that precious Scripture take hold of her Heart, *2 Cor.* xii. 9, *And he said unto me, My grace is sufficient for thee.* More than twenty years after, I have heard her tell how sweet and comfortable that Place was to her. But to return: the *Indians* laid hold of us, pulling me one way and the Children another, and said, *Come, go along with us.* I told them they would kill me. They answered, *If I were willing to go along with them, they would not hurt me.*

O the doleful Sight that now was to behold at this House! *Come, behold the works of the Lord, what desolation he has made in the earth.* Of thirty seven Persons who were in this one House, none escaped either present Death or a bitter Captivity, save only one, who might say as he, *Job* i. 15, *And I only am escaped alone to tell the news.* There were twelve killed, some shot, some stabb'd with their Spears, some knock'd down with their Hatchets. . . . It was a solemn Sight to see so many Christians lying in their Blood, some here and some there, like a company of Sheep torn by Wolves; all of them stript naked by a company of hell-hounds, roaring, singing, ranting, and insulting, as if they would have torn our very hearts out; yet the Lord, by his Almighty power, preserved a number of us from death, for there were twenty-four of us taken alive; and carried Captive.

I had often before this said, that if the *Indians* should come, I should chuse rather to be killed by them than taken alive; but when it came to the trial my mind changed; their glittering Weapons so daunted my Spirit, that I chose rather to go along with those (as I may say) ravenous Bears, than that moment to end my daies.

sioning the Planters to stragle to such remote distances when they cannot find land neerer to seat themselves but by being Tenants which in a Continent they think hard." Nothing was done, however, to remedy that situation. Rather than create a society in which power and wealth were distributed more evenly, in which Virginia once again would offer opportunity to poor Englishmen, the planter elite began importing more enslaved Africans. Bound for life and restricted by laws, black slaves could not demand farms or a voice in government. With settlement in New Jersey, Carolina, and Pennsylvania during the 1670s and 1680s, immigrants had better options than Virginia.

Popé's Rebellion

Four years after Bacon's Rebellion, across the continent in New Mexico, the Pueblos drove out the Spanish—and kept them out for thirteen years. The

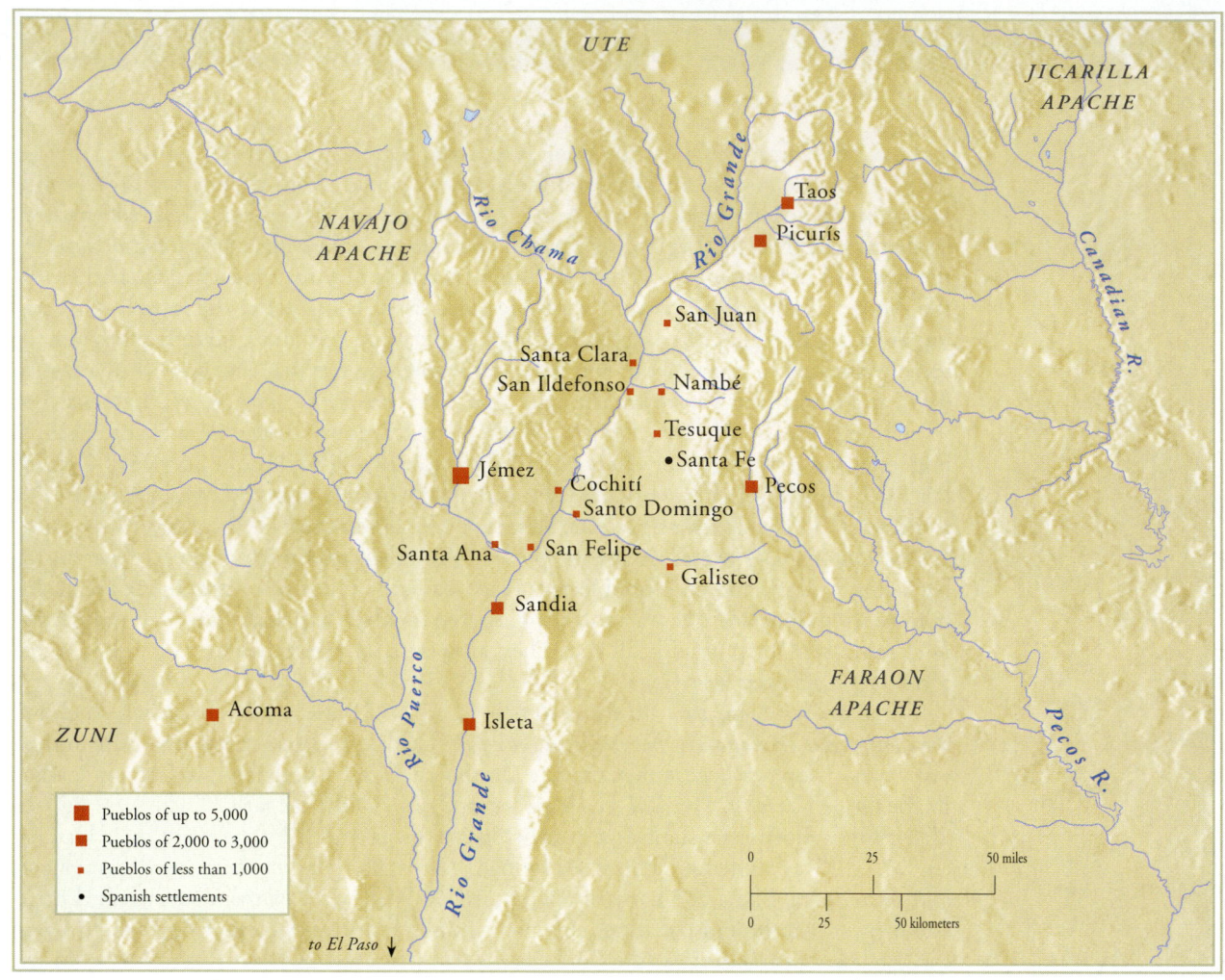

UTE

JICARILLA APACHE

Rio Grande

Taos

Picurís

NAVAJO APACHE

Rio Chama

San Juan

Santa Clara

San Ildefonso

Nambé

Tesuque

• Santa Fe

Jémez

Cochití

Santo Domingo

Pecos

Santa Ana

San Felipe

Galisteo

Sandia

FARAON APACHE

Rio Puerco

Acoma

ZUNI

Isleta

Rio Grande

Canadian R.

Pecos R.

■ Pueblos of up to 5,000
■ Pueblos of 2,000 to 3,000
▪ Pueblos of less than 1,000
• Spanish settlements

0   25   50 miles

0   25   50 kilometers

to El Paso ↓

MAP 3.2 | NEW MEXICO, CA. 1680

Pueblos had the advantage of a much smaller white population in New Mexico—2,800—than in New England or the Chesapeake. The Spanish hold over the missions was tenuous, for native fighting men greatly outnumbered Spanish troops. Nevertheless, the Hispanic settlers and priests demanded forced labor and strict adherence to Christianity from the Pueblos. A number of Indian towns had rebelled during the previous half century, but most failed to win autonomy because they fought the Spanish individually instead of combining with other villages.

The Pueblos became more desperate and enraged during the 1670s, when New Mexico endured severe drought. As famine persisted, Apaches and Navajos attacked the Pueblos. According to one missionary, "a great many Indians perished of hunger, lying dead along the roads, in the ravines, and in their huts." The Pueblos became convinced that the root of their troubles lay in their rejection of ancient gods, the *katsina*. To bring rain and renewed prosperity, some presented gifts to the katsina and performed dances that the Spanish had outlawed. When punished for abandon-

ing Catholicism—as in 1675, when the Spanish government executed three Pueblo priests and whipped 43 others—the Indians felt even greater resentment, leading to revolt.

The leader of the 1680 rebellion was Popé, a medicine man of the village of San Juan, north of Santa Fe. When the katsina told him that the Spanish must be driven from the land, he organized a general insurrection, sending knotted ropes to allied villages, indicating when the uprising should start. On August 10, 1680, a day earlier than planned because the Spanish governor, General Antonio de Otermín, had been warned of the impending revolt, the Pueblos launched a full-scale attack, killing 400 colonists and twenty-one priests. Strategically, the Indians confiscated or destroyed the settlers' chief means of transportation, their horses and mules. When Santa Fe fell to the rebels on September 21, the whites escaped south, settling in the area of present-day Ciudad Juárez, Mexico. Some Spaniards explained the revolt as God's punishment for their sins (much as the Puritans had understood Metacom's War), while others blamed the harsh labor and efforts to repress native religions. As Popé supervised, the Pueblos destroyed churches, broke up church bells, and burned images of Christ and the saints. According to one witness, "in order to take away their baptismal names, the water, and the holy oils, [the Indians] were to plunge into the rivers and wash themselves."

Several times during the next few years, the Spanish attempted without success to retake New Mexico. The rebellion spread south into northern Mexico, where Native Americans demolished settlements and missions. But by 1692, as famine continued, the Pueblo alliance fell into disarray, with resulting war over scarce supplies of corn. The new Spanish governor of New Mexico, Don Diego de Vargas, marched north to Santa Fe with 160 troops. Though many Indians resisted, the Spanish reestablished control over the province. In December 1693, after a three-day siege, Vargas's troops took Santa Fe, killing all of the Indian men and making slaves of the women and children. The Spanish subsequently retained a foothold in New Mexico, but not without further struggle. The Pueblos rejected the Franciscan missionaries, revolting once again in 1696, killing five priests and destroying churches. Some Pueblos fled from New Mexico while others submitted as Vargas systematically conquered the Indian towns once again. After 1696, the Spanish and Pueblos lived together in relative peace, but only

because the Hispanics eased requirements for tribute, forced labor, and adherence to Christianity.

WILLIAM PENN'S "HOLY EXPERIMENT"

In England, in the same year as Popé's Rebellion, the Quaker leader William Penn approached Charles II with a petition to establish a new colony in America, one that would avoid bloodshed by dealing justly with the Indians. While the Pueblos had not yet driven out the Spanish, Penn knew of Metacom's War and Bacon's Rebellion. He was determined to do things differently in Pennsylvania, to create a model society, but one that was distinct from the Puritan "city upon a hill."

Plans for Pennsylvania

William Penn had inherited a £16,000 debt owed to his father by the king, but had little hope for repayment in cash, so he requested a colony on the west bank of the Delaware River. Charles's brother James, the duke of York, governed the territory, which was inhabited by a small number of Dutch, Swedes, and Delaware Indians. The king approved Penn's request in 1681, granting him a charter for Pennsylvania which was more restrictive than either Lord Baltimore's or the duke of York's, in part because the English government was attempting to assert greater control over its colonies, in part because Penn was a Quaker. The new proprietor received the right to enact laws and impose taxes with the consent of the freemen, but was required to submit all laws for approval to the home government within five years of passage. And to protect the status of the Church of England, the charter stipulated that twenty Anglican inhabitants could request a minister from the bishop of London.

In establishing Pennsylvania, Penn hoped to provide a haven for Quakers where they could practice their religion and raise their families without harassment. Like New England Quakers, those in England confronted persecution as an outlaw sect. English Friends refused to pay tithes for church support or

William Penn was a wealthy Quaker who sought to create a model, peaceful society in Pennsylvania.

and colonists to resolve conflicts peacefully. He paid the Delawares a much lower price than he in turn charged the settlers, however, and failed to consider ways in which the Indians might be incorporated into Pennsylvania society. As in other colonies, the Pennsylvanians assumed the Indians would leave after they sold their land.

Like Lord Baltimore, Penn intended to make a fortune from Pennsylvania, summing up his goals: "the service of God first, the honor and advantage of the king, with our own profit." Despite Penn's strong Quaker convictions, which for some suggested a simple life, he appreciated fine food, drink, and accommodations. He was a gentleman who was chronically in debt. He possessed large landholdings in southern England and Ireland, retained many servants, and enjoyed such delicacies as salmon, partridges, saffron, and chocolate. Urgently needing money, he thought the sale of millions of acres in America would solve his financial problems.

attend Anglican services, and instead held their own meetings, which the government considered illegal "conventicles." Even more, Quakers refused to give oaths, arguing that one should always tell the truth, so they could not legally pledge allegiance to the king. They adopted pacifism as one of their central beliefs. Friends also professed to live according to the doctrine that all were equal in the eyes of God; they refused to follow certain customs, such as removing one's hat in the presence of superiors. For practicing their faith, they were jailed and fined, and when they refused to pay, local English officials took their property.

William Penn conceived of his colony as a "holy experiment," a place where Quakers could exercise their beliefs without interference, where everyone would live in harmony, and the government would operate like a Quaker meeting, acting in unison as it followed God's will. Penn also intended to reverse the pattern of Anglo-Indian relations in North America by consistently paying the Delaware Indians for tracts of land and setting up arbitration panels of Native Americans

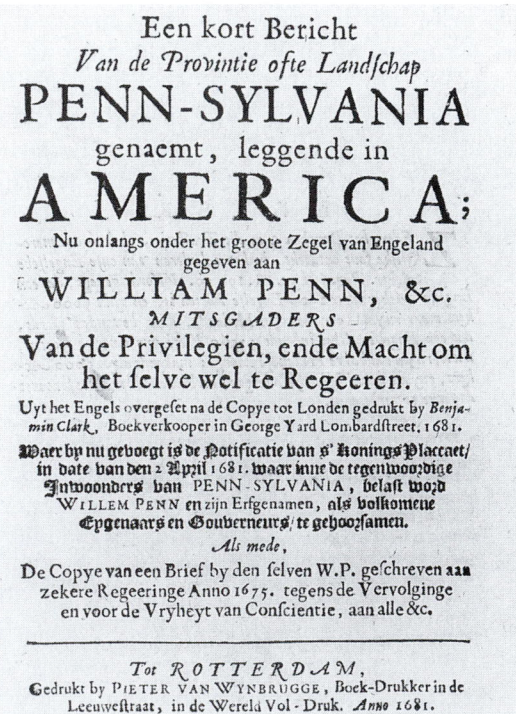

Title page of the Dutch edition of William Penn's promotional pamphlet, Some Account of the Province of Pennsylvania.

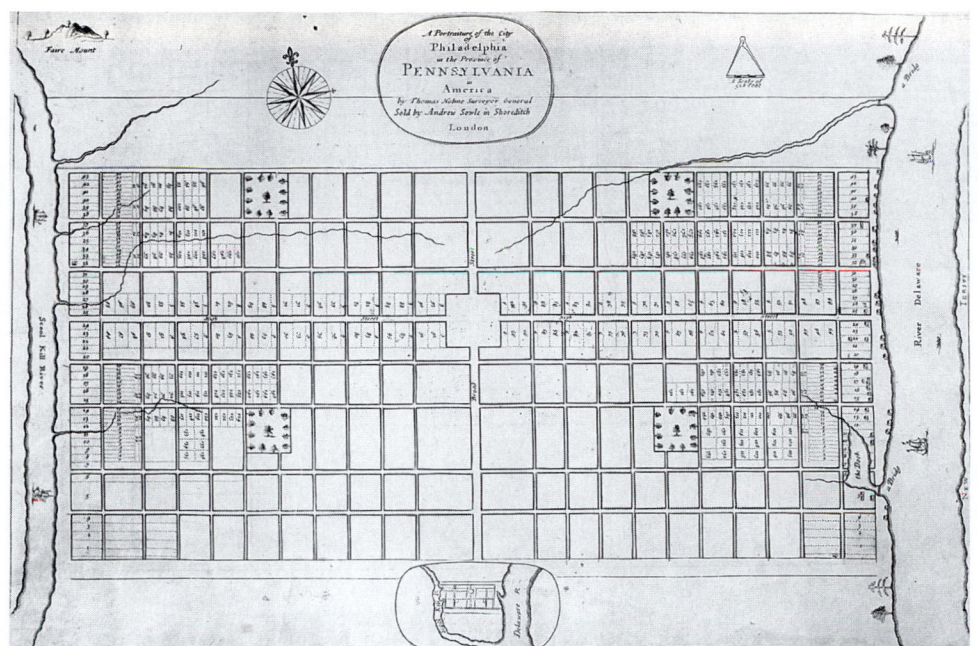

William Penn's plan of Philadelphia, which his surveyor-general Thomas Holme rendered in 1683 as A Portraiture of the City of Philadelphia. *During the colonial period, the city developed along the Delaware River (to the right), not on the Schuylkill River (to the left).*

Penn spent a great deal of time planning the colony. His scheme of government was quite progressive for its time, for it established an assembly with two houses, both elected by the freemen. In some colonies, such as Virginia, members of the upper house, or council, were appointed by the governor. Freemen included adult males who owned at least fifty acres of land or paid taxes on other property. During the early decades, when servants received fifty acres at the end of their terms, nearly every man in Pennsylvania could vote. Penn did not extend that right to women, even to those who owned property, nor did he alter the common law restrictions on married women. Though women Friends took an active role in their meetings as ministers, missionaries, and supervisors of discipline, their legal status in the Quaker commonwealth was similar to that in other colonies. Penn's laws stood out in another respect, however, requiring capital punishment for just two offenses, treason and murder, whereas other governments prescribed the death penalty for many more crimes.

The proprietor's planning went beyond politics, for he also drew up specifications for his capital city and the division of lands. In designing Philadelphia, in taking on the role of city planner, Penn was unique among early English colonizers. He conceived the city as a large "green country town," with wide streets in a grid pattern, public parks, ample lots, and brick houses, to avoid the conditions that had contributed to the London fire of 1666. He failed to fulfill his plan completely because he could not obtain enough acreage to build Philadelphia as he wanted. Dutch and Swedish residents already owned the land along the Delaware River, so Penn decided to buy a site of just 1,200 acres between the Delaware and Schuylkill rivers. His plan remained orderly, with the grid design and parks, but with lots of one-half to one acre instead of one hundred acres for those who purchased "proprietary shares" of 5,000 acres, which Penn was most eager to sell. Like the proprietors of other colonies, Penn discovered that buyers of large acreages were scarce, so he sold much smaller tracts. To maintain a constant income from the colony, landowners would pay annual quitrents.

A Diverse Society

Penn used his Quaker connections in England, Scotland, Ireland, and Holland to promote the colony, but

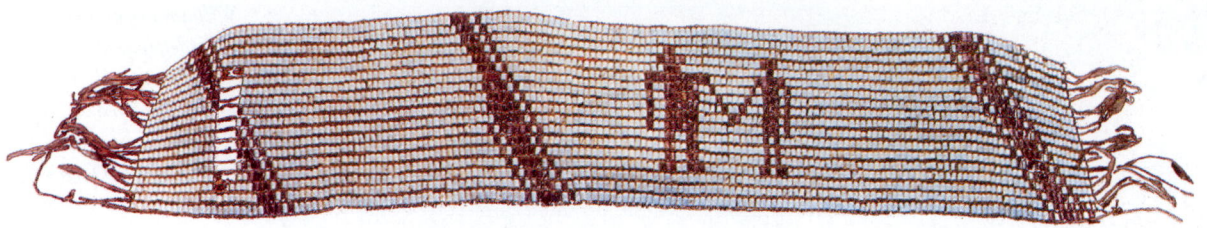

Wampum belt, which according to legend the Lenape gave to William Penn in 1682. It has become a symbol of Penn's efforts to preserve peace with the Indians of Pennsylvania.

did not restrict recruitment to Friends. He sold land briskly, as 600 people bought 700,000 acres within four years. Most of the buyers were Quaker farmers, merchants, artisans, and shopkeepers from England, though many also originated from Scotland, Ireland, Wales, Europe, the West Indies, Maryland, and New York. Their goals were both religious and economic: They wanted freedom to worship as well as opportunity to succeed in farming or trade.

Penn's settlers had a number of advantages, for they moved into an area inhabited by the Delaware, or Lenape, Indians, who were peaceful, sedentary Algonquians, and by Swedes, Finns, and Dutch, who served as intermediaries with the Indians. Both groups gave advice on adjusting to the new environment. The Delawares, who farmed, hunted, and fished, had welcomed trade with the Dutch as early as 1610 and yielded land to the whites. Because Dutch and Swedish settlements remained small, relatively few violent incidents occurred. By the time Penn arrived with thousands of colonists, the Lenape had declined significantly from disease, so they had little choice but to sell their lands and move away if they wanted to remain autonomous. In deeds negotiated between 1682 and 1684, the Delaware sachems sold tracts along the Delaware River from Christiana Creek in northern Delaware to the falls of the river in Bucks County, Pennsylvania. They received wampum, blankets, guns, ammunition, tools, rum, and other goods in return for their land.

By contrast, the European "old residents" integrated with the new arrivals, though not without friction. Some earned money by selling land and provisions, or serving as guides and interpreters. One local Swede, Captain Lasse Cock, in 1682 translated for the

Indians and English, arranged food, drink, and trade goods for the Delawares during negotiations, and traveled to the Susquehanna and Lehigh rivers as Penn's emissary. The Swedish, Dutch, and Finns continued to worship in their own congregations, but became naturalized as English subjects and some served in the assembly and local government. The old residents made up a large part of the population in the Lower Counties (later Delaware), leading to conflict as the different interests of the Lower Counties and Pennsylvania became clear. In 1704, after two decades of wrangling over the appointment of judges and the distance Lower County legislators had to travel to meetings, the three southern counties obtained their own separate Delaware assembly.

Pennsylvania got a boost from its late arrival on the colonial scene because its merchants could tap existing networks in the Atlantic economy. Substantial traders came from New York, the Chesapeake, and the West Indies, bringing their connections and capital to build breweries, tanneries, warehouses, wharves, and ships. Farmers found a market for wheat, livestock, and lumber in the West Indies trade. The Pennsylvanians faced nothing like the "starving times" or bloody conflict that had occurred in early Virginia, Plymouth, and Massachusetts. By 1700, Philadelphia became a thriving port town, with 700 houses and more than 3,000 people.

But for William Penn, his colony was deeply disappointing, as land sales reaped smaller profits than he had hoped and the costs of administering the colony soared. When purchasers refused to send him quitrents, he went more seriously into debt, even spending time in debtors' prison. Penn traveled to his colony twice, but stayed a total of only four years, in

part because he had to defend his charter at Court. While the province became prosperous and quite successful as a tolerant, diverse society, he reckoned it a failure.

THE GLORIOUS REVOLUTION AND ITS AFTERMATH

The founding of Pennsylvania coincided with the English government's effort to tighten colonial administration and enforce the Navigation Acts. Since the Restoration in 1660, Charles II's advisors, English merchants, and especially the king's brother James, the duke of York, pressed for greater control over the American colonies. They recognized the economic value of West Indian sugar, Chesapeake tobacco, and a burgeoning colonial population that promised a welcome market for manufactured goods. Compared to the Spanish empire, with its colonial government centralized under the Council of the Indies, English administration was a hodgepodge. The Privy Council at first appointed temporary committees to address colonial concerns, then in 1675 formed a permanent committee, the Lords of Trade, which met sporadically. Even after 1696, when the more formalized Board of Trade and Plantations was established, this body could gather information and give advice, but lacked authority to appoint colonial officials or enforce laws. These powers belonged to a host of governmental offices, including the secretary of state, the Treasury, and the War Office.

Dominion of New England

While experimenting with these committees, the Crown made other efforts to rein in the colonies. Most vulnerable was the Massachusetts Bay Colony, both for its unrestrictive charter and the perceived intransigence of Puritan leaders. Metacom's War proved to be only the first of a series of trials for the holy commonwealth. In 1678, Charles II required Massachusetts to send agents empowered to renegotiate the

charter. He specifically wanted the New Englanders to comply with the Navigation Acts and apologize for having coined their own money. The colonists delayed action, though they sent regrets for having passed laws contrary to the laws of England. They offered to renounce any "except such as the repealing whereof will make us to renounce the professed cause of our first coming hither." Half a century after settlement, Massachusetts leaders jealously guarded their autonomy and the mission of the founders.

Impressed by neither the Puritans' arguments nor the speed of their response, the English government brought legal proceedings against the Massachusetts Bay Company for "usurping to be a body Politick," and revoked the charter in 1684. The colony's assembly, the General Court, was prohibited from meeting. In February 1685, before a royal governor could be appointed, Charles died and the duke of York became king. James II quickly took advantage of events to move toward centralizing the colonies. With the Privy Council's consent, in 1685, he combined Massachusetts, New Hampshire, and Maine under the Dominion of New England, added Plymouth, Rhode Island, and Connecticut in 1686, and New York and New Jersey in 1688. Apparently, James's plan for the colonies was to create two large dominions, one north of the fortieth degree of latitude (the approximate location of Philadelphia) and one to the south. These dominions would supersede colonial charters, eliminating the confusing diversity of laws and political structures. Representative government would end. Before the Glorious Revolution of 1688, which removed James from the throne, he established the northern dominion, but not the southern.

For Massachusetts Puritans, who felt the force of James's scheme most harshly, the Dominion of New England was a disaster. James's governor-general, Sir Edmund Andros, made sweeping changes that undercut the Puritan notion of a covenanted community. He levied taxes without the approval of a representative assembly, restricted the power of town meetings, mandated religious toleration (a positive change by modern standards but not to the Puritans), and confiscated a Boston church for use by Anglicans. Andros enforced the Navigation Acts, favored his own cronies over the Puritan elite in distributing patronage, required landowners to obtain new land titles from the Crown, demanded payment of quitrents, and took control of common lands, portioning some to his

James II at the time of his accession in 1685, by Godfrey Kneller. An opponent of representative government, James was quickly deposed in the Glorious Revolution of 1688.

A nineteenth-century rendering of Sir Edmund Andros's unpopularity in Boston, by Howard Pyle. Through Andros, James II disbanded colonial governments in New England and New York, creating his Dominion of New England.

friends. A number of colonists rebelled, refusing to pay taxes without a voice in their passage, but were jailed and fined.

Revolutions of 1689

Governor Andros managed to avoid serious revolt until the spring of 1689, when news of James's removal from the throne reached Massachusetts. The king's rule had been as heavy-handed in England as in the colonies. A Roman Catholic, he installed his friends in office and defied Parliament. Protestants feared James would make England a Catholic nation under authoritarian rule. Thus, parliamentary leaders forced him into exile in France, inviting his Protestant daughter Mary and her husband William of Orange, the leader of the Dutch, to take the throne. The Glorious Revolution, though bloodless, had long-lasting results in England: It permanently limited the king's power by establishing parliamentary control of taxation, supremacy of law, and autonomy of the courts.

In the morning of April 18, 1689, many of Boston's populace left their homes, armed, and formed companies with the militia. The rebels, who included several Puritan ministers and some wealthy merchants, arrested Andros and his supporters. Numbering more than one thousand by afternoon, the insurgents deposed the dominion government. They interpreted the revocation of the charter and James's

illegal taxation and expropriation of lands as part of a "popish plot" that Protestant New England must help destroy.

With the dominion gone, Plymouth, Rhode Island, and Connecticut reactivated their charters, but Massachusetts, which had lost its charter under Charles II, had to negotiate a new one. The colonists' arguments for the charter were based less on the old covenant theory than on the fundamentals of the Glorious Revolution, especially the right of English people to representative government. The resulting 1691 Massachusetts charter, which annexed Plymouth to the Bay Colony, established a royal province with an elected assembly and a governor appointed by the king. The charter required freedom of worship and forbade religious restrictions on voting. Massachusetts Bay thus lost the constitutional basis for the theocracy of the founders, which had limited political participation to God's "elect."

Revolutions also took place in New York and Maryland in the wake of James II's fall. New York, which had been James's proprietary colony and part of the Dominion of New England, fell into turmoil with news of William and Mary's ascent to the throne in England and Andros's arrest in Boston. The reports unleashed opposition to Lieutenant Governor Francis Nicholson, who headed the dominion's government in New York. Residents of the colony, especially New England Puritans who had established towns on Long Island, had chafed for decades under the duke of York's arbitrary rule. They too defined the struggle in religious terms, as a crusade to destroy the "papist" threat.

In the city of New York, insurgents included merchants and artisans who had been denied economic privileges to trade and mill flour under James's government. In 1689, with Jacob Leisler, a German-born merchant and militia captain in the lead, they forced Nicholson back to England and elected a Committee of Safety to replace James's council. When Henry Sloughter, the new governor appointed by William and Mary, arrived in 1691, however, he reinstalled James's councilors, executing Leisler for treason. Despite Leisler's early proclamation of the new monarchs in 1689, his enemies had better connections in London.

In Maryland, simmering resentment of Protestants against the Roman Catholic proprietor erupted in the summer of 1689. Charles, Lord Baltimore, had

Charles Calvert, third Lord Baltimore, by Sir Godfrey Kneller. A Roman Catholic, Calvert lost control of the Maryland government in the wake of the Glorious Revolution.

departed the province in 1684 to defend at Court his northern boundary against William Penn. Baltimore's troubles intensified when his nephew, George Talbot, president of the provincial council, murdered the king's customs collector "with a dagger newly prepared and sharpened" aboard a royal ship. This event rocked the colony, so Baltimore sent a man he thought would provide strong leadership as governor, William Joseph, a Roman Catholic and adherent of James II. Upon arriving in 1688, Joseph proceeded to alienate Maryland's assemblymen, calling them adulterers and drunks. When he required them to renew their oaths of fidelity to the proprietor, they refused.

In July 1689, when Lord Baltimore still had not proclaimed the new monarchs, a handful of Maryland

THE TRIAL OF BRIDGET BISHOP, AN ACCUSED WITCH, SALEM, 1692

This report of Bridget Bishop's trial, published by Cotton Mather in *Wonders of the Invisible World,* shows the grounds on which Massachusetts courts convicted women and men of practicing witchcraft, including spectral evidence. In Goody Bishop's case, her accusers said her "shape" had attacked them. They also testified that Bishop's specter had tried to compel them to sign the devil's "book."

I. She was indicted for bewitching of several persons in the neighborhood, the indictment being drawn up, according to the form in such cases usual. And pleading, not guilty, there were brought in several persons, who had long undergone many kinds of miseries, which were preternaturally inflicted, and generally ascribed unto a horrible witchcraft. There was little occasion to prove the witchcraft; it being evident and notorious to all beholders. Now to fix the witchcraft on the prisoner at the bar, the first thing used was, the testimony of the bewitched; whereof, several testified, that the shape of the prisoner did oftentimes very grievously pinch them, choke them, bite them, and afflict them; urging them to write their names in a book, which the said specter called, ours. One of them did further testify, that it was the shape of this prisoner, with another, which one day took her from her wheel, and carrying her to the riverside, threatened there to drown her, if she did not sign to the book mentioned; which yet she refused. Others of them did also testify, that the said shape, did in her threats, brag to them, that she had been the death of sundry

leaders formed the Protestant Association. Aroused by rumors that Catholics were plotting with the Indians to destroy the Protestants, the Association raised troops, defeating the proprietary government without a shot. The rebels obtained articles of surrender that banned Catholics from provincial offices; sent a message to William and Mary informing them of the takeover and requesting a Protestant government; and elected an assembly—the "Associators' Convention"—which ruled Maryland for the next two and one-half years. Baltimore desperately tried to retain the colony. Though he kept proprietary rights to the soil and quitrents, in 1690 he lost the privilege to govern. The Calverts regained Maryland's government only in 1715, after Benedict Leonard, Charles's son, became an Anglican.

The three provincial revolutions of 1689, in Massachusetts, New York, and Maryland, had similarities to England's Glorious Revolution in the relative absence of bloodshed and the recurring theme of "popish plots." They failed, however, to bring about permanent change in the constitutional relationship between England and its colonies. The provincials, lacking delegates in Parliament, continued to endure taxation and mercantilist regulation without their assent. The colonial revolts of 1689 resembled Bacon's Rebellion of 1676, as they mobilized out-of-power elites, and their less affluent confederates, against those who controlled the colonial governments. In 1676, in Virginia, the insurgents had manipulated landless discontents by appealing to hatred against Native Americans as well as grievances against Berkeley's government. In

persons, then by her named; that she had ridden a man, then likewise named. Another testified, the apparition of ghosts unto the specter of Bishop, crying out, you murdered us! About the truth whereof, there was in the matter of fact, but too much suspicion.

II. It was testified, that at the examination of the prisoner, before the magistrates, the bewitched were extremely tortured. If she did but cast her eyes on them, they were presently struck down; and this in such a manner as there could be no collusion in the business. But upon the touch of her hand upon them, when they lay in their swoons, they would immediately revive; and not upon the touch of anyone's else. Moreover, upon some special actions of her body, as the shaking of her head, or the turning of her eyes, they presently and painfully fell into the like postures. And many of the like accidents now fell out, while she was at the bar. One at the same time testifying, that she said, she could not be troubled to see the afflicted thus tormented.

III. There was testimony likewise brought in, that a man striking once at the place, where a bewitched person said, the shape of this Bishop stood, the bewitched cried out, that he had tore her coat, in the place then particularly specified; and the woman's coat, was found to be torn in that very place.

IV. One Deliverance Hobbs, who had confessed her being a witch, was now tormented by the specters, for her confession. And she now testified, that this Bishop, tempted her to sign the book again, and to deny what she had confessed. She affirmed, that it was the shape of this prisoner, which whipped her with iron rods, to compel her thereunto. And she affirmed, that this Bishop was at a general meeting of the witches, in a field at Salem Village and there partook of a diabolical sacrament, in bread and wine then administered!

1689, the leading rebels employed the twin specters of authoritarianism and Catholicism, with rumors of impending French and Indian attack, to gain support from the populace.

Witchcraft in New England

In May 1692, Governor William Phips arrived in Boston harbor with the new Massachusetts charter in hand. He found the colony in disarray after three years without stable government. Symptomatic of the Massachusetts state of affairs was the witchcraft hysteria that had erupted months earlier in Salem Village, a farming community north of Boston. Since 1675, the Bay Colony had one crisis after another—Metacom's War, loss of the charter, Andros's dominion, the Revolution of 1689, and the long period of uncertainty awaiting the new charter. Accompanying this turmoil were structural changes in the society, as traditional, religious authority yielded to elites whose power rested on mercantile wealth and imperial connections. The Salem witch mania was a tragic holdover from a passing culture. Its fury was aggravated by the psychological reaction of traditionally-minded folk to the new, more commercial, secular society of turn-of-century New England.

Belief in witchcraft was embedded in European and Anglo-American culture, though, ironically, it was losing force by the time of the outbreak in Salem. The colonists, like their contemporaries in the Old World, believed that both God and Satan influenced everyday

events. When something bad happened that they could not explain, people turned to supernatural explanations, including the possibility that an individual had compacted with the Devil to do evil deeds. In England, witchcraft had been a capital offense since the time of Henry VIII in the early sixteenth century, with many prosecutions; colonial governments followed suit in condemning those who gave "entertainment to Satan." Over the seventeenth century, the Puritan governments charged many more men and women with witchcraft than did other English colonies: Three hundred and fifty New Englanders were accused during the years 1620 to 1725. Of this number, the Salem episode accounted for almost 200. The southern and middle colonies tried few accused witches and executed none.

The witchcraft cases of Salem in 1691–1692 at first resembled those in other places and times. Several girls experimented with magic, aided by a slave woman Tituba and her husband John, who together baked a "witch cake" of rye meal and urine, feeding it to a dog. The girls, who included nine-year-old Betty Parris, the daughter of Salem Village's minister, started having fits, presumably caused by witches. According to one report, the girls began "getting into holes, and creeping under chairs and stools, and to use sundry odd postures and antic gestures, uttering foolish, ridiculous speeches, which neither they themselves nor any others could make sense of." Possession spread to other village girls, leading to the arrest of three women as witches—Tituba; a poor beggar, Sarah Good; and an ailing elderly woman, Sarah Osborne.

These three alleged witches were the sort of people traditionally prosecuted for the crime. Generally, in witchcraft cases, the accused were women past menopause, who in various ways deviated from expected roles. They had fewer children than the average woman their age. Lacking sons, a significant number were heirs or potential heirs of estates, with greater economic autonomy than most New England women. Some accused witches claimed the power of a "cunning woman" to heal and foretell the future; many had been convicted of assaultive speech at a higher rate than women not accused of witchcraft; and they often were involved in conflict within their families and neighborhoods. Revealingly, men of the same age group and troublesome character were much less likely to be identified as witches. These assertive old women went beyond the accepted bounds of female behavior. As a result, they became vulnerable to prosecution as witches.

Hanging of witches in England c. 1650. No similar image exists of the Salem hangings.

While the Salem craze commenced in the time-worn pattern, it soon engulfed people of all social levels, though still many more women than men. Accusations descended upon prosperous church members, a minister, a wealthy shipowner, and several town officials. Hysteria spread from Salem throughout Essex County. Over three-quarters of the alleged witches were women; half of the accused men were their relations. Of those executed, fourteen women and five men were hanged on "Witches Hill" and another man was crushed to death with stones. Only one of the dead was of high status—the Puritan minister George Burroughs. Governor Phips, supported by influential clergymen, had allowed the prosecutions to proceed after his arrival, but put a stop to them when the accusers pointed to people at the highest levels of society, most significantly, to his own wife, Mary Phips. It had become clear, to many besides the governor, that the situation was out of control, that the evidence presented by the possessed was unreliable and quite likely the work of the Devil. After Salem, witchcraft no longer assumed its earlier importance in colonial society.

WARS AND RIVALRY FOR NORTH AMERICA

From 1680 to 1713, the Spanish, English, French, and many Indian nations battled for control of territory in

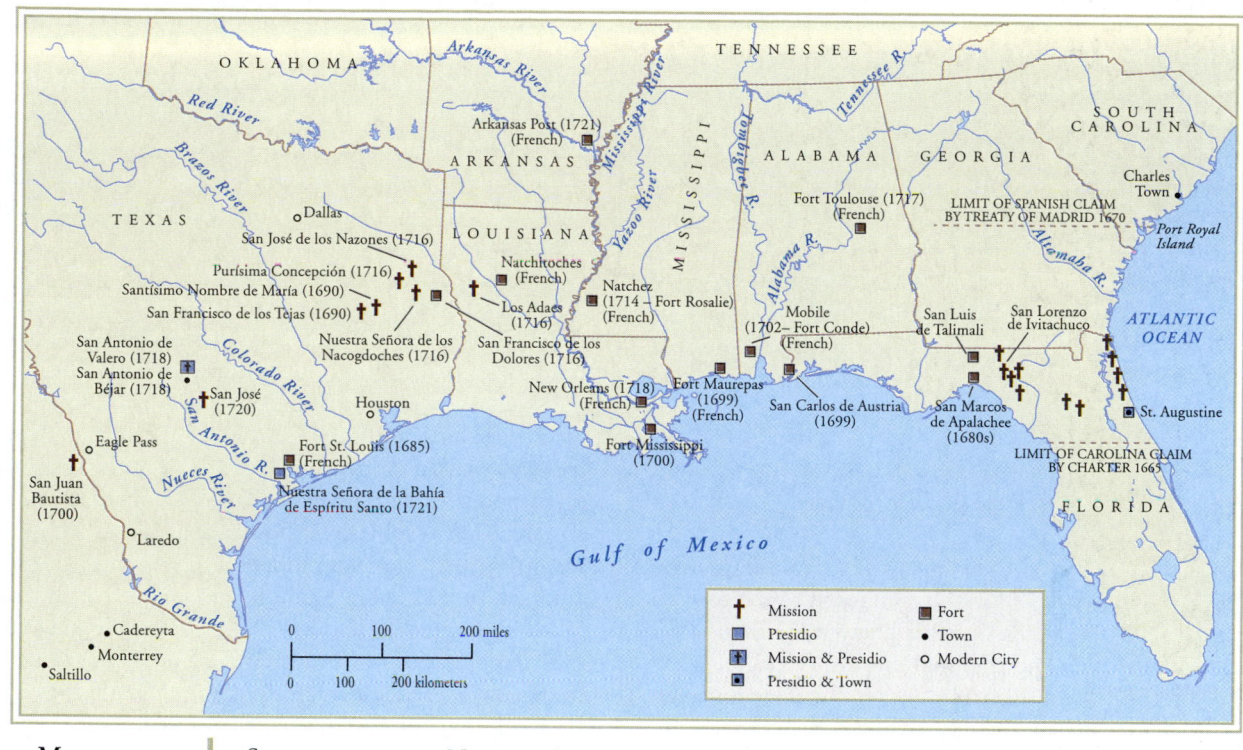

MAP 3.3 — SOUTHEASTERN NORTH AMERICA IN THE EARLY 18TH CENTURY

North America. Despite the political and social turmoil of the 1680s and early 1690s, the English settlements, stretching from New England to South Carolina, were the largest and most dynamic European colonies on the continent. By the mid-1680s, New France had approximately 10,000 settlers, compared with more than 70,000 in New England alone. Spanish Florida was comprised chiefly of missions, run by forty Franciscan priests, and the fortified town of St. Augustine, which held about 1,400 Hispanic, African, and Indian residents. Despite declining populations, many Native American peoples remained powerful in eastern North America, in particular the Five Nations of the Iroquois in New York. To defend their territory and control the fur trade, Indian tribes fought one another as well as the invading whites.

In the late seventeenth century, the three primary areas of dispute on the continent were Florida and Guale (later Georgia), Louisiana and Texas, and Canada. Conflict occurred against the backdrop of two long European wars, the War of the League of Augsburg, 1689–1697, and the War of the Spanish

Succession, 1702–1713 (respectively known as King William's War and Queen Anne's War to the English colonists).

Florida and Guale

Beginning in 1680, the English colonists of South Carolina decided to take advantage of smoldering unrest among the mission Indians of Guale and Florida to attack the Spanish colony. The Native Americans had rebelled against forced labor and efforts to stamp out their traditional religions. They killed Spanish missionaries and destroyed property, but had not closed the missions altogether. The Carolinians raided Guale and Florida from no humanitarian motives to assist the Indians. In fact, a chief reason for attacking the Spanish missions was to capture Native Americans to sell as slaves in the West Indies. The English also wanted to control the deerskin trade in the southeast.

By 1686, the Carolinians thrust the missionaries out of Guale. Then in 1704, during Queen Anne's

War, an army under former Carolina governor James Moore crushed the missions in Apalachee, killing and enslaving hundreds, if not thousands, of Indian men, women, and children. The Carolinians obtained help from their trading partners, the Yamassees, and from many of the mission Indians, who resented Spanish oppression. Moore's troops inflicted brutal torture, burning people alive. The surviving Apalachees dispersed, losing their identity as a nation. The Spanish retained St. Augustine and a fort they built at Pensacola in 1698, but lost control of Guale and most of Florida.

Louisiana and Texas

The Spanish erected their fort at Pensacola Bay in response to French efforts to establish a colony in Louisiana. At risk, the Spanish knew, were their silver mines in Mexico and domination of the Gulf of Mexico. In 1682, René Robert Cavelier, Sieur de La Salle, had explored the Mississippi River from New France to the gulf, claiming its entire watershed and naming the territory Louisiana in honor of King Louis XIV. La Salle sailed to France, then returned to set up a colony from which to attack New Spain. His expedition was an utter failure, as he miscalculated the location of the Mississippi, instead building Fort St. Louis in Texas, near Matagorda Bay. The colony quickly dissolved from disease, loss of ships, and attacks by Karankawa Indians; in 1687, La Salle was murdered by his men.

Despite its quick and grisly end, the French incursion in the Gulf of Mexico inspired the Spanish to expand its settlements in the borderlands. Reconquest of New Mexico from the Pueblos was part of this effort. The Spanish in 1690 founded missions among the Caddo people of eastern Texas and western Louisiana, from whom they took the Caddo word, Tejas or Texas, meaning "friends." Three years later, when the Caddos blamed the friars for bringing smallpox, they escaped, burying their church bells. The Spaniards abandoned Texas until the French once again entered the area.

In 1699, Pierre LeMoyne, Sieur d'Iberville resumed the French search for an opening to the Mississippi River, which was difficult to locate in the muddy Mississippi Delta. Iberville found the river's mouth by accident, then built forts at Biloxi Bay and on the Mississippi to establish French possession. Spain might have forced the French out of Louisiana with quick action, but in 1700, the grandson of French King Louis XIV took the Spanish throne; the two nations became allies against the English, Dutch, and Austrians in the War of the Spanish Succession. In fact, the French helped the Spanish defend St. Augustine and Pensacola against the English and they jointly tried but failed to conquer Charleston.

Although the French-Spanish alliance gave Louisiana a chance to develop without interference from New Spain, the colony grew slowly for lack of immigrants. In 1708, about one hundred white soldiers and settlers lived in Louisiana. They obtained food, deerskins, and the right to occupy the land from local Native Americans by exchanging firearms and other goods. Relations between the French and Indians were not trouble-free, however, as rivalries among various tribes, the Carolinians, and French created conflict. In 1715, for example, after Natchez Indians killed four French traders, the colonists literally demanded the assassins' heads. When the Natchez failed to execute all of the perpetrators, the French murdered Indian hostages and required the Natchez to accept a fortified trading post on their land. The Louisiana settlers also established trade with Caddo Indians in western Louisiana, prompting the Spanish to renew their missions in Texas and build a presidio (or fort) at San Antonio.

Canada

Conflict developed in the north when the Iroquois confederation attacked New France to stop French fur trading in the Ohio Valley and Illinois. The Iroquois defeated New France in 1683, but war continued as the English, French, and Native Americans struggled over trade routes and territory. The outbreak of King William's War in 1689 fueled the contest, as the Five Nations attacked settlements in Canada, while the French and their Indian allies destroyed English frontier outposts from New York to Maine. New England troops, under Sir William Phips, took Port Royal in Acadia, but failed to conquer Quebec. In the Atlantic, the war interrupted trade, as French privateers harassed English fleets carrying tobacco and sugar. Though the European belligerents agreed in the Peace of Ryswick (1697) to return to prewar status in North

America, the Canadians won an important victory over the Iroquois and their English allies. The Five Nations, badly beaten, decimated by disease, and their fur trade disrupted, signed a neutrality treaty in 1701. Frustrated by New York's failure to provide reinforcements, they ended their alliance with the English. New France then developed trade, religious missions, and agricultural settlements in the Great Lakes and Illinois Territory.

The renewal of hostilities between the English and French in 1702, with Queen Anne's War, again brought raids on the New England frontier. In 1704, the Canadians and Native Americans attacked Deerfield, Massachusetts, burning houses and barns, killing inhabitants, and taking many captives. The English once again took Port Royal, after several unsuccessful tries, but called off an attack on Quebec when they lost 900 men in storms on the St. Lawrence River. This time, however, the peace treaty gave the victory to England (which had joined with Scotland in 1707 to form Great Britain). In North America, the Treaty of Utrecht (1713) ceded Nova Scotia (formerly Acadia), Newfoundland, and control of the Hudson Bay territory to the British. Yet they had failed to oust France from North America. What can be called the Second Hundred Years' War between France and England, from 1689 to 1815, resumed a generation later in the 1740s.

THE ENTRENCHMENT OF SLAVERY IN BRITISH AMERICA

Despite wars, rebellions, and witch hysteria, the most significant development in British North America during the late seventeenth and early eighteenth century was large-scale investment in enslaved Africans. The decisions of thousands of individual colonists to purchase men, women, and children who had been seized from their homelands in Africa left an indelible imprint on American society and culture. The slave buyers could not foretell the monumental effects of their actions. They responded to economic conditions: their need for workers, the declining availability of white servants, and the developing Atlantic slave trade.

Adopting Slavery

How could people who increasingly prized their own freedom—who had braved a treacherous ocean voyage to find opportunity in a new land—deprive other human beings of liberty, and often life itself? The answer lies in traditional English culture and the colonists' perceived economic needs.

The English, like other Europeans, believed that hierarchies existed in human society and, indeed, all of nature. Humans were superior to animals; Christians superior to "heathens." English language and culture also differentiated sharply between white and black, with whiteness suggesting purity and good, blackness imbued with filth and sin. The English compared their light skin with the Africans' darker brown color, judging the latter to be inferior. In African religion, social customs, dress, and political organization, the Europeans found serious deficiencies, just as they had found deficiencies among Native Americans. The people of sub-Saharan Africa, the English thought, were lower on the scale of humanity and could justifiably be enslaved. The example of the Portuguese, Spanish, and—most recently—the Dutch, who had fabricated the Atlantic slave trade over the previous two centuries, made the decision to buy Africans seem natural. The mainland English colonists could also look to their countrymen in the West Indies, where thousands of African slaves toiled in sugar fields, outnumbering whites.

Despite this cultural context, colonists viewed their investment in slaves as an economic decision. In Virginia and Maryland, planters purchased Africans because they needed large numbers of workers to grow tobacco. Chesapeake settlers had learned that Native Americans, who easily escaped enslavement and died in catastrophic numbers, would not fill their labor needs. White servants filled the gap until about 1675. Many young Englishmen, and fewer women, willingly signed up to work for three or more years in return for passage and rights to fifty acres of land. In the last quarter of the century, however, the supply of English servants declined in Maryland and Virginia. Economic conditions improved in England, while good tobacco land became scarce. Bacon's Rebellion taught Chesapeake elites the danger of importing thousands of white servants under these circumstances. With the founding of the Carolinas, New Jersey, and Pennsylvania, where land was plentiful, servants had a wider range of options.

Chesapeake planters searching for an alternative labor supply turned to African slaves. Population figures for Virginia and Maryland demonstrate graphically the result of individual decisions. In 1660, only 900 blacks resided in the Chesapeake, some of whom had come as servants and were free. Two decades later, their number had grown to 4,300; by 1720, blacks comprised one-fifth of the population. A similar increase occurred in the Carolinas (primarily South Carolina), where 38 percent of the residents in 1720 were African slaves. The situation was different in New England, where only 2 percent of the population was enslaved, and in the Middle Colonies (New York, New Jersey, Pennsylvania, and Delaware), where about one resident in ten suffered perpetual bondage.

The Slave Trade

English entry into the Atlantic slave trade helped spur the transition to an African workforce. Though smugglers like John Hawkins had interloped earlier in the Spanish trade, England officially became involved in selling human beings in 1663. Charles II granted a monopoly to supply captives to the English colonies first to the Company of Royal Adventurers, then in 1672 to the Royal African Company. When the companies could not meet the demand of labor-hungry colonists, smugglers got involved, so in 1698, the Crown abandoned the monopoly, opening the slave trade to any English merchant who wanted to participate. As a result, the supply of Africans in the English colonies soared and slave prices declined, thus encouraging colonists to invest in even more black labor.

The experience of enslavement and transport across the Atlantic Ocean was dehumanizing and perilous. Probably one-half of the persons sold into slavery died before reaching the New World. Approximately three-quarters of those taken to English North America came from the area of West Africa between Senegambia and the Bight of Biafra, with the remainder coming mostly from Angola. Slaves were "black gold"—prisoners of war and kidnapped children and young adults—whom African merchants collected for sale. As European sea captains made successive trips to the coast, African traders had to reach farther and farther into the continent to find enough people to enslave. Some captives marched 500 miles or more to the sea in "coffles," the term given to the files of shackled pris-

Theodor de Bry's illustration of a Dutch ship trading on the coast of West Africa. The people in the canoe, indicated with "B," represent African merchants who traded human beings to the Europeans for goods such as cloth, rum, and firearms.

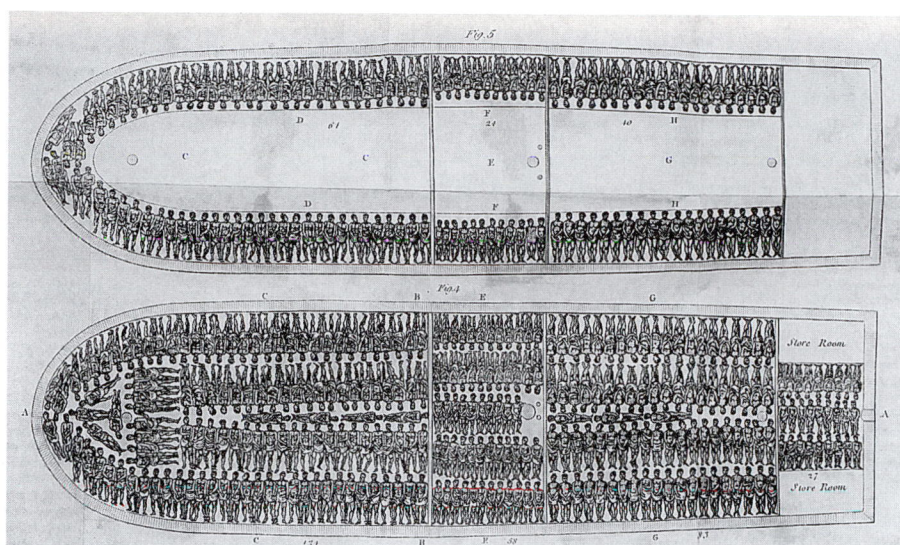

Diagram showing the tight packing of enslaved Africans during the "middle passage."

oners. On the coast, they were confined in enclosures called barracoons, often exposed for long periods to the sun without adequate food and drink. When a ship arrived, according to a Dutch trader, Willem Bosman, in 1700, the Africans were lined up on shore,

> where, by our surgeons . . . they are thoroughly examined, even to the smallest member, and that naked both men and women, without the least distinction or modesty. Those that are approved as good, are set on one side; and the lame or faulty are set by as invalids, which are here called *mackrons:* these are such as are above five and thirty years old, or are maimed in the arms, legs or feet; have lost a tooth, are grey-haired, or have films over their eyes; as well as all those which are affected with any venereal distemper, or several other diseases.

The Africans were treated like any other commodity offered for sale, at best as livestock sold at auction. The process of enslavement, of turning autonomous people into property, required nothing less.

For the Africans chosen for transport, the horror had only begun. The Europeans branded them with the insignia of the company—for example, slaves of the Royal African Company had their skins burned with the letters "DY," for James, duke of York. Then followed the voyage across the Atlantic, called the "middle passage," which could take from three weeks to more than three months, depending upon the weather and destination. Ships normally carried rations for three months, so bad storms could mean starvation. Weather permitting, the captives spent their days on deck, the men in chains, the women and children unrestrained. At night, and around the clock if weather was bad, slaves occupied spaces about the size of coffins in the hold of the ship, where sanitation and ventilation were poor. Temperatures could reach extremely high levels. Disease was often rampant, the experience altogether dehumanizing. Some slaves attempted suicide by jumping overboard or refusing to eat: The latter was so common that traders invested in a tool called the *speculum oris* to force open a person's mouth.

Africans also rebelled violently, attacking the white captain and crew, occasionally taking over the ship. Because they were unfamiliar with ocean navigation, mutineers had the best hope for success when the ship was still in African waters and large numbers could carry out the revolt, escaping to shore. When rebels failed, punishment was swift and brutal. The slave trader Bosman described an incident when a sea captain placed an extra anchor in the ship's hold. The enslaved Africans,

> unknown to any of the ship's crew, possessed themselves of a hammer, with which, in a short time they broke all their fetters in pieces upon the anchor: After this, they came above deck, and fell upon our men, some of whom they grievously

wounded, and would certainly have mastered the ship, if a French and English ship had not very fortunately happened to lie by us; who perceiving by our firing a distressed-gun, that something was in disorder on board, immediately came to our assistance with shallops and men, and drove the slaves under deck: notwithstanding which, before all was appeased, about twenty of them were killed. The Portuguese have been more unlucky in this particular than we; for in four years they lost four ships in this manner.

Upon arrival in America, the Africans faced the ordeal of sale by auction or prearranged contract. They were stripped naked once again and examined for disease and physical defects. Because the greatest need was for strong field hands who would provide years of labor, plantation owners paid the highest prices for healthy young men in their prime. Buyers paid less for women, children, and older men, from whom they expected less production. For both the Africans and their owners, who had just invested a large sum, the year following debarkation was most critical. During this period of seasoning, Africans endured serious illness and high mortality from the new disease environment.

Systems of Slavery in British North America

As more and more Africans arrived, colonial assemblies instituted black codes to define slavery and control the black population. The result was legal entrenchment of the institution. Before 1660, Maryland had officially sanctioned perpetual bondage, but Virginia moved more slowly. While its assembly forbade Africans from bearing arms, it remained silent on the subject of slavery. Enough flexibility existed in Virginia society to allow black servants to gain freedom, earn their livelihoods, and in some cases acquire land. In the 1660s, however, Virginia joined Maryland in enacting laws that recognized differences in the terms of white servants and African slaves. By law, slavery lasted a person's entire lifetime, descended from mother to child, and was the normal status of blacks, but never whites.

In the late seventeenth and early eighteenth century, both Virginia and Maryland created clearly articulated caste systems based on perceptions of race. A person's skin color denoted status: all Africans and their descendants encountered severe discrimination, whether enslaved or free. The Virginia assembly ruled that any master who killed a slave during punishment was not guilty of a felony. Conversely, no black person, slave or free, could strike a white, even a bound servant—even in self-defense. Virginia lawmakers made emancipation difficult to obtain, specifying that conversion to Christianity would not free a slave. Evolving black codes banned interracial marriage, forbade owners from releasing their slaves except in special cases, and restricted enslaved blacks from traveling without permission, marrying legally, holding property, testifying against whites, or congregating in groups. Over the course of the eighteenth century, other British colonies passed similar codes that ranged from fairly moderate New England laws to a harsh regime in Carolina, keyed in large part to the density of the black population.

In the life of an African slave, these laws had force, but more direct was the power of the master over work and family. To be a slave meant that someone else possessed your body and could command your daily activities. The owner chose your job; he or she decided whether your children would stay with you or be sold away. During off-hours, Africans generally maintained autonomy in religion, social customs, and family life, but the law and the master's will remained dominant.

The work Africans and native-born African Americans performed varied from one region to another. In the Chesapeake and the Carolinas, with labor-intensive staple crops, most slaves spent long hours planting, weeding, and harvesting tobacco, corn, and rice. A farm's production depended largely upon the number of workers tending the crop. Masters apparently felt no concern about requiring black women to do hard physical labor in the fields, for it was there that they would yield the greatest return. Over time, as the southern black population increased naturally and importation continued, the supply of labor became more plentiful. Plantation owners assigned slaves to different tasks, though most still raised the staple crop. Some men became drivers and artisans; some women served as nurses, cooks, and spinners. Both women and men performed domestic service. At the same time, female slaves were responsible for the household needs of their own families, including food preparation, laundry, and sewing.

Agricultural production in the middle colonies and New England centered on grains and livestock, which demanded less labor than tobacco or rice, so most parts of the northern countryside had relatively few

slaves. Exceptions included New York and neighboring eastern New Jersey, which had difficulty attracting European immigrants; thus, well-to-do farmers purchased large numbers of Africans to work their land. The largest slaveholder in New Jersey was probably Colonel Lewis Morris of Shrewsbury, who employed more than sixty slaves at his plantation and ironworks. In Rhode Island's Narragansett region, some plantation owners held as many as fifty blacks. Most northern slaves lived in the port towns, however, where women worked as cooks and household servants, and men labored at crafts, domestic service, and as shipbuilders and sailors. Boston, New York, and Philadelphia merchants imported Africans as part of the West Indies trade. In New York City, blacks were about one-fifth of the population; in Boston and Philadelphia they comprised about one-tenth.

A source of comfort to slaves who had lost their African homelands and kin was to establish new families in America. Slaves achieved some autonomy from their masters by creating families and kinship networks. All knew, however, that owners could destroy loving relationships by selling away spouses, children, brothers, and sisters. The ability of blacks to form families changed over time and varied from one region to another. High mortality and a skewed sex ratio prevented many African-born men from marrying and having children. In the disease-ridden West Indies and northern cities like Philadelphia, mortality was so high that colonists had to keep importing Africans to avoid population decline. In the Chesapeake colonies, however, natural population growth began with the first generation of native-born slaves. African American women had more children than their African mothers, creating communities of slaves on large plantations. Whereas most of the first Africans dwelled in white households with just a few blacks, their offspring, known as "country-born" slaves, lived with parents, brothers, and sisters. The third generation lived with grandparents and cousins as well. After 1720, in the Chesapeake, almost one-half of slaves resided on plantations with more than twenty blacks.

Resistance and Rebellion

While for many slaves family and kin helped to reduce their feelings of despair, for others nothing relieved the pain of lifetime bondage. Many resisted their masters'

power by staging slowdowns, pretending illness, destroying crops and tools, committing theft, arson, assault, and murder. Newly arrived Africans were especially likely to rebel against their new status, often running away, sometimes to live with Native Americans. Slaves who were sold away from their families frequently escaped to join them once again. Men ran away in greater numbers than women, who, as mothers, found it difficult to escape with children in tow. If motivated by the threat of punishment or rape to absent themselves from the plantation, women became truants, hiding in nearby woods.

While slaves in the English West Indies often rebelled, blacks in the mainland colonies rarely took the ultimate step of armed insurgency, primarily because they were so outnumbered by whites. Before 1713, West Indian blacks staged seven full-scale revolts; their large population made success seem possible. In Barbados, in 1675, for example, conspirators planned to take over the island, installing an elderly slave Cuffee as king. When whites got wind of the plot, they burned alive or beheaded thirty-five blacks. On the mainland, just one slave revolt occurred by the early 1700s. In New York City, in 1712, about twenty slaves set fire to a building, attacking the white men who came to extinguish it. Nine whites were killed; terror spread up and down the Atlantic coast. As in the case of later slave revolts and conspiracies, the revenge wreaked upon the black community surpassed any violence the rebels had committed. White authorities did not care whether everyone they punished had actually been involved. In the wake of the New York revolt, thirteen slaves were hanged, three burned at the stake, one tortured on the wheel (an instrument used to stretch and disjoint its victims), and another starved to death in chains; six committed suicide to avoid such treatment. The town fathers expected, with these barbarous punishments, to prevent further insurrection.

Early Abolitionists

As slavery became entrenched in the American colonies, a few white colonists questioned its morality. They feared slave rebellions and abhorred the violence needed to enslave Africans, transport them to the colonies, and keep them in bondage. Slavery was morally repugnant, they believed, because all humans are equal in the eyes of God. One of the American opponents of perpetual bondage was Samuel Sewall, a

Boston judge, who wrote in 1700, "It is most certain that all Men, as they are the Sons of Adam . . . have equal Right unto Liberty, and all other outward Comforts of Life."

Quakers also spoke out publicly against the institution. Certainly not all Friends were abolitionists—in Pennsylvania and New Jersey before 1720 a large proportion of the Quaker elite owned slaves—but a few interpreted Quaker ideals to mean that human bondage reeked with sin. According to John Hepburn of New Jersey, for example, slavery violated the Golden Rule to do unto others as you wish others to do unto you. He abhorred slavekeeping. While owners got rich without physical labor, wore fine-powdered wigs and greatcoats, and their wives and children similarly lived well, slaves endured beatings, wore rags, and slept in the ashes of the fire. In the context of rising importation throughout the colonies, however, the protests of Sewall, Hepburn, and a few other critics had little effect.

ECONOMIC DEVELOPMENT IN THE BRITISH COLONIES

While the southern colonies employed slave labor much more extensively than the north, every British province was implicated in the institution. Despite differences in agriculture, labor, and commerce from one region to another, the mainland colonies were all part of the Atlantic economy, dominated by the staple crops, sugar, tobacco, and rice. The developing mercantile economies of New England and the mid-Atlantic region depended heavily upon the slave system, because their chief market was providing food for the multitudes of blacks laboring on West Indies sugar plantations.

Northern Economies

Family farms and dependence on the sea characterized New England's economy. When its agriculture failed to provide a lucrative staple crop, traders turned to fishing and shipping to earn credits to buy imports. With rocky, generally poor soil and a cool climate, the region could not grow a profitable commercial crop

like tobacco or sugar, so rural New England families raised livestock, wheat, rye, Indian corn, peas, other vegetables, and fruit. They ate most of what they produced—a fairly monotonous diet of brown bread, boiled or baked peas, boiled meat and vegetables, and dark beer or apple cider—within their families and communities.

Fishing and shipping developed as important industries during the seventeenth century. The New Englanders replaced English fishermen who had come to the Grand Banks for cod since the 1400s. The New England fishers initially sold their catch, in return for manufactured goods such as shoes, textiles, glass, and metal products, to London merchants, who sent the fish to Spain, Portugal, and the Wine Islands, off the coast of Africa.

The fishing industry spurred the growth of maritime trade, as New England merchants recognized even greater profits to be made by trading directly with the Wine Islands and the West Indies. They formed partnerships among themselves and with English merchants, encouraging a local shipbuilding industry. The New Englanders exported fish, barrels, and other wood products to the islands. They imported wine, fruit, and salt from the Wine Islands, and rum, molasses, sugar, dyes, and other goods from the Caribbean. Soon, aided by the Navigation Acts, they were the chief carriers of goods along the North American coast, exchanging enslaved Africans and rum distilled from West Indies molasses for Pennsylvania wheat and livestock, Chesapeake tobacco, North Carolina tar and turpentine, and South Carolina rice. The credits they earned in shipping were as significant as the value of New England products sold in the trade.

The economy of the Middle Colonies resembled New England's in a number of ways, but was much more prosperous agriculturally. With plenty of good land, farmers raised wheat and livestock commercially, purchasing servants and some slaves to supplement family labor. The region had two ports: one at New York City, which served New York, western Connecticut, and eastern New Jersey; and the other at Philadelphia, which served Pennsylvania, western New Jersey, Delaware, and northern Maryland. Though neither city matched Boston in population or commercial importance before 1750, both quickly surpassed the Massachusetts seaport after that date. New York merchants maintained links with Amsterdam, the Dutch West Indies, and New Spain even after the English takeover in 1664. Philadelphia Quakers exploited their

connections with Friends in other ports, especially in England and the West Indies. Before 1750, Philadelphia primarily exported food, livestock, and barrel staves to the Caribbean for credits to buy English manufactures.

Life in the Seaports

Maritime trade encouraged the development of port cities in the British provinces: Boston, New York, Philadelphia, and Charleston. Until 1750, merchants of Boston and other seaport towns in Massachusetts (Salem, Marblehead, and Newbury) and Rhode Island (Newport and Providence), dominated colonial trade. The ports thrived because they forged commercial links between farmers and external dealers, housing the markets through which imports and exports flowed. The maritime industry itself created demand for shipbuilders, suppliers of provisions, rope and sailmakers, carters, dockworkers, and sailors.

Commercial growth brought social change, distinguishing an urban lifestyle from the countryside. Some merchants became fabulously wealthy from transat-

Cod fishing was an early industry of Europeans in the North Atlantic. This illustration depicts a dry fishery on the Newfoundland coast in which cod were lightly salted and dried for sale in southern Europe.

lantic and coastal trade. They spent their income conspicuously, building costly mansions, purchasing enslaved Africans as household servants, and wearing expensive clothes. They lived comfortably, with servants and slaves to do their menial chores. Other city dwellers were much less fortunate, because they earned minimal wages or lacked employment. Port cities stimulated both affluence and dire poverty. A much wider range of wealth developed there than in rural areas of the north, where most families owned farms of moderate size. The seaport cities attracted many people who hoped to make their fortunes, or at least a decent living, but died with little more than the clothes on their backs. Maritime commerce frequently suffered disruption from war, bad weather, and economic downturns. Seamen and artisans, dependent on overseas trade, could expect little work during the winter, when few ships sailed. City folk were also at greater risk of death than those who lived in the country, as some arriving ships spread smallpox and other diseases to the dense urban populations. The towns lacked adequate sanitation facilities, so garbage and waste cluttered streets, polluting the water supply. With insufficient food and firewood, the poor endured the highest rates of illness and death, but no one was immune to the fevers and dysentery that repeatedly afflicted urban residents.

As trade expanded, sailors became an important segment of the labor force. They were a varied lot. Some men, particularly those who lived along the coast, went to sea only part-time, to supplement the income of their farms. Others chose seafaring as a career, joining a fraternity who divided their time between shipboard and the taverns and boardinghouses of port towns throughout the Atlantic world. Some had no choice in the matter at all, for they were enslaved Africans whose masters purchased them to man the ships. Sailors led a difficult and dangerous life. Crews on ordinary merchant ships were small, so seamen worked long hours loading and unloading the ship, maintaining the rigging and sails, and pumping water from the bilge, an especially backbreaking job. The organization of labor on board was hierarchical, with power descending from the captain to mate, to specialists like ship carpenter and surgeon, to seamen. Discipline could be harsh. The crewmen had little hope of moving up through the ranks, for captains were generally from affluent families, often merchants and part-owners of their ships. Instead, the more common fate of an ordinary "Jack Tar" was early death or disability from shipwreck, combat with enemies or

pirates, and such occupational hazards as falling over-board, broken bones, scurvy, rheumatism, and hernia, or the "bursted belly" as they called it.

When conditions on ship became insufferable, the seamen rebelled, sometimes refusing to work until their grievances were redressed, sometimes deserting the ship at the next port. Most radically, men mutinied and, if successful, sometimes became pirates, or robbers at sea. They plundered merchant vessels and port towns, sharing the proceeds evenly among themselves, electing officers, and recruiting much larger crews than could be found on merchant ships. With eighty or more men on a pirate ship of average size, compared with fifteen on a comparable merchant vessel, each had much less work to do. One pirate, Joseph Mansfield, admitted in 1722 that "the love of Drink and a Lazy Life" were "Stronger Motives with him than Gold."

Plantation Economies in the Chesapeake and South Carolina

From 1675 to 1720, tobacco remained king in Maryland and Virginia, as planters increasingly purchased enslaved Africans instead of white servants. The wealth of plantation owners grew with each child born to a slave mother. At the same time, the richest planters bought up the land of small farmers who found it difficult to compete with the slaveholders. The wealthiest man in early eighteenth-century Virginia was Robert Carter of Lancaster County, called "King" Carter. As a slave trader and land speculator, he parlayed his inheritance of £1,000 and 1,000 acres into an estate of £10,000 in cash, 300,000 acres of land, and over 700 slaves. Carter, with his relatives and friends, formed a tightly knit group of Chesapeake gentry, who consolidated their wealth in land, commerce, and slaves.

In 1720, and throughout the eighteenth century, Chesapeake society was hierarchical. At the bottom of the social structure were African and country-born slaves, who owned no property and had little hope for freedom. Above them were the non-landholding whites, perhaps 40 to 50 percent of white families, whose living conditions were rough. They rented land, owned a horse or two, some cows, a few pigs, tools, and some household goods, but rarely held bound servants or slaves. They lived in shanties and ate from wooden dishes rather than pottery. Their incomes from tobacco were so meager that they had trouble

paying taxes and rent. Often they were in debt to the local merchant-planter for needed manufactured goods, such as ammunition, fabric, shoes, and tools. Next higher were small landholders whose incomes allowed them to live more comfortably, with pottery, more furniture, and nicer (though still quite small) homes. If they owned several slaves, which few did before 1720, they worked alongside them in the fields and house.

In the upper 5 percent were the gentry, who owned many slaves, large acreages, and usually acted as merchants as well. They served as intermediaries for smaller planters, selling tobacco abroad and importing manufactured goods. As such, they became creditors of their poorer neighbors, who often owed them substantial debts. In Maryland and Virginia, the merchant-planters conducted trade without the development of port cities. Ships docked at their plantations along the many tributaries of the Chesapeake Bay to load casks of tobacco and unload imported goods. Tobacco required little processing: planters dried the leaves in sheds and packed them in casks made by local coopers. Merchant-planters and rural artisans, including slaves, provided goods and services for the community without centralizing their activities in towns. Even the two capitals, Williamsburg and Annapolis, remained small throughout the colonial period.

Situated in a semi-tropical climate, South Carolina developed a plantation economy that was linked to, and in many ways resembled, the West Indies. Most early settlers, both black and white, came from the English colony of Barbados, where land was in short supply and almost entirely devoted to sugar cultivation. White planters claimed Carolina headrights, then sold corn, salt beef, salt pork, barrel staves, firewood, and Native American slaves to the islands. South Carolinians enslaved the Indians they captured in raids throughout the American southeast and also obtained them in exchange for guns, ammunition, and cloth from native traders. Native Americans also supplied deerskins, which found a ready market in England, though they were not valued quite so highly as Canadian furs.

As with the northern fur trade between Europeans and Indians, the Carolinians used English trade goods to establish alliances with native groups. However, such major trading partners as the Yamassees quickly discovered that white merchants used theft, violence, rum, and false weights to gain unfair advantage. In 1715, in league with the Creeks, the Yamassees attacked white settlements, nearly destroying the colony.

The whites saved themselves by getting help from the Cherokees, who at first vacillated but then accepted the promise of continued European trade. The Yamassees and Creeks were defeated, their people killed, enslaved, or forced to migrate from the coastal area. White South Carolinians then expropriated their lands.

The settlers wanted the new territory because they had found an export that became much more lucrative than provisions, enslaved Indians, or deerskins. Planters had experimented with a variety of crops—tobacco, cotton, sugar, silk, wine grapes, and ginger—but rice proved most successful in the wet lowlands of the Carolina coast. Also significant were the skills in rice production that many Africans brought to America. Rice exports expanded rapidly in South Carolina, reaching 1.5 million pounds per year by 1710 and nearly 20 million pounds by 1730. The chief markets for rice were Europe and the West Indies. Carolinians first sent their crop directly to Portugal, but in 1705 Parliament added rice to the list of enumerated products that had to be shipped to England first, taxes paid, and then reexported to Europe. The colonists argued that, in the case of southern Europe, this detour made their crop arrive too late for Lent, when much of it was consumed. In response, Parliament allowed South Carolina after 1731 to trade directly with Spain, Portugal, and Mediterranean Europe, but the larger share of the rice crop, which went to northern Europe, still required transit through Britain.

The conversion to rice transformed South Carolina society, affecting the black population with special force. Before planters adopted full-scale rice production, slaves had performed a variety of jobs in crafts, timber, livestock, and agriculture. Their workloads were moderate, especially in comparison with the West Indies; with the first generation of African Americans, natural increase of the population had begun. Rice monoculture changed this situation altogether, as planters imported thousands of Africans. In the coastal areas north and south of Charleston, blacks reached 70 percent of the population in the 1720s (38 percent of the Carolinas overall). With high importation and harsher working conditions, death rates surged. As in the Chesapeake, wealthy planters bought up neighboring farms while investing heavily in slaves. They created large rice plantations, worked by growing numbers of African slaves, not unlike the sugar regime of Barbados. Small planters moved to the periphery, where they raised grain and livestock for the rice dis-trict and the Caribbean. The rice planters found the Carolina lowlands isolated and unhealthy, so they left their plantations part of the year to make social contacts and escape the oppressive heat and disease. However, the Carolinians supervised their plantations directly—unlike British West Indian sugar planters who fled to England, leaving management in the care of overseers.

Charleston, where the rice planters spent at least several weeks each year, was the fourth largest city in the British colonies. The port channeled the trade in provisions, deerskins, rice, slaves, and English manufactures. Charleston remained smaller than Boston, Philadelphia, and New York because British and New England shippers controlled its trade. Without a strong merchant community, the South Carolina seaport lacked the impetus for shipbuilding and associated crafts.

CONCLUSION

Between 1675 and 1720, the people of North America shed their blood over territory, trade, and political autonomy. As English, French, and Spanish settlers expanded into new regions, they established commerce, but also spread smallpox and fostered conflict among the Indians. Despite ardent defense of homelands and the temporary successes of the Pueblos and the Iroquois, Native Americans throughout the continent, weakened by disease and war, yielded to the Europeans.

By the turn of the eighteenth century, the Spanish reconquered New Mexico and infiltrated Texas, France had started Louisiana, and the English were pushing out in many directions. To develop their economies, the British colonists imported Africans in large numbers, creating rigorous slave regimes to control their new, rebellious laborers. With the growth of plantation slave economies in the South and maritime commerce in the North, British North America developed distinctive regional characteristics. Yet in 1720, the Atlantic seaboard colonies had much in common: their settlement by enterprising men and women, regard for English rights of property and representation, and governance within the British imperial system. During the next half century, the importance of these commonalities, as well as the contradictions that emerged from them, would become clear.

RECOMMENDED READINGS

Many of the sources listed for Chapter 2 are useful for the period from 1675 to 1720 as well.

Demos, John. *The Unredeemed Captive: A Family Story from Early America* (1994). The evocative tale of a Puritan minister's daughter who was held captive by the Mohawks and refused to return home.

Dunn, Mary Maples, et al., eds. *The Papers of William Penn*, 5 vols. (1981–1987). Basic documents, with scholarly introductions, on the founding and early development of Pennsylvania.

Innes, Stephen, ed. *Work and Labor in Early America* (1988). Insightful essays that demonstrate the range of labor systems and working conditions in the British colonies.

Jordan, Winthrop D. *White over Black: American Attitudes Toward the Negro, 1550–1812* (1968). Basic source on the construction of ideas about race in Anglo-America.

Karlsen, Carol F. *The Devil in the Shape of a Woman: Witchcraft in Colonial New England* (1987). Convincing argument about the significance of gender in witchcraft trials.

Lovejoy, David S. *The Glorious Revolution in America* (1972) The best introduction to the colonial revolutions of 1689.

McCusker, John J., and Menard, Russell R. *The Economy of British America, 1607–1789, With Supplementary Bibliography* (1991). An excellent survey of economic and demographic development.

Pestana, Carla Gardina. *Quakers and Baptists in Colonial Massachusetts* (1991). Contrasts the experience of two persecuted sects in early New England.

Usner, Daniel H., Jr. *Indians, Settlers, and Slaves in a Frontier Exchange Economy: The Lower Mississippi Valley Before 1783* (1992). A history of colonial Louisiana and West Florida, focusing on relations between Europeans and Native Americans.

Religious Change and Witchcraft in New England

Ahlstrom, Sydney E. *A Religious History of the American People* (1972).

Bonomi, Patricia U. *Under the Cope of Heaven: Religion, Society, and Politics in Colonial America* (1986).

Boyer, Paul and Nissenbaum, Steven. *Salem Possessed: The Social Origins of Witchcraft* (1974).

Demos, John Putnam. *Entertaining Satan: Witchcraft and the Culture of Early New England* (1982).

Hall, David D., ed. *Witch-Hunting in Seventeenth-Century New England: A Documentary History, 1638–1692* (1991).

Pope, Robert. *The Half-Way Covenant: Church Membership in Puritan New England* (1969).

Worrall, Arthur J. *Quakers in the Colonial Northeast* (1980).

Founding of Pennsylvania

Dunn, Richard S., and Dunn, Mary Maples, eds. *The World of William Penn* (1986).

Lemon, James T. *The Best Poor Man's Country: A Geographical Study of Early Southeastern Pennsylvania* (1972).

Nash, Gary B. *Quakers and Politics: Pennsylvania, 1681–1726* (1968).

Schwartz, Sally. *"A Mixed Multitude": The Struggle for Toleration in Colonial Pennsylvania* (1987).

Soderlund, Jean R., et al., eds. *William Penn and the Founding of Pennsylvania, 1680–1684: A Documentary History* (1983).

Weslager, C. A. *The Delaware Indians: A History* (1972).

Imperial Relations and the Revolutions of 1689

Archdeacon, Thomas J. *New York City, 1664–1710: Conquest and Change* (1976).

Carr, Lois Green, and Jordan, David William. *Maryland's Revolution of Government, 1689–1692* (1974).

Hall, Michael Garibaldi. *Edward Randolph and the American Colonies, 1676–1703* (1960).

Olson, Alison Gilbert. *Anglo-American Politics, 1660–1775: The Relationship Between Parties in England and Colonial America* (1973).

Webb, Stephen Saunders. *The Governors-General: The English Army and the Definition of the Empire, 1569–1681* (1979).

Entrenchment of Slavery

Davis, David Brion. *The Problem of Slavery in Western Culture* (1966).

Higginbotham, A. Leon, Jr. *In the Matter of Color: Race and the American Legal Process, the Colonial Period* (1978).

Kulikoff, Allan. *Tobacco and Slaves: The Development of Southern Cultures in the Chesapeake, 1680–1800* (1986).

Littlefield, Daniel C. *Rice and Slaves: Ethnicity and the Slave Trade in Colonial South Carolina* (1981).

Soderlund, Jean R. *Quakers and Slavery: A Divided Spirit* (1985).

Walvin, James. *Black Ivory: A History of British Slavery* (1993).

Regional Development

Bushman, Richard L. *From Puritan to Yankee: Character and the Social Order in Connecticut, 1690–1765* (1967).

Clemens, Paul G. E. *The Atlantic Economy and Colonial Maryland's Eastern Shore: From Tobacco to Grain* (1980).

Hann, John H. *Apalachee: The Land Between the Rivers* (1988).

Heyrman, Christine Leigh. *Commerce and Culture: The Maritime Communities of Colonial Massachusetts, 1690–1750* (1984).

Kross, Jessica. *The Evolution of an American Town: Newtown, New York, 1642–1775* (1983).

Landsman, Ned C. *Scotland and Its First American Colony, 1683–1765* (1985).

Nash, Gary B. *The Urban Crucible: Social Change, Political Consciousness, and the Origins of the American Revolution* (1979).

Rediker, Marcus. *Between the Devil and the Deep Blue Sea: Merchant Seamen, Pirates, and the Anglo-American Maritime World, 1700–1750* (1987).

Shammas, Carole. *The Pre-Industrial Consumer in England and America* (1990).

Wacker, Peter O. *Land and People: A Cultural Geography of Preindustrial New Jersey: Origins and Settlement Patterns* (1975).

Weber, David J. *The Spanish Frontier in North America* (1992).

BENJAMIN FRANKLIN AND LIGHTNING

Benjamin Franklin Drawing Electricity from the Sky, by Benjamin West, c. 1805. Franklin's kite experiment demonstrating the electrical nature of lightning, along with his various activities promoting social welfare, placed him in the forefront of the American Enlightenment.

Chapter 4

THE EXPANSION OF COLONIAL BRITISH AMERICA, 1720–1763

IN 1721, SMALLPOX hit Boston viciously, infecting about 6,000 residents and killing 844. Business stopped for several months, as almost every family battled the contagion. In many respects, this epidemic was unremarkable in the British American colonies: Settlers and Native Americans alike had previously experienced the ravages of disease. But this time, one Puritan minister took an unprecedented step. Cotton Mather, who thirty years earlier had helped aggravate the Salem witch hysteria, encouraged a Boston doctor, Zabdiel Boylston, to test inoculation. Mather had learned from Onesimus, his African slave, and from English scientific papers that inoculation was used in Africa and Turkey to prevent smallpox epidemics. An experiment would be risky, for the procedure involved introducing the smallpox virus into the body, thereby giving the person what was usually (but not always) a mild case of the disease. Many doctors, as well as much of Boston's populace, condemned the proposal, fearing further contamination. Nevertheless, Dr. Boylston inoculated about 250 persons over the course of a year. Those who submitted to the procedure had a much lower death rate than Bostonians who contracted the disease naturally.

Cotton Mather was far ahead of his time in advancing the theory that disease was caused by an invasion of the body by viruses, which he called invisible "worms." Significantly, it was a minister, rather than a physician or scientist, who advanced this hypothesis. During the eighteenth century, science lacked the rigid boundaries of complexity and specialization that would later separate it from other fields of intellectual endeavor. American theologians and philosophers, as well as doctors, naturalists, and astronomers, read the latest scientific literature from England and Europe. The great divide between science and religion did not yet exist, in either university training or intellectual pursuits. Like many other theologians, Mather understood epidemics as God's punishment for sin. But he also believed inoculation was a divine gift, that people should use any means available to combat disease.

Mather's support for inoculation has been called the greatest contribution to medicine by an American during the colonial period. Certainly it represented change, as the Enlightenment, a new intellectual movement, spread from Britain to the colonies. During the years 1720 to 1763, the British provinces experienced intellectual, religious, and social ferment as they continued to expand through North America. As new knowledge, beliefs, and consumer goods arrived from Europe, colonists from Maine to Georgia (founded in 1732) increasingly lived within a

CHRONOLOGY

1720	Theodore Jacob Frelinghuysen begins revivals in New Jersey
1721–1722	Smallpox inoculation in Boston
1732	Founding of Georgia
	Hat Act
1733	Molasses Act
1734	Jonathan Edwards starts revivals in Northampton, Massachusetts
1737	Walking Purchase in eastern Pennsylvania
1739	Stono Uprising in South Carolina
1739–1740	George Whitefield tours northern colonies
1739–1744	War of Jenkins's Ear
1740	James Oglethorpe leads invasion of Florida
1741	British attack on Cartagena
1744–1748	King George's War
1745	New Englanders conquer Louisbourg
1747	Boston riot against impressment
1750	Iron Act
1754	Defeat of Virginia militia at Fort Necessity
	Albany Congress proposes plan for colonial unity
1754–1763	French and Indian War
1755	Braddock's defeat near Fort Duquesne
1758	British capture Louisbourg
1760	British conquer Montreal, seizing control of Canada
1763	Pan-Indian war begins in Ohio Valley and Great Lakes region
	Proclamation of 1763 outlaws white settlement west of the Appalachians
	Paxton Boys revolt in Pennsylvania

common cultural framework. With rising wealth, colonial elites supported colleges, and purchased books and luxury goods. This common culture had important ties to England, yet was not altogether English, for immigrants from Scotland, Ireland, and the continent of Europe, and slaves from Africa brought ideas and practices from their native lands.

Immigration into the British colonies also promoted regional diversity, as the newcomers from Europe settled on the frontier from Pennsylvania to Georgia, and the numbers of enslaved Africans grew to 40 percent of the southern population. The Europeans came looking for land: When they set up farms in contested territory, they provoked conflicts with the Native Americans, French, and Spanish, resulting in a series of wars that lasted a quarter century. When the French and Indian War ended in 1763, the British colonies took a great deal of pride in their contribution to the victory, offering it as evidence of their economic and political maturity within the empire.

INTELLECTUAL TRENDS IN THE EIGHTEENTH CENTURY

The willingness of Mather and Boylston to try inoculation showed important changes in the way people viewed their world. The Puritan clergyman's personal journey from witch hunter in 1692 to medical investigator in 1721 reflected the growing inclination to find natural rather than supernatural causes for unexplained events. The Enlightenment blossomed first in Europe and then in America, encompassing political theory and philosophy as well as science. Though primarily intellectual, the Enlightenment had far-reaching effects, inspiring new technology as well as concepts of human freedom. For Americans, its greatest significance lay in the acceptance of natural rights philosophy, which paved the way for independence and republican government.

Newton and Locke

In the late seventeenth century, two English theorists, Sir Isaac Newton and John Locke, had challenged traditional notions that humans had no role in determining their fate, that they could only trust in God to rule the universe, even if divine will seemed inscrutable. They confronted this older view without denying the existence of God. Newton discovered universal laws that predictably govern the motion of planets, moons, and comets, the motion of falling bodies on earth (gravity), and the ebb and flow of tides. His work demonstrated that the universe operated according to fixed principles, which humans are capable of detecting and understanding. Locke built upon Newton's breakthrough in his extraordinarily influential *Essay Concerning Human Understanding* (1690). Locke argued against the accepted belief in innate knowledge, that infants are born with ideas implanted by God in their minds. He contended that all knowledge is gained by experience, not preordained at birth. Humans are born with the ability to learn, to use their acquired knowledge to benefit society.

Locke, and the Enlightenment thinkers he inspired, believed in freedom and the possibility of human progress, in the right of people to improve the conditions in which they live. Science, of course, was an important means of such improvement. The English philosopher also had a major impact upon eighteenth-century politics, in particular providing a theoretical basis for the American Revolution and the Constitution. In *Two Treatises on Civil Government* (1690), published to justify the Glorious Revolution in England, he argued that humans, according to natural law, had rights to life, liberty, and property. By social contract, they formed governments to guarantee those rights. If a state failed in its obligation, the people had the duty to rebel and establish a new government.

Education in the British Colonies

Throughout British North America, formal education beyond basic reading, writing, and arithmetic was rare, so few read the works of Locke and Newton directly. After 1720, however, as newspapers became more available and reprinted articles from London, provincial readers gained greater familiarity with Enlightenment thought. Many colonists learned to read, though boys and girls spent much of their time in apprenticeships, or with their parents, learning the occupations they would pursue as adults. Daughters learned housewifery and spinning, while sons mastered husbandry (farming) or a craft such as carpentry or printing. The availability of formal schooling varied widely by region, class, and gender. Nowhere did a system of

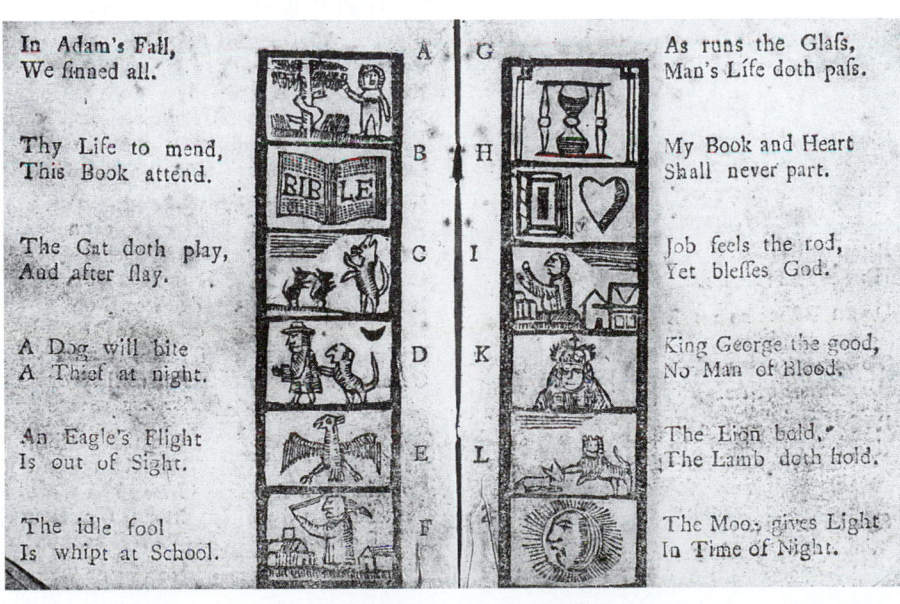

The New England Primer, *first published in the 1680s, taught children moral lessons along with their alphabet and spelling.*

universal, free, public education exist, though New England had some tax-supported schools. Everywhere, schools emphasized moral behavior and used religious texts.

New England made the greatest effort of the British colonies to educate its populace. In 1642, the Massachusetts legislature required parents and ministers to teach all children to read so they could obtain direct understanding of the Bible and the colony's laws. In 1647, the assemblymen took another step, ordering towns with at least fifty families to establish petty (elementary) schools, and those with one hundred families to maintain Latin grammar (secondary) schools. Connecticut and Plymouth passed similar legislation. Towns financed the schools in a variety of ways, through taxes, donations, bequests, and tuition. Though some towns ignored the laws, most New England children learned to read, whether from their parents, at the town school, or at dame schools, where women in their homes taught young girls and boys for a fee. Writing was considered a separate skill, less crucial for girls to learn. The percentage of New England females who could write and do arithmetic was significantly lower than for males, especially in rural districts. Girls, on the other hand, commonly learned sewing and knitting. Boys who planned to enter college attended grammar school from about age seven to

In colonial America, children—especially girls—were less likely to learn to write than to read. Many people could not write their signatures so they made a mark on legal documents, then someone else wrote their name next to the mark.

fourteen, studying Latin, elementary Greek, and sometimes Hebrew. Latin was necessary for the professions, including law, medicine, and the ministry, and to be considered a gentleman.

South of New England, the colonies lacked the common religious and educational values that impelled the Puritans to require town schools. In the Middle Colonies, churches and private teachers offered instruction. Affluent Quaker and Anglican boys were most likely to obtain formal education, though after 1750 girls and poor boys, including African Americans, had better access to schools. As in Massachusetts, females were much less likely to learn to write than males, especially if they lived outside New York and Philadelphia. In the Chesapeake, with dispersed settlement, neither Maryland nor Virginia had many schools. Upper-class boys and girls had private tutors, while middling families in some localities pooled their resources to establish schools. Overall, sons received much more instruction than daughters, and large numbers of poor whites obtained no education at all. Very few slaves learned to read and write, for owners thought these skills would breed discontent and enable them to forge passes, facilitating escape.

New England also surpassed other regions in higher education, as the Puritans established Harvard College in Massachusetts in 1636, and Yale College in Connecticut in 1701. William and Mary, founded in Virginia in 1693, was the only other college in the British colonies before the 1740s. None of the colonial colleges admitted women. The Puritans intended Harvard to preserve classical learning and civilization in what they considered a wilderness, provide liberal education to the region's male elite, and ensure a supply of well-educated ministers. Its faculty would transfer from England the goals and ideals of higher education, perpetuating them from one generation to the next. Harvard offered a curriculum of ethics, religion, logic, mathematics, Greek, Hebrew, rhetoric, and natural history (biology and geology). Most early graduates became clergymen, while others went into medicine, public service, teaching, commerce, and agriculture.

Harvard alumni in Connecticut established Yale to provide advanced education closer to home. Yale had a tentative beginning, but gained more stability by 1720, after receiving funds from Elihu Yale and about 800 volumes for its library, including the books of Locke, Newton, and other Enlightenment figures. The College of William and Mary in Virginia also struggled at first. Chartered by the Crown to train Anglican

The College of William and Mary in Virginia, designed by Christopher Wren.

clergy, educate young men in religion, and convert Native Americans, the school failed to offer college-level courses until the 1720s. Many elite families in the southern provinces continued to depend upon private tutors, trips to Britain, and northern colleges to educate their sons. No college existed in the Middle Colonies until the mid-eighteenth century, when the Great Awakening stimulated a surge in college founding (discussed later in this chapter).

The Growth of Science

After 1720, influenced by Scottish universities that quickly absorbed Enlightenment thinking into their curricula, American colleges expanded their coursework to include French, English literature, philosophy, and science. They offered mathematics and what was then called natural philosophy—astronomy, physics, and chemistry. The colleges hired some of their faculty from Scotland and purchased scientific apparatus, including telescopes, sextants, clocks, and orreries, which demonstrate the motion of planets and moons within the solar system.

American professors of natural philosophy were part of a larger community of scholars centered in the prestigious Royal Society of London, which published a journal, *Philosophical Transactions,* of the latest scientific ideas and knowledge. This transatlantic community included academics like John Winthrop of Harvard College, a descendant of the early Massachusetts governor, as well as largely self-taught men like Benjamin Franklin and John Bartram. More than thirty

colonists belonged to the Royal Society. Scientists took from the Enlightenment a commitment to experiment and observe natural phenomena to obtain information that would lead to human progress. The Royal Society's goals for members were to "impart their knowledge to one another, and contribute what they can to the Grand design of improving Natural knowledge, and perfecting all Philosophical Arts, and Sciences. All for the Glory of God, the Honour and Advantage of these Kingdoms, and the Universal Good of Mankind." John Winthrop was the most renowned professor of natural philosophy in British America, with research interests in such wide-ranging subjects as sunspots, mathematics, earthquakes, and the weather. A member of the Royal Society, he published numerous papers in *Philosophical Transactions.* In the 1760s, Winthrop participated in an important international scientific effort to calculate the distance between the earth and sun, made possible by the transit of the planet Venus across the face of the sun. Venus had last crossed the sun in 1639, when no useful measurements had been made. In 1761, Winthrop was the only American scientist to participate, as he journeyed to Newfoundland to observe the transit. His data, combined with observations from the Cape of Good Hope, were inexact, but eight years later, scientists—including Winthrop—had another chance. This time, at least part of the transit could be viewed in the mainland British colonies. The stakes were high, as observers set up telescopes in Massachusetts, Pennsylvania, and elsewhere, because another transit would not occur for 105 years. The data were again imprecise, but when combined with measurements from around the globe, yielded results very close to the accepted

BENJAMIN FRANKLIN DESCRIBES HIS EXPERIMENTS ON ELECTRICITY 1755

In this letter, Franklin answers some queries from John Lining of Charleston, South Carolina, a physician who had published his own scientific work. Franklin's description of his experiments and explanation of how he came to the conclusion that lightning was electrical exemplify the scientific method. His use of men as guinea pigs in one experiment, however, is shocking in more ways than one.

Sir,   Philadelphia, March 18, 1755

I send you enclosed a paper containing some new experiments I have made, in pursuance of those by Mr. Canton that are printed with my last letters. I hope these, with my explanation of them, will afford you some entertainment.

In answer to your several enquiries. The tubes and globes we use here, are chiefly made here. The glass has a greenish cast, but is clear and hard, and, I think, better for electrical experiments than the white glass of London, which is not so hard. There are certainly great differences in glass. A white globe I had made here some years since, would never, by any means, be excited. Two of my friends tried it, as well as myself, without success. At length, putting it on an electric stand, a chain from the prime-conductor being in contact with it, I found it had the properties of a non-electric; for I could draw sparks from any part of it, though it was very clean and dry. . . .

As to the difference of conductors, there is not only this, that some will conduct Electricity in small quantities, and yet do not conduct it fast enough to produce the shock; but even among those that will conduct a shock, there are some that do it better than others. Mr. Kinnersley has found, by a very good experiment, that when the charge of a bottle hath an opportunity of passing two ways, i.e. strait through a trough of water ten feet long, and six inches square; or round about through twenty feet of wire, it passes through the wire, and not through the water, though that is the shortest course; the wire being the better conductor. When the wire is taken away, it passes through the water, as may be felt by a hand plunged in the water; but it cannot be felt in the water when the wire is used at the same time. Thus, though a small vial containing water will give a smart shock, one containing the same quantity of mercury will give one much stronger, the mercury being the better conductor; while one containing oil only, will scarce give any shock at all.

distance of 93 million miles between the earth and sun.

Other colonists, with less formal education, contributed to understanding the physical world. Though Benjamin Franklin never attended college, he performed important experiments in electricity. Perhaps best known for his diplomacy and political leadership during the Revolutionary era, he has become a symbol of the American Enlightenment for his efforts to improve society through science, inventions, and civic organizations. Franklin was born in Boston, ran away at age seventeen from an apprenticeship with his older brother, and arrived in Philadelphia nearly penniless. He built a highly successful printing business, publishing a newspaper, books, and *Poor Richard's Almanack,* which gained a readership throughout the colonies. He became wealthy

Your question, how I came first to think of proposing the experiment of drawing down the lightning, in order to ascertain its sameness with the electric fluid, I cannot answer better than by giving you an extract from the minutes I used to keep of the experiments I made. . . . By this extract you will see that the thought was not so much "an out-of-the-way one," but that it might have occurred to any electrician.

"Nov. 7, 1749. Electrical fluid agrees with lightning in these particulars: 1. Giving light. 2. Colour of the light. 3. Crooked direction. 4. Swift motion. 5. Being conducted by metals. 6. Crack or noise in exploding. 7. Subsisting in water or ice. 8. Rending bodies it passes through. 9. Destroying animals. 10. Melting metals. 11. Firing inflammable substances. 12. Sulphureous smell. The electric fluid is attracted by points. We do not know whether this property is in lightning. But since they agree in all the particulars wherein we can already compare them, is it not probable they agree likewise in this? Let the experiment be made." . . .

The knocking down of the six men was performed with two of my large jarrs not fully charged. I laid one end of my discharging rod upon the head of the first; he laid his hand on the head of the second; the second his hand on the head of the third, and so to the last, who held, in his hand, the chain that was connected with the outside of the jarrs. When they were thus placed, I applied the other end of my rod to the prime-conductor, and they all dropt together. When they got up, they all declared they had not felt any stroke, and wondered how they came to fall; nor did any of them either hear the crack, or see the light of it. You suppose it a dangerous experiment; but I had once suffered the same myself, receiving, by accident, an equal stroke through my head, that struck me down, without hurting me: And I had seen a young woman that was about to be electrified through the feet, (for some indisposition) receive a greater charge through the head, by inadvertently stooping forward to look at the placing of her feet, till her forehead (as she was very tall) came too near my prime-conductor: She dropt, but instantly got up again, complaining of nothing. A person so struck, sinks down doubled, or folded together as it were, the joints losing their strength and stiffness at once, so that he drops on the spot where he stood, instantly, and there is no previous staggering, nor does he ever fall lengthwise. Too great a charge might, indeed, kill a man, but I have not yet seen any hurt done by it. It would certainly, as you observe, be the easiest of all deaths. . . .

I am, &c. B.F.

enough to retire from his print shop at age forty-two. Throughout his life, Franklin put the Enlightenment ideal of human progress into action. He founded a debating club to discuss politics, morals, and natural philosophy, and helped establish the first American lending library, a hospital, and the College of Philadelphia. Franklin's experiments in electricity yielded information about its properties, including the basic concepts of "plus" and "minus." His inventions, which applied scientific principles to improving daily life, included bifocal eyeglasses, the lightning rod, and an iron stove that was more efficient than colonial fireplaces.

John Bartram, also of Pennsylvania, was the most energetic of American naturalists, whose chief contribution to science was collecting specimens of New World plant life. In return for a yearly pension from

the king and payment for seeds he sent to wealthy collectors in England, Bartram traveled all over the eastern seaboard searching for new plants and animals. His efforts greatly expanded botanical knowledge of the Western Hemisphere, for he sent specimens to such scholars as Carl Linnaeus, the Swedish author of the modern classification system.

Another prominent American naturalist was Cadwallader Colden, a Scot who immigrated to the colonies after receiving his medical degree. Like many well-educated doctors, Colden had broad interests in science. While serving as surveyor-general and lieutenant-governor of New York, he collected and classified plants in the neighborhood of his estate. He corresponded with European botanists, sending them specimens and descriptions. As their demands became overwhelming, Colden taught his daughter, Jane, how to classify according to Linnaeus' scheme. Her accurate descriptions and drawings earned high praise from Linnaeus, Bartram, and other naturalists. Cadwallader Colden also ventured into the field of physics, publishing a pamphlet in which he attempted unsuccessfully to explain the causes of gravity.

Changes in Medical Practice

Just as Colden and other university-trained doctors were interested in many scientific fields, the practice of medicine itself attracted people of widely different backgrounds. Medicine was beginning to develop as a profession. During the colonial period, men with formal medical education comprised a small proportion of the people who provided care for disease, physical injury, and childbirth. Having completed formal coursework abroad—the first medical school in the British colonies, located in Philadelphia, did not open until 1766—educated physicians were at the top of their profession, and charged the highest fees. Consequently, they practiced primarily in the cities, with a wealthy clientele. Below them were men who learned their craft as apprentices; though they assumed the title of doctor in the colonies, they were actually akin to the surgeon-apothecaries of Great Britain. As surgeons, they performed emergency procedures such as setting bones, amputating limbs, and removing superficial tumors, but no major surgery. As apothecaries, they prepared and prescribed drugs for a variety of illnesses.

Female midwives traditionally attended childbirth, treated the ill, and prescribed herbal remedies. Having learned their skills through informal apprenticeships and from witnessing the childbirths of neighbors and relatives, they received payment for their services. During the colonial period, childbirth was the province of women. As an expectant mother's labor began, she called together a group of women, presided over by the midwife, who assisted in the birth. In the early stages of her labor, the woman provided special refreshments, called "groaning beer" and "groaning cakes." The attendants helped her walk around and offered herbal teas or liquor to relieve the pain. In normal deliveries, the mother squatted on a "midwife's stool" or remained standing while supported by several women. If complications occurred, the midwife manipulated the infant manually, but would not perform a Caesarean section. In the worst cases, the midwife had to kill the child; sometimes the mother died. Without modern antibiotics, women constantly faced the threat of infection during pregnancy and in the weeks following delivery.

In the last half of the eighteenth century, the practice of obstetrics changed. In 1762, Dr. William Shippen, Jr., returned from studying medicine in England and Scotland to give lectures in anatomy to Philadelphia midwives and doctors. Soon he accepted only male students; physicians in Boston and New York followed his example. Shippen established an obstetrical practice of his own, quickly attracting well-to-do patients who expected, in return for his higher fee, a more elevated level of care than they received from midwives. Affluent urban women were convinced that the male physicians offered a better chance for a safe, less painful delivery. The doctors' obstetrical training, their use of opiates and instruments such as forceps, spelled progress to these women, inducing them to abandon the traditional woman-dominated rituals of childbirth. That the new obstetrics brought improvement is doubtful. The male doctors, faced with taboos against observing the private parts of ladies, attended their clients in darkened rooms, with the woman lying in bed under covers. The physicians also lacked the means to prevent infection; their use of blood-letting and opium could impede safe delivery. Success still depended primarily upon the skill and experience of the practitioner, whether midwife or physician. In any case, midwives continued to attend the great majority of women, those who lived in rural areas and the poor who could not afford the doctors' fees.

THE GREAT AWAKENING

As Enlightenment ideas gained sway among British colonial elites and in the colleges by 1720, many Protestant ministers embraced Christian rationalism, a theology influenced by Locke and other theorists. Stressing moral, rational behavior and the free will of individuals to lead their lives and achieve salvation, they argued that one could "follow God and obey Reason" at the same time. Some rationalists spoke of an impersonal God who had long ago created the universe to operate according to natural laws, rather than a loving or angry God who controlled a person's daily life. For many, the rationalist religion was comforting, because it included in the church all who tried to live decent Christian lives, not just those who believed they were saved. To others, however, Christian rationalism was heretical, for it rejected the Calvinist belief that salvation came from grace, as the gift of God, and that people must be saved to be full members of the church.

From the 1720s to the 1760s, ministers from various denominations called for the renewal of these beliefs in a series of revivals, known as the Great Awakening. Several of the most important Awakeners brought the impetus for revival from Europe and Great Britain. Religious ferment convulsed British North America, spreading from the churches to threaten social and political authority.

Religious Diversity Before the Great Awakening

In 1720, the British provinces varied widely in religious and ethnic makeup. New England was the most homogeneous, for Massachusetts, New Hampshire, and Connecticut remained predominantly Puritan and of English descent. The established Puritan churches received tax support, but Anglicans, Baptists, and Quakers could also worship freely. Rhode Island, which still embraced the principles of religious liberty and separation of church and state, was home to various denominations, including Quakers, Baptists, and Separatists.

From their founding, the Middle Colonies offered an open door to people of various backgrounds, as both the Dutch West India Company and the duke of York tried to attract settlers. In the late seventeenth century, according to one report, residents of New York City spoke eighteen different languages, including Dutch, Swedish, various African languages, English, German, and French. In eastern New Jersey, Scottish Presbyterians, Dutch Reformed, New England Puritans, Baptists, and Quakers settled towns and plantations, and farther south, on both sides of the Delaware River, Native Americans, Dutch, Swedes, and Finns met the Quakers who accompanied William Penn. Philadelphia and its environs in the 1720s boasted organized meetings of Swedish Lutherans, Quakers, Mennonites, Baptists, Anglicans, Presbyterians, Dunkards, German Reformed, Dutch Reformed, German Lutherans, and Roman Catholics. Though disputes occasionally arose between churches, the Quaker government upheld liberty of conscience throughout the colonial period.

With few towns in the Chesapeake, the Anglican church, which had been established in Virginia since 1607 and in Maryland since 1702, suffered from southern rural conditions. With large parishes, ministers in Virginia faced serious obstacles in meeting the spiritual needs of their scattered congregations. Only half of the Anglican churches had regular preachers. Few planters were interested in converting their African slaves, who kept—and passed on to their children—many traditional African beliefs. The colony's laws against nonconformity prevented most dissent, so only a few Presbyterians and Quakers worshiped openly. In Maryland, many Quakers and Roman Catholics retained their faith, but suffered legal disabilities.

The established Church of England in South Carolina was in better condition than in Virginia; some prosperous parishes could pay adequately their dedicated, well-trained clergy. Even so, Presbyterians, Baptists, Huguenots, and Quakers worshiped freely, for the proprietors had actively recruited dissenters from England, Scotland, and France to increase population and obtain their political support.

The Great Awakening shattered the existing church structure of the colonies, as congregations wakened to the teachings and vigorous preaching style of revivalist, or New Light, ministers. Religious diversity grew in provinces where established churches, with government support, dominated religious life—especially Puritan churches in Connecticut and Massachusetts, and the Anglican establishment in Virginia. As a result of the revivals, these colonies became more like Rhode

Island, New York, New Jersey, Pennsylvania, and South Carolina, where many denominations already flourished.

Early Revivals in the Middle Colonies and New England

In 1720, New Jersey felt the first stirrings of the Great Awakening, when Theodore Jacob Frelinghuysen emigrated from Holland to serve four churches in the Raritan Valley. He had been educated in Dutch Reformed pietism, which emphasized the importance of conversion and personal religious experience (or piety). Using an emotional, revivalist preaching style, he led many people to experience salvation. But Frelinghuysen offended members of his congregations by refusing communion and baptism of their children to the unconverted. He created a split in the Dutch Reformed churches of New Jersey between his followers, who believed a person must experience God's saving grace before participating in church sacraments, and his opponents, who thought that a commitment to living a godly life was sufficient. This was the fundamental conflict between those who supported and opposed the Great Awakening.

Next, revivals engulfed Presbyterian churches in New Jersey, as they adopted doctrines preached by Gilbert and John Tennent, the sons of William Tennent, a Scots-Irish immigrant and Presbyterian minister. The younger Tennents, convinced by their father of the importance of religious piety and conversion, took pulpits in New Brunswick and Freehold, close to Frelinghuysen's congregations. Impressed by the Dutch Reformed pastor's style of preaching, they inspired revivals of their own. Meanwhile, in Neshaminy, Pennsylvania, the elder Tennent established a seminary, called the "Log College" by his critics, where many New Light ministers received training.

In New England, revivals began in 1734, when minister Jonathan Edwards of Northampton, in the Connecticut River valley of western Massachusetts, preached a series of sermons on salvation, inclining many of his parishioners to believe they were saved. They went through the process of self-judgment—first feeling despair as sinners who were damned to hell, then rejoicing in the conviction that God rescued them from this fate. Edwards wrote to a colleague that "this town never was so full of Love, nor so full of Joy,

Reverend Gilbert Tennent, son of the founder of the "Log College," was an avid New Light minister during the Great Awakening.

nor so full of distress as it has lately been." Over the next few years, the revival spread to other towns along the Connecticut River.

Revivalism Takes Fire

Beginning in 1739, the Great Awakening spread throughout the British mainland colonies after a young Anglican minister, George Whitefield, arrived from England to tour the Middle Colonies. Called the Grand Itinerant, he had a magnificent voice, ranging from a whisper to a roar, that could be heard by large crowds in fields and city streets. Benjamin Franklin described one of these occasions in Philadelphia, as Whitefield

> had a loud and clear voice, and articulated his words and sentences so perfectly that he might be heard and understood at a great distance, especially as his auditories, how-

George Whitefield, the itinerant English evangelist, had a spellbinding effect on his listeners, as portrayed here by John Wollaston.

ever numerous, observed the most exact silence. He preached one evening from the top of the courthouse steps, which are in the middle of Market Street and on the west side of Second Street, which crosses it at right angles. Both streets were filled with his hearers to a considerable distance.

Franklin calculated that 25,000 people could easily hear the spectacular preacher at one time.

Whitefield told enthusiastic audiences that they must change their ways and seek God. He found adherents across denominational lines and among native-born Americans and immigrants alike—English, Scots-Irish, African Americans, Dutch, Germans, and Welsh. In 1740, Jonathan Edwards invited Whitefield to Northampton, prompting the itinerant to travel through New England, where he attracted crowds as large as 8,000 in Boston. Other New Light ministers followed, including Gilbert Tennent and James Davenport, a Puritan preacher of Southold, Long Island. Davenport took the Awakening to extremes, harshly attacking other pastors as "unconverted." In 1743, he instigated the burning of books written by well-known clergymen; a year later he repented this excess.

The full force of the Awakening hit the south later than New England and the Middle Atlantic. During the 1740s, Presbyterian missionaries—men who received their education at Tennent's Log College—worked successfully among Scots-Irish immigrants to set up churches on the southern frontier. The new settlements were a fertile field for the revivalists because few regular clergy had migrated west. The more explosive Baptist revivals began a decade later, in the 1750s, when itinerants traveled through Virginia and North Carolina making converts and forming churches. The Baptists believed in adult baptism—that individuals should be saved before they are baptized. With their emotional religious style and challenge to the Anglican establishment in Virginia, they appealed particularly to ordinary white farmers and enslaved African Americans. Followers called each other "Sister" and "Brother," whether slave or free, affluent or poor. They refused to attend their local parish services and condemned many aspects of gentry culture, including horseracing, cockfights, elegant dress, and entertaining on Sunday. Lacking formal churches, Baptists met in fields and homes. The ministry was open to all, even women and slaves, with no requirement for college training.

The Awakening's Impact

The revivals proved to be socially divisive, as many communities split into two groups, the "New Lights" and the "Old Lights." The style of most New Light preachers was to give impassioned, extemporaneous sermons that contrasted dramatically with the closely reasoned sermons of their opponents, the rationalist Old Light ministers. New Lights believed that salvation was more important than religious training; they required a "saved" ministry, with a dynamic preaching style that helped to demonstrate one's conversion. Congregations responded by fainting, shrieking, and shedding tears. Old Light clergymen, who defended their advanced education in theology, Greek, Hebrew,

NATHAN COLE DESCRIBES GOING TO HEAR REVEREND GEORGE WHITEFIELD, 1740

This Connecticut farmer's account of Reverend George Whitefield's visit to Middletown vividly portrays how people throughout the countryside heard of the New Light evangelist's arrival and flocked to hear him preach. Cole's last sentence shows the effectiveness of Whitefield's message that salvation came from God, not from an individual's good works.

Now it pleased God to send Mr. Whitefield into this land; and my hearing of his preaching at Philadelphia, like one of the old apostles, and many thousands flocking to hear him preach the Gospel, and great numbers were converted to Christ, I felt the Spirit of God drawing me by conviction; I longed to see and hear him and wished he would come this way. I heard he was come to New York and the Jerseys and great multitudes flocking after him under great concern for their souls which brought on my concern more and more, hoping soon to see him; but next I heard he was at Long Island, then at Boston, and next at Northampton. Then on a sudden, in the morning about 8 or 9 of the clock there came a messenger and said Mr. Whitefield preached at Hartford and Wethersfield yesterday and is to preach at Middletown this morning at ten of the clock. I was in my field at work. I dropped my tool that I had in my hand and ran home to my wife, telling her to make ready quickly to go and hear Mr. Whitefield preach at Middletown, then ran to my pasture for my horse with all my might, fearing that I should be too late. Having my horse, I with my wife soon mounted the horse and went forward as fast as I thought the horse could bear; and when my horse got much out of breath, I would get down and put my wife on the saddle and bid her ride as fast as she could and not stop or slack for me except I bade her, and so I would run until I was much out of breath and then mount my horse again, and so I did several times to favour my horse. We improved every moment to get along as if we were fleeing for our lives, all the while fearing we should be too late to hear the sermon, for we had twelve miles to ride double in little more than an hour and we went round by the upper housen parish. And when we came within about half a

and ethics, resented accusations that they were unsaved. In turn, they charged the revivalists with being unlearned.

As congregations broke apart, bitter disputes ensued over church property and tax support, spilling what had begun as a religious controversy into the courts and politics. Where strong established churches existed—as in Massachusetts, Connecticut, and Virginia—the New Lights challenged political as well as religious authority. In response, the Connecticut As-

sembly, for example, passed an Anti-Itinerancy Act, which made it illegal for a clergyman to preach in another's parish without his permission and repealed the 1708 law permitting religious dissent. While this heavy-handed approach prevailed in the short run, it generated long-term support for freedom of worship.

Higher education in the British colonies also felt the flames of revivalistic fervor. Yale College was at the center of the intense religious and political battles in Connecticut, as George Whitefield, Gilbert Tennent,

mile or a mile of the road that comes down from Hartford, Wethersfield, and Stepney to Middletown, on high land I saw before me a cloud of fog arising. I first thought it came from the great river, but as I came nearer the road I heard a noise of horses' feet coming down the road, and this cloud was a cloud of dust made by the horses' feet. It arose some rods into the air over the tops of hills and trees; and when I came within about 20 rods of the road, I could see men and horses slipping along in the cloud like shadows, and as I drew nearer it seemed like a steady stream of horses and their riders, scarcely a horse more than his length behind another, all of a lather and foam with sweat, their breath rolling out of their nostrils every jump. Every horse seemed to go with all his might to carry his rider to hear news from heaven for the saving of souls. It made me tremble to see the sight, how the world was in a struggle. I found a vacancy between two horses to slip in mine and my wife said "Law, our clothes will be all spoiled, see how they look," for they were so covered with dust that they looked almost all of a colour, coats, hats, shirts, and horse. We went down in the stream but heard no man speak a word all the way for 3 miles but every one pressing forward in great haste; and when we got to Middletown old meeting house, there was a great multitude, it was said to be 3 or 4,000 of people, assembled together. We dismounted and shook off our dust, and the ministers were then coming to the meeting house. I turned and looked towards the Great River and saw the ferry boats running swift backward and forward bringing over loads of people, and the oars rowed nimble and quick. Everything, men, horses, and boats seemed to be struggling for life. The land and banks over the river looked black with people and horses; all along the 12 miles I saw no man at work in his field, but all seemed to be gone. When I saw Mr. Whitefield come upon the scaffold, he looked almost angelical; a young, slim, slender youth, before some thousands of people with a bold undaunted countenance. And my hearing how God was with him everywhere as he came along, it solemnized my mind and put me into a trembling fear before he began to preach; for he looked as if he was clothed with authority from the Great God, and a sweet solemn solemnity sat upon his brow, and my hearing him preach gave me a heart wound. By God's blessing, my old foundation was broken up, and I saw that my righteousness would not save me.

Jonathan Edwards, and James Davenport all stopped at New Haven on their preaching tours. When the New Haven church separated, a large number of students, many of them studying for the ministry, followed the New Lights. They skipped classes to attend revivals, challenged Yale's curriculum, and questioned whether their teachers were saved. To suppress the student rebellion, Thomas Clap, head of the college, obtained permission from the Connecticut Assembly to expel any student who attended New Light services.

Clap's opposition to the Awakening was not permanent, however, for by 1753 he himself had become a New Light. In 1764, George Whitefield preached in the college chapel. As in many congregations, people eventually found ways to heal the bitterness and division that the Great Awakening had caused.

A more lasting effect of the revivals was the founding of new colleges. Until the mid-1740s, only Harvard, William and Mary, and Yale—all with ties to established churches—existed in the British colonies.

The revivals created a need for ministerial training, for despite their emphasis on a converted ministry, most New Lights believed that preachers should have advanced education. Between 1746 and 1769, the revivalists founded the College of New Jersey (now Princeton), the College of Rhode Island (Brown), Queen's College (Rutgers) in New Jersey, and Dartmouth College in New Hampshire. Anglicans established King's College (Columbia) in New York City, while a group of civic leaders, headed by Benjamin Franklin, started the College of Philadelphia (University of Pennsylvania) on a nonsectarian basis. Though each of these new schools except the College of Philadelphia was tied to a specific religious denomination, they all accepted young men of various faiths. These new colleges taught traditional subjects, including classical languages, but also adopted the new curricula in mathematics, science, and modern languages.

IMMIGRATION AND EXPANSION

Between 1720 and 1760, the population of British North America grew by more than 1 million people, from 472,000 to 1,600,000. Much of this growth came from natural increase, as the creole (or native-born) sons and daughters of white immigrants and enslaved Africans married younger and had more children than their parents. But new arrivals also spurred population growth, as thousands of Germans and Scots-Irish immigrated, and slave traders continued to import blacks.

The newcomers brought ideas, religious beliefs, skills, and ways of life that significantly altered the cultural mix of the British colonies. Some played important roles in spreading the Enlightenment, while others started the Great Awakening. The immigrants from the European continent and the British Isles sought a new beginning in "the best poor man's country": Many disembarked in the Middle Colonies, traveling west to settle the backcountry from Pennsylvania south through the Shenandoah Valley to the Carolinas. Others went directly to Georgia, which reformers started in 1732 as a haven for the poor. The population explosion and demand for new lands brought the British colonists face to face with the Spanish in

Florida, the French in Canada and the Ohio Valley, and Native Americans all along the frontier. The result was war—a series of struggles lasting over twenty years.

German and Scots-Irish Immigrants

More than 100,000 Germans left their homelands for America during the century after 1683; most of them immigrated between 1727 and 1756. Some were forced out by religious persecution, oppressive regulations, and the devastation of war; others pulled up stakes to find economic opportunity. Promoters called "newlanders" told Germans of cheap fertile land and mild government in the British colonies. Many immigrants paid their own passage. Those who could not signed on as "redemptioners," the equivalent of indentured servants, whose labor would be sold for a number of years upon arrival, often to Germans already living in the colonies. Immigrants went to ports from New York to Georgia, with most entering the Delaware Valley. Some Germans remained in Philadelphia, but the majority headed for the Pennsylvania hinterland and south through the backcountry of Maryland, Virginia, and the Carolinas. By 1775, Germans comprised one-third of the population of Pennsylvania and one-tenth of the people of the mainland British colonies.

German-speaking immigrants found the freedom they sought in North America, congregating in distinct communities, building separate churches and schools, and maintaining German language and culture. Pennsylvania was the heart of German America, as the colony's religious freedom allowed a multitude of sects and churches to flourish—the Mennonites, Amish, Brethren, Moravians, Schwenkfelders, Lutheran, and Reformed.

Cultural exchange between the Germans and English enriched American society. German churches introduced the sophisticated choral music of their homelands, installing organs in Philadelphia, Germantown, and Lancaster, Pennsylvania. The printer Christopher Saur reprinted German hymnals along with his German-language newspaper and almanac. Congregations founded schools in which children learned both German and English. Immigrants retained the old tongue in their churches and homes, but used English in business, the courts, and politics. In material culture, they transported Old World tradi-

tions, then created new forms of expression as they responded to British culture and the new environment. German American decorative arts proliferated by the 1740s, in house ornaments, furniture, and elaborately illustrated documents, such as marriage certificates, with gothic *Fraktur* lettering.

German farm women did much heavier fieldwork than most English wives, but otherwise played a similar role in maintaining domestic culture. Germans favored the more efficient European stoves over English fireplaces, and pewter over tinware. In diet, they ate relatively little meat, and preferred coffee to tea. But like their English neighbors, German women served as midwives and dispensed herbal remedies.

Though some German immigrants engaged in politics and law, most remained uninvolved in government before the Revolution. The majority of Germans lived many miles from the provincial capitals located near the seaboard, making political participation difficult. As non-British immigrants with little wealth, they needed time to become naturalized, learn the language and political culture, and establish themselves economically. As exiles from persecution, high taxes, and war, Germans were grateful for the high degree of freedom that they found in the new land.

Large numbers of Scots, Scots-Irish, and Irish Catholics also came during the eighteenth century, settling in New York, Pennsylvania, Delaware, western Maryland, and the southern backcountry. Most were Ulster Scots (or Scots-Irish as they were called in America), Presbyterians whose families had migrated during the 1600s from Scotland to northern Ireland in search of economic opportunity. There they had combined tenant farming and weaving until the early eighteenth century, when their leases expired. Because landlords raised rents exorbitantly, many Ulster Scots left with

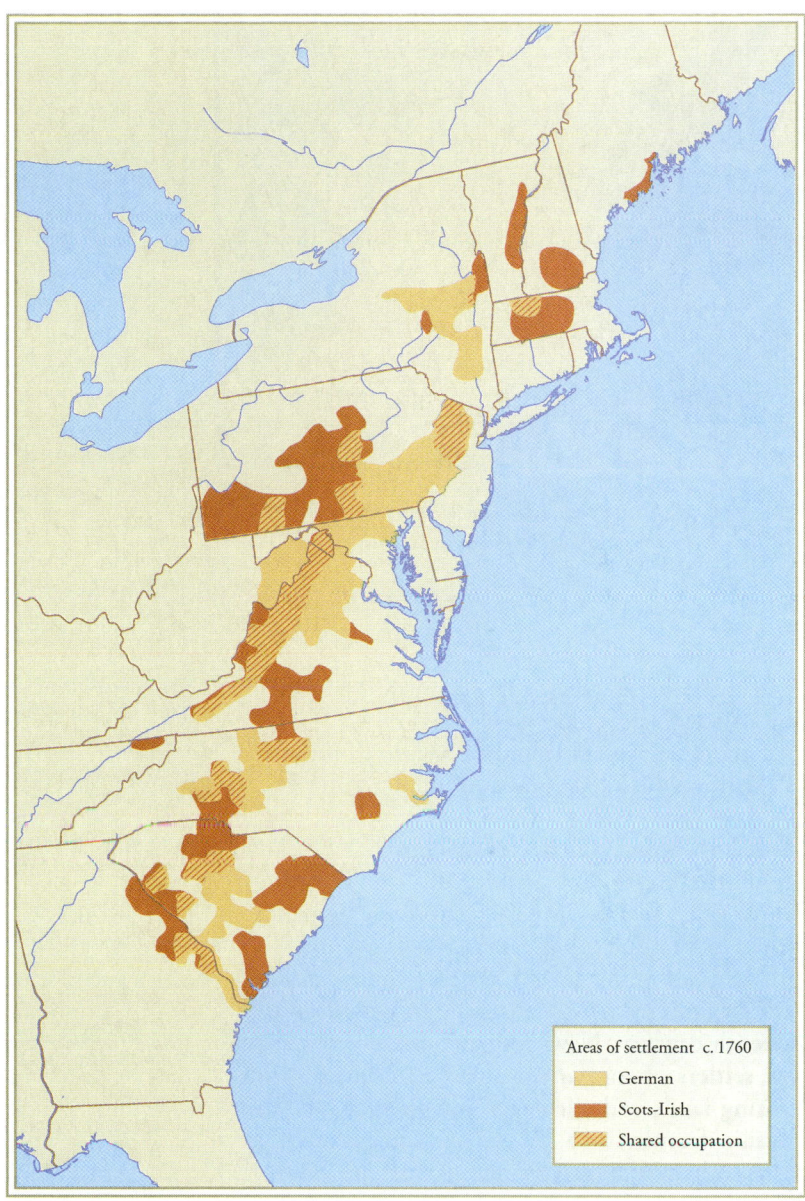

Areas of settlement c. 1760

	German
	Scots-Irish
	Shared occupation

MAP 4.1   GERMAN AND SCOTS-IRISH SETTLEMENTS IN COLONIAL BRITISH AMERICA, CA. 1760

their families for the colonies. The first large wave of immigrants departed during 1717–1718; poor harvests and downturns in the linen industry impelled successive groups toward America. Smaller numbers of Irish Catholics, mostly single young men, migrated from southern Ireland throughout the pre-Revolutionary period.

The baptismal certificate is an example of German-American "fraktur," or documents illustrated with color designs and drawings.

In the colonies, the Scots-Irish achieved a reputation as tough defenders of the frontier. As relatively late arrivals, they had to stake out farms on the edges of existing white settlements to obtain enough good land to raise grain, livestock, and the flax they needed to weave linen cloth. The combination of agriculture and linen manufacture was a distinctive contribution of the Ulster Scots to the colonial economy. As frontier inhabitants, the Scots-Irish came into frequent contact with Native Americans, often with tragic results. Like the English colonists of seventeenth-century New England and Virginia, the new settlers often marked out their farms on Indian hunting lands without negotiating a sale. One Pennsylvania frontiersman, not recognizing the Indians' rights, echoed the early Puritans when he argued that it was contrary to "the laws of God and nature, that so much land should be idle, while so many Christians wanted it to labor on, and to raise their bread."

The Founding of Georgia

The last of the British mainland colonies, Georgia (named for King George II, who governed from 1727 to 1760), lured many German and Scots-Irish immigrants, as well as Scots and English. Animated by Enlightenment ideals of human progress and freedom,

James Oglethorpe and John Viscount Percival, members of the Associates of the Late Doctor Bray, a philanthropic society, sought a charter for the colony. After studying the deplorable conditions of debtors' prisons in England, they were convinced that something had to be done to help the poor. They also argued that the settlement could serve as a buffer between Spanish Florida and South Carolina. The English had craved the region since the late seventeenth century when Carolinians destroyed the Spanish missions of Guale. George II granted the charter, placing control of the colony in the hands of trustees, or proprietors, who could neither receive financial benefits from the province nor own land within its bounds.

The double function of Georgia as a haven for the poor and military outpost shaped the terms under which settlers immigrated. The trustees intended to create a peaceful, moral society of small farmers in which everyone, except indentured servants, worked for themselves. The proprietors wanted to avoid duplicating lowland South Carolina where large plantation owners lived off the toil of their slaves. The Georgia Trustees, led by Oglethorpe, set three significant policies: They prohibited importation of hard liquor, banned slaveholding, and limited land ownership to 500 acres or less. Each free male immigrant was granted land at no charge, but no one could buy or sell real estate, and only men could inherit land. The trustees hoped to keep Georgia as a refuge for small farmers who, coincidentally, would defend the southern frontier. The rule that only men could inherit land, a carryover from the Middle Ages called "tail-male," meant that each farm must be owned by a man who, at least ideally, could fight.

The settlement of Georgia held promise, for in February 1733 the ship *Anne* with approximately one hundred passengers arrived at a site on the Savannah River. Here they built the first town, Savannah, on a high bluff overlooking the river. Oglethorpe purchased land from the Native Americans and pledged to prevent price gouging in trade, a significant complaint of the Indians against South Carolina merchants. He established alliances with Lower Creeks, Cherokees, and Chickasaws against Spanish Florida, not least because English traders offered better merchandise than their rivals. The congenial negotiations boded well for the new colony.

But many settlers in Georgia believed that the prohibitions on liquor, land sales, and slavery were unrea-

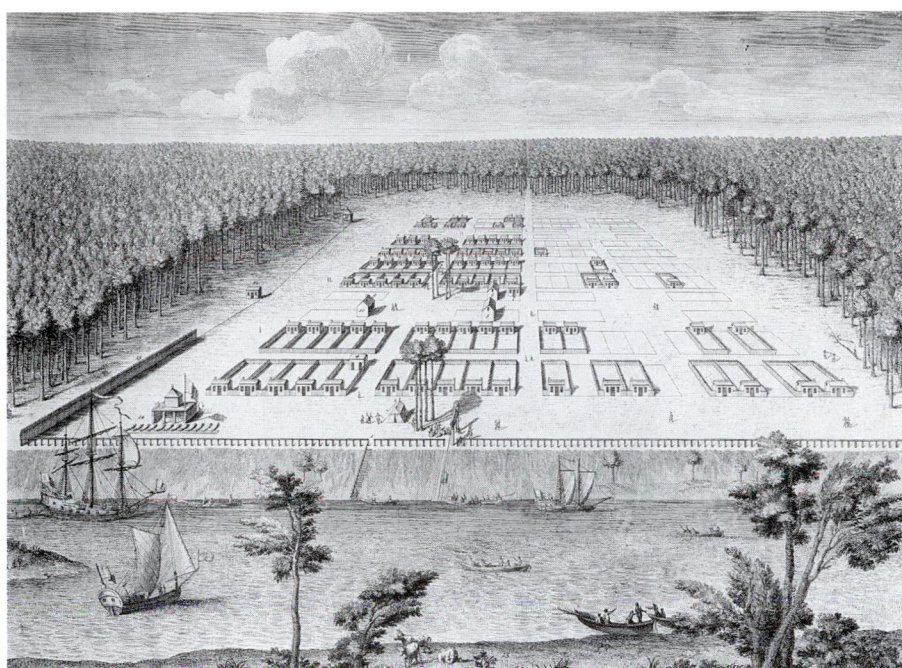

A view of Savannah as it stood on the 29th of March 1734.

sonable. They could do little to change the colony's direction because they lacked an elective assembly. The colonists knew that the embargo on rum, a major Caribbean commodity, prevented expansion of trade with the West Indies, a ready market for their abundant lumber. The bans on slavery and large landholdings were also unpopular with many settlers, who coveted the grander lifestyle of planters north of the Savannah River, in South Carolina.

In consequence, Georgia grew slowly, as some settlers left almost immediately. Of an estimated 5,000 people who arrived in Georgia before 1751, fewer than one-half remained. The trustees gradually recognized their failure, allowing the importation of rum in 1742, and land sales and slavery in 1750. Preparing to turn the colony over to the Crown, in 1751 they called together Georgia's first elected assembly, which obtained legislative powers three years later when the royal government took control. The Georgia population swelled as South Carolinians migrated across the Savannah River, transforming Georgia into a slave society. By 1773, the province had 33,000 inhabitants, of whom 45 percent were enslaved blacks.

Despite its halting start before 1750, Georgia attracted settlers of a variety of nationalities and religions. The colony tapped the eighteenth-century flow of European immigrants, including a group of Spanish and German Jews who settled in Savannah, and German-speaking Lutherans who founded Ebenezer and other farming communities. One of the Lutheran ministers described their satisfaction with the new land: "Every year God gives them what they need. And since they have been able to earn something apart from agriculture, through the mills which have been built and in many other ways, they have managed rather well with God's blessing, and have led a calm and quiet life of blessedness and honesty." Another group of German Protestants, the Moravians, were less content in Georgia, where they hoped to convert the Native Americans. Led by Count Nikolaus Ludwig von Zinzendorf, they arrived in 1735 and were gone five years later, because as pacifists, Moravian men could not serve in the militia. When the threat of Spanish invasion intensified in the late 1730s, most of the Moravians departed for Pennsylvania, which required no military service. In contrast were the Scottish Highlanders, whom the trustees recruited in 1735 for their reputation as rugged soldiers. They agreed to settle at an outpost on the Altamaha River to provide defense against Spanish Florida.

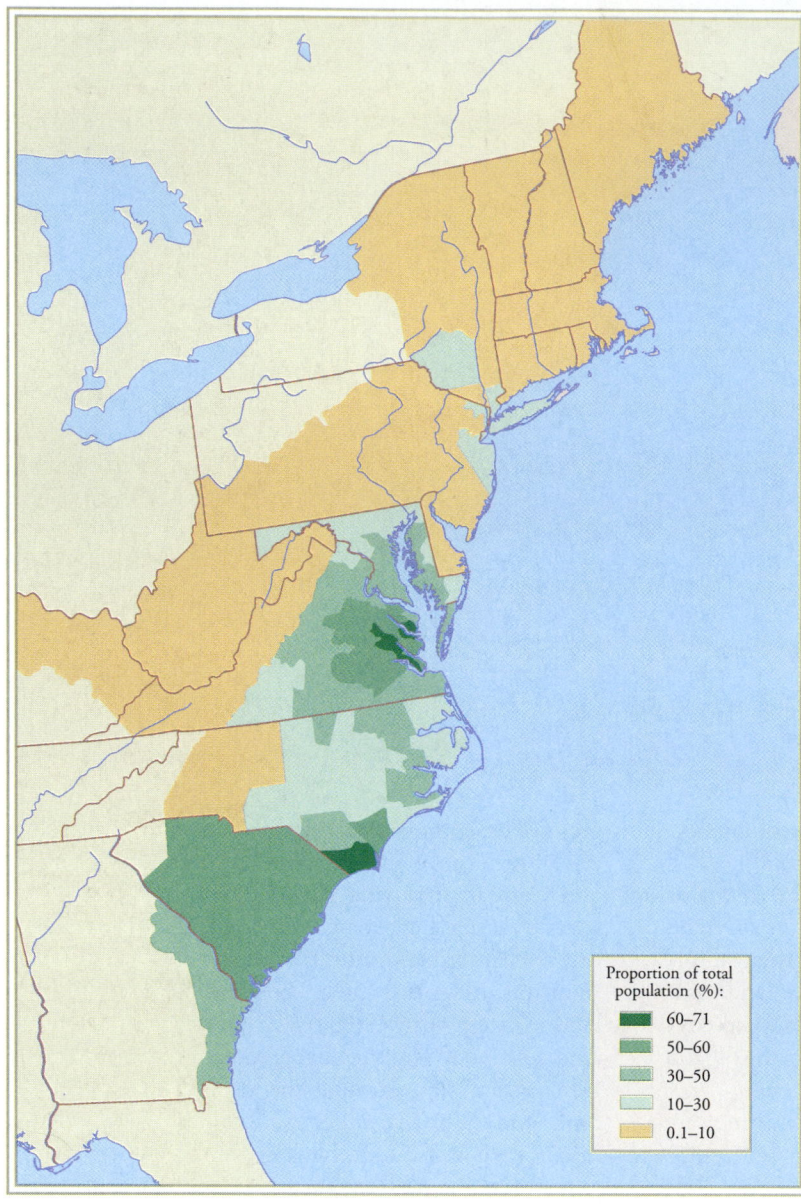

MAP 4.2 AFRICAN-AMERICAN POPULATION IN COLONIAL BRITISH AMERICA, CA. 1760

Proportion of total population (%):

- 60–71
- 50–60
- 30–50
- 10–30
- 0.1–10

Nowhere—not even in Quaker Pennsylvania—did significant abolitionism exist before 1750. Like the Germans and Scots-Irish, Africans helped diversify the American population and shape its culture. Though the number of African Americans grew naturally in many places, especially in the Chesapeake, slave traders imported over 200,000 people between 1720 and the Revolution, most from West and Central Africa, from Senegambia to Angola. In 1750, blacks comprised one-fifth of the population of the mainland colonies, including about 40 percent in the Chesapeake and the Lower South. In comparison, enslaved Africans were 90 percent in the British West Indies, where much larger numbers were imported each year to replace people who died from harsh working conditions and a lethal disease environment.

As the number of African Americans increased and slave societies matured on the mainland, blacks created patterns of community, work, and culture. Extended kinship networks structured community life on large plantations, and even in places where slaves lived in small numbers, such as in northern urban households, family ties remained paramount. Blacks were most successful in perpetuating African language and customs in regions where they were most numerous, particularly the South Carolina low country and, later, Georgia. Because they came from hundreds of societies in Africa, with many different cultural attributes, they had difficulty keeping traditional ways intact. They melded African and European forms together, and in the process, influenced evolving mainstream cultures, especially in the south.

The opportunity of slaves to engage in independent activities varied with the amount of time they had to spend working for their master. In South Carolina, blacks labored by the task; each slave received a certain

The Growth of the African American Population

The failure of the trustees to create a free society in Georgia was symptomatic of the entrenchment of slavery in America, as Africans labored throughout the British mainland colonies in perpetual bondage.

This vivid painting, The Old Plantation, *by an unknown artist, portrays social life among enslaved Africans on a southern plantation. The banjo is just one of the African instruments that became incorporated into American music.*

amount of work to perform each day—a field to hoe, thread to spin, a fence to build. Those who completed their assignments quickly had time to raise their own crops and livestock. Consequently, Carolina slaves participated in trade, selling their production at the "Negro market" in Charleston on Sundays. As in Africa, women were responsible for marketing the family's goods. In the Chesapeake, most slaves on plantations labored for a specified number of hours rather than by the task. They planted, weeded, or harvested in gangs until the overseer told them to stop. As a result, they had little time to work for themselves.

The persistence of African culture, and its influence on white Americans, was conspicuous in language, food, music, dance, and religion. Some newly arrived Africans knew Dutch, Spanish, Portuguese, French, or English from former contacts in Africa or the West Indies, but to communicate with other slaves and with Europeans, most adopted creole speech, a combination of English and African languages. In the Lower South, for instance, the creole tongue known as Gullah evolved from English and various languages from southern Nigeria, the Gold Coast, Angola, and Senegambia. African Americans retained black dialect from creole, contributing to a group identity separate from their masters. For example, most blacks used the word *buckra,* from the African word meaning "he who governs," to refer to white men. Africans also influenced white speech patterns, when white children and immigrants sometimes adopted African American dialect. One British traveler complained that plantation owners allowed "their children . . . to prowl amongst the young Negroes, which insensibly causes them to imbibe their manners and broken speech." Some African words became part of American vocabulary, including cola, yam, goober (peanut), and toting (carrying) a package.

Blacks contributed to the food and material culture of British America, popularizing new foods such as okra, melons, and bananas. They made clay pipes,

pottery, and baskets with African designs, and carved eating utensils, chairs, and other useful objects from wood. They built houses on African models rather than European. In music, they introduced the use of percussion instruments—cymbals, tambourines, and drums—to British military bands. While masters discouraged Africans from drumming because of the potential to call others to revolt, whites enjoyed the music of black fiddlers. Slaves helped create the Virginia "jig," a fusion of African and European elements, accompanied by banjos and fiddles.

Along with whites, during the Great Awakening, Africans shaped the forms of worship in southern Baptist churches, as they responded with enthusiasm to traveling missionaries. Blacks retained traditional African concepts of the hereafter, where the deceased reunited with ancestors, combining these beliefs with European views of heaven. Funerals remained important to African Americans throughout the colonies, as mourners buried the dead facing Africa, with traditional rituals, music, and dance. In Philadelphia, for example, the blacks' burial ground was the focus of community activities where they gathered on Sundays and holidays, "dancing after the manner of their several nations in Africa, and speaking and singing in their native dialects." Blacks also passed down African medical practice, a combination of physical and psychological treatment including magic. More women than men were African American doctors, practicing midwifery as well as nursing and providing cures.

Despite cultural exchange and indications of human understanding, the antagonism and economic exploitation inherent in slavery poisoned relationships among whites and blacks. Whites believed that African Americans were an inferior race; masters used their power in the slave system to control their human property with harsh punishments. Nevertheless, blacks refused to accept their subordinate position, as increasing numbers ran away or were truant for weeks at a time.

Some enslaved Africans took more violent means, killing their masters or setting fire to fields and homes. In 1739, a group of more than fifty bondmen mounted an armed revolt near the Stono River in South Carolina. For most of a day, they marched with drums and banners from one plantation to another, killing about twenty whites. When armed planters defeated the rebels in battle, some of the slaves regrouped and headed for St. Augustine, Florida. But the South Carolina militia pursued the insurgents, putting to death everyone suspected of being involved. By one account, they placed the heads of the revolu-

Colonial newspapers regularly published advertisements of enslaved Africans for sale and notices of escaped servants and slaves. These advertisements often provide detailed information about the skills, health, and living conditions of African Americans.

tionaries on mileposts as a warning to other slaves contemplating rebellion. The Stono Uprising sent shock waves throughout the American colonies. The South Carolina legislature enacted a harsh slave code in an effort to prevent future revolts and limited slave importation for a decade. Most of the core group who planned the Stono Rebellion were African-born slaves, who hoped to escape to Florida, where Spanish authorities offered them religious sanctuary and freedom as a way to bolster the colony's population and undermine stability in the English settlements. By 1740, about one hundred former Carolina slaves had built the village of Gracia Real de Santa Teresa de Mose, called Mose, two miles north of St. Augustine.

During the eighteenth century, newly arrived Africans, often called "salt-water Negroes," were more likely to rebel or run away than creole, or "country-born" slaves. Predominantly male, imported Africans often lacked wives and children to root them to a plantation. Finding slavery intolerable, some fled as soon as they arrived. With Native Americans and runaway

white servants, escaped slaves created maroon societies in frontier areas of Virginia, the Carolinas, and Georgia. They farmed, raised livestock, hunted, and fished. In the Great Dismal Swamp, on the North Carolina-Virginia border, communities numbering perhaps 2,000 people took refuge from colonial authorities. The Dismal Swamp settlements grew from small groups of Native Americans who survived the seventeenth-century English invasion of Virginia to include Indians and whites from the Carolinas, and increasing numbers of escaped Africans. Outlaw maroon communities on the southern frontier remained hostile to outside whites, often raiding nearby plantations for supplies.

WARS FOR EMPIRE

The Spanish offer of refuge and the Stono rebels' goal to reach Florida were part of the ongoing conflict between Britain and Spain in the southeast. The War of Jenkins's Ear (1739–1744) heralded a quarter century of hostilities among Europeans and Native Americans for domination of North America. The War of Jenkins's Ear, King George's War (1744–1748), the French and Indian War (1754–1763), and the Indian war for autonomy in the Ohio Valley (1763–1765) required British colonists to participate more actively in defending the empire, bringing them into greater contact with the British imperial government and armed forces.

The Southern Frontier

The colonies along the southern tier—from east to west, British South Carolina and Georgia, Spanish Florida, French Louisiana, and Spanish Texas and New Mexico—competed for trade with Native Americans and control of territory. Except for war between Georgia and Florida in the early 1740s, the most important battles along the southern rim were commercial, a competition the British traders often won because they had more plentiful and cheaper goods. They exchanged tools, clothing, scissors, guns, ammunition, and rum, in return for slaves, deerskins, and furs from the Indians, who allied militarily with the British to sustain this commerce. In comparison with the English provinces, the Spanish and French colonies remained small and badly supplied by their parent nations. In 1760, Florida had approximately 3,000 Hispanic settlers, Texas had 1,200, and New Mexico

about 9,000, while Louisiana counted 4,000 whites and 5,000 enslaved Africans. In contrast, in the same year, South Carolina and Georgia had a population of about 45,000 whites and 59,000 black slaves.

Governor James Oglethorpe of Georgia tried to use the outbreak of the War of Jenkins's Ear, which developed from trade disputes, to eject the Spanish from Florida. As part of the 1713 Treaty of Utrecht, Britain had obtained the right to sell a specified number of African slaves and commodities to the Spanish provinces. This opening led to British smuggling, which the Spanish, zealously protecting their mercantilist hold on colonial trade, countered with heavy-handed searches of British ships. Accounts of Spanish brutality inflamed the British public, especially when Captain Robert Jenkins displayed one of his ears, which he claimed the Spanish cut off when they caught him smuggling. In 1740, Oglethorpe attacked Florida with seven ships and 2,000 troops, including regiments from Georgia and South Carolina and Native American allies. They captured several Spanish forts and Mose, the village of escaped Carolina blacks, but failed to conquer Fort San Marcos, where the residents of St. Augustine and Mose took cover. Though the European population of Florida was small, a large percentage were soldiers, since the main purpose of the colony was to guard Atlantic shipping lanes. When Hispanic and black soldiers slipped out of the fort and recaptured Mose, and then the fort was resupplied by Cuba, Oglethorpe retreated.

In 1741, a force of 3,600 colonists participated in the British expedition against the Spanish fort at Cartagena, in what is now Colombia. The campaign, the largest British effort of the war, ended bitterly, with heavy losses from battle and smallpox. One-half of the provincial soldiers died, a fact the British colonists long remembered. The following year, the Spanish took revenge for the invasion of Florida by attacking St. Simon's Island, Georgia, but withdrew before conquering it. After some minor skirmishes, both sides gave up, bringing calm to the Georgia-Florida border.

King George's War

The British avoided further conflict with Florida because in 1744, they began hostilities with France in the War of the Austrian Succession, known to the colonists as King George's War. Thus the hundred-year struggle between these two European powers continued.

The war began in Europe, but spilled into North America when, provoked by French attacks on Nova Scotia, Governor William Shirley of Massachusetts organized an offensive against the French fort at Louisbourg, which controlled access to the St. Lawrence River. New Englanders rallied to the cause, intending to drive Catholic France from the continent, while Pennsylvania and New York contributed £11,000. In April 1745, untrained in formal warfare but supported by the British navy, 4,000 New England farmers and fishermen assaulted Louisbourg. The French garrison held out against the badly organized offensive until June, then surrendered. New Englanders considered Louisbourg a great victory, even after many of their troops succumbed to disease and the war degenerated into a series of debilitating border raids. The Canadians and their Indian allies ravaged Saratoga, New York, and northern New England. In spring 1746, a fleet of seventy-six ships left France to retake Louisbourg, but after fighting disease and Atlantic storms for three months, with a loss of 3,000 men, they returned to France empty-handed.

Despite this reprieve, New Englanders had little to celebrate, for they faced another threat—from their own imperial navy. During the war, Parliament permitted naval officers to impress sailors without the permission of colonial authorities. The Royal Navy used impressment, or involuntary recruitment, because many seamen fled the harsh conditions on naval vessels. Indeed, the brutality could make impressment the equivalent of a death sentence. In 1747, several thousand Bostonians protested when a British press gang from the fleet of Admiral Charles Knowles swept up men along the waterfront. The crowd demanded release of the sailors, taking hostage several British officers. The mob surrounded the governor's house and burned a British barge in his courtyard. When the governor called up the militia, the troops refused to move. Knowles threatened to shell the town, but after negotiations lasting several days, he released the impressed men instead.

Though crowd action occurred at other times in Anglo-America, as in the 1750s and 1760s when impressment continued, Bostonians particularly resented Knowles's press gang in view of their sacrifice at Louisbourg. But as the colonists became more involved in imperial politics, they learned that their interests held little sway. To their shock, the British government restored Louisbourg to the French in the Treaty of Aix-la-Chapelle (1748), as the combatants agreed to return all North American territories seized during the war.

Despite heavy human and financial costs, the war brought no change in the power balance between Great Britain and France in North America.

Native American Worlds in the Mid-Eighteenth Century

The conflict ended in 1748 for neither the European colonists nor the Native Americans who contested the continent. With bulging population growth and immigration, the British settlements pushed into the Appalachians, forcing Native Americans once again to rearrange their lives.

Some Indian survivors of earlier struggles remained within the British provinces, called by white Americans, "Settlement Indians," "domestic Indians," or "little Tribes." They worked as servants, slaves, day laborers, artisans, and tenant farmers, assimilating some parts of English culture, but rejecting others. Some continued to hunt, peddling venison and turkeys to the colonists. Dr. Alexander Hamilton, a recent immigrant from Scotland, recorded many encounters with Indians in 1744 as he traveled through the settlements from Maryland to Maine. The Native Americans he met varied greatly in status, from an Indian sachem who had established himself as a wealthy planter, to those on the margins, who tried to hold on to native traditions within an alien culture. In Rhode Island, he approached the large plantation of

> an Indian King named George . . . upon which he has many tennants and has, of his own, a good stock of horses and other cattle. The King lives after the English mode. His subjects have lost their own government policy and laws and are servants or vassals to the English here. His queen goes in a high modish dress in her silks, hoops, stays, and dresses like an English woman. He educates his children to the belles letters and is himself a very complaisant mannerly man. We pay'd him a visit, and he treated us with a glass of good wine.

During worship in a Boston church, Hamilton sat near several Native Americans. But he also met natives who retained at least some of their customs, like the Indian at Princeton who saluted him with "How' s't ni tap." In New York, Hamilton watched "about ten Indians fishing for oysters . . . stark naked" near his tavern. While most Indians who stayed in white settled areas had given up political autonomy, they had not surrendered all of their traditions. Many spoke English in addition to their native language, but did not learn to

read and write. One Rhode Island woman knew only one English word, "broom." The Great Awakening converted many settlement Indians who had long resisted Christianity. The dynamic preaching of New Light ministers, who welcomed enthusiastic response from their listeners, was attractive to Native Americans who had retained traditional rituals and dance.

Many Indians tried to preserve their political independence by moving west, a strategy that worked temporarily. From 1660 to the 1740s, for example, Iroquois, Shawnees, and Delawares moved into the eastern part of the Ohio Valley, from the Allegheny River in western Pennsylvania to west-central Ohio. Wyandots inhabited the lands to the west, at Sandusky and near the French fort at Detroit. Some Iroquois migrated from western New York, while Delawares and Shawnees moved from eastern Pennsylvania under pressure from white settlers. Some of the Delawares left the east as a result of the "Walking Purchase" of 1737, when two of William Penn's sons, the proprietors, used an alleged 1686 deed to cheat the Indians out of their last stronghold on the Pennsylvania side of the Delaware River. The deed, of which only a copy survived, ceded lands as far as a man could walk in one and a half days. Coerced by an alliance between the Penns and the Iroquois, the Delawares agreed to comply. The Penns sent runners in relay to cover almost sixty miles of land in a day and a half, a deception the Delawares could not fail to remember; with the outbreak of war in 1754, they sought revenge.

The Ohio Valley became the focus of conflict in the 1740s as the British and French competed for trade. Following the Delawares and Shawnees west, some Pennsylvania traders took up residence in the multi-ethnic towns such as Chiningue (or Logstown), where Iroquois, Delawares, Shawnees, Ottawas, and other Indians lived. The Ohio Valley, as one Indian leader said, was "a country in between" the English and the French, unfortunately a country that the Europeans craved. From 1754 to 1814, the Native Americans fought the British and Americans to keep their lands and native religions, forging pan-Indian alliances to meet the Anglo threat.

The French and Indian War

During King George's War, the British and Iroquois had evicted French traders from the Ohio Valley. The Canadians returned, however, backed by a government that was determined to force out the British. The French built forts to stop the incursion of Anglo-American traders and to block Virginia's claim to the territory, which dated from its charter. In 1754, after the British government granted half a million acres to the Ohio Company, the Virginia governor sent a young militia officer, George Washington, with 160 troops to expel the French. The Virginians were defeated at Fort Necessity by a superior force of French and Indians.

Recognizing that war was imminent, seven colonies sent delegates to a congress at Albany, New York, where they negotiated unsuccessfully with the Iroquois for an alliance against the French. The Albany Congress also supported a plan devised by Benjamin Franklin to unite the colonies for common defense. When the delegates returned home with the proposal for an inter-colonial government empowered to tax, pass laws, and supervise military defense, not one of the assemblies approved. The provincial elites were unready to surrender their political power, even in the face of a dangerous war. Nor did the imperial government approve unification by its provinces.

Instead, the British decided to destroy French forts in what they considered their territory, even before a formal declaration of war. In early 1755, Major General Edward Braddock landed in the colonies with two British regiments. Joined by hundreds of provincial soldiers, the army of 1,400 marched through the Virginia backcountry to capture Fort Duquesne, the French outpost near the site of present-day Pittsburgh. The British troops were unprepared

Benjamin Franklin published his "Snake Device" just before the Albany Congress in 1754. Considered the first political cartoon in the colonies, it later became an important symbol of American resistance to Britain.

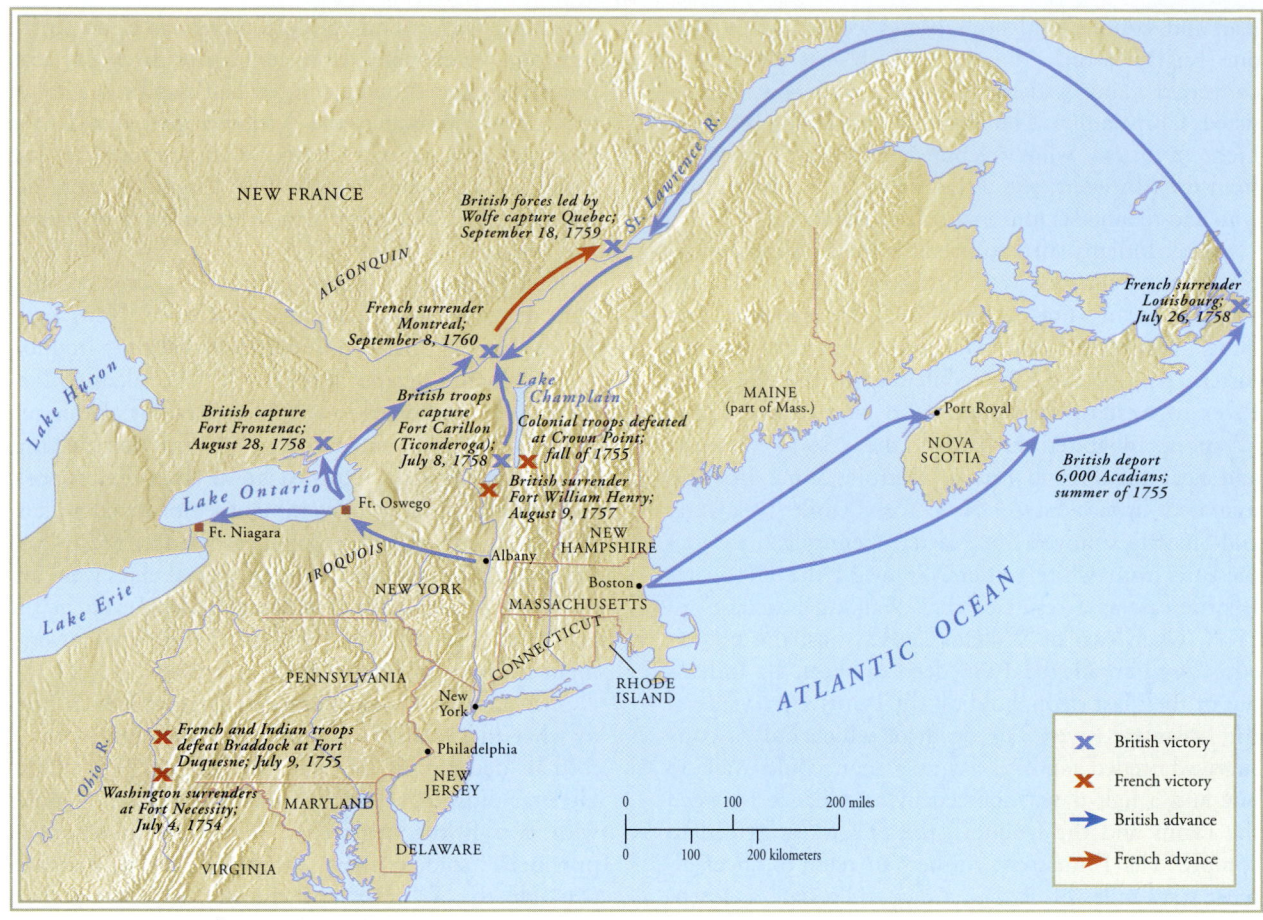

Map 4.3 | Seven Years' War in North America

for frontier fighting, but thought their mission was easy because the garrison had only 250 French troops. Ten miles short of Fort Duquesne, however, the French and allied Indians ambushed Braddock's army, killing or wounding two-thirds of the British force. The general himself lay dead. George Washington, his uniform ripped by bullets, led the retreat.

The 650 Native Americans who fought with the French included their traditional allies and some Delawares and Iroquois of the Ohio Valley who had previously supported the British. By 1754, some Ohio Indians were convinced that Britain and its colonies posed the greatest threat to their lands; with the defeat of Braddock, many more joined the French. Between 1755 and 1757, Delawares, Shawnees, Iroquois, and many others attacked the white frontier from Pennsyl-

vania to Virginia, burning settlements and killing or capturing thousands of colonists. The settlers streamed eastward, seeking military help. After seventy years of relative peace, Quaker Pennsylvania was at war with Native Americans.

But help for the westerners was slow in coming. In 1756, the struggle in North America became part of the larger European conflict known as the Seven Years' War, in which Great Britain supported Prussia against Austria, Russia, and France. Through 1757 and half of 1758, in America, the British and provincials lost one battle after another. They tried but failed to take Louisbourg and the French forts on Lake Ontario. Even worse, the French penetrated into New York, seizing Fort William Henry and 2,000 soldiers at Lake George. The tide changed after the British statesman

William Pitt took command of the war effort. He poured money and men into the American theater, expecting colonial legislatures to do the same. The new generals Jeffery Amherst and James Wolfe, with an army of almost 10,000 men, captured Louisbourg in July 1758. The French then pulled their troops out of the Ohio Valley to protect Quebec and Montreal, allowing the British to take control of the west. Without French supplies and devastated by smallpox, the Native Americans ended their war on the frontier, entering negotiations with the Pennsylvania government for peace.

In 1759, the British and provincial armies had even greater success, leading some of the Iroquois of New York to abandon neutrality to join their side. The British reestablished control of New York, while from Louisbourg, General Wolfe sailed up the St. Lawrence to Quebec, where after several months he finally pierced the defenses of the well-fortified city. The next year, Amherst's army seized Montreal, thus ending French control of Canada.

While the defeat of Canada marked the end of the French and Indian War in North America, the Seven Years' War continued off the coast of France, in India, and in the West Indies. The British military took a number of French sugar islands, including the richest, Guadeloupe. When Spain entered the war as France's ally in 1762 in return for the promise of lands west of the Mississippi River, the British captured Manila in the Philippines and Havana, Cuba. Provincial troops participated in the campaign against Cuba, but, reminiscent of the siege of Cartagena twenty years before, approximately one-half died from disease.

The victory at Quebec came with the loss of one of the commanders who helped win the war in North America for the British. The Death of General Wolfe *by Benjamin West.*

During the French and Indian War, thousands of colonists joined the harshly disciplined British army, and many more served in the provincial forces. The experience brought ordinary settlers into close contact with the imperial authorities—and many loathed the experience. The British army contained professional soldiers drilled rigorously in military tactics, cleanliness, and order. Small numbers of women served in the field, generally soldiers' wives who cooked, washed, and nursed. British officers, from the upper classes, maintained discipline with punishments of death for major offenses such as desertion, and up to 1,000 lashes—which could also kill—for lesser crimes. The British officers disdained the colonial units, which submitted to much lighter discipline and sometimes elected their superiors. Because the provincials failed to keep their camps and clothing clean, many died from disease. Many also deserted, confident that they would be protected from military justice in their communities. For their part, the colonial soldiers thought the British regulars were immoral, profane men who needed to be controlled with brutal discipline. On both sides, this disrespect later contributed to the worsening relationship between Great Britain and its North American colonies.

In the short run, however, the British colonists welcomed the Treaty of Paris in 1763, which finally ended the war. They benefited to a much greater extent than the parent country from the peace terms, which granted lands east of the Mississippi River to Great Britain. Under the treaty, France lost all of its territory in North America, but retrieved the valuable sugar islands of Guadeloupe and Martinique. Spain relinquished Florida to get back Cuba and the Philippines and, because the British lacked interest in the region, acquired French territory west of the Mississippi and New Orleans, located on the east side of the river. The Treaty of Paris gave the British colonists security from France and Spain, while the home government received two unprofitable colonies, Canada and Florida. The provincials celebrated the victory with patriotic fervor, as New York City raised a statue of George III, who had taken the throne in 1760 at age twenty-two. Many colonists, especially New England ministers, had interpreted the war as a fight against Catholicism and tyranny. They viewed the victory as a sign that God favored Britain and its colonies. One Massachusetts clergyman preached,

Safe from the Enemy of the Wilderness, safe from the griping Hand of arbitrary Sway and cruel Superstition; Here shall be the late founded Seat of Peace and Freedom. Here shall our indulgent Mother [Britain], who has most generously rescued and protected us, be served and honoured by growing Numbers, with all Duty, Love and Gratitude, till Time shall be no more.

The Indians Renew War in the Ohio Valley

For Native Americans, the Treaty of Paris was a disaster that failed to resolve the struggle for eastern North America. The agreement ended the conflict among European powers, but not for them. Indeed, the defeat of France worsened the situation of tribes in the Ohio Valley, for they could no longer play one European nation off the other. East of the Mississippi, the British alone supplied European goods, so they could set prices and the terms of trade. They ended the custom of giving annual presents, charged high prices, stopped selling rum, and reduced the amount of ammunition sold. Further, with the end of the French and Indian War, white settlers streamed west into Indian lands, as wealthy land speculators and poor squatters alike ignored treaties that colonial governments had made with the Native Americans.

The altered British trade policies, refusal to offer gifts, and land grabbing drove many Delawares, Shawnees, Iroquois, and others to renew the fighting. They gained spiritual unity from the Delaware prophet Neolin, one of a line of spiritual leaders among the Delawares and Shawnees, who preached that Indians must reject Christianity and European goods, particularly rum. They should revitalize their ancient culture, asserting autonomy and resistance. Neolin called on Native Americans to drive the Europeans out, demanding: "Whereupon do you suffer the whites to dwell upon your lands? Drive them away; wage war against them. I love them not." He warned his followers, "if you suffer the English among you, you are dead men. Sickness, smallpox, and their poison will destroy you entirely."

Many Indians throughout the Ohio Valley adopted Neolin's strategy, boycotting the fur trade by hunting only for their own food and personal needs. The Delaware councils called for a gradual return to mili-

of ammunition and succumbed to smallpox, fighting continued for two more years.

In addition to armed force, the British government tried to end the war by keeping white settlers out of the Ohio Valley. The king issued the Proclamation of 1763, which drew a line along the crest of the Appalachian Mountains from Maine to Georgia, requiring colonists to move east of the line. Colonial governors were instructed to prohibit surveys or land grants west of the Proclamation line; only authorized agents of the Crown could buy lands from the Indians. The proclamation failed in its purpose, however, as land speculators continued their operations and immigrants demanded farms. The British government, weighed down by debt from the Seven Years' War, failed to supply manpower to enforce the law. The government withdrew troops from the Ohio Valley and Great Lakes region, while provincial governments, dominated by speculators, ignored encroachment on Indian lands.

THE BRITISH PROVINCES IN 1763

The end of the French and Indian War brought pivotal changes in British North America. For over a century and a half, Europeans had crossed the ocean to trade with the Native Americans, build farms and businesses, and develop networks of Atlantic commerce. The colonies had dealt with crises, from economic slumps to rebellions, becoming ever more confident of their position as semi-independent societies. During the last quarter century, with greater involvement in imperial affairs and rising importation of consumer goods, the provincials felt more a part of the British empire—more English—even as they created a separate identity as Americans. Most importantly, they believed that they were equal to the residents of Great Britain, that they possessed the rights of English people.

The Economy

In 1763, the mainland provinces still operated within the system of British mercantilism, which consisted of

Chief Pontiac, *by Jerry Farnsworth. When whites streamed west at the end of the Seven Years' War, Indians allied under Pontiac's leadership to attack British forts and settlements in the Ohio Valley and Great Lakes region.*

tary skills with bow and arrow and adopted a ritual tea, which caused vomiting, to cleanse themselves of the "White people's ways and Nature." In 1763, Indians from western Pennsylvania through the Great Lakes region launched a pan-Indian assault on British garrisons, often called Pontiac's War. A follower of Neolin and leader of the Ottawas, Pontiac laid siege unsuccessfully to the British fort at Detroit. Other Indians defeated thirteen British outposts, though not Forts Niagara or Pittsburgh. While the British army established military dominance in the Ohio Valley by the end of 1763, after the Native Americans ran short

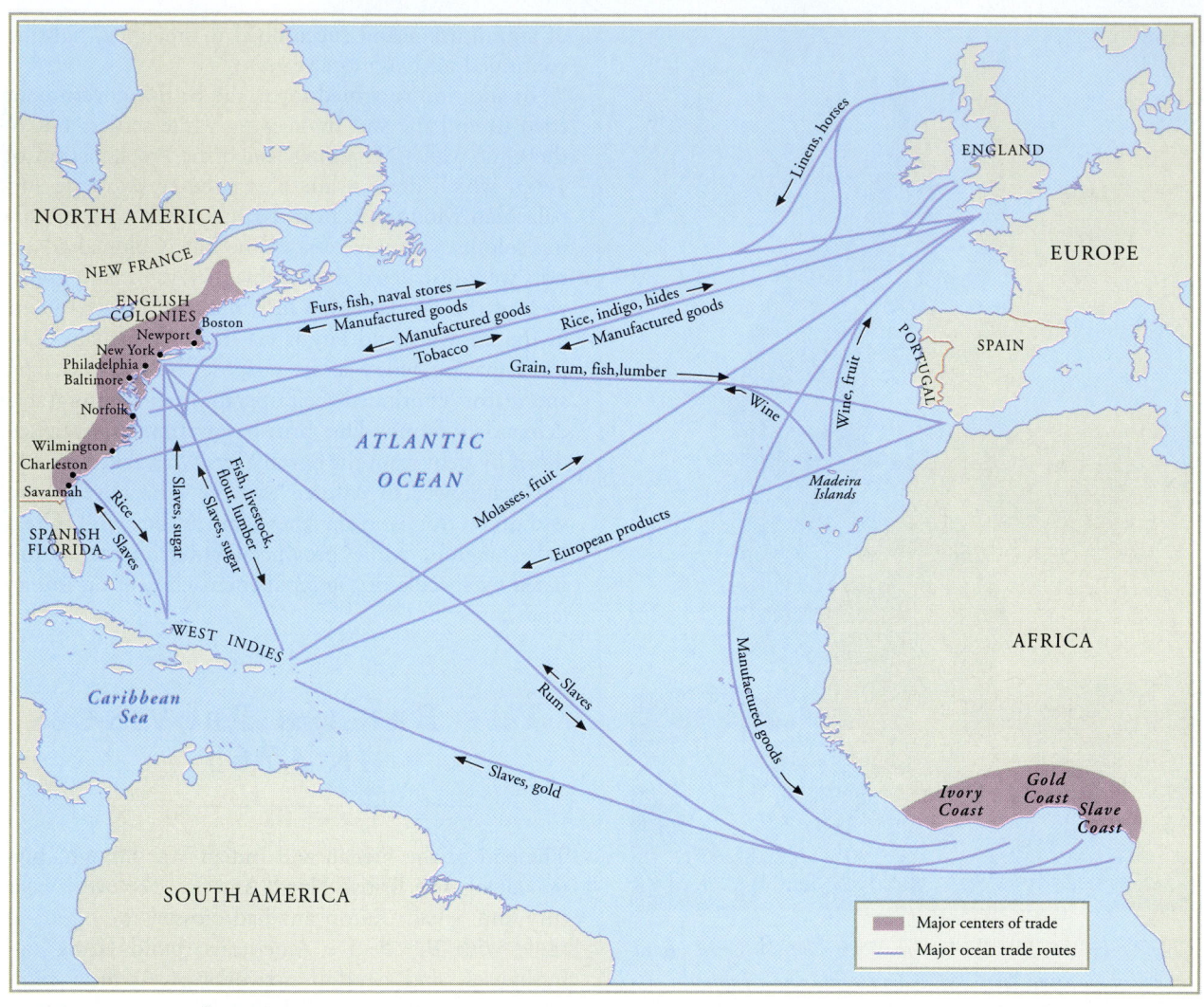

MAP 4.4 | COLONIAL OVERSEAS TRADE

regulations on colonial trade and manufactures. For mercantilism to work to Britain's benefit, the colonies had to produce raw materials and agricultural staples needed by the home economy and serve as a market for its manufactured goods. Such colonial products as sugar, molasses, tobacco, cotton, certain wood products, copper, and furs were "enumerated," meaning that they could be shipped only to Britain or British colonial ports, not to foreign countries such as France and Spain. The basic laws establishing the British mercantilist system were the seventeenth-century Naviga-

tion Acts, which Parliament supplemented from time to time. Though most colonial trade conformed to the law by the eighteenth century, smuggling occurred often enough to prompt demands within the British government for strict enforcement. In particular, colonial shippers bribed customs officials to ignore the Molasses Act (1733), which levied prohibitive duties on foreign sugar products, including a tax of sixpence per gallon on molasses. The British West Indies planters had pushed for the act to create a monopoly for themselves, lowering the cost of provisions and raising the price of

their exports. If the Molasses Act had been enforced, it would have severely damaged the economies of New England and the Middle Colonies, who traded with the French, Spanish, and Dutch West Indies as well as the British islands. The mainland colonies exported food and lumber in return for sugar and molasses, from which distillers produced rum.

Other laws passed by Parliament prior to 1763 had a significant but uneven impact on colonial economic growth. British legislation, combined with lack of investment capital, limited the development of most manufactures. The Woolen Act (1699) and the Hat Act (1732) banned the export of American-produced woolen products and hats from one colony to another. Other laws prohibited the export of machinery and the migration of skilled craftsmen from Britain to America. The Iron Act (1750) allowed duty-free import of colonial bar iron into Britain, but forbade fabrication of iron goods in the colonies. Nevertheless, crude iron production received substantial investment, as did shipbuilding and rum distilling. Unhampered by mercantilist regulation, North American shipbuilders produced nearly 40 percent of vessels in the British-owned merchant fleet.

Despite these laws, the wealth of the British colonies increased between the 1720s and 1760, as trade flourished with the West Indies and, after 1750, with southern Europe, where crop failures and population growth swelled demand for wheat and flour. The Middle Colonies, already expanding with German and Irish immigration, were well situated to supply new markets. Philadelphia became the largest city in the British colonies: Its wealthy merchants invested in ships, built mansions, purchased coaches and other luxuries, and speculated in western lands from the profits of trade. Artisans, shopkeepers, and farmers prospered from the European and West Indies markets and from demand during the Seven Years' War for ships, clothing, boots, food, rum, and other supplies. To the south, large planters in the Chesapeake and Carolinas accumulated great estates, while ordinary farmers more modestly improved their standard of living. All along the eastern seaboard, after 1750, white families indulged in what has been called a "consumer revolution." Not only could they purchase cloth, clothing, carpets, paper, gloves, mirrors, clocks, silverware, china tea sets, pottery, and books, but they had more choices in the specific kind of cloth or paper or gloves they could buy. In New York City in the 1750s, for instance, merchants advertised gloves of various colors—purple, orange, white, and flowered—as well as different sizes and materials, including chamois, silk, "Maid's Lamb Gloves," and "Men's Dog Skin Gloves." This is just one example of the wide variety of consumer goods that became available in mid-century.

The colonies became major markets for textiles, metalware, and other items, which under the Navigation Acts they could import only from Britain. The consumer revolution made the British more attentive to their North American provinces, while at the same time, the imports helped to create in America a more standardized English culture. Affluent colonists became aware of the latest fashions in England, and complained when they received out-of-date merchandise. The young George Washington groused in 1760, for example, "that instead of getting things good and fashionable in their several kinds we often have Articles sent Us that coud only have been usd by our Forefathers in the days of yore."

The economic upswing of the 1750s gave way to a depression after 1760, as the Seven Years' War moved to the Caribbean and military spending dropped. The seaport towns, having attracted workers during the wartime boom, faced deepening poverty and rising demands for relief. With depressed wages and long periods of unemployment, families found survival difficult. The resumption of immigration from Europe after the war intensified economic hardships and contributed to unrest on the frontier.

Politics

In late 1763, after months of Indian attacks in the Ohio country, a band of western Scots-Irish Pennsylvanians used violence to force the Quaker-dominated assembly to provide military protection. The "Paxton Boys" of Lancaster County murdered a number of Christian Indians at Conestoga, then marched on Philadelphia. By the time the rebels reached the capital, the legislature had passed a bill raising 1,000 troops to defend the frontier. The westerners returned home without attacking the city. At the heart of their revolt was the belief that they were poorly represented in the provincial government. As the backcountry population exploded, eastern politicians in Pennsylvania and other colonies guarded their power by

Grey's Inn Creek Shipyard, *by an unknown artist, c. 1760. Shipbuilding, at this Maryland shipyard as well as in northern seaports, was a major industry in the British colonies.*

allotting fewer assembly seats to outlying counties than they deserved. Unfair representation stimulated a series of uprisings from the North Carolina Regulator movement in the 1760s to the Whiskey Rebellion three decades later.

The Paxton Boys revolt signaled the end of an era of political stability as both the western farmers and imperial government put pressure on colonial elites. Since the late 1720s, the British mainland provinces had enjoyed relative peace in their capitals, if not

The Paxton Expedition, *by Henry Dawkins, depicts the threat by western "Paxton Boys" against Philadelphia, demanding frontier defense during Pontiac's War.*

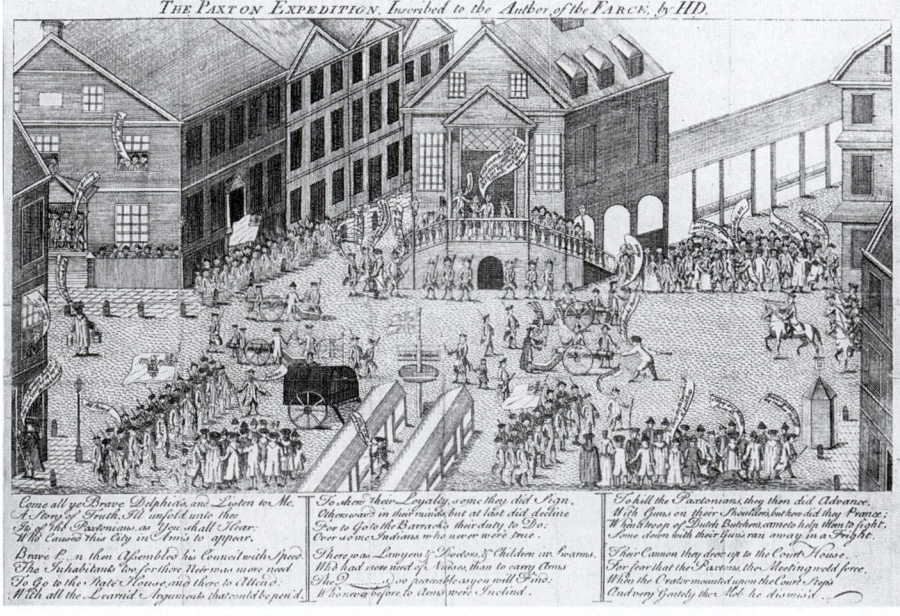

along their frontiers. The period of stability contrasted markedly with earlier decades, before 1720, when Bacon's Rebellion, the revolutions of 1689, and constant strife between governors and assemblies, and among factions of assemblymen, characterized politics.

As part of Britain's empire, the eighteenth-century colonists believed themselves among the most fortunate people on earth. The Glorious Revolution of 1688–1689, which removed James II, had ended the long, bitter contest between king and Parliament. The monarch's power was subsequently limited by the national legislature, comprised of the House of Lords, which represented the aristocracy, and the House of Commons, which in theory represented everyone else. As a result of the 1689 settlement, Parliament's consent was necessary for taxes, new courts, raising an army in peacetime, and foreign invasions. It gained control over its own meetings and, after 1707, the Crown lost veto power over legislation. The balance of powers, political theorists argued, prevented domination by a single segment of society, the monarch, aristocracy, or common people. Thus, the British avoided forms of government considered destructive of liberty: rule by a single despot (tyranny); corrupt and self-serving rule by a group of aristocrats (oligarchy); and uncontrolled rule by the mob (democracy). In their provincial governments, the British

colonists expected to find a similar balance, one that would protect their rights. Indeed, the prevailing structure of governor, appointed council, and elected lower house of assembly reflected the English model. The British provinces were the only European settlements in North America where ordinary people had representative legislatures. Further, an estimated 50 to 75 percent of white men were qualified to vote in the British colonies, the result of much broader property ownership than in England, where about 15 to 30 percent of adult males had the franchise. According to English political theory, a person needed a "stake in society," a certain amount of property, to vote or hold office. Servants, slaves, children, and unpropertied men were beholden to someone else, so could not make independent decisions. Giving them suffrage would award their owner, father, or employer another vote, the theorists claimed, especially in many places where people voted orally, in public. By tradition, women also lacked the franchise, whether or not they owned property or were married. Though part of the reason was the dependency theory that wives would follow the lead of their husbands, not all women had spouses. Denial of the vote to all females arose from the general belief that they were intellectually and morally inferior to men and thus should have no formal role in government.

King George III, *at the time of his coronation in 1760, by Allan Ramsay.*

houses of prostitution, and stop the British navy from impressing men into the king's service, as with the 1747 Knowles riot in Boston.

The most important and sustained political development in British America during the first half of the eighteenth century was the rise of the elected lower houses of assembly. The legislatures acquired greater power and assumed more functions, most significantly, the right to initiate bills to raise taxes and disburse public funds—the "power of the purse." They also gained the authority to initiate other legislation, choose their own leadership, and settle disputed elections.

The political stability and rise of the assemblies that marked the mid-eighteenth century resulted from a number of factors, including the long period of economic growth that began in the 1720s. Prosper-

The Governor's Palace at Williamsburg, Virginia, built in the early eighteenth century. At a time when most Virginians lived in rough-hewn, one-room dwellings, the elegant mansion symbolized the king's authority in America.

The colonists often required their legislators to live in the area from which they were elected and to advocate the interests of their constituents, unlike England, where members of the House of Commons did not have to reside in their electoral districts. The British believed that Parliament represented all of the people of the empire whether they elected delegates or not, a concept known as virtual representation.

Beyond suffrage, English political theory also recognized the right of common people to resort to crowd action to withstand tyranny and require authorities to protect them from harm. The people had this right, theoretically, as long as violence was limited—directed at property rather than persons. At various times, colonial mobs protested to prevent grain from being exported when food was in short supply, destroy

ity supported the formation of cohesive, politically adept elites—mostly second, third, and fourth generation Americans with inherited wealth and large estates, enslaved Africans or servants to meet their domestic needs, and (consequently) sufficient leisure time for politics. They formed a class of skilled politicians, men who learned from their fathers how to govern, then elaborated the art. Many studied the law: The growth of the colonial bar accompanied the professionalization of politics. Economic prosperity inclined ordinary whites to defer to the elites as long as opportunity was good and they had crops to tend or other work to do. Their deference to social and economic superiors became most visible after 1725, when participation at the polls declined among eligible voters, and incumbent assemblymen won reelection year after year.

The provincial elites also benefited after 1720 from the British decision to administer the colonies with a light touch, allowing royal governors to accommodate the assemblies. And while riots occurred during the 1740s and 1750s over land claims and impressment, none threatened social disorder on the level of the seventeenth-century rebellions. Indeed, most ordinary whites feared attacks by Native Americans and slave revolts more than misuse of governmental power by elites.

CONCLUSION

By the end of 1763, the British colonists of North America had reason to be optimistic about their future, despite the pan-Indian assaults in the Ohio Valley and postwar economic downturn. The British army had withstood the worst attacks in the west and colonists could expect a return to prosperity. After a quarter century of war, they celebrated the withdrawal of Spain and France east of the Mississippi, and looked forward to peace and semi-autonomy within the empire. Free colonists appreciated the benefits of being British—their liberties and right to participate in government as well as access to advanced learning and consumer goods. At the same time, the Americans were creating societies quite different from the English, with greater ethnic and religious diversity, dependence on enslaved labor, and wider opportunity to acquire land (even if it meant pushing out the Indians). After 1763, the London

government shocked the American colonists with its effort to rein in the empire, to make them surrender some of their accumulated rights. In turn, the British were unprepared for the coordinated fury with which the thirteen mainland provinces greeted their "reforms."

RECOMMENDED READINGS

Anderson, Fred. *A People's Army: Massachusetts Soldiers and Society in the Seven Years' War* (1984). An influential study of the origins and motives of ordinary soldiers.

Bailyn, Bernard, and Morgan, Philip D., eds. *Strangers Within the Realm: Cultural Margins of the First British Empire* (1991). Important essays on specific groups, including Native Americans, Scots-Irish, African Americans, Germans, and Dutch.

Carson, Cary, et al., eds. *Of Consuming Interests: The Style of Life in the Eighteenth Century* (1994). Excellent essays on topics ranging from housing and art to consumer behavior.

Isaac, Rhys. *The Transformation of Virginia, 1740–1790* (1982). Uses anthropological methods to explore cultural and political change in eighteenth-century Virginia.

Jedrey, Christopher M. *The World of John Cleaveland: Family and Community in Eighteenth-Century New England* (1979). Shows continuity of family strategies over the colonial period.

Merrell, James H. *The Indians' New World: Catawbas and Their Neighbors from European Contact Through the Era of Removal* (1989). Shows how South Carolina Indians created a new nation and identity in the wake of European settlement.

Morgan, Philip D. *Slave Counterpoint: Black Culture in the Eighteenth-Century Chesapeake and Lowcountry* (1998). A comprehensive study of African-American work and culture in the South.

Steele, Ian K. *Warpaths: Invasions of North America* (1994). Examines the Seven Years' War as one of a series of European invasions of Indian territory during the colonial period.

Ulrich, Laurel Thatcher. *A Midwife's Tale: The Life of Martha Ballard, Based on Her Diary, 1785–1812* (1990). The prize-winning account of a Maine midwife within the context of eighteenth-century society.

Enlightenment, Science, and Medicine

Bailyn, Bernard. *Education in the Forming of American Society* (1960).

Cassedy, James H. *Medicine in America: A Short History* (1991).

Cremin, Lawrence A. *American Education: The Colonial Experience, 1607–1783* (1970).

Hindle, Brooke. *The Pursuit of Science in Revolutionary America, 1735–1789* (1956).

Leavitt, Judith Walzer. *Brought to Bed: Child-Bearing in America, 1750 to 1950* (1986).

Leavitt, Judith Walzer, and Numbers, Ronald L., eds. *Sickness and Health in America: Readings in the History of Medicine and Public Health* (1978).

May, Henry F. *The Enlightenment in America* (1976).

Scholten, Catherine M. *Childbearing in American Society: 1650–1850* (1985).

Shryock, Richard Harrison. *Medicine and Society in America 1660–1860* (1960).

Ulrich, Laurel Thatcher. *Good Wives: Image and Reality in the Lives of Women in Northern New England, 1650–1750* (1982).

Great Awakening

Ahlstrom, Sydney E. *A Religious History of the American People* (1972).

Bonomi, Patricia U. *Under the Cope of Heaven: Religion, Society, and Politics in Colonial Amerca* (1986).

Gaustad, Edwin Scott. *The Great Awakening in New England* (1957).

Goen, Clarence C. *Revivalism and Separatism in New England, 1740–1800: Strict Congregationalists and Separate Baptists in the Great Awakening* (1962).

Lovejoy, David S. *Religious Enthusiasm in the New World: Heresy to Revolution* (1985).

Stout, Harry S. *The Divine Dramatist: George Whitefield and the Rise of Modern Evangelicalism* (1991).

Westerkamp, Marilyn J. *Triumph of the Laity: Scots-Irish Piety and the Great Awakening, 1625–1760* (1988).

Immigration and Cultural Diversity in British Colonies

Berlin, Ira. "Time, Space, and the Evolution of Afro-American Society in British Mainland North America," *American Historical Review* 85 (1980):44–78.

Fogleman, Aaron Spencer. *Hopeful Journeys: German Immigration, Settlement, and Political Culture in Colonial America, 1717–1775* (1996).

Herskovits, Melville J. *The Myth of the Negro Past* (1958).

Hoffman, Ronald, et al., eds. *Through a Glass Darkly: Reflections on Personal Identity in Early America* (1997).

Klepp, Susan E., ed. *The Demographic History of the Philadelphia Region, 1600–1860* (1989).

Klepp, Susan E., and Smith, Billy G., eds. *The Infortunate: The Voyage and Adventures of William Moraley, an Indentured Servant* (1992).

Lemon, James T. *The Best Poor Man's Country: A Geographical Study of Early Southeastern Pennsylvania* (1972).

Piersen, William D. *Black Yankees: The Development of an Afro-American Subculture in Eighteenth-Century New England* (1988).

Roeber, A. G. *Palatines, Liberty, and Property: German Lutherans in Colonial British America* (1993).

Schwartz, Sally. *"A Mixed Multitude": The Struggle for Toleration in Colonial Pennsylvania* (1988).

Sobel, Mechal. *The World They Made Together: Black and White Values in Eighteenth-Century Virginia* (1987).

Wolf, Stephanie Grauman. *As Various as Their Land: The Everyday Lives of Eighteenth-Century Americans* (1993).

Wood, Peter H. *Black Majority: Negroes in Colonial South Carolina from 1670 Through the Stono Rebellion* (1974).

Southern Frontiers

Bannon, John Francis. *The Spanish Borderlands Frontier, 1513–1821* (1970).

Davis, Harold E. *The Fledgling Province: Social and Cultural Life in Colonial Georgia, 1733–1776* (1976).

Landers, Jane. "Gracia Real de Santa Teresa de Mose: A Free Black Town in Spanish Colonial Florida," *American Historical Review* 95 (1990): 9–30.

Usner, Daniel H., Jr. *Indians, Settlers, and Slaves in a Frontier Exchange Economy: The Lower Mississippi Valley Before 1783* (1992).

Weber, David J., ed. *New Spain's Far Northern Frontier: Essays on Spain in the American West, 1540–1821* (1979).

Weber, David J. *The Spanish Frontier in North America* (1992).

Economy and Politics in the British Colonies

Bailyn, Bernard. *The Origins of American Politics* (1968).

Doerflinger, Thomas M. *A Vigorous Spirit of Enterprise: Merchants and Economic Development in Revolutionary Philadelphia* (1986).

Gilje, Paul A. *The Road to Mobocracy: Popular Disorder in New York City, 1763–1834* (1987).

Greene, Jack P. *The Quest for Power: The Lower Houses of Assembly in the Southern Royal Colonies, 1689–1776* (1963).

Maier, Pauline. *From Resistance to Revolution: Colonial Radicals and the Development of American Opposition to Britain, 1765–1776* (1972).

McCusker, John J., and Menard, Russell R. *The Economy of British America, 1607–1789, With Supplementary Bibliography* (1991).

Nash, Gary B. *The Urban Crucible: Social Change, Political Consciousness, and the Origins of the American Revolution* (1979).

Olson, Alison Gilbert. *Making the Empire Work: London and American Interest Groups, 1690–1790* (1992).

Shy, John. *Toward Lexington: The Role of the British Army in the Coming of the American Revolution* (1965).

—1764 TO 1814—

During the American Revolution, sixteen-year-old Dicey Langston of the South Carolina frontier left home in the middle of the night, by herself, to warn her brother's unit about tory troop movements. As a historian later described Langston's journey,

Many miles were to be traversed, and the road lay through woods, and crossed marshes and creeks where the conveniences of bridges and foot-logs were wanting.

She walked rapidly on, heedless of slight difficulties; but her heart almost failed her when she came to the banks of the Tyger—a deep and rapid stream, rendered more dangerous by the rains that had lately fallen. . . . But the energy of a resolute will, under the care of Providence, sustained her.*

PASSAGES

POPULATION OF THE UNITED STATES AND OF EACH STATE OR TERRITORY ENUMERATED IN 1790: 1790 TO 1900.

State or Territory	1790	1800	1810	1820	1880	1840	1850	1860	1870	1880	1890	1900
United States	3,929,625	5,308,483	7,239,881	9,638,453	12,866,020	17,069,453	23,191,876	31,443,321	38,558,371	50,189,209	62,979,766	76,303,387
Area enumerated in 1790	3,929,625	5,247,355	6,779,308	8,293,869	10,240,232	11,781,231	14,569,584	17,326,157	19,687,504	23,925,639	28,188,321	33,553,630
New England	1,009,206	1,233,011	1,471,973	1,660,071	1,954,717	2,234,822	2,728,116	3,135,283	3,487,924	4,010,529	4,700,749	5,592,017
Maine	96,643	151,719	228,705	298,335	399,455	501,793	583,169	628,279	626,915	648,936	661,086	694,466
New Hampshire .	141,899	183,858	214,460	244,161	269,328	284,574	317,976	326,073	318,300	346,991	376,530	411,588
Vermont	85,341	154,465	217,895	235,981	280,652	291,948	314,120	315,098	330,551	332,286	332,422	343,641
Massachusetts ..	378,556	422,845	472,040	523,287	610,408	737,699	994,514	1,231,066	1,457,351	1,783,085	2,238,947	2,805,346
Rhode Island ...	69,112	69,122	76,931	83,059	97,199	108,830	147,545	174,620	217,353	276,531	345,506	428,556
Connecticut ...	237,655	251,002	261,942	275,248	297,675	309,978	370,792	460,147	537,454	622,700	746,258	908,420
Middle states	1,017,087	1,466,838	2,087,376	2,772,594	3,664,412	4,604,345	5,990,267	7,571,201	8,935,821	10,643,486	12,874,713	15,639,413
New York	340,241	589,051	959,049	1,372,812	1,918,608	2,428,921	3,097,394	3,880,735	4,382,759	5,082,871	6,003,174	7,268,894
New Jersey	184,139	211,149	245,562	277,575	320,823	373,306	489,555	672,035	906,096	1,131,116	1,444,933	1,883,669
Pennsylvania ...	433,611	602,365	810,091	1,049,458	1,348,233	1,724,033	2,311,786	2,906,215	3,521,951	4,282,891	5,258,113	6,302,115
Delaware	59,096	64,273	72,674	72,749	76,748	78,085	91,532	112,216	125,015	146,608	168,493	184,735
Southern states ...	1,903,332	2,547,506	3,219,959	3,861,204	4,621,103	4,942,064	5,851,201	6,619,673	7,263,759	9,271,624	10,612,859	12,322,200
Maryland and District of Columbia	319,728	355,641	404,569	440,389	486,874	513,731	634,721	762,129	912,594	1,112,567	1,272,782	1,466,762
Virginia and West Virginia ..	747,610	880,200	974,600	1,065,366	1,211,405	1,239,797	1,421,661	1,596,318	1,667,177	2,131,022	2,418,774	2,812,984
North Carolina .	395,005	478,103	555,500	638,829	737,987	753,419	869,039	992,622	1,071,361	1,399,750	1,617,949	1,893,810
South Carolina .	249,073	345,591	415,115	502,741	581,185	594,398	668,507	703,708	705,606	995,577	1,151,149	1,340,316
Georgia	82,548	161,414	201,937	226,739	233,831	231,681	272,151	299,411	327,490	441,659	526,052	640,538
Kentucky	73,677	220,955	406,511	564,317	687,917	779,828	982,405	1,155,684	1,321,011	1,648,690	1,858,635	2,147,174
Tennessee	35,691	105,602	261,727	422,823	681,904	829,210	1,002,717	1,109,801	1,258,520	1,542,359	1,767,518	2,020,616
Added area		61,128	460,573	1,344,584	2,625,788	5,288,222	8,622,292	14,117,164	18,870,867	26,263,570	34,791,445	42,749,757

UNEXPLORED
Hudson Bay
CREE
BLACKFEET
ATSINA
SALISH
NEZ PERCÉ
OJIBWA
Lake Superior
ALGONQUIN
OTTAWA
Quebec
St. Lawrence R.
Montreal
CROW
MANDAN
TETON SIOUX
MENOMINEE
Fort Michilimackinac
Fort Frontenac
Falmouth
Portsmouth
KLAMATH
MODOC
SHOSHONE
CHEYENNE
SANTEE SIOUX
SAUK
LeBaye
Lake Huron
L. Ontario
IROQUOIS
Boston
Plymouth
Providence
NORTHERN PAIUTE
FOX
Fort Niagara
Hartford
New Haven
MAIDU
POMO
WASHO
OGLALA SIOUX
KICKAPOO
Lake Michigan
Fort Detroit
L. Erie
New York
PAWNEE
IOWA
St. Joseph
DELAWARE
Philadelphia
Wilmington
Baltimore
Annapolis
COSTANOAN
SALINAN
UTE
OTO
ILLINOIS
MIAMI
ARAPAHO
KANSA
MISSOURI
Vincennes
St. Louis
Richmond
Williamsburg
Norfolk
Ste. Genevieve
Ohio R.
SHAWNEE
Kaskaskia
CHUMASH
MOHAVE
HOPI
NAVAJO
PUEBLO
Taos
KIOWA
Edenton
OSAGE
Santa Fe
SERRANO
Albuquerque
CHEROKEE
New Bern
CHICKASAW
Mississippi R.
Wilmington
APACHE
Columbia
CATAWBA
Arkansas Post
COMANCHE
CREEK
Charleston
Fort Toulouse
Savannah
PACIFIC OCEAN
CHOCTAW
ATLANTIC OCEAN
PIMA
MESCALERO
WICHITA
Natchitoches
Natchez
OPATA
El Paso
Mobile
Pensacola
St. Augustine
Rio Grande
San Antonio
New Orleans
Chihuahua
SEMINOLE
English
Spanish
Russian
Proclamation Line of 1763
Gulf of Mexico
Monterrey
Saltillo
Durango

DICEY LANGSTON's effort, like those of thousands of Americans, was emblematic of her country's passage from a collection of British provinces in 1764, to a stable republic with some international standing a half century later. The thirteen mainland colonies, proud of their contribution to victory in the French and Indian War, were stunned by Britain's program to curtail their rights. Stretching from the mountains of northern New England to the rice fields of coastal Georgia, diverse in economics, religion, ethnicity, and politics, they mustered enough unity to organize a revolutionary Congress, stop British imports, raise an army, obtain help from France, and win the war.

HAMILTON

The states refused to create a unified nation, however, and instead established, under the Articles of Confederation, thirteen separate republics joined loosely by a representative Congress. Without power to tax or raise troops, the Congress faced severe postwar problems in

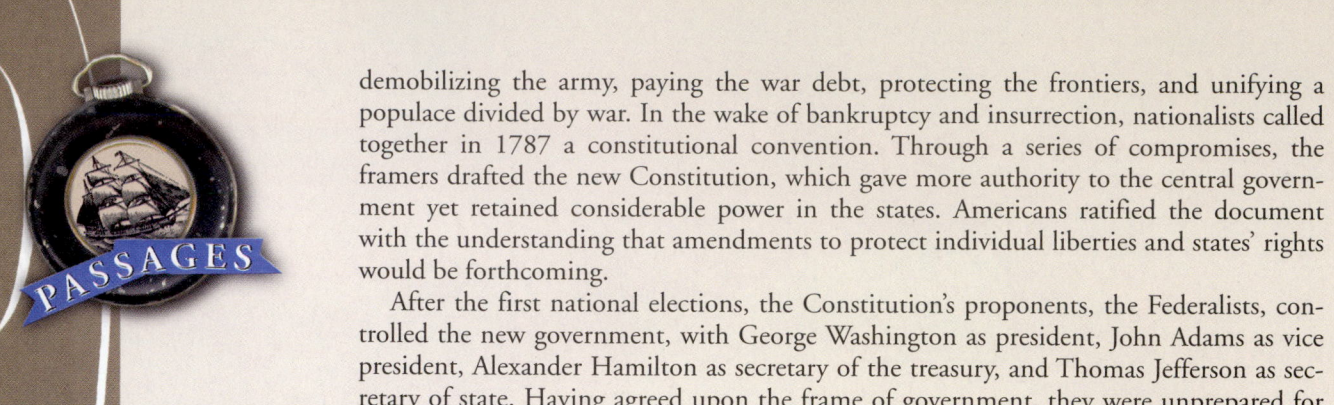

demobilizing the army, paying the war debt, protecting the frontiers, and unifying a populace divided by war. In the wake of bankruptcy and insurrection, nationalists called together in 1787 a constitutional convention. Through a series of compromises, the framers drafted the new Constitution, which gave more authority to the central government yet retained considerable power in the states. Americans ratified the document with the understanding that amendments to protect individual liberties and states' rights would be forthcoming.

After the first national elections, the Constitution's proponents, the Federalists, controlled the new government, with George Washington as president, John Adams as vice president, Alexander Hamilton as secretary of the treasury, and Thomas Jefferson as secretary of state. Having agreed upon the frame of government, they were unprepared for the bitter factionalism that forged political parties in the 1790s. Nor were they ready for the foreign entanglements that resulted from two decades of war between Great Britain and post-revolutionary France. Only after the United States declared war on the British in 1812 and held its own as the conflict ended in stalemate, did the nation finally demonstrate its independence. By 1814, most of the men who led the American Revolution had passed from power—though James Madison would remain president for several years—and a new generation was taking control.

The heroic story of the young nation surmounting difficulties— two wars against Great Britain, a constitutional crisis, several internal rebellions, an undeclared conflict with France, and constant fighting

Map Labels

British North America

Hudson Bay

Cree

Ojibwa

Algonquin

Ottawa

Quebec

Montreal

St. Lawrence R.

Blackfeet

Salish

Atsina

Nez Percé

Crow

Mandan

Teton Sioux

Santee Sioux

Territory disputed by Russia, Spain, and Britain

Klamath

Modoc

Shoshone

Northern Paiute

Cheyenne

Oglala Sioux

Spanish Louisiana

Iowa

Menominee

Fort Michilimackinac

Sauk

LeBaye

Fox

Kickapoo

Fort Detroit

Lake Superior

Lake Michigan

Lake Huron

Huron

Fort Frontenac

Fort Niagara

L. Ontario

Iroquois

L. Erie

Falmouth

Portsmouth

Boston

Plymouth

Hartford

Providence

New Haven

New York

Maidu

Washo

Pomo

San Francisco

Costanoan

Monterey

Salinan

Chumash

Santa Barbara

Los Angeles

San Diego

Ute

Pawnee

Oto

Arapaho

Kansa

Missouri

St. Joseph

St. Louis

Ste. Genevieve

Kaskaskia

Illinois

Miami

Vincennes

Delaware

Baltimore

Annapolis

Wilmington

Philadelphia

Shawnee

Richmond

Williamsburg

Norfolk

United States

Cherokee

Edenton

New Bern

Mohave

Hopi

Navajo

Pueblo

Taos

Santa Fe

Albuquerque

Kiowa

Osage

Chickasaw

Catawba

Columbia

Wilmington

Serrano

Apache

Comanche

Spanish North America

Wichita

Choctaw

Creek

Fort Toulouse

Charleston

Savannah

Pima

El Paso

Mescalero

Opata

San Antonio

Nacogdoches

Natchitoches

Natchez

Appalachee

Mobile

Pensacola

St. Augustine

Atlantic Ocean

Chihuahua

Rio Grande

New Orleans

Spanish Florida

Seminole

Pacific Ocean

Mississippi R.

Ohio R.

Gulf of Mexico

Monterrey

Saltillo

Durango

The map shows forts, cities, settlements, and outposts across North America with the following labels:

OREGON COUNTRY

BRITISH AMERICA

Fort de la Reine (1738)
Fort Maurepas (1734)
Fort Rouge (1738)
Fort St. Pierre (1731)
Fort Michipicton (1730)
Quebec
Montreal
Fort Chequaiegon (1718)
Fort Rouille (Toronto) (1749)
Green Bay
Portsmouth
Boston
Providence
Detroit (1701)
New York
Trenton
Philadelphia
Fort Duquesne (Pittsburgh) (1754)
Fort Miami (1704)
Baltimore (1729)

LOUISIANA PURCHASE

San Francisco (1776)
San Carlos de Monterey (1770)
San Luis Obispo (1772)
Santa Barbara (1782)
Los Angeles (1781)
San Juan Capistrano (1776)
San Diego (1769)

Santa Fe

Fort Orléans (1722)
Fort Vincennes (1724)
Louisville (1778)
Lexington (1779)
Harrodsburg (1774)
St. Louis (1764)
Fort Massac (1758)
Nashville (1780)
Richmond (1742)
Norfolk (1705)
New Bern (1710)
Wilmington (1730)

Memphis

Charleston

PACIFIC OCEAN

Tucson (1709)
San Xavier del Bac (1732)
El Paso del Norte
Nacogdoches (1791)
Natchitoches (1714)
Fort Toulouse (1714)
Savannah (1733)

SPANISH POSSESSIONS

Fort Rosalie (1716) (Natchez)
Mobile (1710)
St. Augustine

Presidio del Norte
San Antonio de Bejar (1718)
San Francisco de la Espada (1730)
New Orleans (1718)

ATLANTIC OCEAN

Laredo (1755)

Gulf of Mexico

Legend:
- Forests
- Settled areas (non-Indian)
- Cities, settlements, outposts
- Forts
- Louisiana Purchase

on the frontier—masks other narratives, those of women, African Americans, and Native Americans, who failed to achieve autonomy. Though Dicey Langston was just one of thousands of sisters, mothers, and wives who risked their lives during the Revolution, they gained little as a result of their efforts. In the new republic, women still lacked basic legal and political rights to hold property after marriage, vote, and take part in government. And while Revolutionary rhetoric against slavery resulted in abolition in the north and many private manumissions in the Chesapeake region, most African Americans remained enslaved, a condition perpetuated by the new Constitution and development of cotton. Even most free blacks had little opportunity to acquire property and were denied suffrage and participation in government.

For Native Americans, the success and growth of the new nation meant their decline. Despite revitalization movements to restore traditional cultures led by Neolin, Handsome Lake, Tenskwatawa, and many others, and destructive wars to defend their homelands in Alabama, Tennessee, Kentucky, and Ohio, by 1814 the United States dominated most of the territory east of the Mississippi River. Native Americans tried various routes to survive and retain as much of their autonomy as possible—adoption of white culture, cession of some lands for the promise they could keep others, alliances with Great Britain and Spain, raids on white settlements, and pan-Indian war. In the face of unremitting westward movement of new settlers and the continuing effects of disease, the Indian peoples of eastern North America became remnants of formerly powerful nations.

* Elizabeth F. Ellet, *Domestic History of the American Revolution* (1850), p. 234.

POLITICS & DIPLOMACY

1765: Stamp Act protest
1766-1771: Regulator movements in North and South Carolina
1767: John Dickinson's "Farmer" letters against Townshend Act
1768: Non-importation movement
1769: Spanish colonize California
1770: Boston Massacre
1772: Committees of Correspondence
1773: Boston Tea Party
1774: Coercive Acts; port of Boston closed
First Continental Congress
1775: Battles of Lexington and Concord
Lord Dunmore's proclamation to servants and slaves

1776: Thomas Paine's *Common Sense*
Declaration of Independence
1777: Burgoyne surrenders to Americans at Saratoga
1778: Alliance with France
Iroquois attacks in New York and Pennsylvania
1780: Pennsylvania law for gradual abolition of slavery
1781: Articles of Confederation ratified
Surrender of Cornwallis at Yorktown
1783: Treaty of Paris

1787: Shaysites attack Springfield, MA, arsenal
Northwest Ordinance
Constitution sent to states for ratification
1789: Inauguration of President George Washington
1791: Bill of Rights ratified

SOCIAL & CULTURAL EVENTS

1765: First American medical school
1766: Queens College (Rutgers)
New Southwark Theatre in Philadelphia
1769: *The American Magazine* (Philadelphia) published
Benjamin West's *Death of General Wolfe*
American scientists observe transit of Venus
1770: Equestrian statue of George III installed in New York
1771: Benjamin Franklin starts *Autobiography*
c. 1772: John Singleton Copley's portrait of Samuel Adams
1773: Phillis Wheatley's *Poems on Various Subjects, Religious and Moral*

1776: Jemima Wilkinson becomes Public Universal Friend
1779: John Murray's American Universalist Church
1780s: Northern black separate churches and societies
1783: Noah Webster's American spelling book
First daily newspaper, *Pennsylvania Evening Post*
1784: Judith Sargent Murray begins essays on women's status

1786: Virginia statute for religious liberty
Gilbert Stuart's portrait of Joseph Brant
1791: Charles Willson Peale's *Thomas Jefferson*
c.1793: Mary Wollstonecraft's *Vindication of the Rights of Women* circulates in the U.S.

ECONOMICS & TECHNOLOGY

1760s: British American traders cross Mississippi River
1764: Sugar and Currency Acts
1776: Adam Smith's *An Inquiry into the Nature and Causes of the Wealth of Nations*
1778: Captain James Cook explores the Pacific Northwest
1779: Continental money becomes nearly worthless

1780s: Rapid settlement of Kentucky and Tennessee
Oliver Evans automates grist mills
1781: Bank of North America in Philadelphia
1783: Great Britain closes West Indies to American ships
1784: Spain closes port of New Orleans to Americans
1784: Debt crisis spurs protests in U.S.

1788: Pennsylvania Society for the Encouragement of Manufactures and the Useful Arts introduces spinning jennies
1790: Samuel Slater builds first U.S. water-powered textile mill
Congress passes patent law
1791: Bank of the United States
Excise tax on whiskey
Alexander Hamilton's plan for promoting manufactures
1793: British blockade of French West Indies
Eli Whitney's cotton gin

1794: Whiskey Rebellion
1795: Jay Treaty
1798: Alien and Sedition Acts
   Quasi-war with France
1799: Fries Rebellion

1800: Washington, D.C., becomes national capital
   Gabriel's Rebellion
   Jefferson elected President
1803: *Marbury v. Madison* case
   Louisiana Purchase
1804: Lewis and Clark expedition

1809: Tecumseh organizes pan-Indian confederacy
1812: U.S. war with Great Britain
1814: Treaty of Ghent

1795: Philadelphia Quaker women establish first female benevolent society in U.S.
1797: Second Great Awakening begins in New England
1799: Rise of Handsome Lake as Seneca prophet
   Charles Brockden Brown's *Wieland*

1800s: Tenskwatawa, the Shawnee Prophet, inspires following
1800: Library of Congress
1801: Cane Ridge, Kentucky, camp meeting
1805: Pennsylvania Academy of Fine Arts

1795: Great Britain opens West Indies to U.S. trade
1796: Spain opens navigation on Mississippi River
   Alexander Hamilton's industrial town in New Jersey fails
1798: Eli Whitney attempts to manufacture guns with interchangeable parts
1790s: U.S. international trade soars with European conflict
   Cotton expands Southern slavery
   Northern cities become magnets for African Americans

1802: Oliver Evans's high pressure steam engine
1806: Non-Importation Act
1807: Embargo Act
1808: Federal ban on international slave trade
1809: Giles's Enforcement Act
   Embargo repealed; replaced with Non-Intercourse Act

1811: Charter of national bank expires

BURNING THE GASPÉE

Burning of Gaspée, *by Charles De Wolf Brownell. The seizure and burning of the British customs ship* Gaspée *by Rhode Island merchants in June 1772 moved the colonies closer to revolution.*

Chapter 5

WARS FOR INDEPENDENCE, 1764–1783

THE TREATY OF 1763 forced Spain and Great Britain to reassess their North American colonies. Both nations had new kings, as Charles III took Spain's throne in 1759 and George III became the British monarch in 1760. For the Spanish, the borderlands in North America were of secondary importance, serving as a buffer to protect the Mexican silver mines. For Britain, however, the mainland provinces had become increasingly significant as a source of revenue and market for consumer goods. The Seven Years' War marked Britain's ascendancy to world power, but resulted in a national debt of £130 million. Annual interest payments alone amounted to £4.5 million, equal to more than half of the government's yearly expenditures prior to the war.

When Parliament imposed levies on the American colonies to help pay expenses, the colonists protested vehemently that they should not be taxed without their consent. They complained that they had no representatives in Parliament, that only their elected provincial assemblies could constitutionally tax them. Beginning in 1764, the Americans petitioned, rioted, boycotted British goods, destroyed tea, and ultimately defied George III and parliamentary leaders when they sent troops. The colonists' belief that they possessed the same rights as the English was something for which many were willing to fight.

Nevertheless, the consensus to declare independence did not come quickly, nor was the war to defend independence easily won. Americans who disagreed that the British actions warranted insurrection remained loyal to the king. These loyalists, also called tories after the pro-monarchy faction in England, tried to subvert the revolutionary governments and formed loyalist militia units to fight alongside British troops. They found allies in many Indians and African Americans who conducted wars of independence of their own. Other colonists remained neutral, whether from principled opposition to violence or from sheer indifference. The Revolution touched everyone, Native Americans, women, and enslaved blacks, as well as the white men who served as military and civilian leaders and comprised most of the armed forces. The cause of the patriots—or whigs, as the American revolutionaries called themselves after the English party that had led opposition to the Crown—depended upon the efforts of many people, those who supplied and supported the troops, as well as those who fought.

CHRONOLOGY

1764	Sugar and Currency Acts
	St. Louis founded
1765	Stamp Act provokes widespread colonial protest
	Stamp Act Congress
1766	Parliament repeals Stamp Act, passes Declaratory Act
	Spanish governor arrives in Louisiana
1766–1771	North Carolina Regulator movement
1767	Passage of Townshend Act
	John Dickinson publishes "Farmer" letters
1767–1769	South Carolina Regulator movement
1768	Massachusetts assembly sends "circular letter"
	Non-importation movement against Townshend duties
	British troops stationed in Boston
	Louisianans expel Spanish governor
1769	Spanish reestablish control of Louisiana
1770	Boston Massacre
	Partial repeal of Townshend Act
1772	Burning of *Gaspée*
1772–1773	Committees of Correspondence established
1773	Boston Tea Party
1774	Passage of Coercive Acts; port of Boston closed
	Quebec Act
	First Continental Congress
	Congress organizes Continental Association
1775	Battles of Lexington and Concord
	Second Continental Congress
	Battle of Bunker Hill
	Congress authorizes invasion of Canada
	Lord Dunmore's proclamation to servants and slaves

1776	Thomas Paine publishes *Common Sense*
	British evacuation of Boston
	Declaration of Independence
	Cherokee War on the southern frontier
	Americans defeated on Long Island; British occupation of New York City
	Battle of Trenton
1777	Battle of Princeton
	British occupy Philadelphia after defeating Washington at Brandywine
	Battle of Germantown
	Burgoyne surrenders to Americans at Saratoga
	Congress approves Articles of Confederation; sends document to states for ratification
1778	Alliance with France
	Iroquois and loyalist attacks in New York and Pennsylvania
	British withdraw from Philadelphia
	Whig frontiersmen take settlements in the Illinois country
	British invade Georgia
1780	Americans surrender at Charleston
	Battle of Camden
1781	Battle of Cowpens
	Articles of Confederation ratified
	Battle of Guilford Courthouse
	Southern army reconquers most of South Carolina and Georgia
	Surrender of Cornwallis at Yorktown
1782	Massacre at Gnadenhutten
1783	Signing of Treaty of Paris

REALIGNMENTS IN THE SPANISH BORDERLANDS

The peace of 1763 required Spain to withdraw from Florida, assume the government of Louisiana, and rethink its defenses in Texas and New Mexico. With Britain's enhanced power, especially in light of its recent victories in Cuba and the Philippines, safeguarding the Mexican silver mines took high priority. The Spanish also considered the soaring population of the British colonies a dangerous, if future, threat to their American empire.

Florida and Louisiana

Spain ordered all of its subjects to leave Florida when Britain took control. Though the British promised religious freedom to the Catholic Floridians, some 200 Christian Indians, 79 free African Americans, 350 slaves, and nearly all of the 3,000 Hispanics departed from St. Augustine to Cuba, and from Pensacola to Mexico. Most of the Spanish colonists served in the military or were dependent on government funds, so they had little choice but to leave. They sold their property at a loss to British bargain hunters. The free blacks of Mose, near St. Augustine, could expect enslavement by the English, so took Spain's offer of homesteads in Cuba. They received some tools and money from the government, but faced hard times because they never received adequate compensation for their property in Florida. The British, who would hold the province for only twenty years, created two administrative districts, East and West Florida.

Acquisition of Louisiana, including all French territory west of the Mississippi River and New Orleans, on the east bank, gave Spain an extensive region to administer. Spain needed to win the loyalties of French inhabitants and Native Americans, and hoped to keep the British colonists out. The concern about British expansion became all too real as interlopers spanned the Mississippi River to trade with Indians on the Great Plains. The Spanish feared that the traders would lay the basis for a British takeover of Louisiana, increasing the vulnerability of the Mexican mines. British colonists moved quickly to the Gulf Coast and eastern shore of the Mississippi (West Florida), where, within a decade, 4,000 whites and 1,500 African American slaves were living.

The more immediate challenge for Spanish authorities in Louisiana, however, was asserting political control of the province. Unlike the Floridians, most settlers stayed in Louisiana, hoping that the French government would return. In fact, for several years, French government remained; even after the first Spanish governor, Antonio de Ulloa, arrived in 1766, he tried to govern jointly with the last French governor. Adhering to Charles III's instructions, Ulloa left the French administration and legal system intact, even allowing the French flag to fly over the capital.

Ulloa did not extend this leniency to commerce, however, for his mission was to pull Louisiana under Spanish mercantilism. He tried to stop business with France and Great Britain and restricted the Native American trade to certain dealers. New Orleans merchants, who had enjoyed little regulation under the French, feared loss of markets and lower prices for their tobacco, indigo, sugar, deerskins, and lumber. Like the thirteen British provinces on the Atlantic coast, at about the same time, the merchants protested the new restrictions, then in October 1768 issued a declaration of loyalty to the king of France. With few Spanish troops at his disposal, Governor Ulloa left for Cuba. When the French refused to intervene, the colony became independent, but only for a year.

The Spanish regained Louisiana when General Alexander O'Reilly arrived in 1769 with more than 2,000 soldiers. An Irishman with a successful career in the Spanish army, O'Reilly arrested the rebels, put five of them to death, but pardoned most who had participated in the uprising. He raised the Spanish flag and within a year ended French government, changed the legal system, made Castilian the official language, and outlawed trade with other nations. Despite the merchants' fears, the economy flourished as smuggling continued with Britain, and Spanish markets welcomed their goods. St. Louis, established in 1764, became the thriving center of trade for beaver, buffalo, and deerskins with Native Americans of the Illinois and Missouri countries. Louisiana remained culturally French, as the numbers of French settlers far surpassed the Spanish. During the 1760s, some French moved into Louisiana from the east bank of the Mississippi, and at least 1,000 Acadians, who had

been forced out of Nova Scotia by Britain, settled in the colony.

Fortifying the Southwest

With ownership of Louisiana, the Spanish could alter their defenses along the frontier in Texas and New Mexico. They removed several forts from East Texas. By the 1760s, the most immediate danger in the southwest came from the Apaches and Comanches, who defended their freedom from Hispanic slave catchers and attempted to drive the Spanish back into Mexico. Skillfully adopting the European horse and gun, they refused to submit to Spanish rule or Christianity. Spain gave up trying to convert them through missions, emphasizing military defense instead. The Apaches and Comanches raided settlements and pack trains, stole horses, mules, cattle, and supplies, killing Pueblos and white settlers alike.

During the 1760s and 1770s, in the face of constant Indian assaults that killed hundreds of settlers in New Mexico and Texas, Spain—like Great Britain in its colonies—tried to reform administration and improve defense. From 1766 to 1768, the Marqués de Rubí, a high-level military official from Spain, inspected the fortifications and missions of the southwest. He discovered badly located presidios (or forts) and soldiers suffering from lack of food and clothes because of their commanders' greed. At one Texas presidio, Rubí found sixty troops without shoes or uniforms and, among them, only two muskets that worked. He recommended building new presidios and relocating others to create an orderly cordon of military bases situated about a hundred miles apart. The presidios would extend from the Gulf of California to the Gulf of Mexico, along a line that was close to the present boundary between the United States and Mexico. The purpose of the cordon was to protect Mexico. Small numbers of Spanish troops would hold garrisons at Santa Fe and San Antonio, north of the cordon, to help defend Hispanics and allied Indians in New Mexico and Texas. The borderlands officials also received more autonomy to deal with local problems, but lacked sufficient troops to conquer the Apaches and Comanches. The settlements remained open to attack with such long distances between presidios.

THE BRITISH COLONIES RESIST IMPERIAL REFORM

In Britain's colonies, which experienced few restrictions before 1763, trouble began when George III appointed George Grenville as first minister, with responsibility for solving the debt crisis. Grenville decided that Americans should pay more taxes because they benefited from the Seven Years' War and continued to drain the government's budget for administrative and military costs. Because the British at home were highly taxed, Grenville's plan to make the colonies pay their way seemed reasonable to many. The Americans saw it differently, however, because they were proud of their role in the war and expected better treatment, so moved quickly to the brink of revolt.

The Sugar and Currency Acts

Grenville began his program in 1764 with the Sugar Act, which initiated a new policy of charging duties primarily to raise revenue rather than to regulate trade. It reduced the duty on foreign molasses from sixpence (under the Molasses Act of 1733) to threepence per gallon, which was further reduced to one penny in 1766. Grenville assumed merchants would pay the lower tariff rather than go to the risk of smuggling and bribery. The law also added timber, iron, and hides to the list of enumerated goods. To make smuggling more hazardous, the act gave increased powers to the vice-admiralty courts, which had been established earlier to hear maritime cases. Because these courts lacked juries, the government expected easy convictions for smuggling. In addition, the law expanded the use of writs of assistance (search warrants), empowered the Royal Navy to inspect ships, and required endless bureaucratic paperwork from colonial shippers. Parliament also passed the Currency Act (1764), which had the potential to cause further hardship by forbidding colonies from issuing paper money, thus creating a shortage of currency.

Coming in the midst of an economic depression, this legislation stirred up colonial protest. Provincial assemblies sent petitions to England requesting relief.

Most urgently, merchants feared that if imports of foreign molasses were cut off, their provision trade to the Spanish and French West Indies would be lost and the rum industry destroyed. Without foreign credits, they could not pay for British manufactures. The Americans slowed down their orders from Britain and encouraged home industry, arousing opposition to Grenville's policies from English businessmen. One colonial merchant wrote to associates in England that if the government deprived Americans of paper currency, "we shall not be able to export Provisions &c. in the same Degree as formerly, and if we are not on any Terms allow'd a Trade to get Money from abroad, we shall have none to pay you for Goods, and then unless you will send them Gratis our Dealings must end."

The Stamp Act

Passed by Parliament in 1765, the Stamp Act provoked an even greater storm of protest. The law departed entirely from the confines of mercantilist policy, for its purpose was to raise an internal revenue, which would be used to pay troops in the colonies. The act required individuals to purchase stamps for official documents and published papers, including deeds, liquor licenses, bills of lading, court documents, wills, passports, playing cards, newspapers, and pamphlets. All publications and official transactions were to be subject to this special tax, which increased with the value of a land sale or the size of a pamphlet. The tax could be paid only in specie, an onerous requirement because colonists generally used paper money and credit instead of the scarce gold and silver. The vice-admiralty courts would enforce the act, confiscating any land or property involved in transactions conducted without the stamps.

Colonists of all walks of life found the Stamp Act offensive. Everyone who engaged in public business, whether to buy a newspaper or sell property, would have to pay the tax. Because Parliament, not their provincial assemblies, passed the act, Americans considered it a violation of their rights as British subjects. As they understood the British constitution, the people must consent to taxes through their representatives. The provinces could not send delegates to Parliament, so that body should not tax them to raise revenue. As one Philadelphia merchant said succinctly, "the point in dispute is a very Important one,

Paul Revere's engraving of the hanging in effigy of an American-born member of Parliament, John Huske, an alleged Stamp Act supporter.

if the Americans are to be taxed by a Parliament where they are not nor can be Represented, they are no longer Englishmen but Slaves." Only tariffs to regulate trade such as the 1733 duty on molasses, many colonists believed, were constitutionally valid.

Recognizing Parliament's attack on their powers, provincial assemblies protested the Stamp Act. In the Virginia House of Burgesses, the newly elected Patrick Henry, only twenty-nine years old, introduced fourteen resolves against the tax. The Virginia assembly refused to accept all of Henry's proposals, for members considered some too radical, but in June 1765, approved the more moderate resolutions that defended the colonists' right to tax themselves.

When newspapers spread word of Virginia's action, other provinces responded. Rhode Island instructed its officials to ignore the stamp tax; Massachusetts,

Connecticut, New York, New Jersey, Pennsylvania, Maryland, and South Carolina passed resolves similar to Virginia's. In October 1765, representatives from nine colonies traveled to New York City to attend the Stamp Act Congress. In resolutions and petitions to Parliament, the congress upheld the power of representative assemblies, not Parliament, to tax the colonists. Further, the congress defended trial by jury, which the expanded authority of the vice-admiralty courts threatened. By issuing resolves and organizing the Stamp Act Congress, the colonial elite challenged British efforts to assert control. The wealthy merchants and planters who sat in provincial assemblies condemned Grenville's assault on their political and economic power.

Ordinary colonists recognized the threat as well. They drew upon the tradition of the mob to protest what they considered tyranny, just as residents of port cities had earlier resisted naval impressment. Crowds in the seaport towns were at the heart of the swelling revolutionary movement, as they blocked implementation of the odious law. The anti-Stamp Act riots began in Boston on August 14, 1765, when a group who called themselves the Loyal Nine organized a demonstration to hang in effigy the appointed stamp collector for Massachusetts, Andrew Oliver. The crowd destroyed a partially constructed building they thought he intended as his stamp office, then damaged his home. Oliver resigned his commission. Twelve days later, a Boston mob attacked the houses of several other officials, gutting the mansion of Lieutenant Governor Thomas Hutchinson.

Protesters all along the Atlantic seaboard mobilized to prevent stamp distribution, scheduled to begin November 1. News of Oliver's resignation prompted anti-Stamp Act mobs in other cities to demand the same from their appointed stampmen. The strategy seemed sensible: if the distributors quit, the stamps could not be sold. In some colonies, rioters forced stamp officials to relinquish their commissions. In others, just the threat of disorder was effective. By the end of 1765, distributors in every colony except Georgia had resigned.

The men who led the crowds called themselves Sons of Liberty, at first informally, then in organized resistance groups. They were mostly propertied men—small merchants, shopkeepers, and craftsmen—from neither the wealthiest nor the most destitute rungs of society. The activists were people who needed documents to conduct business, who would regularly feel the pinch of the stamp tax. The Sons of Liberty also established networks to organize boycotts of British goods. Merchants and retailers in New York City, Philadelphia, and Boston signed pacts to stop imports until Parliament repealed the act. By early 1766, the Sons of Liberty coerced customs officials and judges to open the ports and resume court business without stamps. To Thomas Hutchinson, it appeared "the authority of every colony is in the hands of the sons of liberty." In truth, the American resistance aimed to expunge the stamp tax, not end British authority. The movement achieved success in 1766, when Parliament repealed the Stamp Act, after British businessmen from more than twenty cities petitioned for relief. Suffering from postwar economic depression and unemployment, the British textile industry faced even worse times with an American boycott. They clearly understood the growing significance of the colonial market.

Protest Widens in the Lower South

In the Carolinas, the Stamp Act resistance spawned revolts against colonial elites, who in the eyes of African American slaves and many backcountry whites were more serious oppressors than Great Britain. To blacks, the radicals' oft-spoken argument that the English government intended to deprive white Americans of freedom—to make them slaves—seemed ironic. Yet such statements also gave hope, for the revolutionary movement spotlighted the institution of slavery and its immorality and injustice. While African Americans did not need the imperial crisis to know that slavery was wrong, they gained confidence from the political unrest. In January 1766, in Charleston, 1,400 seamen and a group of black slaves threatened serious disorder. The sailors became restless because the customs agents refused to release ships from port without stamped documents. The people of Charleston were even more concerned, however, when a group of enslaved men marched through the town shouting "Liberty!" The city armed itself against a slave revolt, while the South Carolina assembly became so frightened that it restricted slave imports for three years.

The North Carolina Regulator movement also began in 1766, inspired by the uproar against the Stamp Act, but targeted the colonial elite, not Britain. Six thousand western farmers demanded confirmation of land titles and the end of speculators' monopoly of the

VIRGINIA RESOLVES AGAINST THE STAMP ACT, 1765

When news arrived in 1765 that Parliament had passed the Stamp Act, the colonists protested the internal tax. In the Virginia assembly, Patrick Henry introduced resolutions defending the right of "taxation of the people by themselves, or by persons chosen by themselves to represent them" and accusing Parliament of attempting to destroy "American freedom." Newspapers published seven resolutions, of which the Virginia legislators passed the first four listed below, which were more moderate than the rest.

Resolved, That the first adventurers and settlers of this His Majesty's Colony and Dominion of Virginia brought with them, and transmitted to their posterity, and all other of His Majesty's subjects since inhabiting this His Majesty's said Colony, all the liberties, privileges, franchises, and immunities, that have at any time been held, enjoyed, and possessed, by the people of Great Britain.

Resolved, That by two royal charters, granted by King James the First, the colonists aforesaid are declared entitled to all liberties, privileges, and immunities of denizens and natural subjects, to all intents and purposes, as if they had been abiding and born within the realm of England.

Resolved, That the taxation of the people by themselves, or by persons chosen by themselves to represent them, who can only know what taxes the people are able to bear, or the easiest method of raising them, and must themselves be affected by every tax laid on the people, is the only security against a burthensome taxation, and the distinguishing characteristick of British freedom, without which the ancient constitution cannot exist.

Resolved, That His Majesty's liege people of this his most ancient and loyal Colony have without interruption enjoyed the inestimable right of being governed by such laws, respecting their internal polity and taxation, as are derived from their own consent, with the approbation of their sovereign, or his substitute; and that the same hath never been forfeited or yielded up, but hath been constantly recognized by the kings and people of Great Britain.

Resolved therefore, That the General Assembly of this Colony have the only and sole exclusive right and power to lay taxes and impositions upon the inhabitants of this Colony, and that every attempt to vest such power in any person or persons whatsoever other than the General Assembly aforesaid has a manifest tendency to destroy British as well as American freedom.

Resolved, That His Majesty's liege people, the inhabitants of this Colony are not bound to yield obedience to any law or ordinance whatever, designed to impose any taxation whatsoever upon them other than the laws or ordinances of the General Assembly aforesaid.

Resolved, That any person who shall, by speaking or writing, assert or maintain that any person or persons other than the General Assembly of this Colony, have any right or power to impose or lay any taxation on the people here, shall be deemed an enemy to His Majesty's Colony.

best land. The Regulators also protested corrupt local officials, excessive court fees and taxes, and lack of adequate representation for ordinary backcountry farmers in the North Carolina legislature. They called for a secret ballot to reduce the influence of wealthy planters in assembly elections. The North Carolina Regulators refused to pay taxes and closed several courts. In 1771, when the government sent the eastern militia, 2,000 Regulators met them at Alamance Creek but were dispersed.

Most of the grievances of the South Carolina Regulators were different, except that they too lacked fair representation in the provincial government. As in Pennsylvania (with the Paxton Boys revolt) and North Carolina, representation in the assembly had not kept pace with western settlement. In South Carolina, however, the Regulators were planters who wanted to bring order, "to regulate" the backcountry. The legislature had failed to create local government for the westerners, so they had no courts or jails. Everyone had to travel to Charleston to conduct legal business, but even worse, bandits roamed freely, stealing horses and cattle, destroying property, and sometimes torturing and killing their victims. The frontier robbers were mostly propertyless whites and some free blacks and escaped slaves; one report in the *South-Carolina Gazette* noted "a Gang of Banditti, consisting of Mulattoes—Free Negroes, and notorious Harbourers of run away Slaves." The Regulators resorted to vigilante "justice," capturing and whipping suspected felons, taking some to jail in Charleston, and evicting others from the colony. They finally ceased their activities in 1769 when the legislature established a circuit court system for the entire province.

The Townshend Revenue Act

In other British mainland colonies, attention focused on imperial tensions rather than regional disputes. The British government and American radicals emerged from the Stamp Act crisis with conflicting views: While the Americans celebrated the Stamp Act's repeal, convinced that they had won, the British yielded no authority. In the Declaratory Act, passed with the repeal in March 1766, Parliament affirmed its power to tax the colonies, indeed "to make laws and statutes of sufficient force and validity to bind the colonies and people of America, subjects of the crown of Great

Britain, in all cases whatsoever." The act generated little response in the colonies, but should have, for it laid the basis for subsequent restrictions. The government had withdrawn the offensive Stamp Act, but still argued that the colonies must support the army and Crown officials in America.

Thus, in June 1767, Parliament passed three more laws affecting the Americans: an act establishing the American Board of Customs Commissioners to enforce legislation against illegal trade, the New York Restraining Act, and the Townshend Revenue Act. The Restraining Act would have dissolved the New York Assembly for refusing adequate supplies to British soldiers stationed in the province. Instead, the New York legislators gave in, pledging additional funds for the troops. The Townshend Revenue Act was conceived by Charles Townshend, the British chancellor of the exchequer, who wanted the Americans to contribute, over time, an increasing percentage of imperial expenses in North America. The Townshend Act, which placed duties on tea, glass, paper, and paint would be just the beginning, for they would raise about £40,000 per year, less than one-tenth of the colonial administrative and military costs. The revenues would pay the salaries of governors and judges, thus removing their dependence upon the provincial legislatures. The act also required colonial courts to provide customs officials with writs of assistance to search houses and businesses for smuggled merchandise.

To American whigs, the Townshend Act was dangerous for two reasons: It raised revenue without the approval of colonial assemblies and it removed royal officials from the lawmakers' control. If the king rather than the legislatures paid provincial governors, the colonies lost a powerful negotiating tool for obtaining consent to the laws they wanted. While the British saw the Townshend Act as an appropriate way to force the Americans to begin paying their share, the colonists believed it was a step towards tyranny—towards the loss of traditional English rights.

At first, colonial reaction to the Townshend Act was restrained, largely because the impact of the new law seemed limited. Then, in December 1767, a few weeks after the Townshend Act went into effect, John Dickinson, a Philadelphia lawyer and owner of a Delaware plantation, began publishing a series of twelve letters signed "A Farmer." Soon reprinted by newspapers throughout the thirteen colonies and published in pamphlet form as *Letters from a Farmer in Pennsylvania*

John Dickinson inspired opposition to the Townshend Act with his Letters from a Farmer in Pennsylvania. *This engraving shows the right arm of Dickinson's "Patriotic American Farmer" resting on the English Magna Charta.*

(1768), Dickinson's arguments galvanized opposition to the Townshend duties. He warned that the colonies must work together; for lack of support from the other provinces, New York had little choice but to cave in and supply the British troops. He rejected the position that the colonists should accept external taxes (duties) but not internal taxes (like the stamp tax), stating that only elected representatives could legally impose *any* revenue tax. He believed that Parliament could collect duties in the colonies if the purpose was to regulate trade (as with the Molasses Act of 1733), but not to raise revenue. Further, the purpose of the funds collected under the Townshend Act was oppressive, for it eliminated the power of the colonial legislatures over Crown officials. Dickinson predicted that if the Americans failed to have this act repealed, harsher measures would be forthcoming: "If we can find no relief from this infamous situation . . . we may bow down our necks, with all the stupid serenity of servitude, to any drudgery which our lords and masters shall please to command." Dickinson urged the thirteen colonies to petition for repeal; if that failed, they should once again boycott British goods.

Massachusetts responded first and most enthusiastically to Dickinson's call to action. In early 1768, its assembly petitioned George III for redress, then dispatched a "circular letter" to the other twelve colonies suggesting they do the same. The new English secretary of state for the colonies, Lord Hillsborough, realized that the circular letter was a call to unified resistance. He took his job—to bring colonial affairs in America under control—most seriously. In doing so, he fanned rebellion. Denouncing Dickinson's pamphlet as "extremely wild," he targeted the Massachusetts assemblymen as troublemakers, ordering them to rescind their circular letter. They refused. When he ordered colonial governors to dissolve assemblies that responded to the letter, most legislatures sent petitions and were disbanded. Simultaneously, Hillsborough reassigned military units from the Ohio Valley to Florida, Nova Scotia, Quebec, and the mid-Atlantic region where they could be called upon to control the defiant provinces.

In June 1768, when Massachusetts remained unbowed and the customs commissioners demanded protection against rioters, Hillsborough sent British regiments to Boston. The colonial secretary wanted even more drastic measures to punish the colony—to quarter soldiers in private homes and install a provincial government more sympathetic to the Crown—but failed to convince his colleagues that these steps were necessary. Unrest in Ireland and rumors of Spanish expansion in the American west probably made them unwilling to risk revolt. When troops disembarked in Boston in October 1768, they heard cries of protest but met no armed resistance. As months passed, however, the presence of the redcoats created tensions that would eventually erupt in bloodshed.

Between the time Lord Hillsborough ordered the regiments to Boston and their arrival four months later, city residents had signed a non-importation agreement against the Townshend Act. Most Boston merchants pledged to stop importing goods from Great Britain after January 1, 1769, unless the Townshend duties were repealed. The non-importation movement soon spread to New York City, where artisans supported the merchants by agreeing to boycott any retailer who imported British goods. Traders in

The Occupation of Boston, *1768, engraving by Paul Revere(?), illustrates the arrival of British troops on the Long Wharf (center).*

Philadelphia, New Haven, and other northern ports delayed action, however, because they would face economic loss. They waited until 1769 for the imperial government to respond to their petitions, then approved non-importation. In Virginia, George Washington kindled the boycott. He wrote, "At a time when our lordly masters in Great Britain will be satisfied with nothing less than the deprivation of American freedom, it seems highly necessary that some thing should be done to avert the stroke and maintain the liberty which we have derived from our Ancestors."

The boycotts, which were unofficial agreements without the force of law, met uneven success as colonists disagreed over whether to join. Between 1768 and 1769, American imports from England declined fairly substantially, by 38 percent. As the months passed, however, importers wavered as their incomes fell. In contrast, craftsmen—beyond their concern for liberty—often benefited from the boycott because it created a demand for their products. Some artisans organized into street groups to threaten merchants and customs officials who tried to undermine the non-importation pacts.

Women participated both as purchasers of goods and as producers. Many "Daughters of Liberty" gave up imported tea and clothing, signing agreements to avoid the banned goods. The *Boston News-Letter* reported that "a large circle of very agreeable ladies in this town . . . unanimously agreed" not to purchase ribbons and other imports. Instead, throughout New England, women organized spinning bees to produce woolen yarn. In Boston, some impoverished women profited from the temporary demand for American-made cloth, when William Molineaux, a merchant and radical whig, contracted with local artisans to build 400 spinning wheels, which he distributed to women to spin yarn in their homes. With this "putting-out" system, Molineaux and the spinners responded to both their patriotism and economic needs.

Crisis in Boston

During the years 1769 to 1775, while opposition to British policies grew throughout the colonies, Boston became the powder keg of the Revolution. Violence broke out in the summer of 1769 between the Bostonians and British redcoats, as the heavily armed strangers imposed themselves upon a populace hostile to standing armies. The chief responsibilities of the troops were to protect the despised customs commis-

sioners and help them collect duties. The soldiers became even more unpopular when they took jobs at low pay during their off-duty hours, thus throwing city laborers out of work.

The first serious incident occurred in July 1769, when a redcoat, John Riley, was jailed for hitting a local butcher who had insulted him. A near riot followed as twenty of Riley's comrades tried to rescue him from jail. The soldier's commander said that the butcher had gotten what he deserved. Such episodes continued into early 1770, as each side assaulted the other. On March 2, the violence escalated when soldiers seeking revenge for an insult attacked workers at John Gray's ropeworks. Street fights intensified over the next few days, as townspeople and soldiers exchanged angry words and blows. On March 5, the bloodiest incident occurred, the so-called Boston Massacre. A young apprentice taunted the British sentry at the Customs House, who hit the boy with his gun. When a crowd gathered, shouting at the sentry, "Kill him, kill him, knock him down," Captain Thomas Preston led seven soldiers to assist him. The crowd grew larger, throwing snowballs, ice, and sticks at the soldiers, threatening them with clubs, and calling them "bloody backs," lobsters, and cowards. Then someone hit a redcoat with a club, knocking the gun out of his hands. Preston's men fired, killing five townspeople and wounding six. The dead became martyrs, with March 5 commemorated as "Massacre Day" in the years ahead. The incident crystallized the colonists' opposition to standing armies. Nevertheless, when Captain Preston and six soldiers were tried for murder, the jury found two soldiers guilty of manslaughter and cleared the others. The radical whig lawyer John Adams defended them, saying that all Englishmen should have a fair trial.

Just as the crisis in Boston reached its head in spring 1770, the British government decided on partial repeal of the Townshend Act. The duties had raised under £21,000 in revenues, but cost hundreds of thousands of pounds sterling in trade as a result of the non-importation movement. Lord North, the new British leader, recommended removing the Townshend duties on paint, paper, and glass, but keeping the duty on tea. North wanted to help British merchants who had suffered from the American boycott "without giving up that just right which I shall ever wish the mother country to possess, the right of taxing the Americans." So, as in the case of the Stamp Act, British officials backed away from a specific revenue

measure without abandoning their right to levy taxes. Following Parliament's action, merchants in New York City and other colonial ports, eager to resume trade, cancelled their boycotts except on tea. Imports into the thirteen colonies from England rebounded over the next several years, increasing from £1.3 million in 1769 to £4.2 million in 1771, which was twice the value of imports before the boycotts.

The Gaspée Incident

For two years, the conflict between Great Britain and the colonies abated, then flared again in 1772. Trouble began this time in Rhode Island, when more than one hundred men burned the British schooner *Gaspée*, wounding its commander, William Dudingston. Avidly enforcing the Sugar Act, the *Gaspée* had harassed merchant vessels sailing through Narragansett Bay. The Crown named a Commission of Inquiry to locate the perpetrators and send them to England to be tried for high treason. Though the Commission identified none of the *Gaspée*'s attackers, colonists viewed the policy of taking defendants to England for trial as a serious threat to their constitutional rights.

In response, the Virginia assembly reignited the resistance movement by appointing a Committee of Correspondence to monitor British policy and facilitate communication among the provinces. The Virginians recommended to other colonies that they do the same. Within a year, Committees of Correspondence in all thirteen provinces coordinated opposition to Britain's restraints.

The Boston Tea Party

The final showdown began in 1773, when Parliament passed the Tea Act to bail out the nearly bankrupt East India Company. Though some colonists purchased British tea, the boycott on the product was still in effect and many purchased cheaper, smuggled Dutch tea. To sell the company's huge surplus, the government dropped a heavy import duty into England on tea headed for America, but retained the Townshend duty, which Lord North insisted on keeping to uphold Parliament's power to tax. Indeed, he viewed the Tea Act as a way to induce Americans to accept parliamentary authority, since the price of tea would fall. The company also received a monopoly in the colonies,

with the right to choose certain provincial merchants as agents. The company selected consignees in the ports of Charleston, Philadelphia, New York, and Boston, to whom it promptly dispatched nearly 600,000 pounds of tea.

The Tea Act was doubly offensive to American whigs as it renewed opposition to the duty and caused outrage over favoritism and privilege. One radical called the act "a dirty trick" and accused Lord North of "low cunning" for trying to break American resistance by reducing the price of tea. Before the tea ships arrived in Charleston, Philadelphia, and New York, militants convinced the East India Company's agents to resign. The Charleston tea was stored in a customs warehouse, while the ships headed toward Philadelphia and New York turned back to England with their cargo. In Boston, the consignees, two of them sons of pro-British Governor Thomas Hutchinson, declined to quit. When three ships arrived, members of the Boston Committee of Correspondence, led by Samuel Adams, prevented them from unloading. Adams, the cousin of John, had been the chief agitator in Boston since the Stamp Act. A skilled politician and writer, though

Samuel Adams, *portrait by John Singleton Copley. Sam Adams helped make Boston the center of colonial radical resistance from the Stamp Act to the Boston Tea Party and its aftermath.*

failed businessman, he kept the pot simmering against British policies and Governor Hutchinson. Now, with the Boston committee, he brought matters to a head: In a series of meetings, thousands of residents of Boston and surrounding towns met to refuse the tea. On December 16, 1773, when customs officials and Hutchinson denied the ships clearance to leave port, radicals ill-disguised as Mohawks boarded the ships, broke open the tea chests, and dumped them overboard. The destruction cost nearly £10,000.

For the British, the Boston Tea Party required stern action, for once again the Bostonians had defied them. London decided that steps must "be taken to secure the Dependence of the Colonies," and in particular, "to mark out Boston and separate that Town from the rest of the Delinquents." George III believed that the Americans must be forced to submit, because they increasingly assumed the "independency which one state has of another, but which is quite subversive of the obedience which a colony owes to its Mother Country." In 1774, Parliament passed four Coercive Acts that closed the port of Boston until residents of the city paid for the destroyed tea; altered the provincial charter to limit the power of town meetings and make the council the appointees of the Crown instead of elected officials; expanded the governor's control over the courts; provided that trials of royal officials could be moved to England or to another colony; and permitted quartering of troops in private buildings if a colony failed to provide suitable barracks. The Crown appointed General Thomas Gage, commander of the British army in North America, as Massachusetts governor, thus threatening the colonists with military force.

Americans called these the Intolerable Acts and believed that the Quebec Act (1774) was another, though London did not intend it to punish the Bostonians. The Quebec Act provided that an appointed council not an elected assembly make laws, confirmed religious freedom to Roman Catholics in Canada, allowing them to hold public office, and gave control of the Ohio Valley to the Quebec government. The law boded ill for representative government in the colonies. The New Englanders abhorred the act because it extended rights to "papists," while speculators in other colonies bemoaned the loss of western lands.

The First Continental Congress

Though the British government expected the Coercive Acts to isolate Boston and convince other provinces to

Cartoon showing the Americans providing food to Bostonians "caged" by the Boston Port Act, one of the Coercive Acts.

recognize the rights of Americans, but was not ready to declare independence. Some of its leadership, notably Galloway (who later became a loyalist), argued for a moderate course, but the Congress was committed to action. It confirmed the Suffolk County Resolves forwarded to Philadelphia by a local Massachusetts convention. The Resolves blasted the Coercive Acts as "gross infractions of those rights to which we are justly entitled by the laws of nature, the British constitution and the charter of this province." The laws should "be rejected as the attempts of a wicked administration to enslave America." Everyone qualified to fight should learn "the art of war as soon as possible, and . . . appear under arms at least once a week." By endorsing these Resolves, the Congress took a militant stance.

Further, the Continental Congress passed non-importation, non-exportation, and non-consumption resolutions, ending all trade with Great Britain and Ireland, and exports to the West Indies. It also banned importation of slaves. If the British had hoped to divide the colonies by closing Boston, expecting other cities to pick up its trade, the plan backfired when all of the colonies closed their ports. The boycott would

be obedient, the policies actually pushed Americans toward more unified resistance. After the port of Boston closed, residents faced severe unemployment and food shortages. Neighboring towns provided supplies and harbored refugees looking for work. When Sam Adams and the Boston Committee of Correspondence requested an immediate boycott of British trade, instead the other provinces favored a Continental Congress to consider what action to take. The Massachusetts assembly proposed a meeting in Philadelphia on September 1, 1774, to which all of the thirteen colonies except Georgia sent delegates. The fifty-five representatives included Richard Henry Lee, Patrick Henry, and George Washington of Virginia; Sam and John Adams of Massachusetts; and John Dickinson and Joseph Galloway of Pennsylvania.

The primary purpose of the First Continental Congress was to obtain repeal of the Coercive Acts and other restrictions. The Congress wanted Parliament to

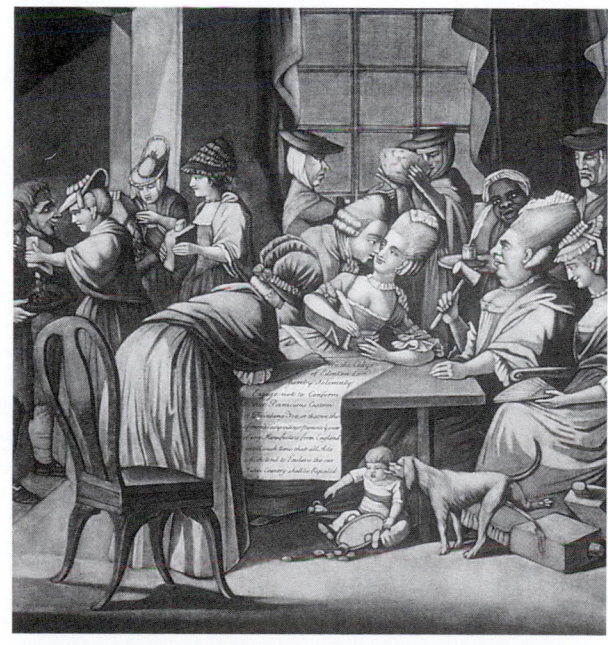

A British cartoon mocking American women who joined the boycott on tea, titled "A Society of Patriotic Ladies at Edenton in N.C."

continue until repeal of the Coercive Acts. Congress set up the Continental Association to enforce the ban on trade through elected local committees, called Committees of Observation and Inspection, or Committees of Safety. The groups would expose violators of the boycott as "enemies of American liberty," publicizing their names and interrupting their business. Almost every town and county in the thirteen colonies elected these committees, which soon took on other functions of local government, including raising militias and collecting taxes. This transfer of authority from colonial governments to the Committees of Observation was revolutionary, for Americans were vesting sovereignty in themselves rather than in Parliament. For its part, the Continental Congress agreed to meet again in May 1775 if the British failed to repeal the acts, thus confirming its role in coordinating the opposition.

RESISTANCE BECOMES A WAR FOR INDEPENDENCE

Over the winter of 1774–1775, the rift widened between the thirteen colonies and Great Britain. George III and his ministers considered the colonies in rebellion, yet the colonists themselves were unprepared to declare independence, a step they delayed for more than a year after hostilities began in April 1775.

Lexington and Concord

The British wanted to quell the revolt quickly, so instructed General Gage to take forceful action. Headquartered in Boston, he decided to seize the patriots'

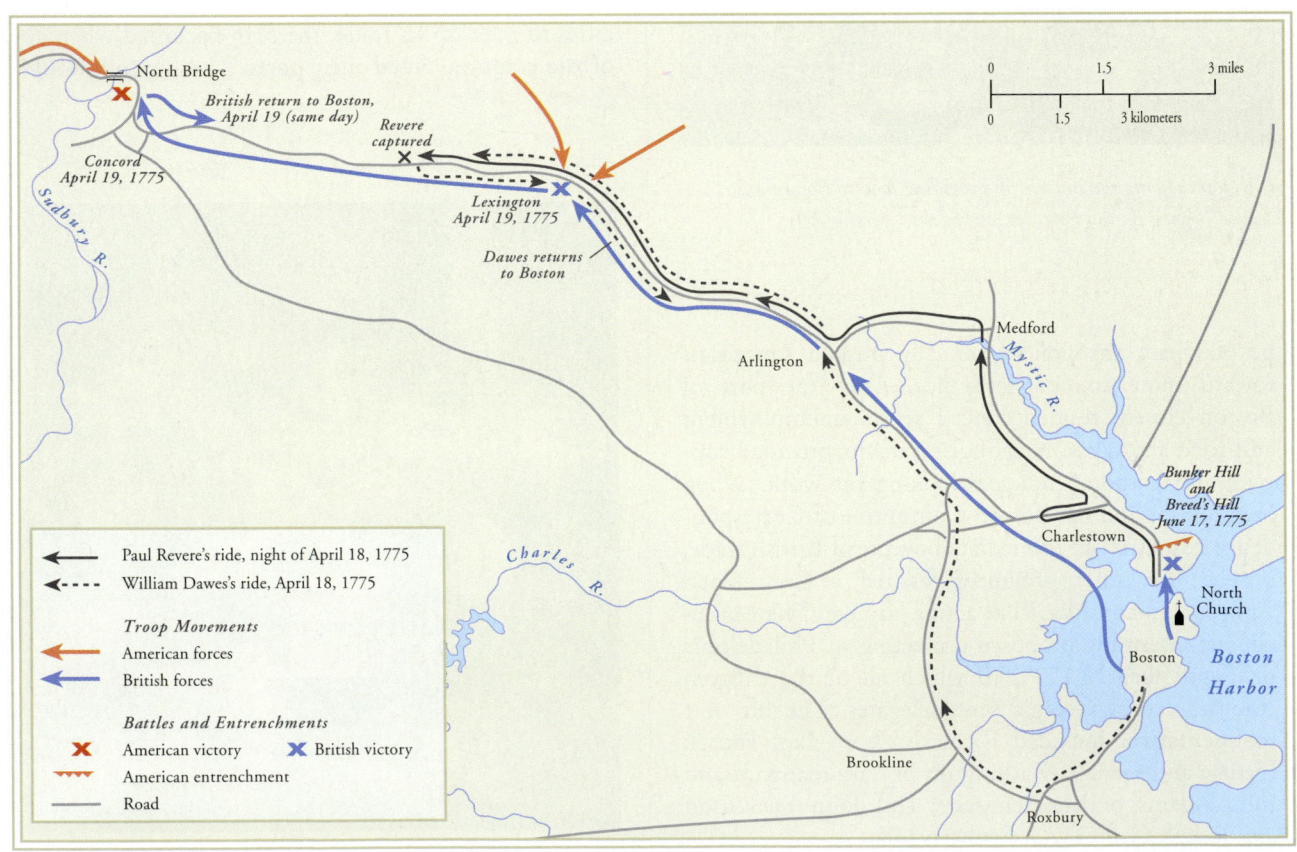

MAP 5.1 | BATTLES IN EASTERN MASSACHUSETTS

Battle of Lexington, *engraving by C. Tiebout after the drawing by E. Tisdale. The artist evokes the confusion and shock of the first battle of the Revolution.*

stores of food and ammunition at Concord, which he had learned about from an informer. Militant Bostonians discovered Gage's plan from their own spies, so were ready to spread the alarm on the night of April 18, 1775, when 700 redcoats mustered on Boston Common. Paul Revere and William Dawes escaped the city to raise the colonial militia and alert leaders Sam Adams and John Hancock, who were staying at Lexington, on the route to Concord. The Massachusetts Provincial Council, just a few weeks before, had resolved to resist any advance by Gage's troops.

As the British marched the sixteen miles to Concord, they heard church bells and saw lights in windows. Soon after sunrise on April 19th they reached Lexington, where they met about seventy armed militia, nearly half of the town's adult males. The Lexington company, led by Captain John Parker, had formed only a few weeks earlier, so their training was incomplete. But they were willing to defend, in the words of their town meeting, their "natural, constitutional and chartered rights." In the face of six companies of British infantry, Captain Parker attempted to disperse his troops. The British officer, Major John Pitcairn, wanted to disarm the Americans, not engage in battle. As the British advanced, a shot rang out, then several shots, and a British volley. Pitcairn tried to stop his troops, but the carnage continued for fifteen to twenty

minutes, leaving eight Lexington men dead and ten wounded. Only one British soldier was wounded and none killed. With the Battle of Lexington, which both commanders tried to avoid, the American war for independence began.

The British reached Concord at about eight o'clock in the morning, long after the patriots had hidden most of their military stores. Following a brief skirmish in which the Americans inflicted more casualties than the British, the redcoats headed back to Boston. The march became a harrowing escape for their lives. Hundreds of colonial militia from throughout the Massachusetts countryside rushed to battle. These farmers ignored standard eighteenth-century European military order of shooting and firing from fixed field positions. Instead, they used guerrilla tactics, shooting from behind trees, walls, rocks, and buildings. The British countered the guerrillas by sending advance parties to clear houses along the route. Using their famed skills with the bayonet, the redcoats killed the occupants and set fire to the homes. By the end of the day, British losses totaled seventy-three dead and 200 wounded or missing, while Massachusetts counted forty-nine killed and forty-three wounded and missing.

In the days that followed the battles of April 19, New England went to arms. Over 20,000 volunteers

streamed to Cambridge from as far away as a hundred miles. A large proportion of these soldiers soon returned home, but many stayed, expecting their wives, mothers, and sisters to work the family farms and defend the towns. One group of thirty to forty women of Pepperell and Groton guarded a bridge on the route British reinforcements might travel from Canada. Dressed in men's clothes and armed with muskets and pitchforks, they met no military action but arrested a tory spy. As Abigail Adams, the wife of John Adams, later wrote, "We are in no wise dispirited here. If our men are all drawn off and we should be attacked, you would find a race of Amazons in America."

Troops from throughout New England besieged Gage's redcoats in Boston. Nathanael Greene, a young ex-Quaker who later demonstrated his brilliance as a military strategist in the southern campaign, led 1,500 troops from Rhode Island. Connecticut promised 6,000 men and New Hampshire sent 2,000. From these earliest days of conflict, African American men served in the militia units. Without a unified army, each colony separately raised troops, selected officers, and secured provisions. By May 1775, the New England forces surrounding Boston numbered about 17,000, as the patriots considered themselves at war. Ethan Allen and his Green Mountain Boys of Vermont captured Fort Ticonderoga, the British garrison on Lake Champlain in northern New York. They commandeered the fort's heavy artillery, with plans to draw by sled the cannon east to Boston when snow fell the next winter.

George Washington, *by James Peale. In choosing Washington as commander-in-chief, the Continental Congress selected a revolutionary dedicated to republican government. His perseverance and leadership kept the army together despite battlefield reverses and lack of supplies.*

The Second Continental Congress

On May 10, 1775, the day after Allen's victory at Ticonderoga, the Second Continental Congress met in Philadelphia. While the delegates remained unwilling to support independence, they were disappointed by Parliament's refusal to change its course. They faced the prospect of executing a war already in progress, convinced that British troops had fired the first shots and committed atrocities. Congress moved slowly to ensure that all of the colonies backed the war, that it was America's effort, not just New England's. The delegates also wanted Congress to control the military, so to serve both purposes, they appointed George Washington of Virginia as commander-in-chief of the Continental army. Designating a southerner to head the military, which in June 1775 consisted of New Eng-

landers, broadened the appeal of the Massachusetts cause. At the same time, Washington was himself a delegate to Congress and steadfastly committed to civilian control of the armed forces. Despite his limited military experience, and early failures in the field, Washington proved to be an excellent choice. Indeed, for many he became the symbol of the American cause. His military bearing, determination, dignity, physical stamina, and ability to learn from his mistakes suited his role as commander-in-chief.

To serve under Washington, Congress appointed thirteen generals. Its four major generals were Artemas Ward of Massachusetts, the less than energetic commander of the troops surrounding Boston; Philip Schuyler of New York; Israel Putnam of Connecticut; and Charles Lee, a veteran officer of the British army

and recent immigrant to Virginia. The adjutant general was Horatio Gates, also a veteran British officer and Virginia planter. The brigadier generals included seven New Englanders and one New Yorker, reflecting the regional origins of men in arms at that time.

"An Open and Avowed Rebellion"

Before Washington could arrive in Massachusetts, his troops engaged in the Battle of Bunker Hill. Learning that the British planned to seize the hills overlooking Boston, a detachment of the patriot army began to fortify the Charlestown heights. By mistake, the men built defenses on Breed's Hill rather than on the higher and less exposed Bunker Hill. This lapse might

Battle of Bunker Hill *(1786) by John Trumbull of Connecticut, who had fought for American independence. This is one of a series of paintings by Trumbull on the Revolution.*

have isolated the detachment from the rest of the army had the British moved more quickly. Instead of attacking immediately, however, General Gage and the man who would soon replace him as commander of British forces, William Howe, foolishly allowed the Americans to complete their fortifications and obtain reinforcements. The British regulars lined up in proper European formation to storm Breed's Hill. Boston residents climbed to their roofs to watch. While the redcoats shot as they advanced up the hill—to little effect—the patriots waited until the enemy was within range of their guns. The Americans refused to engage the British in standard European warfare. The redcoats failed on their first two assaults, losing many officers and troops, then with reinforcements took the hill when the Americans' ammunition gave out. The patriots retreated, pounded by artillery from British ships. While the British won the battle, their losses were staggering, as over 40 percent of their combatants were killed or wounded.

During the year following Bunker Hill, while the British and American governments moved toward the ultimate break, many colonists became whigs. The lives lost on battlefields in eastern Massachusetts undercut advocates of restraint. Still, given opposition from many delegates, the Continental Congress could not declare independence. During the summer of 1775, Congress pursued two strategies: It asked the king for peace while preparing for war. In July, it approved a petition to George III, called the Olive Branch Petition, asking that he resolve their dispute with Parliament. Upon receipt of the petition in August, outraged by the colonists' armed resistance, the king proclaimed the thirteen provinces in "an open and avowed rebellion." In December, Parliament cut off all trade with the colonies, making American ships and any vessels engaging in commerce with the mutinous provinces subject to confiscation. For many Americans, these actions proved that the British government meant to crush the colonies militarily and economically. For militant whigs, there was no turning back.

The Continental Congress further alienated the British by ordering General Philip Schuyler to invade Canada. The congressmen hoped to make Canada the fourteenth British colony in rebellion. They expected to obtain help from French Canadians and perhaps even France itself, but even more, they wanted to prevent a northern attack. The American invasion of Canada was a failure from the start. Schuyler, suffering

from illness and indecision, assembled troops and provisions too slowly, wasting valuable summer days. In September, much too late, Brigadier General Richard Montgomery took charge and moved the army north via Lake Champlain, but as Montgomery said, a "winter Campaign in Canada! Posterity won't believe it!" Compounding this mistake, the enlistments of many of the soldiers would expire at the end of the year.

Concurrently, Washington dispatched a small army under Benedict Arnold and Daniel Morgan, two talented officers, over a rugged route through Maine. Their march took so much longer than predicted that the men had to eat their dogs and soap. When the combined American forces finally attacked Quebec in a blinding December snowstorm, they were defeated with heavy casualties, including Montgomery dead and Arnold wounded. The army remained in Canada until May 1776 when British reinforcements arrived, pushing the patriots back into New York. For Congress, the campaign was a tragic error. The thirteen colonies lost 5,000 troops to battle, desertion, and disease and an enormous amount of supplies, which would prove difficult to replace in coming months.

Taking Sides

The deepening conflict forced colonists to decide whether or not to support the revolutionary whigs. Some people remained neutral, either because they cared little about the issues involved or because, like the pacifist Quakers, they were opposed to violence on religious grounds. Loyalists rejected the Revolution for a variety of motives. Some, out of principle, believed that the king and Parliament were right, or at least had reason to expect the colonists to pay their share toward imperial administration. During the course of the war, about 80,000 loyalists departed for Britain or other British colonies. Many more, numbering perhaps several hundred thousand, continued to live among their patriot neighbors. Tories included Crown officials, Anglican clergy, and merchants with close ties to Britain. Some of the best known loyalists were wealthy gentlemen and officeholders: Governor Thomas Hutchinson and Chief Justice Peter Oliver of Massachusetts; Joseph Galloway, speaker of the Pennsylvania Assembly; and Frederick Philipse, landlord of a 50,000-acre manor in New York, whose tenants reported him as a tory to the whig authorities.

Many tories were not rich or intimately tied to Great Britain, for the Revolution became a power struggle within American society, not just one between the colonies and London. The tenants of New York manors, for example, took the opposite side of their landlords. Thus, residents of Frederick Philipse's manors became whigs, while tenants of the patriot Livingstons and Schuylers supported the British. In Maryland, the loyalists gained widespread backing in Eastern Shore counties where farmers, suffering from economic decline and lack of political power, regarded the patriot elite as their enemies. The South Carolina backcountry divided along lines drawn during the 1760s, with the more affluent former Regulators supporting the whigs, and their opponents, the "lower sort," casting their lot with the British.

Of considerable concern to white Americans, especially those living in the south, were the loyalties of enslaved African Americans. Of the 2.5 million people in the thirteen colonies in 1775, about 500,000 were blacks, most living in the Chesapeake and Lower South. As the rhetoric of revolution reached African American slaves, increasing numbers escaped. On Maryland's Eastern Shore, loyalist whites made common cause with the bondpeople of whig planters: In fall 1775, a Dorchester County committee reported that "the insolence of the Negroes in this county is come to such a height, that we are under a necessity of disarming them which we effected on Saturday last. We took about eighty guns, some bayonets, swords, etc. The malicious and imprudent speeches of some among the lower classes of whites have induced them to believe that their freedom depended on the success of the King's troops."

A chief source of unrest, the patriots believed, was the November 1775 proclamation of Lord Dunmore, royal governor of Virginia, declaring "all indented [sic] servants, Negroes, or others [owned by rebels] free, that are able and willing to bear arms, they joining His Majesty's Troops." Whigs considered this proclamation foul play, an attempt to start an insurrection. They increased slave patrols, tried to convince blacks that the British would sell them to West Indies planters, and warned of harsh punishments to those who ran away or took up arms against their masters. The penalty for slave rebellion, of course, was death. Nevertheless, African Americans aided the British by joining the army and employing their firsthand knowledge of Chesapeake Bay. Some served as pilots along its tribu-

Baron Ludwig von Closen's sketch of American army uniforms reflects the military role of African Americans.

taries, while others delivered fresh provisions to the British ships by foraging plantations at night.

African Americans also supported the Revolution, but received little welcome from the whigs. As the Americans created an army from volunteer forces besieging Boston, they excluded slaves and even free blacks from participating. From 1775 through much of 1776, when white enlistments seemed adequate, the patriot leaders, many of them slaveowners, were unwilling to exchange freedom for military service. Whites feared the results of arming slaves. By 1777, however, when recruiters found it difficult to fill their quotas, the states north of Virginia began accepting free blacks and slaves. Officially, Virginia took only free African Americans, but some masters sent slaves as substitutes for themselves. An estimated 5,000 African Americans served in the Continental army and state militias or at sea on American privateers. They fought side by side with whites, not in segregated units. At the end of their service, many but not all of the enslaved African Americans who fought for indepen-

dence received freedom. Some masters who had pledged liberty to their slaves if they served as substitutes broke the promises after the war.

Estimates of the total number of Americans who joined the whig forces range from 100,000 to 250,000. Because most signed up for tours of duty lasting several months or a year, not for the duration of the war, the exact number of troops is impossible to determine. An ardent Boston patriot, for example, a poor shoemaker named George Robert Twelves Hewes, served at least six different stints for a total of twenty months. Ordinary people like Hewes did their best to support both the patriotic cause and their families. Thus, Washington and his generals constantly faced the problem of expiring enlistments, a condition that severely hampered execution of the war. The inability of Congress to pay soldiers adequately also hindered recruitment and retention of troops. As time went on, the American troops became more professional, better trained, and disciplined, but originated from less privileged rungs of society. By 1778, most of

Deborah Sampson, *by Joseph Stone, 1797. After the Revolution, Sampson gave public lectures about how she disguised herself as a man and enlisted in the Continental Army.*

the states had to adopt conscription to fill their quotas. Men were drafted by lottery, but could pay a fine or hire a substitute, loopholes that contributed to disproportionate service by the poor.

Women took part in the American war effort by operating farms and businesses in their husbands' absence, defending their homes and families against marauding enemy soldiers, supplying food and clothing for the troops, and joining the army. Perhaps several hundred women put on uniforms to become soldiers. These troops included Deborah Sampson of Massachusetts, who enlisted under the name Robert Shurtleff. She fought in battle, but was discovered when she received a wound; after the war she collected an army pension. Another took the name of Samuel Gay, attained the rank of corporal, then according to the record was "discharged, being a woman, dressed in men's clothes. August 1777." Others performed unofficial short-term service as spies. The most substantial contribution of women to the American military was that of the Women of the Army, as George Washing-

ton called them. Numbering perhaps 20,000 over the course of the war, they served as nurses, cooks, laundresses, and water carriers. They were regular members of the army who drew rations and were subject to military discipline. Some saw action in battle, particularly women in artillery crews who carried water to swab out the cannon after each firing. The story of "Molly Pitcher" evolved from women like Mary Hayes of Carlisle, Pennsylvania, who took the place of fallen soldiers.

Independence and Confederation

During the winter and spring of 1776, fighting continued between Great Britain and the thirteen colonies. Though the Canada campaign was a disaster, the Americans gained success in their siege of Boston. They sledged the heavy guns from Fort Ticonderoga about 300 miles, installing them in March 1776 on the Dorchester Heights. Instead of storming the artillery, the British withdrew from the city, sailing to Nova Scotia in preparation for an invasion of New York City, which General William Howe considered a more central location for defeating the rebels. About a thousand tories left Boston with Howe's troops, a pattern that was repeated in British evacuations throughout the war.

In 1776, London undertook a huge effort to put down the revolt. It sent across the Atlantic Ocean 370 transports with supplies and 32,000 troops, of whom many were German mercenaries (called Hessians because the largest proportion came from the principality of Hesse-Cassel). The British intended these soldiers to join William Howe's 10,000 troops from Nova Scotia, take New York City, and destroy Washington's army. The British navy, with seventy-three warships and 13,000 sailors in American waters, would bombard seaports and play havoc on colonial shipping. The British expected considerable assistance from the loyalists.

As the British military descended upon New York in midsummer 1776, the Continental Congress finally declared independence. The force of events propelled most moderate delegates to cast their vote for a complete break. In January 1776, Thomas Paine, a recent immigrant from England, had published *Common Sense.* Though his arguments were familiar to Congress and readers of political tracts, Paine convinced the American public of the need for independence.

Thomas Paine, *by John Wesley Jarvis. A superb propagandist, the recent English immigrant convinced many Americans, "'tis time to part"—to declare independence.*

Common Sense sold over 100,000 copies within a few months, reaching hundreds of thousands of people as copies changed hands and nonreaders listened to Paine's words read aloud. An equivalent press run in the United States today would be over 12 million copies. In Philadelphia, according to a report, the tract was "read to all ranks." Paine used language that appealed to ordinary Protestant Americans, employing biblical arguments that churchgoing farmers and craftspeople could appreciate, and avoiding Latin phrases and classical references known only to well-educated elites. He wanted to demonstrate that the time for compromise had passed, that the proper course was to shed the British monarchy and aristocracy to create an American republic. "We have it in our power to begin the world over again . . . ," he wrote, "the birthday of a new world is at hand." The bloodshed that began at Lexington justified rejection of the king: "No man was a warmer wisher for a reconciliation than myself, before the fatal nineteenth of

April, 1775, but the moment the event of that day was made known, I rejected the hardened, sullen-tempered Pharaoh of England for ever; and disdain the wretch, that with the pretended title of Father of his People can unfeelingly hear of their slaughter, and composedly sleep with their blood upon his soul." Pragmatically, Paine argued that the colonists must break their ties with London if they expected aid from France and Spain. He pointed out the importance of American exports, which "will always have a market while eating is the custom in Europe." He exclaimed, "'TIS TIME TO PART . . . there is something very absurd, in supposing a continent to be perpetually governed by an island."

Through the spring of 1776, sentiment for independence increased. News that the British had engaged German mercenaries heated the debate. The provincial assemblies of Georgia, South Carolina, and North Carolina gave their delegates in Congress permission to support the break, while Rhode Island declared independence on its own. Virginia proposed that Congress separate from Britain, taking measures "for forming foreign alliances and a confederation of the colonies." But in June, the New York, Pennsylvania, Delaware, and Maryland assemblies, controlled by moderate factions that feared a radicalization of politics, were still not ready to condone a split. Nevertheless, Congress appointed a committee to draft the Declaration of Independence, of which Thomas Jefferson, a wealthy thirty-three-year-old Virginia planter and lawyer, was the principal author. A graduate of the College of William and Mary and a serious intellectual, he had been an active opponent of British policies since first elected to the Virginia assembly in 1769.

The Declaration set forth Congress's reasons for separating from the government of George III; the revolutionaries focused on the king's offenses because they had already denied the sovereignty of Parliament. It held "these truths to be self-evident: That all men are created equal; that they are endowed by their Creator with certain unalienable rights; that among these are life, liberty, and the pursuit of happiness." (See the Appendix for full text.) Employing the philosophy of John Locke and other Enlightenment writers, Jefferson continued, "that, to secure these rights, governments are instituted among men, deriving their just powers from the consent of the governed; that whenever any form of government becomes destructive of these ends, it is the right of the people to alter or to

In this painting, The Declaration of Independence *by John Trumbull, the drafting committee stands at center: from left to right, John Adams, Roger Sherman, Robert Livingston, Thomas Jefferson, and Benjamin Franklin.*

abolish it, and to institute new government." Congress placed the blame for the breach on the king, on his attempt to establish "an absolute tyranny" over the colonies. It listed his misdeeds: refusing to approve necessary laws passed by the colonial assemblies, dissolving legislatures and courts, stationing a standing army, interrupting trade, and imposing taxes without colonial consent. Most recently, Congress announced to the world, George III had declared "us out of his protection and wag[ed] war against us. He has plundered our seas, ravaged our coasts, burned our towns, and destroyed the lives of our people. He is at this time transporting large armies of foreign mercenaries to complete the works of death, desolation, and tyranny already begun." In reference to Lord Dunmore's proclamation, the congressmen accused the king of exciting "domestic insurrection among us." For these reasons and more, Congress declared the thirteen colonies, now to be called the United States of America, "free and independent states" having "full power to levy war, conclude peace, contract alliances, establish commerce, and do all other acts and things which independent states may of right do."

On July 2, 1776, all delegations to Congress approved independence except New York's, which had not received new instructions so was forced to abstain. Completing revisions two days later, Congress adopted the Declaration. For many Americans, independence ended the problem of fighting a government that they continued to recognize as sovereign. When the Continental troops heard the Declaration read on July 9, they cheered, as did civilians throughout the states. However, the battles to defend this independence still lay ahead. General Washington cautioned "every officer and soldier . . . that now the peace and safety of his Country depends (under God) solely on the success of our arms."

To mount sufficient military force to win the war, the states needed unity. In mid-July 1776, Congress began debating the Articles of Confederation, a plan for permanent union, which it approved and sent to the states for ratification over a year later. The chief disagreement among the congressmen was one that remained central to American politics for two centuries, the power of the national government versus that of individual states. The Articles permitted less central-

ized authority than would the Constitution, which was drafted a decade later. Under the Articles, Congress had responsibility to conduct foreign affairs, make war and peace, deal with Native Americans residing outside the states, coin and borrow money, supervise the post office, and negotiate boundary disputes between states. The "United States" meant thirteen sovereign states joined together by a Congress with specific functions. Article 1 established the "confederacy" to be called the United States of America, not a sovereign nation. Article 2 held that "each State retains its sovereignty, freedom and independence, and every power, jurisdiction, and right, which is not by this confederation expressly delegated to the United States, in Congress assembled." The Congress could neither tax nor raise troops, but could only assess quotas on the states, a serious disadvantage in time of war. Even so, the Articles failed ratification until 1781, when the last of the thirteen states finally approved. Conflict over state claims on western lands held up ratification. In the meantime, Congress attempted to govern within the limits of the unratified Articles, but its inability to raise revenue and draft troops obstructed the American war effort, creating huge shortages of supplies and men.

WAR IN THE NORTH, 1776–1779

For the American patriots, the Revolution was a defensive war. It lasted eight years, from 1775 to 1783, longer than any other in United States history until the Vietnam War. The Continental army was often outmatched, for it remained smaller than General Washington wanted; his troops constantly needed training as veterans left and new recruits arrived. But as the theater of war moved from one region to another, American generals obtained reinforcements from state militias and local volunteers, as men rose to defend their territory. The British, despite considerable assistance from tories, lacked enough reserves to subdue the rebellious North American seaboard. The sheer expanse of the thirteen states and the 3,000-mile distance from England made the British army's task extremely difficult, despite its formal training and Britain's larger population and wealth.

Invasions of New York

To conquer New York, and thus divide New England from the rest of the states, in July 1776, British troops landed on Staten Island. In August, they attacked Washington's army at Brooklyn Heights. The redcoats defeated the Americans badly, pushing them back to Manhattan Island, and then to White Plains. Still, in this series of advances, General William Howe and his brother, Admiral Richard Howe, missed one opportunity after another to deal the blow that might have won the war in 1776. They failed to take advantage of Washington's mistakes, which could have allowed them to surround his troops. In November, however, the British did hand Washington a humiliating defeat by capturing the 2,900 defenders of Manhattan's Fort Washington.

The Continental army retreated across New Jersey with the British and German allies at its heels. The patriots crossed the Delaware River into Pennsylvania, allowing the British to occupy New Jersey towns. The Howes gathered tory support by offering a pardon to anyone who would take a loyalty oath within sixty days. For the whigs, as Thomas Paine wrote, these were "times that try men's souls." The army was in retreat, the New Jersey government had dispersed, and citizens who were skeptical of Washington's abilities rallied to the British. Even Congress, afraid that Howe could easily take the capital, fled Philadelphia for Baltimore.

Before the end of the year, however, fortunes changed. British and Hessian plundering across New Jersey turned indifferent farmers into radical whigs, who became guerrilas, ambushing the enemy and stealing supplies. Meanwhile, Washington devised a plan that bought him time, acting before the enlistments of a large proportion of his army would expire on December 31. He attacked 1,400 Hessians at Trenton on Christmas night, in the midst of a winter storm. Taking the enemy by surprise, the Americans captured more than 900 men. In early January, Washington took the offensive once again, having convinced many of his soldiers to extend their terms for six weeks. Pennsylvania and New Jersey militia, inspired by the victory at Trenton, reinforced his troops. Washington eluded a superior British army under Lord Cornwallis, then defeated a smaller force at Princeton. General Howe withdrew most of his army to New York, leaving troops in just two eastern New Jersey towns. Though Washington's army shrank as

BRITISH NORTH AMERICA (CANADA)

Montreal

St. Lawrence R.

ST. LEGER

Lake Champlain

BURGOYNE

MAINE (Massachusetts)

Fort Ticonderoga July 5, 1777

Hudson R.

Lake George

Lake Ontario

Fort Oswego

Fort Stanwix Aug. 23, 1777

ARNOLD

Fort Edward

NEW HAMPSHIRE

Oriskany Aug. 6, 1777 (victory contested)

Mohawk R.

Saratoga Oct. 17, 1777

GATES

NEW YORK

Albany

MASSACHUSETTS

Boston

CONNECTICUT

RHODE ISLAND

White Plains

Morristown

New York

LONG ISLAND

PENNSYLVANIA

Delaware R.

Princeton

Trenton

Brandywine Creek Sept. 11, 1777

Philadelphia

York

NEW JERSEY

MARYLAND

HOWE

DELAWARE

Chesapeake Bay

VIRGINIA

ATLANTIC OCEAN

Legend:
✕ British victories
✕ American victories

British troop movements
1776   1777   1778

American troop movements
1776   1777   1778

Inset map:

NEW YORK

Hudson R.

Delaware R.

Morristown Winter quarters, Jan.–May, 1777

WASHINGTON

MANHATTAN ISLAND

New York

White Plains Oct. 28, 1776

LONG ISLAND

CORNWALLIS

Brooklyn Heights Aug. 27, 1776

PENNSYLVANIA

Princeton Jan. 3, 1777

WASHINGTON

STATEN ISLAND

Valley Forge Winter quarters, 1777–78

WASHINGTON

Trenton Dec. 26, 1776

Monmouth Court House June 28, 1778

Brandywine

CLINTON

Brandywine Creek Sept. 11, 1777

Philadelphia

NEW JERSEY

ATLANTIC OCEAN

DELAWARE

0   25   50 miles
0   25   50 kilometers

MAP 5.2 | NORTHERN CAMPAIGNS, 1776-1778

Battle of Princeton, *1777, painted by William Mercer ten years later. The battles at Trenton and Princeton, New Jersey, renewed hope for the Patriot cause.*

militia units returned home and enlistments of Continental soldiers expired, it had demonstrated its ability to win. In the words of one British officer, the Americans had "become a formidable enemy."

In 1777, as the British made plans to suppress the rebellion once and for all, their strategy for the upcoming campaign became confused. William Howe intended to take Philadelphia, not by crossing New Jersey, but by means of his brother's fleet. At the same time, London organized an invasion from Canada, to win back Fort Ticonderoga and divide the states. The campaigns were not coordinated and neither commenced before June, when British General "Gentleman Johnny" Burgoyne led his force of over 7,000 British regulars, German mercenaries, Native Americans, and Canadians by boat down Lake Champlain. True to his reputation, Burgoyne overburdened his troops with baggage, including thirty cartloads of personal clothing and champagne. Burgoyne easily took Fort Ticonderoga, then headed for Albany. The American forces under Philip Schuyler felled trees and rolled boulders into the path of Burgoyne's heavy column. Covering twenty-three miles of terrain that was difficult even without American sabotage took the British army twenty-four days. Short on supplies and

horses, Burgoyne sent 800 troops to Bennington, Vermont, where General John Stark and his militia ambushed them by pretending to be tories. Reinforcements under British officer Barry St. Leger returned to Canada when they heard that Benedict Arnold was headed west to intercept them. The rebel forces, on the other hand, burgeoned with volunteers as British soldiers pillaged the countryside. In September, near Saratoga, Burgoyne encountered the American army under General Horatio Gates, who had replaced Schuyler. The Americans surrounded the enemy, firing upon them day and night. Burgoyne sent for help from New York City, but Howe had long since sailed with most of his troops to Philadelphia. Burgoyne's 5,800-man army thus surrendered at Saratoga on October 17, 1777.

The British Occupy Philadelphia

As Burgoyne marched toward disaster in New York, General Howe more successfully reached Philadelphia. Still, his campaign fell short of triumph. In July, his 13,000 soldiers departed from New York City aboard a fleet of 260 ships, but instead of disembarking

within a week along the Delaware River, they sailed south to the Virginia capes then up the Chesapeake Bay to Head of Elk. Their voyage lasted over a month, costing Howe valuable time that might have permitted him to assist Burgoyne. Washington tried unsuccessfully, with an army of 11,000 at Brandywine, to block Howe's advance through southeastern Pennsylvania. The British occupied Philadelphia, dividing their forces between Germantown and the capital. On October 4, 1777, Washington attacked the British encampment at Germantown, inflicting serious damage though he was once again defeated. Elizabeth Drinker, a Quaker resident of Philadelphia, in her diary reported significant losses on both sides. She wrote, "this has been a sorrowful day at Philadelphia and much more so at Germantown and thereabouts." She recorded news of the Continental army's movements, fearing that the troops would carry the battle to her city. "The apprehensions of their entering," she believed, "will render this night grievous to many." Washington did not attack Philadelphia, so the enemy retained control of the capital until they withdrew the next June.

Even so, in 1777, the British had failed to put down the American rebellion during yet another season of war. Upon hearing that Burgoyne's army had surrendered, the Howe brothers resigned. General Henry Clinton, who had repeatedly advocated a more forceful execution of the war, became the new commander of British forces in North America. The redcoats wintered in relative comfort at Philadelphia while Washington's troops nearly starved and froze to death at Valley Forge, to the west of the city. In February 1778, Continental soldiers lacked adequate clothing and received just three pounds of bread and three ounces of meat to last a week. Some ate only "fire cakes," baked from a paste of flour and water. Nevertheless, they became a disciplined army at Valley Forge, under the Prussian officer Baron von Steuben, who rigorously trained the Americans in the European art of war.

Alliance with France

While February 1778 brought despair to the Americans, it also brought hope—in the form of an alliance with France. Already supporting the United States with economic and military assistance, the French government hoped to recoup the international status it had lost during the Seven Years' War. Convinced by the victory at Saratoga that the former colonies could win the war, the French signed two pacts with the United States. The first was the Treaty of Amity and Commerce, in which France recognized American independence and both nations pledged "a firm, inviolable and universal peace" and most-favored-nation status in each other's ports. The second was the military Treaty of Alliance, in which they agreed to fight Great Britain jointly until the Americans had won independence, pledged not to negotiate a separate peace, and confirmed their defensive alliance "forever." France renounced claims to its former colonies in North America, but could retain any of the British West Indies that it conquered.

In supporting the Americans, the French renewed their long struggle with Great Britain that had been suspended in 1763. France's entry widened the war, placing greater focus on the West Indies, whose sugar production made them more valuable than the North American mainland to the British. The following year, Spain allied with France, but refused to recognize or assist the American insurgents beyond providing limited financial aid. Unlike France, which denied interest in North America, the Spanish viewed the Americans as potentially dangerous competitors.

The Wartime Economy

Despite France's economic assistance of over $8 million and Spain's smaller contribution of about $600,000, the United States had grave economic problems during the war. The loss of British markets devastated farmers, merchants, and fishermen, as the embargo closed crucial ports in the West Indies and British Isles. The Royal Navy attempted to prevent colonial trade with other nations; it attacked and blockaded American harbors and ravaged ships at sea. On land, the armies laid waste to farms and towns, confiscating livestock, crops, and supplies.

For Congress, the chief economic problem was paying for the war. Without the power to tax, it printed money, a total of almost $200 million in paper bills by 1779. The states printed a similar amount, despite their ability to tax, primarily because printing money was easier than trying to collect revenues from a financially strapped populace. Unfortunately, as the war continued year after year, the demand for military equipment, food, medical supplies, clothing, and sol-

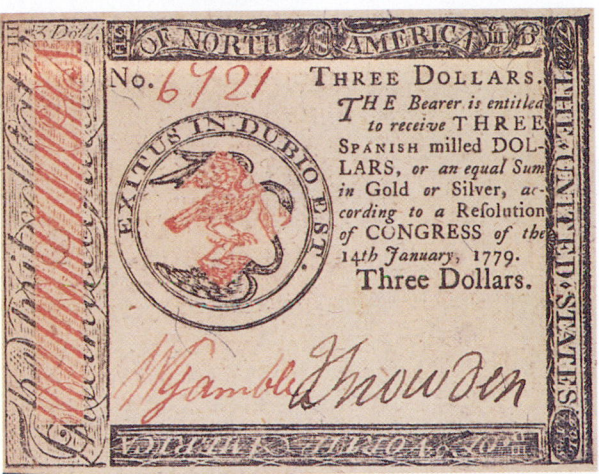

Continental currency depreciated in value as Congress attempted to fund the war with paper money.

diers' wages persisted. This extraordinary demand for provisions coupled with the continuing emission of paper money sent prices soaring. By 1779, the paper money was nearly worthless, inspiring the slogan "not worth a Continental." Pennsylvania and neighboring states were hardest hit by inflation because most military activity took place there from 1776 to 1779.

The depreciation of currency resulted in popular unrest in the American capital, as a group of Philadelphia militia in 1779 demanded a more equitable military draft and regulation of food prices. They were angry that the burden of militia service fell disproportionately on the poor because others could pay fines to avoid the draft. At the same time, the prices of food and firewood skyrocketed. In just two months, August and September 1779, the price of beef, flour, and molasses rose by more than 80 percent. The protesters, according to one broadside posted along the streets, blamed "a few overbearing Merchants, a swarm of Monopolizers and Speculators, an infernal gang of Tories" for the spiraling costs.

In what has been called the "Fort Wilson Incident," armed members of the Philadelphia militia met at Burns's Tavern on October 4, planning to capture and exile from the city four suspected tories. Several hundred militiamen marched their prisoners through the streets to the fife and drum of the Rogue's March, ordinarily played by the military when a soldier was discharged dishonorably. The militia was ridiculing the reputed tories, all four of them wealthy citizens. When rumors raced through the capital that the militia planned to arrest others, about thirty gentlemen who thought they might be targets armed themselves and gathered at the house of lawyer James Wilson. Though a member of Congress, Wilson, like other conservative whig leaders, was suspect because he opposed price regulation. The militia marched past "Fort Wilson," gave three cheers, then shots rang out. Though it is unknown who shot first, both sides subsequently exchanged fire. After cavalry broke up the battle, six people lay dead and seventeen wounded, the majority of them militia.

The Fort Wilson Incident terrified many people because lower-class patriots had directed armed force against the whig elite, protesting the policies of their own government. Henry Laurens, a wealthy South Carolina merchant and member of the Continental Congress, thought the events of October 4 were ominous. He wrote, "we are at this moment on a precipice, and what I have long dreaded and often intimated to my friends, seems to be breaking forth—a convulsion among the people."

THE WAR MOVES WEST AND SOUTH

The failure of the British army to defeat Washington's troops and entry of France into the war led the imperial government to rethink its military strategy. Protection of Caribbean sugar islands from the French navy gained top priority. With redeployment of forces to the West Indies, British General Clinton had to consolidate his army, so in June 1778, he pulled his occupation forces out of Philadelphia, marching across New Jersey toward New York. Washington's army caught up with Clinton at Monmouth Courthouse, where the battle, fought in traditional European style, was indecisive. The British escaped to New York.

The Frontier War

In the west, from New York to Georgia, fighting devastated the backcountry. The Native Americans had not expected the conflict between the American provinces and Great Britain since, as recently as 1774, the whites had cooperated to defeat, in Lord

Dunmore's War, a coalition of militant Delawares, Shawnees, and Iroquois for Kentucky. When the Revolution broke out, many Indians supported the British, who still held garrisons in the west and had more gunpowder and provisions than the patriots. Yet Native Americans responded in various ways to "this dispute between two brothers," as neutral Iroquois called the Revolution in 1775. "The quarrel seems to be unnatural," they said; "you are two brothers of one blood." Just as colonists divided among radical whigs, tories, and neutrals, so did the Native Americans, even within some tribes, separate into factions who favored the British or the Americans, or wanted to avoid any involvement. The militant Indians who sided with Great Britain considered the threat of white settlers crossing the Appalachians as most dangerous to their future. Many attempted to form pan-Indian alliances to fight their own wars of independence against land grabbers from the east. Over the course of the Revolution, the pro-British factions garnered strength from the neutral camp, the result of murders of noncombatants by white frontiersmen and Congress's failure to provide supplies.

Beginning in 1776, Indians attacked Anglo-Americans from the Georgia frontier to the Great Lakes. The Cherokees raided the southern backcountry and planned a major assault on Tennessee, but ran short of gunpowder and were defeated by whig militia in fall 1776. Many Cherokees, Choctaws, Creeks, Shawnees, Iroquois, and others did not give up, however, but rather planned in 1779 "a general invasion of the Frontiers" coordinated by Henry Hamilton, the British lieutenant governor of the Illinois country. George Rogers Clark, a surveyor, who the year before with about 175 frontier soldiers had captured Kaskaskia and Cahokia from the British, heard of plans for the Indian and British offensive. To Patrick Henry, he wrote, "the Case is Desperate but Sir we must Either Quit the Country or attack Mr. Hamilton." In 1779, with a small force, Clark assaulted Fort Vincennes, obtained the British surrender, captured supplies intended for the Indians, and sent Hamilton to a Virginia jail, thus ending the pan-Indian campaign.

Despite Clark's victory at Vincennes, the Kentucky-Ohio frontier remained embattled throughout the war. The same was true of Pennsylvania and New York, where after 1777 most Iroquois and Delawares abandoned their neutrality to ally with the British. In 1778 and 1779, Major John Butler, his son Captain Walter

Joseph Brant, *by Gilbert Stuart. The Mohawk leader, who was educated among whites and traveled to Great Britain in 1775, convinced many Iroquois to ally with the British.*

Butler, and the Mohawk leader Theyendanegea, also known as Joseph Brant, led tory and Native American forces against white settlements. Theyendanegea had visited England and believed that British help was needed to keep white Americans out of Indian lands. The loyalists and Iroquois burned houses, barns, fields, and orchards, ran off livestock, and killed or captured settlers over a swath of frontier ranging from fifty to a hundred miles wide. In summer 1779, General Washington sent General John Sullivan with 4,000 troops, who retaliated by burning Iroquois villages, orchards, and fields of corn. At Newtown, New York, in the one battle of the campaign, Sullivan defeated a contingent of about 700 loyalists and Indians. His scorched-earth policy seriously damaged most of the Iroquois towns; displaced Indians suffered through the winter of 1779–1780 on short rations. But the next spring, they renewed their raids, as the frontier remained aflame until the end of the war and after.

Because many Anglo-Americans had trouble distinguishing between Indian friends and foes, Native

Americans who allied with the United States or remained neutral throughout the war fared little better with the whigs than those who sided with the British. By 1781, for example, killings by Americans and loss of lands had driven most of the Coshocton Delawares of Ohio into the arms of the British. Then in March 1782, frontier militia massacred ninety-six pacifist Indian men, women, and children at the Moravian mission of Gnadenhutten, near Coshocton. More successful, the 500 surviving Catawbas of South Carolina, who lived on a reservation adjacent to white settlements, performed extensive service for the patriots. They searched for loyalists and escaped slaves, supplied food to the rebels, fought the Cherokees in 1776, and battled the British, who destroyed their village in retaliation. After the war, the South Carolina assembly compensated the Catawbas for their loyalty and livestock, refusing to abet the governor's plan to lease out their reservation. The Mahicans of Stockbridge in western Massachusetts were less fortunate after fighting in the American army, for they returned home to find that whites had taken over their town.

The Southern Campaigns

While the Revolution ravaged the frontier, the main theater of war remained east of the Appalachians, where in 1778, the British inaugurated a new strategy. Retaining troops in New York City, they invaded the south, counting on loyalist support in Georgia, the Carolinas, and Virginia to restore colonial governments to the Crown. The British also expected the large numbers of enslaved African Americans in the south to weaken the patriots' defenses. In November 1778, General Clinton sent 3,500 troops under Lieutenant Colonel

MAP 5.3   SOUTHERN CAMPAIGNS, 1778–1781

Archibald Campbell to Georgia, where they joined 2,000 soldiers from Florida. They captured Savannah and Augusta, but had trouble conquering the backcountry. Then, with 10,000 troops, the British turned to Charleston, where in May 1780 they compelled the American general Benjamin Lincoln to surrender 5,500 men, the most serious U.S. loss during the Revolution. The British fanned out through South Carolina, as many residents pledged their loyalty to the

THE NARRATIVE OF MARY JEMISON, 1775–1779

Mary Jemison was a white woman who had been captured by Indians and spent most of her life among the Senecas. Her journal provides the view of an Iroquois woman, as her adopted people tried to maintain neutrality during the Revolution. But they became embroiled in the war and lost their villages and stocks of food when the American general John Sullivan conducted his scorched earth policy.

Thus, at peace amongst themselves, and with the neighboring whites, though there were none at that time very near, our Indians lived quietly and peaceably at home, till a little before the breaking out of the revolutionary war, when they were sent for, together with the Chiefs and members of the Six Nations generally, by the people of the States, to go to the German Flats, and there hold a general council, in order that the people of the states might ascertain, in good season, who they should esteem and treat as enemies, and who as friends, in the great war which was then upon the point of breaking out between them and the King of England.

Our Indians obeyed the call, and the council was holden, at which the pipe of peace was smoked, and a treaty made, in which the Six Nations solemnly agreed that if a war should eventually break out, they would not take up arms on either side; but that they would observe a strict neutrality. . . .

About a year passed off, and we, as usual, were enjoying ourselves in the employments of peaceable times, when a messenger arrived from the British Commissioners, requesting all the Indians of our tribe to attend a general council which was soon to be held at Oswego. The council convened, and being opened, the British Commissioners informed the Chiefs that the object of calling a council of the Six Nations, was, to engage their assistance in subduing the rebels, the people of the states, . . .

The Chiefs then arose, and informed the Commissioners of the nature and extent of the treaty which they had entered into with the people of the states, the year before, and that they should not violate it by taking up the hatchet against them.

The Commissioners continued their entreaties without success, till they addressed their avarice, by telling our people that the people of the states were few in number, and easily subdued; and that on the account of their disobedience to the King, they justly merited all the punishment that it was possible for white men and Indians to inflict upon them; and added, that the King was rich and powerful, both in money and subjects: That his rum was as plenty as the water in lake Ontario: that his men were as numerous as the sands upon the lake shore:—and that the Indians, if they would assist in the war, and persevere in their friendship to the King, till it was closed, should never want for money or goods. Upon this the Chiefs concluded a treaty with the British Commissioners, in

which they agreed to take up arms against the rebels, and continue in the service of his Majesty till they were subdued, in consideration of certain conditions which were stipulated in the treaty to be performed by the British government and its agents.

As soon as the treaty was finished, the Commissioners made a present to each Indian of a suit of clothes, a brass kettle, a gun and tomahawk, a scalping knife, a quantity of powder and lead, a piece of gold, and promised a bounty on every scalp that should be brought in. Thus richly clad and equipped, they returned home, after an absence of about two weeks, full of the fire of war, and anxious to encounter their enemies. Many of the kettles which the Indians received at that time are now in use on the Genesee Flats. . . .

Previous to the battle at Fort Stanwix, the British sent for the Indians to come and see them whip the rebels; and, at the same time stated that they did not wish to have them fight, but wanted to have them just sit down, smoke their pipes, and look on. Our Indians went, to a man; but contrary to their expectation, instead of smoking and looking on, they were obliged to fight for their lives, and in the end of the battle were completely beaten, with a great loss in killed and wounded. Our Indians alone had thirty-six killed, and a great number wounded. Our town exhibited a scene of real sorrow and distress, when our warriors returned and recounted their misfortunes, and stated the real loss they had sustained in the engagement. The mourning was excessive, and was expressed by the most doleful yells, shrieks, and howlings, and by inimitable gesticulations. . . .

In one or two days after the skirmish at Connissius lake, Sullivan and his army arrived at Genesee river, where they destroyed every article of the food kind that they could lay their hands on. A part of our corn they burnt, and threw the remainder into the river. They burnt our houses, killed what few cattle and horses they could find, destroyed our fruit trees, and left nothing but the bare soil and timber. But the Indians had eloped and were not to be found.

Having crossed and recrossed the river, and finished the work of destruction, the army marched off to the east. Our Indians saw them move off, but suspecting that it was Sullivan's intention to watch our return, and then to take us by surprise, resolved that the main body of our tribe should hunt where we then were, till Sullivan had gone so far that there would be no danger of his returning to molest us. . . .

The weather by this time had become cold and stormy; and as we were destitute of houses and food too, I immediately resolved to take my children and look out for myself, without delay. With this intention I took two of my little ones on my back, bade the other three follow, and the same night arrived on the Gardow flats, where I have ever since resided. . . .

. . . The snow fell about five feet deep, and remained so for a long time, and the weather was extremely cold; so much so indeed, that almost all the game upon which the Indians depended for subsistence, perished, and reduced them almost to a state of starvation through that and three or four succeeding years.

king. In July 1780, General Horatio Gates arrived to build a new southern army. Disaster struck once again, when Gates placed too much responsibility on untrained militia in action against Lord Cornwallis at Camden. The battle was a rout, because even the regular Continentals were dispersed, and Gates—the hero of Saratoga—was disgraced.

The tide turned after General Nathanael Greene, the ex-Quaker from Rhode Island who had joined the American cause immediately after Concord, replaced Gates as commander of the southern army. The British contributed to the turnaround, as they became more insistent in demanding oaths of allegiance from Carolinians who preferred to keep out of the fray. This provoked a backlash, particularly because the British army stretched itself so thin that it withdrew protection from the people who took the oaths, thus exposing them to punishment by the whigs. The redcoats and tories also plundered, outraging many southerners

Nathanael Greene, *by Charles Willson Peale. A former Quaker, Greene used both guerrila tactics and formal military methods to wage his successful southern campaign.*

and pushing them into the American camp. Most notorious was Banastre Tarleton's Tory Legion, which executed prisoners of war and destroyed houses and fields, leaving many families homeless. "Bloody" Tarleton created new revolutionaries, who joined Greene's army or the smaller irregular brigades led by Thomas "The Gamecock" Sumter, Colonel Andrew Pickens, and Francis Marion, "the Swamp Fox." During 1780 and 1781, Greene rebuilt the southern army using both traditional and guerrila forces.

While not welcome as soldiers in South Carolina and Georgia, African American slaves, who comprised about 40 percent of the population, played an important role in the southern campaigns. Knowledgeable of the terrain, they acted as spies and counterspies for each side. One man, Antigua, received freedom by act of the South Carolina assembly for himself, his wife Hagar, and child in reward for "procuring information of the enemy's movements and designs." Throughout the south, African Americans provided much of the supporting labor for both armies, as they built fortifications, worked in lead mines, constructed and repaired roads, produced arms and ammunition, and drove wagons. American officers complained about the chronic shortage of black laborers, because whig slave-owners jealously guarded their strongest and most talented slaves to work on their plantations. Further, thousands of African Americans took advantage of General Clinton's 1779 proclamation offering freedom to those who joined the king's service. The slaves of loyalists, while subject to confiscation by the whig governments, were often taken by their masters behind British lines.

One practice of rebel leaders that highlighted their ability to dissociate their own fight for liberty from the plight of enslaved African Americans was to offer recruits enlistment "bounties" in slaves, much as other states promised bounties in land. In South Carolina, Thomas Sumter offered one African American bondman or woman to each private who would enlist for ten months. A colonel would receive three mature blacks and one child. The practice was adopted by Andrew Pickens as well, and supported by General Greene, who expected to pay the bounties from slaves confiscated from loyalist estates. Because sufficient numbers of African Americans owned by tories were lacking, regiments reported "pay" in arrears, some with grotesque precision. One payroll noted a deficit of 93 3/4 mature slaves and "Three Quarters of a Small Negro."

In fall 1780, Lord Cornwallis decided to head north, for while the British had destroyed two American armies and taken control of South Carolina and Georgia, the time had come to conquer the entire south. As his forces marched toward North Carolina, however, they met heavy resistance. In several battles, the conflict became a civil war, as Americans fought on both sides. In October 1780, just to the south of the state line at King's Mountain, whig frontier units defeated an enemy force, of which only Patrick Ferguson, the commander of the loyalists, was British. In January 1781, at Cowpens, an area where Carolinians grazed their cattle, General Daniel Morgan crushed Tarleton's Tory Legion by making the most of his sharpshooting frontiersmen. Morgan lined up the riflemen in front of his disciplined Continentals. The sharpshooters, who were untrained for sustained combat, fired several volleys at Tarleton's troops then withdrew to back up the regulars, who took the brunt of the fighting.

When Cornwallis learned that Tarleton's legion was lost, he chased the Americans into North Carolina, abandoning most of his equipment and supplies to move quickly. In March, Cornwallis met Greene at Guilford Courthouse, where the American general used Morgan's Cowpens tactics, though less effectively because his successive lines of irregulars and Continentals were spread too far apart. Though the battle ended indecisively, one-fourth of Cornwallis's troops lay wounded or dead. Having discarded tents, medical equipment, and food—and cut off from his base in South Carolina—the British general withdrew to the North Carolina coast where he sought naval support.

Meanwhile, Greene moved south to reconquer South Carolina and Georgia, where the British still had 8,000 men in arms. Because these troops were spread out in numerous towns and forts, Greene's 1,500 Continental soldiers and the guerrilla brigades of Sumter, Pickens, and Marion could pick off the garrisons one by one. Greene wrote to Washington in May 1781 that if the enemy "divide their force, they will fall by detachments, and if they operate collectively, they cannot command the country." By July, the Americans had pushed the redcoats and tories back to a narrow strip of territory between Charleston and Savannah, which the British held until their evacuation the next year. Despite initial disastrous defeats, the whigs prevailed in the Carolinas and Georgia by recruiting irregular forces and employing them strategically. The great sweep of territory controlled by the former thirteen colonies proved impossible for the British army to subdue.

Surrender of Lord Cornwallis, *by John Trumbull. Their loss at the Battle of Yorktown convinced the British that retaining the thirteen rebellious colonies was not worth the cost.*

Preliminary Peace Negotiations with Great Britain, *by Benjamin West. This unfinished portrait of the American diplomats includes, from left to right, John Jay, John Adams, Benjamin Franklin, Temple Franklin (Franklin's grandson who served as the commission's secretary), and Henry Laurens (who was not present to sign the final treaty).*

The surrender of Cornwallis at Yorktown in October 1781 effectively ended the war. The general had moved into Virginia, replacing Benedict Arnold as commander of the British forces there. Arnold, the former American officer, had turned traitor, joined the British army, and most recently captured Richmond. With an army of about 8,000 men, Cornwallis intended to concentrate British military efforts in Virginia, so requested more troops from New York. General Clinton refused. Their squabbling and delay allowed the Americans and French to surround by land and sea Cornwallis's camp on the Virginia peninsula. Several times before, the French forces had collaborated with the Americans, but their joint efforts had resulted in failure. This time, soldiers under the Comte de Rochambeau and French fleets commanded by the Comte de Grasse and Comte de Barras played a decisive role in defeating Cornwallis. Washington's army marched south from New York to join American and French troops assembled in Virginia. The operation was a marvel of military cooperation for the eighteenth century; it included even the construction of bake ovens outside New York City to camouflage Washington's departure. With 17,000 men and heavy artillery, the American and French forces won the British surrender, finally placing the seal on American independence.

The Peace Settlement

In negotiating the peace, the United States had to reckon with both its adversary Great Britain and its ally France, which in turn was beholden to Spain. American peace commissioners Benjamin Franklin, John Jay, and John Adams, whom Adams called "militia diplomats," shrewdly worked one European nation against the other to obtain a desirable settlement. They ignored Congress's instructions to take advice from France because they understood that French and Spanish goals were different from their own. France

had little interest in a strong American nation; Spain particularly feared the territorial expansion of the fledgling United States. Thus, in violation of the 1778 treaty with France, the American diplomats negotiated separately with the British, obtaining recognition of independence and most other provisions they requested.

The British and American peacemakers approved preliminary articles of peace on November 30, 1782; the Treaty of Paris signed on September 3, 1783 was essentially unchanged. The new nation would extend from approximately the present United States–Canada boundary on the north, to the Mississippi River on the west, to the thirty-first parallel on the south. The American diplomats also secured fishing rights off Newfoundland and the St. Lawrence River, of particular interest to New Englanders. Further, the British agreed to evacuate their troops promptly from the United States "without causing any destruction or carrying away any Negroes or other property of the American inhabitants." For its part, Congress would urge state governments to return confiscated property to the loyalists. Prewar debts owed by citizens of each country to citizens of the other would be honored: They should "meet with no lawful impediment to the recovery of the full value in sterling money."

The treaty was a success on paper for the United States, but left France and Spain dissatisfied and pro-British Native Americans "Thunder Struck." In coming decades, the Americans would struggle diplomatically and on western battlefields to enforce its provisions. The French gained little from the war except the separation of the mainland colonies from Great Britain and a huge debt. The Spanish had wanted to keep the Americans out of the Mississippi Valley and hoped to obtain the return of Gibraltar from the British. They instead accepted East and West Florida and the Mediterranean island of Minorca. Native Americans, who had not been conquered, were furious that their British allies, without consultation, had signed away their lands.

While U.S. possession of the trans-Appalachian region remained disputed for decades, the provision that most immediately caused trouble was the one dealing with enslaved African Americans. Even before the final treaty was signed, American slaveowners claimed that the British military forces were taking their "property." The situation was complicated, for thousands of African Americans had fled behind British lines to find freedom and some had fought against their former masters. The British ruled that blacks who sought refuge before the signing of the provisional treaty in November 1782 could not be considered the property of Americans because they were already free, but slaves who escaped after that date would be returned to their masters. General Washington, Congress, and state governments tried but failed to convince the British to return all blacks to their former masters. At least 20,000 African Americans, including those who accompanied loyalist owners as well as the ex-slaves of whigs, left with the British military. Some went to Nova Scotia, where they received a generally unfriendly welcome from white residents, while many others were transported to Florida and the West Indies. In the sugar islands most of the newly freed blacks were quickly re-enslaved.

CONCLUSION

The War for Independence was a success as American whigs cast off a monarchy to create a new republic in which many people, not a king and nobility, held power. They rejected the British government's efforts to restrict representative government, calling the "reforms" tyranny and arguing they would not be slaves. Against many odds and with the help of France, the thirteen British colonies won independence, created a confederation of sovereign states, and obtained rights to the vast trans-Appalachian territories. They avoided military dictatorship, preserved individual rights for white Americans, and established the framework for a future democratic society. Yet the changes of the revolutionary era were less than promised by the ideals of the Declaration of Independence, "that all men are created equal; that they are endowed by their Creator with certain unalienable rights." Though some African Americans attained freedom, the vast majority remained enslaved, and women's political and legal status was essentially the same. The Treaty of Paris ignored the territorial rights of Native Americans. As state governments retained property requirements for voting and holding office, political power stayed in the hands of affluent white men. The War for Independence had given birth to a new republic, but failed to extend the rights of "life, liberty, and the pursuit of happiness" to large numbers of Americans.

RECOMMENDED READINGS

Buel, Joy Day, and Buel, Richard, Jr., *The Way of Duty: A Woman and Her Family in Revolutionary America* (1984). The detailed biography of a Connecticut woman from the colonial period through the Revolution.

Foner, Eric. *Tom Paine and Revolutionary America* (1976). A readable "life and times" of the author of *Common Sense*.

Gross, Robert A. *The Minutemen and Their World* (1976). An interesting study of how revolutionary fervor developed in Concord, Massachusetts.

Higginbotham, Don. *The War of American Independence: Military Attitudes, Policies, and Practice, 1763–1789* (1971). Straightforward military history of the Revolution.

Hoffman, Ronald, and Albert, Peter J., eds. *Women in the Age of the Revolution* (1989). Very good essays on women's status and contributions to the War for Independence.

In Search of Early America: The William and Mary Quarterly, 1943–1993, comp. Michael McGiffert (1993). Compilation of classic essays published in the foremost journal of early American history.

Morgan, Edmund S., and Morgan, Helen M. *The Stamp Act Crisis: Prologue to Revolution,* 2d ed. (1996). A close examination of a crucial episode in the prerevolutionary decade.

Nash, Gary B. *The Urban Crucible: Social Change, Political Consciousness, and the Origins of the American Revolution* (1979). Evaluates the role of urban unrest in leading to the Revolution.

Quarles, Benjamin. *The Negro in the American Revolution,* 2d ed. (1996). The classic text on African Americans during the war.

Young, Alfred F., ed. *The American Revolution: Explorations in the History of American Radicalism* (1976). Important essays on the role of ordinary Americans in the Revolution.

Events Leading to the American Revolution

Bailyn, Bernard. *The Ideological Origins of the American Revolution* (1967).

Doerflinger, Thomas M. *A Vigorous Spirit of Enterprise: Merchants and Economic Development in Revolutionary Philadelphia* (1986).

Knollenberg, Bernhard. *Growth of the American Revolution, 1766–1775* (1975).

Labaree, Benjamin Woods. *The Boston Tea Party* (1965).

Maier, Pauline. *From Resistance to Revolution: Colonial Radicals and the Development of American Opposition to Britain, 1765–1776* (1972).

Ryerson, Richard Alan. *The Revolution Is Now Begun: The Radical Committees of Philadelphia, 1765–1776* (1978).

Shy, John. *Toward Lexington: The Role of the British Army in the Coming of the American Revolution* (1965).

Smith, Billy G. *The "Lower Sort": Philadelphia's Laboring People, 1750–1800* (1990).

Revolutionary Politics

Countryman, Edward. *The American Revolution* (1985).

Crow, Jeffrey J., and Tise, Larry E., eds. *The Southern Experience in the American Revolution* (1978).

Greene, Jack P., ed. *The American Revolution: Its Character and Limits* (1987).

Greene, Jack P. *Peripheries and Center: Constitutional Development in the Extended Polities of the British Empire and the United States, 1607–1788* (1986).

Hoffman, Ronald, et al., eds., *An Uncivil War: The Southern Backcountry During the American Revolution* (1985).

Klein, Rachel N. *Unification of a Slave State: The Rise of the Planter Class in the South Carolina Backcountry, 1760–1808* (1990).

Middlekauff, Robert. *The Glorious Cause: The American Revolution, 1763–1789* (1982).

Wills, Garry. *Inventing America: Jefferson's Declaration of Independence* (1978).

Wood, Gordon S. *The Creation of the American Republic, 1776–1787* (1969).

Wood, Gordon S. *The Radicalism of the American Revolution* (1992).

Young, Alfred F., and Fife, Terry J. *We the People: Voices and Images of the New Nation* (1993).

Military Affairs and Diplomacy

Bemis, Samuel Flagg. *The Diplomacy of the American Revolution* (1957).

Dull, Jonathan R. *A Diplomatic History of the American Revolution* (1985).

Hoffman, Ronald, and Albert, Peter J., eds. *Peace and the Peacemakers: The Treaty of 1783* (1986).

Rosswurm, Steven. *Arms, Country, and Class: The Philadelphia Militia and "Lower Sort" During the American Revolution, 1775–1783* (1987).

Royster, Charles. *A Revolutionary People at War: The Continental Army and American Character, 1775–1783* (1980).

Shy, John. *A People Numerous and Armed: Reflections on the Military Struggle for American Independence* (1976).

Native Americans, African Americans, and Women

Applewhite, Harriet B., and Levy, Darline G., eds. *Women and Politics in the Age of the Democratic Revolution* (1990).

Berlin, Ira, and Hoffman, Ronald, eds. *Slavery and Freedom in the Age of the American Revolution* (1983).

Calloway, Colin G. *The American Revolution in Indian Country: Crisis and Diversity in Native American Communities* (1995).

Dowd, Gregory Evans. *A Spirited Resistance: The North American Indian Struggle for Unity, 1745–1815* (1992).

Frey, Sylvia R. *Water from the Rock: Black Resistance in a Revolutionary Age* (1991).

Gundersen, Joan R. *To Be Useful in the World: Women in Revolutionary America, 1740–1790* (1996).

Hatley, Tom. *The Dividing Paths: Cherokees and South Carolinians Through the Era of Revolution* (1993).

Kerber, Linda K. *Women of the Republic: Intellect and Ideology in Revolutionary America* (1980).

Nash, Gary B. *Race and Revolution* (1990).

Norton, Mary Beth. *Liberty's Daughters: The Revolutionary Experience of American Women, 1750–1800* (1980).

Trigger, Bruce G., ed. *Handbook of North American Indians* Vol. 15: *Northeast* (1978).

Wallace, Anthony F. C. *The Death and Rebirth of the Seneca* (1970).

GREAT SEAL OF THE U.S.

The Great Seal of the United States, adopted by Congress in 1782, incorporated as symbols of the new nation: the thirteen stars and stripes, the eagle with the olive branch of peace and arrows of war, and the motto E Pluribus Unum, *Latin for "Out of Many, One."*

Chapter 6

TOWARD A MORE PERFECT UNION, 1783–1788

THE AMERICAN PATRIOTS had won victory on the battlefield and, at least on paper, in negotiating the peace. The new country soon discovered, though, that independence brought severe challenges as well as opportunities. In 1786, Benjamin Rush of Philadelphia, a physician, whig, and promoter of female education and the abolition of slavery, summarized in a pamphlet the tasks facing the United States:

> There is nothing more common than to confound the terms of *the American revolution* with those of *the late American war*. The American war is over: but this is far from being the case with the American revolution. On the contrary, nothing but the first act of the great drama is closed. It remains yet to establish and perfect our forms of government; and to prepare the principles, morals, and manners of our citizens, for those forms of government. . . .

Having fought for liberty and self-government, Americans now had to create an effective political framework to protect those rights. Their first government was a confederation of small republics in which property-holding white men, the minority of the population defined as having a "stake in society," elected representatives. But questions remained about how to avoid the opposite evils of tyranny and anarchy, questions that inspired fiery debates and even rebellion during the 1780s. Indeed, Rush's pamphlet was part of that dispute, as he argued for a stronger national government.

American leaders had understood since 1776 that the task of creating a workable government lay before them. They were less prepared for other problems that arose soon after the peace. With limited powers under the Articles of Confederation, the Congress faced challenges in demobilizing the army, conducting trade outside the confines of British mercantilism, paying the war debt, finding a way to coexist with the neighboring Spanish colonies in Louisiana and Florida, dealing with Native Americans, and supervising white settlement in the west. Despite Congress's competent action on some of these issues, the need for a more powerful central government became clear. Just four years after the conclusion of peace, delegates from the states met in Philadelphia to draft the new Constitution, which became law upon ratification in 1788. Though the product of political maneuvering as well as high-minded theory, this Constitution has endured, with relatively few amendments, for over two centuries.

THE LIMITS OF REVOLUTIONARY CHANGE

In contrasting "the American revolution" with "the late American war," Rush made a distinction that

CHRONOLOGY

1783 Protest of Continental Army officers at Newburgh, New York

Great Britain closes British West Indies to American ships

Massachusetts Supreme Court finds slavery unconstitutional

1784 Rhode Island and Connecticut pass gradual abolition laws

Spain closes port of New Orleans to Americans

Spain signs treaty of alliance with the Creeks

United States forces Iroquois to cede rights in Northwest Territory with Treaty of Fort Stanwix

1785 Native Americans yield lands in Ohio with Treaty of Fort McIntosh

Congress passes land ordinance for the Northwest Territory

1786 Shawnees sign Treaty of Fort Finney

Country Party takes control of Rhode Island assembly

Virginia statute for religious liberty

Annapolis Convention fails

Western Confederacy rejects treaties ceding lands in the Northwest Territory

Massachusetts farmers close county courts

1787 Shaysites attack the federal arsenal at Springfield, Massachusetts

Constitutional Convention meets in Philadelphia

Congress passes Northwest Ordinance

Constitution signed and sent to the states for ratification

1787–1788 Publication of *The Federalist* essays

Ratification of the Constitution by eleven states

---

many people have debated since the 1780s. Rush thought the revolution had to continue because the government was not yet "perfect"—the states had too much power, leading to disunity and inertia. Others have framed the question in a different way: To what extent did the War of Independence bring about basic changes in politics and society? Though Americans won the right to rule themselves from the British and incorporated in their state constitutions many of the English liberties they had fought for, the definition of the electorate remained the same. The war was revolutionary for propertied white men, but less so for women, African Americans, religious minorities, and the poor.

Republican Politics

Under the Articles of Confederation, ratified in 1781, the United States consisted of thirteen sovereign states rather than one nation. In framing the Confederation, representatives from the states had refused to transfer sovereignty to a central government. Only state assemblies, elected by the voters, could impose taxes; the central government, or Congress, would be an agent of the states. This decision was based on republican theory, that only in a small republic could representatives act according to the will of its citizens. If the territory was large, the interests and desires of the people would be too diverse, making harmony impossible. The states feared that a too-powerful national government would be dominated by factions whose interests conflicted with their own. And local leaders cherished their power. Thus, the Articles formed a confederacy of sovereign states, with a weak Congress as the only organ of national government. Comprised of delegates from each of the states, "appointed in such manner as the legislature of each State shall direct," Congress had responsibility to conduct foreign affairs, declare war and peace, and coin money, but could not levy taxes

or raise troops. Each state had an equal vote in Congress. During the 1780s, its dependence on the states for funds brought the Confederation to a standstill. For years, Congress sought an amendment of the Articles to permit a national tax, but failed to obtain the required unanimous agreement of the states.

The structure of the state governments, where sovereignty lay, reflected their framers' concept of republicanism. Most of the state constitutions resembled the old colonial governments, but incorporated changes that made them more responsible to the people. Most had two-house legislatures and a governor, but gave the largest share of power to the lower house of assembly, elected annually by the voters. The radical Pennsylvania constitution of 1776, more democratic than others, dropped the office of governor and the upper house of assembly, or senate, which was designed to represent the wealthier segment of society. Georgia also excluded the upper house and denied its governor any power. Fearing executive power, given their experience with George III, even states that retained the governor prevented him from appointing many officials or dissolving the assembly. They eliminated the governor's veto over legislation or allowed the assembly to override with a two-thirds vote. All of the states produced written constitutions as a protection against the kind of changes they believed the British had made in their unwritten constitution before the Revolution.

During the late 1770s and 1780s, as Americans formulated and revised state constitutions, they also developed the method by which frames of government were written and approved, the constitutional convention. Pennsylvania radicals called the first state convention in 1776, explaining that its members would be "invested with powers to form a plan of government only, and not to execute it after it is framed; for nothing can be a greater violation of reason and natural rights, than for men to give authority to themselves." Then, in 1780, Massachusetts voters demanded a convention to write a new constitution rather than accept a document that assemblymen had prepared. The constitution was ratified by the people (voters), who thus claimed to be sovereign—the ultimate source of political power—because the frame of government originated with them. Within a few years, other states adopted the same process, recognizing that a constitution should not be written by a governmental body—the legislature—that the constitution created. As one theorist argued, "Conven-tions . . . are the only proper bodies to form a Constitution, and Assemblies are the proper bodies to make Laws agreeable to that Constitution." Remarkably, in Massachusetts in 1780, every free man, even those without property, could vote for or against the new constitution. The document they approved limited suffrage to propertied men, despite opposition from the western counties.

State constitutions also provided some protection for the liberties many Americans had defended in the Revolution. Virginia included a model Declaration of Rights that other states copied loosely. Most state constitutions offered freedom of worship, required search warrants, and banned excessive fines and quartering of troops in private dwellings. Only some of the states, however, guaranteed trial by jury and the rights of free speech, press, and assembly. A few opposed monopolies and imprisonment for debt, and New England, Pennsylvania, North Carolina, and Georgia promised public support for schools.

While the state constitutions were radical in the context of eighteenth-century politics, because they vested power in the voters and lower houses of assembly, the definition of who was qualified to cast ballots and hold office remained traditional. John Adams spoke for most politicians of his time when he wrote that only property holders should be counted among the sovereign people who could choose and serve as magistrates because the purpose of government was to safeguard property. "It is dangerous," Adams wrote,

> . . . to alter the qualifications of voters. There will be no end to it. New claims will arise. Women will demand a vote. Lads from 12 to 21 will think their rights not enough attended to, and every man, who has not a farthing, will demand an equal voice. . . . It tends to confound and destroy all distinctions, and prostrate all ranks, to one common level.

Voters, according to republican theory, must have a stake in society. Wives, slaves, servants, and unpropertied laboring men were dependent on others and thus unqualified for suffrage. Yet in most places, women and free African Americans who owned property were also barred from voting, by law or by informal pressure. One exception was New Jersey, where the 1776 state constitution extended the vote to "all free inhabitants" who held sufficient property; in 1807, the legislature fell into line with other states by disenfranchising all women and blacks.

"Keep Within Compass," published during the era of the new republic (c. 1785–1805), warned young women to remain within traditional female roles despite the revolutionary change in government.

Women's Rights

Republican politics brought little change to women's lives. Not only were women excluded from government, but their legal and economic status failed to improve. A married woman was still subject to the English common law that gave control of her property and earnings to her husband and denied her the right, without his permission, to make a will, sign contracts, sue in court, or act as a guardian. Despite independence, the American lawmakers refused to cast off this English tradition. Women were also barred, by custom and insufficient education and capital, from positions of high status. They could serve as ministers among Quakers and some Baptists but in no other churches; they taught school only at the primary level. None were lawyers or wealthy merchants, though some became successful shopkeepers. Women also lost ground in medicine, where they had long played important

roles as midwives. As medical courses at the college level became available to men, doctors with formal training displaced lay practitioners, including some midwives. Change occurred most noticeably in Boston, New York, and Philadelphia, where affluent clients demanded the new college-trained obstetricians.

In the post-Revolutionary years, increased support for female education marked the most positive alteration in women's lives. This change accompanied the more general perception that a republic needed an educated people. Though women were denied entrance to all colleges, including Harvard, Yale, and William

Girl in Green, by an unknown artist, c. 1790. While women's status remained circumscribed in many areas after the Revolution, their access to education improved, as suggested in this rare image of a girl reading a book.

Judith Sargent, *by John Singleton Copley, before her marriage to John Murray. She became a proponent of advanced education for women.*

and Mary, a number of academies opened their doors to provide secondary-level education to well-to-do girls. The school curricula included the three R's, English composition and grammar, geography, music, dancing, and needlework. The young women did not receive instruction in Latin, Greek, and advanced science and mathematics, the courses that their brothers took to prepare for college.

Discussion of the need for better female education became intertwined with ideas about women's roles in the new nation. Beginning in 1784, Massachusetts writer Judith Sargent Murray published a series of essays, later compiled in a book titled *The Gleaner,* in which she argued that young women should prepare to support themselves in case they found no suitable husband or their spouse died. "Our girls," she wrote, "are bred up with one particular view: . . . an establishment by marriage. . . . *An old maid,* they are from infancy taught, at least indirectly, to consider as a contemptible being; and they have no other means of advancing themselves but in the matrimonial line." Murray believed that young women should learn a vocation for independence, but also justified advanced female education on the grounds that girls with developed minds would become better wives and mothers. Dr. Benjamin Rush pointed out that improved school-

ing would help women fulfill their duties in running households and preparing sons to be virtuous, wise leaders of the republic. Carefully avoiding the suggestion that women should participate in politics, he wrote: "The equal share that every citizen has in the liberty and the possible share he may have in the government of our country make it necessary that our ladies should be qualified to a certain degree, by a peculiar and suitable education, to concur in instructing their sons in the principles of liberty and government." Nurturing incorruptible future leaders, or "republican motherhood," was women's principal responsibility under the new government, not voting or holding office.

The Question of Abolishing Slavery

The revolutionary rhetoric of freedom and self-determination unleashed a public debate over the legitimacy of slavery. African Americans fueled the discussion by escaping to the British and serving in the American army. Many took opportunities opened by the Revolution to grasp their own personal liberty. In doing so, African Americans made whites more aware of the hypocrisy of fighting a war of independence while they kept other human beings in chains. In petitions, Massachusetts blacks made the connection explicit during the war, writing that as long as whigs failed to emancipate slaves, they were "chargeable with the inconsistency of acting . . . the part which they condemn & oppose in others. . . . [E]very principle from which America has acted in the course of her difficulties with Great-Britain, pleads stronger than a thousand arguments from your Petitioners."

In the north, the first significant opposition to slavery had developed among Pennsylvania and New Jersey Quakers well before the Revolution. Since the seventeenth century, individual members of the Society of Friends had argued that black bondage violated basic Christian concepts, particularly the belief that all humans are equal in the eyes of God. For decades, these Quaker abolitionists failed to convince their meetings that slavery was wrong because many wealthy, powerful Friends held slaves. But after 1750, the Society of Friends became the first American religion to denounce perpetual bondage as a sin and to prohibit members from holding slaves. The Quakers then spearheaded an emancipation movement that gained strength among other whites in the 1770s and

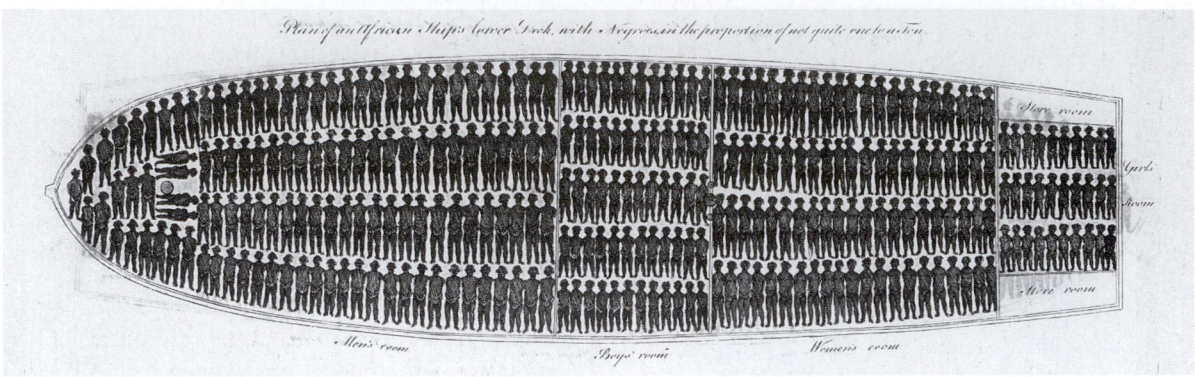

One of the goals of the Pennsylvania Abolition Society was to end the international slave trade. The text of this 1789 tract states that enslaved Africans on slave ships were "packed, side by side, almost like herrings in a barrel, and reduced to the state of being buried alive."

1780s, contributing, along with escapes by African Americans, to the growth of free black communities in Philadelphia, New York, and other northern towns. In addition, by the 1780s, slavery was less important economically in northern states than in the south, thus the combination of religious conviction, natural rights concepts of liberty and equality, and pressure by African Americans could undercut its viability. Prospective owners, already sensitized by guilt, grew wary of purchasing slaves, who were likely to demand emancipation or run away. Instead, northern employers hired workers from among the growing numbers of free laborers in cities and commercial agricultural areas, including many African Americans.

In Pennsylvania and New England, state governments acted against slavery by the mid-1780s. The Pennsylvania assembly passed the first abolition law in 1780, its preamble reflecting the ideas that inspired many abolitionists of the revolutionary era:

> When we contemplate our abhorrence of that condition to which the arms and tyranny of Great Britain were exerted to reduce us, when we look back on the variety of dangers to which we have been exposed, [we are grateful for] the manifold blessings which we have undeservedly received. . . . We conceive that it is our duty, and we rejoice that it is in our power, to extend a portion of that freedom to others.

The act was less comprehensive than its heartiest supporters wished, including radical George Bryan, who probably wrote the initial draft, and Anthony Benezet, the aged Quaker schoolteacher and abolitionist who lobbied every assemblyman for the law. As a result of compromises required for passage, the Pennsylvania act abolished slavery gradually—so gradually that under its provisions no black Pennsylvanian would achieve freedom until 1808. The law provided that children born to slave mothers after March 1780 would be freed when they reached the age of twenty-eight. Slaves who had been born before that date would remain in bondage.

Nevertheless, the Pennsylvania act was more effective than expected, as many enslaved blacks, exasperated that the law failed to free them, escaped their masters, and hundreds of slaveholders conformed to the spirit of the law by manumitting their slaves, regardless of birth date, at about age twenty-eight. Though these owners benefited from the labor of African Americans during their prime years, still, the manumissions helped to bring about the early end of slavery in the state. Also significant was the work of the Pennsylvania Abolition Society, which tested the limits of the 1780 abolition act by providing legal counsel to African Americans to defend their liberty. The PAS, which was dominated by Quaker artisans but also included such luminaries as Benjamin Franklin and Benjamin Rush, kept a record of manumission papers in the event freed men and women were kidnapped into slavery. The number of slaves in Pennsylvania declined from almost 7,000 in 1780, to 3,700 in 1790, and 795 in 1810.

Elsewhere in the north, the Massachusetts supreme court in 1783 decided that slavery was incompatible with the state's 1780 constitution, which said all men are free and equal, though it did not specifically out-

law perpetual bondage. As blacks sued for freedom, the courts ruled on their behalf, and so by 1790, Massachusetts reported no slaves on the federal census. The Connecticut and Rhode Island legislatures in 1784 followed Pennsylvania's example by passing gradual abolition laws, and Vermont and New Hampshire also banned the institution. New York and New Jersey, where slaveholders were more numerous and powerful, passed gradual abolition acts later, in 1799 and 1804 respectively.

During the 1780s, considerable support for abolition also developed in the Chesapeake region, though enslaved African Americans comprised almost 40 percent of the population. Southern states, like their northern counterparts, continued the First Continental Congress' prohibition of the slave trade. Some people expected cessation of the trade to result in the gradual death of slavery in Virginia and Maryland—a mistake because the African American population there grew naturally by reproduction. Involuntary bondage would persist without positive action for abolition.

Thomas Jefferson exemplified the troubled and confused state of mind of many white Americans about slavery. Though he remained a slaveholder throughout his life and held racist beliefs, Jefferson claimed to support a strategy for gradual abolition in Virginia. The plan, never considered by the assembly, would have freed and educated African American children born after the law went into effect and, when adults, remove them to a separate territory. Jefferson, like most whites who lived in areas with large black populations, wanted desperately to ensure that whites kept political control if African Americans gained freedom. Relocation to a new land was one suggestion for abolishing slavery yet maintaining white power.

Efforts for general abolition failed south of Pennsylvania, yet some progress occurred when Virginia (in 1782), Delaware (in 1787), and Maryland (in 1790) made private emancipation easier. New manumission laws permitted slaveholders who were inspired by antislavery beliefs, whether arising from revolutionary ideals or religion, to free their slaves. A private abolition movement took fire in areas of the Upper South where Quakers and Methodists were numerous and planters were changing from tobacco to wheat as their chief crop, thus requiring fewer field hands. Though declining demand for labor played a role in their decision, still, slaveholders had the choice of whether to emancipate or sell their bondpeople. A market for slaves existed in the Carolinas and Georgia, where abolitionist sentiment had little impact.

The rise in the number of free African Americans in the Upper South was a measure of opposition to slavery. The free black population in Delaware rose to 4,000 in 1790, and over 8,000 by the end of the century; in Maryland to 8,000 in 1790, and 20,000 ten years later; and in Virginia, to nearly 13,000 at the turn of the century. Even with impressive numbers of manumissions, however, in 1800 emancipated blacks were just 8 percent of all African Americans in the region. The majority, by far, remained enslaved.

Defining Religious Liberty

Another question that faced the architects of the new state governments was religious freedom. Revolutionary ideals led many to challenge laws that forced people to attend and financially support an established church. Before the Revolution, the colonies had varied widely in the relationship of church and state. Congregational churches were tax-supported in Massachusetts, New Hampshire, and Connecticut, while the Church of England (Anglican) was established in the Carolinas, Virginia, Maryland, and New York. In contrast, Rhode Island, New Jersey, and Pennsylvania protected a great diversity of religions, giving none of them public funds. All of the colonies, however, placed limits on who could serve in political office. In Pennsylvania, for example, anyone who believed in God could live and worship, but only Protestants could participate in government. The British Crown forbade any province from permitting Roman Catholics to vote and hold office.

The break with Great Britain had the greatest impact on the established Church of England, called the Protestant Episcopal church in the United States after the Revolution. With independence, some of its parishes dissolved, as missionaries departed because the church hierarchy in England stopped paying their salaries. Many Anglican clergymen and laypeople in New England and the Mid-Atlantic region became loyalists, helping to fuel the whig movement for disestablishment. All of the states in which the Anglican church was established promptly ended government support except Virginia, where many leading whigs were Anglicans. Virginia finally acted in 1786, when

PETITION OF PHILADELPHIA JEWS FOR EQUAL RIGHTS, 1783

Though Pennsylvania was renowned for religious liberty, its constitution limited election to the state assembly to Christians. As other states broadened religious liberty during the revolutionary era, Philadelphia Jews called for redress of this inequity. The new Pennsylvania constitution adopted in 1790 removed this religious test.

To the honourable the Council of Censors, assembled agreeable to the Constitution of the State of Pennsylvania. The Memorial of . . . the Synagogue of the Jews at Philadelphia, . . . in behalf of themselves and their brethren Jews, residing in Pennsylvania,

Most respectfully showeth,

That by the tenth section of the Frame of Government of this Commonwealth, it is ordered that each member of the general assembly of representatives of the freemen of Pennsylvania, before he takes his seat, shall make and subscribe a declaration, which ends in these words, "I do acknowledge the Scriptures of the old and new Testament to be given by divine inspiration," to which is added an assurance, that "no further or other religious test shall ever hereafter be required of any civil officer or magistrate in this state."

Your memorialists beg leave to observe, that this clause seems to limit the civil rights of your citizens to one very special article of the creed; whereas by the second paragraph of the declaration of the rights of the inhabitants, it is asserted without any other limitation than the professing the existence of God, in plain words, "that no man who acknowledges the being of a God can be justly deprived or abridged of any civil rights as a citizen on account of his religious sentiments." But certainly this religious test deprives the Jews of the most eminent rights of freemen, solemnly ascertained to all men who are not professed Atheists.

May it please your Honors,

Although the Jews in Pennsylvania are but few in number, yet liberty of the people in one country, and the declaration of the government thereof, that these liberties are the rights of the people, may prove a powerful attractive to men, who live under restraints in another country. Holland and England have made valuable acquisitions of men, who for their religious sentiments, were distressed in their own countries.—And if Jews in Europe or elsewhere, should incline to transport themselves to America, and would, for reason of some certain advantage of the soil, climate, or the trade of Pennsylvania, rather

the assembly passed Thomas Jefferson's statute for religious liberty, which stated,

no man shall be compelled to frequent or support any religious worship, place or ministry whatsoever, nor shall be enforced, restrained, molested, or burthened in his body or goods, nor shall otherwise suffer on account of his religious opinions or belief.

Nevertheless, the movement to end discrimination stalled, and in the 1780s, religious tests for political office remained common. Americans, who were over-

become inhabitants thereof, than of any other State; yet the disability of Jews to take seat among the representatives of the people, as worded by the said religious test, might determine their free choice to go to New York, or to any other of the United States of America, where there is no such like restraint laid upon the nation and religion of the Jews, as in Pennsylvania. — Your memorialists cannot say that the Jews are particularly fond of being representatives of the people in assembly or civil officers and magistrates in the State; but with great submission they apprehend that a clause in the constitution, which disables them to be elected by their fellow citizens to represent them in assembly, is a stigma upon their nation and religion, and it is inconsonant with the second paragraph of the said bill of rights; otherwise Jews are as fond of liberty as their religious societies can be, and it must create in them a displeasure, when they perceive that for their professed dissent to doctrine, which is inconsistent with their religious sentiments, they should be excluded from the most important and honourable part of the rights of a free citizen.

Your memorialists beg further leave to represent, that in the religious books of the Jews, which are or may be in every man's hands, there are no such doctrines or principles established as are inconsistent with the safety and happiness of the people of Pennsylvania, and that the conduct and behaviour of the Jews in this and the neighbouring States, has always tallied with the great design of the Revolution; that the Jews of Charlestown, New York, New-Port and other posts, occupied by the British troops, have distinguishedly suffered for their attachment to the Revolution principles; and their brethren at St. Eustatius, for the same cause, experienced the most severe resentments of the British commanders. The Jews of Pennsylvania in proportion to the number of their members, can count with any religious society whatsoever, the Whigs among either of them; they have served some of them in the Continental army; some went out in the militia to fight the common enemy; all of them have cheerfully contributed to the support of the militia, and of the government of this State; they have no inconsiderable property in lands and tenements, but particularly in the way of trade, some more, some less, for which they pay taxes; they have, upon every plan formed for public utility, been forward to contribute as much as their circumstances would admit of; and as a nation or a religious society, they stand unimpeached of any matter whatsoever, against the safety and happiness of the people.

And your memorialists humbly pray, that if your honours, from any consideration than the subject of this address, should think proper to call a convention for revising the constitution, you would be pleased to recommend this to the notice of that convention.

whelmingly Protestant, thought that only Christian men, preferably Protestants, should govern. The success of the republic, they believed, required "a virtuous people"; Protestant Christianity was the glue that would hold them together. State and local laws required observance of the Sabbath, outlawed gambling and other entertainments, and proclaimed days of thanksgiving and prayer. The states most resistant to disestablishment were the old Puritan strongholds in New England, where Congregational ministers had warmly advocated the whig cause. Massachusetts, New Hampshire, and Connecticut required tax

support for Protestant churches well into the nineteenth century.

CHALLENGES TO THE CONFEDERATION

Despite the dominance of the states, the Confederation Congress had important functions that required far more unity and power than it possessed. Of all Congress's difficulties, the inability to tax was most damaging, resulting in the Confederation's quick demise.

Military Demobilization

In the transition to peace in 1783, one of the most remarkable aspects of the American revolutionary experience—in light of revolutions since that time—was the absence of a serious military challenge to civilian control. George Washington was committed to popularly elected government and thus ignored suggestions that he become a military ruler. Even so, Congress faced two problems concerning the armed forces, both arising in part from lack of revenue. During the war, Congress failed to pay or supply the army properly, but had promised generous pensions and bounties to entice men to sign up for the duration of the war. The second question confronting Congress was whether to establish a peacetime army, an issue that had both ideological and financial significance.

For two years after the Battle of Yorktown in 1781, the Continental Army continued to exist, with Washington encamped at Newburgh, New York, where his troops monitored the British army still in New York City. American officers and enlisted men voiced grievances because they needed food, clothing, and wages. Soldiers rioted and insulted their officers, while many simply went home with no compensation except their weapons. Officers at Newburgh drew up a list of complaints for Congress, demanding as much of their back pay as possible and a full reckoning of the entire sum they were owed. The officers suggested that they receive lump sums instead of the promised pensions of half-pay for life. They seemed so disgruntled that Washington remained at Newburgh instead of going home to Mount Vernon as he had planned.

The officers' discontent became more threatening when several politicians, who favored a strong central government, recognized an opportunity to pressure the states into giving Congress the power to tax. In what became known as the Newburgh conspiracy, Robert Morris of Philadelphia and Gouverneur Morris and Alexander Hamilton of New York hatched a plan to use the officers' protests to strengthen the Confederation. Washington would not cooperate, stating that the army was a "most dangerous instrument to play with," even to obtain a national tax. In early 1783, rumors spread that the officers were ready to take "manly" action against the government unless their demands were met. The crisis ended when Washington pledged to negotiate for their back pay and pensions and the officers swore their loyalty to Congress. For its part, Congress agreed to pay troops three months' wages at discharge, while officers would receive pensions of five years' full pay in government bonds. A group of eighty enlisted men stationed at Lancaster, Pennsylvania, found the offer unacceptable, so they mutinied and marched on Philadelphia, barricading the State House where Congress met. Though the soldiers backed down without violence, the frightened congressmen fled to Princeton.

Restitution of military pensions, back wages, and bounties took until the 1790s because Congress lacked the funds to discharge its debts. Soldiers who had been promised land bounties in the west had to wait fifteen years for surveys, in large part because Native Americans refused to give up their territory, which Congress intended to distribute. By the 1790s, most veterans had long since sold their rights to speculators for a fraction of their worth.

The issue of a standing army squared revolutionary ideology against the need for defense. One of the chief causes of the Revolution had been the peacetime quartering in New York and Boston of the British army, which patriots called a "MONSTER of a standing ARMY." But now in the postwar era, the United States faced threats from the Spanish in Florida and Louisiana, the British in Canada, and Native Americans everywhere along the frontier. In April 1783, Congress appointed a committee to consult Washington and other generals on military requirements. The commander-in-chief argued that, despite concerns about armies in peacetime, the United States had to be prepared against its enemies. He suggested retaining 2,600 Continentals in one artillery and four infantry regiments. He also advised Congress to organize a na-

Gouverneur Morris and Robert Morris intended to use the American army's discontent in 1782–1783 to create a strong central government. Portrait by Charles Willson Peale.

tional citizens' militia that would stay in training for ready defense. In 1784, Congress dismissed Washington's plan, stationing a total of eighty men at two forts in New York and Pennsylvania. The following year, it raised another 700 men to supervise the Ohio country, a number that was much too small to support U.S. claims to Indian lands or to force the British from their garrisons. For reasons of principle and finances, the Confederation government virtually disbanded the army during an interval of peace, a pattern the nation would follow well into the twentieth century.

Economic Troubles

The revolution left the United States with a huge debt and an unknown status among trading nations. The Confederation Congress failed to solve the problem of its war debt, which by 1790 amounted to an estimated $10 million owed to other countries and $40 million owed to Americans. During the war, with no power to tax, the government had issued paper currency to pay

for goods and services. It abandoned this policy because of rampant inflation. Congress turned to the states, which refused to contribute sufficient funds, then borrowed from France and from American merchants and farmers for military provisions. It also deferred payment on soldiers' wages. As the principal and interest mounted on these promissory notes and bonds, Congress requested an amendment to the Articles to permit a national duty of 5 percent on all imports. Unanimous agreement of the states was necessary. The legislators tried for five years, but failed on each attempt despite gaining approval from all but one or two states. Through the 1780s the national debt served as the means by which national and state politicians contested power. Nationalists such as Robert Morris and Alexander Hamilton argued for a stronger central government with the power to tax, while state officials used Congress's inability to pay the debt as a reason to ignore the Confederation's authority.

One long-lasting consequence of the war's inflationary crisis was conflict between urban and rural interests over public finance. The spiraling cost of food

and fuel in the late 1770s had hurt city residents much more than farmers. In public debate over currency and credit, farmers wanted access to government loans based on the value of their land and its production, similar to the colonial land banks that had allowed them to use real estate as collateral for loans. Though the provincial currency issued by the land banks had been fairly stable, in the 1780s, merchants and urban artisans recalled the more recent inflation of the Revolution. They believed that paper currency based on real estate would send prices sky-high. At the same time, merchants knew that the economy would stagnate if specie (gold and silver) were required for every transaction, so they embraced an alternative method of generating paper currency, the bank.

The first bank in the United States was the Bank of North America, created in 1781 in Philadelphia. Robert Morris proposed the institution, based on the Bank of England, as a way to help solve the wartime fiscal crisis. Morris obtained support from Alexander Hamilton, Thomas Paine, and a committee of Congress for his plan; both the Congress and state of Pennsylvania chartered the institution. Instead of issuing paper currency through a land office, as farmers wanted, the bank issued currency in the form of short-term loans to merchants. These bank notes were backed by gold and silver plate and coins that investors deposited in return for a share of the bank's profits. The attraction for stockholders was that formerly idle gold and silver assets could now earn interest. The Bank of North America earned regular profits during its first two decades, beginning with an 8.74 percent dividend to investors in 1782. If people doubted the security of the bank, they could redeem their bank notes. Bank advocates believed that once a few people tested its soundness and received specie, others would trust the bank and accept the bank notes as currency.

In fact, the Bank of North America followed a conservative course that kept it solvent financially but made it unpopular with many people. The bank's manager, Thomas Willing, lent money only to good credit risks in the mercantile community, thus angering artisans and farmers who viewed the bank as a monopoly created by Congress to benefit the commercial elite. Also, Willing refused to liberalize the bank's loan policy by taking advantage of confidence in the bank's strength. Instead of expanding the money supply as later banks did, the Bank of North America made loans only up to the amount of specie in its vaults.

The Bank of North America helped the mercantile community through a time of uncertainty. Commerce had suffered during the revolution as merchants lost connections with trading partners in Great Britain and the British West Indies. In 1783, Americans expected to reestablish those ties as well as enter new markets in Europe and the French and Spanish colonies. With their newly won independence, they gained release from the restrictions of British mercantilism.

But being part of the mercantilist system had brought advantages as well as constraints. The British did not allow their former colonies to have the best of both worlds. They closed the ports of the British West Indies to American ships, a sharp blow for New England and the Middle Atlantic states, which before the war had found a major market in the islands for exports of fish, grain, flour, lumber, and livestock. To Great Britain and its colonies, the United States was now a foreign country. Americans could sell provisions in the islands and purchase rum, sugar, and molasses, but everything had to be carried on British ships. West Indies planters complained because this resulted in higher prices; American shipowners had to find new routes. On the other hand, Britain was eager to purchase tobacco from the Chesapeake and sell to Americans all the manufactures they would buy. U.S. merchants had access by treaty to ports in France and the French colonies, but were barred from trading in New Spain. Gradually, Americans developed trade with Germany, the Netherlands, Scandinavia, and even China. Some merchants became involved in the Atlantic slave trade, while others found ways to circumvent the British restrictions in the Caribbean. By the end of the 1780s, U.S. exports recovered to approximately their prerevolutionary level.

The road to recovery was rocky, however, because in the immediate postwar years American demand for British manufactures far outstripped exports. During the revolution, American artisans had attempted to supply metal goods and textiles, but had been unable to match British quality and prices. With peace, British manufacturers extended generous credit to American consumers for clocks, watches, furniture, textiles, clothing, mirrors, and other goods. When depression hit in fall 1783 because of the loss of the West Indies market, American farmers, merchants, and shopkeepers found themselves seriously in debt. In New England, for example, the balance of trade with Great Britain was so uneven that exports covered only 13 percent of imports. While the economy improved

AMERICA TRIUMPHANT and BRITANNIA in DISTRESS

EXPLANATION.

I America sitting on that quarter of the globe with the Flag of the United States displayed over her head; holding in one hand the Olive branch, inviting the ships of all nations to partake of her commerce; and in the other hand supporting the Cap of Liberty.
II Fame proclaiming the joyful news to all the world.

III Britannia weeping at the loss of the trade of America, attended with an evil genius.
IV The British flag struck, on her strong Fortresses.
V French, Spanish, Dutch, &c shipping in the harbours of America.
VIA view of New-York, wherein is exhibited the Traitor Arnold, taken with remorse for selling his country, and Judas like hanging himself.

America Triumphant and Britannia in Distress, *from* Weatherwise's Town and Country Almanack *(1782) illustrates the hopes of Americans for prosperity now that they were free from British mercantilism.*

after mid-1785, many farmers had difficulty escaping from debt.

Indeed, estimates of the gross national product suggest that the revolution had an extended negative impact on the American economy, that liberty came at a high price not only in bloodshed but in financial terms as well. Data available for 1774 and 1790 indicate that income declined by over 40 percent, close to the decrease Americans experienced during the Great Depression of the 1930s.

Foreign Affairs

Though the United States had won both the war and the peace, its leaders soon learned that they received little respect among European nations. Ambassadors Thomas Jefferson to France and John Adams to Great Britain had as much difficulty maneuvering among fellow diplomats as have the representatives of new nations in the twentieth century. Despite the boundary provisions of the Treaty of 1783, Spain and Great Britain took advantage of the Confederation's weakness to trespass on territory in the west. The Spanish and English gained allies among Native Americans who were losing their lands to the steady stream of white settlers crossing the Appalachians.

During the 1780s, the Spanish tried to restrict expansion of the United States, which they considered their chief competitor for North America. With a burgeoning population, the former British colonies rivaled the size of New Spain. The Spanish government had refused to accept the treaty boundaries granting the region between the Appalachians and the Mississippi River to the United States. With settlers rapidly filling the area, Spain feared for its control of Louisiana and East and West Florida; it wanted to extend its territory north from West Florida to the Ohio River. The Spanish pursued this objective in a number of ways. They retained forts north of the 31st parallel, which the United States claimed as its southern border on the basis of the peace treaty. Then, in 1784, the

BRITISH CANADA

Lake Superior

Ceded by VIRGINIA, 1784

Ceded by MASSACHUSETTS, 1785
and VIRGINIA, 1784

Ceded by CONNECTICUT, 1786
and VIRGINIA, 1784

Ceded by
CONNECTICUT,
1800

Ceded by VIRGINIA,
1784

Ceded by VIRGINIA,
1792

Ceded by
SOUTH
CAROLINA,
1787

Ceded by
NORTH CAROLINA,
1790

Ceded by GEORGIA,
1802

Ceded by SPAIN, 1795
Ceded by GEORGIA, 1802

SPANISH
LOUISIANA

Lake Michigan

Lake Huron

Lake Ontario

Lake Erie

Ceded by
MASS.,
1786

Ceded by
CONN.,
1782

Ohio River

Mississippi River

MAINE
(Mass.)

VT
(1791)

NH

NEW YORK

MASSACHUSETTS

RI

CONN.

PENNSYLVANIA

NEW
JERSEY

MD

DE

VIRGINIA

NORTH
CAROLINA

SOUTH
CAROLINA

GEORGIA

SPANISH
FLORIDA

Gulf of Mexico

*ATLANTIC
OCEAN*

States after
land cessions

Ceded territory

Territory ceded by
New York, 1782

MAP 6.1 | WESTERN LAND CESSIONS, 1782–1802

Spanish government closed the port of New Orleans to Americans, apparently hoping to detach from the United States the region that later became Kentucky and Tennessee. Settlers in the trans-Appalachian region protested vigorously because they needed access to the New Orleans market for their goods. Some

threatened to secede from the United States unless Congress convinced Spain to reverse its decision; a few, including James Wilkinson, a former Continental Army officer, actually negotiated with the Spanish. Reporting on a journey in the west, George Washington wrote, "the western settlers (I speak now from my own

observation) stand as it were upon a pivot; the touch of a feather would turn them any way."

Congress directed John Jay, the secretary of foreign affairs and a New Yorker, to negotiate with Spain to reopen the port. The Spanish diplomat, Diego de Gardoqui, under instructions from his government, refused to budge, instead offering to open other Spanish ports to U.S. commerce if Americans would relinquish demands for free navigation on the lower Mississippi. With the permission of Congress, Jay agreed to a treaty that provided commercial advantages for eastern merchants but closed New Orleans to westerners for a generation. The west and south erupted in opposition, blocking approval of the Jay-Gardoqui Treaty. The lower Mississippi River remained closed until 1788 when the Spanish permitted Americans to use New Orleans upon payment of duties.

The Spanish government also cooperated with Native Americans to slow the influx of Anglo-American settlers into contested territory. Spanish colonists in the Floridas remained few, so they depended upon good relations with the Creeks, Choctaws, and Chickasaws who controlled the region. Groups of Creeks who had migrated to Florida, and were called Seminoles by the British, could mobilize at least twice as many soldiers as the Spanish. Contrary to Spain's traditional policy of considering Native Americans as subjects to the Crown, its colonial officials in 1784 signed written treaties of alliance with the Indians.

Most threatening of these pacts to the United States was the one with the Creeks, which their leader Alexander McGillivray arranged. The son of a Scottish trader and French-Creek woman, and educated in Charleston, McGillivray could negotiate his way in both European and Indian societies. To protect Creek lands from settlers streaming in from Georgia, he offered the Spanish "a powerful barrier in these parts against the ambitious and encroaching Americans" in return for an alliance and weapons. The Creeks called the invading Georgians "Ecunnaunuxulgee," or "people greedily grasping after the lands of the red people." With Cherokees and Shawnees to the north, the Creeks battled Anglo-Americans through the 1780s, thus slowing settlement on the southwest frontier.

The Confederation government also had difficulty establishing its claims north of the Ohio River, against the British and the Indians of the Ohio Valley. In the treaty of 1783, the British had promised to remove their troops from forts in the Great Lakes re-

gion, including Detroit, Oswego, and Niagara. Through the 1780s, however, they refused to withdraw, hoping for return of the territory. They barred American ships from the Great Lakes, placed a customs agent at Oswego, and allied with Native Americans who wanted to halt white settlement. British diplomats justified these actions with the excuse that Americans had failed to pay prewar debts to British creditors and return confiscated loyalist property. While some states were slow in executing these treaty obligations, the British would have kept the garrisons regardless.

Though the British forts bolstered Native American resistance, Great Britain's neglect of their Indian allies in negotiating the peace led the U.S. government to treat them as a conquered people. With great bravado, considering the Confederation's small army, American commissioners said to the Ohio Indians, "You are mistaken in supposing that . . . you are become a free and independent nation, and may make what terms you please. . . . You are a subdued people." Other officials announced, "We claim the country by conquest, and are to give not to receive." Under threat of arms, some Native American leaders acquiesced to U.S. demands. A group of Iroquois yielded rights in the Northwest with the Treaty of Fort Stanwix (1784); Wyandots, Delawares, and others ceded Ohio lands in the Treaty of Fort McIntosh (1785); and Shawnees gave up territory in the Treaty of Fort Finney (1786). Many Native Americans refused to recognize these treaties because the Indian negotiators lacked authority and had been forced to sign. Soon, frontier warfare made U.S. officials realize that they were the ones who were "mistaken" in presuming that the Indians had been "subdued." Theyendanegea (Joseph Brant), the pro-British Mohawk leader who led many Iroquois to Canada after the revolution, rallied Indians against white settlement in the Northwest. In 1786, he urged potential allies, "the Interests of Any One Nation Should be the Interests of us all, the Welfare of the one Should be the Welfare of all the others." Their resistance convinced Secretary of War Henry Knox that the United States must change its tactics or risk a general Indian war that the Confederation could ill afford. He suggested that Congress return to the policy of purchasing lands, instead of demanding them by conquest. The congressmen agreed, incorporating into the Northwest Ordinance of 1787 the futile promise that the Indians' land "shall never be taken from them without their consent."

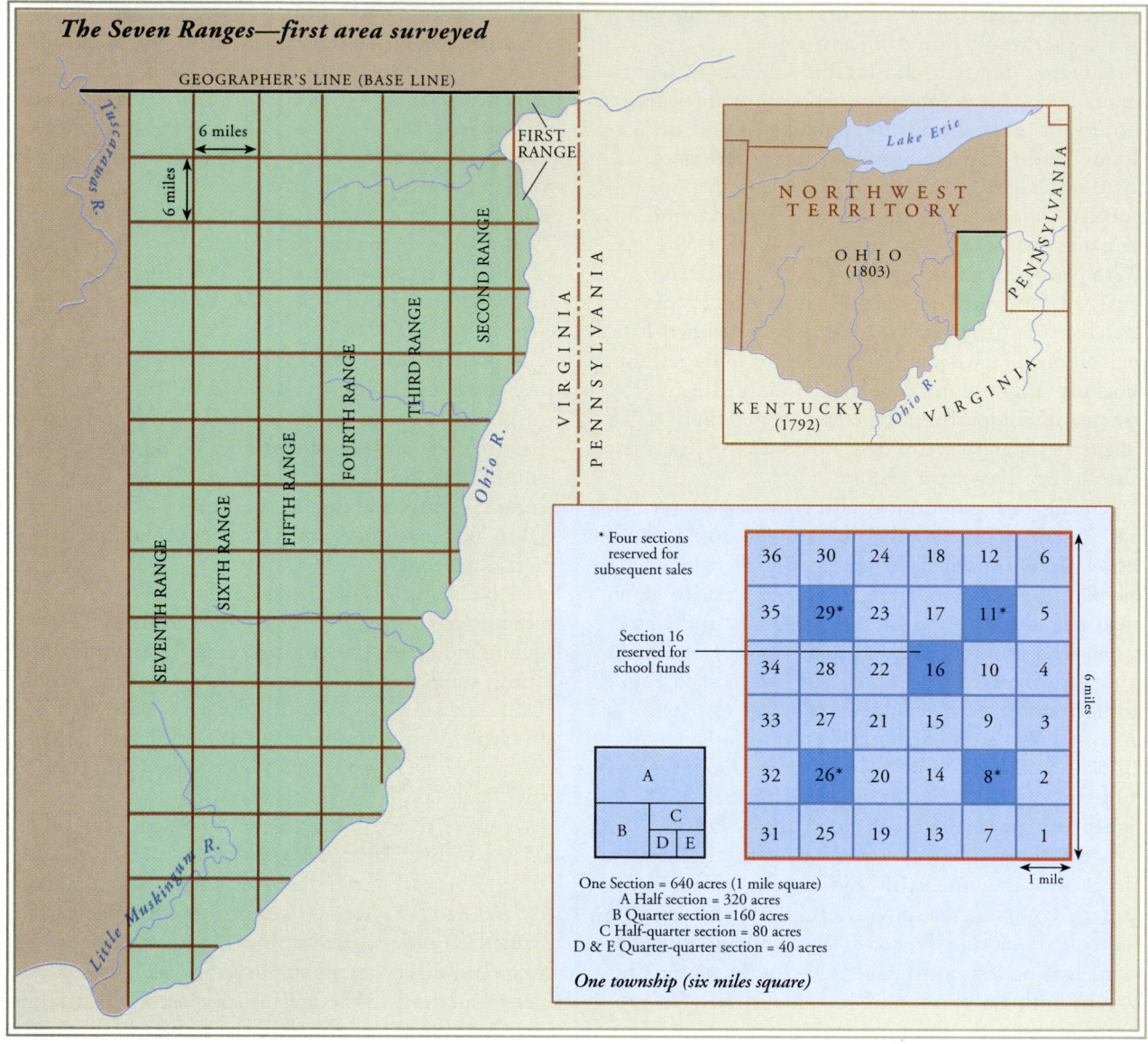

The Seven Ranges—first area surveyed

GEOGRAPHER'S LINE (BASE LINE)

6 miles

6 miles

FIRST RANGE

SECOND RANGE

THIRD RANGE

FOURTH RANGE

FIFTH RANGE

SIXTH RANGE

SEVENTH RANGE

Tuscarawas R.

Ohio R.

Little Muskingum R.

VIRGINIA
PENNSYLVANIA

Lake Erie

NORTHWEST TERRITORY

OHIO (1803)

PENNSYLVANIA

PENNSYLVANIA

KENTUCKY (1792)

Ohio R.

VIRGINIA

* Four sections reserved for subsequent sales

Section 16 reserved for school funds

6 miles

36	30	24	18	12	6
35	29*	23	17	11*	5
34	28	22	16	10	4
33	27	21	15	9	3
32	26*	20	14	8*	2
31	25	19	13	7	1

1 mile

A

B

C

D E

One Section = 640 acres (1 mile square)
A Half section = 320 acres
B Quarter section =160 acres
C Half-quarter section = 80 acres
D & E Quarter-quarter section = 40 acres

One township (six miles square)

MAP 6.2 | LAND ORDINANCE OF 1785

The Northwest Ordinances

Despite war with the Indians and the presence of British troops, the Confederation Congress moved forward with legislation to create the Northwest Territory. The issue of western lands had divided the thirteen states even during the Revolution. Some states claimed territories from their colonial charters, while others, such as Maryland and New Jersey, had never possessed such claims. Titles stood in conflict with one another, as in the case of the region north of the Ohio River, which Virginia claimed in its entirety and Connecticut and Massachusetts claimed in part. States lacking rights to western lands believed that all should be ceded to the Confederation because together the states had won the trans-Appalachian territory in the Revolution. Virginia, whose charter rights were oldest, resolved the issue in 1781 by agreeing to transfer to the United States the region north and west of the Ohio River, the area that later became the states of

Ohio, Indiana, Illinois, Michigan, and Wisconsin. Virginia offered cession on the condition that the territory eventually be divided into states that would join the Confederation on an equal basis with the original thirteen. The trans-Appalachian lands south of the Ohio River remained temporarily under the control of Virginia, North Carolina, and Georgia.

Congress passed three ordinances to establish guidelines for distributing land and governing the Northwest Territory. Wealthy speculators who had purchased rights from Native Americans had significant influence over the shape these ordinances took. Thomas Jefferson was principal author of the first ordinance, which passed Congress in 1784. This law gave settlers a great deal of autonomy in establishing a territorial government. The Northwest would be divided into seven districts, with the settlers of each to govern themselves by choosing a constitution and laws from any of the existing states. When any district reached the population of the smallest of the original thirteen states, it would be admitted as a state to the Confederation on equal terms. Congress retained responsibility for selling the public lands.

The second ordinance, passed in 1785, set the rules for distributing lands. The influence of speculators was apparent, for the minimum price of a lot was $640, payable in specie or its equivalent, a sum far beyond the means of many potential settlers. All property would be surveyed before sale, laid out in townships six miles square. Each lot would contain 640 acres sold at a minimum of one dollar per acre, with better land offered at a higher price. The government retained lots for public schools and for distribution to Revolutionary War veterans. Because of the relatively high cost, Congress found few individual buyers. In fact, many land-hungry squatters simply set up their farms without government approval, sometimes purchasing rights from neighboring Indians, sometimes not. So Congress accepted a deal offered by a group of New England speculators, the Ohio Company, agreeing to sell them 1.5 million acres for $500,000 in depreciated bonds, or less than ten cents per acre in hard money. Given the Confederation's debt, the sale was welcome.

Congress further cooperated with the Ohio Company in drafting the Northwest Ordinance of 1787. In response to speculators' demands, the law established firmer congressional control over the territory, providing settlers less self-government than under the 1784 ordinance. Initially, a governor, secretary, and three judges appointed by Congress would administer the government. When 5,000 adult males resided in the territory, they could elect an assembly, but the governor held a veto over its actions. Men were eligible to vote if they owned at least fifty acres of land. Three to five states would be created from the Northwest Territory, with each state qualified to enter the union when its population reached 60,000. New states would have equal status with the original thirteen. The ordinance of 1787 also included provisions for individual rights that the Congress and the Ohio Company hoped would attract purchasers. They expected many settlers to come from New England. The ordinance protected private contracts, religious liberty, trial by jury, and habeas corpus (protection against illegal imprisonment). It prohibited slavery from the region forever. Thus, while catering to the interests of speculators, the Northwest Ordinance also extended rights won during the Revolution to new settlers in the west. Further, it limited the spread of slavery, and determined that western territories would achieve the status of states rather than remain colonies.

POLITICAL AND ECONOMIC TURMOIL

Political strife under the Articles of Confederation disappointed Americans who had high hopes for their republic. After all, it was a government of their own making, in which everyone was supposed to be represented adequately. But instead of harmony, economic interests clashed; the states failed to satisfy everybody. Many elites thought the United States was becoming too democratic and anarchic, as farmers revolted, government failed to control the violence, and some legislatures approved the insurgents' demands. Corruption seemed to have contaminated their government, just as in the prerevolutionary period it had ruined the British.

Creditors Versus Debtors

As a result of the postwar depression, farmers throughout the United States faced economic hardship. Many had eagerly purchased British manufactures, expecting to pay for the new clothes and consumer goods by

selling their grain and livestock to the West Indies. British merchants offered easy credit to stimulate sales; American merchants and shopkeepers passed the credit on to farm families who would pay with the fall crop.

The house of cards crashed when the British government closed the West Indies to American ships. English mercantile houses called in their debts in specie only, starting a chain of default that extended from London to the frontier. Americans lacked the gold and silver that the British demanded, but merchants refused to accept payment in farm products because they had no market for the goods. So they took farmers to court: In many places, the number of debt cases rose dramatically. For example, in Hampshire County, Massachusetts, from 1784 to 1786, the court heard 3,000 debt cases: Almost one-third of the county's adult males were prosecuted for insolvency.

State governments aggravated the situation by imposing taxes to repay war bonds in full, a policy that worked to the advantage of wealthy speculators who had bought up the bonds from farmers and artisans at a large discount. The Massachusetts government particularly favored mercantile interests, levying on farmers high taxes that also had to be paid in specie. When farmers defaulted, the courts sold their land and cattle, often at only one-third to one-half value. If their assets failed to cover the debts and back taxes, the farmers were imprisoned until they or someone else paid the sum. Often men sat in crowded jails with insufficient ventilation, heat, or food because they owed small debts. Ordinary folk became angry as they feared imprisonment and the loss of their farms.

Farmers Demand Reform

Protesters mobilized as they had in the prerevolutionary period, at first meeting in county conventions to draw up petitions to the state assembly. In Massachusetts, they demanded changes in the state constitution, which many had voted against in 1780, to make the government more responsive to their needs and less costly to run. They wanted abolition of the state senate, which represented the commercial elite; lowering of property qualifications to hold office; and transfer of the capital from Boston to a more central location. Inland towns found it difficult to send representatives to the assembly because expenses were so high. The

farmers also demanded paper money and tender laws, the latter enabling them to settle debts and taxes with goods rather than specie. Both would ease the credit crisis. During the Revolution, the yeomen had benefited from the inflation that resulted from government issued paper money because they received high prices for their produce and were able to pay off prewar debts with cheap dollars. While the farmers stopped short of demanding a return to high inflation, they hoped for a gentle upswing in prices and a larger money supply to help them pay their debts.

When state legislatures emitted paper money or passed tender laws, as in Rhode Island, North Carolina, New York, and Georgia, little unrest ensued. In Rhode Island, political parties channeled conflict, for after the Country party ousted the Mercantile party in spring 1786, the new assembly issued paper money with stiff fines for creditors who refused to accept it. Elites elsewhere referred to "Rogue Island," even suggesting that the state be abolished and divided between Massachusetts and Connecticut.

In other states, mercantile factions maintained control of the government. They detested paper money because debtors would pay in depreciated bills; they opposed tender laws because of the lack of a market for grain and livestock. Merchants argued that paper currency issued as loans on farm property (rather than as notes based on gold and silver deposited in banks) was immoral because it would lose value, allowing debtors to violate contracts by paying back less than they had borrowed. Creditors asserted that their property rights were at risk.

Shays's Rebellion

When state governments failed to help, debtors in New England, New Jersey, Pennsylvania, Maryland, Virginia, and South Carolina protested militantly. Events moved furthest in Massachusetts, where under provocation of the assembly and governor, the farmers rebelled. In fall 1786, armed Massachusetts farmers closed down county courts to prevent further hearings for debt. Perhaps one-fourth of potential soldiers in the state were involved, calling themselves the "Regulators," after the Carolina insurgents of the 1760s. Their opponents first labeled the rebels "Green Bushers" because they wore a sprig of evergreen—the Massachusetts symbol for liberty—then called them Shaysites when Daniel Shays, a forty-year-old veteran

Daniel Shays and Job Shattuck, from the cover of a pamphlet supporting Shays's Rebellion.

of Bunker Hill and Saratoga, emerged as leader. The government, dominated by the eastern elite, frantically requested aid from Congress, which complied by requisitioning $530,000 and 1,340 soldiers from the states. When the states failed to cooperate, the bankruptcy of the Confederation was clear. Congress was powerless, warned those who wanted a stronger central government, even in the face of civil war.

The Massachusetts government acted on its own, taking measures that further alienated angry farmers, inciting greater support for the revolt. The assembly passed the Riot Act, which prohibited armed groups from gathering in public and permitted sheriffs to kill rioters who refused to disband. The legislature also suspended habeas corpus, allowing officials to jail suspected insurgents without showing cause. The farmers refused to back down, as one warned, "I am determined to fight and spill my blood and leave my bones at the courthouse till Resurrection." They protested that the suspension of habeas corpus was "dangerous if not absolutely destructive to a Republican government." Nevertheless, in November 1786, the state government sent 300 soldiers to arrest rebel leaders; when that failed to stop the farmers from closing the courts, Boston merchants raised private funds to outfit 4,400 troops. Residents of Boston and coastal towns who feared the inflationary consequences of paper money filled the ranks. Revolutionary general Benjamin Lincoln commanded the army; in January 1787, they marched to Worcester to protect the county court.

Lincoln's army forced the Shaysites to choose between submission and armed rebellion, for a middle ground of petitions and court closings was no longer

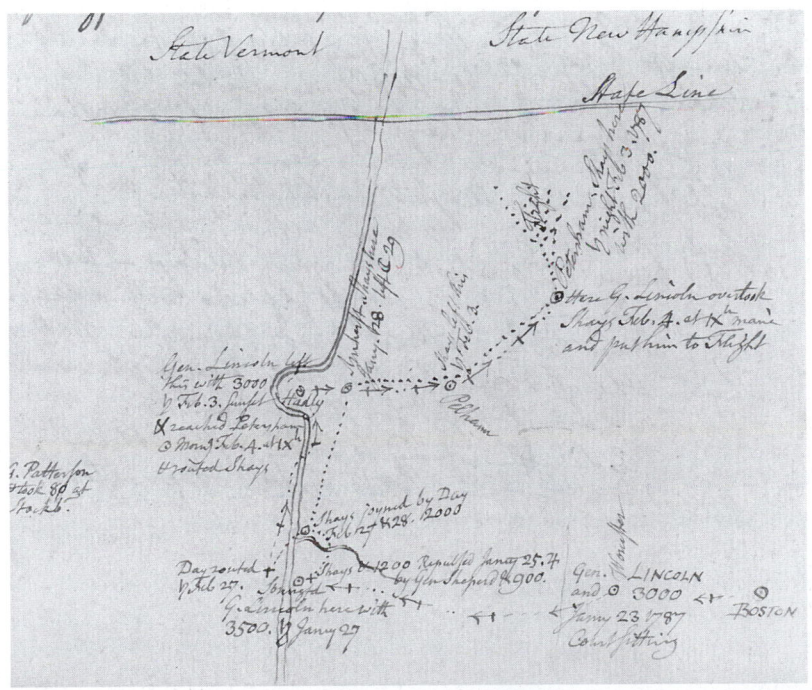

Hand-drawn diagram of the movements of the Shays and Lincoln armies in January–February 1787.

viable. The farmers amassed their own troops, estimated at 2,500 men, with Shays, the former Continental Army captain, in charge of one regiment. They unsuccessfully attacked the federal arsenal at Springfield for weapons to assault Boston, then regrouped to await the merchants' army. Shays was convinced that their cause was just; in a newspaper interview he confidently stated that he "knew General Lincoln was coming against him, but as he would bring with him nobody but shopkeepers, lawyers, and doctors, he could easily defeat him." Lincoln attacked Shays by surprise in a blizzard, dispersing the rebels within half an hour.

The aftermath of Shays's defeat was more divisive and bloody than the engagements between the armies. The assembly declared a state of "open, unnatural, unprovoked, and wicked rebellion," giving the governor the power to treat the Shaysites as enemies of the state. The legislators passed the Disqualification Act, which barred people implicated in the revolt from voting and holding office for three years, teaching school, or keeping inns and taverns. Many of the insurgents escaped to New York and Vermont with their families and possessions. Others, including people who had not been involved, were imprisoned. Militant Shaysites prolonged the conflict by raiding homes and kidnapping merchants, doctors, shopkeepers, and officials who had sided with the government. As a result of the uprising and repression, voter turnout skyrocketed in the April 1787 election. A much greater number of western Massachusetts towns sent delegates to the legislature than they had in previous years, making the new assembly somewhat more responsive to rural debtors. While refusing to approve paper money, it enacted a tender law and quickly restored the civil rights of the insurgents.

THE MOVEMENT FOR CONSTITUTIONAL REFORM

The Confederation's helplessness in response to spreading armed rebellion strengthened the hand of nationalists like Robert Morris and Alexander Hamilton, who had been arguing for a more powerful central government. By 1787, Congress had lost much of its authority, and representatives stopped attending, often preventing action for lack of a quorum. Because it had failed to obtain a national tax and could not force the states to send requisitioned funds, the Confederation was broke. In 1785, Congress stopped interest payments on the French debt and in 1787 ended those on the principal. Nor could it reimburse American creditors. In 1787, Congress transferred responsibility for the national debt to the states.

The Philadelphia Convention

In September 1786, when Shays's Rebellion was still gathering steam, representatives gathered for a convention in Annapolis, Maryland, to discuss amending the Articles to give Congress power to regulate trade. The convention failed when only five state delegations arrived on time. Several of the delegates, including Alexander Hamilton, James Madison, and John Dickinson, called for another convention to meet in May 1787 at Philadelphia to consider a more thorough revision of the Articles. By early 1787, the disorder in Massachusetts and the growing concern about state emission of paper money built support for constitutional reform. In February, Congress endorsed a change. Twelve states—all but Rhode Island where farmers controlled the legislature—sent delegates to Philadelphia.

Though the appointed day was May 14, 1787, the convention failed to start until May 25 when enough representatives finally arrived. State legislatures had delayed choosing their delegations and travel was slow. Among the first were Virginia's representatives, who used the extra time for planning. James Madison, a thirty-six-year-old planter, slaveholder, and intellectual who had served in the Virginia assembly and Congress, came to the convention well prepared. A shy man who avoided public speaking, Madison nevertheless took a dominant role in the proceedings, for which he has been called the father of the Constitution. Propelled by the breakdown of Congress and the problems he witnessed in state government, Madison wanted to reform the Confederation to create a stronger central government. He believed that state constitutions with powerful assemblies were too democratic, giving too much influence to the common people. As a consequence, these legislatures collaborated with debtors by circulating paper money, which Madison considered an attack on property. The people

James Madison, *1783, by Charles Willson Peale. Like most of his fellow delegates, Madison was relatively young when he helped frame the Constitution.*

should be represented adequately, Madison thought, but their power must be constrained. The United States needed a new constitution that would place authority in the hands of well-educated, propertied men. Other Virginia delegates included Governor Edmund Randolph and George Washington, whose popularity and prestige made his support for the convention crucial. Washington presided over the proceedings, but participated little in the debates.

A total of fifty-five men served at the Constitutional Convention between opening day and adjournment four months later. Most were wealthy men, members of the political and social elite. Twenty-one were practicing lawyers, another thirteen had been educated in the law, seven were merchants, and eighteen were farmers or planters; nineteen owned African American slaves. Most were relatively young men under the age of fifty, and many had served in the revolution and had held political office. The elder statesman Benjamin Franklin, now eighty-one years old and ailing, was a member of the Pennsylvania delegation.

Several heroes of the revolution were absent, including Thomas Jefferson and John Adams, who were ambassadors abroad; Samuel Adams, who was not chosen as a delegate; and Patrick Henry, who refused to serve because he "smelt a rat." Most of the delegates supported a plan to place more power in the national government.

The Great Compromise

The convention can be divided into two periods. During the first seven weeks, the matter overshadowing all discussion was the power of "large" versus "small" states. After this issue was resolved, delegations formed blocs in new ways, according to concerns about the executive, slavery, and commerce. The basic question that the convention avoided debating at length was whether to amend the Articles of Confederation or write an entirely new constitution. Madison, who thought the Confederation beyond repair, moved the convention along with a document he had drafted in advance, called the Virginia Plan, which scrapped the Articles. Madison was able to set the convention's agenda because at the outset no other delegate had prepared an alternate design.

The Virginia Plan, which Edmund Randolph presented on May 29, proposed a powerful central government, dominated by a National Legislature of two houses (bicameral). The lower house would be elected by qualified voters and would choose the members of the upper house from nominations by state legislatures. The number of delegates from each state depended upon population. This bicameral National Legislature was empowered to appoint the executive and judicial branches of the central government and to veto state laws.

Several states opposed the Virginia Plan because it gave greater representation in the National Legislature to states with large populations. Delaware, Maryland, New Jersey, and Connecticut feared the power of Virginia, Pennsylvania, and Massachusetts, which together comprised almost one-half of the American people. If the Virginia Plan were adopted, just four states could dominate the legislature and ignore the interests of the rest. In dividing on this issue, states considered the possibility of future population expansion as well as present size. Thus states with unsettled territories mostly

This painting of the Constitutional Convention of 1787 by an unknown artist shows George Washington presiding. Because the convention met in secrecy, the artist used his imagination to paint the scene.

sided with the large states, while those without room for growth chose the opposite camp.

The small states preferred a constitution that retained the structure of the Confederation Congress, but expanded its powers. In mid-June, William Paterson introduced the New Jersey Plan, which proposed a one-house, or unicameral, Congress in which the states had equal representation. Congress would appoint an executive council which in turn would choose a supreme court. As in the Virginia Plan, the authority of Congress was much enlarged, with powers to tax, regulate commerce, and compel states to obey its laws. The large states objected to this plan, arguing that Delaware (population 59,000) should not have as much power as Virginia (population 748,000).

The debate over representation in Congress brought the convention to an impasse. It made little progress toward a new constitution until the issue of state representation was resolved. The large states had the votes in the convention but knew they could never get the document ratified if the Virginia Plan prevailed. The Delaware delegation, as instructed by its legislature, threatened to walk out, until Connecticut put forward its proposal, allowing debate to continue. The "great compromise," as Connecticut's plan be-

came known, established a bicameral Congress, with representation in the lower house based upon population. This house, called the House of Representatives, would be elected directly by the voters and have the sole right to initiate revenue bills. Thus, the idea that people with a stake in society should elect the representatives who taxed them was incorporated into the document. In the upper house, called the Senate, states would have equal representation. According to the Constitution, each state legislature chose two senators to serve six-year terms. The House of Representatives would be elected every two years. The bicameral Congress balanced two different sets of interests: It resolved the division between the small and large states and also satisfied those who wanted to limit the influence of ordinary voters. Senators were expected to come from the wealthier, more established segments of society; their long terms and appointment by state legislators would shield them from public opinion. Both houses of Congress had to approve legislation.

The compromise between the large and small states created a government that was both national and federal. It was *national* because the House of Representatives was popularly elected, with not more than one

representative per 30,000 people. Upon ratification, the United States would become a single nation rather than a confederacy of states. By expanding legislative powers, the sovereign people vested more authority in the central government. Congress received the powers to tax, coin and borrow money, regulate commerce, establish courts, declare war, and raise armed forces. States were specifically forbidden from keeping troops without the permission of Congress, making treaties, coining money, and issuing paper currency. At the same time, the new Constitution established a *federal* government, one in which the states retained rights, including equal representation in the Senate. Congress was forbidden from giving one state preference over another when levying taxes and regulating trade, nor could it impose export duties, prohibit the slave trade until 1808, or carve a new state from any state's territory without permission. Approval by three-fourths of the states would be necessary to amend the Constitution. But despite these provisions, many Americans believed that the states—the small republics—had lost too much power. The struggle for ratification revolved in large part on this issue.

The Executive, Slavery, and Commerce

Once the question of state representation was solved with the "great compromise," the convention made greater headway, amid conflict and further compromise. Factions within the convention shifted from one debate to the next.

The power of the executive was a concern to people living in a world dominated by kings and princes. Delegates wanted to ensure that their government remained a republic, that it would not become a monarchy or dictatorship. At the same time, they believed that the executive branch should serve as a check on the legislature. The convention debated several questions affecting the executive's power. Should there be a single president or an executive board? While some argued that a plural executive could prevent one person from usurping power, the convention chose a single president, expecting to limit his authority in other ways. Length of term also stimulated discussion, for the longer the term the greater a president's autonomy. The convention reached agreement on a four-year term, without specifying the number of times he could be re-elected.

The question of how the president would be chosen was divisive, between those who preferred direct election by the people and those who wanted Congress or the state legislatures to make the choice. Once again, the issue of states' rights reared its head. A committee appointed by the convention devised an ingenious but complicated formula to satisfy all sides—the electoral college. Though the specifics of its operation were subsequently changed by constitutional amendment, presidential elections still occur through this phantom institution. The electoral college was empowered to elect the president and vice president, with each state allotted as many votes as it had representatives and senators. Thus, even the smallest state received three votes and the large states were represented according to population. The state legislatures could determine how to choose the electors, whether by popular election or by the assembly itself. The electoral college would never meet together as a group. The electors of each state gathered within their states to cast votes, which they sent to Congress for counting. If no candidate received a majority, the House of Representatives made the selection from among the five candidates with the most votes.

Of the Philadelphia convention's decisions on the executive, most crucial to the endurance of the Constitution was the balance of power between the executive and legislative branches. The convention gave the president a veto over laws passed by Congress. The legislators could override the veto if two-thirds of both houses approved. Congress also had authority to remove the president by impeachment and trial for treason, bribery, and "other high Crimes and Misdemeanors." Further balancing came in the areas of foreign affairs and the judiciary. While Congress received power to declare war and raise troops, the president served as commander-in-chief. Only with the "advice and consent" of the Senate could the chief executive negotiate treaties and appoint ambassadors, Supreme Court justices, and other officials.

Slavery was a major factor in the convention's deliberations, though the words "slavery," "slave," and "slave trade" appeared nowhere in the 1787 Constitution. African American bondage affected the debates on representation in Congress, the election of the president, and the regulation of commerce. The southern states wanted to include slaves in a state's population when computing delegates to the House of Representatives and votes in the electoral college. Northerners protested that this gave white southerners an unfair

TABLE 6.1	UNITED STATES POPULATION, 1790

	Total (all whites and free African Americans)	Slaves
New England	1,009,206	3,763
Middle Atlantic	1,017,087	45,210
Maryland and Virginia	1,067,338	395,663
Lower South	726,626	237,141

advantage (illustrated in Table 6-1) because enslaved people could not vote. As part of the "great compromise," the convention decided that five enslaved Americans would count as three free persons for apportioning representation and direct taxes among the states. Since three-fifths of slaves living in the Chesapeake and Lower South numbered 380,000 people, the power of white voters south of Pennsylvania was significantly magnified. Later called a "covenant with death" by abolitionists, the "three-fifths compromise" perpetuated slavery in the new republic.

Political bargaining resulted in additional provisions that furthered slavery. The convention approved a fugitive slave clause, which prevented free states from emancipating slaves who had escaped from masters in other states. The delegates also adopted a provision that forbade Congress from prohibiting slave importation for twenty years (with no requirement that it ban the slave trade after that time). North and South Carolina and Georgia demanded the option of importing people from Africa because they expected settlement to continue into western Georgia and the present states of Alabama, Mississippi, and Tennessee. Slaves would be needed, they thought, to work the new plantations. Northern delegates, who might have pushed the convention in the direction of their own states—toward the abolition of slavery—did almost nothing to promote that end.

Instead of trying to eliminate slavery under the new government, the northerners made the regulation of commerce their priority. The Lower South obtained the twenty-year protection of the slave trade when New England delegates promised their support in re-

turn for a compromise on international trade. Because the southern states had different economic interests than the north, they feared giving Congress the power to tax exports and regulate commerce. They suspected that the national government, if dominated by northerners in the future, would place heavy taxes on tobacco, rice, and indigo—the south's main exports. Southerners thought that navigation laws could also work to their detriment, because northern merchants owned most American shipping. If Congress passed legislation requiring that all exports be transported in American ships, southerners would lose the choice of using a foreign, perhaps cheaper, carrier. Northerners, on the other hand, wanted Congress to have the authority to negotiate trade agreements on an equal basis with other nations. Congress could then retaliate if a country imposed restrictions such as closing ports. The convention settled these matters, first by forbidding Congress from imposing export duties, then with a deal that empowered Congress to regulate commerce. In return for South Carolina's vote for the latter provision, New England agreed to extend the slave trade for 20 years.

The Philadelphia convention created a Constitution that shifted important powers to a national government, but still vested a great deal of authority in the states. The framers painstakingly created checks and balances among the branches of government to avoid degeneration of their republic into anarchy or despotism. They required direct popular election of only the House of Representatives, giving that body the right to initiate taxes. The convention incorporated flexibility into the document, which had been

First page of the United States Constitution of 1787.

absent in the Articles of Confederation, by permitting amendment with approval of two-thirds of both houses of Congress and three-fourths of the states. The document shielded some individual rights, though critics argued that many were omitted. The Constitution protected trial by jury in criminal cases and habeas corpus. It banned religious tests for holding office under the United States, ex post facto (retroactive) laws, and bills of attainder, which extinguished a person's civil rights upon sentence of death or as an outlaw. While codifying the principles of self-government and individual liberties, however, the convention—with little dissent—denied them to almost one-fifth of the American population by embedding slavery within the fabric of the new government.

Ratification

After the delegates to the Philadelphia convention signed the Constitution on September 17, 1787, they quickly sent it to the Confederation Congress in New York City. Article 7 of the document required ratification by nine state conventions to establish the new government. States refusing to ratify could remain independent or unite together under another frame of government. The majority of Congress had approved the Constitution as members of the Philadelphia convention, so they forwarded it to the states after little debate. One congressman from Virginia, Richard Henry Lee, tried to bury the document by adding amendments, but was overruled. Advocates of ratification knew that prompt action was necessary to forestall an effective opposition movement.

The group favoring ratification was not particularly well organized but had two advantages over its opponents. One came from the choice of a name, the Federalists, for it undercut the ground on which their adversaries stood. James Madison, Alexander Hamilton, John Jay, and other supporters of the Constitution argued in favor of the federalist provisions that reserved powers to the states as well as the nationalist

Richard Henry Lee, one of the most ardent opponents of the Constitution drafted in Philadelphia during the summer of 1787, tried to kill the document in the Confederation Congress by adding amendments. Here he explains his opposition on the basis that too much power would reside in the central government, which he expected to be dominated by Northerners. Lee thought, in fact, that if the Constitution were ratified without proper amendment, the result could be "Civil War."

I have waited until now to answer your favor of Septr. 18th from Philadelphia, that I might inform you how the Convention plan of Government was entertained by Congress. Your prediction of what would happen in Congress was exactly verified—It was with us, as with you, this or nothing; & this urged with a most extreme intemperance—The greatness of the powers given & the multitude of Places to be created, produces a coalition of Monarchy men, Military Men, Aristocrats, and Drones whose noise, impudence & zeal exceeds all belief—Whilst the Commercial plunder of the South stimulates the rapacious Trader. In this state of things, the Patriot voice is raised in vain for such changes and securities as Reason and Experience prove to be necessary against the encroachments of power upon the indispensable rights of human nature. Upon due consideration of the Constitution under which we now Act, some of us were clearly of opinion that the 13th article of the Confederation precluded us from giving an opinion concerning a plan subversive of the present system and eventually forming a New Confederacy of Nine instead of 13 States. The contrary doctrine was asserted with great violence in expectation of the strong majority with which they might send it forward under terms of much approbation. Having procured an opinion that Congress was qualified to consider, to amend, to approve or disapprove—the next game was to determine that tho a right to amend existed, it would be highly inexpedient to exercise that right, but merely to transmit it with respectful marks of approbation—In this state of things I availed myself of the Right to amend, & moved the Amendments copy of which I send herewith & called the ayes & nays to fix them on the journal—This greatly alarmed the Majority & vexed them extremely—for the plan is, to push the business on with great dispatch, & with as little opposition as possible; that it may be adopted before it has stood the test of Reflection & due examination—They found it most eligible at last to transmit it merely, without approving or disapproving; provided nothing but the transmission should appear on the Journal—This compromise was settled and they took the opportunity of inserting the word *Unanimously,* which applied only to simple transmission, hoping to have it mistaken for an Unanimous approbation of the thing—It states that Congress having Received the Constitution unanimously transmit it &c.—It is certain that no Approbation was given—This constitution has a great many excellent Regulations in it and if it could be reasonably amended would be a fine System—As it is, I think 'tis past doubt, that if it should be established, either a tyranny will result from it, or it will be prevented by a Civil War.

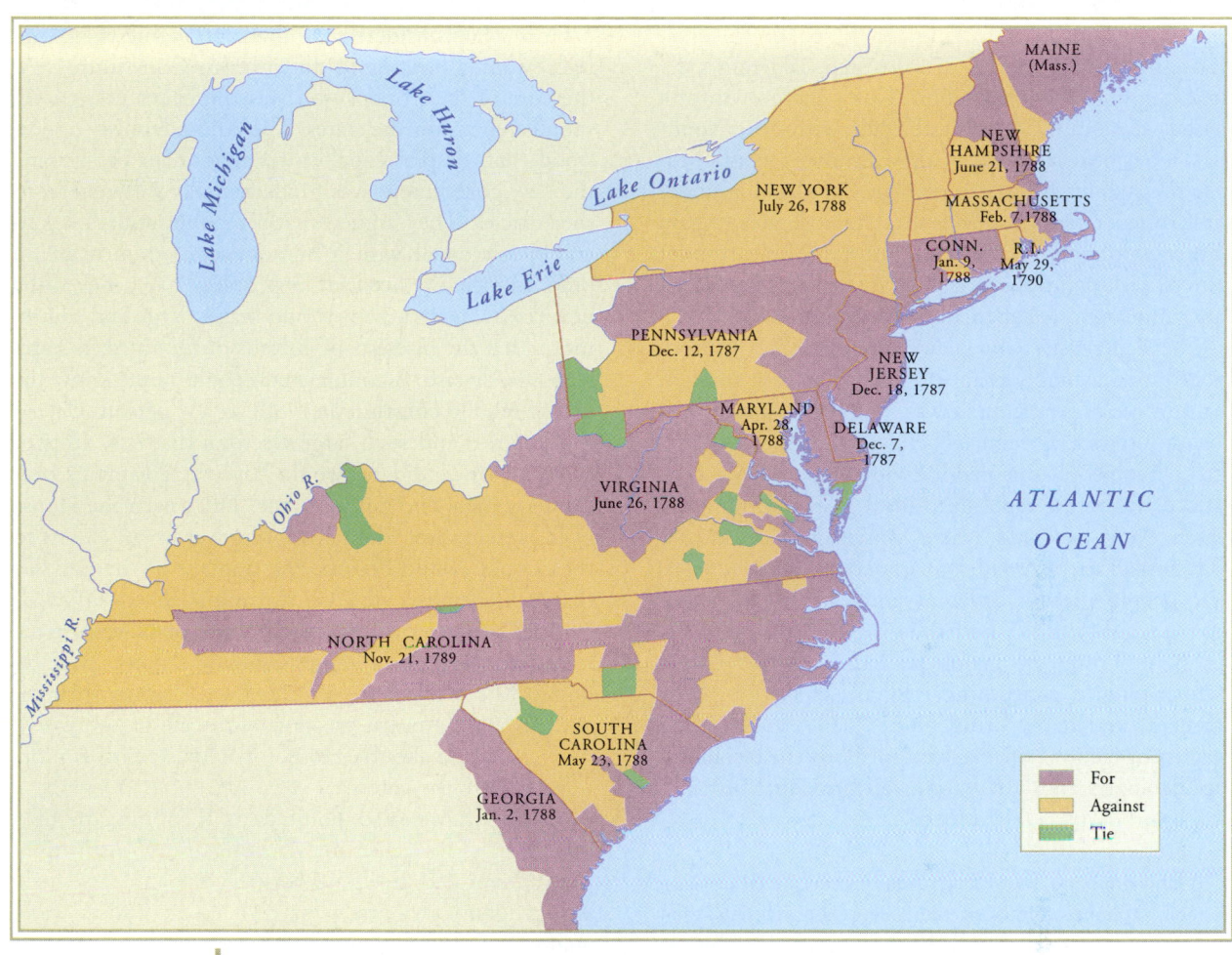

MAP 6.3 | RATIFICATION OF THE CONSTITUTION

elements of the prospective government. While others denounced the Constitution because it transferred too much power to the national government from the states, the Federalists claimed the document provided balance. The critics were obliged to take the negative name of Antifederalists, which misrepresented their position in favor of states' rights. The Federalists also gained advantage from the fact that many advocates of a strong central government resided in the coastal cities and towns, where public opinion was easier to mobilize than in outlying areas. Most newspapers supported the Constitution. For example, in New York, where the ratification battle became intense, Hamilton, Madison, and Jay published in the newspapers a series of eighty-five essays that provided a detailed argument in favor of the Constitution. The essays also gained wide attention outside New York, and in spring 1788, the authors published them in book form as *The Federalist,* which is considered a major work in American political theory.

Americans chose sides over ratification for both political and ideological reasons. Most Federalists gained their livelihoods as merchants, shopkeepers, professionals, artisans, and commercial farmers. As creditors and consumers, many favored the Constitution

because it stopped state emission of paper currency, whose inflationary effects they loathed. Federalists desired a government that would foster the growth of a market economy and facilitate trade with other countries. They believed a national government would provide the stability and strength that were lacking under the Confederation, enabling the United States to gain stature among the nations of Europe. Some frontier settlers, seeking military defense against Native Americans, also supported the Constitution.

The Federalists, who viewed commercial development more favorably than the Antifederalists, thought the purpose of government was to arbitrate among opposing interests. Federalists believed that society benefited when people pursued individual goals. They considered elusive the republican ideal of a community in which everyone could reach consensus because they had similar needs. Madison argued in *Federalist* #10 that people possess different interests because they have unequal abilities and thus varying success in accumulating property. People by nature also have "different opinions concerning religion, concerning government, and many other points." In a free society, they form factions on the basis of both their conflicting ideologies and "the various and unequal distribution of property." He wrote:

> A landed interest, a manufacturing interest, a mercantile interest, a moneyed interest, with many lesser interests, grow up of necessity in civilized nations, and divide them into different classes, actuated by different sentiments and views. The regulation of these various and interfering interests forms the principal task of modern legislation, and involves the spirit of party and faction in the necessary and ordinary operations of the government.

Madison claimed that the Constitution would be beneficial because a large republic contained more safeguards than a small one. In an extended polity, so many factions exist that the ability of a single interest to monopolize power is reduced. With the national government, "you take in a greater variety of parties and interests; you make it less probable that a majority of the whole will have a common motive to invade the rights of other citizens."

Antifederalists disagreed with this analysis, both because they favored small republics and because they feared the actions of men who would likely dominate the central government. Small farmers, many of them

debtors who considered the mercantile elite their enemies, wanted nothing to do with this Constitution. At the core of their opposition was the belief that power should remain in the states. The Antifederalists understood that, despite equal representation in the Senate, the new government was fundamentally different from the Articles. They argued that a republic must be geographically small with a homogeneous population in order to meet the needs of its people. They believed the new central government would be too large and too remote, that the interests of citizens of the thirteen states were too diverse. A congressman could never know the will of 30,000 constituents; with so few persons elected to Congress and such large electoral districts, affluent well-known candidates would have the advantage over ordinary men who ran for office. Thus, even the House of Representatives, the branch of government closest to the people, would become the domain of the rich. To the Antifederalists, the Constitution lacked sufficient barriers against corruption and abuse of power. At the least, term limits on the president and senators were required to prevent these officials from keeping their offices for life. Annual elections (instead of every two years) would make the House of Representatives more responsive to the voters.

Antifederalists also pointed to the omission of a bill of rights as cause for rejecting the Constitution. They advocated freedom of speech, press, assembly, and religion; jury trials for civil cases; judicial safeguards such as the right to a speedy trial and to confront accusers and witnesses; and prohibitions against unwarranted searches and seizures. The Federalists answered that a bill of rights would be superfluous because state constitutions offered these protections (some did, but in no case was protection comprehensive), and because a bill of rights was needed against a powerful king, not when the people themselves were sovereign. This latter argument ignored the vulnerability of the individual to the will of the majority. The Federalists used poor judgment in failing to incorporate a bill of rights into the 1787 Constitution, for the Antifederalists gained momentum as a result. Omitting these rights, for which the patriots had fought, turned many Americans against the proposed frame of government.

Nevertheless, ratification proceeded rapidly at first as state legislatures called elections for the state ratifying conventions. Delaware was the first to ratify when its convention approved the Constitution unani-

mously on December 7, 1787. In Pennsylvania, where resistance was potentially heavy in the backcountry, Federalists moved quickly, securing approval by a two-to-one margin. New Jersey and Georgia then ratified unanimously. When Connecticut accepted the new government in January 1788 by a three-to-one vote, five states had joined the union. All of these states except Pennsylvania were relatively small and recognized the advantages of joining a union in which they had equal representation in the Senate.

Then the conventions became more acrimonious. North Carolina and Rhode Island rejected the document outright and New Hampshire put off its decision. Maryland and South Carolina ratified easily, but the vote in Massachusetts was close, as animosities from Shays's Rebellion colored the debate. Turnout for the Massachusetts convention was huge, as farmers in the central and western regions of the state believed the Constitution represented the interests of the eastern elite. The convention barely ratified the document by a vote of 187 to 168, recommending a series of amendments to protect individual rights and limit the powers of Congress. In June 1788, New Hampshire finally acted, becoming the ninth state to ratify, the number required to establish the new government. Nevertheless, two states remained crucial, Virginia and New York, whose size and economic importance made their approval necessary if the Constitution was to succeed. Virginia ratified in late June after a fierce debate, recommending to the first Congress a series of amendments, including a bill of rights. New York approved in late July, also with recommended changes, after New York City threatened to secede from the rest of the state if rural districts failed to accept the document.

CONCLUSION

With ratification by eleven states, including the most populous and economically dominant, the United States began a new experiment in republican government. The Articles of Confederation had failed to inspire the thirteen states to work together to solve the Confederation's most pressing problems—the national debt, trade, and protection of U.S. borders against Spain and Great Britain. Even Congress's chief success, the legislation for governing and distributing

land in the Northwest Territory, was marred by high land prices, delays in surveying, settlement by squatters, favoritism toward speculators, and conflict with Native Americans. Of course, not all Americans thought the Articles were an utter failure. The Antifederalists preferred a confederacy of sovereign states in which governments stood ready to respond to local needs. But to the Federalists, this had led to paper money and armed rebellion. They demanded a new Constitution, one in which educated, propertied men like themselves would determine national economic policy and foreign affairs. The next challenge for the young United States was to put this new frame of government into effect.

RECOMMENDED READINGS

Beeman, Richard, Botein, Stephen, and Carter, Edward C., eds. *Beyond Confederation: Origins of the Constitution and American National Identity* (1987). These essays provide an excellent introduction to the Confederation period and the making of the Constitution.

Berlin, Ira, and Hoffman, Ronald, eds. *Slavery and Freedom in the Age of the American Revolution* (1983). Important essays on change, or lack thereof, in the status of African Americans during the Revolutionary era.

Doerflinger, Thomas M. *A Vigorous Spirit of Enterprise: Merchants and Economic Development in Revolutionary Philadelphia* (1986). A very good study of Philadelphia merchants and their impact on economic growth in the emergent United States.

Equiano, Olaudah. *The Interesting Narrative of the Life of Olaudah Equiano,* in Henry Louis Gates, Jr., ed., *The Classic Slave Narratives* (1987). Autobiography of a kidnapped African who was enslaved in America, then eventually gained freedom.

Greene, Jack P. *Peripheries and Center: Constitutional Development in the Extended Polities of the British Empire and the United States, 1607–1788* (1986). Links the constitutional structure of Britain and its colonies to the Constitution of 1787.

Hamilton, Alexander, Jay, John, and Madison, James. *The Federalist Papers* (1788). Defense of the Constitution of 1787; seminal treatise of American political thought.

Kenyon, Cecilia M. "Men of Little Faith: The Anti-Federalists on the Nature of Representative Government," *William and Mary Quarterly,* 3rd ser., 12 (1955): 3–43. Insightful essay on the men who opposed ratification of the Constitution of 1787.

Kerber, Linda K. *Women of the Republic: Intellect and Ideology in Revolutionary America* (1980). Evaluates the impact of the revolution on attitudes toward women.

Szatmary, David P. *Shays' Rebellion: The Making of an Agrarian Insurrection* (1980). A detailed study of the western Massachusetts revolt.

Political Ideology, Government, and the Constitution

Appleby, Joyce. *Liberalism and Republicanism in the Historical Imagination* (1992).

Banning, Lance. *The Sacred Fire of Liberty: James Madison and the Founding of the Federal Republic* (1995).

Belz, Herman, Hoffman, Ronald, and Albert, Peter J., eds. *To Form a More Perfect Union: The Critical Ideas of the Constitution* (1992).

Colbourn, Trevor, ed. *Fame and the Founding Fathers: Essays by Douglass Adair* (1974).

"The Constitution of the United States," issue devoted to the Constitution, *William and Mary Quarterly,* 3rd ser., 44 (July 1987).

Greene, Jack P., ed. *The American Revolution: Its Character and Limits* (1987).

Higginbotham, Don. *The War of American Independence: Military Attitudes, Policies, and Practice, 1763–1789* (1971).

Hoffman, Ronald, and Albert, Peter J., eds. *Sovereign States in an Age of Uncertainty* (1981).

Isaac, Rhys. *The Transformation of Virginia, 1740–1790* (1982).

Jensen, Merrill. *The New Nation: A History of the United States During the Confederation, 1781–1789* (1950).

Kurtz, Stephen G., and Hutson, James H., eds. *Essays on the American Revolution* (1973).

Main, Jackson Turner. *The Antifederalists: Critics of the Constitution, 1781–1788* (1961).

Main, Jackson Turner. *Political Parties Before the Constitution* (1973).

Main, Jackson Turner. *The Sovereign States, 1775–1783* (1973).

McDonald, Forrest. *E Pluribus Unum: The Formation of the American Republic, 1776–1790,* 2d ed. (1979).

Miller, William Lee. *The Business of May Next: James Madison and the Founding* (1992).

Morgan, Edmund S. *The Birth of the Republic, 1763–89,* 3rd ed. (1992).

Rakove, Jack N. *The Beginnings of National Politics: An Interpretive History of the Continental Congress* (1979).

Wood, Gordon S. *The Creation of the American Republic, 1776–1787* (1969).

Women and African Americans in Postrevolutionary Society

Berlin, Ira. *Slaves Without Masters: The Free Negro in the Antebellum South* (1974).

Hoffman, Ronald, and Albert, Peter J. eds. *Women in the Age of the American Revolution* (1989).

Gelles, Edith B. *Portia: The World of Abigail Adams* (1992).

Jensen, Joan M. *Loosening the Bonds: Mid-Atlantic Farm Women, 1750–1850* (1986).

Jordan, Winthrop D. *White over Black: American Attitudes Toward the Negro, 1550–1812* (1968).

MacLeod, Duncan J. *Slavery, Race, and the American Revolution* (1974).

McColley, Robert. *Slavery and Jeffersonian Virginia* (1964).

Nash, Gary B., and Soderlund, Jean R. *Freedom by Degrees: Emancipation in Pennsylvania and Its Aftermath* (1991).

Nash, Gary B. *Race and Revolution* (1990).

Ulrich, Laurel Thatcher. *A Midwife's Tale: The Life of Martha Ballard, Based on Her Diary, 1785–1812* (1990).

Zilversmit, Arthur. *The First Emancipation: The Abolition of Slavery in the North* (1967).

Native Americans and the West

Dowd, Gregory Evans. *A Spirited Resistance: The North American Indian Struggle for Unity, 1745–1815* (1992).

McLoughlin, William G. *Cherokee Renascence in the New Republic* (1986).

Onuf, Peter S. *The Origins of the Federal Republic: Jurisdictional Controversies in the United States, 1775–1787* (1983).

Onuf, Peter S. *Statehood and Union: A History of the Northwest Ordinance* (1987).

Wallace, Anthony F. C. *The Death and Rebirth of the Seneca* (1970).

Weber, David J. *The Spanish Frontier in North America* (1992).

White, Richard. *The Middle Ground: Indians, Empires, and Republics in the Great Lakes Region, 1650–1815* (1991).

The Economy and Political Unrest

Ferguson, E. James. *The Power of the Purse: A History of American Public Finance, 1776–1790* (1961).

Foner, Eric. *Tom Paine and Revolutionary America* (1976).

Hall, Van Beck. *Politics Without Parties: Massachusetts 1780–1791* (1972).

Hoffman, Ronald, et al., eds. *The Economy of Early America: The Revolutionary Period, 1763–1790* (1988).

Kulikoff, Allan. *The Agrarian Origins of American Capitalism* (1992).

McCusker, John J., and Menard, Russell R. *The Economy of British America, 1607–1789, With Supplementary Bibliography* (1991).

Merrill, Michael, and Wilentz, Sean, eds. *The Key of Liberty: The Life and Democratic Writings of William Manning, "A Laborer," 1747–1814* (1993).

Pole, J. R. *Political Representation in England and the Origins of the American Republic* (1966).

Rothenberg, Winifred Barr. *From Market-Places to a Market Economy: The Transformation of Rural Massachusetts, 1750–1850* (1992).

Preparation for WAR to defend Commerce.

The Swedish Church Southwark with the building of the FRIGATE PHILADELPHIA.

BUILDING THE *PHILADELPHIA*

Preparation for War to defend Commerce *(1800), illustrating construction of the frigate* Philadelphia. *During the 1790s the United States tried to remain neutral in the European wars while prospering from international trade.*

Chapter 7

THE FEDERALIST REPUBLIC, 1789–1799

AFTER RATIFICATION, THE Federalists took leadership in creating the new government. Everyone expected George Washington to become president, though he was reluctant to assume office. The three authors of *The Federalist,* Alexander Hamilton, James Madison, and John Jay, who had been so important in achieving the Constitution, went on to play a central role in making it work. John Adams and Thomas Jefferson, who were serving as ambassadors in Europe during the convention but supported the document, returned home to become, respectively, vice president and secretary of state.

Though many Federalists disagreed with specific parts of the Constitution, they accepted compromise and knew the weak Confederation had to be replaced. In the flush of victory over the Antifederalists, they set to the task of remedying the nation's ills. Differences soon became clear, however, between Hamilton on the one side, and Madison and Jefferson on the other, as the first administration tackled the national debt and foreign policy. As a result of their conflict over policy, varying interpretations of the Constitution, competition for power, and personal enmity, the nation's first political parties developed.

THE NEW GOVERNMENT

The first national elections went well, from the Federalist point of view, considering the whirlwind of Antifederalist opposition to the Constitution. The great majority of representatives and senators in the first Congress were Federalists. They fulfilled Madison's image of well-to-do men of national reputation and experience in politics. Many had served in the constitutional convention and had signed the document. Most had military or political experience during the Revolution and Confederation period; just a few came from lower-class backgrounds. While the first congressmen were revolutionaries, they were also elites who believed that the country's interests coincided with their own. They wanted a stable government to foster economic growth.

George Washington Becomes President

The choice of George Washington as president was a foregone conclusion, though he would have preferred

CHRONOLOGY

1789	First Congress meets
	Inauguration of George Washington as president
	French Revolution begins
	Judiciary Act of 1789
1790	Site on Potomac River chosen for permanent capital
	Congress approves the funding and assumption plans
	Samuel Slater builds first water-powered textile mill in the United States
	First national census
	Nootka Convention
1791	Bank of the United States is established
	Native Americans of the Ohio Valley destroy Arthur St. Clair's army
	Ratification of Bill of Rights
1793	France declares war on Great Britain and Spain
	Washington begins second term
	Proclamation of Neutrality
	Genêt Affair
	Britain seizes U.S. merchant fleet
	Eli Whitney invents cotton gin
1794	Battle of Fallen Timbers
	Whiskey Rebellion
1795	Senate approves the Jay Treaty
	Treaty of Greenville
	Treaty of San Lorenzo
1797	John Adams becomes second president
1798	XYZ Affair becomes public
	Congress passes Alien and Sedition Acts
	Kentucky and Virginia Resolutions
1798–1800	Quasi-War with France
1799	The Fries Rebellion
	Napoleon takes power in France

to stay at his Mount Vernon estate in northern Virginia. In February 1789, members of the electoral college, selected by popular election in five states, by the governor and council in New Jersey, and by the legislatures of the remaining states, met in their state capitals to cast unanimous votes for the former commander-in-chief. They considered no one else. Washington's leadership during the war, his dignity and character, and his support for republican government made him the obvious choice. He might have tried to grasp power during the shaky Confederation, like a Napoleon or Stalin, but he did not. The first president's commitment to the success of the Constitution ensured the nation's survival during the early years. John Adams, elected vice president, received fewer than half as many votes as Washington.

The president-elect's trip from Mount Vernon to New York City, the temporary federal capital, became an eight-day triumphal march, despite Washington's desire to keep it simple. In large and small towns along his way—Alexandria, Baltimore, Wilmington, Philadelphia—crowds of people, troops of infantry and cavalry, and local officials feted him with ceremonies, cannon fire, and banquets. Philadelphia citizens erected a Roman arch, crowning the Revolutionary hero with a laurel wreath. In New Jersey, throngs saluted his military victories at Trenton and Princeton. On April 23, 1789, Washington crossed into Manhattan on a festooned barge, welcomed by thousands of cheering New Yorkers. He took the oath of office a week later.

The president and Congress, aware that they were setting precedent for the nation, initially placed a great deal of emphasis on titles and the comportment of officials. In this republic, in a world of monarchies, how should they be addressed? Should the president keep his door open and go out to dinner with friends, or should he remain detached? While the questions may

George Washington arrived in New York City for his inauguration as president to the cheers of thousands.

seem trivial, they indicate, at a human level, the novelty of this republican experiment. Sitting as president of the Senate, Vice President Adams, with diplomatic experience in Europe, urged Congress to adopt titles like those of other nations. A Senate committee suggested, for example, that Washington be called "His Highness the President of the United States of America, and Protector of their Liberties." After much debate, Congress dropped the notion of titles, preferring a more republican style. Washington and his successors have been addressed simply as "Mr. President."

For his part, the president wondered how to dignify his office and accomplish his work. He could easily have spent all of his time meeting with visitors, entertaining, and dining out. On the other hand, he did not want complete separation from the people. Washington's personality tended toward aloofness. He decided to hold a one-hour reception once a week, invite a few visitors to dinner, and sometimes attend the theater. In busy New York City, he enforced a distance that nineteenth-century presidents found easier to maintain in more isolated Washington, D.C.

Washington also developed, by trial and error, the way in which the chief executive would deal with Congress. Early in his administration, in advance of negotiating a treaty with the Creek Indians, he attended the Senate to request their "advice and consent," as the Constitution seemed to direct. The senators were unprepared to discuss Washington's proposal, leading to embarrassment on both sides. The president resolved never to consult in formal session again. Instead, he set the precedent of private informal meetings with members of Congress. Heads of executive departments, such as the secretary of the treasury, would attend congressional hearings, not the president. And in the case of treaties, the executive would seek the Senate's consent *after* negotiations were complete, not advice—at least formally—beforehand.

Beyond titles and modes of operating, Congress and the president needed to establish executive departments and courts, and draw up a bill of rights. They filled gaps in the written Constitution. In creating executive departments, which included War, Treasury, State (foreign affairs), and the attorney general, the most crucial constitutional question concerned who would be able to remove the heads of departments from office. The Constitution required that the president appoint officials with the Senate's advice and consent. It said nothing about removal. Some senators hoped to restrict the president's power by requiring Senate approval before officeholders could be fired, thus making them more accountable to the legislature. In rejecting this proposal, Congress clarified one aspect of the Constitution's balance of powers.

The Bill of Rights, 1791

During the debates over ratification of the Constitution, many people argued for increased protection of individual rights, including freedom of religion, speech, the press, assembly, and petition, and judicial safeguards such as the right to a speedy trial and prohibition of cruel punishments. The Bill of Rights, or Amendments 1 through 10, added such provisions to the Constitution.

Amendment I
Congress shall make no law respecting an establishment of religion, or prohibiting the free exercise thereof; or abridging the freedom of speech, or of the press; or the right of the people peaceably to assemble, and to petition the government for a redress of grievances.

Amendment II
A well-regulated militia being necessary to the security of a free State, the right of the people to keep and bear arms shall not be infringed.

Amendment III
No soldier shall, in time of peace, be quartered in any house without the consent of the owner, nor in time of war, but in a manner to be prescribed by law.

Amendment IV
The right of the people to be secure in their persons, houses, papers, and effects, against unreasonable searches and seizures, shall not be violated, and no warrants shall issue but upon probable cause, supported by oath or affirmation, and particularly describing the place to be searched, and the persons or things to be seized.

Amendment V
No person shall be held to answer for a capital, or otherwise infamous crime, unless on a presentment or indictment of a grand jury, except in cases arising in the land or naval

With the Judiciary Act of 1789, Congress put some flesh on the skeleton outlined in Article III of the Constitution, which stated that the "judicial power of the United States shall be vested in one Supreme Court, and in such inferior courts as the Congress may from time to time ordain and establish." The Congress might have created a full-blown national court system, unifying state and federal law. Supporters of states' rights, however, opposed such enhancement of national power. Thus, the Judiciary Act, the result of compromise, established a Supreme Court of six justices and a system of federal inferior courts, which were few in number and restricted primarily to consideration of federal crimes. State courts retained original jurisdiction in most civil and criminal cases, with the U.S. Supreme Court taking appeals from the highest state courts. John Jay, one of *The Federalist* authors, became the first chief justice.

forces, or in the militia, when in actual service in time of war or public danger; nor shall any person be subject for the same offense to be twice put in jeopardy of life or limb; nor shall be compelled in any criminal case to be a witness against himself, nor be deprived of life, liberty, or property, without due process of law; nor shall private property be taken for public use without just compensation.

Amendment VI

In all criminal prosecutions, the accused shall enjoy the right to a speedy and public trial, by an impartial jury of the State and district wherein the crime shall have been committed, which district shall have been previously ascertained by law, and to be informed of the nature and cause of the accusation; to be confronted with the witnesses against him; to have compulsory process for obtaining witnesses in his favor, and to have the assistance of counsel for his defense.

Amendment VII

In suits at common law, where the value in controversy shall exceed twenty dollars, the right of trial by jury shall be preserved, and no fact tried by a jury shall be otherwise re-examined in any court of the United States, than according to the rules of the common law.

Amendment VIII

Excessive bail shall not be required, nor excessive fines imposed, nor cruel and unusual punishments inflicted.

Amendment IX

The enumeration in the Constitution, of certain rights, shall not be construed to deny or disparage others retained by the people.

Amendment X

The powers not delegated to the United States by the Constitution, nor prohibited by it to the States, are reserved to the States respectively, or to the people.

The Bill of Rights

During its first months, Congress took up the question of amending the Constitution to satisfy criticisms voiced during ratification, objections that by the summer of 1789, still kept North Carolina and Rhode Island out of the Union. More than the original document, the first ten amendments, called the Bill of Rights, represented the will of the American people, who demanded protection of individual rights.

The ratification campaign had elicited a mountain of proposals for amending the Constitution. Opponents offered two major grounds for altering the document or abandoning it altogether. Antifederalist leaders believed it took too much power from the states, and from themselves as leaders of state and local governments, while popular opinion feared the loss of

personal freedoms to a strong national government. State ratifying conventions, even as they voted for the Constitution, suggested amendments to ensure freedom of religion, speech, and the press, and safeguards for fair trials.

James Madison became the chief proponent of the Bill of Rights in Congress, despite his earlier advocacy of the Federalist position that the amendments were unnecessary. In order to get elected to the House of Representatives, he had promised his Virginia constituents to obtain the safeguards. Madison took his vow seriously, pushing his reluctant Federalist colleagues to the task. Antifederalist leaders, who wanted to scrap the Constitution entirely, now denied support to the Bill of Rights because they knew protection of individual freedoms would garner popular support.

After much negotiation between the Senate and the House, on September 25, 1789, Congress sent to the states for ratification a total of twelve amendments. By December 15, 1791, three-quarters of the states approved the ten amendments known as the Bill of Rights, thus putting them into effect. Of the two amendments not approved at the time, one was a rule concerning congressional salaries that was not ratified for two centuries, until 1992, and the other was a complicated formula for computing representation in Congress that was never adopted. Of the Bill of Rights, Articles 1 through 8 enumerated basic individual rights, while the intention of Article 9 was to protect any personal freedoms omitted from this list. Article 10 directed that "powers not delegated to the United States by the Constitution, nor prohibited by it to the States, are reserved to the States respectively, or to the people." It addressed concerns that the national government might assume powers that were not mentioned in the Constitution. Passage of the Bill of Rights by Congress attracted enough support to bring in the two remaining states; North Carolina ratified the Constitution in November 1789 and Rhode Island followed suit in May 1790.

The First Census

Congress also promptly ordered a census of the American population, which the Constitution required within three years of Congress's first meeting and every ten years subsequently. The census, the founders expected, would provide an accurate enumeration for apportioning delegates to the House of Representa-

TABLE 7.1 THE U.S. POPULATION, 1790	Total	Slaves
United States	**3,929,625**	**697,624**
New England	**1,009,206**	**3,763**
Maine (part of Massachusetts)	96,643	0
New Hampshire	141,899	157
Vermont	85,341	0
Massachusetts	378,556	0
Rhode Island	69,112	958
Connecticut	237,655	2,648
Middle States	**1,017,087**	**45,210**
New York	340,241	21,193
New Jersey	184,139	11,423
Pennsylvania	433,611	3,707
Delaware	59,096	8,887
Southern States and Territories	**1,903,332**	**648,651**
Maryland	319,728	103,036
Virginia	747,610	292,627
North Carolina	395,005	100,783
South Carolina	249,073	107,094
Georgia	82,548	29,264
Kentucky	73,677	12,430
Tennessee	35,691	3,417

tives and electoral college. Congress set August 1790 as the date for the first census, appointing marshals to complete their work within nine months, which actually stretched to eighteen. The first census was less complicated than later ones, with just six questions: name of head of household, number of free white males aged sixteen years and over, number of free white males under sixteen, number of free white females, number of other free persons, and number of slaves. The census set categories based on race, sex, and age that would be elaborated in later counts. The separate listing of enslaved persons was required by the clause of the Constitution that counted three-fifths of slaves for representation and taxes. The distinction between free whites and blacks came from cultural values rather than some practical use. The census did not include Native Americans who lived outside areas settled by whites.

U.S. Federal Census of 1790

This excerpt from the first U.S. Federal Census shows households on several streets in Philadelphia. The census provides much evidence about urban society in 1790, including the names, occupations, sex, and race of heads of household, but less information on other members of their households. Note that many more free blacks than slaves lived in this part of Philadelphia by 1790.

Name of Head of Family.	*Free White Males of 16 Years and Upward Including Heads of Families.*	*Free White Males Under 16 years.*	*Free White Females Including Heads of Families.*	*All Other Free Persons*	*Slaves.*
PHILADELPHIA CITY—continued.					
North Fifth street from Market to Race street, East side.					
Wheelen, Israel (Grocer)	2	3	7		
Leacock, John (Coroner)	3	2	2		
Howell, Samuel (Brush Mak^{r})	1		3		
Bell, Barbary (Widow)	1		2		
Shaw, John (Carpenter)	2	1	1		
Langdell, Margaret (Spinster)			3		
Snowden, George (Carp^{r})	3		4		
Shea, John (Shoe maker)	2	2	4		
Cruds, George (Breeches Mak^{r})	1	3	2		
Paschall, Stephen (Gent^{e})	1	3	5	1	
Detrick, Michael (Shoemaker)	3	1	1		
Shearer, Peter (Skinner)	2	3	2		
Church Burial Ground					
Gilmore, Daniel (Negroe)				2	
Davison, William (Gent.)	1	1	2	1	
Elton, Thomas (Joyner; S.)					
Gitz, John (plaisterer)	2	3	2		
Kroll, John (Barber)					
Wyman, Jacob (Taylor)	2	2	4		
Dutch Meeting Burial Ground					
North Fifth street from Market to Race street, West side.					
Cochran, Elizabeth (Widow)			1		
Yeager, Adam (Cedar Cooper)	2	2	4		
Boeush, Adam (Reed Mak^{r})	1	5	5		
Facundus, Peter (Shoe Maker)	2		2		
Wolf, Lewis (Barber)	1	2	3		
Clark, Joseph (School Mast.)	1	1	1		
Enk, Jacob (Taylor)	3	1	5		
Wallace, Burton (Brick-layer & Mason)	1		3	1	
Randell, Thomas (Clerk)	1	1	3		
James, John (Merch^{t})	2	1	2		
Ogle, Cath^{e} (Widow)	4		2		
Ritter, Henry (Baker)	1	1	7		
Steines, Frederick (Taylor)	1		3		
Field, Eleanor (Tayloress)			3		
Eckfelt, Jacob (Black Smith)	7	6	8		
Wilson, James (Coach Mak^{r}; S.)					
Clark, Samuel (Board Merch^{t})	2	1	4		
Alexander, Margaret (Spinster)			2		
Sadler, Matthew (Carp^{r}; S.)					
PHILADELPHIA CITY—continued.					
Middle district—Con.					
North Fifth street from Market to Race street, West side—Continued.					
Vandell, George (Negroe)				4	
Whig Quaker Meeting House					
Elwin, Hugh (Shoemaker)	1	1	2		
Weaver, William (Lab^{r})	1	1	2		
Noah, Emanuel (Trader)	1	2	3		
Hartung, William (Scrivener)	1		3		
Robins, Isabella (Widow)	1	1	3		
Dawson, Elias (Merchant)	1	2	4		
Henbury, Thomas (Fish monger)	4		6		
Newman, Frederick (Card maker)	1	1	3		
Kein, Christian (Bl. Smith; S.)	1		3		
Lawrence, Philip (Joyner)	2		2		
Rawlston, George (Custom h^{o} Officer)	1		3		
Ross, Oliver (Comb Mak^{r})	1	1	3		
Dougherty, Daniel (Shoe Maker)	2	1	3		
Wayne, John & Lab^{rs}	3	3	5		
Miller, Jacob (Carter)	1		1		
Robinson, Ebenezar (Brush Mak^{r})	1		2		
Dexter, James (Negroe)				7	
Roe, Thomas (Taylor)	3		3		
Howell, Reading (Surveyor)	4	2	4	1	
Evans, Cadwallader (Merch^{t})	1		3		
Taggart, Robert (Gent.)	1		3		
Evans, Robert (Ho. Carp^{r})	4	2	4		
Hudson, Samuel (Gent^{n})	2		2		
Seyfreid, Jacob (Barber)	1	1	2		
Nail, Henry (Shoemaker)	1		3		
Dennis, John (Shoemaker)	2	1	3		
Meyer, Henry (Inn keeper)	4	3	2		
South Sixth street from Market to Chestnut street, East side.					
Clark, David	7	3	5	1	
Christie, Alexander (painter; S.)	1	2	4		
Gilmore, Samuel (Carp^{r})	1		5		
Hartong, Robert (Lab^{r})	2		1		
South Sixth street from Market to Chestnut street, West side.					
Polk, Adam	1		1		
Ellcott, James (Innkeeper)	1	1	4		
Benge, Samuel (Umbrella M.)	2		1	1	
PHILADELPHIA CITY—continued.					
Middle district—Con.					
South Sixth street from Market to Chestnut street, West side—Con.					
Street, Robert (Shoemaker)	1	1	1		
Welcher, Henry (Lab^{r})	1		2		
Lace, William (Bl. Smith)	1	1	2		
Keen, Reynold. Esqr	4	2	8	2	2
Gray, W^{m} & Joseph (Brewers)	1				
Matthar, Peter (Inn keeper)	1	1	4	2	1
North Sixth street from Market to Race street, East side.					
Donnalson, Joseph (Gent.)	1		4	2	
Redman, Joseph (Doct^{r} P.)					
Simmons, William (Auditors Office)					
Erwin, Robert (Gent^{n})	1	1	1		
Elmsley, Alexander (Carp^{r})	1	1	4		
Link, Frederick (Drayman)	3	3	7		
Albright, Michael (Ced^{r} Cooper)	1	3	2		
Nusshag, Charles Willm (Baker)	1	5	4		
Davis, Sampson (Lab.)	1	3	4		
Hudson, William	4	3	8		
Hawker, Godfrey (Baker)	2	2	4		
Elter, George (Coach Maker; S.)					
Fotter, Matt^{s} (porter)	2		1		
Branger, William (Lab^{r})	1	1	5		
Brinner, George (Taylor)	1		2		
Greer, Jacob (Butcher)	1	1	2		
Walker, Martha (Widow)		1	1		
Miney, Godfrey (Baker)	1	2	5		
Rust, Leonard (Meal Seller & Innkeeper; S.)	1		3		
Gray, Joseph (Brewer)	1	1	3		
Humphries, Amy (Spinst^{r})		1	3		
Harper, John (Bl. Smith; S.)					
Hallowell, Thomas (Joyner)	1	3	2		
Cunningham, Robert (Weaver)	1	1	4		
McConnell, John (Lab)	1		2		
Venables, Robert (Negroe)				4	
Sandiford, Rowland (Coach Mak^{r})	1		3		
Dietz, Henry (Watchman)	2	1	3		
Guest, James (Taylor)	1	1	2		
Lambert, John (Chair Mak^{r})	1		1		
Haseelback, Philip (Shoemaker)	2	2	2		
Hansell, Jacob (Bl. Smith)	1	3	1		

While sketchy and incomplete, the 1790 census served as a baseline for measuring the growth of a dynamic, expanding people. President Washington reported to Congress a total of 3.9 million people, of whom 60,000 were free African Americans and almost 700,000 were slaves. The census covered the territory included in the thirteen original states, and also Vermont, Kentucky, and Tennessee, which became states respectively in 1791, 1792, and 1796. It did not encompass the area north of the Ohio River where at least 4,000 white settlers had taken up land.

During the 1780s, the white population of the country had swelled by an extraordinary 44 percent, mostly through reproduction; in the 1790s, the increase remained high at 36 percent. After the Treaty of Paris, European immigrants had once again begun crossing the Atlantic Ocean, with the majority coming from Ireland. From 1783 to 1799, 156,000 Europeans entered the United States, of whom 69 percent were Irish, 14 percent were English, Scottish, and Welsh, and 6 percent were German. The African American population also grew quickly during the 1780s and 1790s, at a rate of 32 percent per decade.

Especially striking in the 1790 census are the small numbers of enslaved African Americans in New England and Pennsylvania compared with Maryland, Virginia, and the Carolinas, the result in part of northern abolition. This sectional difference would grow in the nineteenth century as the north focused more on commerce and developed a manufacturing sector, while the south cast its fate with agriculture, adopting cotton as its major crop.

OPPOSING VISIONS OF AMERICA

Almost immediately during Washington's first administration, political divisions arose between sides favoring commerce versus agriculture. Two divergent conceptions of the nation's future emerged among leaders who had formerly cooperated in adopting the Constitution. During the early 1790s, two political parties developed, though their leaders were loathe to call them that because most Americans still considered parties as "evil," as detrimental to unified republican government. As events unfolded in foreign and domestic affairs, the two parties contested one issue after

another. Both sides, however, helped to confirm the Constitution by claiming to be its steadfast defenders.

Hamilton Versus Jefferson

Alexander Hamilton, appointed by Washington as secretary of the Treasury, saw the future greatness of the United States in commerce and manufacturing, though in 1790, the country was overwhelmingly agrarian. Born in the West Indies, Hamilton attended King's College in New York City, then served as Washington's aide-de-camp during the Revolution. Highly intelligent, full of energy and enthusiasm, he was a major proponent of the new Constitution. Appointment to the treasury allowed Hamilton to promote his concept of a strong nation, which he modeled on Great Britain for its dominance in international trade, innovations in banking, and burgeoning industry. Hamilton's efforts to foster commerce and manufacturing aroused resistance among former allies, particu-

Alexander Hamilton, *1792, by John Trumbull. The first secretary of the treasury saw Great Britain, with its strong central government and expanding industrial economy, as a model for the new United States.*

larly Madison and Jefferson, leading to bitter partisan disputes.

Hamilton's party, which embraced the name Federalist though it was really nationalist, favored commercial development, a national bank, high tariffs to spur manufacturing, and a strong central government based upon a "loose" interpretation of the Constitution, which allowed expansive powers to Congress and the president. The Federalists favored the British, abhorred the French Revolution after 1792, and were generally suspicious of power wielded by ordinary folk. They were somewhat critical of slavery, however, and gained the allegiance of free blacks. Because their power base lay in New England and the Middle States, the Federalists could generate little enthusiasm for western expansion and sometimes supported the right of Native Americans to retain their lands.

The Republican party, in contrast, favored a "strict" interpretation of the Constitution, opposing a strong central government and federal privileges for manufacturing and commerce. They thought Hamilton's plans for funding the national debt, the bank, and protective tariffs infringed upon states' rights and helped the "few" at the expense of the "many." They disdained the British model and charged Hamilton with advocating a return to monarchy. With their power base in the south, west, and northern cities, the Republicans rejected efforts to abolish slavery and were ardent expansionists on the frontier. They had little sympathy for Indian rights.

Thomas Jefferson became the chief spokesman for the Republican party, though James Madison collaborated in its growth. Jefferson, a wealthy planter and slaveholder, author of the Declaration of Independence, former ambassador to France, and now Washington's secretary of state, argued that Hamilton wanted too much national power. Jefferson rejected the British model of banks and large-scale industry. He believed the root of Britain's effort to destroy American liberty in the 1760s and 1770s had been commercial speculation and greed. Manufacturing in cities created poverty, dependency, and political corruption. Instead, the United States, with limitless land, should foster an agrarian society of small producers. A virtuous republic was one made up of small farmers whose goal was to produce enough to support their families, not make a fortune. Commerce should exist primarily to allow them to sell their surplus in Europe and purchase manufactured goods in return. The farmers should be educated to participate wisely in republican government. Their self-sufficiency and

Thomas Jefferson, *1791, by Charles Willson Peale. The first secretary of state, who favored an agrarian republic, strict construction of the Constitution, and the French, quickly became Hamilton's chief opponent.*

education would make them virtuous, to act for the good of society rather than solely for their own gain.

Paradoxically, a large proportion of the Republicans were not small farmers. Many of the leaders were southern plantation gentry like Jefferson and Madison, or old Antifederalist elites. The party drew together people who had opposed ratification of the Constitution as well as those who favored it but abhorred the government's direction under Washington and Hamilton. The Republicans received solid backing from farmers, especially in the south and west, and from urban craftsmen and small traders who watched wealthy speculators and merchants benefit from Hamiltonian policies.

Funding the National Debt

In becoming secretary of the treasury, Alexander Hamilton's primary challenge, the problem that had helped sink the Confederation, was the Revolutionary war debt. A strong nationalist, he viewed the debt

more as an opportunity to enlarge national power than as a financial hurdle. Because the Confederation had gone bankrupt, the United States had poor credit among international and domestic lenders. The United States owed $10 million to foreigners, particularly the French, and $40 million to Americans. The states also owed $25 million in domestic debts. To continue the War for Independence when funds were depleted, Congress and the states had issued certificates to merchants, artisans, and farmers for supplies and to soldiers for wages. After the war, many ordinary folks could not wait for the government to pay—or lost hope that the money was forthcoming—so they sold their certificates to wealthy speculators for a fraction of face value. Often the sellers received only 10 to 15 percent, rates that reflected the risk speculators were taking during the shaky Confederation period.

In his Report on the Public Credit of January 1790, Hamilton formulated a plan by which the U.S. government would honor at face value all Revolutionary war debts, including those of the states. His "funding" proposal involved the exchange of new federal securities for the old debt certificates. He planned to pay off foreign creditors as soon as possible, but retain the domestic debt, paying only interest and a small amount of the principal each year. A customs duty on imports and an excise tax on whiskey would cover the interest; Post Office income would gradually reduce the principal. Hamilton regarded his funding plan as expedient both financially and politically. It would restore the nation's credit internationally as well as in the eyes of its own citizens. Funding would tie wealthy Americans to the new government through their continuing investment. Hamilton's "assumption" plan, by which the federal government assumed state war debts, expanded this strategy by reorienting the loyalty of investors from the states to the nation.

Congress eventually passed Hamilton's proposal to restore public credit, though with great opposition. Many people, including Madison, thought that repaying the domestic debt at face value was unfair, that speculators received a windfall at the expense of the poor. The split between former allies Hamilton and Madison began over this issue. Critics argued that funding allowed the "few" to benefit from the hardships of the "many," who had lost money when they sold their war bonds and would pay again through import duties and the excise tax. Opponents feared Hamilton's larger purpose, the expansion of national power, and became convinced that the Treasury secretary was upsetting the balance between the central

government and the states. Assumption raised additional questions because some states had more debt remaining than others. Massachusetts and South Carolina were keen on having the federal government assume their large debts, while Virginians opposed the plan, because they had satisfied most of the state's debt. Despite these divisions, the funding and assumption program passed Congress in July 1790, as part of a bargain struck by Hamilton, Jefferson, and Madison to situate the nation's permanent capital on the Potomac River, in Maryland and Virginia.

Planning Washington, D.C.

The choice of the Potomac for the nation's capital was controversial. Delegates from New England and New York thought the place too far away, while Pennsylvanians argued that their state was ideal. Southerners favored the Potomac. While everyone agreed that a central location was necessary, regional interests surfaced as congressmen recognized the economic and political benefits that the seat of government could bestow. They also debated the question of the temporary capital. Should New York City or Philadelphia host the federal government until the permanent site was ready? The complicated negotiations over funding and assumption resulted in moving the temporary capital from New York to Philadelphia as well as locating the new city on the Potomac.

President Washington and his fellow Virginians who had engineered the bargain, especially Jefferson, supervised the development of the capital. The Residence Act of 1790 gave the president authority to select a ten-mile-square location somewhere along the Potomac; he chose, after consulting with Madison and Jefferson, the land on both sides of the river that included Alexandria, Virginia, and Georgetown, Maryland. The federal city would not be built in either of those towns, but on open land on the east bank of the river. Washington appointed a surveyor, three commissioners to manage the project, and Pierre Charles L'Enfant to design the layout of the capital and its major buildings. L'Enfant's grandiose street plan and Greek and Roman architecture expressed an exalted vision of the republic. The commissioners named the federal city "Washington" and the entire district "Columbia."

The president expected to finance construction by selling lots in the capital, thinking that land prices would skyrocket as citizens valued proximity to the

Pierre Charles L'Enfant's intricate design for Washington, D.C., 1791, far outstripped the country's financial resources and interest in creating a national capital.

seat of government. Instead, land sold poorly and lack of money undermined the project. At one of the failed auctions, even the participation of the president and a parade of two brass bands and an artillery troop could not foster sales. When the commissioners suspended construction temporarily for insufficient funds, L'Enfant protested and was fired. His plan for grand boulevards, public squares, fountains, and imposing buildings was retained, but its execution would wait. For a decade the enterprise limped along, saved by grants from Maryland and Virginia. In 1800, when the government moved to Washington, the president's mansion was still unfinished and only one wing of the Capitol had been built.

The National Bank

The cornerstone of Hamilton's new commercial order was a national bank, to be patterned after the Bank of England. The Bank of the United States and its branches, established in selected cities, would hold the federal government's funds. It would also regulate state banks, which had grown in number since the first bank, Philadelphia's Bank of North America, was founded in 1781. The chief purpose of the national bank was to expand the money supply, thereby encouraging commercial growth.

First Bank of the United States, Philadelphia. The imposing structure, designed by Samuel Blodget of New Hampshire, was intended to convey confidence in the bank's financial strength.

The Bank of the United States, which Congress chartered in 1791 for a minimum of twenty years, would have assets of $10 million, including $2 million in government deposits. Private investors could purchase the remaining $8 million in stock. At least one-fourth of their investment had to be in hard currency; investors could pay the other three-fourths in federal securities. As the bank prospered, stockholders would receive dividends on their funds. Thus, Hamilton created a way for wealthy Americans, who had just profited from funding the Revolutionary War debt, to benefit further. Because the government was a major stockholder, it also received dividends that could be used to pay off the national debt. The bank made loans to merchants beyond the value of its stock of gold and silver (specie), thus increasing the supply of money, a critically important move for an economy short of specie. The bank notes circulated as currency; the federal government supported their value by accepting them for taxes. To Hamilton and his commercial backers, the Bank of the United States was essential for economic growth. The majority of the House of Representatives agreed, by a vote of thirty-nine to twenty, but the tally indicated important regional differences that fueled party growth. Among northern congressmen, thirty-three voted for the bank and one against, while only six southern delegates supported and nineteen opposed Hamilton's bill.

The plan had many opponents, who variously considered the bank immoral, monopolistic, or unconstitutional. Some believed that all paper money should be based on gold and silver. "Every dollar of a bank bill that is issued beyond the quantity of gold and silver in the vaults," John Adams said, "represents nothing, and is therefore a cheat upon somebody." The wild frenzy to purchase the bank's stock, in which 25,000 shares sold in two hours and then the shares were bid up to 1,300 percent of their face value, reinforced fears that the national bank would undermine republican virtue. Jefferson called the bank's stock "federal filth." Others charged the bank with monopoly, complaining that merchants could secure short-term loans to finance their commercial ventures, but farmers and artisans could not obtain mortgages for purchasing property or making improvements.

In Congress, Madison opposed the national bank on the constitutional grounds that the federal government lacked the power to create corporations. He argued for a strict interpretation of the Constitution, but failed to convince the majority. In particular, Madison said, the Tenth Amendment denied the central government any power not expressly given. Hamilton and his supporters countered with a loose interpretation, that some powers of the federal government are implied. In the case of the bank, for example, the Constitution delegated to Congress and the president the power to lay and collect taxes, pay debts, regulate commerce, and coin and regulate money. It also provided the authority to "make all laws which shall be necessary and proper for carrying into execution the foregoing powers. . . ." Hamilton argued that the bank was a method by which the United States could fulfill its functions, and because some means was necessary, the power to establish the bank was implied. Though President Washington was initially unsure, he accepted Hamilton's reasoning and approved the bill.

Jefferson, like Madison, was convinced the national bank was unconstitutional, advising Washington with this opinion. By 1791, the secretary of state realized the political and economic consequences of the funding act—channeling more power to the federal government and more money to the rich—and thought the bank could only further these trends. He said he had been "duped" by Hamilton and "made a tool for forwarding his schemes" in accepting the assumption of state debts in return for the capital on the Potomac. He now believed that the Treasury secretary's program "flowed from principles adverse to liberty," Jefferson told the president. It was "calculated to undermine and demolish the republic." For his part, Hamilton chafed at this criticism, stating "that Mr. Madison, co-operating with Mr. Jefferson, is at the head of a faction decidedly hostile to me and my administration; and actuated by views, in my judgment, subversive of the principles of good government and dangerous to the Union, peace, and happiness of the country."

As members of Washington's cabinet, both Jefferson and Hamilton found policy making increasingly difficult as positions hardened, especially because foreign policy, in Jefferson's realm, overlapped with domestic fiscal matters. In particular, Jefferson's pro-French leanings conflicted with Hamilton's need to collect tariffs on British imports for funding the debt. If trade with Great Britain ended, Hamilton's financial system fell apart.

Encouragement of Manufacturing

While the Treasury secretary won congressional support for the bank and funding the national debt, he was much less successful in his plan for industry. In

1791, the United States lacked a solid manufacturing base. Hamilton proposed high protective tariffs on certain goods to discourage Americans from buying imports and thus spur U.S. production. He also advocated bounties, or subsidies, on selected products to encourage entrepreneurs. Hamilton believed that a strong nation needed self-sufficiency in manufactures, especially for military defense, but failed to obtain congressional support. Madison contended that granting bounties would expand the power of Congress, while others argued that they were like monopolies and too expensive. A North Carolina congressman advised, "Establish the doctrine of bounties, [and] . . . all manner of persons—people of every trade and occupation—may enter at the breach, until they have eaten up the bread of our children."

In the 1790s, U.S. manufacturing remained on a small scale. Americans appreciated the quality of British imports; what they did not import, they produced themselves or purchased from neighboring artisans. Industry could not be stimulated overnight, for it required technology and the willingness of businessmen to invest time as well as capital for the long term. While some master craftsmen enlarged their shops and hired more workers, mechanized factories with mass production still lay in the future.

During the colonial and Revolutionary periods, urban entrepreneurs had attempted large-scale textile manufacturing to provide employment for poor women and independence from British imports, but these efforts were short-lived and not mechanized. The "factories" had consisted of workhouses, in which large numbers of impoverished widows produced thread and yarn at traditional spinning wheels. Other businessmen used a "putting-out" system, whereby they distributed flax and wool for spinning at home.

In 1788, the Pennsylvania Society for the Encouragement of Manufactures and the Useful Arts introduced spinning jennies to their textile factory in Philadelphia. The jennies, with forty to eighty spindles each and too heavy for women to operate, threatened to displace home spinners by producing cheaper yarn and thread. In 1790, however, the factory and its wooden jennies went up in flames, as did other early textile mills in the Delaware Valley. While the promoters believed that home spinners were sabotaging the factories, the fires may well have been accidental because the mills were highly flammable.

Samuel Slater, a twenty-two-year-old millworker and recent immigrant from Great Britain, in 1790 instituted a new phase in American cloth production by

Until after 1815, households performed one or more steps in textile manufacturing. Here a family works together, with the wife spinning thread, which the husband then wove on his loom. Women also wove cloth, but men rarely—if ever—used a spinning wheel.

building a textile mill in Pawtucket, Rhode Island, using water power to run the spinning machines. From memory he constructed a spinning frame, a machine that produced stronger threads than the jenny. He had left Britain illegally; to keep its advantage in textile making, the government prohibited emigration of craftworkers or export of drawings of the machines. No satisfactory power loom yet existed, so Slater's mill performed only the first two steps of cloth production: carding, or preparing the cotton fibers for spinning, and spinning the thread. Slater then used the putting-out system of distributing the thread to families, who produced the cloth at home. Though Slater established additional mills in Rhode Island and Massachusetts, his workforce stayed fairly small, with about a hundred millworkers in 1800. His manufacturing process also remained dependent on the traditional home production of weavers.

Alexander Hamilton tried an ambitious industrial program in Paterson, New Jersey, with the Society for Establishing Useful Manufactures. The society hoped to create an industrial town on the Passaic River where skilled craftsmen recruited from Britain would produce a variety of cloth and clothing, blankets, carpets, shoes, hats, pottery, metal wire, and paper. After obtaining a state charter from New Jersey, the society sold stock. As in the case of the national bank, the stock sold quickly and appreciated in value. The project lost capital, however, when major stockholders

Samuel Slater's spinning frame. With his water-powered textile mills, Slater removed part of cloth production from the home—carding and spinning—but relied on families to weave the cloth.

sold their shares to make a fast profit. The managers failed to obtain reliable machinery and workers, closing shop in 1796.

While the results of Hamilton's plans were disappointing, with the society's failure and congressional rejection of the protective tariff and bounties, the United States did make progress during the 1790s toward industrialization. In 1790, Congress passed patent legislation, giving inventors exclusive rights to their work for seventeen years, and Slater initiated water-powered textile manufacture. Then, in 1793, while visiting a Georgia plantation, Eli Whitney, a New Englander, invented the cotton engine, or gin. The device, which separated cotton fibers from husks and seeds, greatly increased the productivity of cotton cultivation, swelling the demand for African American slaves and fertile land in the southwest, and spurring cloth production in the north. Because the gin could be duplicated easily, though, Whitney failed to make a fortune from his invention, despite its economic significance. In 1798, he further laid the basis for industrial growth by attempting to manufacture guns with interchangeable parts. After receiving a government contract for 10,000 weapons, he specified that each part be made identical to its counterparts so that it could be exchanged from one rifle to another, allowing less-skilled workers to build and repair the firearms. At this early date, however, such rigid standards were impossible to meet, and as a result, parts needed filing to fit together smoothly.

An inventor who would have benefited from Hamilton's proposed bounties was the Delaware-born artisan Oliver Evans, who apprenticed as a wagonmaker and became fascinated by machines. In 1772, at age seventeen, he heard that the Scottish inventor James Watt had improved the steam engine a few years earlier. Evans began building his own model but, for lack of money and encouragement, thirty years passed before he actually installed a high pressure steam engine in his gypsum fertilizer factory in Philadelphia. This was the first such application of steam power to an industrial setting. In the meantime, in the 1780s, Evans also developed the idea of automating mills, a concept that has grown in significance over two centuries. He devised water-powered machinery for large grist mills that allowed one worker instead of three to supervise all the steps of producing flour. Evans obtained exclusive rights from the states of Pennsylvania and Maryland to his system of automated elevators, conveyors, and hoppers. With insufficient capital, however, he was unable to pursue many of his designs, including steam carriages and trucks, a machine gun, refrigeration, central heating, and gas lighting.

EXPANSION AND CONFLICT IN THE WEST

While Alexander Hamilton's financial policies aided commerce and made wealthy eastern merchants even richer, dynamic growth also occurred in the west. The

expansion of settlers from east to west challenged the ability of the new government to keep their loyalty. In particular, Hamilton's excise tax on whiskey weighed heavily on westerners, especially in Pennsylvania, leading to a serious rebellion in 1794. The young nation also contended with the Native Americans, whose lands the settlers were taking; the British military, who kept forts in the northwest; and the Spanish, who contested U.S. territorial claims and rights to navigate the Mississippi.

Kentucky and Tennessee

During the 1780s, the region west of the Appalachians and south of the Ohio River developed quickly, as families, many with African American slaves, left Virginia and North Carolina in search of fertile land and lower taxes. Even before the revolution ended, settlers crossed the mountains in large numbers: Kentucky swelled from 150 settlers in 1775 to 61,000 whites and 12,500 enslaved blacks in 1790; Tennessee reported 32,000 whites and 3,500 slaves in the latter year.

White settlement of Kentucky and Tennessee proceeded quickly as state governments, speculators, and frontiersmen defeated the Cherokees, who claimed ancestral rights to the territory. Understanding that they were renting the land rather than selling it, in 1775 a group of Cherokee leaders, including Attakullaculla and Oconostota, traded 27,000 square miles to Richard Henderson and his associates for a cabin of consumer goods. Called Henderson's Purchase, the sale involved most of Kentucky, comprising the hunting lands of the Shawnees and Iroquois as well as the Cherokees, and was illegal in Indian and English law. With the outbreak of the revolution, most Cherokees and Shawnees joined the British, fighting for return of their lands. Receiving little help from Britain, the Cherokees were defeated in 1777 and forced to sign away even more territory.

Young militants led by Dragging Canoe, Bloody Fellow, and others, assisted by loyalist whites who intermarried and became members of the tribe, rejected these land cessions. In the 1780s and early 1790s, the militant Cherokees, called Chickamaugas, allied with Creeks and Shawnees against settlers along the frontier from Kentucky to Georgia. On both sides, fighting was vicious, with men, women, and children burned, scalped, and shot; and, as in so many cases, the whites

failed to distinguish between enemy Indians and those who wanted peace.

The Washington administration attempted to end the hostilities with the Treaty of Holston in 1791, but gave responsibility for negotiating with the Cherokees to Governor William Blount of the Tennessee Territory, a land speculator the Indians called "dirt king" for his greed after land. Blount ignored Washington's promise to the Cherokees that if they ceded territory on which the whites had settled, the United States would guarantee their remaining lands. Instead, Blount required a cession of over 4,000 square miles in return for an annual payment of $1,000 and no guarantee. When Blount surveyed the border without Cherokee witnesses, the treaty fell apart and war continued. In 1794, after Dragging Canoe died and the Spanish stopped supplying the Indians because of war in Europe, the Chickamaugas met defeat.

By the end of the war, parts of Kentucky and Tennessee had passed the initial stages of settlement. Early on, groups of settlers had gathered in frontier stations consisting of two-story log houses connected by a high wall to create a fort against Indian attack. As the population grew and the threat from Native Americans declined, families moved away from the stations. While, at first, subsistence was primary to frontier settlers, access to markets soon became essential. In the early years, all family members worked to provide food, clothing, shelter, and a few amenities such as soap and rough-hewn furniture. They needed to become familiar with their new environment. One Kentucky pioneer described how "the women the first spring we came out, wo'd follow their cows to see what they ate, that they might know what greens to get. My Wife and I had neither spoon, dish, knife, or any thing to do with when we began life. Only I had a butcher knife." The settlers used skills they had learned at home: They grew corn, tobacco, hemp, cotton, vegetables, and fruits; raised cattle, sheep, horses, and pigs; hunted and fished. Soon the settlers produced a surplus to trade for necessities they could not make themselves, such as nails, rifles, ammunition, needles, tools, and salt, as well as to pay taxes and fees. They sold furs, ginseng, agricultural produce, and livestock. As fertile lands such as Kentucky's Bluegrass region yielded bountiful crops, farmers sought markets by way of the Mississippi River and the port of New Orleans. Because transporting crops overland through the mountains was much more difficult and expensive than sending them

downstream, southwestern farmers demanded that the federal government convince Spain to end its restrictions on lower Mississippi shipping.

Even as the number of settlers increased and a market economy developed in the 1790s, the trans-Appalachian region had few schools or church buildings. Most children, if taught at all, learned reading and arithmetic at home. In towns where schools existed, boys might attend for a few months but girls stayed at home. The exception were the children of wealthy families who attended academies with secondary school curricula. One man remembered the experience of most residents of Kentucky in the 1790s: "Our preachers and teachers were, in general, almost as destitute as the people at large, many of whom could neither read nor write, did not send their children to school, and of course, kept no books in the house."

While churches lacked buildings and settled ministers, though, religion was the frontier's chief cultural institution. Throughout the region, Presbyterian, Baptist, and Methodist ministers held services in private homes. Baptist lay ministers farmed beside their neighbors through the week, then led services on Sunday. Methodist circuit riders traveled from one congregation to another, conducting worship services, baptisms, marriages, and prayer meetings. The churches preached a stringent message of salvation and morality. They expected members to avoid sin, including fighting, excessive drinking, adultery, and even celebrating the Fourth of July. If members committed offenses and failed to express sorrow, they were expelled, a serious consequence for people who had few social outlets and whose community revolved around the church. In addition to church, social activities included barn raisings, corn huskings, and log rollings. These events caused trouble when whiskey and frivolity led church members astray, as with one couple a Kentucky Methodist church expelled for "Disorderly Conduct." Another man was "Excluded from this Church for Fighting & Drinking to Excess."

The Ohio Country

White settlement moved more slowly north of the Ohio River than in Kentucky and Tennessee, partly because the U.S. government kept tighter control in the Northwest Territory, but more because Native Americans, with assistance from the British, resisted strongly. Delawares, Shawnees, Iroquois, and many others refused to cede lands that the federal government wanted to sell to land-hungry easterners. In the 1780s, the United States obtained a series of cessions, but from just some of the people who owned the land. Indians who were not party to the agreements rejected them. Forming a confederacy to withstand U.S. invasion, Ohio Indians attacked whites who risked settling in the region. This northern Indian confederacy allied with the Chickamaugas and Creeks in the south, establishing a pan-Indian defensive that gained help from the Spanish in the south and the British in the north. At one meeting in 1787, the Native Americans agreed to merge their forces "for a general defense against all Invaders of Indian rights."

In the early 1790s, President Washington challenged the northern confederacy by sending two expeditions, both of them unsuccessful. Arthur St. Clair, governor of the Northwest Territory, led the second invasion in 1791, in which 600 of his 1,400 men died. Washington believed that the disaster resulted from

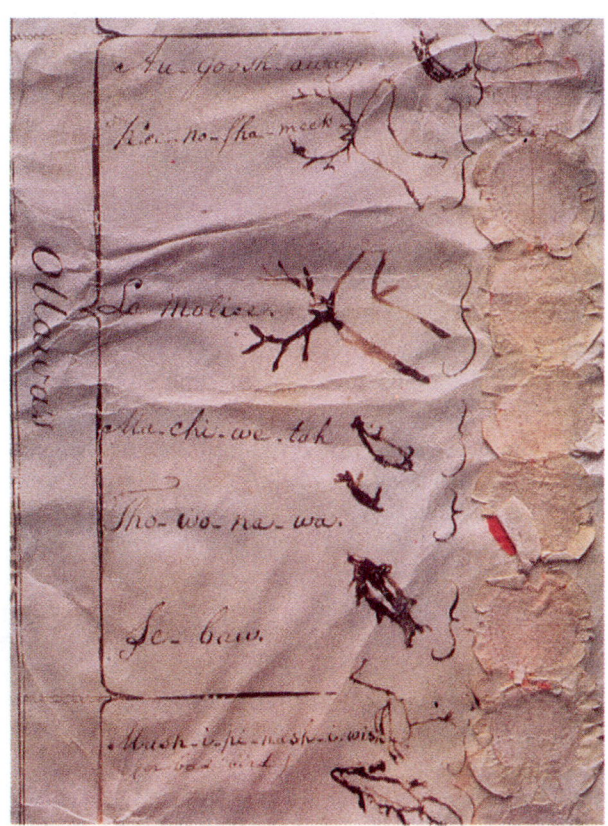

Signatures of Native Americans on the Treaty of Greenville, 1795.

MAP 7.1   CONFLICT IN THE NORTHWEST TERRITORY, 1790-1796

the use of militia, so instructed General Anthony Wayne to raise 5,000 regulars. Wayne trained the troops for two years, then marched west against the Indian confederacy. On August 20, 1794, the U.S. army defeated the Native Americans decisively at the Battle of Fallen Timbers. Though the British had customarily given aid to the Ohio tribes, this time they closed the gates to Fort Miami, denying refuge to the retreating Indians. A year later, when it became clear to the Native Americans that their alliance with the British had ended, they signed the Treaty of Greenville ceding to the United States most of the land in present-day Ohio. Whether this treaty would last when others had failed, however, depended upon British withdrawal from their garrisons.

The Whiskey Rebellion

In the same year, 1794, the Washington administration also sent troops against western Pennsylvania farmers, who since 1791 had resisted the whiskey tax that Congress passed as part of Hamilton's funding plan. For westerners, the excise was unfair because it took money from their pockets to profit eastern speculators who had bought up debt certificates. Washington and Hamilton decided to take advantage of the unrest to demonstrate the power of the new central government. Farmers throughout the west resented the tax on spirits, for distilling whiskey from grain made their produce less bulky, thus less expensive to transport to eastern markets. They also used the whiskey

Indian Treaty of Greenville, *1795, by an unknown artist. Following General Anthony Wayne's victory at the Battle of Fallen Timbers, he negotiated the treaty with the Miami leader Little Turtle and many other Indians, temporarily ending their military resistance to white settlement in the Northwest Territory.*

instead of cash and consumed a good portion of it themselves. In much of the trans-Appalachian region, the federal government failed to collect the excise at all, for under threat of violence from their neighbors, local officials were not inclined to become tax collectors.

The administration found willing officials in western Pennsylvania, however, and there proceeded to enforce the law. The Pittsburgh area farmers resisted in ways reminiscent of the American Revolution. They held protest meetings and refused cooperation with the collectors. They tarred and feathered collaborators,

Pittsburgh in 1790, from a contemporary sketch and later drawing by Seth Eastman. Western Pennsylvania was the center of farmers' protest against Alexander Hamilton's excise tax on whiskey.

burned barns, and destroyed stills of people who paid the tax. The farmers charged that the tax favored large distillers and was collected unevenly. Rebels left notes signed "Tom the Tinker" to warn distillers who registered for the tax that their stills would be "fixed" (that is, ruined) unless they joined the revolt. The insurgents understood their fight as a struggle for "the virtuous principles of republican liberty." But the whiskey tax was only one of the farmers' complaints. Perhaps more important, until August 1794, was the federal government's failure to open up the Ohio country for safe settlement or to convince the Spanish to remove trade restrictions on the Mississippi.

Events came to a climax in July 1794. When officials continued to collect the tax and arrest resisters, 500 men surrounded the excise inspector's home, exchanged gunfire that killed several people, and burned the house. The official and his family escaped. In the days that followed, rebels set more buildings on fire, raised liberty poles, attacked collectors, and rumored secession. In August, 7,000 armed insurgents gathered, some intending to march on the excise headquarters in Pittsburgh, but they stopped before taking further military action. The uprising spread to central Pennsylvania, Virginia, Maryland, and Ohio. Washington sent commissioners to obtain oaths of submission, but the insurrection continued. Hamilton, as acting secretary of war, called up 13,000 eastern troops, who marched west with the president briefly in command. By the time the soldiers reached western Pennsylvania, the revolt was over, as the show of force intimidated the rebels. The administration had demonstrated that armed resistance to federal policies would not be tolerated. Many of the insurgents escaped the grasp of the central government, however, by moving farther west.

The Spanish Frontier

As settlers from the United States migrated across the Appalachians and traders extended their commercial networks, they came into contact with the Spanish. The 1790s marked the high point of Spain's control in North America, its provinces extending from East Florida across the Gulf Coast to Louisiana, Texas, New Mexico, and California. The Spanish government continued to view these borderlands of their empire as a buffer against American and British designs on Mexican silver. Spanish officials recognized the phenomenal population growth of the United States. One warned that Americans were "advancing and multiplying . . . with a prodigious rapidity," while another took a dim view of the American frontier people, whom he considered "nomadic like Arabs and . . . distinguished from savages only in their color, language, and the superiority of their depraved cunning and untrustworthiness."

Nevertheless, the Spanish decided to open their territory to Americans, hoping to bolster the small settler populations of the borderlands. Spain offered free land in the Floridas and Louisiana, and even changed official policy to allow Protestants to keep their religion as long as they took an oath of allegiance to the Crown and had their children baptized Catholic. Spanish mercantilism also broke down, as plantation owners in the borderlands sold their sugar, cotton, and indigo in the United States. Spain could not provide desired consumer goods or adequate markets, so permitted this trade. These new immigration and economic policies facilitated later acquisition of the Floridas and Louisiana by the United States. In 1791, Jefferson said prophetically that Spain had provided "the means of delivering to us peaceably, what may otherwise cost us a war."

Farther west, in New Mexico, the Spanish finally achieved peace with Native Americans during these years. Abandoning their attempt to integrate Comanches and Apaches as subjects of the Crown, Spain signed a treaty recognizing them as sovereign people. The Indians, through military prowess and endurance, had forced the Spanish to set aside the goal of complete domination and to provide such gifts as guns, ammunition, clothing, mirrors, paint, tobacco, and sugar. Still, the Spanish sent prisoners of war to Cuba as forced laborers and settled other Apaches on reservations called *establecimientos de paz,* or peace establishments. The Spanish had not shed their hope of converting and Hispanicizing the natives. Many Apaches refused to live on the reservations, however, steadfastly maintaining their independence. But the fighting stopped, making Texas, New Mexico, and Arizona safer for travel and economic development. Finally, settlers could journey directly between San Antonio, Santa Fe, and Tucson without fear of attack. The region prospered, providing food and clothing to the silver mines of Mexico.

For several decades, fearing Russian and British incursions along the Pacific coast, Spain had expanded settlement in California. The government sent missionaries and soldiers north from Baja California in 1769 to set up missions and presidios along the coast

This sketch by José Cardero in 1791 shows Native Americans and soldiers working outside the presidio of Monterey, California.

from San Diego as far north as San Francisco. José de Gálvez organized the effort, enlisting Junípero Serra, the zealous Franciscan priest, to establish the missions, which soon dominated Spanish California society. Though fewer than 1,000 Hispanics lived in California by 1790, the missions controlled most of the arable land along the Pacific. With military force and by conversion, they put thousands of California Indians to work on mission lands. Before Spanish colonization, the region's native people possessed neither firearms nor horses; they lived in small villages with neither elaborate political structures nor much experience with war. In the earliest years after Spanish settlement, the natives lacked unity to avenge crimes that Spanish soldiers committed—rape, murder, and theft—or to refuse to serve as agricultural laborers. In 1775, however, one group burned the San Diego mission, followed by rebellions of other coastal Indians.

As elsewhere in North America, the California Indians declined sharply in population after contact with Europeans. People who went to work in the missions lived an average of ten to twelve years; their high death rate probably resulted from close quarters and exposure to disease. According to one missionary, "they live well free but as soon as we reduce them to a Christian and community life . . . they fatten, sicken, and die." The native population in the mission region along the Pacific coast declined from approximately 60,000 in 1769 to 35,000 at the end of the century.

The Spanish also looked to the Pacific Northwest, which they investigated in 1774, four years earlier than the British explorer Captain James Cook. After Cook publicized the trade for sea otter furs, however, British and American merchants sailed to Nootka Sound, at Vancouver Island, challenging the Spanish claim to the area north of San Francisco. The traders made huge profits by purchasing the silky black otter pelts from the Tlingit, Haida, Nootka, and Chinook peoples, to sell in China for tea, porcelain, and silk. The Indians had formerly hunted the sea otter on a limited basis for fine clothing and food. The Spanish attempted to enforce their rights to the Northwest coast by seizing two British ships. When England threatened war, Spain signed the Nootka Convention (1790), yielding its sole claim to the area and returning the confiscated vessels. Over the next several years, the two countries tried but failed to negotiate a northern boundary of California. Of more concern to Spain, Great Britain, and the United States during the 1790s, was the outbreak of war in Europe and the Atlantic, in the wake of revolution in France.

Dances held by Native Americans for Alejandro Malaspina at Nootka Sound, 1791. Drawing probably by Tomás de Suria.

FOREIGN ENTANGLEMENTS

As Americans built a new government, differed over which direction it should take, and headed west, events in Europe claimed their attention. In 1789, the United States rejoiced when the French abolished noble privileges and formed a constitutional monarchy. Americans believed that France had followed their example, for during the first phase of the French Revolution, its moderate leaders included friends of the United States, notably the Revolutionary War hero, the Marquis de Lafayette. In 1792, however, radicals took control and executed King Louis XVI the next year. The international situation became perilous when the French Republic declared war on Britain and Spain. The king's execution and thousands of deaths by guillotine during the second phase of the revolution cost the French support in the United States, particularly among Federalists, who feared the consequences of ordinary people, "the mob," taking power. Republicans, while not defending the excesses, remained sympathetic toward France because they hated monarchical Britain more.

Neutrality

The European war presented Americans with a tricky situation, for they had no interest in getting involved in the fray, yet had connections with both France and Britain that were potentially dangerous. The U.S.-France commercial and military alliance of 1778 remained in force. While it did not require the United States to enter the war, the French Republic expected favorable trade policies and informal military assistance. Though Secretary of State Jefferson favored France and hated Britain, he agreed that neutrality was essential. American commerce was closely tied with Britain, whose navy could sweep U.S. ships from the sea. Hamilton was particularly concerned that British imports remain high because tariffs paid the lion's share of interest on the national debt. With all of this in mind, President Washington made the only reasonable decision, issuing his Proclamation of Neutrality in April 1793. The message warned citizens to avoid hostile acts against either side, including sale of weapons and privateering. Washington sought the belligerents' recognition of the U.S. right to trade in nonmilitary goods.

Dramatizing the intense party rivalries of the 1790s, this pro-Federalist cartoon shows President Washington leading troops against French radicals, as Thomas Jefferson and Citizen Genêt try to hold him back. The dog graphically shows its disapproval of a Republican newspaper.

American neutrality quickly hit shoals when the activities of the new French ambassador, Edmond Genêt, became known. Citizen Genêt, as he was called in republican France, had arrived in Charleston several weeks before Washington proclaimed neutrality. Following instructions from home, he began enlisting American mercenaries to man privateers and to organize expeditions against the Spanish garrisons at St. Augustine and New Orleans. While the latter plan fell through when the French failed to pay the soldiers, Genêt obtained ships to sail under the French flag against British shipping. The privateers, with largely American crews, seized British vessels, towing them to U.S. ports. There the French consuls sold the ships and their cargoes, paying the mercenaries with part of the proceeds. The French claimed this right under the 1778 alliance. The Washington administration, fearful of British reprisals and outraged by this violation of U.S. sovereignty, closed the ports to Genêt's privateers and requested his recall. The government established specific rules of neutrality and national sovereignty. It prohibited foreign belligerents from arming vessels in U.S. ports and recruiting U.S. citizens in American territory; set the limit of U.S. territorial waters at three miles; and forbade foreign consuls from holding admiralty courts in U.S. cities to auction confiscated ships.

The Washington administration had greater success protecting the nation's sovereignty from French designs than from the British. The American republic's weakness became all too clear when the Royal Navy began impressing—recruiting by force—U.S. citizens from merchant ships. While the navy's official goal was to reclaim British deserters, the commanders often failed to distinguish among deserters, British immigrants who had become U.S. citizens, and native-born Americans.

Then, in November 1793, the British ordered a total blockade of the French West Indies. Any ship intending to trade there would be confiscated. While partly in retaliation for the Genêt affair, the British timed the blockade to coincide with their invasion of St. Domingue, or Haiti, where enslaved blacks had risen up against their French masters in 1791. The British kept the blockade a secret until after U.S. ships headed for the Caribbean. Over the winter, their navy seized more than 250 American vessels, whether they were aimed for French, British, or neutral ports. The British impounded ships, cargoes, and even the sailors' possessions. Because international correspondence was so slow, especially in the winter and during war, Washington received no intelligence of the blockade and confiscations until March 1794.

The United States and Britain seemed headed for war, a course that Americans could ill afford. Exacerbating the crisis was the British refusal to vacate their forts in the Ohio country, as they had agreed to do in the 1783 Treaty of Paris. Americans knew that Britain helped Native Americans resist settlement in the west. In fact, on practically the same day that Washington heard of the confiscations in the Caribbean, he re-

ceived news that the governor of Canada, Lord Dorchester, had told a group of Indians that they could expect war to break out between the United States and Britain within a year. With British victory, Dorchester promised, the Native Americans could reclaim the lands they had lost north of the Ohio River.

The Jay Treaty

The crisis abated when information soon arrived that the British had ended their total blockade of the French islands, now permitting Americans to trade foodstuffs and consumer goods but not war materiel. Rather than take retaliatory action, the president nominated John Jay, the chief justice of the Supreme Court, to serve as special envoy to the British. Jay's instructions were to convince them to evacuate their forts in the west, pay for African American slaves who had left with the British army after the Revolution, end impressment, open British West Indies trade to American ships, and compensate recent shipping losses in the Caribbean.

Jay completed his negotiations in England in November 1794, obtaining a treaty that was probably as beneficial to U.S. interests as could be expected, given U.S. military weakness. Jay was unable to secure compensation for slaves who departed with the British army over a decade earlier; as a supporter of gradual abolition, he placed low priority on this goal. Nor did he convince the British to stop impressment or to recognize all of the neutral rights that Americans demanded. But Jay actually gained a great deal, including British withdrawal from the western forts by June 1, 1796, payment for confiscated ships in the Caribbean, and the opening of trade in the British West Indies to American vessels of 70 tons or less. He agreed, however, that American shippers would not export from the United States certain tropical products, including cotton, molasses, sugar, coffee, and cocoa, and that Americans would repay British creditors for pre-Revolutionary debts.

Washington received Jay's treaty in March 1795, keeping its contents secret until the Senate debate in June. Twenty Federalist senators voted to ratify while ten Republicans refused. The Federalists struck the provision forbidding U.S. merchants from exporting tropical crops. If they had agreed to this section, American trade would have faced a serious obstacle, particularly with the development of cotton. Thus, the Senate approved the treaty by exactly the two-thirds needed and sent it to the president, who signed the treaty as amended.

When the Jay Treaty became public, Republicans flew into a rage. Their opposition in large part was political: They abhorred *any* treaty with the British and privately bemoaned Jay's success on important issues. Publicly, they complained about his failures on impressment, neutral rights, and compensation for slaves. The Jay Treaty greatly hastened the growth of political parties, as Republicans gained support from former Federalists, particularly in the south. While Hamilton defended the treaty, opponents roared that it surrendered American independence to the former imperial tyrant. John Jay was burned in effigy; mass meetings, petitions, and demonstrations protested the treaty throughout the country.

By spring 1796, however, the tumolt was over, in part because news arrived that Thomas Pinckney had concluded an agreement with Spain the previous October. The Treaty of San Lorenzo opened the Mississippi River to free navigation, allowed Americans to use the port of New Orleans without charge, and fixed the boundary between the United States and West Florida at the 31st parallel as specified in the Treaty of Paris.

Washington Retires

With the threat of war temporarily eased, the west open for settlement and trade, and a flourishing economy, the success of the republic seemed more certain. General Wayne's defeat of the Ohio Indians, the Jay Treaty, and Pinckney's diplomatic success gave westerners—and westward-looking Americans—resolution of their major problems: cession of lands in Ohio, removal of the British from the forts, free access to the Mississippi, and the right of deposit at New Orleans. Eastern merchants and farmers benefited from the lifting of trade restrictions in the British West Indies. Wartime demand for provisions in Europe and the Caribbean drove up farm prices and stimulated production. By the end of the century, American exports and shipping profits were almost five times their 1793 level. As a major neutral maritime nation, the United States assumed a greater place in world trade. With increased transportation profits, merchants invested more heavily in ships. The shipbuilding boom created demand for lumber, rope, and other supplies; wages

for craftsmen and laborers rose, though so did the cost of living. Americans took advantage of their newfound prosperity to buy British imports, which in turn paid tariff income toward the national debt. Hamilton's funding plan was a success—the nation's credit was firm—despite resistance to the whiskey tax.

As the election of 1796 approached, George Washington announced his retirement, raising the question of his successor. The president had served two terms, his health had declined, and the battle over the Jay Treaty left him exhausted and angry. In his Farewell Address, Washington surveyed the accomplishments of his administration and gave the nation advice. The United States should avoid as much as possible becoming entwined in international affairs, he counseled. The European war demonstrated how perilous such involvement could be, and how difficult it was to escape. "The great rule of conduct for us in regard to foreign nations is, in extending our commercial relations to have with them as little *political* connection as possible," Washington urged. "So far as we have already formed engagements let them be fulfilled with perfect good faith. Here let us stop." His other major argument concerned factions. The outgoing president warned against parties based on sectional differences—North against South or East against West. And he cautioned against parties more generally, that the "disorders and miseries which result [from factionalism] gradually incline the minds of men to seek security and repose in the absolute power of an individual." In lamenting "the spirit of party," Washington blamed the Republicans for failing to support his administration. They had undercut his authority and the ideal of a consensual republic.

THE ADAMS PRESIDENCY

In fact, the election of 1796 witnessed further development of partisan politics. Though Washington's successors appreciated the wisdom of his "great rule" of foreign policy, they had less enthusiasm for his advice on factions. In 1796, the parties yet lacked full-scale national organization, and candidates did not campaign. But the contest was very much alive, as Federalists supported the policies of Hamilton and Washington, while Republicans opposed them.

John Adams, elected second president of the United States, had been involved in the Revolutionary movement since the 1760s. He was the sole non-Virginian and the only president to serve a single term among the first five chief executives.

Election of 1796

In the third presidential election under the Constitution, both parties had sufficient cohesion to offer national tickets: The Federalist candidates were John Adams for president and Thomas Pinckney for vice president; the Republicans put up Thomas Jefferson for president and Aaron Burr, a senator from New York, for the second spot. The results of the electoral college vote were close: Adams 71, Jefferson 68, Pinckney 59, Burr 30, and a number of other candidates totalling 48. As specified by the Constitution, Adams became president and Jefferson, vice president. Americans quickly realized the problem of this procedure for electing the executive, as the president represented one party and the vice president the other. The framers of the Constitution had not foreseen the development of political parties. In any event, the Federalists kept control of the presidency, though barely, and they increased their votes in Congress by a small margin, to

64 Federalists versus 53 Republicans. Riding on their foreign policy gains and economic prosperity, the Federalists retained control for another four years.

For many Americans, John Adams possessed credentials from service in the revolution and the new republic that made him a worthy heir to Washington. He had contributed to pre-Revolutionary agitation in Boston, served as a delegate to the Continental Congress, promoted the Continental navy, and assisted Jefferson in drafting the Declaration of Independence. He had helped negotiate the 1783 Treaty of Paris, and in 1785, became the first U.S. ambassador to Great Britain. While Adams was a skilled diplomat, an avid student of government, and entirely honest, he lacked the first president's charisma, military bearing, and understanding of executive leadership. As a lawyer, Adams's style was more intellectual and independent; he had no experience as an executive. He preferred to make decisions on his own, without consulting the cabinet or congressional leaders.

Like Washington, Adams denounced parties, adhering to the ideal of a consensual republic. He began his administration with the hope, soon abandoned, that he might bridge the gulf between Federalists and Republicans. Jefferson rebuffed the chief executive's peace overture and directed the Republican opposition from his post as vice president. After the first few days of the Adams administration, the president and vice president never consulted one another.

"Quasi-War" with France

The second president inherited an international situation that had worsened by the time he assumed office in March 1797. The French, now ruled by a dictatorial executive board called the Directory, declared that the Jay Treaty revoked the 1778 alliance. They confiscated American merchant ships and refused to receive the new U.S. ambassador, Charles Cotesworth Pinckney of South Carolina, Thomas Pinckney's brother. In effect, the Directory cut off diplomatic relations. The situation with France was much like the 1794 crisis with Great Britain. Once again, the United States seemed destined for war.

Called by Adams into special session in May 1797, Congress authorized the mobilization of 80,000 militia, completion of three war vessels, and fortification of harbors. Adams also appointed a commission of three men to negotiate with France: John Marshall of Virginia, Elbridge Gerry of Massachusetts, and the Carolinian, Charles Cotesworth Pinckney. Their assignment was to prevent war, stop the confiscation of American ships carrying nonmilitary cargoes, and

"Cinque-têtes," or the Paris Monster, an American cartoon showing the United States negotiators Elbridge Gerry, John Marshall, and Charles Cotesworth Pinckney refusing the demands for money of the French Directory (the five-headed monster).

The Constellation *Capturing the* Insurgente, *February 9, 1799. In the Quasi-War, the U.S. Navy, with British help, quickly outperformed the French.*

obtain compensation for recent losses. In France, the commission corresponded with French Foreign Minister Talleyrand through three intermediaries, who later became known to the American public as X, Y, and Z. The French agents told the commissioners that, like other petitioners to the Directory, they must pay a bribe even to be heard. The amount specified in this case was $250,000. Pinckney exclaimed, "No, no; not a sixpence!" The Directory also required an apology from Adams for criticizing France, a huge loan, and assumption by the U.S. government of any unpaid debts owed by France to American citizens. The commission refused these conditions and returned home. Their experience became known as the XYZ Affair.

In spring 1798, Adams received delayed correspondence that his envoys had been rebuffed. When he called for additional troops and warships, Congress responded by giving him more than he requested. Jefferson denounced the military buildup as "insane"; Republicans demanded to see evidence of France's treachery. When Adams made the commission's dispatches public, war fever engulfed the nation. The cry in the 1798 congressional elections became, "Millions for defense, but not a cent for tribute." Two patriotic songs "Adams for Liberty" and "Hail Columbia" were widely sung, the latter serving as the unofficial national anthem. Congress expanded the regular army and war fleet, established the Department of the Navy, authorized naval vessels to protect American merchant ships, suspended commerce with France, and revoked the French alliance. George Washington assumed command of the army, with

Alexander Hamilton in charge of field operations. To pay for all of this, Congress levied a direct tax of $2 million on dwelling houses, land, and slaves.

Without declaring war, the United States engaged France in hostilities from 1798 to 1800. In what was known as the Quasi-War, the U.S. navy dominated the French, defeating their warships, sinking privateers, and recapturing at least seventy American merchant vessels. The British navy helped by protecting U.S. carriers. While some congressmen feared a French invasion and thereby justified further military preparations, French naval losses to Great Britain and the United States quickly removed that threat.

The Alien and Sedition Acts

The Federalists rode the crest of patriotism in 1798, using their majority in Congress to pass a series of acts that limited the rights of immigrants and critics of the administration. Though Adams later said that he had not recommended the laws, he signed them. Congressional sponsors argued that they were necessary wartime measures. Their practical purpose, however, sought to destroy the Republicans by undermining their support and closing newspapers. The Federalists tried to take advantage of the Quasi-War to link their opponents with the enemy. This strategy worked in the short term, as the pro-French Republicans lost votes in the 1798 congressional election, but proved suicidal for Adams's party after the fear of invasion had passed.

This Federalist design resulted in four restrictive laws. The Naturalization Act of 1798, which aimed to discourage immigration, lengthened the period of residence needed for citizenship from five to fourteen years. The legislation was intended to stop the flow of Irish immigrants who, because they were anti-British and pro-French, swelled the number of Republican voters. The Alien Enemies Act, a compromise measure that had bipartisan support, did not actually go into effect during the Quasi-War. A permanent statute, it established procedures in the event of declared war or invasion for jailing and deporting citizens of the enemy nation who were considered likely to spy or commit sabotage.

Two additional laws gave wide powers to the president during peacetime as well as in war. The Alien Act, which had a term of two years, allowed the president to deport any non–U.S. citizens "he shall judge dangerous to the peace and safety of the United States, or shall have reasonable grounds to suspect are concerned in any treasonable or secret machinations against the government thereof." Like the Naturalization Act, this law potentially threatened Irish immigrants. But because Adams refrained from using it, the Alien Act's importance was more symbolic than real.

The Federalists did enforce the fourth law, the Sedition Act, with serious results. Its term lasted until March 3, 1801, the day before the next president would be inaugurated. Thus the Federalists ensured that if the next chief executive were a Republican, he would not be able to retaliate without obtaining a new statute. In vague language, the Sedition Act made it illegal for "any persons [to] unlawfully combine or conspire together, with intent to oppose any measure or measures of the government of the United States" or to interfere with the execution of a law. Nor could a person "write, print, utter or publish . . . any false, scandalous and malicious writing or writings against the government of the United States, or either house of the Congress . . . or the President." In effect, this law permitted imprisonment and fines for criticizing the government. It applied to U.S. citizens as well as to aliens. Though individuals charged under the Sedition Act could use the truth of their writings as a defense, the law gave a great deal of latitude in making arrests. It was an obvious infringement upon freedom of speech and freedom of the press.

Nevertheless, the administration enforced the law. Adams believed that the Sedition Act was constitutional, that people who censured his policies threatened the future of the republic. The prime targets for prosecution were Republican newspapers. Among the indicted was Benjamin Bache, the grandson of Benjamin Franklin and editor of the Philadelphia *Aurora,* who was one of Adams's most powerful critics. The official authorized to administer the act was Secretary of State Timothy Pickering, a staunch Federalist, who methodically reviewed the Republican papers for actionable offenses. He even ordered an inquiry into the private correspondence of a Republican congressman who reputedly called Adams a traitor; in this case, however, the investigation was dropped. Under the law, the Federalists indicted and tried at least seventeen people for sedition. They timed cases to reach court in the fall of 1799 or the following spring, with the goal of silencing the Republican press during the 1800 election. Some papers folded and others closed temporarily while their editors were imprisoned. All but one of the cases were prosecuted in New England and the Middle Atlantic states, where the Federalists controlled the courts and could pack juries.

The Republican Opposition Grows

Passage of the Alien and Sedition acts and the jailing of Republican spokesmen shifted the political winds. The war fever from the XYZ Affair subsided with American naval victories and indications that the French were ready to negotiate. In late 1798, the Kentucky and Virginia legislatures approved resolutions that protested the Alien and Sedition acts on the grounds that they were unconstitutional. The Kentucky and Virginia Resolutions, drafted anonymously by Thomas Jefferson and James Madison, respectively, argued that these laws violated the First Amendment and granted powers to the national government not delegated by the Constitution. The Virginia assembly resolved that "in case of a deliberate, palpable, and dangerous exercise of other powers, not granted by the [Constitution], the states . . . have the right, and are in duty bound, to interpose, for arresting the progress of the evil." Virginia and Kentucky sent their resolutions to other legislatures, none of which agreed that states could declare a federal law unconstitutional. Rhode Island, for example, responded that the federal courts held the power to determine constitutionality; "that for any state legislature to assume that authority would be . . . Hazarding an interruption of the peace of the states by civil discord, in case of a diversity of opinions among the state legislatures." Nevertheless, Madison and particularly Jefferson, who drafted yet another set of resolutions for the Kentucky

legislature in 1799, contributed toward a theory of "nullification," the idea that a state had the right to veto a federal law it considered unconstitutional. This theory was based upon the strict interpretation of the Constitution that denied, as in the controversy over the national bank, implied powers to the central government.

With the Alien and Sedition acts, the Federalists made a strategic error, one that gave their rivals the political high ground. Where formerly the Republicans could be branded as a faction creating animosity and disunity, one whose program was primarily negative, they now became legitimate defenders of Revolutionary principles. The Republican party justified its opposition by warning that the Federalists were on the road to tyranny. The Sedition Act, Madison argued in the Virginia Resolutions, impeded free investigation of the actions of government officials and "free communication among the people thereon, which has ever been justly deemed the only effectual guardian of every other right." The administration's effort to destroy its adversaries backfired as the Republicans gained respectability among Americans who had formerly supported the Federalists.

The administration fanned the flames of indignation with its heavy-handed reaction to a tax rebellion among Germans of rural eastern Pennsylvania, a group who had previously favored Washington and Adams or had stayed out of politics entirely. The Republicans took advantage of the Pennsylvanians' aversion to the 1798 federal property tax to win their votes in the congressional election. They circulated petitions against the tax, the defense buildup, and the Alien and Sedition laws, petitions that Congress ignored. By early 1799, the people of Northampton and Bucks counties held public meetings and stopped tax assessors from doing their work. In March, after the U.S. marshal jailed eighteen suspected tax resisters in Bethlehem's Sun Tavern, John Fries, a fifty-year-old auctioneer of upper Bucks County, led a band of 140 armed men to release the prisoners.

The Fries Rebellion ended quickly, as the rebels considered the magnitude of their offense. Fries announced that he would pay the tax and would even welcome the assessor to his house for dinner. Nevertheless, the president decided to make an example of the episode. He dispatched troops that failed to march until almost four weeks after the resistance had ceased. The army descended upon Northampton and Bucks counties, entering houses and arresting sixty men. One

army officer wrote "that every hour's experience confirms me more and more that this expedition was not only unnecessary, but violently absurd." Contrary to the Judiciary Act of 1789, the prisoners were taken to Philadelphia for trial. Fries and two others were found guilty of treason by a Federalist court and sentenced to hang, but were subsequently pardoned by the president. The Republicans added the administration's unwarranted use of force to their arsenal of charges against the Federalists. Jefferson could now count Pennsylvania Germans among his strongest supporters.

━ CONCLUSION ━

George Washington had warned in his Farewell Address that "the spirit of part . . . agitates the community with ill-founded jealousies and false alarms; kindles the animosity of one part against another; foments occasionally riot and insurrection. It opens the door to foreign influence and corruption. . . ." He invoked the ideal of consensual community, challenging his fellow citizens to work together for the good of their country. The flaw of this conception was that Americans could not agree on which policies were best for everyone. The interests of farmers, merchants, and artisans, of residents of the north, south, and west, often diverged. The Federalist and Republican parties grew out of different visions of the nation's future. During the 1790s, the Federalists retained control of the central government, confident that their vision was the correct one. They denounced parties, identifying their government with the republic as a whole. When they tried to eliminate factions by silencing their adversaries with the Sedition Act, ironically they legitimized the party system in the eyes of many Americans.

RECOMMENDED READINGS

Anderson, Margo J. *The American Census: A Social History* (1988). A very good source on the first federal census of 1790.

Charles, Joseph. *The Origins of the American Party System* (1956). Insightful examination of the development of parties in the 1790s.

Cochran, Thomas C. *Frontiers of Change: Early Industrialism in America* (1981). A good introduction to industrialization in the early republic.

Elkins, Stanley, and McKitrick, Eric. *The Age of Federalism* (1993). Detailed narrative of the Washington and Adams administrations.

North, Douglass C. *The Economic Growth of the United States, 1790–1860* (1966). Includes a useful analysis of U.S. trade amid international conflict.

Onuf, Peter S., ed., *Jeffersonian Legacies* (1993). Wide-ranging essays on Thomas Jefferson's character and politics.

Slaughter, Thomas P. *The Whiskey Rebellion: Frontier Epilogue to the American Revolution* (1986). An excellent book on the struggle between Alexander Hamilton and western Pennsylvania farmers over excise taxes.

Smith, James Morton. *Freedom's Fetters: The Alien and Sedition Laws and American Civil Liberties* (1956). Focuses on the Federalists' attempt to curtail civil rights.

White, Richard. *The Middle Ground: Indians, Empires, and Republics in the Great Lakes Region, 1650–1815* (1991). Influential study of Indian-white relations from New France through the War of 1812.

Young, James Sterling. *The Washington Community, 1800–1828* (1966). Interesting work on the development and growth of the new federal capital.

Politics and Diplomacy During the 1790s

Appleby, Joyce. *Capitalism and a New Social Order: The Republican Vision of the 1790s* (1984).

Banning, Lance. *The Jeffersonian Persuasion: The Evolution of a Party Ideology* (1978).

Hoffman, Ronald, and Albert, Peter J., eds. *Women in the Age of the Revolution* (1989).

Beeman, Richard, et al., eds. *Beyond Confederation: Origins of the Constitution and American National Identity* (1987).

Conley, Patrick T., and Kaminski, John P., eds. *The Bill of Rights and the States: The Colonial and Revolutionary Origins of American Liberties* (1992).

Cooke, Jacob E. *Alexander Hamilton* (1982).

Davis, W.W.H. *The Fries Rebellion, 1798–99* (1899).

DeConde, Alexander. *The Quasi-War: The Politics and Diplomacy of the Undeclared War with France, 1797–1801* (1966).

Flexner, James T. *George Washington and the New Nation, 1783–1793* (1970).

Flexner, James T. *George Washington: Anguish and Farewell, 1793–1799* (1972).

Greene, Jack P., ed., *The American Revolution: Its Character and Limits* (1987).

Hoadley, John F. *Origins of American Political Parties, 1789–1803* (1986).

Hofstadter, Richard. *The Idea of a Party System: The Rise of Legitimate Opposition in the United States, 1780–1840* (1969).

Kohn, Richard H. *Eagle and Sword: The Federalists and the Creation of the Military Establishment in America, 1783–1802* (1975).

Kurtz, Stephen G. *The Presidency of John Adams: The Collapse of Federalism, 1795–1800* (1957).

Levy, Leonard. *Legacy of Suppression: Freedom of Speech and Press in Early American History* (1960).

Malone, Dumas. *Jefferson and the Ordeal of Liberty* (1962).

Malone, Dumas. *Jefferson and the Rights of Man* (1951).

Merrill, Michael, and Wilentz, Sean, eds. *The Key of Liberty: The Life and Democratic Writings of William Manning, "A Laborer," 1747–1814* (1993).

Miller, John C. *The Federalist Era, 1789–1801* (1960).

Schwartz, Bernard. *The Great Rights of Mankind: A History of the American Bill of Rights* (1977).

Sharp, James Roger. *American Politics in the Early Republic: The New Nation in Crisis* (1993).

Stourzh, Gerald. *Alexander Hamilton and the Idea of Republican Government* (1970).

Population Growth and the Frontier

Ahlstrom, Sydney E. *A Religious History of the American People* (1972).

Klepp, Susan E., ed. "Symposium on the Demographic History of the Philadelphia Region, 1600–1860," *Proceedings of the American Philosophical Society,* 133:2 (1989).

Rohrbough, Malcolm J. *The Trans-Appalachian Frontier: People, Societies, and Institutions, 1775–1850* (1978).

U.S. Bureau of the Census, *A Century of Population Growth: From the First Census of the United States to the Twelfth, 1790–1900* (1909).

Taylor, Alan. *William Cooper's Town: Power and Persuasion on the Frontier of the Early American Republic* (1995).

Wallace, Anthony F.C. *The Death and Rebirth of the Seneca* (1969).

Weber, David J. *The Spanish Frontier in North America* (1992).

Economic Development and Technology

Browne, Gary Lawson. *Baltimore in the Nation, 1789–1861* (1980).

Doerflinger, Thomas M. *A Vigorous Spirit of Enterprise: Merchants and Economic Development in Revolutionary Philadelphia* (1986).

McGaw, Judith A., ed. *Early American Technology: Making and Doing Things from the Colonial Era to 1850* (1994).

Shelton, Cynthia J. *The Mills of Manayunk: Industrialization and Social Conflict in the Philadelphia Region, 1787–1837* (1986).

Smith, Billy G. *The "Lower Sort": Philadelphia's Laboring People, 1750–1800* (1990).

Tucker, Barbara M. *Samuel Slater and the Origins of the American Textile Industry, 1790–1860* (1984).

SECOND GREAT AWAKENING

Methodist Camp Meeting, engraving by E. Clay. During the Second Great Awakening, itinerant preachers held outdoor revivals that often lasted for several days.

Chapter 8

The New Republic Faces a New Century, 1800–1814

AMERICANS CONFRONTED THE nineteenth century with a variety of fears. For the Federalists, the growing Republican opposition warned that the evils of democracy and anarchy stood on the doorstep, ready to take control after the election of 1800. For the Republicans, the Alien and Sedition acts and Federalist repression of the whiskey rebels and John Fries underscored the need for change. Both parties, still members of the Revolutionary generation, thought in terms of the ideals for which they had fought against the British. They also measured events against what was transpiring elsewhere in the world. By 1800, the radical, then reactionary, phases of the French Revolution and Napoleon Bonaparte's rise to power dismayed Americans. The never-ending European war threatened to involve the United States for twenty years, and finally did in 1812. The revolt by slaves in the French West Indies horrified southern slave owners.

Though Thomas Jefferson's presidency proved to be less revolutionary than many Federalists expected, the new century brought indelible changes to American politics and society. The Federalist party shriveled and died, the Louisiana Purchase expanded the nation's territory to the Rocky Mountains and beyond, slavery became more firmly embedded in the southern economy, and the republic fought once more against Great Britain. The Second Great Awakening, the series of religious revivals that had begun in the late 1790s but gained steam after the turn of the century, influenced the ways in which many people interpreted these events.

RELIGION IN AMERICAN SOCIETY

Politics took a back seat in the lives of most Americans during the first decade of the nineteenth century. In many respects, that was the promise of Jefferson's government: low taxes, a small bureaucracy, minimal intrusion by government into the affairs of citizens, peace, religious freedom. In particular, religion absorbed the energies of many different groups: frontier settlers and Native Americans caught up in revivals, organizations to provide welfare relief in towns and cities, new sects like the Shakers, and free African Americans who built separate churches as the cornerstone of their communities. Many people believed that renewed emphasis on religion would transform the nation through individual faith and communal action.

CHRONOLOGY

1800	Washington, D.C., becomes national capital
	Gabriel's Rebellion
	Convention of 1800 with France
	Jefferson's election as president
	Rise of Handsome Lake as a Seneca prophet
1801	Adams's "midnight appointments"
	John Marshall becomes chief justice
	Tripolitan War
	Cane Ridge, Kentucky, camp meeting
1802	Judiciary Act of 1801 repealed
1803	*Marbury* v. *Madison* case
	Great Britain and France resume war
	Louisiana Purchase
1804	Lewis and Clark expedition departs from St. Louis
	Aaron Burr kills Alexander Hamilton
	Twelfth Amendment ratified
	Haiti founded
	Reelection of Jefferson as president
1805	*Essex* decision in Britain
1806	Non-Importation Act
1807	Burr tried for treason
	Leopard-Chesapeake Affair
	Embargo Act
1808	Federal ban on importation of slaves
	Madison elected as president
1809	Giles's Enforcement Act
	Embargo repealed; replaced with Non-Intercourse Act
	Treaty of Fort Wayne
1810	Annexation of West Florida
1811	Charter of national bank expires
	Tecumseh organizes pan-Indian resistance to land cessions
	Battle of Tippecanoe
1812	U.S. declares war on Great Britain
	Hull surrenders Detroit
	Madison elected to second term
1813	Perry defeats British navy on Lake Erie
	Battle of the Thames
1814	Battle of Horseshoe Bend
	British burn public buildings in Washington, D.C.
	Americans repel invasion on Lake Champlain
	Hartford Convention
	Treaty of Ghent

The Second Great Awakening

As the century began, people throughout the country sought spiritual renewal. Among New England Congregationalists, the revivals spread from one town to another between 1797 and 1801. The national Methodist conference of 1800 held in Baltimore witnessed an outpouring of religious fervor. These flames heralded a series of revivals—the Second Great Awakening—which lasted into the 1830s. Women and men of various denominations started voluntary associations to support missionaries, encourage moral behavior, and provide charity. Many followed the lead of young Quaker women in Philadelphia, who in 1795 had established the first female society to provide food, firewood, and clothing to impoverished city folk. Similar groups soon sprang up throughout the middle states, New England, and parts of the South. In accepting the message of revival, large numbers of Americans embraced evangelicalism—the belief that they

must take their message of salvation to others. They expected to create a more godly nation through conversion and good works.

In particular, eastern clergy worried that people on the frontier, with few churches, would let sin take control of their lives. As Americans streamed west across the Appalachians, by 1810, Ohio had 230,000 settlers, Kentucky and Tennessee had 668,000, and the Mississippi and Louisiana territories had 117,000. New Englanders moved to western New York State and the Midwest, while southerners carved out new plantations in the southern trans-Appalachian region. Evangelical ministers feared for the nation because so many westerners were unchurched. The clerics expressed their dread in terms of millennialism, the belief that the millennium—Christ's second coming—was at hand, as foretold in Revelation, the last book of the Bible. Pastors urged their congregations to prepare for the millennium by supporting missionary efforts in the west. They believed the kingdom of God could extend to the Pacific Ocean and beyond, but Americans throughout the country must embrace Christianity and convert Native Americans and the people of other lands.

Circuit preachers and missionaries traveled throughout the frontier; the churches they started were often the first social organizations in new communities. The great western revivals of 1800–1815, which built upon this work, began when several Presbyterians summoned the first camp meeting, a religious gathering held outside over the course of several days. People came together, miles from their homes, to hear revivalist preachers. The most famous of the early camp meetings took place in August 1801 at Cane Ridge, Kentucky, where Presbyterian, Methodist, and Baptist clergy preached for about a week to a throng numbering about 20,000. From wagons and crude tents, the crowds listened to the spiritual message that Jesus Christ could save everyone from their sins. The wicked could escape eternal damnation. People reacted emotionally and physically to this message, some jerking their heads or entire bodies, others falling to the ground in a faint.

Reminiscent of the Great Awakening in the South during the 1750s and 1760s (see Chapter 4), the camp meetings spread through Kentucky, Tennessee, and southern Ohio, gathering new congregations. The Methodist and Baptist churches, which placed less importance on the fine points of religious doctrine and a well-educated clergy than the Presbyterians, benefited most from the revivals. The Methodists and Baptists saw extraordinary growth among ordinary people, especially in the South, including African Americans and whites. As one minister wrote, "the illiterate Methodist preachers actually set the world on fire, (the American world at least,) while [pastors of other denominations] were lighting their matches!"

Religion was important to black Americans, whether they remained enslaved or had achieved freedom. In the South, where the expansion of cotton culture ended hopes for the abolition of slavery as tobacco declined, African Americans responded enthusiastically to revivalist preachers. The Methodists and Baptists welcomed free and enslaved blacks into their congregations as equals in spirit though not in governing the church. In hostile northern cities, free black communities depended upon separate churches for leadership and communal fellowship.

Growth of Sects

The period around 1800 witnessed the expansion of several dissenting sects: the Shakers, the Society of the Public Universal Friend, and the Universalists. They are called sects, rather than denominations, because they were new and fairly small in number of adherents. These sectarians held distinctive beliefs that set them apart from mainstream religions, yet had a significant influence on intellectual and social movements of their times.

The Shakers, whose official name was the United Society of Believers in Christ's Second Coming (the Millennial church), came to America in 1774, when Mother Ann Lee arrived from Britain with eight disciples. They left England to escape mob attacks and imprisonment. The group grew slowly at first, but expanded after Lee's death in 1784, as they reaped followers from revivals, especially Baptists. The Shakers even converted the three Presbyterians who had organized the Cane Ridge, Kentucky, camp meeting. The sect offered an avenue for people who had been spiritually reborn in the Awakening and sought a distinctive way to represent that rebirth in their lives.

From visions, Mother Lee believed that she embodied Christ's Second Coming, that the millennium had already arrived. As Christ had appeared as a man, and Lee (called Mother of the New Creation) came as a woman, God had both male and female elements. The

The Shakers of New Lebanon — Religious Exercises in the Dining Room. In religious worship, Shakers abandoned their strict, sex-segregated discipline.

Shakers considered themselves a vanguard to lead everyone to the kingdom of God. They believed in salvation by confession of sin, equality regardless of sex or race, opposition to slavery and war, and assistance to the poor. They abstained from sexual relations. In Shaker communities, which by 1809 existed from Maine to Kentucky, men and women ate, slept, and worked separately. They followed a strict discipline and aspired to economic self-sufficiency. Shakers sat on straight-backed chairs, cut their food into square pieces, and walked along paths laid out in right angles. But in religious worship, they abandoned this right-angle order. In a large open space without pulpit or pews, worshippers danced, shouted, and sang. The Shaker communitarian lifestyle, which yielded plentiful food, a comfortable standard of living, and beautifully designed furnishings, influenced other groups to organize communal, utopian experiments during the years after 1815.

A similar but smaller sect was the Society of the Public Universal Friend, founded by Jemima Wilkinson of Rhode Island. Disowned by Quakers in 1776 for joining the Baptists, Wilkinson became ill, believed that she died, and then returned to life as the Public Universal Friend. Her mission was to convince others to repent their sins and prepare for the millennium. Like Mother Lee, Wilkinson preached celibacy, peace, and opposition to slavery. She traveled sidesaddle on horseback, attracting a coterie of believers in New England and Pennsylvania. As one convert said, Wilkinson was "the Messenger of Peace . . . Travelling far & wide to spread the glad tidings & news of Salvation to a lost and perishing & dying World who have all gone astray like Lost Sheep." In 1788, upon gathering over 200 Universal Friends, she organized a community called Jerusalem in western New York. They established the first white settlement at Lake Seneca, then later moved to Keuka Lake. The Universal Friends neither organized a communal economy like the Shakers nor continued to seek new members. Nevertheless, the community survived well past Wilkinson's death in 1819.

Another sect, the Universalists, rejected the Calvinist belief that only a minority of people, the elect, could attain salvation. They preached that "it is the purpose of God, through the grace revealed in our Lord Jesus Christ, to save every member of the human race from sin." The American Universalist Church, established in 1779 by an Englishman, John Murray, found a sympathetic audience among ordinary people caught up in the Second Great Awakening in New England and on the frontier. Its message of universal salvation had wide influence, though the Universalist Church itself remained small.

Revivalism Among Native Americans

While the Second Great Awakening and dissenting sects claimed the imagination and souls of white and black Americans, a new wave of revivals drew together Native Americans. Among the Iroquois living on reservations in western New York and the Shawnees, Creeks, Cherokees, and other nations retaining lands in the trans-Appalachian region, prophets warned of imminent doom unless people changed their ways. Native Americans had continued to lose lands to whites throughout the area from the Appalachians to the Mississippi; by 1812, settlers in the region dwarfed the Indian population by seven to one. Decline in the numbers of fur-bearing animals caused economic hardship, while conflict over whether to cooperate with the United States created political factions within tribes.

Like the Delaware prophet Neolin in the 1760s (see Chapter 4), the new nativists blamed loss of land and power on the Indians' failure to maintain traditional rituals and on their adoption of wicked practices from the whites. Among many prophets, Handsome Lake of the Senecas (a nation of the Iroquois) and Tenskwatawa of the Shawnees wielded the greatest influence in the first decade of the nineteenth century.

Handsome Lake, a respected warrior and leader of the Allegany Senecas, fell ill in 1799, seemed to die, then came back to life saying that he had a vision in which messengers told him to become a prophet. In a series of revelations over several years, Handsome Lake received a message of impending catastrophe and a means to salvation. He told his people to stop drinking alcohol and practicing witchcraft. They should perform ancestral rituals such as the white dog ceremony in which a white dog was strangled, then set on fire as a sacrifice to the Creator, then eaten.

Handsome Lake also advocated peace—among his own people as well as toward white settlers and the U.S. government. He embraced the U.S. acculturation policy by which Quakers tried to convince the Iroquois to adopt white farming methods and gender roles, but he opposed further large-scale land cessions, the whiskey trade, social dancing in couples, and gambling with cards. Other Indians opposed acculturation, which required women to leave the fields and take up spinning, and men to farm rather than hunt. They viewed the policy, accurately, as a way to justify further expropriation of hunting lands.

Handsome Lake served as political leader of the Iroquois only briefly, from 1801 to 1803, but his spiritual message remained strong in the years that followed. Most influential was his drive against liquor. A former heavy drinker himself, Handsome Lake advised, in the words of a white observer, that "the Whiskey is the great Engine which the bad Spirit uses to introduce Witchcraft and many other evils amongst Indians." Many Iroquois abstained from hard drink. One Quaker visitor "noted with satisfaction that in the course of our travels among all the Indians on the Allegheny River . . . we have not seen a Single individual the least intoxicated with Liquor—which perhaps would be a Singular Circumstance to Observe in traveling among the same number of white Inhabitants."

Handsome Lake was one of the most influential Indian prophets of the late eighteenth and early nineteenth century. Another was Tenskwatawa, called the Shawnee Prophet, who became prominent among the people of the Great Lakes and Ohio Valley. With his brother, Tecumseh, he inspired a nativist movement to

Tenskwatawa, the Shawnee Prophet, *painted by George Catlin, 1830. With his brother Tecumseh, Tenskwatawa organized Native American resistance to white settlement in the Great Lakes region.*

resist the U.S. government's acculturation policy and land grabbing. Tenskwatawa saw visions similar to Handsome Lake's but was less accommodating toward whites. To avoid fiery destruction, he warned, Indians must revitalize their traditional ceremonies, avoid liquor, and reject the new gender roles. One of the prophet's visions promised that the whites would be destroyed if his people obeyed these instructions. Tenskwatawa and Tecumseh summoned nativists to oppose the Indian accommodationist leaders who sold land and adopted white farming. During the War of 1812, as will be discussed below, they organized pan-Indian military resistance in alliance with Great Britain against the United States.

AFRICAN AMERICANS

As slavery ended in the north, blacks faced discriminatory practices that kept the racial caste system in place, including segregation in churches and schools, and restriction from politics and many occupations. Despite this racism, northern blacks created new lives, institutions, and communities that offered a potent draw to African Americans in the south. With the St.

Domingue revolution in mind, southern blacks also considered more violent means to end bondage, as in the case of Gabriel's revolt in Virginia.

Free Blacks in the North

By 1800, Pennsylvania, New York, and all of New England had passed gradual abolition acts or ended slavery outright. New Jersey in 1804 became the last northern state to pass a law for gradual emancipation, which, like those of other states, freed children henceforth born to slave mothers, but retained slaves born before that date in perpetual bondage. The black children who benefited from the law would be required to serve their mother's owner until a certain age—in New Jersey, twenty-five for males and twenty-one for females. In effect, these children became indentured servants as compensation to masters for providing support during their early years.

Despite the gradual nature of these emancipation laws, slavery declined rapidly in the northern states. Responding to their slaves' requests for freedom and to the spirit of the abolition acts, owners freed people whom the laws left in bonds. Masters usually required some additional years of service for the promise of freedom. Frequently, blacks negotiated agreements for

TABLE 8.1	NUMBER OF ENSLAVED AFRICAN AMERICANS, 1800 AND 1810	
	1800	*1810*
New England	1,339	418
New York	20,903	15,017
New Jersey	12,422	10,851
Pennsylvania	1,706	795
Delaware	6,153	4,177
Maryland & District of Columbia	107,707	115,056
Virginia	346,968	394,357
North Carolina	133,296	168,824
South Carolina	146,151	196,365
Georgia	59,406	105,218
Kentucky	40,343	80,561
Tennessee	13,584	44,535
Mississippi Territory	3,489	17,088

TABLE 8.2 FREE BLACK POPULATION IN NORTHERN CITIES			
	1790	*1800*	*1810*
Philadelphia	1,849	6,028	8,942
New York City	1,036	3,333	7,470
Boston	766	1,174	1,484

Reverend Richard Allen, a former slave, was founder of the African Methodist Episcopal Church and a leader of the Philadelphia black community.

themselves or family members. In 1805, a New York slave, Margaret, obtained her owner's pledge of freedom in eight years if she behaved "as she always has done in an orderly manner as a servant ought to do." A New Jersey man promised to pay his owner $50 per year for four years in return for his release. When masters proved recalcitrant, blacks often forced the issue by running away.

The northern cities became magnets for escaped slaves, from the surrounding countryside and the Upper South. In addition, humanitarian concerns touched some southern masters, including George Washington, who freed his slaves in his will. Some owners in Delaware and the Chesapeake region, who held more slaves than they needed, emancipated their slaves, then sold them as indentured servants in the north. Between 1790 and 1810, the free black population of Philadelphia and New York City soared, while that of Boston also grew, though more slowly.

Philadelphia and New York City became centers of free African American culture, with churches fostering autonomous community growth. In Philadelphia, responding to hostility, freed men and women organized separate congregations in the 1780s and 1790s. Reverend Richard Allen, for example, led black worshipers from St. George's Methodist Episcopal Church when whites insisted on segregated seating. Allen described the scene as they were forced to move during prayer:

> We had not been long upon our knees before I heard considerable scuffling and loud talking. I raised my head up and saw one of the trustees, H_____ M_____, having hold of the Rev. Absalom Jones, pulling him off his knees, and saying, "You must get up, you must not kneel here." . . . we all went out of the church in a body, and they were no more plagued by us in the church.

Allen purchased a blacksmith's shop, converted it into a church, calling it Bethel, which in Hebrew means "house of God." By 1803, the black Methodist church had 457 members, the result of revivals and Allen's fervent preaching. But while the evangelical message of Methodism appealed to African Americans, and "Mother" Bethel grew, the congregation found relations with the hierarchy of the white Methodist church difficult. In the early decades of the nineteenth century, black Methodists in Philadelphia, Baltimore, Wilmington, and New York struggled against white control, finally seceding to form separate denominations. In 1816, Philadelphia's Bethel became the first congregation of the African Methodist Episcopal church.

Urban black churches, which included the Episcopal, Baptist, and Presbyterian as well as the Methodist, provided mutual aid, fellowship, and avenues for leadership. One benefit of belonging to a New York congregation became obvious to an eighty-year-old woman after a fire destroyed her home. When asked where she would find shelter, she answered, "O a sister

in the church has promised to take me in." Shunned by white organizations, effectively barred from politics, and lacking equal opportunity for employment, African Americans created alternatives through the church. Talented black men became ministers and elders; from these positions they served as spokesmen for their community.

Like white urban residents, freed men and women formed mutual benefit societies. The names African Americans chose for these organizations demonstrated pride in their African heritage. Philadelphians, for example, formed the Free African Society, Daughters of Ethiopia, Angola Society, Sons of Africa, and many others. The official purpose of these societies was to collect dues to provide relief to poor widows and children, but, just as important, the groups facilitated community involvement.

Though most northern blacks remained impoverished, New York and Philadelphia offered a variety of opportunities that could be found nowhere else. With little money or access to capital, few African Americans, perhaps one in ten, scraped together the funds to purchase a house, shop, or farm. In the first decades of the nineteenth century, many blacks were still completing terms of servitude, while others, though free, lived and worked in white households as domestic servants. Even if they established their own households, women generally washed clothes or performed domestic service for others. Most men were mariners or hired as common laborers—digging foundations, wells, and graves; transporting goods on the docks and through the city streets; and sweeping chimneys. The African American community provided additional opportunity by employing its own. Residents supported black shoemakers, carpenters, food retailers, hucksters, barbers, hairdressers, seamstresses, tailors, cooks, bakers, schoolteachers, and ministers. In Philadelphia, a few African Americans achieved considerable wealth and fame. By 1807, James Forten employed thirty men—blacks and whites—to produce sails for the city's shipbuilders. Robert Bogle developed the idea of catering parties, weddings, and funerals, while Frank Johnson became the city's premier musician. He performed on trumpet and violin, composed dance music and songs, and organized a band that played at balls and public events.

Northern blacks faced daily challenges in earning their bread, while keeping their sights on personal goals of economic success and equal status. But they revered their African roots and remembered fellow

Negroes in Front of the Bank of Pennsylvania, Philadelphia *(1814) shows a group of black workers, the male sawyers laboring in a public space and a female domestic caring for a white child.*

blacks held in slavery. The word African in the name of most mutual aid societies and churches testified to their pride of origins, though many of the founders were two, three, even four generations removed from ancestral lands.

African Americans in northern cities also knew of recent struggles by slaves in St. Domingue and elsewhere; a large number of blacks in Philadelphia and New York City had come from the French island with their masters who fled the black revolt. During the 1790s, blacks on St. Domingue led by Toussaint L'Ouverture, a former slave, defeated local whites and the French, Spanish, and British armies. In 1802, Napoleon tried once again to take control of the island, but failed when disease decimated his forces. In 1804, the victorious rebels of St. Domingue established Haiti as an independent nation. Most white Americans dreaded the importation of black revolt. Thomas Jefferson opposed trade with the island, stat-

ing, "We may expect therefore black crews, and super-cargoes and missionaries thence into the southern states. . . . If this combustion can be introduced among us under any veil whatever, we have to fear it."

Slave Rebellion in the South

With more than 850,000 enslaved blacks in the American south in 1800, one-third of the population, whites had reason to be concerned about slave insurgency. After St. Domingue erupted, Georgia and the Carolinas declared black emigrés from the West Indies a threat, prohibiting their entry. South Carolina, in reopening its international slave trade in 1803, made every effort to avoid admitting rebels. The state excluded blacks from the West Indies and South America, and any who had ever lived in the French West Indies. Every man imported from another state needed a certificate indicating that he had not "been concerned in any insurrection or rebellion."

In August 1800, the worst fears of white southerners were nearly realized when an enslaved blacksmith named Gabriel organized an armed march against the capital of Virginia. With about 600 supporters from Richmond and surrounding counties, Gabriel planned a full-scale insurrection. His strategy included seizing guns from an arsenal, taking Governor James Monroe hostage, and forcing concessions from town officials. Gabriel expected poor whites to join him because they, like slaves, lacked political power. The attack failed when a torrential rainstorm washed out bridges, making travel impossible. Efforts to try again another day collapsed when two informers passed word of the conspiracy to authorities who rounded up suspects. Though Gabriel eluded capture for more than three weeks, he was arrested and hanged, as were twenty-six others implicated in the plot.

White Americans, at the beginning of the nineteenth century, still held the Revolutionary belief that all men and women desired freedom. Masters took seriously the threat of slave revolt. After Gabriel's rebellion, Governor Monroe observed about enslaved African Americans, "Unhappily while this class of people exists among us we can never count with certainty on its tranquil submission." In 1802, Virginians discovered additional conspiracies, with rumors of more violence heightening tensions. In 1805, after four whites had been poisoned in North Carolina, officials burned a slave woman alive, hanged three other slaves,

and whipped and cut off the ears of another. Gabriel's plot, the St. Domingue uprising, and what appeared to be an upsurge of murders and arson by blacks convinced southern lawmakers to enact more stringent slave codes. South Carolina and Georgia tightened requirements for slave patrols and defined as treason any collaboration in slave rebellion. South Carolina and Virginia placed restrictions on meetings after dark, and Virginia increased penalties for arson. Hardening attitudes toward slavery snuffed out southern antislavery societies that were already faltering. The Alexandria, Virginia, association died by 1805; the Virginia Abolition Society expressed little hope for its future work. On a more positive note, as the twenty-year constitutional restriction on prohibiting the slave trade expired (see Chapter 6), Congress officially banned the importation of slaves after January 1, 1808.

JEFFERSON'S REPUBLIC

In 1800, the federal government moved from the nation's cultural capital in Philadelphia to an unfinished village on the Potomac: Washington, D.C. The ruling party also changed, as voters voiced their dissatisfaction with the Federalists by electing Thomas Jefferson and a Republican Congress. Jefferson's promise of reduced government and taxes appealed to a populace concerned about other things besides national politics—their finances, their souls, and local communities. Events prevented the young nation from wrapping itself in isolation, however, for its economic prosperity depended a great deal upon international commerce, a trade severely hampered by the ongoing European war.

Election of 1800

Most recently, the United States had been involved in the Quasi-War with France, in which the French navy ravaged the American merchant fleet. Congress had expanded the army, authorized the U.S. Navy to protect commercial ships, and revoked unilaterally the American-French treaty of 1778, which had pledged a mutual defensive alliance "forever." The Federalists swept the congressional elections of 1798 on the crest of anti-French fervor; they tried to use war fever

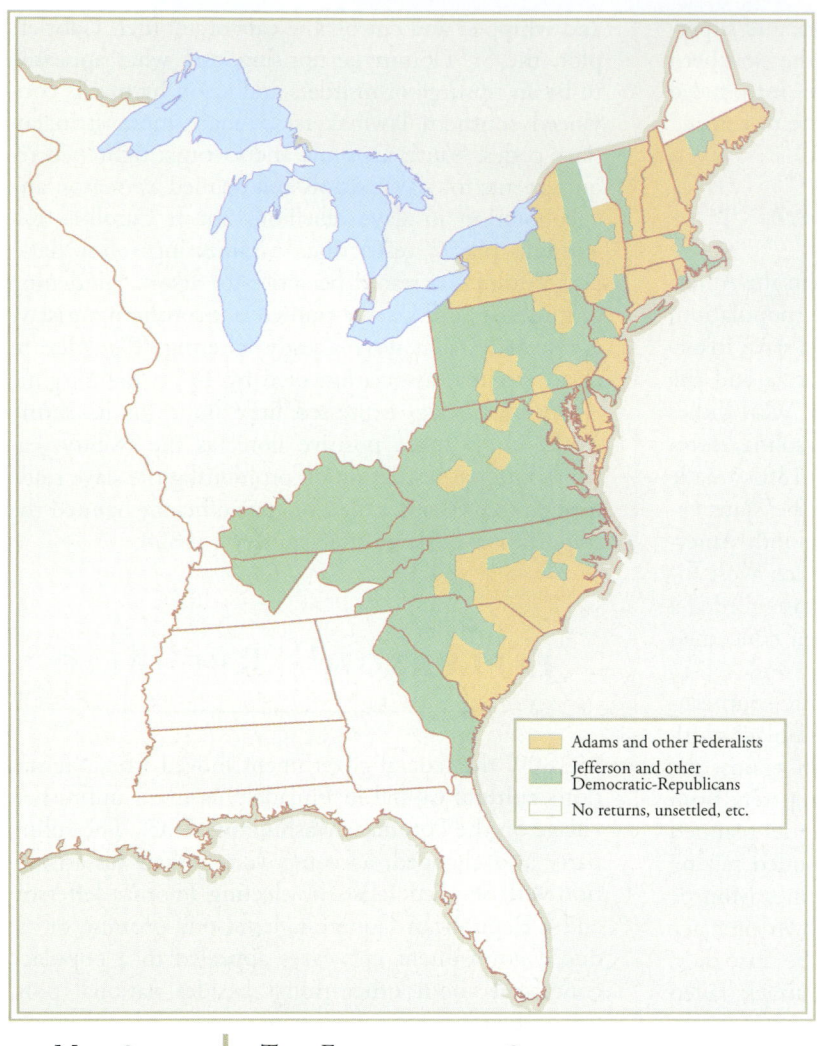

MAP 8.1 | THE ELECTION OF 1800

Legend:
- Adams and other Federalists
- Jefferson and other Democratic-Republicans
- No returns, unsettled, etc.

possible to fulfill: Its mission was to obtain French agreement that the 1778 alliance had ended and indemnities for confiscated American ships. In March 1800, Murray, Ellsworth, and Davie met with Napoleon, who had no intention of paying compensation. The commissioners reached an accord only by ignoring their instructions. The Convention of 1800, signed in France in October and ratified reluctantly by the U.S. Senate in February 1801, echoed provisions of the 1778 commercial treaty in calling for "a firm, inviolable, and universal peace" and recognition of most-favored-nation status between the two nations. The Convention voided the defensive alliance of 1778, however, thus eliminating the French claim to U.S. support against Great Britain. The pact also included a vague confirmation by the French of neutral rights in international trade, but provided no restitution to American shippers, a failing that opponents said made the convention worthless. In fact, it had value in normalizing relations between the two countries and ending the 1778 treaty that had become so dangerous to the United States in the recurring European war.

The chief beneficiary of reduced tensions with France was Thomas Jefferson, named in May 1800 as Republican nominee for president, with Aaron Burr of New York for vice president. John Adams received the Federalist nomination for reelection, with Charles Cotesworth Pinckney of South Carolina as running mate. Many Federalists, including Alexander Hamilton, opposed Adams for making peace with France and for other political reasons. When the electoral votes were tallied, Jefferson and Burr each received 73 votes, Adams had 65, Pinckney 64, and John Jay 1. In lining up votes in the electoral college, the Republicans had failed to take account of the constitutional election procedures that lacked provision for party slates. The drafters of the Constitution had not predicted the development of political parties, so they directed that each elector cast two votes, with the candidate receiving the highest number elected

against the Republicans through the Alien and Sedition acts. Instead, the backlash of concern about civil liberties swelled the opposition, as did suppression of John Fries's rebellion.

As the 1800 election approached, many Federalists expected to take advantage of the unresolved difficulties with France by continuing to paint the Jeffersonian Republicans as pro-French, hence un-American. Nevertheless, to the distress of fellow Federalists, President John Adams moved to end hostilities. He nominated a three-man commission, including William Vans Murray (ambassador to the Netherlands), Chief Justice Oliver Ellsworth, and Governor William R. Davie of North Carolina, to make peace with France. The commission received instructions that proved im-

Aaron Burr, *by Gilbert Stuart. Burr refused initially to follow the script and accept the vice presidency when he tied with Jefferson in the election of 1800.*

president and the runner-up vice president. The electors had no way of designating which candidate they supported for president and which for vice president. The Federalists avoided the difficulty by having one elector vote for John Jay, thus giving Pinckney one less vote than Adams. But the Republicans in the electoral college all cast one vote for Jefferson and one for Burr, resulting in the tie.

If Burr had simply yielded to Jefferson in 1800, the problem would have been resolved without complication. But the New Yorker reached for the presidency, thereby earning the enmity of Jefferson and his party. The tie sent the election to the House of Representatives, which had been elected in 1798 with a Federalist majority. Each state delegation received one vote. Some of the Federalists hatched a plan to support Burr, thinking that they might be able to control him as president. Hamilton, who knew Aaron Burr well, opposed the plot vigorously. To colleagues, Hamilton wrote, "Burr loves nothing but himself; thinks of nothing but his own aggrandizement, and will be content with nothing, short of permanent power in his own hands." The former secretary of the treasury advised his party to make a deal with Jefferson to keep the system of public credit and the navy, retain Federalist appointees in office, and remain neutral in the war between Britain and France. The House of Representatives required thirty-six ballots over six days before the Federalist delegate from Delaware, James A. Bayard, shifted his position to break the tie.

Jefferson's "Revolution"

The third president assumed a conciliatory stance toward the Federalists as he took office. On March 4, 1801, Jefferson delivered his inaugural address to the new Congress, which the Republicans dominated in the House by 69 votes to 36, and in the Senate by an 18–13 majority. He gave the address almost in a whisper, for he was not a good public speaker. The speech reflected his Republican beliefs: emphasis on the power of state governments, freedom of religion and the press, majority rule but protection of minority rights, low government expenditures, and reduction of the federal debt. Jefferson upheld the Convention of 1800 with France implicitly by stating that he desired amity and trade with foreign nations and "entangling alliances with none." His most famous statement, "We are all republicans, we are all federalists," attempted to get beyond the partisan battles that had bedeviled his two predecessors. Jefferson's recapitulation of basic republican principles recalled how recently his generation had fought for these ideals. He later described his election as "the revolution of 1800" that "was as real a revolution in the principles of our government as that of 1776 was in its form; not effected indeed by the sword, as that, but by the rational and peaceable instrument of reform, the suffrage of the people." Despite bitter political enmity, American leaders had created a party system by which power could be contested in elections rather than through bloodshed. With the election of 1800, the Constitution passed a crucial test, with peaceful transfer of power from one party to its opponents.

The new president worked to put his principles into action, to create an agrarian republic in which the federal government kept its role to a minimum. The location in Washington, D.C., seemed the ideal setting for a weak government. In 1800, the town had

THOMAS JEFFERSON'S FIRST INAUGURAL ADDRESS, MARCH 4, 1801

Jefferson wrote this inaugural address, the first given by a president in Washington, D.C., in the two weeks following the confirmation of his election by the House of Representatives. In this speech, the third president sought to heal wounds from the contentious 1800 election and set forth his philosophy of government.

FRIENDS AND FELLOW-CITIZENS Called upon to undertake the duties of the first executive office of our country, I avail myself of the presence of that portion of my fellow citizens which is here assembled to express my grateful thanks for the favor with which they have been pleased to look toward me, to declare a sincere consciousness that the task is above my talents, and that I approach it with those anxious and awful presentiments which the greatness of the charge and the weakness of my powers so justly inspire. A rising nation, spread over a wide and fruitful land, traversing all the seas with the rich productions of their industry, engaged in commerce with nations who feel power and forget right, advancing rapidly to destinies beyond the reach of mortal eye—when I contemplate these transcendent objects, and see the honor, the happiness, and the hopes of this beloved country committed to the issue and the auspices of this day, I shrink from the contemplation, and humble myself before the magnitude of the undertaking. . . .

During the contest of opinion through which we have past the animation of discussions and of exertions has sometimes worn an aspect which might impose on strangers unused to think freely and to speak and to write what they think. But this being now decided by the voice of the nation, enounced according to the rules of the constitution, all will of course arrange themselves under the will of the law, and unite in common efforts for the common good. All too will bear in mind this sacred principle, that though the will of the majority is in all cases to prevail, that will, to be rightful, must be reasonable; that the minority possess their equal rights, which equal laws must protect, and to violate would be oppression. Let us then, fellow citizens, unite with one heart and one mind, let us restore to social intercourse that harmony and affection without which liberty and even life itself are but dreary things. And let us reflect that, having banished from our land that religious intolerance under which mankind so long bled and suffered, we have yet gained little if we countenance a political intolerance as despotic, as wicked, and capable of as bitter and bloody persecutions. . . . We have called by different names brethren of the same principle. We are all republicans; we are all federalists. If there be any among us who wish to dissolve this Union or to change its republican form, let them stand undisturbed, as monuments of the safety with which error of opinion may be tolerated where reason is left free to combat it. I know, indeed, that some honest

fewer than 400 dwellings, which one government official described as mostly "small miserable huts." The Capitol was incomplete, with wings for the Senate and House but no center. What existed was poorly constructed: The acoustics were dreadful, the roof leaked, and the heating "noxious." The president's house was not yet finished in 1814 when the British burned it. Construction materials littered the grounds during Jefferson's administration to the extent that, according to one guest, "in a dark night instead of finding your way

men fear that a republican government cannot be strong, that this government is not strong enough. But would the honest patriot, in the full tide of successful experiment, abandon a government which has so far kept us free and firm on the theoretic and visionary fear that this government, the world's best hope, may, by possibility, want energy to preserve itself? I trust not. I believe this, on the contrary, the strongest government on earth. I believe it the only one where every man, at the call of the law, would fly to the standard of the law, and would meet invasions of the public order as his own personal concern. Sometimes it is said that man cannot be trusted with the government of himself. Can he, then, be trusted with the government of others? Or have we found angels in the form of kings to govern him? Let history answer this question. . . .

About to enter, fellow citizens, on the exercise of duties which comprehend everything dear and valuable to you, it is proper you should understand what I deem the essential principles of this government, and consequently those which ought to shape its administration. I will compress them in the narrowest compass they will bear, stating the general principle, but not all its limitations. Equal and exact justice to all men, of whatever state or persuasion, religious or political; peace, commerce, and honest friendship with all nations, entangling alliances with none; the support of the state governments in all their rights, as the most competent administrations for our domestic concerns and the surest bulwarks against anti-republican tendencies; the preservation of the general government in its whole constitutional vigor, as the sheet anchor of our peace at home and safety abroad; a jealous care of the right of election by the people, a mild and safe corrective of abuses which are lopped by the sword of revolution where peaceable remedies are unprovided; absolute acquiescence in the decisions of the majority, the vital principle of republics from which is no appeal but to force, the vital principle and immediate parent of despotism; a well disciplined militia, our best reliance in peace and for the first moments of war, till regulars may relieve them; the supremacy of the civil over the military authority; economy in the public expence, that labor may be lightly burthened; the honest payment of our debts and sacred preservation of the public faith; encouragement of agriculture, and of commerce as its handmaid; the diffusion of information and arraignment of all abuses at the bar of the public reason; freedom of religion; freedom of the press, and freedom of person under the protection of the habeas corpus, and trial by juries impartially selected. These principles form the bright constellation which has gone before us and guided our steps through an age of revolution and reformation. The wisdom of our sages and blood of our heroes have been devoted to their attainment. They should be the creed of our political faith, the text of civic instruction, the touchstone by which to try the services of those we trust; and should we wander from them in moments of error or of alarm, let us hasten to retrace our steps and to regain the road which alone leads to peace, liberty, and safety.

to the house, you may, perchance, fall into a pit, or stumble over a heap of rubbish." A foreign visitor thought "this parsimony . . . is a disgrace to the country." Cows grazed on what later became the Mall; hogs ran through the city's streets.

Washington, D.C., remained a village in part because the federal government was small, and Jefferson had no interest in seeing it grow. In 1802, federal personnel throughout the country numbered under 10,000, of whom 6,500 served in military posts. Of

The Capitol in Washington was incomplete at the time of Jefferson's election in 1800. With hogs running through the streets, the town seemed an appropriate seat for his agrarian republic.

the nonuniformed officials, fewer than 300 (including the president and Congress) worked in the capital. The president and Supreme Court each had one clerk, Congress employed thirteen, and the Attorney General none. The central government had relatively little to do, for state and local governments or voluntary associations took primary responsibility for keeping law and order, maintaining roads and bridges, supervising the militia, and providing welfare relief and schools.

Jefferson's lack of attention to building Washington, D.C., revealed his approach to the presidency. In contrast to Federalist efforts to reflect the grandeur of European courts and capitals, he adopted informality and frugality. On one occasion, when a senator visited the executive mansion, he found the tall, thin president in a dirty shirt and worn slippers. Jefferson dealt with members of Congress and foreign diplomats personally, inviting small groups for dinner and conversation. He avoided making speeches, sending written messages to Congress. With only one clerk, he handled many documents himself.

The change of political power from the Federalists to the Republicans raised questions about office-holding and political spoils. At the highest level of executive appointments, the cabinet, Jefferson assumed his right to appoint trusted supporters. He named James Madison of Virginia, his closest ally, as secretary of state, and Albert Gallatin of Pennsylvania as secretary

of the treasury. Both were intelligent and reliable. Gallatin was committed to the president's program to pay off the debt. Other members of the cabinet included Levi Lincoln of Massachusetts as attorney general, Henry Dearborn of Massachusetts as secretary of war, and Robert Smith of Maryland as secretary of the navy.

The question of whether or not to retain bureaucrats was more difficult. Jefferson supported the idea of a civil service in which public officers held their positions on the basis of merit; during the election crisis he suggested that he would allow officeholders to keep their jobs. When he learned that Washington and Adams had appointed only six Republicans to about 600 positions, however, the new president replaced about one-half of the Federalists with Republicans. Most infuriating were the "midnight appointments," as Jefferson called them—the appointments Adams made as a lame duck after he knew that the election was lost. In addition, in February 1801, the Federalist Congress had passed a new Judiciary Act creating additional judgeships and other offices, all of which Federalists received. Jefferson cancelled the appointments, calling upon the new Republican Congress to repeal the law.

Jefferson and Gallatin placed high priority in decreasing government expenditures, taxes, and the national debt. Gallatin opposed all spending by the fed-

eral government, including military, because he thought preparedness would incline the nation toward war when a crisis struck. With support of the Republican Congress, the administration cut the defense budget in half and eliminated several ambassadorships in Europe. They repealed all excise taxes, including that on whiskey, relying primarily on import duties for income. Gallatin hoped to pay off the federal debt of $82 million in sixteen years, a goal that was probably impossible even without increased military spending during the War of 1812.

Jefferson's plan to reduce the navy and remain clear of international conflicts hit a snag when Yusuf Karamanli, the leader of Tripoli in North Africa, declared war on the United States. Like the rulers of Algiers, Tunis, and Morocco, Karamanli demanded payments from the United States to "protect" American merchant carriers from pirates. To end this extortion, in 1801 Jefferson sent naval vessels to blockade Tripoli and protect shipping. The United States experienced a major loss when the ship *Philadelphia* ran aground while pursuing pirates, but when a small force of U.S. Marines and Arab mercenaries seized Derna, the Tripolitans agreed to peace. The war had propelled military expenditures upward, however, and convinced Jefferson of the navy's value, thus hindering somewhat the administration's plans for reduced government spending.

The Judiciary

Although the Republicans had captured the presidency and Congress in 1800, the third branch of the federal government, the judiciary, remained firmly in the hands of the Federalists. Adams and the outgoing Congress had tried to solidify their party's power in the courts with the Judiciary Act of 1801, which amended the act of 1789. By appointing additional federal judges, the new law ended the onerous requirement for Supreme Court justices to ride from state to state holding circuit courts twice a year. The act also reduced the number of justices on the Court from six to five, thereby denying Jefferson the opportunity to make an appointment when a seat became vacant. The Republican Congress, in early 1802, repealed this law, reinstating the Judiciary Act of 1789, thus forcing some federal judges out of their jobs and the Supreme Court back to the circuit.

Chief Justice John Marshall, *painted by Ferret de Saint Memin at the time of Marshall's appointment in 1801. During his tenure to 1835, the Chief Justice established federal judicial authority, in particular the court's power to decide the constitutionality of laws.*

Jefferson's bitter relationship with the Supreme Court resulted in part from his antipathy toward Chief Justice John Marshall, his distant cousin, whom Adams had named to the bench in early 1801. Like Jefferson, Marshall was tall, informal in manner, and a native of Virginia. He was educated by tutors, and had joined the patriot forces in 1775, serving until 1781. He attributed his nationalism to that service, saying that he became "confirmed in the habit of considering America as my country, and congress as my government." Marshall began a successful law practice after the war, served as a Virginia assemblyman, supported ratification of the Federal Constitution, then became the leading Federalist in his state. In the legal environment of the new republic, many colleagues appreciated his originality in building cases on logic and natural law rather than depending upon English precedent. On the Supreme Court, too, Marshall followed his own lights, creating the legal basis on which the power of the Court rests. During his long, illustrious career, which lasted until 1835, Marshall solidified the authority of the judicial branch of the federal government.

Marshall's most important decision, *Marbury* v. *Madison* (1803), commenced in a suit by William Marbury, nominated by Adams as a justice of the peace but not commissioned by the Jefferson administration. Marbury sued under the Judiciary Act of 1789, which granted the Supreme Court the power to require Secretary of State Madison to hand over Marbury's commission. Given the partisanship involved, most observers expected Marshall and his Federalist court to direct Madison to comply. Instead, the Chief Justice said that he could not remedy Marbury's situation, though he wished to do so, because the Congress had erred in giving the Court such authority. Marshall declared the provision of the 1789 Judiciary Act unconstitutional, thus establishing the Supreme Court's power of judicial review. Though *Marbury* v. *Madison* was the only case in which Marshall's court struck down an act of Congress, the principle stood.

Jefferson decided that the federal judiciary, still dominated by Federalists and growing in power under his adversary John Marshall, had to be controlled. Because federal judges constitutionally held their seats for life, "during good behavior," the president suggested to congressional Republicans that they start impeachment proceedings against objectionable Federalists. According to the Constitution, officers of the United States should be removed by "Impeachment for, and Conviction of, Treason, Bribery, or other high Crimes and Misdemeanors." The House of Representatives had the duty to impeach, while the Senate's function was to sit in judgment, with a two-thirds vote necessary for conviction. The Republicans impeached John Pickering, an official of the federal district court of New Hampshire, who was an alcoholic and insane, but who had not to anyone's knowledge committed any high crimes. The Senate found him guilty anyway and removed him from his position. Next, in January 1805, the House of Representatives impeached Samuel Chase of Maryland, an associate justice of the Supreme Court and extreme Federalist who castigated Jefferson's administration. But the prosecution failed to convince two-thirds of the Senate that Chase should be expelled from office for misconduct and other charges. Some moderate Republicans refused to adopt Jefferson's strategy to eject troublesome opponents. Thus ended Congress's attempt to remove Federalists from the bench by impeachment. John Marshall probably would have been the next target had the action against Chase succeeded.

Domestic Politics

Jefferson and the Republicans gained in popularity as they steered a course more moderate than the "revolution" of 1800 had promised. The president had reduced taxes and attempted to limit the judiciary, but did not dismantle the Federalist edifice of national power, including the military and the national bank. He mixed republican theory, based upon a nation of small farmers, with practical politics aiding commerce. His policies, combined with booming exports, steadily increased Republican support, as many Federalist voters switched parties. In the election of 1802, the Republicans won 102 seats to the Federalists' 39 in the House of Representatives; the Republican margin in the Senate was 25 to 9.

Looking forward to the next presidential election, Congress acted promptly to avoid the deadlock that had occurred in 1800. The Republicans wanted a formal way (not just an agreement among the electors) to keep the Federalists from conspiring once again to elevate the Republican candidate for vice president to the presidency. The Twelfth Amendment to the Constitution, which required the electors to draw up distinct lists for president and vice president, was ratified by September 1804.

The election of 1804 demonstrated the demise of the Federalists as a national party. They retained power in New England, but Republicans dominated politics elsewhere. Some arch-Federalists, realizing that the nation had moved beyond their control after the Louisiana Purchase (see the next section), briefly plotted to separate the northeastern states from the Union. Jefferson defeated the Federalist presidential candidate, Charles Cotesworth Pinckney, by 162 electoral votes to 14.

Jefferson had replaced Aaron Burr as his running mate with George Clinton, also of New York, thus keeping the ticket balanced geographically. For his part, Burr ran for governor of New York against the Republican candidate, Morgan Lewis. Despite support from Burrite Republicans and some Federalists, the outgoing vice president lost by a landslide. Alexander Hamilton played a decisive role in the defeat by publicly denouncing his longtime enemy. Burr challenged Hamilton to a duel. When the two faced each other at Weehawken, New Jersey, in July 1804, Burr shot Hamilton to death. In doing so, the vice president ended his own political career as well as the life of one of the architects of the American nation-state.

THE LOUISIANA PURCHASE

Jefferson had boosted his popularity prior to the 1804 election with the Louisiana Purchase, which marked the greatest success of his presidency. In pursuing the deal with France, he deviated from one of his beliefs—in limited power of the central government—to obtain land for his agrarian republic. Long interested in the west, he scored a diplomatic coup that doubled the size of the United States and reduced Spain's dominance west of the Mississippi River.

The Bargain with Napoleon

The chain of events leading to the Louisiana Purchase began in 1800, when France signed a secret treaty with Spain for lands in western North America. France would get back the territory it had ceded to Spain in 1763. When Jefferson and Madison heard in 1801 of the impending transfer, they sent the new U.S. ambassador to France, Robert R. Livingston, with instructions to prevent the exchange or at least obtain West Florida. The Americans wanted to prevent France from controlling the Mississippi Valley, for they feared that Napoleon's government would be a greater foe in the west than Spain had been. The dilapidated Spanish empire caused trouble enough. In October 1802, before the French took over the province, the Spanish suspended once again the right of Americans to deposit goods for export at New Orleans. The Americans thought, incorrectly, that Napoleon was behind the ban. Many wanted to take New Orleans by force. Jefferson wrote to Livingston, "The day that France takes possession of N. Orleans . . . we must marry ourselves to the British fleet and nation." Jefferson pushed for negotiations, however, not war.

In response to Livingston's overtures, Napoleon decided to sell the entire Louisiana Territory to the United States. The French leader's zeal to construct an American empire had cooled with the loss of his army in St. Domingue; Louisiana would be too difficult to defend against a hostile United States. And Napoleon needed money, as he was at war with Great Britain once again. In documents dated April 30, 1803, the United States agreed to pay France $15 million, to recognize the rights of the French and Native Americans living in the territory, and to recognize the French residents as American citizens. Spain was furious because

Napoleon had promised not to sell the region to the British or the Americans. Jefferson ignored the Spanish objections, but worried, as a strict constructionist, that the Louisiana Purchase was unconstitutional because the federal government had no specific power to acquire territory. He put aside these concerns, confident that it was right to avoid war and add vast lands for expansion of the American republic. "By enlarging the empire of liberty," the president argued, the nation could maintain its agrarian foundations, thus avoid descent into vice, luxury, and decay. A successful republic was dependent upon broad property holding, for virtuous, independent, middling farmers made ideal citizens. The Louisiana Purchase, Jefferson believed, would extend the life of the republic by providing space for generations of ordinary planters. While some Federalists disagreed, most Americans celebrated the end of friction over the Mississippi River and New Orleans. Western farmers could get their products to market; eastern merchants prospered from the trade.

Disputes with Spain

When U.S. officials gained formal possession of Louisiana in December 1803, the Spanish had only recently transferred control to the French. The ceremonies took place in New Orleans, a city of 8,000 that had been reconstructed in Spanish style since several great fires a decade earlier. With a cathedral, theater, impressive city hall, and mansions, New Orleans served as the cultural and economic center of the lower Mississippi Valley. In population, it was larger than other towns of the Spanish borderlands, including St. Augustine and San Antonio, which each had 1,500 residents; Santa Fe, with 6,000; and Los Angeles, with 850. The entire white population of the Louisiana Territory was approximately 50,000, including French, Spanish, Germans, English, and Americans.

Beyond Spain's objection to the U.S. purchase of Louisiana, the two nations also disputed the territory's boundaries, because the treaties transferring ownership were vague. Thomas Jefferson pushed for the most generous interpretation for the United States. He demanded West Florida, with an eastern boundary at the Perdido River, the present boundary between Alabama and the Florida panhandle. The president also thought his new acquisition extended in the southwest to the Rio Grande, incorporating all of Texas and part of

Plan of New Orleans in 1801, just before the Louisiana Purchase.

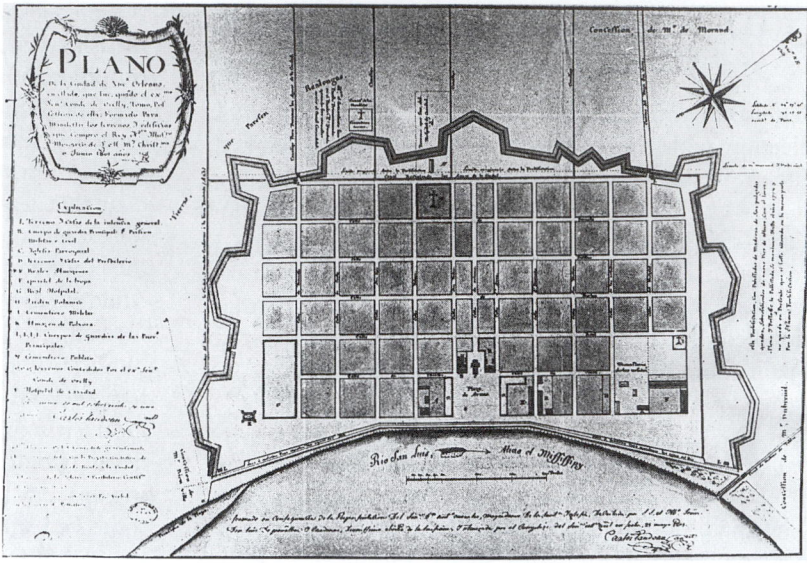

New Mexico, and in the northwest to the Rocky Mountains. Spain, on the other hand, said the Louisiana Territory included only a constricted region along the west bank of the Mississippi from northern Missouri to the Gulf of Mexico.

In 1804, Jefferson sent troops to West Florida, hoping to convince Spain by threat of force to give up or sell the province. Americans already outnumbered Spanish residents in the territory, which later comprised parts of Mississippi, Alabama, and Louisiana. Jefferson also wanted East Florida. He decided not to attack, and instead attempted to purchase the Floridas over the next several years, but failed.

The Lewis and Clark Expedition

To strengthen U.S. claims to the west, Jefferson sponsored an exploratory mission to the Pacific Ocean. Several times since 1783, he had tried to organize expeditions for scientific knowledge and to promote American interests in the region. As president, he now had the authority and financial resources to support this major undertaking. By the early nineteenth century, however, others had surveyed parts of the territory. In 1792, an American sea captain Robert Gray explored the Columbia River, and George Vancouver, a British naval officer, sailed the northwest coast. A few years later, fur traders working for the Spanish government ascended the Missouri River to present-

day North Dakota, while British traders from Canada began moving west.

Even before buying Louisiana, the president had decided to send an expedition west; the purchase gave the project greater urgency. He appointed his private secretary, Meriwether Lewis, as captain of the enterprise. Lewis chose his friend William Clark, the brother of George Rogers Clark of Revolutionary fame, to be his partner. Meriwether Lewis and William Clark had served in the army together in the old Northwest, so both were familiar with frontier conditions. Jefferson selected Lewis for his scientific interests as well as his wilderness experience. The president wanted "a person who to courage, prudence, habits & health adapted to the woods, & some familiarity with the Indian character, joins a perfect knoledge of botany, natural history, mineralogy & astronomy."

Jefferson had a long list of goals for his explorers. They were to travel to the source of the Missouri River to find the elusive Northwest Passage, fill in huge blanks in geographic knowledge of the West, and bring back descriptions of unknown species of plants and animals. He also hoped they would make peaceful contact with Native Americans to expand commercial networks for fur traders. Lewis and Clark more than fulfilled their assignment, keeping daily journals of their experiences, including descriptions of Indian societies and culture, systematic weather records, and observations of flora and fauna, as well as

Page.26.

Captains Lewis & Clark holding a Council with the Indians

Meeting of the Lewis and Clark expedition with Native Americans on the Missouri River, 1804. Illustration from the journal of Sergeant Patrick Gass, a member of the expedition.

a detailed map of their journey. Their relations with the people of the Northwest were for the most part amicable.

Lewis and Clark received commissions as army officers to lead the Corps of Discovery of about forty men who departed from St. Louis in May 1804. During that summer and fall they traveled up the Missouri River, using poles and tow ropes against the current. They battled the hot sun, diarrhea, and mosquitoes; several men deserted and one died, the only member of the Corps to perish during the entire trip. The adventurers met with the leaders of Indian nations along the way, telling them that the United States had taken possession of the territory from the Spanish. They arrived in the Mandan and Hidatsa villages of what is now North Dakota, where they spent the winter of 1804–1805.

In April 1805, the Lewis and Clark expedition set out with their guide Sacagawea, a Shoshone woman, and her French husband and infant son. They proceeded up the Missouri River, made an arduous crossing of the Rockies, and reached the mouth of the Columbia River before winter. They had journeyed through lands known to Shoshones and Nez Perces, but not previously to Anglo-Americans. On the way back, the corps divided in two, with Clark leading

a party southeast along the Yellowstone River and Lewis taking a northern route through Montana. They joined forces once again in North Dakota, said farewell to Sacagawea and her family, then returned to St. Louis by September 1806. They had been away so long that many assumed they had been killed by the Spanish or Native Americans.

Spies and Infiltrators

Spanish officials in fact had tried to intercept Lewis and Clark, whom they correctly suspected of making allies for the United States among the western Indians. General James Wilkinson, commander of U.S. troops in the west, governor of the Louisiana Territory, and a double agent known to the Spanish as "Agent 13," had tipped off New Spain about the expedition. The governor of New Mexico sent out search parties but failed to find Lewis and Clark. They did stop the mission of Thomas Freeman and Peter Custis, who in 1806 set out from Louisiana to find the source of the Red River. Another Spanish party nearly intercepted Zebulon Pike, whom Wilkinson had dispatched to explore and spy in the region that is now Kansas, Colorado, and New Mexico. Pike became lost in the southern

THE JOURNALS
OF MERIWETHER LEWIS
AND WILLIAM CLARK
1805

The following entries from the journals of the two explorers demonstrate the challenges the Corps of Discovery faced in mid-winter 1805. In the first paragraph, Lewis describes the birth of a son to Sacagawea, the expedition's Shoshone interpreter and guide. Lewis and Clark used their diaries to record information about the Native Americans they met as well as the plants, animals, weather, and landscape along their route.

[Lewis]   *11th February Monday 1805.*

The party that were ordered last evening set out early this morning. the weather was fair and could wind N. W.   about five oclock this evening one of the wives of Charbono was delivered of a fine boy.   it is worthy of remark that this was the first child which this woman had boarn and as is common in such cases her labour was tedious and the pain violent; Mr. Jessome informed me that he had freequently administered a small portion of the rattle of the rattle-snake, which he assured me had never failed to produce the desired effect, that of hastening the birth of the child; having the rattle of a snake by me I gave it to him and he administered two rings of it to the woman broken in small pieces with the fingers and added to a small quantity of water. Whether this medicine was truly the cause or not I shall not undertake to determine, but I was informed that she had not taken it more than ten minutes before she brought forth   perhaps this remedy may be worthy of future experiments, but I must confess that I want faith as to it's efficacy. —

[Lewis]   12th February Tuesday 1805.

The morning was fair tho' could, thermometer at 14° below naught wind S. E.   ordered the Blacksmith to shoe the horses and some others to prepare some gears in order to send them down with three slays to join the hunting party and transport the meat which they may have pocured to this place—. . . .   I directed some meal brands given [to the horses] moisened with a little water but to my astonishment found that they would not eat it but prefered the bark of the cotton wood which forms the principall article of food usually given them by their Indian masters in the winter season; for this purpose they cause the trees to be felled by their women and the horses feed on the boughs and bark of their tender branches. . . . The Indians are invariably severe riders, and frequently have occasion for many days together through the whole course of the day to employ their horses in pursuing the Buffaloe or transporting meat to their vilages during which time they are seldom suffered to tast food; at night the Horse returned to his stall where his food is what seems to me a scanty allowance of wood.   under these circumstances it would seem that their horses could not long exist or at least could not retain their flesh and strength, but the contrary is the fact, this valuable anamall under all those disadvantages is seldom seen meager or unfit for service. —   A little after dark

this evening Capt. Clark arrived with the hunting party—   since they set out they have killed forty Deer, three buffaloe bulls, & sixteen Elk, most of them were so meager that they were unfit for uce, particularly the Buffaloes and male Elk—   the wolves also which are here extreemly numerous heped themselves to a considerable proportion of the hunt—   if an anamal is killed and lyes only one night exposed to the wolves it is almost invariably devoured by them.

[Clark]

I returned last night from a hunting party much fatigued, haveing walked 30 miles on the ice and through of wood land Points in which the Snow was nearly Knee Deep

The 1st day [*Feb. 4?*] I left the fort   proceeded on the ice to *new Mandan* Island, 22 miles & Camped   Killed nothing, & nothing to eat,

The 2d day   the morning verry Cold & Windey, I broke thro the ice and got my feet and legs wet, Sent out 4 hunters thro' a point to Kill a Deer & Cook it by the time the party Should get up, those hunters killed a Deer & 2 Buffalow Bulls   the Buffalow too Meagur to eate, we eate the Deer & proceeded on to an old Indian Lodge, Sent out the hunters & they brought in three lean Deer, which we made use of for food,—walking on uneaven *ice* has blistered the bottom of my feat, and walking is painfull to me—

3rd day   Cold morning the after party of the Day worm, Camped on a Sand point near the mouth of a Creek on the S W. Side we Call hunting Creek, I turned out with the hunters, I Killed 2 Deer the hunters killed an Elk, Buffalow Bull & 5 Deer.   all Meager

4th Day   hunted the two bottoms near the Camp   Killed 9 Elk, 18 Deer, brought to camp all the meat fit to eate & had the bones taken out.   every man ingaged either in hunting or Collecting & packing the meat to Camp

5th Day   Dispatched one of the party our Interpeter & 2 french men with the 3 horses loaded with the best of the meat to the fort 44 miles Distant, the remaining meat I had packed on the 2 Slays & drawn down to the next point about 3 miles below, at this place I had all the meat Collected which was killed yesterday & had escaped the wolves, Raven & Magpie, (which are verry noumerous about this Place) and put into a close pen made of logs to secure it from the wolves & birds & proceeded on to a large bottom nearly opposit the Chisscheter (heart) River, in this bottom we found but little game, Great No. of wolves, on the hills Saw Several parsels of Buffalow.—   Camped. I killed a Buck

6th Day   The Buffalow Seen last night provd to be Bulls.   lean & unfit for to make uce of as food, the Distance from Camp being nearly 60 miles, and the packing of meat that distance attended with much difficuity deturmined me to return and hunt the points above, we Set out on our return and halted at an old Indian lodge 40 miles below Fort Mandan   Killed 3 Elk & 2 Deer—. . . .

I saw Several old Villages near the Chisscheta River   on enquirey found they were Mandan Villages destroyed by the Sous & Small Pox. . . .

MAP 8.2 | WESTERN EXPLORATION, 1803–1807

Rockies, was rescued by Spanish soldiers, arrested, then released.

Both the United States and Spain knew they were playing for high stakes with these activities. The United States could use exploration of the west and alliances with Native Americans to help confirm their claims to broad boundaries of the Louisiana Territory.

The Spanish had by far superior documentation for Texas, New Mexico, Arizona, California, and western Colorado. But they also denied American rights to what is now western Louisiana. Jefferson sent General Wilkinson with troops to the undefined boundary between Louisiana and Texas; the Spanish dispatched Lt. Col. Simón de Herrera to defend eastern Texas. The

two officers avoided fighting by establishing a neutral zone until diplomats could negotiate the border.

Still concerned about protecting their silver mines in Mexico, the Spanish took steps to increase settlement in Texas. They welcomed Indian exiles—Cherokees, Choctaws, and Alabamas—from lands overrun by American settlers east of the Mississippi, but the Hispanic population failed to grow significantly. New Spain officials specifically barred U.S. citizens from Texas, under threat of arrest and imprisonment. The Americans, one Spanish official feared, "are not and will not be anything but crows to pick out our eyes." Anglo-American traders continued to infiltrate Texas, however, to trap animals and bargain for horses with Comanches and other Indians.

The Burr Conspiracy

While Lewis and Clark were reconnoitering the far Northwest, Aaron Burr conceived a plot to create a separate nation in the west. His term as vice president completed, his bid for election as New York governor failed, and indicted for killing Hamilton, Burr contacted the double agent James Wilkinson, various unhappy politicians, and representatives of foreign governments. Burr suggested a variety of plans to those who would listen, including an invasion of New Spain, an attack on Washington, D.C., and secession of the west. Wilkinson cooperated with Burr at first, then turned informer when the conspiracy became public knowledge. Jefferson ordered Burr's arrest for treason, while applauding Wilkinson's "fidelity." Burr tried to escape to Europe, but was captured and taken to Richmond, Virginia, where he was tried in 1807.

The Burr conspiracy case, presided over by Chief Justice Marshall, involved three prosecutors and six defense lawyers, of whom two had served as U.S. attorney general. It might have been called the trial of the century. An unbiased jury could not be found; one juror said before the case was heard that Burr should be hanged. The principal actors in the trial were Marshall, who ignored his responsibility as an impartial judge to favor the defense, and Jefferson, who directed the prosecution from afar. Because Marshall upheld a definition of treason that required actual gathering of troops, not just conspiracy, the case against Burr collapsed. Jefferson blamed Marshall and considered trying to impeach him, but found insufficient congressional support.

MORE FOREIGN ENTANGLEMENTS

While the renewal of war in 1803 between Great Britain and France had impelled Napoleon to sell Louisiana, it also portended trouble for the United States. American merchants flourished, as they took advantage of neutrality and wartime demand for provisions in Europe and the West Indies. But their ships became vulnerable to the British navy and French privateers.

A Perilous Neutrality

Great Britain and France each wanted to prevent the United States from provisioning the other. In particular, the British intended to stop American traders from carrying foreign sugar, coffee, and other tropical products to Europe, even though the merchants conformed technically to British guidelines by taking the goods first to U.S. ports then re-exporting. In the *Essex* case of 1805, British courts stiffened their rules, stating that merely carrying Spanish and French goods to U.S. soil for re-export was insufficient, that only commodities originally meant for sale in the United States, then subsequently redirected to Europe, would be considered exempt from seizure. Few re-exported cargoes met the new guidelines. With the *Essex* rule, the Royal Navy stepped up its confiscations of American ships. Then, in 1806 and 1807, the British and French established blockades of each other's harbors, in combination eliminating neutral trade with Europe and the British Isles. The British Order in Council insisted that neutral ships sail to Britain first for inspection and licensing before trading in Europe. Napoleon's Berlin and Milan decrees banned trade with Britain and threatened neutrals who obeyed the British order with seizure.

After the British destroyed the French and Spanish navies in 1805 at Trafalgar, off the coast of Spain, the British restrictions and impressment of sailors were by far the most troublesome to Americans. Many Federalists and some Republicans cried for war. But Jefferson and the congressional majority looked for ways to avoid hostilities—despite the humiliating British attitude that the United States was still their colony. With a trimmed federal budget and small military, the

The British navy had practiced impressment, or forced recruitment, of American sailors since before the American Revolution. While claiming the men were British deserters, the navy often took native-born Americans, including free blacks.

Republicans were unprepared for war, so looked for alternatives. Congress passed a Non-Importation Act (1806) banning specified British goods, while the president opened negotiations with Great Britain to end impressment and recognize neutral trading rights. No agreement satisfactory to both sides could be reached. Then, in June 1807, the British ship *Leopard* fired upon the American frigate *Chesapeake* for refusing to submit to a search for British deserters. The *Chesapeake,* hit twenty-two times, managed to respond with only one shot. The *Leopard* boarded her, impressing four alleged deserters.

The Embargo of 1807

As Americans briefly clamored for war, Jefferson closed U.S. ports to the British navy and recalled ships from the Mediterranean, where they would have been trapped had war begun. The British refused to stop impressing American sailors, arguing that they only seized British deserters. They challenged Jefferson's port closure by firing on coastal towns in Maine and sailing in Chesapeake Bay. The president resisted a de-

claration of war, but placed military posts and gunboats on alert. He chose economic warfare instead. Unfortunately, this policy destroyed the commercial boom that had meant high prices for farmers and employed thousands of sailors.

At the urging of President Jefferson and Secretary of State Madison, Congress passed the Embargo Act in December 1807. The law prohibited exportation to all other countries. The administration hoped in particular to defang the former parent country by withholding provisions to the British Isles and West Indies. A by-product of non-exportation would be a severe drop in imports of British manufactures, of which the United States purchased about one-third of total production. Jefferson and Madison saw the embargo as an act of coercion, one they hoped would be as effective as war. They argued that the boycott would hurt all warring parties, but Britain worst. During 1808, the administration faced difficulty enforcing the embargo because ships, especially from New England, left harbor pretending to sail to American coastal ports but headed for foreign destinations instead. The trade with the British West Indies continued illegally, with encouragement from the British. Federal agents also had little success in preventing smuggling into Canada. In January 1809, the government resorted to an extreme measure, Giles's Enforcement Act, which empowered the president to use the militia against smugglers. The act effectively ended trade.

Despite infractions, the embargo had considerable impact on the U.S. economy. Agricultural prices declined, leading to farm foreclosures. According to official records, exports declined by 80 percent in 1808, though smuggling certainly lessened the effect. The U.S. Treasury suffered a loss in customs revenue, its chief source of income. The embargo stimulated further technological development of the textile industry, particularly in weaving cotton cloth with power looms.

With stern enforcement under Giles's Act, New Englanders became more strident in their demands for termination of the embargo. Jefferson became convinced that civil war was possible, but refused to support repeal at a time when the embargo was starting to work. Republicans in Congress moved anyway, on March 1, 1809, replacing the embargo with a Non-Intercourse Act, which reopened trade with all countries except Great Britain and France. If either of the two belligerents changed its policy to favor neutral rights, the United States would resume commerce with that nation as well. While the new law banned

trade with major markets, loopholes offered generous opportunities for smuggling.

Congress made this shift just days before the close of Jefferson's presidency. He was disappointed that the embargo did not have time to succeed; in fact, the British government, under pressure from manufacturers, had come close to easing its restrictions. Thus, Jefferson ended his administration without solving the nation's international troubles, which Americans increasingly defined as an effort by Britain to subjugate its former colonies. As he returned to Monticello, however, the president could reflect favorably upon the goals he had achieved—lower taxes and national debt, smaller government, open doors to immigrants, and peace. He also took pride in an accomplishment he had not foreseen in 1801, the purchase of the Louisiana Territory. Jefferson's administration was remarkable for what it did—and for what it did not do, considering his opposition to Hamiltonian policies in the 1790s. Under Jefferson, the Republicans left intact the national bank, the federal administrative structure, and armed forces. Considering the war-torn world in which the young nation found its way, however, the Republican commitment to minimal government left the United States militarily unprepared.

James Madison, *painted by Gilbert Stuart, a few years before he became the fourth U.S. president. Called the "Father of the Constitution," Madison also helped develop the two-party system through opposition to the Federalists in the 1790s.*

MADISON AND THE WAR OF 1812

When Britain continued to impress American sailors and seize ships, Jefferson's successor had two choices: accept humiliation as a third-rate power with near colonial status, or declare war on Great Britain. The British argued that they acted from necessity, as Napoleon conquered Europe. Americans, despite their aversion to the dictator of France, upheld their rights as neutrals to sell provisions to both sides. They considered British impressment of 6,000 seamen as a violation of national sovereignty and human rights. Between 1809 and 1812, these conflicts developed into war.

Election of 1808

Despite the embargo, Jefferson retained enough popularity to win a third term, had he chosen to run. When he withdrew, he designated James Madison, the secretary of state, as his successor. James Monroe, who had served as governor of Virginia and ambassador to Britain, challenged Jefferson's choice; but congressional Republicans, meeting in caucus, endorsed Madison. Dissenting Republicans, called the Quids, gave Monroe some support, but his candidacy died quickly. George Clinton accepted renomination for vice president. The Federalists put up Charles C. Pinckney and Rufus King, hoping that the effects of the embargo might reverse their party's decline.

The Federalists improved upon their performance in 1804 and 1806, gaining twenty-four seats in Congress, but still had much less than a majority. The electoral vote for president was 122 for Madison and 47 for Pinckney. While Americans suffered from the embargo, most were unprepared to desert the Republicans. In electing the new president, citizens ratified Jefferson's political philosophy and policies, which Madison had helped formulate. The third and fourth presidents had jointly founded and nurtured the Republican party; together they had adjusted their ideals to meet the practical needs of the expanding nation. The country could expect a continuation of Jeffersonian

Dolley Payne Madison, *by Gilbert Stuart. From a Quaker family, she met and married James Madison in 1794 while he was serving as congressman in Philadelphia. As first lady she brought elegance to the president's mansion.*

policies, though the retiring president withdrew entirely from decision making.

In another way, however, the new administration presented a real departure. Madison brought his elegant wife Dolley Payne Madison with him to the executive mansion, which was still unfinished when they arrived. They made a remarkable couple, as one observer noted:

> Mr Madison was a very small man in his person, with a very large head—his manners were peculiarly unassuming; and his conversation lively, often playful. . . . Mrs. Madison was tall, large and rather masculine in personal dimensions; her complexion was so fair and brilliant as to redeem this objection, in its perfectly feminine beauty. . . . There was a frankness and ease in her deportment, that won golden opinions from all, and she possessed an influence so decided with her little Man.

The first lady transformed the president's house into a proper executive mansion. She served as hostess to frequent teas and dinner parties, inviting Federalists and Republicans to socialize together.

Heading for War

After Madison's election, the European struggle continued to embroil the United States. While both Britain and France were hostile to free trade, the British dominated the seas, and as a consequence had substantial impact on U.S. commerce. Over the period to 1812, as Napoleon pushed across Europe, invaded Russia, and met defeat, he became inconsequential as a threat to the Americans. Indeed, his attempt to install his brother Joseph Bonaparte as king of Spain in 1808 undermined Spanish control in the New World. In West Florida, Anglo-Americans who had earlier pledged allegiance to Spain, in 1810 commandeered the Spanish fort at Baton Rouge, declared independence, and petitioned Madison for annexation by the United States. The president promptly claimed West Florida as part of the Louisiana Purchase. American troops occupied Baton Rouge but unsuccessfully attacked Mobile, which remained in Spanish hands. When Louisiana became a state in 1812, it included the western part of West Florida from Baton Rouge to the Pearl River.

In 1811, Madison appointed James Monroe, his former rival for the presidency, as secretary of state. Monroe, who had earlier negotiated a still-born treaty with the British, took office hoping to reach an accord, but soon decided that they wanted nothing less than to put the United States back into its colonial yoke. Great Britain adhered to its Order in Council that American exports go to England before shipment to Europe; the Royal Navy continued to impress American seamen. When Napoleon partially lifted his blockade in 1811, the United States resumed trade with France. Madison tried to convince the British to drop their restrictions as well, but instead they pounced on American ships headed for French ports.

Events in the west also intensified anger toward Britain, because Anglo-Americans believed that the British in Canada were stirring up Native American discontent. In fact, while some Indians traded with the British, many natives distrusted the whites of both Canada and the United States. An alliance between militant Indians and the British took time to evolve, as

Tecumseh in 1811 attempted to unite northern and southern Indians to defend their remaining lands east of the Mississippi River. Portrait from Benjamin Lossing's Pictorial Field Book of the War of 1812 *(1869).*

Failing that, the Indian leader went south to seek support from the Creeks, Cherokees, and Choctaws. He found allies among militant factions of Creeks and Seminoles, called the Red Sticks (from their war clubs). The Red Sticks opposed the accommodationists among their own people who sold land to the United States and adopted Anglo-American ways of life. Tecumseh's effort to create a pan-Indian movement throughout the trans-Appalachian west ultimately failed, however, because by 1811, large white populations in Tennessee, Kentucky, and Ohio formed a barrier between north and south. In the fighting of 1811 to 1815, Indian militants battled the United States on two fronts—in the Great Lakes and in the Mississippi Territory and West Florida.

In November 1811, William Henry Harrison decided to cut short Tecumseh's efforts for unity. The governor did not believe the Indian leader's assurance that whites were "unnecessarily alarmed at his measures—that they really meant nothing but peace—the United States had set him the example by forming a strict union amongst all the fires that compose their confederacy." Harrison led a force against Prophetstown (Tippecanoe), the village that Tenskwatawa had founded several years before. Before Harrison struck, the Prophet attacked the encamped soldiers at night, but suffered casualties and withdrew. Harrison also lost men, but burned the town and claimed victory in what became known as the Battle of Tippecanoe. The nativists subsequently rebuilt their settlement; Harrison's action had little effect except to drive them closer to the British.

The War of 1812 Begins

When news of the battle reached Washington, many officials interpreted it as evidence that a British-Indian alliance already existed. The outcome, they mistakenly believed, showed that the British were weak, incapable of sustaining their allies. "War Hawks" in Congress, including the newly elected Speaker of the House Henry Clay of Kentucky and Representative John C. Calhoun of South Carolina, advocated preparations for war. They represented a new generation who had not participated in the revolution and perceived Britain's actions as restoring colonial status. In Calhoun's words, his generation had to prove to "the World, that we have not only inherited that liberty

each group moved independently toward war with the Americans. As a result of the Louisiana Purchase, expanding white settlement, and sales by accommodationist Indian leaders of a large proportion of native lands still remaining east of the Mississippi, the nativist message of Tenskwatawa, the Shawnee Prophet, and his brother Tecumseh found widespread support. Their call to resist white encroachment resonated most clearly in what later became Illinois, Michigan, and Wisconsin, among Chippewas, Potawatomis, and Winnebagos, who could predict that their territory would soon be threatened. Establishment of American forts in the region told the tale.

The cession that spurred nativists into action was the Treaty of Fort Wayne (1809), which turned over 2.5 million acres to the United States. Tecumseh met with William Henry Harrison, governor of the Indiana Territory, to request that the treaty be annulled.

MAP 8.3 | THE WAR OF 1812

which our Fathers gave us, but also the will and power to maintain it." By April 1812, President Madison agreed. The Federalists, only one-fourth of Congress and primarily from New England, opposed conflict with Great Britain in part to obstruct administration policy, in part for commercial interests. The Republicans were divided. Opponents claimed that Madison intended to wage war for territorial expansion in Canada and Florida.

Congress authorized a 25,000-man regular army and borrowing $11 million. Still, the nation was ill-prepared when Madison issued his war message on June 1. Military funding would prove difficult because the charter of the national bank had been allowed to expire in 1811 due to politics and state banking interests, leaving state banks but no central agency as a source of loans. Lack of federal taxes beyond import duties, which fell sharply when the British blockaded the Atlantic coast, further limited the country's resources. The failure of New England leaders to provide their share of funds—indeed merchants' provisioning of the enemy and the desire of some New Englanders for a separate peace—severely hampered the war effort. The governors of Massachusetts and Connecticut refused to send their militia. Not everyone in New England opposed the war, however, for the majority of representatives from Vermont, New Hampshire, and Maine (still part of Massachusetts) voted in favor of the June 1812 declaration of war. Large numbers of the region's young men enlisted in the army. Former President Adams and his son, John Quincy Adams, also supported what many of their neighbors derisively called "Mr. Madison's War."

Despite military deficiencies and lack of national unity, the Madison administration pushed forward into battle, even after news arrived in August that the British government had lifted, though only for a year, its most odious restrictions on neutral trade. Madison offered an

armistice if the British stopped impressment, but they refused. Canada, with only 5,000 regular soldiers, seemed the logical target. The redcoats there had little hope for reinforcements as long as Napoleon marched through Europe.

U.S. military leaders planned three advances, one from Lake Champlain to Montreal, a second at the Niagara River, and the third from Fort Detroit east through Upper Canada. With American victories, they hoped, Canada would fall, forcing Britain to recognize U.S. rights. The Americans moved first in the west, where they expected more support from local militia than from New England. Both the Canadians and the United States needed control of the Great Lakes to retain access to lands farther west. General William Hull received orders to lead about 2,000 troops against Fort Malden, opposite Detroit, under command of British General Isaac Brock and reinforced by Tecumseh and his men. Hull dawdled long enough to allow more British soldiers to arrive. He failed to take Fort Malden and surrendered Detroit. The British and Native Americans then took control of much of the region by capturing Fort Michilimackinac, to the north, and Fort Dearborn, at the present site of Chicago. Another blow came for the United States in October, when the army lost the Battle of Queenston, opposite Fort Niagara, after the New York militia refused to leave American soil to assist the regular troops. William Henry Harrison, commissioned a general, reinforced Fort Wayne against Indian attack. The Americans held Fort Harrison (Terre Haute, Indiana) and other points along a line from Sandusky, Ohio, to St. Louis, and undermined Tecumseh's war effort by destroying Indian towns and cornfields in Ohio, Indiana, and Illinois.

During this frustrating campaign against Canada, James Madison stood for reelection. Some critics claimed that he had started the conflict to win another term. Heading the Federalist ticket was DeWitt Clinton, a New York Republican and nephew of the vice president. Clinton tried to gain support from both political parties by advocating peace to the Federalists while telling the Republicans that Madison had failed to prosecute the war hard enough. The president won by an electoral tally of 128 to 89. Clinton's votes came from New York, New Jersey, part of Maryland, and all of New England except Vermont. Madison received his mandate from Pennsylvania, the south, and west; he obtained substantial Republican majorities in the House and Senate.

In contrast to the army's failures in 1812, the tiny U.S. fleet had surprising success against the mighty

Fort Harrison in 1812, near present-day Terre Haute, Indiana.

Royal Navy. U.S. naval officers, unlike the generals Madison placed in charge of the Canada campaign, proved to be capable leaders. The *Constitution* sank the British *Guerrière* in August; two months later the *United States,* captained by Stephen Decatur, took the *Macedonian;* in December the *Constitution* destroyed the *Java.* While British ships also won some rounds, the American defeats of an enemy considered master of the seas greatly bolstered public opinion.

Victories and Losses, 1813–1814

On land, however, 1813 began with another disaster for the Americans, as the British and Native Americans killed and captured nearly an entire force of 900 troops at Frenchtown, south of Detroit. The United States managed to hold Fort Meigs and Fort Stephenson in northern Ohio. But to destroy British control of Lake Erie and territory to the west, the army needed naval support. The United States began building ships at Presque Isle, Pennsylvania (now Erie), and on September 10, 1813, Oliver Hazard Perry defeated the British squadron at Put-in-Bay, establishing American dominance of the lake. This naval victory cleared the way for General Harrison to attack Fort Malden, from which the British and Indians hastily retreated toward Niagara. The Americans caught up with them at Moraviantown on October 5, winning a decisive victory known as the Battle of the Thames.

Battle of Lake Erie, *painted by an unknown artist, c. 1820, commemorates the victory of Oliver Hazard Perry against the British at Put-in-Bay. The painting shows Perry moving to another vessel when his flagship became disabled.*

Tecumseh died on the battlefield; his brother Tenskwatawa continued to fight alongside the British during the rest of the war, but with little success. To the east, the U.S. Army had burned York (Toronto), the capital of Upper Canada. But the Americans met defeat in an offensive against Montreal and lost Fort Niagara.

In the Mississippi Territory, the nativist Red Sticks waged civil war against Creek leaders who accommodated Anglo-American demands for land. The fratricidal conflict became a war against the United States in July 1813 when 180 American militia struck a much smaller group of Red Sticks. A month later, the nativists killed about 250 settlers who had taken cover in a stockade called Fort Mims. The Red Sticks, with 4,000 warriors but lacking adequate arms, faced overwhelming odds against the combined forces of U.S. troops, accommodationist Creeks, and Cherokee allies. Three armies entered Red Stick territory, destroying homes and dispersing families. The turning point came in March 1814, when General Andrew Jackson, with 3,000 militia and Indian allies, defeated 1,000 Red Sticks in the Battle of Horseshoe Bend, killing 800. The surviving militants escaped to Florida, where they joined nativist Seminoles and continued to fight.

Despite the fact that accommodationist Creeks assisted Jackson's troops in the battle, the United States subsequently forced them to cede one-third of their lands.

In the summer of 1814, the British turned greater attention to the war in America, having defeated Napoleon in April. They sent 10,000 experienced redcoats to Canada, promising trouble for the defense of New York, until the American naval victory on Lake Champlain in September cut short the British invasion. Britain also sent forces to Chesapeake Bay, where in August they attacked the nearly defenseless Washington, D.C. Redcoats burned the Capitol and the president's mansion, shortly after the Madisons fled. The president and Mrs. Madison saved official documents, their own valuable possessions, and the Gilbert Stuart portrait of George Washington. The enemy promptly left the capital, and the U.S. government returned.

The British then assaulted Baltimore, which had time to prepare. Despite heavy bombardment of Fort McHenry by the Royal Navy, the redcoats failed to take the city. James Monroe, who was by then secretary of war as well as secretary of state, took credit for Baltimore's stand. Francis Scott Key memorialized the scene of flaming rockets and exploding bombs in his poem, "The Star Spangled Banner," which was later set to the tune of a popular English song and, in the early twentieth century, became the national anthem. The British sailed south to the Gulf Coast, intending to block off the Mississippi River. In late 1814, Andrew Jackson captured Pensacola, Florida, then organized the defense of New Orleans.

The Hartford Convention

Over the course of the war, sentiment had grown in New England for secession, as the British tightened their blockade of the region and occupied the Maine coast. The Massachusetts governor secretly contacted the British about a separate peace. In late 1814, a group of Federalists organized the Hartford Convention to find a more moderate course to remedy their loss of power within the Union. The convention issued a report supporting the right of states to declare federal laws unconstitutional (similar to the Virginia and Kentucky Resolutions of 1798) and arguing that states should be responsible for their own defense. The Hartford delegates called for significant amendments to the Constitution: removal of the three-fifths clause

"The Fall of Washington or Maddy in full flight," an anonymous English cartoon, 1814. Two British sailors ridicule President Madison and Secretary of State Monroe as they escape the burning capital with state documents.

that counted slaves in apportioning delegates in the House of Representatives and electoral college; a two-thirds majority in Congress to declare war and admit new states; a one-term limit on the president and ban on residents from the same state succeeding one another in the office (obviously targeted at Virginia); and prohibition of naturalized citizens—who were largely Republican—from federal positions. These proposals, calculated to damage Republican power bases in the south and west and among new immigrants in the cities, fell on deaf ears when news of the peace treaty arrived from Europe.

The Treaty of Ghent

Peace came as both the British and the United States recognized that the end of the twenty-year struggle in Europe eliminated the rationale for war in America. The defeat of Napoleon removed Britain's need to regulate neutral trade and impress seamen. Both sides could also see that they had little hope of victory. Britain might continue its blockade and smother U.S. commerce, but to what purpose? Conquest of the former colonies, now expanded into the west, would require huge expenditures of manpower and funds. Victory at New Orleans would plug the Mississippi, but

in late 1814 success was still uncertain. News arrived, as the British considered terms for peace, that the Americans had repelled the offensives at Lake Champlain and Baltimore. While some Britons desired revenge, more wanted to resume trade.

Madison authorized John Quincy Adams, Albert Gallatin, Henry Clay, and two others, to meet the British peace delegation at Ghent, Belgium, in August 1814. After several months of stalemate, the negotiators agreed on Christmas Eve, 1814, to return to the status quo at the outbreak of war. The British dropped their demands for part of Maine and an independent Indian territory north of the Ohio River, while the Americans stopped insisting that the British renounce impressment, which had ceased.

CONCLUSION

With its simple provision to reinstate the *status quo ante bellum,* the Treaty of Ghent might appear to make the War of 1812 meaningless. The loss of lives and dollars, and disaffection of New England, all seem for nothing. Yet most Americans celebrated the peace, knowing that they had withstood Britain's attempt to treat them as colonials. True, the end of the European war had solved the problems of impressment and

neutral trade. Still, a second generation of Americans had proven that they could survive a struggle with what was probably the world's most powerful nation. In addition, the United States had defeated Tecumseh's pan-Indian movement in the west, effectively ending Native American power east of the Mississippi.

Much had changed during the first decade and a half of the nineteenth century. The Federalists transformed themselves from the architects of the national government in the 1790s to advocates of narrow sectional interests in 1814. Thomas Jefferson and James Madison, the Republican authors of the Virginia and Kentucky Resolutions, which had upheld states' rights, moved in the opposite direction during their administrations. Without denying their commitment to limited government, a skeleton military, low taxes, and republican principles, they expanded "the empire of liberty" by purchasing Louisiana and forcing Native Americans from their lands. Jefferson and Madison used every means short of armed conflict to protect commerce, then went to war when all else failed. In purchasing Louisiana, Jefferson relaxed his philosophy of strict interpretation of the Constitution in hope that the additional territory would extend the life of his agrarian republic. Madison facilitated the growth of nationalism—despite New England's lapse—by exacting respect from Great Britain. With the Atlantic world at peace once again, residents from Maine to Louisiana concentrated on making money and building their communities, all with a greater sense that they belonged to an American nation.

RECOMMENDED READINGS

Brant, Irving. *James Madison.* 6 vols. (1941–61). Excellent, detailed biography of the fourth president.

Coles, Harry L. *The War of 1812* (1965). A readable, one-volume study.

Dowd, Gregory Evans. *A Spirited Resistance: The North American Indian Struggle for Unity, 1745–1815* (1992). Demonstrates the significance of religion in Native American resistance.

Horsman, Reginald. *The Causes of the War of 1812* (1961). A good discussion of the circumstances leading to war.

McCoy, Drew R. *The Elusive Republic: Political Economy in Jeffersonian America* (1980). Insightful exploration of Jeffersonian politics and thought.

Malone, Dumas. *Jefferson and His Time.* 6 vols. (1948–81). The benchmark biography of Thomas Jefferson.

Moulton, Gary E., ed. *The Journals of the Lewis and Clark Expedition.* 7 vols. (1983–91). Most comprehensive edition of manuscript maps and journals.

Nash, Gary B. *Forging Freedom: The Formation of Philadelphia's Black Community, 1720–1840* (1988). Insightful study of the challenges of freedom for one community of African Americans in the North.

Smelser, Marshall. *The Democratic Republic, 1801–1815* (1992). A useful, lively overview of the period.

Religion
Ahlstrom, Sydney E. *A Religious History of the American People* (1972).

Bloch, Ruth H. *Visionary Republic: Millennial Themes in American Thought, 1756–1800* (1985).

Butler, Jon. *Awash on a Sea of Faith: Christianizing the American People* (1990).

Hatch, Nathan O. *The Democratization of American Christianity* (1989).

Heyrman, Christine Leigh. *Southern Cross: The Beginnings of the Bible Belt* (1997).

Marini, Stephen A. *Radical Sects of Revolutionary New England* (1982).

Native Americans and the West
Ambrose, Stephen E. *Undaunted Courage: Meriwether Lewis, Thomas Jefferson, and the Opening of the American West* (1996).

Edmunds, R. David. *Tecumseh and the Quest for Indian Leadership* (1984).

McLoughlin, William G. *Cherokee Renascence in the New Republic* (1986).

Rohrbough, Malcolm J. *The Trans-Appalachian Frontier: People, Societies, and Institutions, 1775–1850* (1978).

Wallace, Anthony F. C. *The Death and Rebirth of the Seneca* (1969).

Weber, David J. *The Spanish Frontier in North America* (1992).

White, Richard. *The Middle Ground: Indians, Empires, and Republics in the Great Lakes Region, 1650–1815* (1991).

African Americans
Berlin, Ira, and Hoffman, Ronald, eds. *Slavery and Freedom in the Age of the American Revolution* (1983).

Egerton, Douglas R. *Gabriel's Rebellion: The Virginia Slave Conspiracies of 1800 and 1802* (1993).

Jordan, Winthrop D. *White over Black: American Attitudes Toward the Negro, 1550–1812* (1968).

Nash, Gary B., and Soderlund, Jean R. *Freedom by Degrees: Emancipation in Pennsylvania and Its Aftermath* (1991).

White, Shane. *Somewhat More Independent: The End of Slavery in New York City, 1770–1810* (1991).

Zilversmit, Arthur. *The First Emancipation: The Abolition of Slavery in the North* (1967).

Politics and Foreign Policy

Adams, Henry. *History of the United States During the Administrations of Thomas Jefferson and of James Madison.* Reprint, 2 vols. (1986).

Banner, James M., Jr. *To the Hartford Convention: The Federalists and the Origins of Party Politics in Massachusetts, 1789–1815* (1970).

Banning, Lance. *The Jeffersonian Persuasion: Evolution of a Party Ideology* (1978).

DeConde, Alexander. *This Affair of Louisiana* (1976).

Ellis, Joseph J. *American Sphinx: The Character of Thomas Jefferson* (1997).

Ellis, Richard E. *The Jeffersonian Crisis: Courts and Politics in the Young Republic* (1971).

Fischer, David Hackett. *The Revolution of American Conservatism: The Federalist Party in the Era of Jeffersonian Democracy* (1965).

Hickey, Donald R. *The War of 1812: A Forgotten Conflict* (1989).

Kerber, Linda K. *Federalists in Dissent: Imagery and Ideology in Jeffersonian America* (1970).

Ketcham, Ralph. *James Madison: A Biography* (1990).

Levy, Leonard W. *Jefferson and Civil Liberties: The Darker Side* (1989).

McDonald, Forrest. *The Presidency of Thomas Jefferson* (1976).

Onuf, Peter S., ed. *Jeffersonian Legacies* (1993).

Rutland, Robert Allen. *The Presidency of James Madison* (1990).

Stagg, J.C.A. *Mr. Madison's War: Politics, Diplomacy, and Warfare in the Early American Republic, 1783–1830* (1983).

Young, James Sterling. *The Washington Community, 1800–1828* (1966).

— 1815 TO 1855 —

The United States redefined itself during the forty years after 1815. The boundaries of the nation, the character of its population, the nature of its economy, and the religious beliefs of its people all took new shape. Some of the changes confirmed what the architects of the young nation had expected several decades before; other changes proved to be surprises and the bitterest of disappointments. The speed and scale of transformation astonished everyone.

IN 1815, THE YOUNG United States held only eighteen states, with Louisiana standing exposed at the western boundary, Florida in the hands of the Spanish, and an unsettled line between Canada and the United States. The western half of the continent remained only vaguely known to Anglo-Americans and seemed too far away to be of importance any time soon. Even within the country's sketchy borders, American Indians populated large and rich areas in both the north and the south.

Four decades later, the continental boundaries of the nation had expanded beyond recognition. Florida had come into the Union from Spain. War with Mexico had brought in vast territories from Texas to California. Negotiation with Great Britain had defined the northern boundary from Maine to Oregon. Military and economic pressure on the American Indian nations had driven them across the Mississippi River. A new state entered the Union about every two and a half years; by the end of the 1850s thirty-three

TOTAL POPULATION OF THE U.S.

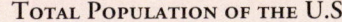
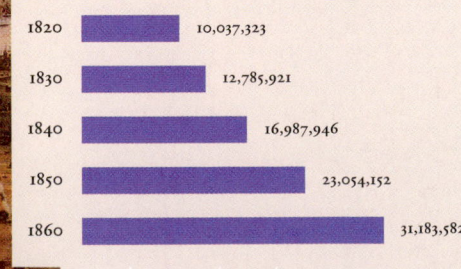

Year	Population
1820	10,037,323
1830	12,785,921
1840	16,987,946
1850	23,054,152
1860	31,183,582

states—including two on the Pacific coast—claimed a place in the nation.

The population exploded. The number of Americans grew from 8.4 million in 1815 to 31.4 million by the end of the 1850s. Nearly 4 million of those people were held in slavery, while 3 million people had crossed the Atlantic from Europe in a mixture of hope and desperation. People spread out across the expanse of the burgeoning country, establishing farms and towns far from the older cities of the east. About half the population of an average town moved every ten years. By the end of the period the United States claimed 5 million more people than England and the new country boasted eight cities of more than 150,000 inhabitants—more than any other country in the world.

Large changes altered the scale of life, tying people together as few could have imagined in 1815. Steamboats transformed water transportation in the 1810s, canals boomed in the 1820s, and railroads arrived in the 1830s. The United States claimed over 35,000 miles of railroad track by the end of the era. In the 1840s,

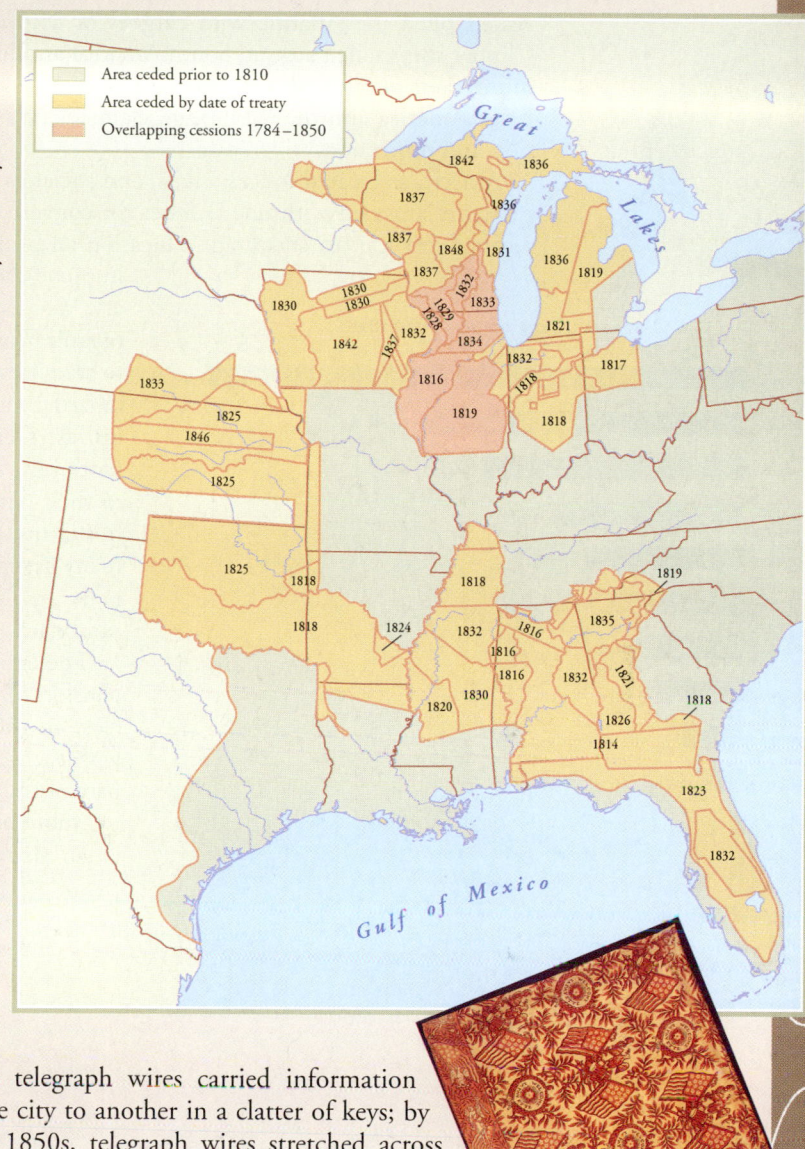

the first telegraph wires carried information from one city to another in a clatter of keys; by the late 1850s, telegraph wires stretched across the Atlantic Ocean. Novels sold tens of thousands of copies in a few months. Newspapers, confined to just a few major cities in 1815, became staples of American life in the 1830s and 1840s, read and published in hundreds of communities of every size. Daguerreotypes and colorful lithographs decorated homes that had been empty of pictures a generation earlier.

The United States became integrated ever more tightly into the international economy. The capacity of ships arriving in American ports doubled in the 1830s, doubled again in the 1840s, and then again in the 1850s. American

PASSAGES

vessels plied the Atlantic with cargoes of cotton and wheat for England and Europe. Clipper ships sailed around South America and into the Pacific, carrying prospectors and immigrants along with tea. The United States, anxious about European intervention in Latin America and the Caribbean, claimed the hemisphere as a place under its jurisdiction and protection.

Americans created lodges, clubs, and societies of every sort. Baptists, Methodists, and Presbyterians vied with one another for converts. Reform groups emerged to stamp out alcohol and war, to encourage education and humane treatment of the unfortunate, to improve diet and health, to bring the end of slavery. Women accounted for many members of these organizations, lending their energy and intelligence to activities beyond the home. Political parties mobilized nearly all adult white men, sweeping them up as Democrats, Whigs, Free Soilers, Know Nothings, and Republicans. Men swore allegiance to their party, expressing their passions and beliefs in slogans, songs, and parades. On election days, as many as eight out of ten eligible voters went to the polls, publicly proclaiming their support for their candidates.

The expansion of the United States was the expansion of the largest and most powerful slave society in the modern world. Slavery grew stronger with each passing decade, embracing an ever larger part of the continent to the south and west, holding more people within its bonds, accounting for a larger share of the nation's exports. As the years

TOTAL NUMBER OF SLAVES IN 1820

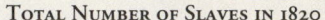

VIRGINIA	425,153
SOUTH CAROLINA	251,783
NORTH CAROLINA	205,017
GEORGIA	149,656
KENTUCKY	126,732
MARYLAND	107,398
TENNESSEE	80,107
LOUISIANA	69,064
ALABAMA	47,449
MISSISSIPPI	32,814
MISSOURI	10,222
NEW YORK	10,088
NEW JERSEY	7,557
DELAWARE	4,509
ILLINOIS	917

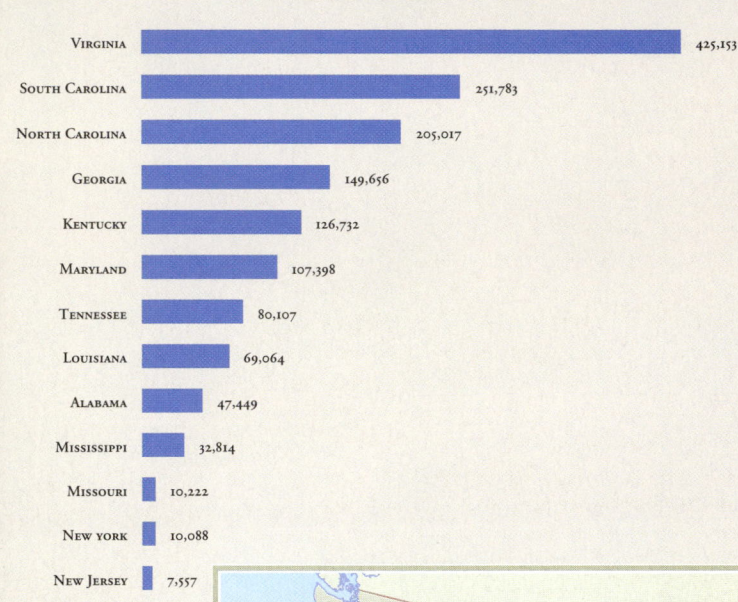

CANADA

WASHINGTON TERRITORY
(Part of Oregon Territory 1848–53)

OREGON TERRITORY
1848–59

MINNESOTA TERRITORY
1849–58

WISCONSIN
1848

MICHIGAN
1837

MAINE
1820

NEBRASKA TERRITORY
1854–61

IOWA
1846

VT

NH

MA

NEW YORK

RI
CT

UTAH TERRITORY
1850–61

ILLINOIS
1819

INDIANA
1816

OHIO

PENNSYLVANIA

NJ

DE

MD

KANSAS TERRITORY
1854–61

MISSOURI
1821

VIRGINIA

CALIFORNIA
1850

NEW MEXICO TERRITORY
1850–61

INDIAN TERRITORY
(Unorganized)

KENTUCKY

NORTH CAROLINA

ARKANSAS
1836

TENNESSEE

Gadsden Purchase
1853

Ceded to U.S. by Texas 1850

MISSISSIPPI
1817

SOUTH CAROLINA

GEORGIA

PACIFIC OCEAN

TEXAS
1845

LOUISIANA
1812

ALABAMA
1819

ATLANTIC OCEAN

MEXICO

Gulf of Mexico

FLORIDA
1845

Legend:
- States previously admitted
- New states admitted
- Territories
- Ceded and purchased lands

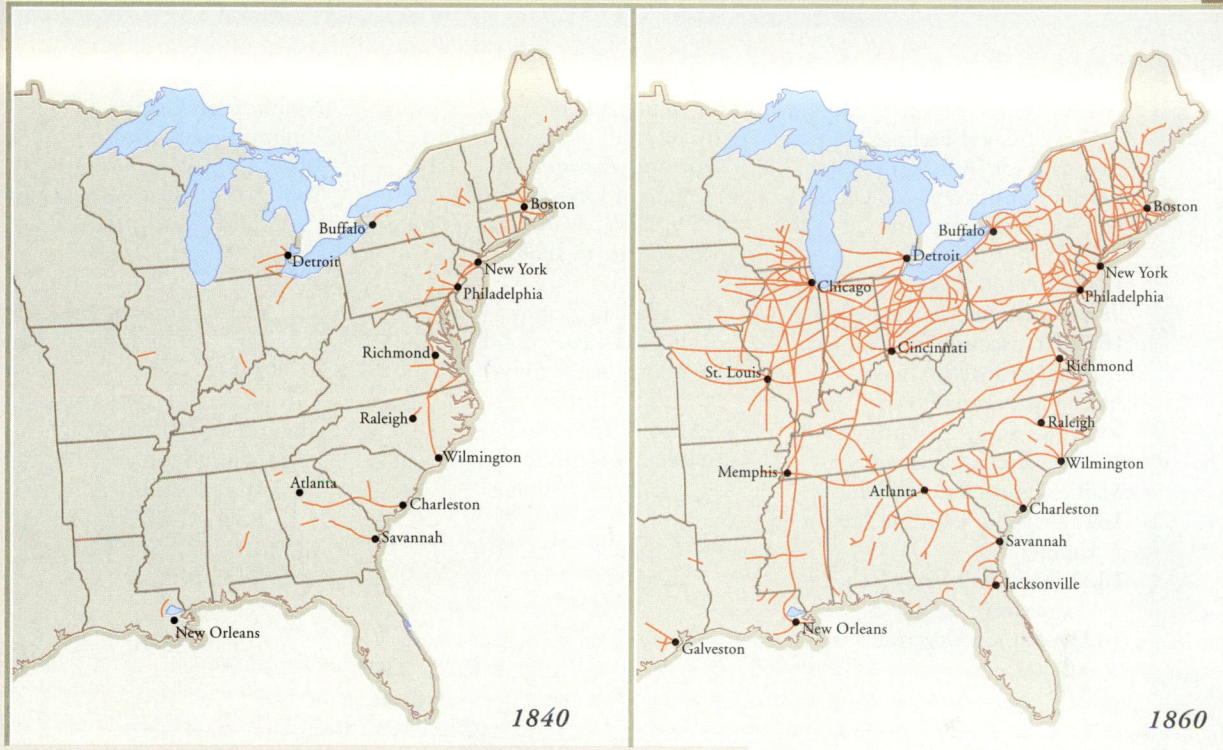

1840

1860

Aggr. Number of Slaves in 1860

State	Number
Virginia	490,865
Georgia	462,198
Mississippi	438,631
Alabama	435,060
South Carolina	402,406
Louisiana	331,726
North Carolina	331,059
Tennessee	275,719
Kentucky	225,483
Texas	182,588
Missouri	114,931
Arkansas	111,115
Maryland	87,189
Florida	61,745
Delaware	1,798
New Jersey	18
Nebraska	15
Kansas	2

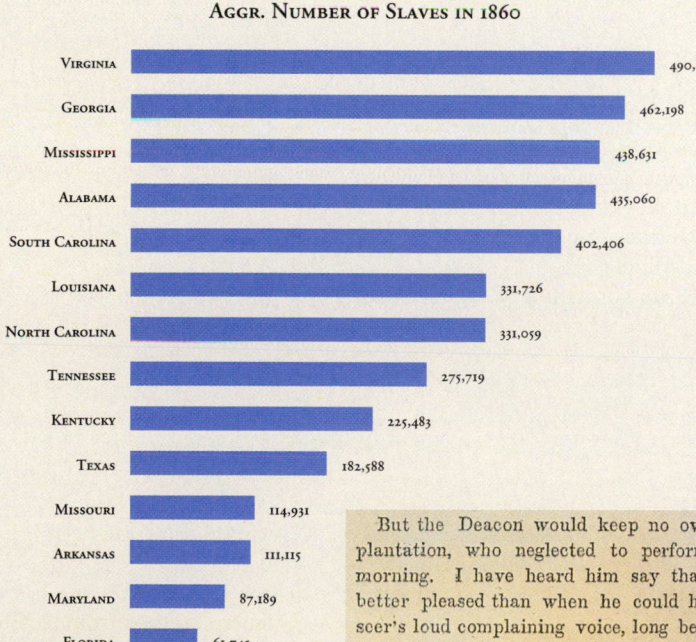

But the Deacon would keep no overseer on his plantation, who neglected to perform this every morning. I have heard him say that he was no better pleased than when he could hear the overseer's loud complaining voice, long before daylight in the morning, and the sound of the driver's lash among the toiling slaves.

passed, the discussions in the churches, the reform organizations, and the political parties increasingly turned to sectional conflict. Rivalry and distrust between the North and the South infected everything in the public life of the country.

The years between 1815 and 1855, then, did not witness a smooth passage through an "industrial revolution" or "growth of the common man" or "westward expansion." Rather, these years marked a passage filled with rapids and countercurrents and waterfalls. Panics and depressions, internal and external wars, massive migration and immigration, freedom and slavery—all came tumultuously.

POLITICS & DIPLOMACY

1815: Battle of New Orleans
1816: Monroe elected president; "Era of Good Feelings" begins
Clay calls for "American System"
Indiana admitted to the Union
1817: Mississippi admitted to the Union
1818: Jackson invades Florida
Illinois admitted to the Union
1819: Transcontinental (or Adams-Onís) treaty with Spain
Alabama admitted to the Union
1820: Missouri Compromise
Monroe elected president
Maine admitted to the Union
1821: Missouri admitted to the Union
1822: Denmark Vesey Rebellion, Charleston
1823: Monroe Doctrine announced

1824: Contested election of John Quincy Adams
1828: Tariff of Abominations
Calhoun's *Exposition*
Election of Jackson
1829: David Walker's *Appeal*
Mexico tries to abolish slavery in Texas
1830: Indian Removal Act
Antimasonic party holds first national party convention
1831: Nat Turner's rebellion
Garrison's *The Liberator*
Jackson reorganizes cabinet, Van Buren over Calhoun

1832: Bank War begins
Nullification Crisis
Virginia debates over slavery
Jackson reelected
1833: Force Bill against South Carolina
Compromise Tariff
Slavery abolished in British Empire
1834: Whig party organized
1835: Arkansas admitted to the Union
Revolution breaks out in Texas
Abolitionists' postal campaign
War against Seminoles and runaway slaves in Florida
1836: Congress imposes gag rule
Texas Republic established; Battle of the Alamo

SOCIAL & CULTURAL EVENTS

1816: American Colonization Society founded
American Bible Society founded
1819: Auburn penitentiary established
1824: Lafayette's visit
American Sunday School Union founded

1825: American Tract Society founded
1829: David Walker's *Appeal*
1830: *Book of Mormon*
Finney's revivals begin in Rochester
1831: Garrison's *The Liberator*
Mormons migrate from New York to Ohio
1833: Formation of American Anti-Slavery Society

1837: Grimké sisters lecture to mixed audiences
Horace Mann becomes first secretary of Massachusetts State Board of Education
Ralph Waldo Emerson, "The American Scholar"
1839: Daguerreotypes introduced to the United States

ECONOMICS & TECHNOLOGY

1815: *Enterprise* first steamboat from New Orleans to Pittsburgh
1816: Second Bank of the United States chartered
1817: Mississippi admitted to the Union
1818: Erie Canal begun
National Road completed
1819: *Dartmouth College Case* and *McCulloch* v. *Maryland*
Financial panic and depression

1824: *Gibbons* v. *Ogden*
1825: Completion of Erie Canal
1828: Tariff of Abominations
1831: John Bull begins railroad operation
1832: Bank War begins
1833: Compromise Tariff
1834: National Trades Union formed
Cyrus McCormick patents reaper

1837: Financial panic
Charles River Bridge v. *Warren Bridge* decision
1839: Depression worsens
Daguerreotypes introduced to the United States

1838: John Quincy Adams successfully defeats attempt to annex Texas

1840: Congress passes Independent Treasury Act

Harrison elected president

Frederick Douglass escapes from slavery

American Anti-Slavery Society splits

James G. Birney runs for president as candidate for Liberty party

1841: Harrison dies; John Tyler becomes president

Amistad case heard before the Supreme Court

1844: James K. Polk claims the United States's claim to "all Oregon"

1845: Texas and Florida admitted to the Union

1846: Mexican War begins; Stephen Kearny occupies Santa Fe; Zachary Taylor takes Monterey

Border between Canada and United States established at 49th parallel

Wilmot Proviso ignites sectional conflict

Bear Flag Republic in California proclaimed by John C. Frémont

1847: Taylor defeats Santa Anna at Buena Vista; Winfield Scott captures Vera Cruz and Mexico City

1848: Treaty of Guadalupe Hidalgo

Attempts to buy Cuba from Spain

Free Soil party runs Van Buren for president

Seneca Falls Convention

Zachary Taylor elected president

1849: California seeks admission to Union

1850: Nashville Convention attempts to unify South

Fugitive Slave Law

Taylor dies; Millard Fillmore becomes president

Compromise of 1850

1851: Maine adopts prohibition

Women's rights convention in Akron, Ohio

Indiana state constitution excludes free blacks

1852: Franklin Pierce elected president

1853: Gadsden Purchase

1854: Know-Nothings win unexpected victories

Whig party collapses

Republican party founded

Kansas-Nebraska Act

Ostend Manifesto encourages acquisition of Cuba

1840: Washingtonian temperance movement emerges

1841: Brook Farm founded

P.T. Barnum opens the American Museum

Amistad case heard before the Supreme Court

1842: Edgar Allan Poe, "The Murders in the Rue Morgue"

1844: Methodist Episcopal church divides over slavery

Edgar Allan Poe, "The Raven"

1846: Hiram Powers completes statue "The Greek Slave"

1847: Mormons reach Great Salt Lake Valley

1848: Seneca Falls Convention

Oneida Community established

Mormons settle in Great Basin

1850: Nathaniel Hawthorne, *The Scarlet Letter*

1851: Herman Melville, *Moby-Dick*

Maine adopts prohibition

Women's rights convention in Akron, Ohio

1852: Harriet Beecher Stowe, *Uncle Tom's Cabin*

1854: Henry David Thoreau, *Walden*

1840: Congress passes Independent Treasury Act

1841: California sees arrival of first wagon train

Oregon fever

1843: Oregon sees arrival of first wagon trains

1844: Baltimore-Washington telegraph line

Samuel F. B. Morse patents the telegraph

1848: Gold discovered in California

Regular steamship trips between Liverpool and New York City

1849: "Forty-Niners" race to California

Cotton prices invigorate South

1854: High-point of immigration

Railroad reaches Mississippi River

VALUE OF COTTON EXPORTS AS A PERCENTAGE OF ALL U.S. EXPORTS, 1800–1860
By 1840 cotton accounted for more than half of all U.S. exports.

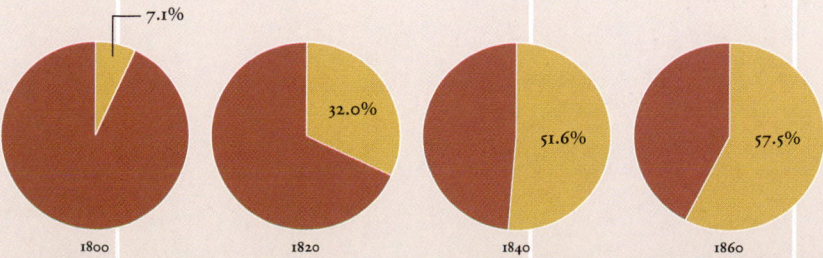

7.1%   32.0%   51.6%   57.5%

1800   1820   1840   1860

THE BATTLE OF NEW ORLEANS

The surprising victory of the United States over Britain in 1815 catapulted Andrew Jackson to prominence and bolstered the confidence of the young republic.

Chapter 9

EXPLODED BOUNDARIES:

1815–1826

THE MILITARY hardships, diplomatic entanglements, political quagmires, and sudden climax of the War of 1812 surprised everyone. Ever since its beginning, even the leaders of the United States had wondered whether a large and lightly governed republic could long endure. Miraculously, the new country did not lose the war. Indeed, upon the war's unexpected end the United States entered upon a period of economic growth and territorial expansion no one could have foreseen. White settlers, newly freed from concern about the British and their American Indian allies, pushed west in remarkable numbers, taking enslaved African Americans with them in the South. Throughout the country, steamboats, canals, and turnpikes tied the countryside to the cities and the cities to one another.

Such rapid growth did not come without a cost. An economic depression suddenly ground the economy to a halt, political crisis emerged out of this time of apparent peace, and slaves staged a revolt. Many Americans worried that their society was changing too fast, that the virtuous time of the Revolution had passed and a time of selfishness had taken its place. Only a resolute determination to redefine the family and to spread the word of God, many believed, would save America.

THE AFTERMATH OF WAR

The United States had little reason to celebrate as 1815 began. For more than two years, bickering grew along with defeats and stalemate. Washington lay in ruins, burned by the enemy. Rumor had it that delegates from the Hartford Convention would soon arrive in the capital threatening to remove New England from the Union unless Congress revised the Constitution. People lost faith in President James Madison and other leaders.

War's End

Throughout the summer and fall of 1814 American and British delegations in the Belgian city of Ghent labored to construct a peace. Britain had just won a long and costly war against France and was eager to bring the hostilities in North America to a close. The United States, for its part, sought to end the fighting and with it the taxation and social division that war bred. After months of deadlock, the two delegations agreed simply to end the war, restoring the previous borders

CHRONOLOGY

1815	Battle of New Orleans
	Enterprise first steamboat from New Orleans to Pittsburgh
1816	Monroe elected president; "Era of Good Feelings" begins
	Clay calls for "American System"
	Second Bank of the United States chartered
	Indiana admitted to the Union
	American Colonization Society founded
	American Bible Society founded
1817	Mississippi admitted to the Union
1818	Jackson invades Florida
	Erie Canal begun
	Illinois admitted to the Union
	National Road completed
1819	Transcontinental (or Adams-Onís) Treaty with Spain
	Dartmouth College Case and *McCulloch* v. *Maryland*
	Financial panic and depression
	Alabama admitted to the Union
	Auburn penitentiary established
1820	Missouri Compromise
	Monroe elected president
	Maine admitted to the Union
1821	Missouri admitted to the Union
1822	Denmark Vesey Rebellion, Charleston
1823	Monroe Doctrine announced
1824	Contested election of John Quincy Adams
	Lafayette's visit
	Gibbons v. *Ogden*
	American Sunday School Union founded
1825	Completion of Erie Canal
	American Tract Society founded

between U.S. and British territories. Both sides, relieved to be rid of the war, quickly adopted the agreement.

Though the treaty was signed in December, bad weather in the Atlantic delayed until February the ship bringing news of the peace negotiations between the Americans and British. In the meantime, British forces, unaware of the decisions made thousands of miles away, prepared to move against the United States's Gulf Coast. A fleet of sixty ships and 14,000 men planned to attack Mobile, seize control of the coast and the rivers, then move against New Orleans.

Such a plan posed a serious threat to the United States. New Orleans, distant and disconnected from the cities of the east coast, lay vulnerable to invasion. Once the British established a foothold there, American leaders worried, troops could move up the Mississippi River. The United States would be surrounded and harassed by its bitter enemy. Moreover, a British invasion threatened to bring free and enslaved African Americans, French and Spanish settlers, Native Americans, and even pirates into the conflict throughout the Gulf territories, igniting rebellions against white farmers and traders.

The commander in charge of the American forces, Andrew Jackson, was especially sensitive to the dangers settlers faced on the Gulf Coast. Jackson, a Tennessee lawyer, planter, and militia leader, had capped a tumultuous career by defeating and then enforcing harsh terms on Creek Indians in the early spring of 1814. Jackson pushed the Creeks into ceding 23 million acres of territory to the United States, including most of what was to become Alabama and a fifth of present-day Georgia. Jackson's soldiers shoved the Creeks into the less productive lands of northeastern Alabama, while reserving the fertile black belt for white farmers. Jackson, with the strong support of the governors of the Gulf territories, prepared to continue the war against other groups of Creeks who had fled to Span-

ish West Florida. After a victory over the British at Mobile, Jackson raced to New Orleans to fight yet more British troops. The American general got there first, in December of 1814. Six hundred free blacks volunteered to help defend the city and Jackson gratefully accepted their offer.

A series of attacks by the British damaged the American forces but did not take New Orleans. The British general in charge, Sir Edward Pakenham, unleashed a frontal assault on January 8, 1815. Two Congreve rockets, launched by the British to signal the beginning of the assault and to frighten their opponents, screamed into the air. Jackson's troops, dug in behind earthworks, fired directly into the charging British troops; wave after wave of the onslaught fell as American troops took turns firing and reloading. In less than an hour it was over: Pakenham and two of his generals lay dead, along with over 2,000 of their troops. The Americans suffered only thirteen dead and a few dozen wounded or missing. Nearly a month later, word of Jackson's remarkable success reached the nation's capital. "ALMOST INCREDIBLE VICTORY!!!," headlines trumpeted. Nine days later word of the Treaty of Ghent, ratified two weeks before the Battle of New Orleans, arrived in Washington.

The Era of Good Feelings

The United States, insecure about its standing in the world of nations, now boasted a new sense of integrity and identity. President Madison announced that the Constitution had proven itself able to "bear the trials of adverse as well as prosperous circumstances." The northern borders of the United States, fluid and in doubt throughout the nation's brief history, took on greater solidity. The Rush-Bagot Treaty of 1817 between the British and the United States calmed conflict on the Great Lakes, while the Convention of 1818 fixed the border with Canada at the 49th parallel.

The War of 1812 suggested to some that the federal government might play a constructive role in American society. Leading members of the Republican party, long known for their opposition to federal power, began to view the central government more favorably. Young Republicans such as Henry Clay of Kentucky and John C. Calhoun of South Carolina urged Congress and the president to encourage the growth of enterprise with the aid of the government, creating

Henry Clay of Kentucky articulated the American System, a plan to encourage national economic growth.

roads, canals, a strong navy, and a national bank. In their eyes, the war with Great Britain had shown the dangers of a sprawling American nation, its resources scattered, its defenses thin. The future of the country, Clay and Calhoun believed, lay in commerce and industry; the government should ally itself with the forces of trade. Although these nationalists called their vision the "American System," representatives from New England objected to projects that seemed so expensive and threatening to local power. Outgoing President James Madison, while unwilling to support all of Clay's and Calhoun's ambitious plans, did decide to support a national bank.

The man who succeeded Madison to the presidency, James Monroe—another in a long line of Virginia Republicans—faced a brief challenge within his party in 1816 but won the national election easily. Monroe was considered an honest man, less intellectually distinguished than Jefferson or Madison, but dependable. He and his wife set a new tone for the presidency, with greater emphasis on etiquette, style, and

Later famous as a defender of states' rights, John C. Calhoun of South Carolina first became famous as a leading nationalist in Congress.

James Monroe of Virginia, president of the United States between 1817 and 1825, presided over the so-called "Era of Good Feelings" after the War of 1812.

entertaining, on embodying and celebrating the new national stature of the United States. The Monroes had the Executive Mansion painted a brilliant white to cover the smoke stains from its burning during the war with England; it became known as the "White House." After his election, Monroe toured the Northeast, including New England. A journalist there, impressed, talked of a budding "Era of Good Feelings," an era without party rancor—a strong contrast to the bitter conflict of earlier decades.

President Monroe relished the role of peacemaker and conciliator. Adopting John C. Calhoun's ideas for encouraging commerce and industry, Monroe urged Congress to use protective tariffs to protect American manufacturing, to build roads to tie the newly expanded markets and farms together, to connect the abundant rivers and lakes in the United States with a system of canals "the whole coast from its southern tip to its northern extremity in one continued inland navigation." Monroe hoped his plan would be supported by a broad and nonpartisan consensus; he downplayed party divisions and waited for agreement to develop.

The emerging Era of Good Feelings, Monroe assumed, would let the nation move forward without political strife or bitterness.

Native Peoples of the South

Relations with American Indians demanded considerable attention in the years following the peace with England. The war had redefined the relationship of the United States with the native peoples of the southeast. By this time, the American Indians had lived in contact with European culture for more than two centuries. They had long combined their ancient practices with newer ones, especially commercial hunting. Expeditions covered ever-expanding territory to kill enough animals to satisfy the white trading partners

upon whose goods the American Indians increasingly depended. Trade networks stretched over thousands of miles. Indians' clothing reflected the combination of cultures, as they combined moccasins with woolen breeches, imported cloth turbans, and jewelry made of melted silver coins. The intermingling worked both ways, for considerable numbers of English and Scots traders lived among the Indians. Many adopted parts of Indian dress and language and married into native families. African Americans, too, often took refuge with the Creeks and Seminoles, so that by 1815 mixed ancestry was common among the people of the southeast.

The removal of the British troops dealt a strong blow to the hopes of the natives of the Gulf Coast. Alliances with the British—both actual and threatened—had been an effective way to hold back the white Americans. Now that that alliance disappeared, the United States quickly sought to exert firm control over the eastern half of the continent. Andrew Jackson

was placed in charge of negotiating with the Creek, Cherokee, Chickasaw, and Choctaw nations of Alabama, Florida, and Mississippi after the peace of 1815. He used heavy-handed treaties to force Indians from their former lands. Many of the natives resisted the removal, objecting that the treaties extracted by Jackson had been signed by men who had no authority to make such concessions. Although the various native peoples, identifying themselves by the location of their villages, their languages, and their traditional enemies, often fought with one another, whites insisted on lumping these diverse people into groups that could be more easily dealt with. Jackson and other officials left the Indians, lacking powerful allies and often in debt to white traders, little choice but to accept bribes and annual grants of money in return for their lands.

As soon as Jackson managed to secure lands from the Creeks, Cherokees, and Chickasaws, white settlers rushed into the territories, hungry for the fertile land

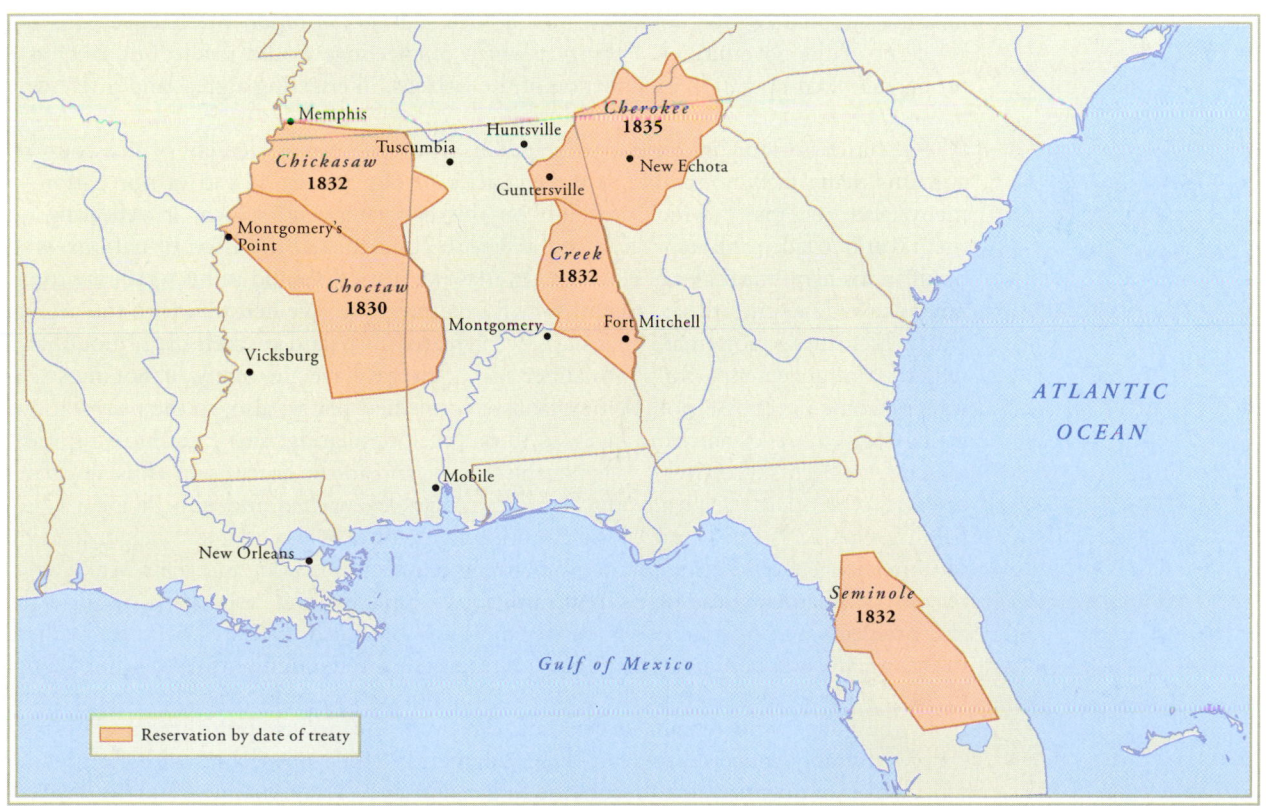

MAP 9.1 | SOUTHERN INDIAN NATIONS AFTER CESSIONS

American Society for Improving Indian Tribes, *The Blessings of Civilization* 1824

In this address to Congress, a prestigious religious group argues that the American Indians have suffered for generations at the hands of the United States. The only way to atone for these "national sins," the commissioners argue, is to educate the Indian people in the ways of white Americans. The document shows the good will that many white Americans held toward the Indians and the limitations of their understanding of the Indians' own desires.

In fulfillment of our commission, we beg leave, respectfully, to state to your honorable body, that a prominent object of the board we represent is, to extend the blessings of civilization and Christianity, in all their variety, to the Indian tribes within the limits of the United States. In carrying on this work of benevolence and charity, we are happy to acknowledge, with much gratitude, the aid received from the government, in making and supporting the several establishments made for accomplishing their purpose. The object of the government and of the Board is one, and, indeed, is common to the whole community. We trust, therefore, that the measure adopted by our board will not be deemed an improper interference with the concerns of the government, a thing at which our feelings would revolt; but, only as a proper act of co-operation of a portion of the citizens, in effecting a great and interesting *national* object.

The history of our intercourse with Indians, from the first settlement of this country, contains many facts honorable to the character of our ancestors, and of our nation—many, also, too many, which are blots on this character; and which, in reflecting on them, cannot fail to fill us with regret, and with concern, lest the Lord of nations, who holds in his hand the scales of equal and everlasting justice, should in his wrath say to us, "As ye have done unto these Indians, so will I requite you." We here allude to the neglect with which these aboriginal tribes have been treated in regard to their civil, moral, and religious improvement—to the manner in which we have, in many, if not most instances, come into possession of their lands, and of their peltry: also, to the provocations we have given, in so many instances, to those cruel, desolating, and exterminating wars, which have been successively waged against them; and to the corrupting vices, and fatal diseases, which have been introduced among them, by wicked and unprincipled white people. These acts can be viewed in no other light, than as national sins, aggravated by our knowledge, and their ignorance; our strength and skill in war, and their weakness—by our treacherous abuse of their unsuspicious simplicity, and, especially, by the light and privileges of Christianity, which we enjoy, and of which they are destitute. In these things we are, as a nation, verily guilty, and exposed to the judgments of that just Being, to whom it belongs to avenge the wrongs of the oppressed; under whose perfect government the guilty, who remain impenitent, can never escape just punishment. The only way, we humbly conceive, to avert these judgments, which now hang, with threatening aspect, over our country—to secure the forgiveness and favor of Him whom we have offended, and to elevate our national character, and render it exemplary in view of the world—is happily, that which has been already successfully commenced, and which the

government of our nation, and Christians of nearly all denominations, are pursuing with one consent, and with their combined influence and energies. The American Board of Commissioners for Foreign Missions view these facts as highly encouraging; and it is their earnest desire that the God of nations would speed the course so auspiciously commenced, and give direction, and his blessing, to our joint efforts; add numbers and strength to those already engaged in this good work; convince, and reconcile to the object, those who are now opposed to it; and, ultimately, crown our labors with the desired success.

The work in which we are engaged, we are sensible, is not only noble, and god-like, and worthy to command the best energies of our nature, but it is also a great, arduous, and difficult work, requiring patience, forbearance, perseverance, and unremitted and long continued efforts. Here is scope enough to employ the wisdom, the means, and the power of the nation; and the object is of sufficient magnitude and interest, to command the employment of them all.

We are aware of the great and only objection, deserving notice, that is made to our project, and which has been made by some men of distinction and influence in our country, whose opinion on other subjects is entitled to respect; and this is, that "it is *impracticable;* that Indians, like some species of birds and beasts, their fellow inhabitants of the forest, are *untameable;* and that no means, which we can employ, will prepare them to enjoy with us the blessings of civilization." In answer to this objection, we appeal to facts; facts not distant from us—not of a doubtful nature; but which exist, and are fast multiplying among us, under our own eyes and observation—to facts which cannot be doubted, and in such number and variety, as furnish indubitable evidence of the practicability of educating Indians in such manner, as to prepare them to enjoy all the blessings, and to fulfill all the duties, of civilized life. . . .

It being admitted, then, that the Indians within our jurisdiction *are* capable of receiving an education, which will prepare them to participate with us in all the blessings which we enjoy, these questions will naturally arise: Is it desirable that they should receive such an education? Are they willing to receive it? Have we the means of imparting it to them? These questions, your memorialists conceive, may, with confidence, be answered in the affirmative. It *is* desirable that our Indians should receive such an education as has been mentioned, we conceive, because the civilized is preferable to the savage state; because the Bible, and the religion therein revealed to us, with its ordinances, are blessings of infinite and everlasting value and which the Indians do not now enjoy. It is also desirable as an act of common humanity. The progress of the white population, in the territories which were lately the hunting grounds of the Indians, is rapid, and probably will continue and increase. Their game, on which they principally depend for subsistence, is diminishing, and is already gone from those tribes who remain among us. In the natural course of things, therefore, they will be compelled to obtain their support in the manner we do ours. They are, to a considerable extent, sensible of this already. But they cannot thus live, and obtain their support, till they receive the education for which we plead. There is no place on the earth to which they can migrate, and live in the savage and hunter state. The Indian tribes must, therefore, be *progressively civilized,* or *successively* perish.

SOURCE American Board of Commissioners for Foreign Missions, Memorial to the Senate and the House of Representatives, in American Society for Improving Indian Tribes, *First Annual Report,* 1824, pp. 66–68.

and the fortunes it could build. Such incursions occurred across millions of acres in North Carolina, Kentucky, and Tennessee as well as in Alabama, Mississippi, and Georgia; in each state, the Indians were pushed to the hilly and mountainous lands least desirable for farming. The U.S. government made it easy for white settlers to buy land and sold about a million acres a year throughout the next decade. Not surprisingly, tensions steadily mounted between the ancient residents of the land and those who now claimed it.

While tens of thousands of American Indians continued to live in the southeast, their position grew less tenable each year as white settlers moved onto their hunting lands. The Indians strove to adapt to white ways while maintaining their identity; the Cherokees, in particular, won praise for their "civilized" customs. One Cherokee, Sequoyah, devised an alphabet in his people's language in 1821. The wealthiest Cherokees purchased African American slaves and built substantial cotton plantations. No matter what accommodations they made, the American Indians suffered re-

peated conflicts with whites who considered themselves the rightful owners of the land.

The Spanish in Florida

Like the American Indians, the Spanish who remained in Florida after 1815 had become vulnerable. Without the assistance of the British, they found it nearly impossible to resist American incursions into their territory. White Americans, for their part, felt they had a right, even an obligation, to drive the Spanish from the mainland, in part because Protestants had long distrusted the Catholic, monarchical Spanish. Many Americans thought it inevitable that Florida and Mexico would become part of the United States. To make relations even more volatile, sixty miles from the southern border of the United States stood the so-called "Negro Fort," occupied by runaway slaves and their Indian allies. In the spring of 1816 Jackson warned the Spanish commandant of Pensacola that the

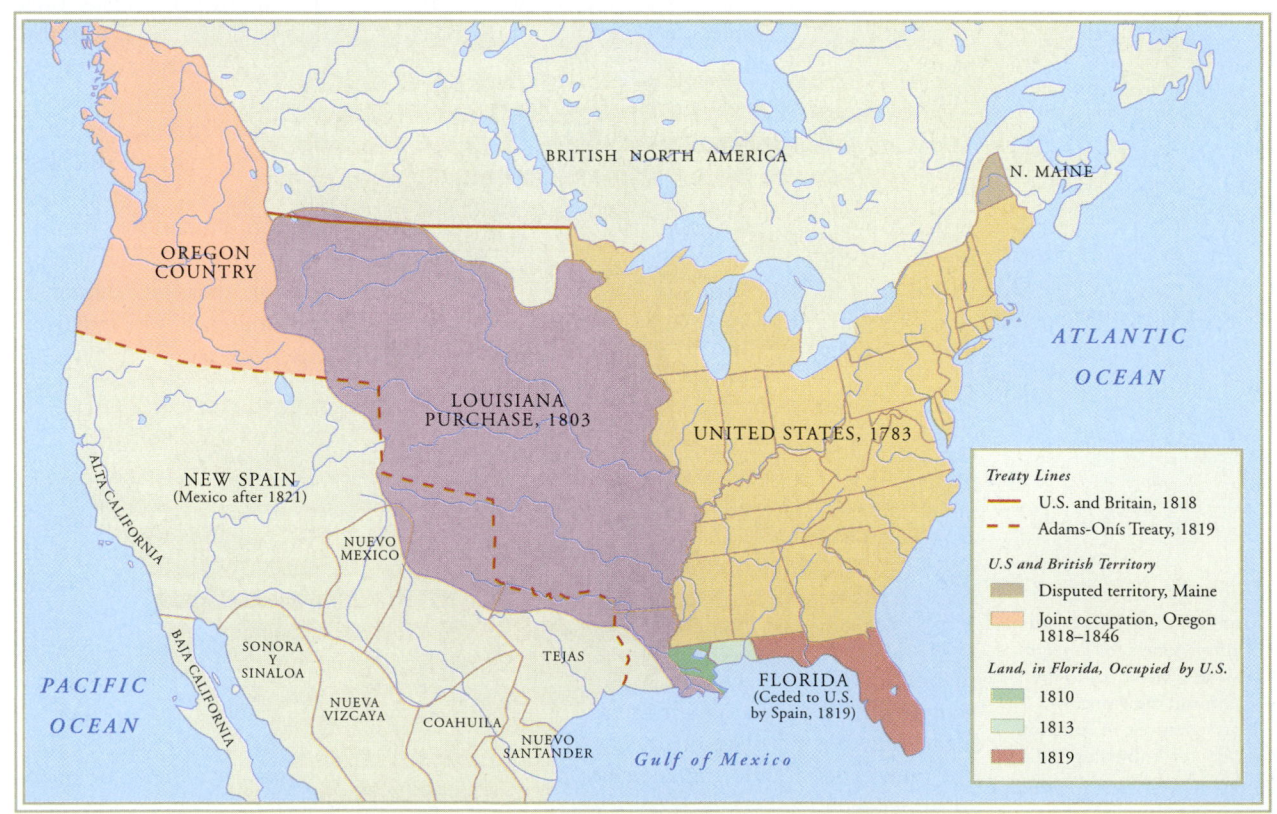

MAP 9.2   REDRAWING THE NATION'S BOUNDARIES

stronghold was "occupied by upwards of two hundred and fifty negros many of whom have been enticed away from the service of their master—citizens of the United States." The fugitives would "not be tolerated by our government," Jackson warned, "and if not put down by Spanish Authority will compel us in self Defence to destroy them." Spain was eager, in fact, to be rid of the fort as well, but did not have the military power to overthrow it. The Spanish feared, correctly, that Jackson would use the refuge as a pretext to invade Florida. Indeed, the Americans sent an expedition against the fort; a projectile hit a powder magazine, killing 270 of the men, women, and children inside.

In 1818, Jackson's forces also punished groups of Seminoles, who, with their Creek allies, had launched raids of white settlers in south Georgia and then fled into Florida. The American soldiers burned a Seminole town, only to see their foes retaliate by attacking a boat of soldiers, women, and children on the Apalachicola River, killing all but a few on board. Though his authorization from Washington was doubtful, Jackson proceeded to invade Spanish territory, execute a Creek prophet and two British men he accused of abetting the Indian cause, and overrun the weak Spanish presence in the most important outposts. Some in Congress wanted to punish Jackson for what they considered his unauthorized attack. Jackson rushed to Washington to defend himself and his honor. Many white Americans thronged the cities where Jackson appeared along the way, celebrating him as a decisive hero rather than castigating him for being the military despot Henry Clay claimed. The congressional hearings on Jackson's behavior in the war had little effect except to make Jackson suspicious of the men in power in Washington.

Meanwhile, American and Spanish officials negotiated. The U.S. delegation was led by the brilliant and tenacious John Quincy Adams, son of the former president. With Jackson's military victories giving force to his words, Adams held out until the Spanish, in return for 5 million dollars in compensation of private claims, ceded to the United States all territories east of the Mississippi River. In this, the Adams-Onís Treaty of 1819, the Spanish kept the vast territory from Texas to present-day California, while the United States claimed a northern border that ran unbroken to Oregon and the Pacific Ocean. Adams called his handiwork the Transcontinental Treaty, for it stretched the borders of the United States from the Atlantic to the Pacific.

THE TIDES OF TRADE

The end of the Napoleonic Wars in 1815 unleashed the economics of Europe and the countries that dealt with them, including the United States. American prosperity grew as the population boomed, as people moved across the expanse of the continent, and as transportation leaped forward. Slavery expanded along with free labor, farms along with factories, the East along with the South and the West. People made their livings in new ways and participated in an economy of ever-expanding scope.

Banks, Corporations, and Law

No country needed credit more than the United States. Because far too little cash spread across the vast and growing landscape, much business within the country rested on nothing more than trust and promises. Credit relations became tangled and fragile; the fall of one borrower could bring down a chain of lenders. Throughout the years before and during the War of 1812 states chartered banks to help alleviate the problems caused by a shortage of cash. More than 200 such banks had been founded by 1815 and nearly 400 by 1818, issuing notes that served as currency in cash-starved areas. Thomas Jefferson worried that "our citizens are clamoring for more banks, more banks."

Many influential men, including the recently elected President Monroe, supported a new national bank to stabilize the economy and distribute scarce money more uniformly. Advocates of the bank argued that the notes of state banks varied far too much in soundness and value, making the economic system dangerously unstable. The expanding country's economic system needed a central institution to coordinate the flow of money. Accordingly, in 1816 Congress chartered the Second Bank of the United States. Based in Philadelphia, it was authorized to establish branches wherever it wished. The new national bank was an amalgam of public and private enterprise: the federal government deposited its funds in the bank and appointed a fifth of the directors, but the bank ran as a private business. For the privilege of being the only such institution authorized to operate on a national basis, the bank handled, without fees, the funds of the federal treasury. The bank pumped large amounts of paper currency into the system in an

The Second Bank of the United States announced its solidity and strength with its austere classical architecture.

attempt to feed the voracious hunger of the postwar economy, especially in the new states of the West.

The local, state, and federal courts of the United States encouraged the growth of business in the years after the peace of 1815. Courts increasingly favored market forces over custom and stability in property relations, shifting the advantage from farmers and landowners to developers. Those who wanted to dam rivers for factories or build roads enjoyed increasing precedence over those threatened by floods, fires, or disruption caused by development. The courts assumed that the public good from the growth of business outweighed the stability favored by older notions of justice. Because many people bitterly protested this shift in emphasis, state legislatures sometimes sought to curb the power of business interests.

The Supreme Court under Chief Justice John Marshall issued a number of important decisions following

In the absence of a paper currency, notes such as this helped fuel the expansive growth of the American economy in these decades.

the War of 1812 that weakened the power of the states to curb economic development. By establishing a more uniform legal environment that transcended the restrictions of particular states, the court hoped to unleash the beneficial effects of business growth. One decision of 1819 made bankruptcy laws more uniform across the country; another, *Dartmouth College v. Woodward,* sheltered corporations from legislative interference; yet another 1819 ruling, *McCulloch v. Maryland,* established the constitutionality of the Bank of the United States and protected it from state taxation. A fourth case in this period, *Gibbons v. Ogden* (1824), limited the rights of states to interfere in commerce with either special favors and monopolies or restrictive laws. "In all commercial regulations," Marshall pronounced, "we are one and the same people." In this new legal environment, increasingly emulated by state courts and legislators, business flourished in the years immediately following the end of war.

Roads and Canals

Americans threw themselves into a frenzy of road and turnpike building after 1815. New York alone chartered 300 companies that began construction of 5,000 miles of gravel roads. Investors, states, and even the federal government built thousands of miles of private roads—turnpikes—charging tolls to offset the roads'

notoriously high maintenance costs. Some road builders laid logs side-by-side to provide a durable surface, though these so-called "corduroy roads" took a heavy toll on horse, wagon, and rider and wore out quickly besides. In 1818 the U.S. government opened the "National Road," connecting the Potomac River at Cumberland, Maryland, with Wheeling, [West] Virginia, on the Ohio River. The road was the best that technology could provide at the time, with excellent bridges and a relatively smooth stone surface. The road attracted so much business, however, that traffic jams slowed movement to a crawl and the road quickly fell into poor condition. Even on good roads, it often cost more to move bulky items such as corn or wheat than the products could bring at market.

Businesses and state governments began to plan dependable canals with controllable locks and a steady flow of water. Because Baltimore and Philadelphia enjoyed close connections with the West, benefiting from heavily used turnpikes, New York City merchants worried that their dominant position in the East would be lost if they did not establish fast and inexpensive connections as well. Fortunately for New York, a flat passage broke through the Appalachian Mountains within the state's borders. New Yorkers believed that a canal through this area, connecting the Hudson River to Lake Erie, would far surpass any other kind of transportation. Such a canal would be ten times longer than any other canal then in

Corduroy roads, while offering some relief from mud and stones, proved poor competition with newer kinds of transportation such as canals and steamboats.

OHIO BOARD OF CANAL COMMISSIONERS, *ANNUAL REPORT* 1828

The commissioners of Ohio struggle here with a key question of an era when new kinds of transportation were rapidly growing: what role should state and federal government play in economic development? Should the government actively sponsor development, stay out of the way while private businesses competed among themselves, or try to regulate and coordinate private efforts? Here, the Ohio commissioners argue that it is more democratic for the government to take on the responsibility.

An important question may present itself for the consideration of the [Ohio] General Assembly, as connected with the proposed improvements; whether the contemplated canals should be made under the authority, and at the expense of the state, or charters should be granted to private companies for that purpose? The commissioners are of opinion, that the work should be undertaken by the state; chartered companies, possessing exclusive privileges, have always been popular in monarchical governments, because their powers and advantages were so much carved out of the sovereign power for the benefit of subjects—so much in fact gained from the monarchy. The judicial tribunals, influenced doubtless by the popular feeling upon this subject soon found means to secure them to the grantees—gave them a character of *immortality;* changed granted privileges, from the sovereign, into a contract between equals, and placed them beyond the reach of his power, under the protection of that ingenious fiction. Our jurisprudence which borrows its principles and reasonings from England, has very gravely adopted this doctrine of immortality in corporations; naturalized and established it as law in our free governments, and stretched over its dogmas, the aegis of

existence: 364 miles through swamps and solid rock, through places where virtually no white settlers had bothered to migrate.

The mayor of New York City and future governor of the state, De Witt Clinton, became the foremost advocate of the canal, certain it would make his city "the great depot and warehouse of the western world." People scoffed at the money thrown away in "Clinton's Big Ditch." But the largely untrained engineers learned as they went along. Aqueducts had to span rivers and gorges, aqueducts tight and strong enough to withstand the weight of the water and the boats they carried. Locks had to be constructed of heavy timbers and even heavier stone. The canal, 4 feet deep and 40 feet wide at the top, was dug by hands, backs, and shovels. Thousands of laborers, many of them foreign-born, moved with the canal, enlivening and sometimes frightening the more sedentary settlements on the route. Year after year, the canal edged toward Lake Erie, transforming the countryside along the way; by 1819, the canal stretched for seventy-five miles. As soon as workers completed a segment, boats crowded upon its waters, the tolls they paid financing the portions yet unfinished.

Steamboats

Canals, though useful and exciting, reached only a limited part of the vast North American continent.

the Constitution, so that in effect, whatever is granted to a private company by the legislature is holden to be intangible and irrevocable. A grant made under erroneous impressions, and which in its operation is found detrimental to, or even destructive of the public welfare, whether it involves the exercise of sovereign powers or not is, according to established principles of law, altogether irrevocable. The present generation may in this way not only bind themselves, but their posterity forever; and government, instead of being at all times administered for the benefit of the people and in accordance with their will; may be parcelled out into monopolies, swallowing up their interests and counteracting their wishes. How long a free people will sanction such principles, or how consonant they are to the fundamental maxims of our social fabric, it is not our purpose to inquire; the existence of them, we remark, as evincing the risk and danger of granting to private companies any control over matters of public and general interest. Nothing can be more interesting to the whole community, than great navigable highways through the state, from the Lake [Erie] to the Ohio river, on the routes proposed; it does not consist with the dignity, the interest or the convenience of the state, that a private company of citizens or foreigners (as may happen), should have the management and control of them; the evils of such management cannot be fully foreseen, and therefore cannot be provided against; for experience is the only safe guide in legislation and of the operation of such grants we have no experience. Besides, such works should be constructed with a view to the greatest possible accommodation of our citizens; as a public concern, the public convenience is the paramount object; a private company will look only to the best means of increasing their profits, the public convenience will be regarded only as it is subservient to their emolument. We think therefore, that it would be extremely hazardous and unwise, to entrust private companies with making those canals, which can be made by the state.

SOURCE: [Ohio] Board of Canal Commissioners, *Third Annual Report, Civil Engineer* (August 16, 1828), pp. 138–40.

Rivers offered faster and cheaper travel, especially along the Mississippi, Missouri, and Ohio. But their limitations were obvious as well. The rivers could be dangerously fast in some seasons and so slow as to be impassable in others. They often froze for months in the winter. Strong currents ran in only one direction. Those who wanted to transport goods northward had to push their boats against the current, sometimes with poles, sometimes by dragging the boats with ropes as the crews walked along the shore, sometimes merely by grabbing trees and bushes on the banks. It took three or four months to drag a boat upstream. Others simply sold their craft for scrap in New Orleans and walked back to Ohio or Illinois, a long and arduous trip.

Not surprisingly, people dreamed of using steam engines to drive riverboats. Robert Fulton's steamboats had traversed the quieter waters of the Northeast since 1807, but he did not manage to build one for the rigors of the Mississippi until 1811. The War of 1812 slowed development of the steamboats, since engines could not be imported from England, but innovation resumed with the war's end. As soon as Jackson won New Orleans in 1815, the *Enterprise* churned its way upriver from Louisiana all the way to Louisville, Kentucky. Dozens of other craft soon joined, competing with one another. In 1817, the journey from New Orleans to Louisville took twenty-five days; in 1819, fourteen days. "If any one had said this was possible thirty years ago," a journalist marvelled, "we should

have been ready to send him to a mad-house." Though the shallow, high-powered, and top-heavy steamboats showed a dangerous propensity to explode, run aground, and slam into submerged obstacles, no one thought of going back to the old way of travel.

The increasing speed and frequency of the steamboats encouraged the growth of villages and towns along the rivers. Huge stacks of wood carted in from the countryside appeared wherever the steamboats regularly stopped for fuel; new stores sold the goods transported on the river; muddy villages dreamed of becoming major cities. Indeed, the populations of Louisville, Pittsburgh, and Cincinnati doubled or more than doubled between 1815 and 1825, developing into centers not only of trade but also of meatpacking and flour milling.

The Growth of the Plantation South

The demand for cotton in England took off after 1815, when cotton became, for the first time, the clothing of choice for large numbers of the world's people. Cotton clothes were cheaper, easier to create, and more comfortable in warm weather than those made from wool or linen. No place in the world was as prepared to supply the burgeoning demand for cotton as the American South. Small farmers as well as planters from the older states of the southern seaboard saw opportunity in the new states of Alabama and Mississippi, especially now that Andrew Jackson had opened Mobile as a port for southern Alabama. Many white farmers also moved to western Tennessee and parts of Louisiana. The steamboat and the cotton gin gave southern planters powerful new tools, while slaves could clear and cultivate land for new plantations far more quickly than would have been otherwise possible. Slaveowners in the older states of the Atlantic seaboard, faced with what they considered a surplus of labor, eagerly sold slaves to planters moving to the "new" lands.

The movement west was not a simple march from the east, but rather followed the geographic and political contours of the areas recently acquired from the American Indians. The first settlements began along the rivers that made it possible to transport cotton to market and in those places where the Creeks and other Indians exercised no claims. The new plantation districts were disconnected from one another, centering on Montgomery in Alabama, Jackson in Mississippi,

The Erie Canal, connecting the Hudson River with Lake Erie, demanded a monumental engineering effort. It soon paid its way, however, as shippers and farmers rushed to use the new waterway.

Steamboats began to ply the Mississippi River and other major waterways in the 1810s and 1820s, accelerating trade and fueling the growth of cities along the way.

and Memphis in Tennessee, all areas taken from the natives of the region since 1814. Small farmers occupied the land farthest from the rivers, supporting themselves with hunting and foraging as well as with growing small amounts of cotton. Young lawyers and editors headed out for the Southwest as well, eager to make their mark in the river towns and county seats growing up across Alabama and Mississippi.

"The *Alabama Feaver* rages here with great violence and has *carried off* vast numbers of our Citizens," wrote one North Carolina planter in 1817. "I am apprehensive, if it continues to spread as it has done, it will almost depopulate the country." The fever proved contagious, "for as soon as one neighbour visits another who has just returned from the Alabama he immediately discovers the same symptoms which are exhibited by the person who has seen the allureing Alabama." Even established men in the older states put their plantations up for sale; others saw the new

states as a place for their grown children to get a fresh start. The combined population of Alabama, Mississippi, and Louisiana more than tripled between 1810 and 1820, growing from 117,000 people to 357,000.

Some ambitious young men from northern states moved to the new cotton lands, the place in the United States, it seemed, where the greatest fortunes could be made in the shortest amount of time. Virgin land could produce a cotton crop in only one year; in two years, a plantation could be in full production. But most of the new residents came from older plantation states. Young southern men were especially eager to move and make their mark. Their wives, mothers, and daughters were often much less enthusiastic about migrating to Mississippi or Alabama, for it meant being removed from the kin who gave those women much of their happiness. The lure of the Southwest overrode concerns husbands may have felt for their wives' opinions, however, for the new states offered a chance at the independence they considered synonymous with manliness. They sought to build a world as much as possible like those of Virginia or Carolina, only more prosperous.

The expansion of the cotton kingdom broadened and deepened the slave trade. Many planters in the East took advantage of the opportunity to sell slaves "down south," especially as the price of slaves — stagnant or declining before 1815 — began to rise. Hundreds of thousands of slaves endured forcible migration to the new states of the Southwest in the 1810s and 1820s; some moved in groups along with their owners to new plantations, but many were sold as individuals to slave traders in the east, who then shipped or marched them to slave markets in New Orleans, Mobile, and other cities to the southwest. The families of many enslaved African Americans were broken apart, as slave traders eagerly bought those in their teens for the hard work of clearing land for plantations from virgin forest.

The new plantations concentrated on cotton at the expense of everything else. Southerners who had just come into the vast and apparently inexhaustible lands of the Creeks and Seminoles worried little about conservation. The finest plantations clung to the rivers, for water offered the only way to get the ever-expanding cotton crop to market. Flatboats carried the bulky product to barges waiting at the docks of Natchez and Vicksburg on the Mississippi or to ships waiting in the bays of Mobile and New Orleans. Food and other provisions for the plantations came down the rivers from

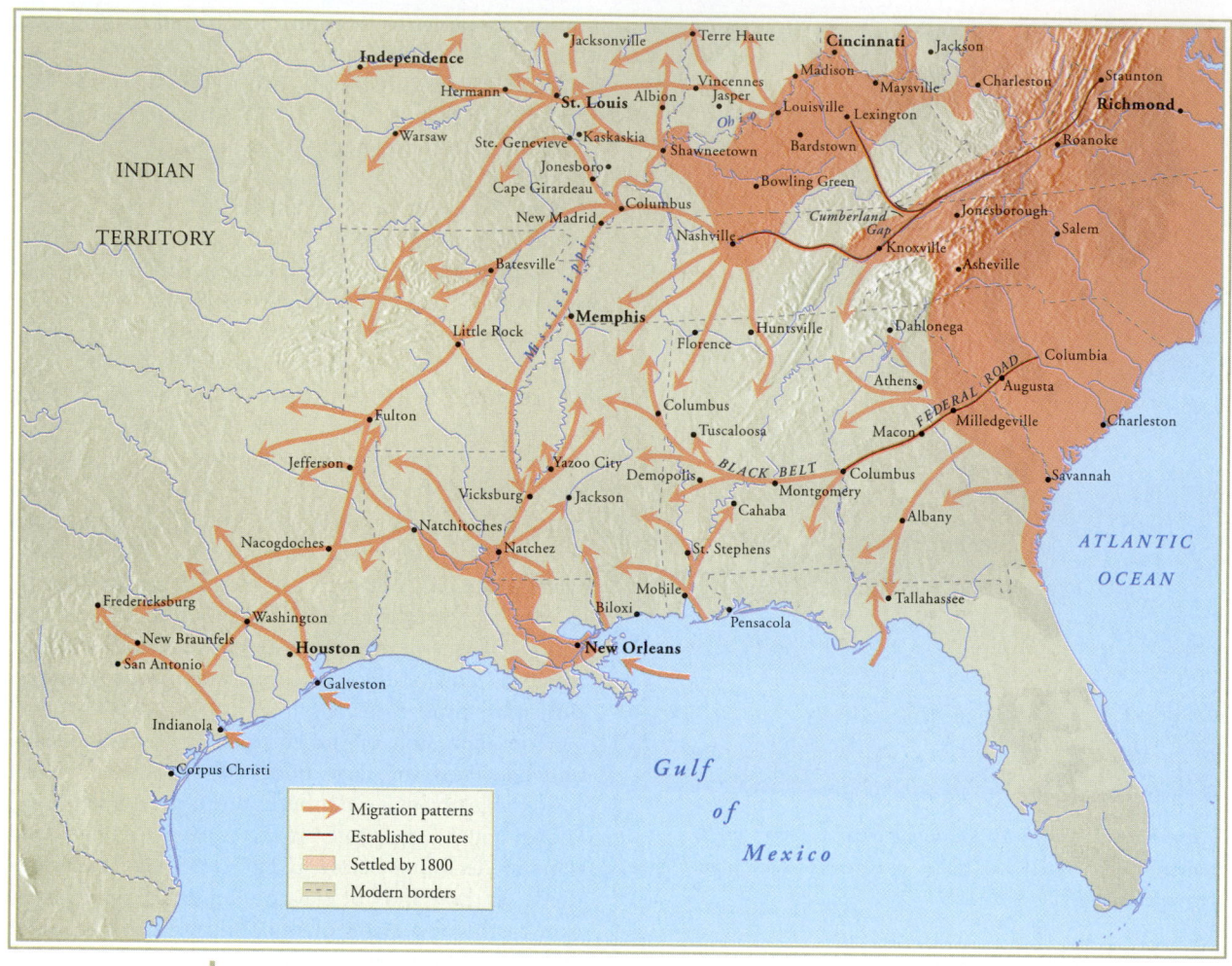

MAP 9.3 | THE PATHS OF SOUTHERN MIGRATION

the new farms and cities to the north. A new national economy knitted together the enormous expanse of the young United States.

Emergence of the Northwest

The area west of the Appalachians, north of the Ohio, and east of the Mississippi—the "Northwest"—was growing at an even faster pace than the Southwest. "Old America seems to be breaking up, and moving westward," one man wrote in 1817 as he watched people move down the Ohio River. The 280,000 white settlers of 1810 in Ohio, Indiana, and Illinois grew to 784,000 ten years later. This immigration in the North bore considerable similarities to its southern counterpart. First of all, many of the settlers to the Northwest came from the states of the upper South; large parts of southern Ohio, Indiana, and Illinois were settled by people from Virginia, Kentucky, Tennessee, and North Carolina. Some southern migrants to the North professed themselves eager to move out of states with slavery, while others merely followed the easiest routes to good land. People from New England and New York filled the towns and farms of the northern parts of the new states of the Northwest.

As in the South, young people dominated migration to the Northwest. Migrants to both regions abandoned areas back east where land had become too expensive, crowded, or depleted. As in the Southwest, settlers to the Northwest did not move in a simple westward wave, but rather flowed up the rivers and

Slave trader, Sold to Tennessee,

Arise! Arise! and weep no more dry up your tears, we Shall part no more. Come rose we go to Tennessee, that happy Shore to old virginia never — never — return.

the Company going to Tennessee from Staunton, Augusta County, — the law of virginia Suffered them to go on. I was Astonished at this boldness, the carrier Stopped a moment, then Ordered the march, I Saw the play it is Commonly in this State, with the negro's in droves Sold,

The rapid spread of cotton plantations to the west fueled the domestic slave trade. This coffle of slaves marched from Virginia to Tennessee.

spread from there, sometimes back towards the East. People often emigrated in groups, whether of families or of larger communities. "We are seldom out of sight, as we travel on this grand track towards the Ohio," one traveller noted, "of family groups behind, and before us, some with a view to a particular spot, close to a brother perhaps, or a friend who has gone before, and reported well of the country." Family farms clustered closer together in the Northwest than in the Southwest because the absence of a large slave work-

force meant that landholdings remained relatively small.

As in the South, white settlement in the Northwest was made possible by the subjugation of the native peoples. After northern Indians' disastrous losses in the War of 1812, they posed little threat to white settlers. The U.S. government quickly established a series of forts throughout the Northwest to intimidate any American Indians and to make sure that the British and Canadians did not regain a foothold. The growing

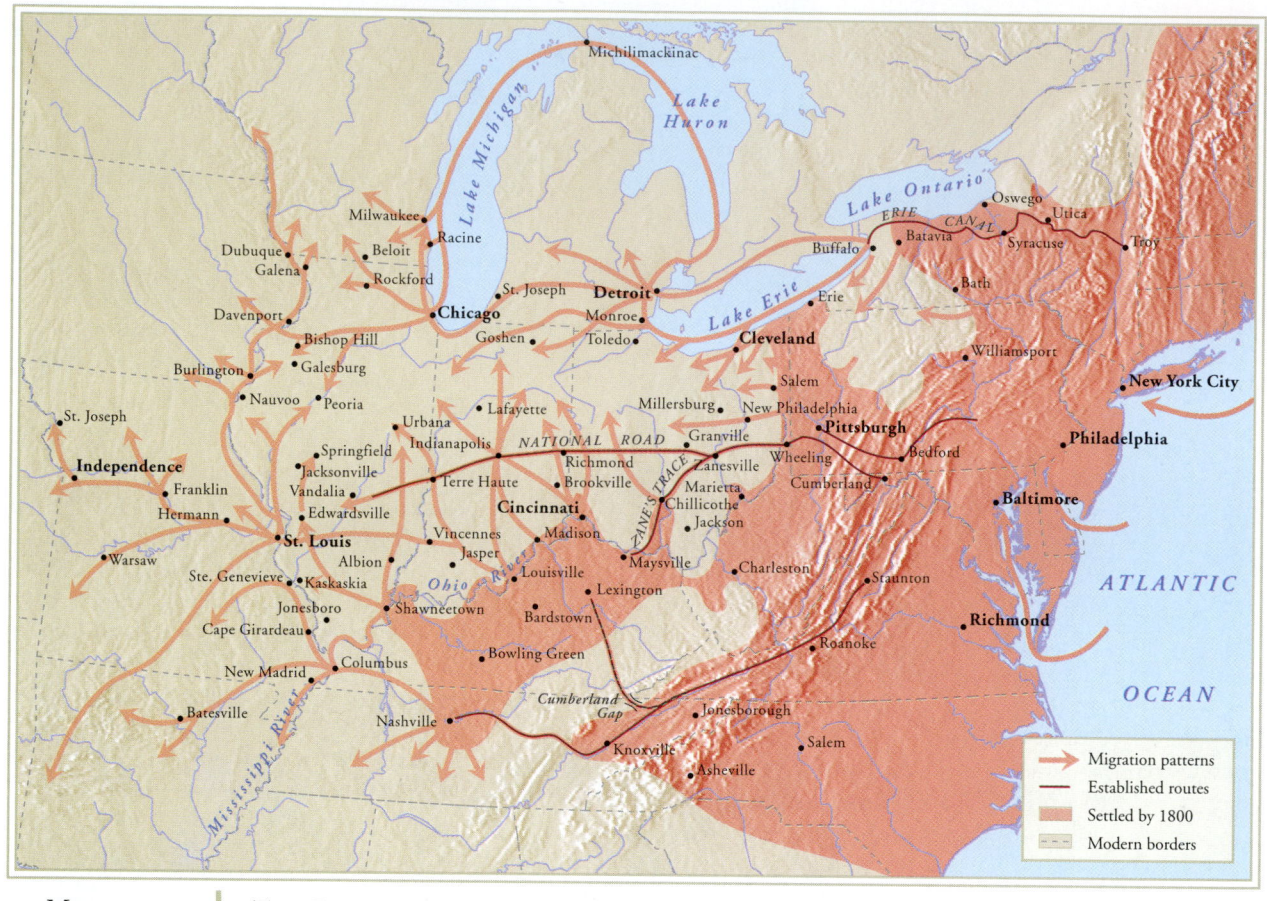

MAP 9.4 | THE PATHS OF NORTHERN MIGRATION

numbers of white farmers made it difficult for Native Americans to hunt for a living. President Monroe exulted in the "rapid and gigantic" spread of white settlers into the Northwest, an expansion the "rights of nature demand and nothing can prevent." The president argued that "the earth was given to mankind to support the greatest number of people of which it is capable, and no tribe or people have a right to withhold from the wants of others more than is necessary for their own support and comfort." Whites who moved to the Northwest confronted only scattered remnants of native peoples, trading with white merchants for food, sometimes begging from homesteaders.

Most white settlers proved dissatisfied with the first land they claimed, for about two out of three migrants moved again within a few years. Rumors always circulated about richer land a bit farther west, about a new town certain to be a major city, about opportunity just over the horizon. Many people who had moved once found it easy to move again. Those who remained in a

community became its "leading citizens," consolidating land into larger farms, setting up grist mills and sawmills, running for office, establishing the small towns that served as county seats and trading centers. In many cases, storekeepers were among the first to arrive and among those whose fortunes flourished best. Storekeepers became the bankers and wholesalers of their communities, often buying considerable amounts of land along the way, boosting the towns growing around the stores, churches, and schoolhouses. Courthouses were built early on to formalize land sales and taxation.

Farm and Factory in the Northeast

While the economies of the West and the South were being transformed by settlers and slaves, the economy of the East underwent its own fundamental change. Since the colonial years, people outside the major cities—more than nine out of ten Americans—had

made in their own homes much of what they needed. This local production grew stronger when trade dried up during the war with England; in the war's wake, more than two-thirds of the clothes Americans wore were made in their own homes. The year of 1815, in fact, saw the peak of household manufacturing. Local blacksmiths, tailors, cobblers, and other artisans supplied what families could not produce for themselves, while local gristmills and sawmills processed crops and lumber.

Farms averaged a little over a hundred acres, about half improved and the other half occupied by wood lots for fuel and timber. Forests often dominated the farms of younger families while mature families proudly claimed large areas of cultivation, the products of years of labor. Women and men, children and adults, shared and divided the work among themselves. Farm families cleared their fields at spring thaw, manuring, plowing, and planting as soon as danger of frost passed. Livestock and poultry needed constant attention; sheep had to be washed and sheared and geese plucked in the spring. Farm families reaped flax in June, enjoyed a brief respite in August, and then pushed hard for the fall harvest. In winter, men and boys cut wood while women and girls spun thread and wove cloth for clothes. The garden and dairy were the responsibility of women and girls, the cash crops the responsibility of men. Farmers, chronically short of cash, bartered among themselves and with merchants.

After 1815, the farms in many parts of New England, New York, and Pennsylvania would be tied ever more tightly into the economies of the towns and cities. Farm families produced more cash crops and bought more things with money rather than through barter. Women, especially widows and other single females, worked in their homes to produce palm hats, portions of shoes, or articles of clothing that merchants from nearby cities gathered and had assembled in workshops. These women added such work to their farm work, laboring in the evenings and throughout the winters. With so many young men leaving New England for the west, many communities found themselves with considerable numbers of young women who might never marry as well as older women who could not count on the support of sons. Piecework offered these women a chance to contribute to the economies of their households in a way the older farm economy had not, bringing in scarce cash. It was important to everyone in their families that those wage-earning women did not have to leave home to earn those wages.

The expanded cash economy thus overlapped with and conflicted with an older, more self-contained economy. Families sought opportunity in new jobs and new markets even as they feared that the increasingly dense networks of trade would depress the value of their crops, make seasonal farm labor even more difficult to acquire, entice young people from the farm, and undermine local artisans. Rural folk both welcomed and worried over the changes. Although it would be generations before cities and factories dominated the economies of the North, in the meantime, farms, towns, and small factories grew ever more interconnected.

The textile industry of New England stood as the most dramatic example of industrial growth. The cost of cotton clothing fell faster than the cost for any other product as machinery and cheaper cotton lowered the price. Francis Cabot Lowell of Boston

Women provided much of the workforce for the new textile factories that emerged in New England.

MAP 9.5 | LOCATION OF COTTON MILLS, 1820S

designed a power loom in 1813, recreating from memory a machine he had seen on a recent trip to England. The same year, Lowell and a partner, Nathan Appleton, spent over $400,000 to open the first factory in the United States that could integrate all the steps of making cloth under a single roof: the Boston Manufacturing Company, in Waltham, Massachusetts, where a waterfall with a ten-foot drop offered free power. An expanded group of investors in the enterprise—the Boston Associates, they were called—pooled the resources of the city's most prominent merchant families.

Unlike earlier factories, that of the Boston Associates used unskilled labor and machines even for weaving, the most expensive part of the process. Lowell and Appleton, concerned that the introduction of factories

into the United States might create the same alienated and despised working class they saw in England, recruited young New England farm women and girls as operatives. Young females had experience in producing yarn and cloth at home and they would work hard for low wages. Many were eager to earn money for themselves, to move out of crowded homes, and to send money back to their families. As Appleton put it, the young women supplied "a fund of labor, well educated and virtuous" for the factory.

The operatives, considering millwork a three- or four-year commitment before they married and began families of their own, worked fourteen hours a day, six days a week. When they signed a contract with the agents who received a dollar a head for each worker they could recruit, the young women agreed to stay

with the mill for at least twelve months or to be put on a blacklist that would prevent them from getting a job elsewhere. The factory was unlike anything the young women had ever confronted: "You cannot think how odd everything seemed," one mill girl recalled; even those who had spun and woven for years could not be prepared for the "frightful" sight of "so many bands, and wheels, and springs in constant motion." Leaving the factory in the evening, an operative could still hear the noise of the mill in her head, "as of crickets, frogs and jewsharps, all mingled together in strange discord."

The social and economic ground for industrialization had been broken in the northeast. Mills, most of them small, grew up along the streams of Connecticut and the Delaware Valley of Pennsylvania and New Jersey, turning out not only textiles but also metal and wood products. These mills, like their bigger and more visible counterparts in Lowell, depended on low wages paid to workers without many other options. Many potential workers, competitors, and outside observers worried about the effects of the factories, even as investors and other supporters saw in the new buildings the hope for a richer and more productive American society.

THE PRICE OF EXPANSION

The prosperity of the immediate postwar years faltered badly in 1819. Apparently boundless growth stopped dead in its tracks. The enlarged scale of the new American economy entangled a far larger number of people than had ever been caught in economic hard times before. Meanwhile, the enlarged boundaries of the American nation brought troubles of their own as the North and the South fought over new territories in the West. Looking out over the world, slaves felt emboldened to revolt and political leaders declared the determination of the United States to control its hemisphere.

The Panic of 1819

A series of events in 1819 abroad and at home conspired to bring a sudden halt to some of the growth in the economy of the United States. Cotton lands in the southeast, the most sought-after property in these years, saw prices skyrocket as world demand for cotton cloth increased every year. Prices for southern cotton rose to such an extent that in 1818 and 1819 British manufacturers turned to cotton from other sources, especially India. The price of American cotton tumbled, along with the price of the land that produced it. And cotton was not the only crop whose price rapidly declined: the price of tobacco plummeted from 40 cents a pound to 4 cents, wheat fell from $2.41 a bushel to 88 cents. State banks built on inflated, even fraudulent, credit wavered and then crashed. The Panic of 1819 had begun.

The panic proved a sudden and sobering reminder of just how complicated and interdependent the economy of the nation was becoming. The cities were hit the hardest. About half a million workers lost their jobs as business ground to a halt. Americans shuddered to see "children freezing in the winter's storm—and the fathers without coats and shoes." The streets where new goods had been piled now displayed people without homes or food. Charitable groups opened soup kitchens. Wherever they could, families who had moved to towns and cities returned to the countryside to live with relatives. Things were not much safer in the country, however, where the failure of banks meant that apparently prosperous farmers saw household goods, farm animals, and the people they held as slaves sold in humiliating auctions.

Many people, including congressmen, began to call for the revocation of the charter of the Second Bank of the United States. States had chafed throughout the two years of the Bank's life at what they considered its dictatorial power. Several states tried to limit that power by levying extremely high taxes on the branches of the Bank of the United States in their states, but it was at this point that the Supreme Court ruled in *McCulloch* v. *Maryland* that the laws of the federal government "form the supreme law of the land."

Despite the panic, James Monroe was reelected to the presidency in 1820 in one of the quietest and most lopsided elections in the nation's history. The Federalist party, fatally crippled by its opposition to the War of 1812 and its support of the Hartford Convention, offered no effective opposition. Neither did Monroe face an organized contest from others within his own Republican party, which was divided along sectional lines. He received every electoral vote but one. Most Americans seemed to blame someone other than President Monroe for the Panic of 1819 and the lingering hard times that followed it. The Era of Good Feelings

somehow managed to survive in the White House—though, it turned out, not in the halls of Congress.

The Missouri Compromise

The recent admission of the new states of the Southwest and Northwest had left a precarious balance in the Senate between slave states and free, though northern states held a strong, and growing, preponderance in the House of Representatives. The Missouri territory posed a special challenge to the balance. Slavery had quickly spread in Missouri, stretching along the richest river lands. If Missouri were admitted with slavery—as its territorial legislature had decreed—then the slave states would hold a majority in the Senate. Slavery in Missouri, an area of the same latitude as much of Illinois, Indiana, and Ohio, seemed to violate the assumption long held by many people in the North that slavery, if it grew at all, would expand only to the south.

The three-fifths clause of the Constitution, northerners complained, gave the slave states twenty more members of Congress and twenty more electors for the presidency than they would have if only white population were counted. The South seemed to be getting extra representation unfairly.

The debates over slavery in Missouri in 1819 and 1820 were not debates between fervent abolitionists in the North and fervent proslavery advocates in the South. Neither of those positions had yet been defined. Instead, white northerners and southerners of all political persuasions agreed that as many blacks as possible should be shipped to Africa. White Americans who could agree on little else about slavery did agree that blacks and whites could not live together in the United States once slavery had ended. That was the message of the American Colonization Society, founded in 1816 and based in Washington, D.C. The society bought land in Africa—naming the new country "Liberia"—and sent about 12,000 African Americans there over the next fifty years. Disease took a terrible toll, however, and many died. Fewer African Americans migrated. In Philadelphia, they even staged protests against the notion of colonization.

In the meantime, slavery caused problems for the political system. A New York congressman, James Tallmadge, Jr., introduced an amendment to the bill that would admit Missouri as a state only if Missouri admitted no more slaves and if those slaves in the territory were freed when they became twenty-five years old. More than eighty of the North's congressmen supported the Tallmadge amendment and only ten opposed it. In the Senate, though, the slave states prevailed by two votes. A deadlocked Congress adjourned in March of 1819 to meet again in December.

During the months in between politicians worked behind the scenes to prepare for the debates and decisions of December. The Union, so celebrated and expansive in the wake of the war with Britain, so peaceful for whites since the Creeks, Seminoles, and Cherokees had been quelled, now seemed in danger of breaking apart from within. Both northern and southern politicians talked openly of ending the Union if need be. Simmering northern resentment, held in check for decades, was suddenly announced, even celebrated. Southerners felt betrayed. In their eyes, slavery was a thing they had inherited, something for which they bore no blame, an institution that would fade away naturally if it were left alone. White southerners thought northerners irresponsible and unrealistic to attack as the Tallmadge amendment did. The denial of Missouri statehood seemed to southerners nothing less than an assault on their character.

In northern states, where abolitionist societies had been relatively sedate, people suddenly announced the depth of their distaste for the institution. Furious meetings erupted in towns and cities across the North, turning out petitions and resolutions in large numbers. Slavery, these petitions thundered, was a blot on the nation, a violation of the spirit of Christianity, an abomination that must not spread into places it had not already ruined. The antislavery advocates of the 1820s expected colonization and abolition to occur simultaneously and gradually. But they also determined to stop the spread of slavery toward the northern part of the continent.

After weeks of debate, a compromise emerged from the Senate: Missouri, with no restriction on slavery, should be admitted to the Union at the same time as Maine, thereby ensuring the balance between slave and free states. Slavery would be prohibited in all the lands acquired in the Louisiana Purchase north of the southern border of Missouri at 36° 30′ latitude. Such a provision excluded the Arkansas territory, where slavery was already established, but closed to slavery the vast expanses of the Louisiana Territory—the future states of Iowa, Minnesota, Wisconsin, the Dakotas, Nebraska, and Kansas. Any slaves who escaped to the free states would be returned. Many of the northern

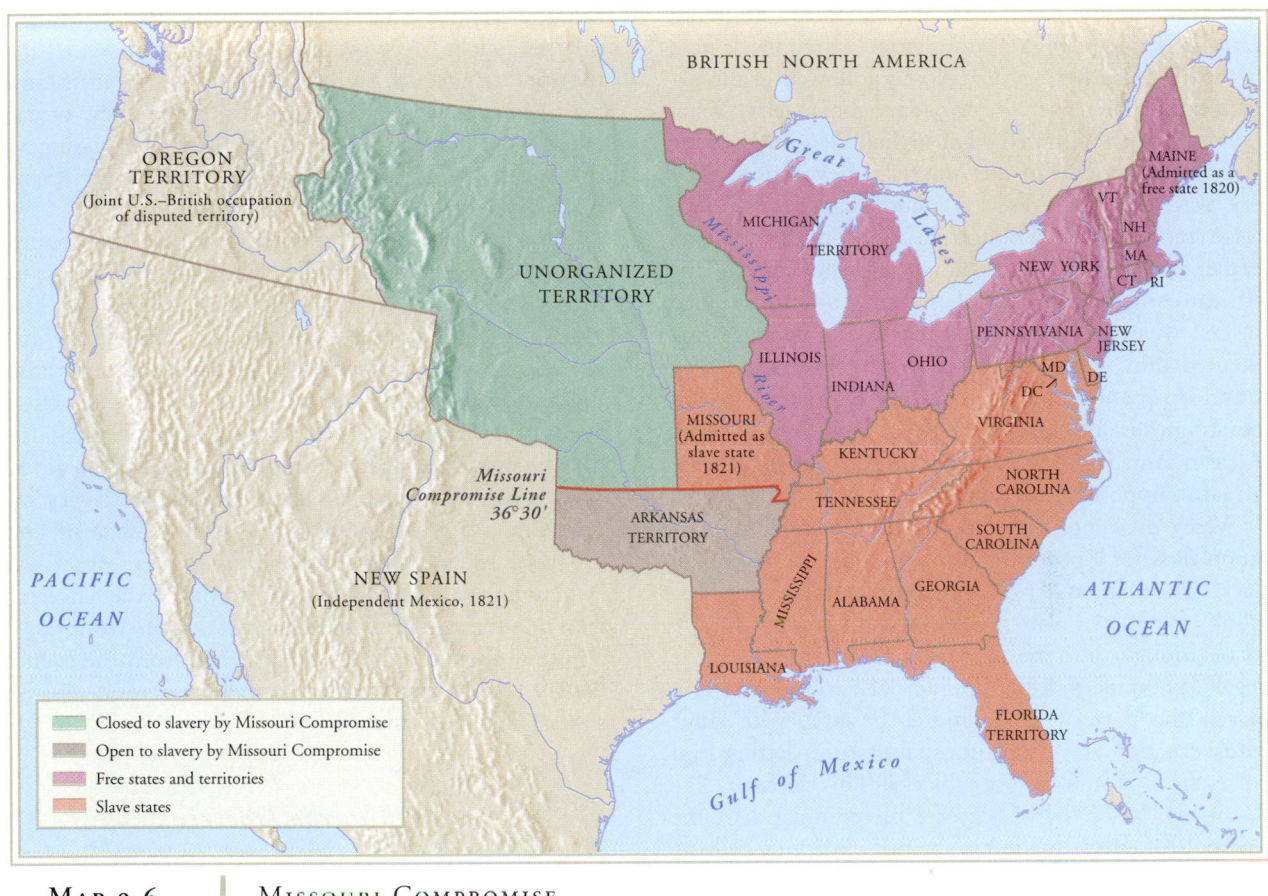

Closed to slavery by Missouri Compromise
Open to slavery by Missouri Compromise
Free states and territories
Slave states

MAP 9.6   MISSOURI COMPROMISE

men who voted for the measure found themselves burned in effigy back home and defeated when it came time for reelection. The South was no more satisfied than the North, furious to hear itself vilified in the national capital it had long dominated.

The debate broke out again when the Missouri constitutional convention not only authorized slavery but decreed that the state legislature could never emancipate slaves without the consent of their masters; the proposed constitution also pronounced that free blacks would never be permitted to enter the new state. The national House of Representatives refused to admit Missouri under this document and the denunciation by both sides began again where it had paused. Finally, in early 1821, Henry Clay managed to fix a majority in the House in favor of a bill that would admit Missouri as long as the new state promised to pass no law barring the entry of a citizen from any other state. Exhausted, Congress ratified the law.

Northern and southern states had become wary and distrustful of one another as they had never been before. In a real sense, the debates over slavery in Missouri created "the North" and "the South," uniting the new states of the Northwest with the states of New England, New York, and Pennsylvania as they had not been united earlier, forging a tighter alliance between the new states of the Southwest and Virginia, the Carolinas, and Georgia. To the North, the South seemed greedy and corrupt; to the South, the North seemed greedy and hypocritical. The country became polarized as never before.

Vesey's Revolt

An event in 1822 in Charleston, South Carolina, forced white Americans, North and South, to pay greater attention to the people who lived under

slavery's dominion. In that city, the heart of South Carolina's richest plantation district, a free black man named Denmark Vesey had closely followed in the papers the debates over the Missouri controversy. What he read there reinforced what he had seen in the Bible and the documents of the American Revolution: Slavery was immoral. Vesey, a middle-aged mulatto of large stature who had bought his freedom twenty years earlier, stood as a commanding presence among the African American people of the low country. He had several wives and many children whose bondage tormented him. A skilled carpenter and preacher, Vesey traveled up and down the coast and into the interior, berating those blacks who accepted racial insult. Many African Americans were attracted to him; most were afraid to oppose him regardless.

Vesey drew not only upon his own strengths, but upon those of a powerful ally, a man known as Gullah Jack. This man, an Angolan, had arrived in South Carolina near the turn of the century, one of the 40,000 slaves brought into the state right before the end of the legal slave trade in 1807. Gullah Jack still looked very much the part of the conjurer he was, with huge whiskers, tiny arms, and unusual gestures setting him apart from American-born blacks. This sorcerer, like Denmark Vesey, hated slavery; his command of the symbols of Africa made his alliance with Vesey all the more powerful. The two men found their most eager audience among the artisans and house slaves of Charleston who had the greatest amount of freedom. Vesey and Gullah Jack found it relatively easy to meet with slaves receptive to their message. Allies in charge of stables and stores gave Vesey access to horses and weapons.

Vesey planned to launch an attack on white Charleston at midnight on a Saturday, when slaves from the countryside came to the city to sell produce. The conspirators hoped to seize the city's poorly protected guardhouse, stores, and roads before the whites could gather themselves in opposition. House slaves would kill their white owners. Once Charleston was secure, the rebels, Vesey planned, would sail to Haiti, where Toussaint L'Ouverture had staged a black rebellion decades earlier and where slavery had been abolished. But the plan met serious difficulties, especially since so many people had to be let in on the secrets. A house servant broke under the pressure and alerted Charleston whites to the danger only two days before the revolt planned for June 16, 1822. The governor

ordered out five military companies and Vesey called off the attack. Over the next two months, white authorities hanged thirty-five alleged conspirators and banished thirty-seven more from the state. Few of the rebels would reveal the names of their allies, going to their deaths with the secrets of the revolt secure. Denmark Vesey was one of those killed.

Though many details remained murky, white South Carolinians believed that they had, by the narrowest of margins, avoided an unimaginable rebellion. The rebels came not from the ranks of the slaves living under the most brutal conditions but from among those most trusted by their owners, those who lived in close association with white women and children. South Carolinians, and white southerners in general, blamed Vesey's Rebellion on the agitation against slavery by northern congressmen in the Missouri debate. "The events of 1822," a leading South Carolinian observed, "will long be remembered, as amongst the choicest fruits of the agitation of that question in Congress." White southerners drew a clear lesson from the events between 1820 and 1822: Northern agitation against slavery invited disaster.

The Monroe Doctrine

The instability of the Spanish regime in Europe, exacerbated by the Napoleonic Wars, sent aftershocks into the colonies in the New World. Throughout the first and second decades of the nineteenth century, one struggle after another disrupted Latin America. Seeing Spain vulnerable in Europe and abroad, leaders in the colonies of the Western Hemisphere—Simón Bolívar in Venezuela, José de San Martín in Argentina, and Miguel Hidalgo in Mexico—pushed ahead with their long-simmering plans for national independence. By 1822, Chile, Mexico, Venezuela, and the Portuguese colony of Brazil had all gained their independence.

Neither the United States nor Great Britain wanted to see France fill the vacuum left by Spain in the New World. A French or Russian empire would pose a potentially dangerous economic and military threat much greater than any posed by the fading Spanish regime. Accordingly, in March of 1822 President Monroe urged Congress to recognize the new republics of Latin America. Throughout the next year, as the French army invaded Spain, the U.S. minister in England proposed that the United States and England

John Quincy Adams was Secretary of State under James Monroe and the author of the so-called "Monroe Doctrine," which announced American opposition to European colonization in the Western Hemisphere.

what would eventually become known as the Monroe Doctrine: "[T]he American continents, by the free and independent conditions which they have assumed and maintained, are henceforth not to be considered as subjects for future colonisation by any European power." The North American republic had exerted its first claim to recognition by the great powers of the world, making a show of acting independently even though Great Britain was the real power. The Russians and Spanish denounced the American policy as "blustering," "arrogant," "indecent," and "monstrous," meriting only "the most profound contempt." They tolerated the doctrine because the European powers, exhausted by wars among themselves, had little desire to expand their involvement on the other side of the world. The leaders of the Latin American revolts welcomed the warning to the European powers, but were less certain about the United States's own intentions toward Latin America. The Monroe Doctrine, after all, did not say that the United States would not interfere in the Western Hemisphere, only that it would not permit European countries to do so.

THE SWIRL OF PUBLIC LIFE

Two events of 1824 threw into sharp relief the accomplishments and dangers of the emerging nation. The first event was the thirteen-month tour of the United States by one of the heroes of the American Revolution: the Marquis de Lafayette. The second event was the presidential election of 1824. While Lafayette's visit tied the country together with bonds of memory and celebration, the election showed that Americans had become far more divided than had seemed possible only four years earlier.

Lafayette's Return

Lafayette sailed into New York and was met, fittingly enough, with a steamboat, symbol of the strides the United States had made since Lafayette's departure decades earlier. He spent tumultuous and tearful days in New York, where old comrades and young admirers poured out to see the living embodiment of the

jointly declare that neither country would annex any part of the tottering empire of Spain, nor permit any other power to do so. Encouraged by former presidents Jefferson and Madison, Monroe wanted to make the joint declaration, but Secretary of State John Quincy Adams persuaded him that it would be more fitting and dignified for the United States to declare its policy independently instead of coming "in as a cockboat in the wake of the British man o'war." Adams's policy was directed more against outside intervention in Latin America than in favor of the new republics, which he considered weak and unlikely to endure an attack by a major power.

Accordingly, in December of 1823 the president used his annual message to Congress to announce

sacrifices and bravery of the Revolutionary War. Then Lafayette, along with his son, George Washington Lafayette, and his traveling companion, a radical young Scotswoman named Frances Wright, set out to see the rest of the United States. They went first to New England, visiting with John Adams, then down the coast to Philadelphia, Baltimore, Washington, Charleston, and then New Orleans. From there, they went up the Mississippi and on to Nashville, where he met Andrew Jackson. Everywhere Lafayette traveled, the people tried to outdo what had been done before; the hero met with booming guns, torchlight parades, thousands of children dressed in the colors of France, beautiful young women, illuminated pictures, banquet after banquet, speech after speech. Some moments stood out: when the general cried, alone, at the grave of Washington at Mount Vernon, and when he traveled to Monticello to meet with Jefferson. Congress, knowing that the marquis was in serious financial difficulties, presented him with a gift of $200,000 (an enormous sum at the time) and a township of public land. Lafayette met with Cherokees in Georgia. Slaves, hearing of the patriot's opposition to slavery, lined the roads wherever he went to cheer him on.

A toast announced what Americans most admired in Lafayette, "the great apostle of liberty whom the persecutions of tyranny could not defeat, whom the love of riches could not influence, whom popular applause could never seduce." The Frenchman, in other words, was admired for his selflessness at the time of the American Revolution, for putting the cause of liberty before his own self-interest, for putting himself at risk in the pursuit of freedom. Such a posture of noble self-sacrifice was what Americans valued most in their public men and what they expected of those to whom power was given. In Lafayette, they could celebrate the best in themselves.

The Election of 1824

Many people felt, on the other hand, that they saw the worst of the country in the presidential election going on while Lafayette toured the country. Few eligible voters had bothered to cast a ballot four years earlier when James Monroe had won the presidency without opposition, for his election seemed foreordained. But politicians and observers expected a more interesting contest in 1824. Many thought the next president

would be William Crawford, secretary of the treasury, a Georgian and apparent heir to the Virginia dynasty. Others focused on John Quincy Adams, an experienced statesman, New Englander, and the secretary of state—the office from which many presidents had come. Others looked to John C. Calhoun of South Carolina, an impressive secretary of war and advocate of a strong government. Yet others placed their bets on Henry Clay of Kentucky, speaker of the House of Representatives for many years and one of the most visible members of Congress. Finally, Andrew Jackson of Tennessee hoped to parlay the widespread fame he won in the wars against the English and the Indians into the presidency.

Several of these men realized they did not command sufficient national support to win the election outright. They hoped, however, to prevail if the election went into the House of Representatives, where the top three candidates would vie if no candidate won in the electoral college. Cliques spread rumors and alliances of convenience flourished. Openly partisan newspapers sang the praises of their man and published lacerating rumors about his opponents. While the Marquis de Lafayette serenely toured the United States, local and state politicians worked feverishly in taverns, caucuses, and newspaper offices. Many American voters seemed disenchanted with the crass politicking, though, and relatively few voted in 1824. Jackson's popular vote nearly equaled that of Adams and Crawford combined, but the election was thrown into the House of Representatives because no candidate received a plurality in the electoral college. The House could choose among the top three candidates: Jackson, Adams, and Crawford.

Since his fourth-place finish put him out of the running, Clay, the speaker of the House, sought to strike the best deal he could with the other candidates, assuring himself of maximum power, visibility, and opportunities in subsequent elections. Clay, considering Jackson unworthy of the post and a potential military despot, discussed his future with Adams. When the vote came to the House of Representatives in early 1825, Adams won the presidency—taking the three states Clay had won in the electoral college. Two weeks later, Henry Clay received the appointment of secretary of state. "So you see," Andrew Jackson fumed, "the *Judas* of the West has closed the contract and will receive the thirty pieces of silver." Throughout the muddy little city of Washington, people specu-

Martin Van Buren helped invent modern politics in the 1820s, combining publicity and patronage into a powerful machine that would soon be emulated across the country.

lated about the promises the upright John Quincy Adams had made to win the presidency. People often mentioned the cold sweat that broke out on his face when he received word of his election.

Adams wanted a stronger national government, internal improvements, and a tariff to protect American industry. But he could not mobilize support for his positions, either within Washington or among the voters. Adams refused to use patronage to persuade or coerce people to go along with his plans. His administration bogged down into factionalism and paralysis, always with the shadow of his supposed "corrupt bargain" with Clay darkening his reputation. Things seemed far removed, indeed, from the glorious days when Lafayette sacrificed for the American Revolution.

New York politicians sought to harness ambition into useful and organized forms in the 1820s, pioneering the development of the party system. Aaron Burr converted a simple patriotic club in New York City, the Society of Saint Tammany, into the beginnings of a major political machine. De Witt Clinton invented the "spoils system," in which it became the expectation that an incoming officeholder would remove those appointed by his predecessor and put his own supporters in their place. Martin Van Buren, a young lawyer and politician from New York, combined the city machine and the spoils system into a powerful statewide organization. He used newspapers in Albany and New York City to spread the word of the party to the fifty small newspapers he controlled throughout the state, which also published vast numbers of hand bills, posters, and ballots at election time. He built a large network of party men, many of them lawyers who traveled widely in the state and knew many of their counterparts. Van Buren's goal was to combine party unity with personal advancement for party members, creating a powerful and self-reinforcing cycle.

Martin Van Buren opposed John Quincy Adams in the presidential contest of 1824 because Adams's nationally sponsored canals, roads, education, and other services would cut into the power of state government and state politics, elevating what Van Buren saw as dangerous federal power over power closer to home. Partly for this reason, Van Buren cast his lot in 1824 and the years thereafter with Andrew Jackson, who shared Van Buren's preference for localized power. As the next presidential election came closer, Van Buren, now a senator, worked ever more energetically for Jackson, hoping to spread the model of New York politics to the nation as a whole.

CHARACTER DEVELOPMENT

For generations before 1815, Americans had relied on authority and reputation to keep their families and communities stable. Young men and women remained in their parents' households well into their twenties, subordinate to the demands and expectations of their fathers. Workingmen served for years as apprentices and journeymen to master artisans, slowly learning the craft and gradually working toward independence. Men and women carefully cultivated their reputations, projecting a polished image of themselves. Churches

aided stability, encouraging deference to the authority of God and institution.

The decade after 1815 saw a new emphasis in American life, a new focus on what people called "character." In a society so mobile, so disconnected from traditional sources of stability and identity, people felt the need for new ways of ensuring appropriate behavior. Americans looked to new kinds of institutions suited for a new age, institutions that could better deal with strangers, new people, those cut off from older forms of social stability. Americans turned first to families, imparting to them primary responsibility for creating virtuous children and husbands.

Women at Home and Beyond

Women had long been recognized as the foundation of a good family. Women directly produced a large portion of the food farm families consumed, while town-dwelling families depended on women for running the household—especially hard work in the days before indoor plumbing and electricity. During the era of the Revolution and early republic, women had been encouraged to raise virtuous children befitting a nation of free people. Churches had long depended on women as the source of spiritual energy and admirable role models.

Women became central in yet another way during the decades following 1815. As Americans looked about them, they became concerned that little seemed to be holding their society together. People moved far beyond the reach of government and beyond the eyes of their parents. Men and women married at younger ages and left home far earlier than their parents had. The opening of land in the West undermined one of the principal forms of control exercised by fathers in earlier generations: the promise of passing on the family farm to sons who stayed at home. Now, sons could acquire land in the West with or without the support of their parents. Daughters might marry earlier and begin families of their own. The American population skyrocketed as so many young families established themselves.

The new economy, too, caused concern for many. Increasingly, men and women seemed pulled in different directions, away from a sole focus on the family farm or family artisan shop. Men found new opportunities in town, in businesses that kept offices or shops in a central area. Young men often worked for wages for a number of employers rather than serving for many years with one master. Middle-class women, too, saw their lives change, especially in towns and cities. Bakeries, butcher shops, clothiers, and candlemakers began to offer, more easily and cheaply, some of the things that women had long labored to produce at home. Schools and academies became more common, providing a place for children to receive education beyond the bounds of the home. Young women from poorer backgrounds came into cities looking for jobs as maids and laundresses, taking away some of the household burden for women well off enough to hire them. Families in towns and cities had fewer children with each passing decade. Women's lives remained hard, as each birth threatened serious illness or death, but those lives began to change in important ways.

As ministers, journalists, and other opinion makers looked upon the changing nature of the households of the Northeast, they began to articulate an ideal of what has been called "domesticity." Families should seize the opportunities provided by the new situations, they said, and help lessen some of the costs created by the new order. Women could put their minds to higher purposes, focusing more on nurturing their children in spirit and mind as well as in body. Women would become the moral center of the household, the guardians of good thoughts, clean living, and a sense of safety for children and husbands. While the world beyond the household seemed increasingly threatening and disorienting, women could make the home a place of refuge and renewal.

Many middle-class women welcomed this message and this mission. It fit well with their own experiences and their own aspirations. In a time when public life made almost no provisions for female participation and when women found virtually no well-paying jobs open to them, the elevation of the home promised an elevation of women's role. Men believed what they said: they thought women naturally better than themselves, more moral and feeling, more intuitive and spiritual. Men worried about the coarseness and callousness of the tumultuous marketplace even as they enjoyed the sense of freedom, excitement, and possibility it offered. Middle-class fathers wanted their children shielded from the hard world as long as possible, if only so they would be better able to handle the world when they emerged after their nurture at home.

Depictions such as this portrait of Catherine Wheeler Hardy and her daughter celebrated the quiet domestic space shared by children and presided over by the mother.

Domesticity asked something of men as well. If the home were to be a haven, the center of society, men would have to make a greater investment in those homes than had their fathers. Men needed to respect the feelings of their wives more, speaking in tones of respect and affection, respecting their wishes about sex and children. Fathers were expected to spend more time with their children, providing a firm male model to accompany the softer nurture of their wives. Drinking and cursing had no place at home.

Such models of domesticity did not emerge overnight, of course. The early 1820s saw only the beginnings of a crusade to make all American homes fit this model. The effort began in towns and cities, making only gradual inroads into the raw and growing countryside. It was stronger in the Northeast than in the South and in the West. Working-class families could not afford this idealized model even if they wanted to follow its example. Women who had to work for others all day had little time to devote to their own families. Women who worked in their own homes mingled the market and the household in a way the creators of the domestic ideal deplored. Men who could not be certain of their next day's wages could not afford to keep children out of the workforce into their late teens. Slave families struggled to stay together in any way they could and could only imagine what it might be like to live in the homes held up as ideal in these years. Nevertheless, that ideal was celebrated and elaborated with each passing year, growing along with the booming towns and cities of the North.

Stirrings of Reform

The same Americans who promoted the Christian, middle-class home as their ideal looked to other institutions and reforms in the early 1820s to help remake

Penal reformers placed great faith in silence, order, and work, helping put the United States in the forefront of the growing penitentiary movement.

American society. They sought to extend the ideals of character, self-control, and education to those who seemed to fall beyond the good effects of family and household. Reformers tapped the domestic impulses of improvement for the society as a whole.

The Panic of 1819 and its aftermath made a deep impression on many town and city dwellers. Wherever they looked in those years, they saw hungry children, desperate fathers, and distraught mothers. They noticed increasing numbers of women selling themselves on the city streets. They decried bulging jails and streets full of people without homes. They worried over the many young men and women who seemed adrift in this rootless new society.

Activist people in the Northeast sought to counter these problems. Some of their efforts grew out of the churches, while others grew out of the ideals of the American Revolution and the marketplace. The churches launched an ambitious drive to put Bibles in every American home, distributing a million Bibles each year. The American Sunday School Union, formed in 1824, wrote and published materials for children to be used in Sunday schools across the country. Those schools, while based in churches, taught reading and writing as well as religion. They

put the churches at the center of community life, giving children beyond the reach of traditional schooling a chance to learn some of the skills and attitudes necessary for spiritual and economic success. The American Tract Society, created in 1825, produced millions of short inspirational pamphlets to reach those who might not set foot in a church or pick up a Bible. The new organizations prided themselves on being national in reach, extending to the Northwest and Southwest, knitting Americans together with a common faith. They preached nothing controversial, claiming only to spread the good news of the Protestant Christian faith. They depended on the hard work of women, who filled the membership rolls and helped raise funds.

Another reform movement of these years took a different kind of strategy. While the idea of the penitentiary had been discussed in Europe and the United States for several decades, support for that institution grew quickly after 1819. In a penitentiary, unlike a common jail, criminals would be locked in individual cells, free from the contamination of others, alone with their conscience and the Bible. There, reflecting on their crimes, they would become "penitent" and would emerge as better people. They would undergo

some of the moral nurture they had obviously missed as children and would be ready to take their place in the economy of wages, self-discipline, and delayed gratification growing in the United States.

The most prominent penitentiaries were built in New York and Pennsylvania between 1819 and 1829. Reformers argued over whether prisoners should be isolated at all times, the Philadelphia model, or whether they might be allowed to work together in silence, as they did at Auburn in New York. In either case, Americans were proud of their penitentiaries, among the first in the world, holding them up as examples of what the enlightened new nation could do. Almost every state in the nation, South as well as North, soon built its own penitentiary.

Alongside those institutions appeared other buildings designed to house other kinds of people who could not keep up with rapidly changing American society. Asylums for the deaf and blind, for the insane, for orphans, and for the poor began to appear in the 1820s, replacing more informal kinds of care. Each institution placed its faith in strict order, in moral teaching, and in faith in the inherent good of human nature. The results were not immediately apparent—indeed, many of the inmates of every kind of asylum resisted and protested—but the hope endured.

Reformers launched one other crusade in the 1810s and 1820s, one that many thought might make all the other reforms effective. Many people, religious and otherwise, saw alcohol as the scourge of American life. "You cannot go into hardly any man's house," an English visitor wrote in 1819, "without being asked to drink wine, or spirits, even in the morning." Men drank at work, farmers routinely turned their grain into whiskey, and rum was a major part of New England commerce. Everyone knew the costs of such drinking and groups around the country mobilized locally to slow the drinking, to be more "temperant" in their use of ardent spirits.

The temperance movement slowly stewed until 1825, when Lyman Beecher, a prominent minister delivered and then published six stirring sermons. Beecher argued that temperance was not enough, that only complete abstinence would remove the stain of alcohol from the United States. Drinkers must make a total and immediate break with their addiction. The next year supporters of abstinence formed the American Temperance Society and adopted the strategies of the American Bible Society, spreading the crusade among the Protestant churches of the country. Thou-sands joined, women as well as men, foreshadowing a flood of activity over the next century.

～ CONCLUSION ～

The United States saw enormous economic change between 1815 and 1826. As embargo and war ended, as the new nation's armies conquered and contained diverse peoples among the Native Americans, new states in both the Southwest and the Northwest pushed into the national and international economies. Cotton flowed out of Alabama and Mississippi in ever-growing amounts while food flowed from Indiana and Illinois. Banks proliferated with the expanding population and the Second Bank of the United States lent stability to the system. The major ports along the east coast grew as they had never grown before, connecting the expanding United States with the economies of England and Europe. New factory buildings went up along the streams and rivers of Massachusetts, Connecticut, Rhode Island, and Pennsylvania, producing by water power what hands had made only a few years earlier. Turnpikes and roads covered the country in an increasingly dense network. Coming on the heels of the Treaty of Ghent, such change seemed to mark the beginning of a new kind of security and prosperity for the United States.

The completion of the Erie Canal in 1825 demonstrated that Americans could accomplish great things. The constructors of the canal, bragged one speaker, "have built the longest canal, in the least time, with the least experience, for the least money and to the greatest public benefit." Soon after De Witt Clinton ceremoniously poured water from Lake Erie into the Atlantic, thousands of boats were traveling along the canal between Buffalo and New York City, pumping half a million dollars of tolls into the state coffers, sending a surge of prosperity along its route. Other states, busy with their own plans and excavations, looked enviously upon the glorious Erie Canal.

Accompanying this rapid expansion of boundaries of every sort, however, grew considerable anxiety that American society threatened to spin out of control. The government held little power and people worried that many Americans had moved beyond the influence of church, family, school, or employer. The centrifugal forces of the society threatened to pull it apart. No sooner had the postwar boom begun than some Americans began to suggest ways to contain the

consequences of change. They offered political compromise, reform societies, and new ideals of the home as ways to counteract what they saw as chaos. But no one expected things to remain settled for long.

RECOMMENDED READINGS

Cashin, Joan E. *A Family Venture: Men and Women on the Southern Frontier* (1991) tells the story of the southwestern migration in a compelling way.

Davis, David Brion. *The Problem of Slavery in the Age of Revolution, 1770–1823* (1975) gives a magisterial overview of the international struggles with slavery.

Horwitz, Morton J. *The Transformation of American Law, 1780–1860* (1977) puts forward a strong and controversial argument about the law and commerce.

Mathews, Jean. *Toward a New Society: American Thought and Culture, 1800–1830* (1990) offers a subtle interpretation of cultural history of this period.

May, Ernest. *The Making of the Monroe Doctrine* (1976) is a solid overview.

Dangerfield, George. *The Awakening of American Nationalism, 1815–1828* (1965) is a classic interpretation of the postwar era.

Freehling, William W. *The Road to Disunion: The Secessionists at Bay, 1776–1854* (1990) portrays the drama of sectional conflict throughout this era.

Sellers, Charles G. *The Market Revolution: Jacksonian America, 1815–1846* (1991) offers a stirring portrayal of the period with economic change at the center.

Sheriff, Carol. *The Artificial River: The Erie Canal and the Paradox of Progress, 1817–1862* (1996) gives a compelling account of the canal's origins, building, and effects.

Rohrbough, Malcolm J. *The Trans-Appalachian Frontier: People, Societies, and Institutions, 1775–1850* (1978) tells this complex story well.

Public Affairs
Fehrenbacher, Don. *The South and Three Sectional Crises* (1980).

Hargreaves, Mary W. M. *The Presidency of John Quincy Adams* (1985).

Moore, Glover. *The Missouri Controversy, 1818–1821* (1953).

Nagel, Paul C. *John Quincy Adams: A Public Life, a Private Life* (1997).

Peterson, Merrill. *The Great Triumvirate: Webster, Clay, and Calhoun* (1989).

Robinson, Donald L. *Slavery in the Structure of American Politics, 1765–1820* (1971).

Young, James Sterling. *The Washington Community, 1800–1828* (1966).

Economic and Legal Change
Bruchey, Stuart. *Enterprise: The Dynamic Economy of a Free People* (1990).

Cochran, Thomas C. *Frontiers of Change: Early Industrialism in America* (1981).

Dublin, Thomas. *Transforming Women's Work: New England Lives in the Industrial Revolution* (1994).

Faulkner, Robert K. *The Jurisprudence of John Marshall* (1968).

Shaw, Ronald E. *Erie Water West: A History of the Erie Canal, 1792–1854* (1966).

Steinberg, Theodore. *Nature Incorporated: Industrialization and the Waters of New England* (1991).

Taylor, George R. *The Transportation Revolution, 1815–1860* (1951).

White, G. Edward. *The Marshall Court and Cultural Change, 1815–1835* (1991).

American Indians
Green, Michael D. *The Politics of Indian Removal: Creek Government and Society in Crisis* (1982).

Finger, John R. *The Eastern Band of Cherokees, 1819–1900* (1984).

McLoughlin, William G. *Cherokee Renascence in the New Republic* (1986).

Perdue, Theda. *Slavery and the Evolution of Cherokee Society, 1540–1866* (1979).

Perdue, Theda. *Cherokee Women: Gender and Culture Change, 1700–1835* (1998).

Washburn, Wilcomb. *The Indian in America* (1975).

Wright, J. Leitch, Jr. *Creeks and Seminoles: The Destruction and Regeneration of the Muscogee People* (1986).

Westward Movement
Atack, Jeremy and Bateman, Fred. *To Their Own Soil: Agriculture in the Antebellum North* (1987).

Bartless, Richard A. *The New Country: A Social History of the American Frontier, 1776–1890* (1974).

Faragher, John Mack. *Sugar Creek: Life on the Illinois Prairie* (1986).

Moore, John Hebron. *The Emergence of the Cotton Kingdom in the Old Southwest: Mississippi, 1790–1860* (1988).

Tadman, Michael. *Speculators and Slaves: Masters, Traders, and Slaves in the Old South* (1989).

Wade, Richard C. *The Urban Frontier: The Rise of Western Cities, 1790–1830* (1964).

Lafayette's Visit
Somkin, Fred. *Unquiet Eagle: Memory and Desire in the Idea of American Freedom, 1815–1860* (1967).

Loveland, Anne. *Emblem of Liberty: The Image of Lafayette in the American Mind* (1971).

Early Reform

Andrew John A., III. *From Revivals to Removal: Jeremiah Evarts, the Cherokee Nation, and the Search for the Soul of America* (1992).

Hirsch, Adam J. *The Rise of the Penetentiary: Prisons and Punishment in Early America* (1992).

Meranze, Michael. *Laboratories of Virtue: Punishment, Revolution, and Authority in Philadelphia, 1760–1835* (1996).

PRESIDENT ANDREW JACKSON

Andrew Jackson of Tennessee seemed to many people an inspiring leader. Others, however, saw him as a "military chieftain" dangerous with the power of the presidency.

Chapter 10

THE YEARS OF ANDREW JACKSON: 1827–1836

Tumultuous change came to the United States in the years Andrew Jackson served as president. Elections became broad public events that involved men of every class. Voters and leaders hotly debated and contested the role of government in American life. Religious revivals swept up entire communities in devotion and prayer. Working people created labor unions and abolitionists launched a bold crusade against slavery.

Growing democracy was not the full story of these years, however. The people of the Creek, Choctaw, Cherokee, Seminole, Sac, and Fox nations were driven from their homes in the South and in the old Northwest. A crisis threatened to ignite a military struggle between South Carolina and the federal government. The revolt of Nat Turner and debates over slavery in Virginia unleashed a proslavery reaction throughout much of the South. The defeat of Mexico in Texas opened a vast new territory to slavery as well as to the settlement of free Americans. Few decades in American history witnessed more important and more sweeping changes.

THE TRANSFORMATION OF AMERICAN POLITICS

John Quincy Adams had been elected in a fractious election that cast politics in a poor light. The squabbling of leading men over votes in the electoral college seemed clear evidence that the age of the Revolutionary leaders had passed and that a less worthy age had taken its place. As people called for a more democratic kind of politics, states across the Union lowered property requirements for voting and made judges elected rather than appointed officials. Voters seemed restless, hungry for someone to give direction and force to public life. Such a man emerged, along with a new kind of politics.

The Adams Twilight

The second half of John Quincy Adams's administration proved unhappy and unproductive. Neither

CHRONOLOGY

1828	Tariff of Abominations
	Calhoun's *Exposition*
	Election of Jackson
1829	David Walker's *Appeal*
	Mexico tries to abolish slavery in Texas
1830	Indian Removal Act
	The Book of Mormon
	Finney's revivals begin in Rochester
	Anti-Masonic party holds first national party convention
1831	Nat Turner's rebellion
	Garrison's *The Liberator*
	Jackson reorganizes cabinet, Van Buren over Calhoun
	Mormons migrate from New York to Ohio
1832	Bank War begins
	Nullification Crisis
	Virginia debates over slavery
	Jackson reelected

1833	Formation of American Anti-slavery Society
	Force Bill against South Carolina
	Compromise Tariff
	Slavery abolished in British Empire
1834	Whig party organized
	National Trades Union formed
1835	Arkansas admitted to the Union
	Revolution breaks out in Texas
	Abolitionists' postal campaign
	War against Seminoles and runaway slaves in Florida
1836	Congress imposes gag rule
	Texas Republic established; Battle of the Alamo
	Treaty of New Echota
	Election of Martin Van Buren

Adams's talents and devotion to the Union had faded, but the public mood seemed little interested in either. The "corrupt bargain," in which Henry Clay allegedly conspired to hand the presidency to Adams, still hung over the White House in 1827. In the eyes of many, Adams had proven himself unfit for office, not only with his reputed bargain, but also, false rumor persisted, by procuring a young American girl for the czar when Adams served as a fourteen-year-old member of the U.S. diplomatic corps in St. Petersburg. The president's elite education and even his purchase of a billiard table and chess set for the White House made him a symbol of "aristocracy." Adams's many and diverse opponents organized against him and his policies almost from the beginning of his administration. It soon became clear that the president would be able to accomplish little of his ambitious agenda of internal improvements, a national university, and western ex-

ploration, ideals that might have won support in earlier years.

Supporters of Andrew Jackson of Tennessee, John C. Calhoun of South Carolina, and William Crawford of Georgia gradually joined forces in anticipation of the election of 1828, when they hoped to unseat Adams and his vision of an active and centralized government. The struggle, Calhoun wrote to Jackson, was between "*power* and *liberty.*" The champion of power had had his turn, Adams's opponents believed; now it was time for the champions of liberty to step forward. After some jockeying, Andrew Jackson emerged as the man to challenge Adams.

Adams supporters warned of the dangers of electing a raw and rough "military chieftain" such as Andrew Jackson to the presidency. Jackson's opponents distributed a handbill marked with eighteen coffins, each one representing a man Jackson had supposedly killed in a

Mrs. Jackson found herself the center of a humiliating scandal as her husband ran for president in 1828. She died soon after the election—the victim, her husband felt certain, of gossip mongers.

duel or ordered executed under his military command. The most incendiary charge, however, was that Jackson had married a woman married to another man, leading her to commit both bigamy and adultery in the process. The facts of the case were unclear—it appears that Rachel Jackson was a religious woman, trapped in a bad marriage, who thought she had received a divorce when she married Jackson—but the anti-Jackson forces made the most of any suspicions to the contrary.

Antimasons

Charges of conspiracy and corruption raged throughout American politics in the 1820s. Some of the suspicions seemed confirmed by events in New York. As the economy of that state prospered along with the Erie Canal, so did fraternal organizations of every sort. The Ancient Order of Masons did especially well, claiming almost 350 lodges in the state. The Masons' exclusive society, surrounded by elaborate ritual and strict secrecy, many non-Masons felt, contradicted American ideals of democracy and openness, taking men away from their families and undermining organized religion. Since Masons were obliged to show business or political preference to a brother over "any other person

in the same circumstances," some of those outside the order feared that Masons might win undue influence in their town, state, or country. As proof, they pointed out that every New York governor but one between 1804 and the late 1820s belonged to the Masons.

Suspicion of the Masons exploded when a brother named William Morgan turned against the order and decided to publish its secret rituals. Local Masonic leaders used their influence with county officials to harass and jail Morgan, who was later kidnapped. He disappeared; many said he had been murdered. The investigation soon stalled, however, as Masonic law enforcement officers and others dragged their feet. Despite twenty trials and three special prosecutors, only a few convictions resulted and those convictions brought only minor jail terms. Fury against the Masons soon spread from New York to the rest of the country, forcing one lodge after another to dissolve.

By 1827, nearly a hundred "Morgan committees" had met and formed in New York and began to spread across the entire northern half of the country. The

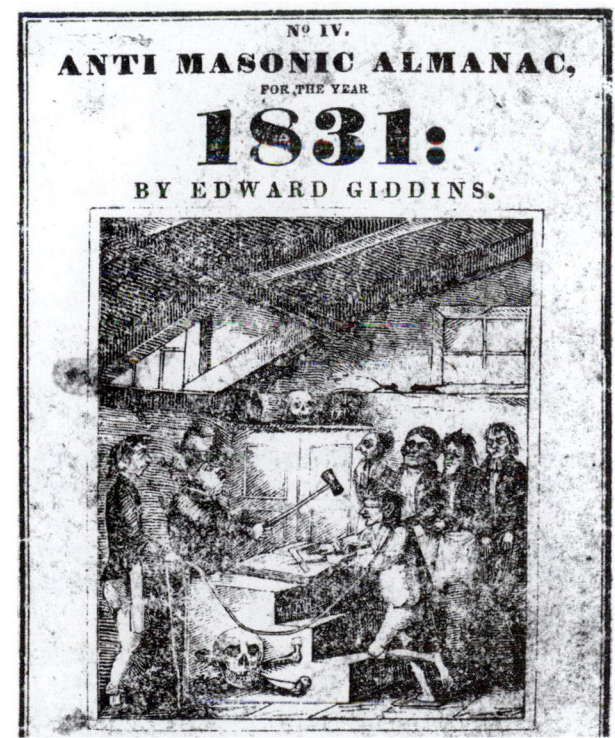

Titillating depictions of the supposed Masonic rituals marked a flood of publications from the Antimasons in the late 1820s and early 1830s.

cess, in fact, that the movement's leaders dreamed of creating a new party to purify and energize American politics.

Birth of the Democrats

Even while the struggle over the Masons unfolded, Senator Martin Van Buren of New York was building a political coalition behind Andrew Jackson. Van Buren traveled throughout the United States, hammering out a new coalition of ambitious state politicians willing to back Jackson. The members of the coalition called themselves "Democratic Republicans," eventually to be shortened to "Democrats." Their candidates did extremely well in the off-year congressional elections of 1827, exploiting people's disapproval of the ineffectual Adams administration. The Democrats controlled both the House and the Senate.

Throughout 1827 and 1828, Van Buren and the other party leaders organized voters as they had never been organized before. Although Jackson himself was a prominent Mason, Van Buren adopted techniques not unlike those pioneered by the Antimasons in these same years. Using every strategy at their disposal—bonfires, speeches, barbecues, parades, professional writers, and the first campaign song—these Jacksonians claimed that they had found a true man of the people to strip the office from the aristocratic Adams. In towns across the country, "Old Hickory"—Jackson was supposedly as tough as that toughest of trees—was celebrated with hickory poles, brooms, sticks, and trees. The National Republicans, as Adams supporters became known, sniffed at what they considered the unseemly display that diverted attention from real issues, but they could not deny the power of the new methods to win voters' attention.

Voting turnout in 1828 doubled that of the 1824 election. The dramatic confrontation of men and styles contributed to widespread voter interest, while politicians at every level and on both sides made sure

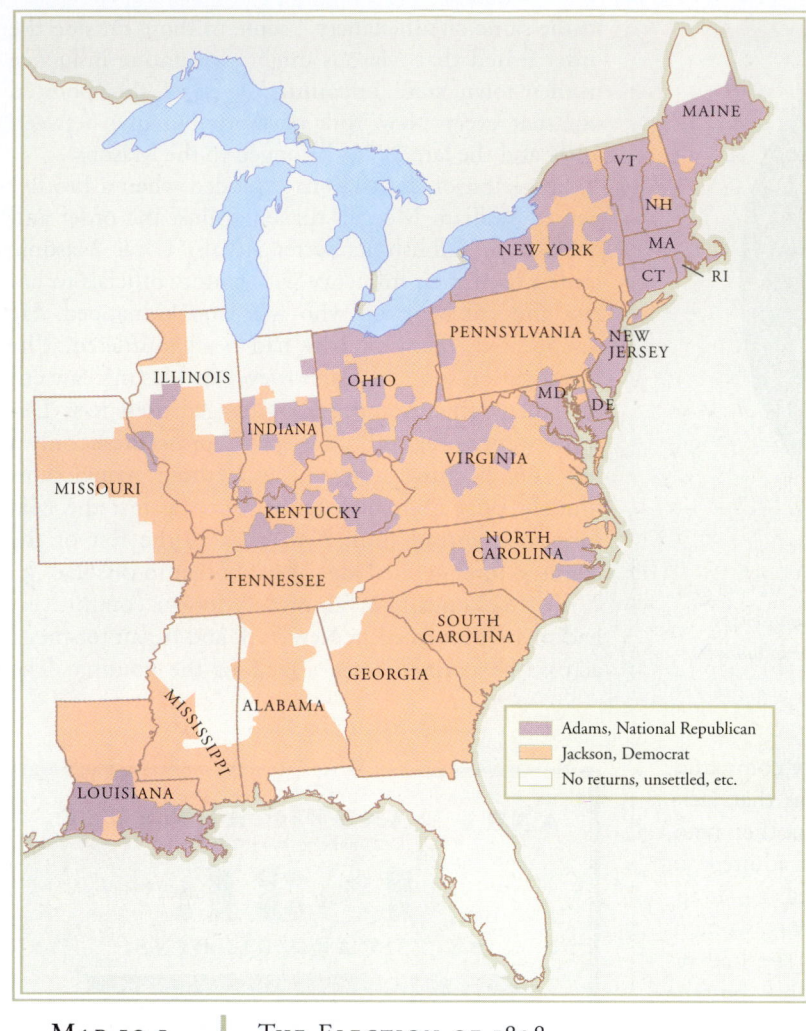

MAP 10.1 | THE ELECTION OF 1828

Legend on map:
- Adams, National Republican
- Jackson, Democrat
- No returns, unsettled, etc.

movement gathered around it much of the anger and many of the anxieties of people who resented the growing power of merchants, manufacturers, lawyers, and a new class of professional politicians. Within two years, the "Antimasons" had established more than a hundred newspapers. They held public meetings and launched lobbying campaigns, bypassing local elites and inventing new means of pressuring legislatures directly. Unlike earlier reform organizations, such as those that supported Sunday schools and the distribution of Bibles, the Antimasons thrived on controversy. They devoted themselves to changing public opinion, to mobilizing people against a powerful entrenched force. They succeeded: Masonry lost more than half its members and created virtually no new lodges for the next fifteen years. So great was the Antimasons' suc-

voters went to the polls. Jackson won easily over Adams, capturing the critical mid-Atlantic states and all the states of the South except Louisiana and Kentucky. The election proved bittersweet for Jackson, though, for his wife died soon afterward. Jackson blamed the slanderers of the other party for Rachel's death, for she had fallen ill after seeing an editorial denouncing her. The president-elect passed the weeks before his inauguration in sadness and bitterness.

The People's President

Andrew Jackson, still dressed in black in mourning for Rachel, traveled by steamboat from Nashville to Washington in the winter of 1829 to begin his presidency. Ensconced in a hotel suite, Jackson assembled his cabinet, balancing North, South, and West. Van Buren, to no one's surprise, became secretary of state, a position traditionally reserved for the man next in line for the presidency. Vice President Calhoun, ambitious for the

presidency himself, chafed at the appointment but could do little to change it; he and his wing of the party had to satisfy themselves with the appointment of one of their number as secretary of the Treasury. The most controversial appointment, however, proved volatile for reasons that had little to do with political partisanship. Jackson wanted a close friend in the cabinet, someone in whom he could confide, and he chose an old Tennessee associate, John Eaton, as his secretary of war.

Eaton, a widower in middle age, had married Peggy O'Neal Timberlake, an attractive and witty twenty-nine-year-old daughter of a well-known innkeeper in Washington. She was rumored to have driven her last husband to suicide, forcing him to defraud the government to pay debts she had run up. She was also rumored to have had sex with Eaton before their marriage—along with, one contemporary smirked, "eleven doz. others!" Eaton had asked Jackson's opinion of the marriage beforehand, receiving the old general's blessing; the president liked outspoken women

The young wife of Secretary of War John Eaton became the center of a scandal that rocked Washington during Andrew Jackson's first term.

In a scene that soon grew legendary, celebrants at Jackson's inauguration overwhelmed the capacity of the White House to contain their numbers or their rambunctiousness.

and knew from bitter experience the power that unfounded rumors could hold. Jackson, in a gesture of friendship and support as the gossip flew, offered Eaton the cabinet position, apparently hoping he would decline. Unfortunately for Jackson, Eaton accepted. The decision electrified Washington.

Despite his rambunctious youth, Jackson disdained official Washington's fondness for strong drink, endless banquets, and overheated social life. He had witnessed that high life during his time as senator from Tennessee and he held it in contempt when he returned to the capital; he preferred instead to attend the city's churches. Jackson considered himself an outsider despite his power and popularity, an outsider determined to reform Washington, to make the city worthy of the nation it was supposed to serve.

As the inauguration day of March 4 neared, Washington's population doubled as men who considered themselves important in General Jackson's election arrived in the city to claim their fair share of glory, excitement, and jobs. They drank all the whiskey the city had to offer, slept five to a bed, and generally offended the more genteel residents of the capital. At the inauguration, 30,000 people crowded in to see the new president. After Jackson's brief address, members of the excited audience followed him back to the

White House—as one observer put it, "country men, farmers, gentlemen mounted and dismounted, boys, women and children, black and white, carriages, waggons and carts all pursuing him." They surged into the White House, spilling barrels of orange punch, standing with muddy boots on expensive chairs to get a better look at the proceedings, smashing thousands of dollars worth of china. Servants attracted the mob outside by moving the liquor. Jackson, literally suffocated by admirers and disgusted by the scene, climbed out a rear window and went for a steak at his boardinghouse.

Jackson Takes Charge

Many people in Washington were as appalled at the events that followed the inauguration as they were with the inauguration itself. As the new administration got under way, Jackson and his advisors cleaned house in the federal government, removing those officials whose competence, honesty, or loyalty to Jackson and the Democrats were suspect. While such a policy had become established practice in several major states, including Van Buren's New York, Jackson was the first president to make such sweeping changes on

the federal level. He envisioned himself purging an arrogant bureaucracy of corruption, establishing the democratic practice of "rotation in office." As officeholders quaked and fretted, Jackson's lieutenants decided which custom houses and federal offices would be cleansed. Some of the incumbents clearly deserved to lose their jobs, having served jail terms, embezzled funds, or succumbed to drink, but others were guilty only of being active partisans for the other side in the recent election.

Jackson removed about 900 of 10,000 men from their offices and removed them in an especially brash spirit. One Jackson supporter unwisely announced to the Senate that the Jacksonians saw "nothing wrong in the rule that to the victors belong the spoils of the enemy." This proclamation gave an enduring notoriety to what from then on would be called the "spoils" system, a system that Jackson envisioned as reform, not cynical politics. Jackson further infuriated opponents by appointing partisan newspaper editors to important posts, leading to charges that Jackson was corrupting rather than cleansing American government. One key appointment, the collector of the Port of New York, did indeed prove disastrous, as the man eventually fled the United States with $1.2 million of the people's money. Yet over the course of Jackson's two terms he replaced only about 10 percent of all officeholders, not many more than his predecessors had. As with so much else in the Jackson administration, symbolism seemed to count as much as anything.

The festering conflict within the administration over the so-called "Eaton affair" proved just how important matters of symbolism could be. The wives of the other cabinet members, Vice President Calhoun's wife, and even Emily Donelson—Jackson's daughter-in-law and hostess of the White House—refused to be in the same room with Peggy Eaton. But Jackson would not be swayed in his support for John and Peggy Eaton. The new cabinet found itself bitterly divided between pro-Eaton and anti-Eaton factions. Jackson labored to mend fences, calling an influential pastor to the White House and trying to find evidence to prove Mrs. Eaton's virtue. Nothing proved effective, though, and Jackson decided that the real villain of the story was Vice President Calhoun and his unbending wife Floride. By contrast, Martin Van Buren, a widower, cemented his friendship with the president by treating Mrs. Eaton with ostentatious respect. Jackson, embittered by the refusal of his other advisors to stand by Mrs. Eaton, largely abandoned his official cabinet and relied instead on an informal group of advisors, his so-called "kitchen cabinet," and on Van Buren, the only winner in the Eaton episode.

Though Andrew Jackson saw his cleansing of federal officeholders as a reform, many critics saw it only as thinly disguised greed.

STRUGGLES OVER SLAVERY

The years around 1830 saw several issues surrounding slavery come to a head. Southern states, worried about the rapidly growing population and power of the North, sought to define the limits of federal power. Feeling themselves neglected and abused by northern interests, South Carolina leaders tried to secure greater autonomy. At the same time, free blacks in both the

North and South worked to replace the colonization movement with a campaign to end slavery and create freedom for African Americans in America. Even as these public struggles unfolded, the largest slave revolt in the history of the United States erupted in Virginia. Combined, these events demonstrated that slavery and the issues on which it touched would bedevil the confident and boisterous young country.

Nullification

Before the election, Martin Van Buren and other Democrats had sought to broaden support for Jackson, whose strength lay in the South, by passing a tariff favorable to the economic interests of New Englanders and westerners. After elaborate deal making, the Democrats enacted a major tariff in early 1828. But it came with a high cost: Southerners were furious with what they called this "tariff of abominations," for it raised the price they would have to pay for manufactured items and threatened markets abroad for southern cotton. John C. Calhoun, like other South Carolina planters, feared not only that the tariff would bleed the state dry economically but that it would set a precedent for antislavery forces who might gain control of the federal government at some future date.

Accordingly, in the summer and early fall of 1828, a few months before he would take office as Jackson's vice president, Calhoun sought to find a principled way to reconcile his national ambitions and his local concerns. Rather than argue only against the tariff itself, Calhoun asserted the general rights of individual states within the Union. To do so, he returned to what he called "the primitive principles of our government," the foundations on which everything else rested. Calhoun insisted that interests had become so diverse in the United States that laws appropriate for one state or section might well harm another. Rather than merely letting the majority run roughshod over the minority, Calhoun believed, it made more sense to let a state "nullify" a national law within its own borders. Such nullification was constitutional, he said, because the federal system did not locate sovereignty in any one place, but rather divided it among the states and the nation. Should three-fourths of the states agree that a law must apply to all the country, then that clear majority could overrule the nullification. Calhoun thought he was finding a way to preserve order in an increasingly contentious Union. The document in

which he laid out his ideas, the *South Carolina Exposition,* appeared in December of 1828; the pamphlet was published anonymously because it was too politically dangerous for the vice president of the United States to be publicly on record for nullification.

As Calhoun's position in the Jackson administration deteriorated under the influence of the "Eaton malaria," and as white South Carolinians grew increasingly angry at their helplessness in the face of the tariff, Calhoun remained silent in public on the issue. His dreams of succeeding to the presidency seemed to hang in the balance. Meanwhile, the pressure built. In early 1830 Calhoun's handpicked spokesman, Senator Robert Hayne of South Carolina, engaged in a debate with Massachusetts Senator Daniel Webster over the power of the federal government. The debate was to remain famous for generations, the first clear conflict between the states' rights argument and the defense of what Webster called "liberty and Union, now and forever, one and inseparable." Calhoun, whose position as vice president made him the presiding head of the Senate, could only watch from the podium. Hayne made Calhoun's argument well enough, but most observers agreed that Daniel Webster dominated the debate; the Massachusetts senator's fame sky-rocketed, as people throughout the North gloried in his defense of the Union. Calhoun could not remain in the background much longer; he would have to make his position known.

Calhoun's declaration of principles came at a celebration of Thomas Jefferson's birthday at the Indian Queen Hotel in Washington. Southern and western Democrats hoped that the gathering would reveal the strength of the alliance between the two sections, both of which wanted greater autonomy from the federal government. President Jackson, Vice President Calhoun, and Secretary of State Van Buren were all present. Van Buren urged the president to make clear his own position on nullification and states' rights. No one was really sure what Jackson thought on the issue, since he was identified as a Southerner but had made his reputation fighting for the Union against the British. As the officeholders went around the table, one toast after another proclaiming the rights of the states, Jackson became ever more steely. When it was his turn, the president stood, lifted his glass, and — staring at Calhoun — pronounced words filled with a meaning obvious to those present: "Our Federal Union — it must be preserved." Van Buren climbed on a chair to see how Calhoun would respond to this

As Daniel Webster of Massachusetts speaks, Robert Hayne of South Carolina (front and center, with his hands together) listens. Vice President Calhoun, working with Hayne behind the scenes, presides. The women who fill the galleries show the fascination of the entire country with this constitutional debate. Courtesy Boston Art Commission, 1998.

rebuke. "The Union—next to our liberties the most dear," he retorted, his glass trembling, "may we all remember that it can only be preserved by respecting the rights of the states and distributing equally the benefits and burdens of the Union." There was no going back.

South Carolina planters persuaded themselves that they would have to do something soon. They watched with growing alarm as the newspapers told of the success of British abolitionists in ending slavery in the British West Indies—the place from which many white South Carolina families had come generations earlier. With the memory of Denmark Vesey's plan of 1822 and an 1829 revolt in the low country still fresh in their memory, white Carolinians felt they could display no weakness on the slavery issue. Unlike other southern states, where stark geographic differences between low country and hill country often divided voters and encouraged party differences, South Carolina witnessed broad agreement among its electorate on this crucial issue. Throughout the state, raucous

crowds gathered to call for a fight against the federal government on the tariff. Those South Carolinians who favored a more conciliatory stance toward the federal government could not generate nearly as much support for their position.

When the toasts at the Indian Queen Hotel revealed that President Jackson had no sympathy for the nullificationist position, the leaders of the movement in South Carolina were surprised and disappointed. After all, Jackson, like them, was a planter and slaveholder and would suffer economically along with the South Carolinians. While he supported the rights of the states when only their own welfare seemed to be at stake, Jackson considered the tariff to be for the good of the nation as a whole. The tariff provided money for defense and prevented federal debt. The South Carolina challenge would limit the power of the U.S. government to make law for the country in matters that transcended state boundaries. Jackson did not believe the United States could afford to permit such

divisiveness to impair its strength in the world of nations. Jackson, the old general, would tolerate no opposition on such matters.

Free Blacks and African-American Abolitionism

Even as the white leaders of South Carolina struggled to define the extent of their powers within the Union, free blacks and slaves struggled to define their freedom. The end had come gradually, fading away in New York only as elderly slaves died. Communities of several thousand free blacks had emerged in every major northern city, establishing their own churches, newspapers, school, and lodges.

Even more numerous were free African Americans in the upper South slave states, especially Maryland and Virginia. Some had been emancipated during the decades after the Revolutionary War, when slavery seemed to be dying and when the ideals of the new nation and Christianity persuaded some masters to free their slaves. Although free blacks in the upper South scattered throughout smaller towns and rural areas, they generally tended to gather in cities as they did in the North. The cities strung along the Atlantic and Gulf coasts—Norfolk, Savannah, Charleston, Mobile, and New Orleans—all contained several thousand free blacks. Outside of Louisiana, few free blacks lived in the deep South.

Free African Americans stayed in the South to be closer to family members held in slavery and because, ironically, southern cities held out greater economic opportunity than the North. Because whites deemed many jobs in the South "nigger work," below the dignity of whites, black Southerners dominated some fields of work. Black men constituted most of the barbers and teamsters, for example, while black women found work as laundresses and domestics. Free blacks in the South had to be careful, making sure that local officials kept records of their freedom, but they could acquire property and educate their children. They stayed in contact with African Americans in the North through newspapers, letters, and word passed by the many black sailors who plied the eastern seaboard.

Free blacks throughout the country debated the merits of leaving the United States altogether, as many whites encouraged them to do. The colonization movement struggled in the 1820s. Few black Americans were willing to be shipped to a place they had never seen; only about 1,400 black Americans went to Liberia in the 1820s. African Americans came to see in colonization an attack on their hard-won accomplishments in the United States, for their leaders insisted that people of color had earned a place in this country. Rather than spending moral energy and money on removing black people, they argued, Americans should work instead on making the United States a fairer place.

David Walker proved to be an important figure in this movement. Walker had lived in Charleston at the time of Denmark Vesey's conspiracy, becoming familiar with the long tradition of revolt and resistance in the Carolina low country. After the suppression of Vesey, Walker moved to Boston. There, he established a used-clothing store, one of the few businesses open to African Americans in the North. Walker did well in the business, bought a home, joined the African Methodist church, and became a black Mason, an organization that fought against slavery and the slave trade. He gave his support to *Freedom's Journal,* an anticolonization paper published by black people in Boston and New York City between 1827 and 1829.

In 1829 Walker released his *Appeal to the Colored Citizens of the World.* Americans, whatever their skin color, had never read such a document. Walker denied that slaves felt or owed any bond to their masters. He called for black spiritual self-renewal, starting with African Americans' recognition of just how angry they were with their lot in the United States. They needed to channel that anger with God's love, Walker urged, making a group effort to end slavery immediately. He did not call for violence but for black Americans to be full Americans in both government and economy.

Within weeks of its publication, Walker's *Appeal* appeared in Savannah, where it was seized, and then in Milledgeville, Georgia (the state capital), then in Virginia, North Carolina, South Carolina, and New Orleans. The *Appeal* created panic and repression wherever it appeared. Southern whites worried at this evidence of invisible networks of communication and resistance among the slaves, free blacks, and, perhaps, sympathetic whites in their midst. Events in Virginia bore out their worst suspicions.

The Crisis of Slavery in Virginia

Nat Turner was a field hand, born in 1800, who felt that God had called him for more than the lot of a

slave. Well known even in his youth for his intellectual abilities and his effectiveness as a preacher, on Sundays Turner traveled throughout the countryside around Southampton County, Virginia, coming to know most of the slaves and free black people who lived there. Praying and fasting, Turner saw visions: drops of blood that formed hieroglyphics on leaves, black shadows across the white moon. These things, he became certain, foretold a slave revolt, of the time "fast approaching when the first should be last and the last should be first." Turner, unlike Gabriel in Richmond in 1800 and Vesey in Charleston in 1822, chose to build his revolt around a small group of select lieutenants rather than to risk spreading the word broadly. Their plan was to begin the rebellion on their own and then attract compatriots along the way.

On August 22, 1831, Turner and his band began their revolt. They moved from one isolated farmhouse to the next, killing all the whites they found inside, including children. They gathered horses and weapons. Turner rode at the end of the group, praying for guidance on what plan they should follow. As the night went on, Turner's men had killed about seventy people, starting with the family of Turner's master. By morning, word had rushed to Richmond of the unimaginable events in Southampton. Whites huddled together in Jerusalem, the county seat, and troops arrived to put down the revolt. Blacks, many of whom had no connection with the rebellion, were killed by infuriated and frightened whites hundreds of miles away from Southampton. Turner's troops were all captured or killed, but he managed to escape and to hide in the woods of the county for two months. Once captured, Turner narrated a remarkable "confession" in which he told of his visions and prophecies. He had no regrets and no doubts that God would stand in judgment of the people who held other people in slavery. At his hanging in November, he showed no signs of remorse.

White Southerners saw in Nat Turner their worst nightmares. Here was a literate slave, allowed to travel on his own, allowed to spread his own interpretation of the Bible to dissatisfied slaves eager to listen to Turner's prophecies. The crackdown was not long in coming, as delegates to the state assembly gathered in Richmond a month after Turner's execution. In a series of remarkable debates, these white Virginians, some of them sons and grandsons of Thomas Jefferson, John Marshall, and Patrick Henry, openly admitted the debilitating effect of slavery on Virginia. They worried most about slavery's influence on whites, worried that slavery kept the economy from developing as it did in the North. Delegates from western Virginia, where relatively few slaves lived, expressed their

Nat Turner launched the largest slave revolt in the history of the United States, assembling a devoted band of lieutenants who kept secret the plans of the revolt.

DAVID WALKER,
*APPEAL . . . TO THE
COLORED CITIZENS OF
THE WORLD* (1829)

David Walker, a free black man, argues with Thomas Jefferson's assertion that slavery in the United States was more benign and beneficial than in ancient Greece and Rome, places to which educated Americans looked for the measure of true civilization. In Walker's eyes, the connection between the ancients and modern whites shows a strain of cruelty that runs throughout the history of western culture. He attacks the un-Christian behavior of slavetraders and slaveholders even as he looks to God for ultimate judgment.

I have been for years troubling the pages of historians to find out what our fathers have done to the *white Christians of America,* to merit such condign punishment as they have inflicted on them, and do continue to inflict on us their children. But I must aver, that my researches have hitherto been to no effect. I have therefore come to the immovable conclusion, that they (Americans) have, and do continue to punish us for nothing else, but for enriching them and their country. For I cannot conceive of any thing else. Nor will I ever believe otherwise until the Lord shall convince me.

The world knows, that slavery as it existed among the Romans, (which was the primary cause of their destruction) was, comparatively speaking, no more than a *cypher,* when compared with ours under the Americans. Indeed, I should not have noticed the Roman slaves, had not the very learned and penetrating Mr. Jefferson said, "When a master was murdered, all his slaves in the same house or within hearing, were condemned to death." — Here let me ask Mr. Jefferson, (but he is gone to answer at the bar of God, for the deeds done in his body while living,) I therefore ask the whole American

misgivings most freely, but even large slaveholders from the East admitted slavery's negative effects. Petitions flowed into Richmond urging the legislators to take a decisive step to rid Virginia of slavery. Defenders of slavery warned that the debates, published in the newspapers and discussed on the streets and in the shops and homes across the state, might result in more revolts. Enslaved Virginians were not an "ignorant herd of Africans," one delegate warned, but an "active, intelligent class, watching and weighing every movement of the Legislature, with perfect knowledge of its bearing and effect."

Some delegates urged that the state purchase all slaves born after a certain date—1840 was proposed—and colonize them in Africa or sell them to plantations farther south. Others argued that the state could not afford such a step, that the Virginia economy would collapse without slavery, that slaves born before the date of freedom would revolt, that property rights guaranteed in the Constitution made it ridiculous to talk about taking slaves from their owners. Others went much further, arguing that slavery was not wrong at all but rather God's plan for civilizing Africans otherwise lost to heathenism and barbarism. The disparate regions of Virginia found themselves in deep conflict; some discussed separating themselves from the rest of the state if one policy or another were followed. The lawmakers, starkly divided, ultimately decided that it was "inexpedient" to take any step at all against slavery at that time, that it would be left for subsequent legislatures to begin the process that would free Virginia from slavery. In the meantime, they

people, had I not rather die, or be put to death than to be a slave to any tyrant, who takes not only my own, but my wife and children's lives by the inches? Yea, would I meet death with avidity far! far!! in preference to such *servile submission* to the murderous hands of tyrants. Mr. Jefferson's very severe remarks on us have been so extensively argued upon by men whose attainments in literature, I shall never be able to reach, that I would not have meddled with it, were it not to solicit each of my brethren, who has the spirit of a man, to buy a copy of Mr. Jefferson's "Notes on Virginia," and put it in the hand of his son. For let no one of us suppose that the refutations which have been written by our white friends are enough—they are *whites*—we are *blacks.* We, and the world wish to see the charges of Mr. Jefferson refuted by the blacks *themselves,* according to their chance: for we must remember that what the whites have written respecting this subject, is other men's labors and did not emanate from the blacks. I know well, that there are some talents and learning among the colored people of this country, which we have not a chance to develop, in consequence of oppression; but our oppression ought not to hinder us from acquiring all we can.—For we will have a chance to develop them by and by. God will not suffer us, always to be oppressed. Our sufferings will come to an *end,* in spite of all the Americans this side of *eternity.* Then we will want all the learning and talents among ourselves, and perhaps more, to govern ourselves.—"Every dog must have its day," the American's is coming to an end.

But let us review Mr. Jefferson's remarks respecting us some further. Comparing our miserable fathers, with the learned philosophers of Greece, he says: "Yet notwithstanding these and other discouaging circumstances among the Romans, their slaves were often their rarest artists. They excelled too in science, insomuch as to be usually employed as tutors to their master's children; Epictetus, Terence and Phaedrus, were slaves,—but they were of the race of whites. It is not their *condition* then, but *nature,* which has produced the distinction." See this, my brethren! ! Do you believe that this assertion is

(continued)

passed harsher laws to limit the movement and gathering of free blacks and slaves.

REVIVAL AND REFORM

The power and influence of Protestant churches surged to a new level in the Jacksonian era. Far more than in any previous generation, the Jacksonian years saw the churches take leading roles in every facet of life and in every part of the Union. Revivals pulled in scores of new members, firing them with the desire to remake their lives. Many of those who experienced the spiritual rebirth of the revivals sought ways to demonstrate their faith and their hope for America. A radical new movement against slavery gathered force with stunning speed. At the same time, other Americans sought purer forms of religion itself, listening to prophets who spoke of new churches and new possibilities. Everywhere in the late 1820s and early 1830s, religion seemed on people's lips.

Revivalism

Since the late eighteenth century, revivals led by the major Protestant denominations had periodically inflamed the United States. In those revivals, people who had never declared their faith in Jesus Christ or who had fallen away from the church made public

swallowed by millions of the whites? Do you know that Mr. Jefferson was one of as great characters as ever lived among the whites? See his writings for the world, and public labors for the United States of America. Do you believe that the assertions of such a man, will pass away into oblivion unobserved by this people and the world? If you do you are much mistaken—See how the American people treat us—have we souls in our bodies? Are we men who have any spirits at all? I know that there are many *swell-bellied* fellows among us whose greatest object is to fill their stomachs. Such I do not mean—I am after those who know and feel, that we are MEN as well as other people; to them, I say, that unless we try to refute Mr. Jefferson's arguments respecting us, we will only establish them.

But the slaves among the Romans. Every body who has read history, knows, that as soon as a slave among the Romans obtained his freedom, he could rise to the greatest eminence in the State, and there was no law instituted to hinder a slave from buying his freedom. Have not the Americans instituted laws to hinder us from obtaining our freedom? Do any deny this charge? Read the laws of Virginia, North Carolina, etc. Further: have not the Americans instituted laws to prohibit a man of color from obtaining and holding any office whatever, under the government of the United States of America? Now, Mr. Jefferson tells us that our condition is not so hard, as the slaves were under the Romans ! ! ! !

. . .

The whites have always been an unjust, jealous, unmerciful, avaricious and blood thirsty set of beings, always seeking after power and authority.—We view them all over the confederacy of Greece, where they were first known to be any thing, (in consequence of education) we see them there, cutting each other's throats—trying to subject each other to wretchedness and misery, to effect which they used all kinds of deceitful, unfair and unmerciful means. We view them next in Rome, where the spirit of tyranny and de-

expressions of their faith. Thousands of people gathered in the North, South, and West, in town and countryside, to pray and hear ministers tell them of God's love and forgiveness. Hearing of these gifts, and aware of their own sinfulness, men and women sometimes fell to the ground as if stricken. Others cried and screamed. The churches that devoted themselves to spreading the Gospel—known as "evangelical" churches because they sought to bring others to their faith in Scripture—periodically experienced revivals or "awakenings" when numbers of people expressed or renewed their faith. This revivalism burst out again in the mid-1820s.

Many ministers and churches across the country were swept up in the awakening, but one man embodied its new and aggressive spirit: Charles Grandison Finney. Finney, a young attorney from Utica, New York, who had not regularly attended church until encouraged to do so by his fiancée, in 1821 suddenly found himself struck with the power of God's love. "An overwhelming sense" of his wickedness brought Finney to his knees. "I wept aloud like a child [and] the Holy Spirit descended upon me in a manner that seemed to go through me body and soul," he recalled. "I could feel the impression like a wave of electricity, going through and through me." Finney spread the word of the Bible in the plain and straightforward language of everyday life. He told people that they had it within their power to take the first step toward God, that God would listen. Finney told people to seek out salvation, to throw themselves open to the mercy of Jesus.

ceit raged still higher.—We view them in Gaul, Spain and in Britain—in fine, we view them all over Europe, together with what were scattered about in Asia and Africa, as heathens, and we see them acting more like devils than accountable men. But some may ask, did not the blacks of Africa, and the mulattoes of Asia, go on in the same ways as did the whites of Europe? I answer no—they never were half so avaricious, deceitful and unmerciful as the whites, according to their knowledge.

But we will leave the whites or Europeans as heathens and take a view of them as christians, in which capacity we see them as cruel, if not more so than ever. In fact, take them as a body, they are ten times more cruel, avaricious, and unmerciful than ever they were; for while they were heathens they were bad enough it is true, but it is positively a fact that there were not quite so audacious as to go and take vessel loads of men, women and children, and in cold blood and through devilishness, throw them into the sea, and murder them in all kind of ways. While they were heathens, they were too ignorant for such barbarity. But being christians, enlightened and sensible, they are completely prepared for such hellish cruelties. Now suppose God were to give them more sense, what would they do. If it were possible would they not *dethrone* Jehovah and seat themselves upon his throne? I therefore, in the name and fear of the Lord God of heaven and of earth, divested of prejudice either on the side of my color or that of the whites, advance my suspicion of them, whether they are *as good by nature* as we are or not. Their actions, since they were known as a people, have been the reverse, I do indeed suspect them, but this, as I before observed, is shut up with the Lord, we cannot exactly tell, it will be proved in succeeding generations.—The whites have had the essence of the gospel as it was preached by my master and his apostles—the Ethiopians have not, who are to have it in its meridian splendor—the Lord will give it to them to their satisfaction. I hope and pray my God, that they will make good use of it, that it may be well with them.

SOURCE David Walker, *Appeal, in Four Articles; Together with a Preamble to the Colored Citizens of the World. . . .* (Boston: September 28, 1829. 3rd ed. Boston: D. Walker).

By the winter of 1825–1826 Finney found in the young cities of western New York a receptive audience among young men, on their own in a rapidly changing America, and among women of every age. The churches, these people believed, had grown cold in the hands of the established ministry and needed a revival of spirit. They wanted a Christianity of activity, of prayer meetings, of spreading the word any way they could. Finney's influence grew in strength and numbers as women prayed with one another. The district of upstate New York that lay along the path of the Erie Canal became known as "The Burned-Over District," as one revival after another surged through its towns and farms.

The revivals took on a new scale and urgency in 1830 as they ignited Rochester. Like other rapidly growing towns and cities along the Erie Canal, Rochester was ripe for revival. Many people worried that the people of the young city barely knew one another, that husbands and wives, workers and employers, rich and poor, were drifting apart. Politics appeared a morass of selfishness; alcohol seemed to drown hopes of social progress and family happiness; men seemed more concerned with their businesses, lodges, and politics than with their souls. When Finney came to town in 1830, accordingly, he was met by a populace hungry for something to stir them up, hungry for a new message.

Women's prayer groups met daily and traveled from home to home in efforts to bring the word of Jesus. Women pleaded with their husbands to listen to the Reverend Finney. Employers made it clear to the men

This engraving depicts Charles Grandison Finney's moment of conversion as he described the scene in his memoirs.

SAVED IN THE LORD'S OWN TIME AND PLACE.

who worked under them that it would be noticed whether or not they attended the revival. These efforts, combined with Finney's masterful sermons and hopeful message, transformed Rochester, bringing hundreds of people into the church who had not come before and reclaiming many who had strayed. All the Protestant denominations worked together, setting aside for a while their differences on baptism and other doctrines.

Such a powerful revival seemed evidence to many people that America could be changed by faith. As they watched saloons shut down, families brought together, and shops and stores closed while the revival was in progress, it appeared that the way was being prepared for God's kingdom on earth. If the United States could be adequately reformed, these people believed, the day of redemption could be hastened. It was up to Americans themselves to purge their country of sin, to make themselves better and then to help others see the way as well. Such faith bred a demand for immediate reforms. When the means of change lay so close at hand, only a prayer away, delay seemed a rejection of God's love.

Abolitionism

Religious ferment stirred some evangelicals to take immediate steps toward improving American society. They believed that they could help prepare the way for God's rule on earth by ridding their society of its numerous evils. While the great majority of white Northerners (and Southerners) thought Christians should seek holiness mainly in their own hearts, others were equally certain that society itself could and should be changed. To many, slavery seemed the place to start.

William Lloyd Garrison was the key person in the emergence of the new antislavery movement. Garrison

William Lloyd Garrison played a key role in persuading many Northern whites that slavery was morally wrong and should be brought to an immediate end.

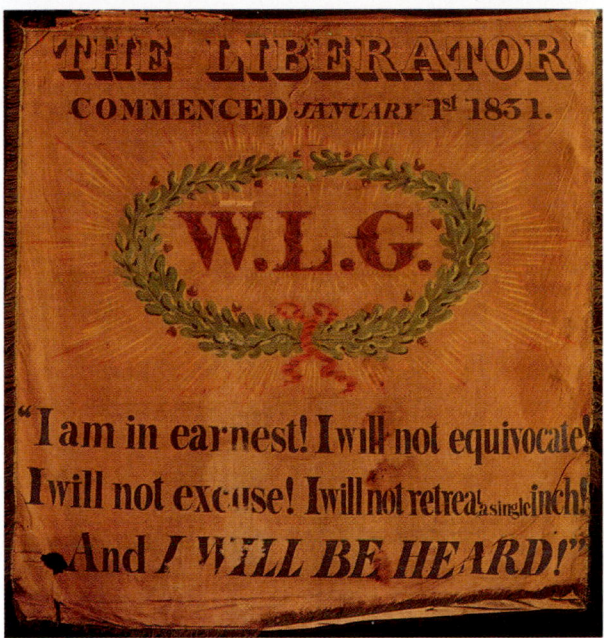

William Lloyd Garrison's abolitionist newspaper made no compromises, as this celebratory banner proclaims.

had grown up hard, abandoned as an infant by his sea captain father and apprenticed to masters in one craft after another. At twelve, he found himself working in a print shop, where he quickly achieved skill in composing type and writing. At the age of twenty-two, he became the editor of the first newspaper dedicated to the prohibition of alcohol. Believing in the necessity of ending slavery as well as drunkenness, Garrison joined the colonization movement and soon became editor of its paper as well.

In the late 1820s Garrison attended the anticolonizationist meetings held by African Americans in eastern cities, including the group that published the first antislavery newspaper, *Freedom's Journal.* He experienced a mounting desire for a more aggressive antislavery crusade as he saw the limitations of the colonization movement and as he witnessed the passion of people such as David Walker. The balding and bespectacled young Garrison sought out other financial supporters and a partner to launch a paper of his own: *The Liberator.* It called for the immediate start toward emancipation, explicitly rejecting colonization. In 1831, the paper's first year, it had only six subscribers, but it acquired fifty-three by the following year, most of them African American. "I *will* be as harsh as

truth," Garrison announced, "and as uncompromising as justice. On this subject, I do not wish to think, speak, or write, with moderation. . . . I am earnest—I will not equivocate—I will not excuse—I will not retreat a single inch—AND I WILL BE HEARD." He was.

Two hundred antislavery societies emerged in the early thirties. Ground that had been prepared by the evangelical crusades of the preceding few years proved fertile for the antislavery cause. Some northern church members argued that it was the duty of good Christians to cast out slaveholders and to work for immediate emancipation, to use the enormous power of the church as a force for freedom. These "immediatists" called for slaveholders to recognize the truth of what the abolitionists were saying, to free their slaves immediately, hire them as free workers, and help repay the former slaves for their years of unpaid toil. These early abolitionists hoped to convert the slaveholders by persuasion and prayer, by church and newspaper—not by law and force.

The American Anti-slavery Society formed in Philadelphia in 1833. Looking to the example of Great Britain, where the major denominations supported the antislavery movement that was at that moment triumphing over slavery in the British West Indies, the members of the society expected American church leaders to take the lead against American slavery. The North would have to be converted before it could expect the South to follow. To convert the North, antislavery organizations held out the prospect of a free South, where 2 million freed slaves would constitute an "immense market" for the products of Northern "mechanics and manufacturers." These abolitionists expected the former slaves to remain in the South; they spoke little of the competition the freedpeople might provide to the workers of the North. Similarly, the antislavery people believed a free South would prosper, with planters and free whites flourishing as they had never flourished before; the South, they claimed, would "exhibit the flush of returning health, and feel a stronger pulse, and draw a freer breath."

The antislavery organizations proved volatile inside as well as out. Far more than any other organizations in the United States at this time, the antislavery cause brought together male and female, black and white, patrician and working class, Quaker and Unitarian, Baptist and Methodist, radical and moderate, political and anti-political people. Each of these groups had its

own vision of how the abolitionists should spend their energies and influence. Black abolitionists, in particular, wanted the organizations to do more to help black communities in the North.

The antislavery societies used pamphlets, leaflets, and other literature as their major weapons. Rapid innovations in printing lowered the cost of producing such materials, which flooded post offices and streets. The postal campaign reached its peak in 1834 and 1835, when a million pieces went out through the mail, much of it to the South, where the abolitionists hoped to appeal directly to ministers and others who might be willing to listen to their pleas. That literature, white Southerners furiously protested, virtually invited slaves to follow Nat Turner's example. Georgia slaveholders offered a $12,000 reward for the capture of wealthy merchant Arthur Tappan, who, along with his brother Lewis, funded much of the postal campaign against slavery. Arthur received a slave's severed ear in the mail.

The pamphlets infuriated people in much of the North as well. Mobs, led by some of the wealthiest merchants of northern towns but constituted in large part by white working people, rose up violently against the abolitionists. In 1835 mobs destroyed the home of African Americans, pelted antislavery speakers, and dragged William Lloyd Garrison himself through the streets of Boston at the end of a rope. The leaders of that mob announced that they had assaulted Garrison "to assure our brethren of the South that we cherish rational and correct notions on the subject of slavery." Many white Northerners believed the abolitionists to be hypocrites who cared nothing for America and everything for their own sanctimonious souls. Antislavery speakers risked a mob every time they spoke; one man counted over 150 attacks made on him. Abolitionists' churches were blown up and their school buildings dragged into swamps.

The persecution, ironically, strengthened the abolitionist cause. Denunciation and harassment only made the abolitionists more certain of the need for their efforts, of the moral decay caused by slavery. The 200 antislavery societies of 1835 grew to over 500 in 1836. The reformers flooded Congress with petitions calling for the end of slavery in the District of Columbia, sending over 300 petitions signed by 40,000 people. The acceptance of these petitions by the House, Southerners argued, besmirched slaveholders' honor and threatened to incite slaves to rebellion. The petitions should be rejected out of hand. Congress sought to avoid conflict by merely tabling the petitions, but

the compromise pleased no one. Over the next decade, Northerners of even a mild antislavery bent chafed at this "gag rule," what they saw as a clear violation of American freedom in the interests of slavery.

The Birth of Mormonism

Like so many American families of these years, that of Joseph Smith could not find a secure place. His father dreamed of bringing his family out of poverty, moving them from one community to another. Young Joseph, like hundreds of other people in upstate New York, looked for treasure rumored to have been buried long ago in the mountains; he watched with concern for his soul, too, as revivals came and went without his conversion. Smith reported that he felt the presence of an angel, however, who told him "that God had work for me to do, and that my name should be for good and evil among all nations, kindreds, and tongues. He said there was a book deposited, written upon gold plates, giving an account of the former inhabitants of this continent, and the source from which they sprang. He also said that, the fullness of the everlasting Gospel was contained in it." Smith claimed that the angel directed him to the location of the sacred writings.

In 1827, Smith began to transcribe what he had found; sitting in a tent divided by a partition, he read the plates to an assistant on the other side. *The Book of Mormon* took shape, telling of a struggle between the chosen ones and their persecutors, of a promised land reserved for the righteous. North America, the book said, had been visited by Jesus in the distant past but the people had lost their way and fallen into disputation. Those people had been cursed by God for their sins and marked with dark skins; their descendants were the American Indians, who had forgotten their lost paradise.

Joseph Smith and several followers traveled throughout New York selling copies of what they called the "Gold Bible." They were met with hostility virtually everywhere they went, but they slowly gathered converts to their Church of Jesus Christ of the Latter-Day Saints. Many of the new members were poor, including some free blacks, but others had considerable resources. The most important converts were two brothers, Brigham and Joseph Young. As the movement gathered momentum, hundreds of people joined the church; entire congregations of churches of other faiths joined the Mormons and gladly contributed everything they owned to the church's common fund. The faithful

Joseph Smith was the founder of the Church of Jesus Christ of the Latter-Day Saints, also known as the Mormons.

moved first to Ohio and then to what Smith believed to be the original Eden: Missouri. But other settlers made no secret of their disapproval of the Mormons, firing shots, throwing stones through windows, and burning the crops of the Latter-Day Saints. The Mormons found no peace for the next decade. They were constantly harassed by non-Mormons who feared the growing number of converts and the local economic power that came from the church members' pooled resources and hard work.

POLITICAL TURMOIL

Andrew Jackson made fervent enemies as well as devoted followers throughout his presidency. No one could be neutral about him. Politics quickened in preparation for the election of 1832 as voters and leaders mobilized in opposition or support, latching on to a wide range of issues. Jackson, furious at any resistance, lashed out, determined that his work not be wasted. The nation had not seen such political conflict for decades, as citizens debated issues of the economy, states' rights, and morality.

Taking Sides

In September 1831 the first national political convention in U.S. history met in Baltimore. It was convened by the Anti-Masons. Despite their origins and their name, the Anti-Masons were concerned with the state of American politics in general, not merely with the threat posed by the Masons. They attracted an impressive list of ambitious and accomplished young men to their convention, including many who believed the Jackson White House was too pro-Southern and too callous with the American Indians. The Anti-Masons found little appeal in John Quincy Adams's National Republicans, for that party seemed to be stuck in the past and hapless against the strong Jacksonian Democrats. The Anti-Masons promised to become a powerful third party, a wild card in an already tumultuous American politics.

The Jacksonians held their own convention the following spring. Jackson, fed up with the controversy over Peggy Eaton and alienated from Calhoun, early in 1831 asked all the members of his cabinet to resign. When the president reconstituted the cabinet, he replaced pro-Calhoun men with men more to his own liking. Van Buren, who had suggested the purge as a way of cleaning house before the election of 1832, was nominated by Jackson to be the new ambassador to Great Britain. Calhoun, in a final act of revenge, cast the Senate vote that rejected Van Buren's appointment. Van Buren and Jackson got the last laugh when the convention of 1832 filled the vice presidential slot with Van Buren and removed Calhoun from the ticket. Calhoun, it became clear, would never be Jackon's choice for president; Van Buren had supplanted him as heir apparent.

The radicals in South Carolina, their last connection to the presidency broken, reacted with fury when Jackson signed another high tariff in early 1832. Advocates of nullification won control of the South Carolina legislature and oversaw the election of a state convention. Such a convention, Calhoun and his allies

declared, could nullify the U.S. Constitution because state conventions had been elected before the first national constitutional convention and authorized delegates to write a national document in the first place. The South Carolina convention announced that the federal tariffs passed in 1828 and 1832 were null, without force in South Carolina. Any state official who attempted to enforce the tariff, in fact, would be removed from office; South Carolina would secede if the U.S. government turned to arms to enforce the tariff. Calhoun resigned the vice presidency before his final few months in the office expired. He became senator from South Carolina, now free to defend openly the state's resistance to the federal government.

The Bank War

Despite the tariffs intended to serve their interests, most people in the Northeast felt they had received little from Andrew Jackson's first term. They viewed him with distrust and growing anger, perceiving in Old Hickory an enemy to moral and commercial progress, a defender of the backward South and West against the East. The fate of the Second Bank of the United States stood as the key issue in this regard. Many merchants and others deemed it a stabilizing force in the American economy, holding an otherwise decentralized money system in place. It was the job of Nicholas Biddle, the president of the Bank of the United States, to make sure that state banks kept plenty of metal currency—specie—on hand with which to pay the national bank when asked to do so. Such rules kept the state banks from putting out too many notes, from inflating the currency with paper money unsupported by gold or silver. When the economy fell into trouble, on the other hand, Biddle and the Bank of the United States would lessen their demands on the state banks, preventing panics and deflation.

While businessmen appreciated this role of the bank, many other Americans distrusted it. In their eyes, this largely private institution enjoyed far too much power for its own good or the good of the country. Why should privileged stockholders in the bank,

To opponents of the Bank, it seemed a "monster"— unnatural, and hard to kill.

GENERAL JACKSON SLAYING THE MANY HEADED MONSTER.

they asked, profit from the business of the federal government? Why should the national notes be allowed to depress the value of state notes, with their origins closer to home?

For many voters, objections to the Bank of the United States were as much objections to banking and commerce in general as to any specific policies of the national bank. The whole business of banking seemed suspect, with its paper money, its profits seemingly without labor, its government-supported monopolies, its apparent speculation with public money. Andrew Jackson shared these feelings of mistrust. As a young man, he had lost a considerable amount of money to a speculator and nothing he saw as president changed his mind about those who dealt in the mysteries of currency. He disliked monopoly, he disliked paper money, and he disliked the Bank of the United States.

The issue came to a head in 1832 as Henry Clay and other National Republicans, joined by South Carolina nullifiers such as Calhoun, sought to use the bank as a way to defeat Jackson for the presidency. A few months before the election in the fall, the bank's supporters steered its application for rechartering through Congress. Jackson heard of the news while he was ill in bed. "The bank," he told Martin Van Buren, "is trying to kill me, *but I will kill it!*" He vetoed the recharter, proclaiming that the bank was "unauthorized by the constitution, subversive of the rights of the States, and dangerous to the liberties of the people."

Jackson's opponents, in turn, saw the president, not the bank, as the usurper of American rights. How dare he singlehandedly overturn what the people, in the form of Congress, had declared to be their will? Henry Clay and other opponents argued that his action posed a far greater threat to the American people than did the bank. If the president could force his way into the lawmaking process, the division of powers laid out in the Constitution would be violated and the Union would risk falling under the despotic rule of a president who would be king.

Jackson on the Offensive

The election of 1832 turned around these broad issues about the fate of the nation. Jackson portrayed himself as the champion of the common man fighting against a bloated aristocracy of privilege and monopoly. Clay, the candidate of the National Republicans, portrayed himself as the defender of the Union against an arrogant and power-hungry president, a man who had shown a disregard for morality and justice in his dealing with the American Indians and the spoils system as well as with the Bank. William Wirt, the candidate of the Anti-Masons, declared himself the opponent of conspiracies, corruptions, and subversions larger and more insidious than the bank, all the more dangerous for not being clearly defined.

Despite the challenges on the bank and by the Anti-Masons, Jackson won by a considerable margin, losing South Carolina to a nullifier, Vermont to the Anti-Masons, and the rest of New England and a few other states to Clay. Emboldened by his majority at the polls, the president went on the offensive. Before the bank could deploy its enormous financial resources to gather the two-thirds' majority necessary to override his earlier veto, Jackson quickly moved all federal funds from the Bank of the United States to state banks. The newly appointed secretary of the Treasury followed Jackson's plan and put the government deposits in seven state banks—promptly dubbed "pet banks" by opponents of the new strategy. Congressmen of both parties denounced Jackson's move. Biddle and his bank's supporters fought on for two more years, but without the government's deposits they had little leverage. Jackson's lieutenants efficiently mobilized the votes they needed in Congress to prevent the renewal of the Bank's charter. The Bank of the United States, deprived of government support, began a slow death.

Even as the bank war raised one set of questions about the Constitution and the separation of powers, the nullification crisis brought another constitutional crisis to a climax. Nullification, Jackson announced soon after his reelection, would not be tolerated. He could not have been any clearer: Nullification was "incompatible with the existence of the Union, contradicted expressly by the letter of the Constitution, unauthorized by its spirit, inconsistent with every principle on which it was founded, and destructive of the great object for which it was formed." Disunion was treason, he warned, and would be treated as such; Congress passed a "Force Bill" to permit him to use military power to keep South Carolina in line. Recent opponents of Jackson such as Henry Clay and Daniel Webster were pleased—and surprised—at Jackson's nationalism; they had not expected such convictions from a Tennessee planter. Southerners in general were caught in a difficult position, disapproving of South

Workers from a broad range of jobs found that membership in a union offered them independence and pride as well as economic benefit.

Carolina's radicalism but distrustful of the centralizing precedent of the Force Bill.

Congress twisted and turned on the issue, not wanting South Carolina to get its way but unwilling to see Jackson use arms. After much debate, Congress, under the leadership of Henry Clay, offered compromise in early 1833: The tariff would be slowly but steadily lowered over the next decade, giving northern manufacturers time to adapt. South Carolina, secretly relieved, declared itself the victor and accepted the compromise tariff; in a final display of states' rights defiance, though, the Carolinians nullified the Force Bill. Jackson ignored them, recognizing the emptiness of the gesture.

Those opposed to Jackson began to call themselves "Whigs." Like their British namesakes, the American Whigs saw themselves as the counterbalance to otherwise unchecked monarchical power—in this case "King Andrew I," "the most absolute despot now at the head of any representative government on earth." The men who moved into the Whigs—former National Republicans, former Anti-Masons, and even former Democrats—shared little at first except their opposition to Jackson and his use of power. As the fight against Jackson continued, however, they would find more common ground and become a powerful enemy against Jackson and his party.

Working People

Not everyone prospered during the "flush times" of the 1820s and 1830s. Since prices and rents rose much more quickly than wages, urban working people found themselves falling behind. For generations, artisans and others who worked with their hands prided themselves on their contribution to America. They saw themselves as the bedrock of the republic, the people whose dedication helped win the Revolution, whose sweat helped make the young United States an economic wonder in the world. These working men and women felt their contributions slighted in the new economy, however, their labor no longer bringing the recognition and rewards it deserved. Business owners, eager to bring products to market as quickly and cheaply as possible, increasingly divided the steps of

production. Rather than having a journeyman construct an entire shoe for a single customer, for example, merchants employed one set of workers to make only soles and heels, another to stitch uppers to soles, and another to finish the shoes. Such people labored in homes where working and living conditions were abominable, where the lack of light and sanitation destroyed eyes and health.

Workers formed unions to defend their rights. After a failed strike for a ten-hour day by journeymen carpenters in Philadelphia in 1827, artisans pooled their efforts in the Mechanics' Union of Trade Associations, the first citywide federation of workingmen's groups. Members of fifteen different trades joined. In the early 1830s trades' associations appeared in New York, Boston, Baltimore, Washington, and Louisville. They sponsored newspapers, lobbied legislatures, and supported one another during strikes. By the mid-1830s, between 100,000 and 300,000 men and women belonged to unions.

A number of labor and political leaders, recognizing the power of such numbers, sought to mobilize the organized workers into politics. While union members generally liked Andrew Jackson's blows against monopoly, they thought he pulled up short in his attack on privilege. It was not only the Bank of the United States that used power unfairly, they argued, but also large businesses and property holders. They sought to push the political system into doing more to protect working people. Some unions became deeply engaged in politics and put forward their own candidates. Such workingmen's parties seemed full of promise. In 1834, at the movement's high point, workers formed the National Trades Union to "unite and harmonize the efforts of all the productive classes of our country." It appeared that a self-conscious urban working class might become a potent factor in American political life.

THE INDIAN PEOPLES AND THE MEXICAN NATION

The most important "foreign relations" of Andrew Jackson's administration were with the native peoples of North America. The American Indians held immense areas of the South and the West when Jackson took office, land that many whites wanted and demanded. The southwestern border of the United States remained dangerously ambiguous as well. Mexico governed its Texas province loosely and many white Americans coveted that land. Both of these situations would undergo explosive change under Andrew Jackson.

Jackson and the American Indians

Andrew Jackson had announced, and acted upon, his attitudes toward the Indians years before he took office as president. The steady pressing of white population onto the rich lands of the Cherokee, Chickasaw, Creeks, Seminoles, and Choctaws, he thought, left the people of those nations with two choices. They could either become "industrious Citizens" who accepted the sovereignty of the states that claimed the lands on which they lived, or they could "remove to a Country *where* they can retain their ancient customs, so dear to them, that they cannot give up in exchange for regular society." If they could adapt themselves to agriculture and law, they might remain where they were, protected by the laws they pledged to obey; if they could not adapt, they would have to leave. Their only other choice, Jackson thought, was extinction.

White people had mixed feelings about the Indians. Americans of European descent considered the Indians admirable in many ways, dignified and free, able to learn and prosper. Not a few "white" and "black" families were proud to claim some Indian ancestry. Andrew Jackson, for his part, adopted a Creek infant, Lyncoya, educated him, and brought him to live with him and his wife. In fact, the death of Lyncoya from tuberculosis in 1828, at age sixteen, hastened Rachel Jackson's heartbreak and decline. Many other white Americans, including some in Congress, had long contributed time and money to the Indians, helping to build and staff schools, sending seed and agricultural implements to ease the transition to farming.

By the late 1820s the "civilized tribes" had adapted themselves to the dominant society. Many of the tribes were led by chiefs of mixed descent, leaders who lived in cabins, houses, and even mansions. The wealthiest Indians, especially the Cherokee, bought African-American slaves. The children of the Indian leaders and others went to schools established by white missionaries, who persuaded a considerable number of Indians to convert to Christianity. The Cherokees

MEMORIAL AND PROTEST OF THE CHEROKEE NATION (1836)

The Cherokee nation, even while the federal and state governments prepared to force them from their homes in the South, desperately reminded Congress of the treaties struck between the two peoples. The Cherokee pleaded that they had done exactly what white Americans had urged them to do: assimilate, progress, and prosper. The arguments had little effect; the Trail of Tears soon commenced.

The undersigned representatives of the Cherokee nation, east of the river Mississippi, impelled by duty, would respectfully submit, for the consideration of your honorable body, the following statement of facts: It will be seen, from the numerous subsisting treaties between the Cherokee nation and the United States, that from the earliest existence of this government, the United States, in Congress assembled, received the Cherokees and their nation into favor and protection; and that the chiefs and warriors, for themselves and all parts of the Cherokee nation, acknowledged themselves and the said Cherokee nation to be under the protection of the United States of America, and of no other sovereign whatsoever: they also stipulated, that the said Cherokee nation will not hold any treaty with any foreign power, individual State, or with individuals of any State: that for, and in consideration of, valuable concessions made by the Cherokee nation, the United States solemnly guar-

published a newspaper that included articles in both their own language and in English.

Despite these adaptations, the Indians of the Southeast showed no desire to leave the land on which they lived in the late 1820s. In their view, they had already given up more land than they should have—millions of acres over the preceding twenty years—and were determined to hold on to what remained. "We would not receive money for land in which our fathers and friends are buried," they declared. Most whites, especially those who lived nearby and coveted the rich cotton lands under the Indians' control, bristled at the continuing presence of the native inhabitants. Many white people longed to banish the American Indians to land on the other side of the Mississippi River, where, it seemed, whites would not want to live for a very long time, if ever.

In 1827, the Cherokees held a national convention and drew up a written constitution, patterned on that of the United States. They desired both to declare their sovereignty over their lands and to show whites just how devoted they were to American values. But the new constitution, U.S. courts ruled, violated the law of both the nation and the state of Georgia, which petitioned the federal government to remove the Cherokees. An already volatile situation worsened when gold was discovered on the Indian lands and white prospectors rushed in. The Georgia legislature declared the Cherokees' laws null and void, placing Georgia law into effect instead. The Cherokees suddenly found themselves even more vulnerable than before. White settlers invaded northern Georgia, taking Cherokee property.

Jackson told the Indians he was their friend, even their "father," but that he could do nothing to stop their mistreatment except to move them beyond the Mississippi River, where, he promised, they would be safe. The Indians and their supporters, mostly

anteed to said nation all their lands not ceded, and pledged the faith of the government, that "all white people who have intruded, or may hereafter intrude, on the lands reserved for the Cherokees, shall be removed by the United States, and proceeded against, according to the provisions of the act, passed 30th March, 1802," entitled "An act to regulate trade and intercourse with the Indian tribes, and to preserve peace on the frontiers." It would be useless to recapitulate the numerous provisions for the security and protection of the rights of the Cherokees, to be found in the various treaties between their nation and the United States. The Cherokees were happy and prosperous under a scrupulous observance of treaty stipulations by the government of the United States, and from the fostering hand extended over them, they made rapid advances in civilization, morals, and in the arts and sciences. Little did they anticipate, that when taught to think and feel as the American citizen, and to have with him a common interest, they were to be *despoiled by their guardian,* to become strangers and wanderers in the land of their fathers, forced to return to the savage life, and to seek a new home in the wilds of the far west, and that without their consent. An instrument purporting to be a treaty with the Cherokee people, has recently been made public by the President of the United States, that will have such an operation, if carried into effect. This instrument, the delegation aver before the civilized world, and in the presence of Almighty God, is fraudulent, false upon its face, made by unauthorized individuals, without the sanction, and against the wishes, of the great body of the Cherokee people. Upwards of fifteen thousand of those people have protested against it, solemnly declaring they will never acquiesce. . . .

SOURCE Memorial and Protest of the Cherokee Nation, June 22, 1836, *Exec. Doc.* No. 286, 24th Cong., 1st sess., pp. 1–2.

religious people in the North, responded bitterly to such claims, arguing that the rights of the Constitution should certainly extend to people who had lived in North America since time immemorial. But the Jacksonians quickly pushed through the Indian Removal Act of 1830. Two Supreme Court decisions in favor of the Cherokees, in 1830 and in 1832, proved to be without effect, since they depended on the federal government to implement them and Jackson had no intention of doing anything of the sort.

In the face of the impending removal, most of the Indian peoples split into pro-assimilation, "progressive" factions and anti-assimilation "conservative" factions. They debated fiercely and sometimes violently among themselves. Missionaries and federal agents dealt primarily with the progressives, but many other Indians resisted, often by moving far into the backwoods. Many thousands of each nation remained behind, either those who had passed into white or black society through marriage or those who lived outside areas of heavy settlement.

Agents, some of mixed blood, swindled the Indians as they prepared for the removal. The Choctaws, the first to move, underwent horrific experiences, suffering greatly and dying in large numbers as they traveled in the worst winter on record with completely inadequate supplies. The Creeks, too, confronted frauds and assaults. The Indians who moved sold whatever they could not take with them, usually at a great loss. Wagons and carts carried the old and the sick, while women and children drove livestock along the trail. Soldiers usually accompanied the Indians, along with an agent to hand out whatever support the government provided. Some of the migrants used steamboats to travel up or down the Mississippi River and then to Oklahoma along the Arkansas or Red River, while others proceeded overland. "To see the remnant of a once mighty people fettered and chained together forced to

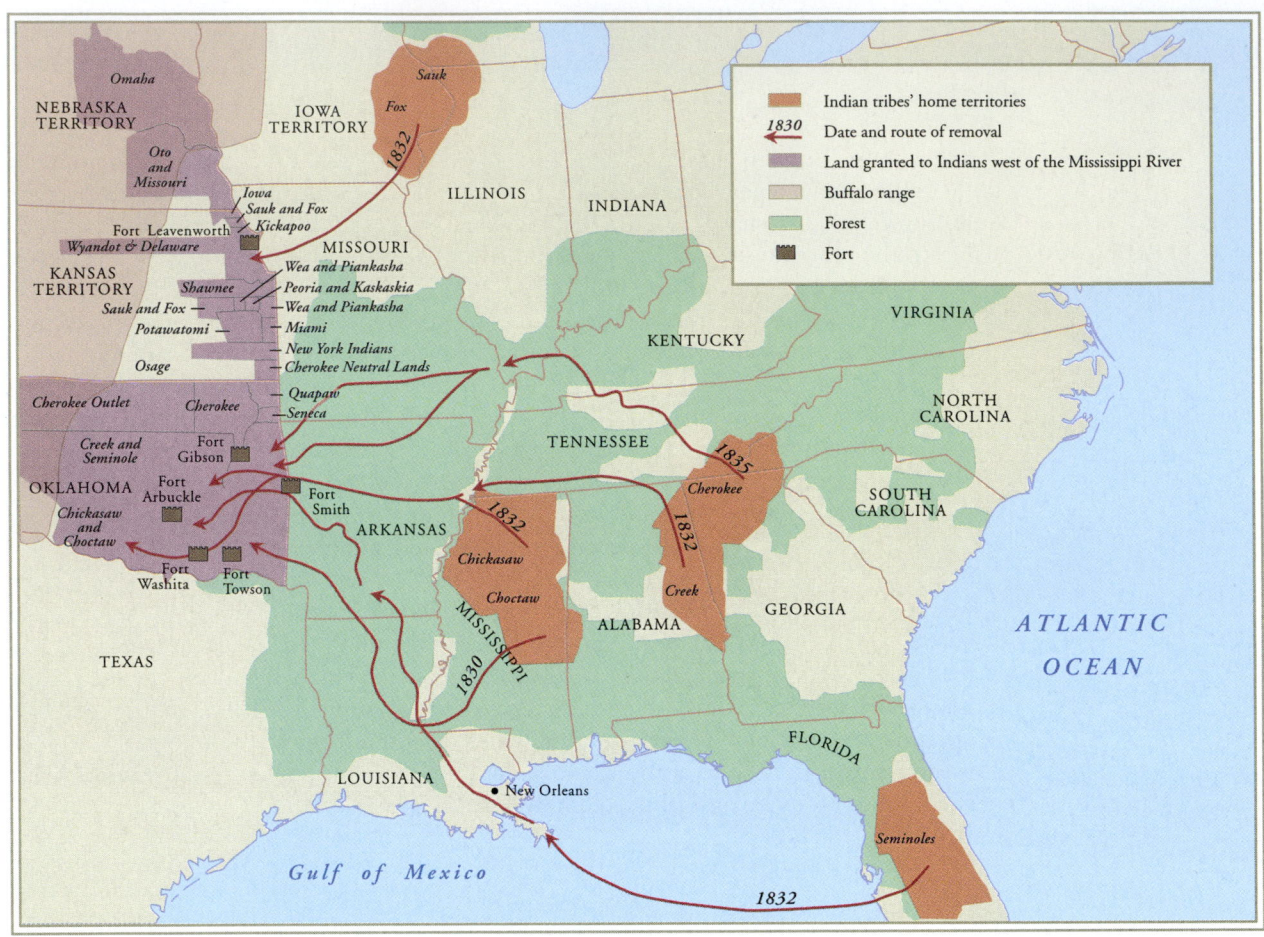

MAP 10.2 | THE REMOVAL OF THE AMERICAN INDIANS

depart from the land of their fathers into a country unknown to them," an Alabama newspaper admitted, "is of itself sufficient to move the stoutest heart."

The Cherokee removal was the most prolonged. After years of negotiating, the government struck a bargain with a small and unrepresentative number of the Cherokee in the Treaty of New Echota in 1836. While groups of several hundred at a time left, including some of the wealthiest, 17,000 refused to leave by the deadline. General Winfield Scott then led 7,000 troops against them, driving people from their homes empty-handed, marching them to stockades and shipping them out by rail and water. About a quarter of all eastern Cherokees died in what they called "The Trail of Tears." Some Cherokees remained in the mountains of North Carolina and Tennessee, but the power of the eastern Indians had been destroyed.

The Seminoles fought against removal as long as they could. Led by Osceola, the son of an English trader and the husband of an escaped slave, the Seminoles tried to break the will of the whites by killing soldiers and civilians and by burning their crops and homes. The Second Seminole War launched by the federal government to remove the 5,000 Indians began in 1836 and dragged on for six years. The conflict proved both unpopular and unsuccessful. About 36,000 U.S. soldiers fought and 1,500 died; many more suffered debilitating disease. The federal government spent $20 million in the fight, even though few white people wanted to settle on the Seminoles' land. The United States captured Osceola only by deception at a supposed peace conference. He died in captivity a few months later, after which some Seminoles finally migrated to Oklahoma. But most of the Seminole

The Cherokee called their forced migration to Oklahoma the Trail of Tears. About 4,000 of the 15,000 Indians forced to move died along the way, as did over 25,000 of the 100,000 southeastern Indians who were driven from their homes in these years.

people, able to use the swampy landscape to hide, were never driven out of Florida.

Fighting also erupted in the Illinois Territory between white settlers and the Sac and Fox Indians. These people, under the leadership of Black Hawk, saw their lands along the Mississippi River taken over by whites while the Indians were on a hunting expedition in 1832. The whites burned the Indians' huts and plowed under their fields. In retaliation, the Sac and Fox destroyed white settlements. A large contingent of volunteers, regular troops, and allied Indians set out after Black Hawk and his people, who also had allies from other Indian nations. Eventually, the whites outnumbered Black Hawk and overran his camp, killing nearly 500 as they tried to cross the Mississippi River. Taken prisoner, Black Hawk refused to repent, telling his captors that he "has done nothing for which an Indian ought to be ashamed. He has fought for his

countrymen, the squaws and papooses, against white men who came, year after year, to cheat them and take away their land." Black Hawk's words and deeds, widely reported in the newspapers of the country, attracted considerable sympathy among whites in the East. Andrew Jackson met with Black Hawk and pardoned him; the chief's autobiography became a bestseller. The United States, using its defeat of the Sac as an example, found it much easier to induce the other Indians of the Old Northwest to cede 190 million acres for $70 million.

Conflict with Mexico

Speculators and settlers from the United States continually moved into Mexican Texas in the 1820s and 1830s. Sometimes the Mexican officials encouraged

A small force of Americans and tejanos *were overwhelmed at the Alamo mission in San Antonio. Although the Mexican army won the battle, their victory unleashed the support of the United States.*

of local officials, improvised laws and took advantage of loopholes to keep slavery in fact if not in name.

American settlers and the Mexican government came into increasing conflict, as provincial officials attempted to collect tariffs and slow immigration into the district. Austin and the other Americans petitioned the Mexican government to let them become a separate Mexican state under its own administration, but they were rebuffed when Antonio López de Santa Anna took control of the government. In Santa Anna's eyes, the Texans were clearly inviting an expansionist United States to take this province away from Mexico; he sent in troops to meet the threat. In 1835, a convention of Texans voted to fight against Santa Anna, offering large amounts of land to all who would come help in the struggle.

Volunteers and money flowed into Texas from throughout the United States, where people had been watching the events in that area with great interest. Southern states in particular sent hundreds of men. Nevertheless, they were greatly outnumbered by the Mexicans, who decimated the Americans at several battles. As the Mexican army sought to occupy San Antonio, 188 rebels—including Davy Crockett of Tennessee, famous for his frontier exploits and for his service in Congress—took refuge in the Mission of the Alamo. Most of the people inside were American, but they were joined by *tejanos,* Mexicans of the province who allied themselves with the revolt for independence. The defenders of the Alamo held out against 3,000 Mexican soldiers for nearly two weeks, until the Mexicans finally stormed the mission and killed all inside except three white women, two white children, and an African-American slave. The Mexicans stripped the bodies of the insurrectionaries and burned them. After the Alamo, support for the rebellion grew rapidly in the United States, where it came to be seen as a moral struggle between the forces of freedom and the forces of autocracy. "Remember the Alamo" became the rallying cry.

Santa Anna seemed on the verge of victory until Sam Houston, the general of the American forces, attacked a much larger Mexican force at San Jacinto in April of 1836. Rushing toward the entrenched Mexicans, the Texans overran the artillery and breastworks, winning a decisive battle in only eighteen minutes. Santa Anna himself was captured a day later. As a prisoner, he signed treaties removing Mexican troops from Texas, granting Texas its independence, and recogniz-

the newcomers; at other times, they sought to slow American settlement. Seeking the end of slavery in Mexico, they wanted settlers but they did not want the slaves white settlers often brought with them. The key leader in the American migration was Stephen F. Austin, a Virginia-born entrepreneur who first arrived in Mexico in 1821 on the heels of Mexican independence. Throughout the 1820s, Austin, negotiating with the changing Mexican governments, oversaw the arrival and settlement of hundreds of Americans. While the Mexican laws on slavery shifted repeatedly, most of the American settlers—the great majority of them Southerners—argued that they had to have slaves if Texas was to develop as they and as Mexican leaders hoped. The Americans, with the tacit approval

The defeat of Santa Anna at San Jacinto brought the fight for Texas independence to a sudden and surprising culmination.

ing the Rio Grande as the boundary. The Mexican Congress, when they heard of this capitulation, announced that they would not be bound by its terms.

Texans and many Americans elsewhere urged the U.S. government to annex the new republic before it could be retaken by the Mexicans. That plea unleashed a heated and protracted debate between advocates of American expansion and those who thought such a step would be immoral and impolitic. Much of the debate raged between Southerners, who saw Texas as a vast new empire, and Northerners, especially abolitionists, who opposed annexation because it would lead to slavery's expansion. The fate of Texas was to be a key political issue for the next decade.

CONCLUSION

The vague and uncertain America of the 1810s and early 1820s became clearer under Andrew Jackson. No longer would politics be a matter of remote personalities in Washington, for now a two-party system mobilized voters and articulated their desires. No longer would slavery be a matter beyond debate, for the nulli-

fication crisis, Walker's *Appeal,* Turner's revolt, and the emergence of an abolitionist movement made slavery a concrete and burning issue. The aggressive young churches of the Second Great Awakening ensured that the Protestant faith became a matter of public action and testimony. After bitter debate and resistance, the power of the American Indians of the eastern United States had been broken and their people removed from homes they had occupied beyond memory. The public culture of the United States had become polarized, sharply conflicted over matters both public and private, full of possibility and full of conflict.

RECOMMENDED READINGS

Feller, Daniel. *The Jacksonian Promise: America, 1815–1840* (1995) offers a recent, upbeat overview.

Freehling, Allison Goodyear. *Drift Toward Dissolution: The Virginia Slavery Debate of 1831–1832* (1982) presents a useful interpretation of the crisis in Virginia.

Freehling, William. *Prelude to Civil War: The Nullification Crisis in South Carolina, 1816–1836* (1966) is the standard account of the subject.

Johnson, Paul. *A Shopkeeper's Millennium: Society and Revivals in Rochester, New York, 1815–1837* (1978) tells the story of revivals in an exciting way.

Laurie, Bruce. *Artisans into Workers: Labor in Nineteenth-Century America* (1989) gives an excellent synthesis of this complicated history.

Roediger, David R. *The Wages of Whiteness: Race and the Making of the American Working Class* (1991) boldly interprets the uses the white working class made of the notion of "race."

Walters, Ronald. *American Reformers, 1815–1860* (1996) offers an updated version of a fine analytical synthesis.

Watson, Harry L. *Liberty and Power: The Politics of Jacksonian America* (1990) provides a helpful and balanced interpretation of a subject that has been much debated by scholars.

Weber, David J. *The Mexican Frontier, 1821–1846: The American Southwest Under Mexico* (1982) tells the complex history of this region before war brought it into the United States.

Wiebe, Robert H. *The Opening of American Society: From the Adoption of the Constitution to the Eve of Disunion* (1984) surveys this entire era.

Andrew Jackson

Schlesinger, Arthur, Jr., *The Age of Jackson* (1945).

Ward, John William. *Andrew Jackson: Symbol for an Age* (1955).

Meyers, Marvin. *The Jacksonian Persuasion* (1957).

Pessen, Edward. *Jacksonian America: Society, Personality, and Politics,* rev. ed. (1979).

Remini, Robert. *The Life of Andrew Jackson* (1988).

Wallace, Anthony F. C. *The Long, Bitter Trail: Andrew Jackson and the Indians* (1993).

The Political System and Political Conflict

Baker, Jean H. *Affairs of Party: The Political Culture of Northern Democrats in the Mid-Nineteenth Century* (1983).

Bartlett, Irving. *John C. Calhoun* (1993).

Bullock, Steven C. *Revolutionary Brotherhood: Freemasonry and the Transformation of the American Social Order, 1730–1840* (1996).

Ellis, Richard. *The Union at Risk: Jacksonian Democracy, States Rights and the Nullification Crisis* (1987).

Formisano, Ronald P. *Transformation of Political Culture: Massachusetts Parties, 1790s–1840s* (1983).

Goodman, Paul. *Towards a Christian Republic: Antimasonry and the Great Tradition in New England, 1826–1836* (1988).

Grimsted, David. *American Mobbing, 1828–1861* (1998).

Howe, Daniel Walker. *The Political Culture of the American Whigs* (1979).

Remini, Robert. *Daniel Webster: The Man and His Time* (1997).

Varon, Elizabeth R. *We Mean to Be Counted: White Women and Politics in Antebellum Virginia* (1998).

Watson, Harry L. *Jacksonian Politics and Community Conflict: The Emergence of the American* (1981).

African-American Resistance

Harding, Vincent. *There Is a River: The Black Struggle for Freedom in America* (1981).

Horton, James Oliver, and Horton, Lois E. *In Hope of Liberty: Culture, Community, and Protest Among Northern Free Blacks, 1700–1860* (1997).

Oates, Stephen B. *The Fires of Jubilee: Nat Turner's Fierce Rebellion* (1975).

Hinks, Peter P. *To Awaken My Afflicted Brethren: David Walker and the Problem of Antebellum Slave Resistance* (1997).

Religion and Reform

Abzug, Robert H. *Cosmos Crumbling: American Reform and the Religious Imagination* (1994).

Cross, Whitney. *The Burned-over District* (1950).

Dillon, Merton L. *Slavery Attacked: Southern Slaves and Their Allies, 1619–1865* (1990).

Hambrick-Stowe, Charles E. *Charles G. Finney and the Spirit of American Evangelicalism* (1996).

Hardman, Keith J. *Charles Grandison Finney, 1792–1875: Revivalist and Reformer* (1987).

Johnson, Curtis D. *Redeeming America: Evangelicals and the Road to Civil War* (1993).

Fogel, Robert. *Without Consent or Contract: The Rise and Fall of American Slavery* (1989).

Friedman, Lawrence J. *Gregarious Saints: Self and Community in American Abolitionism, 1830–1870* (1982).

Harrold, Stanley. *The Abolitionists and the South, 1831–1861* (1995).

Mintz, Steven. *Moralists and Modernizers: America's Pre-Civil War Reformers* (1995).

Richards, Leonard L. *"Gentlemen of Property and Standing": Anti-Abolition Mobs in Jacksonian America* (1970).

Stewart, James Brewer. *Holy Warriors: The Abolitionists and American Slavery,* rev.ed. (1996).

Walters, Ronald G. *The Antislavery Appeal: American Abolitionists After 1830* (1976).

Wyatt-Brown, Bertram. *Lewis Tappan and the Evangelical War Against Slavery* (1969).

The Transformation of the Economy and Work

Bushman, Richard. *The Refinement of America: Persons, Houses, Cities* (1992).

Hammond, Bray. *Banks and Politics in America from the Revolution to the Civil War* (1957).

Hindle, Brooke, and Lubar, Steven. *Engines of Change: The American Industrial Revolution, 1790–1860* (1986).

Wilentz, Sean. *Chants Democratic: New York City and the Rise of the American Working Class, 1788–1850* (1983).

Laurie, Bruce. *Working People of Philadelphia, 1800–1850* (1980).

Dublin, Thomas. *Women at Work: The Transformation of Work and Community in Lowell, Massachusetts, 1826–1860* (1979).

The Mormons

Arrington, Leonard. *The Mormon Experience* (1979).

Bushman, Richard L. *Joseph Smith and the Beginnings of Mormonism* (1984).

Hansen, Klaus J. *Mormonism and the American Experience* (1981).

HARD TIMES, 1837

*The irony of a Fourth of July celebration during hard times fills this cartoon, in which
symbols of poverty and decay pile on one another.*

Chapter 11

PANIC AND BOOM:

1837–1845

In 1837 the largest financial panic and depression the nation had ever experienced descended on the United States. Coming after the deep changes of the preceding decade, that depression exerted broad and immediate effects. The hard times shaped reform, literature, politics, slavery, westward migration, and foreign policy, giving a sharp edge to conflict and strong incentives for change. Not surprisingly, these years of economic trouble also saw political turmoil and deep involvement by many aggrieved groups.

These hard years also saw the flowering of the reform spirit that had begun during the heady days of the Second Great Awakening. Men and women energetically championed public education, abstinence from alcohol, antislavery, and a host of other improvements to American life. The popular press also burgeoned, along with art, photography, and literature. A few leading thinkers articulated a bold and distinctive American philosophy, one that bore the marks of its tumultuous time.

DEPRESSION AND INVENTION

The late 1830s and early 1840s produced a surprising mixture of bad and good economic news. The economy fell into prolonged depression, pushing down wages, destroying jobs, eroding labor unions, and undermining confidence in political leaders. At the same time, the creative energies of the American economy persisted. Courts and legislatures fostered an environment favorable to business while inventors and investors plunged ahead despite the hard times. To use a metaphor from the most important innovation of the time, the American economy kept one hand on the brake and the other on the throttle.

Panic and Depression

Andrew Jackson sought to leave a comfortable legacy to his hand-picked successor, Martin Van Buren, but even the inauguration ceremony in March 1837 accentuated the great disparities between the two men. Van Buren had won the election in 1836 against a Whig party that put four different candidates in the field; he hardly enjoyed the sweeping mandate Jackson had claimed four years earlier. While Jackson's gaunt figure symbolized his sacrifices on the frontier and battlefield, Van Buren seemed the plump embodiment of a life spent in political office. While Van Buren's inaugural speech inspired little enthusiasm in the crowd of 20,000, the mere sight of ex-President Jackson roused great cheers. As one observer put it, "the rising sun was

CHRONOLOGY

1837　Financial panic

Charles River Bridge v. *Warren Bridge* decision

Grimké sisters lecture to mixed audiences

Elijah P. Lovejoy murdered in Alton, Illinois

Horace Mann becomes first secretary of Massachusetts State Board of Education

Ralph Waldo Emerson, "The American Scholar"

1838　John Quincy Adams successfully defeats attempt to annex Texas

1839　Depression worsens

Daguerreotypes introduced to the United States

1840　Congress passes Independent Treasury Act

Harrison elected president

Frederick Douglass escapes from slavery

American Anti-Slavery Society splits

Washingtonian temperance movement emerges

James G. Birney runs for president as candidate for Liberty party

1841　Harrison dies; John Tyler becomes president

Brook Farm founded

California sees arrival of first wagon train

Oregon fever

P.T. Barnum opens the American Museum

Amistad case heard before the Supreme Court

1842　Edgar Allan Poe, "The Murders in the Rue Morgue"

1843　Oregon sees arrival of first wagon trains

1844　Methodist Episcopal church divides over slavery

James K. Polk claims the United States's claim to "all Oregon"

Baltimore-Washington telegraph line

Samuel F. B. Morse patents the telegraph

Edgar Allan Poe, "The Raven"

1845　Texas and Florida admitted to the Union

Baptist church divides over slavery

---

eclipsed by the setting sun." Though Van Buren had been a principal architect of the so-called "spoils" system, he replaced few officeholders on the lower levels of government and made few changes in Jackson's cabinet. The new president seemed content to carry on Jackson's work.

Within weeks of Van Buren's inauguration the American economy hit stormy waters. Complicated changes in international trade played a large role in bringing on the crisis. An unprecedented amount of silver poured into American banks in the mid-1830s, fueling rapid and sometimes dangerous investment. England, concerned that the booming American economy was pulling too much gold and silver out of Britain in the form of investments, demanded repayment in specie just at the time that prices for American cotton—the major element in the Atlantic trade—declined because of record production. As a result, a major New Orleans cotton firm failed when it could not make its payments to British banks. That firm's failure, in turn, led to the closure of a number of banks that had loaned it money. The chain of failures stretched from New Orleans to New York.

Despite the role of international trade in bringing on the crisis, many people blamed the problems on a decision made closer to home: Jackson's policy of accepting only specie, not paper money, for the purchase of public lands. They looked to Van Buren to lead the repeal of this strategy, but Jackson made it clear to Van Buren that he did not want to see his work undone. As usual, Van Buren bowed to Old Hickory's wishes. Delegations of merchants came to the White House to plead with Van Buren, but to no avail. A "run" began on the banks; customers withdrew a million dollars in specie in only two days in early May. The Panic of 1837 had begun. Soon it spread to every city of the

REPRESENTATION OF THE INAUGURATION OF M. VAN BUREN, MARCH 4, 1837.

Martin Van Buren had done more than any other person to create the party system that drove American politics, but he could not meet the expectations for the presidency established by Andrew Jackson nor control the consequences of a debilitating economic depression that hit soon after he took office.

country, to every region. "The immense fortunes which we heard so much about in the days of speculation," one diarist noted, "have melted away like the snows before an April sun."

The panic quickly affected working people as well as the rich. Jobs dried up and many urban families had no idea of where they would get their next meal. The soup kitchens and other charities that had been created in the wake of the last panic, eighteen years earlier, stepped up their operations. In New York City, a poster warned that "Bread, Meat, Rent, Fuel—Their Prices Must Come Down. The Voice of the People Shall be Heard, and Will Prevail." Thousands of people gathered for a public meeting in the freezing weather. Told that a nearby warehouse held 50,000 barrels of flour, the protesters stormed the building and broke in; they took what they could and broke open hundreds of barrels more. The riots continued for days until the police managed to regain order. The working people who made up the crowd blamed "Monopolists and Extortioners" for the widespread misery, hoarding goods to drive up the prices.

The American economy surged up and down over the next five or six years. The panic of 1837 was followed by a better year in 1838, then by another panic in 1839. In the wake of that second panic, the stagnation of the economy spread more deeply and more widely, not ending until 1843. Labor unions weakened as workers grew afraid to risk their jobs. States' plans to finance canals, roads, and other public projects crashed. Several states defaulted on the bonds with which they intended to finance those improvements, leading furious European investors to shun American investments. The flood of capital into the young country dried up, wrecking new projects and causing the failure of those that had already been started. Governors and legislators found themselves under attack from voters angry that the states had permitted themselves to go so far into debt.

Van Buren admitted that allowing state banks to hold federal funds had apparently fueled the speculation, but he would not even consider reinstating a national bank. Instead, he proposed what came to be known as the Sub-Treasury Plan or the Independent

This locomotive in New York State, like its other early counterparts, pulled passenger cars based on old-fashioned carriages. The technology evolved quickly in the 1840s, however, and the United States played an important role in that evolution.

Treasury Plan. In that system, public funds would be disbursed by the secretary of the treasury as the economy seemed to dictate and banks would be kept out of the picture. It would be two more years before the plan passed, but by then it could do neither the country nor Martin Van Buren much good. His foes called him "Martin Van Ruin." The Whigs quickly won state-level offices and looked forward to harvesting more. The Van Buren administration drifted.

The Charles River Bridge Case

Even as the panic unfolded, some of the questions raised by the economic changes of the early 1830s worked their way through the American court system. The Charles River Bridge of Boston, for example, like many others in the late eighteenth and early nineteenth centuries, had been granted a franchise by the state legislature. The owners of the bridge charged a toll for everyone who crossed. As the population of Boston and Charlestown grew rapidly, so did the traffic and the tolls on the bridge. The bridge, which cost about $70,000 to build and improve, was bringing in $30,000 a year by the late 1820s. Another bridge also chartered by the state, the Warren Bridge, went up across the Charles, only 260 feet away. No sooner was the new bridge built than the traffic on the older bridge declined by more than half. The managers of the Charles River Bridge sued in court, claiming that

their original charter implied a monopoly that the state had violated by building a competing bridge. Throughout the 1830s, the case proceeded to the U.S. Supreme Court. It was heard in 1837.

The chief justice of the Supreme Court, Roger B. Taney, recently appointed by Andrew Jackson, shared the Jacksonian animosity against monopolies. His decision regarding the Charles River Bridge case held that a state charter did not imply monopoly, that business must be permitted to flourish in competition. Should old charters be permitted to hinder modern improvements, the country "would be obliged to stand still." The charters had perhaps been necessary in the past, he admitted, when the risks of any commercial undertaking were great in the underdeveloped United States, but by the 1830s such props no longer seemed necessary. Taney's decision in the *Charles River Bridge* reflected a growing consensus among Democrats and Whigs that older forms of economic privilege had to make way for innovation and investment.

Railroads

By the 1830s Americans had devised several means for dealing with the vast spaces of their continent. Thousands of miles of canals cut across the East while steamboats plied the waters of the North and South. Such means of transport, while cheap and dependable, remained relatively slow and limited in their reach. In-

land cities longed for fast overland connections with the outside world and they knew of experiments with railroads in England and the United States over the last decade. England, the innovator in railroad technology, enjoyed a head start over America. When New Jersey sponsored a bold rail and canal connection between New York and Philadelphia in 1831 they ordered a custom-built locomotive from the English company—the *John Bull*. The railroad became an immediate success, carrying over 100,000 passengers in 1834.

American companies emulated and improved upon the English designs. By 1841, ten American railroad shops had sprung into existence and they produced 375 of the 500 engines in the United States. Those shops soon began changing the English designs, making the engines more powerful and the rails cheaper, better suited to the rough conditions in the United States. The American shops even exported their engines, including to Britain. Railroad companies quickly grew into some of the largest and most complex American businesses, employing hundreds of people, creating elaborate organizational hierarchies and techniques, pioneering in management as well as engineering. The companies, operating a dangerous business, were among the first to run tight schedules and enforce their rules with fines and firings.

Railroads almost immediately became the key form of transportation in the United States. By 1840, American companies and states had built 3,300 miles of track, matching that of canals; by 1850, the country claimed nearly 9,000 miles of railroad. The trains created whole new industries to serve them, as iron, coal, and steel burgeoned with the railroads' demand. The railroads consumed prodigious amounts of wood for their ties, trestles, and boilers. The trains quickly became integral parts of the American landscape they were doing so much to alter. The railroads gave farmers quick and certain access to markets, permitting them to specialize in certain crops, and towns prospered or died depending on their rail connection. People traveled much farther than they would have imagined before and began to think of themselves as parts of larger networks.

Telegraph poles marched alongside the railroads, speeding the flow of information just as the railroads sped the flow of people and goods. Like the locomotive, the telegraph was the product of inventors in several different countries but received a major impetus from America. Samuel F. B. Morse, the first professor of art in the United States, patented his version of the electronic telegraph in 1840. Morse struggled with the invention—and with poverty—for more than ten years, devising the code of dots and dashes that bears his name as well as ways to make the current travel farther. He finally received support from Congress in 1843, who invested $30,000 to run an experimental line from Washington to Baltimore. Following its success, the telegraph spread across the country with great speed. Americans proudly claimed this invention as their distinctive contribution to the brave new world emerging in the mid-nineteenth century.

CULTURAL FERMENT

A hunger for social– and self–improvement animated many Americans in the 1830s. People were fired by revivals and reform organizations and roused by the hard years of panic and depression. Some took practical routes to progress, focusing their efforts on schools and alcohol, while others explored philosophy and literature. Some used the new printing machinery of the age for entertainment while others turned it to use in the fight against social evils. Each facet of cultural ferment amplified the others, making the late 1830s and early 1840s years of experimentation and excitement.

Public Schools

Many Americans had become dissatisfied with the way young people were schooled in the United States. No state had a statewide school system and local districts ran their own affairs, often wretchedly. The rich attended private schools or employed tutors, while the parents of poorer children had to sign oaths declaring themselves "paupers" before their children could benefit from charity schools. Parents from the middle classes, charged a fee according to the number of children they had, sent their offspring to schools often taught by untrained teachers who enforced rote learning and spasmodic discipline. Many districts, especially in the South, created no schools at all, leaving parents to fend for themselves. Many American children never went to school in the 1820s and 1830s and those who did often attended for only a short time.

Reformers argued that unequal and inadequate education would not suffice in America, a country

Horace Mann successfully championed the idea of tax-supported public schools in Massachusetts, transforming education as a result.

MᶜGUFFEY'S FIRST ECLECTIC READER

REVISED EDITION

AMERICAN · BOOK · COMPANY
NEW YORK · CINCINNATI · CHICAGO

McGuffey's Reader, *the first standardized textbook, offered millions of American schoolchildren moral as well as academic instruction.*

dependent upon informed democracy and economic opportunity. These reformers wanted free schools. Taxes and other state support would make it possible for all children, whatever the wealth of their parents, to go to public schools. The rich would be more likely to send their children to such schools, reformers reasoned, if their tax dollars were supporting them; the poor would be more likely to send their children if they were not stigmatized as paupers. Buildings and teachers could be improved with the increased support.

A Massachusetts lawyer and Whig politician, Horace Mann worked relentlessly to make rich citizens, especially manufacturers, see that a tax in support of schools was a wise investment. Think how much better workers would be, he argued, if they could read and calculate, if they had imbibed regular habits and discipline in schoolrooms. Think to what good use women could be put as teachers, he argued, instilling their virtues of cooperation and peacefulness. Mann gradually persuaded influential people in Massachusetts of the practicability, even the necessity, of com-

mon schools. In 1837 he became the first secretary of the Massachusetts Board of Education.

When Mann took over, about a third of all children in Massachusetts received no schooling at all and many schools were in session for only a couple of months a year. He transformed that system during his tenure as secretary. The minimum school year stretched to six months, buildings and teacher training improved significantly, and teachers' pay increased by more than half. Women teachers became common in the Northeast. Oberlin College in Ohio admitted women in 1837, making it the first coeducational institution in the country. Females attended new "nor-

mal schools" that provided teacher training; they read educational journals, underwent professional supervision, and taught with uniform textbooks. These standards spread throughout the North and the West in the 1840s and 1850s, as did McGuffey's Readers. These books, which sold an astonishing 9 million copies in school districts all over the country between 1836 and 1850, blended Christian piety and the virtues of hard work. Though each book aimed at a specific grade, the underlying message was always the same: "God has given you minds which are capable of indefinite improvement."

Transcendentalism

Leading thinkers saw the possibilities of improvement everywhere. Several of those thinkers came out of Unitarianism, a form of liberal Christianity especially strong in New England. Unitarianism encouraged people to emphasize feeling rather than doctrine, to focus on the heart of religion and not on its trappings. Several young people in the 1830s raised within the Unitarian church took these ideas further than their elders intended, rejecting much Christian doctrine. A belief in the literal truth of the Bible, these youthful critics argued, trapped religion in the past, making those who lived in modern times base their faith on miracles that had happened long ago. Better, the rebellious thinkers said, to appeal directly to the heart from the very beginning. These thinkers wanted religion to transcend churches and denominations.

Women played an active role in this effort, with Margaret Fuller becoming especially important. Fuller had grown up in the Unitarian church in Cambridge, Massachusetts, receiving a fine education. But she felt herself adrift, full of "unemployed force," after her male classmates went on to college. She read widely and taught school with two other important figures in the revolt against Unitarianism: Elizabeth Peabody and Bronson Alcott. These three, like Horace Mann, believed that children were innately good and that education should be designed to let that goodness flourish. They argued that school, like church, should not be permitted to get in the way of people's natural connection with nature and with one another. Fuller, Peabody, Alcott, and others were looking for a new and liberating cause.

They soon took their lead from Ralph Waldo Emerson. Emerson had grown up around Concord, Massachusetts. Though descended from a distin-

Ralph Waldo Emerson was America's first popular intellectual, a combination of poet, lecturer, entertainer, and minister.

guished ministerial family, he was raised by a widowed mother and forced to work his way through Harvard College. Uncomfortable as a minister, dissatisfied as a schoolteacher, and widowed while a young man, Emerson set out for Europe. There he met exciting English intellectuals whose works he had read and whose stirring ideas were to influence him so deeply: Samuel Coleridge, Thomas Carlyle, and William Wordsworth. These writers, along with other thinkers such as the mystic Emanuel Swedenborg, provided Emerson with a perspective far removed from the cool Unitarianism on which he had been raised. Emerson perceived humankind as deeply tied to nature, filled with its rhythms and longings. He published such ideas in his first book, *Nature* (1836), a work that gained him considerable attention from the like-minded young people of New England.

But it was Emerson's address before the Phi Beta Kappa initiates at Harvard in 1837 that announced his arrival to a larger audience. That essay was written with a close eye on the events of the year in which it was delivered. In his private life and private journals Emerson worried over the state of the nation after the Panic of 1837, the "calamitous times," the "loud

HORACE MANN, *ABSOLUTE RIGHT TO AN EDUCATION,* 1846

Horace Mann abandoned his successful law practice and position in the state legislature to become the first secretary of the Massachusetts Board of Education. Mann argued against those who resisted paying taxes to educate the children of others, insisting that every child had an "absolute right" to an education and that the state had an obligation to provide that education for the public good and at the public's expense.

. . . In the district-school-meeting, in the town-meeting, in legislative halls, everywhere, the advocates for a more generous education could carry their respective audiences with them in behalf of increased privileges for our children, were it not instinctively foreseen that increased privileges must be followed by increased taxation. Against this obstacle, argument falls dead. The rich man who has no children declares that the exaction of a contribution from him to educate the children of his neighbor is an invasion of his rights of property. The man who has reared and educated a family of children denounces it as a double tax when he is called upon to assist in educating the children of others also; or, if he has reared his own children without educating them, he thinks it peculiarly oppressive to be obliged to do for others what he refrained from doing even for himself. Another, having children, but disdaining to educate them with the common mass, withdraws them from the public school, puts them under what he calls "selecter influences," and then thinks it a grievance to be obliged to support a school which he [regards with contempt]. . . .

It seems not irrelevant, therefore . . . to inquire into the nature of a man's right to the property he possesses; and to satisfy ourselves respecting the question, whether any man has such an indefeasible title to his estates, or such an absolute ownership of them, as renders it unjust in the government to assess upon him his share of the expenses of educating the children of the community up to such a point as the nature of the institutions under which he lives, and the well-being of society, require.

cracks in the social edifice." The panic directly touched one of Emerson's friends in Concord, Henry David Thoreau, who graduated from Harvard in the panic year and could find no decent job. Emerson, older than Thoreau, had finally achieved some economic security in the summer of 1837 thanks to an inheritance, but he was well aware of the difficulties facing even the Phi Beta Kappa graduates of Harvard during August of that hard year.

Emerson titled his speech "The American Scholar." He argued that the scholar should be a man of action, a man of nature, a man of risk and endeavor. Books and poetry held tremendous power, Emerson admitted, but it was in activity, in striving, that the American scholar became truly American. It was time to set the teachings of Europe aside long enough to find America's own voice, Emerson told the graduates. "We will walk with our own feet; we will work with our own hands; we will speak our own minds."

Emerson developed these ideas throughout the late 1830s, enjoying growing fame and influence through public lectures. Railroads made it feasible for the first time for speakers to cover a large amount of territory. Public speaking generally paid much better than any

I believe in the existence of a great, immortal, immutable principle of natural law, or natural ethics,—a principle antecedent to all human institutions, and incapable of being abrogated by any ordinance of man,—a principle of divine origin, which proves the *absolute right* to an education of every human being that comes into the world; and which, of course, proves the correlative duty of every government to see that the means of that education are provided for all.

. . .

To any one who looks beyond the mere surface of things, it is obvious that the primary and natural elements or ingredients of all property consist in the riches of the soil, in the treasures of the sea, in the light and warmth of the sun, in the fertilizing clouds and streams and dews, in the winds, and in the chemical and vegetative agencies of Nature. In the majority of cases, all that we call *property*, all that makes up the valuation or inventory of a nation's capital, was prepared at the creation, and was laid up of old in the capacious storehouses of Nature. For every unit that a man earns by his own toil or skill, he receives hundreds and thousands, without cost and without recompense, from the all-bountiful Giver. A proud mortal, standing in the midst of his luxuriant wheat-fields or cotton-plantations, may arrogantly call them his own; yet what barren wastes would they be, did not Heaven send down upon them its dews and its rains, its warmth and its light, and sustain, for their growth and ripening, the grateful vicissitude of the seasons!

. . .

SOURCE   Horace Mann, *Tenth Annual Report of the Secretary of the Board of Education* (1846), in *The Life and Works of Horace Mann* (Boston: Lee and Shepard, 1891), Vol. IV, pp. 114–17, 128–29, 131–34.

The claim of a child, then, to a portion of pre-existent property, begins with the first breath he draws. The new-born infant must have sustenance and shelter and care. If the natural parents are removed, or parental ability fails; in a word, if parents either cannot or will not supply the infant's wants,—then society at large—the government having assumed to itself the ultimate control of all property—is bound to step in and fill the parent's place. To deny this to any child would be equivalent to a sentence of death, a capital execution of the innocent,—at which every soul shudders. It would be a more cruel form of infanticide than any which is practised in China or in Africa.

kind of writing, especially in the days before copyright laws. The growth of newspapers and other printing facilitated advertising, getting word of the lectures out beforehand and spreading summaries of the lectures to those unable to attend. People flocked to the lectures. Those who lived in "dreary" towns, one speaker recalled, wanted "to keep pace with the progress of civilization in all its aspects, by informing themselves about the products of literature, the achievements of science, and the aims and appliances of humanitarian movements." In the lecture hall, Emerson exulted, "everything is admissible, philosophy, ethics, divinity, criticism, poetry, humor, fun, mimicry, anecdotes, jokes, ventriloquism. . . ."

Emerson's home in Concord became the gathering place for a group who came to be called the Transcendentalists, who sought to "transcend" the mundane into the mystical knowledge that every human possessed if he or she would listen to it. Margaret Fuller became the editor of the *Dial,* the Transcendentalist magazine, while Elizabeth Peabody opened a bookstore catering to the interests of the group. Bronson Alcott and about eighty others founded Brook Farm, one of the many utopian communities that tried to get

off the ground in the 1830s and 1840s. Brook Farm combined manual and intellectual labor, putting people to work in the fields in the morning and on their books in the afternoon. The community produced both crops and an impressive weekly newspaper. Its schools stood as examples of enlightened education. It encouraged idiosyncratic dress and habits, independent thought and action. The experiment failed economically after a few years, but for a while Brook Farm offered the possibility of combining intellectual excitement, physical work, and social responsibility in a way the Transcendentalists craved.

Henry David Thoreau founded, in essence, a one-man utopian community. Since the Transcendentalists believed that people should establish a close connection to nature, Thoreau decided to conduct an "experiment in human ecology." He wanted to see—and show—how a modern man could live in harmony with nature. He built, from some trees he cut on Emerson's land and some boards from an old shanty, an isolated house in the woods near Walden Pond, carefully calculating the cost of nails and other sup-

Henry David Thoreau, a close friend of Emerson's, embarked on a characteristically American experiment when he went to live alone in the woods at Walden Pond.

plies. He strove to be self-sufficient and self-contained (though skeptics charged that he was not *that* far from Concord, where his mother and his fellow Transcendentalists lived and where he frequently visited). The experiment proved important for the beautiful and affecting book Thoreau eventually wrote about his experience, *Walden: Life in the Woods* (1854).

Art and Popular Culture

The Transcendentalists were not alone in their craving for intensity. American painters found an increasing audience for their works in the 1830s as they evolved a style of their own. The United States had never been very receptive to figurative art. Wealthy people bought portraits, but most other Americans had no pictures at all in their homes. Talented young painters born in the United States generally had to travel to Europe for their training and often for their livings as well. This began to change, however, as Americans developed more of a taste for painting and as remarkable young artists came on the scene.

Thomas Cole was the key figure in the emergence of American painting. Though born in England, he came to the Ohio frontier as a small child. Cole, fascinated with the wild scenes of the landscapes around him, taught himself to paint but went to England and Italy to perfect his art. He returned to the village of Catskill in New York to paint the Hudson River Valley in the late 1830s and early 1840s. Soon, other painters, such as Asher Durand and Frederick Church, joined Cole in their fascination with the stirring American landscape, creating what became known as the Hudson River School. They found that landscape full of meaning, speaking of birth and decay, danger and possibility. Their countrymen greeted such works with enthusiasm, celebrating the emergence of an American style as well as American subjects.

Cole also turned to richly symbolic allegorical painting. His journey to Europe had struck him by its contrasts, "both the ruined towers that tell of outrage, and the gorgeous temples that speak of ostentation." He believed America, by contrast, "to be the abode of virtue." He embodied his notions of the cycles of civilization and personal life in two powerful allegorical series, *The Course of Empire* and *The Voyage of Life.* Engravings of these series became popular fixtures in American homes.

This painting by Thomas Cole of Northampton, Massachusetts, after a thunderstorm reflects a common theme in the work of American painters in these years: the power as well as the beauty of nature.

Other important artists followed their own paths through the American landscape. George Catlin spent much of the 1830s living among the American Indians of the Great Plains, making hundreds of drawings and paintings. Even as the Indian removals drew to a close in the East, white Americans remained fascinated with the native peoples farther west. In Catlin's paintings Easterners thought they might catch the last glimpse of a disappearing people. Audiences could also view vanishing wildlife in the remarkable watercolors of John James Audubon. Audubon, born in Haiti and educated in France, settled on the Kentucky frontier as a merchant after he married. He loved the American wilderness too much to stay in his shop, though, and he launched out on daunting journeys to record the environment and appearance of the birds of the young nation. After ten years of work Audubon produced *The Birds of America, from Original Drawings, with 435 Plates Showing 1,065 Figures* in four immense volumes, completing the project in 1838.

The most famous artistic production of antebellum America was a statue: Hiram Powers's *The Greek Slave,* completed in 1846. Powers grew up in the raw country of Ohio but moved to Italy as he prospered. There, Powers sculpted his statue of a nude young woman bound in chains. Many Americans had not deemed such statues suitable for their chaste republic, but Powers found a way to make such a work not only permissible but even morally improving. The young woman represented, Powers said, a Greek girl captured by the Turks in the Greco-Turkish war. As such, she represented Christianity and whiteness, unbowed by the evil and darkness surrounding her. Powers sought, and received, the endorsement of a group of American clergymen, removing any qualms audiences might have. Indeed, the statue became a national fixation and drew enormous crowds when it toured the United States. *The Greek Slave* served as the model for hundreds of miniature copies that appeared in the drawing rooms of the finest homes.

soon filled the publications coming off the presses. For the first time, illustrations could be produced cheaply. Anyone with enough money could send messages and images far and wide. Not only did the abolitionists and other reformers use these techniques to great effect, but so did a religious movement, the Millerites, who believed that signs in the Bible foretold the Day of Judgment in 1844. To spread the word, they published 4 million pieces of literature.

Seeing the opportunity afforded by this emergence of a popular audience for print, American writers worked hard to fill the hunger. One especially gifted author, Edgar Allan Poe, skillfully navigated between the market and his art. Poe wrote short stories, the kind of writing most in demand for the burgeoning periodical press and the growing ranks of educated readers, but he brought to the form a kind of self-consciousness few had demonstrated before. Poe tapped into a widespread fascination with the occult, seances, and ghosts, filling his work with ruins, shadows, and legends. Works such as "The Murders in the Rue Morgue" marked the first appearance of the detective story. Poe was not a disturbed man writing out of his

Hiram Power's The Greek Slave *became an American sensation, attracting large crowds and many imitators.*

The same drawing rooms also contained a novelty of the age: daguerreotypes. This form of photography developed in France but arrived in the United States soon after its creation. By the early 1840s all the larger American cities boasted daguerreotype studios. Within a few years, more than eighty young photographers practiced their craft in New York City alone. One of these men on the cutting edge of technology was Matthew Brady, who opened a studio in Washington, D.C., where he and his assistants photographed leading people of the period. This early photography was cumbersome and required long periods of stillness before the camera, but the American people hurried to studios to have their portraits done.

As print became a fixture of everyday life in these years, engravings based on paintings and photographs

Edgar Allan Poe experimented with new literary forms, crafting remarkable stories and poems of terror and dread.

own fantasies and horrors, but was rather the consummate artist, inventive and controlled. Throughout the hard decade of the 1840s he published stories such as "The Masque of the Red Death," "The Pit and the Pendulum," and "The Tell-Tale Heart" and poetry such as "The Raven." Plagued by the death of loved ones and ill health exacerbated by drink, however, Poe did not survive the decade.

A very different kind of entrepreneur, P. T. Barnum, a Connecticut storekeeper turned newspaper editor turned purveyor of popular entertainment, opened his American Museum in New York in 1841 and people flocked to see what it offered. Barnum played an elaborate game, displaying oddities that strained the limits of belief but that could not be completely disproved. Unlike earlier museums, full of supposedly uplifting displays of minerals and stuffed animals, Barnum's museum frankly offered entertainment, including magicians and midgets such as the famous Tom Thumb. The fact that the "curiosities" were often attacked as fakes by scientists did not seem to deter visitors; controversy was good for business. Barnum's American Museum flourished for the next twenty years, attracting visitors from all over the country and the world.

The Washingtonians

Americans had long waged campaigns against intemperance, but in the depression years of the late 1830s and early 1840s the fight against drink took on a new urgency. With work hard to find, alcohol seemed all the more threatening to laboring people. While earlier temperance movements had mainly enlisted those who were already opposed to alcohol, the new movement of the late 1830s marked an effort by drinkers to reform themselves. Earlier attempts at temperance had often pitted middle- and upper-class reformers against members of the working class, but the new movement grew among people in the lower ranks of American society. Older reform attempts had been largely the efforts of men, but now women became active. The Washingtonian movement, named in honor of George Washington, gave these efforts great force and visibility.

The Washingtonians began in Baltimore in 1840, when six drinkers, regretting their fondness for whiskey, pledged to one another to quit drinking and to persuade other drinkers to do the same. Word of the new movement quickly spread up the eastern seaboard and by 1841 gained over 200,000 members;

This painting captures the atmosphere of fascination and energy that surrounded everything the great American showman P. T. Barnum produced.

two years later, the Washingtonians claimed millions of adherents. Partly as a result of the new organization, Americans' consumption of alcohol plummeted in the 1840s, when the per capita intake of liquor fell to half of what it had been in the 1820s. The success of the Washingtonians outstripped that of any prior temperance organization.

"Martha Washington" societies, for women only, grew rapidly, challenging the men's movement both in size and in fervor. These female temperance advocates were not well-to-do ladies stooping to help the fallen, but rather the wives of artisans and small businessmen. They helped families in distress to get back on their feet. They also provided a new edge to the temperance crusade, reminding men that drunkenness was more often than not a male failing and that it was the wives and children of drunkards who suffered most from their neglect, cruelty, and even violence. The Washingtonian movement provided one of the first forums in which American women could publicly express their grievances and act to remedy them.

Abolitionism

By the late 1830s the American Anti-Slavery Society claimed over a thousand locals and over a quarter of a million members. The same lecture circuits that carried general-interest speakers such as Ralph Waldo Emerson also carried abolitionists, bringing the battle against slavery into places where it had been only a distant rumble a few years earlier. The first female abolitionist speakers—the Grimké sisters, Angelina and Sarah—were prize recruits into the antislavery ranks, for they were the daughters of a prominent South Carolina slave-owning planter. The sisters developed into powerful writers and speakers. By telling New England audiences of their own experiences with slavery, the Grimkés held a credibility that white northern abolitionists could not match. In 1837, the Grimkés decided to exert their power in a new forum by lecturing to mixed audiences of men and women. While some people strenuously objected to such an elevation of women in the public sphere, the Grimkés spoke to over 40,000 people at eighty meetings in sixty-seven towns and cities in nine months in 1837 and 1838.

As it grew stronger, the antislavery cause met with more determined opposition. When abolitionist Elijah P. Lovejoy offended readers of his religious paper in St. Louis—denouncing a local judge who prevented the trial of a mob who had burned a black man alive—citizens of Alton, Illinois, invited Lovejoy to move to their town. Alton prided itself on being a progressive place of 3,000 people, even permitting black children

Temperance advocates called for total abstinence from drink, demonstrating in illustrations such as this that the very first drink could lead to crime and even suicide.

The murder of Elijah Lovejoy, an abolitionist editor in Illinois, revealed the depth of opposition held by many northern whites to anyone who would speak forcefully against slavery.

in its schools. Soon, however, some prominent members of the community, angered at Lovejoy's paper for its dissemination of "the highly odious doctrines of modern Abolitionism," held a public meeting demanding him to quit printing such ideas. Lovejoy only intensified his attacks on slavery. Mobs destroyed two of Lovejoy's presses, but he persisted, bolstered by the support of other members of the community. In November, a mob killed Lovejoy and shattered his press.

Abolitionists debated the proper response to such opposition. William Lloyd Garrison, identified by many as the country's most militant abolitionist, counseled his allies to offer no resistance to violence. He opposed war, capital punishment, and prisons because of their reliance on violence and expanded his crusade to women's rights and the plight of American Indians. Garrison and his supporters renounced all allegiance to the established parties and churches, which had long since shown themselves tolerant of slavery. Other abolitionists, by contrast, focused on slavery alone and used whatever means they could to bring slavery to an end, including political parties.

The differences among the abolitionists came to a head at the annual meeting of the American Anti-Slavery Society in 1839. They differed most visibly in their attitudes toward the role of women. Women constituted perhaps half of all members of the antislavery organizations but some male abolitionists sought to keep females in a subordinate role. Unable to resolve their differences, the abolitionists split. The more conservative group, based in New York, created the Liberty party to run a candidate for president in the upcoming election of 1840. Garrison's organization maintained a more radical stance on the role of women and the strategies through which abolition should be pursued.

Whatever their differences, abolitionists barraged Congress with petitions demanding that slavery be ended in the District of Columbia. Former President John Quincy Adams, now a congressman from Massachusetts, used all his parliamentary skill to fight the gag rule that prevented Congress from recognizing antislavery petitions; he finally succeeded in getting it overthrown in 1845. Adams also successfully defended Africans who had seized a slave ship bound for Cuba, the *Amistad,* and landed in Connecticut. Supported by a large network of abolitionists, Adams took the case before the U.S. Supreme Court and won not only the acquittal of the Africans for murdering the ship's captain but their freedom as well.

Black antislavery speakers greatly strengthened the antislavery cause. Northern blacks had long struggled for the freedom of slaves, but voices from slavery itself proved even more compelling. Speakers such as Henry Box Brown (who had himself mailed from Richmond to Philadelphia in a specially fitted box), Henry Bibb, Solomon Northup, Sojourner Truth, Harriet Tubman,

and Ellen Craft electrified audiences with their talks and brought readers to tears with their written testimonies. Slavery, they made clear, was nothing like the benign institution portrayed by the defenders of slavery.

While white abolitionists valued the contributions of their black compatriots, white reformers were not always above racial prejudice. They urged black speakers not to make too much of a fuss when confronted—as they were daily—with the insults and indignities faced by black people in the North. African American abolitionists chafed under the restrictions they faced from fellow reformers and enemies alike; they demanded greater rights for northern as well as southern blacks. Their experiences showed the extent to which race was a national problem.

One of the most remarkable Americans of the nineteenth century burst into visibility in the early 1840s. Frederick Douglass had grown up in Maryland, on the border between slavery and freedom. Like other places in the upper South, Maryland's economy was diversifying in the 1830s and 1840s as towns and cities grew, commerce intensified, and railroads spread. Douglass learned to read from his mistress, though it was against the law for her to teach him, and he began to use that ability to remake himself. In a spirit that would have pleased Horace Mann, the young Douglass carried with him a copy of *Webster's Spelling Book* and *The Columbian Orator,* a book of speeches, including a slave's persuasive argument with his master to set him free. Douglass noticed that his owners spoke bitterly of people called "abolitionists" and he discovered why when he read in a local newspaper of John Quincy Adams's fight against the gag rule.

Sent to Baltimore by his owner, Douglass worked in the shipyards, became skilled as a caulker, continued to read widely, and plotted his freedom. After several attempts at escape, Douglass finally borrowed the papers of a free black sailor and, impersonating his friend, rode a train to freedom. Douglass found himself in New York City, alone and without any notion of what he should do or where he should go. A runaway slave had to be careful, for he or she might be hunted down by a slavecatcher for a reward. Fortunately for Douglass, he met a black man who introduced the young runaway to the New York Anti-Slavery Society. After white abolitionists saw the skill with which he spoke, they sent Douglass to travel throughout the North with William Lloyd Garrison. Throughout the early 1840s, Douglass and other African American abolitionists told their stories of slavery, giving faces and names to the suffering.

One of the most influential and famous Americans of the nineteenth century, Frederick Douglass fought tirelessly against slavery and in favor of a wide range of social reforms.

THE SLAVE SOUTH

The South was an integral part of the United States throughout the antebellum period. Southern cotton drove much of the economy, southern politicians held much of the power, southern concerns guided much foreign policy, and Southerners played important roles in the churches and the armed forces. The South was a prosperous place for white people, whose average per capita incomes compared favorably with those of northern whites. Thanks to the rapid expansion of newspapers and telegraph, white Southerners took part in all the national conversations about race, slavery, and politics.

The South had its trains, newspapers, and reform societies; its white people bought the same books and magazines people read in the North; they had their daguerreotypes taken and sent messages on telegraphs. The growing connections between the regions, in fact, emphasized the differences between the North and the

South. As people in each region read the hard words those across the Mason-Dixon line frequently said about them, their distrust of one another grew. As increasing numbers of people such as Frederick Douglass escaped to the North, Northerners became ever more aware of their region's complicity in perpetuating slavery and even abetting its growth. Even as the two societies developed along similar lines, their single profound difference became ever more potent.

African Americans and the South

By the 1830s, slavery had spread over an enormous area stretching from Frederick Douglass's Maryland to the tumultuous lands of Texas. The decade had seen the domestic slave trade grow at a feverish rate, for the new planters of Mississippi, Alabama, and Louisiana eagerly imported slaves to clear land and plant cotton.

The slaves of the Upper South feared and dreaded being "sold south." By the time of the Panic of 1837, Alabama, Mississippi, and Louisiana grew more than half the nation's cotton, outstripping the older states of the Southeast. American slavery became ever more diverse as it expanded. Enslaved people worked in hemp, wheat, rice, corn, sugar, and tobacco fields as well as cotton. They worked with livestock and racehorses. They practiced carpentry and blacksmithing in the growing towns and small cities of the booming Southwest. They labored on the docks of New Orleans, Mobile, and Memphis and in the shipyards of Baltimore. Some slaves lived where their families had dwelled for generations; others cleared new land of cane brakes and cyprus along the Mississippi frontier. Some knew the white people among whom they lived quite well; others belonged to absolute strangers. Some worked in large groups of black people; others worked alone or beside whites.

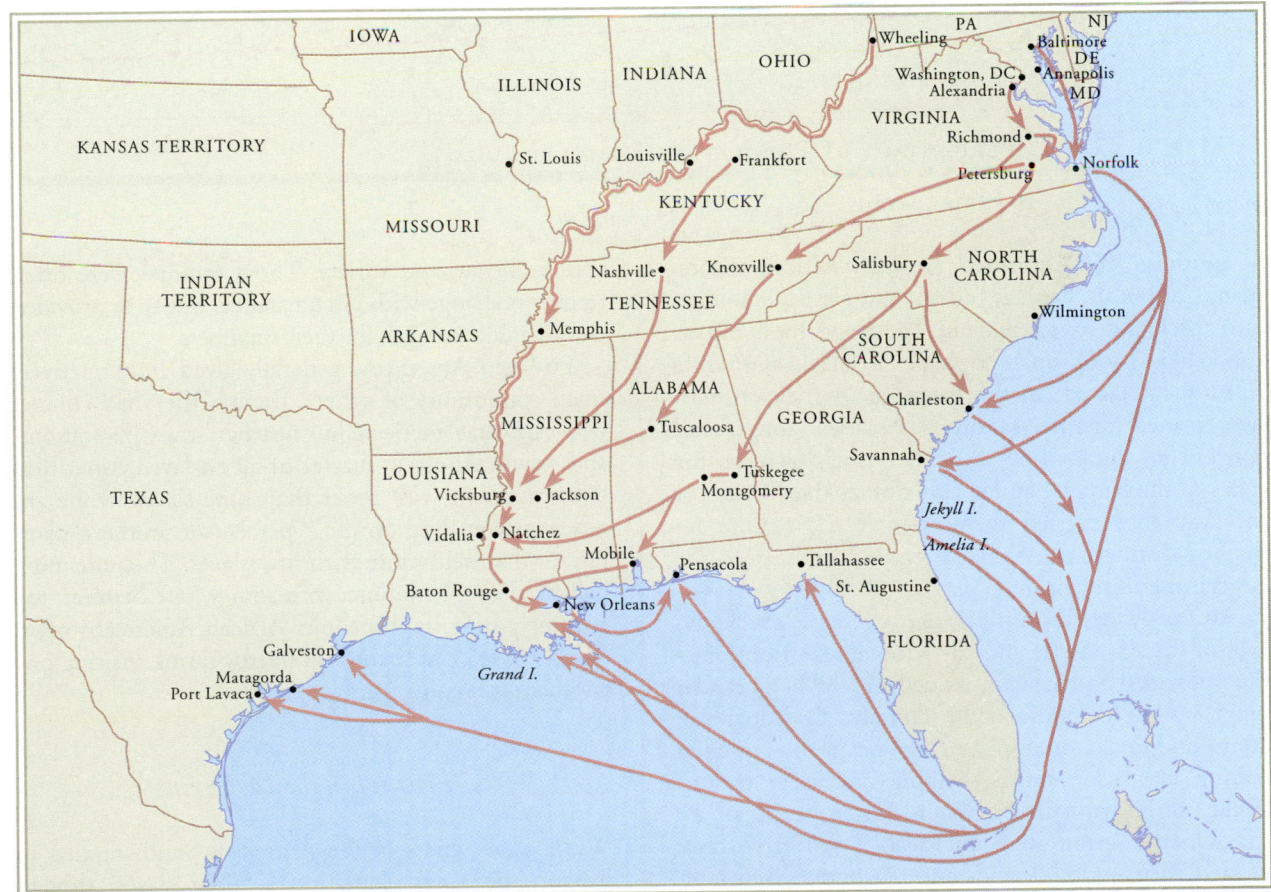

MAP 11.1 | PATHS OF THE SLAVE TRADE

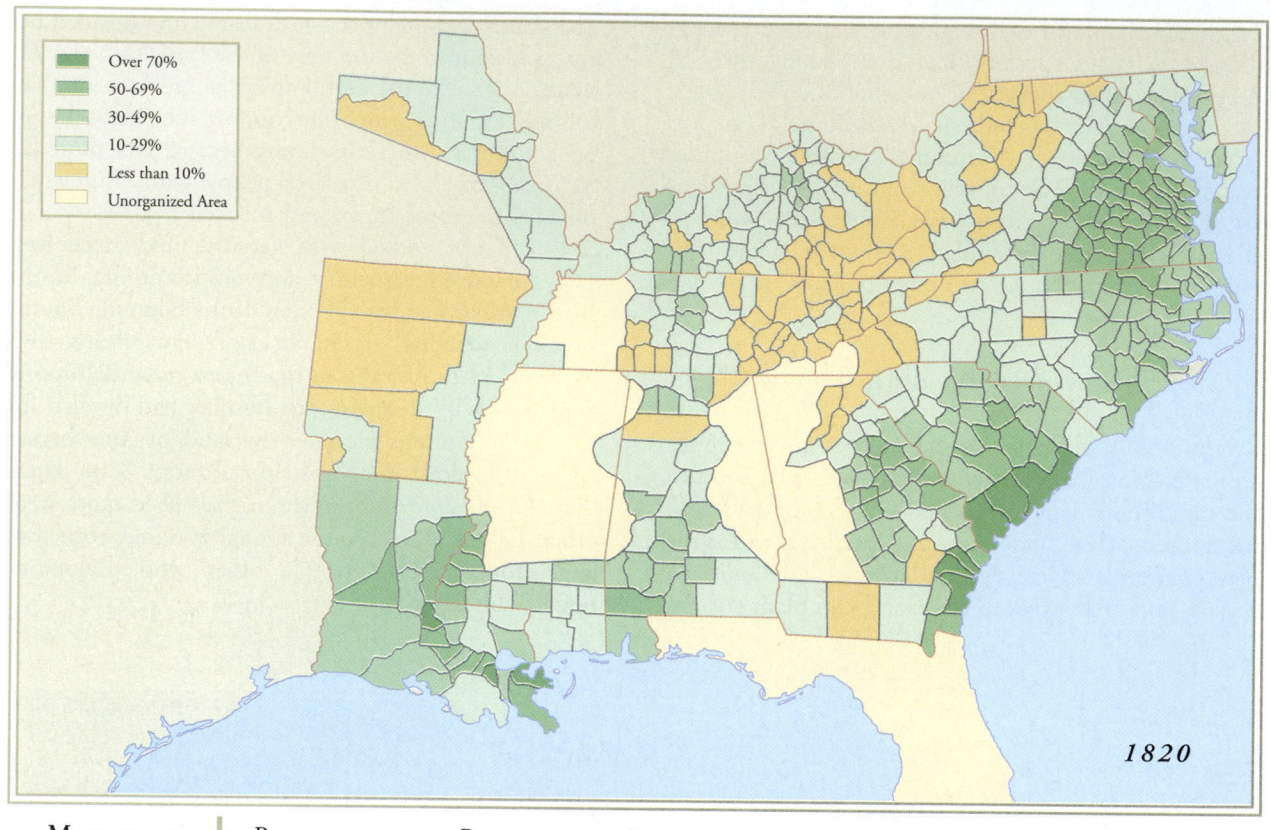

Over 70%
50-69%
30-49%
10-29%
Less than 10%
Unorganized Area

1820

MAP 11.2A | PERCENTAGE OF POPULATION ENSLAVED, 1820

Southern culture mixed English, African, Scots-Irish, Caribbean, French, Indian, and Hispanic sources into a rich and complex blend. Language, food, music, and religion took on new shapes as black and white cultures interacted. In the meantime, African Americans prided themselves on the stories, songs, and dances they knew to be particularly their own, on the styles of the baskets, quilts, and clothes they sewed, or the way they carried themselves. Black culture remained distinct and vibrant even as it influenced the larger American culture.

African-American families, partly because of the ravages of the slave trade and partly because African practices provided a precedent, tended to rely on a broader range of kin than did white families. Grandparents, aunts, and uncles often played significant roles in child rearing in black families, helping out when parents could not be with their children. When people of actual blood relation were unavailable, southern slaves created "fictive kin," friends and neighbors given honorary titles of "brother" or "aunt" and treated as such. These arrangements permitted slave families consider-

able resiliency and variety. Those families were often forced to change with circumstance, but they provided considerable strength for their members.

Enslaved Americans generally lived in a relatively small community of others, though they had contact with African Americans on nearby farms, plantations, and towns. About a quarter of all enslaved Americans lived on farms with fewer than nine slaves, while another quarter lived on the 3 percent of southern plantations that held more than fifty slaves. The remaining half lived on plantations with somewhere between ten and forty-nine bondspeople. African Americans often found wives or husbands on nearby farms, visiting one another on evenings and weekends.

Plantations and Farms

White slaveowners in the American South tended to live on the same plantation as their slaves, though some absentee slaveholders held land in the rich low country of South Carolina and in the sugar planta-

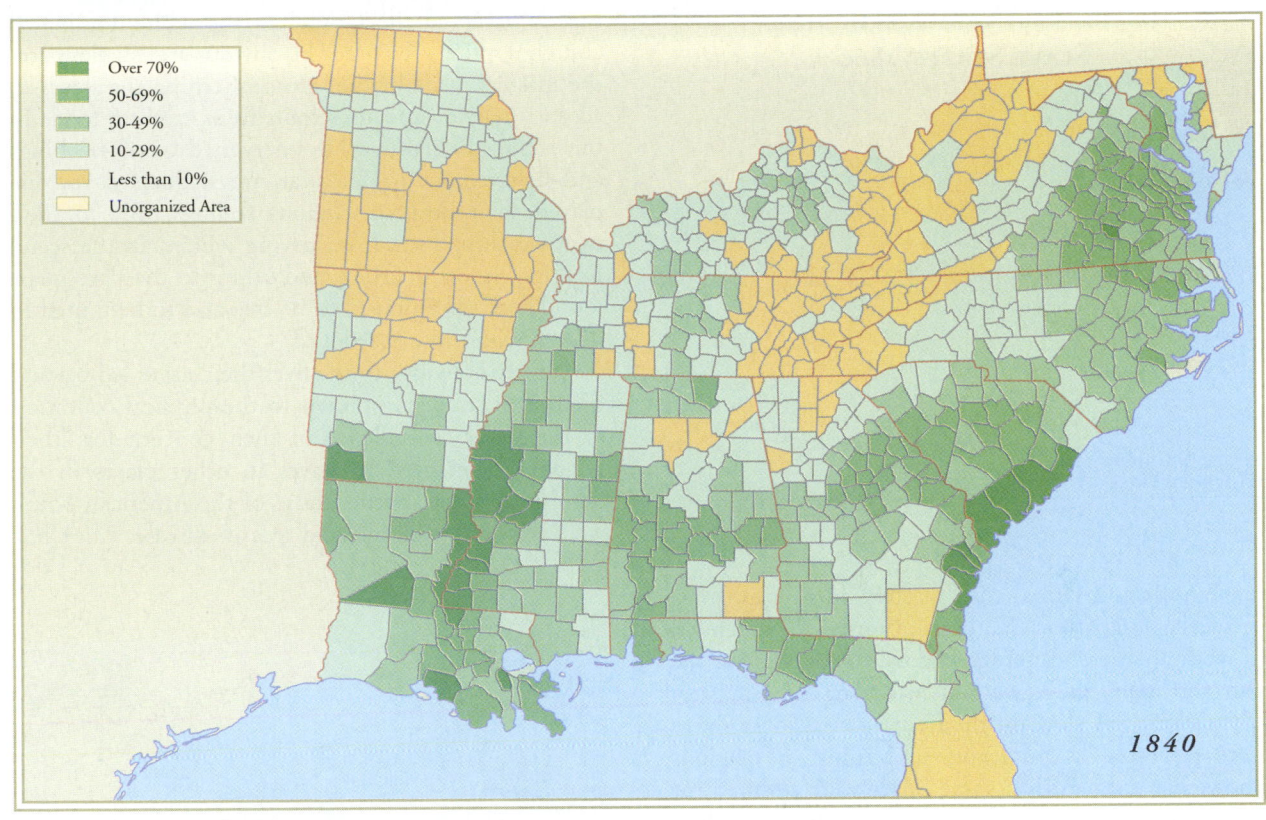

Legend:
- Over 70%
- 50-69%
- 30-49%
- 10-29%
- Less than 10%
- Unorganized Area

1840

MAP 11.2B | PERCENTAGE OF POPULATION ENSLAVED, 1840

tions of Louisiana. Wealthier whites put day-to-day control of their plantations in the hands of professional overseers. These overseers were seldom so-called "poor white trash," for wealthy planters did not hand over property as valuable as their slaves, land, and crops to people of poor reputation. Rather, overseers were often ambitious young men of middling background who used the overseer position as a stepping stone to their own plantation. If the plantation did not run as smoothly and profitably as the slave owner thought it should, the overseer found himself out of a job. Slaves could and did appeal to the owner if they thought the overseer unfair. Since a master might indeed trust a well-known slave more than a new overseer, the position involved tact as well as brute force.

On larger plantations, where slaves often worked in groups called gangs, trusted male slaves served as "drivers." Such drivers tended to be especially strong and skilled, commanding respect from whites as well as blacks. Especially on plantations with both overseers and drivers, the distribution of power was not a simple matter. Although whites held the ultimate threat of

force, they much preferred to keep the work moving smoothly, with as little trouble as possible. The driver could help both sides, protecting fellow slaves from abuse and assuring that the work got done efficiently. Drivers frequently found themselves caught between the two competing sets of demands, however, and slaves often resented or even hated drivers.

The work that enslaved people did varied by farm, by time of the year, and by gender, but about three out of four worked mainly in the fields. Almost all of them went to the fields during the peak times, for only the richest planters kept able-bodied men employed full-time as house servants or coachmen. Women, who worked in the fields alongside men, also served in the house as cooks and domestics. Slaves were well known for controlling the pace of work, proceeding at a rate that seemed appropriate to them, reporting their tools broken or "lost" when they were forced to work too fast or too long. They traditionally had Sundays to garden for themselves, do their domestic chores, or hunt.

Slaves' lives were by no means simple. Lines of power often became complicated and tangled on

AFRICAN AMERICANS IN THE SLAVE STATES, 1860

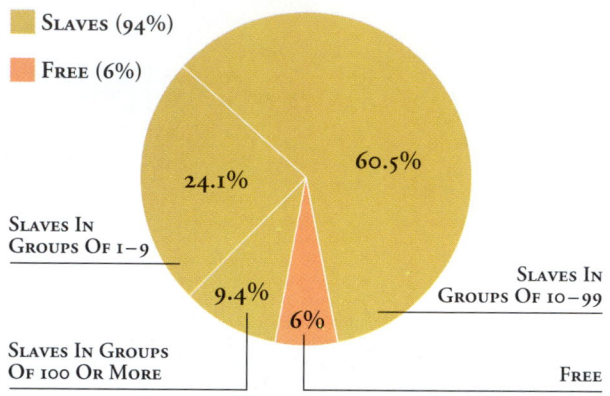

- ■ SLAVES (94%)
- ■ FREE (6%)

24.1% — SLAVES IN GROUPS OF 1–9

60.5% — SLAVES IN GROUPS OF 10–99

9.4% — SLAVES IN GROUPS OF 100 OR MORE

6% — FREE

eagerly accepted the Gospel in the white-dominated churches, others resented the obvious and shallow uses the masters made of the sermons, telling the slaves to accept their lot and to refrain from stealing food. In the eyes of the slaves, whites perverted God's teachings and behaved in un-Christian ways. Such slaves displayed their deepest religious feelings only in their own worship, away from prying whites, in the secret meetings in brush arbors and cabins in the slave quarters. There, they prayed to be free and to be united in heaven with those they loved.

Largely oblivious to the lives their slaves led beyond their sight, masters pointed to the physical condition of the slaves as evidence of their concern for "their people." Compared to slaves in other places in the hemisphere, it was true, those of the American South were relatively well-fed and free of disease. They had

plantations and farms, with masters, mistresses, sons, overseers, and drivers claiming authority. Slaves tended to work at several different jobs over the course of the year and many slaves were hired out to other masters when work was slow on the home place. Some slaves were respected as purveyors of healing or religious knowledge from Africa; some slaves were admired for their musical ability; others won recognition for their ability to read and preach the Gospel. These abilities did not always correspond with the opinions of whites, who frequently underestimated the abilities and character of the people among whom they lived.

Whites told themselves that they knew "their people," that they cared for them and provided them a better life than they would have known in Africa. Indeed, southern masters explained the justice of slavery to themselves and to the North by stressing their Christian stewardship for the slaves and their emotional attachment to them. As one clergyman wrote to his fellow slaveholders in the early 1840s, slaves "were placed under our control . . . not exclusively for our benefit but theirs also." Slaveholders did not want to seem unworthy of the hopeful young nation of which the South was a key part; they did not want to seem antagonistic to spiritual or economic progress.

Throughout the 1830s and 1840s, southern slaveholders and ministers prided themselves on their Christian mission to the slaves, in which thousands of African Americans were inducted into churches along with whites. Most masters would not permit their slaves to learn to read, but they did arrange to have Bible selections read to their slaves. While many slaves

Enslaved people of both genders worked in a variety of demanding tasks throughout the year as they brought the South's valuable cotton crop from seed to bale.

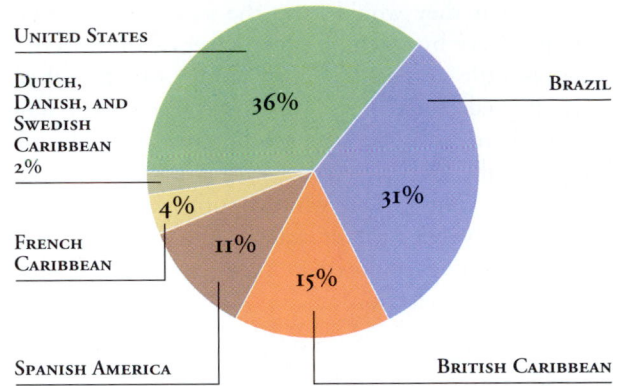

SLAVES IMPORTED, 1500–1870

BRAZIL — 38%
BRITISH CARIBBEAN — 17%
DUTCH, DANISH, AND SWEDISH CARIBBEAN — 6%
UNITED STATES — 6%
SPANISH AMERICA — 17%
FRENCH CARIBBEAN — 17%

PROPORTION OF HEMISPHERE'S SLAVE POPULATION, 1825

UNITED STATES — 36%
DUTCH, DANISH, AND SWEDISH CARIBBEAN — 2%
FRENCH CARIBBEAN — 4%
SPANISH AMERICA — 11%
BRITISH CARIBBEAN — 15%
BRAZIL — 31%

As these two graphs show, the United States accounted for a relatively small proportion of all enslaved people brought from Africa into the Western Hemisphere but, because of the longer lifespans of North American slaves, more than a third of the enslaved population of the New World lived in the United States.

limited and monotonous diets, but generally consumed enough nutrients. Slaves received ineffective or dangerous health care, their houses were small and drafty, and their clothing was limited to a few rough garments per year, but none of these conditions endangered slaves' physical survival. Economic investment as well as community pressure and religious concern helped ensure this minimal support. Slaves in the United States, working in relatively healthy settings and benefiting from a balanced ratio between men and women, generally lived longer than their counterparts elsewhere in the hemisphere.

On the other hand, many slaveowners did not refrain from having their slaves whipped on small provocation, branded, shackled, or locked up in sweltering enclosures. Slave women suffered sexual abuse by overseers, neighboring whites, the owner's sons, or the owner himself. Partly because expectant mothers were often kept in the fields until the last minute, about a third of all black babies died before they reached their first birthday. American slavery, whatever ameliorating features it might have had, was a harsh institution. Its slaves ached for freedom and made the best they could of the hard world into which they were born.

The Politics of the White South

In the South as in the North, the Whigs portrayed themselves as the party of progress and prosperity. The lawyers, editors, and merchants who set up shop in the hamlets and towns of the South proved receptive to such views. The young men who followed such professions eagerly joined organizations such as the Masons, temperance groups, and political parties. They saw themselves as part of the rising generation of Americans and prided themselves on their broad views of national issues. In their eyes, only the Whigs reflected such enlightened perspectives. The large planters on the richest lands were also attracted to the Whigs, for they engaged in trade with northern and English commercial houses, wanted internal improvements, and needed banks and a strong currency. The Whigs drew, too, on the farmers in the mountains of the Upper South, men determined to develop connections to outside markets and to demonstrate their loyalty to the old Union.

The Democrats, on the other hand, found their strongest supporters among the middling farmers and planters of the South. These men tended to be propertied but not wealthy, resentful of the taxes on their lands and slaves. They admired the Democrats' aggressive approach to removing the American Indians and to expanding in the West. Southerners distrustful of Northerners and of commerce found the minimal-government pronouncements of the Democrats appealing and persuasive. Most counties in the South had a substantial number of both Whigs and Democrats; one party tended to breed the other as they built on long-standing rivalries and resentments.

In the South both the Whigs and the Democrats declared themselves the friends of southern slavery, but they differed in their emphases. The Democrats pledged that they would leave the voters alone, protecting slavery by extending the power of the government as little as possible. The Whigs, on the other hand, argued that the best way to protect slavery was for the South to build strong economic and political bridges to the North even as they put a Southerner in the White House. The white South was a touchy democracy. Voter turnout was high and men cared about few things more than they cared about who won in the next election.

THE CHALLENGE OF THE WEST

Americans of every sort kept their eyes to the west. Railroads, telegraphs, canals, and roads strained in that direction; population restlessly flowed there. But thoughtful people recognized that the lack of borders and limits posed threats as well as potential. When everything seemed possible, people placed few checks on their appetites. Every boundary was contested, every obstacle attacked. Politics became a battle between boundless expectation and anxiety.

The Election of 1840

The Whigs should have faced an easy contest in 1840. After all, the Van Buren administration had hardly been a sparkling success. Much of the nation, from the cities of the East to the plantations of the Southwest, remained mired in depression. Van Buren offered little effective leadership during the economic crisis and many people held him to blame for the hard times. But the Whigs were not as strong as they might have been. Their party had been built piece by piece in the 1830s in reaction to Andrew Jackson. As a result, the party was a crazy-quilt of interests and factions. In 1836, the party had even permitted three candidates to run against Van Buren because no one man could command the party's full allegiance. Party leaders vowed that they would not let the same thing happen in 1840. They believed that they would control American politics in the new decade, shaping the country to fit their ideas of what it should be.

The Whigs determined in 1840 to find the one man who stood for the common beliefs that unified Whigs beneath their surface differences. Those beliefs turned around faith in commerce, self-control, Protestantism, learning, and self-improvement. Most important, the Whigs wanted to make an active response to the depression plaguing the nation by putting money in circulation, building internal improvements, and strengthening banks. Such plans appealed to many men appalled at the do-nothing approach of Van Buren and the Democrats. The trick was to find a candidate who embodied their beliefs without appearing to be "aristocratic" or hungry for power, as the Democrats were sure to charge.

The Whigs found such a man in William Henry Harrison. Harrison had made his name as a general—most notably in his defeat of an Indian confederacy in the Battle of Tippecanoe in 1811—and later served in the House of Representatives and in the Senate. Harrison, removed by Andrew Jackson from a position as minister to Colombia, returned to his farm in Ohio, held minor office, and, in his late sixties, expected to live out his days in semiretirement. Harrison had won fame without gathering many political liabilities and was identified with no particular position. The Whigs adopted no platform, not wanting to alienate anyone.

The Whigs sought to balance their ticket with Senator John Tyler of Virginia. This slaveholding Southerner was safe on that issue, but he was also a small-government man. Tyler shared few beliefs with his fellow Whigs, but his embrace of slavery helped mollify Southerners. Moreover, his name made a nice pairing in the phrase that soon became famous: "Tippecanoe and Tyler, Too." One Whig warned that the combination of Harrison and Tyler had "rhyme, but no reason in it." At first, the alliteration seemed reason enough to vote Whig, though, as the party enjoyed a success on the national level that they had never before experienced.

Part of their success grew out of a Democratic blunder. The Democrats were relieved that the Whigs had nominated Harrison. Democrats considered the old general a nonentity; one reporter commented sarcastically that if Harrison were merely given some hard cider and a small pension he would contentedly sit out the rest of his days in a log cabin. The sarcasm backfired, though, for many Americans saw log cabins and home-brewed cider as evidence of American virtue

ALEXIS DE TOCQUEVILLE, *DEMOCRACY IN AMERICA,* 1840

A young French nobleman, Tocqueville came to the United States to observe democracy in action. In the great book from which this selection is drawn, the sympathetic Tocqueville notes a central paradox of American life; all except slaves are free in virtually every facet of their lives and yet that freedom does not seem to bring happiness. Instead, it generates constant anxiety and a ceaseless yearning, as few seem able to grasp all that they can see.

In certain remote corners of the Old World you may still sometimes stumble upon a small district which seems to have been forgotten amid the general tumult, and to have remained stationary while everything around it was in motion. The inhabitants are for the most part extremely ignorant and poor; they take no part in the business of the country, and they are frequently oppressed by the government; yet their countenances are generally placid, and their spirits light.

In America I saw the freest and most enlightened men, placed in the happiest circumstances which the world affords; it seemed to me as if a cloud habitually hung upon their brow, and I thought them serious and almost sad even in their pleasures.

The chief reason of this contrast is that the former do not think of the ills they endure—the latter are for ever brooding over advantages they do not possess. It is strange to see with what feverish ardor the Americans pursue their own welfare; and to watch the vague dread that constantly torments them lest they should not have chosen the shortest path which may lead to it.

A native of the United States clings to this world's goods as if he were certain never to die; and he is so hasty in grasping at all within his reach, that one would suppose he was constantly afraid of not living long enough to enjoy them. He clutches everything, he holds nothing fast, but soon loosens his grasp to pursue fresh gratifications.

In the United States a man builds a house to spend his latter years in it, and he sells it before the roof is on; he plants a garden, and lets it [rents] just as the trees are coming into bearing; he brings a field into tillage, and leaves other men to gather the crops; he embraces a profession, and gives it up; he settles in a place, which he soon afterward leaves, to carry his changeable longings elsewhere. If his private affairs leave him any leisure, he instantly plunges into the vortex of politics; and if at the end of a year of unremitting labor he finds he has a few days' vacation, his eager curiosity whirls him over the vast extent of the United States, and he will travel fifteen hundred miles in a few days, to shake off his happiness. Death at length overtakes him, but it is before he is weary of his bootless chase of that complete felicity which is for ever on the wing.

Among democratic nations men easily attain a certain equality of conditions; they can never attain the equality they desire. It perpetually retires from before them, yet without hiding itself from their sight, and in retiring draws them on. At every moment they think they are about to grasp it; it escapes at every moment from their hold. They are near enough to see its charms, but too far off to enjoy them; and before they have fully tasted its delights, they die. . . . .

SOURCE Alexis de Tocqueville, *Democracy in America,* Vol. II (Boston: C. C. Little & J. Brown, 1841), Second Book, Ch. 13

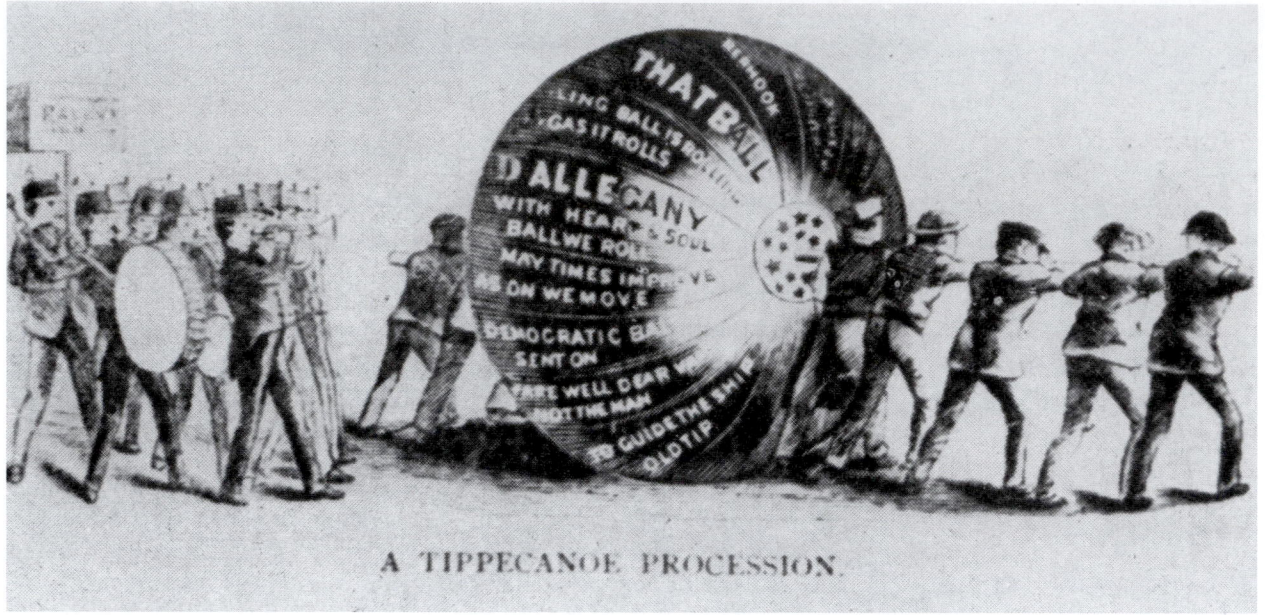

A TIPPECANOE PROCESSION.

Marching to the slogan of "Tippecanoe and Tyler Too," the Whigs determined to keep their momentum strong. They rolled this ball, for example, all the way across Ohio.

and self-reliance. Even though Harrison drank modern distilled spirits and did not in fact live in a cabin, the image stuck. The Whigs, long frustrated at their reputation as snobs and elitists, seized on hard cider and log cabins as symbols of their party's loyalty to the common American.

All over the country, Whig speakers displayed paintings, signs, flags, and models of log cabins while freely dispensing cider to crowds thirsty from singing the boisterous new campaign songs produced by Whig composers. Harrison himself went out on the campaign trail, the first presidential candidate to do so. A new kind of American political style was being forged before people's eyes and with their eager participation. For the first time, women became prominent at these rallies, encouraging their husbands, fathers, and suitors with smiles and waving kerchiefs. The Whigs embraced causes many women supported, such as temperance and allegiance to the church.

The Democrats had no idea of how to respond to the hard cider and log cabin campaign. To a considerable extent, the Whigs had beaten the Democrats at their own game, playing up their democratic impulses and their reverence for the ways of the past. Martin Van Buren proved an easy target for a Whig campaign that emphasized homespun values. The

President's portly figure and penchant for silk vests and doeskin gloves made the Democrats' long-standing claims of representing the common man look hypocritical. Andrew Jackson himself came out to campaign, firing the same charges against the Whigs that had worked so well in the past, charges of elitism, hostility to slavery, and softness on the bank issue. Even these charges failed.

Van Buren received 367,000 more votes than he had four years earlier, but an even higher number of voters cast their ballots for the Whigs. Harrison won nineteen of the twenty-six states, bringing about half a million new voters to the Whigs. Voter turnout surged to a level almost unimaginable just a decade earlier: Eight of every ten eligible voters went to the polls on election day in 1840. Even during the exciting campaigns of the 1820s and 1830s, the turnout had been much lower, between 50 and 60 percent. After 1840, elections would demand the combination of active campaigning, the search for potent symbols, and boisterous public displays that had proven so successful in that year.

Tyler, Webster, and Diplomacy

The Whig celebration did not last long. Harrison, determined to show both his accessibility to the people

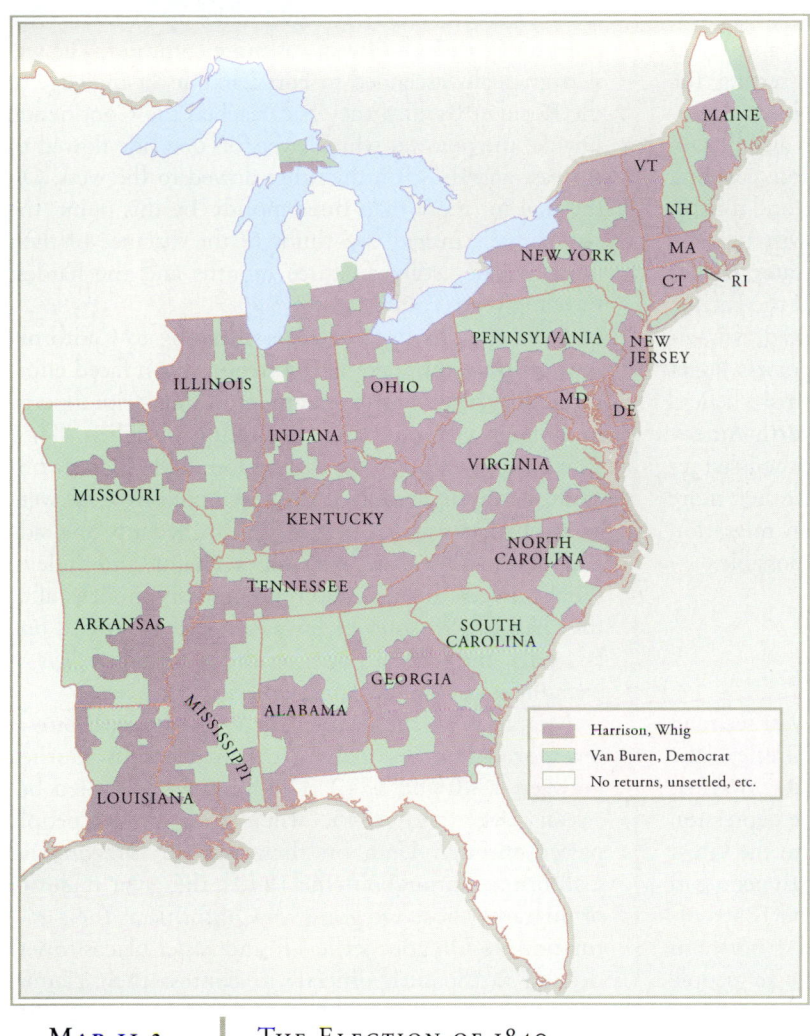

MAP 11.3 | THE ELECTION OF 1840

Legend:
- Harrison, Whig
- Van Buren, Democrat
- No returns, unsettled, etc.

Many Americans still hated the British. Conflicts between the two countries had broken out over the boundary between the United States and Canada, with areas to the north of Maine and Wisconsin in dispute. In 1837 armed men had fought along the border as Americans aided a rebel movement trying to overthrow British control of Canada; later, a Canadian militia burned an American steamboat carrying supplies for the insurgents, killed one of its crew, and set it adrift, generating intense anger in the northern United States. Armed battle also erupted in the "Aroostock War" over the disputed boundary between Maine and New Brunswick.

Conflict had long been building between the British and the Americans, too, over the African slave trade. Because the United States did not provide any funds for the suppression of the trade, which both nations had prohibited, Great Britain insisted that its vessels be permitted to search American ships off the coast of Africa to prevent the transportation of slaves to British colonies. Americans resented the intrusion in its affairs and refused. The issue threatened to explode in 1841, when American slaves seized the slaving ship the *Creole,* which was taking them from Virginia to New Orleans. The slaves steered the vessel to the Bahamas and claimed their freedom under British law. Much to the anger of southern whites, the British gave sanctuary to the slaves though the ship had been on a domestic, not international, voyage.

Daniel Webster sought to quell this volatile situation. He met with the British representative, Lord Ashburton, to settle these issues before they flamed up into a war that neither nation wanted. After extensive debate and attempts to make sense of poorly drawn maps, the United States and Great Britain decided on a new boundary that gave each about half of what they had claimed in Maine and in the area to the west of Lake Superior. The Webster-Ashburton Treaty also quietened the debate over slavery by establishing joint American-British patrols to intercept ships carrying slaves from Africa.

and his own physical toughness, expounded the longest inaugural speech in American history in March 1841. Unfortunately, the weather was bitterly cold; Harrison contracted pneumonia and died within a month of taking office. John Tyler had become president even though he shared few of the prevailing ideals of the Whigs in Congress. Efforts on the part of Henry Clay and other Whig leaders to expand the power and reach of government with tariffs, banks, and internal improvements proved fruitless in the face of Tyler's opposition. All but one of the members of the cabinet Tyler inherited from Harrison resigned in protest.

The only member to stay on, Daniel Webster, the secretary of state, did so only because he was engaged in important negotiations with England and did not think it proper to step down until they were complete.

Oregon also had troubled relations between the two countries. In the 1820s the United States and Great Britain had signed treaties with Russia, setting the southern boundary of Russia's claims in North America at 54°40′. As a result, the United States and Britain shared the Oregon Territory, a vast region covering present-day Oregon, Washington, Idaho, and British Columbia. Both sides agreed that the 49th parallel, the northern boundary of the United States farther east, would be a reasonable dividing line to the Pacific. Depending on where the boundary line was drawn, either the British or the Americans would possess Puget Sound, a coveted deepwater port. The British, believing that overland migration across the North American continent was virtually impossible, let the issue remain unresolved in the early 1840s so that other, more pressing, issues might be settled. American migration to the Pacific, however, soon proved quite possible.

The Wests

The hard times in the East made moving west seem an increasingly attractive option. Horace Greeley, the most influential newspaper editor of the day, warned people looking for a job in the midst of the depression not to come to the city but rather to "go to the Great West." The "West" included many places. To people in New England, migration to the West in the 1840s often meant migration to the lands of the northern plains and surrounding the Great Lakes. To people from Virginia and Kentucky, migration to the West might mean heading to the free states of Ohio, Indiana, or Illinois or, more often, to Mississippi, Louisiana, and Texas. For people from the cities of the East, the destination might be a booming new city such as Indianapolis, Chicago, or Detroit.

One "West" that captured the imagination of Americans in these years lay far beyond the relatively tame plains and forests of today's Midwest. The new dream of the early 1840s resided in Oregon and California, word of whose beauty and wealth had slowly filtered east throughout the preceding decade. Although many people considered it nothing less than suicide to attempt to cross the Rockies and what was considered "The Great American Desert," a growing stream of families decided to take the chance. Most of those who moved to the Pacific coast gathered in northern Missouri or southern Iowa. They set out in early May across undulating plains, with water and firewood easy to find, their wag-

ons pulled by oxen. They could make up to twenty-five miles a day, though fifteen was more common. The settlers gradually ascended to Fort Laramie, at the edge of the Rockies. By July, they had reached the Continental Divide, the point at which rivers on one side flowed to the east and those on the other flowed to the west. On the trail for more than three months by this point, the settlers had covered two-thirds of the distance of their journey. They still had three months and the hardest traveling yet to come.

From the Divide, the settlers heading to California split off from those going to Oregon. Both faced enormous difficulties in the remainder of their trip: deserts, mountains, fatigue, and dwindling supplies. They raced the weather, for early mountain snowstorms could be deadly. Some of the mountainous areas were so steep that wagons had to be dragged up one side and let down the other with ropes, chains, and pulleys. Finally, by October, 2,000 miles and six months after they had left Missouri or Iowa, the settlers crossed one last ridge and looked down on the sparkling valleys of Sacramento or the Willamette River.

Migration to the Pacific began slowly, with only a few dozen families making the treacherous journey between 1840 and 1842. The numbers mounted between 1843 and 1845, when over 5,000 people passed through Utah on their way to Oregon and California. Throughout the 1840s, the great majority of migrants chose Oregon over California as their destination. In Oregon, settlers found easier places to settle and no Spanish officials to contest their claims. Oregon came to seem a respectable place for literate and upright Protestant families to settle while California seemed a gamble, attractive mainly to single men willing to take their chances in a boom economy that could go bust.

Manifest Destiny

In 1842, the Great United States Exploring Expedition, sent out by the federal government, returned from a journey of 87,780 nautical miles. It had circumnavigated the globe, located Antarctica, and explored the Pacific coast. The captain of the expedition reported that Oregon was a treasure trove of "forests, furs, and fisheries" and that the United States could not afford to give up its claim to any of it. If the United States did not use its military to occupy the territory all the way to the 54°40′ boundary it would

MAP 11.4 | DISPUTE OVER OREGON BOUNDARY

The Democrats in Congress and President Tyler supported this expansion, focusing first on Texas. Texas appeared destined to play a key role in the future of the United States, one way or another. If the United States did not quickly annex Texas, Democrats believed, it might fall under the sway of the British. Under British control, they warned, Texas would become not only a barrier to further American migration but also a bastion of antislavery and a haven for runaways. If, by contrast, the United States acted quickly, Texas could become a safety valve for slavery. The vast new territory could attract not only slaveholders and their slaves but also emancipated slaves, pulling them toward their "natural" home in Mexico and Central America, keeping them away from the North and the other attractive lands such as California and Oregon. Midwestern Democrats, for their part, agreed that expansion was essential to the American future. The country simply could not afford to have major ports and potential markets sealed off if it was to avoid another depression such as the one that had recently wracked the country. These Democrats had their eye on Oregon.

James K. Polk, a former governor of Tennessee and an ardent expansionist, got the Democratic nomination for president after an acrimonious convention and nine ballots. The Democrats made their stance: "[O]ur title to the whole of the territory of Oregon is clear and unquestionable." They appealed to both Northerners and Southerners with a program of aggressive expansion, attempting to counter fears of slavery's growth not by rejecting Texas but by embracing Oregon. The first dispatch ever sent by telegraph and then published in a newspaper was a message from this convention about the "Oregon question."

The Election of 1844

In 1844 the Whigs nominated Henry Clay for president on a program explicitly opposed to expansion, expansion that would be "dangerous to the integrity of the

be risking much more than the Oregon territory itself. California might throw off the light Mexican rule under which it rested and join with an independent Oregon to create a nation "that is destined to control the destinies of the Pacific." The Tyler administration sought to downplay this report, not wanting to disrupt negotiations still pending on the boundary of Maine and Wisconsin.

The forces of expansion proved too strong for the administration to contain, however. With increasing numbers of settlers in Oregon, California, and Texas, the issue heated up. In 1845, newspaper editor John Louis O'Sullivan announced that it was the "manifest destiny"—the clear and unavoidable fate—of the United States "to overspread the continent allotted by Providence for the free development of our yearly multiplying millions." In other words, God intended white Americans to fill in every corner of the continent, including all of Canada, Mexico, and Cuba, pushing aside American Indians, Mexicans, English, or anyone else.

Union." The apparently clear-cut choice between Clay and Polk soon became complicated, however. Clay discovered that most white Americans thought westward expansion desirable. He began to waffle on the issue, announcing that he would not oppose Texas annexation if it could be done peacefully and by consensus. Such a strategy backfired, attracting few advocates of expansion but alienating antislavery people in the North.

Meanwhile, the early 1840s witnessed bloody battles over religion that fueled political conflict. A growing stream of immigrants from Ireland, the great majority of them Catholic, flowed into northern cities such as New York, Boston, and Philadelphia. In Protestant eyes, the Roman Catholic Church posed a direct threat to American institutions. That church's hierarchy was undemocratic, critics charged, the concentration of young girls in convents dangerous, the role of nuns and priests suspicious. In 1844 the largest anti-Catholic riot of antebellum America broke out in Philadelphia when Protestants and Irish immigrants erupted into conflict; several Catholic churches burned to the ground while authorities stood by. Because the Democrats proved far more sympathetic to the Irish than did the largely Protestant Whigs, the political differences between the parties now became inflamed with ethnic conflict.

Slavery, too, became an even more explosive issue in the early 1840s. In 1844 the Methodist church divided over slavery and the Baptists split the following year. Though the northern churches had explicitly renounced abolitionism, southern church leaders were angry that many of their northern brethren refused to believe that American slavery was part of God's plan. Five hundred thousand Southerners formed the Methodist Episcopal Church, South, while Baptists from nine southern states created the Southern Baptist Convention. These were the first major splits between Northerners and Southerners.

The conflicts over slavery exerted immediate political consequences. While the abolitionist Liberty party had received only about 7,000 votes in its debut four years earlier, it won 62,000 voters in 1844. In New York, in fact, the Liberty party's strong showing took enough votes from Clay to give the state to Polk. And those electoral votes proved the difference in the national election, as Polk won the presidency by the narrowest of margins thanks to the votes cast in New York.

The Democrats acted on their slim mandate even before Polk took office. The Senate, along party and regional lines, voted to annex Texas, an independent republic since 1836, as soon as Texas consented. Texas gave its approval in the fall of 1845 and won its vote in Washington at the end of that year. The Democrats sought to quiet concerns among Northerners by also annexing Oregon while the fevers of expansion burned. Though some Americans clamored for all of Oregon to its northernmost boundary with Russian territory, chanting "Fifty-four Forty or Fight," neither the United States nor the British proved eager to fight. The boundary was soon set at the 49th parallel, an extension of the northern U.S. boundary from the east.

CONCLUSION

The years between 1837 and 1845 bore the imprint of the largest economic depression in the nation's history up to that time. On the political front, the depression upset what had appeared to be a Democratic stranglehold on the presidency, making Martin Van Buren appear ineffectual and out of touch. Widespread dissatisfaction with the Democrats' handling of the economy laid the foundation for the remarkable Whig victory of 1840, when William Henry Harrison—and Tyler, too—campaigned under the banner of the log cabin and cider, claiming that they stood against economic privilege and corruption. The depression also drove settlers to the West and drove politicians to focus the energies and anxieties of the country on faraway opportunities and dangers.

In a seeming paradox, these same years witnessed American culture at its most ebullient. Painters, philosophers, and poets spoke in a confident new American vernacular. Reformers pushed hard for improvements in education, temperance, antislavery, and much else. Popular culture such as novels, magazines, and Barnum's museum attracted thousands of people. Many Americans focused so much on the future that they often refused to acknowledge the immediate problems surrounding them.

RECOMMENDED READINGS

Genovese, Eugene. *Roll, Jordan, Roll: The World the Slaves Made* (1974) stands as the most powerful portrayal of American slavery.

Kaestle, Carl F. *Pillars of the Republic: Common Schools and American Society, 1780–1860* (1983) is the most thorough and balanced account of education reform.

Kolchin, Peter. *American Slavery, 1619–1877* (1993) offers a nuanced synthesis of much of the recent work.

Rose, Anne C. *Voices of the Marketplace: American Thought and Culture, 1830–1860* (1995) gives a compelling interpretation of cultural history.

Perry, Lewis. *Boats Against the Current: American Culture Between Revolution and Modernity, 1820–1860* (1993) is a stimulating interpretation.

Stevenson, Brenda E. *Life in Black and White: Family and Community in the Slave South* (1996) paints a potent picture of both white and black Southerners.

Thornton, J. Mills, III. *Politics and Power in a Slave Society: Alabama, 1800–1860* (1978) conveys the way democracy and slavery interacted in the South.

Unruh, John I. *The Plains Across: Overland Emigrants and the Trans-Mississippi West, 1840–1860* (1979) tells this story with memorable detail.

Vance, James E. Jr., *The North American Railroad* (1995) shows how the railroad developed in Europe and the United States.

Economic and Political History

Cole, Donald B. *Martin Van Buren and the American Political System* (1984).

Cutler, Stanley. *Privilege and Creative Destruction: The Charles River Bridge Case* (1971).

Holt, Michael. *Political Parties and American Political Development from the Age of Jackson to the Age of Lincoln* (1992).

Howe, Daniel Walker. *The Political Culture of the American Whigs* (1979).

Kohl, Frederick. *The Politics of Individualism: Parties and the American Character in the Jacksonian Era* (1989).

Niven, John. *Martin Van Buren and the Romantic Age* (1983).

Peterson, Norma Lois. *The Presidencies of William Henry Harrison and John Tyler* (1989).

Rezneck, Samuel. "The Social History of an American Depression, 1837–1843," *American Historical Review* (1935).

Temin, Peter. *The Jacksonian Economy* (1969).

Cultural History

Brown, Richard D. *Knowledge Is Power: The Diffusion of Information in Early America, 1700–1865* (1989).

Buranelli, Vincent. *Edgar Allan Poe* (1977).

Cmiel, Kenneth. *Democratic Eloquence: The Fight over Popular Speech in Nineteenth-Century America* (1990).

Emerson, Ken. *Doo-dah! Stephen Foster and the Rise of American Popular Culture* (1997).

Harris, Neil. *Humbug: The Art of P.T. Barnum* (1973).

Laderman, Gary. *American Attitudes Toward Death, 1799–1883* (1996).

Lerner, Gerda. *The Grimké Sisters from South Carolina: Pioneers for Woman's Rights and Abolition* (1967).

Mendelowitz, Daniel M. *A History of American Art* (1970).

Messerli, Jonathan. *Horace Mann* (1972).

Novak, Barbara. *Nature and Culture: American Landscape Painting, 1825–1875* (1980).

Porte, Joel. *Representative Man: Ralph Waldo Emerson in His Time* (1979).

Rose, Anne C. *Transcendentalism as a Social Movement, 1830–1850* (1981).

Tyrrell, Ian R. *Sobering Up: From Temperance to Prohibition in Antebellum America, 1800–1860* (1979).

Zboray, Ronald J. *A Fictive People: Antebellum Economic Development and the American Reading Public* (1993).

The South and Slavery

Blassingame, John., ed., *Slave Testimony: Two Centuries of Letters, Speeches, Interviews, and Autobiographies* (1977).

Boles, John. *Black Southerners, 1619–1869* (1984).

Collins, Bruce. *White Society in the Antebellum South* (1985).

Fox-Genovese, Elizabeth. *Within the Plantation Household: Black and White Women of the Old South* (1988).

Joyner, Charles. *Down by the Riverside: A South Carolina Slave Community* (1984).

Malone, Ann Patton. *Sweet Chariot: Slave Family and Household Structure in Nineteenth-Century Louisiana* (1992).

Martin, Waldo E. *The Mind of Frederick Douglass* (1985).

McFeely, William S. *Frederick Douglass* (1991).

Oakes, James. *The Ruling Race* (1982).

Parish, Peter J. *Slavery: History and Historians* (1989).

Raboteau, Albert J. *Slave Religion: The "Invisible Institution" in the Antebellum South* (1978).

Rose, Willie Lee, ed., *A Documentary History of Slavery in North America* (1976).

White, Deborah Gray. *Ar'n't I a Woman?: Female Slaves in the Plantation South* (1985).

The West and the War with Mexico

Faragher, John Mack. *Women and Men on the Overland Trail* (1979).

Johannsen, Robert W. *To the Halls of the Montezumas: The Mexican War in the American Imagination* (1985).

Merk, Frederick. *History of the Westward Movement* (1978).

Schroeder, John H. *Mr. Polk's War: American Opposition and Dissent, 1846–1848* (1973).

Stephanson, Anders. *Manifest Destiny: American Expansion and the Empire of Right* (1995).

West, Elliott. *The Way to the West: Essays on the Central Plains* (1995).

Winders, Richard Bruce. *Mr. Polk's Army: The American Military Experience in the Mexican War* (1997).

SAN FRANCISCO IN THE DAYS OF THE GOLD RUSH

Ships filled the harbor of the small town of San Francisco as "forty-niners" descended on nearby gold fields.

Chapter 12

EXPANSION AND REACTION:
1846–1854

THE YEARS OF territorial expansion, population growth, and prosperity that accompanied victory in the Mexican War also proved to be years of unprecedented danger and foreboding for the United States. Every hopeful change seemed to bring a reaction. Heightened expectations of a transcontinental empire led to political conflict. Massive immigration from Europe fueled social conflict and sped the disintegration of the party system. Literature took on a more pessimistic tone, expressing doubts about the natural goodness of people and nature. Female activists dicovered that progress for women would come only as a result of prolonged effort. The attempt to open the West to settlement divided Southerners and Northerners against one another. The stopgap compromise on slavery both sides reluctantly signed at the end of all this turmoil satisfied neither side.

WAR WITH MEXICO

Mexico had been a major concern in American foreign policy and politics for generations. Throughout the 1820s American leaders had struggled with the promise and danger posed by the annexation of Texas; throughout the 1830s and 1840s Americans had aided Texans in their fight against the Mexican army. The United States longed for the territories Mexico controlled in western North America, but Mexico pledged to keep those lands. Because the American military remained untested and the battlefields lay far from the centers of population and supplies on the east coast, no one could be sure that the United States could defeat Mexico in a large-scale war. But the United States seemed determined to find out.

The United States at War

No one expected Mexico to accept American annexation of Texas without a struggle. The Mexican government had never recognized the independence of Texas, which Texans claimed as a result of their defeat of Santa Anna in 1836. President James K. Polk made matters worse by insisting that the border between Texas and Mexico lay at the Rio Grande, not at the Nueces River farther north, previously recognized by both nations as the boundary. Even before the formal annexation of Texas took effect in 1845, Polk ordered American troops under the command of General

CHRONOLOGY

1846 Mexican War begins; Stephen Kearny occupies Santa Fe; Zachary Taylor takes Monterey

Border between Canada and United States established at 49th parallel

Wilmot Proviso ignites sectional conflict

Bear Flag Republic in California proclaimed by John C. Frémont

Hiram Powers completes statue "The Greek Slave"

1847 Taylor defeats Santa Anna at Buena Vista; Winfield Scott captures Vera Cruz and Mexico City

Mormons reach Great Salt Lake Valley

1848 Gold discovered in California

Treaty of Guadalupe Hidalgo

Attempts to buy Cuba from Spain

Free Soil party runs Van Buren for president

Zachary Taylor elected president

Seneca Falls Convention

Oneida community established

Regular steamship trips between Liverpool and New York City

Mormons settle in Great Basin

1849 California seeks admission to Union

"Forty-Niners" race to California

Cotton prices invigorate South

Cholera epidemic returns

1850 Nashville Convention attempts to unify South

Fugitive Slave Law

Taylor dies; Millard Fillmore becomes president

Compromise of 1850

Nathaniel Hawthorne, *The Scarlet Letter*

First land-grant railroad: Illinois Central

John C. Calhoun and Henry Clay die

1851 Herman Melville, *Moby-Dick*

Maine adopts prohibition

Woman's rights convention in Akron, Ohio

Indiana state constitution excludes free blacks

1852 Franklin Pierce elected president

Harriet Beecher Stowe, *Uncle Tom's Cabin*

Daniel Webster dies

1853 Gadsden Purchase

Nativism increases

1854 Know-Nothings win unexpected victories

Whig party collapses

Republican party founded

Kansas-Nebraska Act

Ostend Manifesto encourages acquisition of Cuba

Henry David Thoreau, *Walden*

High-point of immigration

Railroad reaches Mississippi River

Zachary Taylor to cross the Nueces; soon, they were proceeding toward the Rio Grande.

Polk had his eyes not only on the border with Texas but on larger prizes still: the sale of California and New Mexico. Polk ordered John C. Frémont, leading an army expedition to map rivers within U.S. borders, to California. Frémont proceeded to support the "Bear Flag Rebellion," an armed struggle by American set-

tlers against the Mexican government. Disrupted, the Mexican provinces might be sacrificed more easily and more cheaply to the United States.

The president prepared for war in Texas, seizing on a skirmish between Mexican and American troops north of the Rio Grande as a convenient excuse. With no apparent sense of irony, Polk declared that "not withstanding all our efforts to avoid it," Mexico had

MAP 12.1 | THE MEXICAN WAR

started a war when it "invaded our territory and shed American blood on the American soil." Even though northern Whigs continually denounced the war and its motives, Whig congressmen believed they had to support appropriations for the soldiers in the field.

American troops under the leadership of Colonel Stephen Kearney took Santa Fe in New Mexico with no casualties late in the summer of 1846. California proved to be a greater struggle, partly because Mexican settlers there put up more of a fight, partly because

battle lines there were confused, and partly because Frémont seemed to provoke fights where resistance might not otherwise have appeared. In any case, the American forces won control of California a few months after they had taken New Mexico. The United States Army, under Zachary Taylor and Winfield Scott, achieved a series of victories in Mexico itself in 1846 and 1847, including an impressive amphibious landing at Vera Cruz by Scott's forces that ended in the conquest of Mexico City and "the halls of Montezuma."

Though the Mexicans outnumbered the Americans, the U.S. forces were much better equipped and supplied and enjoyed innovative and impressive leadership from their officer corps. The Mexican War familiarized Americans with names they would come to know all too well a little more than a decade later: Ulysses S. Grant, Jefferson Davis, Robert E. Lee, George McClellan, Joseph Johnston, William T. Sherman, Braxton Bragg, James Longstreet, Thomas Jonathan Jackson, and George Meade. The United States Army proved remarkably effective and won the respect of more established military powers in Europe. But Polk distrusted his two leading generals—Taylor and Scott—suspecting, correctly, that they harbored ambitions of winning the presidency under the Whig banner by capitalizing on their military success.

The Consequences of War

Many Northerners worried about the expansion of slavery and the increased power of the slave states that might accompany victory over Mexico. To put such concerns to rest, David Wilmot, a Pennsylvania Democrat in favor of the war, made a bold move: When a bill to appropriate additional funds for American troops in Mexico came before Congress in 1846, Wilmot offered a "proviso," a condition, that declared that slavery could not be established in any territory the United States might win from Mexico as a result of the war. Wilmot was no abolitionist and no friend of black people—he acted, he said, to protect his party and people of his own skin color—but his proviso became a central topic of debate in the heated battle over slavery. Votes for and against the proviso followed sectional lines to an alarming degree. The Wilmot Proviso went down to defeat and the war proceeded, but from 1846 on the opponents of slavery increasingly distrusted Polk and southern political leaders.

Henry David Thoreau protested the war with Mexico. As he wrote in his essay "On Civil Disobedience," Thoreau considered the Mexican War "the work of comparatively few individuals using the government as their tool." Thoreau decided to signal his disgust with the American government by claiming the higher law of individual conscience and refusing to pay his taxes. He spent only one night in jail before his friends paid his taxes for him, but Thoreau's essay proved influential later in American history when protesters looked for inspiration and justification. Throughout the North, from New England through the old Northwest, many people expressed their disgust with the war.

The war with Mexico limped to an end in late 1847 and the beginning of 1848. American troops controlled Mexico City, the Gulf Coast, and all the northern provinces claimed by the United States, but the Mexican government refused to settle on terms of peace. President James K. Polk, General Winfield Scott, and peace commissioner Nicholas Trist bickered over the treaty. Whigs argued with Democrats even as conflict churned within both parties. Northerners and Southerners viewed one another with undisguised distrust and distaste, as did abolitionists and their many opponents. Some Americans urged Polk to lay claim to all of the conquered country while others insisted that the United States should seize no territory at all from the war. Trist, on his own in Mexico, finally signed a treaty in Guadalupe Hidalgo that brought the negotiations to an end in February 1848.

Mexico, for $15 million and the abandonment of American claims against the Mexican government and its people, agreed to sell California, New Mexico, and all of Texas above the Rio Grande. When the treaty finally appeared before Congress for ratification the following month, many doubted that it would pass, so bitter was the opposition to the war, to Polk, and to expansion. The various cliques, however, found a way to swallow their disagreements long enough to ratify the treaty in March so that the war could end. A prominent newspaper pronounced the treaty "a peace which every one will be glad of, but no one will be proud of." The Mexicans signed the treaty in May and the war finally closed.

War and Politics

James K. Polk, chronically ill and wearied from the presidency, decided not to seek reelection in 1848.

The Democrats, scrambling to find someone to unite the northern and southern branches of the party, decided on Lewis Cass of Michigan. Cass, a rather colorless man except for his red wig, spoke for the majority of northern Democrats who sympathized with white Southerners in their determination to keep black people enslaved and in the South. Antislavery Democrats walked out of the Democratic convention that nominated Cass and called their own convention in New York; there, they nominated Martin Van Buren for the presidency.

Abolitionists who had supported the Liberty party exulted at a candidate who might win a substantial number of votes. Antislavery "Conscience Whigs," watching with disgust as their fellow Whigs fell over one another to decide which general from the Mexican War to nominate, also threw their support behind Van Buren. These various groups forged a working alliance

Zachary Taylor's fame from the war with Mexico translated into votes for the Whig party—even though that party had opposed the war from its outset.

for the election of 1848, declaring their solidarity behind the name of the Free Soil party and its stirring motto: "Free soil, free speech, free labor, and free men." Leading figures such as Charles Francis Adams and Charles Sumner denounced slavery and its defenders.

The mainstream Whigs found themselves in an awkward spot, for they had fervently opposed the Mexican War but now sought to capitalize on the popularity of General Zachary Taylor. Nevertheless, Taylor had several advantages as a candidate. He had no troubling political past; indeed, he had never before cast a ballot in any election. Though he was a slaveholding planter, he had opposed the war with Mexico before he had been sent there to lead American troops. Just what he thought about anything was quite unclear. That lack of clarity suited the Whigs, who counted on repeating their success of 1840 when another vague general, William Henry Harrison, had led them to victory.

Taylor won the election in the electoral college, but the popular vote revealed little consensus. Taylor won eight slave states and seven free ones, while Cass won eight free states and seven slaveholding ones. While Van Buren won over 290,000 votes and came in second in several important states, he did not win enough votes to cement the identity of the new Free Soil party. Free Soilers began drifting back to the Democrats and the Whigs. The election had not clarified the issues that concerned most voters.

AMERICANS ON THE MOVE

Americans, always restless, moved in massive numbers and on a continental scale in the years around 1850. As the economy lifted, transportation developed, boundaries became settled, and gold beckoned, people flooded to the states of the old Northwest and the old-Southwest as well as to Texas, Oregon, and California. The suffering of Ireland and political conflict within Germany drove millions across the Atlantic, filling the cities and farms of the East. Nothing seemed settled or permanent.

Rails, Sails, and Steam

The late 1840s and early 1850s saw the emergence of the fastest-growing rail lines and the fastest ships in

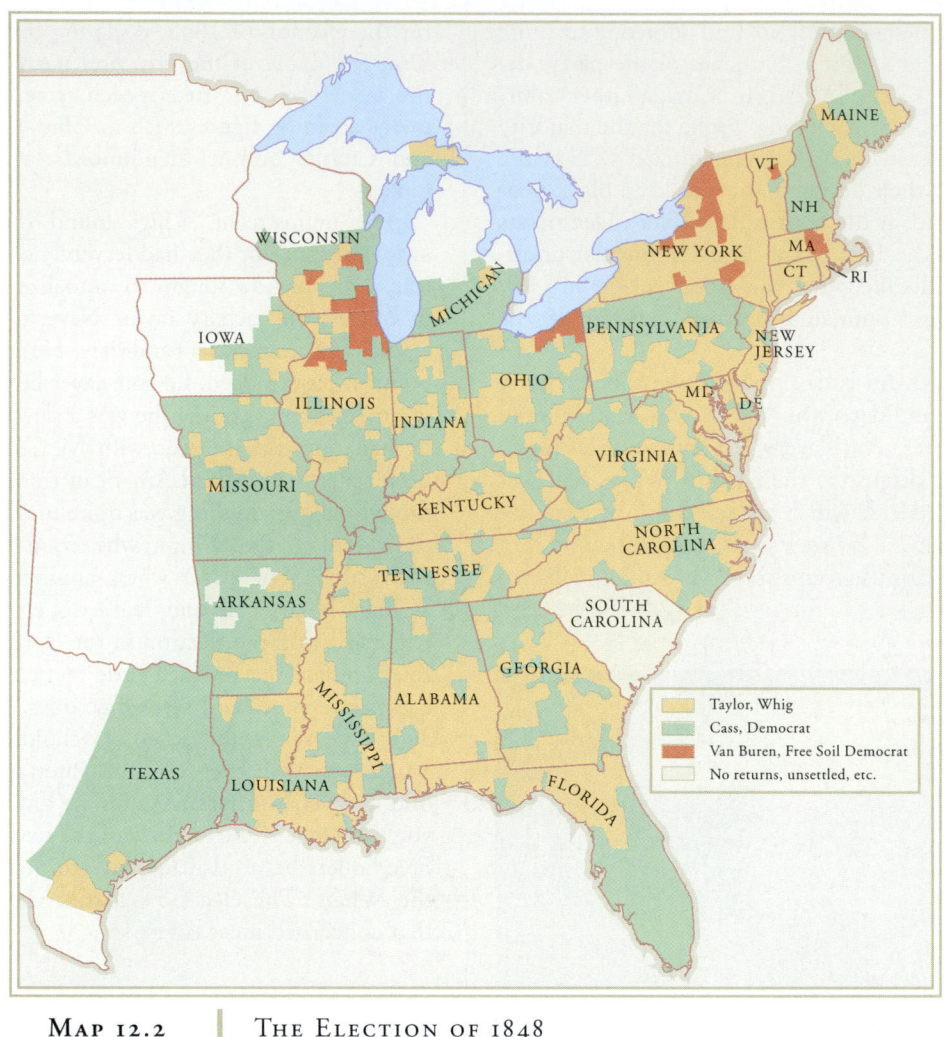

MAP 12.2 | THE ELECTION OF 1848

the world. The nation's rail network, slowed by the depression of the late 1830s and early 1840s, burgeoned with the return of prosperity. Private investors poured tens of millions of dollars into rail expansion. The federal government aided railroads with free surveys, friendly tariffs, and vast grants of land. The major cities of the eastern seaboard competed against one another to attract as many rail lines as possible. Smaller cities and towns fought to contribute land and cash. Owners of mines and factories subsidized new railroads, as did Wall Street speculators and investors from Great Britain.

Railroads proved more important for some parts of the country than for others. Railroads flourished in New England and New York, where the density of population and manufacturing permitted the new technology to work most efficiently. Midwestern states such as Ohio, Illinois, and Indiana also showed themselves well-suited to the railroads, for their vast flat distances and absence of good river transportation made the extension of the steel rails both necessary and relatively easy. Chicago had no railroads at all in 1850 but by 1860 twelve lines converged in the city, making it the undisputed rail center of the nation—indeed, of the world. Three of those lines stretched from Chicago all the way to New York City; a trip that had taken ten days before the railroad now took only a day and a half.

Overland Mail Routes

.... Independence to Salt Lake City

– – – – Salt Lake City to California

– – – – Independence to Santa Fe; Kansas City to Stockton

– – – – San Antonio to Santa Fe

– – – San Antonio to San Diego

– – – – Butterfield Overland Mail

.... Neosho to Albuquerque

.... Leavenworth and Pike's Peak Express

———— Railroads in operation December 1850

MAP 12.3 RAILROADS AND OVERLAND MAIL, 1850

Rural areas as well as cities immediately felt the effects of the railroad. Farmers now found it profitable to ship their produce to a city a hundred miles away. Farmers specialized, becoming dairymen, vegetable growers, and fruit producers. Steel plows and mechanical reapers drew huge harvests from the rich soil of the upper Mississippi Valley. Corn, wheat, hogs, and cattle flowed out of Ohio, Illinois, Indiana, and Wisconsin. The older farms of New England, New York, and Pennsylvania, facing the competition of the new states of the West, turned to specialty products such as cheese, maple sugar, vegetables, and cranberries. These products, along with thousands of others, rode the railroad tracks to market, tying countryside and city together.

Because the relatively sparse population of the South could not sustain much railroad traffic and because the South's natural system of rivers carried cargo so cheaply throughout the year, railroad building trailed off in the South in the 1840s and did not pick up again until the late 1850s. The South relied instead on the steamboats that plied the Mississippi and other major rivers. The riverboats grew in size, number, and ornateness throughout the period, becoming floating hotels decorated with blazing lights, glittering mirrors, and flying flags. The 1850s marked the glory days of these riverboats, with cotton bales stacked on every square inch of deck.

Elsewhere, packet steamships carried mail, freight, and passengers up and down the eastern seaboard,

Graceful and fast, American clipper ships raced around South America and across the Pacific.

over the Great Lakes, and, increasingly, across the Atlantic Ocean. Beginning in 1848, Americans could count on regular steam travel between New York and Liverpool, England. These innovations in transportation, exciting as they were, came at a steep cost. "I never open a newspaper that does not contain some account of disasters and loss of life on railroads," one diarist observed. "They do a retail business in human slaughter, whilst the wholesale trade is carried on (especially on Western waters) by the steamboats. This world is going on too fast."

Clipper ships enjoyed a brief but stirring heyday in the late forties and early fifties. Clippers used narrow hulls and towering sails to attain speeds that have yet to be reached by any other sailing vessels of their size. The clippers carried expensive tea from China to England, fortune seekers to a gold rush in Australia, and Americans from the east coast to the west. They sailed from New York to San Francisco, all the way around South America, in less than a hundred days. Shipbuilders constructed the vessels as fast as they could and the ships sometimes paid for themselves on their very first voyage. Although they were to be displaced after 1855 by uglier and more efficient steamships, for a few exciting years the clipper ships thrived on the high prices, small cargoes, long voyages, and desperate speed fueled by remarkable discoveries in California.

The Gold Rush

The natives of California had long known of the gold hidden in the rocks and creeks of that vast territory, as had the Mexicans who governed the region. White American settlers, too, had found gold deposits in the early 1840s, when a trickle of men had sought their fortune in California rather than in the more popular destination of Oregon. But it was a discovery in January of 1848 that changed everything.

John Sutter had been one of the first non-Spanish white men to settle in California. In 1839 he had emigrated from Switzerland to the area that became Sacramento, where he established a large fort, trading post, and wheat farm. Sutter hired a carpenter named James Marshall to build a mill on the American River. While working on the project, Marshall happened to notice "something shining in the bottom of the ditch." He realized that the nugget, about half the size of a pea, was gold. Sutter, Marshall, and the other men on the place tried to keep the find a secret, but word leaked to San Francisco. There, sailors abandoned their ships and clerks left their shops to look for gold along the American River. By the end of 1848 such men had gathered nuggets and dust worth about $6 million.

Back east, people remained calm, even skeptical, about the discovery until 230 ounces of almost pure

A diverse population of men rushed to the California gold fields in 1849. Recent immigrants from China worked alongside Indians, whites, and African Americans.

gold went on display in Washington. The Gold Rush began: "The coming of the Messiah, or the dawn of the Millennium could not have excited anything like the interest," one newspaper marvelled. By the end of 1849 over 700 ships carrying over 45,000 Easterners sailed to California. Some of the ships went around South America; others transported their passengers to the Isthmus of Panama, which they crossed by foot and canoe. These trips could be horrific, in part because 1848 and 1849 saw cholera break out across the United States. Once the disease began on board a ship, death swept through the crew and passengers.

About 55,000 settlers rejected the ships and instead followed the overland trails cut across the continent. Some traveled alongside the continuing stream of settlers to Oregon, others followed trails directly to the gold fields from destinations as far south as Mexico. Whether they went by sea or land, the participants in the Gold Rush were quite different from other immigrants to the West. The "Forty-Niners" tended to be either single men or groups of men from the same lo-

cality. In sharp contrast to the Oregon migration, women and children rarely appeared among those rushing to get the gold, accounting for only about 5 percent of all those who came to California in the frantic early days. Most of the men who flooded into California, unlike the Oregon settlers, had little interest in settling there permanently. They intended to find their share of the gold and move on. Once in California, men of all classes, colors, and nations worked feverishly alongside one another in the streams and mountainsides during the day; the miners included Mexicans, Chileans, Frenchmen, Englishmen, Hungarians, and other Europeans. Disease and miserable living conditions hounded all of them, sending thousands to their deaths.

When some Chinese men returned home from California flush with American riches and stories of the "Golden Mountain," the fever spread in Asia as it did in Europe and America. About 70 percent of the Chinese immigrants came from Guangdong Province, where many peasants and artisans had become impoverished and desperate enough to launch the dangerous journey. Young men, in particular, thought California might offer a way to attain the wealth they needed to acquire a farm and a wife back in China; they did not intend to stay long in the alien land. Migrants could buy tickets from brokers on credit, with high interest. Upon their arrival in California, the Chinese immigrants discovered that they had to borrow yet more money from Chinese merchants in San Francisco to be transported to the gold fields. The miners worked continuously in hopes of paying off that debt, fueling resentment and persecution by white miners, but the costs seemed worth the potential reward.

California held out hope for African Americans, too. News of the gold rush spread not only by word of mouth but also through black newspapers and the abolitionist press. Most of the black migrants to California left from the coastal cities of New England. California—unlike Ohio, Illinois, and Indiana—held out the promise of an American West where color really might not matter so much, where a hard-working black man might enjoy the fruits of his own labor. Although abolitionists, black and white, warned that even California might not be safe for black migrants, several thousand African Americans decided to take the chance.

Whatever their race, few miners discovered a fortune. The average miner in 1848 found about an ounce of gold a day, worth around $20. Even though

the cost of living was exorbitant in gold-rush California, this $20 was about twenty times what a laborer back east made with a daily wage. As the number of competing miners skyrocketed over the next few years, however, the average take declined until it reached about $6 a day in 1852. Mining became more mechanized and concentrated in fewer hands. Soon, the biggest profits went not to lucky individuals but to companies that assaulted the river beds and ravines with battalions of workers, explosives, and crushing mills.

Although miners of every background went bust, California as a whole flourished. Within four years over $220 million in gold came out of the state. Towns appeared wherever people gathered to look for the gold, and in those towns' stores, physicians, saloons, lawyers, bordellos, and newspapers absorbed the ready cash. Men who tired of mining turned to farming instead, or teaching school, or building houses. San Francisco was the big winner: A dull village before

1848, within a couple of years it had grown into a brash and booming city of 35,000 diverse residents.

The Mormons' Great Migration

A different kind of westward movement was already in full force as the California Gold Rush got underway. These migrants were members of the Church of Jesus Christ of Latter-day Saints, or Mormons. In the face of relentless persecution Joseph Smith, the founder of the church, had led his flock to Illinois. There they established the town of Nauvoo and flourished; by the mid-1840s Nauvoo, with 15,000 residents, had become the largest city in Illinois. But the peace was not to last. Conflict erupted within the church itself when Smith decreed that polygamy was God's will, that men within the church would marry several wives. When Smith ordered the destruction of a Mormon newspaper that opposed the new practice, the paper's owners

Persecuted in Illinois in the 1840s, the Mormons launched a mass migration to the Great Salt Lake in the state they called "Deseret."

signed warrants for his arrest. A mob of non-Mormons broke into the jail where Smith was being held and killed both him and his brother. The Mormons of Nauvoo feared for their lives as vigilantes roamed the area.

The Mormons turned to one of their elders, Brigham Young, to lead them in this time of trial. Young, believing that their church would not be tolerated within settled areas, decided to move to a place beyond the reach of the Mormons' many enemies. Young knew from reading guidebooks for settlers to Oregon and California about the Great Salt Lake, a place of rich land and good water cut off from the east by mountains and from the west and south by deserts. The Mormons carefully planned their migration, sending out scouts and establishing way stations for those who would follow. They abandoned Nauvoo in the spring of 1846. In a well-coordinated migration, 15,000 Mormons moved in stages to the Great Salt Lake. When they first arrived, in 1847, the valley presented a daunting picture of rock and sagebrush but the settlers irrigated the land, turning it into a thriving community.

When frosts, insects, and drought ruined much of the crops in the spring of 1848, Young announced that the Mormons would follow a new strategy: They would pool their labor and their resources even more than before. They designed an ambitious city on the shores of the Great Salt Lake, with wide streets surrounding a temple that would "surpass in grandeur of design and gorgeousness of decoration all edifices the world has yet seen." Young concentrated control of the city and its farms in his own hands and in those of his fellow church leaders. Few Mormons left with the fortune seekers when the gold rush brought thousands of travellers through their new settlement; rather, the Mormons did a profitable business with the forty-niners.

As some non-Mormons settled at the Great Salt Lake, Young decided that a form of government other than the church must be established. He oversaw the creation of a state called "Deseret," a Mormon term meaning "honeybee." The Mormons began a successful campaign to attract new converts from Europe, Asia, and Latin America; thousands of people prepared to move to the new refuge at the Great Salt Lake. In 1849 the residents of Deseret petitioned Congress for admission into the Union as a new state and awaited the decision, knowing that many Americans viewed them with contempt and suspicion.

The High Tide of Immigration

Even as Americans moved west, a vast immigration from Ireland surged into the eastern United States in the late 1840s and early 1850s. Irish immigration itself was not new; about a million people had left Ireland for the United States between 1815 and 1844, though many of those early migrants were Protestant Scots-Irish. The situation in Ireland changed much for the worse beginning in 1845, when the potato harvest failed. A blight suddenly struck healthy fields, turning the leaves black almost overnight and filling the air with "a sickly odor of decay." This, the Great Potato Famine, which would last for nearly a decade, destroyed the basic food for most of the Irish people and created suffering on an immense scale. Over a million people died; another 1.8 million fled to North America as their only hope for survival. In all, about a fourth of the island's population departed, with more people leaving in the eleven years after 1845 than in the preceding 250 years combined. The year of 1854 marked the high point of immigration to the United States before the Civil War.

The Irish emigrants tended to be young, single, poor, unskilled, and Catholic; a large number spoke Irish rather than English; they came over in the dead of winter and with virtually no money or property. While some Irish immigrants spread throughout North America, from Ontario to New Orleans to San Francisco, most congregated in the cities of the North and Midwest. They lived from day to day on whatever money they could earn, moving frequently in hopes of bettering their condition. Most men worked on docks, others in canal and railroad construction, often in competition with free blacks and even slaves, always for the lowest wage. Women worked as domestics and as unskilled laborers in textile mills. Desperately poor, easily identified, widely despised, and often subsisting on the bare edge of starvation, the Irish figured prominently in arrest reports and on penitentiary rolls.

The high tide of Irish immigration occurred simultaneously with the peak of German immigration. Over a million Germans came to America between 1846 and 1854, many of them dislocated by a failed revolution in Germany in 1848. The Germans were much better off financially than the Irish. They tended to be farmers who brought some property with them and established farms in the Midwest. The Germans, more than the Irish, were divided by wealth, generation,

IMMIGRATION TO THE UNITED STATES, 1820–1860

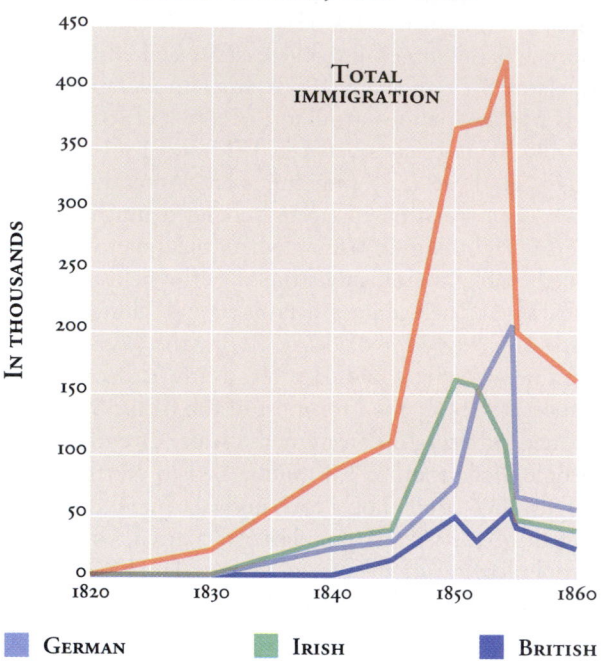

TOTAL IMMIGRATION

IN THOUSANDS

■ GERMAN   ■ IRISH   ■ BRITISH

politics, regional background, and religion. Combined, the Irish and German immigrants accounted for almost 15 percent of the entire population of the United States; in some cities, the foreign-born and their children constituted a majority of the population.

In the eyes of many white Protestants, the new arrivals appeared impossible to assimilate, marked, it seemed, by drink, strange languages, and clannishness. The immigrants threatened to drive down wages because they were willing to work for so little. They also threatened to thwart enforced temperance. That movement gained momentum in 1851, when Maine, in reaction to the new immigrants, became the first state to enact statewide prohibition of alcohol. The immigrants often received the vote in state and local elections soon after they landed and they voted heavily against prohibition. Protestants saw in the large numbers of new immigrants an immediate threat to American political institutions.

In the face of such challenges to their values and power, "native Americans" organized against the immigrants. The most powerful manifestation of nativism

Hounded by poverty, Irish people gathered in their villages in search of transportation to America in the late 1840s and early 1850s.

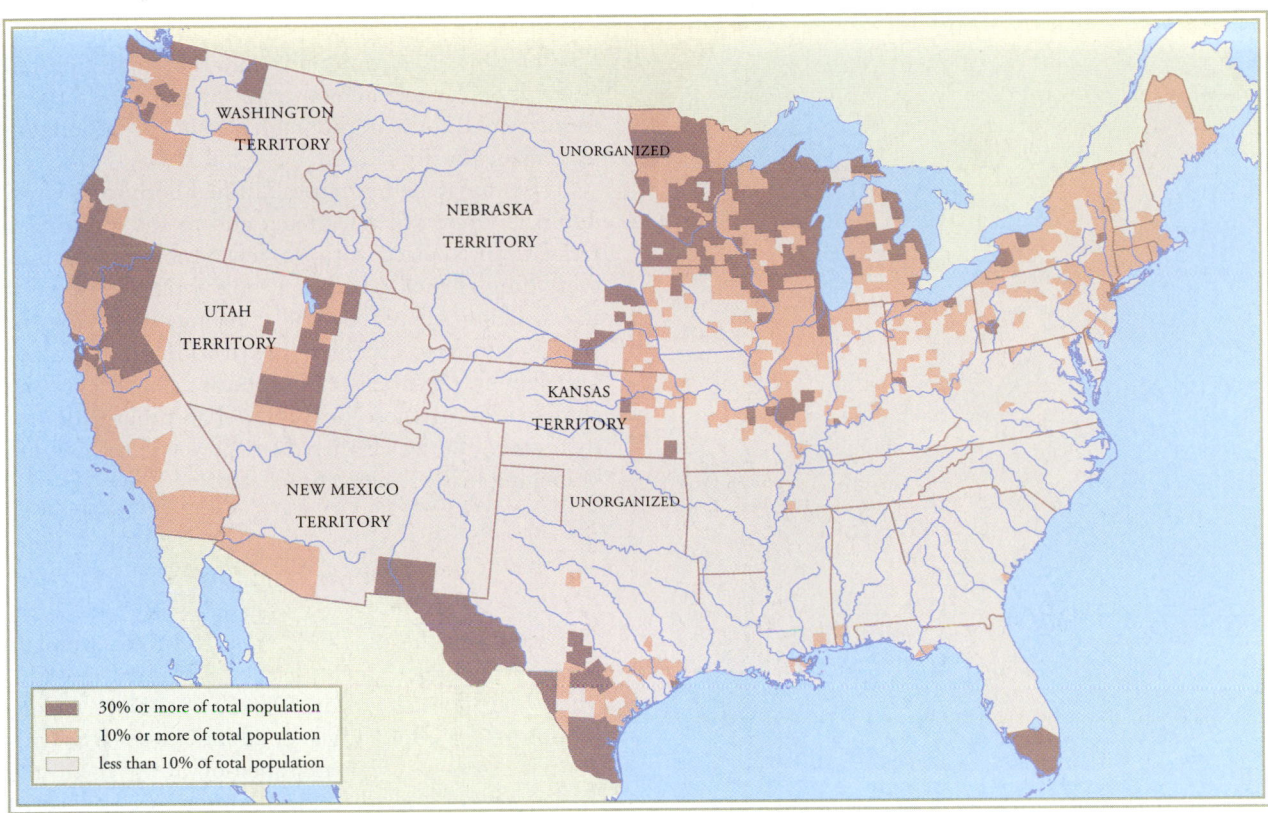

30% or more of total population
10% or more of total population
less than 10% of total population

MAP 12.4 | FOREIGN-BORN POPULATION, 1840-1860

appeared in New York City in 1849, when Charles Allen founded the Order of the Star Spangled Banner. Its membership was restricted to native-born white Protestants sworn to secrecy. When asked about the order by outsiders, members were instructed to say "I know nothing"—and thus they became popularly known as the "Know-Nothings." The order grew slowly at first, but it drew on deeply held and deepening prejudices. No one knew what the movement might become.

ACTION AND REFLECTION

The late 1840s and early 1850s, though relatively peaceful and prosperous, led a number of people to protest the drift of American life. Some became so disenchanted that they established communities set aside from the rest of society, places where they could experiment with alternative ways of organizing labor, power, and sexuality. Others launched a crusade to make the United States consistent with its highest ideals, defining women as well as men as full citizens. Yet others wrote novels and poetry that reflected, sometimes obliquely and sometimes directly, on the whirl of American life.

Perfect Communities

Most of the hundred or so utopian communities created in the United States between the Revolution and the Civil War were founded in the 1840s. Some communities were secular in origin and some religious, some boldly experimental and others reactionary. They all insisted that people truly dedicated to social improvement had to flee corruption and compromise. Though several prophets and leaders emigrated from Europe to the New World in hopes of establishing

John Humphrey Noyes founded the Oneida community in upstate New York, proclaiming sexual freedom in "complex marriage."

religious utopias, most of the idealistic communities grew directly from American origins.

The most notorious American communal experiment emerged in 1848. It was in that year that John Humphrey Noyes and his 250 followers created the Oneida Association in upstate New York. Noyes, educated as a minister and a lawyer, had become convinced years before that it was possible for humans to be "perfected," made free of sin. Most controversial, he argued that people in a state of perfection should not be bound by conventional monogamous marriages; all belonged to one another sexually in "complex marriage." He gathered a small group of disciples around him who put such beliefs into action, practicing birth control by having males withdraw during intercourse. Without fear of pregnancy, Noyes argued, sexual intercourse could become "a joyful act of fellowship."

Oneida experimented not only with sex but also with economic cooperation. Everyone performed the full range of labor, with few distinctions based on gender. The women of the group cut their hair, wore pantaloons rather than skirts, and played sports with their male compatriots. Unlike other utopian communities,

Oneida focused its energies on manufacturing rather than farming. The community produced an improved and profitable steel animal trap. Later, Oneida transformed itself into a profitable business corporation specializing in silverware.

The utopian communities testified both to the freedom the United States offered and to the yearning it created. In a place with so few visible constraints, everything seemed possible. People took advantage of the isolation offered by the enormous space of the young country to experiment with communities based on religious, sexual, or philosophical principles, or any combination of those principles. The proliferation of such communities also testified, however, to how full of longing many Americans seemed.

Woman's Rights

The seeds for the organized movement for woman's rights in the United States had been planted in 1840, when women attending the World's Anti-Slavery Convention in London, England, found themselves consigned to seats in a separate roped-off area. One of the delegates was Elizabeth Cady Stanton, a well-educated young woman, twenty-five years old, on her honeymoon with her husband, a political abolitionist. Listening to the debates over the place of women in antislavery, Stanton felt "humiliated and chagrined, except as these feelings were outweighed by contempt for the shallow reasoning of the opponents and their comical pose and gestures." Stanton discovered an important ally at the London meeting: Lucretia Mott, twenty-two years Stanton's senior, a devout and activist Quaker and feminist. The two women vowed that they would start a movement back in the States for woman's rights, but they did not soon find the opportunity they sought. Stanton devoted her time to raising her family in Boston, participating only marginally in reform. In 1847, she moved with her family to Seneca Falls, New York, for her husband's health.

While living in Seneca Falls, Stanton revived the idea of holding a convention on woman's rights. She grew frustrated with the narrowness of life in a small town and the limitations placed on women there. Meeting with Lucretia Mott again, Stanton told her friend how miserable she had become. They renewed their determination to start a conversation in the United States over the place of women. The two women joined with three of Mott's Quaker friends to plan a convention in July in Seneca Falls, although

Elizabeth Cady Stanton, one of the founders of the woman's rights movement, about the time of the Seneca Falls Convention of 1848.

people might attend the meeting—held in an obscure town during a busy season for farmers—but over a hundred people came, including a considerable number of men. Of those men the most prominent was Frederick Douglass. Douglass's newspaper, the *North Star,* was one of the few papers to give the convention a positive notice; the rest ridiculed the very notion of equal rights for women.

Despite the skepticism, Stanton and the other organizers of the Seneca Falls Convention succeeded in their major role: getting Americans to talk about woman's rights. Word of the Declaration spread among the many women's groups working in other reform organizations. Stanton, Mott, and their allies determined that they would hold a convention each year to keep the momentum going. Meetings in Rochester, Akron, Worcester, and Syracuse convened over the next decade.

At the Akron meeting in 1851 a black woman spoke, despite the opposition of some who feared that

only Mott had had any experience in organizing a reform meeting. Stanton recalled that they "felt as helpless as if they had been suddenly asked to construct a steam engine." The five women "were neither sour old maids, childless women, nor divorced wives, as the newspapers claimed them to be," Stanton argued; it was not that they themselves had suffered so much, but rather that they had "souls large enough to feel the wrongs of others."

Casting about for a way to express their grievances most effectively, they decided to model their "Declaration of Rights and Sentiments" on the Declaration of Independence. It began with a ringing statement: "The history of mankind is a history of repeated injuries and usurpations on the part of man toward woman, having in direct object the establishment of an absolute tyranny over her." The Declaration drew on the strategies and rhetoric of other reform efforts. It demanded the right to vote and insisted on women's full equality with men in every sphere of life, including property rights, education, employment, divorce, and in court. The organizers worried about how many

Sojourner Truth, a former slave from New York, embodied for many people the pride and strength of black women, for she spoke out for both her gender and her race.

"DECLARATION OF SENTIMENTS" OF THE WOMAN SUFFRAGE MOVEMENT 1848

Sixty-eight women and thirty-two men signed this declaration, produced at Seneca Falls in 1848. Modeled on the Declaration of Independence, this document provided a touchstone for the woman's movement throughout the rest of the century and beyond.

The history of mankind is a history of repeated injuries and usurpations on the part of man toward woman, having in direct object the establishment of an absolute tyranny over her. To prove this, let facts be submitted to a candid world.

He has never permitted her to exercise her inalienable right to the elective franchise.

He has compelled her to submit to laws, in the formation of which she had no voice.

He has withheld from her rights which are given to the most ignorant and degraded men—both natives and foreigners.

Having deprived her of this first right of a citizen, the elective franchise, thereby leaving her without representation in the halls of legislation, he has oppressed her on all sides.

He has made her, if married, in the eye of the law, civilly dead.

He has taken from her all right in property, even to the wages she earns.

He has made her, morally, an irresponsible being, as she can commit many crimes with impunity, provided they be done in the presence of her husband. In the covenant of marriage, she is compelled to promise obedience to her husband, he becoming, to all intents and purposes, her master—the law giving him power to deprive her of her liberty, and to administer chastisement.

He has so framed the laws of divorce, as to what shall be the proper causes, and in case of separation, to whom the guardianship of the children shall be given, as to be

---

her appearance would identify the woman's rights movement too closely with abolition. She had escaped slavery in New York in 1827, freed her son in Alabama, and supported her family by working as a domestic. In 1843, she had a vision in which she was commanded to carry the word of God; she renamed herself "Sojourner Truth." In Akron she rebuked the white ministers who had come to argue against the advocates of woman's rights. Those ministers urged women to accept the fact that they were special creatures who should be protected and who should stay in their restricted sphere. "Look at me!" Truth commanded them. "I have ploughed, and planted, and gathered into barns, and no man could head me! And a'n't I a woman? I could work as much and eat as much as a man—when I could get it—and bear de lash as well! And a'n't I a woman?" She had seen most of her thirteen children sold into slavery, and "when I cried out with my mother's grief, none but Jesus heard me! And a'n't I a woman?"

The campaign for woman's rights, as it evolved, developed a complex relationship to abolition and to African Americans. The movement might offer a rare opportunity for women such as Sojourner Truth to be heard, but white woman's rights advocates generally phrased their demands for equal rights in terms of education and refinement that neglected black women and their needs.

Not all activist women, moreover, dedicated themselves to woman's rights. More conservative women,

wholly regardless of the happiness of women—the law, in all cases, going upon a false supposition of the supremacy of man, and giving all power into his hands.

After depriving her of all rights as a married woman, if single, and the owner of property, he has taxed her to support a government which recognizes her only when her property can be made profitable to it.

He has monopolized nearly all the profitable employments, and from those she is permitted to follow, she receives but a scanty remuneration. He closes against her all the avenues to wealth and distinction which he considers most honorable to himself. As a teacher of theology, medicine, or law, she is not known.

He has denied her the facilities for obtaining a thorough education, all colleges being closed against her.

He allows her in church, as well as state, but a subordinate position, claiming apostolic authority for her exclusion from the ministry, and, with some exceptions, from any public participation in the affairs of the church.

He has created a false public sentiment by giving to the world a different code of morals for men and women, by which moral delinquencies which exclude women from society, are not only tolerated, but deemed of little account in man.

He has usurped the prerogative of Jehovah himself, claiming it as his right to assign for her a sphere of action, when that belongs to her conscience and to her God.

He has endeavored, in every way that he could, to destroy her confidence in her own powers, to lessen her self-respect, and to make her willing to lead a dependent and abject life.

Now, in view of this entire disfranchisement of one-half the people of this country, their social and religious degradation—in view of the unjust laws above mentioned, and because women do feel themselves aggrieved, oppressed, and fraudulently deprived of their most sacred rights, we insist that they have immediate admission to all the rights and privileges which belong to them as citizens of the United States.

SOURCE Elizabeth Cady Stanton, et al., *History of Woman Suffrage*, Vol. 1 (Rochester, N.Y.: Fowler & Wells, 1889), 58–59.

often socially prominent, had for several decades devoted their energies to acquiring public funds for orphanages, shelters for "fallen" women, and the poor. They continued with these practices throughout the 1840s, using their connections to important men in state legislatures, on city boards, and in prosperous businesses to raise money and garner support. Such women did not hesitate to raise and circulate petitions, gathering the signatures of hundreds of thousands of women. They asked for laws to criminalize seduction and to change property laws, to oppose Indian removal, restrict slavery, and stop the sale of liquor. They often proved successful and effective with these indirect means and saw little need for agitating for the vote for women. American women, in other words,

were as politically diverse as the men in their households.

Hawthorne, Melville, and Whitman

Whereas the 1830s and 1840s had been the time of transcendentalism, the 1850s saw American writers grappling with themes very much attuned to their time and place. While Nathaniel Hawthorne's *The Scarlet Letter* and Herman Melville's *Moby Dick* were ironic, dark, and complex allegories, Walt Whitman's *Leaves of Grass* evoked a determinedly hopeful vision. All three captured a key part of the American mood in the 1850s.

A writer deeply engaged with the history of his native New England, Nathaniel Hawthorne wove powerful allegorical stories of sin and regret such as The Scarlet Letter.

Nathaniel Hawthorne's father died at sea and left his family to do the best it could with limited resources and memories of once being a leading family of Massachusetts. Hawthorne went to Bowdoin College despite the family's reduced circumstances and then returned to his mother's home and set up as a writer. Quiet and ambitious, he did not marry until he was thirty-eight years old, devoting his energies to his work. He read almost indiscriminately, gulping down popular crime fiction as well as the latest literary products of Europe. Though he himself was not morose, Hawthorne was fascinated by the lingering consequences of sin, perhaps because one of his ancestors had been a judge in the notorious Salem witch trials. He turned to the history of New England as the setting for his best work, finding there an allegory for the struggles of his own age.

Hawthorne became an active supporter of the Democratic party, largely because of his friendship with an old college friend, Franklin Pierce, a rising figure in the party. Hawthorne wrote for the Democratic papers and won a job in the Salem customs house as measurer

of salt and coal. Hawthorne's political experiences in the late 1840s embittered him, however, for his Whig opponents not only sought to remove Hawthorne from his post but also charged him with corruption. It was at this point that Hawthorne wrote *The Scarlet Letter,* a symbolic story about revenge and its costs. Though set in the colonial era, the novel opened with a biting portrayal of the Salem customs house and its petty (Whig) politicians. The novel propelled Hawthorne into literary fame.

After the arrival of Hawthorne's long-delayed prosperity, he and his family moved to Lenox, Massachusetts, in the Berkshire Mountains in 1850. There he met a younger writer, one who admired Hawthorne for his willingness to write complicated stories of guilt. The young author was Herman Melville. He had left school at the age of fifteen, tried his hand at writing, but, in need of work that paid better and more certainly in the hard times of the late 1830s, went to sea. His experiences on ship, in port, and on the Pacific island where he lived among friendly cannibals gave him the subjects for most of his writing. His first two

Herman Melville became famous as a writer of sea stories but found little public interest in his 1852 masterpiece, Moby-Dick.

books, *Typee* and *Omoo,* adventure stories of the sea, did quite well and made a name for the young author. But Melville was not satisfied to write such books; he envisioned nothing less than an American epic.

Melville's masterpiece, about a ship captain's search for the great white whale "Moby-Dick," created a peculiarly American idiom: part Old Testament, part adventure story, part how-to book, part encyclopedia, part meditation on the enormous and reckless entity that the United States had become by the early 1850s. Good and evil swirled together in *Moby-Dick,* bonded and switched. Unlike *The Scarlet Letter, Moby-Dick,* published in 1852, did not do well on the market. Melville, disenchanted, made his work more cynical and biting. His novel *The Confidence-Man,* published six years after *Moby-Dick,* dwelt on the swindling, corruption, and self-deception that seemed at the heart of the United States in the 1850s, a time when everyone seemed to be on the make. Few people at the time noticed Melville's bold experiments and he gradually fell silent.

Walt Whitman also labored on an epic work, *Leaves of Grass,* throughout the early 1850s. The long poem reflected America at mid-century in all its diversity, roughness, innocence, and exuberance. This poetry of democratic origin and impulse included everything and everyone, speaking in a language stripped of classical allusion and pretension. As Whitman wrote in the preface to this book, anyone who would be a poet in the mid-nineteenth century must "flood himself with the immediate age." Whitman had done just that throughout his entire adult life.

Whitman took the raucous city of New York as his subject. For him, as for so many Americans in these years, cities were frontiers, full of democracy and possibility. Whitman participated fully in the life of the city, writing as a partisan Democratic journalist, running a shop, working as a building contractor, walking the streets, spending days in the public library reading books of science and travel and religion, moving from one editing job to another, attending boisterous political meetings—all the while jotting notes for a new kind of epic poetry taking shape in his head.

As he invented a poetical style to match his kaleidoscopic vision of American life, Walt Whitman also invented an image of himself as the poet who would take in and express everything. Both his life and his poem would be "A Song of Myself." He had his photograph taken, showing him tanned and bearded, shirt open at the collar. Whitman's book was literally self-made; in 1855 he set some of the type and hired

Walt Whitman, exuberant poet of New York and America, gloried in his connection to common people.

friends—printers of legal work—to publish the book for him.

Leaves of Grass came out to no public recognition whatsoever. Whitman sent a few copies to people he admired, however, including Emerson. The reply could not have been more heartening: "I find it the most extraordinary piece of wit and wisdom that America has yet contributed. . . . I greet you at the beginning of a great career. . . ." But most readers of the book, including several leading literary figures who read it on Emerson's recommendation, considered it vulgar, even obscene, shapeless, and crude. The hopeful words of *Leaves of Grass* soon became lost in years when a darker vision of the United States prevailed.

RACE, SLAVERY, AND POLITICS

The decade of the 1850s began with many signs of change and progress. The economy kicked into high

gear. People flooded to the recently acquired territories of California and Oregon as well as to the upper and lower Mississippi region. Clipper ships, steamships, and railroads expanded their reach. Abolitionists, perfectionists, and feminists worked for the improvement of American society. Despite the generally positive turn of events, however, a persistent undercurrent of fear and anxiety wore at even the most privileged Americans, a sense that things were becoming undone, going wrong. Even the West, so full of promise, seemed full of threat.

The Crisis of 1850

Some of Americans' anxiety emanated from the new golden land of California. With so many men fighting over access to gold, water, land, and liquor, lawlessness became rampant. The men who had left everything back east or in Europe to come to the goldfields showed little respect for the property rights—and even lives—of the Mexicans, Indians, or white men who were there before. In the eyes of many, anarchy threatened if California could not form a government quickly. A territorial convention created such a government in 1849, helping to restore order, but one of the provisions of the new constitution created great disorder of another kind back in the United States. The new constitution declared that "neither slavery nor involuntary servitude . . . shall ever be tolerated in this state."

This straightforward statement exacerbated conflicts that had been brewing in Washington ever since the Wilmot Proviso three years earlier. The Democrats and Whigs were so divided by region that the House of Representatives could barely elect a speaker. White Southerners of both parties considered the admission of a free California a grave threat to their own status in the Union, giving the Senate a free-labor majority. John C. Calhoun, who had been the most vocal and extreme spokesman for the South ever since the days of the nullification crisis almost twenty years earlier, urged his fellow white Southerners to band together. If they did not cooperate, Calhoun argued, they would be overwhelmed by the numbers and the energy of the free states of the North and the West, abandoned within the Union they had helped create. To lose California was to lose the future. Southern congressmen talked of commercial boycotts, even of secession.

Southern Whigs had put Zachary Taylor forward for the presidency in 1848 assuming that, as a Southerner himself, he would support the expansion of slavery. To their disbelief and disgust, Taylor urged that California be admitted as it wished to be admitted, without slavery. He believed that letting the people of a territory decide their own laws was the surest route to peaceful growth of the country. But Taylor's support of the proposed California constitution unleashed a bitter debate in Congress that many feared would result in disunion or armed conflict. White Southerners argued that to bottle up slavery was to risk war between the races and that to deny the South an equal representation in the Senate was to risk war between North and South. To give in on California, the South's defenders argued, was to lose the sectional balance on which their very safety rested. The most aggressive white Southerners wanted to go on the offensive before Northerners in Congress had time to act; in late 1849 they called a convention of the southern states, to meet in Nashville in June of 1850. Several states agreed to send delegates to the convention.

A fabled session of Congress occurred as a result. In January 1850 the three most famous legislators of the first half of the nineteenth century—John C. Calhoun, Henry Clay, and Daniel Webster—assumed leading roles in the great national drama, drawing the last bits of strength from their aged bodies. Calhoun played the role of the protagonist, delivering fiery warnings and denunciations on behalf of the white South; Clay reprised the role of the Great Compromiser that had made him famous almost exactly three decades earlier in the Missouri controversy; Webster played the role of the conciliator, persuading the angry North to accept, in the name of the Union, the South's demand for respect. Clay and Webster rehearsed their lines in a private meeting before Clay presented his bill to Congress.

Clay's bold plan addressed in one inclusive "omnibus" bill all the issues tearing at the United States on the slavery issue. Balance the territory issue, he suggested, with other concerns that angered people about slavery. Leave slavery in the District of Columbia but abolish the slave trade there. Provide a stronger law to capture fugitive slaves in the North and return them to their owners in the South, but announce that Congress had no power to regulate the slave trade among the states. Admit California as a free state, but leave undetermined the place of slavery in the other territories won from Mexico. Advocates on both sides hoped the compromise would buy time for passions to cool;

In the Great Debate of 1850, Henry Clay, the "Great Compromiser," holds forth while the United States Senate listens. John C. Calhoun sits at a desk on his right, and Daniel Webster to his left, his hand to his ear.

after all, no more new territory remained to fight over that was not covered by either the new compromise or by the Missouri Compromise.

Clay made his plea in January, before a jam-packed Congress, with his characteristic eloquence and power. The eloquence appeared to be to little effect, however, for the same bitter arguments went on for months after Clay's speech. In March, Calhoun gave an address in which he conceded nothing; three days later, Webster claimed to speak "not as a Massachusetts man, nor as a northern man, but as an American. . . . I speak to-day for the preservation of the Union." Webster found himself widely denounced in the North as a traitor, buckling under to the slave mongerers. Moreover, President Zachary Taylor, like Clay and Webster a Whig, refused to support their compromise. William Seward of New York denounced the compromise as "radically wrong and essentially vicious." The "higher law" of God, Seward argued, overruled any human law, including the Constitution.

The Nashville Convention of southern states, meanwhile, turned out to be ineffective, since six states sent no representatives and the representatives who did come disagreed on the proper course of action. While all of them believed in southern rights, most of them did not believe in disunion. The convention took no stand on the pending compromise; they waited to see its provisions.

The omnibus bill appeared doomed. The debates dragged on in committees, the bill torn apart. A series of unanticipated events, however, aided the compromise. Both Calhoun and Taylor died—Calhoun after a long decline, Taylor unexpectedly a few days after a ceremony inaugurating the construction of the Washington Monument. Millard Fillmore was now president. A New Yorker of low visibility before his choice as vice-presidential candidate to balance the Southerner Taylor, Fillmore supported the omnibus bill. Clay and Webster faded from view as younger, less prominent, members of Congress steered the various components of the compromise through committees and votes. The compromisers were led by Stephen A. Douglas, a promising young Democrat of Illinois. The majority of northern and southern senators and

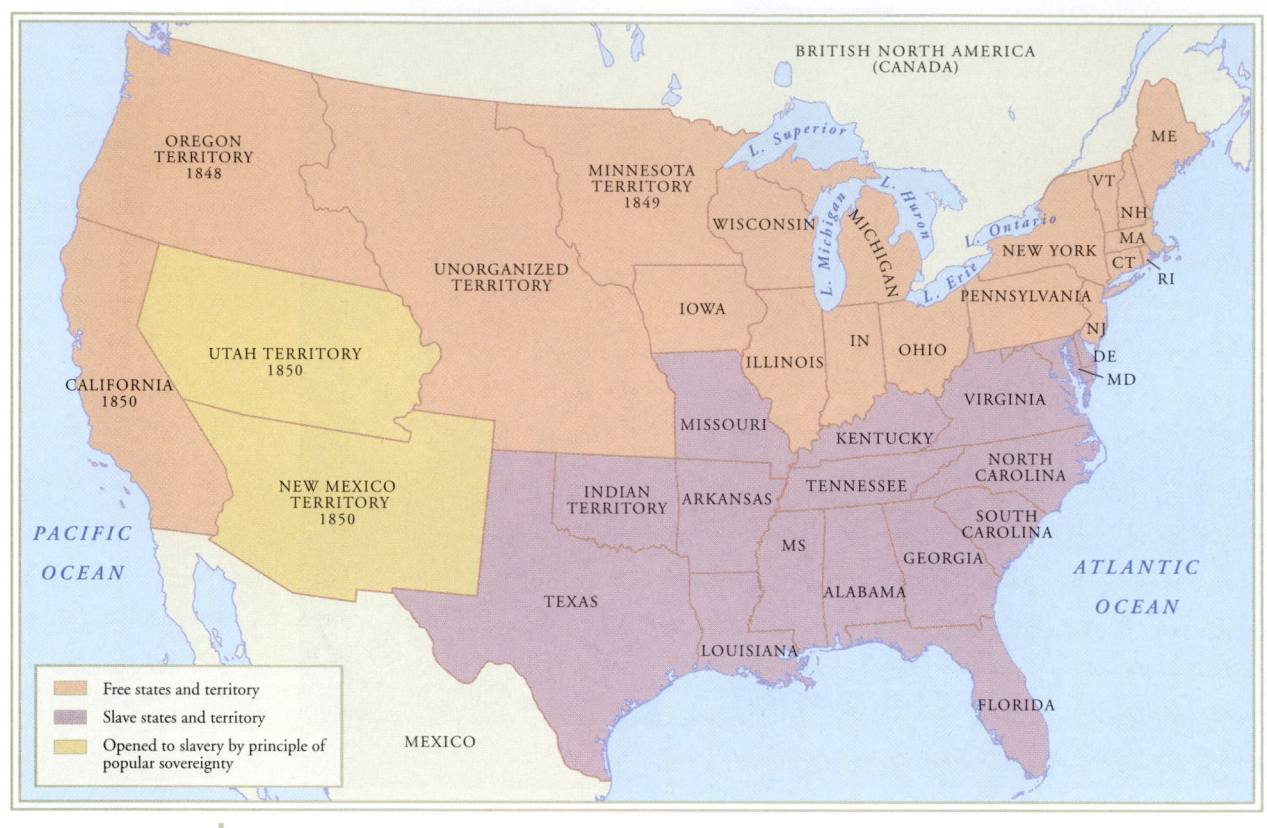

MAP 12.5 | THE COMPROMISE OF 1850

Representatives tenaciously voted against one another, but each part of the compromise passed because a small group of conciliatory congressmen from each side worked together. By September the various components of the compromise of 1850 had become law. "Let us cease agitating," Douglas urged, "stop the debate, and drop the subject." People wanted to forget about the problem of slavery.

The problem of slavery, of course, would not go away merely because of a political compromise. The fugitive slave component of the Compromise of 1850 proved especially troubling. Unlike other parts of the Compromise, provisions regarding fugitive slaves did not concern theoretical issues but rather living and breathing people who risked their lives to escape slavery and flee to the North. The Fugitive Slave Act directly implicated white Northerners and insulted them with blatantly unjust provisions. The commissioners who decided the fate of black Americans accused of being runaway slaves, for example, received ten dollars if an accused fugitive were returned to his or her master but only five dollars if freed. Marshals and sheriffs could force bystanders to aid in the capture of an accused fugitive; if bystanders refused, they faced a substantial fine or even jail term. The alleged runaway could not even testify in his or her own defense or call witnesses. There would be no jury trial. Perhaps most horrifying of all was this provision: No matter how many years before slaves had escaped, no matter how settled or respectable they had become, they could be captured and sent back into bondage. All free blacks stood continually at risk from kidnappers.

Most northern whites offered no opposition and most of the two or three hundred alleged fugitives prosecuted under the law were ruled to be runaways and sent south. But abolitionists raged at the Fugitive

PRACTICAL ILLUSTRATION OF THE FUGITIVE SLAVE LAW.

This cartoon ridicules the law that required Northerners to help capture and return runaway slaves. It glorifies William Lloyd Garrison and assails Daniel Webster, who voted in favor of the law as part of the Compromise of 1850.

Slave Law and they were not alone. Many Northerners, even those unconcerned about slavery in the South, were furious. Armed opposition to the slave catchers immediately arose in cities across the North; it cost $5,000 to capture one fugitive in Boston; mobs broke into jails to free ex-slaves; one slaveowner who came north to claim his property was shot. The Fugitive Slave Law, far from calming the conflict between North and South, made it more bitter.

The White North and African Americans

The years surrounding the crisis of 1850, ironically, were also the years in which black minstrel shows reached their peak of popularity. The traveling troupes of minstrels constituted the most popular form of public entertainment in these years, offering the strange ritual of white men in blackface simultaneously ridiculing and paying homage to the creativity of African-American culture. While white people of all classes and backgrounds attended the minstrel shows, the quick-paced, humorous, and flashy skits and songs held special appeal for members of the white working class. Over the preceding decades, those workers had seen the value of their skills eroded by mechanization, their wages lowered by depression and competition, their organizations undercut by employers. In their eyes, the minstrel shows offered both a comforting dramatization of their own racial superiority and a way to associate imaginatively with carefree and fun-loving "black" people.

White Northerners revealed their ambivalences about African Americans in other ways as well. Whites who argued that the new territory of the West must be free soil frequently insisted on the exclusion of free blacks as well. Indiana's constitution of 1851, like that of other states in the Midwest and West, specifically barred free blacks from entering the state. Whites in cities associated black people with poverty and crime. A considerable majority of northern whites showed little interest in attending antislavery rallies or reading Frederick Douglass's *North Star.*

White men in blackface mimicked southern slaves for white audiences in this era, acting out ambivalent feelings of contempt and envy.

Harriet Beecher Stowe, the author of Uncle Tom's Cabin, *wove Christianity and the domestic ideal into a powerful fable of slavery and its consequences.*

Harriet Beecher Stowe's *Uncle Tom's Cabin* helped change white attitudes toward African Americans. Stowe, the daughter of one of the most prominent ministers of the era, had been writing throughout her life, but had not not become prominent. In 1849, when Stowe was thirty-eight years old, her infant son died of cholera in Cincinnati; the next year she moved back to the Beechers' native New England to try to build a new life. There, people talked angrily of the new Fugitive Slave Law and the brutalities it bred. "You don't know how my heart burns within me at the blindness and obtuseness of good people on so very simple a point of morality as this," she wrote to her brother Henry Ward Beecher, a noted minister and an outspoken foe of the new law.

Stowe put her objections to the law and its effects into a story printed serially in a moderate antislavery newspaper over forty issues in 1851. Stowe based her portrayals of black people on the African Americans she had known in Cincinnati, where they worked for her as domestic servants. They told Stowe of their own experiences, of the terrors of being sold south to Louisiana, of their vulnerability to sexual exploitation. Stowe also drew on firsthand narratives of escape, narratives that had long been prominent in the antislavery movement. She switched the usual roles of the freedom narratives, however, making a woman—Eliza—the active heroine and a man—Uncle Tom—the one left behind to endure slavery with Christian suffering and fortitude. The love of a mother for her children drove the story. The image of Eliza crossing the partially frozen Ohio River, baby in her arms, grew into one of the most powerful and familiar scenes of American culture in the nineteenth century and beyond.

This book not only helped mobilize the white North's opinions on slavery, but it also proved an immediate and persistent bestseller.

The novel sold 300,000 copies in 1852 alone and became the subject of the most popular play in American history. Readers and theatergoers who had never picked up an antislavery newspaper were shocked at scenes that had long been commonplace in the antislavery press, stories of cruelty, violence, and sexual abuse. Stowe used techniques commonly found in domestic novels—the sanctity of the family, the power of religion, the triumph of endurance—to show that black people had the same feelings as white people, that they experienced the same happiness and despair, that slavery bred misery.

That *Uncle Tom's Cabin* and minstrel shows reached their peak of popularity at the same time gives some idea of the confusion and ambivalence with which white Northerners viewed African Americans in the early 1850s. The most popular cultural icon of the northern United States, Stowe's story, was based on an antislavery message, but thousands of whites laughed at other whites in blackface. Only events could force Northerners to decide what they really thought.

The Know-Nothings

Franklin Pierce, the Democratic candidate for president in 1852, was a Northerner friendly to the white South, a mediocre officer in the Mexican War, and a man known to drink. Fortunately for the Democrats, Pierce's opponent—Winfield Scott—proved to be even less impressive despite his fame as a general in the war with Mexico. The death of Henry Clay in 1850 and Daniel Webster in 1852 left the Whigs, always dependent on strong national leadership, adrift and directionless. Pierce, his campaign biography written by his friend Nathaniel Hawthorne, crushed Scott in every state except four. "General opinion seems to be that the Whig party is dead and will soon be decomposed into its original elements," one diarist commented in the wake of the election. "Shouldn't wonder. Where is its leader or leaders[?]"

Many influential Whigs took the 1852 election as a sign that their party could never win, that the Democrats would always succeed by appealing to the lowest common denominator. The real, substantive issues that had originally shaped the two parties—banks, the tariff, and internal improvements—no longer distinguished them from one another because both the Whigs and the Democrats had moved to the middle on those issues. Neither did slavery and sectional issues sharply define the two parties, for each tried to appease both the North and the South. Even the broader cultural orientation of the two parties had blurred in 1852, as the Whigs appealed to the burgeoning foreign-born vote and the Protestant nativists that had been at the heart of the party grew disgusted with the Whigs.

The Know-Nothings, growing steadily since their emergence in 1849, moved into politics in 1854, but in a way few Democrats or Whigs expected. The Know-Nothings did not announce their candidates beforehand, but rather wrote them in on the ballots, taking incumbents by complete surprise. The Know-Nothings won virtually all the seats in the Massachusetts legislature with this strategy and registered strong showings in New York and Pennsylvania. By 1855, the Know-Nothings dominated New England and displaced the Whigs as the major opponents to the Democrats through the Middle Atlantic states, in much of the South, and in California.

No one in the major parties had anticipated such a turn of events. The Whigs, after all, had long attracted the nativists, fervent Protestants, and temperance

HARRIET BEECHER STOWE, *UNCLE TOM'S CABIN,* 1852

Stowe's remarkable novel captured the moral energy of the antislavery movement. In this episode, the evil New England-born Simon Legree is confronted by the unbending Christian strength of Uncle Tom.

"And now," said Legree, "come here, you Tom. You see I told ye I didn't buy ye jest for the common work; I mean to promote ye and make a driver of ye; and tonight ye may jest as well begin to get yer hand in. Now, ye jest take this yer gal and flog her; ye've seen enough on't to know how."

"I beg Mas'r's pardon," said Tom, "hopes Mas'r won't set me at that. It's what I an't used to—never did—and can't do, no way possible."

"Ye'll larn a pretty smart chance of things ye never did know before I've done with ye!" said Legree, taking up a cowhide and striking Tom a heavy blow across the cheek, and following up the infliction by a shower of blows.

"There!" he said, as he stopped to rest, "now will ye tell me ye can't do it?"

"Yes, Mas'r," said Tom, putting up his hand to wipe the blood that trickled down his face. "I'm willin' to work night and day, and work while there's life and breath in me, but this yer thing I can't feel it right to do; and, Mas'r, I *never* shall do it—*never!*"

Tom had a remarkably smooth, soft voice, and a habitually respectful manner that had given Legree an idea that he would be cowardly and easily subdued. When he spoke these last words, a thrill of amazement went through everyone; the poor woman clasped her hands and said, "O Lord!" and everyone involuntarily looked at each other and drew in their breath, as if to prepare for the storm that was about to burst.

Legree looked stupefied and confounded; but at last burst forth—

"What! ye blasted black beast! tell *me* ye don't think it *right* to do what I tell ye! What have any of you cussed cattle to do with thinking what's right? I'll put a stop to it! Why, what do ye think ye are? May be ye think ye're a gentleman, master Tom, to be a telling your master what's right and what an't! So you pretend it's wrong to flog the gal!"

advocates to which the Know-Nothings now appealed. But these disgruntled voters proved extremely receptive to the Know-Nothing appeal. The Know-Nothings, unlike the Whigs, left control of the party close to the grassroots; there were no Clays or Websters cutting deals in Washington, no Winfield Scotts appealing to Catholics. The Know-Nothings offered a revitalized political party, one more receptive than the Whigs to the desires of its constituents and one that would attack problems rather than compromise on them. Young men, in particular, seemed drawn to the Know-Nothings, for the new party offered a fresh start, a place for new men. Many rural districts voted heavily for the Know-Nothings as a way to get back at the cities that had dominated the major parties for so long. For such reasons, the Know-Nothings made strong showings in the South as well as the North.

The appearance of the Know-Nothings reflected a deep-seated change in the American political system, a change that destroyed the delicate balance of power between the two well-established parties. The American party system began disintegrating at the local and state level, with the Whigs fading in some states as early as 1852 and in others not until three years later. Voters defected from the Whigs to both the Know-Nothing and Free Soil parties, depending on which alternative party was strongest in their locality.

"I think so, Mas'r," said Tom, "the poor crittur's sick and feeble; 't would be downright cruel, and it's what I never will do, not begin to. Mas'r, if you mean to kill me, kill me; but as to my raising my hand agin anyone here, I never shall—I'll die first!"

Tom spoke in a mild voice but with a decision that could not be mistaken. Legree shook with anger; his greenish eyes glared fiercely and his very whiskers seemed to curl with passion; but, like some ferocious beast that plays with its victim before he devours it, he kept back his strong impulse to proceed to immediate violence and broke out into bitter raillery.

"Well, here's a pious dog, at last, let down among us sinners!—a saint, a gentleman, and no less, to talk to us sinners about our sins! Powerful, holy crittur, he must be! Here, you rascal, you make believe to be so pious—didn't you never hear out of yer Bible, 'Servants, obey yer masters'? An't I yer master? Didn't I pay down $1,200 cash for all there is inside yer old cussed black shell? An't yer mine, now, body and soul?" he said, giving Tom a violent kick with his heavy boot. "Tell me!"

In the very depth of physical suffering, bowed by brutal oppression, this question shot a gleam of joy and triumph through Tom's soul. He suddenly stretched himself up, and, looking earnestly to heaven, while the tears and blood that flowed down his face mingled, he exclaimed—

"No! no! no! my soul an't yours, Mas'r! You haven't bought it—ye can't buy it! It's been bought and paid for by one that is able to keep it—no matter, no matter, you can't harm me!"

"I can't!" said Legree, with a sneer, "we'll see—we'll see! Here, Sambo, Quimbo, give this dog such a breakin' in as he won't get over this month!"

The two gigantic Negroes that now laid hold of Tom, with fiendish exultation in their faces, might have formed no unapt personification of the powers of darkness. The poor woman screamed with apprehension and all arose as by a general impulse while they dragged him unresisting from the place. . . .

SOURCE Harriet Beecher Stowe, *Uncle Tom's Cabin* (Boston: J. P. Jewett, 1852), pp. 419–423.

Dreams of Expansion

The same forces of commerce and transportation that tied together the vastly expanded United States in the late 1840s and early 1850s pulled Americans into world affairs. The steamships and clipper ships that connected New York and San Francisco crisscrossed the oceans of the world. American ships set out not only for Liverpool, but also for South America, Asia, Australia, New Zealand, and Tahiti. The ships carried lumber and hides, tea and silks, missionaries and scientists. American whaling ships restlessly and relentlessly patrolled the South Pacific, stopping for fuel and food at islands scattered over a vast territory. Some entrepreneurs even rushed to mine mountains of bird droppings piled up on remote Pacific islands. The droppings, called guano, offered a nitrogen-rich fertilizer much in demand on the farms and plantations of the eastern United States. American traders eager to break into the Asian market—led by Commodore Matthew C. Perry—appeared in Japanese ports and bargained with the skeptical Japanese.

These exchanges in far-off ports often depended on the Hawaiian Islands as way stations, strategically placed by wind and currents to attract much of the Pacific trade. On a single day in 1852, for example, 131

The Know-Nothings, a party of resentment, secrecy, and violence, attracted criticism as well as voters in the mid-1850s.

whaling ships and eighteen merchant ships tied up in Honolulu. Such trade, while lucrative for some, came at a horrifying cost to the native population because of disease brought by American, Asian, and European ships. Over the seventy-five years since the first contact with outsiders in the late eighteenth century, the Hawaiian population had declined from about 300,000 residents to only about 73,000. Around 2,000 foreigners lived in Hawaii by the early 1850s, a good many of them Americans, both businessmen and missionaries. Though politicians and editors talked of annexing the islands for the United States, opposition on the islands and in Washington postponed any action. Besides, expansionists' main focus lay elsewhere.

Some well-placed Americans gazed at yet more Mexican territory with covetous eyes, urging the Pierce administration to acquire Baja California and other parts of northern Mexico. Mexico was not inter-

As these three sketches by an American visitor show, European and Polynesian cultures existed side by side in the capital of Hawaii. Protestant and Catholic churches stand beside consulates and native homes.

ested, though, and many Northerners in the United States opposed further acquisitions. Proponents of expansion had to settle for much less than they had wanted: After long wrangling and somewhat inept bargaining, in 1853 the United States paid $15 million for a strip of Mexico to use as a route for a southern transcontinental railroad. This was the Gadsden Purchase, named for the American diplomat who negotiated it. The purchase defined the final borders of the continental United States.

Cuba seemed the most obvious place for further expansion, for it stood as both an opportunity and a threat. It seemed to many Americans that Cuba should be part of the United States, that Havana should stand as the Gibraltar to the entrance of the Gulf of Mexico, a sort of American lake. Cuba was rich and growing, its slave trade flourishing even in the middle of the nineteenth century after the slave trade to the United States had ended. Abolitionists and others talked of freeing Cuba both from slavery and from the Spanish, while white Southerners talked of adding this jewel to the slave empire. Cuban exiles worked in New Orleans and New York to encourage American intervention.

The United States offered to buy Cuba from Spain in 1848, but met a rude rebuff from the weakening European power. Franklin Pierce, pressured by the Southerners in his party and in his cabinet, in the early 1850s renewed the effort to "detach" Cuba from Spain. Southern planters argued that the United States had to act quickly, for they feared that the Spanish would free Cuba's slaves, who would then revolt, take over the island, and threaten the American South. American diplomats in Europe created a furor when they wrote the "Ostend Manifesto," a statement of the policy they wanted the administration to follow: Gain

Cuba one way or the other to prevent its "Africanization." The United States would be justified in this action "on the very principle that would justify an individual in tearing down the burning house of his neighbor if there were no other means of preventing the flames from destroying his own home." When the "manifesto" was leaked to the press, the Pierce administration was widely vilified at home and abroad. Pierce publicly renounced any intention of taking over Cuba. The movement to expand the United States into the Caribbean came to a temporary halt.

The Kansas-Nebraska Act

As the Cuban episode revealed, Franklin Pierce proved to be an ineffectual president and party leader, permitting conflicts within the party to overwhelm him. The best hope for the Democrats, Stephen A. Douglas determined, was to deflect attention to the West. Douglas called for two kinds of action: organizing the territories of the West, especially the Kansas and Nebraska area to the west of Iowa and Missouri, and building a railroad across the continent to bind together the expanded United States. The two actions were interrelated, for the railroad could not be built through unorganized territory. Partly to get southern votes for the territorial organization and partly because he believed that slavery would not survive in the northern territories, Douglas agreed to back a bill invalidating the Missouri Compromise line. He proposed that the people of the new territories decide for themselves whether or not their states would permit slaves and slaveholders. Calling this policy "popular sovereignty," Douglas put it forward in the Kansas-Nebraska Bill.

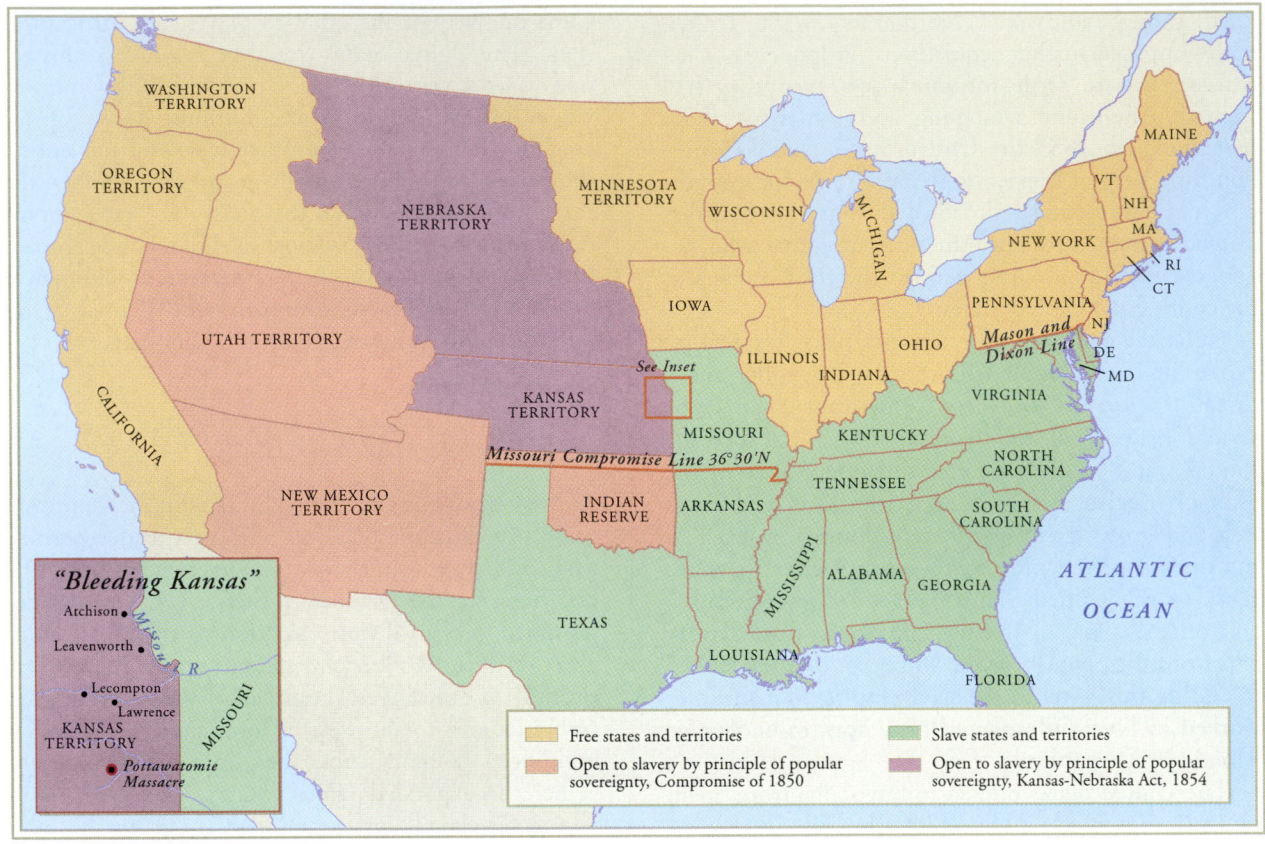

Free states and territories

Slave states and territories

Open to slavery by principle of popular sovereignty, Compromise of 1850

Open to slavery by principle of popular sovereignty, Kansas-Nebraska Act, 1854

MAP 12.6   KANSAS NEBRASKA AND SLAVERY

Douglas's plan, by reopening the question of slavery in the territories, unleashed political and sectional resentments that had been bottled up by prior compromises. Six prominent Free Soil senators, including Salmon P. Chase, Charles Sumner, and Joshua Giddings, denounced the plan as a plot by a "Slave Power" to make Nebraska a "dreary region of despotism, inhabited by masters and slaves." Northern ministers publicly protested the pending legislation, while newspapers throughout the North scornfully attacked the proposal. Despite the widespread opposition, however, the opponents of the Kansas-Nebraska Bill could not coordinate their efforts sufficiently to stop its passage, supported as it was by virtually all southern congressmen and the Pierce administration.

The fight over Kansas-Nebraska inflamed northern resentment as never before. Many Northerners deter-

mined that they could no longer trust Southerners to keep a bargain and that Northerners were no longer obligated to enforce the Fugitive Slave Act because the Kansas-Nebraska Act had nullified the Compromise of 1850. In the wake of the debate in Congress, attempts to arrest and extradite Anthony Burns, a fugitive slave in Boston, created such a turmoil that the mayor called out 1,500 militia to line the streets along the route between the courthouse and the ship that was to take Burns back to slavery in Virginia.

The Kansas-Nebraska Act sparked a chain reaction. It divided the Democratic party across the North; it upset the fragile balance of power between North and South in Congress; it provided a set of common concerns and language to unite disgruntled Northern Whigs, Free Soilers, and abolitionists. At this juncture, moreover, the Know-Nothings attained their new

This illustrations tells the story of Anthony Burns's sales, escape, arrest, and return to slavery in Virginia. His highly publicized case further inflamed the conflict between the North and the South in the mid-1850s.

prestige and power, pulling voters to their program of nativism and temperance. The Know-Nothings took advantage of the widespread disillusionment with the two major parties to work along lines apparently unrelated to slavery.

Over the next two years the northern political system churned as voters looked for a party that would reflect their concerns and also have a chance of winning power. Each northern state fell into its own kind of confusion and conflict, as politicians and voters jumped from one party to another. The Know-Nothings began to fade almost as quickly as they had emerged. Their descent had several causes. The Know-Nothings came to seem just another political party led by ambitious politicians, violent gangs that terrorized immigrants under the Know-Nothing banner alienated many voters, and Know-Nothing legislators proved unable to control or punish Catholics as they had promised.

The rise of yet another party also pulled voters away from the Know-Nothings. In 1854 a party was founded in Wisconsin to unite disgruntled voters. The new party appealed to former Whigs, Free Soilers, Know-Nothings, and even Democrats fed up with the pro-Southern party. This new party called itself the "Republican" party. Its platform announced that "no man can own another man" and it would not permit slavery in the territories or in new states. Whether such a bold party could unify the many disaffected voters of the North remained to be seen.

CONCLUSION

The late 1840s and early 1850s saw the United States energized by victory over Mexico and the acquisition of vast new territories, by prosperity in the North and the South, by railroads and clipper ships, by westward migration, and by the arrival of millions of immigrants. As northern family farms spread during the good times, however, so did southern slavery. The gold of the West brought not only wealth but also lawlessness and environmental destruction. The cities of the Atlantic coast seemed full to overflowing with immigrants from Ireland and Germany, while the cities of the Pacific burgeoned with immigrants from China and restless men from back east. Politicians seemed helpless in the face of these changes. Each political compromise only seemed to make things worse. The parties that had held the country together for a quarter of a century began to buckle under the stress.

RECOMMENDED READINGS

Anbinder, Tyler. *Nativism and Slavery: The Northern Know-Nothings and the Politics of the 1850s* (1992) provides a full and balanced account.

Fellman, Michael. *The Unbounded Frame: Freedom and Community in Nineteenth-Century American Utopianism* (1973) offers a helpful overview of perfectionist communities.

Griffith, Elisabeth. *In Her Own Right: The Life of Elizabeth Cady Stanton* (1984) tells the compelling story of this crucial leader of the woman suffrage movement.

Hedrick, Joan D. *Harriet Beecher Stowe: A Life* (1994) paints a detailed portrait of the author of *Uncle Tom's Cabin.*

Hietala, Thomas R. *Manifest Design: Anxious Aggrandizement in Late Jacksonian America* (1985) ties the war with Mexico into the larger patterns of life in the United States.

Lott, Eric. *Love and Theft: Blackface Minstrelsy and the American Working Class* (1993) is an original and challenging analysis.

Miller, Kerby A. *Emigrants and Exiles: Ireland and the Irish Exodus to North America* (1985) gives a full account of the origins and impact of this migration.

Potter, David M. *The Impending Crisis: 1848–1861* (1976) is a superb overview of American politics from the wake of the Mexican War to the outbreak of the Civil War.

Reynolds, David S. *Beneath the American Renaissance: The Subversive Imagination in the Age of Emerson and Melville* (1988) is a brilliant exploration of the "classic" era of American literature.

Rohrbough, Malcolm J. *Days of Gold: The California Gold Rush and the American Nation* (1997) offers a fresh and exciting account of its subject.

Politics and Sectional Relations

Ashworth, John. *Slavery, Capitalism, and Politics in the Antebellum Republic. Volume 1: Commerce and Compromise, 1820–1850* (1995).

Campbell, Stanley. *The Slave Catchers* (1968).

Carwardine, Richard J. *Evangelicals and Politics in Antebellum America* (1993).

Gara, Larry. *The Presidency of Franklin Pierce* (1991).

Gienapp, William E. *The Origins of the Republican Party, 1852–1856* (1987).

Johannsen, Robert W. *Stephen A. Douglas* (1973).

Johannsen, Robert W. *The Frontier, the Union, and Stephen A. Douglas* (1989).

Peterson, Merrill D. *The Great Triumvirate: Webster, Clay, and Calhoun* (1987).

Rayback, Joseph G. *Free Soil: The Election of 1848* (1970)

Transportation and Its Effects

Alvarez, Eugene. *Travel on Southern Antebellum Railroads, 1828–1860* (1974).

Faragher, John Mack. *Sugar Creek: Life on the Illinois Prairie* (1986).

Fishlow, Albert. *American Railroads and the Transformation of the Antebellum Economy* (1965).

Hahn, Steven and Prude, Jonathan eds., *The Countryside in the Age of Capitalist Transformation: Essays in the Social History of Rural America* (1985).

Stover, John. *American Railroads* (1961).

Taylor, George Rogers. *The Transportation Revolution, 1815–1860* (1951).

The Gold Rush

Billington, Ray Allen. *The Far Western Frontier, 1830–1860* (1956).

Lapp, Rudolph M. *Blacks in Gold Rush California* (1977).

Saxton, Alexander. *The Indispensable Enemy: Labor and the Anti-Chinese Movement in California* (1971).

White, Richard. *It's Your Misfortune and None of My Own: A New History of the American West* (1991).

Utopian Communities

Bestor, Arthur E. *Backwoods Utopias: The Sectarian and Owenite Phases of Communitarian Utopianism in America, 1663–1829* (1950).

Lockwood, Carden, *Oneida: Utopian Community to Modern Corporation* (1969).

Klaw, Spencer. *Without Sin: The Life and Death of the Oneida Community* (1993).

Kolmerten, Carol. *Women in Utopia* (1990).

Women and Women's Rights

DuBois, Ellen C. *Feminism and Suffrage: The Emergence of an Independent Women's Movement in America, 1848–1869* (1978).

Hoffert, Sylvia D. *When Hens Crow: The Woman's Rights Movement in Antebellum America* (1995).

Ginzburg, Lori D. *Women and the Work of Benevolence: Morality, Politics, and Class in the Nineteenth-Century United States* (1990).

Hewitt, Nancy. *Women's Activism and Social Change: Rochester, New York, 1822–1872* (1984).

Lebsock, Suzanne. *The Free Women of Petersburg: Status and Culture in a Southern Town, 1784–1860* (1984).

Painter, Nell Irvin. *Sojourner Truth: A Life, a Symbol* (1996).

Ryan, Mary P. *Women in Public: Between Banners and Ballots, 1825–1880* (1990).

Sklar, Kathryn Kish. *Catherine Beecher: A Study in American Domesticity* (1973).

Stansell, Christine. *City of Women: Sex and Class in New York, 1789–1860* (1986).

Yellin, Jean Fagan. *Women and Sisters: The Antislavery Feminists in American Culture* (1989).

The American Renaissance

Callow, Philip. *From Noon to Starry Night: A Life of Walt Whitman* (1992).

Halttunen, Karen. *Confidence Men and Painted Women: A Study in Middle-Class Culture in America, 1830–1870* (1982).

Kirby, David. *Herman Melville* (1993).

Mellow, James R. *Nathaniel Hawthorne in His Times* (1980).

Rogin, Michael Paul. *Subversive Genealogy: The Politics and Art of Herman Melville* (1983).

Zweig, Paul. *Walt Whitman: The Making of the Poet* (1984).

Immigration

Knobel, Dale T. *Paddy and the Republic: Ethnicity and Nationality in Antebellum America* (1986).

Ripley, LaVern J. *The German-Americans* (1976).

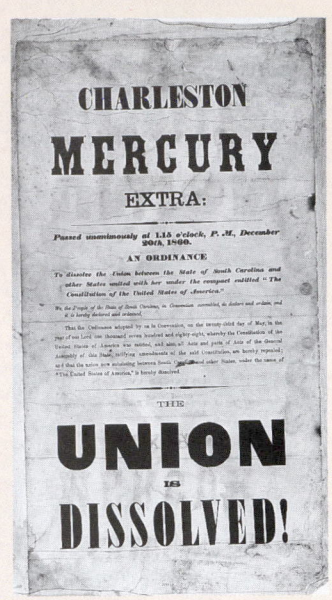

AMERICANS OF THE 1850s had no idea that the Civil War awaited them. They could not imagine that a vast war, larger than any Europe had known, could overwhelm the new republic. New farms and plantations, after all, spread rapidly in expectation of more boom years like the 1850s. Villages and work- shops spread throughout the North while cities, fed by millions of immi- grants from Europe, grew rapidly at harbors and along railroads and rivers. In the South, cotton and slavery created a per capita income for white Southerners higher than that of any country in Europe except England. Slavery, it was clear, would not collapse of its own contradictions any time soon; the institution had never been more profitable. Telegraphs, newspapers, steamboats, and railroads tied the North and South together more tightly every year.

The two sections viewed each other as aggressive and expansionist, intent on making the nation all one thing or another. The North claimed that the slaveholder South would destroy the best government on earth rather than accept the results of a fair election. The white South claimed that the arrogant and greedy North would destroy the nation rather

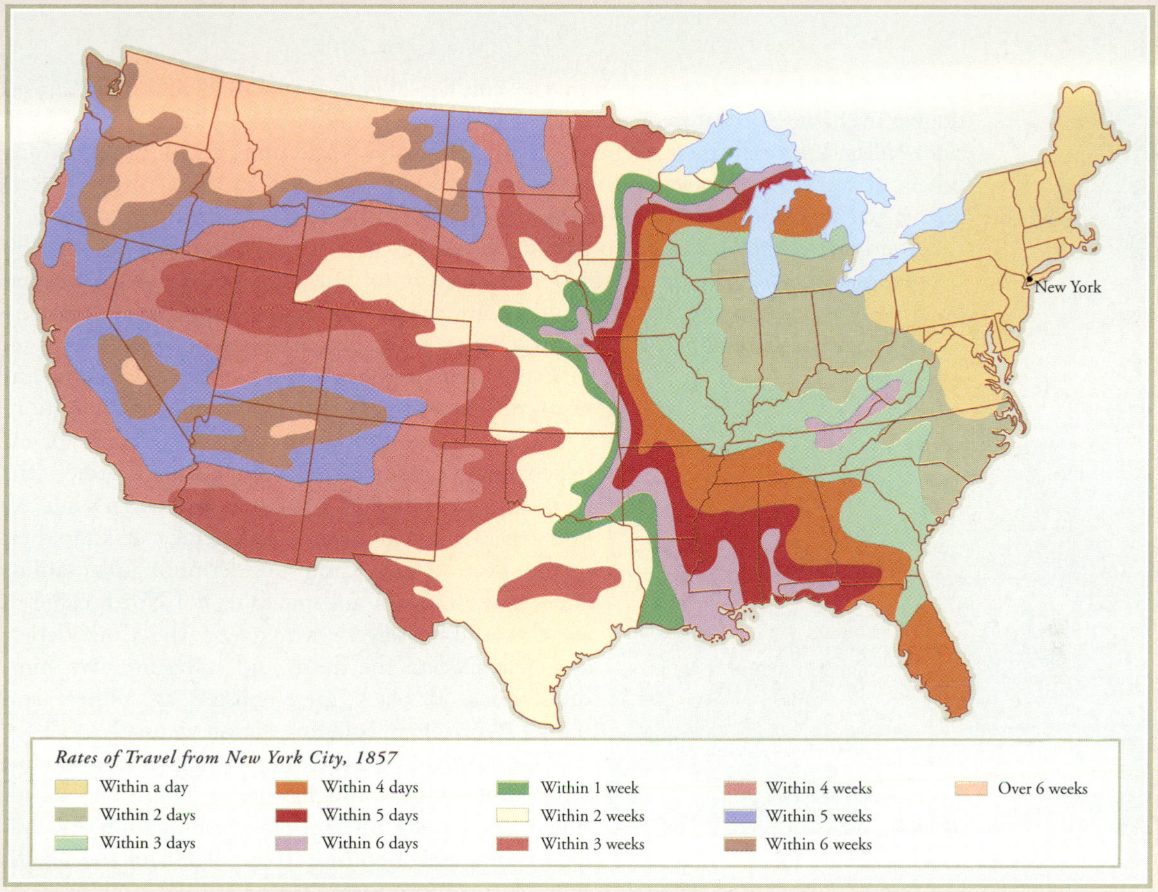

Rates of Travel from New York City, 1857

- Within a day
- Within 2 days
- Within 3 days
- Within 4 days
- Within 5 days
- Within 6 days
- Within 1 week
- Within 2 weeks
- Within 3 weeks
- Within 4 weeks
- Within 5 weeks
- Within 6 weeks
- Over 6 weeks

than acknowledge what the Constitution had established. Both sides were filled with righteous rage, accepting violence to gain the upper hand, whether that involved capturing fugitive slaves or applauding John Brown's failed insurrection. Americans could not stop the momentum they had themselves created. Despite desperate efforts at compromise and delay, the war came.

Once the war could no longer be avoided,

most people threw themselves into the conflict alongside their neighbors, whatever doubts they had held before. Confident that the war would be brief, young men on both sides enlisted to teach their enemies a lesson. Both the North and the South proved excellent at war. They innovated freely and successfully, fought relentlessly, discovered effective generals, and mobilized women as well as men. Indeed, the North's strengths and the South's strengths balanced so that the war went on for four years, killing 630,000 people, a proportion of the population equivalent to 5 million people in the United States today and a number larger than the country was ever to sacrifice in another war.

Throughout the conflict, from Lincoln's election to his death, the role of slavery remained both powerful and unclear. Lincoln announced that the war was for Union, not abolition. The Confederacy announced that the war was for independence, not merely slavery. Enslaved Americans in the South, however, forced slavery as an issue on both the Union and the Confederacy, risking their lives to flee to Union camps, undermining plantations and farms. Lincoln and much of the North came to see that ending slavery would end the Confederacy and help redeem the death and suffering. Two hundred thousand black men enlisted as soldiers and played a key role in bringing Union victory.

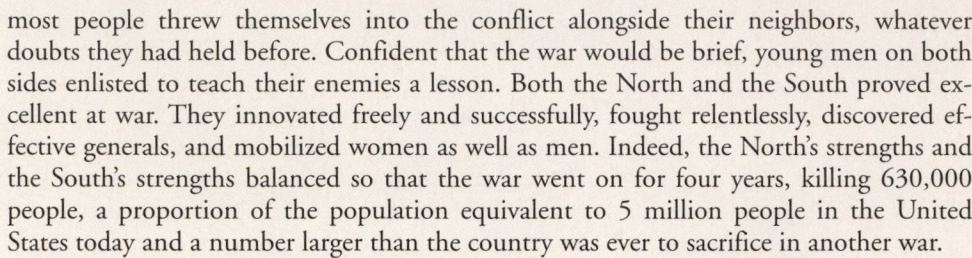

The North and the South struggled with themselves even as they fought one another. The North broke apart along lines of class, ethnicity, party, and locale. By 1864 a considerable portion of the northern population wanted the war to end, with compromise if necessary. The opponents of Lincoln expected to overwhelm him in the election that fall and even Lincoln shared that expectation. The white South broke apart along lines of class, locale, and gender. Poor soldiers deserted; upcountry communities shielded deserters and resisted the Confederate government; impoverished white women rioted and resisted. Slaves rushed to the Union army at the first opportunity, every escape weakening the southern economy and Confederate morale.

Events on the battlefield, through 10,000 conflicts large and small, exerted their own logic and momentum. The Union army grew stronger as the Confederate army thinned and weakened. The victories of Grant and Sherman in 1864 destroyed the South's best hope of a negotiated peace. The relentless spread of the Union army throughout the South divided the Confederacy into smaller and smaller pieces, each helpless to aid the other. When Lee's army fell into defeat the Confederate nation dissolved almost immediately.

Whatever Lincoln's plans for reuniting the nation, those plans ended at Ford's Theater in April of 1865. His successor, Andrew Johnson, took the most cautious route possible, limiting the scope of black freedom in every way he could. The white South's resolve, indeed, seemed greater than any power the Union wielded in the South. African Americans struggled to make their freedom real: they mobilized politically, founded churches and schools, and reconstituted families. They demanded rights as Americans and did all they could to secure those rights. Black Southerners found many white northern allies but many more white southern enemies who quickly turned to violence, as well as white Northerners who supported or tolerated the violence. The years of 1866 and 1867 were full of a promise and a terror no one could have imagined ten years before. In many ways, the Civil War had not yet ended; its consequences had hardly begun.

CIVIL WAR LOSSES

Civil War deaths compared with U.S. deaths in other wars (estimated)

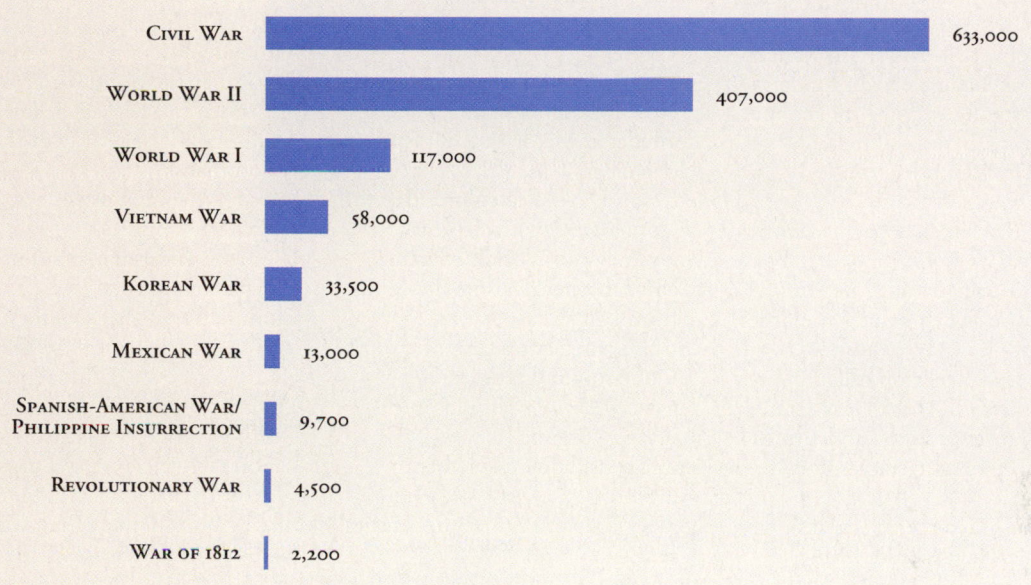

CIVIL WAR	633,000
WORLD WAR II	407,000
WORLD WAR I	117,000
VIETNAM WAR	58,000
KOREAN WAR	33,500
MEXICAN WAR	13,000
SPANISH-AMERICAN WAR/ PHILIPPINE INSURRECTION	9,700
REVOLUTIONARY WAR	4,500
WAR OF 1812	2,200

For the next decade, Reconstruction in the South gradually receded. The process left blacks with greater political rights in law because of the Fourteenth and Fifteenth Amendments, but a more limited role in the day-to-day process of governing. The presidency of Ulysses S. Grant was a disappointment because the hero of the war proved unable to provide effective leadership, sectional reconciliation, or honest government. An

economic collapse in 1873 helped the Democrats restore the national political balance and hasten the end of Reconstruction. The disputed election between Rutherford B. Hayes and Samual J. Tilden in 1876 saw the abandonment of black southerners to the rule of those who believed in white supremacy. The Civil War had preserved the Union and abolished slavery, but the unsettled problem of race cast a long shadow into the future.

	1855	1861	1862	1863
POLITICS & DIPLOMACY	**1855:** Proslavery and free-soil forces clash in Kansas Massachusetts desegregates public schools **1856:** John Brown's raid in Kansas James Buchanan elected president Congressman Preston Brooks canes Senator Charles Sumner **1857:** *Dred Scott* decision Lecompton Constitution Hinton R. Helper, *The Impending Crisis of the South* **1858:** Lincoln-Douglas debates **1859:** John Brown's raid on Harpers Ferry Vicksburg convention calls for reopening of African slave trade Kansas ratifies free-soil constitution **1860:** Democratic convention divides Abraham Lincoln elected president South Carolina secedes from the Union **1861:** Mississippi, Florida, Alabama, Georgia, Louisiana, and Texas secede	Montgomery Convention creates Confederate States of America Lincoln inaugurated Firing on and surrender of Fort Sumter Arkansas, Tennessee, Virginia, and North Carolina secede Confederate victory at Bull Run (Manassas) Jefferson Davis elected president of Confederacy with six-year term Union navy seizes Confederate commisioners Mason and Slidell from British ship *Trent* **1862:** Confederates surrender Fort Donelson to Grant *Virginia* v. *Monitor* in Hampton Roads, Virginia Grant wins dramatic victory at Shiloh New Orleans surrenders to Admiral Farragut Jackson's Shenandoah Valley Campaign Lee takes command of Army of Northern Virginia	Lee drives McClellan from Richmond in Seven Days' Battles Confederate victory at Second Bull Run (Manassas) Battle of Antietam (Sharpsburg) First Emancipation Proclamation Burnside replaces McClellan as commander of Army of the Potomac Lee overwhelms Burnside at Fredericksburg **1863:** Second Emancipation Proclamation Culmination of Lee's victory over Hooker at Chancellorsville Grant's successful campaign in Mississippi Death of Stonewall Jackson Union victory at Gettysburg Vicksburg surrenders to Grant Black troops fight at Fort Wagner, South Carolina Lincoln's Gettysburg Address Union victory at Chattanooga
SOCIAL & CULTURAL EVENTS	**1857:** Mass revivals **1858:** Frederick Law Olmsted begins design for Central Park in New York City			**1863:** Lincoln's Gettysburg Address
ECONOMICS & TECHNOLOGY	**1857:** Financial panic and depression Baltimore–St. Louis rail service completed **1861:** Suspension of specie payments Mathew Brady begins photography of Civil War		**1862:** Legal Tender Act in North authorizes "greenbacks" Homestead Act passed by Union Congress *Virginia* v. *Monitor* in Hampton Roads, Virginia	**1863:** Confederate Congress passes Impressment Act Union Congress passes National Bank Act Bread riot in Richmond

1864: Grant assumes command of all Union forces

Battle of the Wilderness in Virginia

Union victory at Cold Harbor

Sherman captures Atlanta

Lincoln re-elected president

Beginning of Sherman's march from Atlanta to the Atlantic

1865: Congress passes Thirteenth Amendment, abolishing slavery

Congress creates Bureau of Refugees, Freedmen, and Abandoned Lands (Freedmen's Bureau)

Lincoln's second inauguration

Fall of Richmond to Union

Lee surrenders to Grant at Appomattox Court House

Lincoln assassinated; Andrew Johnson becomes president

Former Confederate states hold constitutional conventions through December; pass "black codes"

Thirteenth Amendment to Constitution ratified, abolishing slavery

1866: Congress passes Civil Rights Act and Freedmen's Bureau renewal over Johnson's veto

Riots in New Orleans and Memphis

Congress approves Fourteenth Amendment

Ku Klux Klan formed

1867: Congress passes Reconstruction Act and Tenure of Office Act

Johnson dismisses Secretary of War Stanton, triggering impeachment proceedings

First elections in South under Reconstruction Act

Passage of Reconstruction Act

Alaska Purchase negotiations

1868: Andrew Johnson impeached and acquitted

U.S. Grant elected President

1869: Fifteenth Amendment passes Congress

Woman suffrage starts in Wyoming Territory

1870: Ku Klux Klan conducts terror raids in South

1871: Tweed Ring exposed in New York City

1872: Grant reelected

1873: Salary Grab and Credit Mobilier Scandals

1874: Democrats gain in congressional elections

1875: Civil Rights Act passes Congress

1876: Hayes and Tilden in disputed election

1877: Hayes declared president after compromises settle election dispute

---

1865: First woman professor of astronomy appointed at Vassar College

1866: American Equal Rights Association founded to seek black and woman suffrage

1867: Horatio Alger begins publishing series of books for young boys

1868: Louisa May Alcott publishes *Little Women*

1869: Licensing of women lawyers begins

First intercollegiate football game played between Princeton and Rutgers

1870: First Greek letter sorority, Kappa Alpha Theta, founded

1871: Cable car invented

1872: American Public Health Association starts

1873: Mark Twain and Charles Dudley Warner publish *The Gilded Age*

1874: Women's Christian Temperance Union founded

1875: Smith and Wellesley College open to provide higher education for women

1876: Centennial Exposition in Philadelphia

1864: Confederate Congress assumes new powers of taxation, impressment of slaves

George Pullman invents sleeping car

1866: National Labor Union organized

1867: Patrons of Husbandry (Grange) founded

1868: First 8-hour day for federal workers

1869: Gold Corner scheme of Jay Gould and Jim Fisk

Transcontinental Railroad completed

1870: Standard Oil Company of Ohio organized

1871: Chicago fire burns center of city

1872: Adding machine invented

1873: Panic of 1873 starts depression

1874: Sale of typewriters begins

Tomkins Square riot of unemployed in New York City

1875: First dynamo for outdoor lighting constructed

1876: Heinz tomato ketchup marketed

1877: National railroad strike

"BORDER RUFFIANS"

The northern press depicted what they took to be the seedy character of the proslavery men who came over the border from Missouri into Kansas to support slavery.

Chapter 13

Broken Bonds:

1855–1861

THE UNITED STATES had never seemed stronger than at the beginning of 1855. The economy was booming, settlers pushed into the West, steamers and clippers plied the oceans of the world, railroads spread at a relentless rate, and immigrants streamed into American farms and factories. Churches, schools, asylums, and reform organizations grew faster than ever. Many people believed that the nation was entering upon its brightest day.

But the signs of danger were not hard to see. The conflict between the North and the South grew more bitter with each passing political crisis. Those crises came in a stunning succession in the late 1850s and early 1860s, every year bringing a clash more divisive than the one before. The battle between North and South broke out in the Kansas territory, in state politics, in the village of Harpers Ferry, and finally in the contest for president. The party system, weakened by nativism and loss of faith by voters, seemed powerless to stop the disintegration.

SECTIONAL CONFLICT

Conflict between the North and the South had been a staple of American politics for decades before 1855. Territories proved a persistent problem, but Northerners and Southerners also argued over the tariff, nominees for high office, and religion. They sometimes confronted the issue of slavery head-on, but more often they talked around it. The arguments grew hot, but eventually calmed down until the next outbreak. Events of the late 1850s, however, broke the pattern. New crises came before the old ones could dissipate. The crises embroiled every political, economic, moral, and practical difference between the North and the South.

Bleeding Kansas

The Kansas-Nebraska Act, steered through Congress in 1854 by Senator Stephen A. Douglas of Illinois, declared that settlers would decide for themselves, in their "popular sovereignty," what kind of society they would create. But partisans from both the North and the South determined to fill the territory with settlers of their own political persuasion. "Come on, then, Gentlemen of the slave States," New York's Senator William H. Seward proclaimed soon after the Kansas-Nebraska Act passed. "Since there is no escaping your challenge, I accept it in behalf of the cause of freedom. We will engage in competition for the virgin soil of Kansas, and God give the victory to the side which is stronger in numbers as it is in right."

CHRONOLOGY

1855   Proslavery and free-soil forces clash in Kansas

Massachusetts desegregates public schools

1856   John Brown's raid in Kansas

James Buchanan elected president

Congressman Preston Brooks canes Senator Charles Sumner

1857   Financial panic and depression

Dred Scott decision

Lecompton Constitution

Baltimore–St. Louis rail service completed

Hinton R. Helper, *The Impending Crisis of the South*

Mass revivals

1858   Lincoln-Douglas debates

Frederick Law Olmsted begins design for Central Park in New York City

1859   John Brown's raid on Harpers Ferry

Vicksburg convention calls for reopening of African slave trade

Kansas ratifies free-soil constitution

1860   Democratic convention divides

Abraham Lincoln elected president

South Carolina secedes from the Union

1861   Mississippi, Florida, Alabama, Georgia, Louisiana, and Texas secede

Montgomery Convention creates Confederate States of America

Lincoln inaugurated

Firing on and surrender of Fort Sumter

The Massachusetts Emigrant Aid Company announced that it planned to dispatch $5 million and 20,000 settlers to Kansas to ensure that the embattled territory became a free state. Though the Emigrant Aid Society only managed to send about 1,200 settlers to Kansas under its sponsorship, and about a third of those soon left, advocates of slavery in Kansas believed that the forces of abolition would overwhelm the territory before slaveholders could move there. The abolitionist press, building on over thirty years of experience, encouraged the impression that the antislavery settlers constituted a formidable foe.

Proslavery advocates across the Kansas border in Missouri fought what they saw as Yankee invaders. On election day, these Missourians flooded across the border to vote in support of the proslavery candidates for the territorial legislature. This illegal and inflammatory action by the "border ruffians," as the northern press quickly labeled them, was not necessary, for Southerners already accounted for six of every ten men settled in Kansas by 1855. In any case, the proslavery forces triumphed and took control of the territorial legislature in Lecompton. There, they passed a series of aggressive laws against free-soil advocates. Forbidding antislavery men to serve on juries or hold office, the legislature also decreed the death penalty for any person who assisted a fugitive slave. Ironically, only about 200 slaves lived in Kansas.

Faced with the blatant acts of the proslavery legislature and encouraged by their allies back east, antislavery Kansans decided that their only recourse was to establish a rival government. They worked through the summer and fall of 1855 in Topeka to write a constitution of their own. Over the winter, the free-soil advocates "ratified" the constitution—though they had no legal authority to do so—and elected their own legislature and governor. The free-soil delegates felt justified by the obvious injustice of their proslavery opponents. Both sides were certain that the future of the country lay in their hands.

Antislavery forces in New England and New York, including church congregations, sent rifles to Kansas

These settlers in Topeka, Kansas, armed themselves against their proslavery adversaries.

to arm what they saw as the side of righteousness. Southerners, in turn, organized an expedition to reinforce their comrades. Not surprisingly, this volatile situation soon exploded into violence. On May 21, 1856, a group of slave-state supporters, angered by free-state newspapers and rumors of military drills by their opponents, marched into the free-soil stronghold of Lawrence, threw printing presses into the river, and fired cannon at the Free State Hotel, which, they believed, had been established as a free-soil fortress. The cannon shot proving inadequate, the slave-state men burned the hotel to the ground. Free-soilers labeled the episode the "sack of Lawrence."

The very next day, in Washington, D.C., Representative Preston Brooks of South Carolina searched out Senator Charles Sumner of Massachusetts. Sumner had delivered a series of bitter speeches against slavery, the last one focusing on the "crime against Kansas." Sumner attacked Brooks's relative and fellow South Carolinian, the elderly Senator Andrew P. Butler, for taking "the harlot, slavery" as his "mistress" and ridiculed the old man for spitting when he talked. Brooks, defending the honor of his family and his

state, demonstrated his contempt for Sumner by striking him repeatedly about the head with a heavy rubber cane. Sumner, seated at a Senate desk screwed to the floor, ripped the chair from its moorings as he tried to rise. He did not return to his seat for two and a half years, the victim of shock. The empty seat became a symbol in the North of southern brutality, even insanity, on the slavery issue; the incident became a symbol in the South of the only sort of response the arrogant North would respect. Supporters from across the South sent Representative Brooks dozens of new canes to replace the one he had broken on their behalf.

The next day, an event back in Kansas intensified the already volatile conflict. The episode swirled around one John Brown, a free-soil emigrant to Kansas. Brown was fifty-six years old, a man who had failed in twenty different businesses in six states. He had been a supporter of abolitionism since 1834 and followed five of his sons to Kansas in 1855. There, he became furious at the proslavery forces and entered into the fight against them. Brown accompanied a group of free-staters to defend Lawrence, but they heard of the hotel's destruction before they arrived.

Preston Brooks's attack on Charles Sumner in the United States Senate electrified the nation in the spring of 1856.

SOUTHERN CHIVALRY — ARGUMENT versus CLUB'S.

Brown persuaded four of his sons and a son-in-law, along with two other men, to exact revenge for the defeat. Sharpening their broadswords to razor-like edges, the band set out for Pottawatomie Creek. There, acting in the name of the "Army of the North," they took five men from three houses and, after questioning them, split open their skulls. The men who were killed had been associated in some way with the territorial district court, but no one was, or is, sure of Brown's precise motives. He was never punished for the killings, though his responsibility was widely reported.

In the wake of the "sack of Lawrence," the caning of Sumner, and the "Pottawatomie Massacre"—exploding in just a three-day period in May of 1856—the territory became known as "Bleeding Kansas." A new governor finally helped quieten the conflict in September and Kansans seemed eager to settle the conflict and get to work building farms and towns. But the legitimacy of the territorial government remained an issue of heated contention both in Kansas and in Washington. The South, as it had in recent years with the Fugitive Slave Act and the Kansas-Nebraska Act, won a hollow victory when it seized the first election for the territorial government in Kansas. That government would soon pass, but the symbolic value of Bleeding Kansas would long endure.

The Election of 1856

The events in Kansas proved a disaster for the Democrats. In one state after another, Democratic senators lost office in the off-year elections of 1855. To many Southerners, the Democrats seemed a mere tool of Stephen Douglas and his northern allies; to many Northerners, it seemed that Douglas's call for popular sovereignty was a cover for greedy slaveholders. President Franklin Pierce seemed incapable of leadership, many in his party decided, and they set about looking for a new candidate for the fall election. The Democrats, needing someone who had not been tarnished by the events of the preceding two years, turned to James Buchanan to run in 1856. As minister to England, Buchanan had conveniently been out of the country during the entire Kansas mess.

The Know-Nothings alienated voters on both sides of the slavery issue by refusing to address the territorial problem directly. Southerners who had voted with the Know-Nothings had nowhere to turn but to the Democrats, but Northerners could devote their attention to the new Republican party. While many Republicans viewed the extreme nativism of the Know-Nothings with distaste, the Republican party did not denounce the anti-immigrant movement. They bypassed their

most outspoken antislavery men for the 1856 nomination and turned to John C. Frémont, famed as an explorer of the West and expander of liberty's empire in California. He had taken almost no public positions and had accumulated almost no political experience. The Republicans thought they had found just the sort of vague candidate who would give few potential voters a reason to vote against him.

The new Republican party was antislavery but not pro-black; Republicans avoided talking about race at all if they could help it. What they did talk about was the goodness of the North: its free labor, its free speech, its free soil. The North, they argued, was everything the South was not, a place where hardworking white men could build a life for their families free from the threat of arrogant, powerful, and greedy slaveholders.

The Republicans talked of the "Slave Power," a political conspiracy of the most powerful slavehold-

The Republicans, putting forward John C. Frémont for president, depicted themselves as the party of free-soil prosperity.

ers. Republicans saw everything from the three-fifths clause to the Missouri Compromise to the gag rules to the war with Mexico to the bloodshed in Kansas as the fruit of the Slave Power. How else to explain the long list of southern victories at a time when the North grew more populous and wealthy? Kansas and the caning of Sumner showed that the Slave Power, a Cincinnati paper raged, "cannot tolerate free speech anywhere, and would stifle it in Washington with the bludgeon and the bowie-knife, as they are now trying to stifle it in Kansas by massacre, rapine and murder." By speaking of the Slave Power, the Republicans could denounce the South without calling for the end of slavery and could rail at the richest slaveholders without denouncing the majority of southern whites.

Republicans attacked Catholics as well, repeating the charges that nativists had made for decades. Ironically, rumors that Frémont was a Catholic quickly surfaced and refused to subside, undercutting his support. Moreover, Frémont refused to give direction to the national campaign. To make matters worse, Millard Fillmore, the former president, ran under the banner of the American party, as the Know-Nothings called themselves, appealing to those nativists for whom the Republicans seemed too weak. Fillmore and his diehard supporters hoped that the three-way election would split the electorate so that the final decision would rest with the House; there, Fillmore thought, he would appear as a compromise candidate.

On election day in 1856, 83 percent of the eligible voting men went to the polls, one of the highest turnouts of the era. Although Buchanan won all of the South except Maryland, he received only 45 percent of the popular vote in the country as a whole. A difference of a few thousand votes in a few states would have denied Buchanan the election. The Democrats had won, but were filled with anxiety; the Republicans had lost, but they were filled with confidence. It was clear to everyone that the American political system was in flux and transition. No sooner was the 1856 election over than political leaders and editors began planning for the next one.

Observers of all political persuasions believed that James Buchanan had it within his power to strengthen the Democrats in both the North and the South. His party, after all, still controlled both houses of Congress and the Supreme Court as well as the presidency. The Republicans, moreover, had drawn much of their power from the chaos in Kansas. Should that situation

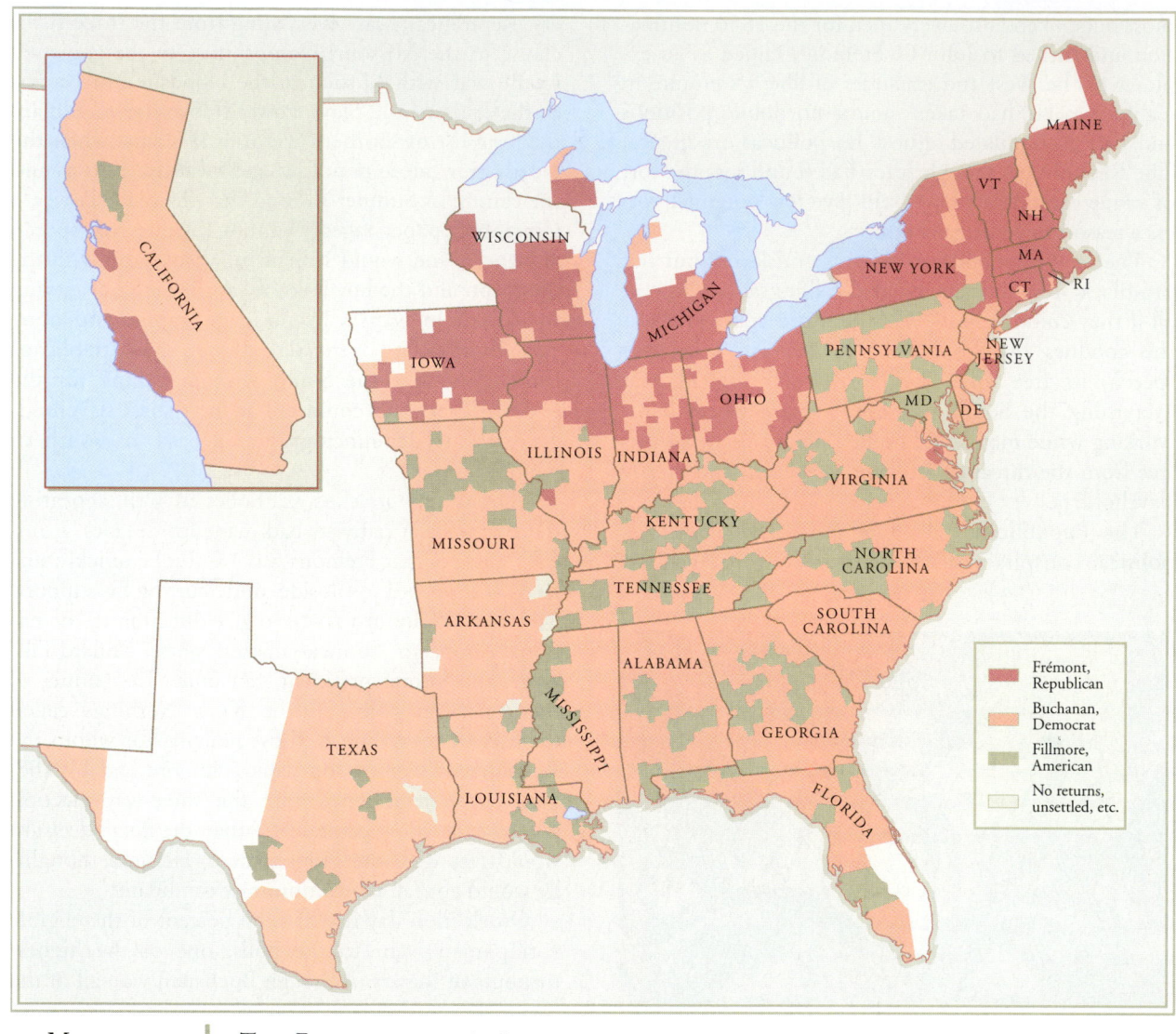

MAP 13.1 | THE ELECTION OF 1856

---

stabilize, the Republicans would lose their most effective weapon. Once Kansas had peacefully entered the Union as a free state under the banner of popular sovereignty, Democrats happily observed, no other territory awaited in which similar conflicts might be expected. Slavery, everyone seemed to agree, had no chance in Oregon, Nebraska, Minnesota, Washington, Utah, or New Mexico. The territorial issue that had torn at the country since 1820 might finally die down. When it did, moderates on both sides hoped, reason would return to American politics.

Dred Scott

In his inaugural address, James Buchanan mentioned a case pending before the Supreme Court, the case of Dred Scott, a slave. That case had moved its way through various levels of courts for more than a decade. Scott, born in Virginia around 1800, had in the 1830s been taken by his master, an army surgeon named John Emerson, to territories far in the upper Midwest. Scott had married Harriet Robinson, the slave of a federal Indian agent. Dr. Emerson bought

Harriet and thus owned the two daughters she bore with Scott. When Emerson died in 1843, Scott and his family became the property of Emerson's widow, who moved to St. Louis. Scott pleaded with her to let him hire out his own time—to work for wages and pay her from his earnings, as many urban slaves did—but Mrs. Emerson refused. In 1846 the Scotts petitioned for their freedom, claiming that their residence in the free territory entitled them to free status.

Suits such as the Scotts' had been brought successfully before Missouri courts in years past and at first there seemed nothing remarkable about their case. A long series of postponements and delays dragged the case on into the early 1850s, however, when the legal environment had become much more divided by political controversy over slavery. Democratic judges and lawyers worked to deny the Scotts their freedom on the grounds that such a precedent would undermine the right of Southerners to take slaves, constitutionally protected property, into the territories. A Republican lawyer agreed to carry the Scotts' case before the Supreme Court to counter the Democrats' aggressive claims. Unfortunately for the Republicans and the Scotts, five southern Democrats sat on the court, along with two northern Democrats, one northern Whig, and one northern Republican. Presiding was Chief Justice Roger B. Taney (pronounced "tawney"), an eighty-year-old Marylander first appointed to the court by Andrew Jackson in 1835, well known for his determination to defend slavery at every opportunity.

The *Dred Scott* case came before the Supreme Court during the superheated months of 1856, when Kansas, the Brooks/Sumner affair, and the presidential election commanded the country's attention. Although the case could have been decided on relatively narrow grounds, the Democratic members of the court wanted to issue a sweeping pronouncement that would settle once and for all the question of slavery in the territories. President-elect Buchanan pressured a fellow Pennsylvanian on the court to side with the Southerners. Two days after Buchanan took office in March of 1857, the court announced its decision in the *Dred Scott* case. It took Chief Justice Taney two hours to read the opinion. What he read shook the nation.

Taney spent half his time denying that Scott had the right to bring a case in the first place. Black people, Taney decreed, could not become citizens of the United States nor exercise the rights of citizenship because "they were not included, and were not intended

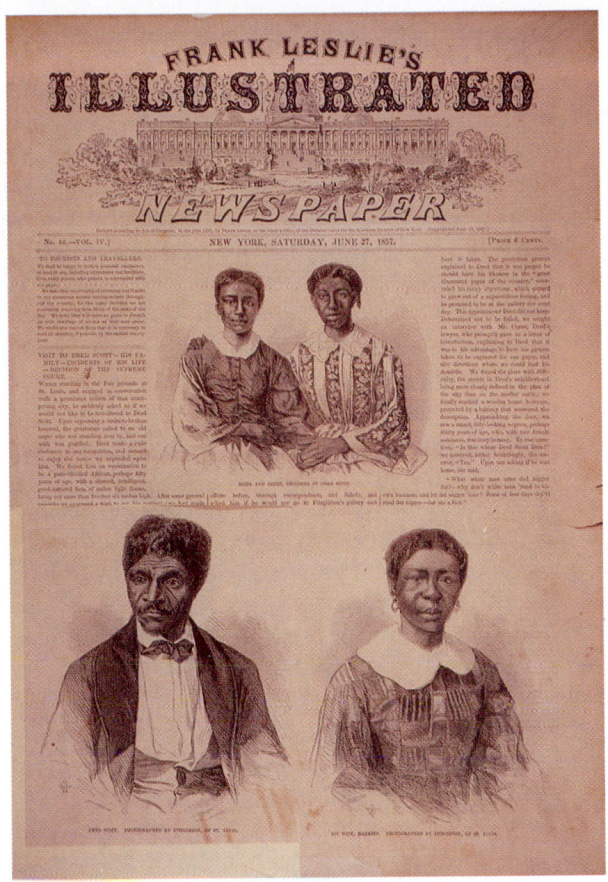

The Dred Scott *case attracted the attention of the entire country in 1856. This northern newspaper depicted Scott and his family sympathetically, emphasizing family ties and the women of the family.*

to be included, under the word 'citizens' in the Constitution." In chilling language and with distorted history, Taney declared that at the time the Constitution was written, throughout the "civilized and enlightened portions of the world," members of the "negro African race" were held to be "altogether unfit to associate with the white race . . . and so far inferior, that they had no rights which the white man was bound to respect; and . . . might justly and lawfully be reduced to slavery for his benefit." Therefore, Dred Scott had never been a citizen of Missouri and had no right to sue his mistress. Taney also decreed that Congress had never held a constitutional right to restrict slavery in the territories and that therefore the Missouri Compromise of 1820 was invalid. Two justices dissented from the majority's opinion, but the decision stood as the law of the land. In the meantime, a descendant of

Dred Scott's original owner bought the slave and set him free; Scott died the next year.

White Southerners exulted that they had been vindicated by the *Dred Scott* decision, that the Supreme Court was on their side, that the Republicans' demand for territories free of slavery was simply unconstitutional. The Republicans, however, sneered at the decision, which they saw as one more corrupt act by the Slave Power Conspiracy. A New York newspaper held that the court's decision was "entitled to just so much moral weight as would be the judgment of a majority of those congregated in any Washington barroom." The Republicans reprinted the dissenting opinions in the *Dred Scott* case and denounced the decision in the state legislatures they controlled throughout the North. They argued that the Founding Fathers had never intended slavery to be a permanent part of the United States, that the founders had carefully avoided using the word "slavery" in the Constitution and merely tolerated bondage because they expected it to die of its own weight. If the *Dred Scott* decision were followed to its logical conclusion, these northern Republicans warned, the United States would reopen the slave trade with Africa and even extend slavery into northern states where it had been banned.

The Republicans thought the court's audacious statement "the best thing that could have happened" to the Republican party. As an abolitionist newspaper put it, the "fiercer the insult, the bitterer the blow, the better." The Republicans expected the *Dred Scott* decision, like the events in Kansas and the caning of Sumner, to "galvanize" their party, to make it stronger. The Republicans needed to sweep the government in 1860, they argued, to clean out corruption and conspiracy from top to bottom.

Arguments over Slavery

Slavery had never been stronger in the United States than it was in 1857. The three and a half million slaves of the South extended over a vast territory stretching from Delaware to Texas. Four hundred thousand slaveowners possessed slaves worth $3 billion. Theorists devised ever more elaborate and aggressive defenses of slavery, no longer depicting it merely as a necessary evil or an unfortunate inheritance from the English or a burden that had to be shouldered with Christian forbearance. Rather, they claimed, slavery was an instrument of God's will, a progressive force in the world, a means of civilizing and Christian-

izing Africans otherwise lost to barbarism and heathenism. Southern physicians went to great lengths to prove that Africans and their descendants were physically and intellectually inferior to whites, dependent upon white guidance for their very survival.

Some defenders of slavery argued that slavery was *better* than free labor, more humane and Christian. If

THE NEGRO IN HIS OWN COUNTRY.

THE NEGRO IN AMERICA.

This proslavery cartoonist imagined an Africa of cannibalism and an America of refinement to claim that slavery was a force for good in the world.

the hypocritical and self-righteous men of the North would admit it, white Southerners argued, free labor exacted a great cost. Men, women, and children went hungry when unemployment, ill health, or old age struck because no one in the North felt any responsibility for anyone else. In the South, by contrast, theorists such as George Fitzhugh of Virginia insisted in *Cannibals All!* of 1857, slaveholders cared for their slaves even when those slaves had grown too old or feeble to work. The South's relative lack of schools, orphanages, asylums, and prisons, the defenders of the region insisted, testified not to backwardness but to a personalized society where individual responsibility replaced impersonal institutions. Compare the status of free blacks in the North and the South, white Southerners challenged, and you will find that white Northerners showed much less concern for the black people who lived in their own communities than they did for slaves they never saw.

Some white Southerners in the late 1850s argued for the expansion of American territory in Cuba or Central America, places where slavery could flourish. William Walker, a young Tennesseean, dreamed of personal glory, an isthmian canal, and a new territory for slavery. After several attempts at "filibustering," small-scale military efforts, in Mexico, Walker took advantage of a civil war to gain power in Nicaragua in 1855 and 1856, attracting great attention and 2,000 American settlers. But Central American leaders united against him, cholera wiped out his army, and the United States rejected his claims to legitimacy. White Southerners enthusiastically supported several attempts by Walker in the late 1850s to take Nicaragua, but he failed repeatedly. Finally, a firing squad in Honduras put an end to Walker's crusade by executing him.

Despite the highly publicized adventures of the filibusters and the agitation of a few editors and politicians for the reopening of the African slave trade, most white Southerners wanted above all to keep and protect what they had, not jeopardize slavery by brashly expanding it. Not only would a renewed slave trade with Africa ignite the opinion of the world against the South, they recognized, but it would also drive down slave prices and create new problems of discipline and revolt. The white South prided itself on having created a stable and prosperous society during its two and a half centuries of slavery and did not want to endanger that society.

Moreover, the slave economy boomed in the late 1850s. Planters took advantage of improved cotton gins, river boats, railroads, and new kinds of seed to double, in the 1850s alone, their production of cotton. The claim of southern politicians that "Cotton is

The southern cotton economy boomed in the late 1850s even as the sectional crisis grew more threatening.

SCENE ON A COTTON PLANTATION. GATHERING COTTON.

HINTON HELPER,
*THE IMPENDING CRISIS
OF THE SOUTH,*
1857

This book, a lacerating critique of slavery by a racist white Southerner, proved even more incendiary in the South than had Harriet Beecher Stowe's *Uncle Tom's Cabin.* The Republican party seized on the book as a revelation from inside the slave power's empire, arguing that it revealed the secret resentments of the white majority. To the Republicans' surprise and dismay, however, the book bred anger against the North instead of Republican recruits in the South.

It is a fact well known to every intelligent Southerner, that we are compelled to go to the North for almost every article of utility and adornment, from matches, shoepegs and paintings, up to cotton-mills, steamships and statuary; that we have no foreign trade, no princely merchants, nor respectable artists; that, in comparison with the Free States, we contribute nothing to the literature, polite arts and inventions of the age; that, for want of profitable employment at home, large numbers of our native population find themselves necessitated to emigrate to the West, while the Free States retain not only the larger proportion of those born within their own limits, but induce, annually, hundreds of thousands of foreigners to settle and remain amongst them; that almost everything produced at the North meets with ready sale, while, at the same time, there is no demand, even among our own citizens, for the productions of Southern industry; that, owing to the absence of a proper system of business among us, the North becomes, in one way or another, the proprietor and dispenser of all our floating wealth, and that we are dependent on Northern capitalists for the means necessary to build our railroads, canals and other public improvements; that if we want to visit a foreign country, even though it may lie directly south of us, we find no convenient way of getting there except by taking passage through a Northern port; and that nearly all the profits arising from the exchange of commodities, from insurance and shipping offices, and from the thousand and one industrial pursuits of the country, accrue to the North, and are there invested in the erection of those magnificent cities and stupendous works of art which dazzle the eyes of the South, and attest the superiority of free institutions!

. . .

And now that we have come to the very heart and soul of our subject, we feel no disposition to mince matters, but mean to speak plainly and to the point, without any equivocation, mental reservation, or secret evasion whatever. The son of a venerated parent, who, while he lived, was a considerate and merciful slaveholder, a native of the South, born and bred in North Carolina, of a family whose home has been in the valley of the Yadkin for nearly a century and a half, a Southerner by instinct and by all the influences of thought, habits and kindred, and with the desire and fixed purpose to reside permanently within the limits of the South, and with the expectation of dying there also—we feel that we have the right to express our opinion, however humble or unimportant it may be, on any and every question that affects the public good. . . .

And now to the point. In our opinion, an opinion which has been formed from data obtained by assiduous researchers and comparisons, from laborious investigation, logical reasoning, and earnest reflection, the causes which have impeded the progress and pros-

perity of the South, which have dwindled our commerce and other similar pursuits, into the most contemptible insignificance; sunk a large majority of our people in galling poverty and ignorance, rendered a small minority conceited and tyrannical, and driven the rest away from their homes; entailed upon us a humiliating dependence on the Free States; disgraced us in the recesses of our own souls, and brought us under reproach in the eyes of all civilized and enlightened nations—may all be traced to one common source, and there find solution in the most hateful and horrible word, that was ever incorporated into the vocabulary of human economy—*Slavery.*

. . .

In making up these [statistical] tables we have two objects in view; the first is to open the eyes of the non-slaveholders of the South to the system of deception that has been so long practiced upon them, and the second is to show slaveholders themselves—we have reference only to those who are not too perverse, or ignorant, to perceive naked truths—that free labor is far more respectable, profitable, and productive, than slave labor. In the South, unfortunately, no kind of labor is either free or respectable. Every white man who is under the necessity of earning his bread, by the sweat of his brow, or by manual labor, in any capacity, no matter how unassuming in deportment, or exemplary in morals, is treated as if he were a loathsome beast, and shunned with disdain. His soul may be the very seat of honor and integrity, yet without slaves—himself a slave—he is accounted as nobody, and would be deemed intolerably presumptuous, if he dared to open his lips, even so wide as to give faint utterance to a three-lettered monosyllable, like yea or nay, in the presence of an august knight of the whip and the lash.

. . .

The lords of the lash are not only absolute masters of the blacks, who are bought and sold, and driven about like so many cattle, but they are also the oracles and arbiters of all the non-slaveholding whites, whose freedom is merely nominal, and whose unparalleled illiteracy and degradation is purposely and fiendishly perpetuated. How little the "poor white trash," the great majority of the Southern people, know of the real condition of the country, is, indeed, sadly astonishing. The truth is, they know nothing of public measures, and little of private affairs, except what their imperious masters, the slave-drivers, condescend to tell, and that is but precious little, and even that little, always garbled and one-sided, is never told except in public harangues; for the haughty cavaliers of shackles and handcuffs will not degrade themselves by holding private converse with those who have neither dimes nor hereditary rights in human flesh.

Whenever it pleases, and to the extent it pleases, a slaveholder to become communicative, poor whites may hear with fear and trembling, but not speak. They must be as mum as dumb brutes, and stand in awe of their august superiors, or be crushed with stern rebukes, cruel oppressions, or downright violence. If they dare to think for themselves, their thoughts must be forever concealed. The expression of any sentiment at all conflicting with the gospel of slavery, dooms them at once in the community in which they live, and then, whether willing or unwilling, they are obliged to become heroes, martyrs, or exiles. . . .

Non-slaveholders are not only kept in ignorance of what is transpiring at the North, but they are continually misinformed of what is going on even in the South. Never were the poorer classes of a people, and those classes so largely in the majority, and all inhabiting the same country, so basely duped, so adroitly swindled, or so unpardonably outraged.

SOURCE Hinton R. Helper, *The Impending Crisis of the South* (New York: A. B. Burdick, 1859), pp. 25–26, 28–29, 40, 42–43.

King" proved no empty boast. Even though northern factories and farms grew rapidly in the 1850s, cotton still accounted for fully half of all U.S. exports. Without cotton, many thousands of northern and British workers would have had no jobs, along with a large number of merchants, lawyers, bankers, insurance agents, dock workers, and clerks.

The prosperity created by the cotton boom resonated throughout the southern economy. Small towns emerged in the 1850s and southern cities grew quickly, attracting immigrants and businesses. Although the South could not keep up with the North—one of the most rapidly developing economies in the world—the South actually did quite well by international standards. Considered as a separate economy, the South stood second in the world in the number of miles of railroad, sixth in cotton textile factories, and eighth in iron production. The South was roughly the equal of France, Germany, or Austria-Hungary in its level of industrial output. Slaves proved to be adaptable both to factories and cities. The number of slaves in cities declined in the 1850s mainly because the demand for slaves in the countryside was so strong.

The southern economy, then, was not weak or weakening in the 1850s. Slavery and cotton had never been more profitable. On the other hand, the South was not urbanizing or industrializing nearly as quickly

as the North. The South did not create a large class of entrepreneurs or skilled workers, nor did the region invest much money in machinery to make its farms and plantations more efficient; the purchase of a slave was a more certain investment. The southern plantation economy, in effect, was too profitable for its own good. The short-term gains of the 1850s dissuaded wealthy Southerners from investing in businesses that held greater potential for long-term development, businesses that were not as dependent on other regions and countries for their continued prosperity.

Northerners considered the southern economy the mirror image of the North: sick rather than healthy, backward rather than dynamic, inegalitarian rather than democratic. Critics of the South argued that slavery victimized not only slaves but also "poor whites." In the antislavery portrayal, the Slave Power's domination began at home, where haughty self-proclaimed aristocrats lorded over ignorant whites, bullying them into supporting parties and policies that worked against their own interests. Antislavery people charged that slaves degraded white labor in the South, made manual labor shameful, and substituted a cheap sense of racial superiority for actual accomplishment.

The most effective criticism of the South in this vein came from a Southerner: Hinton Rowan Helper, the son of a small slaveholding farmer in western North Carolina. In 1857, a northern press published

Graph 13-1 Extent of Slaveholding in the South
Population of 7,981,000

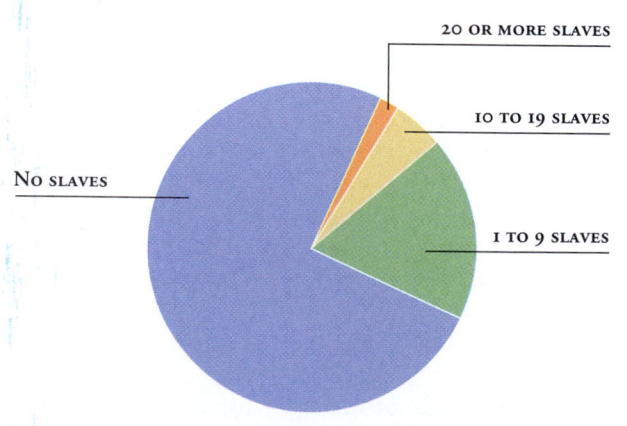

20 OR MORE SLAVES
10 TO 19 SLAVES
NO SLAVES
1 TO 9 SLAVES

Graph 13.2 Patterns of Slaveholding in the South, 1850
347,525 Families

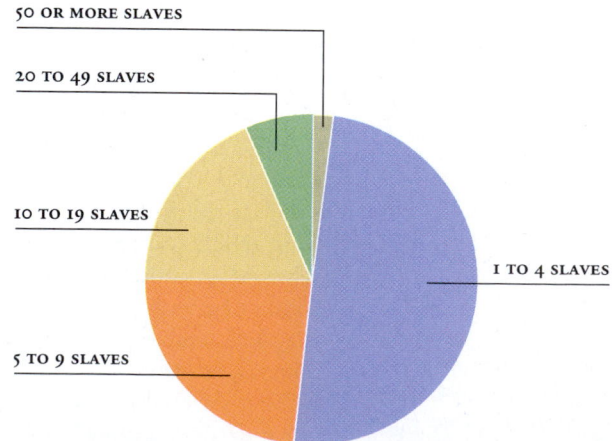

50 OR MORE SLAVES
20 TO 49 SLAVES
10 TO 19 SLAVES
5 TO 9 SLAVES
1 TO 4 SLAVES

More than half of all slaveholders owned four or fewer slaves in 1850.

Helper's book, *The Impending Crisis of the South,* which argued that the South's growth, prosperity, and cultural development were being held back by slavery. He charged that "the lords of the lash are not only absolute masters of the blacks . . . but they are also the oracles and arbiters of all non-slaveholding whites." Helper deployed statistics from the census to prove his case, showing that land values, literacy levels, and manufacturing rates in the South were substantially lower than those in the North. Helper, no friend to black Southerners, proposed that slaveholders be taxed to colonize all free blacks in Africa or Latin America.

Though many Northerners believed that Helper spoke for a large number of yeomen farmers in the South, there is little indication that many southern whites agreed with Helper's assessment of their status. Most whites saw slavery as an avenue for their own advancement, not a hindrance. Many men and women bought a slave before they bought land, even if only to rent the slave to other whites. Slaveowners included women, shopkeepers, industrialists, lawyers, ministers, and even a few free blacks. No investment seemed to offer a more certain return than a slave, especially in the 1850s when slave prices rose rapidly. While that rise in prices meant that a growing proportion of white people would be unable to afford a slave—so that the percentage of whites who owned slaves declined from about a third in 1840 to about a quarter in 1860— most nonslaveholding whites apparently reconciled themselves to their situation or determined that they, too, would eventually join the slaveowning ranks.

Southern Solidarity and Differences

Politics reinforced the sense among southern white men that they lived in a fair and democratic society. While many nonslaveholders in mountainous districts across the South voted against the large slaveholding districts, most southern white men voted in concert with the richest men in their immediate neighborhoods. And in every county in the South, including the mountains, those richest men were slaveholders. In the eyes of the poorer men, their wealthy neighbors could act as spokesmen and brokers for the community in the state capital. Common people identified themselves as members of communities, congregations, and parties.

Southern whites identified themselves most of all as white people, tied to other whites by blood and her-

itage, transcending obvious differences of wealth and background. Whites held black people in contempt despite their knowledge that many African Americans were more intelligent, hard-working, and Christian than many whites. To be white was to be the inheritor of all the accomplishments of the ancients, of Christendom, and the modern world. It was to be inherently, undeniably, free. Such attitudes were reinforced at every level, from the daily rituals of life to the writings of leading thinkers from Europe. White Southerners railed against the Republicans because that party threatened this bond of race between the white North and the white South. When southern whites called the Republicans "Black Republicans," they seized on the most charged and degrading language they could imagine.

Despite the solidarities of racial thinking, important political differences divided Southerners. At one extreme were the so-called "fire-eaters," virulent defenders of the South and slavery. These men were diverse in age, wealth, occupation, slaveholding, and

Edmund Ruffin of Virginia was a "fire-eater"—a proponent of southern independence—as well as a proponent of agricultural reform. He hoped that both would make the South stronger.

James D. B. DeBow, "The Interest in Slavery of the Southern Non-Slaveholder" 1860

DeBow used his statistical expertise as a former Superintendent of the United States Census to refute arguments such as Hinton Helper's in the preceding document. DeBow argued that the South was actually more democratic in property holding than the North and that slavery actually helped the non-slaveholding white Southerner in many ways.

. . . WHEN IN CHARGE of the national census office, several years since, I found that it had been stated by an abolition Senator from his seat, that the number of slaveholders at the South did not exceed 150,000. Convinced that it was a gross misrepresentation of the facts, I caused a careful examination of the returns to be made, which fixed the actual number at 347,255, and communicated the information, by note, to Senator Cass, who read it in the Senate. I first called attention to the fact that the number embraced slaveholding families, and that to arrive at the actual number of slaveholders, it would be necessary to multiply by the proportion of persons, which the census showed to a family. When this was done, the number was swelled to about 2,000,000.

Since these results were made public, I have had reason to think, that the separation of the schedules of the slave and the free, was calculated to lead to omissions of the single properties, and that on this account it would be safe to put the number of families at 375,000, and the number of actual slaveholders at about two million and a quarter.

Assuming the published returns, however, to be correct, it will appear that one-half of the population of South Carolina, Mississippi, and Louisiana, excluding the cities, are slaveholders, and that one-third of the population of the entire South are similarly circumstanced. The average number of slaves is nine to each slaveholding family, and one-half of the whole number of such holders are in possession of less than five slaves.

It will thus appear that the slaveholders of the South, so far from constituting numerically an insignificant portion of its people, as has been malignantly alleged, make up an aggregate, greater in relative proportion than the holders of any other species of property whatever, in any part of the world; and that of no other property can it be said, with equal truthfulness, that it is an interest of the whole community. Whilst every other family in the States I have specially referred to, are slaveholders, but one family in every three and a half families in Maine, New Hampshire, Massachusetts and Connecticut, are holders of agricultural land; and, in European States, the proportion is almost indefinitely less. The proportion which the slaveholders of the South, bear to the entire population is greater than that of the owners of land or houses, agricultural stock, State, bank, or other corporation securities anywhere else. No political economist will deny this. Nor is that all. Even in the States which are among the largest slaveholding, South Carolina,

party affiliation. Some lived in cities, others on plantations. Some, such as J.D.B. DeBow, wanted to make the South more industrial and modern, while others rejected such development as a Yankee blight on the rural South. Whatever their differences, these men saw themselves as the voice of honesty. They did not consider themselves hotheads. Men such as Robert Barnwell Rhett and Edmund Ruffin argued that the abolitionists and their Republican supporters intended to destroy the South. The only sane response, they be-

Georgia and Tennessee, the land proprietors outnumber nearly two to one, in relative proportion, the owners of the same property in Maine, Massachusetts and Connecticut, and if the average number of slaves held by each family throughout the South be but nine, and if one-half of the whole number of slaveholders own under five slaves, it will be seen how preposterous is the allegation of our enemies, that the slaveholding class is an organized wealthy aristocracy. *The poor men of the South are the holders of one to five slaves, and it would be equally consistent with truth and justice, to say that they represent, in reality, its slaveholding interest.*

[How does slavery benefit the non-slaveholding white man?]

1. The non-slaveholder of the South is assured that the remuneration afforded by his labor, over and above the expense of living, is larger than that which is afforded by the same labor in the free States.

2. The non-slaveholders, as a class, are not reduced by the necessity of our condition, as is the case in the free States, to find employment in crowded cities and come into competition in close and sickly workshops and factories, with remorseless and untiring machinery.

3. The non-slaveholder is not subjected to that competition with foreign pauper labor, which has degraded the free labor of the North and demoralized it to an extent which perhaps can never be estimated.

4. The non-slaveholder of the South preserves the status of the white man, and is not regarded as an inferior or a dependent.

5. The non-slaveholder knows that as soon as his savings will admit, he can become a slaveholder, and thus relieve his wife from the necessities of the kitchen and the laundry, and his children from the labors of the field.

6. The large slaveholders and proprietors of the South begin life in great part as non-slaveholders.

7. But should such fortune not be in reserve for the non-slaveholder, he will understand that by honesty and industry it may be realized to his children.

8. The sons of the non-slaveholder are and have always been among the leading and ruling spirits of the South; in industry as well as in politics.

9. Without the institution of slavery, the great staple products of the South would cease to be grown, and the immense annual results, which are distributed among every class of the community, and which give life to every branch of industry, would cease.

10. If emancipation be brought about as will undoubtedly be the case, unless the encroachments of the fanatical majorities of the North are resisted now the slaveholders, in the main, will escape the degrading equality which must result, by emigration, for which they would have the means, by disposing of their personal chattels: whilst the non-slaveholders, without these resources, would be compelled to remain and endure the degradation.

SOURCE "The Non-Slaveholders of the South," in DeBow and others, *The Interest in Slavery of the Southern Non-Slaveholder. The Right of Peaceful Secession. Slavery in the Bible.* (Charleston: Evans & Cogswell, 1860), pp. 3–5, 7–12.

lieved, was to face the issue squarely and aggressively, to agitate the slavery issue constantly, to refuse to yield an inch in the territories or anywhere else. The fire-eaters were calling for secession as early as 1857. They sought to keep secessionism in people's minds so they could act quickly when events drove the two regions apart once again.

At the other end of the political spectrum in the South were the former Whigs and Know-Nothings. They considered the Democrats, especially the

fire-eaters, great threats to the future of the South and slavery. The Democrats' relentless calls for southern rights and the expansion of slavery, they argued, did as much as the abolitionists to inflame northern sentiment against the South. Former leaders of the Whigs and the nativist American party did their best to pull their allies into a new party opposed to the Democrats and attractive to a "thoughtful, sedate, constitution-abiding, conservative class of men." The many Unionists in the upper South, in cities, and even in some of the richest plantation districts felt drawn to this position. The editors of the former Whig and American papers chided the Democrats for continually agitating the slavery question. They warned voters that the Democrats would sell out the South in Kansas, that the Democrats talked a tough game but always ended up caving in to the North.

In the North, too, the major parties had to contend with activists on the fringes of respectable opinion. By 1857, the abolitionists had become both entrenched and somewhat discouraged. They had succeeded in making slavery detested throughout the North and had created much of the anti-southern energy that flowed into the Republican party. But abolitionists distrusted that party. The Republicans seemed interested only in the welfare of the white North, in keeping the territories open to northern men. Republicans denied any intention of ending slavery in the South, the very reason the immediate abolitionists had come into being over a quarter of a century before. The Republicans even resurrected talk of colonization, the movement the abolitionists had abandoned twenty-five years earlier. The Republicans, while better than the pro-southern Democrats, still dissatisfied the abolitionists.

A SOCIETY IN CRISIS

The American economy boomed in the mid-1850s. Not only did cotton do well, but so did the farms, factories, railroads, and cities of the North and West. People cheered the laying of a telegraphic cable all the way across the Atlantic Ocean, an incredible feat. New York City began the construction of its glorious Central Park. Currier and Ives prints became the rage, brightening homes across the country with charming scenes of American life. The sale of newspapers, books,

and magazines surged, including an impressive new publication, *Atlantic Monthly*. Working people's organizations staged a comeback. Churches and schools spread with remarkable speed. The mileage of railroads tripled, to more than 30,000 miles. The United States had become a marvel of the modern world.

But underlying this prosperity ran a deep current of unease. Some people were uncomfortable with the prosperity itself, worried that Americans were growing soft and self-indulgent. Others felt guilt that as the economy boomed slavery became stronger. Others despaired at the state of American politics, which seemed in disarray under the control of selfish men who cared for nothing other than their own advancement. The conflict between the North and the South embodied all these anxieties, focusing them, giving them concrete shape.

Financial Panic and Spiritual Revival

Late in the summer of 1857, people warned that there had been too much speculation recently, that companies and individuals had borrowed too much money. The end of the Crimean War in Europe seemed ominous for the United States, for now the countries of the Old World could turn their energies toward growing their own food, undermining the heavy demand for American farm products that had buoyed the economy for several years. When a major insurance company went under in 1857, a panic spread among New York banks and railroad stocks plummeted along with western land values. Soon, banks and companies across the country began to fail.

Working people of all ranks lost their jobs. Not only unskilled laborers, domestics, and millworkers found themselves without work, but so did educated bookkeepers and clerks. Not only were recent Irish immigrants homeless, but so were white Protestant native-born workers. Across the North, hundreds of thousands of people had no income and many were forced to rely on charity to feed and clothe themselves. Workers tried to organize, but employers shut down the mills and factories. As winter approached, many people wondered whether their families would survive through the cold months. Others worried that the poor would rebel against the rich.

The white South used the panic for rhetorical advantage. Southerners blamed northern financiers for bringing on the Panic of 1857, for dragging the pros-

The sudden financial panic of 1857 seemed to many Americans a sign of moral corruption and social decay.

perous South into depression. Though the white and free black working people of southern cities suffered along with their counterparts to the north, white Southerners bragged that their region quickly recovered from the panic, showing the greater stability of their agrarian social order. They also bragged that their slaves, unlike white workers, never starved or went without a roof over their heads. Slaveholders, unlike employers, could not—would not, they said—abandon their workers when hard times arrived.

Throughout the country, the panic and depression of 1857 caused people to pause and take stock of their situation. How could it be, they asked, that the country could go so quickly from prosperity to poverty? Some said that the political system had betrayed the country, that selfish politicians had allowed banking to become too loose or the tariff too strict—or vice versa, since no one could be certain. Others warned that Americans had grown too rich and lazy for their

own good, borrowing and spending too freely, becoming too wrapped up in their material welfare at the expense of everything and everyone else.

A wave of religious revivals emerged in response to the panic and the moral failures it reflected. Almost as soon as the crisis began in the fall of 1857, revivals commenced. They lasted for over a year, sweeping back and forth across the country. Unlike earlier revivals, the religious spirit emerged not in rural districts or in raw new canal towns but in the largest cities of the Northeast. Unlike earlier revivals, too, those of 1857 attracted a conspicuously large number of men as well as women. Both businessmen and workingmen attended sermons and prayer meetings on their lunch hour. The revivals also witnessed the first active participation of denominations such as the Episcopalians and Unitarians. It seemed to many people, in fact, that the revivals were the most heartening and significant in American history, showing that the

people in the forefront of modern America were trying to change their ways. And as people read their newspapers they saw plenty that needed to be changed — especially in Kansas, where events in the fall of 1857 reclaimed the front page from both the hard times and the revivals.

Kansas — Again

Most of the settlers who had arrived in Kansas in 1856 and 1857 were nonslaveholding migrants from the upper South. They did not appear eager to establish slavery in Kansas. An open election, therefore, would likely install a constitutional convention in favor of free soil at the time Kansas became a state. The proslavery legislature elected in the earliest days of the territory, however, still controlled Kansas in 1857 and a prosouthern Democrat still sat in the White House. Free state advocates fought back, touring the North, preaching their cause, and raising money for the struggle against the Slave Power. Leading abolitionists, as well as leading thinkers such as Henry David Thoreau and Ralph Waldo Emerson, warmly supported John Brown for what they saw as his bravery in Kansas.

As the curtain opened in Kansas in November of 1857, the small band of unregenerate proslavery delegates who still controlled the legislature proposed a new constitution. Kansas had to produce a constitution that the U.S. Congress would accept. The legislature, after a drawn-out and drunken convention, provided that voters would choose between the constitution with slavery or without slavery. In either case, slaveowners already in Kansas would be permitted to keep their slaves. The Republicans portrayed the constitution as one more audacious act of the Slave Power, but in fact the "Lecompton Constitution" posed a serious problem for the Democrats. Northern members of the party could not support it without appearing too sympathetic to the South and losing already queasy constituents to the Republicans; they could not oppose it without alienating the southern Democrats that made up the bulk of the party's strength.

Stephen Douglas refused to endorse the Lecompton Constitution as a violation of popular sovereignty but President Buchanan, the other leading Democrat, urged its adoption. He persuaded himself that the constitution was in fact a moderate compromise, letting Kansas enter the Union as a free state in the long run while protecting the slaveholders who were already

James Buchanan, a Pennsylvania Democrat, became the object of contempt among many Northerners for his sympathy for the South in the political struggles of the late 1850s.

there. Once Kansas was a state, he reasoned, its legislature could decide what to do with those slaves without dragging all of Congress into the conflict. Most northern voters saw the matter differently: though it was obvious that the great majority of Kansans wanted to enter the Union as a free state, those antislavery Kansans would be forced to accept slavery in their midst.

Republicans could hardly believe that Buchanan had handed them such an easy way to portray him as a tool of the South. And neither could Stephen Douglas, who recognized that Buchanan's actions would create enormous problems for the Democrats, for popular sovereignty, and for Stephen Douglas. The Democrats fought bitterly among themselves for months, Douglas denouncing the president and seeking to use the Senate to block the Lecompton Constitution,

Buchanan using the powers of the presidency to mobilize senators against Douglas. Southern senators sneered at Douglas and called him a traitor to the party, even as they delivered blustering proslavery arguments from the Senate floor.

Moderate southern and northern Democrats warned that the South, drunk with its power on the Supreme Court, in Congress, and in the White House, was destroying its only hope for continued success: a strong Democratic party in the North. When Kansas voters overwhelmingly rejected the Lecompton Constitution in the spring of 1858, they rejected Buchanan and the South as well. The Democrats suffered widespread defeat in the state elections that spring and lost control of the House. The prospects were not much better for the fall. Douglas himself faced a tough election battle and Buchanan did everything he could to destroy this rival in his own party. Running against a promising Republican candidate, Abraham Lincoln, Douglas needed all the help he could get.

The Lincoln-Douglas Debates

Abraham Lincoln, though possessing considerable political assets, was still very much the underdog in the Illinois senatorial race of 1858. As a Whig in a heavily Democratic state, Lincoln had not found it easy to win or hold office in the 1840s and 1850s. He had lost repeatedly, occupying national office for all of two years: elected to the House of Representatives in 1845, Lincoln lasted only one term. He opposed the war with Mexico, an unpopular stance in Illinois, and was sent back to his law office in Springfield. There, Lincoln made a good living for himself and his family, drawing on his own abilities and the connections that came with his marriage to Mary Todd, a member of a prominent family in the booming town. Lincoln's modest beginnings on the Kentucky and Illinois frontier, where he had received only one year of formal education, lay comfortably in the past. Still, he longed for a major public office.

Though the short, portly, experienced, pragmatic, and famous Stephen Douglas seemed the opposite of the tall, thin, inexperienced, principled, and obscure Abraham Lincoln, the two men in fact shared a great deal. Douglas, too, had grown up poor and Douglas too had made himself into what he had become by the late 1850s. Douglas, although the most prominent Democrat in the country, was actually four years younger than Lincoln, who had watched Douglas with some envy over the preceding two decades. Both Lincoln and Douglas identified quite easily with the voters of Illinois, sharing their constituents' moderate positions on most national issues.

Illinois held within its borders a considerable share of American diversity, its population composed of many New England migrants in the northern half of the state, upcountry southern migrants in the bottom half, and German and Irish immigrants in Chicago. Both the factories and the farms of Illinois prospered in the 1850s, as did abolitionists, Know-Nothings, Whigs, and southern-leaning Democrats. The Illinois senatorial election of 1858 promised to throw all these groups into contention. "The battle of the Union is to be fought in Illinois," a Washington newspaper announced. At stake was this question: Could the Democrats survive as a national party, with Douglas as their leader, or were they doomed to become a party of the South?

Douglas traveled by private railroad car from Chicago to Springfield, the state capital and Lincoln's base. All along the way, Douglas gave speeches to thousands of people, telling them that he was the voice of experience, principled compromise, and popular sovereignty. He also told them that Lincoln, while "a kind-hearted, amiable, good-natured gentleman," held "monstrous revolutionary doctrines" of abolitionism. To Douglas's great annoyance, Lincoln followed the senator to rebut his arguments and charges, sometimes appearing in the crowd, sometimes arriving the next day. Douglas, though reluctant to give the relatively unknown Lincoln a share of attention, finally agreed to hold seven joint debates in the late summer and early fall. The candidates took turns opening and closing the debates, every word transcribed by reporters from across the country.

Lincoln was far from an abolitionist, refusing to join the antislavery Liberty and Free Soil parties and staying with the Whigs far longer than most of the men who became Republicans. Unlike the abolitionists, Lincoln venerated the Constitution and the spirit of compromise it embodied. He repeatedly brought up the Dred Scott decision from the previous year, however, arguing that it was a corruption of the Constitution. The Supreme Court decision, Lincoln warned, would permit slavery to spread into lands where Illinois men or their sons would otherwise migrate. Douglas offered what he saw as practical, commonsense responses to such charges, arguing that slavery would not spread anywhere the majority of the

Abraham Lincoln and Stephen Douglas vied for a U.S. Senate seat from Illinois in 1858, debating the most troubling issues that faced the entire nation.

white population did not want it to. A far greater and more immediate threat, Douglas argued, was that the Republicans would force the South into desperate acts by dragging moral issues into political contexts where they could not be resolved. Let the sovereign white people of each state decide for themselves, in the fullness of time, whether they would have slavery or not, Douglas counseled. Douglas did not defend slavery—which he hoped and expected would eventually fade away through natural causes—but he declared that "I care more for the great principle of self-government, the right of the people to rule, than I do for all the negroes in Christendom."

Lincoln charged that Douglas's strategy merely postponed an inevitable reckoning between the slave states and the free states. He argued that "a house divided against itself cannot stand. . . . Either the opponents of slavery will arrest the further spread of it, and place it where the public mind shall rest in the belief that it is in the course of ultimate extinction, or its

advocates will push it forward till it shall become alike lawful in all the States, old as well as new, North as well as South." Notwithstanding Douglas's efforts to dismiss the morality of slavery as beside the point in a northern senatorial campaign, that morality repeatedly surfaced in the debates. Lincoln argued that he, not Douglas, was the one defending true self-government. Douglas's policy permitted the forces of slavery to grow stronger and more aggressive, while Lincoln's would place slavery on the path toward "ultimate extinction." It would likely be several generations before that extinction occurred, Lincoln believed, and it would probably need to be accompanied by the colonization of the former slaves out of the United States, but the process could begin in 1858.

Lincoln made a distinction between different kinds of rights. African Americans, he thought, had economic rights: "In the right to eat the bread, without leave of anybody else, which his own hand earns, he is my equal and the equal of Judge Douglas, and the

equal of every living man." But Lincoln did not believe in social equality between blacks and whites. He would not grant black men the right to intermarry with whites, serve on juries, or vote, but he did believe that black people had the right not to be slaves. Lincoln, though not offering a coherent or consistent vision of African-American freedom, took the offensive, making Douglas appear more of a defender of slavery than at heart he was.

The election was close, the Douglas Democrats defeating the Republicans by about 4000 votes out of 250,000 cast. The state legislature, which elected U.S. senators in these decades, went to the Democrats and they returned Douglas to Washington. But Abraham Lincoln had won as well. He had become nationally famous, identified as the spokesman for a principled yet restrained antislavery. All across the North, in fact, the Republicans made impressive gains in 1858. In every state, many people—perhaps the majority of whites—wanted the conflict to quieten, wanted the nation to find some compromise. But the political environment did not have a chance to calm in 1859, for it was then that John Brown returned to the national scene.

John Brown and Harpers Ferry

John Brown had become famous in the three years since he had burst into prominence in Bleeding Kansas in 1855. Antislavery people back east, assured by journalists that Brown had not personally killed anyone at Pottawatomie, admired the hard man for his firsthand opposition to slaveholders. He acted on what other antislavery people only talked about. Thus, as he toured New England in search of funds to carry on the cause, he found willing listeners and open hands. Antislavery advocates were eager to contribute to the fight against slavery in Kansas, not realizing they were contributing to a fight against slavery much closer to home.

Throughout 1857 and 1858 Brown planned for an attack on the federal arsenal at Harpers Ferry, Virginia. He had a thousand iron pikes forged to arm the slaves he believed would rise in rebellion once he and his men triggered the revolt. He revealed his plans to black ministers and to the so-called "Secret Six," leading white abolitionists who helped fund his attack on slavery where it lived. He tried to win the support of Frederick Douglass, who while sympathetic thought

The campaign launched by John Brown and twenty-one black and white allies in 1859 failed in its immediate aims of unleashing a rebellion of the enslaved but succeeded in heightening the moral and political debate over slavery.

the plan doomed logistically. But Brown pressed on. One of his lieutenants moved to Harpers Ferry and even established a family there, preparing the way for the attack. In the meantime, Brown continued the fight against slavery in the West, freeing eleven slaves in Missouri, killing their master and leading them into Canada. Such exploits, though illegal, only heightened Brown's visibility and appeal in New England, where he was welcomed by leading industrialists and politicians.

The assault on Harpers Ferry started in earnest in the summer of 1859, when Brown rented a farm seven miles away and assembled his men and munitions. To his disappointment, he could recruit only twenty-one men, five of them African Americans. Brown's sons accounted for three of the number, while runaway slaves, free blacks, abolitionist editors, and college students made up the rest. Most of them were quite young, in their twenties.

The raid began easily enough on Sunday, October 16, as Brown's men quickly seized the arsenal and a rifle-manufacturing plant. Rather than merely taking the weapons and freeing local slaves, however, Brown and his men occupied the small armory building and waited for word to spread among the slaves of Virginia that their day of liberation had come. The word spread instead among local whites, who quickly surrounded the armory and Brown's men, killing or capturing eight of them. Militia from Virginia and Maryland arrived the next day, followed soon after by federal troops under the command of Robert E. Lee and J. E. B. Stuart. The troops rushed the armory, easily overwhelming Brown's men. Ten of the abolitionist forces were killed, five (including Brown) wounded, and seven escaped to Canada or the North. Brown was tried within two weeks and found guilty. He was sentenced to be hanged exactly a month later, on December 2.

The entire episode, from the raid to Brown's execution, took only about six weeks in late 1859 to unfold. Yet those six weeks saw opinion in both the North and the South change rapidly. Contradictory reports and rumors eventually settled into an accepted narrative of events. Public opinion in the North and South, mixed at first, crystallized into sharply opposing viewpoints. Even those Northerners who were appalled at the violence were also appalled at the speed with which Brown was tried and condemned. Even those Southerners who read with reassurance early denunciations of Brown in the North were appalled when they realized that many Northerners refused to condemn the raid and even applauded it.

The rhetoric surrounding John Brown showed none of the careful phrasing and hedging that had marked the Lincoln-Douglas debates, none of the calculation about votes that might be won or lost. Rather, the rhetoric seemed almost cathartic, as both Northerners and Southerners said the worst they could imagine about the other. The many people of moderate sympathies on both sides watched, appalled, as common ground eroded beneath their feet, as whatever goodwill that had survived Bleeding Kansas, the Fugitive Slave Law, and *Uncle Tom's Cabin* disappeared.

Brown had not set out to become a martyr. He fully expected to unleash a massive slave rebellion, bringing the end of American slavery. While his precise plans remain obscure, maps in his possession marked places where slaves outnumbered their masters and might overwhelm them with force. Brown wanted to play the role of Moses, leading the oppressed and chosen out of captivity. Once captured, however, Brown seemed to fit another role, that of Christ, selflessly dying for the salvation of others. No longer the Old Testament figure of blood and vengeance, Brown now appeared to many in the North as a New Testament figure of suffering and dignified sacrifice. The metaphorical struggle did not end with that resolution. Many Northerners came to believe that John Brown's body could be redeemed only with a return to the stern violence he had championed. Even pacifist abolitionists began to think that the time for a more direct attack on slavery had come.

THE FIRST SECESSION

Everyone knew the election of 1860 held enormous meaning for the United States, but no one could be sure what that meaning might be. Would this be the election that brought everyone to their senses so that the conflict between North and South could be resolved? Would the border states be able to control the election, putting men of moderation in the White House? Would northern voters suddenly realize the South meant what it said and pull back? The actual events proved far more threatening than most Americans had believed possible.

The Election of 1860

White Southerners automatically linked John Brown with the Republican party, though leading Republicans explicitly denied any connection and even denounced Brown. The Republicans, hoping to win support from the nonslaveholders in the South, arranged for the distribution of Hinton Helper's *Impending Crisis of the South*. The book had little effect in the South, however, and the Republicans realized that they would be a purely northern party. Not only had any southern base of support disappeared, but Harpers Ferry had made the Republicans far more attractive in the North than before.

The Democrats, more determined than the Republicans to remain a national party, also felt the effects of Brown's raid. Meeting in Charleston in April 1860 to

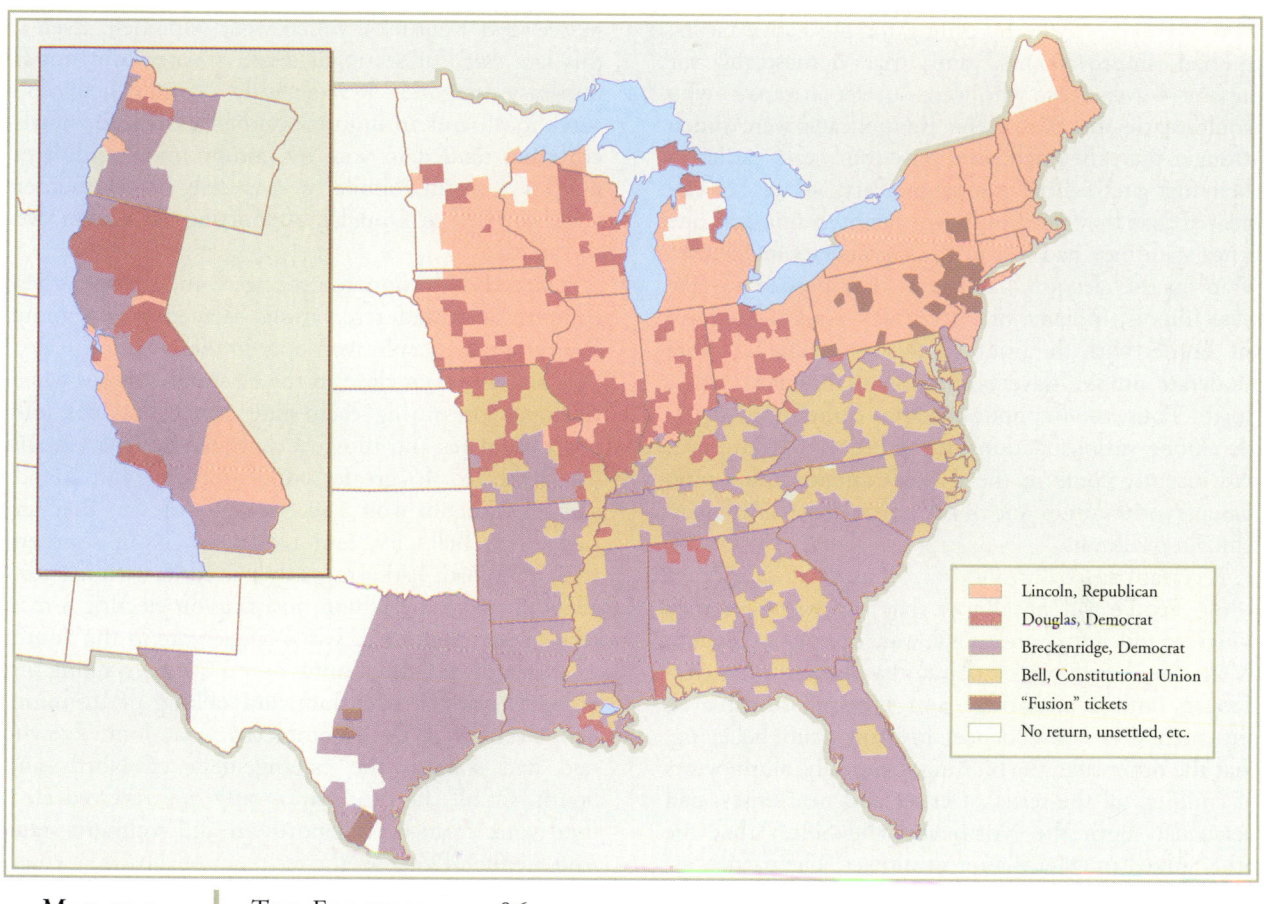

Lincoln, Republican
Douglas, Democrat
Breckenridge, Democrat
Bell, Constitutional Union
"Fusion" tickets
No return, unsettled, etc.

MAP 13.2 | THE ELECTION OF 1860

decide on their presidential nominee for the fall election, the northern Democrats attempted to carry out the strategy everyone expected: nominating Stephen Douglas and popular sovereignty. The northern Democrats saw this as a compromise with the South. But southern Democrats, outraged at the northern response to Dred Scott, Kansas, and John Brown, demanded that the party explicitly support the rights of slaveholders to take their slaves into the territories. Northern Democrats, already besieged by the Republicans in the North, could not afford to make that concession and still have a chance to win back home. The Southerners proved heedless of this plea, however, and walked out of the convention. Several weeks later, the Northerners met in Baltimore and nominated Douglas. The Southerners, meeting in Charleston, nominated John C. Breckinridge of Kentucky.

Before the two Democratic conventions met again in June, Unionists in both the North and the South tried to avert catastrophe by nominating a compromise candidate, a candidate who would strictly follow the Constitution as it was interpreted by the Supreme Court. Calling themselves the Constitutional Union party, they settled on John Bell of Tennessee. Many of these Unionists were former Whigs who no longer had a political home. They counted on the other candidates to create a deadlock that would have to be settled in the House of Representatives. There, the Unionists hoped, cooler heads would prevail and legislators would gratefully turn to their compromise candidate.

As the Democrats tore themselves apart, the Republicans met in Chicago. There, in efforts to put southern concerns at rest, the Republicans denounced the John Brown attack on Harpers Ferry and announced their belief in the right of each state to decide for itself whether it would have slavery. The Republicans cemented their appeal to voters unconcerned

with the slavery issue by calling for protective tariffs, internal improvements, and free homesteads for anyone—even those who were not yet citizens—who would settle the West. The Republicans were much stronger than they had been only four years earlier in their first presidential campaign. Party strategists calculated that they need only win Pennsylvania and one other state they had lost to the Democrats in 1856 to wrap up the election. The states they needed to take were Illinois, Indiana, or New Jersey—all of them on the border with the South and all of them far more moderate on the slavery question than states farther north. Thus, the Republicans, after tumultuous struggle among various factions, turned to a moderate who had recently come to the nation's attention and who was a favorite son of one of the crucial states: Abraham Lincoln of Illinois.

A certain air of unreality surrounded the election of 1860. People did not know that the way that they voted would bring on a civil war, or even secession. While Stephen Douglas constantly warned of such a danger, both Breckinridge and Lincoln downplayed any such dire consequence, insisting, and believing, that the other side was bluffing. Ironically, all the years of conflict, all the series of crises and near-crises, had persuaded both the North and the South that the other talked tougher than it would act. The parties, especially the Republicans, staged loud and raucous political events that proved long on emotion and short on clearly defined positions. Lincoln said nothing and stayed close to home while his party leaders displayed split fence rails and touted his honesty.

Northerners and Southerners were willing to believe the worst of each other because the election of 1860 was actually two separate elections, one in the North and one in the South. Lincoln made no attempt to explain himself to the South; Breckinridge made little attempt in the North. They never met face to face, either in cooperation or in debate. Bell spoke mainly to the already converted. Douglas, speaking from New England to Alabama and everywhere in between, tried to warn people what could happen if they voted along sectional lines, but few were willing to believe their opponents would have the nerve to act on their threats.

On election day, November 6, Lincoln won in every northern state except New Jersey, which divided between Douglas and Lincoln. Douglas won outright only in Missouri, and that barely. Breckinridge won all the South except the border states of Virginia, Ten-

nessee, and Kentucky, which went with Bell. Even at this late stage of sectional division voters did not fit into easy categories. It was hardly a contest between a rural South and an industrial urban North, for northern cities tended to vote for compromise candidates, not for Lincoln. Similarly, over half of Southerners voted for Bell or Douglas, supporting the Union over the South.

Once the election returns were in, though, these complications and reservations seemed to evaporate. Even though Lincoln won only in the North, the election was not even close in the electoral college, where electors representing each state cast ballots for only two candidates and thus concentrated their votes, and where the North's greater population gave him an advantage. Lincoln won 180 electoral votes to Breckinridge's 72, Bell's 39, and Douglas's 12. In southern eyes, the North had arrogantly placed its own interests above those of the Union, insisting on electing a man who made no effort to win a single vote in the South. In northern eyes, the South was to blame, walking out of nominating conventions and talking of disunion. The election of 1860 completed what John Brown's raid had started: the estrangement of North and South. Of all the candidates, only one received electoral votes from both a northern and southern state. And Stephen Douglas, the recipient of those few votes, soon died.

The Quest for Southern Independence

Some white men in the South had talked for years about what they would do if an avowed enemy of slavery became president. These fire-eaters declared Abraham Lincoln's 1860 victory a sign that the North valued neither the Union nor the Constitution on which it was based. The South, they said, had every right, every incentive, to leave the Union. Although the Republicans claimed to work within the political system, Southerners charged, Lincoln's supporters had violated an honored tradition of compromise necessary for the country's survival.

Even though the Democrats still controlled Congress and the Supreme Court, Southerners believed that Lincoln would use the patronage of the federal government to install Republican judges, customs collectors, federal marshals, and postmasters throughout the South. Such officials could undermine slavery from within, Southerners worried, eroding the author-

THE POLITICAL QUADRILLE
Music by Dred Scott

As "Dred Scott" fiddles, the four candidates of 1860 dance to the tune of slavery. While Lincoln is accompanied by a black woman, Breckenridge, in the upper left, dances with the devil in the form of secessionist William L. Yancey, Stephen Douglas cavorts with an Irishman in the lower left corner, and John Bell solemnly steps with an American Indian—all references to supposed liabilities each candidate carried with him.

ity of slaveowners and permitting abolitionist literature to circulate. For years, Lincoln had talked of "a house" that had to be unified, of a nation that had to be all one thing or all another, all slave or all free. Would he not act to undermine slavery now that he was in power?

The nation's eyes turned to South Carolina. Influential men there, after all, had talked of secession since the nullification crisis nearly thirty years earlier. The same states that had created the Union, they believed in 1861 as they had believed before, could also dissolve that Union when it no longer served their purposes. South Carolinians remembered that they had lost the nullification struggle, however, and did not want to act alone again. Therefore, the South Carolina legislature met on the day after Lincoln's election but did not secede immediately. Its members called for an election two months later to select delegates who would then decide the course the state should follow. In the meantime, they hoped, support for secession would grow and other southern states would join South Carolina in leaving the Union. One South Carolina lawmaker, scoffing at the idea that the North would offer military resistance, laughingly offered to drink all the blood shed over secession.

States of the Deep South quickly lined up behind South Carolina, as secession rallies erupted across the region. Carolina leaders, heartened by the response, seceded earlier than they had planned, on December 20. By February 1, Mississippi, Florida, Alabama, Georgia, Louisiana, and Texas had joined the secession movement. On February 9, delegates from these states met in Montgomery, Alabama, and created a provisional constitution, similar to that of the United States except in its explicit guarantee of slavery and states' rights. On February 18, the convention inaugurated a provisional president, Jefferson Davis of Mississippi, and vice president, Alexander H. Stephens of Georgia. Davis, long a national figure, was a moderate, a strong states' rights advocate but not a fervent secessionist. The states of the new Confederacy portrayed themselves as a calm and conservative people, not wild-eyed revolutionaries.

Though the South appeared united against the North, it was not. The advocates of secession knew they had to strike while Lincoln remained more image than substance. Two bad things could happen if they waited to see what the new president did once in office. He might either attack the South by force or he might prove to be as moderate as he claimed to be. In

On December 20, 1860, South Carolina declared its connection to the Union dissolved. Within six weeks, six other southern states joined in the dissolution.

Jefferson Davis, of Mississippi, a former U.S. Senator and Secretary of War, became the first—and only—president of the Confederate States of America in 1861.

the latter case, secessionists feared, white Southerners would let the moment pass, giving the North time to build its strength and the Republicans time to tighten their hold on the nation.

Divisions over Secession

Many thousands of white Southerners, some of them quite powerful and influential, resisted secession.

Some argued that secession was treason. Others warned that the South was committing suicide. Others argued that slavery would be far safer within the Union than in a fragile new country bordered by an antagonistic United States. Other opponents of immediate secession argued that the southern states should wait until they could cooperate with one another more formally and fully. By presenting a united front to the North, these "cooperationists" insisted, the South would not need to secede at all. The North, recognizing that the South really was not bluffing, would grant concessions protecting slavery forever.

The arguments against immediate secession appealed to a large portion of Southerners. Even in the southern states that rushed to secede in January of 1861, almost half of all votes went to delegates who had not supported immediate secession. The opposition to secession proved stronger still in the upper

South, in Virginia, North Carolina, Tennessee, Kentucky, and Maryland. Under the name of Douglas Democrats, Constitutional Unionists, or simply the Opposition, men of moderate impulse in the upper South mobilized to resist immediate secession. These upper-South moderates warned that their states would bear the brunt of any conflict between the lower South and the North, whatever form that conflict might take. And voters listened: more than a month after the first seven states seceded, secession lost in Virginia by a two-to-one margin. The secessionists were stymied, too, in Tennessee, North Carolina, and Arkansas. The leaders of these border states believed they could bargain between the Gulf Confederacy and the North, winning the concessions the South wanted while maintaining the Union.

Northerners, too, remained quite divided at the beginning of 1861. Many recent immigrants from Ireland and Germany viewed the conflict between the North and the South as none of their business. Northern Democrats loathed Lincoln and feared his policies. They called for conciliation with the South, for a quieting of the rhetoric. Many black Northerners urged caution, warning that a war for Union alone did not deserve black support. A war to end bondage would be worth fighting, such African-American spokesmen argued, but in 1861 only the most aggressive white abolitionists, few in number, spoke of such a cause.

People had plenty of opportunity to air their opinions, for events did not move quickly after Lincoln's election. After the first flush of secessionist victory at the beginning of 1861, people throughout the nation watched and waited to see what would happen when the new president officially assumed office on March 4. In the meantime, no one appeared to be in charge. James Buchanan, as lame-duck president, could not do much, and neither could the lame-duck Congress. Lincoln, for his part, remained at home in Illinois, saying little.

Most Republicans, including Lincoln, viewed the rhetoric and even the votes for southern secession as negotiating strategies rather than actual steps toward dissolving the Union. The Republicans showed no inclination to bargain with the South over what remained the key question: federal support for slavery in the territories. The tensions that had built up in the 1850s, Lincoln thought, could no longer be avoided. There had to be some sort of conflict and resolution before the nation could move forward. "The tug has to come," he argued, "and better now, than any time

hereafter." If the North postponed action, Lincoln and other Republicans thought, the South would step up its efforts to gain new slave territories in the Caribbean and Central America, dragging the United States into war and perpetuating human bondage far into the future. Like the secessionists, Lincoln did not think the "tug" between North and South would require bloodshed.

The Situation in Charleston

While Americans fixed their attention on political leaders in the winter of 1861, the center of the conflict gradually shifted to two obscure forts in the harbor of Charleston, South Carolina. A Kentucky-born U.S. army officer, Major Robert Anderson, worried that secessionists would attack his small federal force at Fort Moultrie in Charleston and force him either to surrender or to fire on American citizens. Determined to avoid a war, on December 26 Anderson moved his small garrison from Fort Moultrie to Fort Sumter, a facility still under construction but occupying a safer position in the center of the Charleston harbor. Anderson hoped that his strategic retreat would prevent an attack on the federal fort. When South Carolina guns drove away a ship President Buchanan had sent with supplies for Anderson and his men, Buchanan chose not to force the issue; like the rest of the nation, he would wait for Lincoln's inaugural. Meanwhile, South Carolina troops strengthened their position around the Charleston harbor. Anderson's food reserves began to run dangerously low.

Men from both the North and the South worked frantically, but fruitlessly, to find a compromise during these weeks. Some urged the passage of a new constitutional amendment that would permit slavery forever; some urged the purchase of Cuba to permit slavery to expand; some urged that war be declared against another country to pull the United States together again. All the compromises were designed to placate the South, to draw it back into the Union with guarantees of its safety. Abolitionists viewed such maneuvering with disgust and told their countrymen to let the South go, purifying the country and hastening the end of slavery in the process. "If the Union can only be maintained by new concessions to the slaveholders," Frederick Douglass argued, "if it can only be stuck together and held together by a new drain on the negro's blood, then . . . let the Union perish."

Such views were not popular. Mobs blamed the abolitionists for the South's secession and attacked antislavery advocates throughout the North.

On February 11, Abraham Lincoln began a long and circuitous railway trip from Illinois to Washington, pausing frequently along the way to speak to well-wishers. At first, he played down the threat of secession—"Let it alone," he counseled, "and it will go down of itself." But as the train rolled on and the Confederate convention in Montgomery completed its provisional government, Lincoln became more wary. Warned of attempts on his life, Lincoln slipped into Washington under cover of darkness.

Lincoln Assumes Office

Lincoln assembled his government under the growing shadow of war. He sought to balance his cabinet with men of various temperaments, backgrounds, and strategies. The two most formidable cabinet members were Secretary of State William H. Seward, a moderate Republican who still dreamed of compromise, and Secretary of the Treasury Salmon P. Chase, a radical Republican inclined to take a harder line with the South. Fort Sumter stood as the most pressing issue facing the new administration. Any show of force to reclaim the fort from South Carolina, southern Unionists warned, and the secessionists would sweep border states such as Virginia into the Confederacy.

Lincoln, with Seward's advice, toned down the speech he delivered at his inauguration in March. As sharpshooters stood on nearby rooftops to watch for assassins, Lincoln told the South that he had no intention of disturbing slavery where it was already established, that he would not invade the region, that there would be no shedding of blood, that he would not attempt to fill offices with men repugnant to local sensibilities. But he also warned that secession was illegal, "the essence of anarchy." It was his duty to maintain the integrity of the federal government, and to do so he had to "hold, occupy, and possess" federal property in the states of the Confederacy, including Fort Sumter. Lincoln pleaded with his countrymen to move slowly, to take their time, to let passions cool. "We must not be enemies. Though passion may have strained it, it must not break our bonds of affection."

People heard in Lincoln's inaugural what they chose to hear. Republicans and Unionists in the South thought it a potent mixture of firmness and generosity.

Lincoln took over the presidency at a time when the sectional conflict had reached a crisis; he had little time or room in which to maneuver as the federal soldiers in Fort Sumter ran out of food and had to be abandoned or supplied.

Skeptics in the North, South, and Europe, on the other hand, focused on the threat of coercion at Fort Sumter. If Lincoln attempted to use force of any kind, they warned, war would be the inevitable result. Lincoln did not plan on war; he was trying to buy time, hoping that southern Unionists could gather their strength and that compromisers in Washington would come up with a workable strategy.

The Crisis at Fort Sumter

But there was less time than Lincoln realized. On the very day after Lincoln's speech, Major Anderson reported to Washington that he would be out of food within four to six weeks and that it would take at least 20,000 troops to resupply the fort. After weeks of lis-

South Carolina troops fire cannon at the federal forces under the command of Captain Robert Anderson. Although no one was killed in the assault, the shots opened the Civil War.

tening to various counsellors, Lincoln finally decided that he had to act: he would send provisions but not military supplies to Fort Sumter. By doing so, Lincoln would maintain the balance he promised in his inaugural speech, keeping the fort but not using coercion unless attacked first.

The president recognized that this distinction would not matter to the Confederacy. Jefferson Davis and his government, goaded by impatient editors and would-be soldiers, had decided a week earlier that any attempt to reprovision the fort would be in and of itself an act of war, a violation of the territorial integrity of the Confederacy. Davis recognized that no foreign power would respect a country, especially one as new and tenuous as the Confederate States of America, if it allowed one of its major ports to be occupied by an-

other country. The Union's resupply of the fort would mean they still controlled it.

The Confederate government decided that their commander in Charleston, P.G.T. Beauregard, should attack Fort Sumter before the relief expedition had a chance to arrive. On April 12, at 4:30 in the morning, Beauregard (a former student of Major Anderson's at West Point) opened fire on the Union garrison. The shelling continued for thirty-three hours. Anderson held out for as long as he could, but when fire tore through the barracks and his ammunition ran low he decided the time for surrender had come. Although no one on either side died in the battle, Northerners, even those who had little faith in their new president or his policies, agreed that the events in South Carolina could not go unanswered. Southerners, even those

who resented South Carolina for precipitating the war, agreed that they would have no choice but to come to that state's aid if the North raised a hand against their fellow Southerners.

CONCLUSION

It was no accident that the slave states and free states experienced mounting animosity and distrust in the late 1850s. The rapid expansion of both the North and the South led people to focus their eyes on the West; the struggles in Kansas, Washington, Illinois, and state capitals would determine the character of the American nation. The struggles carried great symbolic weight, testifying to the worth of the northern and southern people, to their justice and courage.

Watching the events of those years unfold, however, it is clear that the conflict could most certainly have taken other forms. Had Kansas been handled more adroitly by Buchanan and the Democrats, had Preston Brooks not caned Charles Sumner, had Chief Justice Taney not issued the *Dred Scott* decision, and had John Brown not given violence a martyr's sanction, the election of 1860 would not have become the watershed it did. This cascade of events washed the United States toward dissolution. Another cascade of events would soon push it into war.

RECOMMENDED READINGS

Crofts, Daniel W. *Old Southampton: Politics and Society in a Virginia County, 1834–1869* (1992) provides a wonderfully detailed account of the way politics worked in communities.

Fehrenbacher, Don E. *The Dred Scott Case: Its Significance in American Law and Politics* (1978) is the classic account of this complicated episode.

Finkelman, Paul, ed., *His Soul Goes Marching On: Responses to John Brown and the Harpers Ferry Raid* (1995) contains fascinating articles about this much-interpreted event.

Foner, Eric. *Free Soil, Free Labor, Free Men: The Ideology of the Republican Party Before the Civil War* (1970) masterfully demonstrates the power of free labor ideology.

Holt, Michael F. *The Political Crisis of the 1850s* (1978) stresses the dynamics of the two-party system in bringing on the Civil War.

Morrison, Michael A. *Slavery and the American West: The Eclipse of Manifest Destiny and the Coming of the Civil War* (1997) is a subtle and up-to-date survey of this critical topic.

Stampp, Kenneth. *America in 1857: A Nation on the Brink* (1990) shows the advantages of examining the simultaneous processes and events of this period.

Wyatt-Brown, Bertram. *Southern Honor: Ethics and Behavior in the Old South* (1982) is a bold and powerful interpretation of white southern culture.

Zarefsky, David. *Lincoln, Douglas, and Slavery: In the Crucible of Public Debate* (1990) recasts our understanding of these famous political debates.

Political Crisis

Cooper, William J. Jr., *The South and the Politics of Slavery, 1828–1856* (1978).

Dykstra, Robert R. *Bright Radical Star: Black Freedom and White Supremacy on the Hawkeye Frontier* (1993).

Fehrenbacher, Don E. *Prelude to Greatness: Lincoln in the 1850s* (1962).

Finkleman, Paul, *An Imperfect Union: Slavery, Federalism, and Comity* (1981).

Forgie, George B. *Patricide in the House Divided: A Psychological Interpretation of Lincoln and His Age* (1979).

Kelly, Robert. *The Cultural Pattern in American Politics: The First Century* (1979).

Knupfer, Peter. *The Union As It Is: Constitutional Unionism and Sectional Compromise* (1991).

Levine, Bruce. *Half Slave and Half Free: The Roots of Civil War* (1992).

Oates, Stephen B. *To Purge This Land with Blood: A Biography of John Brown* (1970).

Rawley, James A. *Race and Politics: Bleeding Kansas and the Coming of the Civil War* (1969).

Gupta, Gunja Sen. *For God and Mammon: Evangelicals and Entrepreneurs, Masters and Slaves in Territorial Kansas, 1854–1860* (1996).

Sewell, Richard. *A House Divided: Sectionalism and the Civil War, 1848–1865* (1988).

Smith, Elbert B. *The Presidency of James Buchanan* (1975).

Stampp, Kenneth. *The Imperiled Union* (1980).

Summers, Mark W. *The Plundering Generation: Corruption and the Crisis of the Union, 1849–1861* (1987).

Von Frank, Andrew. *The Trials of Anthony Burns: Freedom and Slavery in Emerson's Boston* (1998).

Walther, Eric H. *The Fire-Eaters* (1992).

The White South

Ayers, Edward L. *Vengeance and Justice: Crime and Punishment in the Nineteenth-Century American South* (1984).

Burton, Orville Vernon. *In My Father's House Are Many Mansions: Family and Community in Edgefield, South Carolina* (1985).

Ford, Lacy K. Jr., *Origins of Southern Radicalism: The South Carolina Upcountry, 1800–1860* (1988).

Harris, J. William. *Plain Folk and Gentry in a Slave Society: White Liberty and Black Slavery in Augusta's Hinterlands* (1985).

Huston, James L. *The Panic of 1857 and the Coming of the Civil War* (1987).

Inscoe, John C. *Mountain Masters: Slavery and the Sectional Crisis in Western North Carolina* (1989).

Jaffa, Harry. *Crisis of the House Divided: An Interpretation of the Issues in the Lincoln-Douglas Debates* (1959).

McCardell, John. *The Idea of a Southern Nation: Southern Nationalists and Southern Nationalism, 1830–1860* (1979).

Owsley, Frank L. *Plain Folk of the Old South* (1949).

Takaki, Ronald T. *A Pro-Slavery Crusade: The Agitation to Reopen the African Slave Trade* (1971).

Wright, Gavin. *The Political Economy of the Cotton South: Households, Markets, and Wealth* (1978).

ROBERT E. LEE

*Lee rejected Lincoln's offer of command of the Union armies before he resigned his U.S. commission
and swore allegiance to the Confederacy, dramatizing the divided loyalties of many Americans at the beginning of the war.*

Chapter 14

Descent into War,
1861–1862

At the beginning of 1861, Americans could not imagine anything like the war that soon consumed their nation. Events piled on one another in ways that few would have wished and that no one could have predicted. The men who voted for Lincoln did not think the South would secede, the architects of secession did not think the North would resist, and neither side thought the other would or could fight for long. Events proved no more predictable once the war began. Last-minute reinforcements and retreats changed the outcome of battles; news from the battlefield shaped every political and diplomatic decision. Circumstance and timing shaped everything.

WAR BEGINS: APRIL 1861 TO JULY 1861

Neither the Union nor the Confederacy was ready for conflict in the spring of 1861. A number of states had yet to declare their loyalties and other states, communities, and families found themselves divided against themselves. In a matter of months, both the North and the South had to prepare for war and throw themselves into the first battle.

Lincoln Calls for Troops

Two days after the Confederate flag went up over Fort Sumter on April 15, President Lincoln declared South Carolina in rebellion against the United States and called for 75,000 militiamen from states north and south to help put the rebellion down. Lincoln could have called up far more troops, for men clamored to serve throughout the North. But the president sought to appear restrained in his response. He still hoped that Unionists in southern states besides South Carolina would rally to the nation's defense if he showed that he was no extremist. Lincoln also acted cautiously because he had not received the approval of Congress, which would not convene until July.

Lincoln's attempt to blend firmness and conciliation failed. Southern states saw the call to the militia as an act of aggression against South Carolina and state sovereignty. The upper South states replied with defiance to Lincoln's requests for their militia. "Tennessee will furnish not a single man for the purpose of coercion," its governor responded, "but fifty thousand if necessary for the defense of our rights and those of our Southern brothers." Virginia seceded two days later. Although many people in Virginia, especially in the mountainous western counties, still clung to hopes of avoiding war, two delegates to every one voted for

CHRONOLOGY

1861

April	15	Lincoln calls for 75,000 militia
	17–20	Arkansas, Tennessee, Virginia, and North Carolina secede
May	29	Richmond becomes capital of Confederacy
July	21	Confederate victory at Bull Run (Manassas)
	25	Frémont takes command in the West
	27	McClellan takes command of Union forces near Washington
August	30	Frémont declares martial law, and frees slaves, in Missouri
September	6	Kentucky remains in the Union
November	1	McClellan assumes command of all Union armies
	6	Jefferson Davis elected president of Confederacy with six-year term
	7	Union capture of Port Royal, South Carolina
	8	Union navy seizes Confederate commisioners Mason and Slidell from British ship *Trent*
	19	Halleck replaces Frémont as Union commander in West
December	26	Union government releases Mason and Slidell
	30	suspension of specie payments

1862

February	6	Union captures Fort Henry on Tennessee River
	16	Confederates surrender Fort Donelson to Grant
	22	Inauguration of Jefferson Davis
	25	Legal Tender Act in North authorizes "greenbacks"
		Confederates evacuate Nashville
	27	Confederate Congress authorizes martial law and suspends habeas corpus
March	8–9	*Virginia* v. *Monitor* in Hampton Roads, Virginia

secession on April 17. These Virginians, like white Southerners of all inclinations and temperaments, refused to permit northern troops to march through their states to defeat South Carolina. Southerners considered this an invasion by an arrogant central government, the very sort of coercion that had triggered the American Revolution. Recognizing the importance of Virginia's addition to their ranks, the Confederacy immediately voted to move their capital to Richmond in May of 1861.

The States Divide

Arkansas, Tennessee, and North Carolina, despite the continuing vitality of the Unionist cause in all three states, quickly followed Virginia's example. The Oklahoma Territory, too, aligned itself with the Confederacy. There, leaders of the Five Civilized Tribes, slaveholders themselves, used the opportunity to fight against the U.S. government that had dispossessed them from their homes three decades earlier. The leaders of other Indian nations sided with the Union, however, and began to fight for control of the Indian Territory. The Pamunkey of Virginia and the Lumbee of North Carolina aided the Union behind Confederate lines, while the Eastern Cherokee and Catawba fought hard for the Confederates among whom they lived.

State leaders elsewhere frantically struggled with one another. In Maryland, rioters attacked Massachusetts troops as they marched through Baltimore two days after the secession of neighboring Virginia—spilling the first blood of the war when twelve civil-

CHRONOLOGY

	17	McClellan begins move to James River Peninsula
April	5	McClellan begins siege of Yorktown
	6–7	Grant wins dramatic victory at Shiloh
	16	Confederacy passes Conscription Act
	25	New Orleans surrenders to Admiral Farragut
May	8–9	Jackson's Shenandoah Valley Campaign
	20	Homestead Act passed by Union Congress
	31	Lee takes command of Army of Northern Virginia
June	6	Confederates evacuate Memphis
	26	Lee drives McClellan from Richmond in Seven Days' Battles
July	11	Halleck appointed general-in-chief of Union armies
	12	Border states reject Lincoln plan for gradual emancipation

	17	Second Confiscation Act
	22	Cabinet hears Lincoln's draft of emancipation proclamation
August	3	Union decides to evacuate McClellan's troops from peninsula
	29–30	Confederate victory at Second Bull Run (Manassas)
September	4–6	Lee invades Maryland
	17	Battle of Antietam (Sharpsburg)
	22	First Emancipation Proclamation
October	3–4	Union victory at Corinth
November	7	Burnside replaces McClellan as commander of Army of the Potomac
		Republicans lose widely in mid-term elections in North
December	13	Lee overwhelms Burnside at Fredericksburg
	16–20	Crisis in Lincoln's cabinet
	27–29	Sherman defeated near Vicksburg

ians and four Union soldiers died in the gunfire. Maryland bitterly divided along lines of geography and sentiment, the southern portion of the state sympathizing with the Confederacy, Baltimore and the western portion generally supporting the Union. Should the United States lose Maryland, the District of Columbia would be completely surrounded by Confederate territory. Accordingly, Lincoln acted quickly to keep Maryland in line, jailing secession advocates before they could persuade others and suspending the writ of habeas corpus so those leaders could not be released.

Kentucky, after months of determined attempts to remain neutral, narrowly decided for the Union in September. Missouri, after chaotic bloodshed reminiscent of the events in Kansas seven years earlier, officially remained in the Union but was ravaged from within for the next four years. Dissension took different form in the mountains of western Virginia. In June, delegates from fifty counties met in Wheeling to renounce the Virginia secession convention, begin the gradual abolition of slavery, and declare their loyalty to the Union. After a complicated series of conventions and elections, the state of West Virginia came into being in 1862 and joined the Union the following year. As in Maryland and Kentucky, the presence of Union troops in western Virginia provided protection against Confederate forces and sympathizers.

As it turned out, the Union and the Confederacy divided about as evenly as possible. Virginia, Tennessee, North Carolina, and Arkansas, all of which went into the Confederacy, might well have decided to remain with the Union; had they done so, the Confederacy would have had little hope of sustaining a

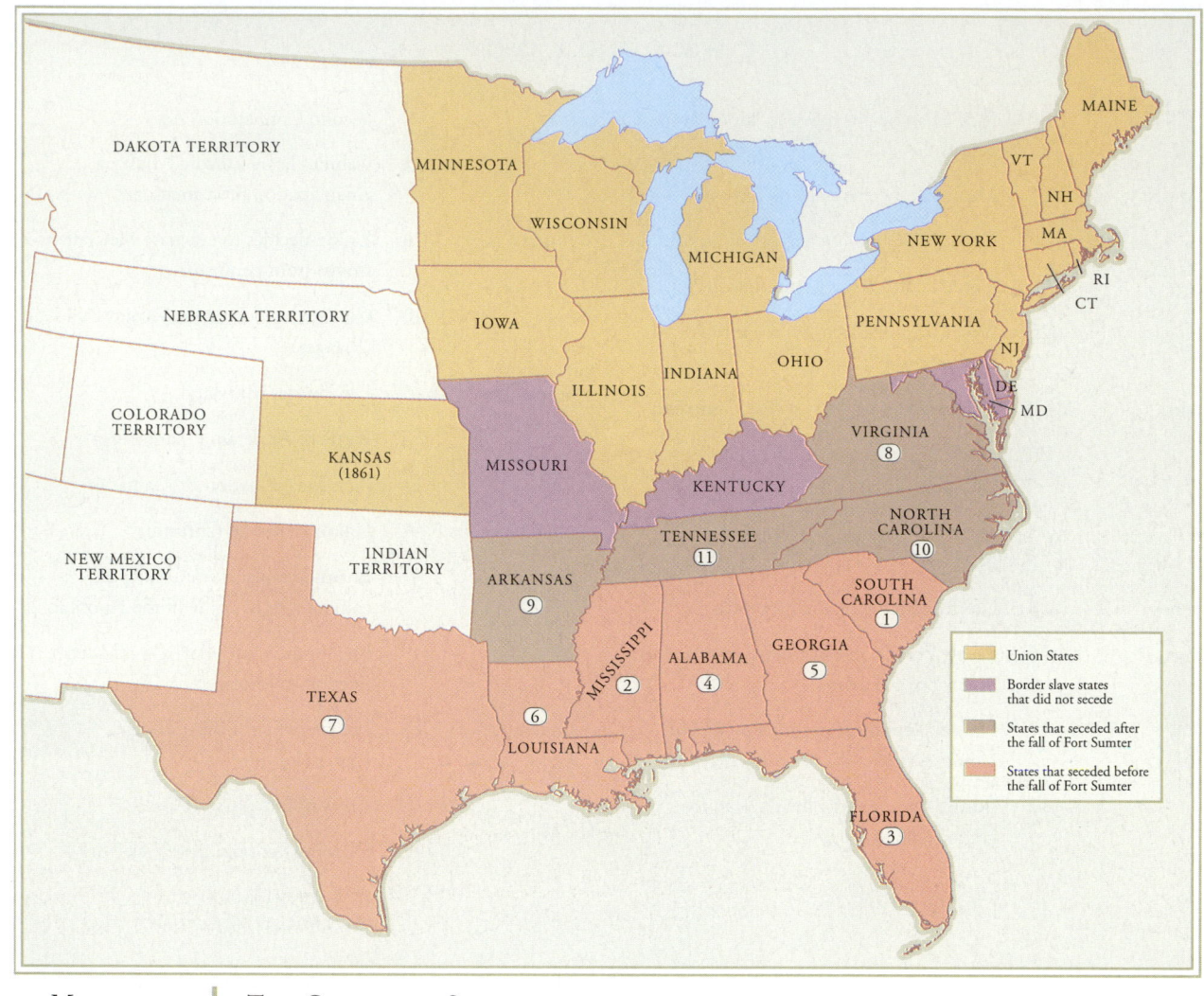

	Union States
	Border slave states that did not secede
	States that seceded after the fall of Fort Sumter
	States that seceded before the fall of Fort Sumter

MAP 14.1 | THE COURSE OF SECESSION

successful war against the North. Those states, the three most populous in the South among them, accounted for half of all manufacturing and half of all food production in the Confederacy. Maryland, Kentucky, and Missouri, on the other hand, might well have joined the Confederacy; had they done so, the Union cause would have been weakened, perhaps fatally. Kentucky and Missouri, possessing white populations and economic resources larger than those of any Confederate state except Virginia, occupied crucial positions along the major rivers that led into the South. Even the dissidents balanced out. About 100,000 men

from these border states that went with the Union ended up fighting for the Confederacy. About 90,000 men—half of them white, the other half black—of the border states that went with the Confederacy ended up fighting for the Union.

Although Abraham Lincoln was criticized from every angle in these months—for acting too arrogantly and for acting indecisively, for taking too much power into his hands and for not taking enough—he managed to bring into the Union fold the states he had to win. Had he lost these struggles, he might well have failed in all the other struggles that awaited him.

The Numbers

Looking back, knowing that the war dragged on for four years, the cards seem heavily stacked in the North's favor. The Union, after all, had vastly greater industrial capacity, railroads, canals, food, draft animals, ships, and entrepreneurial talent, all the things a mid-nineteenth-century war required. The Union could also claim four times as many white residents as the South—22 million versus 5.5 million. And while the 3.5 million enslaved people who lived in the Confederacy were extraordinarily valuable to the South, everyone recognized that the slaves could become equally valuable allies for the North under the exigencies of war.

Since the South acknowledged the North's advantages, many people then and since assumed that the Confederates must have been driven either by irrational rage or heedless bravery. Neither the Confederates nor the North, however, expected the secession crisis to turn into a full-fledged war, much less a four-year war of attrition and endurance. When Lincoln called for the 75,000 militia he called them for only ninety days' service. When southern boys and men rushed to enlist for the Confederacy in the spring of 1861, they assumed they would be back home in time to harvest their crops in the autumn.

Southerners considered themselves natural soldiers, comfortable on horseback and with a rifle, caricaturing their new enemies as clerks and factory workers. Though the Union did have more city men and immigrants than the South, most Northerners, like Southerners, were young men raised on farms. Since both sides believed that the other was bluffing and that their opponents were weak and divided, Northerners and Southerners thought the conflict would likely come to a swift, and peaceful, resolution. In such a struggle, sheer numbers did not seem nearly as important as they eventually became.

The Strategies

The military strategies of both sides sought to minimize actual fighting. The South saw itself as purely on the defensive; it would wait for northern armies to invade and then defeat them with the determination of people defending their own homes and farms. The North, for its part, counted on what became known as the "Anaconda Plan," named after the snake of that name that slowly squeezes its prey to death. That plan depended on sending an overpowering force down the Mississippi River, both by water and by land, dividing the South in two. At the same time, the Union navy would seal off the South from outside supplies. The goal, general-in-chief Winfield Scott said, was to "envelop the insurgent states and bring them to terms with less bloodshed than any other plan." Ground troops and land battles would be kept to a minimum.

The Confederacy, from the perspective both of its own strategy and that of the North, possessed considerable military advantages. It occupied an enormous area, larger than today's United Kingdom, France, Italy, and Spain combined. It possessed dozens of harbors and ports, connected by an excellent system of rivers and an adequate network of railroads. The Confederacy's long border with Mexico made it difficult to seal off outside supplies. The Confederacy could wage a defensive war, drawing on its own resources, fighting on its own land, moving its troops internally from one point to another while the Union had to move around the perimeter. The many country roads of the South, known only to locals, would provide routes for Confederate surprise attacks or strategic retreats. Every white Southerner could be a spy or an ally when a fellow Confederate needed food or medical aid.

For a model of how such a defensive plan might work, Southerners looked to the American Revolution, when the thirteen colonies absorbed everything the powerful British army and navy could throw at them. Like the American colonies eighty years earlier, the Confederates did not have to win every battle nor conquer northern territory. Southerners thought they had only to keep fighting long enough for the North to lose heart, for the North's political, economic, regional, and ethnic divisions to overwhelm its temporary unity. Indeed, the Confederacy enjoyed advantages the American colonies had not enjoyed. The new southern nation covered twice as much territory as the colonies and the North possessed nowhere near the military power of the British at the time of the Revolutionary War.

Leadership

There was also the matter of leadership. In 1861, many observers would have given the advantage to the Confederates in this regard. Abraham Lincoln, after all, had held public office for only two years before he assumed

Lincoln's Cabinet: seated from the left, Secretary of State William H. Seward; Secretary of the Treasury Salmon P. Chase; Secretary of War Edwin M. Stanton; Postmaster General Montgomery Blair; Secretary of the Navy Gideon Welles. Lincoln is seated at the head of the table.

the presidency, and his only military service had been a brief battle against Indians. Jefferson Davis, by contrast, had graduated from West Point and distinguished himself in the war with Mexico. He had been secretary of war under Franklin Pierce and had served in the United States Senate. Davis, unlike Lincoln, directed his forces' military strategy with the confidence born of firsthand knowledge and experience.

At the beginning of the war, too, it appeared that the South had the better generals. The southern generals certainly had more experience: the average age of the Union generals in 1861 was thirty-eight; of Confederate generals, forty-seven. At the outbreak of hostilities, Lincoln actually offered Robert E. Lee of Virginia command of the Union army. Lee had graduated second in his class at West Point in 1829 and had served as an engineer, an officer in the Mexican War in the 1840s, and superintendent of West Point in the late 1850s. He had opposed secession. But Lee was descended from a long line of distinguished Virginians and had married into another prominent Virginia family. He declined the Union generalship and then resigned his U.S. military commission altogether;

within a week he had accepted command of Virginia's forces. Lee made the same tortured decision so many Southerners made when secession finally came: "With all my devotion to the Union and the feeling and loyalty of an American citizen, I have not been able to make up my mind to raise my hand against my relatives, my children, my home."

After Lee rejected overall command of the Union troops, Lincoln decided to forego a single commander for the time being. The Confederacy, with Jefferson Davis in the presidency, also felt no need for a commanding general. Many lesser generals still had to be named quickly, however: 126 by the Union and 89 by the Confederacy. Military experience and ability did not always prove to be the major considerations in these appointments, as both Lincoln and Davis used generalships to cement the loyalty and support of politically important men. About a third of Union generals and half their Confederate counterparts had not been professional soldiers, though most had undergone some military training; overall, the North and the South placed roughly similar proportions of professional soldiers in command. Lincoln, forced to

unify a people far more divided than the white population of the Confederacy, chose generals from the ranks of various constituencies he needed to appease: abolitionists, Democrats, Irish, and Germans. The northern generals, not surprisingly, tended to have more business experience than their southern counterparts, expertise that proved useful in the modern warfare then emerging.

Neither the Union nor the Confederacy enjoyed a clear advantage in civilian leadership. Both Lincoln and Davis assembled cabinets that balanced geography, political faction, personality, and expertise; both leaders continually rearranged their cabinets as dissension broke out, incompetence became obvious, or politics demanded. The Confederates had to create a government from scratch, including the design of flags, stamps, and money. Davis ran through several secretaries of war and secretaries of state before finding the two men on whom he felt he could rely, James A. Seddon and Judah P. Benjamin, respectively.

The Union enjoyed a head start in such matters—it at least had a flag and office furniture—but the Republicans had never been in federal power before and had many problems to iron out. Several of Lincoln's cabinet members—Seward and Chase, in particular—let it be known that they considered themselves better qualified for the presidency than Lincoln. Office-seekers besieged Washington at the very time Lincoln was trying to keep the South in the Union; he felt like an innkeeper, he said, faced with customers demanding rooms in one wing while he tried to put out a fire in another wing. Lincoln's cabinet ended up containing men whom he barely knew and upon whom he was not always sure he could rely.

The First Conflicts

Battles began before anyone was ready, even before the alignment of states was complete. On the day following Lincoln's call for troops in April, federal officers in charge of the arsenal at Harpers Ferry and the naval yard in Norfolk, Virginia, sought to destroy the weapons under their command before secessionists could seize them. Despite their efforts, Virginia troops managed to recover valuable gun-making machinery, artillery, and ships for the Confederate cause. At almost exactly the same time, southern sympathizers in Missouri raided the arsenal at St. Louis. A few weeks later, battles broke out along the B&O Railroad in what would become West Virginia, with Robert E. Lee, the new general for Virginia, leading an unsuccessful and embarrassing chase of troops under the command of George McClellan. Meanwhile, nearly four thousand Confederates, most of them from Texas, pushed into New Mexico. They hoped to win the mineral riches of Colorado and perhaps even California for the southern cause.

All these struggles showed both sides to be far from ready to fight a war in 1861. Not only were guns and uniforms scarce, but so were combat experience and even battlefield training. Even those men who had attended West Point had learned more about engineering than they had about tactical maneuvers; many of the men who were to become leading generals over the next few years had left the army for civilian pursuits in the years before the war. The United States Army contained only about 16,000 men, and most of them were scattered across the vast territory west of the Mississippi River. Neither side had accurate maps of the terrain on which they would be fighting. The militiamen who first responded to the calls of the Union and Confederacy had scarcely been trained at all. Militia companies had long been famous for drinking and socializing, not teaching men how to fight.

Mobilization

Both sides took immediate steps to create new armies, organized within local communities and led by local men. The Confederate Congress authorized 400,000 volunteers in May of 1861, only weeks after the secession of the upper South states. In its special session beginning in July of 1861, the Union Congress authorized 500,000 troops, each signing on for three years; 700,000 eventually enlisted under this law. Much mobilization took place on the local level. Prominent citizens often supplied uniforms, guns, and even food for the troops from their localities. Men signed on in communities and for communities, their official names identifying their states, their nicknames identifying their town or county. Units elected their own officers. States competed to enlist the largest numbers of men. Governors chose military leaders who could strengthen political bonds, satisfy calls for patronage, and assuage enemies. Local newspapers sought to make sure that state-level leaders dealt fairly with local troops and officers.

Some Northerners wondered whether their society had grown too rich and soft to fight the South, whether the many divisions among classes, occupations, religions, and ethnic groups would hinder the Union war effort. Such doubters took heart at the response to the crisis of 1861. Both workingmen and wealthy men eagerly signed up, even in places recently divided by labor conflict. Members of ethnic groups took pride in forming their own units; the Irish and Germans, recent immigrants to the United States, supplied over 150,000 men each. Northerners congratulated themselves that patriotism and self-sacrifice had not been killed, as many feared, by the spirit of commerce so strong in the land.

Southerners, too, found reason to be proud in 1861. The leaders of the South had secretly worried that some of what the abolitionists had said was true, that when push came to shove the nonslaveholders would not fight for a cause that many identified with the defense of slavery. But southern boys and men were activated by the same impulses that drove their northern counterparts: idealized images of the American Revolution, dreams of glory, youthful self-confidence, and a burning desire to impress family, friends, and young women with their bravery. At this point in the war, white southerners talked less about slavery than they had before or than they would later. In their eyes, they fought to defend their farms and homes from "foreign" invaders. That helped account for the fact that four-fifths of military-age white men in the South fought in the army or navy, compared to about half of those in the North.

Editors, politicians, and citizens of both the North and the South, impressed with the outpouring of volunteers, impatiently demanded that the conflict be wrapped up immediately. Confident of victory, such people on both sides itched for the fight that would settle things once and for all.

The First Battle

Northerners soon grew impatient with the passive Anaconda Plan of cutting the South off from the outside. "Forward to Richmond," one influential New York paper trumpeted day after day in June and July of 1861. With so many men eagerly signing on to fight, Northerners thought they should get the war over with early, before the South had time to consolidate its forces—maybe even before the Confederate

Congress met on July 20. The Union already had 35,000 men poised in northern Virginia, about twenty-five miles away from a Confederate force of 20,000 under the command of P. G. T. Beauregard. Beauregard's troops protected an important rail junction at Manassas, along Bull Run (a "run" is a stream). Confederate and Union troops also watched one another warily in the Shenandoah Valley, about fifty miles to the west.

These troop deployments reflected a primary goal of each side in the early stages of the war: capturing the capital of their enemies. Both Washington and Richmond seemed tantalizingly vulnerable to their enemies. Union leaders thought that if they could win Richmond, the industrial, commercial, and administrative center of the South, the rest of the Confederacy would soon follow. Confederate leaders thought that if they could conquer the capital of the United States, forcing Lincoln and his cabinet to flee, European powers would recognize the Confederacy's sovereignty and legitimacy. Each side's men and resources arrayed around the two capitals.

The officers of both the Union and the Confederacy had learned their strategy at West Point, a strategy based on the experience of European armies in the Napoleonic Wars of several decades earlier. These officers usually attempted to concentrate their force in hopes of overwhelming the enemy at the point of attack. The Union tried to take advantage of its greater numbers of men and resources; the Confederacy sought to use its interior lines, its knowledge of the Virginia landscape, and aggressive maneuvers to gain an advantage. Both sides knew what the other hoped and planned to do, making it difficult for either to strike the decisive blow.

In the first major battle of the war, the South's advantages outweighed the North's. Both sides attempted to coordinate their troop movements near Washington and in the Shenandoah Valley. The valley, shielded from the east by the Blue Ridge Mountains, had long served as a major corridor between the North and the South. If that corridor was left unprotected by the Union, Confederate forces could rush up the valley and capture Washington. But if too many troops protected the valley, the North would tie up men and resources that could be used more effectively elsewhere. The Confederacy employed cavalry, under the command of the flamboyant young colonel James E.B. (Jeb) Stuart, to move quickly up and down the valley, keeping the North off balance.

Despite his flamboyant appearance and cavalry tactics, J. E. B. Stuart, like a number of other Confederate generals, adhered to a strict religious discipline that prohibited drinking and swearing.

Early in the war, Thomas J. "Stonewall" Jackson was the most beloved Confederate leader, admired for his military daring and his devout religious belief.

The Union, under the command of General Irvin McDowell, tried to concentrate most of their forces at Manassas by moving them from the valley. On July 21 the northern troops were finally ready to attack. Congressmen and other spectators drove their carriages out from Washington to "see the Rebels get whipped." At first, it appeared that the ladies and gentlemen would see what they came for. Union troops flooded over the battlefield, fording the creeks, flanking the strongest points in the Confederate lines. The southern forces fell back to more defensible positions. When it looked as if the Confederates were to be routed, a southern general found inspiration in the actions of a unit under the command of Thomas J. Jackson. "Look!," the general pointed out to his men, "There is Jackson standing like a stone wall! Rally behind the Virginians!" The man who made the plea was soon killed, but "Stonewall Jackson," until recently an undistinguished mathematics professor at the Virginia Military Institute, had been christened.

Confederate reinforcements that poured off the train at Manassas gave Beauregard a renewed spirit. The Union forces, spent from days of marching and long hours of fighting, suffered confusion when the lack of a common uniform led some Northerners to mistake Confederates for their own troops. They began to pull back and then to run, throwing away their equipment along the way. Some civilian carriages got caught in the panicked flood of troops rushing back to Washington; the Confederates gleefully captured a congressman.

The South had claimed its first victory. Each side had engaged about 18,000 soldiers, making Bull Run by a considerable margin the largest battle ever waged in the United States up to that time. Both the North and the South lost about 600 men. Although each side had about an equal number of soldiers and although defending ground was much easier than taking it offensively, the humiliating rout confirmed the Confederate belief that one Rebel could whip ten Yankees.

Key parts of Confederate lore emerged from Bull Run as well: the rebel yell and the Confederate battle flag. The yell was not merely a scream or a roar, but a high wail, unnerving and strange. No one knew where

The first major battle of the war, at Manassas, Virginia, on July 21, 1861, suddenly turned into a rout of Union forces when confusion and Confederate reinforcements abruptly turned the tide.

it came from—fox-hunting, perhaps—but it served as the rallying cry for southern troops for the rest of the war. Union soldiers admitted that it affected them, for "there is nothing like it this side of the infernal region." The first flag of the Confederacy, the "Stars and Bars," looked a great deal like that of the United States, leading to confusion in the heat of battle. After Bull Run, Beauregard designed a new flag—a square banner, red with a blue cross and white stars—to ensure that southern troops did not fire on one another. It was that battle flag, never the official flag of the Confederacy, that later generations came to consider synonymous with the South.

For the next two years, the Battle of Bull Run emboldened southern forces who fought in Virginia. The Confederacy, feeling itself invulnerable, fought aggressively, even recklessly, in the east. The Union fought cautiously, even tentatively, in Virginia. Neither side forgot this conflict even though they called it by different names. Northern forces generally named battles after physical features such as rivers and mountains; thus, they deemed this the Battle of Bull Run. Southerners usually named battles after nearby towns or villages; they called this one Manassas. Later, after tens of thousands more had died, both the Union and the Confederacy would have to change their name for this

The Confederate battle flag, on the right, was adopted after Bull Run because the official flag—the so-called "Stars and Bars" (at left)—looked too much like the U.S. flag and led to deadly confusion in battle.

battle, adding a "first" to distinguish it from blood later poured on the same battlefield.

Women and War

Women North and South had avidly studied the debates over the elections and secession being waged in the newspapers. They had expressed their opinions in private conversation, in their letters, and in their diaries. Many had listened to the speeches on all sides, applauding the speakers they liked and avoiding those they did not. They had counseled their sons and husbands, sometimes resisting the drift of opinion and sometimes urging their men on to join others of their community. They had worn cockades displaying their loyalties and had sung the latest songs. The testimonials and tributes that officials and soldiers offered to women were not hollow gestures, but heartfelt. Men believed they were fighting for their families.

Once the speeches, songs, and toasts had come to an end and the fighting begun, women became even more active. Since neither the Union nor the Confederacy had prepared for a fight, the women had much to do. Within two weeks of the war's beginning, women on the two sides had formed 20,000 aid societies. These societies devoted themselves to supplying the armies' needs, especially clothing and medical supplies. One such organization in Alabama provided, in just one month, "422 shirts, 551 pairs of drawers, 80 pairs of socks, 3 pairs of gloves, 6 boxes and one bale of hospital supplies, 128 pounds of tapioca, and a donation of $18 for hospital use." Such women's groups in the South worked independently of one another, but in the North the United States Sanitary Commission coordinated their efforts, producing supplies worth over $15 million.

With the first battles, women claimed positions as nurses even though men had served before as military nurses. Despite some initial grumbling by men and gossiping by cautious women, women converted themselves immediately into competent and devoted nurses. Wounded men poured into Washington and Richmond after First Manassas, with only women in private homes and institutions to take care of them. Dorothy Dix, long known as the champion of the mentally ill and neglected people in the antebellum era, took matters in hand for the North. She became superintendent of nurses for the Union army, organizing 3,000 women who volunteered to serve. Concerned both about the effectiveness and propriety of

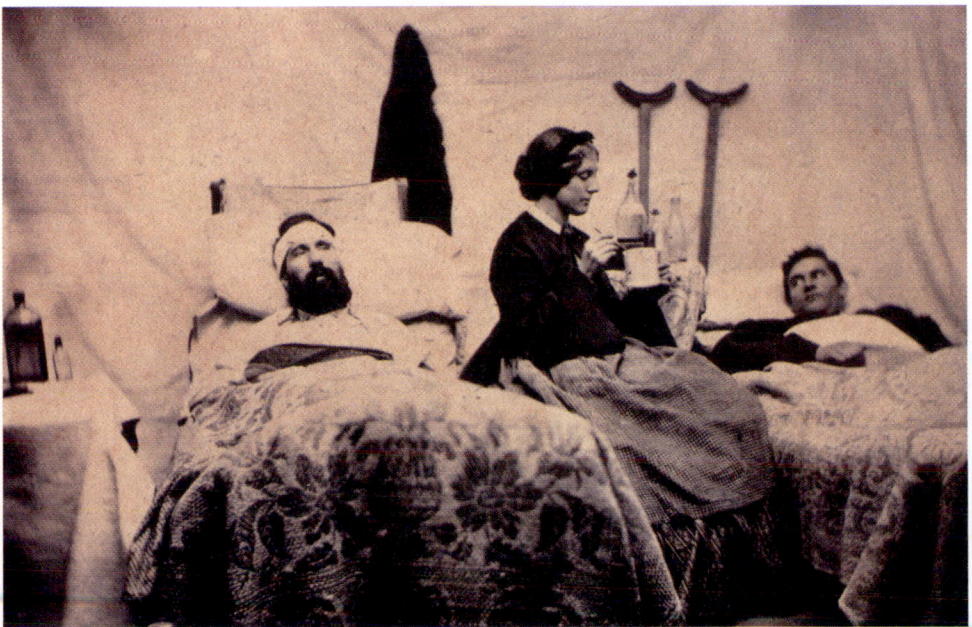

Women in both the North and South quickly stepped forward, sometimes against opposition, to save lives and relieve suffering.

LOUISA MAY ALCOTT, "JOURNAL" APRIL 1861

Thirty years old in 1862, Alcott, who had lived in her father's home her entire life, applied to become a nurse. She had no formal training, though she had cared for her dying sister. Her journal tells of her feelings at the beginning of her service, "full of hope and sorrow, courage and plans." She threw herself into the work, but grew ill with typhoid fever and endured mercury poisoning from the medication she received. She had to come home for the duration of the war. Alcott became a best-selling author with her enduring novel, *Little Women*, published in 1868.

April. [1861]—War declared with the South, and our Concord company went to Washington. A busy time getting them ready, and a sad day seeing them off, for in a little town like this we all seem like one family in times like these. At the station the scene was very dramatic, as the brave boys went away perhaps never to come back again.

I've often longed to see a war, and now I have my wish. I long to be a man, but as I can't fight, I will content myself with working for those who can. . . .

September, October. [1862]— . . . War news bad. Anxious faces, beating hearts, and busy minds.

I like the stir in the air, and long for battle like a warhorse when he smells powder. The blood of the Mays is up! . . .

November.—Thirty years old. Decided to go to Washington as a nurse if I could find a place. Help needed, and I love nursing, and *must* let out my pentup energy in some new way. Winter is always a hard and a dull time, and if I am away there is one less to feed and warm and worry over.

I want new experiences, and am sure to get 'em if I go. So I've sent in my name, and bide my time writing tales, to leave all snug behind me, and mending up my old clothes,—for nurses don't need nice things, thank Heaven!

December.—On the 11th I received a note from Miss H. M. Stevenson telling me to start for Georgetown next day to fill a place in the Union Hotel Hospital. Mrs. Ropes of

women ministering to young male strangers, Dix decreed that she wanted only "plain" women, women over thirty, and women who would dress in brown and black. Such women did come forward in large numbers, but so did women of other descriptions as well. Patriotism and mercy activated them, but the forty-cents-a-day wage was certainly welcome too during these harsh days.

Women's efforts soon became legendary, North and South. Women labored until they could no longer stand, until their long dresses trailed blood from amputations and wounds, until they had watched one young man after another die. Kate Cumming and Phoebe Pember played leading roles in the Confederacy, and Clara Barton, formerly a clerk at the Patent Office in Washington, took her aid to the front lines of the Union and later founded the American Red Cross. Most women stayed closer to home, working in factories or doing piecework in their households under ever harsher circumstances.

Boston was matron, and Miss Kendall of Plymouth was a nurse there, and though a hard place, help was needed. I was ready, and when my commander said "March!" I marched. Packed my trunk, and reported in B.[oston] that same evening.

We had all been full of courage till the last moment came, then we all broke down. I realized that I had taken my life in my hand, and might never see them all again. I said, "Shall I stay, Mother?" as I hugged her close. "No, go! and the Lord be with you!" answered the Spartan woman, and till I turned the corner she bravely smiled and waved her wet handkerchief on the doorstep. Shall I ever see that dear old face again?

So I set forth in the December twilight, with May and Julian Hawthorne as escort, feeling as if I was the son of the house going to war.

Friday, the 12th, was a very memorable day, spent in running all over Boston to get my pass, etc., calling for parcels, getting a tooth filled, and buying a veil,—my only purchase. A. C. gave me some old clothes, the dear Sewalls money for myself and boys, lots of love and help, and at 5 P.M., saying "goodby" to a group of tearful faces at the station, I started on my long journey, full of hope and sorrow, courage and plans.

A most interesting journey into a new world full of stirring sights and sounds, new adventures, and an evergrowing sense of the great task I had undertaken.

I said my prayers as I went rushing through the country white with tents, all alive with patriotism, and already red with blood.

A solemn time, but I'm glad to live in it, and am sure it will do me good whether I come out alive or dead.

All went well, and I got to Georgetown one evening very tired. Was kindly welcomed, slept in my narrow bed with two other room-mates, and on the morrow began my new life by seeing a poor man die at dawn, and sitting all day between a boy with pneumonia and a man shot through the lungs. A strange day, but I did my best, and when I put mother's little black shawl round the boy while he sat up panting for breath, he smiled and said, "You are real motherly, ma'am." I felt as if I was getting on. The man only lay and stared with his big black eyes, and made me very nervous. But all were well behaved, and I sat looking at the twenty strong faces as they looked back at me,— hoping that I looked "motherly" to them, for my thirty years made me feel old, and the suffering round me made me long to comfort every one. . . .

SOURCE Alcott's journals are located at Houghton Library, Harvard University, and have been published in Joel Myerson and Daniel Shealy, editors, *The Journals of Louisa May Alcott* (Boston, 1989).

WAR TAKES COMMAND: AUGUST 1861 TO MARCH 1862

The war spread across the continent in the fall, winter, and spring of 1861–1862. Armies consolidated command and launched campaigns thousands of miles from headquarters. Governments transformed their economies, invented or reinvented navies, conducted diplomacy, and cemented the loyalties of those at home. Families steeled themselves for a war longer than they had been willing to imagine.

McClellan Assumes Control

The North, while embarrassed by Bull Run, took from that defeat a determination to fight more effectively.

Early in the war, Lincoln and the rest of the North placed great faith in the "Young Napoleon," General George B. McClellan. Events would later lessen their admiration.

Volunteers flooded into recruitment offices. Lincoln removed the leaders responsible for that battle and replaced them with George B. McClellan. McClellan was the logical choice. Although short of stature and only thirty-four years old, he exuded great authority. He was known as the "young Napoleon." McClellan had distinguished himself in the Mexican War, studied military tactics in Europe, and served as a railroad president. Moreover, he had already frustrated Confederate forces with Robert E. Lee in western Virginia. Drawing on all these experiences, McClellan threw himself into reorganizing and reenergizing the Union troops under his command.

McClellan's men loved him and the press lavished praise on the young general. Already inclined toward grandiose visions of his abilities, McClellan developed an exalted sense of himself. The cocky commander considered Lincoln an "idiot" and his cabinet incompetent "geese." McClellan ignored, avoided, and in-

sulted those men at every opportunity. A Democrat deeply suspicious of abolitionists and Republicans, McClellan wanted only to restore the Union, not to dislodge slavery in the South or to damage his prospects as a presidential candidate in 1864. As a result, McClellan wanted to make his army perfectly prepared before he risked it, and his reputation, in battle against Confederates whose numbers his spies consistently exaggerated. Meanwhile, months dragged by. Lincoln and newspaper editors became furiously impatient but McClellan would not be moved. Everyone in the east waited for McClellan to attack the Confederates in Virginia.

The War in the West Begins

There was to be no waiting in the West, where troops fought on a smaller but more vicious scale. Four days after the battle at Bull Run, the Union installed a new commander in charge of the forces in Missouri: John C. Frémont, the "pathfinder of the West" and unsuccessful Republican candidate for president in 1856. While the situation in Virginia unfolded slowly, the situation in Missouri burst into chaos in July and August of 1861. Guerilla forces ranged throughout the state, sharply divided between northern and southern partisans. Confederate armies built up on the southern border, ready to attack in both the eastern and western parts of the state. Frémont decided that he had to protect the Mississippi River in the East and therefore left a weak force in the West. That force, outnumbered by the Confederates, staged a desperate attack, with terrible losses, at Wilson's Creek. As at Bull Run, the lack of a standard uniform color created deadly confusion; Union troops withheld fire against men in blue only to realize, too late, that they were Confederates. The northern units fell into ragged retreat, exposing Missouri to Rebel incursions.

Not only had Frémont lost much of Missouri, but he faced problems McClellan, back in the East, never confronted. With the army desperate for war materiel and supplies so far from Washington, contractors took advantage of the situation, selling substandard goods to the Union army at inflated prices. With the populace of Missouri so divided in its loyalties, Frémont did not know whom to trust; spies and guerillas seemed everywhere. Frantic, he declared the entire state under martial law, decreed the death penalty for captured guerillas, and seized the slaves and other

property of all Confederate sympathizers. While anti-slavery advocates in the North applauded Frémont for doing what they thought Abraham Lincoln should be doing for the entire South, slaveholders in the border states of Kentucky and Maryland threatened to throw their allegiances to the South if Lincoln did not overrule Frémont. The president, desperate to keep the border states within the Union, publicly reprimanded his general. When Frémont resisted, Lincoln felt that he had no choice but to remove Frémont from his post. Missouri, like Bull Run, embarrassed the Union in the summer of 1861.

Events on the battlefield in the earliest stages of the war proved to be a poor guide to the long term. Although the North had been shaken by Bull Run and Missouri, it had lost neither Washington nor the border states. Although the South had apparently won at Bull Run, the Confederate forces, exhausted and bogged down in mud, had not taken advantage of the situation to attack the Union capital. Although the Confederacy had driven Union troops from much of Missouri, that state was eventually to supply 100,000 men to the North and only 30,000 to the South. Although slaveholders in the border states fumed at the Union government and military leaders, they remained in the Union. As a result, the South was deprived of a key strategic advantage: access to the Ohio River and a defensible border with the North. With the Union army able to move up and down the Ohio at will, the Confederates had to defend a vast, vague, and shifting border in Kentucky and Tennessee.

To virtually everyone's surprise, the war was not to be won by a decisive battle within a few months of the war's start. Instead, slower and less dramatic processes proved decisive. Armies and navies had to be built from scratch; economies had to be converted to wartime demands; politics had to be reoriented; diplomacy had to adjust to the complexities of the battlefield and the international order; households and families had to absorb growing sacrifices. These transformations began in earnest in the summer of 1861.

Paying for War

The Civil War, involving so many men over such an enormous territory, immediately became breathtakingly expensive. It was by no means clear how either side was going to pay. Although the Union and the Confederacy were, by any international standard, rich societies, neither had ever supported a large army or an active government. Taxes on imported goods and the sale of apparently endless public lands paid for what government there was. Ever since the Bank War of the 1830s the federal and state governments did little to manipulate the currency. As a result, when the war came, the men responsible for paying for it had only a few options—loans, new taxes, or the creation of paper money—all of them long suspect in America.

Loans met the least resistance in both the North and the South, but this borrowing could provide only a third of the cost of the war. Taxes proved even less effective, never supplying more than a small portion of the funds despite considerable effort to raise them. The Confederacy, enjoying far fewer resources than the North, quickly decided that it had no choice but to turn to paper money. As soon as they could find adequate engravers and printing presses, the South began producing millions of dollars in the new currency in an ever-growing stream. Catastrophic inflation began to grow as early as the winter of 1861–1862.

The situation was not quite as bad in the North, where taxes and bonds carried much more of the burden of financing the war, but the Union, too, was forced to issue paper money by the first winter of the war. As the secretary of the treasury warned, *"immediate action is of great importance. The treasury is nearly empty."* People hoarded gold in anticipation of the deprivations a widened war would cause. New York banks felt they had no choice but to suspend specie payments in December of 1861. The Union Congress, faced with strong warnings from constituents and colleagues, reluctantly decided in February of 1862 that it had no choice but to create paper money as well. The Legal Tender Act of that month permitted the treasury to release up to $10 million of the new currency, quickly dubbed "greenbacks." The paper money provided critical fuel for the northern economy and for the burgeoning military.

The Confederate Homefront

Southerners, black and white, watched helplessly as armies stripped their farms of food and livestock. They cowered as rifle and cannon shot ripped through their homes. They ministered to the bleeding young men dragged into their parlors and bedrooms. The residents of places where both Unionists and

Much of the Civil War turned around conflicts such as the one depicted in this painting, in which small groups of soldiers confronted one another and civilians far from the scenes of major battles.

Confederates remained strong—such as Missouri and eastern Tennessee—became caught in internal civil wars that pitted roving gangs of thugs against one another and against those who happened to be in their path. Governors received letters from women, their husbands and sons gone, who worried that they faced starvation if they did not get help soon.

Inflation ate away at the Confederacy like a cancer. The rapid rise in prices made currency worth less every day, food and cotton worth more. Speculators could make money simply by buying up supplies and holding them while prices escalated. Farmers faced the temptation to grow cotton despite the needs of the armies in the fields. Cotton stored well and everyone knew that cotton would fetch a high price after the war, no matter who won. As a result, land and labor that could have grown food bent under the weight of cotton.

White Southerners began to worry that the slaves would rise in rebellion if permitted to grow ever more "insolent." Confederate leaders worried that the plantations could not produce the food the armies so desperately needed if white men did not force the slaves

to work. African Americans wanted to hunt, fish, or work for themselves and their own families rather than to labor for the white people. Plantation mistresses often discovered, to their fury and fear, that slaves would not work when the master—and the overseer, whips, and guns he wielded—no longer hung over the slaves. Accordingly, the Confederate Congress passed what became known as the "twenty negro law," exempting from the draft one white man on every plantation that had at least twenty slaves. That a government in such need of every available soldier felt compelled to write such laws revealed how central slavery and its control remained even in the midst of war.

The twenty slave law came at additional cost as well: to many poorer Southerners, the law was another in a growing list of grievances against the rich and the Confederate government. Resentment against wealthy men and women, mediated during peacetime by family ties, common church membership, careful manners, and democratic politics, quickly came to the surface in the context of war. Common people were quick to notice when plantation slaves labored over cotton rather than

corn, when mistresses appeared in public in their finery, when the well-to-do hoarded gold or dodged taxes. Wealthy young men sometimes entered the Confederate army as privates—Robert E. Lee's son did so—but others considered an officer's commission, preferably in the cavalry, their just due as gentlemen. Scions of plantation fortunes often did little to disguise their disgust or amusement at the speech or clothing of the poorer men alongside whom they fought. The poorer soldiers noticed, as did their wives.

Navies

The navies of the North and South had to adapt most quickly. In the mid-nineteenth century, water vied with railroads as the most vital means of transportation. Just as many battles, starting with Bull Run,

broke out at rail junctions, so did the leaders on both sides recognize the centrality of ports and rivers. The North's Anaconda Plan depended on control of the waterways, stopping the shipment of the South's immensely valuable cotton crop, cutting the region off from importations of weapons and other manufactured goods, and dividing the Confederacy along the Mississippi River. While ground troops back east dug in for the winter of 1861–1862, the navies of both sides struggled for control of the seas and rivers.

The Union enjoyed a great initial advantage in its number of ships, but at the time of the war many of those ships were scattered around the globe. It took months to track them down and bring them home. Moreover, most of the Union's vessels were deep-sea ships, not very useful for the sort of river and port fighting the war was likely to bring. With remarkable speed, however, the Union naval department built new

The Confederacy depended on English shipyards, such as this one in Liverpool, to construct vessels to run the Union blockade, attack Union ships on the seas, and defend their ports.

craft and deployed them against the South. The skilled workers of the shipbuilding towns of the east coast produced hundreds of ships and boats.

Although a number of naval officers resigned their Union commissions to join the Confederacy, the South had virtually no ships at the beginning of the war. The Confederacy immediately contracted with large shipbuilding companies in England to produce craft the South did not have the time or facilities to make for itself. Jefferson Davis also authorized sailors to attack northern ships on the high seas and turn them in for a share of the booty. For a few months these "privateers" preyed on any unguarded ship they could find, but the Union navy quickly shut them down. The Confederates then used their naval officers to man ships that would attempt to sink rather than claim enemy ships. One intrepid officer, Raphael Semmes, escaped through the blockade in 1861 and seized eighteen Union ships before he was trapped at Gibraltar on the other side of the Atlantic and forced to sell his ship and escape to England.

In the meantime, the North pushed its advantage. Larger ships began to blockade 189 harbors and ports from Virginia to Texas, patrolling 3,500 miles of coastline. Such enormous territory obviously proved difficult to control, especially because northern ships periodically had to travel to ports hundreds of miles away for supplies and fuel. When Union craft left for such journeys, southern blockade runners rushed into the unprotected ports. The Union navy decided to seize several southern ports for use as supply stations. The federal ships moved first in August, at Cape Hatteras in North Carolina, shelling the forts there and cutting off the supplies that dozens of blockade runners had brought into the Confederacy. The northern navy also took a station near Biloxi, Mississippi, from which they could patrol the Gulf of Mexico. The most valuable seizure, however, was Port Royal, South Carolina. Not only did that place offer an excellent harbor, but it stood midway between the major southern ports of Charleston and Savannah. In November of 1861, the Union navy overwhelmed Confederate forts on the Sea Islands that stretched along the coast. The federal army and navy now had invaluable bases of operations.

Diplomacy and the Trent Affair

On the day after the capture of Port Royal, another event on the seas drew attention on both sides of the Atlantic. A Union ship stopped a British mail packet, the *Trent,* as it traveled from Cuba to St. Thomas. The *Trent* carried James Mason and John Slidell, Confederate commissioners sailing to London and Paris to negotiate for the support of the British and French governments. The captain of the Union ship, Charles Wilkes, after firing two shots across the bow of the British vessel, boarded it and seized the Confederate emissaries. When Wilkes arrived in Boston to deposit Mason and Slidell in prison, he met with a hero's welcome. A northern public that had been frustrated by the inability of its leaders to achieve success on the battlefield roared its approval of Wilkes's bold and decisive action. Congress ordered a medal struck in his honor.

The excitement began to wane, however, when people realized the possible repercussions of Wilkes's actions. Despite the growth of the Union navy, Great Britain still ruled the oceans—and Great Britain was furious at the boarding of their ship by the Americans. British newspapers and politicians called for war against the arrogant Americans. The *Trent* affair reflected the uneasy state of international relations created by the war. The Confederacy hoped that England or France, even both, would come to its aid. The importance of cotton in the international marketplace was such, Southerners argued, that the industrial powers of Europe could not long afford to allow the northern navy to enforce its blockade. Moreover, many Southerners—and Northerners, for that matter—expected the European powers to take advantage of the American war for their own purposes. The United States had been growing with daunting speed in population, territory, and trade; surely it would benefit France and England to support the Confederacy and weaken the Union.

The situation in the winter of 1861–1862 proved more complicated than people had expected, however. International law did not offer a clear ruling on whether Captain Wilkes had acted legally. And neither did self-interest offer a clear guide to whether England should declare war on the United States or aid the Confederacy. The factories of Britain had stockpiled cotton in expectation of the war and did not clamor for intervention as Southerners had hoped. France and England watched one another warily, neither country eager to upset the fragile balance of power between themselves by taking the first step in America. Besides, the United States seemed to be doing a good job of destroying itself without the intervention of Europe.

Public opinion within England and France divided, for it was by no means clear to most Europeans in this first year of the war which side had the better claim to their sympathies. Lincoln repeatedly declared that the war was not a war against slavery. That declaration, Lincoln believed, was necessary to cement the support of the border states and dubious Democrats, but it undercut the support of English and European abolitionists for the Union cause. The Confederates claimed to be fighting for self-determination, a cause with considerable appeal in Europe, but potential supporters often viewed southern slaveholding with disgust and distrust. Both the English and the French waited for events on the battlefields of North America to clarify issues.

The *Trent* affair, however, had to be settled at once. Its settlement came through diplomatic evasion and maneuvering. The U.S. officials decided that, despite the enthusiasm with which Wilkes's actions were greeted by Congress, he had acted on his own, unauthorized by the government of the Union. Mason and Slidell were freed from prison and permitted to continue their journey to London and Paris. The English, eager for a solution, put the incident behind them. Although the Confederacy was jubilant at having "won," the underlying situation had not changed. Mason and Slidell, along with the Confederate emissaries to other countries, found that though many powerful people elsewhere were sympathetic to the rebellious Southerners and hopeful of their success, they were unwilling to go to war against the United States.

The international situation remained tense and unsettled throughout the war. Leaders of both the North and the South could imagine situations in which England or France would intervene with weapons and supplies, tipping the balance of the war. Foreign intervention remained a fervent hope for the Confederacy and a great fear of the North. Abraham Lincoln and Jefferson Davis would always pay close attention to Europe.

The Rivers of the West

The Union felt starved for victories at the beginning of the hard winter of 1862. Northern troops remained bogged down in the eastern theater, where George McClellan lay immobile with typhoid fever, but Union generals in the West moved aggressively. Deprived of control of the Ohio River when Kentucky

Ulysses S. Grant distinguished himself in key battles in Tennessee and Mississippi in 1862. Many months and battles would pass, however, before Grant would assume command in the East.

sided with the Union, the Confederates under Albert Sidney Johnston desperately needed to stop the Union in the West. Troops under the command of Ulysses S. Grant, a relatively obscure general from Illinois, confronted a Confederate line of defense across southern Kentucky, based at the most important railroad junctions. Grant decided to use the rivers rather than the railroads for his assault, however. Employing the Union's new river gunboats to great effect, Grant pushed down both the Tennessee and the Cumberland rivers across the Kentucky border into Tennessee.

Important Confederate forts stood on both these rivers, but Grant hoped to overwhelm them by combined attacks on water and land. He assaulted Fort Henry on the Tennessee River in early February, easily overcoming the fort's defenses with the big guns on his river craft. The Union now commanded a river that flowed all the way through Tennessee into northern Alabama. Grant, buoyed by this remarkable victory, sent his boats steaming back up the Tennessee River to

MAP 14.2 | THE CIVIL WAR IN THE WEST, 1861-1862

the Cumberland while he marched his men overland to Fort Donelson. There, the Confederates enjoyed a more strategic position for their fort and fought desperately, destroying several of the gunboats that had seemed so indestructible only a few days earlier. Despite the Confederacy's efforts, however, Grant pressed his advantage and overwhelmed southern troops that attempted to break out of the fort and retreat to nearby Nashville.

When the Confederate general in charge of the 13,000 troops who remained in the fort attempted to negotiate with Grant (an old friend) for their surren-

der, Grant brusquely responded: "No terms except an unconditional and immediate surrender can be accepted. I propose to move immediately upon your works." Grant's phrase soon echoed through northern newspapers, jokes, and even mildly risqué love letters. Grant's first two initials, northern newspapers crowed, actually stood for Unconditional Surrender. Within days, Union troops pushed into nearby Nashville, the capital of Tennessee, making it the first great conquest of the war. Europe noticed: One of the Confederate emissaries released after the *Trent* affair morosely reported from London that "the late reverses at Fort

The Union's use of river boats provided a decided advantage when they quickly overran this fort on the Tennessee River in February 1862.

Henry and Fort Donelson have had an unfortunate effect on the minds of our friends here."

The Monitor *and the* Virginia

Even as Grant's troops seized their victories on the rivers of Tennessee, the Union navy continued its relentless attack on the eastern seaboard of the Confederacy. A well-planned amphibious attack allowed the northern navy to consolidate its control of the North Carolina coast, sealing off every city except Wilmington. The blockade steadily tightened.

Despite the Union's success, the southern navy had reason for hope in early 1862. Confederate Secretary of the Navy Stephen Mallory—a former U.S. senator quite experienced in naval affairs—had created an effective and innovative department. Mallory sought to take advantage of recent developments in shipbuilding and naval warfare such as steam power, the screw propeller, and armor. The Confederacy eagerly experimented, too, with mines in their harbors.

Most important, the South examined the possibilities of iron-plated ships. In the years immediately preceding the Civil War, the French and British had been experimenting with such vessels but the United States remained far behind. The Confederacy began building an ironclad almost from the very beginning of the war, converting a Union ship captured in Norfolk in April of 1861. They added walls of two-feet-thick solid oak, covered with four-inch-thick iron plate, and installed an iron ram on the front to rip through the wooden hulls of enemy ships. It carried ten heavy guns. The Confederacy changed the ship's name from the U.S.S. *Merrimack* to the C.S.S. *Virginia.*

The Union, for its part, hired a Swiss inventor to design a different kind of ironclad; his innovative plan called for a ship most of which would be submerged except for a rotating turret on top. The result resembled "a tin can on a shingle," one observer commented, and it was by no means clear how such a craft might work in battle. No one was even sure it would stay afloat, much less fight effectively with its two guns. It was called the *Monitor.*

On March 8, 1862, with the Union navy consolidating its control of the eastern seaboard, the Confederates decided the time had come to unleash their new weapon. The *Virginia* attacked several Union ships occupying the harbor at Hampton Roads, Virginia. The ironclad overwhelmed two wooden ships and drove

In one of the most memorable episodes of the war, the U.S.S. Monitor *and the C.S.S.* Virginia *bruised one another in the harbor of Hampton Roads, Virginia, in March 1862. Though neither ship won, the Union's* Monitor *proved the superior vessel.*

THE FIRST BATTLE BETWEEN IRON SHIPS OF WAR.
The *Monitor* 2 Guns and *Merrimac* 10 Guns.
The *Merrimac* Was crippled and the whole Rebel Fleet driven off.

three others aground; their guns proved useless against the heavy iron sheathing. The Confederates looked forward to the next day, when they planned to finish off the grounded ships.

In one of the more dramatic episodes of the young war, however, the Union happened to be sending its own ironclad to a Virginia port thirty miles away on the morning after the *Virginia* launched its attack. Hearing the sound of the guns in Hampton Roads, the *Monitor* steamed down and arrived just in time. The two vessels pounded one another for hours, the cannonballs bouncing off both ships. The imposing southern ironclad had been neutralized and the blockade would continue. Although neither iron ship actually won the battle of March 9, the advantages of the northern *Monitor* quickly became evident. Not only did that craft provide a much smaller target and a more maneuverable set of guns, but the *Monitor* required only half as much water in which to operate. The *Virginia* proved too big to retreat into rivers and too unwieldy for open seas; it would pose no threat to Washington or New York. The Union began a crash campaign to build as many ironclads as possible, using the *Monitor* as their model.

THE UNION ON THE OFFENSIVE: MARCH TO SEPTEMBER 1862

The Union strategy had long pivoted around the effort to take Richmond. With their most illustrious general in command and enjoying apparently unlimited resources, Northerners expected to make quick work of Virginia. Although the Confederacy had put up a surprisingly effective campaign, the Union expected to win the war in the spring and summer of 1862. As with all things in this war, however, events followed directions no one could foresee.

The Peninsular Campaign Begins

On the very day that the C.S.S. *Virginia* emerged at Hampton Roads, Abraham Lincoln gave his approval of General George McClellan's long-delayed plan to win the war in the East. Rather than fighting in northern Virginia, McClellan would attack on the peninsula

MAP 14.3 | THE CIVIL WAR IN THE EAST, SPRING 1862

between the James and York rivers farther south, using the Chesapeake Bay as a supply route. By moving the war away from Washington, McClellan argued, he would lessen the threat to the nation's capital and find better roads from which to attack Richmond. His army, after months of marching and polishing (and criticism from the northern public, press, and president), was finally ready to do its job.

Four hundred watercraft of every description began transferring Union soldiers to the tip of the peninsula at Fortress Monroe, about seventy miles from Richmond. The march that McClellan envisioned would, ironically, push through two of the most famous places in American history: Jamestown and Yorktown. The

transfer of 100,000 men took weeks to unfold. McClellan required several more weeks to arrange them just so in preparation for what he expected to be his triumphant march into Richmond.

Shiloh

In the meantime, U. S. Grant and his fellow general William T. Sherman pushed their troops ever deeper into Tennessee. The Confederates, under the leadership of Albert Sidney Johnston, had retreated to Corinth, Mississippi, where they regrouped and joined with other units. They planned to attack Grant to

regain momentum if not the enormous territory and strategic rivers they had lost at Fort Henry and Fort Donelson. Grant established his own base of operations only twenty miles away, at Pittsburgh Landing, Tennessee. To the surprise of the Union, Johnston attacked the larger Union force at Shiloh Church on April 6.

The area around Shiloh was no classic battlefield of sweeping vistas and high ground. Rather, its scattered woods and rough terrain turned the battle into a series of brutal fights among desperate groups of scattered men with little coordinated leadership. Johnston, killed leading an attack, was replaced by Beauregard, who succeeded in pushing the Union men back two miles. The Confederates' dominance proved short-lived, however, for 25,000 northern reinforcements arrived overnight. The Southerners received no new men. The next day saw Grant and his men regain the ground they had lost, driving the Confederates back to Corinth. Though the southern forces had been badly hurt, the northern forces were themselves too exhausted and shaken to pursue.

The carnage at Shiloh exceeded anything anyone had ever seen. The bloodiest battle in the hemisphere up to that point, Shiloh exacted a horrible toll: about 1,700 killed and 8,000 wounded on each side. About 2,000 of the wounded men in both the Union and the Confederacy forces would soon die. Sherman wrote of the "piles of dead soldiers' mangled bodies . . . without heads and legs. . . . The scenes on this field would have cured anybody of war." Newspapers and generals debated the outcome of the battle for months, trying to decide the hero and the loser, but it eventually became clear that the southern attempt to halt northern momentum in the Mississippi Valley had failed. It also became clear that commanders on both sides would fight desperately, and with enormous costs, when cornered.

In one of the bloodiest days of fighting in the war, the troops of Grant and William T. Sherman clashed with those of Albert Sidney Johnston and P. G. T. Beauregard. Johnston was killed and the Union forces seized a desperate, last-minute, and costly victory.

The fleet of David Farragut accomplished what the Confederates considered impossible, pushing past the elaborate defenses of New Orleans. Using the cover of darkness, much of the fleet managed to survive a thundering artillery assault.

New Orleans

The Federals' success in Tennessee, along the Carolina coast, and in Hampton Roads in the spring of 1862 heartened Union supporters who had begun to doubt the success of their cause. Yet another drama played itself out in New Orleans. There, a Union naval force under David Farragut—a sixty-year-old Tennessean married to a Virginian—determined to do what Confederates considered impossible: overwhelm their largest city and largest port from the Gulf. Confederates recalled that the mighty British of 1815 had been unable to take New Orleans and fully expected the same fate to befall the Yankees. The city lay under the protection of two forts claiming 115 guns as well as a river blocked with logs and thick cables. So safe did they consider New Orleans that Confederate troops abandoned the city to fight at Shiloh, leaving the port protected only by militiamen.

Farragut had his own weapons, however: 20 mortar boats, 17 ships with 210 guns, and 15,000 soldiers.

The Union navy pounded the forts for days with the mortars, unsuccessfully. Frustrated, on April 24 Farragut audaciously led his ships, single-file, past the forts and past Confederate ships that tried to ram the Union craft or set them on fire with flaming rafts. Once they had run this gauntlet, the Union ships had clear sailing right up to the docks of New Orleans. There, they confronted no resistance, only thick smoke from the bales of cotton the Southerners had set on fire to keep out of Yankee hands. Troops under the command of Benjamin Butler occupied New Orleans while Farragut continued to drive up the Mississippi River. He took Baton Rouge and Natchez, but Vicksburg held Farragut off, thanks to its position on bluffs high above the river. River boats coming from the north soon took Memphis as well, giving the Union control of all the Mississippi River except the area near Vicksburg. Northern forces used the river as a major supply route. Rather than a highway uniting the upper and lower South, the Mississippi became a chasm separating one half of the Confederacy from the other.

SARAH MORGAN, "DIARY" MARCH 1864

Sarah Morgan was a high-spirited teenager when the Civil War broke out, the daughter of a respected judge. Though she and her father supported the Union during the secession crisis, both invested their loyalty in the Confederacy once the Civil War began. This part of her diary, begun in 1862, records the grief that struck the hundreds of thousands of American families who lost sons, brothers, and fathers in the war. Despite her sense of helplessness, Morgan went on to write for a leading newspaper in South Carolina after the war.

March

Dead! dead! Both dead! O my brothers! what have we lived for except you? We who would so gladly have laid down our lives for yours, are left desolate to mourn over all we loved and hoped for, weak and helpless; while you, so strong, noble, and brave, have gone before us without a murmur. God knows best. But it is hard—O so hard! to give them up without a murmur!

We cannot remember the day when our brothers were not all in all to us. What the boys would think; what the boys would say; what we would do when the boys came home, that has been our sole thought through life. A life time's hope wrecked in a moment—God help us! In our eyes, there is no one in the world quite so noble, quite so brave, quite so true as our brothers. And yet they are taken—and others useless to themselves and a curse to their families live on in safety, without fear of death. This is blasphemy. God knows best; I will not complain. But when I think of drunken, foolish, coarse Will Carter with horses and dogs his sole ambition, and drinking and gambling his idea of happiness, my heart swells within me. He lives, a torment to himself and a curse to others—he will live to a green old age as idle, as ignorant, as dissipated as he is now.

And Gibbes, Harry, and George, God's blessings he bestowed on us awhile—are dead. My brothers! my dear brothers! I would rather mourn over you in your graves, remembering what you were, than have you change places with that man. Death is nothing in comparison to dishonor.

If we had had any warning or preparation, this would not have been so unspeakably awful. But to shut ones eyes to all dangers and risks, and drown every rising fear with "God will send them back; I will not doubt his mercy," and then suddenly to learn that your faith has been presumption—and God wills that you shall undergo bitter affliction—it is a fearful awakening! What glory have we ever rendered to God that we should expect him to be so merciful to us? Are not all things His, and is He not infinitely more tender and compassionate than we deserve?

We have deceived ourselves willfully about both. After the first dismay on hearing of Gibbes' capture, we readily listened to the assertions of our friends that Johnson's Island was the healthiest place in the world, that he would be better off, comfortably clothed and under shelter, than exposed to shot and shell, half fed, and lying on the bare ground

during Ewell's winter campaign. We were thankful for his safety, knowing Brother would leave nothing undone that could add to his comfort. And besides that, there was the sure hope of his having him paroled. On that hope we lived all winter—now confident that in a little while he would be with us, then again doubting for awhile, only to have the hope grow surer afterwards. And so we waited and prayed, never doubting he would come at last. He himself believed it, though striving not to be too hopeful lest he should disappoint us, as well as himself. Yet he wrote cheerfully and bravely to the last. Towards the middle of January, Brother was sure of succeeding, as all the prisoners had been placed under Butler's control. Ah me! How could we be so blind? We were sure he would be with us in a few weeks! I wrote to him that I had prepared his room.

On the 30th of January came his last letter, addressed to me, though meant for Sis. It was dated the 12th—the day George died. All his letters pleaded that I would write more frequently—he loved to hear from me; so I had been writing to him every ten days. On the third of February I sent my last. Friday the fifth, as I was running through Miriam's room, I saw Brother pass the door, and heard him ask Miriam for mother. The voice, the bowed head, the look of utter despair on his face, struck through me like a knife. "Gibbes! Gibbes!" was my sole thought; but Miriam and I stood motionless looking at each other without a word. "Gibbes is dead" said mother as he stood before her. He did not speak; and then we went in.

We did not ask how, or when. That he was dead was enough for us. But after a while he told us uncle James had written that he had died at two o'clock on Thursday the twenty first. Still we did not know how he had died. Several letters that had been brought remained unopened on the floor. One, Brother opened, hoping to learn something more. It was from Col. Steedman to Miriam and me, written a few hours after his death, and contained the sad story [of] our dear brother's last hours. He had been in Col. Steedman's ward of the hospital for more than a week, with headache and sore throat; but it was thought nothing; he seemed to improve, and expected to be discharged in a few days. On the twenty first he complained that his throat pained him again. After prescribing for him, and talking cheerfully with him for some time, Col. Steedman left him surrounded by his friends, to attend to his other patients. He had hardly reached his room when someone ran to him saying Capt. Morgan was dying. He hurried to his bedside, and found him dead. Capt. Steedman, sick in the next bed, and those around him said he had been talking pleasantly with them, when he sat up to reach his cup of water on the table. As soon as he drank it he seemed to suffocate; and after tossing his arms wildly in the air, and making several fearful efforts to breathe, he died.

O Gibbes! Gibbes! When you took me in your arms and cried so bitterly over that sad parting, it was indeed your last farewell! My brothers! my brothers! Dear Lord how can we live without our boys?

Sewed to the paper that contained the last words we should hear of our dear brother, was a lock of hair grown long during his imprisonment. I think it was a noble, tender heart that remembered that one little deed of kindness, and a gentle, pitying hand that cut it from his head as he lay cold and stark in death. Good heart that loved our brave brother, kind hand that soothed his pain, you will not be forgotten by us!

SOURCE   *The Civil War Diary of Sarah Morgan,* Charles East, ed. (Athens: University of Georgia Press, 1991), pp. 597-600.

The Confederate Draft

The end of April, then, seemed to promise the early end to the war that people had expected at its outbreak. Although many of the battles had been close that spring, they all seemed to turn out in favor of the North. The first year-long enlistments in the Confederate army were running out in April, just when the southern army met its worst defeats. Many soldiers, deciding they had done their part, left for home. Jefferson Davis and the Confederate Congress, fearful that their armies would be short of men as the Union stepped up its attacks in the late spring and summer, decided that they had no choice but to initiate a compulsory draft, the first centrally administered draft in American history. All white men between the ages of eighteen and thirty-five were required to fight for three years. Those soldiers who had been fighting for the last year would have to fight for three more. If men enlisted or reenlisted within the thirty days following passage of the law, they could choose the unit with which they fought and bear the proud title of volunteer. If they waited, they would have no such options.

Although the Confederacy eventually abolished substitution, in which men with enough money could pay a substitute to fight in their place, it still permitted men from many occupations to claim an exemption from military service. Governors, resentful of the power of the Confederacy, appointed many men to positions in their state governments and militia so that they would be exempted from the draft. Within a few months, the Confederacy, concerned about the productivity and safety of the South's plantations, also exempted one white man for every twenty slaves he supervised in the twenty negro law. Conscription ran against everything the South saw itself fighting for: freedom, a weak state, manly bravery, a common cause that would unite all white southern men. The draft, necessary though it was—providing a fifth to a third of all Confederate soldiers—divided Southerners more profoundly than anything else in the Civil War.

The Seven Days

"Every blow tells fearfully against the rebellion," a New York newspaper declared at the end of May. "The rebels themselves are panic-stricken or despondent. It now requires no very far reaching prophet to predict the end of this struggle." From the viewpoint of the battlefields in Tennessee and Mississippi, and from the viewpoint of the ports of Norfolk and New Orleans, the war did indeed seem to be nearing its end. And in Virginia George McClellan's troops, the pride of the Union and 100,000 strong, had pushed their way up the peninsula toward Richmond. By the end of May only five miles separated them from their destination.

Not that it would be easy for the Union troops to take Richmond. The river assaults that had worked so well two months earlier in Tennessee failed in Virginia. The Confederates were able to attack the river gunboats from the heights of Drewry's Bluff, raining artillery and rifle shot down on the craft below. Even the *Monitor,* fresh from its impressive showing in Hampton Roads, proved ineffectual when faced with an enemy one hundred feet above. Moreover, the Confederates, knowing that the Union would try to take their capital, had established imposing defenses around Richmond and concentrated many of their troops in the vicinity.

Defensive positioning proved more important in the American Civil War than in any prior conflict, including the war with Mexico, in which so many of the generals on both sides of the Civil War had gained their experience of battle. Defenders gained their advantage from a new kind of weapon: the rifle. A rifle, unlike a musket, used a spiral groove in the barrel to put spin on a bullet, like a football pass, giving the bullet much greater stability and accuracy. A musket had been accurate at only about eighty yards but a rifle could hit a target at four times that distance. While the benefits of rifling had long been recognized, it was not until the 1850s that a French inventor, Charles Minie, devised a way to make it possible for a rifled gun to fire without requiring the grooves to be cleaned. While the rifles still had to be loaded from the end of the barrel, preventing even the most skillful soldiers from firing more than three times a minute, rifles nevertheless made it much more difficult for attacking troops to overwhelm a defense. Far more northern troops than southern troops had rifles in 1862, but the Confederates around Richmond still benefited from the trenches and walls of their defenses.

Lincoln and McClellan believed that Washington faced a direct threat from Confederate troops in the Shenandoah Valley under the command of the increasingly impressive Stonewall Jackson. Jackson had already developed a reputation as a general who fought cleverly, quickly, and unpredictably. For three months

in the spring of 1862, Jackson maneuvered his men back and forth, up and down the valley, creating the impression that his forces were larger than they were and that they could attack anywhere, any time. As a result, the Union divided its forces, depriving McClellan's invasion of tens of thousands of soldiers that would have otherwise been available for the assault on Richmond.

The Union and the Rebel forces tested one another around Richmond in May and June, inflicting heavy casualties in battles that settled nothing. Robert E. Lee replaced Joseph Johnston, wounded in battle, as general of the Confederate forces in Virginia. Lee had no towering reputation at that point; the South did not exult nor did the North tremble. But Lee quickly proved himself aggressive and daring, much like Jackson. He almost immediately planned an attack against the larger force under McClellan's command. Lee sent out J. E. B. Stuart, his cavalry leader, who rode all the way around McClellan's troops, reconnoitering their position, stealing their supplies, and humiliating them with his skill and bravery. Stuart reported that part of McClellan's troops were vulnerable to attack. Lee brought Jackson and his men to join in an assault. The resulting prolonged conflict around Richmond, which became known as the Seven Days' Battles, did not distinguish either side. The Confederates' offensive did not work as planned and Jackson failed to carry out his part of the assault. For the North's part, McClellan, though possessing far more troops than his opponents, believed himself outnumbered and sacrificed his advantage. Thirty thousand men had been killed and wounded.

Slavery Under Attack

By the summer of 1862 the war seemed to have reached a stalemate, strength against strength. Both the Union and the Confederacy claimed important victories and both believed a decisive battle could still win the war. The North took heart because Union ships controlled the coasts and rivers on the perimeter of the South even as Union troops pushed deep into Tennessee and Mississippi. The Confederacy took comfort because vast expanses of rich southern farmland and millions of productive slaves remained beyond the reach of Union control.

President Lincoln, while detesting slavery personally, feared that a campaign against bondage would di-

vide the North and undermine his administration. As the war dragged into its second year, however, even Northerners who did not oppose slavery on moral grounds could see that slavery offered the South a major advantage. Slaves in the fields meant more white Southerners on the battlefields; slaves in the cooking tents and at the reins of wagons meant more Confederate soldiers shouldering guns. Most important, black Southerners themselves pressed slavery as a problem on the Union armies. Wherever those armies went, slaves of every description fled to the Federals as refugees. The Union called the black people who made their way to the Union ranks "contrabands," a word usually used to describe smuggled goods. The term revealed the confusion among white Northerners about the status of the black people in their midst. Were they fugitive slave property or people who had made themselves free by escaping bondage? While some Union officers returned the slaves to their owners, other officers seized the opportunity to strike against slavery.

Northern leaders confronted such issues most directly near Port Royal, South Carolina. When the Union forces overran the Sea Islands along the coast in 1862, the relatively few whites who lived there fled, leaving behind 10,000 slaves. Almost immediately, various groups of Northerners began to vie for the opportunity to reshape southern society as they thought it should be shaped. The Sea Islands claimed some of the largest and richest plantations in the South, growing rare and expensive long-staple cotton. Union leaders felt it crucial that freed slaves prove they would work willingly and effectively. Female abolitionist schoolteachers journeyed down from New England, while men mixing motives of profit and reform came from New York City and the Northwest to demonstrate that plantations run on the principles of free labor could be both productive and humane.

The black South Carolinians who lived on the islands both welcomed and struggled with these white Northerners. While the former slaves valued the opportunity to learn to read and write and wanted land of their own, they did not always appreciate lessons from the newcomer whites about religion and agriculture. Black people knew how to farm and knew their God. Not only in South Carolina, but wherever the Union army penetrated, officers and civilians sought to control black labor and rich land. Sometimes, federal officials decreed that the freed people could sign contracts with whomever they chose—but they had to sign contracts with someone. In other times and

The Sea Islands of South Carolina quickly became a testing ground for northern ideals. Missionaries and teachers of both genders came to the islands to instruct the newly liberated residents in matters both secular and religious.

places, Union leaders followed bolder experiments, permitting black people to take responsibility for some of the land they had worked as slaves. Some white Northerners, including military leaders, proposed seizing land from former slaveholders to give to the former slaves.

General David Hunter, a man of abolitionist sympathies, took advantage of his position in Port Royal in the late spring of 1862 to organize a number of black military units and to declare slavery abolished in South Carolina, Georgia, and Florida. Lincoln revoked Hunter's proclamation, however, determined that he, not generals in the field, would control the volatile issue of slavery. Lincoln did not envision the immediate emancipation decreed by Hunter, with no compensation to slaveholders and with former slaves living alongside their former masters. Lincoln thought that sectional reunion demanded that slavery end in the United States as it had elsewhere in the Western Hemisphere: gradually, with payments to the slaveholders for their loss of property. Ideally, Lincoln argued, the former slaves would be colonized beyond the borders of the United States, perhaps in Haiti or Liberia.

Lincoln also resisted those members of his party and his cabinet who thought that black men should be enlisted into the Union army. Such Republicans, often called "Radicals" for their support of black rights, did all they could to turn the Union cause into an antislavery cause. The Radicals passed laws that forbade northern commanders to return refugee slaves to their former masters and they ended (albeit gradually and with compensation) slavery in the District of Columbia. Many northern Democrats bitterly opposed such expansion of the war's purposes and means, warning that abolition would only embitter and embolden the Confederates, making peace that much more difficult to attain. Democrats sympathetic to the South, called "Copperheads" by their opponents, marched under the motto "The Constitution as it is and the Union as it was." They wanted slavery to remain in place so that the South would come back into the nation and the bloodshed would stop.

Lincoln sought to steer a course between the Radicals and the Copperheads, between the immediate abolitionists on the one hand and those who would leave slavery entrenched in a reunified United States on the other. But in the summer of 1862 he moved closer to an assault on slavery. The Union army had strengthened its position in Kentucky and Missouri and it no longer appeared that the border states could effectively align themselves with the Confederates, no matter how disgruntled they might be with the Union. Similarly, Lincoln came to see that the southern

Unionists, upon whom he had pinned so many hopes in 1860 and 1861, could not or would not organize effective opposition to the Confederacy from within. Lincoln decided that to win the war he would have to hit slavery. "It may as well be understood, once for all," Lincoln announced, "that I shall not surrender this game leaving any available card unplayed."

On July 22, 1862, Lincoln and his cabinet authorized Federal military leaders to take whatever secessionist property they needed and to destroy any property that aided the Confederacy. That meant that Union officers could protect the black men and women who fled to northern camps, using them to work behind the lines. Lincoln decided to wait for a victory on the battlefield before announcing the most dramatic part of his plan: that as of January 1, 1863, he would declare all slaves in areas controlled by the Confederates free. While this proclamation would free no slaves under Union control in the border states, it ruled out compromise that would end the war and bring the South back into the Union with slavery. Knowing that this announcement would unleash harsh criticism in the North, Lincoln wanted to wait until the North was flush with confidence before he announced this Preliminary Emancipation Proclamation. When and where that victory might occur, however, was by no means clear in July of 1862.

Second Manassas and Antietam

Confidence actually ran higher in the Confederacy than in the Union during the second summer of the war. The Union, after all, could draw little solace from McClellan's sluggish performance in the ferocious Seven Days' Battles outside of Richmond in June. His insistence in the battles' aftermath that no Virginia property, including slaves, should be confiscated showed that he was out of step with the Republican leadership. Lincoln placed Henry Halleck, who advocated a more aggressive stance toward southern civilians and their slaves, in charge of all Union troops. The president put John Pope, who had been fighting in the West, in charge of the new Army of Virginia. Pope prided himself on his harshness toward Confederate property, spies, and guerillas. McClellan still commanded troops, but his role had been restricted.

The new Union leaders decided to remove McClellan's troops from the peninsula of Virginia and consolidate them, under the joint command of Pope, with troops from the Shenandoah Valley. The forces began to move from the peninsula in August, transported by water to an area closer to Washington. Lee watched this process with a mixture of excitement and concern. Even though a massive unified army in northern Virginia posed a long-term threat of considerable consequence, the withdrawal created a temporary opportunity for the Confederacy. Lee decided to attack Pope's troops while McClellan's were withdrawing. Lee hoped to occupy as much territory as possible, resting and re-supplying his troops while complicating Union efforts to unify their forces.

Lee's plan worked better than he could have expected. Stonewall Jackson attacked Pope's men and pillaged a large federal supply depot at Manassas—on virtually the same ground where the first battle of that name had been fought a long year before. Pope then fell under attack by James Longstreet's troops, who drove the new Yankee commander back into Washington. With McClellan no longer threatening Richmond and Pope posing no danger to northern Virginia, Lee decided to seize the advantage and push into Maryland. He believed that large numbers of Marylanders would rush to the Confederate cause, showing the North that the Confederacy could not be defeated. Lee had another audience in mind as well: England and France. In the wake of Union indecision and defeat in the summer of 1862, leaders in both countries were leaning toward recognition of the Confederacy. A major victory in northern territory, Lee felt certain, would prove that the South deserved the support of the major powers.

Lee acted so confidently because he knew he would face George McClellan again. On September 17, the two old adversaries fell into battle once more, this time at Antietam Creek, near Sharpsburg, Maryland. The Confederates had 35,000 men to McClellan's 72,000, but the Southerners held the defensive ground. The terrible battle ended as so many had ended in the eastern battlefields over the preceding months, in confusion and stalemate. More men were killed, wounded, or declared missing on this day than on any other day in the Civil War: 13,000 for the Confederacy and 12,000 for the Union. Lee had lost nearly a third of his army; McClellan, despite his numerical advantage, had been unable to destroy the enemy.

Neither side could be satisfied with the battle's outcome, but the North made the best of the situation. Lincoln decided that Antietam represented enough of

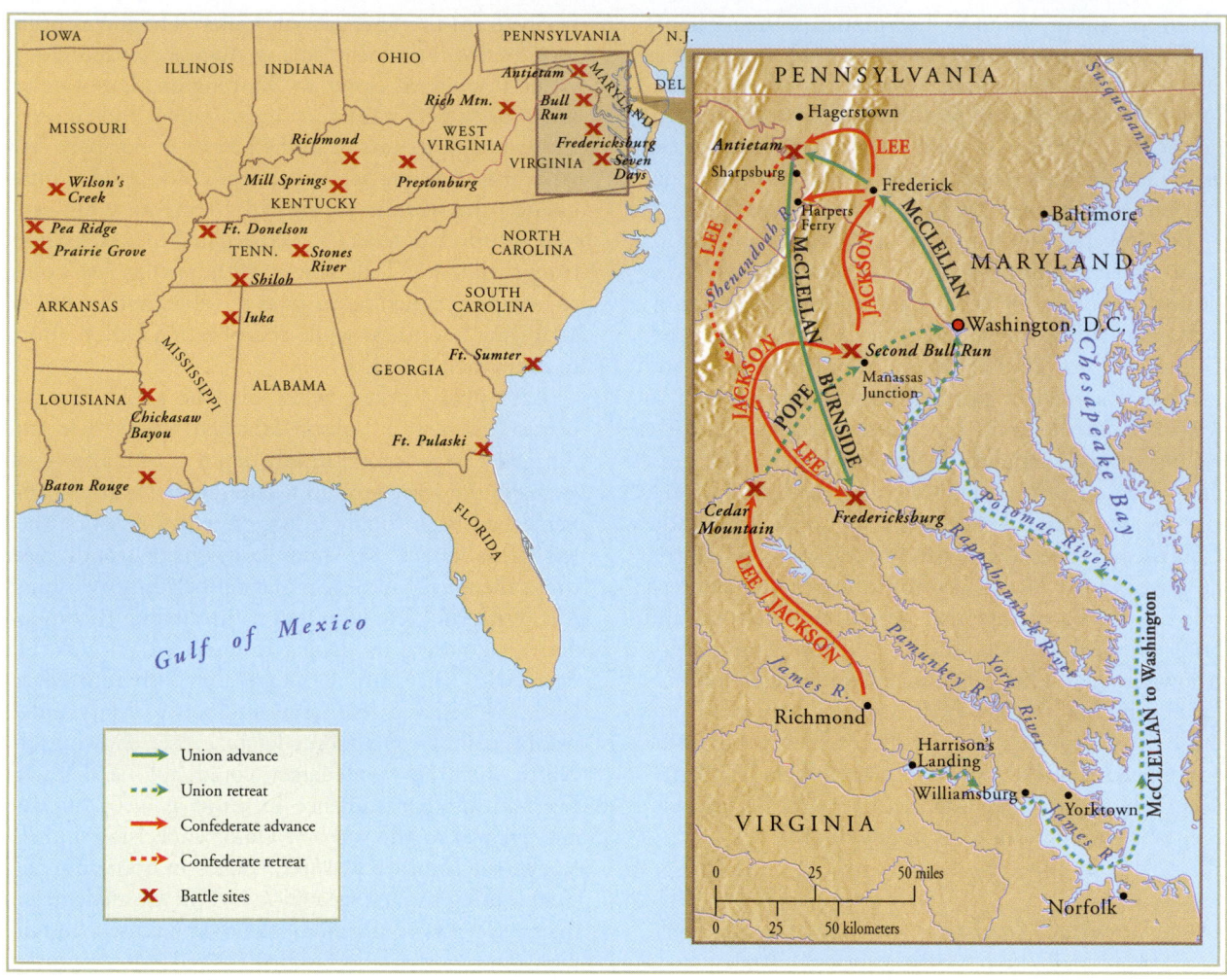

Map 14.4 | The Civil War in the East, Summer and Fall 1862

a victory to justify his announcement of the Preliminary Emancipation Proclamation. The European powers decided that they would withhold their support for the Confederacy for the time being. The Confederacy decided that they would pull back into Virginia to fight another day. Things could have turned out very differently at this juncture. Had McClellan destroyed Lee's army—and it appears in retrospect that he might have done so—the Confederacy might have given up its claims for independence before slavery had been ended. Had Lee merely held his ground in Virginia after driving McClellan away from Richmond and Pope back into Washington, on the other hand, England and France might have offered mediation—

and the North might well have accepted, again without the end of slavery. As it was, however, both the North and the South would fight again and again.

Stalemate

While Northerners and Southerners slaughtered one another in Maryland with little clear advantage gained by either side, troops also ranged over Kentucky and Tennessee. Southern forces under the command of Braxton Bragg pushed far into Kentucky in the fall of 1862, determined to regain ground lost early in the war. Confederates believed that Kentuckians, like

The sunken road where Confederates battled Union soldiers on this Maryland battlefield became known as "Bloody Lane." Bodies piled up six deep on the bloodiest single day of the Civil War.

Marylanders, would rush to the southern flag if given a chance. Both in Kentucky and in Maryland, sympathy for the Confederacy did not lead people to enlist or even to share their food or horses. People had little confidence that the Confederates could prevail in Kentucky and did not want to risk all they had in support of a losing cause. Although the Confederates never suffered sharp defeat in Kentucky, they had too few men to occupy the state. Rather than risk losing his army, Bragg pulled his men into a more defensible position in Tennessee. As in Maryland at about the same time, bold Confederate offensives had ended without any tangible gain.

By the summer and fall of 1862, many men had died to little apparent purpose. Lincoln decided that generals in both the East and the West must be removed; George McClellan and Don Carlos Buell seemed too slow to react, too cautious—and perhaps too inclined to side with the Democrats. Lincoln replaced Buell with William S. Rosecrans and replaced McClellan with Ambrose E. Burnside, an appealing man uncertain that he was qualified for the job entrusted to him. His doubts proved to be well founded.

In November, Burnside decided to establish a new base for yet another assault on Richmond. He moved his troops to Fredericksburg, Virginia, and launched an attack on a virtually impregnable Confederate position at Marye's Heights. With Southerners able to fire down on them at will from protected positions, over 12,000 Union soldiers died as they tried repeatedly to ford the Rappahannock River and storm the heights. At battle's end, both armies remained where they had been at the battle's beginning.

The North fell into mourning, humiliation, and anger at this sacrifice. Officers as well as enlisted men made no secret of their loss of faith in Burnside, complaining bitterly through official and unofficial channels. In Tennessee, Rosecrans felt that he had to move against Bragg to demonstrate Union resolve and power. The two armies clashed on the last day of 1862 at Stones River near Murfreesboro, ending the year with a battle like so many others in this year. The two sides, losing about a third of their men each, the worst proportion in the entire war, fought to a virtual draw.

The winter of 1862–1863 saw the North and the South precariously balanced, both against one another

After the slaughter at Marye's Heights in December 1862, Confederates stripped the bodies of Union soldiers of their boots and uniforms. Here, northern burial parties inter their dead.

and within their own societies. On the battlefield, the South had made impressive showings at Fredericksburg and at Second Manassas, but the northern army had held Kentucky and Maryland. The Confederacy still possessed Vicksburg, high on a bluff on the Mississippi River, but Grant and Sherman were planning ways to take the city. Slaves ran to Union armies at every chance and plantations decayed. The Preliminary Emancipation Proclamation had given the Union effort a new purpose and new credibility with liberals in Europe, especially in England, but Lincoln faced mounting criticism within his own party and a growing threat from disgruntled Democrats. The North needed victories. Everything depended on the men in the field.

CONCLUSION

The bloody sacrifice without decisive victory of the Seven Days and Antietam fed disillusionment on both sides. The governments in both the North and the South found themselves the objects of bitter criticism from political opponents, newspapers, the public, and even former supporters. Military officers squabbled among themselves and with civilian leaders. The only thing people could agree on was that the war would

not end soon, that the death and suffering would continue.

The preceding year and a half had seen events and changes no one could have predicted, warfare on a scale no one could have imagined. Eighteen months after Lincoln had begun his journey to Washington to become president, war had become a way of life. The boundaries between the Union and the Confederacy had been firmly drawn. The governments of both sides had begun to function effectively. The first volunteer units of both armies had been mobilized and had seen action. Both the South and the North had claimed military victories. The Confederacy recalled the battle at Manassas with pride, while the Union took comfort in the steady success of its navy. The first international crisis, the *Trent* affair, had passed without dragging a major European power into the conflict. But in late 1862 both the North and the South felt that their cause must be clarified and given greater purpose if the war were to be anything more than sheer carnage.

RECOMMENDED READINGS

Boritt, Gabor. *Why the Civil War Came* (1996) gives a useful overview of recent thinking on this much-debated historical topic.

Crofts, Daniel W. *Reluctant Confederates: Upper South Unionists in the Secession Crisis* (1989) analyzes the crucial border states with keen insight.

Jones, Howard. *The Union in Peril: The Crisis over British Intervention in the Civil War* (1992) provides a fresh interpretation of a critical episode.

McPherson, James M. *Battle Cry of Freedom: The Civil War Era* (1988) is the fullest one-volume account of the Civil War.

Paludan, Phillip Shaw. *A People's Contest: The Union and the Civil War, 1861–1865* (1988) paints a full portrait of the North during war.

Parish, Peter J. *The American Civil War* (1975) offers an elegant synthesis.

Royster, Charles. *The Destructive War: William Tecumseh Sherman, Stonewall Jackson, and the Americans* (1991) is an original and disturbing meditation on war.

Simpson, Brooks D. *America's Civil War* (1996) is a fine brief interpretation with a useful bibliography.

Thomas, Emory M. *The Confederate Nation, 1861–1865* (1979) is the standard account.

Overviews

Catton, Bruce. *The Centennial History of the Civil War,* vol. 1: *The Coming Fury* (1961); vol. 2: *Terrible Swift Sword* (1963); and vol. 3, *Never Call Retreat* (1965).

Freehling, William W. *The Reintegration of American History: Slavery and the Civil War* (1994).

McPherson, James M. *What They Fought For, 1861–1865* (1994).

Nevins, Allan. *The War for the Union,* 4 vols. (1959–1971)

Foote, Shelby. *The Civil War: A Narrative* (1958–1974).

Secession and the South

Barney, William L. *The Secessionist Impulse: Alabama and Mississippi in 1860* (1974).

Channing, Steven A. *A Crisis of Fear: Secession in South Carolina* (1970).

Davis, William C. *"A Government of Our Own": The Making of the Confederacy* (1994).

Faust, Drew Gilpin. *The Creation of Confederate Nationalism: Ideology and Identity in the Civil War South* (1988).

Johnson, Michael P. *Toward a Patriarchal Republic: The Secession of Georgia* (1977).

Klein, Maury. *Days of Defiance: Sumter, Secession, and the Coming of the Civil War* (1997).

Rable, George C. *The Confederate Republic: A Revolution Against Politics* (1994).

Snay, Mitchell. *The Gospel of Disunion* (1993).

Biographies

Davis, William C. *Jefferson Davis: The Man and His Hour* (1991).

Fellman, Michael. *Citizen Sherman: A Life of William Tecumseh Sherman* (1995).

McFeely, William S. *Grant: A Biography* (1981).

Oates, Stephen B. *A Woman of Valor: Clara Barton and the Civil War* (1994).

Paludan, Phillip Shaw. *The Presidency of Abraham Lincoln* (1994).

Robertson, James I. Jr., *Stonewall Jackson: The Man, the Soldier, and the Legend* (1997).

Sears, Stephen W. *George B. McClellan: The Young Napoleon* (1988).

Simpson, Brooks D. *Let Us Have Peace: Ulysses S. Grant and the Politics of War and Reconstruction, 1861–1868* (1991).

Thomas, Emory M. *Robert E. Lee: A Biography* (1995).

The Border States

Curry, Richard O. *A House Divided: A Study of Statehood Politics and the Copperhead Movement in West Virginia* (1964).

Fellman, Michael. *Inside War: The Guerilla Conflict in the Civil War* (1989).

Harrison, Lowell. *The Civil War and Kentucky* (1975)

Naval History

Fowler, William M. Jr., *Under Two Flags: The American Navy in the Civil War* (1990).

Merrill, James M. *Battle Flags South: The Story of the Civil War Navies on Western Waters* (1970).

Wise, Stephen R. *Lifeline of the Confederacy: Blockade Running During the Civil War* (1988).

Foreign Policy

Crook, David P. *The North, the South, and the Powers, 1861–1865* (1974).

Owsley, Frank L. *King Cotton Diplomacy* (1959).

Warren, Gordon H. *Fountains of Discontent: The "Trent" Affair and the Freedom of the Seas* (1981).

Paying for War

Ball, Douglas B. *Financial Failure and Confederate Defeat* (1990).

Hammond, Bray. *Sovereignty and the Empty Purse: Banks and Politics in the Civil War* (1970).

The War in the West

Hauptman, Laurence M. *Between Two Fires: American Indians in the Civil War* (1995).

Josephy, Alvin M. Jr., *The Civil War in the American West* (1991).

THE WOUNDED

Many of the men waiting to be taken to the hospital tent would not emerge alive.

Chapter 15

Blood and Freedom:

1863–1867

IT WAS NOT clear in 1863 or even 1864 that the North was going to win the Civil War. Over the course of those years, people on both sides believed that Lincoln might not be reelected, that European powers might intervene, that the North might lose its will to fight, that one key battle could swing the outcome in the favor of the South. The Civil War enveloped the entire nation, home front and battlefield alike. The outcome of a battle could win an election or trigger a riot, while events at home affected the leaders' decisions of when and where to fight. In the North, the strong political opposition to Abraham Lincoln and his policies exerted a constant pressure on his policies and his conduct of the war. In the South, slaves abandoned plantations and white families' hardship led soldiers to rethink their loyalties. Those struggles continued after the guns had fallen silent.

PEOPLE AT WAR: SPRING 1863

Both Northerners and Southerners expected the spring of 1863 to bring the climax of the Civil War. Much had been decided, organized, and mobilized over the preceding two years. The generals and the battlefields determined the outcome of battles, but perhaps the wives, slaves, workers, bureaucrats, draft dodgers, and politicians behind the lines would determine the outcome of the war.

Life in the Field

Soldiers eventually got used to the miseries of sleeping on the ground, poorly cooked food, driving rain, and endless mud. They might even become adjusted to the lice and dirt that flourished in the camps of both the Union and the Confederacy. They learned to adapt to gambling, drinking, cursing, and prostitution, either by succumbing to the temptations or by steeling their resolve against them. They could toughen themselves to the intermittent mails and the arrival of bad news from home. Confederates managed to march with shoes falling off their feet. Over time, veterans could even learn to absorb the deaths of men with whom they had shared so much.

But even the most stalwart of soldiers could not adapt to the constant threat of diseases such as diarrhea, dysentery, typhoid, malaria, measles, diphtheria,

CHRONOLOGY

1863

January	1	Second Emancipation Proclamation
	25	Hooker replaces Burnside as commander of Army of the Potomac
February	25	Union Congress passes National Bank Act
		Grant unsuccessfully looks for "back door" to Vicksburg
		Trans-Mississippi area comes under command of Confederate General Kirby Smith
March	3	Union Congress passes Conscription Act
	26	Confederate Congress passes Impressment Act
April	2	Bread riot in Richmond
May	1	Confederate Congress gives more power to War Department
	5	Clement Vallandigham, "copperhead leader," arrested
	6	Culmination of Lee's victory over Hooker at Chancellorsville
	1–18	Grant's successful campaign in Mississippi
	10	Death of Stonewall Jackson
June	3	Lee begins advance to North
	15	Lee's army crosses Potomac
	28	Meade replaces Hooker as commander of Army of Potomac
July	1–3	Union victory at Gettysburg
	4	Vicksburg surrenders to Grant
	8	Port Hudson surrenders to Union
	13–14	Lee retreats across Potomac into Virginia
	13–16	New York City draft riots
	18	Black troops fight at Fort Wagner, South Carolina
September	8	Union captures Fort Wagner
	19–20	Rosecrans defeated by Bragg at Chickamauga
		Confederate congressional elections go against Jefferson Davis
October	17	Grant assumes control of Union forces in West
		Elections show Republicans growing stronger
November	19	Lincoln's Gettysburg Address
	25	Union victory at Chattanooga
December	8	Lincoln proclamation of amnesty and proposals for reconstruction

1864

January		Widening rift between Lincoln and Congress on reconstruction
February		Confederate Congress assumes new powers of taxation, impressment of slaves
March	9	Grant assumes command of all Union forces
	16	Alexander Stephens attacks "despotism" of Davis administration
April	12	Confederate general Nathan Bedford Forrest captures Fort Pillow, Tennessee; allegedly massacres African-American troops
May	4	Union begins offensive in Virginia and Georgia
	5–6	Battle of the Wilderness in Virginia
June	3	Union victory at Cold Harbor
	7	Lincoln renominated by Republicans; Andrew Johnson as vice president

CHRONOLOGY

	15–18	Union fails in attack on Petersburg; begins nine-month siege
	27	Sherman defeated at Kennesaw Mountain, Georgia
July	4	Lincoln pocket vetoes Wade-Davis Reconstruction bill
	17	Hood replaces Johnston as Confederate commander in Atlanta
	30	Union failure at Battle of the Crater near Petersburg
August	5	Union victory at Mobile Bay
		Republicans discuss removal of Lincoln as candidate
	29	Northern Democrats nominate McClellan for president
September	2	Sherman captures Atlanta
	19–22	Sheridan's victories in Shenandoah Valley
October	19	Union victory at Cedar Creek, ending Confederate threat in Shenandoah
	23	Union victory in Missouri ends fighting west of the Mississippi
November	8	Lincoln reelected president
	15–16	Beginning of Sherman's march from Atlanta to the Atlantic
	30	Union victory at Franklin, Tennessee
December	15–16	Union victory at Nashville
	21	Savannah falls to Sherman
1865		
January	31	Congress passes Thirteenth Amendment, lending federal sanction of slavery
February	1	Sherman begins march through Carolinas
	6	Lee becomes commander of all Confederate forces
	17	Columbia, South Carolina, burned; Confederates evacuate Charleston
March	3	Congress creates Bureau of Refugees, Freedmen, and Abandoned Lands (Freedmen's Bureau)
	4	Lincoln's second inauguration
		Sherman completes march through Carolinas
	13	Confederate army authorizes recruitment of slaves into army
	30	Grant begins final assault in Virginia
April	2	Fall of Petersburg to Union
	3	Fall of Richmond to Union
	4	Jefferson Davis's last appeal to people of the South
	9	Lee surrenders to Grant at Appomattox Court House
	14–15	Lincoln assassinated
	26	Joseph E. Johnston surrenders in North Carolina
May	10	Jefferson Davis captured
	26	Edmund Kirby Smith surrenders trans-Mississipp region, bringing the war to formal end
		Former Confederate states hold constitutional conventions through December; pass "black codes"
		African Americans hold conventions in South
December	18	Thirteenth Amendment to Constitution ratified, abolishing slavery

CHRONOLOGY

1866	
February	Johnson vetoes Freedmen's Bureau Bill
April	Congress passes Civil Rights Act and Freedmen's Bureau renewal over Johnson's veto
May	Riots in New Orleans and Memphis
June	Congress approves Fourteenth Amendment
	Ku Klux Klan formed
	Most ex-Confederate states reject Fourteenth Amendment

1867		
March	2	Congress passes Reconstruction Act and Tenure of Office Act
		Constitutional conventions in southern states
August	12	Johnson dismisses Secretary of War Stanton, triggering impeachment proceedings
		First elections in South under Reconstruction Act

and scarlet fever. As bloody as the battles were, disease killed twice as many men as died from the guns of the enemy. Many doctors of the Civil War era used the same instruments of surgery on soldier after soldier, unwittingly spreading disease to patients already suffering from amputation or bullet wounds. After every battle, screams filled the night as surgeons sawed off legs and arms, feet and hands, in often vain hopes of stopping gangrene.

Purposes

The North fought for ideals of union and democracy; the South fought for ideals of self-determination. But soldiers fought for more personal purposes as well. Men acted courageously not only because they believed in the official political purposes for which they were fighting, but also because they wanted to be admired by the people at home, because they wanted to be manly, because they wanted to do their part for their comrades, because they wanted to bring the war to a quicker end, and because they grew to hate the enemy.

Soldiers enlisted in their communities, as members of communities. Many men fought alongside their brothers, uncles, cousins. A steady stream of letters flowed back and forth between the units and the families and neighbors back home. Gossip, praise, and condemnation flourished, as acts of bravery or cowardice became magnified through distance and repetition. Any soldier who planned to return home knew that his deeds in the war would live with him the rest of his life. As a result, even fearful or halfhearted soldiers might throw themselves into battle to demonstrate their courage.

While about three-fifths of Civil War soldiers were over twenty-one at the age of enlistment—considerably older than the armies of the twentieth century—the largest single group of soldiers was eighteen. They came of age during the war, defined themselves during the war. For those who passed the birthdays of their late teens or early twenties on the battlefields, the transition to manhood became inseparable from the war. To be manly meant more than the simple ability to inflict violence on the enemy. It meant pride, responsibility, loyalty, and obedience. Every battle became a test of manhood, which could not be won once and forever but had to be proven every time it was challenged under fire. Some of the bravery and sacrifice of the war grew out of boys' desperate desire to be thought men.

Courage developed, too, out of hatred. While neither the Union nor the Confederacy developed effective twentieth-century style propaganda machinery, people on both sides spread the worst stories and rumors about one another. Newspapers printed exaggerated or fabricated atrocity reports about the enemy.

The longer the war went on the more people felt they had to hate one another to justify so much bloodshed. Violence, on the battlefield and against property and civilians, was often sheer vengeance.

The sermons men heard in the camps told them they were fighting on the side of the right. The Old Testament afforded rich imagery and compelling stories of violence inflicted for good causes. Many Americans believed that God enacted His will directly in human affairs. As the war ground on, the leaders, the soldiers, and the civilians of both sides came to feel that events were more than the product of human decision or even courage. Surely, they told themselves, so much suffering and sacrifice had to be for a larger purpose.

The Problems of the Confederate Government

Convinced that greedy merchants were holding supplies of flour until prices rose even higher, in the spring of 1863 poor women in Richmond rushed into the streets of the Confederate capital. They broke open the stores of merchants accused of hoarding the precious staple, taking what they needed and what they considered fairly to be theirs. Jefferson Davis went to plead with the angry women. The threat of being arrested and the promise of free supplies broke up the riot, but similar events occurred in several other southern cities. No one could tell when even larger riots might erupt again.

The rioters were not the only ones who took what they needed. Confederate officers in the field took— "impressed"—what their troops required. The officers forced reluctant farmers to accept whatever prices the army offered, in an increasingly worthless currency. In the spring of 1863, the Confederate government attempted to curb the worst abuses of this practice in the Impressment Act. If a farmer did not think the prices he or she received were fair (and they were almost never as high as they could get through private sale), the case could be appealed before local authorities. In practice, however, this cumbersome system failed. Farmers hid their produce from officers and resented it when they were forced to sell. Impressment, like the draft and the "twenty negro law," eroded civilian support for the Confederate government.

The southern government could not afford to lose this or any other kind of support, for its power, weak at the beginning of the conflict, became even weaker over time. While the absence of political parties originally appeared to be a sign of the South's consensus, that absence eventually undermined what original consensus the Confederacy had enjoyed. Jefferson Davis, without a party mechanism to discipline those who spoke out against him, could not remove enemies from office or threaten them with loss of party patronage. Davis's own vice president, Alexander Stephens, turned against the president soon after the war began. Stephens became a persistent and outspoken critic of the Confederate president throughout the rest of his term, actively undermining support for Davis and even allying with avowed enemies of Davis and his policies.

The Confederate government faced a fundamental dilemma. The whole point of secession had been to move political power closer to localities, protecting slavery in particular and self-determination in general. States' rights had been the rallying cry. The government of the Confederacy, however, had to centralize power in order to protect the states. If the armies were to be fed and clothed, if diplomats were to make a plausible case for the Confederacy's nationhood, if soldiers were to be mobilized, then the Confederate government had to exercise greater power than its creators had expected or intended. Jefferson Davis continually struggled with this tension. For every Southerner who considered Davis too weak, another considered the president dangerously powerful.

The Northern Homefront

In the North, the war heightened the strong differences between the Democrats and the Republicans. The Democrats won significant victories in congressional elections throughout much of the North in the fall and winter of 1862, testifying to the depth and breadth of the opposition to Lincoln and his conduct of the war. Wealthy businessmen in the cities of the northeast were eager to reestablish trade with their former southern partners, while Irish immigrants wanted to end the risk of the draft and competition from freed slaves. Some Democrats in the northwest talked of seceding from both the South and the East, which they saw as the base of the rich and the Republicans. Many citizens of Ohio, Indiana, and Illinois, whose families had come from the South, wanted to renew the southern connections that had been broken by the war.

Black men had called for their inclusion in the U.S. Army from the beginning of the war. In the spring of 1863 the U.S. Colored Troops were formed and over 180,000 African-American men fought for the Union over the next two years.

The Union passed its Conscription Act in March of 1863 because disease, wounds, and desertion had depleted the ranks faster than they could be replaced. When drafted, a man could appear for duty, hire a substitute to fight in his place, or simply pay a fee of $300 directly to the government. State and federal governments often paid bounties—signing bonuses—to those who volunteered. More than a few men, struck by the possibilities of such ready cash, took the bounties and then promptly deserted and moved to another locality to claim another bounty.

The opposition to the Lincoln government raised crucial issues. How much dissent could a wartime government tolerate? With the North claiming to fight for liberty, what limitations on freedom of speech and protest could it enforce? A Democratic congressman

from Ohio, Clement Vallandigham, tested those limits in the spring of 1863. Hating both secessionists and abolitionists, Vallandigham refused to obey a general's orders to stop criticizing the Lincoln administration. He was arrested, tried before a military court, and sentenced to imprisonment for the rest of the war. Lincoln was dismayed by these events. They fueled the charge common throughout the North that he was a tyrant, trampling on the rights of Americans. The president commuted Vallandigham's sentence, sending him to the Confederates in Tennessee, hoping to make Vallandigham appear a southern sympathizer rather than a martyr to the cause of free speech. Vallandigham quickly escaped to Canada, however, where he continued his criticisms. Ohio Democrats defiantly nominated Vallandigham for governor in the elections to be held in the fall of 1863. If things

continued to go badly for the Union, who knew what kind of success a critic of Lincoln might find?

African-American Soldiers

Though northern civilian and military leaders remained deeply divided and ambivalent about black freedom, it became clear to everyone that freed slaves could be of great value to the Union. In May 1863, the War Department created the Bureau of Colored Troops. White men of abolitionist leanings sought to become officers for these units, eager to show what they and their men could do. Generals in the field accepted into service many southern black men who had traveled to northern camps.

At first, black recruits found themselves restricted to noncombat roles and a lower rate of pay: ten dollars a month versus the thirteen dollars a month and three-fifty clothing allowance given white soldiers. Black men, though eager to serve, protested that they could not support their families on such amounts and that their lives were worth just as much as their white compatriots. African Americans knew, and coveted, the rights and privileges of other Americans. They wrote petitions and appealed to higher authorities, often in the language of the Declaration of Independence and the Constitution.

Confederate officials who expected black soldiers to make reluctant or cowed fighters soon discovered otherwise. In May of 1863 two black regiments stormed, seven times, a heavily fortified Confederate installation at Port Hudson, Louisiana. Soon thereafter, black soldiers found themselves on the other side of the barricades. At Milliken's Bend, Louisiana, they fought Confederates hand-to-hand, desperately wielding swords and bayonets against white men. Northern newspapers echoed the words of praise from generals in the field: "No troops could be more determined or more daring."

African-American men in the North rushed to the recruiting tables. Frederick Douglass, the leading spokesman for black Americans, celebrated the enlistments: "Once let the black man get upon his person the brass letters, *U.S.*; let him get an eagle on his button, and a musket on his shoulder, and bullets in his pocket, and there is no power on earth which can deny that he has earned the right to citizenship in the United States." From Rhode Island to Ohio, black troops prepared to head south. Even more African-

American units formed in the states of the occupied South, as formerly enslaved men became soldiers of the United States Army.

THE BATTLEFIELDS OF SUMMER: 1863

Everything seemed in place for a climactic culmination of the war in the summer of 1863. The Union had almost severed the western half of the Confederacy from the eastern; the Union army received a relentless flow of men and arms; the Union had penetrated deep into Tennessee and stood on the threshold of Georgia. On the other hand, the Confederate army had toughened itself to its disadvantages and learned to make the most of the advantages it enjoyed. It appeared to be strength against strength as the mud dried and the fighting season began.

Vicksburg and Chancellorsville

Union leaders needed all the help they could get in early 1863, for pivotal battles clearly loomed in the summer to come. Grant and Sherman remained frustrated in their goal of seizing Vicksburg; Rosecrans faced Bragg in Tennessee; Lee's army had yet to be decisively defeated despite the men, resources, and determination thrown into battle against him. Lee would face General Joseph Hooker. Lincoln, in one more attempt to find an effective leader, had chosen Hooker to replace Ambrose Burnside. Throughout the spring, "Fighting Joe" Hooker energized his men and repaired some of the damage to morale and readiness inflicted at Fredericksburg. But no one knew if he would be able to handle Lee.

The Northern public was especially impatient with Grant and Sherman, who, it seemed, would be stranded forever outside Vicksburg. Grant knew the delays threatened his command. Vicksburg, heavily fortified by both geography and the Confederates, seemed most vulnerable to attack from the southeast, but to get there Grant would have to find a way to move his men across the Mississippi River without landing them in swamps that could swallow an army. Throughout the long wet winter, Grant had tried one experiment after another, including digging canals. Nothing worked.

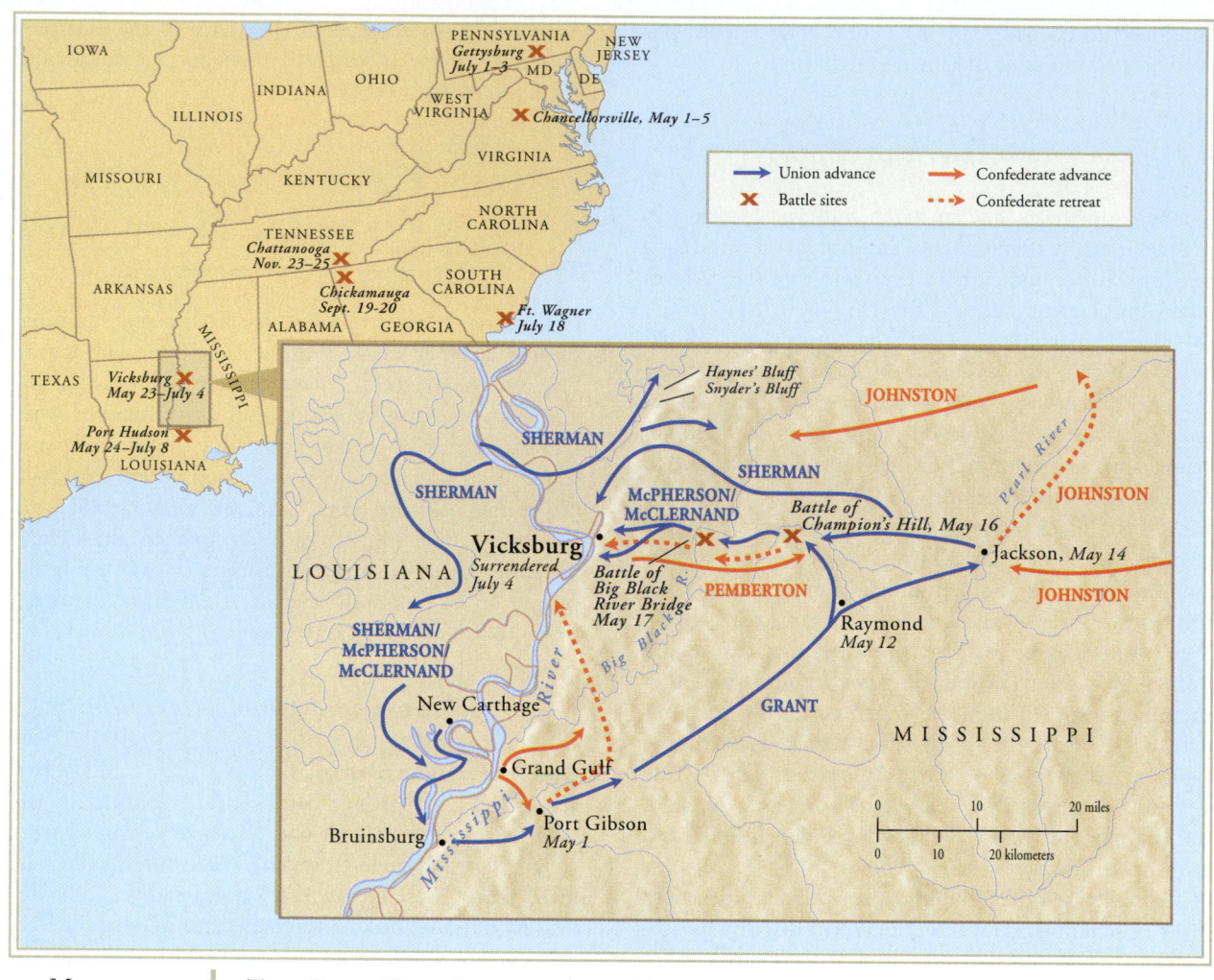

Union advance　Confederate advance
Battle sites　Confederate retreat

IOWA
PENNSYLVANIA
Gettysburg
July 1–3　MD
NEW JERSEY
DE
ILLINOIS
INDIANA
OHIO
WEST VIRGINIA
X Chancellorsville, May 1–5
MISSOURI
KENTUCKY
VIRGINIA
NORTH CAROLINA
TENNESSEE
Chattanooga
Nov. 23–25 X
ARKANSAS
Chickamauga
Sept. 19–20 X
SOUTH CAROLINA
ALABAMA
GEORGIA
X Ft. Wagner
July 18
TEXAS
Vicksburg
May 23–July 4 X
MISSISSIPPI
Port Hudson
May 24–July 8 X
LOUISIANA

Haynes' Bluff
Snyder's Bluff
JOHNSTON
SHERMAN
SHERMAN
McPHERSON/
McCLERNAND
SHERMAN
Battle of
Champion's Hill, May 16
JOHNSTON
Pearl River
Vicksburg
Surrendered
July 4
LOUISIANA
Battle of
Big Black
River Bridge
May 17
PEMBERTON
Jackson, May 14
JOHNSTON
SHERMAN/
McPHERSON/
McCLERNAND
Raymond
May 12
New Carthage
Big Black R.
GRANT
MISSISSIPPI
Grand Gulf
Mississippi River
Port Gibson
May 1
Bruinsburg

0   10   20 miles
0   10   20 kilometers

Map 15.1 | The Civil War, Summer 1863: Vicksburg

Grant finally set aside his complicated engineering plans and decided on a bold move: he would run a flotilla of gunboats and barges past Vicksburg under the cover of night to ferry his men across the Mississippi south of the city, where the land was better. The guns of Vicksburg stood two hundred feet above the river, ready to fire down on any passing craft, but the Union men covered their boilers with sacks of grain and bales of cotton to protect them from the shelling. Most of the boats made it through. Grant, now equipped with means of transport and supply, took the advice of a local slave about the best place to land his men on the other side of the river. He had Sherman create a diversion far away from Grant's landing place, confusing the Confederates, and then ferried his

entire army across the Mississippi. Grant's army remained vulnerable, cut off from his allies and his major supply base, but by late April he was finally where he wanted to be.

In the same week Grant made his landing near Vicksburg, Hooker began his attack on Lee, still based in Fredericksburg. Hooker commanded 130,000 men, the largest army in the war thus far. Unlike Burnside, however, Hooker intended to outsmart Lee rather than try to overwhelm him with numbers and bravery. A large Union force would sweep around Lee and attack him from behind even as another force attacked from the front. To keep from being bottled up in Fredericksburg, Lee would have to emerge from his well-entrenched defensive

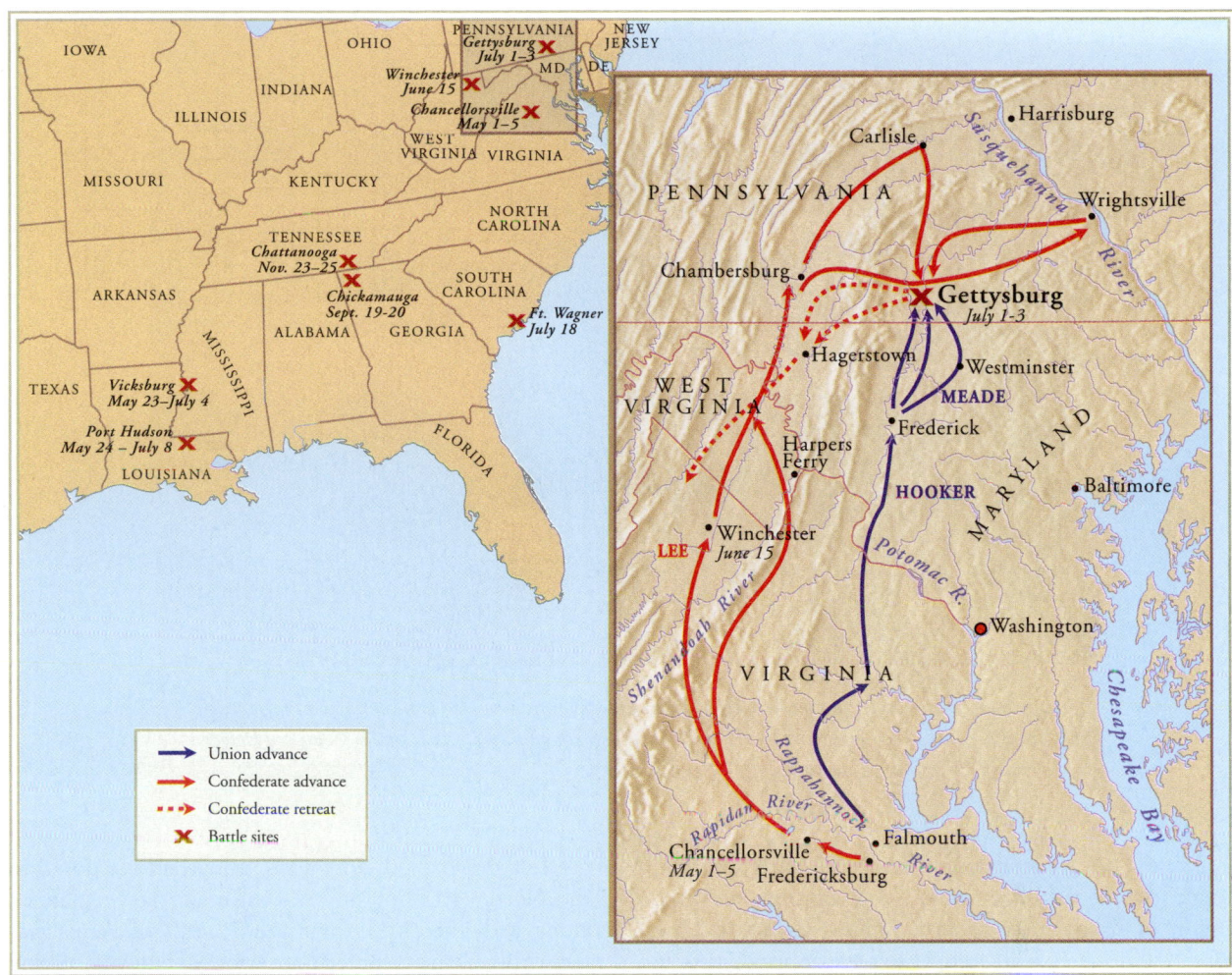

MAP 15.2 | THE CIVIL WAR, SUMMER 1863: VIRGINIA AND PENNSYLVANIA

position, either fighting in the open or retreating to Richmond. Lee met this bold move with an even bolder one. He would divide his forces, already much smaller than Hooker's, and send Stonewall Jackson to attack Hooker's men from the rear, outflanking Hooker's own flanking maneuver.

On May 2, Jackson assaulted Hooker's troops near Chancellorsville. The outnumbered Confederates defeated the surprised and indecisive Hooker, achieving a major victory. Southern jubilation, though, ended the very night of their triumph, for nervous Confederate soldiers accidentally shot Stonewall Jackson while he surveyed the scene near the front lines. The surgeons removed his arm that evening and hoped that he might live.

While Jackson lay in his tent, fading in and out of consciousness, Lee managed to contain another assault on Fredericksburg and to push the Union troops away from their positions. The losses had once again been staggering, for the South even more than for the North, but Lee had overcome a larger opponent. After the last battles quieted, however, Jackson died. His death took with it Lee's most trusted general and a kindred spirit, a quiet man who loved the attack.

Gettysburg

Despite his victory at Chancellorsville, Lee recognized that the Confederacy was in trouble. Rosecrans still

A battle in an obscure town in southern Pennsylvania, Gettysburg, provided some of the most memorable struggles of the entire war, especially the Confederate charge up an unprotected slope to Cemetery Ridge, where massed Union troops awaited.

threatened to break through Tennessee into Georgia, Grant clawed his way closer to Vicksburg, and the Union blockade drew an ever tighter net around the coast. While the North seemed to have an inexhaustible supply of men, the South did not. The Confederacy could not fight everywhere at once. Some of his generals urged Lee to rush with his troops to Tennessee to defend the center of the Confederacy and pull Grant away from Vicksburg. But Lee decided that his most effective move would be to invade the North again, taking the pressure off Virginia and replenishing his troops, heartening the South and disheartening the Union. A successful strike into the North might even yet persuade Britain and France to recognize the Confederacy.

In early June, Lee began to move up through the Shenandoah Valley into southern Pennsylvania. Hooker seemed confused, certain that Lee had the Union outnumbered even though he did not. When, after a minor dispute, Hooker offered his resignation to Lincoln, the president quickly accepted and put General George Meade in charge. Meade, while experienced, knew little of Hooker's plans and even less of Lee's. He quickly had to decide how best to stop the

greatest threat the Confederate army had yet posed to the North. Washington and Baltimore lay in danger, along with the cities, towns, and farms of Pennsylvania. There, the Confederate troops enjoyed taking food and livestock from the rich land.

Although Lee and his men moved unchecked across the Potomac and deep into Pennsylvania, they found themselves in a dangerous situation. Lee had permitted Jeb Stuart's cavalry, his "eyes," to range widely from the main army; as a result, the Confederates had little idea where the Union army was or what moves they were making. For their part, Meade and his fellow officers decided to pursue Lee, but not too aggressively, looking for a likely time and place to confront the enemy. Neither side had a clear plan or desire to fight immediately; both waited to see what the other would do.

On June 30, units from the Confederacy and the Union stumbled over one another at a small town neither side knew or cared much about: Gettysburg. Ironically, the Confederates flowed down from the northwest while the Union soldiers came in from the southeast. On July 1 they began to struggle for the best defensive position near the town, fighting over the highest and

most protected land. It appeared at first that the Southerners had the better of the first day's battle, but as the smoke cleared both sides could see that late in the day the Union army, larger in any case, had consolidated itself on the most advantageous ground. Meade's men, after fierce fighting at the ends of their line, occupied a fishhook-shaped series of ridges and hills that permitted them to protect their flanks and to repel the Confederates spread around them. The second day saw the Confederates slowly mobilize their forces for assaults on those positions and launch attacks late in the afternoon. The resulting battles in the peach orchard, the wheat field, Little Round Top, and the boulder-strewn area known as the Devil's Den proved horrific—with 35,000 men dead or wounded—but left the Union in control of the high ground.

Despite the Union's superior position and some misgivings by his generals, Lee decided on a frontal attack the next day. The Confederates hoped their artillery would soften the middle of the Union lines. The Confederates did not realize how little damage their guns had done until well-entrenched Union troops decimated waves of an attack led by George E. Pickett. Only a few southern men made it to the stone wall that protected the Northerners, and even those Confederates quickly fell. It proved a disastrous charge and a disastrous three days for Lee and the Confederacy. They lost 23,000 men through death or wounds, about a third of their entire force. While the Union lost similar numbers of men, they had more to lose. The Northerners and their new general had fought a conservative, defensive battle; the southern side, short on supplies and men, had gambled, somewhat desperately, on an aggressive assault. The strategic and political consequences of the battle remained to be seen on the evening of July 3, when men lay dead or dying all across the somber fields of Gettysburg.

The next morning, a thousand miles away, Vicksburg surrendered to Ulysses S. Grant. Unlike Gettysburg, where the battle had been fought in a place no one would have foretold and which no one considered strategically important, Vicksburg held enormous tactical and psychological importance. It had been the symbol of Confederate doggedness and Union frustration. After six weeks of siege, after six weeks of near starvation behind the Confederate defenses, Vicksburg fell. The Mississippi River now divided the Confederacy while it tied the Union to the Gulf of Mexico.

Some Southerners, including Jefferson Davis, did not perceive Gettysburg as a defeat. In their eyes, Lee and his men had pushed deep into the Union, inflicted heavy losses, and damaged northern morale without being trapped there. Northerners at the time often agreed, pronouncing themselves more frustrated than satisfied with Meade, who had not destroyed Lee's army despite his greater numbers and the friendly terrain. During the Confederate retreat to Virginia the Southerners found themselves caught between a swollen Potomac River and pursuing Federal troops. Meade, his army exhausted and weakened from losing tens of thousands of men, chose not to fight against the defenses Lee's men hurriedly put up against their pursuers. Meade could not know that the condition of the southern troops was even worse than his own, full of demoralization and desertion. Fortunately for the Confederates, the river soon calmed enough that they were able to escape back into Virginia. Meade could have ended the war at the Potomac, Lincoln felt certain, but "as it is, the war will be prolonged indefinitely."

The New York City Draft Riots

On the very day that Lee struggled across the Potomac to safety, riots broke out in New York City. Northern working people held complicated feelings about the war. Many of those who labored in the North's factories, mines, farms, and railroads had come to the United States in the last few years. These people, mostly Irish and Germans, valued the opportunity the American economy offered as well as the nation's avowed commitment to freedom. They volunteered in large numbers, often in units comprised solely of immigrants from their country, to fight for the Union cause. Immigration to the North continued to flow heavily even during the war, as men and women eagerly filled the jobs vacated by those who fought.

On the other hand, many of the immigrants viewed black Americans with dread and contempt, seeing them as competitors for jobs and housing. Urban labor organizations divided over Lincoln's election and over the response to secession. Many Irishmen, almost all of them Democrats, proclaimed that they had no quarrel with white Southerners and that they resented the federal government's draft. The conspicuous success of northern businessmen and the obvious effect of inflation on the wages of workers created strong resentments as well. Working people sneered at those men who had enough money to hire substitutes to

fight in their place. Three hundred dollars, after all, constituted half a year's wage for a workingman.

Irish immigrants despaired at the losses among Irish-American units in the field. When their regiments were decimated at Fredericksburg, Gettysburg, and elsewhere, Irish people began to wonder if commanders valued their lives as highly as those of the native-born. When word came, just as the draft lottery was to take place in New York City on July 11, 1863, of the 23,000 men lost at Gettysburg, the fury of working people rose. On July 13, it exploded. Mobs began by assaulting draft officials, then turned their anger on any man who looked rich enough to have hired a substitute, then on pro-Lincoln newspapers and abolitionists' homes. Most viciously, they turned on black citizens. The rioters burned a black orphanage and assaulted any African Americans they encountered on the streets.

The police struggled for three days to control the riot, the largest the United States had ever seen. Eventually, troops (including all-Irish units) rushed from the battlefields of Pennsylvania to aid the police. The troops fired into the rioters; over a hundred people, most of them protesters, died and another 300 were injured. The working people got some of what they wanted: more welfare relief, exemptions from the draft for those whose families would have no other means of support, and an exodus of black people who feared for their lives. Resistance to the draft and to blacks erupted, too, in the mining districts of Pennsylvania, in the immigrant sections of Chicago, and in the quarries of Vermont. As in the South, women rioted alongside men. The war threatened to pull the North apart in 1863 even as it attempted to save the Union.

Ironically, a few days after the New York draft riots scores of black troops died during a bold nighttime assault on Fort Wagner near Charleston, South Carolina. Despite the bravery of the African Americans, the assault failed. The Confederates made a point of burying the African-American soldiers in a mass grave along with their white officer, Robert Gould Shaw, intending to insult him and his memory. Instead, they elevated him as a northern martyr.

Chickamauga

After Gettysburg, Vicksburg, and the New York riots in July, events slowed until September, when Union

General William Rosecrans left Chattanooga, near the Georgia border, and began moving toward Atlanta. His opponent, Braxton Bragg, was reinforced by Longstreet from Virginia and hoped to entice Rosecrans into dividing his forces so that they could be cut off. They confronted one another at Chickamauga Creek—a Cherokee name meaning "river of death." The Confederates took advantage of Union mistakes on the heavily wooded battlefield, inflicting harrowing damage and driving Rosecrans back into Chattanooga. The Union troops were trapped there, the Confederates looming over them on Lookout Mountain and Missionary Ridge, with few routes of escape and limited supplies. The Northerners had gone from a position of apparent advantage to one of desperation.

Lincoln, judging Rosecrans "confused and stunned" by the battle at Chickamauga, used this opportunity to put Grant in charge of all Union armies between the Appalachian Mountains and the Mississippi River. In the fall of 1863, Grant traveled to Chattanooga, where Sherman joined him from Mississippi and Hooker came from Virginia. Lincoln had growing faith in Grant, the man who had taken the Tennessee and Mississippi rivers for the Union. Now the president trusted Grant to save Chattanooga, a crucial outpost on the Union's drive into Georgia.

The Gettysburg Address

The North's victories in the summer of 1863 aided Lincoln's popularity. The draft riots in New York City damaged the reputations of Democrats while the bravery of black soldiers on the battlefields of Louisiana and South Carolina led white Northerners to rethink some of their prejudices. In the fall of 1863, the Republicans won major victories in Pennsylvania and Ohio, the latter especially sweet because the Democrats had nominated Clement Vallandigham, the Copperhead whom Lincoln had exiled from the state only a few months earlier. Lincoln determined to make the most of these heartening events, for the good fortune might not last.

When Lincoln received an invitation to speak at the dedication of the cemetery at Gettysburg on November 19, he saw it as a chance to mend political fences, offer words of comfort to grief-stricken parents and wives, and persuade reluctant governors to give

ABRAHAM LINCOLN "THE GETTYSBURG ADDRESS," 1863

Perhaps the most influential and memorable brief passage in American history, Lincoln's "remarks" at the opening of the Gettysburg battlefield in November of that year articulated the highest ideals with which the war could be associated: a government "of the people, by the people, for the people." The "new birth of freedom" Lincoln invoked proved, however, to take generations to come to pass.

Four score and seven years ago our fathers brought forth on this continent, a new nation, conceived in Liberty, and dedicated to the proposition that all men are created equal.

Now we are engaged in a great civil war, testing whether that nation, or any nation so conceived and so dedicated, can long endure. We are met on a great battle-field of that war. We have come to dedicate a portion of that field, as a final resting place for those who here gave lives that that nation might live. It is altogether fitting and proper that we should do this.

But, in a larger sense, we can not dedicate—we can not consecrate—we can not hallow—this ground. The brave men, living and dead, who struggled here, have consecrated it, far above our poor power to add or detract. The world will little note, nor long remember what we say here, but it can never forget what they did here. It is for us the living, rather, to be dedicated here to the unfinished work which they who fought here have thus far so nobly advanced. It is rather for us to be here dedicated to the great task remaining before us—that from these honored dead we take increased devotion to that cause for which they gave the last full measure of devotion—that we here highly resolve that these dead shall not have died in vain—that this nation, under God, shall have a new birth of freedom—and that government of the people, by the people, for the people, shall not perish from the earth.

even more to the Union cause. The event had not been planned with him in mind and the president was not even the featured speaker. Edward Everett, a scholar and famed lecturer, had been asked weeks before to give the main address. But Lincoln, seeing a chance to impart a sense of direction and purpose to the Union cause, recognized that a battlefield offered the most effective backdrop for the things he wanted to say.

Burial crews had been laboring for weeks to inter and reinter swollen and stinking remains on the Gettysburg battlefield. Thousands of horse carcasses had been burned; thousands of human bodies had been hastily covered with a thin layer of soil. Speculators hurriedly bought up land in expectation of government-sponsored cemeteries. Pennsylvania purchased seventeen acres and hired a specialist in rural cemetery design to lay out the burial plots so that no state would be offended by the location or amount of space devoted to its fallen men. Only about a third of the reburials had taken place when Lincoln arrived; caskets remained stacked at the station.

Lincoln, contrary to legend, did not dash off his speech on the back of an envelope. He had reworked and polished it for several days. The "remarks," as the program put it, lasted three minutes. Lincoln used

those minutes to maximum effect. He looked beyond the muddy fields, the decaying bodies, the shattered hopes for a decisive northern victory. He said virtually nothing about the details of the scene surrounding the 20,000 people at the ceremony. Neither did he mention slavery directly. Instead, he spoke of equality as the fundamental purpose of the war. He called for a "new birth of freedom."

Lincoln was attempting to shift the purpose of the war from Union for Union's sake to Union for freedom's sake. He spoke as if all the white Union men who died at Gettysburg had willingly given their lives for black freedom and even equality, though he knew that many had not. Lincoln sought to salvage something from the deaths of the 50,000 men at Gettysburg. Democratic newspapers rebuked Lincoln for his claim, arguing that white soldiers had "too much self-respect to declare that negroes were their equals." But other Northerners accepted Lincoln's exhortation as the definition of their purpose. They might not believe that blacks deserved to be included as full participants in a government of, by, and for "the people," but they did believe that the Union fought for liberty broadly conceived. As battles and years went by, the words of the Gettysburg Address would gain force and resonance as Americans looked back to see the war's purposes portrayed in their most flattering light.

Just four days after Lincoln's speech, Grant gave the North new reason to believe their ideals might triumph. On November 23, Grant's men overwhelmed the Confederates on Lookout Mountain outside Chattanooga; two days later, Union soldiers accomplished the improbable task of fighting their way up Missionary Ridge because Confederate artillery could not reach opponents coming up directly from below. The Union, now in control of Kentucky and Tennessee, had a wide and direct route into Georgia. Lincoln had finally found in Grant a general who seemed to value action over preparation.

England and France finally determined in late 1863 that they would not try to intervene in the American war. England even decided against delivering two powerful ships being built there for the Confederacy. The northern public, encouraged by events on the battlefield, supported Republican candidates in the congressional elections of 1863 more vigorously than had seemed possible just a few months before, when the New York draft riots and Chickamauga had thrown shadows over the Union purpose.

THE WINTER OF DISCONTENT: 1863-1864

The battles of the summer had been horrific; more men had died than anyone had thought possible. Both sides held their victories close to their hearts and brooded over their losses. The resolve and fury of summertime faded into the bitterness and bickering of winter. As the cycle rolled around again, people grew profoundly weary of the sacrifice but steeled themselves for a final push.

Politics North and South

Lincoln hoped to end the war as soon as possible, using persuasion as well as fighting to entice white Southerners back into the national fold. In early December 1863, Lincoln issued his proclamation of amnesty and reconstruction. To those who would take an oath of loyalty to the Union, Lincoln promised a full pardon and the return of all property other than slaves. Though he excluded Confederate leaders and high officers from this offer, Lincoln tried to include as many white southern men as possible. As soon as 10 percent of the number of voters in 1860 had sworn their loyalty to the Union, he decreed, the Southerners could begin forming new state governments. Slavery would come to a gradual end. Education and apprenticeship programs would aid former slaves in the transition to full freedom. He did not provide for African-American participation in the new governments of the South. Though he did comment that some "very intelligent" black men, including veterans, might be permitted to vote, Lincoln would not risk alienating an already skittish white northern electorate with radical plans for the postwar world.

Abolitionists and their allies attacked Lincoln's reconstruction plan as far too lenient to the rebel masters and not helpful enough for the former slaves. "To free the slave, and then to abandon him . . . betwixt bondage and manhood, is not this as cruel as slavery?" asked one critic. In the Wade-Davis bill of February 1864, Republican congressmen attempted to institute more stringent demands on former Confederates and offer more help to former slaves. They wanted to use the power of the national government to enforce a standard set of laws across the South. Just as Lincoln

feared that too strong a plan of reconstruction would galvanize white Southerners against peace, Republicans in Congress and in his cabinet feared that too weak a plan would permit former slaveowners and Confederates to negate much of what the war might win. Congressmen and Secretary of the Treasury Salmon P. Chase worked behind the scenes in opposition to Lincoln's plan.

While Jefferson Davis did not have to worry about his own re-election in late 1863—the Confederacy had established the presidential term at six years—he did have to worry about congressional elections. They did not go well: forty-one of the new 106 representatives expressly opposed Davis and his policies, while he held only a slight majority in the Senate. Just as northern Democrats called for compromise and peace, so did some Southerners. When Davis took a hands-off policy, he was criticized for doing too little. When he tried to assert more control, he found himself called "despotic" by his own vice president. When he tried to use slaves to the South's advantage, he was criticized for meddling with the very institution the war was supposed to protect. When he tried to use the power of the Confederate government to coordinate the war effort, he was criticized for undermining the rights of the states in whose name the war was being fought.

The Confederacy stumbled through the winter and into the spring of 1864, arguing with itself, desperately watching for signs that the North might be losing heart.

Prisons

Early in the Civil War, both sides had exchanged prisoners of war rather than spend men and resources maintaining prisons. Such arrangements worked well enough into 1863, but then things began to break down. Not only did the battles of that year fill the ramshackle prisons of both sides to capacity and beyond, but the Confederates decreed that any former slave captured would be executed or reenslaved, not taken prisoner. The Union, as a matter of principle, refused to participate in any exchanges so long as this policy remained in effect. Prisoners began piling up on both sides and stories of mistreatment became more frequent and more horrifying. Men spent months in abandoned warehouses or exposed to the elements in the roughest of camps.

Northerners who heard of the Confederate camp at Andersonville, Georgia, became livid. The camp was built early in 1864 when the Confederates decided to

The Confederate prisoner of war camp in Andersonville, Georgia, witnessed great brutality and appalling death rates from disease and hunger.

move prisoners from Richmond. Not only would they be less likely to be rescued by northern troops farther south, but they could more easily be supplied by railroad away from the heavy fighting in Virginia. The camp, built for 10,000 men, soon became overcrowded; it held 33,000 by August. The prisoners, without shade, had to drink polluted water. Gangs of northern soldiers controlled daily life within the prison, routinely beating and robbing new arrivals. Of the 45,000 men eventually held at Andersonville, 13,000 died. Even higher proportions died at smaller camps in North Carolina. While Confederates held in northern prisons were better supplied, even their death rates reached as high as 24 percent. Overall, about 16 percent of northern soldiers died in prison, 12 percent of Southerners. Many in the North criticized Lincoln for refusing to reinstitute exchanges, but Lincoln would not sacrifice the former slaves. Moreover, he knew that exchanges helped the soldier-starved Confederacy more than they did the North. Lincoln wanted to push the war to the earliest possible conclusion, even if that meant, much to his regret, that suffering would have to increase before it could end.

Union Resolve

In March 1864 Lincoln gave new direction and purpose to the Union effort by putting Ulysses S. Grant in charge of all northern forces. By then, with victories stretching from Fort Donelson to Vicksburg to Chattanooga, Grant had gained confidence both in himself and from others. He and Lincoln agreed that the Union had to use its superiority in materiel, manpower, and navy to attack the Confederacy on every front at once, forcing the South to decide what terri-

African-American men worked at a wide range of tasks for the Union army, both behind the lines and at the front.

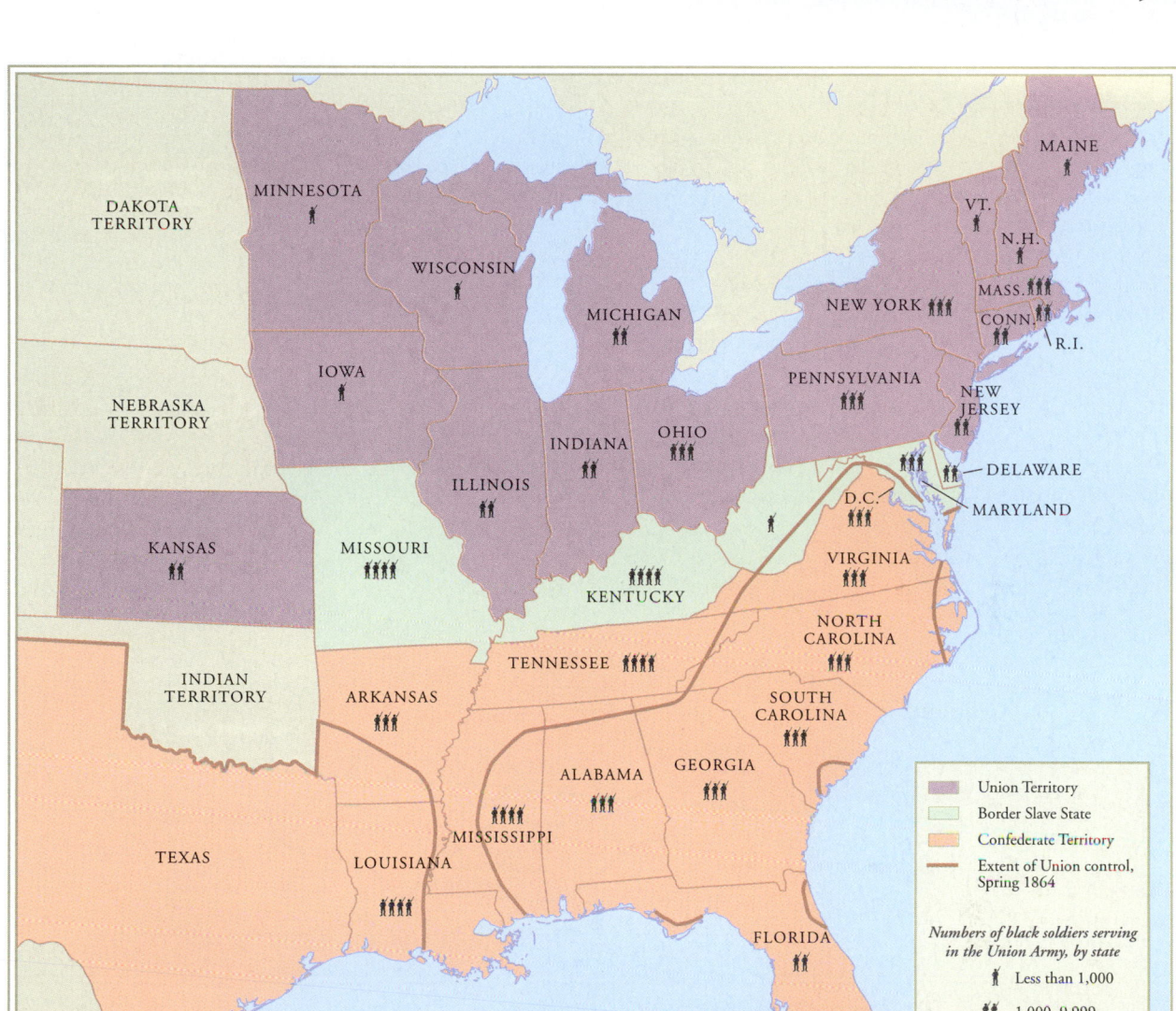

MAP 15.3 | ORIGINS OF AFRICAN-AMERICAN SOLDIERS

tory it would sacrifice. While Grant would fight in Virginia, he left William T. Sherman in charge in Chattanooga. Sherman would attack the young railroad center of Atlanta, cutting the Gulf South off from the Upper South. With the trans-Mississippi South lost to the Confederacy since 1863 and much of Louisiana, Tennessee, Mississippi, western Virginia, and Alabama under Union control, the loss of Atlanta

would chop the Confederacy into pieces too small to resist the northern army.

In retrospect, knowing how the war turned out, the events of 1864 may appear anticlimactic. Lee and the Confederates seemed to face overwhelming odds. Yet Southerners recognized that everything turned around holding the Northerners off until the presidential election in the North. Many Northerners

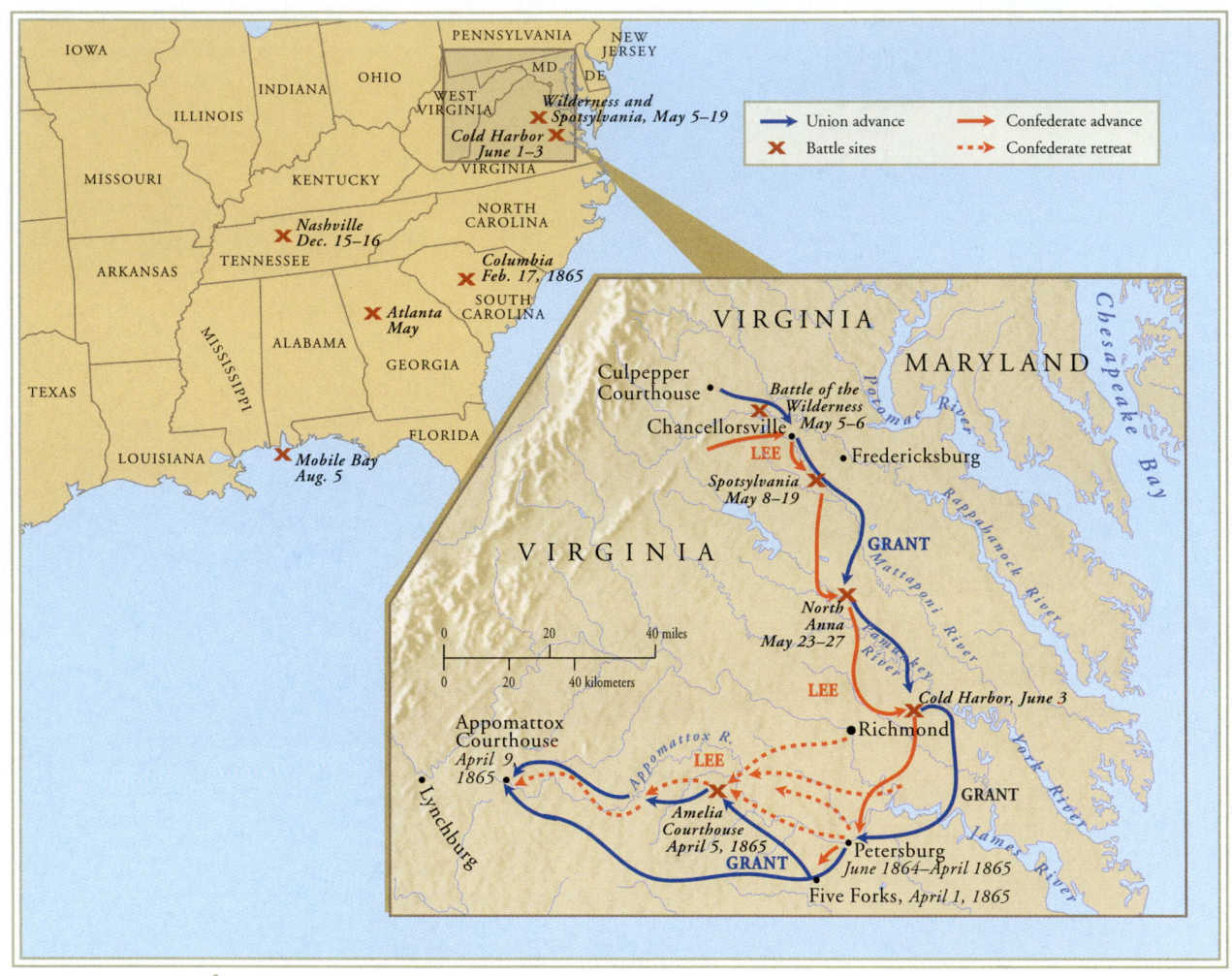

MAP 15.4 | THE CIVIL WAR, 1864-1865

called for peace and compromise. If the Southerners could inflict enough damage on the Union army, Northerners might elect someone willing to bring the war to an end through compromise and recognition of Southern independence. The Confederates knew, too, that the three-year terms of the most experienced veterans in the Union army expired in 1864. More than half of those veterans, willing to let someone else fight the Rebels, chose to leave the army even though the war was not over. They would be replaced with soldiers younger, less seasoned, and perhaps less committed to the Union cause. The Confederates also realized that Grant, new to his command, would be confronting Robert E. Lee, who was fighting with an experienced army on battlefields where he had already

seized victory. All things considered, it was by no means clear in 1864 that the Union would win Virginia or the war.

African Americans played an increasingly large role in Union plans, for over 180,000 black soldiers enlisted just when the North needed them most, upon the departure of so many men who had enlisted for three years. By the spring of 1864, the means of recruitment, training, and pay for these soldiers had become well established. The Confederates, however, refused to recognize the same rules of warfare for black soldiers that they acknowledged for whites. In April of 1864, at Fort Pillow in western Tennessee, Confederate cavalry under the command of Nathan Bedford Forrest shot down black Union soldiers who at-

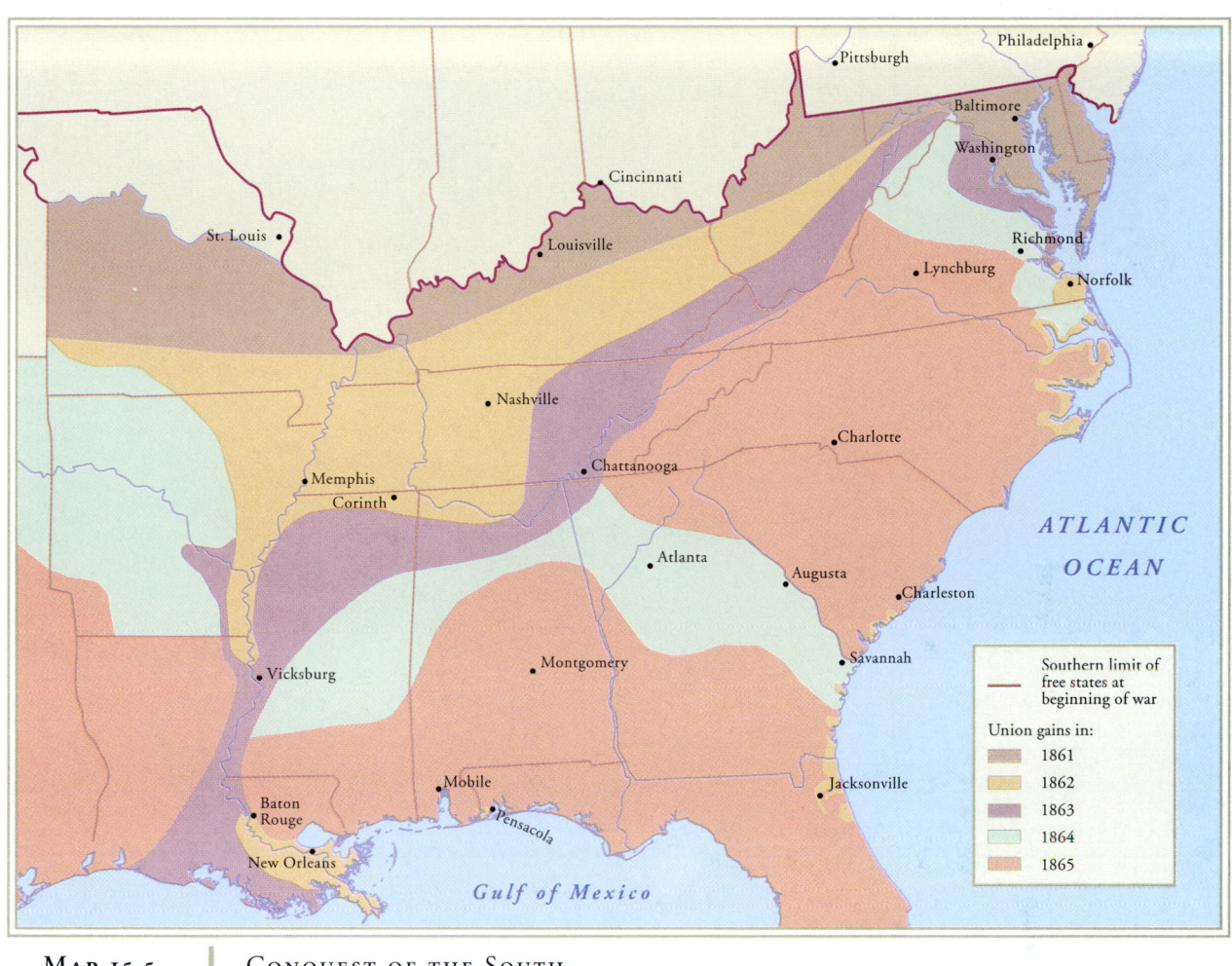

MAP 15.5 | CONQUEST OF THE SOUTH

tempted to surrender. More than once thereafter, the Confederates would hear black soldiers yell "Remember Fort Pillow!" as they attacked.

With the election clock running, Grant set out in May 1864 to destroy Lee's army. The Battle of the Wilderness near Chancellorsville, close to the site where Stonewall Jackson had died a long year before, saw brutal fighting and horrible losses. Fire in the tangled woods trapped wounded men, burning them alive. Grant lost more men than Hooker had in the battle of the previous year, but whereas Hooker treated such losses as a decisive defeat, Grant pushed on, relentlessly pressuring Lee's men.

The two armies fought again and again over the next two months in the fields of Virginia, the casualties mounting in a sickening spiral. The Confederates turned the Union army back to the east of Richmond

and rushed up the Shenandoah Valley to threaten Washington itself. The North repulsed the invasion and dispatched Philip Sheridan to the valley to make sure the Confederates did not regroup. With the Confederates pinned down in Petersburg, near Richmond, Pennsylvania coal miners volunteered to tunnel under the fortifications and plant explosives. Throughout July, they dug; finally, at the end of the month, they detonated a charge and blew an enormous crater in the Confederate lines. The attack that followed the explosion, however, failed. Union soldiers piled into the crater, where the rallying Confederates trapped them. Petersburg did not fall. Once again, Virginia had seen desperate fighting but few decisive results.

Fortunately for Lincoln, things were going better farther south. Throughout June and July, Sherman pushed relentlessly through north Georgia toward

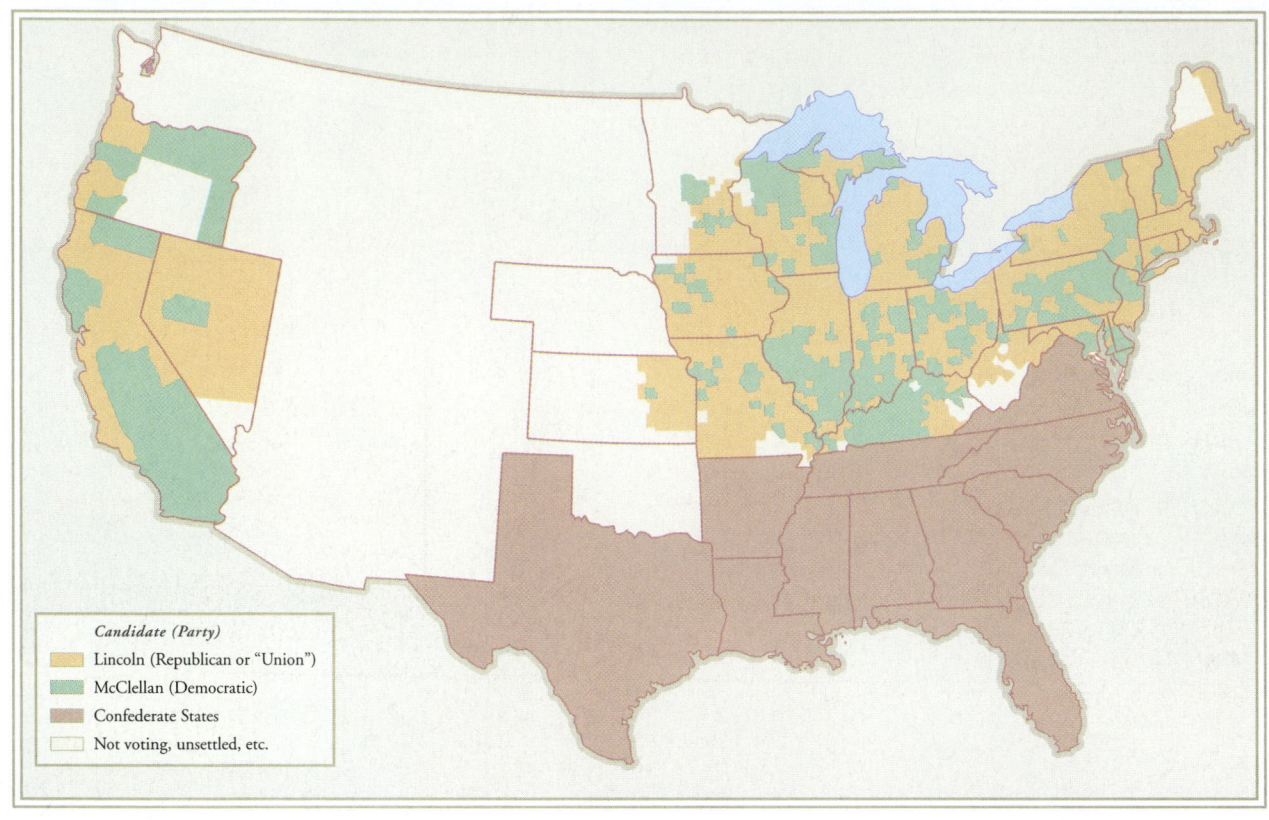

MAP 15.6 | THE ELECTION OF 1864

Candidate (Party)
- ▨ Lincoln (Republican or "Union")
- ▨ McClellan (Democratic)
- ▨ Confederate States
- ☐ Not voting, unsettled, etc.

Atlanta. By the end of July, the southern army had fallen back into Atlanta, preparing to defend it from siege. It seemed only a matter of time before the Union triumphed. But how much time? The offensives by Grant and Sherman had come at the cost of high casualty rates. How many more tens of thousands would the North sacrifice? How many more months under the leadership of Abraham Lincoln?

The Northern Election of 1864

The president had to fight off challenges even within his own party, for some Republicans called for Chase, Frémont, or even Grant to carry the banner in 1864. Some party leaders considered Lincoln too radical; others considered him too cautious. Through adroit use of patronage, however, Lincoln managed to win renomination in June. The Republican party tried to broaden its appeal to Democrats by nominating An-

drew Johnson, military governor of Tennessee and a former Democrat, to the vice presidency.

In the meantime, the Democrats confidently moved forward. They knew that many Northerners distrusted, even hated, Lincoln. In the eyes of his critics, Lincoln had caused the war, trampled on constitutional rights, consolidated too much power, and refused to end the war when he had a chance. The Democrats intended to take full advantage of such criticisms, especially by nominating George McClellan as their candidate. McClellan retained great renown as a general and demonstrated that a person could oppose Lincoln's political purposes of the war without being a coward or traitor. McClellan and the Democrats portrayed themselves, not the Republicans, as the truly national party, for they were determined to restore the United States to its prewar unity and grandeur. McClellan said he would end the war if the South would reenter the Union—bringing slavery with it. It was a bargain that appealed to many in the North.

Just when it appeared that the Democrats would unseat Lincoln, however, news from the battlefield changed everything. Sherman swung around Atlanta and began destroying the railroads that made the small city an important junction. The Confederates, afraid they would be encircled and trapped within the city, set much of Atlanta on fire and abandoned it. Sherman and his army marched into the city on September 2. Two weeks later, Sheridan attacked the Confederates in the Shenandoah Valley, pushing them far beyond any threat to Washington and systematically destroying the valley's ability to support them again.

Even with these victories, and even with the heavy support of Lincoln by men in the army, Lincoln won only 55 percent of the popular vote. He did much better in the electoral college, sweeping every state except three. The Republicans also elected heavy majorities to both houses of Congress. For the time being, the Republicans closed ranks.

The March to the Sea

A week after Lincoln's election Sherman judged that he could not remain in Atlanta, where he could be cut off from his supply line. He decided to set out across Georgia, provisioning his army along the way, taking the war to the southern people themselves. Such a march would be as much a demonstration of northern power as a military maneuver, proving to the Confederate populace that they could no longer resist. The triumphant army of 60,000 made its way across the state throughout the fall of 1864, living off the land. Large numbers of deserters from both sides, fugitive slaves, and outlaws took advantage of the situation to inflict widespread destruction and panic. Sherman arrived at Savannah on December 21. "I beg to present to you, as a Christmas gift, the city of Savannah," Sherman buoyantly telegraphed Lincoln.

FROM WAR TO RECONSTRUCTION: 1865–1867

Americans had lived with war for four years; they had learned how to hate. As the war ground to a halt in

This picture, taken four days before his assassination, shows the toll four years of war had taken on the 56-year-old president.

early 1865, Americans had to wonder if they remembered how to share a country with their former enemies. They had to wonder, too, how different the country would be with African Americans no longer as slaves. Of all the changes the United States had ever seen, emancipation stood as the most profound.

War's Climax

Events moved quickly at the beginning of 1865. In January, Sherman issued Special Field Order 15, which reserved land in coastal South Carolina, Georgia, and Florida for former slaves. Those who settled on the land would receive forty-acre plots. Four days later, the Republicans in Congress passed the Thirteenth Amendment, abolishing slavery forever—a bill

The mountains of Tennessee, North Carolina, and Georgia saw brutal fighting far from the front lines. Here, guerillas attack Confederate cavalry pursuing deserters and Union sympathizers.

that had failed only seven months before. The law-makers may have been influenced by petitions from the Women's National Loyal League with 400,000 signatures in favor of the amendment. At the begin-ning of February, Sherman's troops began to march north into the Carolinas. Columbia, South Carolina, burned to the ground, with both Confederate and Union troops contributing to the conflagration. Growing numbers of Confederate soldiers deserted from their armies to return to their homes. Lincoln met with Confederate officials to try to bring the war to an end, offering slaveowners compensation for their freed slaves if the Southerners would immedi-ately cease the war. Jefferson Davis refused and Lin-coln's cabinet persuaded him never to speak of com-pensation again.

At the beginning of March, Lincoln was inaugu-rated for his second term. Rather than gloating at the impending victory on the battlefield, Lincoln called for his fellow citizens to "bind up the nation's wounds." That same month, Congress created the Bu-reau of Refugees, Freedmen, and Abandoned Lands to ease the transition from slavery to freedom, helping destitute whites as well as blacks. Nine days later, the Confederate government, after hotly debating whether to recruit slaves to fight as soldiers if their owners agreed, finally decided to do so after Lee, desperate for men, supported the measure.

Appomattox and Assassination

The Confederates' slave recruitment law did not have time to convert slaves to soldiers, however, for Grant soon began his final assault on Confederate troops in Virginia, systematically cutting off the rail lines that offered reinforcements and supplies. Petersburg fell on April 2, Richmond the next day. Jefferson Davis vainly appealed for southern resolve. Lee hoped to lead his army to the train station at Appomattox Court House to resupply them, but on April 9 Grant intercepted Lee's men just short of their destination. Lee, with

While John Wilkes Booth had been killed by Union troops twelve days after Lincoln's assassination in April of 1865, it was not until July that four of the eight convicted co-conspirators—including a woman—were hanged.

nowhere else to go and no ally to come to his aid, surrendered.

A number of Confederate armies, scattered from North Carolina to Texas, had yet to surrender, and Jefferson Davis had yet to be captured, but it was clear that the war had ended. Lee refused the pleas of some of his men to fight the Yankees as guerrillas. Grant permitted the Confederates to keep their animals for farming. The Southerners began to straggle home. Two days later, Lincoln addressed a Washington audience about what would come next for the freedmen. He admitted that Northerners differed "as to the mode, manner, and means of Reconstruction" and that the white South was "disorganized and discordant."

Lincoln did not live to take part in the planning, for he was assassinated on April 14 by John Wilkes Booth, a failed actor and southern sympathizer. Booth attacked Lincoln while the president sat with Mrs. Lincoln at Ford's Theater in Washington, shooting him in the back of the head and then leaping to the stage. Lincoln lingered for the night but never recovered consciousness; he died early the next morning. After a long and frantic search, Booth was captured and killed in a burning barn. Several conspirators, including a female accomplice, were executed several months later.

The Costs and Consequences of the War

The North lost almost 365,000 men to death and disease in the Civil War, the South 260,000—a fifth of its adult white male population. Another 277,000 Northerners were wounded, along with 195,000 Southerners. Many of these wounded men carried the legacy of the war through the rest of their lives; empty sleeves, blank stares, disfigured faces, and incessant pain continued long after the armies had gone home. Black Americans lost 37,000 men in the Union Army and another 10,000 men, women, and children in the contraband camps. Widows and orphans, black and white, northern and southern, faced decades of struggling without a male breadwinner. Many people found their emotional lives shattered by the war, unable to forget what they had seen and done. Alcohol, drug abuse, crime, and violence became widespread problems in postwar America.

The southern economy fell to its knees. Major southern cities had been reduced to ash. Railroads had been ripped from the ground, engines and cars burned. Fields had grown up in weeds and brush, drainage ditches choked. Farm values fell by half. Livestock, tools, barns, and fences stolen or destroyed by

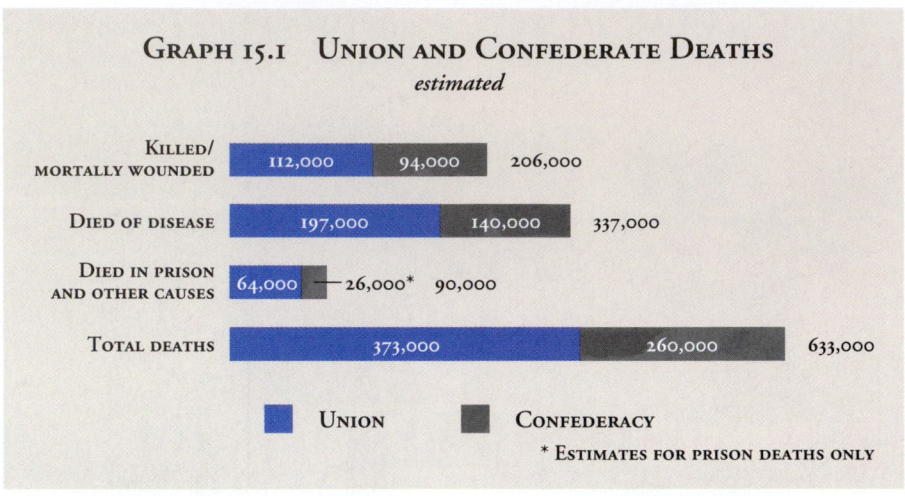

GRAPH 15.1   UNION AND CONFEDERATE DEATHS
estimated

	Union	Confederacy	Total
KILLED/ MORTALLY WOUNDED	112,000	94,000	206,000
DIED OF DISEASE	197,000	140,000	337,000
DIED IN PRISON AND OTHER CAUSES	64,000	26,000*	90,000
TOTAL DEATHS	373,000	260,000	633,000

■ UNION   ■ CONFEDERACY

* ESTIMATES FOR PRISON DEATHS ONLY

the armies of both sides would take years to replace. Just as damaging in the long run, lines of credit had been severed. Before emancipation, planters had used slaves as collateral for loans. Now, without that basis, few people outside the South were willing to loan money to planters or other investors. Moreover, during the war Congress had passed banking acts that favored the North at the expense of the South, directing capital away from the credit-starved South. Southerners who had supported the Confederacy by purchasing its bonds and currency found that they had lost the inheritance of generations.

The Civil War did not mark a sudden turn in the northern economy, but it did accelerate processes already well underway. The nationalization of markets, the accumulation of wealth, and the dominance of larger manufacturing firms all became more marked after 1865. Greenbacks, bonds, and a national banking system regularized the flow of capital and spurred the growth of business. The Republicans used the opportunity of the war years to enact their vision of progress, passing the Department of Agriculture Act, the Morrill College Land Grant Act, the Homestead Act, and the Union Pacific Railroad Act, all using the power of the federal government to encourage settlement of the West, strengthen public education, and spur economic development. Northern farmers saw prices for their products remain high, as the demands of the war coincided with poor harvests in Europe. Despite the prosperity in the North, the hundreds of thousands of veterans faced many dislocations and

readjustments as they returned to the farms, factories, and shops they had left months or years before.

Emancipation and the South

As the battles ground to a halt, slaves became former slaves. For some, the process proved dramatic and sudden, while for others freedom emerged only gradually. Some, especially the young, greeted freedom confidently, while others, especially the elderly, could not help but be wary of anything so strange, no matter how long and how much they had prayed for it. Some seized their freedom at the first opportunity, taking their families to Union camps or joining the army. Others celebrated when the Yankees came to their plantations, only to find that their owners and white neighbors retaliated when the soldiers left. Others bided their time, waiting to make sure the war had really ceased and their bondage had come to an end. Some refused to believe the stories of freedom at all until their master or mistress called them together to announce that they were indeed no longer slaves.

Upon hearing the news, the freed people gathered to discuss their options. For many, the highest priority was to reunite their families. Such people set off on journeys short or long, south or north, in desperate efforts to find a husband, wife, child, or parent sold away in earlier years. For others, sheer survival was the highest priority. Freedom came in the late spring,

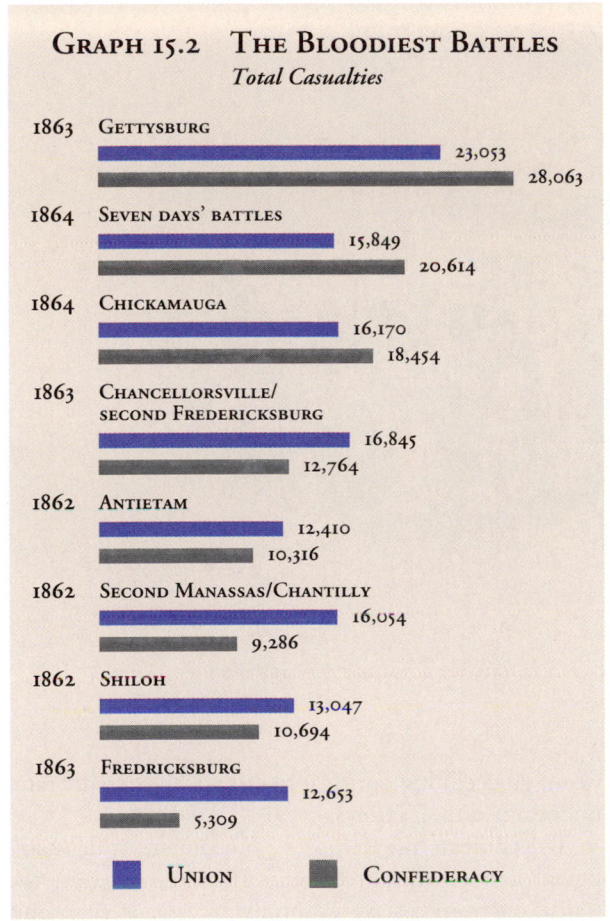

GRAPH 15.2   THE BLOODIEST BATTLES
Total Casualties

Year	Battle	Union	Confederacy
1863	GETTYSBURG	23,053	28,063
1864	SEVEN DAYS' BATTLES	15,849	20,614
1864	CHICKAMAUGA	16,170	18,454
1863	CHANCELLORSVILLE/ SECOND FREDERICKSBURG	16,845	12,764
1862	ANTIETAM	12,410	10,316
1862	SECOND MANASSAS/CHANTILLY	16,054	9,286
1862	SHILOH	13,047	10,694
1863	FREDRICKSBURG	12,653	5,309

■ UNION   ■ CONFEDERACY

After four years of war, little remained in the besieged cities of the Confederacy.

barely in time to get crops in the ground. Some former slaves argued that their best bet was to stay where they were for the time being. They had heard rumors that the government would award them land in the South just as it had given lands in the West to northern settlers. Between July and September of 1865, however, those dreams died. Union officers promised land to former slaves in Virginia, Louisiana, Mississippi, and South Carolina, but then Washington revoked the promises. The land would be returned to its former owners. Black people would have no choice but to strike bargains with white Southerners.

Former slaveowners also responded in many different ways. Some, unable to conceive of living in a South without slavery, fled to Latin America. Others tried to keep as much of slavery as they could by whipping and chaining workers to keep them from leaving. Other former masters and mistresses attempted to keep as much of slavery as possible by of-

fering to let former slaves stay in their cabins and work for wages. Some callously evicted older and less productive slaves even as others assured the elderly that they had a home on the plantation for the rest of their lives.

Plantation owners came to realize that all the land in the world was worthless without someone to work it. African Americans had no choice but to compromise with white landowners. At first, in the spring of 1865, planters insisted that the former slaves work as they had worked before emancipation, in "gangs." In return for their work, they would receive a portion of the crop, shared among all the workers. Many black people chafed at this arrangement, preferring to work as individuals or families. In such places, landowners found that they had little choice but to permit black families to take primary responsibility for a portion of land. The former slaves provided the labor and received part of the crop as a result. Planters, though

Black Southerners took advantage of the presence of Union troops to leave the farms and plantations on which they had been held. Many set out to find family members.

reluctant to give up any control over the day-to-day work on their land, realized they had few choices. They possessed little cash to pay wage workers and no alternative labor. The black families who worked the land often found themselves in debt despite their hard work, as declining cotton prices and high credit rates undermined their efforts.

The Bureau of Refugees, Freedmen, and Abandoned Lands—the Freedmen's Bureau—oversaw the transition from a slave economy to a wage economy.

The Freedmen's Bureau, created in the spring of 1865, adjudicated conflicts between white landowners and black workers.

Black Southerners established schools for themselves across the region, often at considerable sacrifice.

Much of the work of its agents, military officers, involved keeping people alive in the ravaged South. They dispensed medicine, food, and clothing from the vast stores of the federal government to white and black alike. The Bureau created courts to adjudicate conflicts and to draw up labor contracts between landholders and laborers. It established schools and coordinated female volunteers who came from the North to teach in them. While many white Southerners resented and resisted the Freedmen's Bureau, it helped smooth the transition from slavery to freedom, from war to peace, in 1865.

Black Mobilization

Black Southerners mourned and feared the loss of Abraham Lincoln. He had helped bring their freedom, a freedom that remained new and tenuous. Without his leadership, former slaves rightly worried, the forces of reaction might overwhelm their freedom. Southerners of both races watched to see what Andrew Johnson might do.

African Americans in the South quickly mobilized. Throughout the South, former slaves and former free blacks gathered in conventions to announce their vision of the new order. They paraded and petitioned, making the case for their full citizenship. They wanted, above all else, equality before the law and the opportunity to vote. The delegates, while insistent, spoke to southern whites in conciliatory terms. By and large, they did not demand confiscation of land nor did they speak extensively of economic concerns in general. Let us have our basic rights before the courts and at the ballot box, they said, and we will take care of ourselves. Such concerns and confidence reflected the perspective of the conventions' leadership: former free blacks, skilled artisans, ministers, and teachers. The great mass of southern blacks—former slaves desperate for a chance at some economic independence in the countryside—found their concerns neglected.

Black Southerners agreed on the centrality of two institutions, however: the church and the school. At the very moment of freedom, they began to form their own churches. For generations, African Americans had been forced to worship alongside whites, sitting in

"Letter to the Union Convention, 1865"

Black Citizens of Tennessee

In this petition by black Tennesseans to their white Unionist couterparts in the waning days of the Civil War, the themes of the Gettysburg Address receive eloquent endorsement. The fifty-nine men who signed the petition articulated the highest ideals of the American nation. There is no record of a response.

[Nashville, Tenn., January 9, 1865]

To the Union Convention of Tennessee Assembled in the Capitol at Nashville, January 9th, 1865:

We the undersigned petitioners, American citizens of African descent, natives and residents of Tennessee, and devoted friends of the great National cause, do most respectfully ask a patient hearing of your honorable body in regard to matters deeply affecting the future condition of our unfortunate and long suffering race.

First of all, however, we would say that words are too weak to tell how profoundly grateful we are to the Federal Government for the good work of freedom which it is gradually carrying forward; and for the Emancipation Proclamation which has set free all the slaves in some of the rebellious States, as well as many of the slaves in Tennessee.

After two hundred years of bondage and suffering a returning sense of justice has awakened the great body of the American people to make amends for the unprovoked wrongs committed against us for over two hundred years.

Your petitioners would ask you to complete the work begun by the nation at large, and abolish the last vestige of slavery by the express words of your organic law.

Many masters in Tennessee whose slaves have left them, will certainly make every effort to bring them back to bondage after the reorganization of the State government, unless slavery be expressly abolished by the Constitution.

We hold that freedom is the natural right of all men, which they themselves have no more right to give or barter away, than they have to sell their honor, their wives, or their children.

We claim to be men belonging to the great human family, descended from one great God, who is the common Father of all, and who bestowed on all races and tribes the priceless right of freedom. Of this right, for no offence of ours, we have long been cruelly deprived, and the common voice of the wise and good of all countries, has remonstrated against our enslavement, as one of the greatest crimes in all history.

We claim freedom, as our natural right, and ask that in harmony and cooperation with the nation at large, you should cut up by the roots the system of slavery, which is not only a wrong to us, but the source of all the evil which at present afflicts the State. For slavery, corrupt itself, corrupted nearly all, also, around it, so that it has influenced nearly all the slave States to rebel against the Federal Government, in order to set up a government of pirates under which slavery might be perpetrated.

In the contest between the nation and slavery, our unfortunate people have sided, by instinct, with the former. We have little fortune to devote to the national cause, for a

hard fate has hitherto forced us to live in poverty, but we do devote to its success, our hopes, our toils, our whole heart, our sacred honor, and our lives. We will work, pray, live, and, if need be, die for the Union, as cheerfully as ever a white patriot died for his country. The color of our skin does not lessen in the least degree, our love either for God or for the land of our birth.

We are proud to point your honorable body to the fact, that so far as our knowledge extends, not a negro traitor has made his appearance since the beginning of this wicked rebellion.

Whether freeman or slaves the colored race in this country have always looked upon the United States as the Promised Land of Universal freedom, and no earthly temptation has been strong enough to induce us to rebel against it. We love the Union by an instinct which is stronger than any argument or appeal which can be used against it. It is the attachment of a child to its parent.

Devoted as we are to the principles of justice, of love to all men, and of equal rights on which our Government is based, and which make it the hope of the world. We know the burdens of citizenship, and are ready to bear them. We know the duties of the good citizen, and are ready to perform them cheerfully, and would ask to be put in a position in which we can discharge them more effectually. We do not ask for the privilege of citizenship, wishing to shun the obligations imposed by it.

Near 200,000 of our brethren are to-day performing military duty in the ranks of the Union army. Thousands of them have already died in battle, or perished by a cruel martyrdom for the sake of the Union, and we are ready and willing to sacrifice more. But what higher order of citizen is there than the soldier? or who has a greater trust confided to his hands? If we are called on to do military duty against the rebel armies in the field, why should we be denied the privilege of voting against rebel citizens at the ballot-box? The latter is as necessary to save the Government as the former.

The colored man will vote by instinct with the Union party, just as uniformly as he fights with the Union army. . . .

If colored men have been faithful and true to the Government of the United States in spite of the Fugitive Slave Law, and the cruel policy often pursued toward them, will they not be more devoted to it now than ever since it has granted them that liberty which they desired above all things? Surely, if colored men voted without harm to the State, while their brethren were in bondage, they will be much more devoted and watchful over her interests when elevated to the rank of freemen and voters. If they are good law-abiding citizens, praying for its prosperity, rejoicing in its progress, paying its taxes, fighting its battles, making its farms, mines, work-shops and commerce more productive, why deny them the right to have a voice in the election of its rulers?

This is a democracy—a government of the people. It should aim to make every man, without regard to the color of his skin, the amount of his wealth, or the character of his religious faith, feel personally interested in its welfare. Every man who lives under the Government should feel that it is his property, his treasure, the bulwark and defense of himself and his family, his pearl of great price, which he must preserve, protect, and defend faithfully at all times, on all occasions, in every possible manner.

This is not a Democratic Government if a numerous, law-abiding, industrious, and useful class of citizens, born and bred on the soil, are to be treated as aliens and enemies, as an

continued next page

inferior degraded class, who must have no voice in the Government which they support, protect and defend, with all their heart, soul, mind, and body, both in peace and war.

This Government is based on the teachings of the Bible, which prescribes the same rules of action for all members of the human family, whether their complexion be white, yellow, red or black. God no where in his revealed word, makes an invidious and degrading distinction against his children, because of their color. And happy is that nation which makes the Bible its rule of action, and obeys principle, not prejudice.

Let no man oppose this doctrine because it is opposed to his old prejudices. The nation is fighting for its life, and cannot afford to be controlled by prejudice. Had prejudice prevailed instead of principle, not a single colored soldier would have been in the Union army to-day. But principle and justice triumphed, and now near 200,000 colored patriots stand under the folds of the national flag, and brave their breasts to the bullets of the rebels. As we are in the battlefield, so we swear before heaven, by all that is dear to men, to be at the ballot-box faithful and true to the Union.

The possibility that the negro suffrage proposition may shock popular prejudice at first sight, is not a conclusive argument against its wisdom and policy. No proposition ever met with more furious or general opposition than the one to enlist colored soldiers in the United States army. The opponents of the measure exclaimed on all hands that the negro was a coward; that he would not fight; that one white man, with a whip in his hand could put to flight a regiment of them; that the experiment would end in the utter rout and ruin of the Federal army. Yet the colored man has fought so well, on almost every occasion, that the rebel government is prevented, only by its fears and distrust of being able to force him to fight for slavery as well as he fights against it, from putting half a million of negroes into its ranks.

The Government has asked the colored man to fight for its preservation and gladly has he done it. It can afford to trust him with a vote as safely as it trusted him with a bayonet. . . .

balconies and listening to sermons exhorting slaves not to steal. For many ex-slaves, one of their first acts of freedom was to form their own churches with their own ministers. People who owned virtually nothing somehow built churches across the South. Those churches often served as schools as well. Hundreds of northern white women aided black Southerners in their quest for an education in 1865 and 1866, but the former slaves did not wait for outside help before creating their own schoolhouses and choosing teachers from among themselves.

Andrew Johnson

In the meantime, events in Washington undermined the efforts of black Southerners to build a new world for themselves. Andrew Johnson wanted to attract moderates from both the North and the South to a party that would change as little as possible; he was willing to sacrifice black Southerners to create that alliance. Johnson had been selected to run for the vice presidency because he was a Southerner who had remained true to the Union. As a result, both Northerners and Southerners

One other matter we would urge on your honorable body. At present we can have only partial protection from the courts. The testimony of twenty of the most intelligent, honorable, colored loyalists cannot convict a white traitor of a treasonable action. A white rebel might sell powder and lead to a rebel soldier in the presence of twenty colored soldiers, and yet their evidence would be worthless so far as the courts are concerned, and the rebel would escape. A colored man may have served for years faithfully in the army, and yet his testimony in court would be rejected, while that of a white man who had served in the rebel army would be received. . . .

There have been white traitors in multitudes in Tennessee, but where we ask, is the black traitor? Can you forget how the colored man has fought at Fort Morgan, at Milliken's Bend, at Fort Pillow, before Petersburg, and your own city of Nashville?

When has the colored citizen, in this rebellion been tried and found wanting? . . .

In this great and fearful struggle of the nation with a wicked rebellion, we are anxious to perform the full measure of our duty both as citizens and soldiers to the Union cause we consecrate ourselves, and our families with all that we have on earth. Our souls burn with love for the great government of freedom and equal rights. Our white brethren have no cause for distrust as regards our fidelity, for neither death nor life, nor angels, nor principalities, nor powers, nor things present, nor things to come, nor height, nor depth, nor any other creature, shall be able to separate us from the love of the Union.

Praying that the great God, who is the common Father of us all, by whose help the land must be delivered from present evil, and before whom we must all stand at last to be judged by the rule of eternal justice, and not by passion and prejudice, may enlighten your minds and enable you to act with wisdom, justice, and magnanimity, we remain your faithful friends in all the perils and dangers which threaten our beloved country.

SOURCE   *Free at Last: A Documentary History of Slavery, Freedom, and the Civil War.* Ira Berlin, et al., eds. (New York: New Press, 1992) pp. 497–505.

[*59 signatures*]
And many other colored citizens of Nashville

distrusted Johnson. A longtime Democrat before the crisis of the Union, Johnson maintained a limited, Jacksonian view of government in opposition to the rapid expansion in the power of government in the war years. The new president's well-known disdain for the wealthy planters of the South appealed to equally disdainful Republicans in Washington. Unlike them, however, Johnson held little sympathy for black people and little interest in promoting their interests. Johnson saw himself following Lincoln's plan and pursuing Lincoln's highest goal: reuniting the Union. Johnson believed that reunification should start by winning the support of white Southerners.

Johnson could hardly have been placed in a more difficult position and could hardly have made worse of it. Congress was not in session at the time of Lincoln's death and would not be for seven months, so Johnson used the opportunity to implement his vision of reunion. In what became known as "Presidential Reconstruction," Johnson offered amnesty to former Confederates who would take an oath of loyalty to the Union, restoring their political and civil

Andrew Johnson attempted to forge a new alliance between white Northerners and white Southerners, callously abandoning black Southerners in the process.

flaunted their opinions of the North. Some refused to fly the American flag, some refused to ratify the Thirteenth Amendment, some even refused to admit that secession had been illegal. Former Confederates filled important posts in state governments throughout the South. Georgia elected Alexander H. Stephens, the ex-vice president of the aborted nation, to Congress. Johnson personally pardoned such men, reasoning that reunion could best be served by acknowledging the decisions of the white South.

The North erupted in outrage when the new state governments enacted the so-called "black codes," laws for the control of the former slaves. The southern white legislatures granted only the barest minimum of rights to black people: the right to marry, to hold property, to sue and be sued. Most of the laws decreed what African Americans could not do: move from one job to another, own or rent land, practice certain occupations. When the members of Congress convened in December of 1865, they reacted as many of their constituents did—with fury. To Northerners, even those inclined to deal leniently with the South, the former Confederates seemed to deny all the war had decided. And many Northerners blamed the man who had overseen this travesty, Andrew Johnson.

Johnson and the Radicals

It was not that most Northerners, even most Republicans, wanted the kind of policies promoted by Radicals such as Thaddeus Stevens, who called for land to be seized from wealthy planters and given to the former slaves, or of Charles Sumner, who wanted immediate and universal suffrage for blacks. But neither did they want the sort of capitulation that Johnson had tolerated. Moderates tried to devise plans that would be acceptable to both sides, that would protect black freedom while still permitting white Southerners to reclaim a place in the nation.

The moderates sought to continue the Freedmen's Bureau, which was not only saving people, white and black, from starvation in the South but was also providing for schools and at least some measure of justice for the former slaves. The Bureau was understaffed and underfunded—only about 900 agents covered the entire South—but it offered some measure of

rights and immunizing them against the seizure of their property or prosecution for treason. While Johnson withheld such amnesty from political leaders of the rebellion, the Confederate military, and the largest planters, he soon began to grant pardons to such men when they applied to him personally. Johnson's plans for political reunion made no provisions at all for black voting. Indeed, his plan threatened to return the South to even greater national power than it had held before because the entire African-American population would now be considered when the number of representatives was calculated, not merely as three-fifths of a people as before the war.

White Southerners could hardly believe their good fortune, for they had told themselves to expect harsher peace terms. The state conventions elected in 1865

Thaddeus Stevens, a congressman from Pennsylvania, was among the leaders of the Radical Republicans.

hope for former slaves. The Bureau, under the leadership of the deeply religious General O. O. Howard, saw itself as a mediator between blacks and whites. It insisted on the innovation of formal contracts between laborer and landlord, specifying the duties and responsibilities of all involved. Although these contracts infuriated southern white men, who resented the implied challenge to their honor and who resisted treating former slaves with such dignity, the Freedmen's Bureau ended up supporting landowners as often as black laborers. The moderates also attempted to institute a Civil Rights bill to define American citizenship for all those born in the United States, thereby including blacks. Citizenship would bring with it equal protection under the laws, though the bill said nothing about black voting and gave African Americans only the most rudimentary guarantees of freedom.

Republicans of widely varying perspectives supported the Freedmen's Bureau and Civil Rights bills as the starting place for rebuilding the nation. But Johnson vetoed both bills, claiming that they violated the rights of the states and of white Southerners who had been excluded from the decision making. Republicans, furious and determined, closed ranks to override Johnson's veto. Recognizing their ability to overrule any presidential vetoes, in fact, the Republicans proceeded to neutralize Johnson altogether.

To prevent any future erosion of black rights, the Republicans proposed the Fourteenth Amendment, which, as eventually ratified, guaranteed citizenship to all American-born people and equal protection under the law for those citizens, making it illegal to deprive any person of life, liberty, or property without due process of law. The amendment decreed that any state that abridged the voting rights of any male inhabitants who were twenty-one and citizens would suffer a proportionate reduction in its congressional representation. (It did not simply guarantee universal male suffrage because all but five northern states still refused black men the right to vote.) Johnson urged the southern states to refuse to ratify the amendment, advice they promptly followed.

Throughout the second half of 1866 the North watched, appalled, as much that the Civil War had been fought for seemed to be brushed aside in the South. Not only did the southern men who met in the state conventions refuse to accept the relatively mild Fourteenth Amendment, but they made clear their determination to fight back in every way they could against further attempts to remake the South. The spring of that year saw riots in Memphis and New Orleans in which policemen and other whites brutally assaulted and killed black people with little or no provocation.

It was in 1866, too, that the Ku Klux Klan appeared. This group was the strongest and most visible of many paramilitary organizations created by whites after the war. Founded in Tennessee, the Ku Klux Klan dedicated itself to maintaining white supremacy and everything it associated with that supremacy: law and order, Christian morals, and home rule. The Klan dressed in costumes designed to overawe the former slaves, hiding behind their anonymity to avoid retaliation from the black community and from government authorities. The Klan became in effect a military wing of the Democratic party, devoting much of its energy to warning and killing white and black men who dared associate with the Republicans.

Johnson toured the country in the fall of 1866 to denounce the Republicans and their policies. The

In the Memphis riot of July 1866, southern whites killed thirty-seven blacks and three white supporters after a Republican meeting.

tour was a disaster. The voters rejected both Johnson and the Democrats, as the governorship and legislature of every northern state came under the control of the Republicans. The Republicans who returned to Congress in December of 1866 felt they held a mandate to push harder than they had before. They had only a few months, however, until their term ended in March, to decide what to do and how to do it. They bitterly disagreed with one another over the vote, land distribution, the courts, and education. Some wanted to put the South under military control for the indefinite future while others sought to return things to civilian control as soon as possible. Finally, on March 2, 1867, as time was running out on the session, they passed the Reconstruction Act.

The Reconstruction Act

The Reconstruction Act, coming two tumultuous years after the end of the war, placed the South under military rule. All the southern states except Tennessee, which had been readmitted to the Union after it ratified the Fourteenth Amendment, were put

in five military districts. The military commander of each district held broad power to punish those who imperiled the rights or property of others. Once order had been instituted, then the states would proceed to elect conventions to draw up new constitutions. The elections for those conventions would include black voters, but not former Confederates who had been disfranchised. The constitutions written by those conventions had to accept the Fourteenth Amendment and provide for universal manhood suffrage. Once a majority of the state's citizens and both houses of the national Congress had approved the new constitution, the state could be readmitted to the Union. White Southerners resisted the plan as tyrannical, but submitted to it when it became clear they had no choice.

To ensure that Andrew Johnson did not undermine this plan—which soon became known as "Radical Reconstruction"—Congress sought to curb the president's power. With no threat of his veto after the 1866 elections, the Republicans could do much as they wanted. Congress decreed that it could call itself into special session. There, they limited the president's authority as commander-in-chief of the army and, in the Tenure of Office Act, prevented him from removing

officials who had been confirmed by the Senate. Some Republicans were queasy about such steps, but they had no intention of letting Johnson undermine Reconstruction.

Johnson, characteristically, did not quietly accept such restrictions of his power. He saw the Republicans as power-hungry tyrants, writing unconstitutional laws, and he determined to challenge them. When he intentionally violated the Tenure of Office Act by removing Secretary of War Edwin Stanton in the summer of 1867, many in Congress decided that Johnson warranted impeachment. Matters stewed throughout the fall, while the first elections under the Reconstruction Act took place in the South.

Reconstruction Begins

Secession and the war had dissolved the old party system in the South, forcing former Whigs and former Democrats into awkward and testy alliances. Whites argued openly with one another about the best route to restoring their former power. Some called for cooperation with the North while others called for resistance. Some called for cooperation with blacks, while other whites declared themselves dedicated to a party of unalloyed white supremacy.

After word of the Reconstruction Act circulated in the spring and summer, both black men and white claimed leadership roles within the Republican party. Black Northerners came to the South to use their educations in the service of Reconstruction, looking for appointive and elective office. Ambitious black Southerners, many of whom had been free and relatively prosperous before the Civil War, put themselves forward as the natural leaders of the race. Such men became the backbone of the Republican party in black-belt districts, giving speeches, visiting with voters, often risking their lives to mobilize former slaves into citizens.

White Southerners sneered at white Northerners who supported the Republican cause. They called them "carpetbaggers." These men, according to the insulting name, were supposedly so devoid of

The Ku Klux Klan emerged in 1866, devoting itself to the maintenance of white supremacy in all its forms.

African-American men could vote in the South during Reconstruction, but often risked their livelihoods or their lives to do so.

connections and property in their northern homes that they could throw everything they had into a carpetbag—a cheap suitcase—and head south as soon as they read of the opportunities created by Radical Reconstruction. The majority of white Northerners who became Republican leaders in the South, however, had in fact moved to the region long before Reconstruction began. Many were former Union soldiers who had decided to try their lot in the South at war's end, becoming planters or merchants. Many had been well educated in the North before the war and many held property in the South. Like white Southerners, however, the northern-born Republicans found the postwar South a difficult place in which to prosper. Black people were no more inclined to work for low wages for white Northerners than for anyone else and southern whites often went out of their way to avoid doing business with the Yankees. As a result, when Reconstruction began, a considerable number of Northerners took up the Republican cause as a way to remake

the South and find a place for themselves in the new order.

White southern Republicans, labeled "scalawags" by their enemies, risked being called traitors to their race and region. Few white Republicans emerged in the plantation districts, because they endured ostracism, resistance, and violence for violating white unity in the face of Radical Reconstruction. In the upcountry districts, however, former Whigs and Unionists asserted themselves against the planters and Confederates. The Republican party became strong in the mountains of east Tennessee, western North Carolina, eastern Kentucky, north Alabama, and northern Georgia. Many whites in these districts, though unwilling to join with low country African Americans or their white leaders in true party feeling or common purpose, struck alliances of convenience with them. Black voters and white voters generally wanted and needed different things. Blacks, largely propertyless, called for an activist government

to provide schools, orphanages, and hospitals. Most whites, on the other hand, owned land and called mainly for lower taxes.

Throughout the South, most whites watched, livid, as the Republicans mobilized black voters in enormous numbers in the fall of 1867. While many white Democrats boycotted the elections, the Republicans swept into the constitutional delegate positions. Most white Republicans came from the upcountry, but about a sixth of the delegates were of white northern background. Although many black men voted, African-American delegates made up only a relatively small part of the convention's delegates. They held the majority in South Carolina and Louisiana, but much smaller proportions elsewhere. About half of the 265 African Americans elected as delegates to the state conventions had been free before the war, about forty had served in the Union army, and most were ministers, artisans, farmers, and teachers. Over the next two years, these delegates would meet to write new, much more democratic, constitutions for their states.

At the very moment of the success of the southern Republicans, however, ominous signs came from the North. Republicans were dismayed at the election returns in the North in 1867, for the Democrats' power surged from coast to coast, reducing by three-quarters the gains the Republicans had made just the preceding year. Many white voters thought that the Radicals had gone too far in their concern with black rights and wanted officeholders to devote their energies to problems closer to home. The Republicans in Washington heard the message. They began scaling back their support for any further advances in Reconstruction. No sooner had the experiment in the South begun, in other words, than the North began to undermine it.

CONCLUSION

The Civil War changed the United States more deeply than any other event in the nineteenth century. The conflict brought the deaths of over 625,000 soldiers and the shattering of families North and South. It saw bitter rioting in the streets and the first assassination of a president. It saw fortunes made and lost. It brought a major shift in the balance of power among the regions and an expansion of the federal government. Most important, the war brought what few Americans, regardless of their region or their color, could have imagined at the end of 1860: the immediate emancipation of 4 million enslaved people.

Freedom emerged from the war through a circuitous route. The war began as a war for Union. As the deaths mounted and African Americans seized freedom at every opportunity, abolitionists and Republicans increasingly insisted that the war become a war to end slavery. Many white Northerners supported emancipation because it seemed the best way to end the war, crippling the Confederate ability and will to fight. Abraham Lincoln worked desperately to keep the support of both the advocates and foes of emancipation, knowing that moving too quickly would shatter the fragile support that kept him in office. The New York City draft riots and the close elections of 1863 demonstrated that many Northerners resisted the continuation of the war and its embrace of black freedom. Only Union success on the battlefield in late 1864 permitted Lincoln's reelection. His assassination made an already confused situation far more so, ending slavery and restoring the Union without a blueprint and without leadership. The end of the war resolved the question of secession and the continuance of slavery, but it left much undecided.

The end of the fighting saw the conflict shift in the South, as people struggled to determine what freedom would mean. For black Southerners, the goal was autonomy and respect, a chance to work for themselves and enjoy the fundamental rights of American citizens. For white Northerners, the goal was to reconstruct the South in an idealized image of the North, with orderly free labor and the rule of law at its heart. For white Southerners, the goal was the reassertion of the power they had held before the war, especially power over the black people in their midst. Such goals could not be reconciled. The era of Reconstruction would be devoted to the struggle among them.

RECOMMENDED READINGS

Berlin, Ira, Barbara J. Fields, Steven F. Miller, Joseph P. Reidy, and Leslie S. Rowland, eds., *Freedom,* (1985–) is a fascinating multivolume documentary collection.

Donald, David. *Lincoln* (1995) stands as the most elegant biography.

Faust, Drew Gilpin. *Mothers of Invention: Women of the Slaveholding South in the American Civil War* (1995) offers a challenging and interesting interpretation.

Fellman, Michael. *Inside War: The Guerilla Conflict in Missouri During the American Civil War* (1989) makes palpable the internal struggles in the border areas.

Foner, Eric. *Reconstruction: America's Unfinished Revolution, 1863–1877* (1988) is a magisterial interpretation of the struggle over black freedom.

Gallagher, Gary W. *The Confederate War: How Popular Will, Nationalism, and Military Strategy Could Not Stave Off Defeat* (1997) explores why the Confederacy could fight as long as it did.

Harris, William C. *With Charity for All: Lincoln and the Restoration of the Union* (1997) offers a fresh assessment of Lincoln's attitudes toward the white South.

Hattaway, Herman, and Jones, Archer. *How the North Won: A Military History of the Civil War* (1983) authoritatively describes strategy and tactics.

Litwack, Leon. *Been in the Storm So Long: The Aftermath of Slavery* (1979) beautifully evokes the conflicting emotions and motives surrounding freedom.

Roark, James L. *Masters Without Slaves: Southern Planters in the Civil War and Reconstruction* (1978) describes the war from the perspective of those who lost the most in southern defeat.

Rose, Willie Lee. *Rehearsal for Reconstruction: The Port Royal Experiment* (1964) is a classic account of the first efforts to create northern policy toward the freed people.

Interpretations

Aaron, Daniel. *The Unwritten War: American Writers and the Civil War* (1973).

Beringer, Richard E. Herman Hattaway, Archer Jones, and William N. Still, Jr., *Why the South Lost the Civil War* (1986).

Frederickson, George. *The Inner Civil War: Northern Intellectuals and the Crisis of Disunion* (1965).

Vinovskis, Maris A. *Toward a Social History of the American Civil War: Exploratory Essays* (1990).

Warren, Robert Penn. *The Legacy of the Civil War* (1961).

Wills, Garry. *Lincoln at Gettysburg* (1992).

Wilson, Edmund. *Patriotic Gore: Studies in the Literature of the American Civil War* (1962).

Battles

Castel, Albert. *Decision in the West: The Atlanta Campaign of 1864* (1992).

Cozzens, Peter. *The Shipwreck of Their Hopes: The Battles for Chattanooga* (1994).

Glatthaar, Joseph T. *The March to the Sea and Beyond: Sherman's Troops in the Savannah and Carolina Campaigns* (1985).

Hennessy, John H. *Return to Bull Run: The Campaign and Battle of Second Manassas* (1993).

Kennett, Lee. *Marching Through Georgia: The Story of Soldiers and Civilians During Sherman's Campaign* (1994).

Rhea, Gordon H. *The Battle of the Wilderness, May 5–6, 1864* (1994).

Sears, Stephen W. *Landscape Turned Red: The Battle of Antietam* (1983).

Sears, Stephen W. *Chancellorsville* (1996).

Sword, Wiley. *Shiloh: Bloody April* (1974).

Tucker, Glenn. *Chickamauga: Bloody Battle in the West* (1961).

Northern Politics and Leadership

Klement, Frank L. *Clement L. Vallandigham and the Civil War* (1970).

Neely, Mark. *The Fate of Liberty: Abraham Lincoln and Civil Liberties* (1991).

Richardson, Heather Cox. *The Greatest Nation on the Earth: Republican Economic Policies During the Civil War* (1997).

Silbey, Joel H. *A Respectable Minority: The Democratic Party in the Civil War Era, 1860–1868* (1977).

Waugh, John C. *Reelecting Lincoln: The Battle for the 1864 Presidency* (1997).

The Homefronts

Ash, Stephen V. *Middle Tennessee Society Transformed, 1869–1870* (1988).

Ash, Stephen V. *When the Yankees Came: Conflict and Chaos in the Occupied South, 1861–1865* (1995).

Bernstein, Iver. *The New York City Draft Riots: Their Significance for American Society and Politics in the Age of the Civil War* (1990).

Cook, Adrian. *The Armies of the Streets: The New York City Draft Riots of 1863* (1974).

Durrill, Wayne K. *War of Another Kind: A Southern Community in the Great Rebellion* (1990).

Grimsley, Mark. *The Hard Hand of War: Union Military Policy Toward Southern Civilians, 1861–1865* (1995).

O'Connor, Thomas H. *Civil War Boston: Home Front and Battlefield* (1997).

Sutherland, Daniel E. *Seasons of War: The Ordeal of a Confederate Community, 1861–1865* (1995).

Soldiers' Experiences

Cornish, Dudley Taylor. *The Sable Arm: Negro Troops in the Union Army, 1861–1865* (1956).

Glatthaar, Joseph T. *Forged in Battle: The Civil War Alliance of Black Soldiers and White Officers* (1990).

Hess, Earl J. *The Union Soldier in Battle: Enduring the Ordeal of Combat* (1997).

Linderman, Gerald F. *Embattled Courage: The Experience of Combat in the Civil War* (1987).

Marvel, William. *Andersonville: The Last Depot* (1994).

McPherson, James M. *For Cause and Comrades: Why Men Fought in the Civil War* (1997).

Mitchell, Reid. *Civil War Soldiers* (1988).

Mitchell, Reid. *The Vacant Chair: The Northern Soldier Leaves Home* (1993).

Trudeau, Noah Andre. *Like Men of War: Black Troops in the Civil War, 1862–1865* (1998).

Wiley, Bell I. *The Life of Johnny Reb* (1943).

Wiley, Bell I. *The Life of Billy Yank* (1952).

Women's Experiences

Clinton Catherine, and Nina Silber, eds., *Divided Houses: Gender and the Civil War* (1992).

Massey, Mary E. *Bonnet Brigades* (1966).

Rable, George C. *Civil Wars: Women and the Crisis of Southern Nationalism* (1991).

Rose, Anne E. *Victorian America and the Civil War* (1992).

Venet, Wendy Hamand. *Neither Ballots nor Bullets: Women Abolitionists and the Civil War* (1991).

Emancipation and Aftermath

Carter, Dan T. *When the War Was Over: Self-Reconstruction in the South, 1865–1867* (1985) .

Cimbala, Paul A. *Under the Guardianship of the Nation: The Freedmen's Bureau and the Reconstruction of Georgia, 1865–1870* (1997).

Fields, Barbara Jeanne. *Slavery and Freedom on the Middle Ground: Maryland During the Nineteenth Century* (1985).

Holt, Thomas. *Black over White: Negro Political Leadership in South Carolina During Reconstruction* (1977).

McFeely, William S. *Yankee Stepfather: General O. O. Howard and the Freedmen* (1966).

Mohr, Clarence L. *On the Threshold of Freedom: Masters and Slaves in Civil War Georgia* (1986).

Perman, Michael. *Reunion Without Compromise: The South and Reconstruction, 1865–1868* (1973).

Ransom, Roger L., and Sutch, Richard. *One Kind of Freedom: The Economic Consequences of Emancipation* (1977).

THE FIFTEENTH AMENDMENT ADOPTED

When the Fifteenth Amendment was approved in 1870, a lithograph artist depicted the moment when race, color, and having been a slave were no longer barriers to male voters. The prominent individuals shown include the most famous African American of the day, Frederick Douglass, in the group at the top of the illustration.

Chapter 16

RECONSTRUCTION ABANDONED,

1867–1877

After 1867 the nation continued to struggle over the gains that black Americans had earned during the Civil War. The battle raged in the minds of Northerners and in the halls of Congress, but it was fought with the greatest intensity in the South. There, whites sought to recapture as many of the features of slavery as they could. Violence, brutality, election fraud, and economic intimidation ended the experiment in multiracial politics known as Reconstruction.

Racial prejudice was at the heart of the problem, but other circumstances hastened the abandonment of Reconstruction. Settlement of the West claimed the energies of many people. In the mid-1870s an economic depression made civil rights seem less relevant. White Americans worried that the national government was becoming too powerful, and they reverted to traditional beliefs in localism and state rights. For many in the North, the issue of race seemed a dreary and hopeless legacy of the war, a commitment easier to forget than to fulfill. The hum of industry, the spread of railroads, the rise of cities, all seemed more in tune with an era of progress than preserving the rights of former slaves. Slowly, painfully, the nation retreated from the principles for which the Civil War had been fought. In 1877 an informal sectional compromise sealed the return to white rule in the South.

Outside the political arena, industrialization transformed the economy. The completion of the two transcontinental railroads in 1869 symbolized the rapid pace of technological change. Four years later, however, the Panic of 1873 demonstrated that progress did not always move forward along an unbroken path. The 1870s produced social unrest and deprivation for many.

A PERIOD OF UNREST

The waning of Reconstruction left African Americans and Indians further removed from the mainstream of society. As the drive to expand freedom for black Americans stalled, white dominance in the South hardened. Military defeat of the Indians confined them to reservations. Women of all colors and ancestries found that their future remained subject to the wishes of a male-dominated nation. After the upheaval of the Civil War, the 1870s were a time to pause and react, a time of political mediocrity and governmental caution.

CHRONOLOGY

1867   Alaska purchase treaty signed

1868   Andrew Johnson impeached and then acquitted

         Purchase of Alaska completed

         Ulysses S. Grant wins presidency

1869   Ulysses S. Grant inaugurated as president

         Transcontinental railroads link up

         Licensing of women lawyers begins

         Fifteenth Amendment passes Congress

         "Gold Corner" scheme of Jay Gould and Jim Fisk

         Woman suffrage enacted in Wyoming Territory

1870   Santo Domingo annexation treaty defeated

         Ku Klux Klan terror raids in the South

         First Greek letter sorority (Kappa Alpha Theta) founded

1871   Ku Klux Klan Act passes Congress

         Tweed Ring exposed in New York City

         Chicago fire burns three and a half miles of the city

1872   Liberal Republican movement challenges Grant

         Grant wins reelection over Horace Greeley

1873   Panic of 1873 starts economic depression

         Salary Grab and Crédit Mobilier scandals

         Mark Twain and Charles Dudley Warner publish *The Gilded Age*

1874   Women's Christian Temperance Union founded

         Democrats make substantial gains in the congressional elections

         Sale of typewriters begins

         Chautauqua movement for summer education starts

1875   Civil Rights Act passes Congress

         Smith College and Wellesley College open to provide higher education for women

1876   Custer defeated at Little Big Horn

         Heinz tomato ketchup is marketed

         Centennial Exposition opens in Philadelphia

         Tilden and Hayes are candidates in presidential election which remains contested as year ends

1877   Hayes declared winner of the presidency after series of compromises settles disputes

         Reconstruction comes to an end

The Impeachment of Andrew Johnson

As President Andrew Johnson sought to block the Radical Reconstruction program, sentiment to impeach him grew among Republicans in Congress. The president's effort to oust Secretary of War Edwin M. Stanton in August 1867 also resulted in demands for his impeachment. The Republicans could do little until December when Congress reassembled. By that time, impeachment efforts had faltered, and it appeared that the political momentum had turned toward Johnson. After the Senate refused to accept his dismissal of Stanton in January 1868, Johnson replaced him anyway—an act of defiance that Republicans claimed was a clear breach of the Tenure of Office Act (see Chapter 15).

Emboldened by Johnson's action, the solidly Republican House voted for his impeachment and brought eleven charges against him. None of the charges involved violations of criminal law; they dealt instead with Johnson's Reconstruction policies. The trial got underway in March. Two months later the Senate failed to produce a two-thirds' vote to convict the president.

The impeachment attempt failed for several reasons. Moderate Republicans feared that if a president were impeached and convicted on political grounds a bad precedent would be set. Johnson temporarily eased obstructive tactics and the situation in the South became more favorable to the Republicans. The approach of the 1868 election also made ousting Johnson seem less urgent.

Although he was acquitted, Johnson did not become more conciliatory; he opposed Reconstruction until the end of his term. His intransigence encouraged southern whites and contributed to the resistance against African-American equality that marked the 1870s. Few presidents have done less to capitalize on their historic opportunities than Andrew Johnson.

The Purchase of Alaska

During the months that Andrew Johnson's impeachment case dominated the headlines, the Congress also moved to complete a major territorial acquisition. In March 1867 the Russian minister to the United States hinted to Secretary of State William H. Seward that the tsarist government in St. Petersburg would respond favorably to an American offer to purchase Alaska. The Russians knew that they could not defend their northern possession against the British in Canada, and they worried about a potential American occupation. The Russian diplomat and Seward worked

out a treaty that was signed on March 30, 1867. The United States paid $7,200,000 for Alaska. On April 9, the Senate gave its approval by a vote of thirty-seven to two.

Paying for the Alaska purchase required an appropriation from the House. The members did not take up the subject until July 1868, after the House had impeached the president. Faced with a *fait accompli* in that the occupation of the territory had occurred a year earlier, the House approved the money solidly on July 14, and the measure became law two weeks later. The purchase of Alaska represented a major strategic and geographic victory for the country, but it would be another twenty-five years before overseas expansion once again took place.

The Election of 1868

The leading candidate for the Republican nomination was Ulysses S. Grant. His association with the Union victory gave him a popularity that transcended

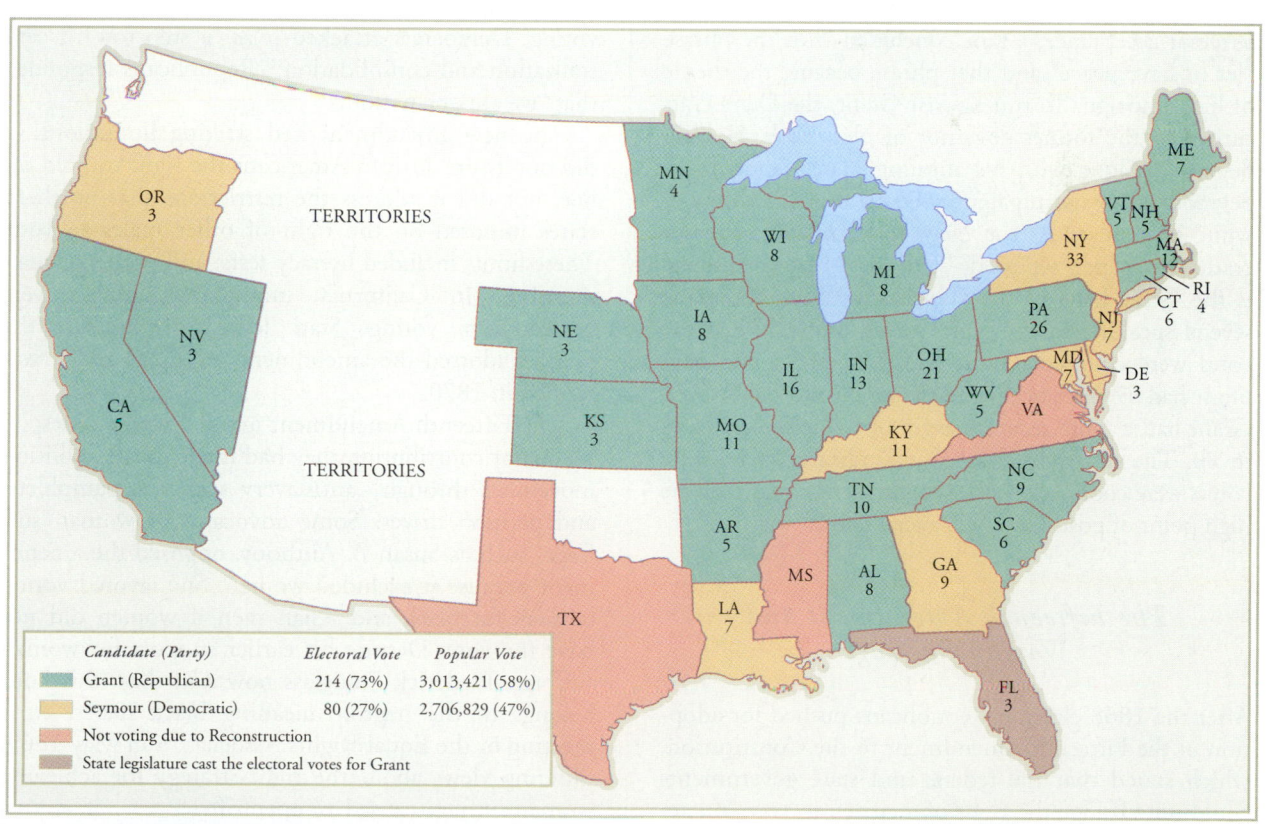

Candidate (Party)	Electoral Vote	Popular Vote
Grant (Republican)	214 (73%)	3,013,421 (58%)
Seymour (Democratic)	80 (27%)	2,706,829 (47%)
Not voting due to Reconstruction		
State legislature cast the electoral votes for Grant		

MAP 16.1 | THE ELECTION OF 1868

THE FIFTEENTH AMENDMENT 1870

The last of the three Reconstruction amendments, the Fifteenth Amendment said that race or color could not be a reason for denying a citizen the right to vote.

Sect. 1. The right of citizens of the United States to vote shall not be denied or abridged by the United States or by any State on account of race, color, or previous condition of servitude.

Sect. 2. The Congress shall have the power to enforce this article by appropriate legislation.

partisanship and would draw key Democratic votes in what shaped up to be a close election contest. In his letter of acceptance, Grant concluded with the phrase "let us have peace" and that phrase became the theme of his campaign. To run against Grant, the Democrats turned to the former governor of New York, Horatio Seymour. Along with his running mate, Frank Blair, Seymour made a campaign based on the philosophy of white supremacy. As the New York *Herald,* a Democratic newspaper, reported, "Universal Nigger Suffrage is the Great Issue of the Campaign." Seymour made several speaking tours; Grant stayed home. When the votes were counted, Grant had 53 percent and Seymour had 47 percent. In the electoral college, however, Grant had a more secure margin of 214 electoral votes to 80. The relatively close result indicated that white voters were cooling toward Reconstruction and that the high point of post–Civil War racial reform was past.

The Fifteenth Amendment and Woman Suffrage

After the 1868 election Republicans pushed for adoption of the Fifteenth Amendment to the Constitution, which stated that the federal and state governments could not abridge the right of a citizen to vote "on account of race, color, or previous condition of servitude." Legislative approval came in February 1869.

Because the amendment reduced the legal ability of the southern states to exclude African Americans from voting, Democrats attacked it as "a step toward centralization and consolidation." Republicans responded that "we are one nation."

The new amendment had striking limitations. It did not assure African Americans the right to hold office, nor did it address the restrictions that northern states imposed on the right of other males to vote. These limits included literacy tests, and property qualifications. In California, immigrant Chinese were barred from voting. State legislatures outside the South endorsed the amendment promptly and it was ratified in 1870.

The Fifteenth Amendment ignored women, despite the major contribution they had made to the abolition movement through antislavery societies, pamphlets, and petition drives. Some advocates of woman suffrage, such as Susan B. Anthony, opposed the amendment because it excluded women. She favored voting barriers for black and Asian men if women did not have the vote. Despite his earlier support for woman suffrage, Frederick Douglass now said that "this hour belongs to the negro," meaning black males. At a meeting of the Equal Rights Association in May 1869, differing views about the right strategy for achieving woman suffrage caused an open rift.

The split led to the formation of two distinct groups. The National Woman Suffrage Association

Susan B. Anthony was a leading advocate of a woman's right to vote in the post-Civil War era. Her connection with that reform continued throughout the late nineteenth century.

(NWSA) reflected the position of Susan B. Anthony and Elizabeth Cady Stanton who believed that the Fifteenth Amendment should not be supported until it included women. The American Woman Suffrage Association (AWSA), led by Lucy Stone and Alice Stone Blackwell, endorsed the amendment and focused their suffrage efforts on the states. The new territory of Wyoming granted women the right of suffrage in 1869. The goal of the Wyoming legislature was to advertise its underpopulated territory, not to expand women's rights, but a small step forward had nonetheless been taken. The discord between the two suffrage organizations lasted for two decades, however, and slowed the progress toward reform.

GRANT'S FIRST TERM

The new president entered the White House with little political experience. He intended to administer the government rather than promote new programs. "I shall on all subjects have a policy to recommend," he said in his inaugural address, "but none to enforce against the will of the people."

Grant's limited view of the presidency meant that Congress played a dominant role during his adminis-

tration. Republicans did not look to the White House for leadership in developing programs or shaping policy. As a result, the office of the presidency lost some of the authority it had acquired during the Civil War. A generation passed before the balance shifted back toward the executive branch.

The new administration faced hard choices. Southern Republicans wanted help from Washington against resurgent Democrats. A growing number of northern party members questioned whether continuation of Reconstruction was wise or practical. Some had backed off from the commitment to African Americans that Reconstruction implied. Within the Republican ranks, party reformers wanted to limit the power of the leaders to dole out patronage. They wanted to adopt a merit system for appointing officials; this was referred to as "civil service reform." Party regulars hoped that Grant would side with them against the reformers and recognize the power of congressional leaders.

At first Grant tried to avoid partisan battles. For example, he had no clear policy on appointments. In selecting his cabinet he did not follow the advice of influential Republicans but relied instead on men who shared his cautious governing style. Cabinet officers

When he took office, President Grant was seen as a constructive change from the turmoil of Andrew Johnson's administration. In office, he found that politics was more of a challenge to him than military success in the Civil War.

were given free rein in using merit rather than political connections to staff their departments. Some worked with Congress; other did not.

In the South, the Democrats endeavored to split the Republicans. They collaborated with party members who had become alienated from the Republican leadership. Playing down their dislike of black voters, they centered their arguments on whether former Confederates should be allowed to cast ballots. The elections in 1869 produced mixed results. Republicans did well in Mississippi and won narrowly in Texas while Democrats prevailed in Virginia and Tennessee. The latter outcomes foreshadowed an erosion of Republican electoral strength as the Democrats reestablished their power in the South. Grant's passive style meant that Republicans and their black allies in the South found themselves at a disadvantage.

The Railroads Meet

While politics dominated Washington, an event in Utah captured the attention of the rest of the nation. Throughout the 1860s two transcontinental railroads had been laying track across the country. The Union Pacific had built westward and the Central Pacific eastward. The competing lines faced significant obstacles of money and geography. The Central Pacific had

In the work of building the transcontinental railroad, the grueling labor of Chinese workers was indispensable. They worked for low pay in difficult conditions in a society that scorned them and often subjected them to harsh discrimination.

crossed the heights of the Sierra Nevada mountains through rocky gorges and treacherous rivers. Several thousand Chinese laborers did the most dangerous work. They tunneled into snowdrifts to reach their work sites and then toiled on sheer cliffs with picks and dynamite. On the Union Pacific side, more than 10,000 construction men, many of them Irish immigrants, laid track across Nebraska and Wyoming.

On May 10, 1869, the two rail lines met at Promontory, Utah. The occasion was marked by a dramatic ceremony. Engine 119 of the Union Pacific stood with its cowcatcher touching the cowcatcher of the Central Pacific's Engine No. 60. A gold spike was driven into the ground with a silver sledgehammer, though railroad executives failed to hit the spike on their first few tries. The transcontinental lines had been built so quickly in part because of loans and subsidies from the federal government to the rail companies. The process by which the financing had occurred would soon become one of the more notorious scandals of the Grant presidency.

The completion of the first transcontinental railroad in 1869 ushered in a period of railroad construction in which the nation developed one of the best and most comprehensive transportation systems in the world. It meant that the opening of the entire

The completion of the transcontinental railroad at Promontory, Utah, in 1869 symbolized the joining together of the nation's two coasts. As the presence of photographers indicates, it also became an important media event.

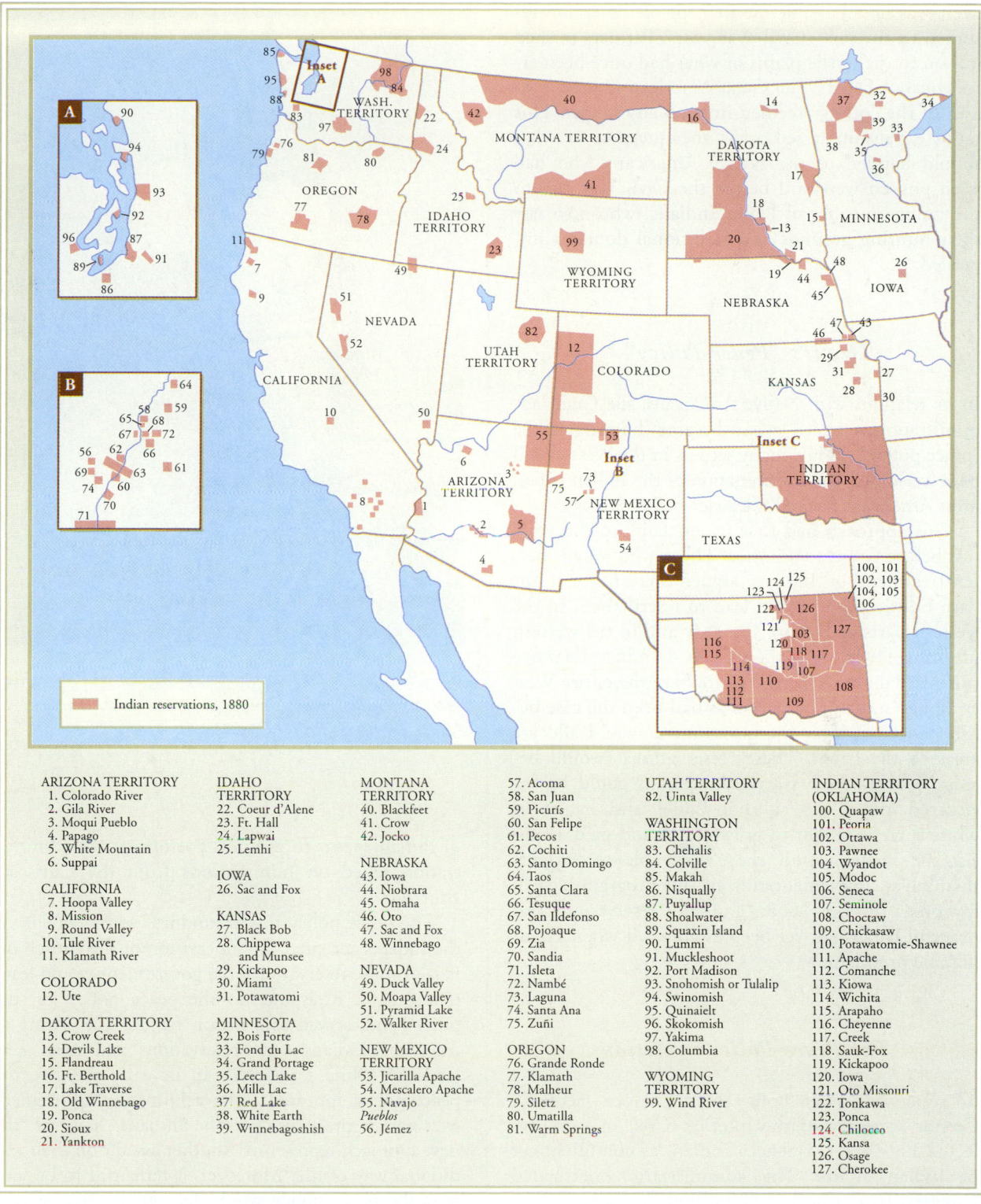

Indian reservations, 1880

ARIZONA TERRITORY
1. Colorado River
2. Gila River
3. Moqui Pueblo
4. Papago
5. White Mountain
6. Suppai

CALIFORNIA
7. Hoopa Valley
8. Mission
9. Round Valley
10. Tule River
11. Klamath River

COLORADO
12. Ute

DAKOTA TERRITORY
13. Crow Creek
14. Devils Lake
15. Flandreau
16. Ft. Berthold
17. Lake Traverse
18. Old Winnebago
19. Ponca
20. Sioux
21. Yankton

IDAHO TERRITORY
22. Coeur d'Alene
23. Ft. Hall
24. Lapwai
25. Lemhi

IOWA
26. Sac and Fox

KANSAS
27. Black Bob
28. Chippewa and Munsee
29. Kickapoo
30. Miami
31. Potawatomi

MINNESOTA
32. Bois Forte
33. Fond du Lac
34. Grand Portage
35. Leech Lake
36. Mille Lac
37. Red Lake
38. White Earth
39. Winnebagoshish

MONTANA TERRITORY
40. Blackfeet
41. Crow
42. Jocko

NEBRASKA
43. Iowa
44. Niobrara
45. Omaha
46. Oto
47. Sac and Fox
48. Winnebago

NEVADA
49. Duck Valley
50. Moapa Valley
51. Pyramid Lake
52. Walker River

NEW MEXICO TERRITORY
53. Jicarilla Apache
54. Mescalero Apache
55. Navajo
Pueblos
56. Jémez

57. Acoma
58. San Juan
59. Picurís
60. San Felipe
61. Pecos
62. Cochiti
63. Santo Domingo
64. Taos
65. Santa Clara
66. Tesuque
67. San Ildefonso
68. Pojoaque
69. Zia
70. Sandia
71. Isleta
72. Nambé
73. Laguna
74. Santa Ana
75. Zuñi

OREGON
76. Grande Ronde
77. Klamath
78. Malheur
79. Siletz
80. Umatilla
81. Warm Springs

UTAH TERRITORY
82. Uinta Valley

WASHINGTON TERRITORY
83. Chehalis
84. Colville
85. Makah
86. Nisqually
87. Puyallup
88. Shoalwater
89. Squaxin Island
90. Lummi
91. Muckleshoot
92. Port Madison
93. Snohomish or Tulalip
94. Swinomish
95. Quinaielt
96. Skokomish
97. Yakima
98. Columbia

WYOMING TERRITORY
99. Wind River

INDIAN TERRITORY (OKLAHOMA)
100. Quapaw
101. Peoria
102. Ottawa
103. Pawnee
104. Wyandot
105. Modoc
106. Seneca
107. Seminole
108. Choctaw
109. Chickasaw
110. Potawatomie-Shawnee
111. Apache
112. Comanche
113. Kiowa
114. Wichita
115. Arapaho
116. Cheyenne
117. Creek
118. Sauk-Fox
119. Kickapoo
120. Iowa
121. Oto Missouri
122. Tonkawa
123. Ponca
124. Chilocco
125. Kansa
126. Osage
127. Cherokee

MAP 16.2   INDIAN RESERVATIONS IN THE WEST

West was now possible. Settlement of the region resumed in the post–Civil War years. Farmers pushed out on to the fertile plains of what had once been erroneously labeled "The Great American Desert." No area of the country seemed isolated any longer. This rapid expansion raised anew the question of what should happen to the Native Americans who had been pushed westward before the Civil War and to the nomadic tribes of Plains Indians, who now saw their hunting grounds and traditional domains imperiled.

Grant's "Peace Policy"

In its relations with Native Americans, the Grant administration pursued what became known as the "peace policy." While many settlers in the West would have welcomed the extermination of the Indian tribes, most Americans favored the peace policy strategy.

This approach had first taken shape in the years just before Grant took office. Those who sought better treatment of Indians argued that negotiations with hostile tribes would lead to resettlement in the western parts of Dakota Territory and in the western portion of what was then dubbed Indian Territory (now Oklahoma). Instead of treating the entire West as a huge Indian reservation as had been the case before the Civil War, the government would allocate areas to the tribes. These "reservations" would become places where Native Americans could be instructed about the cultural values and habits of white society, taught to grow crops, and paid a subsistence income until they were able to support themselves. Implementation of this program lagged, however, during 1868, and no reservations for peaceful tribes had yet been established when Grant became president.

The Peace Policy in Action

To supervise Indian policy, Grant named Jacob D. Cox as secretary of the interior. Cox, in turn, selected Ely Parker, a Seneca Indian, as commissioner of Indian affairs. The administration persuaded Congress to appropriate $2 million for Indian affairs and to set up a Board of Indian Commissioners to distribute the money. Instead of leaving the selection

Chief Red Cloud of the Sioux sits for a photographer in his regalia. Fear and fascination were mingled in popular attitudes toward Native Americans after the Civil War.

of Indian agents to political patronage, the administration relied on nominations from the Christian churches.

The peace policy mixed kindness with coercion. If the Indians accepted the supervision of the church officials on the reservations, the government would leave them alone. Resistance to the peace policy, on the other hand, served as a reason for the U.S. Army to drive the Indians onto reservations and open new lands for white settlement. In its early months, the peace policy appeared to be a humane improvement over earlier practices. For the Indians, however, the new approach represented another assault on their traditional way of life. Moreover, it remained to be seen how the peace policy would fare in the face of economic and political pressures that continued white settlement generated.

AN ERA OF SCANDALS

Scandals plagued the Grant administration from the outset. In the summer of 1869, two speculators, Jay Gould and Jim Fisk, sought to manipulate the market in gold so as to achieve huge profits. Their efforts caused a rise in the price of gold that produced financial turmoil on September 24, 1869, when investors who had contracted to sell gold at lower prices faced ruin. The government ordered the sale of its own gold supplies, and the crisis eased when the price returned to its normal level. The details of the controversy soon faded away but the administration was embarrassed by revelations that some members of Grant's family, along with an official in the Treasury Department, had aided Gould and Fisk in carrying out their plan. Some critics suggested that First Lady Julia Grant had participated. Even though Grant and his wife were not implicated, the episode raised serious doubts about the ethical standards of his presidency.

To this impression of corruption the Grant administration also added a sense of confusion and incompetence. In foreign policy, there was talk of confronting Spain in an attempt to acquire Cuba. Secretary of State Hamilton Fish forestalled that potential crisis.

The railroad operator Jay Gould was a favorite subject of cartoonists who derided his financial schemes and treated him as a menace to the welfare of society. Gould's sharp dealings gave his enemies ample ammunition for their attacks.

Grant also wanted to annex the Dominican Republic (Santo Domingo). A presidential agent negotiated an annexation treaty with Santo Domingo's rulers, and the pact was sent to the Senate. Grant pushed hard for approval of the treaty, but the Senate, fearful of the influence of speculators and lobbyists, was suspicious of the president's goals and balked at endorsing what Grant had done with the treaty.

One diplomatic area in which Grant had some success was in the resolution of American claims for maritime losses against Great Britain over the *Alabama,* one of several Confederate merchant raiding ships that had been constructed in Great Britain during the Civil War. The *Alabama* had sunk numerous Union vessels. Charles Sumner, chair of the Senate Foreign Relations Committee, wanted to use the claims as leverage in an effort to acquire Canada. In 1871, Secretary of State Fish negotiated a treaty that led to an amicable settlement of the issue but left Canada undisturbed.

Grant and the Congress

Other issues troubled Grant's relations with Congress. Congressional Republicans split on a number of economic issues such as the protective tariff and the currency question. The mainstream of the party now believed that a tariff policy to "protect" American industries against foreign competition would be in the best interests of the business community, workers, and the Republican party. A minority of party members viewed the protective policy as unwise economically and a potential source of corrupt influence from protected industries. On the currency question, eastern Republicans favored the gold standard and what was known as "hard money"; western colleagues advocated an expansion of the money supply, government use of paper money or "greenbacks," and even some reliance on silver dollars as an alternative to gold.

Equally divisive was the issue of civil service. Calls for reform in the way government employees were selected intensified as the movement for a nonpartisan civil service gathered momentum. Republicans who wanted to reduce the tariff, implement the civil service, and treat the South more leniently defected from the administration and formed what they called Liberal Republican alliances with Democrats in such states as West Virginia and Missouri. In the 1870s, "liberal" meant a person who favored a smaller government, lower tariffs, and an end to Reconstruction.

Grant and His Party

Faced with a series of challenges to his presidency during 1870, Grant displayed greater reliance on the Republican party and its leaders in Congress. These Republican regulars had little taste for civil service reform, lower tariffs, or an end to Reconstruction. The president's turn to traditional politicians made sense, but it alienated Liberal Republicans. The possibility of a split in the party increased.

The president's resolve to depend more on regular Republicans strengthened after the Senate defeated his treaty with Santo Domingo during the summer of 1870. Following this episode, Grant knew that he could not work with Republican opponents of his presidency or satisfy the clamor for milder Reconstruction policies, civil service reform, and a less active national government. The Democrats could always outbid him on those issues, and courting them would only weaken the Republicans further. Failure to maintain good relations with his own party would mean political disaster. Grant was not an astute politician, but he could read that lesson clearly.

Toward the 1870 Elections

As a result, in 1870 Grant turned to groups within the party that could ensure his renomination and reelection two years later. He made conciliatory gestures toward the party mainstream. When Secretary of the Interior Jacob D. Cox complained about the practice of compelling government employees to make campaign contributions, Grant dismissed him. The president nominated his attorney general, Ebenezer R. Hoar, for the Supreme Court. When the Senate rejected him, Grant decided that Hoar too should leave the cabinet. To succeed him, he chose Amos T. Akerman, a southern Republican.

In the 1870 elections the Grant administration aligned itself with Republicans who defended Congress and the White House. Officeholders who supported Liberal Republican candidates or Democrats were removed. Despite these actions, the fall elections produced a setback for the president and his party. Liberal Republicans won in West Virginia and Missouri. Nationwide, the Democrats gained forty-one seats in the House of Representatives as the members from all the southern states rejoined the Congress. The Republicans retained control, however. The Demo-

crats also gained six seats in the Senate, although the Republicans still held a decisive edge in that chamber as well. Given Grant's relatively narrow victory in 1868, the enemies of the president looked forward to the 1872 election with some optimism.

The Ku Klux Klan in the South

By the summer of 1870 reports reached Washington of growing violence against blacks as well as white Republicans in the South. Roving bands of whites calling themselves the Ku Klux Klan (see Chapter 15) were responsible for the attacks. Throughout the South the Klan repressed any challenge to white dominance. One Republican in Louisiana said that "murder and intimidation are the order of the day in this state."

The Klan and its offshoots, such as the Knights of the White Camellia and the White Brotherhood, acted as paramilitary agents of the Democratic party to stamp out Republicanism through any means available. In Tennessee a black Republican was beaten after he won an election for justice of the peace. His

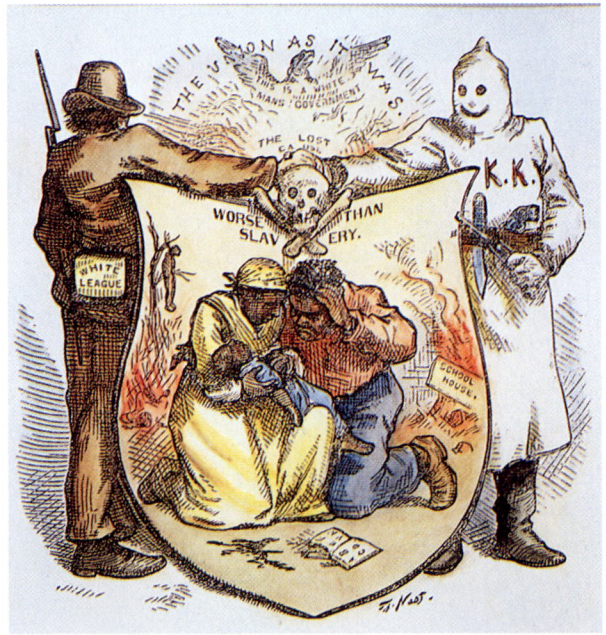

A cartoon attacks the Ku Klux Klan and the "white leagues" of the South for their terrorist tactics toward the African-American population. The result for the freed slaves is a condition that is "worse than slavery."

assailants told him "that they didn't dispute I was a very good fellow . . . but they did not intend any nigger to hold office in the United States."

The Klan would stop at nothing to eliminate its opponents. Leaders of the Republican party were hunted and killed. Campaign rallies sparked terror raids. In an incident in Alabama, in October 1870, four blacks died in a Klan attack on an election meeting. A "negro chase" in South Carolina left thirteen blacks dead.

The Klansmen rode in white robes and hoods; their aim, they said, was to frighten their racial foes. The disguises also hid their identity as white leaders employing extralegal violence to subvert the democratic process. Throughout 1870 a wave of shootings and brutality swept across the South, undermining the Republican party's chances of surviving below the Mason-Dixon line.

The Government and the Klan

During the 1870 election, the Klan violence had a devastating impact on Republicans in the South. In North Carolina, Georgia, Florida, and Alabama, the Klan's terror tactics intimidated voters and demoralized the party's leadership. In county after county the night riders attacked and murdered local black leaders. After the elections the Klan, emboldened by its success, became more active than ever.

By 1871 the Republicans had less stomach for military intervention in the political affairs of the South. As an Illinois newspaper put it, "the negro is now a voter and a citizen. Let him hereafter take his chances in the battle of life." Republican leaders asked themselves whether the cost of helping to maintain party organizations in the South justified the effort and time that had to be expended in the face of resolute Democratic opposition.

The Klan's violence, however, presented a challenge that could not be ignored. If violence could not be stopped, the Republican party in the South might simply vanish and the achievements of Reconstruction would be nullified. As a result, Congress adopted legislation to curb election fraud, bribery, and coercion in elections. When these measures proved inadequate, the lawmakers passed the Ku Klux Klan Act of 1871. This legislation outlawed conspiracies to deprive voters of their civil rights and prohibited efforts to bar any citizen from holding public office. If the Klan in-

In the aftermath of the Civil War, the old labor system of slavery and the plantation gave way to other forms of agricultural labor that kept African Americans tied to the land. Sharecropping meant that farmers had to provide a substantial portion of their crops to the white owner of the land.

terfered with equal protection of the laws, it could be prosecuted. The government received expanded powers to deal with such actions through the use of federal district attorneys to override state laws and, as a last resort, through military force.

The Democrats labeled these laws an unconstitutional interference with the rights of the states. Their passage was the "crowning act of centralization and consolidation," said one critic. A Republican countered by saying: "Tell me nothing of a constitution which fails to shelter beneath its rightful power the people of a country."

Breaking the Klan's Power

Events in the South renewed the Republicans' resolve to end the law-breaking and violence that the Klan represented. Attorney General Akerman argued that the threat the Klan posed to democratic government amounted to war. Akerman and his solicitor general,

Benjamin H. Bristow, were now part of the Department of Justice, which had been established in 1870, and they mobilized federal district attorneys and U.S. marshals to enforce prosecutions against the Klan.

During 1871 the legal offensive against the Klan went forward. In state after state indictments came down against Klan leaders. In North Carolina, hundreds of men faced trial; many went to prison. Similar prosecutions began in Mississippi and South Carolina. Federal troops assisted the Justice Department's work in South Carolina. The Klan was discredited as a public agent in southern politics and its violence became more covert and less visible. Although the Klan prosecutions showed that effective federal action could force the southern states to comply with the rule of law, in the North sentiment for such stern measures was ebbing. Soon the popular mood would move toward virtual abandonment of Reconstruction.

Scandals and Corruption: New York's Tweed Ring

The willingness to use national power that had marked the Reconstruction era receded in part because Americans increasingly believed that politics everywhere had become hopelessly corrupt. The most celebrated example of corruption in this period was the Tweed Ring, which dominated New York City during the late 1860s.

The leader of the ring was William Magear Tweed, Jr., who had risen through various city offices such as alderman and supervisor of elections and by the early 1870s had won a seat in the state senate. He was closely identified with the Democratic party organization which met at a political clubhouse called Tammany Hall to plan electoral strategy. The expanding cities of the post–Civil War years offered politicians countless chances to profit from the allocation of lucrative contracts and official services. Tweed and his allies turned these new opportunities to their personal advantage. They padded the city's accounts, and extracted kickbacks from contractors doing business with the city.

"Boss" Tweed's power rested on the votes of the city's heavily Democratic population. Long loyal to the Democrats who shared their suspicion of Republican efforts to regulate moral behavior, Irish Catholic immigrants supported the party that spoke to their needs and was receptive to their lifestyle and religious

Few individuals were more notorious in the 1870s than William M. "Boss" Tweed of New York City. The Tweed Ring and the lavish expenditures of money that it made in New York City came to symbolize the corruption and boss rule that many Americans associated with the rise of the city.

values. Their votes were crucial if the party expected to carry the state in a presidential contest. Tammany Hall also made sure that city services and jobs were available to those who supported them at the polls. By the end of the 1860s, Tweed seemed to hold New York City's political destiny in his hands.

In fact, Tweed's moment at the top of New York politics was very brief. He came under assault from the *New York Times,* which devoted endless columns to exposing the misdeeds of the Democratic party and its leaders. More significant from a national perspective, a cartoonist named Thomas Nast used artistic skill to make Tweed an object of derision. Nast's drawings depicted Tweed as the leader of a band of criminal freebooters, a money-grabbing scoundrel, a ludicrous caricature of an official in a democratic society. Tweed was

aware of the damage the cartoons did to his reputation and political standing. As he told one editor, "I don't care a straw for your newspaper articles. My constituents don't know how to read, but they can't help seeing them damned pictures."

In mid-1871, a resentful member of the Tweed Ring, angered at being left out of the spoils, gave city account books to a reporter. The revelation of how much had been spent on city projects stunned the population. A courthouse that had been projected to cost $250,000 came to $13 million. Other reports of corruption abounded as Tweed's pursuers closed in. Within a year, Tweed had been indicted, ousted from his position at Tammany Hall, and placed on trial. He escaped conviction in his first trial but was later retried and found guilty on 204 counts. He fled the country and took refuge in Spain. Arrested there when an official recognized him from a Nast cartoon, he returned to New York a broken man and died in 1878.

For many fearful Americans Tweed's story symbolized the decline in ethical standards that they believed had followed the Civil War. They had short memories. American politics in the 1850s had not been famous for the honesty and moral standards of those who led the nation. Nonetheless, citizens began to think that the expanded power of the state and the extension of the franchise to all white males and many freed slaves threatened the nation's political future. "We are in danger of going the way of all Republics," said one critic of the existing system. "First freedom, then glory; when that is past, Wealth, vice, corruption." A North Carolina newspaper echoed this sentiment: "As things go, the thieves will soon be in the majority."

The Liberal Republican Challenge to Grant

Restoring "higher" ethical standards was the stated purpose of the Liberal Republicans, who sought a presidential candidate to run against President Grant in the 1872 election. Their political creed included ending Reconstruction, returning good men like themselves to national power, and curbing the influence of political patronage through expanded use of the merit system. The leaders of the campaign were Senator Carl Schurz, a Missouri Republican, Edwin L. Godkin, editor of *The Nation,* and Charles Francis Adams, the son of former President John Quincy Adams.

Liberal Republicans believed in smaller government. "The Government," wrote E.L. Godkin, "must get out of the 'protective' business and the 'subsidy' business and the 'improvement' business and 'development' business. . . . It cannot touch them without breeding corruption." Such Republican programs as the protective tariff appalled them. Most of all, they saw Reconstruction as a failed experiment in racial democracy that should be abandoned. As Grant's one-time secretary of the Interior, Jacob D. Cox, contended: "the South can only be governed through the part of the community that embodies the intelligence and the capital." In effect, black Americans in the South would have to look to whites in that region for protection of their rights and privileges.

The Liberal Republicans lacked a national candidate with the stature to challenge a popular president whose reputation had not been diminished by the problems of his first term. Although many party leaders were unhappy with the policies of the Grant administration, few were commanding political figures. Senator Carl Schurz had been born in Germany and therefore was ineligible under the Constitution. Other presidential hopefuls included Charles Francis Adams, Senator Lyman Trumbull of Illinois, and Horace Greeley, the editor of the New York *Tribune*.

In May 1872, the Liberal Republicans gathered in Cincinnati. According to the *Tribune,* "there had never been a better class of men gathered on such an occasion." The balloting revealed that the contest lay between the colorless Adams and the well-known and eccentric Greeley. Greeley won the nomination on the sixth ballot.

The sixty-one-year-old editor was an odd choice. He favored the protective tariff, which most reformers disliked, and was indifferent to civil service reform. Once a harsh critic of the South, he had mellowed and now favored ending Reconstruction. A lifetime of passions for such offbeat remedies as vegetarianism and the use of human manure in farming made him seem a political oddball in the eyes of many Americans. "That Grant is an Ass no man can deny," said one Liberal Republican, "but better an Ass than a mischievous idiot."

The 1872 Election

The Republican convention renominated Grant and chose Henry Wilson of Massachusetts to be his running mate. In its platform the party stressed the

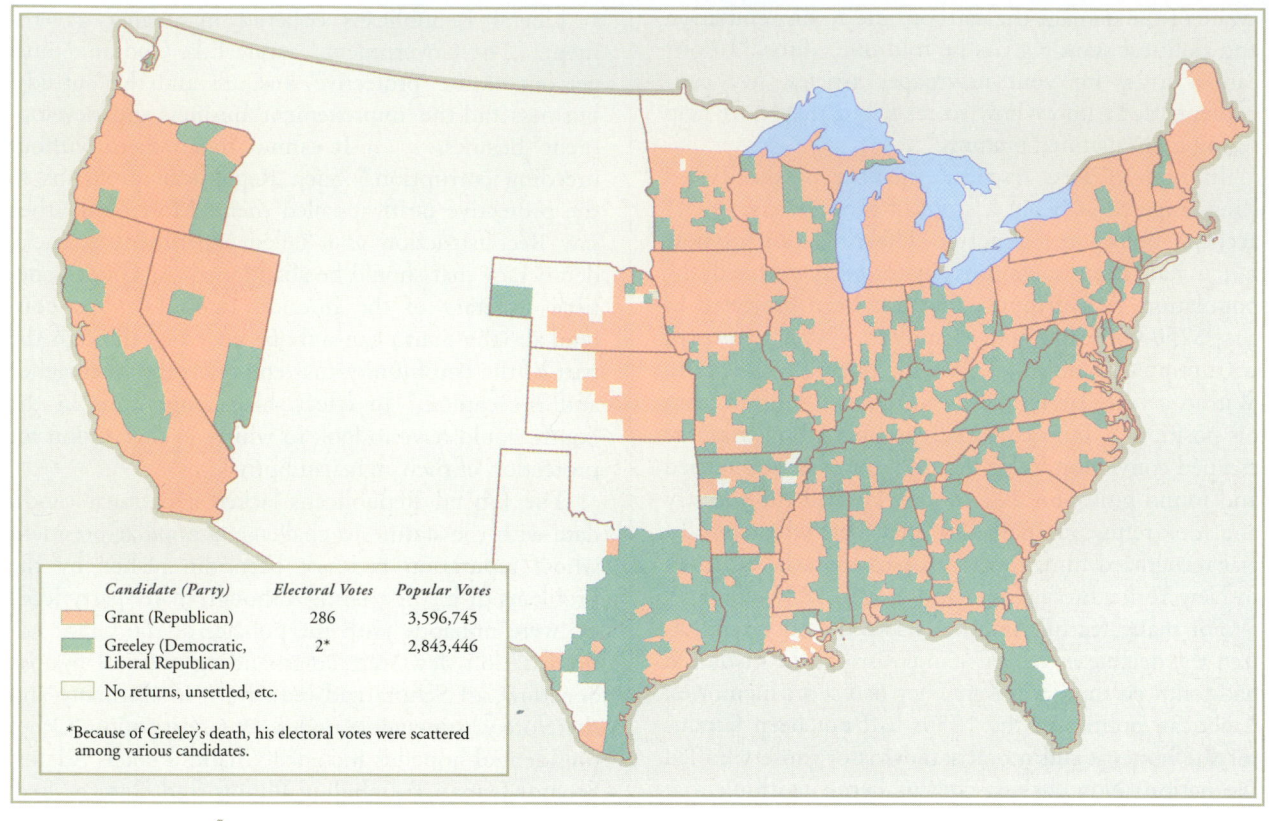

MAP 16.3 | THE ELECTION OF 1872

Legend:

Candidate (Party)	Electoral Votes	Popular Votes
Grant (Republican)	286	3,596,745
Greeley (Democratic, Liberal Republican)	2*	2,843,446
No returns, unsettled, etc.		

*Because of Greeley's death, his electoral votes were scattered among various candidates.

continuing problem of Reconstruction. The black leader Frederick Douglass said of the impending contest: "If the Republican party goes down, freedom goes down with it." The Republican appeal urged voters to preserve what had been achieved during the Civil War. One Republican orator told the crowd that they could either "Go vote to burn school houses, desecrate churches and violate women or vote for Horace Greeley, which means the same thing."

When the Democrats held their national convention in early July, they faced a dilemma. If they failed to nominate Greeley, they had no chance of winning. Nominating him, however, would alienate southern voters. In the end the delegates accepted Greeley as their only alternative. The Liberal Republican-Democratic nominee made a vigorous campaign while Grant observed the tradition in which an incumbent president did not campaign actively. Grant did, however, influence the campaign from behind the scenes.

The outcome was a decisive victory for Grant and his party. The president swamped Greeley in the popular vote and in the electoral tally. There were still enough Republicans in the South to enable Grant to carry all but five of the southern states. Worn out by the rigors of the campaign, Greeley died in late November 1872. Because of Greeley's ineptitude and divisions within the party, the election marked a low point for the Democrats. Grant would continue as president, but his second term would prove to be even more difficult and scandal-ridden than his first administration.

Recurrent Scandals

As the excitement of the 1872 election died down, political attention turned to sensational allegations of corruption in Congress. The first scandal concerned the efforts of the Crédit Mobilier Company (named

after a French company) to purchase influence with lawmakers during the late 1860s. The directors of the Union Pacific Railroad had established Crédit Mobilier to raise money to build the transcontinental line. By paying themselves to construct the railroad, the participants in the venture made large profits and the company's shareholders did as well. The only problem was that much of the money in effect came from the federal government through loans and guarantees.

To forestall a congressional probe into the company, Crédit Mobilier's managers gave leading Republicans in Congress a chance to buy shares in the company at prices well below their actual market value. When the lawmakers sold their shares, they pocketed the difference—the equivalent of a bribe. One beneficiary was a future president, James A. Garfield, of Ohio, but he sold his stock soon after he received it and made a profit of only $329. When a newspaper broke the story in late 1872, an investigation followed. The inquiry produced a few scapegoats but cleared most of the lawmakers involved. Nevertheless, the episode damaged the credibility of public officials.

Another embarrassing episode occurred in February 1873. At the end of a congressional session, a last-minute maneuver gave senators and representatives a retroactive pay increase. The public denounced the action, calling it the "Salary Grab." The Chicago *Tribune* said it was "nothing more nor less than an act of robbery." When Congress reconvened in December 1873, repeal of the salary increase sailed through both houses in a burst of political contrition. These two incidents generated widespread calls for reducing government expenditures and rooting out corruption. As Mark Twain said, "It could probably be shown by facts and figures that there is no distinctly native American criminal class except Congress."

Twain himself captured the spirit of the times in his novel, *The Gilded Age*. The main character, Colonel Beriah Sellers, was an engaging confidence man who embodied the boosterism and economic looseness of the postwar years, along with the healthy amount of fraud and chicanery that accompanied the rapid growth of business. In time, the title of Twain's book came to be used as a label for the entire era between the end of Reconstruction and the start of the twentieth century. "The Gilded Age" was, however, a richer and more complex time than the stereotype of corrupt politicians and fraudulent entrepreneurs that Twain portrayed.

THE PANIC OF 1873 AND ITS CONSEQUENCES

The sense of national crisis deepened in September 1873 when the banking house of Jay Cooke and Company failed. The disaster was triggered by the bank's inability to market the bonds of the Northern Pacific Railroad, in which it had invested heavily. An economic downturn ensued that rivaled similar panics that had occurred in 1819, 1837, and 1857; however, the Panic of 1873 was worse than any of them.

The immediate effects of the downturn lasted until 1879. In fact, an extended period of economic hard times had begun that would extend through the 1890s. A hallmark of the "Great Depression," as it was then called, was declining prices for agricultural products and manufactured goods. Americans grappled with the consequences of an economy in which falling prices placed the heaviest burdens on people who were in debt or who earned their living by selling labor. An abundance of cheap unskilled labor proved a boon for capitalists who wanted to keep costs down. For the

Cartoonists reacted when the Panic of 1873 began with the failure of the Northern Pacific Railroad and Jay Cooke's banking interests. Here the "Northern Pole R.R." and the "Bank of Inflation" are consumed in the general collapse.

TABLE 16.1 RAILROAD MILEAGE, 1869–1876	
1869:	46,844
1870:	52,922
1871:	60,301
1872:	66,171
1873:	70,268
1874:	72,385
1875:	74,096
1876:	76,808

poor, however, it meant that they had little job security and could easily be replaced if they protested against working conditions. Industrialization went forward at a substantial human cost.

The panic occurred because of a speculative post–Civil War boom in railroad building that produced an overexpansion of transportation facilities. In 1869, railroad mileage stood at about 47,000 miles; four years later it had risen to 70,268 miles. The new railroad lines employed tens of thousands of workers and extended across a far larger geographical area than any earlier manufacturing enterprises. Bigness in railroad operations portended the future expansion of the industrial sector. When large railroads such as the Northern Pacific failed because of their overexpansion and inability to pay their debts, the resulting impact rippled through society. Economic activities such as car making, steel rail production, and passenger services, which were dependent on the rail lines, declined as well. Layoffs of employees and bankruptcies of businesses followed. More than 10,000 companies failed in 1878, the worst year of the depression.

The Plight of the Unemployed

Americans who were thrown out of work during the 1870s had no system of unemployment insurance to fall back on. In some cities up to a quarter of the labor force looked for work without success. Tramps roamed the countryside. The conventional wisdom held that natural forces had to operate to restore prosperity; any form of political intervention would be futile and dangerous. When President Grant proposed that the national government generate jobs through public works, the secretary of the Treasury informed him: "It is not part of the business of government to find employment for people."

Those who were out of a job during the mid-1870s could not afford such a philosophical attitude. Laborers in the Northeast mounted a campaign calling for

The hard times that arose from the Panic of 1873 produced labor unrest in many cities. Here an artist recreates the riot in Tompkins Square in New York in 1874.

"Work or Bread" that included large public demonstrations in major cities. The marchers asked city and state governments to sponsor projects to create parks and construct streets, thereby providing work. In January 1874 a demonstration at Tompkins Square in New York City pitted a crowd of 7,000 unemployed laborers against police. Many marchers were arrested; others were injured in the confrontation.

Labor unrest marked the first half of the decade. Numerous and prolonged strikes occurred in 1874 and 1875. In Pennsylvania the railroads used their control of police and strikebreakers to put down the "Long Strike" of coal miners and their supporters. Twenty alleged members of a secret society called the Molly Maguires were hanged. Conservative Americans feared that the nation was on the verge of revolution.

Distress and Protest Among the Farmers

In agricultural regions, the drop in farm prices also produced discontent. The price of wheat stood at $1.16 per bushel in 1873; it fell to ninety-five cents a bushel a year later. The price of corn reached a high of sixty-four cents a bushel in 1874 but had slipped to forty-two cents a bushel in 1875. The resulting decline in income meant that debts on land and equipment were a greater burden on the hard-pressed farmers. Faced with the economic power of the railroads and grain merchants, the farmer was "a mere bushwhacker, confronting organized and well-equipped armies."

Farmers' protests were led by the Patrons of Husbandry, also known as the Grange. Created in 1867, the nonpartisan Grange focused on complaints about the high mortgages farmers owed, the prices they had to pay to middlemen such as the operators of grain elevators, and the discrimination that they suffered at the hands of railroads that charged high rates for shipping agricultural commodities.

Regulating the Railroads

The answer to the railroads' power, the angry farmers argued, lay in using the power of state governments to force the railroads to end their discriminatory practices. That meant the creation of state railroad commissions with the power to establish equitable rates and prevent unfair treatment of those who shipped agricultural products. Shippers of manufactured goods in many states added their political clout to the campaign for state commissions. In 1870 Illinois adopted a new state constitution that mandated that the legislature "pass laws establishing maximum rates of charges for the transportation of passengers and freight." The legislature responded a year later, giving the Illinois Railroad Commission wide powers. Neighboring states such as Iowa, Minnesota, and Wisconsin followed suit in the next several years. Railroad companies challenged some of these laws in the courts, and a case involving the constitutionality of the Illinois law began working its way toward the Supreme Court under the title *Munn* v. *Illinois*.

The pressure for regulatory legislation affected Congress in 1873–1874. An Iowa Republican introduced legislation in the House to establish a national railroad commission. As an anonymous spokesman for the West told a journalist, "Sir, you will never make me doubt that a government which could put down that mighty Rebellion can regulate the details of a few tariffs of some railroad corporation." The bill passed in the House, but the Senate never acted upon it. Federal legislation would not be enacted until 1887.

The decline in consumer prices and the burden of debt on farmers and businessmen in the South and West stimulated pressure for laws to put more money in circulation. That would make debts easier to pay. The Treasury Department's decision to end the coinage of silver in 1873 aroused particular ire among southern and western advocates of inflation; they called it the "Crime of 1873." Proponents contended that an overabundance of silver in the marketplace required the move to a gold standard. By coining silver into money at a price above its market levels, the government was in effect subsidizing American silver production and cheapening the currency. Opponents of the change, however, were suspicious of the dominance of eastern bankers over financial policy.

An effort to inject a modest amount of inflation into the economy came in 1875. A currency bill cleared both houses of Congress, providing some $64 million in additional money for the financial system. President Grant considered signing the bill, but he encountered economic conservatism among eastern Republicans. Their advice led him to veto the bill in April 1875, and Congress failed to override his action. The federal government would not intervene in the deepening economic crisis.

WOMEN IN THE 1870S

Amid the male-dominated political scenes that marked this period, occasional episodes reminded the nation that women were not allowed to play a direct part in public life. Susan B. Anthony sought the opportunity to address the Liberal Republican and Republican national conventions in 1872, but without success. On election day she and fifteen other women registered and voted at their polling place in Rochester, New York. Anthony and the voting officials were arrested. Her trial in federal court led to a $100 fine, which she refused to pay. Rather than giving Anthony a reason for appealing the case to a higher court, authorities did not collect the fine against her.

Another champion of woman's rights was Victoria Claflin Woodhull. A faith healer and spiritualist from Ohio, she and her sister Tennessee Claflin came to New York, where in 1870 Victoria announced her candidacy for president of the United States. She published a weekly newspaper that endorsed the right of women to practice free love outside of marriage. In 1872 she denounced one of the nation's leading ministers, Henry Ward Beecher, for having had an affair with a member of his congregation. The exposé led to one of the most sensational public trials of the nineteenth century. The proceedings ended in a hung jury, and Victoria Woodhull and her sister fled to England to escape from public outrage. Woodhull's experience and social disgrace demonstrated the perils that faced women who defied the strict social conventions of the post–Civil War era.

Overcoming Barriers to Equality

For women from the middle and upper classes the 1870s brought expanding educational opportunities. The number of women graduating from high school stood at nearly 9,000 in 1870, as compared with 7,000 men. Aware of these trends, state universities and private colleges opened their doors to women students in growing numbers. The University of Minnesota, the University of Kansas, and Indiana University did so in 1869; universities in Missouri, California, and Michigan followed suit a year later. By 1872 nearly one hundred institutions of higher learning admitted women. This process went forward despite the fears of male academics. Edward Clarke, a retired Harvard medical professor, warned in 1873 that when women expended their "limited energy" on

The spread of industrialism brought new products into the home that were advertised as labor-saving devices for women. The reality was that the amount of work women did expanded as a result of the new machinery for domestic use.

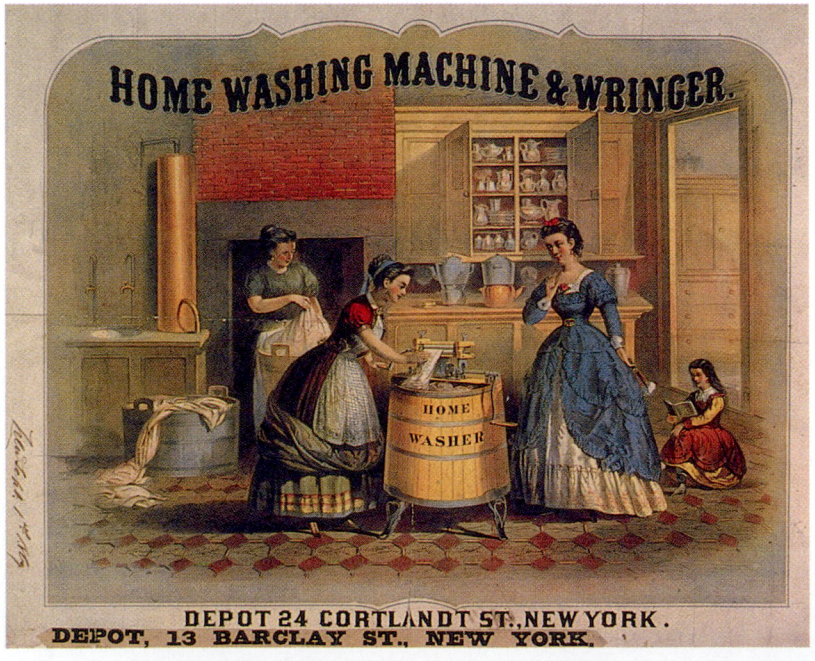

higher education, they put their "female apparatus" at risk. Nevertheless, Cornell University began accepting women applicants in 1875.

One of the first female students at Cornell was M. Carey Thomas, who received her B.A. at Cornell in 1877. Five years later she received her Ph.D. at a German university. By the 1890s she had become the president of Bryn Mawr, a woman's college outside Philadelphia. Like other women in male-dominated institutions, she endured rudeness and indifference from her male colleagues. She later recalled that "it is a fiery ordeal to educate a lady by coeducation."

Obtaining an education did not ensure access to male-dominated professions, however. Myra Bradwell tried to become a lawyer in Illinois, but the state bar association rejected her application. She sued in federal court, and in 1873 the U.S. Supreme Court ruled that the law did not grant her the right to be admitted to the bar. One Justice said that "the paramount destiny and mission of woman are to fulfill the noble and benign offices of wife and mother." That decision gave the Illinois legislature the authority to deny women the chance to practice law. In fact, in 1870 there were only five female lawyers in the entire country.

The Supreme Court also rebuffed efforts to secure woman suffrage through the courts. Virginia Minor, president of the Woman Suffrage Association in Missouri, tried to vote in the 1872 election, but the registrar of voters turned her away. She sued on the grounds that the action denied her her rights as a citizen. In the case of *Minor* v. *Happersett* (1875) the Supreme Court ruled unanimously that suffrage was not one of the rights of citizenship because "sex has never been made one of the elements of citizenship in the United States." To achieve the right to vote, women would have to amend the Constitution or obtain the right of suffrage from the states, a process that took another four decades to complete.

The Rise of Voluntary Associations

Blocked off from politics, women created a public space of their own through voluntary associations. Notable in this process were the efforts of black church-women, who established missionary societies to work both in the United States and abroad on projects to assemble funds and create institutions such as Spelman College in Atlanta, founded in 1881. Clubs and literary societies sprang up among white women as well.

In New York City women created Sorosis, a club for women only, after the New York Press Club barred women from its membership. In 1873 delegates from local Sorosis clubs formed the Association for the Advancement of Women. The New England Woman's Club, located in Boston, represented "the social force of the women of New England." Its members succeeded in the early 1870s in changing local laws to allow women to serve on the School Committee. Later the club founded the Women's Education Association to expand educational opportunities for their sex. During the two decades that followed, the women's club movement established strong roots in all parts of the nation.

Despite their inability to vote, women made their presence felt in public affairs in an unexpected way in 1873. Protests against the sale and use of alcohol erupted among women in New York, Ohio, and Michigan. Their anger was a response to the growing number of liquor dealers in these states and the spread of saloons and bars. Women marched in the streets and demanded that saloons and liquor dealers close their establishments. They also exhorted drunkards to reform. Middle-class women went down on their knees in front of bars and smashed barrels of liquor in public. "The women are in desperate earnest," said a Missourian who witnessed one of these crusades. The temperance movement was not limited to women, but the upsurge of activity among women gave the crusade a new militance.

The Woman's Christian Temperance Union

As their successes grew, women sought to make their campaign more than a transitory episode. In August 1874 a group of temperance leaders assembled at Lake Chautauqua, New York, where they called for a national meeting that developed into the Woman's Christian Temperance Union. During the next five years temperance leagues and local organizations of the WCTU crusaded against intoxicating beverages. By the end of the 1870s a thousand unions had emerged, with an estimated 26,000 members. In 1879, Frances Willard became president of the Union. Under her leadership, the WCTU went beyond its original goal of temperance and ventured into broader areas of social reform such as woman suffrage and the treatment of children.

Minor v. Happersett 21 Wallace, 162 1875

This case involved the question of whether women were entitled to vote as citizens under the Fourteenth Amendment.

WAITE, C. J. The question is presented in this case, whether, since the adoption of the Fourteenth Amendment, a woman, who is a citizen of the United States and of the State of Missouri, is a voter in that State, notwithstanding the provision of the constitution and laws of the State, which confine the right of suffrage to men alone. . . .

It is contended that the provisions of the Constitution and laws of the State of Missouri, which confine the right of suffrage and registration therefore to men, are in violation of the Constitution of the United States, and therefore void. The argument is, that as a woman, born or naturalized in the United States and subject to the jurisdiction thereof, is a citizen of the United States and of the State in which she resides, she has the right of suffrage as one of the privileges and immunities of her citizenship, which the State cannot by its laws or constitution abridge.

There is no doubt that women may be citizens. They are persons, and by the Fourteenth Amendment "all persons born or naturalized in the United States and subject to the jurisdiction thereof" are expressly declared to be "citizens of the United States and of the State wherein they reside." But, in our opinion, it did not need this amendment to give them that position. Before its adoption the Constitution of the United States did not in terms prescribe who should be citizens of the United States or of the several States, yet there were necessarily such citizens without such provision. . . .

For convenience it has been found necessary to give a name to this membership. The object is to designate by a title the person and the relation he bears to the nation. For this purpose the words "subject," "inhabitant," and "citizen" have been used, and the choice between them is sometimes made to depend upon the form of the government. Citizen is now more commonly employed, however, and as it has been considered better suited to the description of one living under republican government, it was adopted by nearly all of the States upon their separation from Great Britain, and was afterwards adopted in the Articles of Confederation and the Constitution of the United States. When used in this sense it is understood as conveying the idea of membership of a nation, and nothing more. . . .

Women at Work

The 1870s also brought greater economic opportunities for women in sales and clerical work. The typewriter was developed in the early 1870s and young, college-educated women were an abundant source of skilled labor to operate the new machines. E. Remington and Sons, which produced the typewriter, said in 1875 that "no invention has opened for women so broad and easy an avenue to profitable and suitable employment as the 'Type-Writer.'" At the end of the decade women accounted for 40 percent of the total number of stenographers and typists in the country. The developments of the 1870s laid the foundation for the growth in

. . . Sex has never been made one of the elements of citizenship in the United States. In this respect men have never had an advantage over women. The same laws precisely apply to both. The Fourteenth Amendment did not affect the citizenship of women any more than it did of men. In this particular, therefore, the rights of Mrs. Minor do not depend upon the amendment. She has always been a citizen from her birth, and entitled to all the privileges and immunities of citizenship. . . .

If the right of suffrage is one of the necessary privileges of a citizen of the United States, then the constitution and laws of Missouri confining it to men are in violation of the Constitution of the United States, as amended, and consequently void. The direct question is, therefore, presented whether all citizens are necessarily voters.

The Constitution does not define the privileges and immunities of citizens. For that definition we must look elsewhere. In this case we need not determine what they are, but only whether suffrage is necessarily one of them.

It certainly is nowhere made so in express terms. The United States has no voters in the States of its own creation. The elective officers of the United States are all elected directly or indirectly by state voters. . . .

The [Fourteenth] Amendment did not add to the privileges and immunities of a citizen. It simply furnished an additional guaranty for the protection of such as he already had. No new voters were necessarily made by it. Indirectly it may have had that effect, because it may have increased the number of citizens entitled to suffrage under the constitution and laws of the States, but it operates for this purpose, if at all, through the States and the state laws, and not directly upon the citizen.

It is clear therefore, we think, that the Constitution has not added the right of suffrage to the privileges and immunities of citizenship as they existed at the time it was adopted. This makes it proper to inquire whether suffrage was co-extensive with the citizenship of the States at the time of its adoption. If it was then it may with force be argued that suffrage was one of the rights which belonged to citizenship, and in the enjoyment of which every citizen must be protected. But if it was not, the contrary may with propriety be assumed.

When the Federal Constitution was adopted, all the States, with the exception of Rhode Island and Connecticut, had constitutions of their own. . . . Upon an examination of these constitutions we find that in no State were all citizens permitted to vote. . . .

(continued)

numbers of female office workers during the rest of the nineteenth century. For most women, however, these opportunities remain edelusive.

The most typical experience of American women was toil. Black women in the South labored in the fields alongside their husbands who were tenant farmers or sharecroppers. They did "double duty, a man's share in the field, and a woman's part at home." In the growing cities, immigrant and native-born women worked in textile factories or became domestic servants. Women accounted for more than a quarter of the workforce in Philadelphia at the end of the 1870s. Many urban women took in boarders; their routine equalled that of a small hotel.

In this condition of the law in respect to suffrage in the several States it cannot for a moment be doubted that if it had been intended to make all citizens of the United States voters, the framers of the Constitution would not have left it to implication. . . .

It is true that the United States guarantees to every State a republican form of government. . . . The guaranty is of a republican form of government. No particular government is designated as republican, neither is the exact form to be guaranteed, in any manner especially designated. Here, as in other parts of the instrument, we are compelled to resort elsewhere to ascertain what was intended.

The guaranty necessarily implies a duty on the part of the States themselves to provide such a government. All the States had governments when the Constitution was adopted. In all the people participated to some extent, through their representatives elected in the manner specially provided. These governments the Constitution did not change. They were accepted precisely as they were, and it is, therefore, to be presumed that they were such as it was the duty of the States to provide. Thus we have unmistakable evidence of what was republican in form, within the meaning of that term as employed in the Constitution.

As we have seen, all the citizens of the States were not invested with the right of suffrage. In all, save perhaps New Jersey, this right was only bestowed upon men and not upon all of them. Under these circumstances it is certainly now too late to contend that a government is not republican, within the meaning of this guaranty in the Constitution, because women are not made voters. . . .

Certainly if the courts can consider any question settled, this is one. For nearly ninety years the people have acted upon the idea that the Constitution, when it conferred citizenship, did not necessarily confer the right of suffrage. . . .

Being unanimously of the opinion that the Constitution of the United States does not confer the right of suffrage upon any one, and that the constitutions and laws of the several States which commit that important trust to men alone are not necessarily void, we affirm the judgment.

Middle-class women with domestic servants had some assistance, but they still did an incredible amount of work. Sewing machines had become more common, but preparing food, doing laundry, keeping the house warm, and disposing of waste all required hand labor. Mary Mathews, a widowed teacher in the 1870s, "got up early every Monday morning and got my clothes all washed and boiled and in the rinsing water; then commenced my school at nine." Other days of the week passed in the same fashion for her and other women.

To assist women in performing these tasks in the separate sphere of the home and family, manuals about housework became popular in the 1870s, along with private cooking schools and college courses in home economics. Catherine Beecher, who had written about the ways in which women could exercise influence in the domestic aspects of life since the early 1840s, collaborated with her famous sister, Harriet Beecher Stowe, in writing *The American Woman's Home* (1869). In this work, she argued "that family labor and care tend not only to good health, but to the *Highest culture of the mind.*" Women were, she contended, "ministers of the family state." In the new coeducational colleges and universities, home economics programs offered instruction in operating kitchens and dining

As women became more involved in public life after the Civil War, they found outlets for their social concerns beyond the ballot box. One of the most important organizations was the Woman's Christian Temperance Union (WCTU). The artist evokes the imagery of the medieval Crusades to show women attacking the liquor industry and its political connections.

As industrialism took hold, women moved into the workplace. New inventions such as the typewriter gave women a larger place in offices and stores as secretaries and clerks.

rooms in an efficient manner. Cooking schools appeared in large cities with a separate class for "plain cooks" and a "Ladies Class" for affluent women who sought to link "the elegancies of artistic cookery with those economical interests which it is the duty of every woman to study."

The ease with which divorces could be obtained in many states produced a movement to tighten the conditions under which marriages could be dissolved. Laws to limit the sale of birth control devices and restrict abortions reflected the same trend. The New York Society for the Suppression of Vice was formed in 1872 under the leadership of Anthony Comstock. It lobbied successfully for a national law barring obscene materials, including information about birth control and abortion, from the mails. Comstock and

his allies pushed for a similar law in New York and obtained the power to make arrests for violations of the statute. Thus, while women had made some gains after the Civil War, they remained second-class citizens within the masculine political order of the Gilded Age.

POLITICS IN THE GILDED AGE

After the presidential election of 1872, the North's already weakened commitment to the continuation of Reconstruction ebbed more rapidly. The Panic of 1873 distracted attention from the rights of black Americans. The Grant administration was less willing to intervene in southern politics and the Justice Department prosecuted fewer individuals for violations of the Enforcement Acts against the Klan and pardoned some of those who had earlier been convicted of terrorist activity.

Northern support for Reconstruction had fallen away because the experiment in multiracial government

appeared to have failed. Liberal Republicans and northern Democrats used racist propaganda against the political aspirations of southern blacks. The editor of *The Nation*, E. L. Godkin, said that black residents of South Carolina had an "average of intelligence but slightly above the level of animals." White northerners found it easier to believe that the South would be better off when whites were once again dominant. Black Americans should be left "to the kind feeling of the white race of the South."

A damaging setback to African Americans' economic aspirations occurred with the failure of the Freedmen's Savings and Trust Company in Washington, D.C. Since its founding in 1865 the bank had managed the deposits of thousands of former slaves. It was supposed to provide lessons in thrift for its depositors. However, its managers sought larger returns by investing in speculative railroad projects. The Panic of 1873 caused huge losses, and the bank failed in the following year. Some depositors received 60 percent of what they had put in, but many lost their entire accounts.

The Stigma of Corruption

Corruption among southern Republican governments became a favorite theme of critics of Reconstruction. There were some genuine instances of corruption: Black and white Republicans accepted bribes from lobbyists or benefited from government contracts. But these actions were far from widespread or typical. Moreover, the white governments that took over after Reconstruction also displayed lax political ethics and committed more serious misdeeds than their predecessors had. Nevertheless, the corruption issue gave the opponents of black political participation a perfect weapon which they exploited fully during the 1870s. Of course, it would not have mattered if Reconstruction governments lacked any moral flaws. Any government that represented a biracial community was intolerable to white southerners.

While participation of African Americans in southern politics increased dramatically during Reconstruction, their role in the region's public life remained limited compared to whites. Sixteen blacks served in Congress during the period, most only briefly, and several were unseated by white opponents. Many more held offices in the state legislatures, but even their numbers were comparatively modest. In 1868, for example, the Georgia legislature had 216 members, of whom only thirty-two were black. In only one state,

South Carolina, did blacks ever hold a majority in the legislature, and they did so in only one house. One black man, P.B.S. Pinchback, served as governor in Louisiana for a little more than a month. Six African Americans held the office of lieutenant governor in the states of Louisiana, Mississippi, and South Carolina.

Two blacks served in the U.S. Senate. Hiram Revels of Mississippi became the first African American to enter the Senate. His term began in 1870 but lasted only one year. From 1875 to 1881 Blanche K. Bruce represented Mississippi for a full term. Thus, whites retained statewide and national offices throughout the Reconstruction era. By the 1870s blacks had begun to make their presence felt in southern legislatures, but the decline of Reconstruction made that trend a short-lived one.

The Resurgence of the Democrats

The changing political situation across the nation further diminished support for Reconstruction outside the South. Hard economic times arising from the Panic of 1873 worked against the Republicans. Discontented farmers wanted the government to inflate the currency and raise prices on their crops. Factory workers wanted to see more jobs become available. The fate of African Americans in the South became a secondary concern. Accordingly, angry voters turned to the Democrats in the 1874 congressional races. The party used the issue of Republican corruption to regain control of the House of Representatives for the first time in sixteen years, adding seventy-seven seats to their total. Democrats elected 169 members, compared to 109 for their opposition. The Democrats also picked up ten Senate seats. It was a "Tidal Wave" said one happy Democrat.

In the South, the resurgent Democrats "redeemed," as they called it, several states from Republican dominance. They began with Texas in 1873, then took back Arkansas and elected most of the region's members in the U.S. House of Representatives. Louisiana experienced the emergence of the White League, which was determined that "the niggers shall not rule over us." In September open fighting erupted in New Orleans between armed Republicans and more than 3,000 White League partisans. President Grant sent in federal troops to restore calm. In Alabama the Democrats also relied on violence and murder to oust the Republicans. Some blacks who attempted to vote in the Barbour County election were shot; seven were killed and

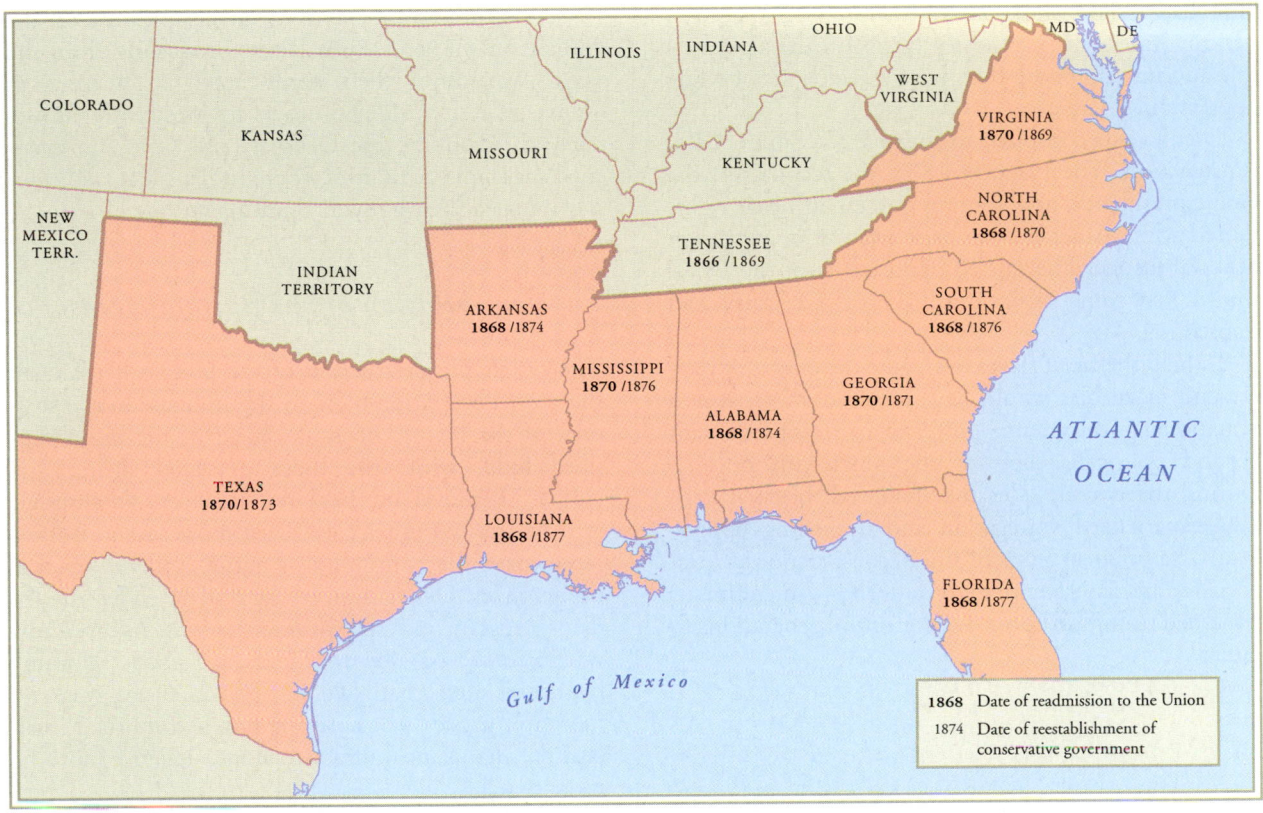

COLORADO

KANSAS

NEW MEXICO TERR.

INDIAN TERRITORY

ILLINOIS

INDIANA

OHIO

MISSOURI

KENTUCKY

WEST VIRGINIA

MD

DE

VIRGINIA
1870 /1869

NORTH CAROLINA
1868 /1870

TENNESSEE
1866 /1869

ARKANSAS
1868 /1874

MISSISSIPPI
1870 /1876

ALABAMA
1868 /1874

GEORGIA
1870 /1871

SOUTH CAROLINA
1868 /1876

TEXAS
1870/1873

LOUISIANA
1868 /1877

FLORIDA
1868 /1877

ATLANTIC OCEAN

Gulf of Mexico

1868	Date of readmission to the Union
1874	Date of reestablishment of conservative government

MAP 16.4 | RECONSTRUCTION IN THE SOUTH

nearly seventy wounded. Given the wide support for the Democratic party among southern whites, honest elections might have produced similar victories for their party at the polls; but intimidation and violence were key elements in the victories that the Democrats secured in the South in 1874.

The Democrats intended to use their control of the House of Representatives afterward to roll back Reconstruction and also prevent any further expansion of black rights. During the lame-duck congressional session of 1874–1875 Republicans enacted a path-breaking civil rights law that gave black citizens the right to sue in federal courts when they confronted discrimination in public accommodations. The law involved an additional expansion of national power; it remained to be seen how the federal courts North and South would rule when black plaintiffs sued to enforce their rights under the new civil rights statute.

Early in 1875 the Grant administration used troops to prevent occupation of the Louisiana state capitol and illegal seizure of the state government by the Democrats in the midst of an election dispute. The action drew widespread protests from many northern Democrats and a growing number of Republicans who argued in favor of allowing the white South to handle its own affairs. Meanwhile, the Democrats used more violence to overturn Republican rule in Mississippi. The state governor, Adelbert Ames, stated that he was "fighting for the Negro, and to the whole country a white man is better than a 'Nigger.'" Without a national consensus behind civil rights and Reconstruction, the fate of black Americans lay in the hands of white southerners who were determined to keep African Americans in economic, political, and cultural subjection.

Why Reconstruction Failed

Reconstruction failed to change American race relations because it challenged long-standing racist arrangements in both the North and South. The Civil

War had called these arrangements into question. African Americans had acted to expand their political role and become more than passive recipients of white oppression or largesse.

Then events conspired to frustrate the hopes of Reconstruction. The Panic of 1873, the scandals of the Grant presidency, and waning interest in black rights caused white Americans to back away from expansion of racial justice. The missed opportunity of the 1870s would not come again until almost a century had elapsed.

To help the freed slaves overcome the effects of slavery and racial bias would have involved an expansion of national governmental power to an extent that went beyond political beliefs of the nineteenth century. During the two decades that followed, black Americans experienced segregation and deepening oppression. The political gains of the Reconstruction era, especially the Fourteenth and Fifteenth Amendments remained unfulfilled promises for future generations to pursue.

THE END OF NATIVE AMERICAN RESISTANCE

While the United States was in the process of abridging its Civil War commitments to African Americans, the long struggle of Native Americans to resist white encroachment also ended. Pressures for white expansion onto Indian lands intensified during the Reconstruction period. Indians' efforts to push back the wave of white encroachment failed, and after 1876 Native Americans lacked the power to determine their own destiny.

During the 1870s Easterners and new immigrants surged westward to the prairies. The census reported over 2,660,000 farms in 1870 and just over 4 million ten years later. The newcomers competed with the Indians for space and resources. The amount of land devoted to wheat cultivation, for example, rose from nearly 21 million acres at the beginning of the decade to 62,545,000 in 1880. An African-American man who moved to Kansas at this time explained what drove him westward: "That's what white men go to new countries for, isn't it? You do not tell them to stay back because they are poor."

The cattle industry exerted further pressure on the Indians in the late 1860s. Texans returning from the Civil War drove their herds north to markets in Kansas. These cattle and others in western territories such as Wyoming, the Dakotas, and Colorado occupied space on the prairies where Indians had traditionally pursued their nomadic hunting culture.

Annihilation of the Buffalo Herds

The systematic destruction of the buffalo herds dealt the most devastating blow to the Indians. In the societies of the Plains tribes, the meat of the bison supplied food, while the hides provided shelter and clothes. Removal of these resources was calamitous, but the cultural impact was even more severe. Buffalo represented the continuity of nature and the renewal of life cycles. Destruction of the buffalo ended the Indians' capacity to resist white incursions. As one Crow warrior observed after the herds had gone, "Nothing happened after that. We just lived. There were no more war parties, no capturing horses from the Piegan and the Sioux, no buffalo to hunt. There is nothing more to tell."

The decline of the buffalo herds began during the 1860s, when drought, disease, and erosion shrank the animals' habitat. Then an expanding eastern market for buffalo robes and such products as pemmican (dried buffalo meat, berries, and fat) spurred intensive hunting of buffalo. As railroads penetrated the region, hunters could transport their products to customers with relative ease. The result was virtual extermination of the buffalo. More than *5 million* buffalo were slaughtered during the early 1870s. Along the Arkansas River, a British traveler reported, "there was a continual line of putrescent carcasses, so that the air was rendered pestilential and offensive to the last degree." Within a decade the once huge buffalo herds had vanished. By the end of the nineteenth century only a few buffalo remained alive.

A Last Stand for Custer and the Indians

During the mid-1870s, as the buffalo vanished and white incursions into Indian territories increased, Native American tribes mounted a last, futile effort to stem the tide that was overwhelming their way of life. The renewed strife on the Plains occurred in spite of

The opening of the West to white settlement in the 1870s produced the extermination of the huge buffalo herds that had roamed the prairies and sustained the Native American tribes. This picture shows some forty thousand hides piled up in a "hide yard" in Dodge City, Kansas.

President Grant's peace policy. The president's original appointees either resigned or left because of political attacks and the churches' influence over the operation of Indian policy receded as corruption and politics again shaped the treatment of Native Americans. Fewer Indians trusted the promises that they would receive fair treatment on the reservations, and the tribes that retained their nomadic way of life confronted ever-increasing numbers of settlers and a hostile military.

Fighting erupted on the southern plains in 1874 when Comanches and Kiowas attacked wagon trains. The Indians were arrested when they returned to their reservations, but raiding continued. A confrontation ensued between U.S. soldiers and Cheyennes, Kiowas, and Comanches that became known as the Red River War. The army did not win on the battlefield. Instead, the Indians' resistance collapsed because of lack of food and supplies.

In the North, the discovery of gold in the Black Hills of Dakota produced a wave of treasure seekers and increased pressure on the Sioux to relinquish the area for white development. The Indians refused, and the U.S. government sent soldiers to protect the miners. The Indian leaders, Crazy Horse and Sitting Bull, rallied their followers to stop the army. Near what the Indians called the Greasy Grass (known to whites as the Little Big Horn), Colonel George Armstrong

Custer led a force of 600 men. With a third of his detachment, he attacked more than 2,000 Sioux warriors. The result was the annihilation of Custer and his force on June 25, 1876. The Indian victory shocked the country, but it was only a momentary success. The army pursued the Indians during the months that followed, and in the process the ability of the Sioux to resist white soldiers declined. By the end of the Grant administration, the only Indians who were able to fight actively against the army were the Apaches in the Southwest. The bad treatment that the Apaches received from the government produced sporadic clashes during the 1880s and the army triumphed by the end of the decade.

One more tragic encounter, the Battle of Wounded Knee in 1890, lay ahead for the Plains Indians. For the most part the Grant presidency brought an end to the centuries of white–Indian warfare that had marked the history of the West in the United States.

THE ELECTION OF 1876

Several themes of late-nineteenth-century American life came together as the 1876 presidential election approached. The centennial of the Declaration of

Independence offered citizens an opportunity to reflect on the nation's progress and the social issues that remained unresolved. The race question confronted leaders and citizens even as the passions and commitments of Reconstruction faded. The contest for the White House seemed unusually important as it would shape the direction of the country during the rest of the century. As a result, the year achieved more than usual significance.

The Continuing Shadow of Scandal

Toward the end of Grant's second term, political corruption continued to cast a shadow over the White House. Attention focused on the "Whiskey Ring" in the Treasury Department. The officials involved took kickbacks from liquor interests in return for not collecting federal excise taxes on whiskey. Grant had appointed a new secretary of the Treasury, Benjamin H. Bristow, a Kentucky Republican who began a campaign to expose the ring. At first Grant said to Bristow: "Let no guilty man escape if it can be avoided." Later he changed his mind. When Bristow's probe discovered that the president's own secretary, Orville E. Babcock, had ties to a leader of the conspiracy, Grant allowed Babcock to avoid prosecution and sought Bristow's resignation. The episode further damaged Grant's credibility.

The final incident involved the secretary of War, W.W. Belknap. For some time Belknap's wife had been receiving regular cash gifts from a man who sold supplies to the army. When these financial ties were revealed, Belknap faced impeachment by a congressional committee. He resigned abruptly, and Grant accepted his hasty departure. The trail of scandal had now touched the White House, or so the president's critics argued. In the end, the most that could be laid at Grant's door was a too-trusting nature and bad judgment in some of his appointments. Grant presided over what became known as one of the most corrupt administrations in the nation's history, but his personal honesty remained unquestioned and his popularity high.

Marking the Centennial

As the nation's one hundredth birthday neared, attention focused on the Centennial International Exhibi-

tion to be held in Philadelphia in May of 1876. It was the second such fair to be held in the United States; New York had held an exposition in 1851. On 285 acres of fairgrounds stood several hundred buildings and pavilions crammed with exhibits, specimens, and artifacts from thirty-seven nations. The fair opened on May 10 with 200,000 spectators, the entire Congress in attendance, and a welcoming address by President Grant. Handel's "Hallelujah Chorus" and a salute from one hundred guns ended the ceremonies. The crowd poured into the buildings to see what had been assembled as evidence of the advance of civilization in the United States.

For spectators the huge Corliss steam engine was a stellar attraction. Standing forty feet tall, it weighed

At the Centennial Exposition in Philadelphia in 1876, one of the great attractions was the Corliss steam engine. To those who flocked into the grounds, the massive machine became a symbol of the promise and the dangers of industrial growth.

700 tons. The engine was shut down at noon each day for one hour; throngs assembled to see it start up again. Seventy-five miles of shafts and belts made the gigantic machine move. This massive example of technology symbolized the nation's faith in its industrial future.

Equally fascinating was the "harmonic telegraph" of Alexander Graham Bell, as the telephone was then called. To help publicize Bell's invention, Emperor Dom Pedro II of Brazil listened to the receiver and heard Bell deliver a soliloquy from "Hamlet" from across the hall. Dom Pedro exclaimed: "I hear, I hear! To be or not to be."

For all its technological marvels, the exhibition did not do justice to the complexity of American life in the 1870s. African Americans had almost no recognition at the fair. Native American cultures were depicted as "curiosities" consisting of totem poles, tepees, and trinkets. The Woman's Pavilion stressed homemaking. The exhibit evoked a protest from Elizabeth Cady Stanton and Susan B. Anthony. On July 4, 1876, they read a "Women's Declaration of Independence" that contrasted their aspirations with the traditional attitudes toward women expressed at the fair.

Nearly 10 million Americans came to the fair during its run, which ended on November 10. There they learned to eat bananas, and hot popcorn became a fad among city dwellers who soon made it a staple at other entertainment and sporting events. Although the fair lost money, its organizers pronounced it a great success. "We had a nation to show," said one U.S. senator. The Centennial exhibition contributed to a sense of national pride and confidence as the nation completed its first one hundred years. The presidential election that marked the year proved to be a more troubling symbol of the problems that the country faced.

The Race for the White House

A key test of the nation's institutions occurred during the election of 1876. The closest result in history produced a dispute that threatened to renew hostilities between North and South. As the election year began, the Democrats were optimistic about their ability to regain power for the first time since 1860. The repudiation of the Republicans in the 1874 elections seemed to foreshadow a Democratic triumph in the race for the presidency. The South would return to its usual Democratic allegiance; the Democrats could also capitalize on unhappiness with the difficult economic times in the North and Midwest.

To run as the Democratic candidate, the party selected the governor of New York, Samuel J. Tilden. Tilden was known as "Whispering Sammy" for his soft-spoken demeanor and as the "Great Forecloser" for his business dealings. He had been an opponent of the Tweed Ring and was regarded as a political reformer. A corporate lawyer, he believed in the gold standard and governmental economy. His platform spoke of a "revival of Jeffersonian democracy" and called for "high standards of official morality." Since Tilden was not in good health, the fact that presidential candidates did not campaign during that era worked to his advantage.

Among the Republicans there was some talk of a third term for President Grant, who remained very popular. The scandals of his presidency, however, made him a political burden rather than an asset. The front-runner for the nomination was the charismatic and exciting James G. Blaine of Maine, a former speaker of the House of Representatives. With the nomination seemingly in his grasp, Blaine encountered questions about his dealings with an Arkansas railroad while he was in the House. He answered the charges vigorously, but the episode raised problems about his ethics at a time when the party wanted to run a "clean" candidate against Tilden.

At the national convention Blaine took an early lead, but as the balloting continued, his candidacy lost momentum. Instead, the Republicans chose Governor Rutherford B. Hayes of Ohio as the nominee. Hayes had a good military record in the Civil War; there were no questions about his honesty; and he been able to carry the key state of Ohio on three occasions. He had all the assets of a man such as Blaine without any of the liabilities. The Republicans chose William A. Wheeler of New York as their candidate for vice president.

In the campaign the Democrats stressed Republican corruption and Tilden's honesty. A campaign song contained this message:

> The night of gloom is gliding out,
> Forth breaks the rosy day.
> And Tilden is the sun of hope,
> That lights the nation's way.

In response, the Republicans used the Reconstruction issue, as they had in the 1868 and 1872 contests.

Americans brought the military experience of the Civil War to their political campaigning in the 1870s. The massive parade of the "Boys in Blue" in 1876 indicates how strong were the memories of the recent war. Many feared that the disputed election in which Hayes finally defeated Tilden might spark a renewal of the fighting.

The rhetoric invoking the Civil War became known as "waving the bloody shirt," in memory of a Republican orator who had held up a bloodstained Union tunic and urged voters to remember the sacrifices of the Men in Blue. As one Republican put it, "Soldiers, every scar you have on your heroic bodies was given to you by a Democrat." Hayes saw the wisdom of this strategy. "It leads people away from hard times, which is our deadliest foe."

When the election results came in, it seemed at first that Tilden and the Democrats had won. With most of the South in his column, the Democratic candidate had also carried New York, Connecticut, and New Jersey. Preliminary counts indicated that Tilden had won 184 electoral votes, one short of the 185 needed for victory. Hayes, on the other hand, had 165 electoral votes, and seemed to have been defeated. Yet three southern states—Louisiana, Florida, and South Carolina—and a disputed elector in Oregon were still in doubt because both Democrats and Republicans claimed victory. They might give Hayes the White House. On election night that seemed an unlikely scenario, but the Republicans acted quickly to build a case for Hayes.

Republican operatives moved to contest the outcome in the three undecided states. Telegrams to party members called for evidence of intimidation of African-American voters. Honest returns from these states, the Republicans argued, would show that Hayes had carried each one; they disputed the results provided by Democratic election officials. The Republicans believed that they held a trump card. In the three states that they were contesting, the Republicans could rely on federal troops to safeguard state governments that were loyal to their cause. Otherwise, Democrats could simply occupy the state capitals and count the election returns their way. Both parties began maneuvering to control how the electoral votes of these three states were recorded.

The Constitution did not specify how a contested presidential election was to be decided. With each of the states in question sending in two sets of election returns, the House of Representatives had the responsibility for electing a president if no one won a majority in the electoral college. At the same time, the Senate had the constitutional duty to tabulate the electoral vote. With Republicans in control of the Senate and Democrats in control of the House, neither

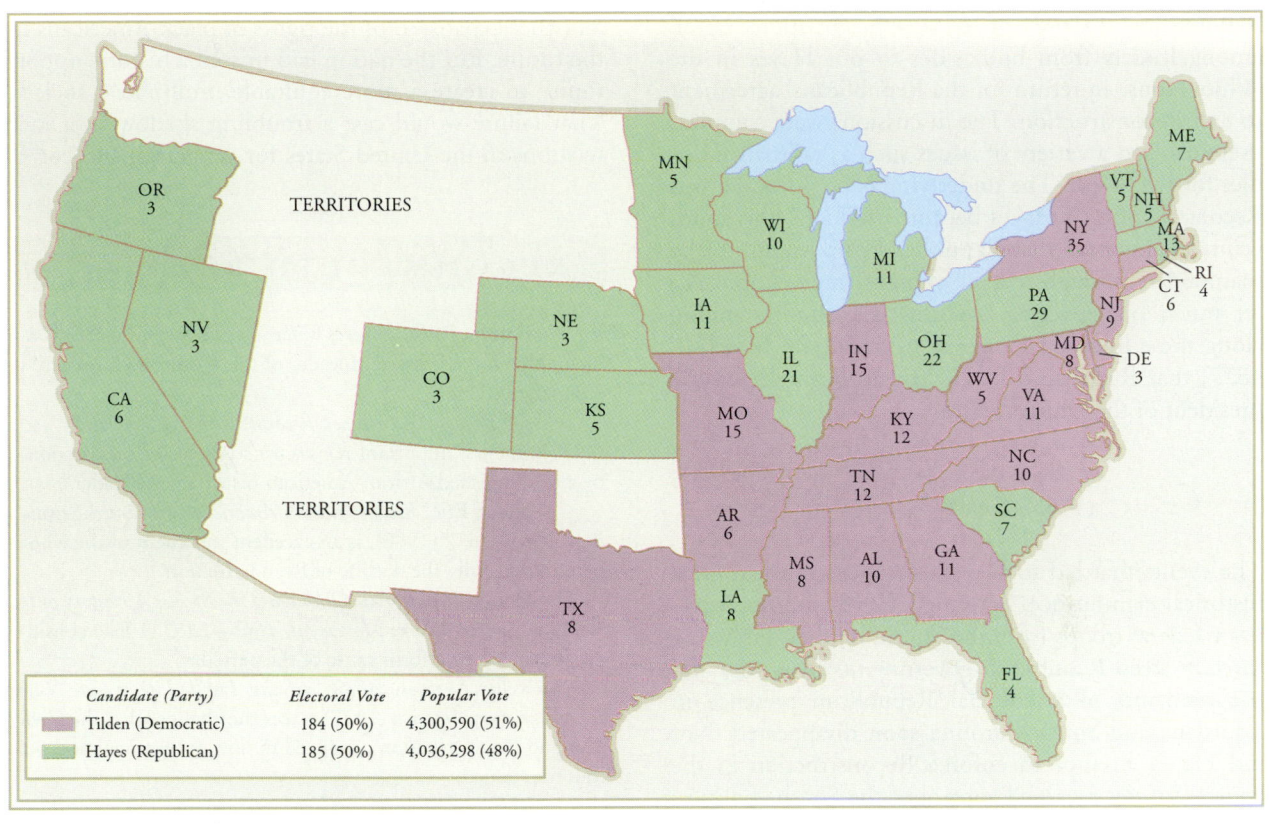

Candidate (Party)	Electoral Vote	Popular Vote
Tilden (Democratic)	184 (50%)	4,300,590 (51%)
Hayes (Republican)	185 (50%)	4,036,298 (48%)

MAP 16.5 | **THE ELECTION OF 1876**

side could proceed without the support of the other. A stalemate ensued.

To resolve the crisis, Congress created an electoral commission of fifteen members, ten from the House and Senate and five from the Supreme Court. As originally conceived, the panel was to have seven Republicans, seven Democrats, and a politically independent Supreme Court justice named David Davis. Then Davis was elected to the U.S. Senate by the Illinois legislature with Democratic votes in a move to defeat a Republican incumbent. Their ploy won a Senate seat, but wounded Tilden's chances. Davis resigned from the commission and a Republican justice took his place. In a series of 8–7 votes along straight party lines, the electoral commission accepted the Republican returns from Louisiana, Florida, and South Carolina, allocated the single disputed Oregon electoral vote to Hayes as well, and declared that Hayes had received 185 electoral votes and Tilden 184.

The question of who had really been elected president depended on the political perspective from which the contest was viewed. Tilden had a margin of 250,000 popular votes over Hayes and had carried sixteen states. Hayes had won eighteen states in addition to the three contested southern states. In Louisiana, Florida, and South Carolina, Tilden had received a majority of the white vote, but black Republican voters had been intimidated and terrorized to such an extent that an honest count was in doubt. Resolving the issue of which man deserved to be president became a matter for political compromise between the two major parties.

Despite the electoral commission's decision, the Democratic House still had to declare Hayes the winner. With the March 4, 1877, inauguration date approaching, the Democrats postponed tallying the electoral vote in an effort either to make Tilden president after March 4 or to extract concessions from the

Republicans. To prevent a crisis, negotiations began among leaders from both sides to put Hayes in the White House in return for the Republicans' agreement to end Reconstruction. The discussions were complex; they involved a variety of issues such as railroad subsidies for the South. The underlying issue, however, was Reconstruction. If Hayes became president, the South wanted assurances that Republican rule would not be maintained through federal military intervention. After much maneuvering, an unwritten understanding along these lines led Congress to decide on March 2, 1877, that Rutherford B. Hayes had been elected the president of the United States.

CONCLUSION

The events that led to Hayes's inauguration had great historical significance. Although Hayes did not withdraw federal troops from the South, neither did he use them to keep Republican governments in power, and the remnants of an official Republican presence in Louisiana and South Carolina soon disappeared. Nor did Hayes attempt to enforce Reconstruction in the courts. Whites regained control of the South's political institutions, while black southerners remained second-class citizens with limited political and economic rights. Reconstruction had ended in name as it had been ending in fact during Grant's second term.

Several powerful historical forces produced that sad result. Pervasive racism in both the North and the South labeled African Americans as unfit for self-government and accepted a return to white rule in the South. Pursuing Reconstruction into the 1880s would have involved giving to the national government more power over the lives of individual Americans than would have been tolerated in that era. Weary of Reconstruction and its moral claims, the generation of white Americans who had fought the Civil War turned their attention to other national problems. In so doing, they condemned black citizens to continued segregation and oppression.

The Civil War and Reconstruction period did have a positive legacy despite the tragic abandonment of African Americans. Slavery was abolished and the Union preserved. Black Americans had demonstrated that they could fight and die for their country, help make its laws, and function as full citizens when given an honest chance to do so. The Fourteenth and Fifteenth Amendments at least contained the promise of a further expansion of the rights of black Americans in the future. But the nation had missed a historic opportunity to create a more equitable, multiracial society. That failure would cast a troubling shadow over race relations in the United States for generations to come.

RECOMMENDED READINGS

Bordin, Ruth. *Frances Willard: A Biography* (1986) is a biography of the important leader of the Women's Christian Temperance Union.

Du Bois, W.E.B. *Black Reconstruction in America* (1935), the first important revisionist study of Reconstruction by a distinguished African-American historian and leader.

Foner, Eric. *Reconstruction: America's Unfinished Revolution, 1863–1877* (1988), is an excellent treatment of the whole period, especially the decline of Reconstruction.

Hoogenboom, Ari. *Outlawing the Spoils: A History of the Civil Service Reform Movement, 1865–1883* (1961) considers an important reform cause of the period.

Keller, Morton. *Affairs of State: Public Life in Late Nineteenth-Century America* (1977) traces the changes that the Civil War and Reconstruction produced in how government and politics functioned.

McFeely, William S. *Grant: A Biography* (1981), a prize-winning biography that examines Grant's life from the perspective of the 1970s.

Sproat, John G. *"The Best Men": Liberal Reformers in the Gilded Age* (1968) is a critical examination of the reformers who disliked the political system of the 1870s.

Summers, Mark Wahlgren. *The Era of Good Stealings* (1993) uses the corruption issue of the 1870s to write the closest thing to a political history of the decade.

Woodward, C. Vann. *Reunion and Reaction: The Compromise of 1877 and the End of Reconstruction* (1951) offers a provocative treatment of the disputed election of 1876.

Politics and Public Policy
Hoogenboom, Ari. *Rutherford B. Hayes: Warrior & President* (1995).

Polakoff, Keith I. *The Politics of Inertia: The Election of 1876 and the End of Reconstruction* (1973).

Summers, Mark. *The Press Gang: Newspapers and Politics, 1865–1878* (1994).

Thompson, Margaret Susan. *The "Spider Web": Congress and Lobbying in the Age of Grant* (1984).

Unger, Irwin. *The Greenback Era: A Social and Political History of American Finance, 1865–1879* (1964).

Women
Beeton, Betty. *Women Vote in the West: The Woman Suffrage Movement, 1869–1896* (1986).

Davis, Margery W. *Women's Place Is at the Typewriter: Office Work and Office Workers, 1870–1930* (1982).

Jeffrey, Julie Roy. *Frontier Women: The Trans-Mississippi West* (1979).

Jones, Jacqueline. *Soldiers of Light and Love: Northern Teachers and Georgia Blacks, 1865–1873* (1980).

Kugler, Israel. *From Ladies to Women: The Organized Struggle for Women's Rights in the Reconstruction Era* (1987).

The West

Ambrose, Stephen. *Crazy Horse and Custer: The Parallel Lives of Two American Warriors* (1976).

Gould, Lewis L. *Wyoming: From Territory to Statehood* (1989).

Lamar, Howard R. *Dakota Territory, 1861–1889: A Study of Frontier Politics* (1956).

Utley, Robert. *The Indian Frontier of the American West, 1846–1890* (1984).

Wooster, Robert. *The Military and United States Indian Policy, 1865–1890* (1988).

The South

Abbott, Richard H. *The Republican Party and the South, 1855–1877: The First Southern Strategy* (1986).

DeSantis, Vincent. *Republicans Face the Southern Question* (1959).

Gillette, William. *Retreat from Reconstruction, 1869–1879* (1979).

Perman, Michael. *The Road to Redemption: Southern Politics, 1869–1879* (1984).

Seip, Terry. *The South Returns to Congress: Men, Economic Measures, and Intersectional Relationships, 1869–1879* (1983).

—1877 TO 1909—

To white Americans during the late 1870s, the sense that the Civil War and Reconstruction were receding into history represented a comforting illusion. African Americans knew best of all citizens how alive and painful the problem of race remained. Yet the popular belief that important forces now reshaped American life also described reality. The national journey was leaving behind an agricultural, rural, underdeveloped economy and culture, and gathering speed as an industrialized nation. The transformation took decades, but its consequences proved decisive in creating the modern United States.

Industry became the way in which more and more Americans made a living during the years from the presidency of Rutherford B. Hayes (1877–1881) through the end of Theodore Roosevelt's administration in March 1909. First came the railroads, but soon followed steel, oil, machinery, telephones and, after 1900, the automobile. The relentless process of industrial growth drew families from the country to the city, changed the look and population of the cities themselves, and made society adapt to the pace of machinery and the factory. Business leaders emerged as national figures—Andrew Carnegie, John D. Rockefeller, and J.P. Morgan. Their fellow citizens wondered about the fate of the average person in the face of such concentrated economic power.

The result of industrialism was material abundance for some and great want for many others. The ability of factories to provide cheaper, standardized goods such as canned foods, sewing machines, tools, and clothes pleased those who could afford to buy them. For those left behind or shut out from society's bounty, the riches of the new system seemed a mockery. Industry knit the country

PASSAGES

together in a shared experience as consumers in a national market; it alienated others who saw their hard work bringing no fair reward for themselves.

Immigration into the United States changed the shape of the nation's population and instilled an even richer diversity in the society. Older residents reacted with suspicion and hostility to the influx of newcomers from Southern and Eastern Europe, and ethnic tensions underlay voting decisions, residence patterns, and social conflict. The immigrants filled the nation's cities, tilled and settled the western plains, and did much of the work of the industrial sector. By the first decade of the twentieth century, pressures mounted for immigration restriction.

Politics struggled to keep pace with accelerating change in the business sector. An even balance between Republicans and Democrats from 1877 to 1894 kept the national government passive and slow to react. An expansion of governmental power took place on the state level despite claims that the era favored noninvolvement in social policy. An economic depression during the 1890s destroyed the national

stalemate, wounded the Democrats, and gave the Republicans a majority of the electorate. A third party, the Populists, failed meanwhile to halt the erosion of the once powerful agricultural sector.

By the end of the 1890s, the United States stepped into the arena of international politics when it acquired an empire from Spain after a war over Cuba. The heyday of imperialism did not last; the consequences of overseas expansion endured. New responsibilities in the Atlantic and Pacific meant a growth in the power of the federal government to fulfill the world role. Currents of isolationism persisted to limit foreign adventures, but the movement toward world power continued.

The nation mixed confidence and doubt as the twentieth century opened. From the small nation of 1800 had emerged a continental giant, the world's largest internal free market, and a functioning experiment in political democracy. All that bred optimism by 1900. Social critics, however, pointed out the other side of the ledger. "We can feed ourselves, we are great and powerful," said a popular newspaperman in 1900, "but we have our own galling Negro problem, our rotten machine politics, our legisla-

Class and population size	1860	1870	1880
Urban territory	392	663	939
Places of 1,000,000 or more	-	-	1
Places of 500,000–999,999	2	2	3
Places of 250,000–499,999	1	5	4
Places of 100,000–249,999	6	7	12
Places of 50,000–99,999	7	11	15
Places of 25,000–49,999	19	27	42
Places of 10,000–24,999	58	116	146
Places of 5,000–9,999	136	186	249
Places of 2,500–4,999	163	309	467

Class and population size	1890	1900	1910
Urban territory	1,348	1,737	2,262
Places of 1,000,000 or more	3	3	3
Places of 500,000–999,999	1	3	5
Places of 250,000–499,999	7	9	11
Places of 100,000–249,999	17	23	31
Places of 50,000–99,999	30	40	59
Places of 25,000–49,999	66	82	119
Places of 10,000–24,999	230	280	369
Places of 5,000–9,999	340	465	605
Places of 2,500–4,999	654	832	1060
Places under 2,500	-	-	-
Rural territory	6,490	8,931	11,830
Places of 1,000–2,499	1,603	2,128	2,717
Places under 1,000	4,887	6,803	9,113

URBANIZATION, 1860–1910

- Represents zero.

tive bribery, our municipal corruption, our giant monopolies, our aristocracy of mere riches, any one of which is a rock on which the ship of state, unless skillfully navigated, may go to its destruction."

The indictment had merit. Too many in the United States—African Americans, Hispanics, Indians, immigrants, and women—did not share in all that the country offered. Looking back, the verdict would be that the late nineteenth century fell short of its historic duties. To Americans who lived through these times, who saw Hayes enter the White House and Roosevelt give way to William Howard Taft, it appeared that they had left the country better than they found it when they first addressed its problems during the 1870s. Their part in the American journey will be the underlying theme of the four chapters that follow.

GROSS NATIONAL PRODUCT, TOTAL AND PER CAPITA, IN CURRENT AND 1958 PRICES: 1869 TO 1909

Year	Current prices		1958 prices		Implicit price index (1958 = 100)
	Total	Per capita	Total	Per capita	
	Bil. dol.	Dollars	Bil. dol.	Dollars	
1869–1878[1]	7.4	170	23.1	531	32.1
1879–1888[1]	11.2	205	42.4	774	26.5
1889	12.5	202	49.1	795	25.4
1890	13.1	208	52.7	836	24.9
1891	13.5	210	55.1	856	24.6
1892	14.3	218	60.4	920	23.6
1893	13.8	206	57.5	859	24.1
1894	12.6	185	55.9	819	22.6
1895	13.9	200	62.6	900	22.3
1896	13.3	188	61.3	865	21.7
1897	14.6	202	67.1	930	21.8
1898	15.4	210	68.6	933	22.4
1899	17.4	233	74.8	1,000	23.2
1900	18.7	246	76.9	1,011	24.3
1901	20.7	267	85.7	1,105	24.1
1902	21.6	273	86.5	1,093	24.9
1903	22.9	284	90.8	1,126	25.2
1904	22.9	279	89.7	1,092	25.5
1905	25.1	299	96.3	1,149	26.1
1906	28.7	336	107.5	1,258	26.7
1907	30.4	349	109.3	1,255	27.8
1908	27.7	312	100.2	1,130	27.6
1909	33.4	369	116.8	1,290	28.6

[1] Decade average.

	1877	1880	1885	1890

POLITICS & DIPLOMACY

1877: Rutherford B. Hayes elected president after disputed election
Nationwide railroad strike
Supreme Court decides case of *Munn v. Illinois*
1878: Bland-Allison Act for silver passed over Hayes's veto
Congress passed Timber and Stone Act
1879: Exoduster movement of blacks to Kansas
1880: James A. Garfield defeats Winfield Scott Hancock in presidential election

1881: Garfield assassinated in July; dies in September
Chester A. Arthur becomes President
1882: Chinese Exclusion Act passed
1883: Supreme Court rules in *Civil Rights Cases* that Civil Rights Act of 1875 does not apply in southern states
Mongrel Tariff law enacted
Pendleton Civil Service Law passed
1884: Grover Cleveland defeats James G. Blaine in presidential election
1885: Ulysses S. Grant dies of cancer

1886: Haymarket Riot in Chicago
Great Southwestern Strike occurs
1887: President Cleveland calls for reform of tariff in annual message
1888: Benjamin Harrison defeats Cleveland in presidential election
1889: Opening of Oklahoma Territory to non-Native American settlement
Jane Addams starts Hull House settlement house program
1890: Passage of Sherman Silver Purchase Act, McKinley Tariff, and Sherman Antitrust Acts
Battle of Wounded Knee
People's Party makes electoral gains in South and West
Republicans suffer major losses in Congressional elections

SOCIAL & CULTURAL EVENTS

1877: New York YMCA offers first typing course for women
1878: President Hayes and his wife Lucy begin tradition of White House Easter egg roll
1879: Henry George publishes *Progress and Poverty*
1880: Metropolitan Museum of Art opens in New York City
1881: Helen Hunt Jackson publishes *A Century of Dishonor* about treatment of Native Americans
Boston Symphony Orchestra established
1882: American Association of University Women founded
1883: Lester Frank Ward publishes *Dynamic Sociology*

1884: Mark Twain's *Huckleberry Finn* is published
1885: William Dean Howell's book *The Rise of Silas Lapham* appears
1886: Death of poet Emily Dickinson
Coca-Cola goes on sale in Atlanta
Statue of Liberty dedicated
1887: William Randolph Hearst begins career as publisher of San Francisco *Examiner*
1888: Edward Bellamy, *Looking Backward* becomes best-seller
1889: Singer electric sewing machine introduced
Safety bicycle enjoys wide popularity

1890: Daughters of the American Revolution founded
Poems by Emily Dickinson published
1891: James Naismith invents basketball
University of Chicago opens
1892: Ida Wells-Barnett begins anti-lynching campaign
Ellis Island in New York opens to receive immigrants
Shredded Wheat created
1893: Mildred Hill publishes song that becomes "Happy Birthday"
Columbian Exposition offers "Great White City" in Chicago
1894: Radcliffe College for Women opens in Cambridge, Mass.

ECONOMICS & TECHNOLOGY

1877: Bell Telephone Company organized
Thomas Edison invents the phonograph
1878: General Assembly of Knights of Labor founded
1879: Thomas Edison invents incandescent lamp
Henry George publishes *Progress and Poverty*
1880: George Eastman patents first successful roll film camera
1881: American Federation of Labor (AFL) formed
1882: Standard Oil becomes first trust
Observance of Labor Day begins

1883: Railroads create national time zones
1884: Bureau of Labor established in federal government
1885: American Telephone and Telegraph Company organized
1886: Southern railroad tracks moved closer together to comply with national standards
1887: Interstate Commerce Act passed to regulate railroads
First electrical streetcar service in Richmond, Virginia
1888: George Eastman perfects Kodak hand camera

1889: Electric sewing machine developed
1890: Sherman Antitrust Act passed
1891: Thomas Edison receives first radio patent in United States
1892: Homestead Strike is broken in Carnegie Steel
1893: Panic of 1893 begins four-year depression
1894: Pullman Strike occurs in midst of economic hard times

1891: Federal Elections Bill to regulate elections in South blocked in the Senate

1892: Cleveland defeats Harrison in 1892 presidential election

Democrats gain control of both houses of Congress

1893: Sherman Silver Purchase Act repealed

1894: Coxey's Army makes protest march to Washington

Republicans make large gains in congressional elections

1895: Venezuelan Crisis with Great Britain

1896: McKinley defeats Bryan in presidential election

Supreme Court upholds segregation in *Plessy v. Ferguson*

1897: Dingley Tariff enacted

1898: Hawaiian Islands annexed

Spanish-American War begins; United States defeats Spain and acquires Philippine Islands

1899: Open Door policy in Far East announced by John Hay

1900: McKinley defeats Bryan again in presidential race

Theodore Roosevelt is McKinley's running mate

1901: McKinley assassinated

Theodore Roosevelt becomes president

1902: Northern Securities Case filed by Justice Department

Anthracite Coal Strike settled

1903: Panama Canal Zone acquired; Canadian boundary dispute settled

1904: Theodore Roosevelt elected president over Alton B. Parker

1905: Roosevelt mediates Russo-Japanese War

1906: Hepburn Act passed to regulate railroads

Pure Food and Drug and Meat Inspection Act passed

1907: Gentleman's Agreement with Japan over immigration policy

1908: William Howard Taft defeats Bryan for presidency

1909: Theodore Roosevelt leaves office; Taft inaugurated president

---

1895: Stephen Crane publishes *The Red Badge of Courage* about Civil War

Booker T. Washington proposes "Atlanta Compromise"

Anti-Saloon League established

1896: Trading stamps offered by stores in the United States

First commercial movie showing occurs

1897: Jell-O is introduced

1898: Condensed soups are offered to consumers

1899: Scott Joplin publishes "Maple Leaf Rag"

Edward Kennedy "Duke" Ellington born in Washington, D.C.

1900: Olds Motor Works begins mass producing cars

1901: Dorothy Dix advice columns begins in New York *Evening Journal*

Jazz trumpeter Louis Armstrong born in New Orleans

1902: Teddy Bear toy developed

Muckraking journalism begins in *McClure's Magazine*

1903: National Woman's Trade Union League formed

"Great Train Robbery," first western movie, premieres

1904: Ice cream cone marketed

1905: Edith Wharton publishes *The House of Mirth* about New York upper class

1906: Theodore Roosevelt attacks muckrakers

1907: Self-contained electric clothes washer developed

1908: Henry Ford introduces Model T automobile

First Mother's Day observed

Jack Johnson becomes heavyweight boxing champion

1909: National Association for the Advancement of Colored People founded

---

1895: Supreme Court ruling in *U.S. v. E.C. Knight* case weakens Sherman Antitrust Act

1896: Gold discovered in Klondike in Canada and helps ease deflation

1897: Depression of 1890s eases

1898: Burst of industrial consolidation as mergers accelerate

1899: Founding of National Consumers League

1900: Gold Standard Act passed

1901: United States Steel created as first billion dollar corporation

1902: Newlands Act passed to promote irrigation in the West

U.S. files suit against Northern Securities Company

1903: Department of Commerce and Labor created

Wright brothers make first airplane flight

1904: In *Northern Securities Co. v. U.S.,* Supreme Court upholds government position against railroad holding company and strengthens Sherman Antitrust Act

1905: In *Lochner v. New York* rules that maximum hours law for bakers is not constitutional

1906: Bureau of Immigration established

1907: Panic of 1907 results in calls for banking reform

1908: In *Muller v. Oregon* U.S. Supreme Court upholds law specifying maximum hours that women can work

1909: Payne-Aldrich Tariff enacted

SYMBOL OF AN INDUSTRIAL AGE

In the 1870s Commodore Cornelius Vanderbilt became one of the symbols of unbridled corporate power for the way he ran his railroads in the Northeast and Midwest. Critics of these railroad owners called them "robber barons" to link them with the tactics of the tyrannical lords of the Middle Ages.

Chapter 17

The Economic Transformation of America, 1877–1887

After the inauguration of Rutherford B. Hayes on March 4, 1877, national interest turned to scientific inventions, the rise of urbanization, and the growth of industry. Politics and public policy struggled with the social issues that emerged from this economic upheaval.

The agenda of social and political problems facing the nation between 1877 and 1887 was formidable. The process of industrialization transformed how Americans lived and worked together. As an economist observed, "civilized society in recent years has become a vastly more complicated machine than before." How the American people grappled with the effects of industrial growth defined the decades between the waning of Reconstruction and the end of the nineteenth century.

RAILROADS AND A "LOCOMOTIVE PEOPLE"

The railroad stood as the most visible example of the complexity that came with industrialization. One British writer noted that "The Americans are an eminently locomotive people." The completion of the transcontinental railroads signalled the energetic pace of rail development. During the 1880s the amount of tracks rose steadily, reaching 167,000 miles in 1890. By that time the United States had a more extensive railroad network than all the European countries combined, even with Russia included.

Creating the Railroad Network

This network of iron and steel drew the nation together as bridges and tunnels removed the obstacles posed by mountains and rivers. Another step toward unification was the establishment of a standard gauge or width for all tracks. Some railroads used the standard gauge of 4 feet 8.5 inches; others relied on tracks as much as 6 feet apart. These inconsistencies translated into extra equipment, higher costs, and lost time. By 1880 the standard gauge dominated, with the South the principal holdout. However, on a single day in 1886, all the southern lines moved their rails to the standard gauge. To put all railroads on the same set of working times, in 1883 the railroads agreed to set up four standard time zones across the country.

Consistency streamlined the operation of the railroads. Freight was moved with greater ease through bills of lading (a statement of what was being

CHRONOLOGY

1877	After wages of railroad workers are reduced, national strike erupts
	Desert Land Act passed
1878	Bland-Allison Act passed to buy silver
	Timber and Stone Act passed
1879	Thomas Edison invents incandescent lamp
	Cash register invented
	Woman suffrage amendment introduced in Congress
	Frances Willard becomes president of the Woman's Christian Temperance Union (WCTU)
	Henry George publishes *Progress and Poverty*
1880	Metropolitan Museum of Art opens in New York City
	James A. Garfield elected president
1881	Garfield assassinated; Chester Alan Arthur succeeds him
	American Federation of Labor (AFL) formed
	Boston Symphony Orchestra begins performances
1882	Chinese Exclusion Act
	Standard Oil Company becomes first trust
	American Association of University Women established
1883	Pendleton Civil Service Act passed
	Railroads create national standard time zones
	Lester Frank Ward publishes *Dynamic Sociology*
1884	Grover Cleveland defeats James G. Blaine for presidency
	Mark Twain's *Huckleberry Finn* published
1885	Death of Ulysses S. Grant
1886	Haymarket Riot in Chicago (May 4)
	Emily Dickinson dies in Amherst, Massachusetts
1887	Dawes Severalty Act passed
	Interstate Commerce Act passed
	Cleveland attacks tariff in annual message
	First electrical streetcar service in Richmond, Virginia

TABLE 17.1
RAILROAD MILEAGE, 1877–1887

1877	97,308
1878	103,649
1879	104,756
1880	115,647
1881	130,455
1882	140,878
1883	149,101
1884	156,414
1885	160,506
1886	167,952
1887	184,935

SOURCE: *The Statistical History of the United States,* p. 427.

shipped), which all lines accepted. Standard freight classifications were developed and passenger schedules became more rational and predictable, especially after the establishment of standard time zones. After the enactment of the Interstate Commerce Act (1887) and the passage of other relevant legislation during the 1890s, all railroads adopted automatic couplers, air brakes, and other safety devices.

Railroad travel also became more comfortable for passengers and more accommodating to food and other perishables. The refrigerator car preserved food for transport to distant consumers. George Pullman pioneered the sleeping car. The railroads built huge terminals through which millions of passengers and countless tons of freight moved each day.

It took a staggering amount of money to construct the railroad system. More than $4 billion was invested by 1877. In comparison, the entire national debt was just over $2.1 billion. To finance this huge commit-

ment of money, the railroads drew upon the funds of private investors both in the United States and Europe. An impressive amount, however, came from government. To aid in the construction of the western transcontinental railroads, for example, the federal government made direct loans of almost $65 million to the rail lines along with millions of acres of land grants. Total federal land grants to railroads exceeded 130 million acres, and state and local governments added another 49 million acres. Other examples of state aid included loans, tax reductions, and issuing of bonds. The total amount of all such assistance approached $500 million.

By 1880 the railroad network had assumed a well-defined shape. East of the Mississippi River to the Atlantic seaboard ran four *trunk* [main line] railroads that carried goods and passengers from smaller towns connected by *feeder* [subsidiary] lines. The trunk lines

were the Pennsylvania Railroad, the Erie Railroad, the New York Central Railroad, and the Baltimore and Ohio Railroad. The transcontinental lines included the Union Pacific/Central Pacific, Northern Pacific, and Southern Pacific. In the South the trunk lines emerged more slowly. During the 1880s and 1890s southern railroads built five trunk lines, including the Southern Railway and the Louisville and Nashville Railroad.

Organizing the Railroad Business

Because they conducted their affairs on a grand scale, railroads were the first big business. Factories in a single location had fewer than a thousand workers; the railroads extended over thousands of miles and

MAP 17.1 | THE RAILROAD NETWORK

employed tens of thousands of workers. Customers flowed in and out of trains and stations in large numbers. The railroads required an immense amount of equipment and facilities; no single individual could supervise it all directly.

New management systems arose to address these problems. Executives set up clear lines of authority. Separate operating divisions purchased supplies, maintained track and equipment, handled freight, dealt with passengers, and transmitted information. Local superintendents took care of day-to-day matters; general superintendents resolved larger policy issues; and railroad executives made the overall decisions. By the 1870s the organizational structure of the railroads included elaborate mechanisms for cost accounting.

Railroads stimulated the national economy. From the late 1860s through the early 1890s, the railroads consumed more than half the nation's output of steel. Railroads also used about 20 percent of the nation's coal production. Their repair shops created a market for industrial workers in midwestern cities such as Chicago and Cleveland.

The United States was becoming a national economic market in which similar goods and services were available to people throughout the nation. The development of a national market also encouraged the growth of big business to meet consumer demand for canned goods, ready-made clothes, and industrial machinery. Thus, the expansion of the railroads was a key element in the dramatic changes brought about by industrialization.

The Railroad as a Political Issue

Because of their economic impact, railroads became a political issue. Land grants affected numerous communities and railroad executives provoked controversy. Cornelius Vanderbilt of the New York Central, Collis P. Huntington of the Southern Pacific, and Jay Gould of the Union Pacific, among others, were renowned for the ruthless methods they employed against their competitors. Their critics called them "robber barons" because their exploitation of the public reminded them of the mercenary nobles of the Middle Ages or the pirates of the high seas.

Industry leaders believed that too much competition caused economic and political problems. Because a railroad ran constantly and had to maintain its equipment, facilities, and labor force on a continuing

basis, its operating costs were inescapable or "fixed." To survive, a railroad needed a reliable and constant flow of freight and passengers. One strategy was to build tracks and add lines in order to gain more business. Each new line required more business to pay off the cost of building it. Railroads therefore waged a constant economic struggle for the available traffic.

One obvious solution was to lure customers, either openly or secretly, with reduced prices. From 1865 to 1900 railroad rates were lowered. Some of the reduction in rates stemmed from the general deflation in prices that marked this period. Other price declines came about because the railroads and their workers found ways to move freight and passengers more efficiently. Greater productivity was a key element in the success of railroads and industry in general.

To maintain their share of the total available business, railroads resorted to a number of secret devices. The *rebate* was a discount on published rates that was given to a favored shipper in the form of cash payments. Other customers had to pay the listed rate or were charged more. When faced with potentially destructive competition, the railroads engaged in price wars or tried to acquire their rivals. Railroads (and other industries) also used the *pool,* a private agreement to divide the available business in an industry or locality. Working together, the railroads hoped to maintain rates at a level that ensured profits for all members of the pool.

Attractive in theory as a means of restraining competition, in practice, pools were impossible to enforce because their secrecy violated state laws against economic conspiracies. Weaker railroads were willing to cheat on the pool if it would bring in more business. Railroad men wanted the federal government to legalize pooling through legislation, an approach that was politically unpopular because it would have endorsed price-fixing and monopolies. By the middle of the 1880s, therefore, the larger railroads moved toward consolidation as a way to deal with the problems created by too many railroads and too much competition.

Regulating the Railroads

While rebates, pools, and consolidation made sense to the railroads, they aroused anger among those who traveled or shipped their goods by rail. Shippers who did not receive rebates regarded the tactic as unfair.

Railroads often charged more for a short haul than for a longer one because fewer exchanges and stops made the long haul cheaper. Shippers claimed that this practice was further evidence of unfair tactics. Because of the advantage they gave to some shippers over others, railroad rates also served the interest of some cities such as Chicago or Kansas City to the detriment of others in the Middle West. To many observers these facts seemed to be evidence of abuses by railroad management. Added to this unease was the danger to the traveling public. In 1888 alone some 5,200 Americans were killed while traveling or working on the railroad. Another 26,000 were injured. Industrial growth came at a significant human cost which led to calls for regulation of the railroads.

Americans debated how society should respond to the political and economic challenge that the railroads posed. The idea of government ownership of some railroads so as to provide a yardstick against which the rates and services of others might be judged, did not achieve public support. The prospect of having legislatures or courts oversee the railroads was not popular either. Instead, Americans developed a middle way between those apparent extremes.

The Railroad Commission

The characteristic response to such dilemmas during this period was the *regulatory commission*. Ideally, such a body, created by the state legislature, was composed of experts who decided issues of rates, finance, and service in a neutral, nonpartisan way. The first railroad commission had been created in New Hampshire in 1844; there were four in existence when the Civil War broke out. After the war, the commission concept spread; there were twenty-eight such agencies by 1896.

Railroad commissions were generally of two kinds. One variety advised railroads of possible violations and publicized information about railroad operations. The most notable example of this kind of commission was the one in Massachusetts. Critics claimed that the Massachusetts commission was weak because it lacked the power to set rates. The second kind of railroad commission was established in Illinois in 1871. It had the power to set rates and put them into effect in 1873. Because of this authority, which other midwestern states adopted, the Illinois model became known as the "strong" form of the railroad commission.

During the 1870s railroads challenged the authority of these state commissions. The most important case involved Illinois, and it reached the U.S. Supreme Court in 1876. The decision of *Munn* v. *Illinois* (1877) ruled that the state did have the power to establish a commission that could regulate railroad rates. Railroads, the court said, were "engaged in a public employment affecting the public interest." Because Congress had not yet acted to regulate interstate commerce in railroad matters, a state could make "such rules and regulations as may be necessary for the protection of the general welfare of the people within its own jurisdiction." The case was a strong assertion of the power of state governments to regulate business in the public interest.

Despite such successes, reservations about the effectiveness of state commissions grew. Critics complained that the railroads had too much influence over the state commissions. There was some corruption, and the process of regulation was often cumbersome. Most important, however, the state commissions could not deal effectively with interstate railroads. In 1886, in the case of *Wabash, St. Louis, and Pacific Railway Company* v. *Illinois,* the Supreme Court ruled that enforcement of the Illinois law infringed on interstate commerce. It was clear that Congress needed to establish a national policy for regulating the railroads.

The Interstate Commerce Act

A number of political and economic forces combined to stimulate the demand for railroad regulation. Western and southern farmers supported such a policy. However, their influence was less significant than that of merchants and shippers on the East Coast, who wanted a government agency to ensure that they received fair treatment from the rail companies. Some railroads preferred federal regulation to the confusion of competing state commissions. Congress responded to these pressures by passing the Interstate Commerce Act in 1887. This law set up an Interstate Commerce Commission (ICC), composed of five members, that could investigate complaints of railroad misconduct or file suit against the companies. The law forbade rebates and pooling. The new regulatory agency was the first of its kind on the federal level. Despite a shaky start for the ICC in its first decade, commissions became a favored means of dealing with the problems of managing an industrial society. They reflected the desire of Americans to preserve the economic benefits

that railroads provided while at the same time preventing the rail companies from exercising excessive economic power.

THE ARRIVAL OF BIG BUSINESS

While the growth of the railroads laid the basis for further industrial expansion, the success of big business came during difficult economic times. The depression of the 1870s ebbed by 1879, but the prosperity that followed was brief. From 1881 to 1885 there was another slowdown, with numerous business failures. Two years of good times preceded another recession during 1887 and 1888. Uncertainly and fear of another "panic" shaped the way business leaders went about increasing the size of their enterprises. A key fact of the economy in the late nineteenth century was that businesses grew larger even though prosperity was elusive.

Throughout these years, deflation brought about by increased productivity, a tight money supply, and an abundant labor force, was a fact of life for businessmen. Companies with high fixed costs, such as railroads, oil, and steel, experienced intense, constant pressure to reduce competition and avoid its impact through arrangements such as pools that divided up the available business. In a few industries it even seemed possible to escape competition and achieve monopoly.

John D. Rockefeller and Standard Oil

The most famous example of such an industry was oil. John D. Rockefeller and Standard Oil became renowned as examples of monopoly power and economic concentration. Rockefeller had been in the oil business since the mid-1860s. From his base in Ohio, he built his company on the principle of expanding as rapidly as possible while watching costs carefully. He founded the Standard Oil Company in 1870. As Rockefeller's oil interests grew, he and his partner, Henry Flagler, used the company's size to secure rebates from the railroads. Able to assure the rail companies a dependable supply of oil to haul, they also obtained a share, or "drawback," of what their compet-

His mastery of the American oil industry in the 1870s and 1880s and his use of the trust device that his lawyers created made John D. Rockefeller one of the most famous and hated men of the time. He saw himself as bringing rationality and order to a chaotic economy. His activities and the behavior of other business leaders sparked a movement to regulate the trusts by the end of the 1880s.

itors paid. Despite these advantages, there were still too many producers in the industry, resulting in a glut of oil.

The creation of Standard Oil was Rockefeller's effort to impose control on a chaotic business. Through rebates, drawbacks, and price-cutting against rivals whose companies he eventually acquired, he sought to gain control over all the supplies of oil. By the end of the 1870s, he controlled about 90 percent of the nation's oil-refining capacity. Economists call this "a horizontal integration" of the oil business.

The Emergence of the Trust

The creation of a virtual monopoly in oil triggered a political response. Under state law, Standard Oil of Ohio could not legally own stock in other oil companies or conduct its business in other states. Yet registering to do business in other states could reveal as-

pects of the company's business to competitors and expose it to legal challenges in the courts for restraint of trade. In 1882, a lawyer for Rockefeller, S.T.C. Dodd, responded to these challenges by formulating a new use for an old legal device. Standard Oil became the first example of the *trust* in American business.

The forty-one stockholders of Standard Oil, entered into an agreement that created a board of nine trustees. In return the board held the company's stock in trust and exercised "general supervision over the affairs of said Standard Oil Companies." The trustees could select the board of directors and set policy for all Standard Oil's subsidiaries in other states. In this way the trust escaped the restrictions of state laws everywhere. The term trust soon lost its legal connotation and became a general label for the rise of big business.

The trust device was used only for a brief period. In the late 1870s several states passed laws that allowed corporations to own branches in other states, to hold the stock of other corporations, and to pursue a policy of consolidation to the extent that their industry and its conditions permitted. The "holding company" law, first enacted in New Jersey and later in Delaware, was more efficient than the trust approach. A large company simply held the stock of its subsidiaries. The spectacle of the trust swallowing up its rivals became ingrained in the popular imagination.

By the end of the 1880s, there were demands for state and congressional action to curb the growth of the trusts and their power. In the 1888 presidential election both major parties denounced trusts that aimed "to control arbitrarily the condition of trade among our citizens," as the Republicans put it. Fourteen states and territories passed laws to curb monopoly power. President Grover Cleveland said in 1887 that "competition is too often strangled by combinations quite prevalent at this time, and frequently called trusts." The political world seemed intent on taking at least symbolic action against large industrial combinations. As a result the heyday of unregulated big business was very brief.

Andrew Carnegie and the Steel Industry

Almost as famous as Rockefeller was Andrew Carnegie. He was one of the few prominent businessmen of the era who had risen "from rags to riches." He came to the United States from Scotland in 1848 and worked first in a textile factory and then as a telegraph clerk. By 1853 he was the private secretary to Thomas A. Scott of the Pennsylvania Railroad. During the 1860s he played the stock market through investments in railroading, oil, and telegraph company securities. By 1873, however, he was focusing on the burgeoning steel industry. He summed up his philosophy with these words: "Put all your good eggs in one basket, and then watch that basket."

Carnegie had selected the best industry in which to make his fortune. In the 1870s the technology of steelmaking relied on the Bessemer process of steel production in which molten pig iron was placed in a receptacle or converter and air was blown across it to remove impurities through oxidization. The result was a flow of steel in about fifteen or twenty minutes, much faster than the earlier process in which an individual "puddler" had worked the molten iron. Eventually the

Rising from poverty to great wealth, Andrew Carnegie made his greatest fortune in the steel business. He cut costs, emphasized control of all steps in the process of making steel, and proved to be a ruthless competitive force in the industry. Later in life he turned to charitable works and preached the "Gospel of Wealth," which said that the rich should use their money for constructive purposes.

A TEXAN
PROTESTS CORPORATE
POWER
1885

During the 1880s, Americans began to worry about the impact on society of the rising power of large corporations. In the South and West, politicians spoke out about the menace that big business posed to traditional values. In a speech in Missouri on June 1, 1885, a Texas lawyer named Alexander W. Terrell addressed what he saw as the injustices of corporate behavior. His language reflected the fears of many citizens as industrialism went forward.

I arraign private corporations as inimical to civil liberty, which is so largely dependent on the virtue of man, because they demoralize from head to foot those who embark in them, and because they educate and indoctrinate their corporators with their heartless principles of action.

I know that we live in an era when home truths like this, such as would have been spoken boldly fifty years ago, without being questioned, are now whispered with bated breath, and that he who speaks plainly of the bad influences of this artificial power among natural persons, incurs the risk of being suspected of communism. But if there is any truth valuable to be known, next to that which will affect us after death, it is that which affects our freedom here; and civil liberty is never in such deadly peril as when men deceive themselves as to its dangers.

No one will deny that the harsh and inflexible rules with which corporate power administers its capital and directs its agencies, are such as no manly and generous mind will sanction. The individual is merged in the money-machine of which he is an integral part, and the morality of its action is the morality of the company, not his; nor is he unhappy over it so long as it produces gain. Thus its reacting influence on the man, corrupts and degrades, until at last a sort of financial self-respect will constrain him first to excuse, and then to defend all the means, no matter how corrupt, which were used to bring him a fortune.

SOURCE "Address of A. W. Terrell on Private Corporations Delivered Before the Literary Societies of the University of Missouri," June 1, 1885, pamphlet in Center for American History, University of Texas at Austin.

open-hearth method of steel-making supplanted the Bessemer technique. In this method the iron ore was heated up and scrap metal was then added to the mixture. Subsequent modifications and refinements of the process allowed steelmakers to use American iron ores. The Bessemer process dominated the construction of steel rails; the open-hearth method proved better for heavy machinery, skyscraper beams, and other uses. By 1890 steel production had risen to 4,277,000 tons annually; it would climb still more, to 10,188,000 tons by 1900.

Carnegie became the dominant figure in steel-making. His philosophy was simple. A steel owner should "watch the costs and the profits will take care of themselves." Between 1873 and 1889 Carnegie cut the cost of steel rail from $58 a ton to $25 a ton. He poured money into new equipment and plowed profits back into the business. During the 1880s steel production at Carnegie's works rose constantly, costs went down, and his profits grew by over a million dollars annually. Carnegie sought to achieve the *vertical integration* of his steel interests; this meant controlling all the steps

TABLE 17.2
STEEL PRODUCTION, 1877–1887

Year	Production
1877	569,618
1878	731,977
1879	935,273
1880	1,247,335
1881	1,588,314
1882	1,736,692
1883	1,673,535
1884	1,550,879
1885	1,711,920
1886	2,562,503
1887	3,339,071

SOURCE: *The Statistical History of the United States*, p. 416.

in the process of making steel. Carnegie therefore acquired mines to ensure that he had raw materials, boats to move ore on rivers, railroads to carry it to his mills, and a sales force to market his many products.

Carnegie's innovations in steel-making were felt throughout the economy. The lower cost of steel spurred the mechanization of industry. As machines became more complex and more productive, machine tools were needed to turn out these labor-saving and cost-cutting devices in sufficient amounts. In such industries as firearms, bicycles, and sewing machines, the use of machine tools spread technological innovations throughout the economy. Carnegie and Rockefeller's managers broke work down into specific, well-defined tasks for each employee. They made everyone in the workplace follow standardized procedures. Finally, they emphasized lower costs for every aspect of the business. In that manner the innovations of Rockefeller and especially Carnegie typified American industry. Mass production and a continuous flow of resources into factories and of goods to the consumers were part of the larger process of industrialization that reshaped the American economy.

The Pace of Invention

Inventions were a hallmark of the period. An average of 13,000 patents were issued each year during the 1870s. In the next twenty years the annual total reached about 21,000. Among the devices that came into use between 1877 and 1887 were the phonograph (1877), the typewriter (1878), the cash register (1879), and the linotype in newspaper publishing (1886). The Kodak camera went on the market in 1888. The process of innovation led to such constructive changes as the twine binder, which made harvesting straw more efficient; time locks for bank vaults; and the fountain pen. As one writer put it, "Our greatest thinkers are not in the library, nor the capital, but in the machine shop."

Two inventors who changed the nature of life in the United States were Alexander Graham Bell and Thomas Alva Edison. A Scottish immigrant from Canada, Bell wanted to transmit the human voice by electrical means. In 1876 he and his assistant, Thomas A. Watson, created a practical device for doing so: the telephone. By 1877 it was possible to make telephone calls between New York and Boston; and New Haven, Connecticut, established the first telephone exchange. Soon President Hayes had a telephone installed at the White House. Long distance service between some cities arrived in 1884. After Bell overcame legal challenges to his patents, the Bell Telephone Company expanded into the American Telephone and Telegraph Company. The industry grew slowly at first, but its potential market was almost unlimited.

The most famous inventor of the time was Thomas Alva Edison, the "Wizard of Menlo Park." Born in 1847, Edison was a telegrapher during the Civil War. By the end of the 1860s he had already patented some of his nearly 1100 inventions. In 1876 he established the first industrial research laboratory at Menlo Park, New Jersey. His goals, he said, were to produce "a minor invention every ten days and a big thing every six months or so." In 1877 he devised the first phonograph, although it would be another decade before he perfected it commercially. More immediately rewarding was the invention of the carbon filament incandescent lamp in 1879. Edison decided to use carbonized thread in the lamp, and it glowed for more than forty-five hours.

For the electric light to be profitable, it had to be installed in a system outside the laboratory. In 1882 Edison put his invention into operation in New York City. The area covered was about a square mile, and after a year in service there were 500 customers with more than 10,000 lamps. Electric power caught on rapidly. Edison's system, however, relied on direct

This photograph shows Alexander Graham Bell, the inventor of the telephone, placing the first telephone call between New York and Chicago in 1892. The telephone was one of the inventions at the end of the nineteenth century that transformed how Americans communicated in business, politics, and private life.

electric current for power. As the distance traveled by the current increased, the amount of usable electric power decreased. One of Edison's business rivals, George Westinghouse, discovered how to use a transformer to make electricity safe at the point where the consumer needed it. This device made possible alternating current, which could transmit higher amounts of electricity.

Electricity had an immediate impact on urban transportation. The electric streetcar was invented in Germany in 1879, and Edison and others adapted it for use in the United States. Granville T. Woods, a black inventor, devised the "third rail" to convey electric power to the cars. By 1882 there were more than 400 streetcar companies in the United States and they moved a total of 1.2 billion passengers annually. Streetcars proved an efficient mode of transportation that dominated cities until the arrival of the automobile.

AMERICANS IN THE WORKPLACE

Industrialization brought many benefits to the people of the United States, but individual Americans often felt the adverse impact of these changes. They

Few individuals better embodied the spirit of invention and innovation that marked the United States in the 1880s than did Thomas Alva Edison. He is shown here listening to one of his stenographic devices in a posture that evokes his slight resemblance to the French leader Napoleon Bonaparte. Edison's inventions of the electric light, the phonograph, and the motion picture camera reshaped the way Americans lived.

struggled to improve their lives within a society that resisted their efforts to lessen the harmful effects of industrial growth on themselves and their families. In 1877 there were 15 million nondomestic workers, more than half in agriculture and another 4 million in manufacturing. The economy was in the fourth year of a depression, stemming from the Panic of 1873, and almost 2 million people were unemployed.

The labor force grew by more than 29 percent during the 1870s. One-fifth of the increase came from immigrants. Four out of every ten of these working immigrants were unskilled; their sweat helped the new industries expand and the cities to rise. Most of the immigrants left from Northern Europe as they had before the Civil War. Irish, Germans, British, and Scandinavians made up the bulk of the newcomers. The growth of the transatlantic steamship business and the aggressive work of emigration agents in Europe helped persuade many to come to the United States; hard times in Europe impelled others to make the trip. Western states and territories hoped that the new arrivals would become farmers, but the majority found work in the cities of the Northeast and Midwest. Soon distinctive ethnic communities grew up in New York, Boston, and Philadelphia.

Skilled Workers

A key development during this period was a change in the position of skilled labor in the new industrial setting. Technology replaced craft skills with machines, and market pressures led businesses to limit their dependence on trained artisans. A more hierarchical system of management stripped skilled workers of much of their autonomy and reduced their control over the workplace. The use of apprenticeship as a way of moving up in industry receded, and the workforce was divided into unskilled and semiskilled employees. All of these trends made workers more vulnerable to corporate power.

Workers resisted these changes through mutual support in times of crisis. In 1882 the Amalgamated Association of Iron and Steel Workers struck for higher pay from the owners of steel rolling mills in Pennsylvania. For five months the union held together against unified management, but finally the workers were forced to go back on the job. Although the strike was unsuccessful, it demonstrated that workers were active participants in efforts to improve their lives.

Women represented another new element in the labor force. They still worked as domestic servants, but they appeared in greater numbers as teachers and office workers, and as salesclerks in the expanding department stores. Eight thousand women worked in sales in 1880; a decade later the total was more than 58,000. Many stores preferred women, especially native-born white women. While many immigrant women toiled as domestic servants, they also found work in the sweatshops of the textile trades. For the most part, the jobs open to women were lower paid, required fewer skills, and offered less opportunity than those open to men.

Real wages for workers increased as the prices of farm products and manufactured goods fell during the deflation that lasted until the late 1890s. The hours that employees worked declined from more than sixty-five hours a week in 1860 to under sixty by 1900. Gradual though they were, these changes represented real gains.

The Dangers of Industrialism

The desperate circumstances of many workers belied these general trends. Steelworkers put in twelve hours a day seven days a week amid the noise, heat, and hazards of the mills. In the coal mines, in the factories, and on the railroads, work was dangerous and deadly. From 1880 to 1900 some 35,000 of the 4 million workers in manufacturing died in accidents each year and another 500,000 were injured.

Workers had almost no protection against sickness, injury, or arbitrary dismissal. If an injury occurred, the courts had decided that the liability often belonged to another worker or "fellow servant" rather than to the company that owned the factory. For a worker who was fired during an economic downturn, there were no unemployment benefits, no government programs for retraining, and little private help. Old age pensions did not exist, and there were no private medical or retirement insurance plans. Child labor reached a peak during this period. Almost 182,000 children under the age of sixteen were at work in 1880 with no health and safety restrictions to protect them.

Workers had few ways to insulate themselves from the impact of harsh working conditions and often cruel employers. There were sporadic attempts at labor organization and strikes throughout the nineteenth century, but unions faced legal and political obstacles.

The law said that a worker and his employer were equal players in the marketplace, one buying labor for the lowest price possible, the other selling labor for as much as could be obtained. Real equality in bargaining power rarely existed. The worker had to take what was offered; the boss set the conditions of employment.

The Rise of Unions

The workers responded to these conditions by creating labor unions. During the 1860s and 1870s skilled craftsmen in cigar making, shoemaking, and coal mining formed unions. The National Labor Union (NLU), a coalition of trade unions, was established in 1866. In 1868 its leader was William Sylvis, the head of the union of craftsmen in the steel industry known as iron-puddlers. Under his direction, the NLU pursued the eight-hour day and other improvements for labor. Sylvis's death in 1869 and the dominance of middle-class social reformers in the organization eroded the influence of the National Labor Union by the early 1870s. Still, the first national labor organization provided a model for others to imitate.

Because of the number of workers they employed, railroads were the first business to confront large-scale labor issues. The professional skills that engineers, firemen, brakemen, and others possessed made it more difficult for railroads to find replacements during a strike. Railroad workers joined unions based around these crafts such as the Brotherhood of Locomotive Firemen and the Brotherhood of Locomotive Engineers. "Unless labor combines," said one engineer, "it cannot be heard at all." The issue, according to one railroad executive, was, "who shall manage the road?" From this difference of opinion flowed the labor disputes that marked the decade from 1877 to 1887 and beyond.

The Railroad Strike of 1877

A bitter railroad strike erupted during the summer of 1877. On July 1, in the middle of an economic depression, the major eastern railroads announced a 10 percent wage cut. Facing their second pay reduction in a year, railroad employees walked off their jobs in an unplanned protest. Strikers disrupted train traffic across Pennsylvania, West Virginia, Maryland, and Ohio. In Baltimore and Pittsburgh there were battles

The walkout of railroad employees in 1877 over low wages led to a series of strikes that convulsed the nation for several months. This painting shows the social violence that erupted when the army was called out to help subdue the labor unrest.

between strikers and state militia. A general strike spread to Chicago, St. Louis, and other large cities. Railroad unions played a relatively small part in starting these walkouts, however; during the depression their membership had declined and their economic impact on the roads had lessened.

The governors of the states where the riots occurred called out the militia. Some militia units refused to fire on their fellow citizens. As violence spread, the Hayes administration sent in the Army. Deaths ran into the hundreds, many more were injured. Newspapers sympathetic to the strike said that "never before has the cause of justice been so thoroughly on the working-man's side." Faced with such overwhelming use of force by the government, the unrest died away rapidly. Nevertheless, the strike had touched most of the nation in some way.

The Knights of Labor

One result of the strike was increased support for a new national labor organization: the Noble and Bold Order of the Knights of Labor. The Knights combined fraternal ritual, the language of Christianity, and belief in the social equality of all citizens. While advancing the cause of labor through unions and strikes where necessary, the Knights wanted government to play a larger role in protecting working people who produced goods and services for the economy. They spoke about the "Commonwealth of Toil" and deplored "the recent alarming development of aggregated wealth." Instead they wanted "a system adopted which will secure to the laborer the fruits of his toil." By the mid-1870s the Knights were established among coal miners in Pennsylvania. After the railroad strike, the Knights' membership grew, reaching 9,000 in 1879 and soaring to 42,000 by 1882.

The leader of the Knights was known as the grand master workman. Terence V. Powderly was elected to that post in 1879, and he soon became the first national labor figure. The Knights also grew because they had few membership requirements, and their ideology reached out to all sectors of the working population. Their ranks soon embraced workers from skilled craft unions, agricultural laborers in the South, and women who were new entrants into the workforce. The willingness of the Knights to include women and blacks set it apart from other unions. By 1885 the union claimed more than 100,000 members. Its message of working-class solidarity and mutual assistance among all producers seemed attractive to many laboring citizens.

The Knights in Decline

Success brought problems of internal strain and union discipline. In 1885 the Knights conducted a strike against a railroad owned by Jay Gould, one of the most hated of the rail executives. They struck his Wabash, Missouri Pacific, and other lines, and achieved a form of official recognition that allowed the Knights to represent the company's employees in relations with management. Since it appeared that the

The leader of the Knights of Labor, Terence V. Powderly, pursued the vision of an all-embracing union that would unite the working classes against organized capital. It proved difficult for him to direct such a diverse coalition effectively, and by the mid-1880s the Knights had fallen victim to a popular backlash against strikes in the Southwest and the Haymarket Riot in Chicago.

Knights had beaten Gould, their popularity exploded among workers. By 1886 there were more than 700,000 members. A second walkout was called against Gould in February 1886, but this time the strike was broken through the use of police and violence against those who had walked out.

The Haymarket Affair

Other events put labor on the defensive. On May 4, 1886, workmen in Chicago gathered in Haymarket Square to protest police conduct during a strike at a factory of the McCormick Company that made farm reaping and harvesting machinery. As a heavy rain began to fall, the police endeavored to break up the meeting. Then a bomb exploded in the midst of the crowd. One police officer was killed; others fired into the throng. Seven policemen and two demonstrators were killed and seventy people were hurt.

Eight alleged participants in a bombing conspiracy were arrested and convicted, although none had taken part in the event itself. Four were executed, one committed suicide, and three others went to prison. The Haymarket affair shocked the nation. Public support for labor's demands for an eight-hour work day and other concessions dried up. In fact, the affair triggered widespread anti-radical hysteria.

These events did most damage to the Knights of Labor. Even though Powderly had questioned the wisdom of strikes, business leaders and conservatives blamed the Knights for the violence and unrest. The union underwent a permanent decline. To some workers, the failure of the Knights demonstrated the need for more violent action. To others, it indicated that Powderly's strategy of a broad, inclusive appeal and an avoidance of strikes had been wrong from the start.

The American Federation of Labor

One vigorous critic of the Knights of Labor was Samuel Gompers. Because a philosophy of "pure and simple unionism" had worked for his own Cigar Makers International Union, he believed that only such an approach could help labor in the long run. The son of a British cigar maker, Gompers had come to the United States in 1863. During his years of employment in the cigar trade, he decided that labor should accept corporations as a fact of life, seek concrete and limited improvements in living and working conditions, and avoid political involvements.

The Knights of Labor had women as full members of their organization, and this picture shows eight delegates to the order's 1886 convention. The woman holding her two-month-old baby in the front is Elizabeth Rodgers. Although men dominated public life in this period, the role of women was expanding in ways that foreshadowed their greater participation after 1900.

Late in 1886 Gompers and others organized the American Federation of Labor (AFL) whose participating unions had 150,000 members. An alliance of craft unions and skilled workers, the AFL did not try to organize the masses of industrial workers. The union opposed immigrant labor, especially of the Chinese on the West Coast, and was cool toward the idea of black members. Nevertheless, the AFL's membership rose to more than 300,000 during its first ten years, and it achieved considerable benefits for its members through judicious use of strikes and negotiations with employers. Most of the men and women who worked as unskilled labor in the nation's factories and shops, however, derived little benefit from the AFL's policies. Their fate lay in the hands of the employers, the courts, and the political system.

Opposed to the inclusive policies of the Knights of Labor, Samuel Gompers, president of the American Federation of Labor (AFL) after 1886, wanted a labor movement that worked for well-defined objectives and better working conditions for its members. The craft unions that Gompers represented did not reach out to the large, unorganized mass of workers, and barred African Americans and Chinese from their ranks. Gompers believed that his strategy was more effective than what the Knights had tried to accomplish.

Social Darwinism

Beginning in 1877 and continuing for a decade thereafter, many commentators praised the material accomplishments of industrialism. Because clothes were now made so cheaply, said one observer, "the very beggars in our metropolitan cities, and the 'tramps' sleeping in our fields or under the roof that shelters our cattle, wear a finer fabric than kings could boast a century ago." One academic contended that John D. Rockefeller had done more good for the world than William Shakespeare.

A more systematic justification for the existing social order was the philosophy that came to be known as *Social Darwinism.* Charles Darwin's famous work *On the Origin of Species,* published in 1859, offered an explanation for why some species survived and others became extinct. Darwin contended that a process of "natural selection" occurs in nature that enabies the "fittest" animals and plants to evolve and develop over time. Darwin did not attach any moral virtue to the ability of one species to survive and reproduce as a result of the process of natural selection. He was simply analyzing the workings of the world as he found it. Advocates of Darwin's ideas, such as the English writer Herbert Spencer, applied them to human existence. If the doctrine of "survival of the fittest" operated in the natural world, Spencer argued, it governed human affairs as well. Since capitalists and the wealthy represented the "fittest" individuals, it was folly to interfere with the "natural" process that produced them. "The law of the survival of the fittest was not made by man and cannot be abrogated by man," said William Graham Sumner, a leading exponent of this doctrine. "We can only by interfering with it produce the survival of the unfittest." Sumner's status as a professor at Yale University, along with the vigor of his ideas, brought him a wide audience. On the other hand, few businessmen looked to Sumner or Spencer for advice about how to succeed in the marketplace where they sought government interference on their behalf through tariffs and subsidies.

These ideas were supported in the "rags to riches" novels of Horatio Alger, a popular writer of the day. Alger's theme was that men of energy and determination (i.e., the "fittest") could triumph in the competitive system even against great odds. He wrote 106 books with such titles as *Brave and Bold* and *Paddle Your Own Canoe.* The central characters were

impoverished young boys who used their natural talents to gain the support of wealthy benefactors and go on to achieve riches and success. The public consumed millions of copies of Alger's books despite repetitive plots. They taught the lessons of self-reliance and personal commitment, even though few corporate leaders started at the bottom as Alger's characters did.

Despite the popularity of Social Darwinism, the impact of these ideas on actual practice was limited. While many Americans applauded Social Darwinism in theory, they also tolerated considerable government intervention in the economy and social relations.

Not everyone accepted the excesses and injustices of industrialism. One of the most famous social critics of the day was Henry George. A California newspaperman, George said that the cause of the gap between the wealthy and the poor was the monopoly of land by the rich and the rents that landowners charged. He expressed his ideas in a book titled *Progress and Poverty* (1879), which sold over 2 million copies in the United States and more worldwide. Rent, he wrote, was "a toll levied upon labor constantly and continuously," and the solution for this social ill was a "single tax" on rising land values. With such a tax, all other forms of taxation would be unnecessary. George's writings enjoyed worldwide influence. Single-tax leagues flourished in the United States, and his ideas promoted social reform among clergymen in the 1890s and early 1900s. What gave *Progress and Poverty* its major impact was the moral intensity of George's analysis of the ills of capitalist society. The single-tax crusade was evidence that not all Americans favored an inactive and passive government.

Another challenge to Social Darwinism came in 1883 when a government geologist, Lester Frank Ward, published *Dynamic Sociology* in which he assailed Social Darwinism's view of evolution as applying to nature and human society and not just to the natural world. Ward attacked Spencer and his followers for having left the human mind out of their philosophy. The process of evolution did not work, he wrote, because of "the unconscious forces of nature, but also through the conscious and deliberate control by man." The idea that government should not interfere with the workings of society reflected the self-interest of those who espoused it. "Those who dismiss state interference are the ones who most frequently and successfully invoke it." Ward's view of what Americans were actually doing was sound. All through this period citi-

His book Progress and Poverty *(1879) made Henry George into one of the leading social reformers of the period. George diagnosed the problems of society in ways that captivated many who did not share his view that a single tax on land would provide the answers to the nation's ills.*

zens asked government at all levels to take action on matters of health, safety, and finance.

THE CHANGING SOUTH AND WEST

Among the most pressing concerns of the 1880s were those that focused on the South and West. In the South, issues of race, industrial development, and agricultural growth were important aspects of what was called the "New South." In the West, the vast spaces beyond the Mississippi Valley still were not fully integrated into the United States. Both of these regions also experienced changes stemming from the industrialization and urbanization of the North.

The Fate of Native Americans

The American West entered a new phase after 1877. The defeat of Custer at the Battle of the Little Big Horn in June 1876 was one of the final flurries of combat on the Great Plains. Some sporadic resistance continued. During 1877 the Nez Percé tribe in Oregon, led by Chief Joseph, resisted attempts to move them to a reservation. During four months of running battles, Joseph led his band of 650 people toward Canada but they were beaten before they could reach safety. "From where the sun now stands," said Joseph, "I will fight no more forever." The Nez Percés were sent to the Indian Territory in Oklahoma, where they fell victim to disease. As one white magazine said of Indian reservations, "If they [the Indians] cannot bear civilization, it will at least kill them decently."

Another famous example of Native American resistance was Geronimo, the Apache chief in New Mexico.

The Apache leader Geronimo eluded capture in the Southwest until he surrendered to the army in 1886. Once in custody, he could be photographed with a rifle and menacing expression as a way of earning money from tourists.

With a small band of followers, he left the Arizona reservation where he had been living in 1881 and conducted raids across the Southwest for the next two years. After brief periods of surrender he resumed his military forays. Finally, in September 1886 he was persuaded to surrender once again and was exiled to Florida.

As Native American resistance ebbed, the national government shaped policy for the western tribes. Many white westerners believed that the "Indian question" could be solved only when the tribes were gone. Easterners contended that Native Americans should become a part of white society through assimilation. Organizations such as the Indian Rights Association lobbied for these policies, and a book by Helen Hunt Jackson, *A Century of Dishonor* (1881), publicized the plight of the Native Americans. Although the westerners had destructive motives toward the Indians while the easterners' policies were more benevolent, their combined efforts were devastating to Indian culture.

The Dawes Act (1887)

Congress passed the Dawes Severalty Act in 1887. Named after Senator Henry L. Dawes of Massachusetts, the law authorized the president to survey Native American reservations and divide them into 160-acre farms. After receiving their allotment, Native Americans could not lease or sell the land for twenty-five years. Any Indian who adopted "habits of civilized life" became a U.S. citizen, but most Indians did not achieve citizenship. Any surplus land left over after this process was finished could be sold to white settlers. For the reformers, this law would push the Indians toward white civilization; for the western settlers it offered a way to obtain Indian land. During the next fifty years, the total land holdings of Native Americans declined from 138 million to 47 million acres. By dividing up tribal land holdings and putting Indians at the mercy of white speculators, the Dawes Act undermined the tribal structure and culture of the Native Americans. The social transformations of the late nineteenth century were a disaster for Indians in the United States.

The Mining Frontier

One impetus for whites to develop the West lay in the mining "booms" that drew settlers to seek riches in a

series of bonanzas, first of gold, later of silver, and eventually of copper in territories and states such as Colorado, Montana, and the Dakotas. The mining camps became notorious for their violence and frenzied atmosphere. More than 90 percent of their inhabitants were men; most of the women were prostitutes.

During the 1870s the western mining industry came to resemble other businesses. Individual miners gradually gave way to corporations that used industrial techniques such as jets of water under high pressure to extract the metal from the ground. The ravaged land left farmers with fouled rivers and polluted fields.

In 1877, Leadville, Colorado, emerged as a major silver mining center and Coeur d'Alene, Idaho, went through a similar process a few years later. In Butte, Montana, the development of the Anaconda Copper Mine would characterize the western mining business from the mid-1880s onward: an industrialized workforce, a company town, and bitter labor relations.

The Cattle Country

White settlement on the Great Plains during the 1880s started with the cattle ranchers, who dominated the open range in Wyoming, Colorado, and Montana. After the Civil War, ranchers in Texas found that their steers had multiplied during their absence. Enterprising cattlemen drove herds north to market at rail lines in Kansas and Nebraska. Up the Chisholm and Goodnight–Loving Trails came Texas longhorns to the cattle towns of Ellsworth, Dodge City, and Abilene. Unlike the mining towns, these communities were not noted for violence and vice; respectable citizens quickly imposed law and order on their temporary guests. Dance halls and bordellos for the visiting cattlemen, though plentiful at first, soon were restricted.

During the late 1870s and early 1880s, cattle raising shifted from Texas to areas nearer the railroads and the Chicago stockyards. The growth of the railroad network gave ranchers access to eastern and foreign markets. Improved breeding and slaughtering practices produced beef for consumers both in the United States and in Europe, and the demand grew. With cattle easy to raise in the open spaces of the West and with an efficient transportation system, entrepreneurs in New York, London, and Scotland wanted to buy cattle cheaply in the West and resell them to eastern buyers at a profit. Money poured into the West and increased the number of cattle on the ranges of Montana and Wyoming.

The Life of the Cowboy

The men who worked the steers were not the glamorous "cowboys" of popular mythology. Life on a ranch was characterized by drudgery and routine. The cowboy's days were fourteen hours long and he could be killed when restless cattle stampeded. Much of what he did—riding the line, tending sick cattle, and mending fences—consisted of grinding physical labor in a harsh environment.

The cowboys reflected American diversity. One of every seven was African American. Former slaves from ranches in Texas or fugitives from the oppression in the South, these black cowboys gained a living but were not granted social equality. Other cowboys included Hispanics and Native Americans, and they also experienced discrimination. From the Hispanic *vaqueros* and the Native Americans, other cowboys learned the techniques of breaking horses and the complex skills of managing cattle. Western development thus involved a subtle interaction of cultures that few whites understood.

The End of the Cattle Boom

The boom years in the cattle business soon ended. As the ranges became overstocked in 1885 and 1886, the prices for western cattle fell. A steer that had brought thirty dollars early in 1886 sold for less than ten dollars several months later. Then came the "hard winter" of 1886–1887, during which blizzards killed thousands of cattle. Before prices rose, investors from the East and Great Britain, including the young Theodore Roosevelt, lost all they had as the remaining stock was dumped onto an already depressed market. There had been 9 million cows in Wyoming Territory in 1886; there were 3 million in 1895. The cattle industry changed from a speculative, high risk venture of part-time capitalists to a more rational, routinized business.

Ranchers in the West faced other challenges. Sheep raisers moved onto the range and discovered that sheep could graze more economically than cattle. Range wars between cattle and sheep growers broke

The actual routine of work in the range cattle business was more deadening than glamorous. Here a group of cowboys makes camp after a long day of herding steers. Low pay and difficult conditions stimulated cowboy strikes on more than one occasion.

out in Arizona and Wyoming. In the long run, however, sheep raising proved to be a viable business, and by 1900 there were some 30 million sheep on western ranges.

Farming on the Great Plains

During the 1880s hundreds of thousands of farmers swept onto the Great Plains. Advertising by the railroad companies drew them from midwestern states and from northern Europe. The picture painted in the ads was one of abundant land, water, and opportunity. The reality was less hospitable.

The Homestead Act of 1862 gave farmers public land, which they could use and eventually own. In practice, the 160-acre unit of the Homestead Act was much too small for a farmer to cultivate successfully on the plains. To make a farm work, a settler had to purchase two or three times that acreage. The Homestead Act also did not give prospective farmers the money they needed to go West, file a claim, and acquire the machinery required for profitable farming. Few laborers in the East became homesteaders. Most of the settlers had some previous experience with farming.

Congress complicated the land system. Cattle ranchers persuaded lawmakers to pass the Desert Land Act (1877), which allowed individuals to obtain a provisional title to 640 acres in the West at twenty-five cents an acre. Before securing a title, they had to irrigate the land within three years and pay a dollar an acre more. This law was easily evaded. Cowboys filed claims for their employer, threw a bucket of water onto the property, and swore that irrigation had occurred.

A year later, lumber interests in the West lobbied for what became the Timber and Stone Act (1878). Directed at lands that were "unfit for cultivation" in Washington, Oregon, California, and Nevada, it permitted settlers to acquire up to 160 acres at $2.50 per acre. Under the act, lumber companies used false entries to gain title to valuable timber holdings.

Land and Debt

Most settlers on the Great Plains obtained their land from the railroads or land companies. Congress had granted the railroads every other 160-acre section of land along their rights of way. Large tracts of land were closed to settlement until the railroads sold the

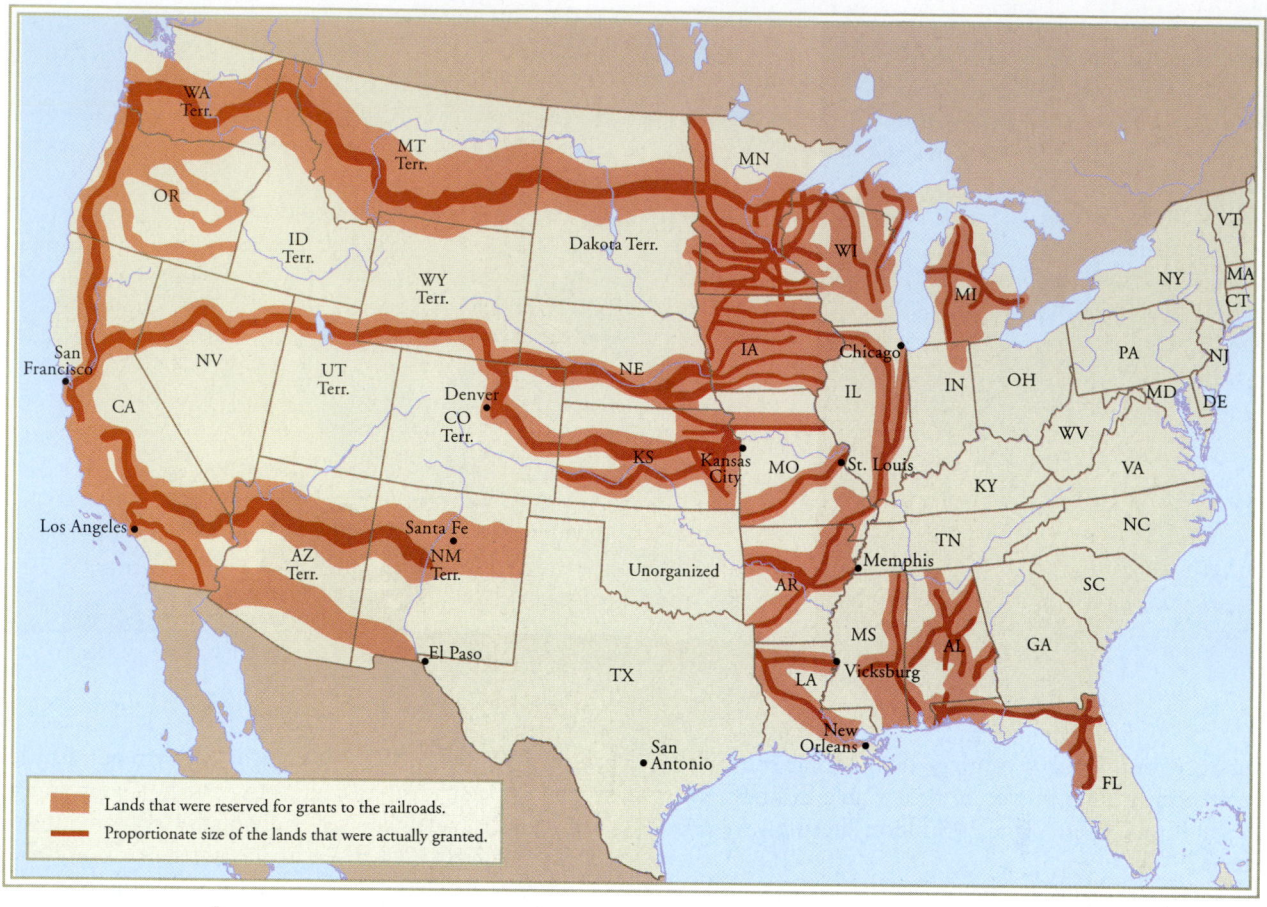

MAP 17.2 | RAILROAD LAND GRANTS

land to farmers. During the period between 1862 and 1900, land companies acquired almost 100 million acres from railroads or the government. Other lands had been granted to eastern states to support their agricultural colleges under the Morrill Land-Grant Act of 1862. These western holdings went into the hands of speculators who purchased the lands, as did the land of Native Americans that had been sold off to white buyers.

Most of the western settlers had to acquire their land at prices that often ranged between five and ten dollars per acre. To buy the land, the farmers borrowed from loan companies in the East and Midwest. Interest rates on the resulting mortgages were as high as 25 percent annually. As long as land values rose and crop prices remained profitable, the farmers made the needed investment. When prices fell, however, they faced economic adversity.

Fences and Water

Industrial growth and technological advances made cultivation possible on the Great Plains. Modern fencing kept cows and crops apart. Joseph Glidden of Illinois devised the practical form of barbed wire in 1873. Soon Glidden's invention came to the attention of the Washburn and Moen Company of Massachusetts which developed a machine to produce barbed wire. By 1880 some 80 million pounds had been produced and the price of fencing stood at ten dollars per pound. Improved plows, the cord binder for baling hay, and grain silos also aided western farming. During the 1880s steam-powered threshers for wheat and cornhusking machines were developed.

Machines alone could not provide enough water for farming. West of the ninety-eighth meridian, which ran through the Dakotas, Nebraska, Kansas, Okla-

homa, and Texas, fewer than twenty inches of rain fell annually. Efforts to irrigate the land with the waters that ran from the Rocky Mountains worked in certain areas, but most of the region lacked adequate rivers. Ordinary wells did not reach the waters far below the surface. Windmills offered a possible solution but the high cost of drilling and installing a windmill made it too expensive for most farmers. The most practical technique was "dry farming," cultivation designed to use water that the land retained after rainfall. These practices made farming possible on the Great Plains when used with mechanical equipment.

Farm Life on the Plains

For the farm families who did the backbreaking work of cultivation, life on the western farms was a grind.

With little wood available, shelter often consisted of a sod house made of bricks of dirt or dried sod. When it rained, the house became a mixture of mud and straw. To keep warm in the winter, the farmers burned buffalo chips [droppings] or dried sunflower plants. Grasshoppers ruined crops, animals trampled fields, and the weather was always uncertain.

The burdens of farm work fell hardest on women. "I never knew Mama to be idle," the daughter of one farm woman recalled. The child of another farm woman remembered "Bake day, mending day. A certain day for a certain thing. That's what I remember, those special days that my ma had." Amid the endless spaces of the Great Plains, women labored on small plots of land, sustained by a network of friends and neighbors. Some women achieved a degree of independence in the male-dominated West. They operated farms, taught school, ran boardinghouses, and participated in politics and cultural life.

Farm women on the Great Plains toiled in a harsh environment where fuel and shelter required constant collection. Buffalo chips could be burned for warmth when wood might be miles away. What this woman and her child did took place every day despite incessant wind and extremes of temperature.

HOWARD RUEDE
SOD-HOUSE DAYS
1877

The settlement of the Great Plains often required the use of unfamiliar materials to create shelter. In this document, a settler in Kansas details for his relatives in Pennsylvania in 1877 how sod houses were constructed. The author, Howard Ruede, does not discuss how the sod house must have smelled to its inhabitants.

Perhaps you will be interested in the way a sod house is built. Sod is the most available material, in fact, the only material the homesteader has at hand, unless he happens to be one of the fortunates who secured a creek claim with timber suitable for house logs.

Occasionally a new comer has a "bee," and the neighbors for miles around gather at his claim and put up his house in a day. . . . The women come too, and while the men lay up the sod walls, they prepare dinner for the crowd, and have a very sociable hour at noon. A house put up in this way is very likely to settle and get out of shape, but it is seldom deserted for that reason. . . .

When the prairie is thoroughly soaked by rain or snow is the best time for breaking sod for building. The regulation thickness is $2\frac{1}{2}$ inches, buffalo sod preferred on account of its superior toughness. The furrow slices are laid flat and as straight as a steady-walking team can be driven. These furrow slices, 12 inches wide, are cut with a sharp spade into 18-inch lengths, and carefully handled as they are laid in the wall, one length reaching across the wall, which rises rapidly even when the builders are green hands. Care must be taken to break joints and bind the corners of the house. "Seven feet to the square" [top of the wall] is the rule, as the wall is likely to settle a good deal, especially if the sod is very wet when laid. The door and window frames are set in place first and the wall built around them. Building such a house is hard work.

At first these sod houses are unplastered, and this is thought perfectly all right, but such a house is somewhat cold in the winter, as the crevices between the sods admit some cold air; so some of the houses are plastered with a kind of "native lime," made of sand and a very sticky native clay. This plaster is very good unless it happens to get wet. In a few of the houses this plaster is whitewashed, and this helps the looks very much. Some sod houses are mighty comfortable places to go into in cold weather, and it don't take much fire to keep them warm. I will have to be contented with a very modest affair for a while, but perhaps I can improve it later.

SOURCE   *The American Heritage History of The Confident Years*, pp. 156–157, taken from Howard Ruede. *Sod-House Days* (Columbia University Press, 1937).

From Territories to States

By the late 1880s some of the western territories were ready for statehood. The territorial system had transferred eastern political ideas and values to the West and integrated settlers into the national political structure. In 1889 and 1890 Congress enacted legislation to admit the Dakotas, Montana, Washington, Idaho, and Wyoming into the Union.

During the decade from 1877 to 1887, one group of newcomers experienced danger and prejudice in the West. Chinese immigrants came to California during

the 1840s and 1850s to work the gold mines. They constructed the transcontinental railroads in the 1860s. Energetic and thrifty, the Chinese soon began engaging in manufacturing enterprises and agricultural pursuits. White Californians reacted with bigotry and violence. Laws were passed to bar the Chinese from professions in which they competed successfully with whites. A movement to ban Chinese immigration gained widespread support. An 1868 treaty with China had guaranteed free access to Chinese immigrants to the United States. In 1880 the United States pressured China to change the treaty to grant it authority to regulate Chinese immigration. The Chinese Exclusion Act of 1882 barred the Chinese entry into the United States for ten years.

Ranchers and settlers had overcome natural obstacles, political difficulties, and economic problems to build new societies on the Great Plains. They had added to the nation's resources in important respects. Their efforts had created an elaborate economic and environmental system that linked the city and the country in mutually interdependent ways. By the end of the 1880s, however, the process of development had created problems as farmers failed to achieve the prosperity they had anticipated. Crop prices for what they grew fell, and the debts that settlers had incurred to pay for their farms became an ever greater burden. The transition to industrialism meant pain and hardship for the West. As a result, the region was politically restive by 1887. Similar pressures were building up in the South.

The New South

The presidential election of 1876 ended what remained of Reconstruction. Democrats took over state governments in South Carolina, Louisiana, and Florida. The program and views of the Democrats in this period had great appeal to many white men in the South. In both the North and the South, the Democrats believed that white supremacy and limited government were the basic principles of political life. The bitter memories of Radical Reconstruction and the need to maintain the South as "white man's country" made the Democrats dominant among white southerners. Not all southerners became Democrats, however. Blacks voted Republican, as did whites in the southern mountain regions. Independents and others cooperated with Republicans against the Democrats.

The men who took over the state governments in the South after Reconstruction believed that they had "redeemed" the region from the mistaken Republican experiment in multiracial politics. Their policies, they claimed, lacked the corruption and waste characteristic of their Republican predecessors. In reality, the record of these politicians was worse than that of Reconstruction. Across the South, scandals and frauds marred the Redeemer administrations.

The Redeemers were a diverse lot. There were plantation owners, a generous assortment of one-time Confederate officers, and aspiring capitalists who wanted to see a more urban and developed South. This coalition dominated the politics of many southern states throughout the 1880s, though they could agree on only the most general (and vague) principles. Slavery had vanished, never to return, but white supremacy remained entrenched.

The hold of the Redeemers on southern politics during the 1880s faced some opposition. In Virginia, the size of the public debt became a central issue, with William Mahone campaigning against using tax money to pay off out-of-state creditors. Mahone and his allies also advocated more money for public schools and other state services. These "Readjusters" attracted even many black voters. As a result they soon faced a counterattack from the Democrats who intimidated black voters from supporting Mahone's party. Within a few years the Readjuster movement had been defeated, in part through the use of rigged elections and stuffed ballot boxes.

A key theme in the South during these years was embodied in the phrase "The New South." This phrase was meant to signify that the South would now welcome industrialization and economic expansion. The most famous advocate of the New South idea was an Atlanta newspaper editor named Henry Grady. He thrilled northern audiences with his speeches about how southerners would build new businesses in the same spirit as their Yankee friends. The South, Grady said in 1886, would soon have "a hundred farms for every plantation, fifty homes for every palace—and a diversified industry that meets the complex needs of this complex age." All over the region there were plans to build steel mills, textile factories, and railroads.

The Industrial South

A substantial expansion of manufacturing capacity occurred in the South between 1870 and 1900. In the major cotton producing states of South Carolina, Georgia, Alabama, Mississippi, and Louisiana, the amount of capital invested in manufacturing increased about tenfold between 1869 and 1889. Southern railroads expanded rapidly during the postwar period; by 1880 there were 19,430 miles of track, double the total that had existed in 1860. Other key industries grew during this decade as well.

Southern forests were cut down to satisfy the growing national demand for lumber. Almost 3 million board feet of yellow pine was produced in 1879 by crews working under dangerous conditions for wages that often came to less than a dollar per day. The region's ample deposits of iron ore stimulated the expansion of the iron and coal industries after the war ended. Production of iron ore rose from 397,000 tons in 1880 to almost 2 million tons twenty years later. Birmingham, Alabama, became a center of the burgeoning southern iron industry. Large amounts of coal were mined in the southern Appalachian region of West Virginia and Virginia.

Before the Civil War tobacco had been popular as something to chew, smoke in a pipe, or as a cigar. During the war, northern soldiers tried the variety of bright leaf tobacco grown in North Carolina, and demand for Bull Durham and other products of the area increased. A significant change in American smoking habits occurred during the 1880s, when James Buchanan Duke began using a practical cigarette-making machine. Production costs fell rapidly, and cigarette use skyrocketed. By the end of the 1880s Duke's company was making more than 800 million cigarettes annually, and Americans were becoming accustomed to smoking as a pervasive and addictive habit.

The cotton textile industry also grew rapidly during this period. The number of people working in the cotton mills rose from about 16,000 in 1880 to more than 36,000 ten years later. Increasing national demand for southern products spurred the industry. Lower labor costs made southern mills highly competitive. Women and children accounted for a high proportion of the labor force in these establishments; often whole families worked to provide basic subsistence.

Industrialism led to greater prosperity for the South. New cities and towns sprang up as the South's economy expanded. But this growth came at a high cost to those who worked in the factories and mills. Wages were often low and conditions crude. Tobacco workers in North Carolina earned around a hundred dollars a year. In the cotton mills an average work-week might be more than sixty hours for wages that could be as low as fifteen cents a day. Influential southerners resisted arguments against child labor, even as others tried to end the practice.

Problems of Southern Agriculture

Agriculture was a way of life for most southerners, but the system of farming that evolved in the aftermath of the Civil War created serious economic problems. The central fact of southern farming between 1877 and 1887 was dependence on cotton. Southern cotton farmers produced 3,111,000 bales of cotton in 1870; ten years later production had risen to 5,709,000 bales. Although newspaper editors and publicists urged farmers to grow other crops in addition to cotton, few took this advice. Cotton growers knew that their crop rarely failed, caused less depletion of the soil, and brought a higher price per acre than any other crop.

World production of cotton was increasing, however, and prices for the South's primary crop fell between 1870 to 1885, rose somewhat at the end of the decade, and plunged again during the 1890s. Unable to increase their productivity enough to make money despite lower prices, cotton farmers became locked in a system of debt and dependence.

To make cotton growing work, farmers needed a reliable supply of cheap labor to pick the crop in an era before machines did this exhausting work. The end of slavery meant that plantations could no longer count on having enough field hands. Whites held most of the land while blacks had less land and were forced to sell their labor. The result was a system that combined sharecropping, tenant farming, and the "furnish merchant," who provided the farmers with the "furnish" (whatever was needed) to get them through the year.

Sharecroppers were workers who received as their wage a designated proportion of the crops they produced. The landlord or owner controlled the crop until some of it was allocated to the sharecropper. Tenant

farmers, on the other hand, owned the crop until it was sold. They then paid to the owner of the property either cash or a fixed amount of the crop or cash. Both tenants and "croppers" depended on a local merchant to provide the food, clothing, farm equipment, and crop supplies that they needed until their harvests were completed. To safeguard the merchant's investment, southern states passed crop lien laws that gave the merchant a claim on the crop if a farmer could not make enough money to pay off his debt. Thus, the farmers in the South, both black and white, were locked in a cycle of debt in which they owed money or crops first to the landlord and then to the "furnish" merchant. In bad years the farmers did not make enough to get out of debt. The interest that the merchants charged was often very high, as much as 50 percent, and they exercised a degree of supervision over the croppers and tenants that reminded some observers of the era of slavery.

A Colonial Economy

Part of the South's problems grew out of the region's financial plight after the Civil War. The South had long lacked adequate capital and losing the war made the situation worse. The National Banking Act of 1863 required banks to have up to $50,000 in capital and to be located in a small town to get a national bank charter. Few southern communities could meet that standard, and so prospective borrowers had to compete for scarce local credit. Since national banks could not make mortgage loans, even those that opened in the South were of little help to the southern farm population. At the same time the national government followed monetary policies that promoted deflation. All of these economic elements taken together meant that the South's lack of capital worsened during the 1880s.

Southern farmers saw themselves at the mercy of a conspiracy of economic forces. The furnish merchant was the most visible agent of a system that had been imposed upon them by northern bankers, international cotton marketing companies, and industrialism. The cotton farmers had to tolerate these conditions because there appeared to be no other way to participate in the South's burgeoning economy. By the end of the decade, however, the problems of perpetual debt were becoming acute. Political discontent grew in the South as a result.

Segregation

Racial segregation evolved slowly but steadily across the South. One obstacle to this trend was the enactment of the national Civil Rights Act in 1875, which prohibited racial discrimination in public accommodations. In the *Civil Rights Cases* (1883), the Supreme Court ruled that under the Fourteenth Amendment Congress could prohibit only *state* actions that violated civil rights. It could not prohibit individual acts of racial discrimination in restaurants, hotels, and other public places. The Court said that it was up to the states to ban discrimination, and, not surprisingly, southern states chose instead to allow and even encourage racial segregation as a preferred policy.

During this period segregation lacked the rigidity and legal power that it acquired later. In some southern states, for example, black citizens could use railroads and streetcars on a roughly equal basis with whites. Elsewhere in the region travel facilities were segregated. Under the regimes of the Redeemers, black men continued to vote in some numbers before 1890, retained the right to hold office, could be members of a jury, and were permitted to own weapons.

Whatever opportunities were open to black citizens existed alongside an overall system of racial discrimination and bigotry. Black men often found their choices at the polls limited to approved white candidates, and if too many African Americans sought to cast ballots, white violence might erupt. By the end of the 1880s growing numbers of white politicians believed that blacks should be barred from the electoral process altogether.

Thus, for African Americans in the South, the fifteen years after the end of Reconstruction began with hopeful signs, but had a bleak outcome. Black families wanted to rent farms and work land for themselves rather than return to anything that resembled the plantation system. They believed that growing cotton in the delta of Mississippi gave them a chance to participate in that region's expanding economy. The area saw an influx of blacks at the end of the 1880s as African-American men competed for new jobs and the opportunity to acquire land of their own. Sharecropping and tenant farming were also present, but in this part of the South for a brief period there was a chance for black economic advancement. African Americans created networks of black churches and endeavored to

educate their children. Booker T. Washington's leadership of the Tuskegee Institute in Alabama, which began in 1881, symbolized what education and training could do for aspiring African Americans. Growing up with no direct experience of slavery, a new generation of southern blacks demanded their legal rights. When older blacks warned of the possible consequences of such behavior, the younger generation answered that "we are now qualified, and being the equal of whites, should be treated as such." The response of southern whites would be further repression in the years that followed.

Some African Americans preferred to get out of the South if they could. At the end of the 1870s rumors spread through the black population that Kansas offered a safer haven. During 1879 some 20,000 blacks, known as Exodusters because they were coming out of bondage as the children of Israel had in the Exodus, arrived in Kansas. More settled in the cities than actually farmed on the prairie. Hundreds of thousands of other blacks left the South in these years. Their willingness to go to areas that offered less oppression and more opportunity than the South testified to the enduring optimism of black Americans.

As the end of the 1880s approached, white spokesmen for the South boasted of the region's progress. The South produced more cotton than ever before; towns were growing throughout the region; industries had developed; and tens of thousands of black Southerners had accumulated property. Yet there were danger signs. State legislatures wrote new laws to segregate first-class railroad passengers by race. Farmers who grew more cotton each year without getting ahead organized to oppose the power of merchants and railroads. Tenants and laborers of both races seemed restless and in constant motion. Racial violence reached unprecedented levels. Although much had changed, many worried that the New South would be little better than the Old.

LIFE AND CULTURE DURING THE 1880s

The daily rhythms of American life were still those of the country and the small town. According to the

1880 census, there were 50,155,783 people in the United States in that year. More than 70 percent of them lived in "rural territory." Another 3.5 million people lived in towns and villages with fewer than 5,000 inhabitants. Of the nearly 10 million households in the nation, the most common family consisted of a husband, a wife, and their three children. The father worked the family farm or at a job in an office or at the factory. The mother stayed at home and did the endless round of cleaning, cooking, sewing, and shopping that kept the home operating. The children attended schools near their home or, in less prosperous families, labored to supplement the family's income.

Their Daily Bread

The meals that Americans consumed daily were large ones. For the middle class breakfast often included fried eggs, biscuits, wheatcakes, potatoes, and steak. By the 1870s, however, makers of breakfast cereals had made some inroads into the traditional diet. In 1878 John Harvey Kellogg invented a mixture of cornmeal, oatmeal, and wheat flour that, when baked into biscuits, became "granola." The afternoon and evening meals were also quite large. Among the upper classes a fancy dinner might provide as many as ten or eleven courses of meats, fish, salads, and starchy foods.

Industrialism changed the way Americans ate. Millions of tin cans were produced each year. Vegetables and fruits were available at the twist of a can opener. In large cities fresh meats became more readily available as the Armour meat company moved beef in iced railroad cars. The saltine cracker, shipped by the National Biscuit Company and other firms, proved that packaged crackers could remain fresh and crisp. Brand names told Americans that "Uneeda" biscuit and a portly Quaker figure appeared on containers of Quaker Oats. "Certified milk," freer from harmful bacteria than natural milk, became a staple of the American diet; by the end of the 1880s milk was being pasteurized. In 1886 an Atlanta druggist named John Pemberton developed a syrup from an extract of the cola nut that he mixed with carbonated water and called "Coca Cola." A year later he sold out to Asa Candler, who made Coca-Cola a household word.

During the 1880s soft drinks became a national diversion, and Coca-Cola used advertising campaigns to spread its message of quick refreshment to consumers. Improved transportation, brand names, and shared personal experiences of leisure activity were part of a country that was being knit together at the end of the nineteenth century.

Power for the Home

In the homes of city dwellers, gas and electricity provided new sources of power. No longer did people have to chop and gather wood, clean fireplaces, and maintain a multitude of candles and lamps. Running water replaced water drawn by hand from a distant pump. Refrigeration reduced the need for daily shopping; ready-made clothing relieved housewives of the task of sewing garments for the family.

While machines reduced the burdens of the husband and children, the duties of the wife were still time-consuming and tiring. However fuel was supplied, she had to prepare the meals. Despite the availability of canned fruits and vegetables, many women did their own canning and preserving. Sewing, cleaning, and household maintenance continued on a daily basis without the assistance of the male members of the family. To a large extent, the wife and mother found herself alone in the house each day as the husband went to work and the children went to school.

The Middle-Class Family

Middle- and upper-class women who could afford to hire domestic servants to perform these chores enjoyed more leisure. Smaller families also meant that women ended their child-rearing years earlier and then had more time for themselves. New magazines catered to this audience, including the *Ladies' Home Journal* in 1883 and *Good Housekeeping* in 1885. For many women their new situation allowed them to join in voluntary associations with other women of their class. Women's clubs spread during the 1870s and 1880s, and in time these groups became important sponsors of middle-class social reform. The Young Women's Christian Association, founded in 1867, the Women's Christian Temperance Union, established in 1874, and the Association of Collegiate Alumnae, formed in 1882, gave tangible expression to these women's desires for association and service.

The children were educated in schools that were locally controlled and designed to instill patriotism and moral values. "We went to school to work," remembered one student; "our playing was done elsewhere." City children attended school for some 180 to 200 days a year. In rural areas, however, the demands of farm work often limited children's school attendance to under one hundred days a year. Courses included arithmetic, the history of the United States, geography, reading, grammar, and spelling. Many students read the famous series of *McGuffey's Readers,* which stressed religion, obedience, and family. In the better school systems, students received instruction in Latin and at least one other foreign language; less attention was given to the sciences. For new immigrants, the school system became a means for them to learn the values of the dominant culture and prepare their children for citizenship.

Although only a small percentage of students attended high schools and even fewer pursued a college degree, the late nineteenth century brought rapid growth for institutions of higher learning. Wealthy businessmen created private universities such as Johns Hopkins in Baltimore (1876), the University of Chicago (1890), and Stanford in California (1891).

State universities expanded in the Midwest and were created in the South. Modeled on the German educational system, these universities established academic departments and stressed research and graduate training as a primary mission of advanced learning. Higher education in the United States became increasingly professionalized as teachers had to possess graduate degrees and prove themselves through research and publication in their discipline.

Leisure in the 1880s

The cultural changes of the 1880s gave rise to new common diversions and entertainments. At Chautauqua meetings (named after the lake in western New York state where the program began), held in the summer, citizens gathered for ten-week sessions, read long lists of suggested and required books and listened to lectures by scholars, prominent public figures, and artists. Participants waved white handkerchiefs as evidence of their enthusiasm.

Appealing to a wider audience were the circuses and Wild West shows. The first three-ring circus debuted in Manhattan in 1883, and P.T. Barnum, with his "greatest show on earth," became the entertainment equivalent to the giants of industry. During the same year William "Buffalo Bill" Cody assembled a troupe of former Pony Express riders, stage coach robbers, and riding artists that toured the United States and Europe. In major cities vaudeville, a form of entertainment consisting of a series of singers, comedians, and specialty acts, was a favorite of urban audiences.

Baseball was already a popular pastime. The National League, founded in 1876, entered an era of prosperity after 1880. Star players like Adrian "Cap" Anson of the Chicago White Stockings became household names. Anson's team won five pennants in ten years; its fastest player was Bill Sunday, later a popular religious evangelist. Baseball fans, known as "kranks," delighted in baiting the umpire. In the 1880s many new rules were adopted, including the three strikes, four-balls format; overhand pitching; and substitutions of players. Attendance figures rose, with as many as 30,000 people turning out for games on Memorial Day. Sunday contests were banned, as was the sale of beer at ballparks. In 1888 Ernest L. Thayer wrote his famous poem "Casey at the Bat," and several generations of schoolchildren learned to recite how there was "no joy in Mudville" when "mighty" Casey struck out at the crucial moment. It was a golden age for baseball.

Literate citizens found an abundance of reading for varied tastes. The magazines of the day, some 3300 in all, carried articles on every possible subject. *Atlantic Monthly, Harper's Weekly, Century, The North American Review,* and *Scribner's* dealt with scientific discoveries, literary trends, and political issues in an informed and thorough way. Americans also read popular novels such as Lew Wallace's *Ben Hur* (1880), an engrossing blend of religion, ancient history, and a good story. The more serious novels of the decade included *The Rise of Silas Lapham* (1885), by William Dean Howells and *The Bostonians* (1885) by William James. Probably the most important literary work of the 1880s was *Huckleberry Finn,* written by Samuel L. Clemens ("Mark Twain") in 1885. In it Clemens used an adventure in which a boy helps a runaway slave to create a chronicle of the nation's experience with slavery, freedom, the wonders of childhood, and the ambiguities of adult life.

Visual arts also fascinated Americans. Private acquisitions of paintings grew; about 150 such collections were in existence in 1880. Museums were founded in St. Louis, Detroit, and Cincinnati between 1879 and 1885, continuing a trend that had begun earlier in Boston, Philadelphia, and New York. Notable artists included Frederic Remington, who had gone west in 1880 to improve his health and arranged to accompany the army on campaigns against the Indians. His evocations of frontier life, published in *Harper's Weekly,* made him famous. Two of the most important figures of the decade were Thomas Eakins and John Singer Sargent. Eakins lived and worked in Philadelphia where he was forced to resign from the Pennsylvania Academy for using a naked male model in a class of female students. His most notable works included *The Swimming Hole* and *The Agnew Clinic.* Sargent became famous for portraits such as *The Daughters of Edward Boit* and *Mrs. Edward Burkhardt and Daughter Louise.*

During this era private institutions, universities, and the federal government encouraged the diffusion of scientific information. One scientist of the time, Josiah Willard Gibbs, had became world famous for his work in theoretical physics and physical chemistry. The American Association for the Advancement of Science resumed operation after the war; other scientific societies expanded after 1877 as well. From the

American art in the 1880s sought to portray the world in realistic terms. Thomas Eakins went into the operating theater of a medical school to show how an operation was conducted. Medicine was becoming scientific and professional, qualities that are shown in the attentive students, the authoritative surgeon, and this team of aides and a nurse in this painting titled The Agnew Clinic.

industrial laboratories of General Electric and other corporate giants to the facilities of research universities, the United States forged a partnership between science and technology that laid the basis for future innovations.

Two symbols of the decade were the Brooklyn Bridge in New York and the Statue of Liberty in New York City. Completed in 1883, the bridge allowed 11 million people to cross the East River from Brooklyn to Manhattan in its first year of operation. It took John A. Roebling and his son Washington Roebling twelve years to construct the longest suspension bridge in the world but the resulting structure demonstrated what the new processes of industrialism could accomplish. The Statue of Liberty was dedicated three years later on October 28, 1886. The work of a French sculptor, Frédéric-Auguste Bartholdi, it was sponsored by a public fund-raising effort in the United States; the statue was placed on Bedloe's Island, now called Liberty Island, at the entrance to New York Harbor. Out of the campaign to raise money came the celebrated poem by Emma Lazarus that promised the "golden door" of opportunity to Europe's "huddled masses yearning to breathe free." The union of liberty and technology was one of the enduring ideas of the 1880s.

POLITICS AND PUBLIC POLICY, 1877–1887

In politics, both of the major parties sought to overcome an electoral stalemate that had developed after 1872. The Republicans won the presidency in 1876, 1880, and 1888; the Democrats triumphed in 1884 and 1892. Neither party controlled both houses of Congress on a regular basis. The Republicans had control twice, from 1881 to 1883 and 1889 to 1891; the Democrats only once, from 1893 to 1895. Outside the South, elections often were decided by very narrow margins.

Americans lavished time on their politics. Only men took part in elections, and most of them were whites. (A few black men voted in the South.) Those who did vote turned out at a record rate. About eight out of every ten eligible voters went to the polls. Women could vote only in Wyoming and Utah. When they were not voting, Americans listened to long speeches by candidates and read about politics in the extended stories that partisan newspapers printed. Coverage of congressional deliberations was much more detailed than would be the case a century later.

Moral and religious values shaped the way that men voted and helped define which party won their support. The prohibition of alcohol, the role of religious and sectarian education in the public schools, and the observance of the Sabbath were hotly contested questions. Republicans favored government intervention to support Protestant values; Democrats thought the government should keep out of such subjects.

The most prominent national issues involved the kind of money Americans used, how the government raised revenue, and who served in the government itself. On the subject of money, some Americans believed that for every dollar in circulation an equal amount of gold should be stored in the Treasury or in banks. Others contended that the government should issue more money by coining silver into currency on an equal basis with gold. Debtors favored inflation, which made their loans easier to pay; creditors liked the deflation that raised the value of their dollars. The South and West wanted inflation; the Northeast and developed portions of the Midwest preferred the existing financial system. Both parties struggled with the issue during the ten years after 1877.

Other major concerns were taxation and the protective tariff. There was no federal income tax; the government raised money from two main sources: excise taxes on alcohol and tobacco, and customs duties (taxes) on goods imported into the United States. The latter method, the *protective tariff,* became a hot political issue. Those who favored a tariff said that high customs duties would protect American industry, help workers, and develop the economy. Republicans championed the protective system, while Democrats countered that tariffs raised prices, hurt the consumer, and made government too expensive. The South liked the Democratic argument, but Republicans found support from business and labor.

At bottom the argument was over the size and role of the national government. Should the government stimulate the economy, as the Republicans wanted, or allow natural forces to operate, as the Democrats advocated? This issue shaped party battles during the 1880s.

Finally, there was the question of who should serve in government. Politicians preferred the "spoils" or patronage system. Allocating government jobs to partisan supporters enabled them to strengthen their party. Critics of the patronage system called it a corrupt and inefficient way to choose government officials. They favored a *civil service,* in which individuals, chosen through competitive examinations, would administer government without being subject to partisan pressure. Civil service reformers urged Congress to write laws to reduce the power of patronage during the 1870s, but incumbents of both parties liked the existing system.

From Hayes to Arthur

The Republicans began the period with Rutherford B. Hayes in the White House. Hayes proved to be a capable chief executive whose moderate policies restored some of the morale that the Republicans had lost dur-

Despite his disputed election victory in 1876, Rutherford B. Hayes was an effective president who restored the integrity of the institution after the difficult years of Andrew Johnson and Ulysses S. Grant. He could not prevent the return of white rule in the South, but he did preserve the authority of the presidency against the claims of Congress for a larger voice in patronage.

ing the first half of the 1870s. He pushed for civil service reform and resisted pressure from Congress to base his appointments on candidates that Congress favored. He vetoed the inflationary Bland-Allison Act (1878) which called for monthly government purchases of silver, but Congress overrode his veto.

Hayes had promised to serve only one term. To succeed him the Republicans nominated James A. Garfield of Ohio, and Chester Alan Arthur of New York as his running mate. The Democratic candidate was a former Civil War general named Winfield Scott Hancock. After an intense campaign that focused on the tariff issue, Garfield won by a narrow plurality in the popular vote and a larger margin in the electoral college.

Garfield's presidency lasted only four months. In the spring of 1881 he made a promising start toward reforming the patronage system but on July 2 he went to the Washington railroad station to leave for a vacation. Presidents were not well guarded at this time, and a crazed assassin shot Garfield. He died on September 19, and Chester Alan Arthur became president. Much to everyone's surprise, Arthur who was widely regarded as a mediocrity, proved a competent chief executive. During his single term, Congress passed the Pendleton Act (1883), which created a civil service system and limited the practice of assessing campaign contributions from federal employees. The act also established rules about where and how government officials could raise campaign funds. Arthur also asked Congress to consider downward revision of the tariff. The lawmakers responded with the Mongrel Tariff of 1883 (so called because it pleased no one), which generally raised protective duties. The president vetoed a Chinese Exclusion Law, but after Congress revised it slightly, Arthur signed it.

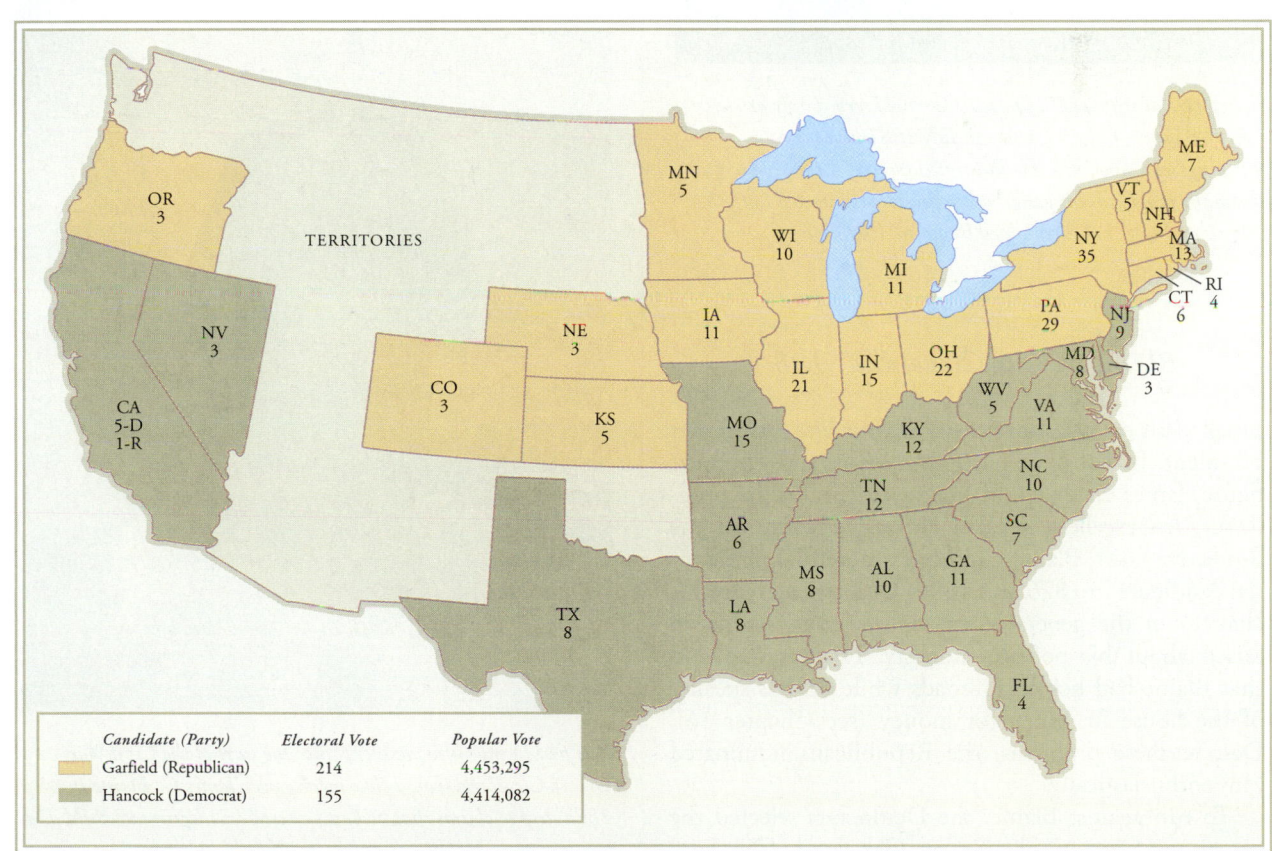

Candidate (Party)	Electoral Vote	Popular Vote
Garfield (Republican)	214	4,453,295
Hancock (Democrat)	155	4,414,082

MAP 17.3 | THE ELECTION OF 1880

Elected president in 1880, James A. Garfield served only briefly before he was shot by an assassin in July 1881 and died the following September. His fate illustrated how close the presidency was to the people in this period when presidents traveled like other citizens and were not surrounded by guards and security.

Blaine Versus Cleveland, 1884

Despite his solid performance, Arthur was a caretaker president. In 1884 the party selected its most popular figure, James G. Blaine of Maine, to run for the presidency. An excellent speaker and an advocate of the protective tariff, Blaine had been a potential presidential candidate in 1876 and 1880. Unfortunately for his chances in the general election, questions had been raised about his political honesty. His enemies said that Blaine had helped railroads while he was speaker of the house in return for money (see Chapter 16). Despite these problems, the Republicans nominated him enthusiastically.

To run against Blaine, the Democrats selected the governor of New York, Grover Cleveland. Cleveland had risen from political obscurity. He was a lawyer in Buffalo, New York, when he was chosen to be the

city's mayor in 1881. A year later he was the Democratic nominee for governor of the Empire State. Elected in a year when the Republicans were disunited and demoralized, Cleveland proved to be a popular state executive who delighted in vetoing bills and lecturing the legislature. The national Democrats wanted a fresh face, and the stocky Cleveland (relatives called him "Uncle Jumbo") was an attractive blend of honesty, conservatism, and independence. His campaign suffered a setback when it was revealed that some years earlier he had accepted responsibility for an illegitimate child in Buffalo. Cleveland acknowledged his part in the episode, however, and his candor defused the issue. Meanwhile, the issue of Blaine's public morality worked against the Republicans.

The first Democratic president since the start of the Civil War, Grover Cleveland won a close victory over James G. Blaine in 1884 despite claims that he had fathered an illegitimate child as a younger man. He then demonstrated that his party could govern at a time of intense partisanship and even balance between the two major parties.

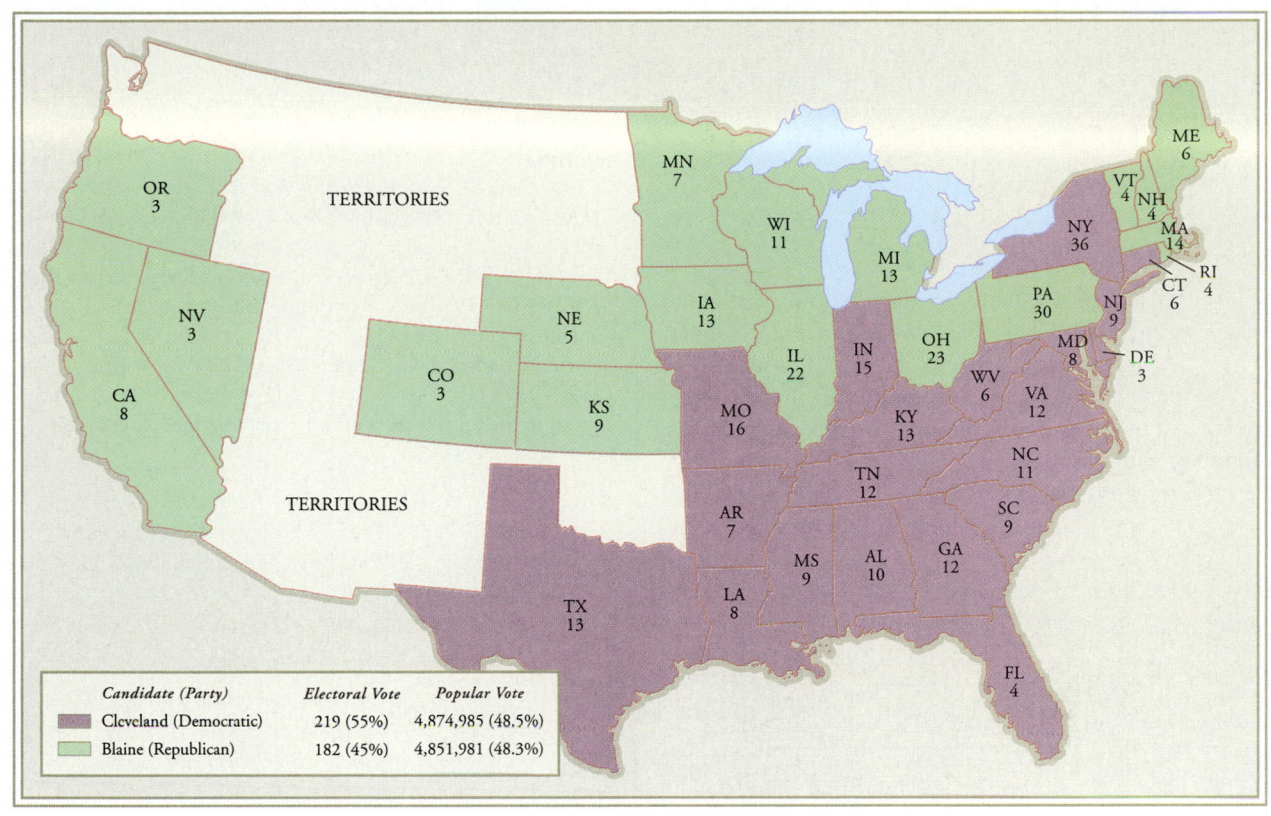

Candidate (Party)	Electoral Vote	Popular Vote
Cleveland (Democratic)	219 (55%)	4,874,985 (48.5%)
Blaine (Republican)	182 (45%)	4,851,981 (48.3%)

MAP 17.4 | THE ELECTION OF 1884

Cleveland was helped by the defection of upper-class Republicans in the Northeast. These voters, calling themselves "Mugwumps" (an Indian word meaning "Big Chief"), threw their support to the Democrats. The outcome of the election was very close, reflecting the even balance of the major parties. Cleveland carried the South, New York, New Jersey, Connecticut, and Indiana, receiving 219 electoral votes to Blaine's 182.

Cleveland in Office

Cleveland took office on March 4, 1885. During his first term, he established that his party could govern, and his political opponents gave him grudging respect. For the Democrats, however, Cleveland proved to be a mixed blessing. He was slow to turn Republican of-

ficeholders out of office, and he alienated many Democrats with his patronage policies. "Faithlessness is a passport to recognition by this mass of presidential fat," said one of his critics. Still, Republicans made few gains in the congressional elections of 1886, and Cleveland seemed to have good prospects for a second term in 1888.

In December 1887, hoping to establish an issue for his reelection campaign, the president made the subject of tariff reform the sole issue of his annual message to Congress (known as the State of the Union message). With a surplus in the Treasury, Cleveland believed that the tariff could be reduced, leading to lower prices for consumers. The Republicans' reaction to Cleveland's move was one of delight. Now the 1888 election could be fought on the issue that united the Republicans and divided the Democrats. With the stage set for the election, the stalemated politics of the

1880s slowly broke up. For the next twelve years American politics would experience one of the most turbulent and decisive periods of change and partisan realignment in the nation's history.

CONCLUSION

The 1880s were lived out in the shadow of the recently concluded Civil War. As one veteran, Oliver Wendell Holmes, Jr., said in 1884, "Through our great good fortunes, in our youth our hearts were touched with fire." Having experienced so much as young people, between 1877 and 1887 they sought harmony, prosperity, and stability. They pursued industrialism and its benefits with intense energy. Their achievements—in terms of railroads and factories built, inventions developed, and society transformed—were striking.

Yet the transformation of the American economy came at a cost. In 1887 the United States was characterized by deep social divisions and economic inequality. Regional differences remained unresolved. Industrialism had produced serious changes in the environment that would imperil the natural resources available to future generations. The animosity between capitalists and workers smoldered behind a facade of calm. The nation had yet to work out the tensions that had accompanied industrial growth. That task would be addressed in the succeeding decade in a setting in which the rise of the American city would grow to be as important a force for change as industrialism had been in the years after 1877.

RECOMMENDED READINGS

Avrich, Paul. *The Haymarket Tragedy* (1984) considers one of the significant episodes of social conflict and labor unrest during the 1880s.

Ayers, Edward. *The Promise of the New South* (1992) is a fine modern treatment of the South in the years after Reconstruction ended.

Chandler, Alfred D. *The Visible Hand: The Managerial Revolution in American Business* (1977) is a detailed examination of how industrial growth occurred.

Garraty, John A. *The New Commonwealth, 1877–1890* (1968) offers an informative discussion of all aspects of the 1880s.

Morgan, H. Wayne. *From Hayes to McKinley: National Party Politics, 1877–1896* (1969) is excellent on the national scene and the political leadership of the time.

Porter, Glenn. *The Rise of Big Business, 1860–1900* (1973) offers a good brief survey of the process of industrial growth.

Saum, Lewis O. *The Popular Mood of America, 1860–1890* (1990) considers how the nation responded to social change.

Utley, Robert. *The Indian Frontier of the American West: 1846–1890* (1984) is a very thorough treatment of Indian–White relations in the 1880s.

Woodward, C. Vann. *Origins of the New South, 1877–1913* (1951) is a classic study of the development of the South in the four decades after Reconstruction.

Politics and Public Policy

Brock, William R. *Investigation and Responsibility: Public Responsibility in the United States, 1865–1900* (1984).

Doencke, Justus. *The Presidencies of James A. Garfield and Chester A. Arthur* (1981).

Keller, Morton. *Affairs of State: Public Life in Late Nineteenth Century America* (1977).

Reitano, Joanne. *The Tariff Question in the Gilded Age: The Great Debate of 1888* (1994).

Welch, Richard. *The Presidencies of Grover Cleveland* (1988).

Women

Blair, Karen. *The Clubwoman as Feminist: True Womanhood Redefined, 1868–1914* (1980).

Degler, Carl. *At Odds: Women and the Family from the Revolution to the Present* (1980).

Jeffrey, Julie Roy. *Frontier Women: The Trans-Mississippi West* (1979).

Kessler-Harris, Alice. *Out to Work: A History of Wage-Earning Women in the United States* (1982).

Turbin, Carole. *Working Women of Collar City: Gender, Class, and Community in Troy, New York, 1864–1886* (1992).

The West

Fite, Gilbert. *The Farmer's Frontier* (1966).

Gressley, Gene. *Bankers and Cattlemen* (1966).

Hoxie, Frederick. *A Final Promise: The Campaign to Assimilate the Indians, 1880–1920* (1989).

Webb, Walter Prescott. *The Great Plains* (1931).

White, Richard. *"It's Your Misfortune and None of My Own": A New History of the American West* (1991).

The South

Davis, Harold E. *Henry Grady's New South: Atlanta, a Brave and Beautiful City* (1990).

Fite, Gilbert. *Cotton Fields No More: Southern Agriculture, 1865–1900* (1984).

Gaston, Paul M. *The New South Creed: A Study in Southern Mythmaking* (1970).

Ransom, Roger, and Richard Sutch. *One Kind of Freedom: The Economic Consequences of Emancipation* (1977).

Wright, Gavin. *Old South, New South: Revolutions in the Southern Economy Since the Civil War* (1986).

THE OKLAHOMA LAND RUSH

When the Oklahoma Territory was opened to white homesteaders in April 1889, a wild land rush ensued. This photograph conveys the frenzy with which prospective settlers hurried to establish their claims to the best holdings.

Chapter 18

URBAN GROWTH AND FARM PROTEST,

1887–1893

As the United States approached its one hundredth birthday in 1889, its burgeoning urban population posed a growing social problem. The new metropolises were characterized by huge gaps between the rich and poor residents. Citizens sought to reconcile traditional rural values of the country with the diversity and turbulence of the cities. The city became a forum for important debates about the future of society. At the local and national level the political system struggled to adjust to the new demands of the urban population.

The farm problems that had simmered throughout the early 1880s also reached a crisis level as the new decade began. In the South and West angry farmers formed a fresh political organization, the People's party, to make their grievances heard. For Indians and African Americans, the 1890s brought further painful reminders of their marginal status and their vulnerability to bigotry and discrimination. The end of the nineteenth century saw renewed questions about the future of the nation as it urbanized and became a world power.

THE NEW URBAN SOCIETY

After Grover Cleveland made tariffs the central issue in the 1888 election, the Republicans united in support of the protective tariff. The Republican candidate, Benjamin Harrison of Indiana, ran a strong campaign, speaking to large crowds from his front porch. Party members distributed millions of pamphlets to voters. In contrast, the Democrats ran a sluggish race. Cleveland won the popular vote, because of his strength in the one-party South, but Harrison won 233 electoral votes (compared to 168 for the incumbent president), did well in the Northeast and Middle West, and gained a majority in the electoral college. The Republicans also gained control of both houses of Congress.

The result of the election proved to have large consequences for national politics. With their hold on the executive and legislative branches, the Republicans intended to move ahead with an ambitious agenda of legislation and activist government. The Democrats

CHRONOLOGY

1888   Edward Bellamy publishes *Looking Backward*

Benjamin Harrison elected president over Grover Cleveland

1889   Oklahoma Territory becomes available for settlement by non-Native Americans

National Farmers Alliance and Industrial Union is organized

Jane Addams establishes Hull House in Chicago

Pan-American Congress held

First electric sewing machine marketed

1890   Congress enacts Sherman Silver Purchase Act, McKinley Tariff, and Sherman Antitrust Act

Mississippi constitutional convention establishes strict segregation laws

William Dean Howells publishes *A Hazard of New Fortunes,* a novel about the Haymarket Affair in 1886

Republicans suffer large losses in congressional elections; Farmers Alliance makes strong showing

National American Woman Suffrage Association set up

Battle of Wounded Knee

Daughters of the American Revolution founded

Poems by Emily Dickinson published

1891   Queen Liliuokalani comes to power in Hawaii

1892   People's party founded

Homestead Strike occurs

Ida Wells-Barnett begins campaigns against lynching

Grover Cleveland defeats Benjamin Harrison in presidential election

Ellis Island opens in New York to receive immigrants

1893   Hawaiian Revolution occurs

Grover Cleveland inaugurated for second term

Mildred Hill publishes song that becomes "Happy Birthday to You"

---

were ready to challenge such initiatives in Congress and at the polls. The stalemated system that had existed since the end of Reconstruction was beginning to break down.

Sooners and Settlement Houses

During 1889 two events occurred in the center of the nation that reflected the contrasting directions of the United States at the end of the decade. Shortly after Benjamin Harrison took office in March 1889 a climactic moment in the settlement of the West took place. Since the 1820s the Five Civilized Tribes of Native Americans had lived in what is now Oklahoma. Other tribes had received land in the region after the Civil War. By the 1880s, however, pressure from white settlers to be given access to the territory proved irresistible in Congress. The Dawes Act of 1887 (see Chapter 17) completed the process of stripping the In-

dians of their rights. President Harrison announced that unoccupied land could be settled beginning on April 22, 1889. One hundred thousand people rushed to acquire the newly available land. Within a few hours the "Sooners," who entered the territory early, and the "Boomers" (a general name for eager settlers) had created towns and staked out farms. Other "rushes" occurred in the following four years until all the available land that the Indians had once controlled was open to white settlement. The scene of surging, land-hungry Americans would not be repeated as the western frontier became more settled after 1890.

A few months later, in August 1889, Jane Addams and Ellen Gates Starr, founded Hull House, a settlement home in a Chicago neighborhood. Like the creators of similar houses that had started in New York a few years earlier, Addams and Starr hoped that solutions to the troubling problems of American city life could be found in their new residence. Americans took their cue from settlement houses in England, and

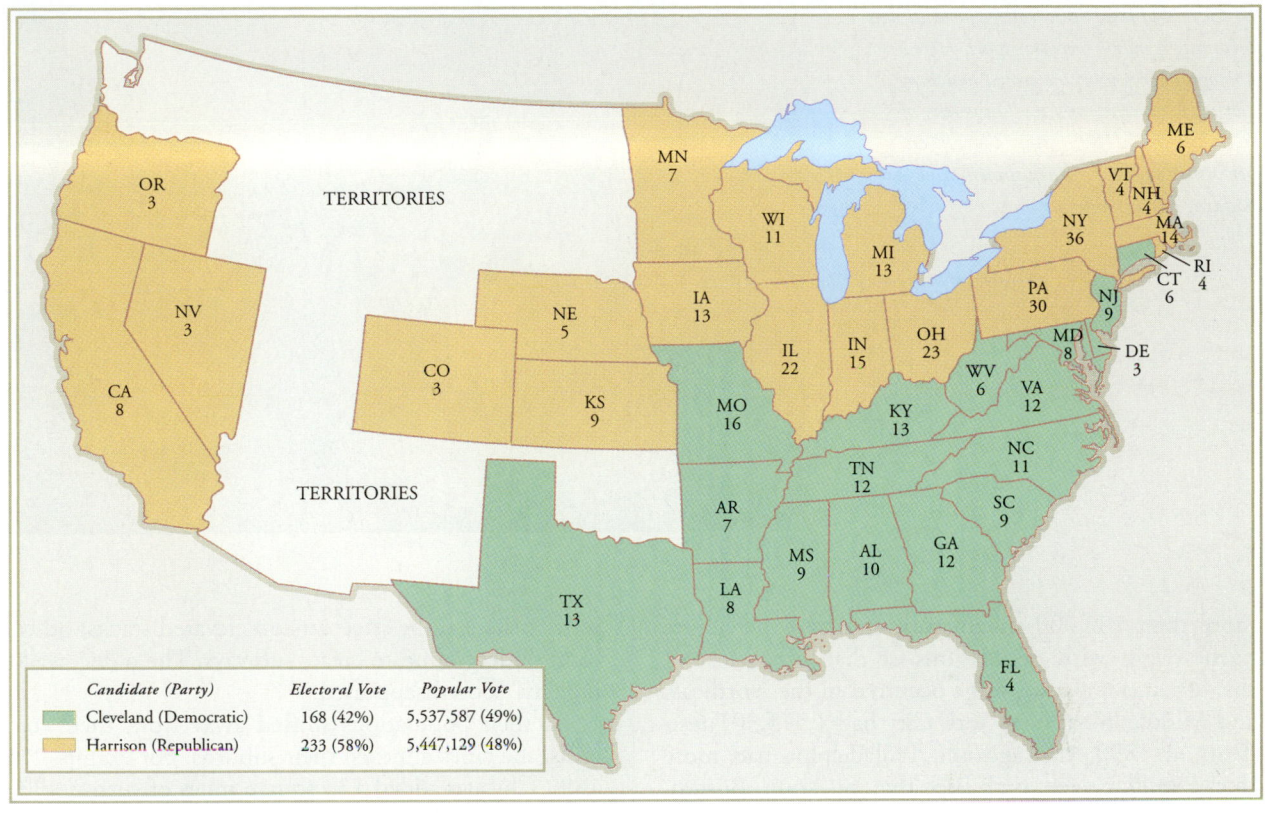

Candidate (Party)	Electoral Vote	Popular Vote
Cleveland (Democratic)	168 (42%)	5,537,587 (49%)
Harrison (Republican)	233 (58%)	5,447,129 (48%)

MAP 18.1 | THE ELECTION OF 1888

precedents from those ventures such as Toynbee House in London guided Addams and Starr in establishing their project. Hull House and Addams became famous as the settlement house idea grew in popularity among socially conscious, middle-class Americans. Her personal commitment to the experiment reflected the views of many Americans that the rapid rise of large cities posed new challenges for the nation. One commentator observed that "the concentration of population in cities" was "the most remarkable social phenomenon" of the nineteenth century. Jane Addams and like-minded Americans believed in the accuracy of that assessment and wanted to be part of making the new cities work.

The New City

The place that Addams and Starr had chosen for their social experiment symbolized what had happened in

urban America since the Civil War. In 1860, Chicago had been the nation's ninth-largest city, with a population of just under 109,000 people living in a seventeen-square-mile area. Thirty years later Chicago was the nation's second largest city, with 1,099,850 people within an area of 178 square miles. Through Chicago ran the major east–west railroads. To its stockyards came beef cattle from the West, to its elevators grain from the prairie, and to its lumberyards wood from the forests of Wisconsin and Minnesota. Chicago had survived the Great Fire of 1871, and from the ashes had risen the skyscrapers that gave it a distinctive skyline and the ethnic neighborhoods whose residents Hull House attempted to serve.

The Exploding Urban Population

Chicago's expansion typified the nation's rocketing urban population growth. In 1869 only nine cities had

By the end of the 1880s, college football was becoming a major spectator sport. Here a photographer records the crowd watching Cornell University and the University of Rochester in an 1889 game. The players performed without the equipment and padding of the modern game.

more than 100,000 inhabitants; in 1890 there were twenty-eight with populations of that size. Most of this urban population surge occurred in the Northeast and Middle West. New York City had 1,515,301 residents in 1890; Chicago and Philadelphia had more than 1 million each, with Brooklyn, St. Louis, Boston, and Baltimore next in order.

Americans moved to the cities to escape the routine of "hard work and no holidays" that dominated rural life. Immigrants from Europe, many of them from cities in Central and Eastern Europe, remained in the large cities after they arrived. Newcomers came to large cities like Chicago and New York, worked there for months and years, and then either moved to other cities, returned to the rural areas, or, in the case of some immigrants, went back to their home country.

The Structure of the City

After 1880 American cities grew dramatically. New forms of transportation such as horse-drawn omnibuses and commuter railroads allowed the cities to grow outward from the center. After the Civil War, the horsecar gave way to cable cars in San Francisco and other hilly cities. However, cable systems were clumsy, expensive, and inefficient, and they were soon replaced by electric streetcars or the trolleys, which ran under overhead wires and moved at speeds of up to ten miles an hour. Across the nation (see Chapter 17), urban transit rapidly became electrified. To avoid traffic jams,

some cities ran the streetcars on elevated tracks; others went underground to create subways. The older "walking city" soon disappeared.

As their populations shifted away from their core areas, the cities annexed their suburbs. For example, in 1889 Chicago added 133 square miles of surrounding communities. Linked by the new streetcars, various parts of the city became distinguished by the race, income level, and ethnicity of their residents. Within the core of the city, race and ethnicity determined where people lived. The more affluent residents moved as far from the center as they could. This dispersal of the population loosened the ties among the city's residents. Each class, racial, and ethnic group had fewer encounters with people in other sections of the city.

At the core of the cities, central business districts emerged. Railroads built terminals; banks and insurance companies located their main offices downtown; and department stores anchored shopping districts. Streetcars brought customers from the suburbs to Macy's in New York, Marshall Field's in Chicago, and Filene's in Boston. In these "palaces of consumption," middle-class women spent their time in leisurely shopping for an array of attractive products. Museums, theaters, and opera houses added to the cultural resources of the industrial city.

Skyscrapers and Tenements

Two new types of structures characterized the new metropolis. Architects created the *skyscraper* as a practical

The clutter and congestion of the city was one of the hallmarks of the urbanizing of the United States. This scene of Dearborn Street in Chicago conveys some of the bustle and energy of the city as the 1890s began. Transportation by carriages and trolleys was common in the decade before the arrival of the automobile.

solution to the need to conduct economic activities in an often compressed central business district. As a Chicago newspaper noted, "Since water hems in the business center on three sides and a nexus of railroads on the south, Chicago must grow upward."

Architects like Louis Sullivan of Chicago developed techniques that made it possible for buildings to rise higher than the five to ten stories that had been the upper limits of tall structures in the past. Passenger elevators, lighter walls reinforced with iron piers, and a framework of structural steel made it feasible to erect buildings with twenty to forty stories or more. The principle, Sullivan wrote, was that "form follows function." The skyscrapers that he and others built enabled the business district to accommodate thousands of office workers each day.

The Tenement and Its Residents

The sheer numbers of people who crowded into Chicago, New York, Boston, and the other expanding cities between 1880 and 1900 strained the available living space. For the middle and upper classes, apartments were a practical answer. Apartment buildings, some of which were quite expensive, began to replace the single-family home in urban areas.

Poorer city residents lived in the *tenement houses,* six- or seven-story houses built on narrow lots. New York had 20,000 such structures, most of them twenty-five feet wide and one hundred feet deep, with windows only at the front and back. During the late 1870s after legislation mandated that at least some ventilation be provided, "dumbbell tenements" appeared; these had tiny, indented windows along the sides and often provided only crude sanitation facilities. In these buildings dozens of people were crowded into small, dark rooms. Daily life often spilled out onto the surrounding streets. The buildings looked decent enough to a passerby, but as the novelist William Dean Howells noted, "To be in it, and not have the distance, is to inhale the stenches of the neglected street, and to catch the yet fouler and dreadfuller poverty-smell which breathes from the open doorways."

Inside the tenement or on the teeming sidewalks, urban residents strained the city's water and sanitation systems. The stench of manure, open sewers, and piled-up garbage filled their nostrils. Smoke from factories and grime from machinery was everywhere. One New York resident said that "the stink is enough to knock you down." Chicago's water systems were taxed to the limit during the 1880s, and residents of Philadelphia described their water as "not only distasteful and unwholesome for drinking, but offensive for bathing purposes."

The Need for Services

The cities expanded their facilities in order to provide better service. New York City created a system of reservoirs that brought water to the residents from surrounding rivers and lakes. Chicago faced immense difficulties in transporting water from Lake Michigan for drinking needs and providing adequate sanitation. By the end of the century, however, much progress had been made. Among other things, park building became a priority of urban machines and reformers alike. Although most of the new parks appeared on the outskirts of the city, away from the poorer sections, the amount of parkland in the larger cities doubled during the years from 1888 to 1898.

American artists incorporated the life of the city into their work in the 1890s. In W. Louis Sonntag, Jr.'s, The Bowery at Night, *the elevated railroads that moved people through the city become a striking visual image for the changes that were reshaping the nation's existence.*

The New Immigration

The cities grew because people flocked to them from the countryside and from other countries. For the twenty years after 1870 net immigration totaled more than 7.5 million people. Unlike the immigrants from Northern and Western Europe who had come during the first seventy-five years of the nineteenth century, these "New Immigrants" were mainly from Southern and Eastern Europe. These Italians, Poles, Hungarians, Russian Jews, and Czechs brought with them languages, lifestyles, and customs that often clashed with those of native-born Americans or earlier immigrants. Marrying within their own ethnic group, speaking their own language, reading their own newspapers, they created distinctive, vibrant communities within the cities.

Many newcomers first saw the United States when they entered New York Harbor. They were processed at Castle Garden at the Battery in lower Manhattan. By the end of the 1880s those immigration facilities had become inadequate; they were closed in 1890 and a new, more extensive immigrant station was opened in 1892 on Ellis Island in New York Harbor. There the new arrivals were passed through a medical examina-

tion and questioned about their economic prospects. Sometimes even their names were changed. One often-told story was that of a German Jew confronted by an inspector who fired a volley of questions at him. When finally asked his name, the man responded in Yiddish: "Schoyn vergessen" (I forget). The inspector heard what the words sounded like and said that "Sean Ferguson" was eligible to enter the United States. Only about 1 percent of potential immigrants were excluded.

Life in the United States

They made their living any way they could. They provided the labor for city construction gangs that built New York City's subways, the steel mills of Pittsburgh, and the skyscrapers of Chicago. Some men sold fruits and vegetables from pushcarts, others worked as day laborers, and increasing numbers built their own small businesses. Italian immigrant women "finished" garments for the clothing industry or made artificial flowers.

Their cultural values and Old World experiences often dictated the jobs that men and women took.

Italians preferred steady jobs with a dependable salary that left time for family life. Greeks joined railroad gangs where they could work in the open. Jews became shopkeepers, merchants, and peddlers, the trades that had been open to them in the anti-Semitic world of Eastern Europe. Some nationalities, Bohemians and Slovaks for example, allowed women to work as domestic servants; others, such as Jews, Italians, and Greeks, barred women from domestic work outside the home.

The Rise of Ethnic Communities

Ethnic neighborhoods appeared. In New York City, immigrants from Naples lived on Mott Street while Sicilians resided on Prince Street. Churches and synagogues shaped community life. Newcomers formed self-help societies to ease the transition for those who came after them—the Polish National Alliance, the Bohemian-American National Council, and the Hebrew Immigrant Aid Society. They built theaters and concert halls, and created schools to educate their children. Some of the newcomers moved away from their ethnic roots as they prospered; other immigrants soon replaced them. In the Tenth Ward of New York, the Jewish immigrant population in 1900 had a density of 900 people per acre, one of the highest in the world.

The Nativist Reaction

As the communities of immigrants grew, older residents expressed fears about the impact of the newcomers on traditional values and customs. Prejudice and religious intolerance flared. Editors of urban newspapers called immigrants "the very scum and offal of the earth." During the 1880s the anti-Catholic American Protective Association recruited those for whom the immigrants were a source of fear or economic competition. Its members resolved to limit the role of Catholics in politics. These sentiments that favored "native" Americans (hence "nativist") led to calls for legislation to restrict immigration through literacy tests for entrance into the United States or quotas based on national origin.

Anti-Semitism permeated American society during the Gilded Age. In addition to the longstanding religious roots of prejudice among Christians against Jews, the struggle over the currency revived notions that Jewish financiers dominated world banking and sought to perpetuate the gold standard. Among academics, social scientists, and historians, quasi-scientific arguments arose to justify exclusion of Jews from universities and businesses. Anti-Jewish stereotypes pervaded popular art and culture.

The Urban Political Machine

Politicians in the large cities grappled with this volatile mix of ethnicity, race, and economic class. Most cities had a mayor-council form of government in which the entire population elected the mayor, while council members represented individual districts or wards. Divided, ineffective government followed as council members traded favors and blocked legislation that hurt their districts. The urban "political machine" led by the "political boss" developed. The machine relied for its existence on the votes of the large inner-city population. They turned out faithfully on election day to support the candidates that the machine had designated.

The organization began in the ward. The machine's representative in the ward got out the vote by supplying his constituents with employment, helping in an economic crisis or brush with the law, and regularly attending the weddings, funerals, and wakes of the neighborhood. A ward leader like George Washington Plunkitt in New York or John F. "Honey Fitz" Fitzgerald in Boston was the man to see when disaster threatened an urban family. "I think that there's got to be in every ward somebody that any bloke can come to— no matter what he's done—and get help," said a Boston ward leader. "*Help, you understand, none of your law and justice, but help!*"

As the city grew, contracts were awarded to businesses to build the streets, install the sewers, lay the gas lines, and erect the trolley lines. There were abundant opportunities for politicians to decide how money was spent and who would benefit. With the power of its votes, the machine profited from the city services it allocated to the business community. Decisions about who built streets, parks, and sewer lines often depended on payoffs and graft to the boss and his associates. The flow of money, much of it based on corruption, enabled the machine to provide the social services that people wanted and a human sympathy for those in trouble.

In the public's mind, the political boss stood at the top of the machine. These men rarely held office and

Many people lived in squalid and dismal conditions in the cities. The noted photographer Lewis Hine here captures how a mother and six children were crammed together in a tenement apartment.

managed affairs from behind the scenes. "Honest John" Kelly and Richard Croker of Tammany Hall in New York City were among the most famous such leaders. Other bosses included George B. Cox of Cincinnati, Ohio; Isaac F. Rasin of Baltimore, Maryland; and Christopher "Blind Boss" Buckley of San Francisco. Their enemies depicted the bosses as unchallenged dictators of the city's destiny. In most cases, however, the bosses were shrewd politicians who balanced factions and interest groups in a constantly shifting political scene. They represented a response to the fragmentation of the city political system because of the coming of industrialism. In that sense they became an important and badly needed institutional innovation.

Reformers constantly challenged the power of the bosses. In their public comments, critics of the urban machine attacked its reliance on graft and corruption to sustain itself. The president of Cornell University said that cities in the United States were "the most corrupt in Christendom." Like-minded members of the middle and upper classes warred on the bosses and their machines throughout the late nineteenth century, seeking to replace them with more efficient, economical government. The machines often defeated the campaigns of the reformers because inner-city residents ap-

preciated what the bosses did for them. Reformers came and went; the machine was always there. As George Washington Plunkitt said, reformers "were mornin' glories—looked lovely in the mornin' and withered up in a short time, while the regular machines went on flourishin' forever, like fine old oaks."

The rank-and-file residents also knew that the reformers wanted to shift power away from the lower classes. The reform programs often involved cutbacks in even the already minimal services that the poorer areas of the city received. On balance, the machines and bosses supplied reasonably good city government. Services were provided and economic opportunity expanded. City residents endorsed the results with their votes. Most cities had water, fire, and health services of a quality that compared with those found in the industrial nations of Western Europe. In the city parks—Central Park in New York, the Boston park system, and the sprawling green spaces of St. Louis and Kansas City—the generation of the 1880s left a positive legacy to future urban residents.

A strong force for improving city life was the settlement houses that Jane Addams and others launched at the end of the 1880s. College-educated young women "settled" in houses in the ethnic communities to school the residents in the ways of American life. They

held citizenship classes, provided training in cultural issues, and offered sports to local youth. Often settlement workers approached the ethnic neighborhood with arrogance and insensitivity. In time, some settlement workers gained a better understanding of the obstacles that the immigrants faced. Their experiences in the ghettos and streets of the cities prepared them for work in subsequent reform campaigns. At the same time, Addams and others also conveyed a strong sense of moralistic paternalism to the people they sought to serve. Their goal was to "build a bridge between European and American experiences" over which the immigrants could pass toward integration into the dominant culture. Despite this paternalistic attitude, the settlement house movement did soften the impact of the urban experience on the new immigrants. Still, the urbanizing process of the late nineteenth century had left the nation with accumulated social problems that would tax leaders and institutions for decades.

A "Billion Dollar Country"

In December 1889 the first session of the Fifty-first Congress assembled in Washington with the Republicans in control of both houses. This session brought the differences between the major parties into sharp focus. To hamper the activism of the Republicans, the Democrats refused to answer their names when roll calls occurred to determine whether enough members were present to do legislative business. Immobility became a virtue to the negative-minded Democrats. To break the deadlock, the Republicans elected a new speaker of the House, the forceful and sarcastic Thomas B. Reed of Maine. When a Democrat boasted, echoing the famous remark of Henry Clay, that he would rather be right than president, the speaker countered that "the gentleman need not worry, he will never be either." Reed counted the Democrats as present even if they did not answer to the roll call. His tactic produced a working Republican majority, and the House embarked on an ambitious program of legislative action.

In line with their commitment to the protective tariff, the Republicans adopted the McKinley Tariff (1890) which raised customs duties. They wrote the Sherman Antitrust Act (1890) which declared any combination (trust) in restraint of trade illegal as a response to popular concern about the growth of big business. They passed the Sherman Silver Purchase Act

(1890) which required the government to purchase 4.5 million ounces of silver each month. The latter law was mildly inflationary and did not satisfy either proponents of gold or silver-based currency. In a last-ditch effort to fulfill the promise of Reconstruction, the Republicans also introduced a Federal Elections bill to protect African American voters in the South, but a coalition of southern and western senators, along with some urban bosses, blocked it.

By the end of the session, the Republicans believed that they had enacted a far-ranging program of constructive legislation. To their surprise, however, they found that the voters were angry at their activism. Since this was the first Congress to appropriate $1 billion, Democrats called it the "Billion Dollar Congress." Speaker Reed responded by pointing out that the nation was a "Billion Dollar Country," but few shared his optimism. The Republicans faced bleak electoral prospects in the 1890 elections.

THE DIMINISHING RIGHTS OF MINORITY GROUPS

The United States was not a very tolerant nation at the end of the 1880s. For African Americans, Chinese immigrants, and Native Americans these were years when their rights were at risk from repressive forces within white society. As a result, the period produced a narrowing of the possibilities for Americans who found themselves in one of these distinct racial minorities.

Native Americans

In the early 1890s the trends toward exclusion and segregation of racial minorities that began after Reconstruction accelerated. For Indians, the end of large-scale armed resistance to white expansion left them with few viable ways to protest the policies that destroyed their traditions and confined them to reservations or government schools. The Dawes Act (see Chapter 17) was already taking away their lands. Bowed down by despair and hopelessness, the Plains Indians were receptive to any leaders who offered them a chance to regain their lost cultural values.

"THE INDIAN
SITUATION"
1891

The battle of Wounded Knee triggered much press comment about how the nation treated the Indians in general and in this tragic incident in particular. The following editorials from the *New York Herald,* January 4, 1891 and the *Detroit Tribune,* January 2, 1891 present contrasting perspectives on what had occurred and what the proper Indian policy should be.

N. Y. Herald, Jan. 4.—This Indian question is intensely interesting and pathetic. There is also an element of tragedy in it from which we recoil.

We have about a quarter of a million of red men on our territory. Their ancestors were originally the possessors of the rich lands which we now occupy. We have multiplied and they have decreased. Only a remnant remains, and we have apportioned to them large areas in different parts of the country—north of Texas, in Dakota, Arizona, Montana and Washington—and told them to stay there and behave themselves.

The continent is none too large for our purposes, and the red man has only a few more years to live. He hasn't kept up with the procession; by little and little he is dropping out and dying on the road side. He can't understand the situation, and once in a while puts on war paint, sharpens his tomahawk and fiercely resists the inevitable.

What a pity that when he meets the multitude in the happy hunting grounds he can't report that we have treated him fairly and kept our promises.

If he tells the truth he will say:—The white man made treaties and broke them. He has lied to me and starved me. When I rebelled he shot me, and here I am.

Our Indian record is wholly brutal and shameful.

Detroit Tribune, Jan. 2.—The present war was unavoidable. The Government and the military did all that was possible to prevent war, but all their efforts were futile. The hostile Indians must be conquered now once for all, and those of them who shall survive the war be forever deprived of all firearms and other war weapons.

Hereafter the only Indian policy that will be acceptable to the people of this country will be one that shall make impossible another Indian outbreak. Grant all that has been said about the wrongs the Indians of previous generations endured, the sentiment of the past cannot come into the situation of the present. For many years the Indians have been most humanely and generously dealt with by the Government and they have been growing more and more restless and treacherous. Doubtless they have sometimes been cheated and wronged by scoundrelly post traders and agents, but the Government has not countenanced such wrongs; it has sought to correct them. The present outbreak was entirely causeless, so far as any fault of the Government or the military is concerned; and the public good demands a speedy and permanent settlement of the war on the basis of everlasting peace.

The Ghost Dance of the Sioux Indians in 1890 promised them relief from the rule of their white captors and led to the Wounded Knee Massacre. Frederic Remington, one of the leading artists of western life in the 1890s, records the Oglala Sioux at the Pine Ridge Indian Agency in South Dakota performing this ceremony.

The appearance of a religious movement, called the Ghost Dance, promised Plains Indians the return of their buffalo herds and an end to white domination. If the Indians performed the rituals of the dance, said a Paiute messiah named Wovoka, the Indian dead would be reborn and the whites would vanish for all time. Apprehensive whites saw the Ghost Dance as a portent of another Indian uprising. When the army moved against the Sioux in December 1890, fighting occurred on Wounded Knee Creek on the Pine Ridge Reservation in South Dakota. Despite bitter hand-to-hand combat, the "battle" was no contest. The army's machine guns cut down the Indians; they suffered 146 dead and fifty-one wounded while army losses were twenty-five killed and thirty-nine wounded. The Battle of Wounded Knee was the last major chapter in the Indian wars.

Mexican Americans

In the Southwest, Mexican Americans were a majority in the territory of New Mexico, and their influence remained strong in southern California. A major political issue in New Mexico was land grants that the Spanish crown had made. Lawyers acquired title to these properties in order to assemble large landholdings of their own. Hispanic residents grazed their cattle on communal lands that all ranchers shared. Anglo ranchers and settlers divided up the land with fences and sold it among themselves. Spanish Americans tried to resist this activity by forming a secret vigilante organization *Las Gorras Blancas* (The White Caps). In 1889 they removed the fences, and burned Anglo property and businesses such as railroads and lumberyards. Thus ethnic and economic tensions led to social violence in the territory.

Chinese Immigrants

The prejudice that the 104,000 Chinese residing in the West faced became more institutionalized in the early 1890s. Congress moved to tighten the restrictions on immigration embodied in the Chinese Exclusion Act of 1882. In 1889 the Supreme Court upheld the constitutionality of such laws and stated that such measures would help in "the preservation of our civilization there." In 1892 Congress extended the Chinese exclusion law for ten years, and by 1900 the number of Chinese living in the United States fell to 85,000. Most of the Chinese Americans lived in cities

where they established laundries, restaurants, and other small businesses that served members of their own community. The Chinese Benevolent Association or "Six Companies" offered support for a Chinese culture that existed in a rich and complex setting of its own.

African Americans

The most elaborate and sustained policy of racial separation was aimed at African Americans in the South. As blacks tried to benefit from their newly acquired rights to take part in politics and to seek wealth and happiness, white southerners created a caste structure to ensure their continued dominance. In the Civil Rights cases (see Chapter 17) the Supreme Court had ruled that the Fourteenth Amendment did not give Congress the power to prohibit discrimination by individuals. That left southern states the opportunity to write segregation laws against their black population.

An important national trend allowed the South to pursue these policies. White Americans in all parts of the nation believed that blacks were inferior to whites. Reconstruction was widely considered to have failed. White southerners, it was argued, should deal with its black population as it deemed best. Northern willingness to abandon the aims of the Civil War and Reconstruction was a key element in the rise of segregation.

With the tacit approval of the North, the white politicians of the South devised segregation laws that covered most spheres of human activity. Blacks were barred from white railroad cars and had to use the inferior and often shabby cars assigned to their race. Whites had their own hotels, parks, hospitals, and schools. Blacks had to make do with either lesser facilities or do without them entirely.

Informal restrictions also shaped the everyday life of blacks. African-Americans were expected to step out of the way of whites, to be respectful and deferential, and never, by look or glance, to display resentment or anger. Courtesy titles for blacks disappeared. A young black man was a "boy" until he became old enough to be labeled "uncle." To call an African-American person either "Mr." or "Mrs." would have implied a degree of individuality that the culture segregation in the South could not tolerate.

TABLE 18.1 IMPACT OF SUFFRAGE RESTRICTION IN THE SOUTH PROPORTIONATE REDUCTION IN OVERALL TURNOUT AND ESTIMATED TURNOUT BY RACE (SIX SOUTHERN STATES IN THE 1890s)

		Percentage Reduction in Voter Turnout		
		Overall Turnout	White Turnout (Estimated)	Black Turnout (Estimated)
Alabama	1892–1896 Governor's Races	19	15	24
Arkansas	1890–1894 Governor's Races	39	26	69
Florida	1888–1892 Governor's Races	61	31	83
Mississippi	1888–1892 Presidential Election	57	34	69
South Carolina	1892–1896 Presidential Election	13	17	51
Tennessee	1888–1892 Governor's Races	19	4	68

Adapted from the chart in J. Morgan Kousser, *The Shaping of Southern Politics* (New Haven: Yale University Press, 1974), p. 240.

The 1890s saw the rise of segregation in the South and an increase in violence directed against black Americans. These events often became social occasions for white Southerners who gathered to see the alleged criminal receive punishment that was swift but less often sure. Members of the crowd often took home grisly souvenirs of the proceedings.

Laws removed blacks from the political process. They could not serve on juries in judgment of whites. Punishments for their crimes were harsher than for white offenders. Although some blacks had voted in elections during the 1880s, laws were passed to make it impossible for African Americans to vote. The South took its cue from Mississippi whose constitutional convention, held in 1890, required that voters demonstrate their literacy and pay a poll tax before they could cast a ballot. An illiterate man had to qualify to vote by demonstrating that he could "understand" a provision of the state constitution when it was read to him. A poll tax had to be paid in advance and a receipt presented at the polls. These laws worked against poor whites and most blacks who found it easier not to vote. In states like Mississippi and Louisiana, the number of registered black voters fell drastically during the early 1890s; the number of white voters declined as well.

If legal restrictions were not sufficient to maintain white supremacy, blacks faced the constant possibility of extralegal violence against themselves and their families. During the ten years after 1889, an average of 187 black Americans were lynched each year. Blacks convicted of crimes were often imprisoned in brutal circumstances in overcrowded penitentiaries or made to work on gangs that the state leased out to private contractors. The convict-lease system produced inmate death rates as high as 25 percent in some states.

In Louisiana, blacks decided to test an 1890 law specifying that they must ride in separate railroad cars. On June 7, 1892, Homer A. Plessy, who was one-eighth black, boarded a train bound from New Orleans to Covington, Louisiana. He sat in the car reserved for whites, and the conductor instructed him to move to the car for blacks. He refused and was arrested. When his case came before Judge Thomas H. Ferguson, Plessy's claim that the law violated his constitutional rights was denied. His case was then appealed to the U.S. Supreme Court. A key legal test of segregation was underway.

Black leaders resisted to the extent they could with their scant resources. The remaining African-American members of southern legislatures argued against discriminatory legislation, but they were easily outvoted. A Richmond Democrat boasted of the tactics used to exclude blacks from elections: "It was well understood that the blacks had to be beaten by hook or by crook—they knew what to expect and they knew who was putting the thing on them but they could not prevent it." By the mid-1890s the South was as segregated as white leaders could make it. The legal and political gains that African Americans had made during Reconstruction had been rendered largely obsolete. For most blacks the constitutional guarantees of the Fourteenth and Fifteenth Amendments existed only on paper. The fate of minorities had a low priority in a society where the values of Victorian life governed everyday existence.

A VICTORIAN SOCIETY

In the late nineteenth century the social customs embodied in the term "Victorian" provided the context in

which most white Americans lived their lives. Like their counterparts in Great Britain, where Queen Victoria ruled between 1837 and 1901, these Americans professed a public code of personal behavior that demanded restraint, sexual modesty, temperate habits, and hard work.

The Rules of Life

The precepts of Victorian morality applied to every aspect of daily life. Relations between the sexes followed precise rules. Unmarried men and women were supposed to be chaperoned when they were together before marriage. A suitor asked a woman whether he might write to her before presuming to do so. A kiss resulted either in an engagement or social disgrace. Premarital sex was taboo. People married for life, mourned a dead spouse for at least a year, and showed fidelity by not remarrying. Some people did not follow these guidelines to their full extent, but many did and social conventions were strong.

Once married, a couple was expected to engage in sexual intercourse only for the purpose of having children. The wife was to tame the husband's baser instincts. She was considered to be naturally pure; he was thought to be dominated by animalistic drives. "The full force of sexual desire is seldom known to a virtuous woman," said one male writer, with the implication that women did not achieve the same pleasure in sex that men did.

In reality, women's desires did not conform to these masculine stereotypes. One mother of four in her thirties remarked that sexual relations "makes more normal people." A survey of married women found that almost three-quarters experienced pleasure during lovemaking. Limits on the frequency of sex may have been to reduce unwanted pregnancies in a time before birth control devices became widespread.

The Moral Code

The role of the man in Victorian society was to do the work of the world. Men spent their days at the factory or office, and their children saw them in the evening and on Sundays. Males displayed the right virtues in what the age called their "character." Men in the middle and upper classes might sow their "wild oats" be-

fore marriage, but after that were expected to adhere to their marriage vows. The rising number of divorces (some 56,000 by 1900) indicated that many did not do so. Society practiced a "double standard." People looked the other way when men patronized prostitutes or had discreet sexual adventures outside marriage. When it became known that a woman followed such a course, she was disgraced.

A strict moral code also governed the raising of Victorian children. Parents sought to instill character in their children. They were required to show respect to their elders. Discussion of sex was rare. Many women knew nothing about it until they were married. Despite the constraints placed on children's behavior, youthful high spirits found an outlet in games and play. Entertainment was centered in the home, where families assembled to play board and card games, sing around a parlor organ or piano, and, for the wealthier Americans, play croquet or lawn tennis.

A Godly Society

Religion permeated society. In 1890 there were 145 different Christian denominations with a total of nearly 22 million members. More than 8 million people were Roman Catholics; Presbyterians, Methodists, and Southern Baptists were the major Protestant denominations. Families reserved the Sabbath for churchgoing, rest, and quiet. Despite fears that religious convictions were waning in the face of growing secularism, thousands responded enthusiastically to the religious revivals of Dwight L. Moody and other celebrated evangelists.

By 1890, Victorian morality was challenged on several fronts: "Doubt is mostly a modern thing," argued one religious writer. Science and the teachings of Charles Darwin had undermined traditional religious precepts. "The human soul shrinks from the thought that it is without kith or kin in all this wide universe," concluded another observer of the intellectual currents of the decade.

Sports and Leisure

While thinkers debated the impact of modern ideas on old-time religious verities, everyday Americans also sought relaxation and recreation in the increasingly popular spectator sports. Among the upper and mid-

dle classes, football had emerged as second only to baseball (see Chapter 17) in its popular appeal. The first intercollegiate football game occurred between Princeton and Rutgers in 1869; the modern form of the game evolved as rules for scoring became established. Walter Camp, the unofficial coach at Yale University and the founder of the "All-American" teams, devised the line of scrimmage and the requirement that a team gain five yards in three attempts in order to retain possession of the ball. Dividing the field into five-yard squares produced the "gridiron."

With regular rules came also recruitment of talented athletes, charges of professionalism, and intense interest in the sport among alumni. By 1890, the game held in New York City on Thanksgiving Day in which teams vied for the unofficial national championship drew crowds of up to 40,000 people. College officials said that football allowed their students to "get together in the old-fashioned democratic way." In fact, football appealed most to those who believed that young men should demonstrate commitment to a strenuous existence in a violent game that tested their masculine courage.

Beyond the Gridiron

Boxing had a wider appeal for the masses. Irish-American boxers dominated the sport, with John L. Sullivan the most famous champion. Some matches were held in secret and continued for as many as seventy-five bloody rounds. The contestants did not use gloves. Gloves and formal rules appeared during the 1880s. Sullivan lost his heavyweight crown in 1892 to James J. "Gentleman Jim" Corbett in the first gloved title fight. African-American fighters appeared in interracial bouts in some divisions, but before 1900 white heavyweight champions observed the "color line."

In 1891, James Naismith, an instructor at the Young Men's Christian Association Training School in Springfield, Massachusetts, wanted to develop a sport that could be played indoors during the winter. He devised an early form of basketball which soon spread across the nation.

Another popular diversion was bicycling, which became a craze after 1890. The bicycle would become "the universally accepted steed of the future," said one prediction. Before the development of the modern "safety" bicycle in the 1880s and the addition of pneumatic tires in 1889, cycling was a sport for those who could master the brakeless "ordinary" bikes with their

Bicycling became a popular fad during the 1890s. Its low cost and convenience made it an attractive recreation for millions of Americans. It also brought men and women together in comfortable and socially approved surroundings.

large front wheels. But once technology put a convenient bicycle within the reach of the masses, the fad was on. Some 10 million bikes were in use by 1900. Cycling led women to adopt looser garments and, according to some enthusiasts, eased childbirth. After the automobile appeared at the beginning of the twentieth century, the passion for bicycles receded and memories of the craze that had marked the early 1890s faded away.

VOICES OF PROTEST AND REFORM

Bicycles were not the only craze that swept the nation at the end of the 1880s. A best-selling book captured

the fancy of the reading public and pointed toward the social upheavals of the decade to come. Edward Bellamy, a former reporter turned novelist, published a novel called *Looking Backward: 2000–1887* in 1888. Its main character, Julian West, had gone to sleep in 1887 and awoke in 2000. In the future he met Doctor Leete who told him how the world had changed during the 113 years he had been asleep. In the new industrial order of "Nationalism," efficiency and discipline had replaced the chaos of the late nineteenth century. Citizens had purpose in their lives. Members of an industrial army, they served the state that in turn provided them with material rewards. Bellamy's argument made sense to many people because it offered the promise of a nation organized for a common purpose in pursuit of abundance without the coercion of government.

Bellamy became an overnight celebrity. *Looking Backward* sold hundreds of thousands of copies. "Nationalist" clubs sprang up to spread his doctrine. The fad ebbed quickly, but Bellamy had struck a chord from a society that was dissatisfied with the way industrialism had changed American life. His evocation of community and cooperative action was appealing in an increasingly competitive, capitalist society. Troubled individuals turned to their faith, to organization, and to political action to deal with their unease about the direction of the nation.

The Social Gospel

Religion offered one answer to the social ills that accompanied industrialism. As businesses grew, many clergymen had defended the inequalities of wealth and status that resulted. However, harsh dogma offended some of the younger members of the ministry who saw the need to improve society rather than to save the souls of individuals. They rebelled against the tenets of Social Darwinism and what they regarded as its indifference to the ills of society. Walter Rauschenbush, a Baptist clergyman in Rochester, New York, had seen at firsthand the hardship and despair experienced by slum dwellers. He believed that it was necessary to "Christianize" the social order so as to bring it "into harmony with the ethical convictions which we identify with Christ." The church, he wrote, must "demand protection for the moral safety of the people."

Rauschenbush's ideas came to be known as the *Social Gospel*. He and other ministers went into the city to preach the Gospel to poor slum dwellers. Washington Gladden spoke out from the First Congregational Church in Columbus, Ohio, and wrote a book entitled *Applied Christianity*, which was published in 1886. "The Christian moralist," he wrote, had to tell "the Christian employer" that the wage system "when it rests on competition as its sole basis is anti-social and anti-Christian." Similar doctrines were promoted within Judaism and Catholicism. The Social Gospel became a strong current in American culture that contributed to the reform tendencies that extended through the 1890s.

Organized Women

Middle-class women spearheaded the reform efforts of the 1890s. The Woman's Christian Temperance Union (WCTU) expanded its role under Frances Willard, its president from 1879 to 1899. Its activities and causes now included missions to the urban poor, prison reform, and protests against male-dominated politics.

During the 1890s social reformers continued their efforts to improve society. Frances Willard of the Woman's Christian Temperance Union sought to unite her organization with the work of the Populists and labor unions in an effort to build a broader coalition for change.

Alcohol reform became a means for many women to engage in other social concerns.

Women who had gained leisure time during the 1880s (see Chapter 17) transformed their literary and discussion clubs into groups with more ambitious agendas. A leading feminist, Charlotte Perkins Gilman, saw clubs as "the first timid steps towards social organization of these so long unsocialized members of our race." In 1890 the General Federation of Women's Clubs (GFWC) was founded, with a core membership of 200 clubs and some 20,000 women on its rolls. The GFWC sponsored cultural and educational activities for working women and homemakers. In Chicago, women's clubs supported the Legal Aid Society and other "child-saving" endeavors to help mothers raise their children in healthier settings.

The campaign to achieve woman suffrage had remained divided after the National Woman Suffrage Association and the American Woman Suffrage Association split over the Fifteenth Amendment and African-American voting rights. The rift was healed through the efforts of Lucy Stone Blackwell, and in 1890 the National American Woman Suffrage Association (NAWSA) was formed. The president was Elizabeth Cady Stanton; Susan B. Anthony succeeded her in 1892. Progress toward suffrage was slow at first. Elections to secure suffrage usually failed, and by the middle of the 1890s only four states (Wyoming, Utah, Colorado, and Idaho) allowed women to vote. Nonetheless, NAWSA provided an important organizational foundation for future growth.

Other reform goals attracted the support of committed women. Josephine Shaw Lowell animated the Charity Organization Society (COS), which sent "friendly visitors" into urban slums to instruct residents and "in great measure prevent the growth of pauperism." Homes were established for the impoverished mother and prostitute where she could obtain "Friends, Food, Shelter and a HELPING HAND by coming just as she is." Florence Kelley of Hull House carried the ideas of the settlement movement into the more ambitious Illinois Women's Alliance in 1892. The New York City Working Women's Society protested harsh working conditions in New York in 1890; its activities led to the formation of Consumers' Leagues in other cities.

While public opinion was not yet ready for a wide-ranging reform movement, these diverse examples of social criticism and constructive action taught lessons about the effects of industrialism that would shape the experience of the coming generation.

LOOKING OUTWARD: FOREIGN POLICY IN THE EARLY 1890S

While some Americans worried about the conditions within the nation's borders, interest in the outside world was also growing. After several decades of internal development, many people thought the United States should play a larger role in world affairs. Their campaign for an expansionist foreign policy gained momentum slowly in the face of ingrained isolationism. Yet the nation could not remain aloof from a world that was becoming more competitive and interdependent. Between 1887 and 1893 the United States took the first steps toward becoming a world power.

In 1889 the United States was not a significant military or diplomatic force. The army was small, consisting of fewer than 25,000 men, who served in isolated posts in the West to protect settlers from the remote possibility of renewed Indian uprisings. The navy was equally insignificant. One congressman called the fleet "an alphabet of floating washtubs." Sails and wooden vessels were the rule until the end of the 1880s when four steel ships were built. During the first Cleveland administration additional modern ships were built and in 1890 Congress appropriated funds for three battleships "designed to carry the heaviest armor and the most powerful ordnance."

Overseas Markets and Foreign Policy

The Census Bureau announced the official closing of the "frontier" in 1890 with the disappearance of a clear line of unsettled territory. As a result, some were concerned that the nation would have to expand internationally. Noting the size of the nation's industrial output, business people and farmers worried about whether the home market could consume everything that factories and farms produced. Perhaps it would become necessary to gain access to overseas markets in order to relieve the pressure. The United States still imported more than it exported; in 1887 exports stood at $810 million, imports at $967 million. Exports fluctuated during the last quarter of the nineteenth century, but the overall trend was gradually upward. By the middle of the 1890s the nation would export more than it imported.

A quest for overseas markets did not drive American foreign policy. While there was much interest in overseas markets, the percentage of the gross national product devoted to exports remained very low. Official economic policy toward foreign trade was protectionist, and proponents of the protective tariff resisted efforts to lower trade barriers in order to expand overseas commerce. Exporters lobbied for expanded foreign trade and reciprocal tariff legislation to lower foreign trade barriers, but their direct impact on policy and diplomatic decisions was less important than the general enthusiasm for a more aggressive policy that they generated.

The Roots of Imperialism

The example of other European powers engaged in a scramble for empire had a greater impact than did economic concerns. As Africa and Asia became colonies and protectorates of Great Britain, Germany, France, and other countries, Americans worried that they would be left behind. Applying the doctrines of Social Darwinism to foreign relations, advocates of empire said that a nation that did not expand would find itself unfit to survive in a competitive and dangerous world.

A leader in the movement for expansion was Captain Alfred T. Mahan of the U.S. Navy. Mahan's research into naval history led to his most important work, *The Influence of Seapower on History, 1660–1783,* published in 1890. More than a military historian, Mahan wanted his country to embark on the path to global greatness, and he believed that seapower was the way to achieve it. Only through naval bases, a powerful battleship fleet, and an aggressive foreign policy could the United States compete in a world of empires. "Whether they will or not," he wrote, "Americans must now begin to look outward." He told policy makers that the United States needed to expand its foreign commerce, construct a strong navy, and acquire overseas bases from which to operate. Of particular concern was a canal across Central America. Secretaries of the Navy from 1889 onward listened to Mahan, as did such future leaders as Senator Henry Cabot Lodge of Massachusetts and Theodore Roosevelt. The admiral enjoyed a worldwide influence for his theories.

The notion of Anglo-Saxon supremacy also fed the new interest in foreign affairs. The Protestant clergyman Josiah Strong contended in *Our Country: Its Pos-*

As secretary of state during the Harrison administration, James G. Blaine pursued an expansionist foreign policy that sought to develop a larger world role for the United States. One of the lasting achievements of his tenure was the Pan-American Union to promote greater unity among the nations of the Western Hemisphere.

sible Future and Its Present Crisis (1885) that "God, with infinite wisdom and skill, is training the Anglo-Saxon race for an hour sure to come in the world's future." The popular author, John Fiske, traversed the country giving a lecture on "Manifest Destiny" that predicted that "every land on the earth's surface" that was not already civilized would become "English in its language, in its religion, in political habits and traditions, and to a predominant extent in the blood of its people." These statements established a context in which expansionism gained popularity.

New Departures During the 1880s

American foreign policy became more activist as the new decade began (see Chapter 16). During the brief administration of James A. Garfield, Secretary of State

James G. Blaine wanted to improve ties with Latin America. One of his goals was to renegotiate the Clayton-Bulwer Treaty (1850) in order to give the United States control over any canal across Central America. Blaine hoped to create a Pan-American system that would promote stability and security in the Caribbean and South America. The end of the Garfield administration took Blaine out of office, and postponed any further action on Pan-Americanism for almost a decade.

The gradual movement toward an expanded foreign policy continued under presidents Chester Arthur and Grover Cleveland. Secretary of State Frederick T. Frelinghuysen pursued treaties for trade reciprocity with nations such as Mexico, Santo Domingo, and Colombia. Much as Blaine had done with South America, Frelinghuysen believed that these treaties would unite the interests of these countries with those of the United States. However, since the pacts involved concessions on the protective tariff policy, Congress declined to act on them.

Under Cleveland, the process slowed as the administration showed less enthusiasm for a canal in Nicaragua or an expanded role around the world. Still, the size and quality of the navy grew during the president's first term. When James G. Blaine returned to the State Department as Benjamin Harrison's secretary of State in 1889, the drive for an expansionist policy resumed.

The Pan-American Impulse

The idea of Pan-Americanism had remained alive during the 1880s, and invitations to a conference were sent out to Latin American countries in 1888. Delegates from nineteen nations gathered in Washington on October 2, 1889, for the first International American Conference. Blaine urged them to support the creation of a customs union and to work out procedures for settling their regional conflicts. Unwilling to accept what seemed to be the dominance of the United States, the conference declined to pursue these initiatives. Instead, they established the International Bureau of the American Republics, which became the Pan-American Union in 1910. Thus, although the conference fell short of Blaine's expectations, it laid the basis for better relations in the Western Hemisphere through the sharing of information and ideas.

Blaine's interest in improving trade with Latin America remained strong. He persuaded his Republi-

can colleagues in Congress to include language allowing for reciprocity treaties in the McKinley Tariff Act of 1890. A number of products were placed on the free list, including sugar, molasses, coffee, and tea, with the understanding that the president could impose tariffs on such items if Latin American countries did not grant the United States similar concessions on its exports. Blaine used the reciprocity clause of the McKinley Tariff to negotiate treaties with South American countries such as Argentina. U.S. exports increased, disproving the claims of critics who warned that it would stifle trade with other nations. Republican protectionists remained cool to Blaine's idea and the Democrats disliked reciprocity as well because it worked within the tariff system. Blaine's initiative indicated how difficult it would be to make an export-driven approach a part of the nation's trade policy.

The Harrison administration pursued a more aggressive foreign policy in two other key areas. Secretary of the Navy Benjamin F. Tracy urged Congress to appropriate money for a battle fleet that would not just protect the coastline of the United States but could engage enemies across the oceans. The lawmakers ultimately authorized four modern battleships, fewer than what Tracy wanted, but nonetheless an expansion of the nation's naval power. Tracy also carried out reforms within the navy that led to more efficient weapons and a better fighting force by the time he left office in 1893.

The Hawaiian Involvement

The United States had long sought to exercise greater influence in Asia. Religious leaders saw China and other Asian nations as sources of potential converts. Business leaders and farmers thought of potential markets for products and crops. In the quest to enter Asia, the Hawaiian Islands seemed a logical stepping-stone. Missionaries had been working in the islands since the 1820s, and their reports fed American fascination with Hawaii. Trade relations between the two countries had become stronger since the Treaty of Reciprocity, signed in 1875, which gave Hawaiian sugar and other products duty-free entry into the United States. In exchange, Hawaii agreed not to grant other countries any concessions that threatened the territorial or economic independence of the islands. Thus, Hawaii had become a virtual American protectorate. The relationship was further strengthened in 1887 when the treaty

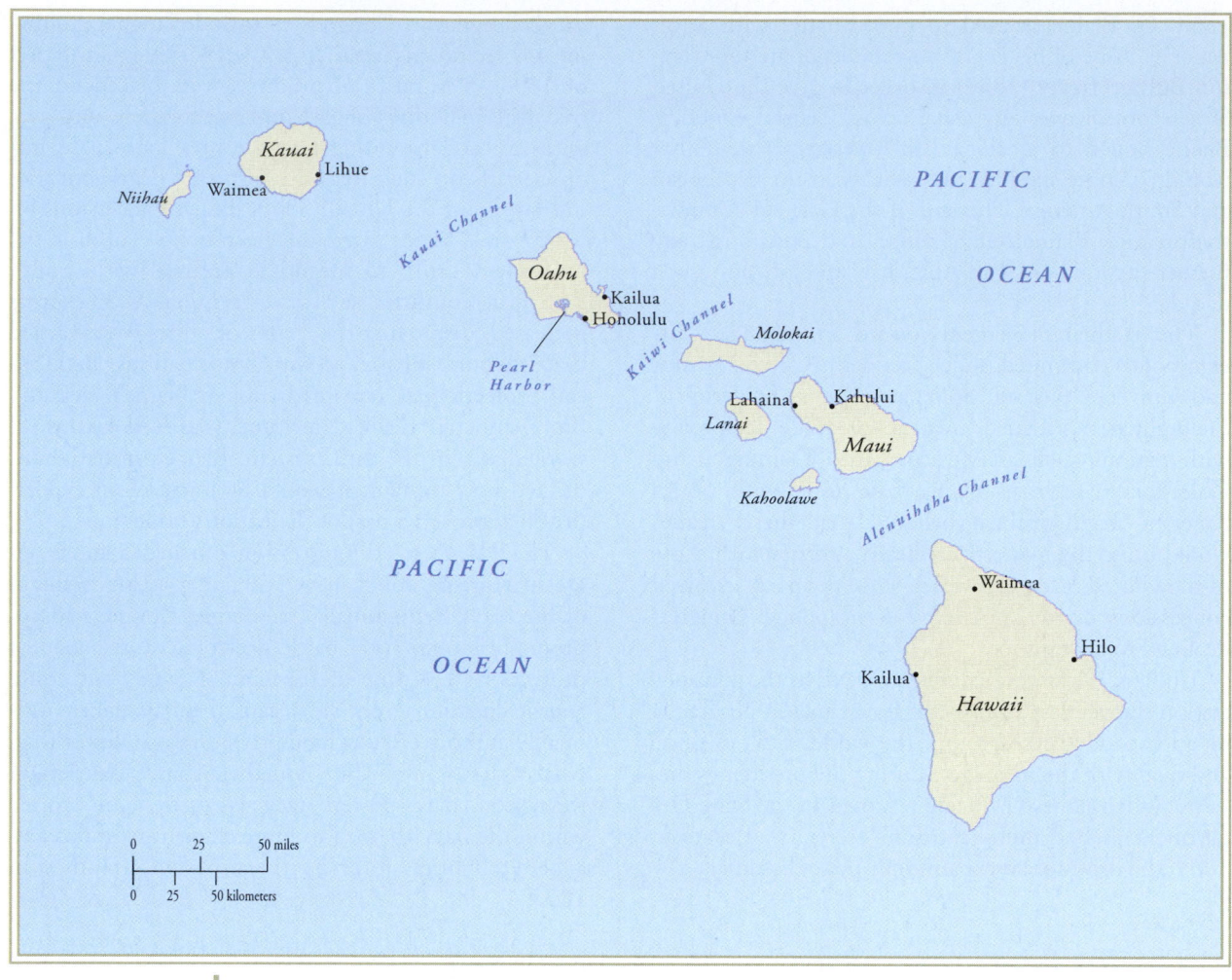

MAP 18.2   HAWAII AND PEARL HARBOR, 1889-1893

was renewed and the United States received the exclusive right to use the superb strategic asset of Pearl Harbor.

Within Hawaii the white settlers and the native rulers clashed over the future of their country. The Hawaiian monarch, King Kalakua, had been inclined to accept the closer ties between the United States and his nation. He died in 1891, bringing to power his sister, Queen Liliuokalani. She resented the American presence in Hawaii and believed that the white minority should not have dominant power.

Hawaiian politics became more complex after the enactment of the McKinley Tariff in 1890 which removed the duty-free status of Hawaiian sugar and granted bounties to American cane producers in

Louisiana and beet sugar growers in the Rocky Mountain states. As a result, the Hawaiian sugar industry slumped and economic conditions on the islands worsened. Americans in Hawaii and in the Congress called for annexation of the islands. Blaine told President Harrison in 1891 that "Hawaii may come up for decision at any unexpected hour, and I hope we shall be prepared to decide it in the affirmative."

The Hawaiian Revolt

The hour came in early 1893. During 1892 the Hawaiian legislature and the queen had argued over the presence and role of foreigners in the country. As

When Americans endeavored to bring the Hawaiian Islands under U.S. control, Queen Liliuokalani led the native Hawaiians in efforts to forestall the end of their independence. Her resistance led the Cleveland administration to block Hawaiian annexation for most of the 1890s.

the new year began, the queen dismissed the legislature and established a constitution that stripped white settlers of many of the powers that they had enjoyed under the existing constitution. Proponents of annexation launched a revolt and called on the U.S. minister (the official representative of the United States in the islands) and the American Navy for help. The coup was successful, helped by 150 U.S. Marines. The queen gave in, and a provisional government was created. "The Hawaiian pear is now fully ripe," said the minister, John L. Stevens, "and this is the golden hour for the United States to pluck it." The United States agreed to a treaty of annexation with the pro-American and predominantly white rebels on February 14,

1893. It looked as if Hawaii would become a possession of the United States. Then the incoming president, Grover Cleveland, said that the treaty should not be ratified until the new administration took office. The Harrison administration ended with the fate of Hawaii still in limbo.

Despite this temporary pause, the extent of American expansion during the Harrison administration was striking. The navy had been increased and its mission broadened. The nation's ties to Latin America had been extended, and the fate of Hawaii seemed to be linked to that of the United States. In the Pacific, the United States had become one of the three participants, with Great Britain and Germany, in a protectorate over the strategic islands of Samoa. Harrison and Blaine had launched the nation on a path of expansion that would be pursued throughout the 1890s. For the moment, however, internal ferment captured the nation's attention as social and political unrest flared in the heartland of the United States.

THE ANGRY FARMERS

Of all the groups who found themselves at odds with the direction of American society between 1887 and 1893, the unhappy farmers of the South and West had the greatest impact on the nation and its political system. The anger of the farm sector first attracted national attention during the elections of 1890.

A Democratic Landslide

In those contests, the Republicans emphasized their achievements in the "Billion Dollar Congress." They confronted an aroused and cohesive Democratic party that took advantage of a host of grievances among voters in the Midwest. Fresh from their victory in the 1888 presidential contest, Republicans in states like Illinois, Wisconsin, and Iowa had pushed an agenda of social change that reflected the party's activist religious sentiments. State legislatures passed laws to implement the prohibition of alcohol. Other measures required that schools chartered by a state teach subjects in English rather than in the languages of immigrant children. Still other laws restricted activities on the

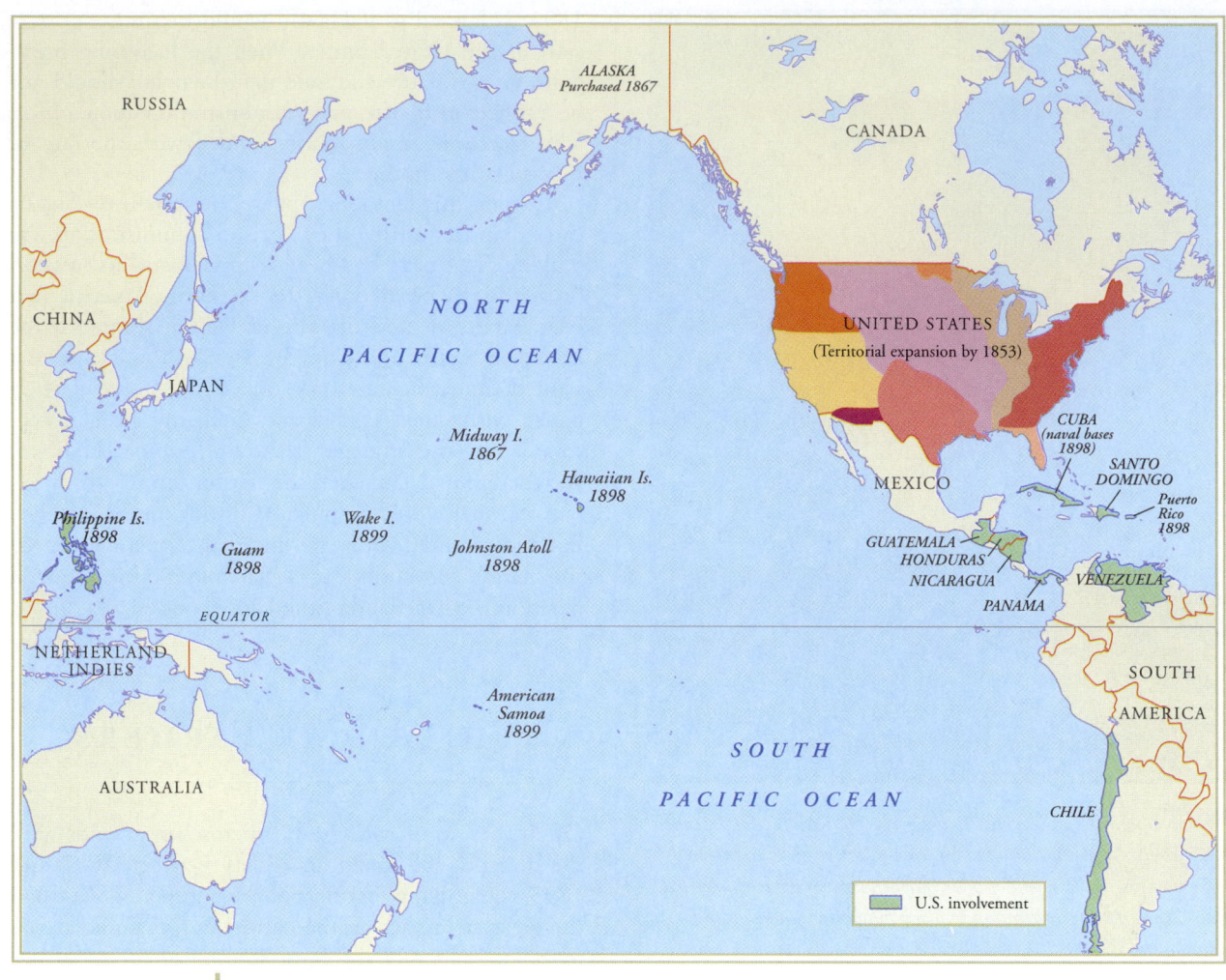

MAP 18.3 | EXPANSION OF THE UNITED STATES

Sabbath. The Democrats realized that they could win the votes of the Catholic and German Lutheran voters who disliked these policies.

An appeal to the pocketbook strengthened the Democratic campaign. Party workers told homemakers that the McKinley tariff would raise the cost of living. The Democrats also tapped into racial fears in the southern and border states about the proposed Federal Elections bill. The results in November 1890 shocked Republicans. Their numbers in the House of Representatives dropped from 166 to 88, while the Democrats controlled 235 seats. Party leaders such as William McKinley of Ohio were defeated, and the chances of President Harrison being reelected in 1892 were jeopardized.

The Rise of the Populists

Political observers, however, noted another striking phenomenon. In addition to the shift in power between the two major parties, a new political force had appeared. Candidates identified with the Farmers Alliance, an agrarian protest group, had made impressive gains in the South and West. When the votes were counted in November 1890, the extent of farmer discontent was clear. Alliance candidates had won nine seats in the House of Representatives; they had also elected two members of the U.S. Senate. In the South, the governors of South Carolina, Georgia, and Tennessee were leaning toward the Alliance. Alliance men dominated a number of southern state legislatures,

POPULIST PARTY PLATFORM 1892

When the Populist Party wrote its platform in 1892, Ignatius Donnelly of Minnesota composed a stringing indictment of the existing political system. His words convey some of the passions that fueled the third party movement during the early 1890s. The reference to isolating voters at the polling places alludes to the use of the secret non-partisan ballot rather than the party-oriented ballots of the earlier years of the Gilded Age.

Preamble

The conditions which surround us best justify our cooperation; we meet in the midst of a nation brought to the verge of moral, political, and material ruin. Corruption dominates the ballot-box, the Legislatures, the Congress, and touches even the ermine of the bench. The people are demoralized; most of the States have been compelled to isolate the voters at the polling places to prevent universal intimidation and bribery. The newspapers are largely subsidized or muzzled, public opinion silenced, business prostrated, homes covered with mortgages, labor impoverished, and the land concentrating in the hands of capitalists. The urban workmen are denied the right to organize for self-protection, imported pauperized labor beats down their wages, a hireling standing army, unrecognized by our laws, is established to shoot them down, and they are rapidly degenerating into European conditions. The fruits of the toil of millions are boldly stolen to build up colossal fortunes for a few, unprecedented in the history of mankind; and the possessors of these, in turn, despise the Republic and endanger liberty. From the same prolific womb of governmental injustice we breed the two great classes—tramps and millionaires. . . .

Assembled on the anniversary of the birthday of the nation, and filled with the spirit of the grand general and chief who established our independence, we seek to restore the government of the Republic to the hands of the "plain people," with which class it originated. We assert our purposes to be identical with the purposes of the National Constitution; to form a more perfect union and establish justice, insure domestic tranquility, provide for the common defence, promote the general welfare, and secure the blessings of liberty for ourselves and our posterity. . . .

and they showed strength in midwestern states such as Kansas, Nebraska, South Dakota, and Minnesota. These gains occurred after fiery campaigns that often resembled "a religious revival, a crusade, a pentecost of politics in which a tongue of flame set upon every man, and each spake as the spirit gave him utterance," according to Elizabeth Barr, a Kansan who was there during the election.

The crisis in southern and western agriculture had been building for decades. The vast expansion of cultivation in the years following the Civil War was a major element in promoting economic hardship. As productivity increased between 1865 and 1885, the prices of farm products declined. A bushel of wheat brought almost $1.20 in 1881 but just under $.70 a bushel in 1889. Cotton was worth almost $.11 a pound in

1881; by 1890 that figure had fallen to $.085 per pound. Farmers had to plant more acreage to cover their costs, but the increased production that resulted further depressed crop prices.

Two other grievances were the debts that farmers owed and the costs of moving their crops to market. During the 1880s western farmers had borrowed from mortgage loan companies in the East to buy land and equipment. Rising land values and stable crop prices made this strategy appear sound. When farm prices declined, however, paying off debts became increasingly difficult. In the South, where sharecropping and farm tenancy tied many farmers to the credit that the "furnish merchants" provided, the slide in cotton prices meant that farmers' debts to the merchant increased each year. Farmers seemed trapped in a cycle of debt and dependence. Their predicament was an international one that was common to farmers in Europe as well during this period. That was scant consolation to those who faced economic ruin.

The Targets of Farm Complaints

Another villain in the eyes of the farmers was the railroad that carried their crops to market. Growers in the plains states complained that the rates they paid were too high and that the railroads discriminated against them in favor of manufacturers and middlemen. The railroads had this power, critics said, because they corrupted the political process. An Alliance orator charged in 1890 that "we are fast becoming entangled in the web of the giant spider which controls our commerce and transportation. We must own the railroads or enough of them to do the necessary carrying."

The system of money and banking also attracted the scorn of western and southern farmers. Every dollar in circulation had to have an equal amount of gold bullion behind it to keep the nation's currency on "the gold standard." Gold was stored in banks and at the U.S. Treasury. International production of gold was static and, as a result, the amount of money in circulation did not keep pace with the growth of the population. The currency became deflated as the value of the dollar appreciated. More and more people were pursuing relatively fewer dollars. Wheat farmers on the plains or cotton growers in the South had to work harder and harder to maintain the same level of income. The thoughts of many farmers naturally turned to ways in which the currency might be inflated — that is, ways of putting more dollars into circulation.

A PARTY OF PATCHES
Grand Balloon Ascension—Cincinnati, May 20th, 1891.

The rise of the Populist party in the South and West puzzled and frightened Americans in the Northeast. A cartoonist for Judge *magazine, a popular journal of the 1890s, depicts some of the leaders of the People's party as engaged in a fanciful balloon ride for their ideas after a meeting in Cincinnati in 1891.*

The complaints of these farmers were genuine and their anger was real. Workable solutions were another matter. Farm prices were low as a result of the expanding acreage under cultivation. One long-term solution was a reduction in the number of farmers and the consolidation of small farms into larger, more efficient agricultural businesses. Such a process would occur later in the nation's history. But at the end of the nineteenth century it ran counter to the widely held belief in the importance of small landowners to the health of a democratic society. Critics of the farm protest movement said that its members overdramatized their plight. While farm prices were dropping, so were those of industrial goods. In many instances the real income of farmers was stable or increasing. However, that was small consolation to a cotton farmer in Texas who lost his property.

The problem of debt was equally complex. Farmers on the plains, for example, had purchased land whose value was expected to increase, and they now faced the ruin of their ventures. Interest rates were not as high as

they believed, nor were mortgage companies as tyrannical as agrarian complaints indicated. The prevailing perception among farmers in the South and West, however, was that they were the victims of a system that took no heed of their needs or interests. "The farmer fed all other men and lived himself upon the scraps," said a sympathetic social critic, Charles Edward Russell. As a result, discontented agrarians looked eagerly at proposals that would relieve them of their debt burden.

The farm protest that began during the late 1880s was not a national movement. In more settled regions of the nation, such as the farm areas of New York, Ohio, or Wisconsin, growers had easier access to markets, more varied crops to sell, and little sense of a shared identity with their counterparts in Kansas or Alabama. Facing competition from Canadian products, these farmers often supported the same tariff policies that were denounced in political rallies in South Dakota or Texas.

The Farmers Alliance

The campaign to improve the lives of southern and western farmers had begun during the 1870s (see Chapter 16) and slowly gathered momentum for more than a decade. The Patrons of Husbandry (the Grange) had been active between the late 1860s and the end of the 1870s when economic recovery from the Panic of 1873 eased the sense of crisis among farmers. The Farmers Alliance had been formed in Texas to stop horse thieves in Lampasas County. After some early troubles, it had emerged as the Texas Farmers Alliance in 1884, and its membership had soon begun to grow. Elsewhere in the South, in Arkansas, Louisiana, and South Carolina, angry farmers had organized into alliances and associations that expressed their grievances.

The proposed solutions went through three broad stages. In the first phase the southern and western farmers looked toward cooperative action. A leader in this effort was a Texan named Charles W. Macune. A self-taught doctor and lawyer, Macune became president of the Texas Alliance in 1886. He wanted to build on local alliances to set up Alliance exchanges and cooperatives across the South. The theory was that these institutions could provide farmers with supplies and equipment at a cost below what the "furnish merchants" and local retailers charged. They would also enable the farmers to gain greater control over the marketplace. To spread the creed of the cooperatives, the Alliance relied on individual organizers or "lecturers" who fanned out across the region. Newspapers that supported the Alliance cause reprinted speeches and letters stating the complaints of agrarians and the merits of cooperation. Countless farm families read these documents, and the Alliance claimed hundreds of thousands of members on its rolls.

Cooperatives proved easier to organize than to sustain. Marketing crops at a time other than harvest season required capital because it was necessary to store the crops until prices rose. The farmers did not have the resources to make such a scheme work. It also proved difficult to obtain the lower prices sought by the cooperatives. A complex distribution system moved goods across the country and that process had certain inherent costs no matter who controlled it. Farm cooperatives lacked the capital to compete with larger wholesalers such as Montgomery Ward and Sears, Roebuck. By 1889 it was evident that cooperatives alone could not solve the problems of the southern and western farmer.

The Rising Tide of Farm Protest

While economic success eluded the Alliance between 1886 and 1890, its political power grew. The ideology of cooperative action appealed to farm families who often were isolated from one another. The Alliance meetings brought farmers together to hear speeches, enjoy entertainment, and share experiences. The Alliance thus built on shared emotion among farmers as the 1890s began. Its members told each other that they were part of a mass movement that could reshape the way the nation treated its rural citizens.

Some members of the Alliance saw African-American farmers as potential allies. The Colored Farmers' National Alliance and Cooperative Union was formed in 1886 and had as many as 250,000 members by 1891. Leaders of the group said that it "is the only thing that will give us protection for our labor and crops." Cooperation between the black Alliance and its white counterpart was uneasy. Whites were usually landowners, even if impoverished ones; blacks tended to be either tenants or farm laborers. The problem was revealed in 1891 when the Colored Alliance tried to get higher wages for cotton picking. A strike for that purpose, organized by a black leader named Ben

Patterson in Lee County, Arkansas, was met with violence. Fifteen of the strikers, including Patterson, were lynched, and the Colored Alliance vanished.

While the Alliance had been growing in the South, it had also put down roots in the states of the Great Plains. As the farm depression worsened during years of drought and falling crop prices, branches of the Alliance gained members in the Dakotas, Nebraska, and especially Kansas. By 1889 it was apparent that concerted national action was a logical next step if the state alliances could join forces effectively. Representatives of these various organizations met at St. Louis in December 1889. Out of their deliberations came the National Farmers' Alliance and Industrial Union. The delegates agreed to leave out the word "white" from the organization's requirements, although state organizations in the South could continue to exclude black members. There was also disagreement over whether secrecy should remain a key element in attracting new members. Nevertheless, three key northern states, Kansas and the two Dakotas, joined the national organization.

The Subtreasury Plan

Charles Macune offered the most important policy proposal of the conference, the *subtreasury plan.* Macune recognized that the major problem that confronted cotton and wheat farmers was having to sell their crops at a time of the year when prices were at their lowest point. To get around this obstacle, he envisioned a system of government warehouses or subtreasuries where farmers could store their crops until prices went up. To bridge the months between storage and selling, the farmers would receive a certificate of deposit from the warehouse for 80 percent of the crop's existing market value. The charge for this service would be a 1 or 2 percent annual interest rate. Farmers would sell the crops for higher prices, repay their loans, and keep the resulting profits.

The subtreasury plan addressed the marketing and currency problems of staple crop farmers, but it had some weaknesses. If a majority of wheat or cotton farmers waited until prices rose and then sold their crops, the market glut would force prices down again. The certificates that the farmers would have received for storing their crops at the subtreasury warehouses would represent another form of paper money. The policy would have led to some inflation of the cur-

rency, but no one could have predicted how much inflation would result. Beyond that, the idea involved a large expansion of governmental power in an era when suspicion of federal power was still strong. Nevertheless, to its agrarian advocates, the subtreasury seemed to be a plausible answer to the harsh conditions they confronted. It would, they claimed, "emancipate productive labor from the power of money to oppress."

The Alliance in the 1890 Election

During the 1890 election, the protest movement poured out its energy in speeches throughout Kansas and other friendly states. The Alliance attracted much attention. In Kansas it represented an entirely new third party that challenged the supremacy of the

The People's party used women to recruit new members and thus gave them a greater opportunity to be heard in political life. One of the most celebrated and controversial figures was Mary Elizabeth Lease of Kansas, here shown in a publicity photo for a lecturing career.

The nature of political campaigning was changing as the 1890s started. In the 1892 election this centerfold from Judge *announces the allegiance of the Republican magazine. The older style of marching men and campaign spectacles was giving way to advertising and the use of magazines to convey political messages.*

Republicans and Democrats. A candidate for Congress, Jeremiah Simpson of Kansas, attacked an aristocratic opponent known as "Prince Hal." Princes, Simpson said, "wear silk socks. I don't wear any." From that moment on he was known as "Sockless Jerry Simpson."

At a time when women took little direct part in politics, the Alliance allowed some female speakers to address audiences. One of them, Annie Diggs, was born in Canada, grew up in the Northeast, and came to Kansas during the 1870s. After some years in the East, she was working for a Topeka, Kansas, newspaper as the 1890 campaign got underway. Her speeches proved crowd-pleasers. Even more charismatic was Mary Elizabeth Lease. Her enemies changed her middle name to Ellen, which rhymed with "Yellin." She coined several phrases that became memorable parts of the agrarian cause. Kansas farmers, she said, should "raise less wheat and corn, and more hell." Whether she actually uttered the words or reporters put them in her mouth did not matter. It was, she later remarked "a right good bit of advice."

The Alliance's success in electing congressmen and state legislators in the South and West led their leaders to consider mounting a third party campaign during the next presidential election. To ponder this important decision, they gathered in Ocala, Florida, in early December 1890. Their platform became known as the Ocala Demands. They included the subtreasury program, abolition of private banks, regulation of transportation facilities, and the free and unlimited coinage of silver into money at a fixed ratio to gold. Other planks asked for an income tax, restrictions on aliens owning land in the United States, and election of U.S. senators by the people rather than by state legislatures. The Alliance did not decide to become a third party. That issue was put off until February 1892 to allow the legislatures that had been elected with Alliance support to show what they could accomplish.

During the ensuing months the economic situation of southern farmers worsened. Cotton prices fell sharply and the Alliance lost members. Facing increasing hostility from Democrats in the South, the Alliance men looked more favorably on the idea of forming a third party. The national meeting scheduled for February 1892 appeared to present an opportunity to assemble a political party to contest the presidency. There was already a name for the new party: the People's party, or Populists.

The People's Party

The delegates met in St. Louis and quickly decided in favor of forming a third party. The Populists' first national convention would be held in Omaha, Nebraska, on a symbolic date, July 4, 1892. Their prospective candidate was Leonidas L. Polk, a North Carolinian who could bridge the gap between northern and southern Populists. But Polk died suddenly on June 11, 1892. His demise left the party without a national figure and "the one man in the country who can break the Solid South." With Polk gone, the Omaha Convention chose James B. Weaver, a long-time third party politician from Iowa. His running mate was James G. Field of Virginia. The ticket was not a strong one, consisting of "old time agitators with new hopes."

The party's platform took a stern view of the state of the nation in 1892. Written by Ignatius Donnelly, a long-time rebel against traditional politics, it proclaimed that "We meet in the midst of a nation brought to the verge of moral, political, and material ruin. Corruption dominates the ballot box, the legislatures, the Congress, and touches even the ermine of the bench." The specific planks echoed what had been said at Ocala. They endorsed the subtreasury, free coinage of silver, and other reform proposals.

From the Subtreasury to Free Silver

By 1892 it was evident that Congress was not going to implement the subtreasury plan. Attention turned instead to another Populist proposal that commanded wide support: free coinage of silver. The deflationary effects of the gold standard had aroused intense resentment. To expand the currency, raise prices, reduce the weight of debt on those who owed money, the best solution, Populists contended, would be to base the nation's currency on both gold and silver. If silver were coined into money at a ratio of sixteen to one with gold, there would soon be ample money in circulation.

The country needed controlled inflation. However, the market price of silver stood at more like twenty-five to one, relative to gold. A policy of free coinage would lift the price of the white metal in an artificial way. As a result, people would hoard gold, silver thus would continue to lose value, and inflation would accelerate. Meanwhile, if the nation went off the gold standard its foreign trade would also suffer because international transactions were handled in gold.

Partisans still made sporting wagers on the outcome of elections. In Joseph Klir's painting, The Lost Bet, *a defeated Republican pulls his victorious Democratic rival through the streets of Chicago while a large crowd of happy Democrats looks on.*

The Populists rejected these arguments. They maintained that "money can be created by the government in any desired quantity, out of any substance, with no basis but itself." The idea of crop supports underlying the subtreasury plan and the manipulation of the money supply that could be achieved through free coinage of silver advocated would become common ideas during the twentieth century. But in 1892 they seemed radical to many Americans.

THE PRESIDENTIAL ELECTION OF 1892

The Republicans and Democrats had watched the emergence of Populism with a mixture of bewilderment and apprehension. They sensed that something important was happening and wondered how to re-

Labor unrest marked the election of 1892. The most famous incident occurred in Homestead, Pennsylvania, in the company town that housed workers of Andrew Carnegie's steel mills.

spond. For the moment, the familiar routines of political life went on. The elections of 1890 had left the Republicans shocked at their losses and aware that President Harrison was not a strong candidate for re-election. His cold personality alienated fellow party members who felt that Republicans should not have to "live four years more in a dripping cave." The alternative to Harrison was Blaine, and he made a brief run at the nomination during the spring of 1892. It was a doomed effort, however, and Harrison was unenthusiastically renominated.

The Democrats felt more confident. Their candidate was Grover Cleveland, who had kept himself in the public eye during his four years out of office. He easily won a third nomination from his party. Although he strongly favored the gold standard, he did not stress the point. Some party leaders in the South and West saw silver as the answer to the depression and the threat of populism. Cleveland muted his real beliefs to keep these Democrats willing to vote for him. In some western states the Democrats and the Populists struck deals and "fused" their two tickets, with Cleveland getting the electoral votes and the Populists electing state candidates.

The 1892 campaign was quiet on the surface. The political tradition at that time said that incumbent presidents should not make a formal reelection campaign. Such an outright seeking of votes would be undignified. As a result, Harrison did not make speeches. That suited his challenger as well, and Cleveland stayed home too. The two parties pitched their appeals more to educated voters who now read pamphlets and avoided rallies. The intense, military-style campaigning of the post–Civil War era, with the ranks of marching men parading through the streets, was passing from the scene. In many states there was talk about an unusually calm election.

The Homestead Strike

One significant event cast doubt on that judgment and revealed the social tensions lying beneath the surface of politics. For workers at Andrew Carnegie's Homestead steel works outside Pittsburgh, Pennsylvania, the summer of 1892 was a time of misery and violence. The manager of the plant, Henry Clay Frick, cut wages and refused to negotiate with skilled workers who had unionized their craft. A strike resulted and violence broke out when Pinkerton detectives stormed through the town of Homestead to allow strikebreakers to retake the mills. Detectives and workers died in the ensuing battle and state troops came in to restore order.

A few weeks later, an anarchist named Alexander Berkman shot and stabbed Frick. The industrialist survived his wounds, however, and the strike was broken. The walkout became a political issue that the Democrats exploited to their advantage. One of their posters said: "The cock will crow in '92, Over Fort Frick and

A Populist leader, Thomas E. Watson of Georgia, argued that blacks and whites in the South should join to fight their common enemies in the early 1890s. Later in life he abandoned his racial tolerance and became an ardent exponent of segregation and racial violence.

the Pinkerton crew." The Homestead strike seemed to many people to embody the tensions between capital and labor that industrialism had fostered.

The Populist Campaign

The Populists tried to make the same argument about the struggle between agriculture and capital. Weaver drew big crowds, but the Democrats in the South subjected him to personal abuse and accused the third party of promoting black rule and a return to Reconstruction. As a result, Weaver and his wife were pelted with rotten eggs and tomatoes; "Mrs. Weaver was made a regular walking omelet by the southern chivalry of Georgia," said Mary Lease. Other Populist campaigners attracted similar attention. Thomas E. Watson of Georgia had emerged as one of the leaders of the cause. Elected to Congress in 1890, he urged black and white farmers of the South to unite to fight

their common enemy. His goal was "to destroy *class rule* and to restore to the people the government."

Democrats in the South turned weapons of intimidation and violence against their Populist foes. Watson's reelection campaign failed when the Democrats stuffed the ballot boxes. In the town of Augusta, his opponent won twice as many votes as there were registered voters. Other Populist candidates were counted out because the Democrats controlled the election machinery. Blacks who might have voted for the People's party candidate as the lesser of two bad choices were coerced to stay away from the polls. When the votes were counted, the Democrats had held the South solid for Grover Cleveland. Populists had won some local

The Columbian Exposition of 1892–1893 marked the 400th anniversary of the landing of Christopher Columbus. The "Great White City" in Chicago symbolized the progress of the nation and its technological accomplishments. The outbreak of the Panic of 1893 dulled the luster of the occasion for many Americans.

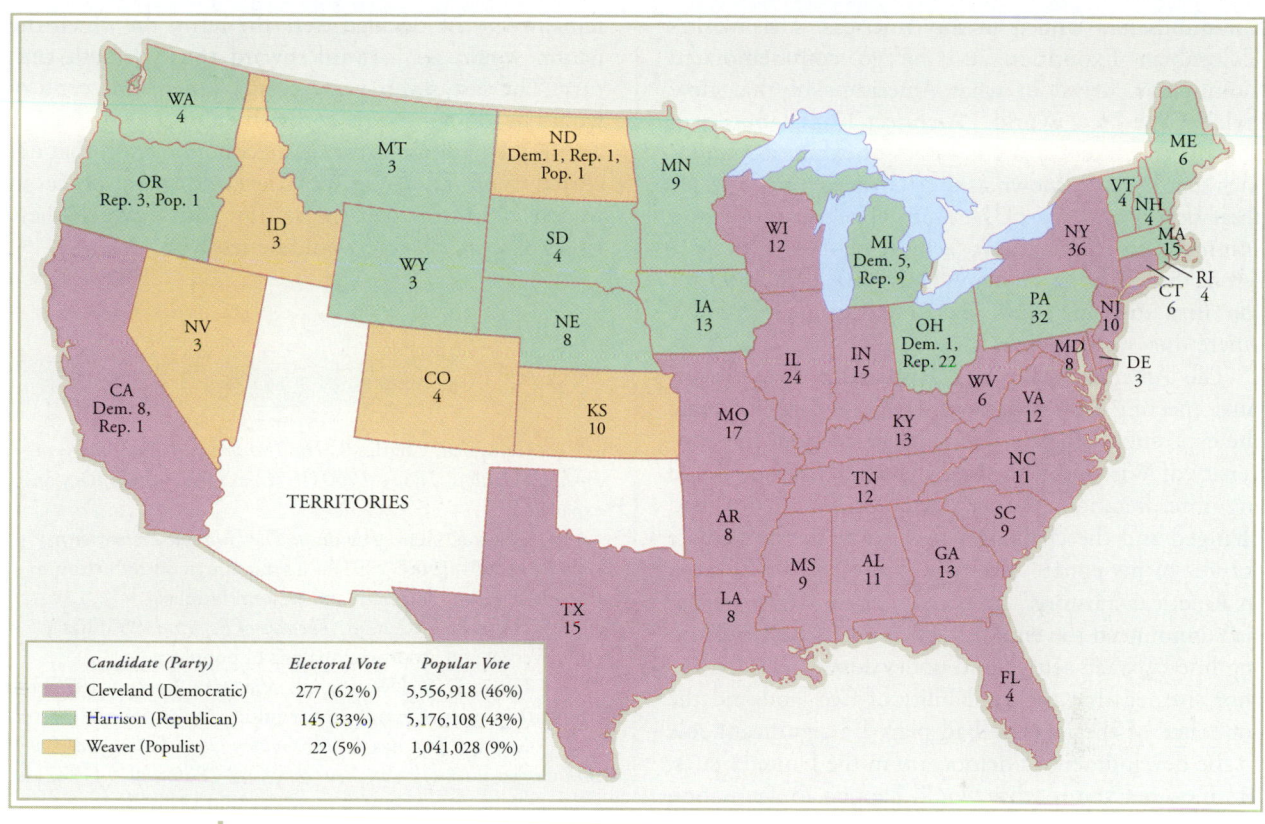

Candidate (Party)	Electoral Vote	Popular Vote
Cleveland (Democratic)	277 (62%)	5,556,918 (46%)
Harrison (Republican)	145 (33%)	5,176,108 (43%)
Weaver (Populist)	22 (5%)	1,041,028 (9%)

MAP 18.4 | THE ELECTION OF 1892

offices in the region, but the Democrats were still dominant.

The Election Results

On the national level, Cleveland gained a second term by a decisive margin. His plurality over Harrison was almost 400,000 votes, and he won in the electoral college with 277 votes to 145 for the Republicans. The Democrats also controlled both houses of Congress for the first time since before the Civil War. Weaver carried three states and won electoral votes in three additional states for a total of twenty-two electoral votes. His popular vote total reached just over 1 million. The spirit that had driven the Populists was far from dead after the 1892 election, but in fact the movement had reached its high-water mark.

For the moment, it appeared as if the Democrats had emerged as the majority party from the long stalemate of 1874–1890. "The Republican party is going,

or at any rate may presently go, to pieces," wrote a college professor named Woodrow Wilson. The Democrats had captured the mood of discontent that was sweeping the country during the early 1890s. They had resisted Republican activism and an expanded role for the federal government. It remained to be seen how Cleveland would carry out the mandate to satisfy the many groups that had deserted the Republicans and appease the restless farmers who had supported Weaver and the Populists.

THE "GREAT WHITE CITY"

The American economy was in trouble at the beginning of 1893. Distracting the nation's attention from the gloomy forecasts was the prospect of a large popular spectacle that would sum up the state of civilization in the United States 400 years after Christopher

Columbus had landed in the Americas. The World's Columbian Exposition in Chicago commemorated Columbus's arrival in what Americans of that time styled "The New World." Architect Daniel Burnham and his coworkers created a series of exhibition buildings that became known as the "Great White City" for their beauty and artistic harmony. The exposition also summed up the nation's achievements. "Chicago," wrote the historian Henry Adams, "asked in 1893 for the first time whether the American people knew where they were driving."

The American Historical Association held its annual meeting in Chicago in 1893 to commemorate the exposition. There a young historian from the University of Wisconsin, Frederick Jackson Turner, offered his interpretation of how the United States had changed and the challenges it faced in the immediate future. In his paper "The Significance of the Frontier in American History," he noted that the 1890 Census had announced the end of the frontier as a clear dividing line between settled and undeveloped areas. Its author stressed that the availability of free land and the influence of the frontier had played a significant role in the development of democracy in the United States. He inquired about what would happen to the nation now that the possibility of free land and a new life in the West was vanishing. Turner's "frontier thesis" became a powerful and controversial explanation of the way the nation had developed.

CONCLUSION

As the 1890s approached their midpoint Americans sensed that the country faced important new challenges. The end of western settlement was one important element. So too was the rise of large cities and the attraction they exerted on the rural countryside. "The tendency is away from the farm and away from the rural districts," said James B. Weaver. "The trend is toward the city, where the needy congregate and where crime becomes organized and where the Republic is stabbed."

By 1893, however, such a simple choice between urban and rural life no longer existed. The country and the city had become interdependent in their need for products and services. There was no returning to the simpler republic for which so many longed. What

remained to be decided were the terms on which the nation would go forward toward the twentieth century. The last seven years of the nineteenth century would be among the most divisive and controversial as any in the nation's history. An economic crash that occurred soon after Grover Cleveland took office in March 1893 provided the setting within which these issues of social change would be resolved.

RECOMMENDED READINGS

Campbell, Charles S. *The Transformation of American Foreign Relations, 1865–1900* (1976) examines diplomacy and expansion.

Clanton, Gene. *Populism: The Humane Preference in America, 1890–1900* (1991) is a sympathetic introduction to the unrest among southern and western farmers.

Hofstadter, Richard. *The Age of Reform* (1955) has a controversial and absorbing analysis of populism.

Howe, Daniel Walker, ed., *Victorian America* (1976) is a stimulating series of essays on the culture of the period.

Kessner, Thomas A. *The Golden Door: Italian and Jewish Immigrant Mobility in New York City, 1880–1915* (1977) is a fine account of how the immigrants adjusted to their new home.

Mohl, Raymond A. *The New City: Urban America in the Industrial Age, 1865–1920* (1985) offers a thorough treatment of the growth of the cities.

Woodward, C. Vann. *The Strange Career of Jim Crow* (1955) became a controversial analysis of the origins of segregation in the South.

Socolofsky, Homer and Spetter, Allan B. *The Presidency of Benjamin Harrison* (1989), looks at events from the perspective of the White House.

Utley, Robert. *The Last Days of the Sioux Nation* (1963) is thorough and moving on the Battle of Wounded Knee.

Williams, R. Hal. *Years of Decision: American Politics in the 1890s* (1993) is an excellent introduction to the decade.

Politics

Calhoun, Charles W., ed., *The Gilded Age: Essays on the Origins of Modern America* (1996).

Jensen, Richard J. *The Winning of the Midwest: Social and Political Conflict, 1889–1896* (1971).

Kleppner, Paul. *The Cross of Culture: A Social Analysis of Midwestern Politics, 1850–1900* (1970).

Kousser, J. Morgan. *The Shaping of Southern Politics: Suffrage Restriction and the Establishment of the One-Party South, 1880–1910* (1974).

McGerr, Michael E. *The Decline of Popular Politics: The American North, 1865–1928* (1986).

Populism

Goodwyn, Lawrence. *Democratic Promise: The Populist Moment in America* (1976).

Hicks, John D. *The Populist Revolt* (1961).

McMath, Robert C. *American Populism: A Social History, 1877–1898* (1989).

McNall, Scott G. *The Road to Rebellion: Class Formation and Kansas Populism, 1865–1900* (1988).

Woodward, C. Vann. *Tom Watson: Agrarian Rebel* (1938).

Cities

Cronon, William. *Nature's Metropolis: Chicago and the Great West* (1991).

Melosi, Martin V., ed., *Pollution and Reform in American Cities, 1870–1930* (1981).

Miller, Zane. *The Urbanization of Modern America: A Brief History* (1973).

Teaford, John C. *The Unheralded Triumph: City Government in America, 1870–1900* (1984).

Warner, Sam Bass. *Streetcar Suburbs: The Process of Growth in Boston* (1970).

Immigration

Dinnerstein, Leonard, Roger L. Nichols, and David M. Reimers, *Natives and Strangers* (1989).

Higham, John. *Strangers in the Land: Patterns of American Nativism, 1860–1925* (1955).

Kraut, Alan M. *The Huddled Masses: The Immigrant in American Society, 1880–1921* (1982).

Takaki, Ronald. *Strangers from a Different Shore: A History of Asian Americans* (1989).

Foreign Affairs

Beisner, Robert L. *From the Old Diplomacy to the New, 1865–1900* (1975).

La Feber, Walter. *The New Empire: An Interpretation of American Expansion, 1860–1898* (1963).

Tate, Merze. *The United States and the Hawaiian Kingdom: A Political History* (1965).

COXEY'S ARMY ON THE MARCH

The industrial armies of out-of-work Americans moved toward Washington during the spring of 1894 to protest the economic conditions arising out of the Panic of 1893. Colonel Jacob S. Coxey is mounted on the white horse on the left as his marchers string out behind him. Note the interested spectators as "army" goes by.

Chapter 19

DOMESTIC TURMOIL AND OVERSEAS EXPANSION, 1893–1901

DURING THE 1890s the social problems accumulating since the Civil War reached crisis proportions. An economic depression that began in 1893 sent shockwaves throughout the country as Americans struggled with the effects of four years of hard times. With millions out of work and faith in the institutions of the nation at a low point, the major political parties looked for solutions that would satisfy voters. In the middle part of the decade, the Republicans emerged as the majority party, with the divided Democrats in disarray and the Populists unable to transform their protest into a viable third party. The election of 1896 brought William McKinley to the White House, the architect of Republican success. He revitalized the presidency after its eclipse since the death of Abraham Lincoln.

As the condition of the economy improved at the end of the 1890s, Americans looked outward to an empire in the Caribbean and the Pacific. A war with Spain brought territorial gains and a debate about whether overseas possessions meant fundamental change. World power seemed alluring and troubling at the same time. By 1900, the United States had assumed a world role. American institutions and leaders faced the challenge of the new responsibilities.

THE PANIC OF 1893 AND ITS CONSEQUENCES

Grover Cleveland began his second term as president on March 4, 1893. In May 1893 the weakened economy went into a collapse that became known as the Panic of 1893. The depression that followed lasted for four years.

Business had expanded during the late 1880s. In 1891 and 1892, investors turned cautious, worried about the soundness of the banking system and the stability of the currency. Banks failed as depositers pulled out their funds and hoarded cash. A decline in export trade further strained the economy. Individuals cut back on purchases and sought to protect their investments. Business activity slowed, workers were laid off, and businesses cut back on production. The devastating effects of bad times spread across the country.

Effects of the Depression

By the end of 1893, some 600 banks had failed and 119 railroads were bankrupt and being run by

CHRONOLOGY

1893 Grover Cleveland inaugurated as president

Panic of 1893 begins four years of depression

Sherman Silver Purchase Act repealed

National League of Colored Women established

1894 Coxey's army marches on Washington

Pullman strike occurs

Republicans make major gains in elections

Radcliffe College for women opens in Cambridge, Massachusetts

1895 Booker T. Washington proposes "Atlanta Compromise"

Coin's Financial School published

Venezuelan crisis brings threat of war with British

Utah adopts woman suffrage

Stephen Crane's *The Red Badge of Courage* published

1896 Republicans nominate William McKinley

William Jennings Bryan delivers "Cross of Gold" speech

Bryan receives Democratic and Populist presidential nominations

Trading stamps are offered by stores in the United States

McKinley wins presidential election

Plessy v. *Ferguson* decision endorses racial segregation

1897 Dingley Tariff enacted

Jell-O is introduced

1898 Battleship *Maine* explodes in Havana harbor

United States and Spain go to war

Treaty of Paris ends war and United States obtains Philippines and Puerto Rico

1899 Insurrection in Philippines begins

Open Door Policy toward China announced

1900 McKinley and Bryan each renominated for presidency

Republicans win presidential election

International Ladies Garment Workers Union founded

Olds Motor Works begins mass producing cars

court-appointed receivers. Estimates were that 15,000 businesses had closed. The stock market lost hundreds of millions of dollars. Most important, by early January 1894, 2.5 million people were unemployed. The economy was functioning at only three-quarters of its capacity.

The depression fell hardest on the average workers and their families. The expansion of industry meant that workers had become more dependent on the jobs that corporations provided. When these jobs vanished, there were no unemployment insurance payments, no government benefits, no temporary jobs programs to bridge the gap between a living wage and poverty.

States and cities endeavored to provide some relief for those out of work. In New York, daily newspapers distributed food, clothing, and fuel to the needy. Charity organization societies in Boston, New York, and Chicago coordinated volunteer efforts. However, these private endeavors did not meet the needs of most of the unemployed. Most well-off Americans believed the federal government should not intervene to alleviate a depression. As a result, people slept in the parks, camped out in railroad stations, and sought food at the soup kitchens that appeared in the big cities. Angry poor people called the soup kitchens "Cleveland Cafés." One newspaper wrote at the end of the first year of the depression "Thank the Lord! 1893 is in the hands of a receiver."

To deal with the economic slump, Cleveland proposed a simple solution: repeal of the Sherman Silver

Purchase Act of 1890. That law had specified that the government buy a fixed amount of silver each month. Cleveland argued that the law produced inflation, undermined business confidence, and caused investors to take money out of the nation's gold reserve at the Treasury Department. If the amount of the reserve fell below $100 million it would be regarded as a sign that the credit of the United States was in danger. In fact, the amount was largely a psychological issue and did not measure the nation's economic condition. To people in 1893, however, it was a crucial symbol of national confidence in the nation's credit. Accordingly, the president regarded repeal of the law as the key to ending the Panic.

In August 1893 Cleveland called a special session of Congress to repeal the Sherman Act. His own party was badly split over the issue of money. In the 1892 presidential campaign Cleveland had left his position on silver unclear; now he had to face the issue directly. Northeastern party members believed in the gold standard with what resembled religious fervor. In the South and Far West, Democrats argued with equally passionate conviction that what the nation needed was more money in circulation through the free and unlimited coinage of silver into money at the fixed ratio to gold of sixteen to one. By asking his party to repeal the Sherman Act, Cleveland was inviting Democrats to wage war against each other. He put off the tariff issue, on which most Democrats agreed, until they had settled the monetary issue, on which disagreement was intense.

The Special Session

Congress convened for its special session in August 1893, with the international economic climate running against silver. All of Europe was on the gold standard. In India the government had shut its mints to silver. Mexico alone allowed silver to be coined freely. Over the protests of his party and with no tolerance of compromise, Cleveland insisted that Congress repeal the Sherman Act. With the aid of Republican votes, he won the battle. The bill repealing the Sherman Act was signed into law on November 1, 1893. The struggle left the Democrats badly split.

Having blamed the Sherman Act for the depression, Cleveland had staked his party's political future on a turnaround in the economy. It did not come.

There were some short-term benefits. Confidence in the dollar grew and the flow of gold out of the country eased somewhat. But prosperity did not return. As the new year approached, there was no evidence of better times ahead. Every indicator seemed headed downward. More railroads failed, more businesses closed, and more people were laid off to join the millions who were already unemployed. "A strange blight fell upon the country," commented one newspaper and "fear spread like a pall over a hitherto prosperous land."

The Tariff Disaster

The Democrats now had to deal with the tariff issue that they had postponed. Their control over Congress was precarious, especially in the Senate. Cleveland had also submitted two unsuccessful Supreme Court nominations and these had worsened his relations with the Senate. As a result, Senate Democrats had to write a tariff bill that in some instances raised customs rates on key products such as sugar, coal, and iron. The law fell far short of the tariff reform that the Democrats had promised in 1892.

Congress finally passed the Wilson–Gorman Tariff Act in August 1894. It reduced rates on wool, copper and lumber, and raised duties on many other items. The measure repealed the reciprocal trade provisions of the McKinley Tariff which had aimed at opening up markets and (easing the political costs of protection). To make up for lost revenues, the Wilson–Gorman bill added a modest tax on personal incomes. Disgusted with the outcome, Cleveland let the bill become law without his signature. Weary Democrats in Congress admitted that the unpopular law was the best that they could do under existing political circumstances.

The Industrial Armies

Outside of Washington, 1894 was a year of unrest. As the hard times lingered, some of the unemployed decided to present their grievances to the nation's leaders. Those out of work wandered across the country seeking some haven where they could find a job or help. Their presence frightened the nervous middle class who saw in these tramps the possibility of violence and revolution.

Some of the unemployed formed "Coxey's Army," uniting behind Jacob S. Coxey, a businessman from Massillon, Ohio. On Easter Sunday 1894 he left for Washington with 300 supporters to petition for a program of road building paid for by $500 million of paper money. Coxey and his son, "Legal Tender Coxey," headed the procession, which included more than forty reporters covering the protest. Slowly and painfully, the "Commonweal Army of Christ" approached Washington.

Across the nation other armies of the unemployed moved toward the capital. They rode the rails, marched through cities, and demanded jobs from the government. The climax for Coxey and his followers came on May 1, 1894, when they reached Capitol Hill and tried to present their demands to Congress. Police intercepted Coxey, clubbed him and then arrested him for trespassing and "walking on the grass." The other armies were discouraged and dispersed. However, the spectacle of so much protest undermined the political credibility of the Cleveland administration.

The Pullman Strike

Even more devastating to the president was the major railroad strike that erupted shortly after the Coxey episode ended. George Pullman, the developer of the railroad sleeping car, had created a model town outside Chicago where his employees were to live in apparent comfort and serenity. Pullman, Illinois, was often cited as an example of how a "company town" could see to every need of the worker and thus eliminate the need for unions or strikes. Employees who lived in Pullman and worked for the Pullman Palace Car Company experienced a reality that was far different from the rosy picture of life in the "model" town. "When we die," a worker observed, "we shall be buried in the Pullman cemetery and go to the Pullman hell." The prices workers paid for services often ran 10 percent above what was charged in other communities.

When Pullman laid off employees and trimmed wages for others, he did not reduce the rents that his workers paid. As a result, in May 1894 the workers

When the U.S. Army went in to control the Pullman Strike in July 1894, the soldiers used force to coerce the strikers. The artist Frederic Remington recorded the military tactics under the pointed title "Giving the Butt."

went out on strike. The strikers asked railroad workers across the nation not to handle Pullman's cars as a gesture of sympathy with the walkout. The response from the American Railway Union (ARU) and its president, Eugene Victor Debs, was cautious at first. But by late June the ARU started a sympathetic boycott and decided not to move trains that had Pullman cars attached to them.

A National Railroad Strike

At its height the strike involved 125,000 men representing twenty railroads. The commerce of the nation stalled as freight shipments backed up in stations and train yards. The ARU did not interfere with the mails lest that action arouse the opposition of the federal government. Their economic power could not match that of the railroads' General Managers' Association, which had influence with Cleveland and his attorney general, Richard Olney, himself a former railroad corporation lawyer. On July 2, 1894, the president and the Justice Department obtained a court injunction to bar the strikers from blocking interstate commerce. Federal troops were ordered to Chicago.

Within several days violence erupted as angry mobs destroyed railroad property and equipment. "We have been brought to the ragged edge of anarchy," Olney told the press. The strikers were not to blame for the episode; the rioters were local people. Police and national guard troops put down the disturbance, but the public gave Cleveland and the federal government the credit. For the moment, the president regained his popularity among conservatives in both parties. His standing with ordinary voters remained low, however.

Debs went to jail for violating the court's injunction, and the U.S. Supreme Court confirmed his sentence in *In re Debs* (1895). By doing so the Court gave businesses a potent way to stifle labor unrest. If a strike began, management could seek an injunction from a friendly federal judge, jail the union leaders, and break the strike. Union power stagnated throughout the rest of the decade. Debs himself decided to cast his lot with members of the Socialist movement who called for more radical change in the nation's institutions.

Politically, the strike divided the Democrats once again. The governor of Illinois, John P. Altgeld, had protested Cleveland's actions. When the president overruled him, the governor resolved to oppose the ad-

Eugene V. Debs was the leader of the American Railway Union that struck in sympathy with the workers in the Pullman Palace Car Company. His experiences in this labor dispute helped persuade Debs to become a leader of the Socialist party.

ministration's candidate in 1896. Across the South and West, bitterness against the president became even more intense. Hate mail flooded into the White House, warning him of death if he crossed the Mississippi River. As one observer said, "If this keeps on long, fire and sword will devastate the country."

1894: A Realigning Election

The first chance for the voters to express themselves on the performance of the political system during the depression came in the congressional elections of 1894. The Democrats were demoralized. The policies of the Cleveland administration had split the party into factions that distrusted each other. In states where sentiment for silver was strong, the president was repudiated and criticized. For the Populists, on the other hand, these elections seemed to offer an excellent chance to establish themselves as a credible challenger

TABLE 19.1	PARTY STRENGTH IN CONGRESS, 1886–1900

House of Representatives

Congress and Year Elected	Republicans	Democrats	Other
Fiftieth (1886)	152	169	4
Fifty-first (1888)	166	159	
Fifty-second (1890)	88	235	9
Fifty-third (1892)	127	218	11
Fifty-fourth (1894)	244	105	7
Fifty-fifth (1896)	204	113	40
Fifty-sixth (1898)	185	163	9
Fifty-seventh (1900)	197	151	9

Senate

Congress and Year Elected	Republicans	Democrats	Other
Fiftieth (1886)	39	37	
Fifty-first (1888)	39	37	
Fifty-second (1890)	47	39	
Fifty-third (1892)	44	38	3
Fifty-fourth (1894)	39	43	6
Fifty-fifth (1896)	47	34	7
Fifty-sixth (1898)	53	26	8
Fifty-seventh (1900)	55	31	4

SOURCE   *The Statistical History of the United States* (Stamford, CT: Fairfield Publishers, 1965)

to the supremacy of the two major parties. Tom Watson said that in 1892 "we were fed upon the ambrosia of Democratic expectations. Today we are gnawing the cobs of Democratic reality."

The Republicans assailed the Democrats for failing to restore prosperity. Republican speakers urged a return to the policy of tariff protection that they had pursued under Benjamin Harrison. Party leaders, such as William McKinley, the governor of Ohio, crisscrossed the Midwest speaking to enthusiastic audiences. Soon the party was confident of victory. Former House Speaker Thomas B. Reed said, "The Democratic mortality will be so great next fall that their dead will be buried in trenches and marked unknown."

Reed's forecast was accurate. The Republicans prevailed in one of the most decisive congressional elections in the nation's history. The Democrats lost 113 seats in the largest transfer of power from one party to another in the annals of the two-party system. The Republicans regained control of the House of Representatives by a margin of 244 to 105. There were twenty-four states in which no Democrat won a federal office; six other states elected only one Democrat. In the Midwest 168 Republicans were elected to Congress, compared with nine Democrats. "There was hardly an oasis left in the Democratic desert."

The significance of this outcome went beyond its immediate results. The stalemated politics of the late nineteenth century had ended in an election that realigned the nation's political alliances. A Republican electoral majority had arisen that would dominate American politics until 1929. Voters outside the Democratic South were inclined to support Republicans unless the party itself split. The decision foreshad-

owed a Republican victory in the presidential contest in 1896.

The Populist Dilemma

The Populists were almost as disappointed as the Democrats with the outcome of the 1894 election. To be sure, the total vote for the Populists had increased over what the party had won in 1892. Much of that rise occurred in the South where the Democrats then used their control of the electoral machinery to deny victory to Populist candidates. The Populist delegation in Congress went from eleven members to seven.

By 1894 the Populists were strongly associated with the free coinage of silver which appealed to the debt-burdened South and West. For industrial workers who had to survive on a fixed or declining income, higher prices arising from this inflationary policy seemed less attractive. The Populists told each other that they would do better in 1896, but they assumed that neither the Republicans nor the Democrats would adopt a free-silver position. In fact, the Populists' failure to mount a significant challenge to the major parties during the 1894 election signaled the end of their assault on the two-party system. The People's party had articulated the grievances of the agrarian United States with force and insight but it had not proved capable of broadening its program to enlist industrial workers, owners of small businesses, and the middle class. The party remained a factor in the 1896 election, but its best days were past.

THE ECONOMIC AND SOCIAL IMPACT OF HARD TIMES

The economic impact of the depression of the 1890s was profound and its effects were far-reaching. By 1894 the economy was operating at 80 percent of capacity. Total output of goods and services was down by some 13 percent. Unemployment ranged between 17 and 19 percent of the workforce.

As the amount of money in circulation dropped, the nation experienced severe deflation. In the South, for example, cotton prices fell from 8.4 cents per

While the national economy deteriorated during the 1890s, African Americans in the South provided the labor to support southern agriculture as crop prices declined. Here a young woman joins others in the labor of harvesting the peanut crop.

pound in 1892 to 4.6 cents per pound in 1894. Since a figure of 10 cents per pound was necessary to break even, southern cotton farmers faced the prospect of disaster. One of them wrote: "If there is nothing done to alleviate the suffering among the people . . . we will have revolution." For people with money, their dollars bought more goods. Among those out of work and without funds, however, lower prices were little comfort when they had no money to pay for the necessities of life. Families in the growing cities depended on wages for their livelihood, and for them the depression of the 1890s was difficult to endure.

With their husbands, fathers, and sons out of work, women joined the workforce in greater numbers during the decade. During the 1890s the total number of women with jobs rose from 3.7 million to just under 5 million. They gained employment in the expanding clerical fields, where they mastered typing and stenography. Traditional occupations such as teaching and

The labor of young women and men became more common in the nation's factories. This woman could spend ten to twelve hours daily at her shoemaking tasks for six days a week. Efforts to regulate child labor were tentative and inadequate during the 1890s.

nursing also attracted more women. In the factories, Irish-American, French-Canadian, and Italian-American women worked in textile and clothing establishments; or they did piecework for tobacco processors and shoemakers. In commercial food production and laundries the number of women employees also grew. The earnings of these women were necessary for the survival of their families. When the male wage-earner brought home only $300 per year, and rents for a tenement dwelling were as much as $200 annually, the contributions of a daughter or wife were vital. However, the wages paid to women were as much as 40 percent below what men earned in industrial jobs.

The depression also brought young children back into the workforce. During the 1880s, the percentage of employed children between the ages of ten and fifteen had fallen from 17 percent to 12 percent. During the 1890s, the percentage rose to 18 percent. By 1900 1,750,000 children were employed. One child worker was thirteen-year-old Fannie Harris, who told government investigators in New York that she earned two dollars for the sixty hours of work she did each week in a necktie shop. When asked what she did with her money, she replied "Gave it to my mamma." She received two cents a week in spending money. By the end of the century thirty states had passed child labor laws, but these were often ineffective. Restricting the practice of child labor became an important social cause after 1900.

Reshaping the Economy

In the economy as a whole, the depression brought important changes. As a result of the downturn, the number of bankrupt businesses had been growing, revealing an obvious economic need for reorganization. In railroads, for example, major systems such as the Union Pacific were in receivership. The investment banker J. P. Morgan refinanced many of these rail lines and consolidated them in order to raise profits and increase efficiency. The thirty-two railroads capitalized at over $100 million controlled nearly 80 percent of the mileage of the nation. Shippers complained that these railroads gave larger customers unfair advantages in the form of rebates. By the end of the decade there were increasing pleas from the South and Middle West to revive and strengthen the Interstate Commerce Commission whose power to oversee railroad rates had been reduced by court decisions.

In the 1890s "finance capitalists" like J. P. Morgan challenged the dominance of the "industrial capitalists" of the 1870s and 1880s who had built large enterprises in steel, oil, and railroads. These financiers launched a wave of corporate mergers that began in 1895 and continued for a decade. An average of 300 companies a year were merged with larger firms. Twelve hundred mergers occurred in 1899. Some states such as New Jersey and Delaware made it easier for firms to locate holding companies there. In New York a market for industrial stocks enabled bankers to raise capital. In the case of *U.S.* v. *E.C. Knight* (1895), the Supreme Court ruled that the Sherman Antitrust Act applied only to monopolies of interstate commerce and not to those solely of manufacturing. This decision made it more difficult to enforce the antitrust laws and, as a result, the government took little action against any of the mergers that occurred during the 1890s.

When the economy began to recover in 1897, the public's attention turned to the growth of large businesses and trusts. Consumers believed that it was unfair for a few men or businesses to dominate a single

industry or control the price of commodities. As the size of corporations grew, their decisions affected the lives of thousands of private individuals. Several railroads employed more than 100,000 people, and Standard Oil was capitalized at almost $125 million in 1900. There was, said newspaper editors, a "growing antagonism to the concentration of capital."

The Revolt against Bigness

The depression of the 1890s caused fear and apprehension across the United States as the hard times went on year after year. No part of the nation escaped the effects of the crisis. The accepted values of earlier generations came under scrutiny as people struggled to make sense of their situation. Writers questioned whether the government should simply promote economic expansion and then allow fate to decide who prospered and who did not. For the first time many argued that government should *regulate* the economy in the interest of social justice. The Populist governor of Kansas in 1893 said that "the survival of the fittest is the government of brutes and reptiles, and such philosophy must give place to a government which recognizes human brotherhood." In discussion clubs in Wisconsin, at political rallies in Texas, and in the streets of New York and Boston, citizens wondered whether their governments at all levels should do more to promote the general welfare.

A growing number of social thinkers suggested that additional government action was necessary. In 1894 Henry Demarest Lloyd published a book entitled *Wealth Against Commonwealth* that detailed what he believed the Standard Oil Company had done to monopolize the oil industry and corrupt the nation. "Monopoly cannot be content with controlling its own business. . . . Its destiny is rule or ruin, and rule is but a slower ruin." Unimpressed with the idea of merely regulating the large corporations, Lloyd called for public ownership "of railroads, telegraphs, and all the monopolies."

The economic hard times strengthened the resolve of the Social Gospel movement (see Chapter 18). The church, said Walter Rauschenbusch in 1893, should be the "appointed instrument for the further realization of that new society in the world about it." Other young people of the day echoed similar themes. Ray Stannard Baker had reported on Coxey's army for his newspaper. He told his editor, "When such an ugly and grotesque fungus can grow so prominently on the body politic there must be something wrong. The national blood is out of order."

Women and Reform in the 1890s

In states like Illinois and New York, bands of women joined together as consumers to push for better working conditions in factories and fair treatment of employees in department stores. Social workers and charity operatives decided that the plight of the poor was not simply the fault of those in need. Better government and more enlightened policies could uplift the downtrodden. As one settlement worker put it, "I never go into a tenement without longing for a better city government."

Women's participation in the process of change was significant. Julia Lathrop and Florence Kelley worked for Governor Altgeld in Illinois improving state charitable institutions and inspecting factories. Ida Wells Barnett rallied African-American women against lynching. Mary Church Terrell led the National Association of Colored Women, founded in 1896, in making the women's clubs in the black community a more effective force for change. The suffrage movement and the women's clubs among white, middle-class women and their black counterparts slowly established the basis for additional reforms after 1900.

A leading voice for a new role for women was Charlotte Perkins Gilman, whose major work, *Women and Economics,* was published in 1898. Gilman advocated that women seek economic independence. The home, she argued, was a primitive institution that should be transformed through modern industrial practices lest it impede "the blessed currents of progress that lead and lift us all." Housework should be professionalized and homes transformed into domestic factories; women would then be free to pursue their own destinies, which could include social reform. Gilman's work influenced a generation of women reformers as well as future feminists.

Liquor Control and Reform

The renewed emphasis on reform during the 1890s also affected the long-standing campaign to control the sale and use of alcoholic beverages. Opponents of alcohol had long sought to prohibit the sale of liquor

Charlotte Perkins Gilman's writings challenged the traditional roles that women occupied in the household. She became an important advocate for a new kind of thinking about how women should function in society.

through local and state laws. Now a new and more effective pressure group tactic appeared. In 1895 the Reverend H. H. Russell established the Anti-Saloon League in Oberlin, Ohio. Its organization relied on a network of local Protestant churches throughout the nation. They aimed to regulate saloons as tightly as possible. The League focused on a single issue, and it became a model for the kind of lobbying that would characterize reform campaigns during the first two decades of the twentieth century.

The prohibition campaigns in the South brought black and white women together in a brief alliance to cripple what they both regarded as an important social evil. In some parts of North Carolina, for example, white women organized chapters of the Woman's Christian Temperance Union (WCTU) among black women. When white volunteers did not appear, black women took over and set up their own organizations. Even as racial barriers rose in the South, women continued to work together to curb drinking until at the end of the 1890s it became politically impossible to do so. Nonetheless, the liquor issue illustrated that black

women played a significant role in southern reform during this period.

To counter the drive for prohibition, brewers and liquor producers created lobbying groups of their own to match the Anti-Saloon League and the persistent militance of the WCTU. Brewing associations appeared in battleground states such as Texas to coordinate strategies in local option elections and to get "wet" voters to the polls. Anti-prohibition sentiment flourished among Irish Americans and German Americans in the cities and towns of the Northeast and Midwest. The struggles over liquor often pitted the countryside dwellers against urban residents who wanted liquor to remain available.

Reform in the Cities and States

Reform also appeared in the cities as the depression dramatized social problems and political injustices. In Detroit, Hazen Pingree had been elected mayor in 1889. During the depression, he decided that city government ought to do more than just stand by while the poor suffered. He constructed his own political machine to pursue social justice through lower utility rates and expanded government services. That brought him into conflict with the streetcar companies and utilities which dominated Detroit politics. In Chicago, a British editor, William T. Stead, visited the city for the Columbian Exposition in 1893. What he saw in the slums led him to write *If Christ Came to Chicago* in 1894. Stead contended that the city needed a spiritual and political revival. He singled out the power of the street railway operator, Charles T. Yerkes, as particularly oppressive because of the high rates and poor service his companies provided. Stead's attack led to the formation of the Chicago Civic Federation, which sought to control gambling, clean up the slums, and limit the power of men like Yerkes. Similar reform groups sprang up in Wisconsin's cities to restrain corporations that provided vital municipal services at an exorbitant cost to taxpayers.

By the mid-1890s these examples of urban reform sparked the creation of groups to address urban problems on a national scale. The National Municipal League came into existence in 1894; in the same year the First National Conference for Good City Government took place. Over the next several years reformers began to diagnose the ills of American cities and recommend solutions. "We are not unlike patients assem-

bled in a hospital, examining together and describing to each other our sore places," said one participant at the Good City Government meeting in 1894. Out of these debates came the ideas that would flourish during the Progressive Era a decade later.

Reform in the States

As the depression worsened, citizens looked to their state governments for answers and instead found political and social problems that rivaled the plight of the cities. Critics complained of corruption, political machines, and a breakdown of democracy. In Wisconsin a Republican politician, Robert M. La Follette, built a political following by attacking the entrenched organization within his own party. He called for primary elections to choose candidates for office rather than leave the decision to the politicians and their rigged meetings. Albert B. Cummins of Iowa attacked the power of railroads in his state and Republicans in neighboring Kansas set up a Boss Busters League to challenge the party hierarchy. After his triumphs in the Spanish-American War, Theodore Roosevelt was elected governor of New York, where he displayed his vigorous leadership skills in publicizing the activities of large corporations and using state power to conserve natural resources.

The work of reform governors and their supporters in the states led to increased authority for these governments and greater reliance on experts and nonpartisan commissions in making decisions about public policy. Railroad commissions, public utility commissions, and investigative boards to oversee key industries were formed. By the end of the decade, however, observers believed that meaningful reform would come only when the federal government shaped national legislation to curb railroads and trusts engaged in interstate commerce.

Resistance from the Courts

Advocates of reform faced many obstacles. Among the most powerful were judges who upheld business interests in their decisions. The doctrine of *substantive due process* gave state and federal judges a way to block legislative attempts to regulate economic behavior. According to this doctrine, the due process clause of the Fourteenth Amendment did not apply only to the is-

sue of whether the procedure used to pass a law had been fair. Judges might consider how the substance of the law affected life, liberty, and property. They could then decide whether the law was so inherently unfair that it would be unjust even if the procedures for implementing the statute were unbiased. This approach gave the judiciary the right to decide whether a law regulating business enterprise was fair to the corporation being supervised.

Judges also interpreted federal laws in ways that limited the effectiveness of efforts to curb corporate power. The same year (1895) that the Court issued the *E. C. Knight* decision, which limited the scope of the Sherman Antitrust Act, it also ruled in *Pollock* v. *Farmers' Loan and Trust Co.* that the income tax provisions of the Wilson-Gorman Tariff were unconstitutional. In labor cases in which they imposed injunctions to bar unions from boycotts and strikes, the courts also acted as barriers to change.

A few jurists and lawyers, however, had doubts about this philosophy of favoring corporations. In Massachusetts, Oliver Wendell Holmes, Jr., had published a book on *The Common Law* in 1881. Holmes contended that "the life of the law has not been logic; it has been experience." By this he meant that judges should not base their rulings on abstract premises and theories but should consider the rational basis of a law in judging whether it was constitutional or not. Such a philosophy would give greater weight to the actions of legislatures in regulating business.

Conservative himself, Holmes was ready to defer to the popular will in legislative matters. If the Constitution did not prohibit a state from building a slaughterhouse or regulating an industry, his response was "God-dammit, let them build it." In Nebraska, Roscoe Pound was evolving a similar reality-based approach to legal thinking that became known as *sociological jurisprudence.* Louis D. Brandeis of Massachusetts was gaining a reputation as the "People's Lawyer" who believed that the legal system should serve small businesses and consumers as well as large corporations.

The Philosophy of Pragmatism

The philosopher William James of Harvard University evolved an explanation for what political and legal reformers were trying to do. He called it *pragmatism.* James wanted to show that truth is more than an abstract concept. He believed that truth must

demonstrate its value in the real world. "What in short is the truth's cash value in experiential terms?" James asked. To James, pragmatism meant *"looking away from first things, principles, 'categories,' supposed necessities; and of looking towards last things, fruits, consequences, facts."* James divided the world into tough-minded people, who based their actions on facts and pragmatic truths, and tender-minded people, who were swayed by abstractions. His philosophy emphasized self-reliance and gritty reality. It appealed to a generation of reformers who sought practical solutions to the problems they saw in their communities and the nation as a whole. They believed that it would be possible to accomplish significant reforms within the moral limits of the world as they knew it.

Another spokesman for reform was a University of Chicago teacher and philosopher named John Dewey. In his major work, *The School and Society* (1899), Dewey contended that schools should undertake the task of preparing students to live in a complex, industrial world. The public school must do more than transmit academic knowledge for its own sake. As an

In his writings about how children should be educated, John Dewey influenced several generations of American teachers. He wanted schools to do more to prepare children to be productive members of society.

institution, it should be a means of instilling democratic values and usable skills. Education, Dewey wrote, "is the fundamental method of social progress and reform."

Literary Naturalism and Realism

During the 1890s writers and artists turned to the world around them for inspiration and subjects. They preached the doctrine of realism and they tried to capture the complexity of a natural world in which science, technology, and capitalism were challenging older values. William Dean Howells, a novelist, examined the impact of capitalism on workers and urban dwellers in New York City in *A Hazard of New Fortunes* (1890). During the depression Howells's novels and essays were sharply critical of the new industrial system. Stephen Crane depicted the ways in which the city exploited and destroyed a young woman in *Maggie: A Girl of the Streets* (1893).

Two noteworthy practitioners of literary naturalism were Frank Norris and Theodore Dreiser. Norris wrote

The Harvard philosopher and psychologist William James advanced his theory of "pragmatism" as a way that individuals could deal with the realities of the world. His work was part of the intellectual ferment of the 1890s.

about California railroads in *The Octopus* (1901) and about the wheat market in Chicago in *The Pit* (1903). In Norris's Darwinian world, humanity was trapped in the impersonal grip of soulless corporations. In *Sister Carrie* (1900), Dreiser described how a small-town girl went to work in Chicago and was consumed by its temptations. These novels reached a large audience, and their depiction of characters caught in an amoral universe intensified the sentiment for reform.

By the 1890s, then, the currents that would come together as the progressive movement of the 1900–1920 period were already forming. Urban reformers, believers in the social gospel, politically active women, candidates angry with the established powers in their state's dominant party—all of these groups shared a pervasive discontent with the state of society. The volatile domestic and international events of the 1890s would prepare the ground for a generation of reform.

African Americans and Segregation

In addition to experiencing the same economic deprivations that the whole nation faced during the 1890s, African Americans confronted the ever-tightening grip of segregation in the South. While blacks had made great strides in building viable communities and economic institutions since Reconstruction, their advancement was not welcomed by white southerners. Instead, they endeavored to return African Americans to a subordinate position, The courts proved unreceptive to the pleas of blacks for equal treatment under the law. A spokesman for blacks emerged in the person of Booker T. Washington, who argued that African Americans should emphasize hard work and personal development rather than rebelling against their condition. Whites applauded Washington's philosophy, but bigotry continued in the form of race riots and lynchings.

Washington believed that African Americans must demonstrate their worthiness for citizenship through their own achievements. In 1895 he reached a national audience when he spoke at the Cotton States and International Exposition in Atlanta. What he said made him the leading black figure in the United States for a generation. His "Atlanta Compromise" told white America what it wanted to hear about African Americans.

"In all the things that are purely social, we can be separate as the fingers," Washington proclaimed, "yet one as the hand in all things essential to mutual progress." To his fellow blacks he said, "it is at the bottom of life we must begin" to create an economic base through hard work: "[C]ast down your bucket where you are" and be "patient, law-abiding and unresentful." Any "agitation of questions of social equality" would be "the extremest folly."

Washington's white audience gave him an enthusiastic response, and white philanthropists funded his school, the Tuskegee Institute (Chapter 17) generously. Behind the scenes, Washington dominated the political lives of blacks and even more secretly he funded court challenges to segregation. In public, however, he came to symbolize an accommodation with the existing racial system.

A year later the Supreme Court put its stamp of approval on segregation as a legal doctrine a year later. Homer A. Plessy's appeal of the Louisiana court's decision upholding segregation of railroad cars had taken four years to make its way to the Supreme Court (see Chapter 18). The court heard oral arguments in the case in April 1896 and rendered its judgment five weeks later. By a vote of seven to one in the case of *Plessy* v. *Ferguson,* the justices upheld the Louisiana law and, by implication, the principle of segregation generally. Writing for the majority, Justice Henry Billings Brown said that the Fourteenth Amendment "could not have been intended to abolish distinctions based on color, or to enforce social, as distinguished from political equality, or a commingling of the two races upon terms unsatisfactory to either." He rejected the argument that "the enforced separation of the races stamps the colored race with a badge of inferiority." In a dissenting opinion, Justice John Marshall Harlan responded that "Our Constitution is color-blind, and neither knows nor tolerates classes among citizens." This ruling determined the legal situation of African Americans for more than half a century.

As the political rights of blacks diminished, whites' attacks on them increased. During the North Carolina elections of 1898, race was a key issue that led to a Democratic victory over the Populists, Republicans, and their African-American allies. Once whites had won, they turned on the black-dominated local government in Wilmington, North Carolina. Several hundred whites attacked areas where blacks lived in December 1898, killing eleven people and driving residents from their homes. Lynchings in the South continued at a rate of more than one hundred per year. Other acts of violence became common and went unreported.

PETITION FROM THE CITIZENS OF NEW JERSEY TO THE U. S. CONGRESS PRAYING FOR CONGRESS TO MAKE THE ACT OF LYNCHING A CRIME IN THE UNITED STATES, 1900

At the end of the nineteenth century, lynchings directed against blacks became a frequent occurrence in the South. Some concerned citizens in the North protested against these crimes, as this petition from individuals in New Jersey shows, but the federal government took no action against this wave of extralegal violence.

We, the undersigned petitioners, citizens of New Jersey, beg most respectfully to represent to your honorable bodies, the Senate and House of Representatives, the alarming state of the country in respect to the appalling prevalence in the Southern States, of that species of lawlessness known as lynching whereby inhabitants of that section are deprived of life without due process of law by gangs of irresponsible and wickedly disposed persons; that the victims of these barbarous outbreaks and outrages are usually members of the Negro race, and that the crimes imputed to them by their self-constituted executioners, but never proved, and for which they suffer death, have ranged all the way from petty larceny to murder; that Negroes have been hanged and shot in the South by lynching mobs on mere suspicion, or because they have incurred the odium of being politically troublesome to the community in which they resided; that human life is frightfully cheap in the South, and that a Negro's life has absolutely no value whatever there when a Southern mob scents his blood; that the local police power offers him under such circumstances no adequate protection and often times are in actual or virtual connivance with his murderers:

WHEREFORE, your petitioners pray your honorable bodies to make the act of lynching a crime against the United States, to provide for its commission the sternest pains and penalties, and to empower the President of the United States and to make it his duty to intervene whenever and wherever necessary with the armed force of the nation to prevent the commission of this atrocious crime, and to rescue any person or persons from the hands of any mob in any state of the Union, and for the better prevention of lynching your petitioners further pray your honorable bodies for the creation of a Central Detective Bureau at Washington with branch offices in various parts of the section or sections subject to this kind of lawlessness, for the purpose of collecting and transmitting information promptly to the President relative to the intentions and movements of lynching bodies, and that such information may be used in subsequent prosecuting proceedings against such individuals in the Courts of the United States for violation of the law made and provided in that behalf.

SOURCE Petition presented to Congress, February 21, 1900, National Archives.

While black Americans faced daunting obstacles in the 1890s, they made substantial progress toward improved living conditions in ways that showed that they were more than simply the victims of white oppression. They founded colleges in the South, created self-help institutions in black churches, and developed pockets of well-off citizens in cities such as Washington, Boston, Baltimore, and Philadelphia. In the South black women pursued social reform in states with impressive determination. The National Association of Colored Women, founded in 1896, sought to become, in the words of its president, Mary Church

In trying to prepare Native Americans for life in mainstream society, institutions such as the Carlisle Indian School sought to take students away from tribal customs and have them emulate white practices. These pictures show a young Indian named Tom Torlino and his friends in their native clothes in 1886 and three years later in their school clothing.

Terrell, "partners in the great firm of progress and reform." African-American resistance to segregation shaped the 1890s as much as did the white drive to subjugate blacks in the South and the North.

Native Americans

In the years after the Battle of Wounded Knee (see Chapter 18), efforts to assimilate the 250,000 Indians into the dominant culture went on. One favored method was to educate Native American children at schools either located on the reservation or many miles distant. The students were required to speak English, wear white people's clothes, and abandon their tribal ceremonies and religions. The most celebrated of these Indian schools was located in Carlisle, Pennsylvania, and was operated by Richard Henry Pratt between 1879 and 1904. "Transfer the savage-born infant to the surroundings of civilization," Pratt said, "and he will grow to possess a civilized language and habit." For many of the Indian children, however, these schools seemed more like a prison. They were malnourished, often treated cruelly and stripped of their individuality. The government was spending more than $2,638,000 on Indian education by 1900 and the schools often competed for these funds in what one administrator called "a regular system of traffic in . . . helpless little red people." The goal of government policy seemed to be the extinction of the Indians' culture in the name of benevolent assimilation.

FOREIGN POLICY AND NATIONAL POLITICS

Amid the political turmoil of the second Cleveland administration, foreign affairs pressed for attention. The

nation stood on the verge of becoming a world power, and national leaders debated how to respond to increasing competition with powerful international rivals and the upsurge of nationalism among colonial peoples.

Diplomatic Problems: Hawaii and Venezuela

The first issue was that of Hawaii, left over from the last days of the Harrison presidency (see Chapter 18). Grover Cleveland was not convinced that the revolution that had occurred in the islands in 1893 represented the will of the Hawaiian people. Holding the treaty of annexation in limbo, he waited for the report of a special commission that he dispatched to Hawaii to investigate conditions. Believing that the native population backed Queen Liliuokalani, he refused to send the treaty to the Senate and asked instead for restoration of the native government. The revolutionary government declined to yield power, however, and in 1894 the administration granted it diplomatic recognition.

Another foreign policy crisis occurred in South America in 1894 when a dispute arose between Great Britain and Venezuela over the precise boundary line that separated Venezuela and British Guiana. The Cleveland administration concluded that the controversy was also a test of the Monroe Doctrine. In 1895 the new secretary of State, Richard Olney, sent a diplomatic note to London that asserted that the United States was "practically sovereign on this continent, and its fiat is law upon the subjects to which it confines its interposition." The British responded slowly, and when their answer finally arrived it rejected the arguments of the Cleveland administration. Newspapers talked of a possible war. The president asked Congress for the power to name a commission to decide the boundary dispute and enforce its decision. The British found themselves in a difficult position. In South Africa they were encountering problems that would eventually lead to the Boer War (1899–1902) and they had few European friends when it came to foreign policy. Accordingly they decided to arbitrate their quarrel with Venezuela through a joint Anglo-American-Venezuelan commission to resolve the dispute, and the crisis passed. From this low point, relations between Britain and the United States improved during the twenty years that followed.

The Cuban Rebellion

The most dangerous foreign policy issue that confronted Cleveland stemmed from the revolution that Cubans launched against Spanish rule in 1895. Discontent had persisted since the previous unsuccessful rebellion between 1868 and 1878. The Wilson-Gorman Tariff had increased import duties on Cuban sugar, damaging the island's economy, which depended on sugar.

Rebels took to the battlefield in February 1895 seeking the end of Spanish control of Cuba. The beleaguered Spanish were unable to defeat the rebels in direct combat; instead, they drove the civilian population into cities and fortified areas. The "reconcentration" camps where these refugees were housed were disease-ridden and overcrowded. The architect of this harsh "reconcentration" policy was General Valeriano Weyler, nicknamed "The Butcher" for his cruelty to the Cubans who came under his control. These events strengthened the will of the Cuban rebels to achieve independence.

The American Stake in Cuba

The American public took a close interest in the Cuban situation. Investments in the island, totalling about $50 million, were threatened by the conflict. Religious denominations saw the brutality and famine of the rebellion as cause for concern and perhaps direct intervention. The press covered the war in detail. Sensational newspapers, known as "the yellow press," because one of them carried a popular comic strip about "The Yellow Kid," printed numerous stories about atrocities in Cuba. William Randolph Hearst, publisher of the *New York Journal,* and Joseph Pulitzer of the New York *World* were the most sensational practitioners of this kind of journalism. The Cubans also established an office in New York from which their "junta" dispensed propaganda to a receptive audience. These efforts aroused pro-Cuban sympathies among the American people. Morality and self-interest reinforced each other to make concern about Cuba a significant element in the nation's foreign policy during the mid-1890s.

President Cleveland tried to assist Spain in subduing the revolution through enforcement of the neutrality laws that limited shipments of arms to Cuba. He did not recognize the Cubans as belligerents, and he

informed the Spanish that they might count on the good offices of the United States in negotiating an end to the fighting. This position suited Spain, which was following a policy of procrastination in the hope of quelling the revolt before the United States intervened. By the end of his administration, the president was trying to press Spain to make concessions to the Cubans, but he never challenged Spain's right to exercise its sovereignty over the island. Congress prodded the president toward more aggressive action, but he refused. As a result, when the end of the Cleveland administration approached early in 1897, his policy toward Cuba had failed.

The Election of 1896

The Cleveland administration did not recover politically from the disasters of 1894. The president's relations with the Democrats worsened. Preferring to work alone and wary of threats on his life, he increased the number of guards around the White House and rarely ventured out to meet his fellow citizens. Newspaper coverage of the presidency proved difficult. As a result, Cleveland became a virtual recluse.

The reserves of gold were still shrinking, despite the repeal of the Sherman Silver Purchase Act in 1893. To bolster the reserves and bring in gold, the White House turned to selling government bonds. The sale that took place in February 1895 was handled by New York banker J. P. Morgan, who made a nice profit from the transaction. Eventually there were four bond sales which supplied needed currency for the Treasury but also further alienated advocates of inflation and free silver within the president's own party. One angry Democratic senator said of the president: "I hate the ground that man walks on."

The Political Lineup

All three political parties confronted important challenges as the 1896 election approached. For the Republicans, who sensed victory after their sweep of the 1894 election, the main task was to nominate a candidate who could lead the party to the White House. Their front-runner was William McKinley of Ohio. A veteran of the Civil War, he had served in Congress between 1876 and 1890 and had been governor of Ohio from 1891 to 1895. He was a popular speaker and was identified with the protective tariff. He delivered 371 speeches during the 1894 elections and emerged from that contest as the most popular figure in the party. With the aid of his close friend Marcus A. Hanna, an industrialist from Ohio, McKinley became the favorite for the Republican nomination. He attracted Republican voters because of his popularity within the party, his moderate record, and his abilities as a politician. His campaign slogan proclaimed him as "The Advance Agent of Prosperity."

McKinley won on the first ballot at the Republican National Convention in St. Louis in June 1896. The only difficult issue was gold and silver. Eastern Republicans wanted the party to endorse the gold standard. The key plank contained that language, but it also conciliated pro-silver Republicans with a promise to seek wider international use of silver. McKinley's running mate was Garret A. Hobart of New Jersey. The Republicans expected to wage a campaign centered on the tariff against a Democratic nominee burdened with the unpopularity of the Cleveland administration.

The Rise of William Jennings Bryan

The Democratic convention, however, took an unexpected turn. After the elections of 1894, the free silver wing of the party dominated the South and West. Literature proclaiming the virtues of silver found a receptive audience. The most popular of these publications was William H. Harvey's *Coin's Financial School,* which appeared in 1895. In the book a young man named Coin showed his elders the merits of silver. At the height of its popularity, the book sold 5,000 copies each day. By 1896, it was clear that an articulate spokesman for the silver cause would appeal to many Democrats at their national convention.

Among the leading candidates for the nomination, however, none possessed the required excitement and devotion to silver. A young politician from Nebraska named William Jennings Bryan saw himself as the "logic of the situation." During 1895 and early 1896 he spoke frequently to Democrats about silver and urged leaders to think of him as a possible second choice should the convention deadlock. By the time the Democratic National Convention opened in Chicago in July 1896, there was a good deal of latent support for Bryan among the delegates.

At the age of thirty-six, William Jennings Bryan was a striking and handsome figure during his first race for the presidency in 1896. His musical voice and ardent advocacy of the silver issue gave him a powerful push in the summer until the effects of the Republican campaign turned the tide for William McKinley.

The Cross of Gold

Bryan's chance came during the debate over whether the party platform should endorse silver. He arranged to be the final speaker on behalf of free silver. He had perfected his speech during his various tours and knew just what his listeners wanted to hear. Bryan had a clear, musical voice that could be heard across the convention hall in the years before modern amplification systems. The speech he gave, entitled the "Cross of Gold," became a classic moment in American political oratory. He asked the delegates whether the party would stand "upon the side of 'the idle holders of capital,' or upon the side of the struggling masses?" His answer was simple. To those who wanted a gold standard, the Democrats would say: "You shall not press down upon the brow of labor this crown of thorns, you shall not crucify mankind upon a cross of gold." His audience was enthralled and enthusiastic.

The next day the convention nominated Bryan for president on a free silver platform. As his running mate, it chose Arthur Sewall of Maine. A wave of support for Bryan swept the country, and the Republicans found their careful plans for the campaign suddenly at risk. Since the Democrats could not raise much in the way of campaign funds, Bryan decided to take his message to the voters in person. He prepared for an extensive nationwide campaign tour to speak on behalf of the common man, a rural nation, and the older agrarian virtues.

The Populists and the Campaign

The nomination of an outspoken advocate of free silver left the Populist party in disarray. They had delayed their national convention until after the two major parties had named their candidates. If the Republicans and Democrats picked men who en-

The Republican magazines in the East attacked Bryan for his use of religious imagery in his famous "Cross of Gold" speech. The cartoon Bryan tramples on the Bible and his followers preach anarchy behind him.

dorsed the gold standard, the People's party would have the only genuine champion of free silver in the contest. Now the Populists faced a dilemma. If they failed to select Bryan as their candidate, they would be accused of depriving silver of any chance of victory. Yet if they went along with Bryan's nomination, there would be no need for their party. Some delegates advised that the party should "fuse" with the Democrats. Others said that the Populists could preserve their identity only by staying "in the middle of the road" between the two major parties.

The Populists wrestled with these problems at their national convention in St. Louis in late July. They ultimately decided to name Bryan as the presidential nominee, with Thomas E. Watson as their vice-presidential choice instead of Sewall. The Democrats refused to accept this awkward compromise; all that Watson's nomination did was confuse the issue.

Bryan Versus McKinley

Bryan set about trying to translate his popular acclaim into victory in the November election. His speaking tours were prodigious efforts. He traveled 18,000 miles and gave more than 600 speeches; his audiences, estimated at a total of 3 million people, turned out to see "The Boy Orator of the Platte River." Less kindly, Theodore Roosevelt called him a "human trombone."

To counter Bryan, the Republicans raised between $3.5 million and $4 million from fearful corporations. The Democrats charged that the Republicans and their business allies were coercing workers to vote for McKinley. Most industrial workers voted Republican because they feared the inflationary effects of free silver. Mark Hanna, who managed McKinley's campaign, used the party's substantial war chest to distribute several hundred million pamphlets to the voters. Republican speakers took to the campaign trail; party newspapers poured out information about the merits of the tariff and the gold standard. Hanna called it "a campaign of education."

The key to the Republican campaign was McKinley. He did not try to match Bryan's tours. "I have to *think* when I speak," he told Hanna. Instead, he stayed home in Canton, Ohio, and let the voters come to him. As the weeks passed, more than 750,000 people stood in McKinley's yard to hear him deliver speeches about the dangers of free silver. "If free coinage of silver means a fifty-three cent dollar, then it is not an

The Republican candidate also came in for newspaper assault. A Democratic magazine ran a cartoon showing a dispirited Uncle Sam having to accept monopoly power in the nation's capital once McKinley was elected.

honest dollar," he said. These addresses were published daily in newspapers across the country. By mid-September the tide turned against Bryan, and there were signs that the Republicans would win in November. "McKinley offers change, but not too big a change, and so McKinley it is," wrote a British reporter.

A Decisive Election

The result was the most decisive outcome since the 1872 presidential contest. McKinley had a margin of 600,000 popular votes and won 271 electoral votes to 176 for Bryan. Bryan ran well in the South, the plains states, and the Far West. McKinley dominated in the Northeast, the mid-Atlantic states, and the Midwest. Despite his appeals to the labor vote, Bryan ran poorly in the cities. Free silver might lead to inflation, an idea that had little appeal to workers on fixed incomes. McKinley's argument that the tariff would restore prosperity also took hold in the more industrialized areas of the country.

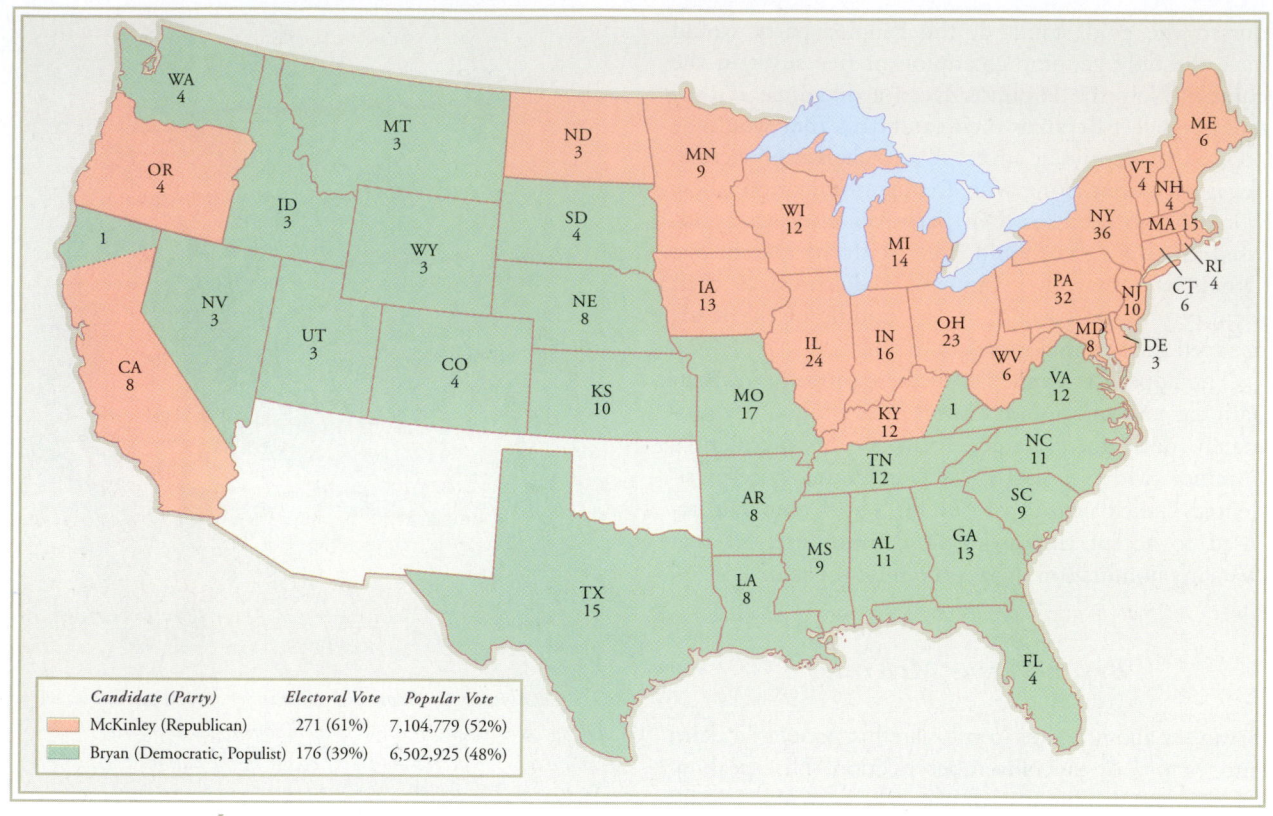

Candidate (Party)	Electoral Vote	Popular Vote
McKinley (Republican)	271 (61%)	7,104,779 (52%)
Bryan (Democratic, Populist)	176 (39%)	6,502,925 (48%)

MAP 19.1 | THE ELECTION OF 1896

The 1896 results confirmed the outcome of the 1894 election. The Republicans had established themselves as the nation's majority party. The South remained solidly Democratic; the industrial North was Republican. By 1896, the nature of national politics was changing. The stalemated politics of the late nineteenth century had ended. The older issue of how much the government ought to promote economic expansion was giving way to the new problem of whether the government should *regulate* the economy so as to relieve injustices and imbalances in the way that society worked. Bryan and the Populists had suggested that government should play a larger regulatory role. The voters had chosen instead to accept the economic nationalism of the Republicans as embodied in the tariff and the gold standard. Once the hard times of the 1890s ended, however, the issue of regulation would arise again.

THE MCKINLEY PRESIDENCY: ACHIEVING WORLD POWER

When Grover Cleveland left office in March 1897, he left a weakened presidency. McKinley revived the office during the four and a half years that followed. He improved relations with the press, which Cleveland had ignored; he traveled extensively to promote his policies; and he used experts and commissions to strengthen the operation of the national government. His personal secretary, George B. Cortelyou, played an important role in making the White House a more efficient governing power.

In domestic policy, McKinley persuaded Congress to enact the Dingley Tariff of 1897, which raised rates

above those that the Wilson-Gorman Tariff contained. He also sought without success to convince European nations to agree to wider use of silver through an international agreement. As a result, when the Republicans gained secure control of both houses of Congress after the 1898 election, the Gold Standard Act of 1900 established gold as the basis of the nation's currency. The silver issue was resolved permanently. The return of prosperity in the second half of 1897 also helped the administration. Gold discoveries in South Africa and Alaska inflated the currency by making more gold available. That change relieved the agricultural tensions of the decade.

The Road to Empire

From the beginning of his presidency, McKinley faced a growing crisis in Cuba. He embarked on a policy de-

signed to secure the eventual withdrawal of Spain from Cuba if its forces could not suppress the rebellion quickly. The administration took the position that any solution must be acceptable to the Cuban rebels. Since they would accept nothing less than the end of Spanish rule, there was little apparent basis for a negotiated settlement. During 1897, however, McKinley tried to persuade Spain to agree to a diplomatic solution through a gradually intensifying pressure on Madrid. The problem was that no Spanish government could stay in power if it agreed to leave Cuba without a fight.

At first it appeared that the president's policy might be working. In the fall of 1897 the Spanish government moved toward granting the Cubans some control over their internal affairs. Foreign policy, however, was to remain in Spanish hands. The practice of moving Cubans into reconcentration camps was abandoned. However, the situation worsened during the

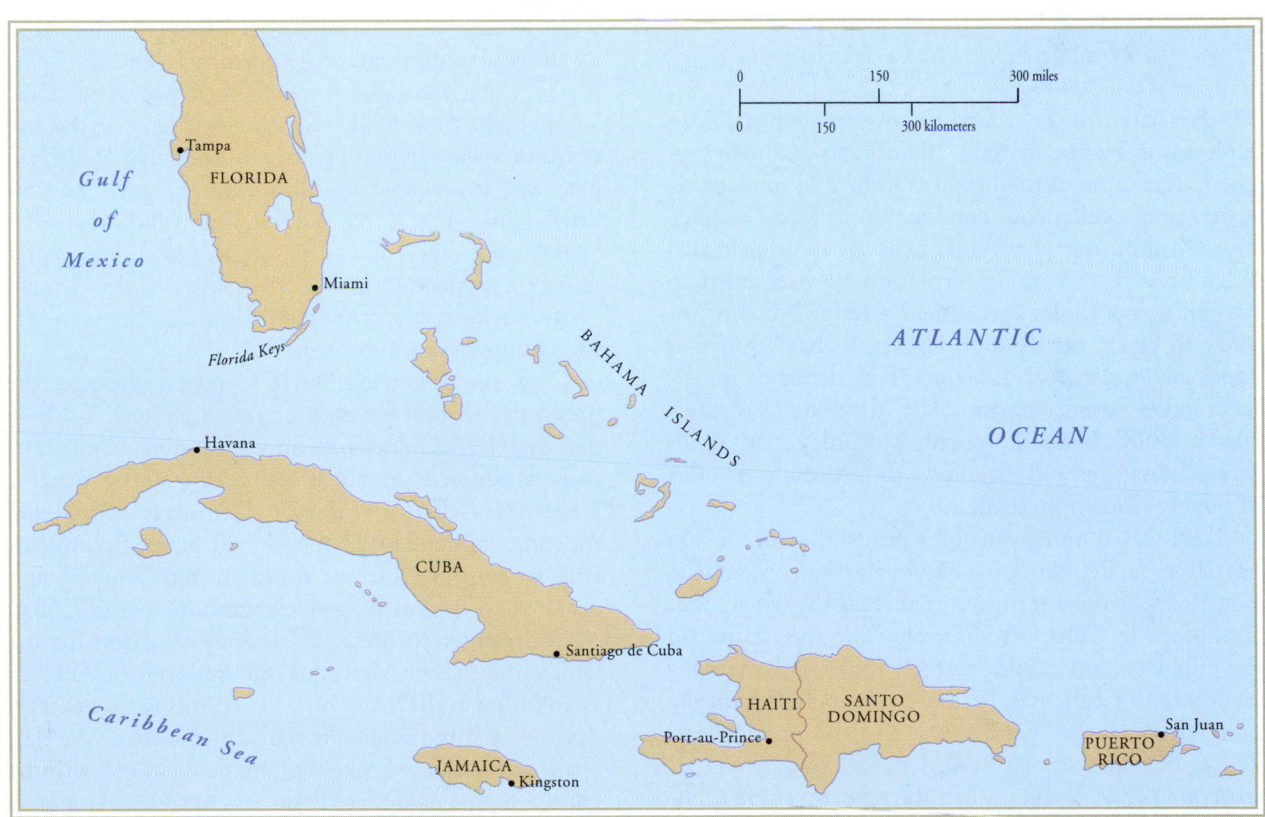

MAP 19.2 | CUBA AND THE CARIBBEAN

early months of 1898 as the rebellion persisted. On January 12, 1898, pro-Spanish elements in Cuba rioted against the autonomy program. The administration worried that Spain would be unable to maintain its promises. To monitor the situation, the White House decided to send a warship to Havana. The battleship *Maine* arrived there on January 25. Spain was pleased at this sign of normal relations, but the diplomatic problem continued. On February 1 Spain insisted that its sovereignty over Cuba must be preserved even if it meant resisting foreign intervention.

On February 9, 1898, newspapers in the United States published a letter written by the Spanish minister to the United States, Enrique Dupuy de Lôme, which the Cuban rebels had intercepted. The letter described McKinley as "weak and a bidder for the admiration of the crowd." These insulting remarks led to de Lôme's recall and resignation. De Lôme's other statements revealed that Spain was playing for time in its negotiations with Washington.

The Sinking of the Maine

Six days later, on February 15, the battleship *Maine* exploded in Havana harbor; 260 officers and men perished. The cause of the blast, according to modern research, was spontaneous combustion in a coal bunker. In 1898, however, the public believed that Spain had either caused an external explosion or had failed to prevent it. McKinley established a naval board of inquiry to probe the disaster. He knew that when that panel made its report, he would face demands for direct action against Spain. The deadline was mid-March 1898. While he waited, McKinley made military preparations and explored unsuccessfully the idea of buying Cuba from Spain.

Time was running out for a peaceful solution. On March 17 a Republican senator who had visited the war, Redfield Proctor of Vermont, told the Senate that conditions in Cuba were horrible. The speech swayed the public toward intervention. Two days later McKinley learned that the naval board had concluded, on the basis of the science of the time and the physical evidence, that an external explosion had caused the destruction of the *Maine*. When the report went to Congress, pressure on the president to intervene in Cuba (which would mean war) would mount.

The Last Drive for Peace

McKinley pushed Spain to agree to an armistice in the fighting that still raged in Cuba, or to permit American mediation that would end in Cuban independence. However, the Spanish were opposed to independence for Cuba directly or through negotiations. Still, McKinley was able to hold off Congress until Spain had another chance to consider its options. When a negative answer arrived from Spain on March 31, 1898, McKinley prepared to put the issue before Congress.

There was one last flurry of diplomatic activity. On April 9 Spain agreed, at the urging of its European friends, to suspend hostilities in Cuba. It was not an armistice, which would have meant formal recognition of the Cuban cause. The idea was for Spain to gain more time to defend Cuba against the United States. The Spanish military commander in Cuba would determine how long the cessation of the fighting would last. There was no agreement on Cuban independence from Madrid. Thus the Spanish had not yielded on the key demands of the United States.

McKinley sent his message to Congress on April 11. It requested presidential authority to end the fighting in Cuba through armed force if necessary. "The war in Cuba must stop," said the president. At the end of his message the president mentioned that Spain had proposed to suspend hostilities, but he gave the idea little significance. Later generations would argue that Spain's acceptance of a suspension of hostilities represented a surrender to the demands of the United States. In fact, the diplomatic impasse between the two countries was unbroken.

Over the following week Congress debated the president's request for authority to intervene. To show that the United States had no selfish motives, the lawmakers adopted an amendment offered by Senator Henry M. Teller, a Colorado Democrat. The Teller Amendment stated that the United States did not intend to control Cuba or annex it. Yet Congress also declined to extend official recognition to the Cuban rebels in order to preserve freedom of action for the United States. For McKinley, the important result was a resolution authorizing him to act; this was passed on April 19 and the president signed it the following day. Spain immediately broke diplomatic relations with the United States; it declared war on April 24. Congress replied that a state of war had existed between the United States and Spain since April 21.

The War Begins

The war between the United States and Spain occurred because both sides believed that their cause was just. McKinley had pursued a diplomatic solution until it became clear that Spain would not agree to a negotiated settlement that would end its reign over Cuba. In the end, Spain preferred to lose Cuba on the battlefield rather than at the bargaining table. Neither of the two powers believed that the Cubans themselves should determine their own destiny without interference. The resulting war set the United States on a path toward world power.

The war began with a stunning naval victory. On May 1, 1898, Commodore George Dewey and the Asiatic naval squadron inflicted a decisive defeat on the Spanish navy at Manila Bay in the Philippine Islands. The U.S. unit was in the waters of the Philippines so that it would be in a position to carry out war plans that had been developed in 1895 and updated as relations with Spain worsened. The goal was to hit the Spanish hard in the Philippines and thus pressure them to surrender Cuba. During February 1898 the assistant secretary of the Navy, Theodore Roosevelt,

had sent Dewey a telegram instructing him to be prepared to execute the war plan. The actual order to attack came from President McKinley on April 24. The triumph at Manila Bay made Dewey a national hero, but it confronted the president with new opportunities and problems in foreign policy.

A Broadening Commitment in the Pacific

To follow up on Dewey's success, the McKinley administration despatched troops to the Philippines. The president wanted the option of acquiring the islands as a result of the war. He thought that a port in the Philippines might be enough, but he intended to maintain flexibility. "While we are conducting war and until its conclusion we must keep all we get," he said in a private memorandum. "When the war is over we must keep what we want."

As the United States's involvement in the Philippines increased, the fate of the Hawaiian Islands gained added importance because of their strategic value. A treaty of annexation had been worked out during 1897, and Congress considered the pact early

MAP 19.3 | THE SPANISH-AMERICAN WAR

in 1898. It proved difficult to obtain the necessary two-thirds majority to adopt the treaty because of the opposition of southern states, whose industries competed with Hawaiian sugar. After the war began, the president and congressional leaders turned to a strategy of annexation by means of a legislative resolution which needed only a simple majority from Congress. Through presidential persuasion, the required votes for the resolution were obtained in July 1898, and Hawaii was annexed.

Meanwhile, U.S. policy toward the Philippines became a source of tension with Filipino leaders, notably Emilio Aguinaldo, who wanted their islands to be independent of all foreign powers. The administration instructed army and navy officers not to have any formal dealings with the Filipinos. The buildup of military strength continued, and the ambitions of the Filipinos were seen as an obstacle to American policy rather than as a legitimate expression of nationalism.

The "Smoked Yankees" and the War with Spain

The main focus of the combat phase of the war was on Cuba. The U.S. Army numbered 25,000 men, so the nation turned to volunteers to raise a larger force. In the first wave of national enthusiasm there were 1 mil-

lion volunteers, far more than the army could handle. Eventually about 280,000 men saw active duty. The size of the force presented logistical problems. Soldiers complained about shortages of ammunition and supplies and the poor quality of the food rations. The army experimented with canned beef, creating an inedible meal and a postwar controversy over the product. The press criticized the army's performance, but by the time the fighting ended, the War Department had settled most of the snags that marked the early days of the war.

In the regular army, an important part of the force that fought the Spanish were the four regiments composed of African-American soldiers, or the "Smoked Yankees" as the Spanish troops described them. Seasoned fighters against Indians, the black soldiers were ordered to move south and prepare to invade Cuba. On their way through the southern states they encountered scorn and segregation. As one black soldier put it, to whites "it mattered not if we were soldiers of the United States, and going to fight for the honor of our country . . . we were 'niggers' as they called us and treated us with contempt."

The African-American soldiers did not endure such treatment quietly. When they boarded segregated railroad cars, they sat wherever they pleased. If they saw signs that barred their presence, they took down the signs. Violence broke out between white and black

Because the war with Spain was fought primarily with U.S. Army regulars, African-American soldiers played a large role in the nation's victory. This detachment of black troops in Cuba was part of the American advance into the island.

The war made Theodore Roosevelt a national hero. He poses with his Rough Riders atop San Juan Hill in Cuba shortly after his successful charge on July 1, 1898. African-American soldiers like those shown in the previous picture helped Roosevelt and his men gain their objective, but Roosevelt gave them little credit later in his career for their timely assistance.

troops in Florida, and men were killed and wounded in the exchanges of gunfire. Seeing all this, one soldier asked poignantly: "Is America any better than Spain?" Once the black regiments reached Cuba, their military contribution was significant. They earned numerous decorations for bravery and five of them won the Congressional Medal of Honor.

Despite the bravery of the "Smoked Yankees," the Spanish-American War worsened the plight of African Americans. The ideology of imperialism that allowed whites to dominate Cubans and Filipinos also supported racial segregation in the South. McKinley's efforts to reconcile the whites of the North and South brought harmony at the expense of black Americans. Northern newspapers wrote that segregation was necessary "under the supreme law of self-preservation."

Victory in Cuba

In late June the U.S. Navy found the Spanish fleet in the harbor of Santiago de Cuba, and army detachments went ashore to engage the Spanish forces holding the city. President McKinley monitored the war closely through a telegraph system that enabled him to issue commands within twenty minutes. On July 1,

the army, commanded by General William R. Shafter, defeated the Spanish defenders at the Battle of San Juan Hill. Theodore Roosevelt and his volunteer regiment of Rough Riders took part in the battle. Roosevelt became a national hero on his way to the presidency, but the Rough Riders might have been defeated had it not been for the timely support they received from their black comrades.

From War to Peace

On July 3 the navy destroyed the Spanish fleet when it tried to escape from Santiago harbor. Negotiations for an armistice began with the French ambassador acting as intermediary. McKinley insisted that Spain relinquish Cuba and Puerto Rico and that the fate of the Philippines be discussed at the peace conference. Spain did not like these terms, but it had no choice but to accept them, which it did on August 12, 1898.

John Hay, soon to be McKinley's secretary of state, called it "a splendid little war." Victory had been achieved at a low cost in terms of combat deaths—only 281 officers and men. However, malaria, yellow fever, and other diseases killed more than 2,500 others. A public outcry arose about the condition of the

In August 1898 the United States and Spain reached an agreement on an armistice to end the fighting. This picture, which shows Secretary of State William Rufus Day signing the peace protocol with President McKinley (standing at right, in bow tie) was posed some days after the actual event for photographers.

army, and McKinley named a commission to investigate the leadership of the War Department and the way the war had been conducted. The commission's report led to reforms such as general staff shakeups and improved organization that enhanced the future fighting ability of the army. The war also strengthened the power of the presidency because of McKinley's expansive use of his role as commander-in-chief of the armed forces. He would be equally assertive in his handling of the peace negotiations.

The Peace Talks

McKinley's first problem was the peace conference with Spain, to be held in Paris. He appointed a commission that included several senators who would ultimately vote on any treaty that they negotiated. The president was aware that Germany and Japan had an interest in the Philippines, and he intended that the

United States should retain control of the islands. American officials did not believe that the Filipinos should determine their own destiny. Within the United States, opponents of such a policy, calling themselves anti-imperialists, aroused public sentiment against the administration.

To build support for his foreign policy, McKinley made effective use of the powers of his office. During October he toured the Midwest. Ordinarily presidents did not take part in congressional election campaigns. However, though billed as a non-partisan event, McKinley's tour helped Republican candidates in the 1898 congressional contest. It also gave the president an opportunity to state the case for a more expansive foreign policy. In a typical address he told an Iowa audience that "we do not want to shirk a single responsibility that has been put upon us by the results of the war." In this way, McKinley shaped the alternatives that the public was considering.

The Philippines were the most divisive issue at the peace conference. On October 25, 1898, the president's commissioners asked him for instructions. On October 28 he responded that he could see "but one plain path of duty—the acceptance of the archipelago." The decision to keep the Philippines was the logical next step in the policy that McKinley had been pursuing since he received word of Dewey's victory in May. The peace treaty was signed on December 10, 1898. The United States gained the Philippines, Guam, and Puerto Rico. Spain gave up its claims to Cuba and received a payment of $20 million for what it had lost. The United States obtained legal sovereignty over the Philippines but would soon face challenges from the island's inhabitants. For the moment, however, attention turned to the Senate, where the peace treaty faced a decisive vote.

Approval of the Treaty

Opponents of imperialism tried to block acceptance of the treaty in the Senate. They had strength in the East, but the treaty had more support in the South and West. To win the necessary two-thirds vote, McKinley used the power of the presidency in new and creative ways. In December he went south to woo Democrats. He used patronage to persuade wavering senators and exerted pressure on the state legislatures, which elected senators. Believing that the Democrats would benefit if the issue was settled before the 1900 elections,

William Jennings Bryan endorsed the treaty. That action divided the opposition at a key point. On February 6, 1899, the Treaty of Paris obtained Senate approval on February 6, 1899, by a vote of fifty-seven to twenty-seven, one more than the necessary two-thirds.

War in the Philippines

As the Senate voted, the nation knew that fighting had erupted in the Philippines between U.S. soldiers and the Filipino troops that Aguinaldo commanded. Relations between the two sides had worsened during December 1898 as it became clear that the United States did not intend to leave the islands. Although the president asserted that his nation had "no imperial designs" on the Philippines, anti-imperialists and the Filipinos were not convinced. For Aguinaldo and his supporters, it seemed that they had ousted the Spanish only to replace them with another imperial master, the United States.

The war that resulted was a difficult and controversial one. During 1899 the U.S. Army defeated the Filipinos in conventional battles, and the administration sent out a commission to work out a civil government under U.S. sovereignty. However, the Filipinos turned to guerilla tactics. Their soldiers hit selected targets and then blended back into the population. Faced with this new threat, the U.S. Army responded by killing some Filipino prisoners and torturing others. The army's purpose was not genocidal, but many soldiers and their officers violated the rules of war and government policy in brutal and inhumane ways. A nation that had denounced such cruel practices under the Spanish in Cuba was now accused of doing the same things in the Philippines. Enthusiasm for further imperialistic adventures ebbed as the controversy raged.

The Battle over Imperialism

During the last two years of McKinley's first term, imperialism became a heated issue. An Anti-Imperialist League was created in November 1898 to unite the opposition against McKinley's foreign policy. Critics of expansionism charged that overseas possessions would damage the nation's democratic institutions. Some

After the war with Spain ended, the United States faced another conflict with Filipino nationalists. The ugly and brutal war dragged on for three years. This picture shows American troops after assaulting an enemy position.

people used racist arguments to block the acquisition of lands where nonwhite populations lived. Others evoked moral concern about imperialism. A number of prominent Americans including Andrew Carnegie, Thomas B. Reed, and the longtime reformer Carl Schurz lent their voices to the anti-imperialist campaign.

Advocates of empire used the ideas of Social Darwinism and Anglo-Saxon supremacy to justify the acquisition of other countries. Theodore Roosevelt, Henry Cabot Lodge of Massachusetts, and other proponents of a "large" foreign policy contended that the nation could not escape the world responsibilities that the war with Spain had brought. By 1900, the consensus was that the gains of empire should be retained and protected but not increased. Anti-imperialism had persuaded public opinion that further overseas growth would be unwise. The resulting examination of the nation's goals and purposes contributed to the mood of reform and renewal that emerged at the turn of the century.

Other foreign policy issues emerged from the outcome of the war. The Teller Amendment blocked the annexation of Cuba, but the McKinley administration wanted to ensure that the island did not become a target of European intervention, most notably from Germany. A military government ran Cuba during 1899. As a civil government developed, the United States insisted on guarantees that Cuba would retain political and military ties with the country that had liberated it. The result of this process was the Platt Amendment of March 1901. Attached to an army appropriation bill, the amendment barred an independent Cuba from allying itself with another foreign power. The United States had the right to intervene to preserve stability. Aimed at preventing what had happened in 1898 and mindful of a possible threat from Germany before 1914, the Platt Amendment became a permanent source of Cuban-American friction because of the way it diminished Cuban sovereignty.

The Open Door in China and Beyond

The acquisition of the Philippines heightened interest about the fate of China, where European powers sought to establish economic and political spheres of influence. Worried about the nation's trade with China and concerned to preserve that country's territorial integrity, in September 1899 the administration, through Secretary of State John Hay, issued what became known as the Open Door Notes. The messages asked European countries that were active in China to preserve trading privileges and other economic rights that gave the United States a chance to compete for markets there. The replies of the powers were noncommittal, but Hay announced in March 1900 that the other nations had accepted the U.S. position in principle. The Open Door Notes became a significant assertion of U.S. interest in China.

When anti-foreign sentiment in China led to the Boxer Rebellion during the summer of 1900, an important test of the Open Door principle occurred. Secret associations known as the "Righteous and Harmonious Fists" (hence "Boxers") launched a series of attacks on westerners in China. Europeans who had taken refuge in Peking were rescued by an international force that included 2,500 U.S. soldiers. President McKinley justified sending the troops into a country with which the United States was at peace as a legitimate use of his war power under the Constitution. Secretary Hay reaffirmed the U.S. commitment to the Open Door policy in a diplomatic circular to the powers that he issued on July 3, 1900. McKinley withdrew the troops rapidly after their rescue mission had been completed, but presidential authority was strengthened still further as a result.

Toward a Canal Across Central America

The Spanish-American War and the expansion of American commitments in the Pacific demonstrated the need for a waterway that would link the two oceans and enable the navy to conduct its growing worldwide responsibilities. The McKinley administration laid the groundwork for a canal across Central America when it renegotiated the Clayton-Bulwer Treaty of 1850 with Great Britain. That document prohibited both nations from exercising exclusive control over any future waterway.

The first treaty that Hay worked out with the British ambassador, Julian Pauncefote, had to be changed when the Senate insisted that it include provisions for a fortified canal under U.S. control. A second along those lines evolved during the last months of McKinley's presidency. The administration also addressed the issue of the boundary between Alaska and Canada, but the problem was left to McKinley's successor.

The 1900 Election

As the presidential election of 1900 approached, the signs seemed to point to McKinley's reelection. Prosperity had returned, and the conflict in the Philippines was being won. McKinley's vice president, Garret A. Hobart, died in November 1899. Theodore Roosevelt, the popular young governor of New York, became McKinley's running mate when the Republican National Convention met in Philadelphia in June 1900. This was a major step on to the stage of national politics for the exciting and dynamic Roosevelt.

To oppose McKinley, the Democrats again turned to William Jennings Bryan. His running mate was Adlai Stevenson who had held the vice presidency under Grover Cleveland. Bryan made another vigorous campaign. He attacked McKinley's policies on imperialism as a threat to the nation's institutions, and he accused the Republicans of being the tools of the trusts and the business community. The Democratic candidate also renewed his pleas for a free silver policy. The anti-imperialists did not trust Bryan, but they preferred him to McKinley. The 1900 contest, said Bryan, was "between democracy on the one hand and plutocracy on the other."

Conforming to the custom of the day in which incumbent presidents did not make speeches, McKinley allowed Theodore Roosevelt to do most of the campaigning. Bryan made so many criticisms that his campaign lacked a clear theme. McKinley increased his margin in the popular vote over what he had achieved four years earlier. The result in the electoral college was 292 for McKinley and 155 for Bryan. "I am now the President of the whole people," said the winner when he heard the election's outcome.

McKinley's Second Term

As his second term began, McKinley gained further victories in foreign policy. Congress set up a civilian government for the Philippines when the insurrection

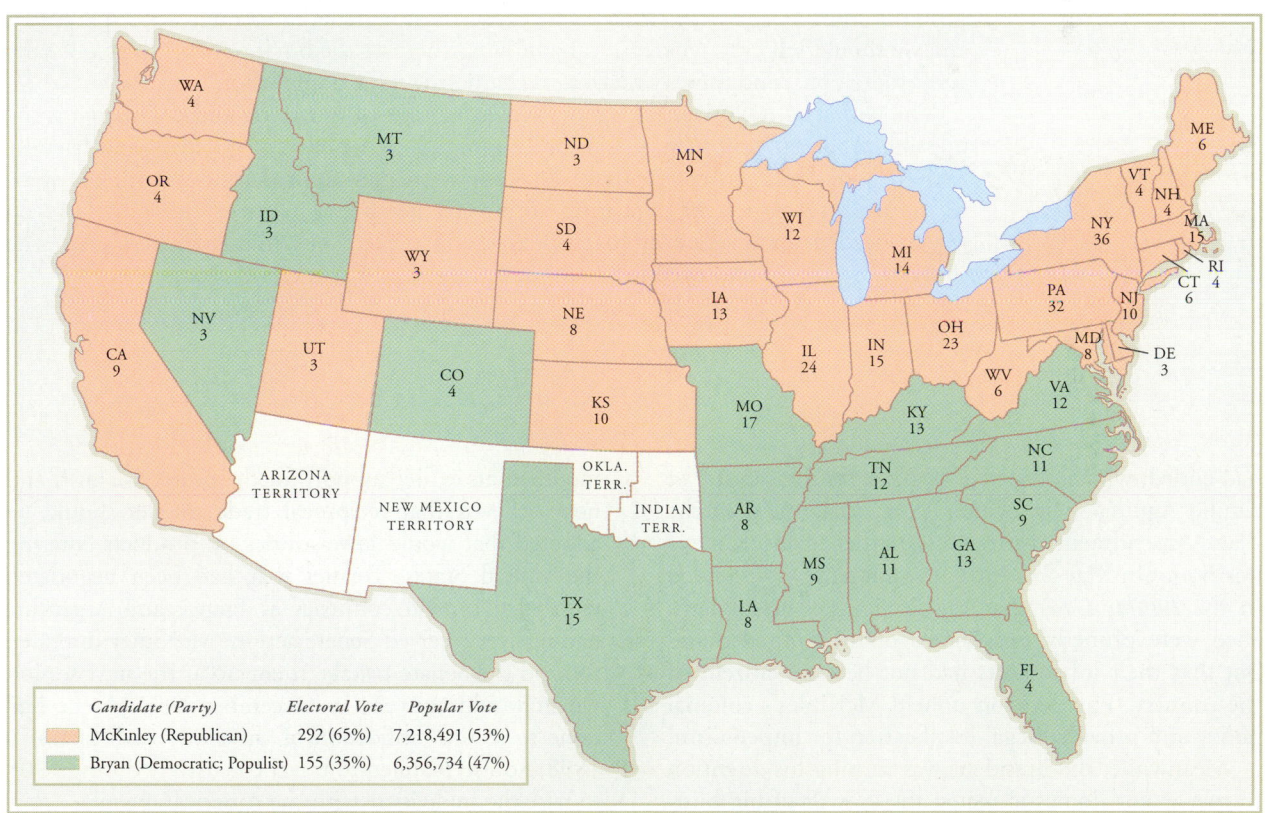

Candidate (Party)	Electoral Vote	Popular Vote
McKinley (Republican)	292 (65%)	7,218,491 (53%)
Bryan (Democratic; Populist)	155 (35%)	6,356,734 (47%)

MAP 19.4 | THE ELECTION OF 1900

WILLIAM MCKINLEY: RECIPROCAL TRADE AGREEMENTS, 1901

As he began his second term, President McKinley was urging his party and the nation to pursue a policy of trade expansion overseas. That theme dominated his last public address on September 5, 1901, where he called for reciprocity with our trading partners. The next day the president was assassinated.

By sensible trade arrangements which will not interrupt our home production, we shall extend the outlets for our increasing surplus. A system which provides a mutual exchange of commodities is manifestly essential to the continued and healthful growth of our export trade. We must not repose in fancied security that we can forever sell everything and buy little or nothing. If such a thing were possible, it would not be best for us or for those with whom we deal. We should take from our customers such of their products as we can use without harm to our industries and labor.

Reciprocity is the natural outgrowth of our wonderful industrial development under the domestic policy now firmly established. What we produce beyond our domestic consumption must have a vent abroad. The excess must be relieved through a foreign outlet, and we should sell everywhere we can and buy wherever the buying will enlarge our sales and productions, and thereby make a greater demand for home labor.

The period of exclusiveness is past. The expansion of our trade and commerce is the pressing problem. Commercial wars are unprofitable. A policy of goodwill and friendly trade relations will prevent reprisals. Reciprocity treaties are in harmony with the spirit of the times; measures of retaliation are not. If perchance some of our tariffs are no longer needed for revenue or to encourage and protect our industries at home, why should they not be employed to extend and promote our markets abroad?

---

had ended, which occurred shortly after the capture of Emilio Aguinaldo in March 1901. Enactment of the Platt Amendment further strengthened McKinley's position. On May 27, 1901, the Supreme Court ruled in the *Insular Cases* that the Philippines and Puerto Rico were properly possessions of the United States but that their inhabitants had not become citizens of the country. The decision upheld McKinley's colonial policy and provided legal justification for imperialism.

Meanwhile, the president was turning his attention to two major domestic issues: the growth of big business and the issue of high tariffs. By 1901 McKinley was persuaded that some action was necessary to enforce the Sherman Antitrust Act of 1890. He had also

modified his earlier support for the protective tariff and now believed that reciprocal trade treaties should be adopted that would lower duties on products entering the United States. Treaties that had been negotiated with such foreign countries as France and Argentina had not yet received Senate action. McKinley intended to prod the Senate to take them up at the next session which would convene in December 1901. As he had done to secure ratification of the treaty with Spain in 1898, he also planned to travel extensively during 1901 to raise the trade issue with the American people.

As the new century began, McKinley had revived the power of the presidency after the decades of congressional supremacy that followed the Civil War. He

had expanded the size of the president's staff, begun to involve the press in the coverage of White House affairs, and personalized the office through his travels. In many respects, McKinley was the first modern president.

THE UNITED STATES ON THE EVE OF THE TWENTIETH CENTURY

The nation saw the arrival of the twentieth century on December 31, 1900, with a mixture of confidence about what the United States had accomplished and apprehension about what the future held. The depression of the 1890s remained a vivid memory for most citizens, even with the return of prosperity after 1897. The shift in attitudes toward government and its role that had occurred during the hard times led many people to advocate programs of social reform. Such people were beginning to think of themselves as "progressives" and of those who disliked change as "conservatives."

Calls for Change

With the end of the century in sight, and the experience of the war with Spain still vivid, there was a flurry of public debate about the direction of the nation. Reformers gathered to discuss campaigns for change. A National Social and Political Conference took place in Buffalo, New York, in 1899 that brought together Eugene V. Debs, Henry Demarest Lloyd, Samuel Gompers, and Hazen Pingree, among others. The delegates called for "equality of economic opportunity and political power" as well as equal access "to all the material and social resources needful for the living of free, righteous, happy, and complete lives." Their goals required a more activist government than had been common in the nineteenth century.

In 1900 other future advocates of change came onto the scene. After a long political battle in Wisconsin, Robert M. La Follette finally won election as governor. Regular Republicans supported him, but his agenda looked toward changes in the way the state government functioned. A devastating hurricane in Galveston, Texas, in September 1900 caused significant damage to that Texas city. Political leaders there turned to a new form of government to deal with re-

Jane Addams reads a book with one of the children at Hull House.

building. Commissioners of fire, water, police and other services replaced the older style of ward leaders. The idea of having officials tied to the workings of city departments rather than representing geographic areas would attract increasing attention after the turn of the new century.

In the academic world, a biting analysis of how Americans used the wealth that they had acquired during the process of industrialization was published. Thorstein Veblen was a professor at the University of Chicago when he wrote *The Theory of the Leisure Class* (1899). In this book he analyzed the ways in which citizens displayed their social status. "Elegant dress serves its purpose of elegance not only in that it is expensive," he wrote, "but also because it is the insignia of leisure." Although his writings offered more diagnosis than solutions, Veblen was a provocative critic of capitalist institutions and practices at a time when his fellow citizens worried about their impact on national life.

As the twentieth century began, Americans were eating more mass-produced foods. In this advertisement for Postum, a substitute for coffee, two women discuss what the drink can do for their complexion and general health.

Miss Nervis Hedake: "I wonder if it really is Coffee that keeps me sallow, skinny and sick most of the time."

Miss Comfort: "I used to do a bit of wondering, too, until I tried it out by quitting Coffee and using **Postum**."

"THERE'S A REASON" for **POSTUM**

Postum Cereal Co., Ltd., Battle Creek, Mich., U. S. A.

At both ends of the economic spectrum, Americans looked to organization to address social ills. In 1900 Italian and Jewish immigrants who worked in the clothing business in New York City united to form the International Ladies Garment Workers Union (ILGWU). The membership was predominantly female, and they used the ILGWU to spread the ideas of unionism to other immigrant workers and to discuss alternatives to the existing system. Also in 1900 the more well-to-do business leaders of the day created the National Civic Federation. Made up of representatives from organized labor, the business community, and the public, the NCF sought to promote harmony between labor and capital. While most people in business remained staunchly anti-union, the Federation suggested that alternative policies might exist.

⟜ CONCLUSION ⟜

A balance sheet on the achievements of the late nineteenth century was a mixed one. Optimists could cite the nation's burgeoning productive capacity, the totals of steel produced and railroad track laid, and the impressive per capita wealth of U.S. citizens. Most of the population could read, and there were more than 2,000 newspapers available covering a staggering variety of subjects. The papers included elaborate coverage of sports and the new advice columns that "Dorothy Dix" and other writers made famous. There was an equally dazzling array of magazines on the newsstands with growing numbers of illustrations of national and world events. Advertisers spent $90 million in 1900 to tempt readers to try their products.

The United States was devoted to education. There were 1,700 libraries in the nation that held more than 5,000 volumes in their collections. Almost 240,000 students attended the nation's 977 colleges and universities at the turn of the century, or a little more than 1 percent of Americans between the ages of fifteen and twenty-five. Eighty percent of these institutions admitted women to their programs, although men received four times as many degrees as women did. Below the college level, 16 million children went to public schools. The educated, literate workforce that resulted was the envy of competing economies in Western Europe.

On the negative side of the balance sheet were the social problems that the nation confronted. An esti-

mated 10 million Americans, or about 13 percent of the population, lived below the poverty line. A visitor to the United States said that half its population was "ill-housed, ill-fed, and ill-clothed." Although the often-anticipated social revolution of the 1890s had not occurred, influential leaders such as Theodore Roosevelt worried about the potential for violence and upheaval if moderate reforms did not take place. In addition, the nation faced the problems of race that had not been resolved since the Civil War. Other issues were the fate of Native Americans, and the place of immigrants in American society. As the century ended, there were ample tasks to be done. Americans turned to these duties with an energy and vigor that made the twenty years between 1900 and 1920 famous as an age of political reform and government regulation.

RECOMMENDED READINGS

Beisner, Robert L. *From the Old Diplomacy to the New, 1865–1900,* 2nd ed. (1986) looks at the foreign policy changes that occurred during the 1890s.

Gould, Lewis L. *The Spanish-American War and President McKinley* (1982) is a brief, interpretive account of the war in 1898 and its consequences.

Hoffman, Charles. *The Depression of the Nineties: An Economic History* (1970) is good for the economic causes of the Panic.

Jensen, Richard Joseph. *The Winning of the Midwest: Social and Political Conflict, 1888–1896* (1971) examines why people voted as they did during the 1890s.

Lofgren, Charles A. *The Plessy Case: A Legal-Historical Interpretation* (1987) considers a key legal step toward a segregated nation.

Morgan, H. Wayne. *From Hayes to McKinley: National Party Politics, 1877–1896* (1969) is a lively look at the political battles of the era.

Schlereth, Thomas J. *Victorian America: Transformations in Everyday Life, 1876–1915* (1991) is strong on the social and cultural changes that occurred during the 1890s.

Thelen, David P. *The New Citizenship: Origins of Progressivism in Wisconsin, 1885–1900* (1972) looks at the ways in which consumers in a key state protested the hard times and corrupt politics of the decade.

Welch, Richard. *Response to Imperialism: The United States and the Philippine-American War, 1899–1902* (1979) provides a balanced and perceptive overview of a central episode in American imperialism.

Williams, R. Hal. *Years of Decision: American Politics in the 1890s* (1993) is the best narrative account of this important decade.

The Depression and Its Impact
Lindsey, Almont. *The Pullman Strike* (1967).
Salvatore, Nick. *Eugene V. Debs: Citizen and Socialist* (1982).
Schwantes, Carlos A. *Coxey's Army: An American Odyssey* (1985).
Welch, Richard E. *The Presidencies of Grover Cleveland* (1988).

Politics
Durden, Robert. *The Climax of Populism: The Election of 1896* (1965).
Glad, Paul. *McKinley, Bryan and the People* (1964).
Gould, Lewis L. *The Presidency of William McKinley* (1980).
Jones, Stanley L. *The Presidential Election of 1896* (1964).
Morgan, H. Wayne. *William McKinley and His America* (1963).

Foreign Policy
Campbell, Charles S. *The Transformation of American Foreign Relations, 1865–1900* (1976).
Healy, David. *U.S. Expansionism: The Imperialist Urge in the 1890s* (1970).
Morgan, H. Wayne. *America's Road to Empire* (1965).
Offner, John L. *An Unwanted War: The Diplomacy of the United States and Spain over Cuba, 1895–1898* (1992).
Young, Marilyn Blatt. *Rhetoric of Empire: American China Policy, 1895–1901* (1968).

Race and Segregation
Gatewood, Willard B. *Aristocrats of Color: The Black Elite, 1880–1920* (1990).
Harlan, Louis R. *Booker T. Washington: The Making of a Black Leader, 1865–1901* (1972).
Meier, August. *Negro Thought in America, 1880–1915: Racial Ideologies in the Age of Booker T. Washington* (1963).

Women
Buhle, Mari Jo. *Women and American Socialism, 1870–1920* (1983).
Eisenstein, Sara. *Give Us Bread but Give Us Roses: Working Women's Consciousness in the United States, 1890 to the First World War* (1983).
Katzman, David M. *Seven Days a Week: Women and Domestic Service in Industrializing America* (1981).
Peiss, Kathy. *Cheap Amusements: Working Women and Leisure in Turn-of-the-Century New York* (1986).

THE ACTIVIST PRESIDENT ON TOUR

Theodore Roosevelt imparted his energy and enthusiasm to the first decade of the twentieth century. Here he sits astride a horse during one of his frequent trips around the United States. His intense smile became one of the trademarks of his public image.

Chapter 20

THEODORE ROOSEVELT AND

PROGRESSIVE REFORM

1901 - 1909

ON SEPTEMBER 6, 1901, President William McKinley was shot during a public reception in Buffalo, New York. A week later he died and Vice President Theodore Roosevelt became president. The eight years that followed were a time of political change that has come to be known as the Progressive Era. Responding to the social and economic impact of industrialism, Americans endeavored to reshape their nation so as to curb the power of large businesses, improve conditions for the consumer, and reform the political parties.

In the process Americans confronted new issues. Citizens argued about whether government should regulate the economy and whether the power to do so should be local or national. The political party became a major source of contention. Its critics contended that the intense partisanship of the late nineteenth century had corrupted government and weakened democracy. Power should be shifted away from the parties and toward the individual voter. Other advocates of change clamored for more voter participation in the electoral system. This would be accomplished by broadening the ability of citizens to propose laws, choose candidates, and overturn judicial decisions. Thus, during a time of prosperity at home and relative peace abroad, the United States went through a decade of political ferment. The issues that Americans debated at the turn of the twentieth century would dominate the agenda of domestic policy for decades to come.

THE AGE OF THEODORE ROOSEVELT

At forty-two, Theodore Roosevelt was the youngest man to become president. He was already famous as an author, hunter, naturalist, soldier, and politician. During the war with Spain he raised a volunteer regiment called the Rough Riders and led them on a dangerous charge in Cuba toward fortified Spanish positions on Kettle Hill. Victory made him a national hero, and he won the governorship of New York in 1898. When he publicized corporate abuses in his state, Republican leaders pushed his name for the vice presidency in 1900 in order to get him out of their way. To the chagrin of party insiders, McKinley's murder thrust Roosevelt into the political spotlight.

"It is a dreadful thing to come into the presidency in this way," he wrote to a friend, "but it would be a far worse thing to be morbid about it." Roosevelt

CHRONOLOGY

1901	United States Steel created
	William McKinley inaugurated for second term
	Theodore Roosevelt becomes president after McKinley's assassination
1902	Antitrust suit filed against Northern Securities Company
	Anthracite coal strike
	Teddy Bear toy introduced
	McClure's Magazine starts muckraking journalism
1903	Elkins Act outlaws railroad rebates
	Alaska Boundary dispute settled
	Panama Canal Zone acquired
	Wright brothers make first successful powered flight
	National Women's Trade Union League founded
1904	Roosevelt elected president but declines to run in 1908
	Roosevelt Corollary to Monroe Doctrine announced
1905	Niagara Movement to improve conditions for African Americans starts
	Portsmouth Conference settles Russo-Japanese War
1906	Algeciras Conference in Morocco
	President Roosevelt attacks Muckrakers
	Passage of Hepburn Act (railroads), Pure Food and Drug Act, Meat Inspection Amendment
1907	Panic of 1907
	Self-contained electric clothes washer developed
	Florenz Ziegfeld begins annual Broadway review called "Ziegfeld Follies"; continues until 1931
1908	Henry Ford introduces Model T automobile
	Election of William Howard Taft
	Supreme Court upholds Oregon law limiting hours of work for women in *Muller* v. *Oregon*
	First Mother's Day celebrated in Philadelphia
1909	Taft inaugurated as president
	National Association for the Advancement of Colored People (NAACP) founded
	Roosevelt leaves for Africa

pledged to continue McKinley's policies and retained the slain president's cabinet. From his first days in office, however, the youthful and vigorous Roosevelt made news in ways that no previous president had done. He changed the official name of the president's residence to the White House and infused energy into its daily routine. His large family—he had six children—captivated the nation. His second wife, Edith Roosevelt, hired a social secretary and played a more visible cultural role as first lady. The president's oldest daughter, Alice Lee, made her debut in the White House, kept a pet snake, and drove around Washington in fast cars. "I can be President of the United States or I can control Alice," Roosevelt told friends who asked him to rein in his daughter. "I cannot possibly do both."

The Roosevelt Agenda

Roosevelt planned to be a strong and forceful president. He wanted to make the government "the most efficient instrument" to help the American people. In time, he decided that the president should be the "steward" of the general welfare. As long as the Constitution did not prohibit executive action, the president should stretch the limits of what was possible. "I did not usurp power," he wrote later, "but I did greatly broaden the use of executive power." Roosevelt built on McKinley's example but he went further, causing the public to see the president as the focus of national authority.

The nation watched him in fascination. When Roosevelt was "in the neighborhood," said a reporter,

the public could "no more look the other way than a small boy can turn his head from a circus parade followed by a steam calliope." Roosevelt reformed college football to make it less violent, pursued simplified spelling of English (*thru* instead of *through,* for example), and waged loud, frequent quarrels with political enemies. Like a preacher in church, he called the White House his "bully pulpit," using it to give sermons to the country about morality and duty.

The new president had a number of goals. He wanted to limit the power of big business in order to avoid pressure for more radical reforms from the Democrats or Socialists. He believed that the nation had to protect its natural resources. Before 1912, he saw the Republican party as the best means to implement his agenda. As a result, he did not challenge the party's leaders on the protective tariff. He cooperated with the conservative Republicans who dominated Congress during his first term. But after 1905 as he became more committed to reform and exerted presidential power more vigorously, his relations with Capitol Hill worsened.

Theodore Roosevelt was the first celebrity president. The spread of newspapers and the emergence of motion pictures made it possible for Americans to follow the nation's leader with greater attention than they had during the nineteenth century. Roosevelt dramatized what went on in Washington. By using the power of his office, he strengthened the presidency to meet future challenges.

The United States at the Outset of the Twentieth Century

In 1901 Americans balanced confidence about the future in a new century with worries about the direction in which their society was moving. There were ample reasons for national pride. The population stood at 76 million, up from 63 million ten years earlier. Immigrants accelerated the growth of the population. New arrivals came in at a prodigious rate during the first decade. There were 449,000 in 1900, 648,000 in 1902, and over 1.1 million in 1906. Like their late-nineteenth-century predecessors, most of these newcomers settled in the nation's growing cities. Israel Zangwill wrote a famous play, *The Melting Pot,* that celebrated the United States as "God's Crucible, the great melting pot where all the races of Europe are

TABLE 20.1 IMMIGRATION INTO THE U.S., 1901–1909	
1901	487,918
1902	687,743
1903	857,046
1904	812,870
1905	1,026,499
1906	1,100,735
1907	1,285,349
1908	782,870
1909	751,786

SOURCE   *The Statistical History of the United States* (1965), p. 56.

melting and reforming!" The reality was less simple and less benign, but Zangwill's vision appealed to many, and the phrase "melting pot" came into widespread use in describing American society.

Most Americans, however, still lived in rural areas or small towns with fewer than 2,500 residents. Not for another twenty years would the population become more urban than rural. As the cities expanded, tensions between rural and urban areas mounted.

A Longer Lifespan

People lived longer in 1900, a trend that accelerated throughout the century. Life expectancy for white men rose from forty-seven years in 1901 to almost fifty-four in 1920. For white women, the increase was from around fifty-one years in 1901 to almost fifty-five in 1920. Life expectancy for members of minority groups rose from thirty-four years in 1901 to just over forty-five in 1920.

The population was young in 1900. The median age was twenty-three; it rose to just over twenty-five by 1920. The death rate for the entire population was seventeen per thousand in 1900. It fell to thirteen per thousand by 1920. For infants in the Progressive Era, the prospects were less encouraging. In 1915, the first

year for which there are accurate numbers, almost sixty-one deaths were recorded for every 10,000 births. The situation worsened during the next several years, and the infant mortality rate reached more than sixty-eight deaths per 10,000 births in 1921. For non-white babies the picture was even worse: There were almost 106 deaths per 10,000 live births in 1915. Some positive changes occurred, however. More and more mothers gave birth in hospitals rather than at home. Improved medical techniques and the antiseptic setting of the hospitals helped reduce the incidence of infant mortality.

Children at Work

The problem of child labor that had developed during the late nineteenth century persisted. In 1900 more than 1,750,000 children between the ages of ten and fifteen worked in the labor force. An example of the situation for these child laborers was the case of Sadie Frowne, an immigrant girl from Poland, who went to work in a sweatshop in New York City's garment district before she was fifteen. She made four dollars a week and reported that "the machines go like mad all day, because the faster you work the more money you get."

In the South, children worked in cotton mills. Conditions were so bad that reformers called the mills and their communities "the poorest place in the world for training citizens of a democracy." Abolishing child labor became a major goal of reform campaigns after 1900.

Changes in the Family

In families whose children did not have to work, child rearing became more organized and systematic. Kindergartens became popular as a way to prepare children for school. There were 5,000 in 1900 and nearly 9,000 twenty years later. The federal government held conferences on child rearing and issued booklets about infant care. Improved methods of contraception led to smaller families. In 1900 the average mother had 3.566 children compared with seven children in 1800. Attention shifted to rearing fewer children more successfully.

The status of women also changed after 1900. Divorce became easier and more common. About four marriages out of every thousand ended in divorce in 1900 but in the ensuing years the divorce rate increased three times faster than the rate of population growth. There were 56,000 divorces in 1900 and 100,000 in 1914. Other women delayed marriage to attend college. Yet opportunities for women to enter law, medicine, or higher education remained limited. In 1920 fewer than one and one half percent of all attorneys were women. In 1910 there were only 9,000 women doctors, about 6 percent of all physicians. Restrictive policies on admissions to medical schools and barriers to staff positions at hospitals posed obstacles to women who sought to become doctors. Nursing and social work were more accessible to women, but they still faced condescension from men. "We don't mind the nurses," said one male medical student. "They are sort of servants, you understand."

Women at Work

Women in factories, mills, and garment sweatshops also saw little improvement in their condition as the new century began. Their workday was ten hours long, and six- and seven-day weeks were common. Men received more pay than women; labor unions regarded women as competitors for jobs held by men. Women set up their own unions, such as the Women's Trade Union League, established in 1903. They also formed the backbone of the International Ladies Garment Workers Union (ILGWU) which led strikes in New York City in 1910 and 1911. Women worked because they had no alternative, and one woman in the cap-making trade spoke for many of her sister laborers when she said: "Work . . . spells no gateway to freedom."

Social trends slowly altered the status of women. Their clothes became less confining and cumbersome. The full skirt was still the fashion in 1900, but soon thereafter petticoats and corsets disappeared. Women began to show their ankles and arms in public. Some more daring young women, such as Alice Roosevelt, smoked in public; others used cosmetics openly. In dance halls and restaurants, young people danced the turkey trot and the bunny hug to the rhythms of ragtime. A nervous magazine worried that "sex o'clock had struck."

The institution of marriage felt the effects of these changes. Marriage ceremonies used the word "obey" less frequently. Women asked more of their husbands,

including companionship and sexual pleasure. Government programs were instituted to encourage family togetherness. In 1913, prodded by advocates of the traditional home (and the florist industry), Congress designated Mother's Day as a national holiday. Throughout the Progressive Era politicians and reformers debated how the government might safeguard the family.

A Nation of Consumers

In 1900, 76 million people in the United States owned 21 million horses. Some forecasters said that the automobile would replace the horse, but in 1903 only a little more than 11,000 cars were sold. During the next decade, however, Henry Ford created the Model T. Ford's goal was to use mass production techniques to build an automobile that could be sold in large numbers. By 1908 the Model T was ready for distribution, priced at about $850. Sales increased rapidly as Ford steadily reduced the car's price. In 1908 5,986 Model T's were sold; by 1912, the total was 78,611. The mass-produced automobile was a key element in the evolution of the consumer society during the Progressive Era.

Standardized food products also gained popular acceptance. For example, Asa Candler's Coca-Cola (see Chapter 17) became available throughout the country when the parent company licensed bottling plants everywhere. There were 241 bottlers by 1905, 493 by 1910, and 1,095 a decade later. In 1912 Procter and Gamble introduced Crisco, a vegetable shortening, as a way of selling its cottonseed oil. The company used marketing campaigns in popular periodicals, held "Crisco teas" at which club women could try out their own recipes, and created cooking schools to spread awareness of the new product. By 1915 its advertising proclaimed that "Crisco is rapidly taking the place of butter and lard for cooking." Other famous brands, such as Kellogg's Corn Flakes, Uneeda Biscuit, and Kodak cameras, relied on mass advertising, billboards, and mail flyers to instill popular desire for these new and convenient consumer goods.

The Role of Advertising

Advertising became a central feature of American culture. Newspapers and magazines gave lower rates to advertisers who used entire pages. Billboards appealed to the new motoring public and outraged garden club

Sponsorship of car racing provided a means for automobile manufacturers such as Henry Ford to publicize their new vehicles. Ford is standing next to the racer that is driven by Barney Oldfield, one of the first of the famous race drivers.

members when they obscured scenic views. Advertising agencies shaped the content of product information. Men were urged to buy Gillette razors because "You Ought to Shave Every Morning." Toothbrush ads proclaimed that Americans should "keep their teeth and mouths clean." The Kodak camera was an essential part of the Christmas season as "your family historian."

To master these markets, advertisers surveyed potential purchasers. Their goal was "to reduce the art of advertising to a science—to develop what may be called the mathematics of advertising." Agencies tracked customers through reports from salespeople, mail surveys, and questionnaires printed in magazines. Coca-Cola, for example, increased its advertising budget annually and in 1913 distributed 5 million metal Coca-Cola signs across the country.

The mail order services of Sears, Roebuck, & Co. became a familiar part of countless American households as the new century began. In this "consumers guide," Sears is instructing its customers about comparing the prices of local shopkeepers with the less expensive goods that can be obtained through the mail.

The Example of Sears

Sears, Roebuck Company was a leader in consumer marketing. Founded during the economic depression of 1893, the company was the brainchild of Richard Warren Sears, who believed in low prices as a selling technique. Beginning with mail-order watches, Sears expanded to general merchandise which was sold in a catalogue published annually. He cut prices for desirable products such as sewing machines and cream separators and soon produced record sales. Sears spent lavishly on advertising—over $1.5 million in 1902—and promised low prices, guarantees of any products and parts, and the opportunity to order merchandise without prepaying. "Send No Money" was the Sears slogan. Volume sales at low prices built a market for Sears; the company sent out more than 1.5 million catalogues in 1902. Americans increasingly thought of themselves as the nation of consumers that people like Sears envisioned.

In many respects, the United States occupied an enviable position. A British visitor said that the standard of American life had reached a height "hitherto unrealized in a civilized society." National income stood at $17 billion; the average American's annual per capita income of $227 was the highest in the world. Innovations promised further abundance to a prosperous population.

Despite these positive trends, citizens worried about the nation's future. The growth of big business, the spread of labor organizations, the corruption in politics, the decline of the individual in a bureaucratic society—all these trends prompted fear that older values and attitudes were under assault. The early twentieth century saw a renewed debate about the purpose and accomplishments of the United States. For white Americans, however, the persistent issue of race and the treatment of minorities did not attract much attention during this period of reform.

Race Relations in the Roosevelt Era

Theodore Roosevelt encountered the race issue soon after he became president. On October 16, 1901, Booker T. Washington dined with the president and his family at the White House. The evening meal was social but the purpose of Washington's visit was political. Since he had emerged as a leading spokesman for

W. E. B. Du Bois on what blacks felt during the age of Roosevelt 1903

SOURCE   W. E. B. Du Bois, *The Souls of Black Folk* (1903)

After the Egyptian and Indian, the Greek and Roman, the Teuton and Mongolian, the Negro is a sort of seventh son, born with a veil, and gifted with second-sight in this American world—a world which yields him no true self-consciousness, but only lets him see himself through the revelation of the other world. It is a peculiar sensation, this double-consciousness, this sense of always looking at oneself through the eyes of others, of measuring one's soul by the tape of a world that looks on in amused contempt and pity. One ever feels his twoness—an American, a Negro; two souls, two thoughts, two unreconciled strivings; two warring ideals in one dark body, whose dogged strength alone keeps it from being torn asunder.

The history of the American Negro is the history of this strife, this longing to attain self-conscious manhood, to merge his double self into a better and truer self. In this merging he wishes neither of the older selves to be lost. He would not Africanize America, for America has too much to teach the world and Africa. He would not bleach his Negro soul in a flood of white Americanism, for he knows that Negro blood has a message for the world. He simply wishes to make it possible for a man to be both a Negro and an American, without being cursed and spit upon by his fellows, without having the doors of opportunity closed roughly in his face.

African Americans during the 1890s (see Chapter 19), Washington had built a political machine among black Republicans in the South. He came to the White House to discuss the new president's nominations for patronage positions in the South. When southern newspapers learned that a black man had eaten with the president, they were furious. A Tennessee editor called the occasion "the most damnable outrage that has ever been perpetrated by any citizen of the United States." Other southern newspapers complained about the episode for months.

Roosevelt saw himself as a friend of African Americans and the heir of Abraham Lincoln. He moved cautiously on race during his first term and conciliated white southerners during his second. Between 1901 and 1905 he defended black appointees to post offices and customs houses who were under attack in the South and he spoke out against lynching. He also resisted attempts by "Lily-White" Republicans to remove blacks from the party in the South. After 1905, however, he criticized African Americans when blacks did not inform southern authorities where accused black criminals might be found. When black soldiers were falsely charged with attempting to kill white residents of Brownsville, Texas, in August 1906, the president discharged their units without a hearing and blocked congressional efforts to reinstate the men.

Black Life in the Early Twentieth Century

For the majority of African Americans in the era of Theodore Roosevelt, segregation was now an ever-present fact of life. "Don't monkey with white supremacy," warned a Mississippi newspaper, "it is loaded with determination, gun-powder, and dynamite." Eight days after Washington and Roosevelt sat down to dinner, a black man named "Bill" Morris was burned at the stake in Balltown, Louisiana. He had allegedly robbed and raped a white woman. Apprehended by a mob, Morris was "taken back to the scene of his crime." No trial occurred. Instead, "pine knots and pine straw were heaped about him and over this kerosene was poured and the whole set on fire."

Between seventy and eighty black citizens of the United States were lynched during each year of Roosevelt's presidency.

Social and economic inequality were the lot of African Americans as well. Conditions had worsened since the passage of segregation laws in the South during the 1880s and 1890s (see Chapters 18 and 19). Nine million southern blacks lived in rural poverty. The field hands sang as they toiled: "Done worked all the summer/Done worked all the fall/And here comes Christmas/And I ain't got nothing at all." Black wage workers received much less per day and per hour than their white counterparts in the same trade. Other black men were industrial or agricultural peasants, virtual slaves who received only food and a place to sleep for their labor.

The system of segregation affected blacks in every aspect of their existence. "The white man is the boss," said one man. "You got to talk to him like he is the boss." Facilities for the races were supposed to be "separate but equal," but this was rarely the case in practice. In Florida, for example, the amount spent on educating white children was $5.92 per capita annually, as compared with $2.27 for black children.

Exclusion from Politics

Blacks no longer voted in significant numbers because of the barriers white politicians had raised during the 1890s and early 1900s. The white primary barred black voters from elections that selected Democratic party candidates. In the one-party South this meant that African Americans had no voice in the political contests that really mattered. They retained some role in the Republican party because their votes helped to choose the delegates to the national convention. A few black politicians in some states of the upper South wielded influence. For the most part, however, the bitter comment of one African-American politician summed up the situation: "The Negro's status in Southern politics is dark as Hell and smells like cheese."

When he dined with Theodore Roosevelt, Booker T. Washington demonstrated to other African Americans that he could deliver the support of white politicians. To keep the president's friendship and to obtain money from wealthy whites, Washington had to accept the existence of segregation and the system it represented. Washington was doing what he had proposed in his speech in Atlanta in 1895 (see Chapter 19). By the time Roosevelt became president, more militant blacks were saying that Washington's methods had failed.

The Stirrings of Militant Protest

Their leader was W. E. B. Du Bois, who had received a doctoral degree from Harvard and who taught sociology at Atlanta University, a black institution. After initially supporting Washington's policy, Du Bois decided that blacks had to confront segregation. "Separate schools for Whites and Blacks are not equal, can not be made equal, and . . . are not intended to be equal," he wrote. In *The Souls of Black Folk* (1903), Du Bois criticized Washington's methods as having

During the first ten years of the twentieth century, the writings and political work of W.E.B. Du Bois provided a more militant alternative to the strategy of Booker T. Washington that accepted publicly the institutions of segregation and white supremacy. Du Bois's agitation led to the creation of the National Association for the Advancement of Colored People.

"practically accepted the alleged inferiority of the Negro."

In June 1905 Du Bois led a delegation of twenty-nine blacks to Niagara Falls, New York, where they issued a call for political and social rights. The meeting denied that "the Negro-American assents to inferiority, is submissive under oppression and apologetic before insult." The Niagara Conference aroused Booker T. Washington's intense opposition, but it laid the basis for more lasting protests about the worsening situation of African Americans.

ROOSEVELT AND THE MODERN PRESIDENCY: THE FIRST TERM

Early in his first term Roosevelt launched a dramatic attack on consolidated economic power. On February 19, 1902, the Department of Justice announced that it was filing suit under the Sherman Antitrust Act (1890) against the Northern Securities Company. That firm, created in late 1901, merged major railroads in the Northwest, including the Great Northern, the Northern Pacific, and the Chicago, Burlington, and Quincy Company. The key leaders in assembling this large company were James J. Hill and E. H. Harriman; their financing came from J. P. Morgan. The stated goal of the merger was to reduce destructive competition among warring railroads and make railroad rates more stable. Opposition to the merger came from states across which the company would operate, most notably in Minnesota. Farmers and business operators in the upper Midwest feared that a giant railroad would raise rates and limit their profits. They urged their governors to file suit against the new company in federal court. Many Americans believed that only the federal government could regulate such unbridled corporate power.

The creation of the Northern Securities Company was part of the trend toward larger economic units that had begun during the 1890s (see Chapter 19). A highly publicized case was that of the United States Steel Company which had been formed earlier in 1901. The steel merger symbolized bigness in business in the same way that the railroad combine did. Indeed, the same forces that led to consolidation in railroads promoted a similar result in steel.

At the turn of the century the Carnegie Steel Company dominated the industry, producing finished steel products at a lower unit cost than its rivals. For J. P. Morgan and the steel companies that he represented, Carnegie's power raised the possibility that competing firms might go bankrupt. The logical answer, Morgan concluded, was to buy out Carnegie and create a steel company that could control the entire industry. Morgan sent an aide to see Carnegie. "If Andy wants to sell, I'll buy," said Morgan. "Go and find his price."

Morgan's agent, Charles M. Schwab, found Carnegie on the golf course. Carnegie sent his answer a day later. In a penciled note, he told Morgan that the price was $480 million. Morgan paused and responded: "I accept this price." The merger was made public on March 3, 1901, the day before William McKinley began his second term. Carnegie Steel joined other firms financed by Morgan such as Federal Steel and the National Tube Company. The half-billion dollars that Carnegie received for his holding was a staggering sum in an era when there was no federal income tax, no capital gains tax, and low inflation. In modern terms, Carnegie probably would have received more than $50 billion.

The Challenge of United States Steel

The new company, United States Steel, was capitalized at $1.4 billion. It had 168,000 employees and controlled 60 percent of the steel industry's productive capacity. Smaller steel companies would have to compete with the vertical integration Carnegie had achieved with the company that Morgan had acquired. Workers in steel now faced a powerful employer that could fix wage levels in any way it chose. The prospect worried outside observers. "We have billion dollar combines," said one editor, "maneuvered by a handful of men who have never been in a plant and think of a factory as just another chip in a gigantic financial poker game."

Theodore Roosevelt worried too. He saw the forces that led to business consolidation as the logical outcome of economic development, but he did not believe that the federal government should passively stand by. The large corporations, Roosevelt decided, should not be destroyed. Firms that were socially beneficial should be encouraged; those that misbehaved should be regulated. At first Roosevelt thought that publicizing the activities of corporations would be enough regulation. He soon concluded that he must

The New York investment banker J.P. Morgan was the most powerful private individual in the United States during Theodore Roosevelt's presidency.

In 1904 the Supreme Court agreed with Roosevelt when the government won its case against the Northern Securities Company. By a 5–4 margin the justices ruled that the railroad company violated the Sherman Act. The case reestablished the power of the national government to use the Sherman Act, which had been called into question in the 1895 case of *U.S.* v. *E.C. Knight.* The American public saw Roosevelt as a "trustbuster" who was willing to curb the power of big business. Having established the principle that the government was supreme over any individual corporation, the president used trust-busting sparingly against "bad" trusts and sought to assist "good" trusts with policies that rewarded their positive behavior.

The Square Deal in the Coal Strike

The nation also applauded when Roosevelt intervened to end a strike in the coal industry during the autumn of 1902. The 140,000 members of the United Mine Workers walked off their jobs in the anthracite (hard coal) fields of Pennsylvania. The miners asked for a pay hike and for the railroads and coal operators to recognize their union in bargaining talks. Having lost an earlier strike in 1900, management wanted to break the strike and the union. As the walkout stretched into autumn, fears grew of coal shortages during the winter. If the voters were cold in November, the Republicans faced political losses in the 1902 congressional elections. Yet neither side in the walkout seemed prepared to yield to the other.

As the crisis worsened, Roosevelt intervened. He brought both sides to the White House in early October. Throughout a day of talks, Roosevelt urged the workers and owners to settle. The union's president, John Mitchell, said that arbitration was acceptable, but the mine owners refused. Roosevelt responded that he might bring in the army to mine coal. Facing that threat, J. P. Morgan and Elihu Root worked out a deal in which a presidential commission was set up to look into the strike. The panel granted the miners a 10 percent pay increase, but the union was not recognized. In 1894, Grover Cleveland had used federal troops to break the Pullman Strike (see Chapter 19). Now, Roosevelt wielded presidential power to treat capital and labor on an equal basis. Roosevelt called his approach "The Square Deal." His actions in the coal strike strengthened the power of the presidency.

establish the power of the federal government to intervene in the economy. The Northern Securities Company was unpopular, so the president acted.

Controlling the Trusts

After the Department of Justice made its announcement in February 1902, the stock market fell. J. P. Morgan hurried to Washington to ask the president if additional lawsuits were planned. No, said Roosevelt, "unless we find out . . . [that other companies] have done something wrong." Roosevelt argued the "trusts are creatures of the State, and the State not only has the right to control them, but it is in duty bound to control them wherever the need of such control is shown."

The United Mine Workers became a controversial labor union especially during the anthracite coal strike of 1902. This recruiting poster stresses the dangers of work in the mines and the need for miners to organize themselves for mutual protection and benefit. It reflects the ideology that lay behind the coal strike of 1902.

Roosevelt's record and his popularity limited Republican losses in the congressional elections. The results virtually assured the president's nomination as the Republican candidate in 1904. During the session of Congress that began in December 1902, Roosevelt endorsed the Elkins Act which would outlaw the rebates railroads gave to favored customers. The law was a prelude to later action to strengthen the Interstate Commerce Commission. Roosevelt also called for a law to create a Department of Commerce. One of the agencies of this new department would be a Bureau of Corporations, which would publicize corporate records and indicate which businesses were behaving in the public interest. Congressional opposition to this proposal melted away when Roosevelt charged that John D. Rockefeller and Standard Oil were lobbying against the legislation. Other laws strengthened the power of the Justice Department to pursue antitrust

cases. Roosevelt now had the weapons he sought to distinguish between businesses that he deemed socially good and those that behaved improperly. He attacked the unpopular meat-packing industry, known as the "Beef Trust," and then left business alone until he was safely reelected in 1904.

Roosevelt and Foreign Policy

Theodore Roosevelt enjoyed the exercise of the president's power in foreign policy. He wanted to complete the work left over from the Spanish-American War and make the United States a force in world affairs. Because the world was increasingly dangerous, military preparedness was a key goal. "There is a homely adage which runs," the president said, "'Speak softly and carry a big stick; you will go far.'" By 1905 he had added ten battleships to the navy and improved its gunnery. While Roosevelt loved to perform on the world stage without having to consult Congress, he always remembered the public's caution about overseas adventures. Except in the Philippines, where the guerilla war sputtered on, during his presidency Roosevelt sent no American forces into armed combat.

He did act vigorously in places where the power of the United States was dominant. In 1902, Germany and Great Britain used their navies to collect debts that Venezuela owed them; Roosevelt sent the U.S. Navy into the region to limit foreign involvement there. Similar problems with the Dominican Republic and its debts two years later led him to pronounce the "Roosevelt Corollary" which he believed was a natural extension of the Monroe Doctrine. In his annual message in 1904, he said that "chronic wrongdoing or impotence" of Latin American nations in paying their debts might lead the United States "to the exercise of an international police power." After 1905 the United States controlled customs revenues and tax services in the Dominican Republic.

Roosevelt also sought better relations with Great Britain. That policy would make it easier to secure a canal across Central America. A possible flashpoint between Washington and London was the boundary between Alaska and Canada. Discoveries of gold in the Yukon region attracted rival miners and speculators and raised the possibility of violence between Canadians and Americans. Roosevelt believed that Canada had no valid claims to the disputed territory of islands and inlets that provided access to the goldfields. He

THE ROOSEVELT
COROLLARY TO THE
MONROE DOCTRINE
1904, 1905

In his Annual Message (State of the Union Message) of 1904, President Theodore Roosevelt announced what became known as the Roosevelt Corollary to the Monroe Doctrine. His remarks emphasized the right and responsibility of the United States to intervene in the affairs of Latin American nations when they failed to fulfill their international responsibilities as Washington defined them. Roosevelt's comments represented a high point of American imperialistic attitude toward neighboring nations to the South.

. . . It is not true that the United States feels any land hunger or entertains any projects as regards the other nations of the Western Hemisphere save such as are for their welfare. All that this country desires is to see the neighboring countries stable, orderly, and prosperous. Any country whose people conduct themselves well can count upon our hearty friendship. If a nation shows that it knows how to act with reasonable efficiency and decency in social and political matters, if it keeps order and pays its obligations, it need fear no interference from the United States. Chronic wrongdoing, or an impotence which results in a general loosening of the ties of civilized society, may in America, as elsewhere, ultimately require intervention by some civilized nation, and in the Western Hemisphere the adherence of the United States to the Monroe Doctrine may force the United States, however reluctantly, in flagrant cases of such wrongdoing or impotence, to the exercise of an international police power. If every country washed by the Caribbean Sea would show the progress in stable and just civilization which with the aid of the Platt amendment Cuba has shown since our troops left the island, and which so many of the republics in both Americas are constantly and brilliantly showing, all question of interference by this Nation with their affairs would be at an end. Our interests and those of our southern neighbors are in reality identical. They have great natural riches, and if within their borders the reign of law and justice obtains, prosperity is sure to come to them. While they thus obey the primary laws of civilized society they may rest assured that they will be treated by us in a spirit of cordial and helpful sympathy. We would interfere with them only in the last resort, and then only if it became evident that their inability or unwillingness to do justice at home and abroad had violated the rights of the United States or had invited foreign aggression to the detriment of the entire body of American nations. It is a mere truism to say that every nation, whether in America or anywhere else, which desires to maintain its freedom, its independence, must ultimately realize that the right of such independence can not be separated from the responsibility of making good use of it.

used his influence with the British to gain a reluctant Canadian acceptance of an Anglo-Canadian-American commission to settle the problem. That body, in turn, gave the United States most of what it wanted in late 1903.

The acquisition of the Panama Canal Zone led to the most heated controversy of Roosevelt's foreign policy. The United States had wanted to see a waterway built across Central America for decades, but disease, mud, and the jungle defeated all construction efforts.

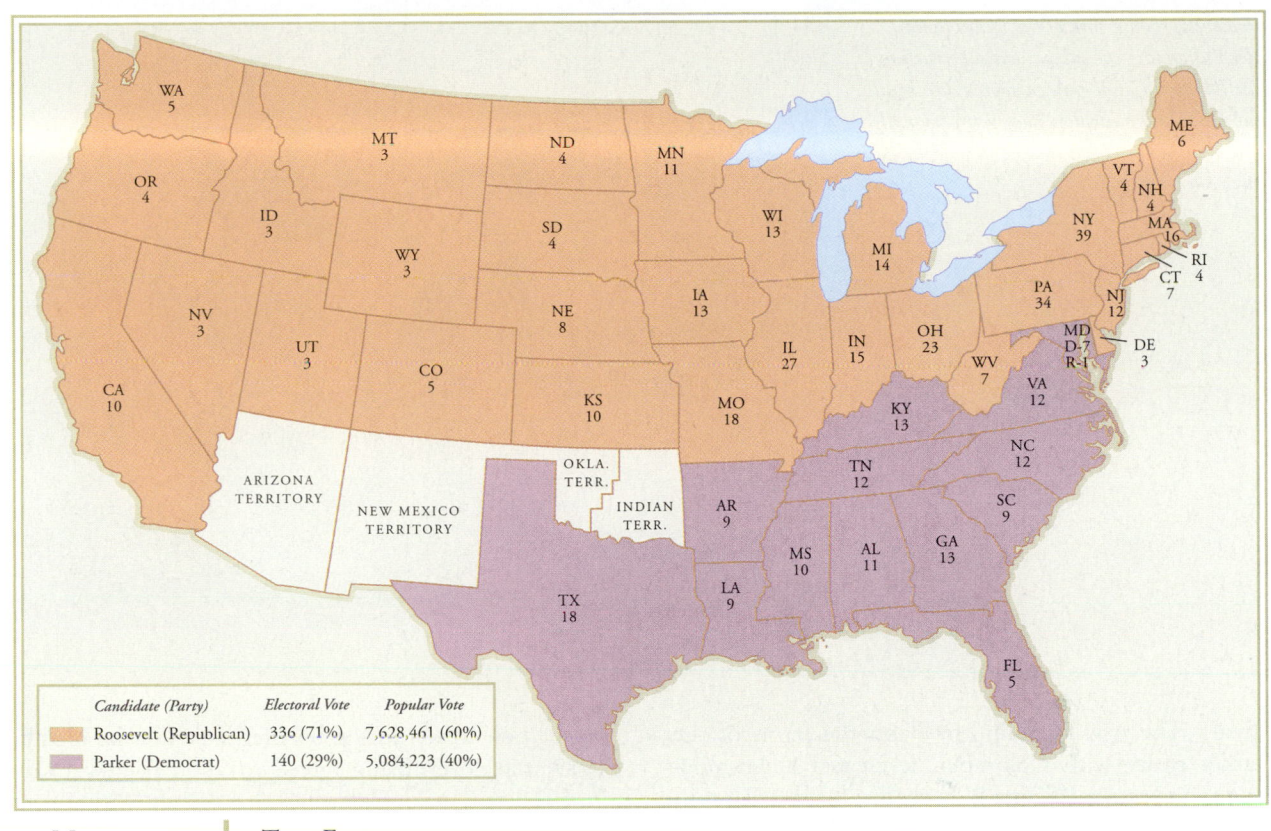

Candidate (Party)	Electoral Vote	Popular Vote
Roosevelt (Republican)	336 (71%)	7,628,461 (60%)
Parker (Democrat)	140 (29%)	5,084,223 (40%)

MAP 20.1 | THE ELECTION OF 1904

The most ambitious project collapsed during the 1880s. The New Panama Canal Company, a French firm, left behind some construction work and large financial debts.

The Spanish-American War reminded Americans of the need for a canal. It took the battleship U.S.S. *Oregon* two months to go from San Francisco Bay around the tip of South America to join the navy near Cuba. The McKinley administration negotiated with the British for the right to build a Central American canal that all nations could use freely. In the Hay-Pauncefote Treaty (1901), Great Britain gave up its rights to participate in a canal project. Congress then decided in 1902 that the best route lay across Panama. Secretary of State John Hay opened talks with Colombia, of which Panama was then a part. In 1903 Hay and a Colombian diplomat concluded the Hay-Herrán Convention. There would be a six-mile-wide canal zone, under American control, with a ninety-nine year lease. The Colombians would receive a $10 million payment

and $250,000 per year in rent. The U.S. Senate quickly ratified the pact.

Colombia was less cooperative. The Colombian Senate believed that the treaty infringed on their country's sovereignty, and the lawmakers wanted more money from the United States. Roosevelt was outraged. Within Panama, opponents of Colombia rule plotted revolution. Lawyers for the New Panama Canal Company lobbied for American intervention if a rebellion broke out. The uprising occurred in November 1903 amid strong signals that Washington supported the revolution. The presence of the cruiser U.S.S. *Nashville* and other American vessels discouraged the Colombians from putting down the rebellion. The United States recognized the new Panamanian government, as did other European and Latin American nations.

In November 1903 discussions with the representative of Panama, a Frenchman named Philippe Bunau-Varilla, led to drafting of the Hay-Bunau-Varilla

Roosevelt's sponsorship of the Panamanian Revolution and the subsequent construction of the Panama Canal gave cartoonists an ideal subject. This one depicts Roosevelt personally shoveling out the locks that became "The Path Between the Seas."

Treaty. The new pact improved on the terms of the earlier treaty with Colombia. It created a ten-mile-wide zone across Panama in exchange for the $10 million payment and the $250,000 annual rent. Within the Canal Zone, the United States could act as a sovereign nation, a provision that subsequent Panamanian governments resented greatly. Construction of the canal proceeded slowly until Roosevelt put the U.S. Army in charge in 1907. Then work moved ahead efficiently. Roosevelt visited Panama himself in 1906, thus becoming the first president to leave the continental United States while in office.

It cost more than $350 million to build the Panama Canal, or the equivalent of several billion dollars in modern funds. Almost 6,000 workers died of disease and accidents during the decade of construction. The official opening took place on August 15, 1914. Theodore Roosevelt regarded the canal as the greatest achievement of his presidency. His strong leadership, he believed, had made the waterway possible. "I took the Isthmus, started the canal, and then left Congress not to debate the canal, but to debate me." Roosevelt's infringement on Colombian sovereignty produced hard feelings in Latin America, however. Years later the Wilson administration signed a treaty with Colombia that gave it $25 million more, accompanied by an expression of "sincere regret" about what had happened. An angry Roosevelt prevented the Senate from acting

on the new treaty during his lifetime. After he died in 1919, the government agreed to another new treaty in 1921 that paid Colombia the money without an apology.

The Election of 1904

Roosevelt's domestic and foreign policy triumphs made him a unanimous choice for the Republican presidential nomination in 1904. The Democrats tried to run to the right of Roosevelt, and turned to Alton B. Parker, a very dull, conservative New York state judge. Parker proved an inept campaigner. Despite last-minute Democratic charges that big business was behind the Roosevelt campaign, the American people voted enthusiastically for the incumbent president. Roosevelt received more than 56 percent of the vote, compared to Parker's 38 percent. The Socialist party and its candidate Eugene V. Debs received a small number of votes. Roosevelt's 336 electoral votes were the most that any presidential candidate had ever won up to that time. It was an electoral landslide. The number of Americans who voted, however, was more than 400,000 below the 1900 figure. Turnout also slipped to under 65 percent of the voters in the North, compared with nearly 72 percent four years before. Popular participation in elections would

drop further in subsequent elections as interest in politics declined.

On the night that he was elected president in his own right, Roosevelt made a dramatic statement. He said that the three years he had already served represented his first term as president. Accordingly, he promised that he would not be a candidate for another term in 1908. By respecting the third-term tradition, he hoped to allay fears that he would use his popularity to remain president for life. Having assured the nation of his respect for this unwritten rule of politics, Roosevelt thought he could embark on a campaign of reform without being accused of personal ambition to stay in office.

In his 1904 annual message, Roosevelt asked Congress to strengthen the power of the Interstate Commerce Commission to regulate the railroads. He pointed to other social problems that the nation needed to address. Roosevelt contended that the power of the federal government should be used to make the whole society more just and equitable. He talked of carrying out the Square Deal he had promised in his campaign. With his gift for understanding where public opinion was going, Roosevelt had caught the spirit of change that came to be called the Progressive Movement. In his second term he put the power of the modern presidency behind the new agenda for reform.

PROGRESSIVE CAMPAIGNS TO REFORM THE NATION

The efforts to improve American life had gotten underway during the 1890s (see Chapter 19) but achieved national significance in the years just after 1904. Responding to the growth of cities, the problems of industrialism, and fears about the nation's future, the American people launched movements to clean up politics and society. The goals of progressivism were sometimes inconsistent and contradictory; its accomplishments were wide-ranging and important.

Consumers and Reformers

Progressivism occurred during a time of relative economic prosperity in which Americans saw themselves more as consumers than producers. A sense of well-being allowed middle-class citizens to address the social and economic problems that had emerged during the depression of the 1890s. After the deflation of the late nineteenth century, rising prices aroused popular concern about the high cost of living. Critics of the Republicans' protective tariff policies charged that customs duties added to inflation. Equally strong were fears of the effects of business consolidation on the smaller companies for which so many people worked. In 1909, 1 percent of firms accounted for 45 percent of manufactured goods.

When Americans focused on the products they bought and used, they listened when investigative reporters said that patent medicines were unsafe. The discovery that meatpacking plants and other food processors tolerated unsafe conditions led to federal regulation in 1906. Pure food and pure drugs were so necessary, reformers argued, that businesses would have to accept more governmental intrusion than ever.

The Currents of Reform

The movement for progressive reform drew upon forces that had been gathering strength for two decades (see Chapters 18 and 19). As the problems of industrialism and urban growth emerged, a coalition of groups proposed fresh answers. Diversity of goals and approach was the striking feature of early twentieth century reform. Nonetheless, shared assumptions united most people who called themselves progressives.

During the years before World War I in 1914, when Europe was at peace and society seemed to be improving, men and women believed that human nature was basically good and could be made better. The human environment could be reshaped, reformers contended. They also said that government at all levels could promote a better society, and the state had a duty to relieve the ills that confronted the nation as a result of industrial growth.

Differing Methods of Reform

The question of how best to accomplish such goals gave rise to two different approaches within progressive reform. One answer for the problems of democracy was more democracy. Proposals for a *direct*

primary to allow voters to choose the candidates of their political parties became popular. The selection of U.S. senators should be taken away from state legislatures and given to the people. The voters themselves should have the right to vote on public issues in *referenda,* to propose laws in *initiatives,* and to remove or *recall* officials or judges whose decisions offended majority sentiment in a city or state.

Another strand of progressivism focused on producing greater order and efficiency in public life. In this view, government had become corrupt, expensive, and clumsy. Accordingly, efforts were made to improve the structure of cities and states in order to make them work more economically and with less confusion. The commission form of city government did away with elected aldermen from local wards and replaced them with officials who were chosen in citywide elections and assigned to a specific department such as utilities, transit, or housing. Regulatory agencies like the Federal Trade Commission and the Interstate Commerce Commission, staffed with experts on the industries they supervised, would see that the marketplace operated in an orderly way without partisan influences. A strong distrust of political parties animated this style of reform.

The Ambiguities of Progressivism

Some aspects of progressivism were later discredited. Some reformers sought programs that emphasized social control of groups and individuals. Prohibition of the use of alcohol, restriction of immigration into the United States, and efforts to shift political power in cities away from the poor and unorganized reflected a desire to compel correct behavior or restrict democracy to native-born white Americans and the "respectable" classes. These coercive aspects of reform became less attractive to later generations.

Despite these failings, progressivism made constructive changes. The regulatory agencies, direct primaries, and other programs did not wipe out all the existing injustices, but they did soften the impact of an industrial social order. The principle that government was responsible for the general welfare of the nation also became well established. Reform did not attack the preeminence of democratic capitalism, but the men and women who joined the crusades for change during the era of Theodore Roosevelt wanted to improve their country, not to revolutionize it.

The Muckrakers

Important figures in progressive reform were a group of journalists who exposed corruption and weaknesses in American society. They published their revelations in numerous monthly and weekly magazines. Selling for as little as ten cents a copy, these magazines gained large circulations and advertising revenues. New printing techniques made these periodicals economical and profitable. There were also more than 2,000 daily newspapers which gave reporters expanding opportunities to probe for scandals and scoops.

The Impact of McClure's Magazine

Samuel S. McClure, publisher of *McClure's Magazine,* helped launch the popular literature of exposure. By 1902 his monthly journal had attracted a wide middle-class audience for its appealing blend of fact and fiction. McClure had larger ambitions, however. He wanted the magazine to address the major issues of the day so as to achieve political and cultural influence. McClure decided that the rise of big business and

The muckrakers became famous as investigative journalists. One of the most celebrated was Ida Tarbell who explored how Standard Oil became such a powerful economic force.

trusts provided the "great theme" he sought. He sent one of his star reporters, Ida Tarbell, to look into "the greatest of them all—the Standard Oil Company." With Tarbell's articles ready to run in the autumn of 1902, McClure decided to expand on an article that another reporter, Lincoln Steffens, had written about municipal corruption in St. Louis. That essay, "Tweed Days in St. Louis," led to a series on city government in the magazine that were published under the title *The Shame of the Cities* (1904). The January 1903 issue of *McClure's* carried articles by Tarbell and Steffens, along with an essay about the anthracite coal strike by Ray Stannard Baker. McClure had found a format that attracted national attention.

Where McClure had led, other magazines soon followed. One writer called it "government by magazine." Samuel Hopkins Adams exposed fraud in patent medicines; his series contributed to the passage of the Pure Food and Drugs Act in 1906. Ray Stannard Baker wrote about unethical railroad practices; his revelations assisted President Roosevelt in his campaign for regulation. For almost five years, the popular press echoed with disclosures of this nature. Then the trend stopped.

The End of Muckraking

In April 1906 Theodore Roosevelt, unhappy with press attacks on the Republican party and conservative senators, used the label "muckrakers" referring to investigative journalists. He was comparing them to a character in John Bunyan's *Pilgrim's Progress* who spent all his time raking the muck on the floor and therefore could not see heaven above him. The label stuck. Muckraking seemed to symbolize a style of reporting that emphasized only the negative. By 1907 popular interest in muckraking waned. Readers wanted a more positive portrayal of life in their magazines. While it lasted, however. muckraking gave progressivism much of its momentum. It supported the view of many reformers that once the facts of an evil situation were revealed, the political system would move to correct them.

Women and Progressive Reform

Women were the crucial foot soldiers of progressive reform; they were responsible for the success of these campaigns. Changes in the status of middle-class women gave them more time to devote to progressive causes. The settlement house movement (see Chapter 18) continued to attract young women who were interested in social service. The number of such houses had risen steadily since the 1890s; and by 1905 there were over 200 of them. Jane Addams of Hull House in Chicago remained in the forefront of the movement. Other women joined Addams to promote urban-oriented reforms. Florence Kelley guided the National Consumers League. Julia Lathrop supported child labor legislation and in 1912 became the first director of the federal Children's Bureau. In New York Lillian Wald used the Henry Street Settlement as a base for work to improve conditions for women and children. She also cooperated with the National Association for the Advancement of Colored People to pursue racial justice. Not all settlement house workers were women, but these institutions gave female reformers a supportive environment and a foundation on which to base their role in society.

Women also figured importantly in the conservation movement. In garden clubs and women's improvement clubs, they criticized the spread of billboards, dirty streets, and neglected parks. They called their efforts "municipal housekeeping." Women joined the Audubon Society, the Women's National Rivers and Harbors Congress, and the Sierra Club. They saved species of birds from extinction, fought against dams and destructive logging in the West, and campaigned for more national parks.

The Continuing Fight for Woman Suffrage

The lack of the right to vote frustrated women, and the campaign for woman suffrage became a central concern. Giving women the ballot, said suffrage leaders, would be a "tool with which to build a better nation." Once they could participate in politics, women would promote progressive causes. Carrie Chapman Catt, president of the National American Woman Suffrage Association, said that "the enfranchisement of women will be the crowning glory of democratic government."

To reach that goal, however, the movement had to overcome substantial problems. In Congress, southern Democrats opposed suffrage because it might lead to votes for African Americans. Liquor interests feared that suffrage would help the prohibitionists. Within

the suffrage campaign, fund-raising problems and organizational disarray limited the effectiveness of the drive for votes.

By 1910 it was evident that the strategy of pursuing a constitutional amendment at the federal level had stalled. Suffragists turned to the states where they devoted themselves to organizing campaigns that appealed to a majority of male voters. The result was a string of victories in western states such as Washington (1910), California (1911), Oregon (1912), Arizona (1912), Kansas (1912), Montana (1914), and Nevada (1914). Woman suffrage was about to become one of the hottest political issues of the Progressive Era.

Reform in the Cities

Progressive reformers made their first important impact in the nation's cities. Two Ohio mayors, Samuel "Golden Rule" Jones of Toledo (1897–1903) and Tom L. Johnson of Cleveland (1901–1909), sought to produce changes in the way that their cities functioned. A wealthy businessman himself, Johnson lowered streetcar fares and introduced an electric lighting plan to show how rates could be kept low. Jones instituted municipal ownership of the trolley system, provided higher wages for city employees than private industry did, and founded free kindergartens for Toledo's children. Some cities, such as Milwaukee, Syracuse, and Minneapolis elected Socialist mayors during the Progressive Era. In Jersey City, the reformers George L. Record and Mark Fagan offered an East Coast variety of municipal uplift.

More typical of urban reform across the country were efforts to change the structure of city government itself. After Galveston, Texas, adopted the commission idea in 1900 (see Chapter 19) and put each commissioner in charge of a separate city department, the "Galveston Idea" attracted national attention. Refined in Des Moines, Iowa, in 1908, commission government was in place in 160 cities by 1911. The shift away from ward representation also restricted the power of local interests in a nonpartisan way, according to its advocates. The new approach, however, sometimes reduced the voting impact of minority groups.

Soon, however, the commission form gave way to the "city manager" idea. Under this arrangement the city council named a nonpartisan executive who was trained to administer the city under policies that the council specified. The plan promised efficiency, cost-cutting, and reduced partisan influence. Smaller and medium-sized municipalities began instituting the city manager form around 1908.

Urban reform achieved positive results in many cities. Reduction of political influence and limits on the role of partisanship did produce better government. The consequences were not always constructive, however. Middle-class reformers who pursued these changes often did so at the expense of residents of poorer areas of the city who now found it harder to get a hearing from city hall. Stressing the interest of the city as a whole did not always translate into fair treatment for the less advantaged and less powerful. In the case of the cities, as in other aspects of progressivism, efficiency and democratic values were not easy to reconcile.

Reform in the States

As urban reformers tried to improve their cities, they often confronted barriers within state government and opposition from state politicians. The constitutions of many states restricted the capacity of a city government to manage its own taxes, regulate its public utilities, or supervise the moral behavior of its citizens. By the beginning of the twentieth century, some cities had obtained "home rule," but frustrated reformers saw state governments as obstacles to change. When progressives looked at their problems on the state level, they detected patterns of corruption and business influence that resembled those they had fought locally. Strong political organizations in many states stood in the way of the goals of reform. Reformers charged that the political party, tied to business interests, prevented meaningful improvements in state government.

At the state level, progressives favored the initiative and referendum because they limited the power of political parties to shape public policy. Allowing the people to propose laws or to vote on laws that had been enacted gave less authority to established political figures and institutions. The initiative and referendum first appeared in South Dakota in 1898; other western states adopted them before 1908. By 1915, twenty-one states had some form of these progressive procedures.

The direct primary spread across most of the nation by 1916; the recall was largely confined to a small

number of western states. The primary was popular because it took the power to make nominations out of the hands of party leaders and gave it to the voters. The recall was more controversial. Angry conservatives charged that an election to remove a judge threatened the independence of the judiciary as a whole.

Increasing Regulatory Power

Greater emphasis on the regulatory power of state government accompanied these procedural reforms. Progressives strengthened the authority of existing state railroad commissions and created new commissions to oversee public utilities and insurance companies. These bodies, which would rely on experts in the field, seemed preferable to the whims of partisan lawmaking.

State government attracted popular and effective leaders during the twenty years after 1900. Theodore Roosevelt was a forceful executive for New York during his one term as governor. Also in New York, Charles Evans Hughes became famous for his probe of insurance companies, which gained him the governorship in 1906. Hughes increased the state's role in regulating utilities and railroads. Woodrow Wilson, elected governor of New Jersey in 1910, limited the power of corporations in that state. Other progressive governors included Hiram Johnson of California, Albert B. Cummins of Iowa, and Herbert S. Hadley of Missouri.

La Follette of Wisconsin

The leading symbol of state reform was Robert M. La Follette of Wisconsin. When Republican party leaders opposed him after he was elected as governor in 1900, he launched a crusade against them. During his two terms as governor, from 1901 to 1905, he established the direct primary, regulated Wisconsin's railroads, and levied higher taxes on corporations. He forged a close relationship between the state government and faculty members at the University of Wisconsin who advised him about policy. This reliance on academic experts was called "the Wisconsin Idea." La Follette possessed much of the moral passion that drove progressivism.

Progressivism drew much of its energy from reformers on the state level. Robert M. La Follette of Wisconsin was one of the most controversial. This cartoon shows what happened to Wisconsin as "Battle Bob" tamed the corporations and created a "model state." La Follette's thick hair made him a favorite of cartoonists.

Progressivism as a National Force

By 1905 progressivism was moving on to the national stage. The issues that reformers faced in the states and cities now seemed to require action by the federal government. Corporations were interstate in character; only Washington could regulate them effectively. To solve the problems of political parties, the Constitution had to be changed. To create a more moral society, progressives contended, the national government had to grant women the vote, regulate the consumption of alcohol, and limit immigration into the United States.

With growth came problems. Where should the balance be struck between the goal of a more democratic society and that of greater efficiency? Efficiency required organization, expertise, and compulsion. Decision making should be left to the experts who knew how to regulate a railroad or a public utility. But that process enabled a well-organized interest group or lobbying campaign to exercise significant influence and sometimes corrupt the system. During this period

professional organizations such as the American Medical Association, the National Association of Manufacturers, and the National Civic Federation played a large role. Advocates of social justice organized their own lobbying groups, including the National Child Labor Committee, the National Conservation Association, and the National Consumers League. A major result of progressivism was more opportunities for organized groups to shape public policy.

The Problems of Reform

The changes that sought to make the political process more democratic sometimes had unexpected results. Conservative groups used the initiative and referendum for their own ends. Well-funded pressure groups could employ the ballot to pursue an issue such as lower taxes or to attack an unpopular idea or group. The initiative could also reduce the electorate to deciding such issues as how long the lunch hour of a fire department might last. The direct primary did not mean that good candidates replaced bad candidates. A scoundrel such as James E. Ferguson of Texas used the primary system to win election as governor there in 1914. A wealthy but less qualified candidate could circumvent the party and achieve success in the primary.

The direct election of U.S. senators, mandated through the Seventeenth Amendment in 1913, took the power of choice away from the state legislatures and gave it to the voters in each state. It meant that candidates had to raise larger amounts of money for their campaigns and gave an advantage to wealthy men such as the conservative Boies Penrose in Pennsylvania in 1914. Meanwhile, lobbying groups simply found new channels for improper influence. One unexpected consequence of these changes was the declining popular interest in voting that became evident in the 1904 presidential election and in later contests. Political parties, for all their weaknesses, had mobilized voters to come to the ballot box. The progressives never found a replacement for that function of the parties.

During the spring of 1905, however, reform was still fresh. Advocates of change believed that limited and gradual measures could improve society. With Roosevelt in the White House, they had a president who also believed that moderate reform was necessary to avoid radical transformations. He pushed for national progressive legislation and the result was a series of turbulent battles during his second term.

ROOSEVELT AND THE MODERN PRESIDENCY: THE SECOND TERM

In the four years after he was elected in his own right, Theodore Roosevelt wielded the powers of the presidency with even more zeal and energy. He traveled widely to promote his programs, built up the bureaucratic machinery of the national government, and pushed Congress to consider a wide range of social problems, from child labor to increased taxation of the wealthy. The president attracted bright young men to Washington to join him, and under Roosevelt the nation's capital became the focus of news and controversy.

Railroad Regulation and the Hepburn Act

Roosevelt began his reform campaign with the railroad regulation he had promised in his 1904 annual message. Strong constituencies supported the proposal. Customers of railroads in the South and West complained that rates were too high. Shippers and politicians maintained that the federal government, not the railroads themselves, should determine whether a rate was fair. To do that, the Interstate Commerce Commission (ICC) should have the power to review railroad rates to ensure that they were reasonable. Roosevelt agreed.

Presidential power had to be used to achieve Roosevelt's goal. During 1905 he gave speeches on behalf of his program across the South and West. The Department of Justice launched well-publicized probes of railroad practices to find out whether railroads were still giving rebates in violation of the 1903 Elkins Act. Roosevelt dangled the threat of revising the tariff to sway Republican leaders in the House to favor his approach. He shared information about railroad misdeeds with sympathetic reporters. When the rail companies started their own public relations effort, it backfired because the public did not believe the railroad claims. Support for reform grew.

Still, getting a bill that the White House wanted through Congress was not easy. Matters went smoothly in the House. The Hepburn bill, named after William P. Hepburn of Iowa, to give the ICC greater authority over railroads and their practices, was passed in February 1906 by a vote of 346 to seven.

The Senate was the main obstacle. A long struggle ensued between Roosevelt and the conservative Republican leader, Nelson W. Aldrich of Rhode Island. The issue was whether the courts should have broad power to review the ICC's rulings. If courts had such authority, they could water down the law. The Senate won some victories on the issue, but Roosevelt obtained what he most wanted. The Hepburn Act was passed in late June 1906. The ICC now had the power to establish maximum rates and to review the accounts and records of the railroads. Most of all, the Hepburn Act showed what a strong president could do to achieve a major legislative goal when he summoned public opinion to support a popular cause.

The Expansion of Regulation

There was more to Roosevelt's regulatory program besides railroads. The public was worried about the condition of the food and drugs that Americans consumed. Muckrakers had revealed that patent medicines sold over the counter were usually ineffective and sometimes dangerous. Led by Dr. Harvey Wiley of the Department of Agriculture, the government conducted experiments on the purity of food that revealed that adulterations and toxic chemicals made many food products unsafe. By early 1906 the clamor for reform had led to the introduction of a bill in Congress to restrict the sale of impure or adulterated food and drugs. The measure was passed by the Senate, but stalled in the House of Representatives.

During the winter of 1906, thousands of Americans read *The Jungle,* a novel about the meatpacking industry in Chicago. Written by a young socialist named Upton Sinclair, the book depicted shocking conditions in the meatpacking plants. The public ignored Sinclair's political message; they were outraged that dirt and filth endangered their meat supply. A newspaper in New York reflected the national mood:

> Mary had a little lamb
> And when she saw it sicken
> She shipped it off to Packingtown
> And now it's labelled chicken.

President Roosevelt was outraged as well. If the government did not take action, he feared that the socialism Sinclair favored might gain followers. The White House supported an amendment to the Agricultural Appropriation Act of 1906 that set up a federal program for meat inspection. The meatpacking industry tried to water down the bill, but the law represented a significant advance in regulatory power.

The controversy over meat inspection cleared the way for House action on the Pure Food Act. Roosevelt "threw his influence into the balance," and roadblocks to the law disappeared. The Pure Food and Drugs Act was passed on June 30, 1906. A happy president called the three regulatory laws passed during that year's congressional session "a noteworthy advance in the policy of securing Federal supervision and control over corporations."

A NAUSEATING JOB, BUT IT MUST BE DONE

The publication of Upton Sinclair's The Jungle *in 1906 angered the nation and led Roosevelt to support meat inspection legislation. A cartoonist depicts the president performing an unpleasant but necessary probe of the issue.*

To achieve that control, Roosevelt placed less emphasis on breaking up large corporations. Instead, he sought to use the Bureau of Corporations to supervise companies that the White House deemed socially responsible. Having decided which businesses and corporate leaders met his standards of morality in the marketplace, he made private agreements with International Harvester and United States Steel. In return for letting the government examine their financial records, these companies would not be subjected to antitrust prosecutions. Firms that Roosevelt disliked, including Standard Oil, would be disciplined by federal lawsuits. The "Roosevelt policies" thus consisted of a mixture of administrative discretion and legal action that rested on the president's expansive interpretation of the power of his office.

Roosevelt and World Politics

Roosevelt matched his activism in domestic policy with equal energy in the conduct of foreign affairs. He carried on secret negotiations without Congress's knowledge, broadened the nation's activities in Asia and Europe, and tried to educate the American people to accept the nation's new role as a world power. The result was a significant expansion of the power of the presidency in foreign affairs. The most notable achievement for Roosevelt was his part in bringing an end to the fighting between Russia and Japan.

Early in 1904 war broke out between Russia and Japan when the Japanese launched a surprise attack. Roosevelt sympathized with Japan because he regarded the Russians as a threat to the Open Door policy in China. As the Japanese won a series of decisive victories, however, the president concluded that a negotiated settlement would best serve the interests of the United States. He was ready to act as an intermediary when the two parties began negotiations.

Though victorious on the battlefield, Japan was financially exhausted. In April 1905 they invited Roosevelt to mediate. Roosevelt summoned the combatants to a peace conference to be held at Portsmouth, New Hampshire, in August. The president's efforts as a peacemaker bore fruit when the two nations agreed to end the conflict; the Treaty of Portsmouth was signed in September 1905. Meanwhile the Roosevelt administration recognized the supremacy of Japan over its neighbor, Korea. In turn, Japan pledged that it had no aggressive designs on the Philippines. In 1906

Roosevelt's diplomatic successes included his successful mediation of the war between Russia and Japan. He summoned delegates from both countries to Portsmouth, New Hampshire. This picture shows the Russians and the Japanese meeting with Roosevelt for what would later be called a "photo opportunity."

Roosevelt received the Nobel Peace Prize for his diplomatic achievement.

The Algeciras Conference

In Europe, Roosevelt sought to reduce the growing tension between Germany and the other major powers, France and Great Britain. Roosevelt sympathized with Britain and France, but he wanted to persuade Germany and its leader, Kaiser Wilhelm II, to be reasonable in its international conduct. During 1905 the Germans made a major issue of French dominance of Morocco. The Kaiser wanted a conference to determine Morocco's status. Roosevelt convinced Britain and France to accept a conference rather than go to war over the fate of the North African country. The president expanded the international role of the United States when he sent delegates to the Algeciras Conference. The resulting settlement was a victory for France and its allies, but Roosevelt had for the moment staved off a European war.

The Gentlemen's Agreement

Later in 1906 the lingering problems in Japanese-American relations flared up again. Japan resented the nativist immigration policies of the United States, which discriminated against Japanese newcomers. On the West Coast the increasing number of Japanese workers and residents intensified nativist and racist sentiments among whites. The San Francisco school board segregated children of Japanese ancestry, and Japan reacted angrily to this slight. Washington and Tokyo eventually worked out the "Gentlemen's Agreement" of 1907. The order of the school board was revoked, and Japan agreed to limit the number of immigrants who left that country for the United States.

The Great White Fleet

To underline his concern about the crisis and to increase funding for the navy, Roosevelt sent the American navy's "Great White Fleet" on a round-the-world tour from 1907 to 1909. When the vessels stopped in Japan in October 1908, the reception was enthusiastic and friendly. A month later the two nations negotiated the Root–Takahira Agreement, which called for the Open Door in China, the independence of that country, and preservation of the status quo in the Pacific.

When he left office in March 1909, Roosevelt expressed pride that the United States was "at absolute peace" with the rest of the world. The president had been an effective diplomat. His policy in the Caribbean had reaffirmed the supremacy of the United States and made possible the construction of the Panama Canal. In Asia he had done his best with the limited power available to him. Roosevelt's involvement in Europe had been positive, but it had not addressed the interlocking alliance systems that would lead to war in 1914. In a time of relative international quiet, Theodore Roosevelt had exercised world leadership in a manner that pleased his fellow citizens.

Labor and Socialists Challenge Roosevelt

As the congressional elections of 1906 approached, the Republican party was still dominant, as it had been since the election of 1894. Some voters were turning away from the Republicans, however, and the Democrats entered the contest "buoyant with hope, and planning for victory." They had a new asset to help them against the Republicans: organized labor. The American Federation of Labor (AFL) had a membership of nearly 1.7 million by 1904. Its leaders hoped for legislation to limit the power of state and federal courts to block strikes through injunctions. When

Roosevelt's order that the American fleet should sail around the world proved to be a natural inspiration for advertising. The Prudential Insurance Company used the vessels to make an appeal to their customers.

Republicans in Congress rejected such a program, the leader of the union, Samuel Gompers, called for the defeat of Republican candidates who were "hostile or indifferent to the just demands of labor."

In addition to the opposition of the AFL, Roosevelt worried about the growing power of the Socialist party and the most radical wing of the labor movement, the Industrial Workers of the World. Founded in 1905, the IWW, or as they were nicknamed "Wobblies," criticized the AFL as timid and called for the overthrow of capitalism. The Socialist party, under the leadership of Eugene V. Debs, also gained strength at the polls. In 1904 Debs won some 400,000 votes. The threat of socialism, with its attacks on private property, disturbed the president. He believed that his reforms were necessary to stave off more sweeping social change. During the 1906 election campaign he sent out members of his cabinet to attack the IWW as violent and dangerous.

The 1906 Elections

The Republicans lost twenty-six seats in the elections, but the campaign of the AFL to unseat Republicans did not do as much damage as Gompers had promised. Nevertheless, the results revealed that the Republicans had significant problems. The protective tariff divided the party. Midwesterners wanted lower duties, whereas Republicans in the East would tolerate no tariff revision. Roosevelt's regulatory policies alienated party conservatives too. During the late nineteenth century Republicans had used government power to promote economic growth, but they were less enthusiastic when Roosevelt regulated railroads, watched over the quality of food products, and attacked large corporations.

Problems with the Supreme Court

One barrier to reform was the Supreme Court. The justices often overturned progressive laws. In the case of *Lochner* v. *New York* (1905), for example, they struck down a New York law that limited the hours employees could work in a bakery. The Court ruled that the law infringed on the right of the bakers under the Fourteenth Amendment to get the best reward for their labor. Sometimes the justices made an exception. In the 1908 case of *Muller* v. *Oregon,* influenced by a brief submitted by Louis D. Brandeis, they upheld an Oregon statute that limited the hours women could work.

In the South, women labored in the cotton mills of the region for long hours with low pay. While the Supreme Court upheld the principle that a state could limit the hours that women worked in Muller v. Oregon, *the decision had little effect in North Carolina where these women worked in the spinning room of the White Oak Cotton Mill in Greensboro.*

In other decisions, that same year, however, the court invalidated the Employers Liabilities Act of 1906 and curbed the power of labor unions in the Danbury Hatters case. Reformers debated various approaches to reducing the power of judges to block progressive ideas.

Roosevelt and Conservation

Roosevelt's campaign for the conservation of natural resources also reflected his presidential activism. He believed that the nation needed to safeguard its natural heritage. Using the power of his office, he created refuges for wild birds, preserved the Grand Canyon against intrusion from development, and set aside national parks. During his first term he worked for passage of the Newlands Reclamation Act (1902), which established a system of irrigation reservoirs in the West that was financed through the sale of public lands. The idea was to increase the amount of land available for agriculture and to preserve the rural way of life. Over the long term, however, the Newlands Act helped large farming corporations more than it did small landowners.

Roosevelt worked closely with Gifford Pinchot of the United States Forestry Service to formulate conservation policy. Neither man thought that natural resources should be locked up and saved for some indefinite future use. Instead, the national parks, coal lands, oil reserves, water-power sites, and national forests in the West should be managed by trained experts from the federal government to achieve the maximum amount of effective use. For Roosevelt and Pinchot conservation did not mean that large corporations should be excluded from developing such resources. In fact, corporations might be the best means of exploiting resources in the wisest possible way. Conservationists who were convinced that the wilderness should be preserved rather than developed opposed the Roosevelt–Pinchot policy. Small landowners and stock growers in the West also disliked federal bureaucrats who favored big business in conservation matters. Roosevelt's conservation program thus produced political divisions during his second term.

In Theodore Roosevelt's campaign for conservation of natural resources, Gifford Pinchot was his right-hand aide as Chief Forester. Wealthy in his own right, Pinchot approached government service with a firm belief in the rightness of his views and the bad motives of his enemies.

Roosevelt had alerted the American people to a serious national problem. He raised important issues about the future of timber, water, wildlife, and mineral resources. He created national parks, including Mesa Verde and Crater Lake, and established four national game preserves, fifty-one bird reservations, and 150 national forests. He could be proud of the National Monuments Act (1906) and the Governors Conference on Conservation (1908). Roosevelt had earned a place in history as the first great conservation president.

His policies did not, however, resemble modern environmental ideas. They required a high degree of control by the federal government and the cooperation of large corporations. In the West there was much resentment of programs that Washington had devised without much local support and implemented over the protests of the westerners themselves.

Deteriorating Race Relations

During his second term Roosevelt showed less sympathy for the plight of African Americans than he had as a candidate for the presidency. He made no public statement about a 1906 race riot in Atlanta, Georgia, in which four blacks were killed and many others injured. Later that year he discharged without a hearing or trial the African-American soldiers who were falsely accused of shooting up Brownsville, Texas, in 1906, and he resisted all efforts to reopen the case of the men involved. Many blacks no longer believed that they had a friend in the White House.

The situation of African-Americans worsened. In August 1908 whites rioted against blacks in Springfield, Illinois, Abraham Lincoln's hometown; two blacks were lynched. A tide of bigotry swept the nation. In 1909 in the face of presidential inaction, prominent white reformers such as Oswald Garrison Villard (grandson of the abolitionist William Lloyd Garrison), Mary White Ovington, and William E. Walling, met with W. E. B. Du Bois, Ida B. Wells, and other blacks to form the National Association for the Advancement of Colored People. They sought an end to segregation, voting rights for blacks, and equal education for all children. Du Bois became the editor of the NAACP's magazine, *Crisis*.

Membership grew among educated members of the black elite. The NAACP's use of the courts to attack segregation soon gave it a leading role in the struggle for racial justice.

A cartoon attacks Roosevelt's anti-business policies as a cause of the Panic of 1907.

"WILL YOU PLEASE HUSH?"
From the *Herald* (New York)

Roosevelt's Last Years of Power

Roosevelt remained popular with the American people during the waning years of his administration. Among conservative Republicans, however, unhappiness with the president mounted. On Capitol Hill, party mem-bers in the House and Senate balked at Roosevelt's as-sertiveness. "That fellow at the other end of the Av-enue," said Speaker of the House Joseph G. Cannon, "wants everything, from the birth of Christ to the death of the devil." When problems in the banking in-dustry led to the Panic of 1907, a momentary collapse

By 1908 William Jennings Bryan made his third unsuccessful run for the White House. The "boy orator" of 1896 had less hair and more flesh, but he retained his capacity to enthrall Democratic voters.

of the financial system and a brief recession followed. Roosevelt's Republican opponents blamed the economic troubles on his regulatory policies. To stem the danger to banks, Roosevelt agreed to let United States Steel acquire the Tennessee Coal and Iron Company, a decision that came back to affect Roosevelt after his presidency.

The issue of Roosevelt's successor became a central problem for Republicans. Hoping to see his progressive policies carried on, the president decided to support his secretary of War, William Howard Taft. Roosevelt's resolve was confirmed when the secretary's major opponent, Senator Joseph B. Foraker of Ohio, attacked the president for his discharge of the soldiers who had been accused in the Brownsville shooting episode. By early 1907 Roosevelt had become the real campaign manager of Taft's drive to win the Republican nomination.

During early 1908 Roosevelt stepped up his assertion of progressive policies. He endorsed more sweeping regulation of corporations, a tax on inheritances of great wealth, and compensation laws for workers.

Congressional Republicans reacted coolly to these proposals and relations between the White House and Capitol Hill worsened throughout 1908. Meanwhile, Taft advanced toward the Republican nomination at the national convention in June.

His selection came on the first ballot, and for his running mate he allowed the convention to pick a colorless and conservative New York congressman, James S. "Sunny Jim" Sherman. In their platform the Republicans promised to revise the protective tariff at a special session of Congress shortly after the new president was inaugurated. The public assumed that any change in the tariff would lead to lower rates. Given the divisions among Republicans over the issue, it would not be easy to reach agreement on a new tariff law.

The 1908 Presidential Election

The Democrats nominated William Jennings Bryan for the third time, and were optimistic about his chances. After all, Roosevelt was not a candidate and

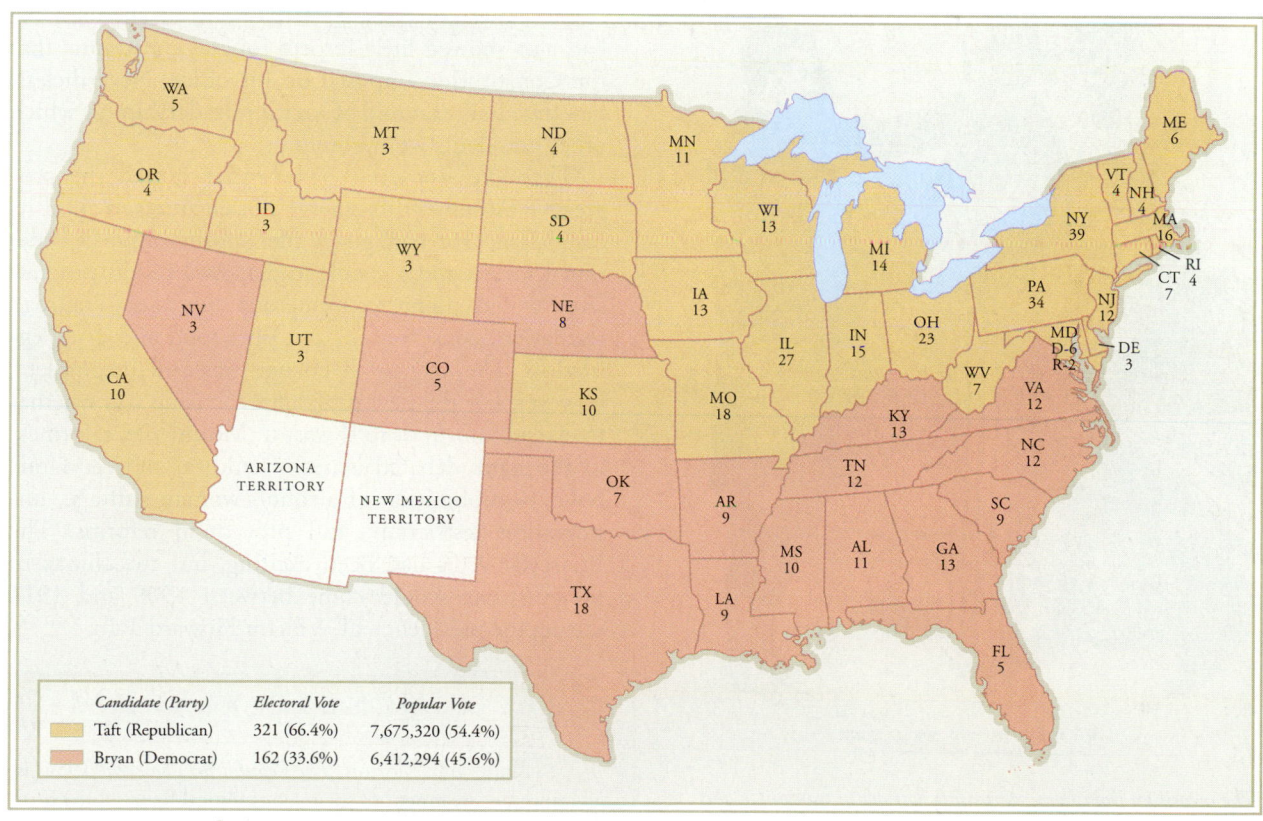

Candidate (Party)	Electoral Vote	Popular Vote
Taft (Republican)	321 (66.4%)	7,675,320 (54.4%)
Bryan (Democrat)	162 (33.6%)	6,412,294 (45.6%)

MAP 20.2 | THE ELECTION OF 1908

Taft had not been tested at the polls. In the early days of the campaign, Bryan ran well. Then Roosevelt threw his support behind Taft in a series of public statements. The secretary of War also proved to be an effective speaker. The Republicans won again: Taft garnered 321 electoral votes to Bryan's 162. The popular vote went solidly for Taft, although Bryan ran much better than Alton B. Parker had in 1904. The election was marked by ticket-splitting in which voters cast ballots for Taft for president and Democrats for other offices. Democrats elected governors in five states that Taft had carried. The partisan allegiances and loyalties of the late nineteenth century were breaking down.

Roosevelt had picked Taft as his successor because he was convinced that Taft would carry on with his reform policies. Shortly after the election, however, tensions developed between Roosevelt and his political heir. Taft's family, especially his wife Helen, encouraged the president-elect "to be his own king." Battles

WELL BEGUN AND WELL DONE
From the *Evening Mail* (New York)

The transition from Roosevelt to Taft was not as tranquil as this cartoon implies.

between Roosevelt and Congress flared as inauguration day approached. As Roosevelt prepared to leave office and embark on a hunting trip to Africa, the Republican party remained divided over its future.

❧ CONCLUSION ❧

The day before Taft took office, a friend of Roosevelt's said: "The great and joyous days are over, we shall never have anything like them again. There is no one like Theodore." Roosevelt had been an important president. Building on the legacy that William McKinley had left him, Roosevelt had expanded the powers of the modern presidency. In domestic policy, he had demonstrated what a chief executive could do to mobilize public opinion behind the policies of the national government. On the world stage, he had involved the nation in European and Asian affairs to preserve international stability.

Not all that Roosevelt did was positive. His handling of race relations was neither consistent nor principled, and he failed to exercise serious leadership on this troubled problem. Sometimes he flirted with excessive power in pursuit of his political enemies. He had also showed little respect for the constraints that the Constitution imposed on his office. Nevertheless, he offered an example of exciting leadership on which other presidents would build.

Theodore Roosevelt had neither caused the progressive movement to emerge nor encouraged all of its campaigns. He had given the reform impulse a national forum and a visible leader. As a result, progressives would point to numerous successes—railroad regulation, conservation, and pure food and drug legislation. The agenda of change was still incomplete, however. For the new president, the issue was whether to extend reform or to thwart it. Meanwhile, reformers in the states debated issues of cultural and economic policy—prohibition of alcohol, woman suffrage, immigration restriction, and procedural reforms. The Roosevelt years had been exciting, but the climax of progressivism would come between 1909 and 1914 during the presidency of William Howard Taft.

RECOMMENDED READINGS

Blum, John Morton. *The Republican Roosevelt* (1954) is an important treatment of the major political figure of the first decade of the century.

Cooper, John Milton., Jr., *The Pivotal Decades: The United States, 1900–1920* (1990) offers an interesting and well-informed account of the first two decades of the new century.

Crunden, Robert M. *Ministers of Reform* (1982) looks at the religious and cultural roots of the reform movement.

Gould, Lewis L. ed., *The Progressive Era* (1974) is a collection of interpretive essays.

Gould, Lewis L. *Reform and Regulation: American Politics from Roosevelt to Wilson* (1996) covers the politics of the era.

Hofstadter, Richard. *The Age of Reform: From Bryan to FDR* (1955) has many thoughtful intepretations about progressivism.

Link, Arthur S. and McCormick, Richard L. *Progressivism* (1983) provides the best overview of the reform sentiment of the early twentieth century.

Mowry, George E. *The Era of Theodore Roosevelt and the Birth of Modern America* (1958) is an older study that is still very useful.

Painter, Nell Irvin. *Standing at Armageddon* (1987) synthesizes older scholarship in a widely used narrative.

Watson, Richard L. Jr., *The Development of National Power: The United States, 1900–1919* (1976) has an abundance of helpful information about the public policy of the period.

Theodore Roosevelt

Beale, Howard K. *Theodore Roosevelt and the Rise of America to World Power* (1956).

Collin, Richard H. *Theodore Roosevelt's Caribbean: The Panama Canal, The Monroe Doctrine, and the Latin American Context* (1990).

Gatewood, Willard B. *Theodore Roosevelt and the Art of Controversy* (1970).

Gould, Lewis L. *The Presidency of Theodore Roosevelt* (1991).

Marks, Frederick W. *Velvet on Iron: The Diplomacy of Theodore Roosevelt* (1979).

Economic Issues

Kolko, Gabriel. *Railroads and Regulation, 1877–1916* (1965).

Martin, Albro. *Enterprise Denied: Origins of the Decline of American Railroads* (1971).

Sklar, Martin. *The Corporate Reconstruction of American Capitalism, 1890–1916: The Market, the Law and Politics* (1988).

Wiebe, Robert. *Businessmen and Reform: A Study of the Progressive Movement* (1962).

Young, James Harvey. *Pure Food: Securing the Federal Food and Drugs Act of 1906* (1989).

Reform in the Cities

Crooks, James B. *Politics and Progress: The Rise of Urban Progressivism in Baltimore, 1895 to 1911* (1968).

Miller, Zane L. *Boss Cox's Cincinnati: Urban Politics in the Progressive Era* (1968).

Mohl, Raymond. *The New City: Urban America in the Industrial Age, 1860–1920* (1985).

Rice, Bradley R. *Progressive Cities: The Commission Government Movement in America* (1977).

Schiesl, Martin J. *The Politics of Efficiency: Municipal Administration and Reform in America, 1880–1920* (1977).

Reform in the States

Abrams, Richard M. *Conservatism in a Progressive Era: Massachusetts Politics, 1900–1912* (1964).

La Follette, Robert M. *La Follette's Autobiography* (1913).

McCormick, Richard L. *From Realignment to Reform: Political Change in New York State, 1893–1910* (1981).

Margulies, Herbert F. *The Decline of the Progressive Movement in Wisconsin, 1890–1920* (1968).

Thelen, David P. *Robert M. La Follette and the Insurgent Spirit* (1976).

1909 TO 1933

Progress seemed everywhere in 1909. Aviators crossed the English Channel for the first time, wireless communication linked ships at sea with their destinations; at home Americans took to the open road in their new Ford automobiles. In such a heady climate of advancing technology and growing economic abundance, writers spoke of an end of war as nations talked out their disputes at the conference table rather than settling them on the battlefield. The path of history seemed well-lit and clear toward a bright future of hope and peace.

Twenty-four years later, in the winter of 1933, the United States lay in the grip of a severe economic depression. Banks had closed, unemployment had soared, and the homeless and destitute roamed the land. Newspapers and magazines ran articles that speculated on whether democracy had failed. To a minority of Americans, the opposing ideologies of communism and fascism seemed alluring. As the nation faced the prospect of a potential social revolution, its citizens looked back with nostalgia to the early years of the century and wondered what had happened to destroy that optimistic and confident world.

The outbreak of a world war in the summer of 1914 did the most to unhinge the sense of progress that then permeated the United States. If advanced nations could ravage each other on European battlefields, who could any longer believe in the perfectibility of humanity? Americans first tried to stay out of the conflict, but by 1917 they entered the war on the side of France and Great Britain.

In less than two years, the experience of World War I accelerated trends toward a more powerful federal government, a more bureaucratic society, and a nation in which large corporations exercised an even greater

MILITARY PERSONNEL ON ACTIVE DUTY: 1909–1933

	Grand total	Army			Air Force			Navy			Marine Corps		
		Total	Officers	Enlisted	Total	Officers	Enlisted	Total	Officers	Enlisted	Total	Officers	Enlisted
Year	904	905	906	907	908	909	910	911	912	913	914	915	916
1970	3,066,294	1,322,548	166,721	1,155,827	791,349	129,803	661,546	692,660	80,761	611,899	259,737	24,941	234,796
1969	3,460,162	1,512,169	172,590	1,339,570	862,353	135,476	726,877	775,869	85,199	690,670	309,771	25,698	284,073
1968	3,547,902	1,570,343	166,173	1,404,170	904,850	139,691	765,159	765,457	85,425	680,032	307,252	24,555	282,697
1967	3,376,880	1,442,498	143,517	1,298,981	897,494	135,485	762,009	751,619	81,902	669,717	285,269	23,592	261,677
1966	3,094,058	1,199,784	117,786	1,081,998	887,353	130,724	756,629	745,205	79,805	665,400	261,716	20,512	241,204
1965	2,655,389	969,066	112,120	856,946	824,662	131,578	693,084	671,448	77,866	593,582	190,213	17,258	172,955
1964	2,687,409	973,238	110,870	862,368	856,798	133,389	723,409	667,596	76,400	591,196	189,777	16,843	172,934
1963	2,699,677	975,916	108,302	867,614	869,431	133,763	735,668	664,647	75,549	589,098	189,683	16,737	172,946
1962	2,807,819	1,066,404	116,050	950,354	884,025	134,908	749,117	666,428	75,302	591,126	190,962	16,861	174,101
1961	2,483,771	858,622	99,921	758,701	821,151	128,793	692,358	627,089	69,981	557,108	176,909	16,132	160,777
1960	2,476,435	873,078	101,236	771,842	814,752	129,689	685,063	617,984	69,559	548,425	170,621	16,203	154,418
1959	2,504,310	861,964	101,690	760,274	840,435	131,602	708,833	626,340	69,795	556,545	175,571	16,065	159,506
1958	2,600,581	898,925	104,716	794,209	871,156	132,939	738,217	641,005	71,560	569,445	189,495	16,741	172,754
1957	2,795,798	997,994	111,187	886,807	919,835	140,563	779,272	677,108	73,703	603,405	200,861	17,434	183,427
1956	2,806,441	1,025,778	118,364	907,414	909,958	142,093	767,865	669,925	71,770	598,155	200,780	17,809	182,971
1955	2,935,107	1,109,296	121,947	987,349	959,946	137,149	822,797	660,695	74,527	586,168	205,170	18,417	186,753
1954	3,302,104	1,404,598	128,208	1,276,390	947,918	129,752	818,166	725,720	77,280	648,440	223,868	18,593	205,275
1953	3,555,067	1,533,815	145,633	1,388,182	977,593	130,769	846,824	794,440	81,731	712,709	249,219	18,731	230,488
1952	3,635,912	1,596,419	148,427	1,447,992	983,261	128,742	854,519	824,265	82,247	742,018	231,967	16,413	215,554
1951	3,249,455	1,531,774	130,540	1,401,234	788,381	107,099	681,282	736,680	70,513	666,167	192,620	15,150	177,470
1950	1,460,261	593,167	72,566	520,601	411,277	57,006	354,271	381,538	44,641	336,897	74,279	7,254	67,025
1949	1,615,360	660,473	77,272	583,201	419,347	57,851	361,496	449,575	47,975	401,600	85,965	7,250	78,715
1948	1,445,910	554,030	68,178	485,852	387,730	48,957	338,773	419,162	45,416	373,746	84,988	6,907	78,081
1947	1,582,999	991,285	132,504	858,781	. . . .	. . . .	. . . .	498,661	52,434	446,227	93,053	7,506	85,547
1946	3,030,088	1,891,011	267,144	1,623,867	. . . .	. . . .	. . . .	983,398	141,161	842,237	155,679	14,208	141,471

	Grand total	Army			Navy			Marine Corps		
		Total	Officers	Enlisted	Total	Officers	Enlisted	Total	Officers	Enlisted
Year	904	905	906	907	911	912	913	914	915	916
1933	243,845	136,547	13,896	122,651	91,230	9,947	81,283	16,068	1,192	14,876
1932	244,902	134,957	14,111	120,846	93,384	9,967	83,417	16,561	1,196	15,365
1931	252,605	140,516	14,159	126,357	93,307	9,849	83,458	18,782	1,196	17,586
1930	255,648	139,378	14,151	125,227	96,890	9,540	87,350	19,380	1,208	18,172
1929	255,031	139,118	14,047	125,071	97,117	9,434	87,683	18,796	1,181	17,615
1928	250,907	136,084	14,019	122,065	95,803	9,401	86,402	19,020	1,198	17,822
1927	248,943	134,829	14,020	120,809	94,916	9,440	85,476	19,198	1,198	18,000
1926	247,396	134,938	14,143	120,795	93,304	9,091	84,213	19,154	1,178	17,976
1925	251,756	137,048	14,594	122,454	95,230	8,918	86,312	19,478	1,168	18,310
1924	261,189	142,673	13,784	128,889	98,184	8,651	89,533	20,332	1,157	19,175
1923	247,011	133,243	14,021	119,222	94,094	8,410	85,684	19,674	1,141	18,533
1922	270,207	148,763	15,667	133,096	100,211	8,334	91,877	21,233	1,135	20,098
1921	386,542	230,725	16,501	214,224	132,827	9,979	122,848	22,990	1,087	21,903
1920	343,302	204,292	18,999	185,293	121,845	10,642	111,203	17,165	1,104	16,061
1919	1,172,602	851,624	91,975	759,649	272,144	19,357	252,787	48,834	2,270	46,564
1918	2,897,167	2,395,742	130,485	2,265,257	448,606	23,631	424,975	52,819	1,503	51,316
1917	643,833	421,467	34,224	387,243	194,617	8,383	186,234	27,749	776	26,973
1916	179,376	108,399	5,175	103,224	60,376	4,022	56,354	10,601	348	10,253
1915	174,112	106,754	4,948	101,806	57,072	3,593	53,479	10,286	338	9,948
1914	165,919	98,544	5,033	93,511	56,989	3,406	53,583	10,386	336	10,050
1913	154,914	92,756	4,970	87,786	52,202	3,273	48,929	9,956	331	9,625
1912	153,714	92,121	4,775	87,346	51,357	3,074	48,283	9,696	337	9,359
1911	144,846	84,006	4,585	79,421	51,230	2,886	48,344	9,610	328	9,282
1910	139,344	81,251	4,535	76,716	48,533	2,699	45,834	9,560	328	9,232
1909	142,200	84,971	4,299	80,672	47,533	2,630	44,903	9,696	328	9,368

role. At the same time, the bitter national and ideological conflicts of Europe spilled over into American life. Racial, ethnic, and sectional tensions produced social unrest and group hatreds that raged between 1917 and 1933.

During the war, however, some aspects of prewar reform reached completion. Women gained the vote in 1920 after three generations of struggle. Their ballots did not transform national politics in the years that followed, but their presence in the process ended centuries of a male monopoly of the elective system. The war years also achieved the temperance dream of a national prohibition of alcohol. Despite this reform success, the nation remained divided over its attitude toward liquor, a condition that raised problems for enforcing the new constitutional amendment.

Save time, energy and money
—don't market every day

GENERAL ELECTRIC
Refrigerator

In the aftermath of World War I, Americans rushed forward to embrace the new world of consumer goods and economic affluence. Automobiles, appliances, and installment buying reshaped attitudes about frugality and the future. The spread of mass media and bigtime sports brought shared cultural experiences to many Americans. The decade seemed vibrant with the wailing of jazz, the roar of the metropolis, and the excitement of flaming youth.

Year	Total Utility and Industrial
1933	102,655
1932	99,359
1931	109,373
1930	114,637
1929	116,747
1928	108,069
1927	101,390
1926	94,222
1925	84,666
1924	75,892
1923	71,399
1922	61,204
1921	53,125
1920	56,559
1917	43,429
1912	24,752
1907	14,121

NET PRODUCTION OF ELECTRIC ENERGY, BY CENTRAL STATIONS, BY CLASS OF OWNERSHIP: 1907 TO 1933

Not all Americans shared in the prosperity or endorsed the headlong embrace of the modern world. Farmers never experienced the prosperity of the decade, and they encountered economic downturns sooner than did their city counterparts. Rural values remained strong even when transplanted to an urban setting. Some dislocated citizens sought the missing sense of community in an organization such as the Ku Klux Klan, which promised ritual, controversy, and social change in equal measure. Many Americans found that fundamentalist religious denominations spoke to their spiritual needs in ways that the modernist churches did not. Strains between the city and country showed themselves in politics in the 1928 presidential election when

Motor-Vehicle Deaths: 1913 to 1933

Year	Total motor-vehicle accidents (1,000)	Traffic deaths[1]					Traffic death rates		
		Total	Non-collision accidents	Collision accidents			Per 100,000 population	Per 10,000 motor vehicles	Per 100 million vehicle miles
				With other motor vehicles	With pedestrians	With fixed objects[2]			
	224	225	226	227	228	229	230	231	232
1933		31,363	8,680	6,470	12,840	900	25.0	13.0	15.6
1932		29,500	7,000	6,070	11,490	800	23.6	12.2	16.1
1931		33,700	7,850	6,820	13,370	870	27.2	13.0	17.0
1930		32,900	8,730	5,880	12,900	720	26.7	12.4	17.4
1929		31,200	8,430	5,400	12,250	620	25.7	11.8	17.3
1928		28,000	7,360	4,310	11,420	540	23.4	11.4	17.4
1927		25,800	7,280	3,430	10,820	500	21.8	11.2	17.7
1926		23,400					20.1	10.6	18.0
1925		21,900					19.1	11.0	17.9
1924		19,400					17.1	11.0	
1923		18,400					16.5	12.2	
1922		15,300							
1921		13,900							
1920		12,500							
1919		11,200							
1918		10,700							
1917		10,200							
1916		8,200							
1915		6,600							
1914		4,700							
1913		4,200							

[1] Totals may not quite equal sums of various types because totals for most types are estimated, and these have been rounded.
[2] Data based on improved reporting procedure; therefore, not entirely comparable with other years.

the urban, Catholic background of Democrat Al Smith turned many in his party toward the Republican nominee, Herbert Hoover.

Throughout the 1920s, the confidence that the economy would move ever upward sustained people even when they lacked wealth themselves. By the end of the decade, however, the prosperity that consumers had built and corporations relished began to totter. Poor distribution of income, corporate excesses, weaknesses in the banking structure, and mounting problems with international finance led to a stock market crash in 1929 and a Depression that grew steadily worse during the early 1930s.

A generation raised on the prospect of burgeoning prosperity found itself confronted with want, destitution, and despair. Organized charity seemed inadequate to the task of relief, and government at all levels also failed to address the economic problems in effective ways. By the winter of 1932, the nation experienced a tightening spiral of gloom and fear. The sunny days of progressivism and reform were only a grotesque echo of an age that had disappeared. In the American passage, the early 1930s seemed as close as any citizen wished to get to the valley of the shadow.

	1909	1912	1915	1918

POLITICS & DIPLOMACY

1909: Ballinger Pinchot controversy over conservation begins
1910: Roosevelt proclaims his New Nationalism
Democrats regain control of House of Representatives in elections
1911: Taft pursues Canadian Reciprocity on tariff but fails
1912: Republican party splits between Roosevelt and Taft
Roosevelt forms Progressive Party
Democrats nominate Wilson for president and he is elected

1913: Wilson address Congress in person, breaking long-time precedent
Underwood Tariff passed
16th Amendment adopted allowing income tax
1914: Clayton Antitrust law passed
Vera Cruz incident leads to intervention in Mexico
World War begins in Europe
1915: *Lusitania* sunk
Leo Frank lynched in Georgia
1916: Germany makes *Sussex Pledge* about submarines
Americans intervene in Mexico to attempt capture of Pancho Villa
Wilson defeats Hughes in presidential election

1917: Zimmerman Telegram released
United States declares war on Germany
1918: Wilson announces Fourteen Points
Armistice ends World War I
Democrats are defeated and Wilson repudiated in congressional elections
1919: Wilson attends Peace Conference, but League of Nations is defeated in Senate
Prohibition adopted
1920: Woman suffrage adopted
Harding defeats Cox and is elected president

SOCIAL & CULTURAL EVENTS

1909: Massachusetts forms first public commission on aging
Motion Picture Trust formed out of early movie companies
1910: Mann White Slave Traffic Act passed to discourage transportation of women across state lines for "immoral purposes"
Jack Johnson defeats James Jeffries ("the Great White Hope") in heavyweight title fight
Boy Scouts of America founded
1911: Harriet Quimby becomes first licensed woman pilot
1912: S.S. *Titanic* hits iceberg and sinks in North Atlantic
Children's Bureau established
Girl Scouts of America begins

1913: Armory Show provides introduction to modern art
Massive suffrage march occurs in Washington, D.C., on March 3.
Brillo pads introduced
1914: President Wilson proclaims first national Mother's Day
Margaret Sanger introduces term "birth control"
New Republic magazine begins publication
1915: "Birth of a Nation" becomes hit movie
Support for woman suffrage grows
Charlie Chaplin becomes movie star
Great Migration of African Americans to north begins

1916: First birth control clinic opens in Brooklyn, New York
National Woman's Party founded
1917: Frozen food processing developed
Woman suffrage advocates jailed for picketing White House
1918: Influenza epidemic sweeps the globe and kills 21 million people
First granulated soap ("Rinso") introduced
1919: Dial telephones introduced
Red Scare about Bolsheviks occurs
1920: Edith Wharton wins Pulitzer Price for her novel *The Age of Innocence*
Miss America beauty pageant begins
Marcus Garvey's United Negro Improvement Association claims more than two million members

ECONOMICS & TECHNOLOGY

1909: Payne Aldrich Tariff enacted
International Ladies Garment Workers Union begins prolonged strike in New York City
1910: Mann-Elkins Act to strengthen railroad regulation passed
1911: Triangle Fire in New York City produces regulation of sweatshop conditions
1912: Lawrence, Mass. Strike occurs in woolen mills
1913: Federal Reserve Act passed and system of twelve regional banks created

1914: Ludlow, Colorado, strike leads to deaths of twenty-one people by state militia
Henry Ford introduces $5 day for auto workers
1915: Preparedness movement and war orders revive American economy
1916: Federal Farm Loan Act passed
Adamson Act creates eight hour day for railroad workers
1917: Production and use of food is regulated through food administration
War Industries Board created

1918: Webb-Pomerene Act passed to promote foreign trade
National War Labor Board established
1919: Economy reverts to peace-time status with little government supervision
Strikes and labor disputes occur nationwide
Inflation becomes problem
1920: Esch-Cummins Act passed to return railroads to private control and broaden powers of Interstate Commerce Commission
Woman's Bureau created in Department of Labor

1921: Harding inaugurated
United States signs separate peace with Germany
1922: Washington Naval Conference
Democrats make gains in congressional elections
1923: Teapot Dome scandal breaks
Harding dies of heart attack
Calvin Coolidge becomes president
1924: Miriam Amanda Ferguson and Nellie Tayloe Ross elected as first woman governors
Democratic convention takes 103 ballots to nominate John W. Davis
Coolidge defeats Davis and third party candidate Robert M. La Follette
1925: Scopes trial on evolution in Dayton, Tennessee

1926: United States membership in World Court fails
Democrats make gains in congressional elections
1927: President Coolidge says he will not run in 1928
Sacco-Vanzetti executed
1928: Hoover defeats Smith in presidential election
1929: Hoover becomes president

1930: London Naval Conference on disarmament
Democrats erase most of Republican House majority in elections
1931: Depression deepens
Hoover declares moratorium on war debts
1932: Bonus Marchers dispersed in Washington
Roosevelt defeats Hoover in election
1933: Roosevelt inaugurated president as Depression hits bottom

---

1921: Immigration laws set quotas for Eastern Europeans
Shepard-Towner Maternity and Infancy Protection Act passed
1922: Sinclair Lewis, *Babbitt,* is published
Radio gains in popularity as stations spread
Reader's Digest begins publication
1923: *Time* magazine is launched
Blues singers such as Alberta Hunter and Bessie Smith become popular
1924: Kleenex is introduced
1925: Red Grange becomes national football hero and signs professional contract
Publication of F. Scott Fitzgerald's *The Great Gatsby*
Harlem Renaissance at height in New York City
New Yorker magazine starts

1926: Publication of Ernest Hemingway's *The Sun Also Rises*
Gertrude Ederle becomes first woman to swim English Channel
1927: Babe Ruth hits sixty home runs
Charles Lindbergh flies across the Atlantic alone
Al Jolson makes talking pictures popular in "The Jazz Singer"
1928: Walt Disney releases his first cartoon, "Plane Crazy"
Eugene O'Neill's play "Strange Interlude" wins Pulitzer Prize
1929: Sales of processed baby food begin
Museum of Modern Art founded in New York City
The first Blue Cross health insurance group starts in Dallas

"Amos 'n' Andy" radio show becomes nationally popular
1930: Sliced bread introduced commercially
First supermarket opens
1931: Southern Commission on the Study of Lynching formed
Empire State Building, world's tallest, opens in New York City
Al Capone, leading mobster, sentenced to jail for tax evasion
1932: Charles Lindbergh's son kidnapped and found dead
Amelia Earhart makes first solo transatlantic flight by a woman
Radio City Music Hall opens in New York City
1933: Prohibition ends

1921: Nation experiences business recession as intense deflation occurs
1922: Fordney-McCumber Tariff Act passed
1923: Supreme Court in *Adkins v. Children's Hospital* invalidates law providing for minimum wage for women in Washington, D.C.
1924: McNary-Haugen Bill to help farmers is introduced
1925: Florida land boom flourishes

1926: Revenue Act produces substantial tax reduction
Florida land boom collapses
1927: Henry Ford introduces Model A car
1928: Federal Reserve raises interest rates to curb speculation
1929: Stock Market crash occurs in September and October

1930: Great Depression begins
Smoot-Hawley Tariff enacted
1931: Hoover administration relief measures address condition of unemployed but do not bring upturn in economy
1932: Reconstruction Finance Corporation created to deal with bank and corporate failures in Depression
Revenue Act cuts government spending
1933: Depression hits bottom as Franklin D. Roosevelt takes office

TAFT: THE UNLUCKY SUCCESSOR TO ROOSEVELT

As Theodore Roosevelt's designated successor, William Howard Taft found the presidency more of an ordeal than a reward. He proved incapable of satisfying the different wings of the Republican party, and he faced a challenge to his renomination from Roosevelt in 1912.

Chapter 21

PROGRESSIVISM AT ITS HEIGHT

1909–1914

When Theodore Roosevelt left the presidency in March 1909, progressivism entered a phase of partisan upheaval. Under William Howard Taft the Republicans split apart as conservatives and reformers struggled for control. The Democrats moved toward a more active role for the national government and away from their heritage of state rights. The Socialists mounted a vigorous challenge from the left. For five years it seemed as though the party system might fragment into more consistent ideological alignments.

Political ferment also revealed the tensions among reformers. Campaigns for woman suffrage, the prohibition of alcohol, restriction of immigration, and social justice created new coalitions that sometimes followed party lines and at other times disrupted them. In the process, progressivism provoked a conservative reaction that limited the possibilities for reform.

The social and economic forces that were producing a consumer society also gathered strength during this period. Henry Ford's low-priced automobile gained greater popularity while other products of industrialism attracted more customers. Women found more opportunities for employment. For minorities, however, these years saw continuing tension and racial strife.

Beyond the nation's borders, international strains in Europe and revolutions in Latin America and Asia made foreign policy more of a national concern than it

had been since the war with Spain. Still, the outbreak of fighting in Europe during the summer of 1914 came as a shock to the government and people of the United States. World War I did not resolve the crisis in which progressivism found itself. Instead, it added new complexity to an already turbulent period.

TAFT'S PRESIDENCY

Soon after William Howard Taft took the oath of office as the twenty-seventh president on March 4, 1909, Theodore Roosevelt left for his hunting safari in Africa. The hope on Wall Street, ran a joke of the day, was that a lion would do its duty. A celebrity as an ex-president, Roosevelt found that his activities were news, even across the ocean. The issues of regulation, social justice, and corporate power with which he had struggled were also on the agenda for his successor. The mood of reform that had accelerated under Roosevelt was still gathering momentum, and the public wondered how Taft would deal with it.

Taft came to the White House facing complex problems. Republican conservatives expected him to slow the movement toward reform. Party progressives, on the other hand, wanted the new president to

CHRONOLOGY

1909 William Howard Taft inaugurated as president

Enactment of Payne-Aldrich Tariff

1910 Ballinger-Pinchot controversy over conservation

Roosevelt returns from Africa, announces New Nationalism

Camp Fire Girls founded

Democrats regain control of House of Representatives in elections

1911 Triangle Fire in New York City kills 146 people

Canadian voters defeat reciprocity agreement with United States

Harriet Quimby becomes first licensed woman pilot

Roosevelt and Taft split over trust policy

1912 Taft defeats Roosevelt for Republican nomination

Bitter strike in Lawrence, Massachusetts, woolen mills

S.S. *Titanic* hits iceberg and sinks in North Atlantic

Roosevelt forms Progressive party

Woodrow Wilson becomes Democratic nominee

Wilson defeats Taft and Roosevelt in presidential race

1913 Suffragettes stage large march on the day before Woodrow Wilson is inaugurated in Washington

Federal income tax adopted

Armory Show of Modern Art held in New York City

Federal Reserve System established

1914 Federal Trade Commission created

Henry Ford announces Five-Dollar Day

Margaret Sanger coins term "birth control"

Fighting occurs at Vera Cruz in Mexico

Outbreak of First World War

---

expand Roosevelt's legacy. The Republicans had promised in their 1908 platform to revise the tariff but had not specified which direction the alterations would take. The president planned to call a special session of Congress to address the issue. Protectionists who wanted no changes and reformers who sought lower rates waited to see what Taft would do.

A native of Cincinnati, Ohio, Taft was fifty-one. He had been a lawyer and a federal judge before heading the Philippine Commission in 1900. He proved to be an adept colonial administrator, but Roosevelt summoned him back to the United States in 1904 to serve as secretary of war.

During Roosevelt's presidency, Taft acted as troubleshooter for the administration. When Roosevelt went on vacation, he told reporters that he felt confident because Taft was in Washington "sitting on the lid." It was widely believed that the two men agreed on almost all issues. As a result, Roosevelt looked forward to a continuation of his policies under the new president.

A Conservative President

Roosevelt had miscalculated. Taft was a conservative man who had taken on some of Roosevelt's reform spirit. He did not agree with the expansive view of presidential power that Roosevelt had advanced. Taft believed that the president should act within the strict letter of the law and the constitutional boundaries of his office. Such a philosophy was bound to disappoint Roosevelt and the progressive Republicans who wanted the president to press the limits of what an aggressive chief executive could do to achieve social justice.

Taft had other political problems as president. He lacked Roosevelt's sense of public relations. He played golf at fashionable country clubs and vacationed with wealthy men at a time when riches were associated with political corruption. He quarreled with the press and often delayed writing speeches until the last minute. The success he had enjoyed as a speaker during the 1908 campaign was soon forgotten as he failed

to sway audiences or committed political gaffes. Taft also depended on the advice of his wife, Helen Herron Taft, in political matters, but during the spring of 1909 she had a serious illness that deprived him of her emotional support. The presidency soon became a personal ordeal for Taft.

The Dilemma of the Tariff

In revising the tariff, Taft confronted the consequences of Roosevelt's postponement of the issue. Tensions had grown among Republicans about whether rates were too high. Progressive Republicans favored reductions in customs duties and a move away from protectionism. Conservatives regarded the tariff as the cornerstone of Republicanism and felt that high rates were justified.

To maintain Republican unity in Congress, Taft supported the reelection of conservative Joseph G. Cannon as speaker of the House. He saw Cannon as central to his plans for a revision of the tariff. If Taft challenged the speaker, who enjoyed the support of a majority of House Republicans, Cannon could easily stall action on the tariff program.

Once Congress assembled in March 1909, Taft sent them a message asking for a new tariff law. In April the House passed a tariff bill that lowered rates on sugar, iron, and lumber and placed coal and cattle hides on the free list. The measure was named the Payne bill after its author, Sereno B. Payne, chairman of the Ways and Means Committee. The bill passed the House.

The bill then went to the Senate where the Republicans had sixty-one members, the Democrats thirty-one. The Republican leader, Nelson Aldrich of Rhode Island, was regarded as a virtual dictator of the Senate.

In fact, Aldrich's position was much more vulnerable than it seemed. Among the Senate Republicans, there were seven to ten midwesterners, such as Robert La Follette of Wisconsin, Albert J. Beveridge of Indiana, and Jonathan P. Dolliver of Iowa, who wanted to see lower tariffs and limits on Aldrich's power. On the other side of the debate, senators from the East and Far West insisted that goods from their states must be protected against foreign competition. The result was that Aldrich did not have a majority of votes for the Payne bill.

To obtain the votes that he needed, Aldrich had the Senate Finance Committee write a bill with 800 amendments, half of which raised rates back toward those of the Dingley Tariff. Senate progressives were infuriated. During the summer of 1909, Dolliver, La Follette, and Beveridge attacked Aldrich's bill. They said that the public expected lower tariffs and they denounced attempts to protect it. The quarrels over the bill on the Senate floor damaged Republican unity. The Aldrich version finally cleared the Senate in early July by a vote of forty-five to thirty-four. Ten Republicans voted against Aldrich.

The Political Consequences

As a House-Senate conference committee hammered out the final version of the bill, both sides looked to Taft for support. The president used his leverage to obtain some concessions, such as lower duties on gloves, lumber, and cattle hides, but he failed to obtain reductions on wool, cotton, and industrial products. Convinced that he had gained all he could, Taft signed the Payne-Aldrich Tariff when it was passed in early August 1909. The battle had split the Republicans. "Our party as a party is no more," said one Republican. "It went to pieces in a panic."

Taft endorsed the new tariff during a tour of the Midwest in September. Speaking at Winona, Minnesota, he called the law "the best tariff bill that the Republican party ever passed." Conservatives applauded his remarks while progressives fumed because he had not praised their fight for lower rates. The president struck back when he refused to appoint individuals whom the progressives recommended for federal offices in their states. Republican harmony thus took a beating throughout the autumn of 1909.

The Battle over Conservation

To make matters worse for the president, he found himself engaged in a battle that threatened to disrupt his friendship with Theodore Roosevelt. Federal government control of natural resources had been one of Roosevelt's favorite policies. His principal aide in this program had been Chief Forester Gifford Pinchot. Taft disliked Pinchot and doubted whether the policies Roosevelt had pursued were legal. The new secretary of the Interior, Richard A. Ballinger, also had little use for Pinchot. The president and Ballinger intended to pursue conservation policies that conformed to

existing laws and allowed less room for presidential initiative. When Ballinger began to open lands for development that Pinchot had closed off to settlers and businesses, Pinchot struck back. He accused Ballinger of acting as an agent for J.P. Morgan and a syndicate trying to sell valuable coal lands in Alaska. After looking into the charges, Taft sided with Ballinger.

Pinchot then leaked information about the episode to the press. In early 1910 he went even further, writing a letter of protest that a senator released to the public. Taft thereupon fired Pinchot for insubordination. In the ensuing controversy, a congressional probe revealed that Taft and Ballinger had not done what Pinchot had charged. But the political damage led to Ballinger's resignation in 1911.

The political consequences were significant. Taft seemed to be attacking a key Roosevelt policy. Friends of the former president said that Taft "is proving a weak man—yielding to those who are really opposed to the great policies upon & for which Taft was elected." Roosevelt, still on safari in Africa, received letters saying that Taft was betraying him. Roosevelt supporters talked of restoring him to the presidency in 1912. In his responses Roosevelt said that perhaps he had made a mistake in picking Taft as his successor.

The congressional session of the spring of 1910 added to Taft's problems. Progressive Republicans in the House saw Speaker Cannon's conservatism and his reputation as a dictator as a liability for the congressional elections to be held that fall. In March House members curtailed Cannon's power to schedule legislation for debate and to determine committee assignments. Because Taft had supported the speaker, the episode was viewed as a rebuke to the president as well. Taft insisted that Republicans should be loyal to his administration or risk reprisals when they sought White House approval of appointments or legislation. This policy increased the tension between the president and Congress.

At the end of the session Taft adopted a more conciliatory tone. Greater harmony led to the enactment of additional progressive legislation. The Mann-Elkins Act broadened the power of the Interstate Commerce Commission beyond that provided by the Hepburn Act (1906). The measure gave the ICC more authority to block railroads from charging higher rates for short hauls, gave it additional power to set rates, and compelled the railroads to justify rate increases. The law also set up a Commerce Court to hear railroad-related cases. The court barely functioned before Congress

THE MEETING

Once Roosevelt returned from his African trip, cartoonists depicted what might happen when he met Taft again. The expressions on their faces and the yipping dog indicate the tension that the public believed existed between the two former friends.

abolished it in 1913. Other legislation included increased appropriations for the navy. Progressives applauded a postal savings law that encouraged private citizens to use federal banks located in post offices as a means of encouraging thrift. Unhappily for Taft, progressive Republicans maintained that these results were achieved in spite of the president rather than because of his support.

Roosevelt's Return

Meanwhile, Theodore Roosevelt had returned to the United States. As he came home, Pinchot and others filled his ears with Taft's alleged misdeeds. Roosevelt concluded that Taft "had not proved a good leader in spite of his having been a good first lieutenant." Roosevelt decided that it was up to him to get the Republican party back on the right course. He received a tumultuous welcome when his ship entered New York Harbor. Guns boomed and fireboats shot water into the air. A crowd of 100,000 people cheered him as he rode up the streets. His popularity seemed as strong as ever.

TABLE 21.1	PARTY STRENGTH IN CONGRESS, 1894–1918

Congress	Year Elected	Republicans	Democrats	Other
SENATE				
Fifty-fourth	(1894)	43	39	6
Fifty-fifth	(1896)	47	34	7
Fifty-sixth	(1898)	53	26	8
Fifty-seventh	(1900)	55	31	4
Fifty-eighth	(1902)	57	33	
Fifty-ninth	(1904)	57	33	
Sixtieth	(1906)	61	31	
Sixty-first	(1908)	61	31	
Sixty-second	(1910)	51	41	
Sixty-third	(1912)	44	51	1
Sixty-fourth	(1914)	40	56	
Sixty-fifth	(1916)	42	53	
Sixty-sixth	(1918)	49	47	
HOUSE				
Fifty-fourth	(1894)	244	105	7
Fifty-fifth	(1896)	204	113	40
Fifty-sixth	(1898)	185	163	9
Fifty-seventh	(1900)	197	151	9
Fifty-eighth	(1902)	208	178	
Fifty-ninth	(1904)	250	136	
Sixtieth	(1906)	222	164	
Sixty-first	(1908)	219	172	
Sixty-second	(1910)	161	228	
Sixty-third	(1912)	127	291	17
Sixty-fourth	(1914)	196	230	9
Sixty-fifth	(1916)	210	216	6
Sixty-sixth	(1918)	240	190	

SOURCE   The information in this table is derived from *The Statistical History of the United States* (Stamford, CT: Fairfield Publishers, 1965).

At first, Roosevelt refrained from public quarrels with the president. The two men met in late June but did not discuss the issues that separated them. Roosevelt was not finding it easy to defer to Taft's leadership. Meanwhile, the Republicans' internal warfare intensified. Taft used his appointment power against the Middle Western progressives in his party; their candidates were not nominated for positions in the federal government. Taft went even further, trying to organize loyal Republicans against reform leaders such as Dolliver, La Follette, and Beveridge. These moves failed, and the president's inability to rally support within his own party emphasized his weakness as a leader. Taft knew that his troubles with Roosevelt were growing. "I do not see how I am going to get out of having a fight with President Roosevelt," he said in July 1910.

Roosevelt and the New Nationalism

Roosevelt sharpened the dispute in a series of speeches during the summer of 1910. He called his program

"The New Nationalism." In doing so he drew in part upon the ideas of Herbert Croly, whose book *The Promise of American Life* had been published in 1909. Croly urged political leaders to advocate a "New Nationalism" that accepted the growth of big business and supplied strong presidential leadership. This message was a natural for Roosevelt. In a speech at Osawatomie, Kansas, he said that "The New Nationalism regards the executive power as the steward of the public welfare." The Square Deal of his presidency should be expanded. The "rules of the game" should be "changed so as to work for a more substantial equality of opportunity and reward for equally good service." He meant that there should be an income tax, inheritance taxes on large fortunes, workmen's compensation laws, and legislation to protect child labor. Roosevelt was advocating the modern regulatory state and wanted to achieve it as president.

The congressional elections of 1910 hurt both the progressives and the conservatives in the Republican party. The Democrats gained control of the House of Representatives when the Republicans lost fifty-eight seats. In the Senate, the Republicans dropped ten seats. They still had a ten-seat majority, but the progressive Republicans often voted with the Democrats. Republicans suffered their biggest losses in the industrial East where twenty-six Republican House members were defeated. Stressing inflation and the high cost of living, Democrats won governorships in New York, New Jersey, Ohio, and Indiana. After years of being the opposition party, they looked forward to the presidential election of 1912. For Roosevelt, the elections proved a major setback. He told friends that he would not oppose Taft in 1912.

PROGRESSIVE VICTORIES

Between 1910 and 1913 the spirit of progressivism reached its high-water mark. In every area of public life the movement for social change gathered momentum. The reformers seemed to have public opinion behind them, and for a brief interval it appeared that conservatives in both parties were on the defensive. This did not prove to be the case in the long run, but in the short term the forces of reform pushed forward.

Woman Suffrage

A leading example of this trend was the campaign for woman suffrage. In April 1910 the National American Woman Suffrage Association (NAWSA) presented Congress with a petition that more than 400,000 people had signed. The document asked for a constitutional amendment allowing women to vote. Although Congress refused to act, one suffrage worker, surprised by the size of the petition, said that her cause "is actually fashionable now."

The petition reflected NAWSA's new vitality. Under the leadership of Anna Howard Shaw, the organization's membership had grown. In states like Washington (1910), California (1911), and Arizona, Kansas, and Oregon (1912), woman suffrage triumphed. However referenda to give women the vote failed in Ohio, Wisconsin, and Michigan. Within the movement, younger women, eager for results, urged the older leaders to concentrate on obtaining a constitutional amendment.

Alice Paul became the main figure of the radical wing of the suffrage movement. She had fought for the vote in England and now she wanted to apply the same militant tactics of picketing and civil disobedience to the United States. Other women joined her, including Lucy Burns and Harriot Stanton Blatch, daughter of Elizabeth Cady Stanton. For a few years Paul and her allies worked on NAWSA's congressional committee. In March 1913, just days before Woodrow Wilson became president, they staged a well-publicized suffrage parade in Washington. Frustrated at what she saw as the cautious tactics of NAWSA, Paul and Lucy Burns left the organization in early 1914 to form the Congressional Union.

Significant obstacles to suffrage remained. The liquor industry feared that women who voted would support Prohibition. White southerners worried that woman suffrage might lead to suffrage for African Americans. Men saw their dominance threatened if women took part in politics. To counter these arguments, NAWSA stressed that female voting would lead to a purer and more honest politics. They also played down the argument that women should have equal political rights. Instead, they contended that woman suffrage would offset the votes of immigrants and racial minorities in large cities. Thus, suffragists would be protecting traditional values against "alien" assaults. Between 1910 and 1914 momentum for suffrage increased.

The militant spirit of the woman suffrage movement was embodied in the young and dynamic leader Alice Paul, who broke away from the National American Woman Suffrage Association to pursue a more aggressive course.

Prohibition

The drive to restrict the use and sale of alcohol also gained increasing support after 1910. The Anti-Saloon League had established a dominant position among prohibitionist organizations since its founding during the 1890s (see Chapter 19). Older groups, such as the Woman's Christian Temperance Union, continued to play an important role in the crusade, but the Anti-Saloon League mastered the techniques of interest group politics. The league sought to limit the power of the liquor industry to sell its product to the public. The first step in its strategy involved elections to give voters in a county or state the "local option" to ban the sale of alcohol. The plan was by a series of such elections to widen gradually the area that dry forces controlled. By 1906, impatient with the slowness of the local option method, the league shifted its emphasis to statewide elections to achieve dry dominance.

Oklahoma adopted Prohibition in 1907. By 1914 eight other states had banned the sale of alcohol. Militant prohibitionists (they were called "drys"; anti-pro-hibitionists were "wets") found the state-by-state process discouraging. The presence of a wet state next to a dry one encouraged drinkers to cross the border to ease their thirst. In 1913, prohibitionists in Congress passed the Webb-Kenyon Act which outlawed the shipment of alcohol into dry states. President Taft vetoed the bill, but Congress overrode his veto. The Anti-Saloon League's next goal was a constitutional amendment to ban the sale of alcohol everywhere in the United States.

Daddy's in There---

And Our Shoes and Stockings and Clothes and Food Are in There, Too, and They'll Never Come Out.
—*Chicago American.*

WANTED--A FATHER; A LITTLE BOY'S PLEA
JULIA H. JOHNSON

A shy little boy stood peering
  Through the door of a bright saloon;
He looked as if food and clothing
  Would be thought a most welcome boon.

And one of the men, in passing,
  As if tossing a dog a bone,
Asked, "What do you want this evening?"
  In a rude and unkindly tone.

"I am wanting"—the boy's lips trembled—
  "I am wanting my father, sir,"
And he gazed at the little tables
  Where the careless onlookers were.

It was there that he saw his father,
  But the man only shook his head,
And the boy, with his thin cheek burning,
  Ran away with a look of dread.

Oh, the fathers—the fathers wanted!
  How the heart-break, and bitter need,
With the longings, deep and piteous,
  For the wandering children plead.

May the children's call arouse them,
  May the fathers arise and go
With the young souls waiting for them,
  For the little ones need them so!

SERIES G. NO. 23.

The American Issue Publishing Co.
Westerville, Ohio

The Anti-Saloon League was one of the primary forces behind the drive for national prohibition. Its use of cartoons and leaflets made it a precursor of modern issue-oriented campaigning for social causes.

Restriction of Immigration

The effort to restrict immigration into the United States also accelerated during these years. The flow of newcomers from southern and eastern Europe remained large. There were more than 1 million immigrants in 1910, nearly 2 million in 1913, and over a million more in 1914, before the outbreak of World War I. In addition, revolutionary upheavals in Mexico drove thousands of Hispanic immigrants into the Southwest.

Ethnic and cultural tensions erupted. Protestants wanted to keep out Catholic and Jewish newcomers. Labor unions feared that immigrants would become strikebreakers; rural residents saw urban populations growing at their expense. Prejudice against the Chinese and Japanese fed nativist sentiments on the West Coast. Diplomatic friction with Japan followed. By 1913 a bill to impose a literacy test on immigrants passed both houses of Congress. President Taft vetoed the measure and Congress was unable to override the veto. Despite this setback, sentiment for immigration restriction spread after the war began.

The campaign for immigration restriction sought to place even tighter controls on such newcomers to the United States as these Chinese entrants photographed during the process of entering the country.

Progressivism and the Immigrant

Progressive reform offered some support to the nativist and racist feelings behind the movement to restrict immigration. Businesses favored a loose immigration policy. Opposition to allowing further immigration was portrayed as a way to help workers already in the United States. A feeling that cultures from southern and eastern Europe threatened traditional values led some progressives to endorse restriction. Thus, reform in this period did not always conform to the principles that later Americans would admire.

A tragic incident in Atlanta, Georgia, in 1913, underlined the tensions that accompanied the drive to restrict immigration. When a young factory worker, Mary Phagan, was murdered, suspicion fell on her superintendent, Leo Frank. A Jew whose parents had come from Russia, Frank was innocent, but he fell victim to anti-Semitism and fear of outsiders. As a "victim worthy to pay for the crime," he was convicted and sentenced to death. After the governor of Georgia commuted his sentence, a mob abducted and lynched him in August 1915. The episode helped to promote the rise of the Ku Klux Klan, a further testament to the strong currents of xenophobia and bigotry that ran beneath the age of reform.

Saving the Children

Amid so many social tensions, Americans worried about the future of their children in a changing world. People spent much time thinking about how youngsters could be nurtured and protected against harmful influences. Three organizations sprang up to address these concerns. In 1910–1911 the Boy Scouts of America, modeled on the British precedent created by Robert Baden-Powell, began training young men in the principles of loyalty and service. Boys twelve through eighteen years of age enrolled to receive instruction in "the military virtues such as honor, loyalty, obedience, and patriotism."

For young women there were the Girl Scouts, founded by Juliette Low in 1912, and the Campfire Girls, founded in the same year. These two groups prepared American girls for future domestic responsibilities. "The homemaker of tomorrow," said one Girl Scout leader, "must be made efficient in her task and happy in it." With the constructive activities that the Girl Scouts, Campfire Girls, and Boy Scouts supplied, delinquency and crime among the young would be reduced, or so their advocates maintained. In the process, members would learn the values that middle-class society cherished.

The struggle against child labor overshadowed all the other drives to improve the condition of children. In 1910 some 200,000 youngsters below the age of twelve labored in mills and factories. Attempts to limit child labor in textile firms in the South brought meager results. In 1912 the reformers succeeded in establishing a Children's Bureau within the federal government, but Congress failed to pass any legislation that directly addressed the child labor problem. Proponents of child labor laws hoped to make it an issue for the parties in the 1912 presidential contest.

Despite the many obstacles that progressive reformers faced, there was a sense that the nation was making genuine progress on social issues. William Allen White, a Kansas newspaper editor and a friend of many of the leading progressives, recalled that "All over the land in a score of states and more, young men in both parties were taking leadership by attacking things as they were in that day." Women, too, experienced feeling a sense of possibility that infused middle-class reform during the years before World War I.

LABOR PROTEST IN A CHANGING WORKPLACE

Despite this sense of progress, conflict prevailed in the relations between labor and capital. There were many strikes. Bitter struggles between workers and employers occurred in the garment unions of New York, among the textile workers of Massachusetts, in the coal mines of Colorado, and in other parts of the nation. Unlike White's middle-class colleagues, American laborers measured their progress in violent and bloody confrontations against harsh conditions in the workplace.

Changes in the Corporation

Unrest grew out of changes in the way that men and women worked. As industrialization spread, factories and businesses grew. In Chicago, Marshall Field had 5,000 salespeople in its many store departments. The meatpacking firm of Swift and Company employed 23,000 people in its seven plants by 1903. A business such as the Amoskeag Company textile mills in Manchester, New Hampshire, dominated the lives of its 17,000 employees with an elaborate system of welfare programs and company organizations.

The nature of these large corporations was changing as well. Important companies applied scientific research techniques and social science procedures in ways that altered the working experience of Americans. The need to develop new products at a regular rate led such corporations as DuPont and General Electric to emulate the example set by German firms. They created industrial laboratories where research and development could go on steadily. General Electric set up links to universities that allowed scientists and engineers on their faculties to address the needs of the corporations in their research. The ties between business and education helped propel economic growth for the rest of the century. Critics charged that it corrupted universities as well, but the trend proved to be irreversible.

New Rules for the Workplace

Within the large factories, relationships between employers and workers became more structured and routinized. The informal dominance that the foreman had exercised during the nineteenth century often gave way to bureaucratic practices. To control costs and ensure steady production, companies set up procedures for regular reporting on expenditures, centralization of purchasing and maintenance, and measurement of worker productivity. The goal, according to one engineering advisor, was "the establishment of standards everywhere, including standard instruction, cards for standard methods, motion study, time study, time cards, records of individual output."

Out of these innovations came a new way to run the factory and workplace. This technique, known as *scientific management* was developed by Frederick Winslow Taylor. As a mechanical engineer in the steel industry, Taylor became convinced that careful study

of how each individual task was conducted would lead to a more efficient workplace. Once the maximum amount of time necessary to do a specific job was established, workers could be instructed on how to complete the task without any wasted motion. Stopwatches measured the speed of work down to the split second. "We use the stopwatch," said one of Taylor's aides, "because the sun dial will not do."

As a concept, Taylorism enjoyed great popularity among business people. Although most employers did not adopt all of Taylor's ideas, the principle of managing factories and shops systematically took hold. Since the core of scientific management meant reducing all jobs to a set of simple steps that required little skill, workers resented practices that made them perform repetitive, routine movements all day long. Henry Ford claimed that "no man wants to be burdened with the care and responsibility of deciding things." Thus, he believed that workers welcomed freedom from mental strain. In fact, however, employees disliked having their work measured by a stopwatch. "We object to being reduced to a scientific formula," said one machinist.

The Limits of Paternalism

While scientific management viewed workers in a detached and bloodless way, some corporations revived the tradition of paternalism in the form of welfare and incentive programs for their employees. Lunchrooms and toilet areas were cleaned up, recreational facilities established, and plans set up for pensions and profit sharing. National Cash Register of Dayton, Ohio, was a leader in the field, along with H. J. Heinz Company, the Amoskeag Mills, and Remington Typewriter. As one steelmaker put it, "We make better steel and more of it by raising flowers and having them in our yards."

Despite these efforts, the situation for most American workers showed only marginal improvement. Businesses used a variety of techniques to block unions and prevent workers from improving their condition. The National Association of Manufacturers (NAM) pushed for laws to outlaw the union shop (mandating membership in a union to work in the plant) in favor of what was called the "open shop" in which unions were not allowed. Blacklists of pro-union employees were circulated, and new workers often had to sign contracts that barred workers from joining a union. (Because they reduced the power of workers below

that of a "yellow dog," these became known as "yellow dog" contracts.) When strikes occurred, employers used nonunion labor (strikers called them "scabs") to end the walkouts. Court injunctions limited the ability of strikers to picket and organize. Violent clashes between workers and police accompanied many strikes. So explosive did the conflict between labor and capital become that Congress created a Commission on Industrial Relations in 1912 to probe the causes of the unrest.

Unorganized Workers

The working classes in the cities faced the ravages of inflation during the early years of the century. While wages rose over the levels of the 1890s, prices accelerated at a faster rate and many consumer products remained out of reach of the average laborer. These workers also encountered difficult and often dangerous conditions in their factories and sweatshops. Many laborers turned to strikes and unions as the best weapons against a callous and unfeeling economic system. In New York City and Philadelphia from 1909 to 1911, the International Ladies Garment Workers Union organized workers within the shirtwaist manufacturing business. Twenty thousand women strikers took their grievances into the streets to demonstrate their solidarity. They managed to wrest some concessions from their employees in the form of union shops and improved working conditions.

Many manufacturers forced their employees to work in deplorable conditions with poor ventilation, dirt and filth, and danger to the lives of those who labored. In March 1911 a fire erupted at the Triangle Shirtwaist Company on New York City's Lower East Side. As the workers fled the flames, they found locked doors and no fire escape routes. The conflagration claimed 146 lives. Many women were killed when they jumped to the pavement below. "The floods of water from the firemen's hose that ran into the gutter were actually stained red with blood," wrote one reporter. The Triangle Fire spurred reform efforts among politicians in the New York Legislature.

Varieties of Labor Protest

Labor unions gained members between 1900 and 1914. The American Federation of Labor, led by

THE NEW YORK *TRIBUNE* REPORTS THE TRIANGLE FIRE, MARCH 26, 1911

The Triangle Fire of March 1911 was a tragic event that dramatized the desperate working conditions that often confronted the poor in an industrial society. The deaths that the fire caused spurred the New York Legislature to consider remedial legislation for workers in the garment district. The news story from the New York *Tribune* conveys some of the drama and tragedy of the episode.

Scores of Girls Leap to Death In Streets Ten Stories Below Them,
Had No Chance For Life
Unable to Reach Elevators or Stairways, Employees Rush to Windows,
Croker Blames Escapes
None on Outside of Building, Says Fire Chief, Saying That is Reason For Fearful Loss of Lives in Disaster,
Elevators Save Hundreds
Frightful Panic as Trapped Workers Fight Like Furies in Cars, Almost The Only Means of Escape, As Flames Sweep Through Workrooms.

Nearly one hundred and fifty lives were lost in a fire that swept through the three upper stories of a ten story factory loft building at the Northwest corner of Washington Place and Green Street at 5 o'clock yesterday afternoon, occupied by the Triangle Waist Company and a clothing house. At midnight 142 bodies had been taken to the morgue.

Fire Chief [Edward] Croker said:

"This calamity is just what I have been predicting. There were no outside fire escapes on this building. I have been advocating and agitating that fire escapes be put on building such as this. This large loss of life is due to this neglect."

Thirteen of the victims were men; 129 were women and girls.

The cause of the fire is unknown. No one has tried to do more than guess at it.

Scenes of almost indescribable horror attended the catastrophe. Scores of girls leaped from windows eight, nine, and ten stories above the street to their death. In one place so many bodies fell that the glass and iron deadlights in the pavement were broken.

A fire escape in a light shaft proved a veritable death trap. More than fifty girls were found dead at the bottom of the shaft.

Samuel Gompers, had several million members. The politics of the AFL had not changed since the end of the nineteenth century. Its craft unions discouraged organization among industrial workers. Women employees received little support from Gompers and his allies. Thus, the majority of workers remained out of the union movement.

The Industrial Workers of the World (IWW) appealed to the unskilled masses. Its ultimate goal was still a social revolution that would sweep away

The tragedy of the Triangle Shirtwaist Fire in New York City killed dozens of women who labored in that sweatshop. Rescue workers lay out the corpses from the disaster.

industrial capitalism. To the IWW's leadership, including William D. "Big Bill" Haywood and Elizabeth Gurley Flynn, violent strikes seemed the best way to promote industrial warfare. "The working class and the employing class have nothing in common," said the IWW in its public statements.

Strikes in Lawrence and Ludlow

The IWW gained national attention when a strike erupted in the textile mills of Lawrence, Massachusetts, in mid-January 1912. After the textile companies announced substantial wage reductions, the workers walked out. "Better to starve fighting than to starve working," they said. Haywood came to Lawrence to support the strike. The children of strikers were sent to live in other cities, a tactic that publicized the walkout and swayed public opinion to the workers' cause. On March 1, the companies granted them a pay hike. Women strikers were key participants in the victory. As one of their songs put it, they sought "bread and roses" by which they meant a living wage and a life with hope. Despite this local success, the IWW did not build a strong following in the East.

Another controversial strike occurred in Colorado. The United Mine Workers struck against the Colorado Fuel and Iron Company in September 1913. The workers complained about low wages and company camps with brutal guards. "The miners get very poor food," said one man, "and some of the children are dressed in gunny-sacks and their fathers are working every day." John D. Rockefeller, who controlled the coal company, asked the governor to call in the National Guard to maintain order. Confrontations between soldiers and miners ended in the "Ludlow Massacre" of April 1914 in which troops fired on miners in a tent city at Ludlow. Five strikers and one soldier were shot, and two women and eleven children died in the flames that broke out in the tents. Federal inquiries followed, and the workers obtained some concessions. Yet, later in 1914 they were forced to end the strike without gaining the union recognition they sought.

Changes in the workplace during the progressive period had benefited the employers far more than they had improved the lot of the people who labored in factories and shops. Some social legislation had been enacted to protect the worker from the effects of industrial accidents. The length of the working day had been reduced somewhat. Compared with Great Britain or Germany, however, the United States still did not provide social insurance when a worker became unemployed, pension benefits for old age, or equal bargaining power on the job.

Dollar Diplomacy

While the nation grappled with problems arising from the struggle between business and labor, its role over-

seas revealed the continuing effects of the expansion that began under McKinley and Roosevelt. In foreign affairs, William Howard Taft and his secretary of state, Philander C. Knox, adopted the policy of "dollar diplomacy" in their relations with Latin America and Asia. They believed that when U.S. corporations traded and invested in underdeveloped areas of the world, peace and stability increased. Instead of military force, the ties of finance and capital would instruct countries in the wise conduct of their affairs. "The borrower is the servant of the lender," said Knox. Military intervention should be a last resort when order needed to be restored.

Latin America seemed to offer an ideal location for applying the principles of dollar diplomacy. No European countries challenged the supremacy of the United States in that region. In 1909 Taft and Knox induced bankers to loan money to Honduras to prevent British investors from achieving undue influence there. In 1911 they compelled the government of Nicaragua to accept another loan from U.S. investors. Unfortunately, some Nicaraguans regarded the scheme as an intrusion in their affairs, and they rebelled against the government that had made the deal. The Taft administration sent Marines to Nicaragua to restore order; the resulting U.S. Military presence continued for several decades as successive presidents pursued political stability there. Such policies left a lasting feeling of bitterness in relations with Latin America.

Taft and Knox also tried to apply dollar diplomacy to China. A newspaper editor called that country "the greatest uncut commercial melon in the world." The government wanted American capitalists to support a railroad in China, first to develop the country and then to offset further intrusion by Japan. Roosevelt had recognized Japanese dominance in the region; Knox wanted to challenge it economically. He envisioned that a syndicate of nations would lend China money to purchase existing railroads in Manchuria. The plan collapsed when the British, Russians, and Japanese rejected the idea in early 1910. Knox "has done himself no good," wrote a British diplomat. Instead of promoting stability in China, he drove the Japanese and Russians to join forces against American interests. The Knox initiative sparked resentment in Japan, and relations between that country and the United States remained tense. Dollar diplomacy proved to be an ineffective way to achieve the kind of world influence that Taft and Knox had sought.

A foreign policy problem closer to home emerged in 1911. Porfirio Díaz had ruled Mexico for almost

PORTRAIT OF A PATIENT OLD GENTLEMAN WAITING FOR UNIVERSAL PEACE.

This cartoon from the Philadelphia Inquirer *of 1911 reflects American attitudes toward overseas involvement during the Progressive Era. Across the Mexican border the bullets fly while revolutions plague other parts of the world.*

forty years. He had attracted American investment because he had maintained apparent calm and stability within his nation. In fact, however, his dictatorial rule bred discontent that eventually erupted in a revolution. Francisco I. Madero, the leader of the revolution, came to power hoping to transform the nation. But he aroused the opposition of conservative forces, including the military, large landowners, and the Roman Catholic church. Shortly before Taft's term ended in 1913, Madero was overthrown and murdered. Mexico's revolutionary ferment would be a continuing problem for the successful candidate in the 1912 presidential race.

REPUBLICAN DISCORD AND DEMOCRATIC OPPORTUNITY

Following the Republican losses in the elections of 1910, Taft and Roosevelt worked out an uneasy agreement not to attack each other during the first half of

1911. Republican progressives still looked for an alternative to Taft in 1912. Robert M. La Follette hinted that he might run against the president and courted support from other reformers. To placate the progressives, Taft eased Ballinger out of the cabinet and named two supporters of Roosevelt as secretary of the Interior and secretary of War. Roosevelt told friends that he would not be a candidate in 1912.

Taft's Embattled Presidency

Taft's troubles with Congress persisted. He negotiated a trade agreement with Canada that was based on reciprocal concessions on tariffs. Neither the Democrats nor the progressive Republicans liked Canadian Reciprocity because it lowered import duties on products that affected their districts. Taft pushed the agreement through Congress, but then Canadian voters rejected the government that had supported it. Taft's trade initiative was dead.

Then the president's fragile friendship with Roosevelt collapsed. Unlike his predecessor, Taft believed in the principle of greater business competition underlying the Sherman Antitrust Act; he was more vigorous in "busting" the trusts than Roosevelt had been. In October 1911 the Department of Justice filed an antitrust suit against United States Steel. One of the practices that violated the law, according to the indictment, was the company's acquisition of the Tennessee Coal and Iron Company during the Panic of 1907 (see Chapter 20). Since Roosevelt had approved the merger, the indictment amounted to a public criticism of his presidency. Roosevelt was furious. He listened more eagerly to friends who told him that he should run against Taft. By the early part of the year, he decided to do so. "My hat is in the ring, the fight is on, and I am stripped to the buff," he said in February 1912, as he opened his campaign against Taft's renomination.

The Struggle Between Roosevelt and Taft

Throughout the spring of 1912 the two former friends waged a bitter battle for the Republican nomination. For the first time, a few states held primary elections to choose delegates to the Republican convention. That change, which would grow in popularity, gave an obvious advantage to Roosevelt, who attracted a ma-

The increasing friction between Taft and Roosevelt appeared in postcards that were sent out in 1911–1912. A bevy of Theodore Roosevelts declare their allegiance to the former president.

jority of these voters. Taft ran strongly among party regulars, who selected their delegates in tightly controlled nominating conventions. As the Republican National Convention opened in Chicago, neither man had a clear majority. Several hundred delegates were contested. The Republican National Committee, which Taft controlled, gave the president 235 of the disputed delegates and left Roosevelt with only 19. When the national convention upheld what the national committee had done, Roosevelt knew that he would not have the votes to become the Republican nominee. He believed that Taft had stolen from him a prize that was rightfully his.

Summoning his followers to leave the convention, Roosevelt denounced Taft's "theft" of delegates and promised that he would fight on. "We stand at Armageddon and we battle for the Lord," he said. For the next two months Roosevelt prepared to run as a third-party candidate, leading the progressive wing of his party against Taft and the Democratic nominee.

At the first convention of the Progressive party in August 1912, Roosevelt put forward a very progressive platform that embodied the New Nationalism he had been advocating since 1910. The party sought more government regulation of big business, minimum wages and maximum hours for workers, government pension programs, and the end of child labor. In many respects, Roosevelt and the Progressives offered a more advanced program of social justice than any other candidate. He told reporters that he was "as fit as a bull moose." Cartoonists quickly made the animal the symbol of Roosevelt's crusade.

The Democratic Opportunity

The Democrats watched with astonishment and glee as the Republicans split apart. To exploit the disarray of their opponents, they needed a credible presidential candidate of their own. After three unsuccessful races, William Jennings Bryan was only a remote possibility. The search for a fresh face began as soon as the election of 1910 was over. One attractive newcomer was the governor of New Jersey, Woodrow Wilson, who had carried that staunchly Republican state by a sizable majority. Soon there was talk of Wilson as a potential candidate for the Democrats.

Woodrow Wilson was fifty-six years old in 1912. Born in Virginia, he grew up in the South and shared its racial views. He attended Princeton University in New Jersey, studied law for a time, and then earned a doctorate in history and political science at Johns Hopkins University. After teaching at several colleges, he joined the Princeton faculty in 1890, was quickly recognized as an outstanding instructor, and became president of the university in 1902. He soon gained national fame as a champion of small undergraduate classes and young, dynamic teachers. After initial successes, he ran into resistance from more conservative alumni and faculty when he opposed class distinctions among the Princeton student body and clashed with a powerful dean. He resigned from the Princeton presidency in 1910. New Jersey Democrats urged Wilson

This advertisement for Roosevelt and Hiram Johnson in 1912 depicts the symbol of the party, the "Bull Moose," and the campaign slogan "Pass Prosperity Around."

to run for state office. Long interested in a career that might take him to the White House, he won the New Jersey governorship in his first try at elective office.

The Wilson Candidacy

Wilson had been a conservative Democrat for much of his life. The experience of his Princeton presidency and his sense of political opportunity led him toward progressivism. His candidacy scared some Democrats who preferred the safer and less inspiring leadership of the speaker of the House, James Beauchamp "Champ" Clark of Missouri. Wilson, Clark, and several other Democratic hopefuls fought for the nomination in primaries and state conventions.

When the national convention met in Baltimore in late June, no candidate was in sight of the two-thirds majority needed for the nomination. Clark was the closest to having a simple majority of the delegates. In

a series of ballots, the convention was deadlocked. After Clark failed to get the needed two-thirds, Wilson gained strength as an acceptable national candidate. He won on the forty-sixth ballot, and Thomas Riley Marshall became the vice-presidential nominee. With the Republicans split between Roosevelt and Taft, prospects seemed excellent for a Democratic victory in 1912.

The Socialist Challenge

There was a fourth serious candidate in the 1912 presidential race. Once again the Socialist party selected Eugene V. Debs as its candidate. Debs had run in every election since 1900, and his total vote had increased each time. In 1908 he had amassed 420,000 votes. The party also made gains at the state and local levels. Seven hundred thousand voters supported Socialist candidates in 1910, and the following year Socialist mayors or city officials were chosen in seventy-four cities. Labor unrest seemed to be growing, especially in the Lawrence, Massachusetts, textile strike that broke out in January. A popular speaker who loved the rigors of campaigning, Debs took his "Red Special" across the country. "Comrades," Debs cried, "this is our year."

Socialism gained followers because the party spoke to the grievances of the agricultural and working poor. In an era when their doctrines were not linked to a foreign nation and did not imply totalitarian methods, socialists seemed to present a tolerable alternative to the major parties. Disputes within their ranks over whether to pursue reform at the ballot box or through more violent means prevented the party from offering a united front. Moreover, since he had little chance of winning, Debs did not have to frame programs with a view to carrying them out in office.

The Creation of the Progressive Party

Among the three major party candidates in 1912, President Taft decided to observe the custom that an incumbent president did not campaign for reelection. Since he expected to lose badly and the Republicans were short of money, it was a wise choice. Many conservative Republicans decided to support Wilson in order to retain control of their party and keep Roosevelt out of the presidency.

Roosevelt campaigned with his usual energy and excitement, and he attracted many reformers to his cause. The Progressive party held its national convention in Chicago during August. The atmosphere mixed the fervor of a revival meeting with the backroom bargaining of a traditional political conclave. Delegates sang "Onward Christian Soldiers" as the theme of the convention. Roosevelt told them that "our cause is based on the eternal principle of righteousness, and even though we who now lead may for the time fail, in the end the cause itself shall triumph."

Some aspects of the Progressive party reflected old politics. To woo the white South, the delegates excluded African Americans from the convention. Roosevelt defended the protective tariff and attacked reciprocity with Canada. The main financial support for the new party came from wealthy newspaper publishers and corporate executives, who liked Roosevelt's attitude toward big business.

At its core, however, the Progressive party's endorsement of expanded social justice legislation made it more forward-looking than either the Republicans or the Democrats. Jane Addams and other social justice reformers joined Roosevelt's crusade for that reason. The party supported woman suffrage, limits on child labor, and a system of "social insurance." The centerpiece of Roosevelt's New Nationalism was the proposal for an "administrative commission" that would "maintain permanent, active supervision over industrial corporations engaged in interstate commerce." This would enable Roosevelt to continue his policy of distinguishing between "good trusts" that served the public interest and "bad trusts" that harmed the public. The judgment of what constituted a good or bad trust would be up to Roosevelt and his administration. As a joke of the time went, the difference between a good trust and a bad trust was that when you tickled a bad trust it said "Tee Hee," and when you tickled a good trust it said "TR."

Enacting Roosevelt's program thus would involve a broadening of national authority and an expansion of the bureaucratic machinery of the federal government. The role of the president would also be expanded to ensure that the public's rights were protected. To that extent, Roosevelt's position in 1912 looked forward to the regulatory and welfare state that emerged later in the twentieth century. Critics at the time warned that in the wrong hands this increased national power could also threaten individual liberty.

The Democrats selected Woodrow Wilson to oppose Roosevelt and Taft in 1912. Seated in the chair, he talks to supporters at a rally.

Woodrow Wilson and the New Freedom

Wilson's initial campaign strategy was to make only a few appearances in important states. As Roosevelt laid out his program, however, the Democratic nominee soon decided that he would have to campaign as actively as his major rival. Wilson told the voters that only a Democratic president could govern effectively with the Democratic Congress that was certain to be elected. He then offered a program of his own to counter Roosevelt's New Nationalism. He called it the New Freedom.

As Roosevelt began his campaign, Wilson consulted with Louis D. Brandeis, a prominent Boston lawyer in Boston and reformist thinker. Brandeis believed that big business was inefficient economically and dangerous to democracy. "The very large unit — is not as efficient as the smaller unit," he wrote. He laid out his critique of bigness and the role of finance capitalism in a book titled *Other People's Money,* which was published in 1914. He told Wilson that the issue Roosevelt was raising could be met with a simple question: Shall we have regulated competition or regulated monopoly? Wilson should emphasize the need for greater competition to control monopoly and call for stricter

enforcement of the antitrust laws. Rather than relying on trusts and large corporations to act in a socially responsible manner, as Roosevelt contended, the government should create conditions in which competition could flourish.

As for social justice, Wilson said that he supported the goals of eliminating child labor, improving wages for women, and expanding benefits for employees, but he questioned whether the federal government should supply these benefits. In that way he appealed to progressives but also prevented southern Democrats from opposing him as an enemy of state rights (and segregation). The New Freedom was, like most campaign slogans, broad and vague. It gave Wilson a mandate for action without tying his hands.

Wilson Victorious

The 1912 election was turbulent down to election day. During a speaking engagement in Milwaukee, Wisconsin, Roosevelt was shot, yet he finished his talk while the bullet was still embedded in the copy of his speech he carried in his pocket. The incident aroused sympathy for Roosevelt but did not change

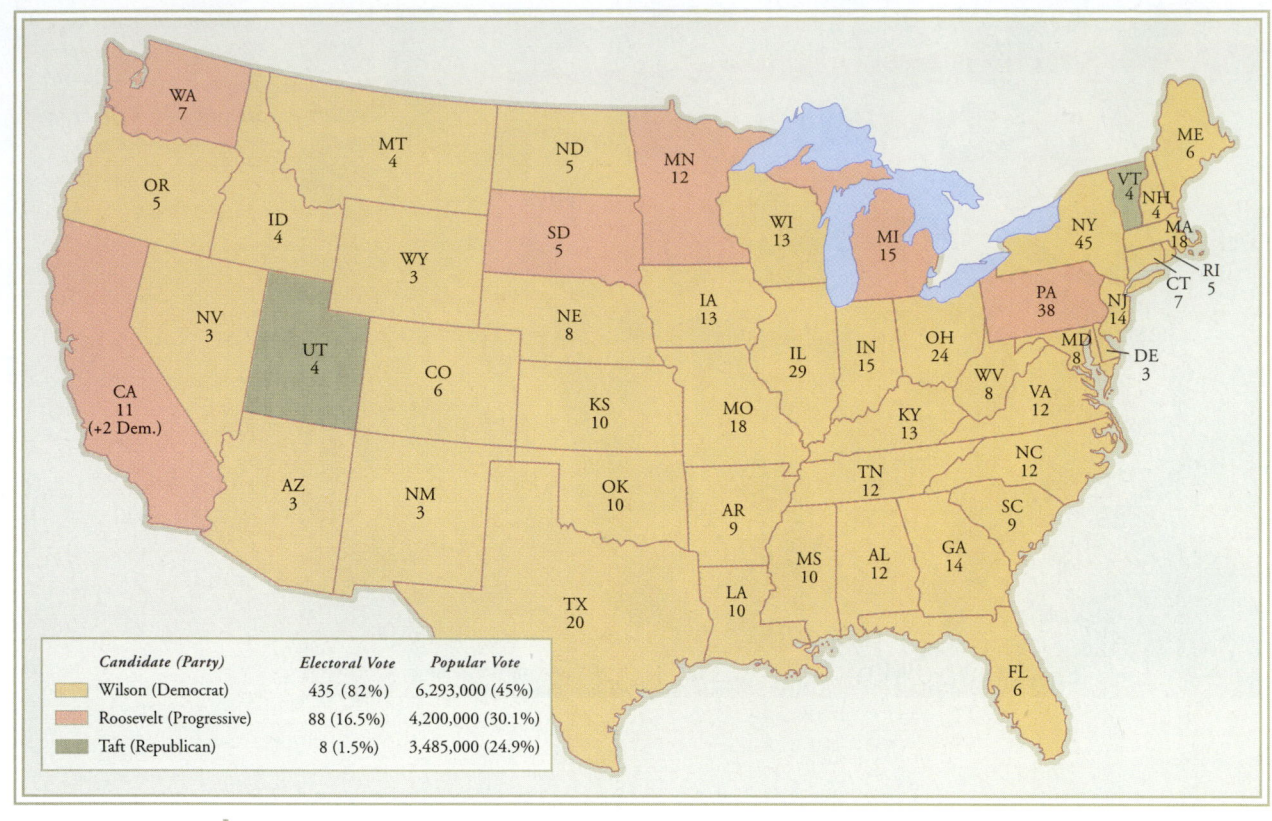

Candidate (Party)	Electoral Vote	Popular Vote
Wilson (Democrat)	435 (82%)	6,293,000 (45%)
Roosevelt (Progressive)	88 (16.5%)	4,200,000 (30.1%)
Taft (Republican)	8 (1.5%)	3,485,000 (24.9%)

MAP 21.1 | THE ELECTION OF 1912

the outcome. From the outset of the campaign it was clear that the Democrats had the electoral advantage over the divided Republicans and Progressives. Wilson received 435 electoral votes to eighty-eight for Roosevelt and eight for Taft. The Democrats swept Congress. They had fifty-one seats in the Senate to forty-four for the Republicans and their margin in the House was 291 to 127. Nevertheless, Wilson was a minority president. He received about 42 percent of the popular vote. Eugene Debs won just over 900,000 popular votes, or 6 percent of the total, and Roosevelt and Taft divided the rest. Voter turnout for the election was lower than it had been in 1908, and the public's interest in the contest seems to have been more limited than the clamor of the campaign suggested. It was now up to Woodrow Wilson to prove that the Democratic party could govern the nation. The Democrats must avoid the mistakes of the Cleveland era and defy Republican predictions that Democrats would split as they had done so often before.

WILSON'S PRESIDENCY

Because of the domestic achievements of his first term and his advocacy of the League of Nations in his second, Woodrow Wilson became one of the most important political leaders of the early twentieth century. He was a brilliant speaker whose moral rhetoric spoke of lofty ideals. He strengthened the power of the presidency, increased the regulatory role of the national government, and led the nation to play a greater part in international affairs. Even more than Roosevelt, he had the capacity to articulate national values in effective and moving language.

With these strong qualities came important limitations. Before he became president, Wilson had suffered a series of small strokes that increased his natural stubbornness and made him reluctant to accept unwelcome advice. Although he often called for open government and sought what he called "common

THE SOCIAL COST OF INDUSTRIALISM

An Excerpt from Woodrow Wilson's First Inaugural Address, March 4, 1913

Woodrow Wilson's first inaugural address on March 4, 1913, offered an eloquent statement of how a major national progressive saw the nation's task in dealing with the social cost of industrialism and rapid change. Wilson's reference to "the groans and agony of it all" may be compared with the earlier document in this chapter on the Triangle Fire.

We see that in many things that life is very great. It is incomparably great in its material aspects, in its body of wealth, in the diversity and sweep of its energy, in the industries which have been conceived and built up by the genius of individual men and the limitless enterprise of groups of men.

It is great, also very great, in its moral force. Nowhere else in the world have noble men and women exhibited in more striking forms the beauty and the energy of sympathy and helpfulness and counsel in their efforts to rectify wrong, alleviate suffering, and set the weak in the way of strength and hope. We have built up, moreover, a great system of government which has stood through a long age as in many respects a model for those who seek to set liberty upon foundations that will endure against fortuitous change, against storm and accident. Our life contains every great thing, and contains it in rich abundance.

But the evil has come with the good, and much fine gold has been corroded. With riches has come inexcusable waste. We have squandered a great part of what we might have used, and have not stopped to conserve the exceeding bounty of nature, without which our genius for enterprise would have been worthless and impotent, scorning to be careful, shamefully prodigal as well as admirably efficient. We have been proud of our industrial achievements, but we have not hitherto stopped thoughtfully enough to count the human cost, the cost of lives snuffed out, of energies overtaxed and broken, the fearful physical and spiritual cost to the men and women and children upon whom the dead weight and burden of it has fallen pitilessly the years through. The groans and agony of it all had not reached our ears, the solemn, moving undertone of our life, coming up out of the mines and factories, and out of every home where the struggle had its intimate and familiar seat. With the great Government went many deep secret things which we too long delayed to look into and scrutinize with candid, fearless eyes. The great Government we loved has too often been made use of for private and selfish purposes, and those who had used it had forgotten the people.

counsel," he kept his decisions to himself and consulted only a few friends about his policies. His righteousness and sense of personal virtue caused his political enemies to develop an intense dislike of his methods and tactics. However, when the tide of events ran with Wilson, as they did during his first term, he was a powerful leader.

Launching the New Freedom Program

Wilson lost no time in demonstrating his intention to be a strong president. In his inaugural address on March 4, 1913, he spoke eloquently of the negative aspects of industrialism. There was "the human cost, the cost of lives snuffed out, of energies overtaxed and

When Woodrow Wilson came to Congress to speak on behalf of tariff reform in 1913, he broke a century and more of tradition that presidents did not deliver their messages in person. His innovation became a commonplace in the years that followed.

broken, the fearful physical and spiritual cost to the men and women and children upon whom the dead weight and burden of it all has fallen pitilessly the years through."

To implement his program, Wilson first asked Congress to take up the issue of the tariff. He called the lawmakers into a special session in April 1913. To dramatize the problem, he decided to deliver his message to Congress in person. No president had done so since Jefferson had abandoned the practice in 1801, but presidential appearances before Congress became more common once Wilson resumed the technique. The move proved to be an important step in expanding presidential influence both on Capitol Hill and in the nation at large.

In the speech itself, Wilson urged the House and Senate to reduce import duties in order to promote "effective competition, the whetting of American wits by contest with the wits of the world." The Democratic House responded with a measure to lower tariffs, named after Oscar W. Underwood, the chairman of the Ways and Means Committee. The Underwood bill cut duties on raw wool, sugar, cotton goods, and silks.

To compensate for the revenue that would be lost, the new tariff imposed a small tax on annual incomes over $4,000 with rates increasing for those who made more than $20,000 a year. Progressives had secured ratification of the Sixteenth Amendment in February 1913, which made the income tax constitutional.

Democrats worried about what would happen when the Underwood bill reached the Senate. They remembered the experience of 1894 and the Wilson-Gorman Tariff, or the Payne-Aldrich Law of 1909, when the Senate changed the House bill in a protectionist way. In fact, the Democrats were relatively unified in 1913, and pressure from large corporations for higher rates had eased. Only smaller businesses, fearing foreign competition, pushed hard for tariff protection. President Wilson added his voice on May 26, when he publicly denounced the "industrious" and "insidious" lobby that was trying to weaken the drive for tariff reform. He said that he would be the people's lobbyist. It was a dramatic gesture, but it was not really necessary. The Democrats stuck together, lowered the duties that the House had set, and passed the bill in August by a vote of forty-four to thirty-seven. The

conference committee's version of the bill passed both houses in October. Wilson signed the Underwood Tariff into law on October 3, 1913. The president and his party had demonstrated that they could provide positive leadership.

The Federal Reserve System

Building on his momentum with the tariff, during June 1913 Wilson turned to another important subject. Since the Panic of 1907, there had been a clear need for reform of the nation's banking system. A modern economy could not function efficiently without a central bank with the capacity to control the currency, meet the monetary needs of different sections of the country, and ensure that the money supply was adequate to the demands of the growing economy. The issue became whether private banking interests or the national government should be in charge of the central bank.

Before Wilson was elected, the National Monetary Commission, headed by Nelson Aldrich, had offered the idea of a system of reserve banks that private bankers would supervise. Wilson initially favored this approach until Secretary of State William Jennings Bryan and his allies in Congress insisted that the federal government must be supreme over the reserve banks and the currency they would issue. At the urging of Louis Brandeis, Wilson accepted Bryan's ideas, and in a message to Congress on June 23, 1913, he said that the new system "must be public, not private, must be vested in the Government itself."

It took six months to get a banking bill through Congress. Wilson had to appease southern and western Democrats, who wanted two changes in the proposed law. These members sought to expand the credit available to farmers, and they wanted to outlaw the practice known as interlocking directorates, in which banking officials served as directors of banks with which they competed. For reformers, such arrangements symbolized the power of finance capital. The president withstood criticism from the banking community itself, and used patronage and persuasion to win over potential opponents among Democrats in the Senate.

Congress completed its action in mid-December, and Wilson signed the Federal Reserve Act on December 27. This act was one of the most important pieces of economic legislation of the first half of the twenti-

eth century. It established the Federal Reserve Board, whose members the president appointed, and created a structure consisting of twelve reserve banks located in different parts of the country. The Federal Reserve had the power to determine the amount of money in circulation, to expand or contract credit as needed, and to respond to some degree to changes in the business cycle.

Wilson and the Trusts

Wilson had now gone a good distance toward fulfilling his campaign pledges to reduce the tariff, reform the banking system, and deal with the problem of trusts. Early in 1914, the president asked Congress to consider trusts in a constructive spirit. "The antagonism between business and government is over," he told them. Some of the legislation passed in that year followed the principles that Wilson had outlined in his campaign. The Clayton Antitrust Act (1914) endeavored to spell out precisely the business practices that restricted competition and then prohibit them.

As time passed, however, the president's thinking shifted. He came to favor the creation of a Trade Commission that would respond to business practices as they evolved, an idea that resembled what Theodore Roosevelt had proposed in 1912. The Federal Trade Commission was established during the fall of 1914. A delighted Wilson said that he had almost completed the program he had promised in his 1912 presidential campaign.

Wilson and the Progressive Agenda

The president's statements left many progressives disappointed. They wanted the Democratic administration to push for social justice legislation. Wilson did not yet believe that Washington should support the demands of progressive interest groups. He also worried about the precedent that might be set by a government that used power to address specific social issues. Such a policy might lead to attacks on racial segregation in the South which Wilson supported. In fact, the Wilson administration expanded racial segregation in the federal government. The color line, Wilson told a black delegation that came to protest such policies, "may not be intended against anybody, but for the benefit of both."

When supporters of woman suffrage sought Wilson's backing in 1913 and 1914, he turned them down. He also opposed federal aid for rural credits, restrictions on child labor through congressional action, and Prohibition. Court decisions had subjected organized labor to the workings of the antitrust laws, and the unions wanted that policy changed through legislation. Again, Wilson declined to act. Worsening economic conditions during the spring and summer of 1914 reinforced Wilson's belief that his administration should remain conservative on social issues. He tried to reassure businesses that the administration was friendly toward them. These gestures did not appease the Republicans or their business supporters, however. There were indications that the Democrats would have a difficult time at the polls in the 1914 congressional elections.

SOCIAL AND CULTURAL CHANGE DURING THE WILSON YEARS

While politicians worked out Wilson's New Freedom programs during 1913 and 1914, social and cultural transformations accelerated. The Victorian era, with its cultural restraints, seemed to be fading. Americans with a literary or artistic bent turned to the ideas of European thinkers, who emphasized greater freedom for the individual in an uncertain world. Some of these principles came to be defined as *modernism*. In the days just before World War I, a sense of optimism and possibility filled the air. "Looking back upon it now," wrote Mabel Dodge Luhan, a sponsor of artists and their work, "it seems as though everywhere, in that year of 1913, barriers went down and people reached each other who had never been in touch before."

Automobiles for a Mass Market

When Wilson went to his inauguration on March 4, 1913, he drove in an automobile. It was the first time a president-elect had traveled to his swearing-in by car. This action symbolized the vast changes that were making the people of the United States more mobile in their daily lives and more eager for the consumer products of an industrial society. In particular, the innovations in both production and marketing of Henry Ford (see Chapter 20) were bringing cars within the reach of the average middle-class American.

If Ford wanted to fulfill his dream of building "a motor car for the great multitude," he had to devise a means of producing cars continually and in even

TABLE 21.2	MANUFACTURING AND MARKETING OF MODEL T FORDS, 1908–1916		
Calendar Year	*Retail Price (Touring Car)*	*Total Model T Production*	*Total Model T Sales*
1908	$850	n.a.	5,986
1909	950	13,840	12,292
1910	780	20,727	19,293
1911	690	53,488	40,402
1912	600	82,388	78,611
1913	550	189,088	182,809
1914	490	230,788	260,720
1915	440	394,788	355,276
1916	360	585,388	577,036

SOURCE   Table is taken from David A Hounshell, *From the American System to Mass Production, 1880–1932* (Baltimore: Johns Hopkins University Press, 1984), p. 224.

greater quantities. He borrowed the concept of the assembly line from the meatpacking industry and his engineers adapted it to carmaking. The Ford plant covered more than sixty-five acres in Highland Park, Michigan. It featured a large belt, fed by smaller belts, that brought the chassis of the car and its windshields, tanks, batteries, and other parts together in a smoothly functioning operation. At first, it took the work force ninety-three minutes to turn out a single Model T. By 1920 the cars were coming off the line at the rate of one per minute. In 1914 the Model T cost under $500 and Ford produced more than 260,000 cars.

On January 5, 1914, Ford proclaimed that he would pay his workers $5 for an eight-hour day. The announcement was headline news across the country, and Ford became a national hero. He was not a serious economic thinker, but he understood that people needed to earn enough money in wages to be able to afford the cars he was making. He realized that he could make more money by selling large numbers of low-priced vehicles than he could by selling a few expensive cars. Ford thus could be described as an apostle of the emerging mass society.

The Five-Dollar Day program was also designed to head off potential unrest among Ford workers. Absenteeism and high turnover among employees hampered production schedules. In addition, unhappiness among workers might lead to the organization of unions. To offset these trends, the new program aimed at sharing profits in a way that would keep workers at their jobs. In addition, Ford developed a "Sociological Department" to instill in employees the values required for efficient mass production. Workers who were productive and cooperative received higher wages. Those who were not were discharged.

The Growing Use of Electricity

The five-dollar day was an apparent sign of progress. Another was the spreading reliance on electricity. Average annual use of electricity doubled during the twenty years after 1912. New products offered homemakers the chance to ease the dull routines of domestic work. General Electric introduced the Radiant Toaster in 1912, which promised "Crisp, Delicious, Golden-Brown Toast on the Breakfast Table." The Hoover Suction Sweeper would "Sweep With Electricity for 3¢ a Week." Newer stoves and washing ma-

Henry Ford's cheap and efficient car became very popular during the first decade of the new century. This photograph gives a good sense of the simplicity and durability of the Model T.

chines also came into use. Women could also buy ready-made clothes and spend less time on the sewing that had occupied much of their time a generation earlier.

Other technological developments were still in their early stages. The Wright Brothers had made the first power flight in 1903, but aviation began in earnest five years later. Harriet Quimby of the United States was the first woman to fly a plane across the English Channel. Meanwhile, the use of wireless telegraphy in marine navigation expanded. The disaster of the *Titanic,* which hit an iceberg in April 1912 and sank with the loss of hundreds of passengers, underlined the need for reliable radio communications for all vessels. Congress enacted a bill mandating the navy to promote radio usage. Within a few years tentative steps would be taken toward broadcasting voices over the airwaves.

Artistic and Social Ferment

Artistic and cultural ferment accompanied the peak years of progressivism. In 1913 the International Exhibit of Modern Art took place at the 69th Regiment Armory in New York City. Quickly dubbed "The Armory Show," it displayed the works of such European painters as Pablo Picasso and Henri Matisse. The modernist paintings offended many critics who attacked them in vicious terms. Marcel Duchamp's work *Nude Descending a Staircase* was labeled "an explosion in a shingle factory." Yet, the public flocked to see the paintings, and American artists were stimulated and challenged to adopt the new forms of expression. As one critic predicted, "American art will never be the same again."

The period also produced innovative literary figures who would become even more famous during the 1920s. Reporters and novelists clustered in New York's Greenwich Village. Among them were Max Eastman, publisher of *The Masses,* a magazine that assailed conventional values and the established political system; Eugene O'Neill, a playwright; and John Reed, a radical journalist. Outside of New York, Theodore Dreiser was continuing a literary career that included *The Financier* (1912), a novel depicting a ruthless tycoon; Sherwood Anderson was a short-story author who criticized middle-class life in the nation's heartland.

Among the influential writers of the day was Walter Lippmann, a Harvard-educated commentator and social critic, who published *A Preface to Politics* (1913) and *Drift and Mastery* (1914). Lippmann sympathized with the New Nationalism of Theodore Roosevelt, and was one of the cofounders, with Herbert Croly, of *The New Republic,* soon a leading journal of political opinion and cultural commentary. Another important critical voice was H. L. Mencken, editor of *Smart Set,* a New York magazine; he assailed the cultural provincialism of much of American culture.

Women, too, sought to gain greater rights and to share the freedoms that men enjoyed. In 1912 women in Greenwich Village founded a club called Heterodoxy whose only demand was that its members should "not be orthodox" in their views. In their discussions and in the public meetings they sponsored, they called their doctrine "feminism," which they defined as an attempt on the part of women to be "our whole big human selves."

Heterodoxy represented only a small proportion of American women, but cultural changes occurred even for those who did not call themselves feminists. Women's skirts had become several inches shorter since the beginning of the century. Bobbed hair became fashionable, and more women smoked openly in public. When movie stars like Mary Pickford became famous, the use of cosmetics spread as women emulated

Greater freedom for women in the Progressive Era brought them into places previously reserved for men. These four women are drinking in the bar of a New York hotel.

the images of feminine beauty that appeared on screen. The "flapper," an image associated with the 1920s, actually made her appearance at about this time. In fact, the years between 1910 and 1920 saw greater opportunities for women in employment and cultural affairs than would occur in the decade that followed.

Americans at Play

The ways in which Americans used their leisure time reflected a trend toward mass entertainment. Boxing was still a major sport. When Arthur John "Jack" Johnson became the first African-American heavyweight champion in 1908, the public clamored for a "white hope" to reclaim the title. Jackson defeated each of his white challengers in the ring, but he had to flee the country when the government accused him of transporting women across state lines for immoral purposes. In 1915 Johnson lost the heavyweight title when he was well past his prime.

The early years of the twentieth century brought baseball to new heights of popularity. The two professional leagues had emerged, and the World Series had become an annual fall ritual in which the "world's champion" was decided. It was a time of few home runs because of the "dead ball" (wrapped and made in such a way as to make it less resilient and less likely to be hit a long distance). Nevertheless, the public avidly absorbed the ample news coverage that baseball received.

Motion Pictures and the Vaudeville Stage

Motion pictures and vaudeville competed for Americans' entertainment dollars. In elaborate vaudeville houses, audiences saw such stars as Fanny Brice, Al

The American painter George Bellows records the teeming life of New York City in 1913 in his painting that reflects the newer currents of art at the time of the Armory Show and the onset of World War I.

Jolson, and Sophie Tucker in well-developed routines aimed at the whole family. A circuit of theaters gave performers a reliable market in which to perfect their craft and maintain their popularity. By the time Wilson became president, however, motion pictures offered a challenge to the dominance of vaudeville. Movies were evolving from short features into real stories of an hour or more in length. The places where patrons saw films were upgraded, while the price of admission remained reasonable. An average family of five could see a movie for less than a half a dollar. In the darkness they followed the feats of the acrobatic Douglas Fairbanks, Sr., or the winsome beauty of Mary Pickford. Within a decade, the movies would emerge as the mass entertainment medium of the nation. They were lively and up-to-date, and conveyed a sense of modern life and spontaneity that made nineteenth-century ideas appear even more dated and obsolete.

NEW FREEDOM DIPLOMACY

Throughout the Progressive Era, the focus of national attention was on domestic political and economic concerns. The newspapers carried full coverage of international news, and readers could follow the unfolding of European diplomacy if they wished to. However, isolated from the tensions of world affairs by two vast oceans, Americans allowed their elected leaders to conduct foreign policy as long as the general policies of isolation and noninvolvement with Europe were observed. For the first two years of his presidency, Woodrow Wilson's foreign policy concerns arose from issues that resembled those his immediate predecessors had faced.

Woodrow Wilson and the World

Woodrow Wilson came to the presidency without any experience in foreign policy. In fact, early in 1913 he remarked to a friend that "[it] would be the irony of fate if my administration had to deal chiefly with foreign affairs." Nevertheless, Wilson had definite ideas about how the nation should behave in world affairs. During his first eighteen months in the White House, Wilson applied his precepts to diplomatic problems in

Asia and Latin America, situations that trained him for the greater trials he would face in World War I.

The president handled most of the business of foreign affairs himself. He appointed William Jennings Bryan as secretary of state, but he never allowed Bryan to have a significant role in shaping policy. Bryan spent some of his time making speeches about public issues and promoting international treaties of conciliation that he thought would end the threat of war. Many countries signed these treaties before the war broke out in 1914; they provided for a "cooling-off" period before countries could begin fighting. Though a noble gesture, these documents had no practical effect.

Wilson's closest advisor on foreign policy was Edward M. House of Texas, an honorary "colonel" who cultivated a friendship with Wilson by agreeing with him on most subjects. House conducted foreign missions for Wilson before and during World War I. As for the rest of the diplomatic corps, Wilson allowed Bryan to select "deserving Democrats" to replace Republican ambassadors and ministers. The quality of American diplomacy suffered in the process.

Wilsonian Ideas in Practice

In foreign affairs, Woodrow Wilson believed that the United States should set an example for the world because of the nation's commitment to democracy and capitalism. "Morality and not expediency is the thing that must guide us," he said in 1913. The United States' economic influence thus was a benefit to all nations. The Wilson administration encouraged American business to seek markets overseas but to do so in a way that did not resemble the "dollar diplomacy" of the Taft years.

In Asia, the Wilson administration stepped back from Taft's commitments, instructing American bankers to withdraw from the Chinese railroad consortium that Taft and Knox had sponsored. The United States also recognized the Republic of China which had come into power following the 1911 revolution that ousted the Manchu dynasty. Wilson and the Democrats put the Philippine Islands on the road toward independence, but their efforts to counter the rise of Japanese influence in Asia proved less successful.

Wilson wanted his policy toward Latin America to be less intrusive and dominant than Roosevelt's had

One of Wilson's closest advisers was the enigmatic and discreet Texan, Edward M. House, who had the honorary title of "Colonel." He made several diplomatic missions for the president, who valued his counsel greatly.

been. To that end, he worked out a treaty with Colombia that apologized for Roosevelt's actions in 1903–1904. The pact outraged the former president and the Senate did not approve the treaty while Wilson was in office. Better relations with Latin America did not, in the president's mind, mean accepting governments that offended his moral values. "I am going to teach the South American Republics to elect good men," he said. That principle led him into the kinds of intervention that he would have preferred to avoid. He kept troops in Nicaragua and extracted further concessions from that country. Other military detachments went to Cuba, Haiti, and the Dominican Republic.

The Mexican Involvement

The most controversial episode in foreign affairs that confronted Wilson was the revolution in Mexico. The Madero government, which had taken over from Porfirio Díaz in 1911, was ousted just before Wilson was inaugurated in March 1913. The man who toppled Francisco Madero was General Victoriano Huerta. Although most European nations quickly recognized Huerta's government, the United States did not. Wilson regarded the Mexican leader as "a diverting brute" and called him a "butcher." To win recognition from the United States, the Mexicans would have to install a

One of the more controversial episodes of Wilson's early foreign policy was the intervention in Mexico in 1914. Marines march through the streets of Vera Cruz to carry out the president's pressure on the Mexicans.

The Mexican leader General Victoriano Huerta, whom Wilson despised and sought to overthrow in implementing his policy south of the border.

government that relied on law rather than "arbitrary and irregular force."

Wilson instead threw the weight of the United States behind Venustiano Carranza, a rebel against the Huerta government, but his offers of cooperation were not accepted. If Carranza agreed to Wilson's insistence on some U.S. economic and political presence in Mexico, he would have been regarded as pro-American, a fatal weakness to the sensitive Mexican populace. The president's policy eventually resulted in an armed confrontation in April 1914.

To block the flow of munitions into Mexico, Wilson had sent the navy to patrol the Gulf of Mexico. Sailors from the U.S.S. *Dolphin* went ashore at Tampico on April 9 without the necessary permission, and Mexican authorities arrested them. Released quickly and without further incident, they returned to their ship. The admiral on the scene nonetheless demanded that the Mexican authorities apologize and make a twenty-one gun salute to the American flag. Huerta's government replied that the Mexican flag should be saluted.

The president went to Congress for authority to use force at a time when a German vessel was unloading arms on the Mexican shore. Wilson ordered troops to occupy the port of Vera Cruz. Heavy fighting erupted in which more than one hundred Mexicans and nineteen Americans died. The reaction in Mexico was immediate and unanimous. All the warring parties denounced the United States. The two countries seemed on the edge of outright war.

At this point Wilson drew back and allowed Argentina, Brazil, and Chile to act as mediators. The negotiations that followed led to the evacuation of Vera Cruz in November 14. Dependent on outside funds to pay his army, Huerta left office when his money ran out in July 1914. Carranza took power, and Wilson promptly recognized his government. Yet the president's troubles with Mexico were not over. A rebellion against Carranza by one of his generals would lead to further confrontations with the United States during the rest of Wilson's first term.

Hispanics in the Southwest

One of the lasting effects of the revolutionary upheavals in Mexico was an increase in the flow of immigrants from that country into the United States after 1910. A mix of social, political, and economic forces had already produced a rising number of Mexican immigrants during the first decade of the century. While many of those immigrants returned to Mexico after working in the United States for several months, some 35,000 to 75,000 Hispanic immigrants stayed on each year. The dictatorial regime of Porfirio Díaz impelled political dissidents and impoverished peasants to travel north of the Rio Grande. Once the revolution began in 1911, the ensuing turbulence and violence drove more Mexicans toward the border. Throughout these years the spread of irrigation agriculture, railroads, and mining in the Southwest increased the demand for inexpensive labor. The closing off of Japanese immigration after 1907 made Mexican laborers an attractive option for Anglo businesses.

The newcomers from south of the border found work in the sugar beet fields of Colorado, the agricultural valleys of south Texas and southern California,

MAP 21.2 | AMERICAN INTERVENTIONS IN LATIN AMERICA

where they picked the lettuce and citrus fruits that grew in irrigated fields, and the towns of Arizona and New Mexico. Other Hispanics labored for daily wages in Los Angeles, El Paso, and San Antonio. They paved streets, built houses, and processed food for the Anglo community. Their wages were low, sometimes under $1.25 per day.

Major centers of Hispanic life emerged in the southwestern cities. Ethnic communities sponsored mutual aid societies and established Spanish language newspapers to ease the immigrants' adjustment to a new culture. Religious prejudice remained strong, however. When Mexican immigrants settled in San Bernadino, California, one longtime resident warned that he "might use a shotgun on these aliens if necessary." In Texas and California, segregation and poverty limited the opportunities open to Mexican Americans.

The international tension between Mexico and the Wilson administration led to periodic "brown scares"

along the border. Anglo residents feared vague conspiracies to reclaim land lost by Mexico during the nineteenth century. Cross-border incursions from Mexico further heightened tensions. By 1915 a violent cultural conflict that claimed hundreds of lives was in progress in south Texas. As a result of these struggles, the Mexican Americans lost much of the land they held in the area. Nevertheless, Hispanics had achieved the basis for a greater presence in the United States during the twentieth century.

WORLD WAR I

By 1914 the major European nations were in a state of barely repressed tension. For several decades a system of interlocking alliances tied nations together with

▮	Central Powers 1914
▮	Neutral countries later aligned with Central Powers
▮	Allies 1914
▮	Neutral countries later aligned with Allies
▮	Allied with Central Powers, declared neutrality at outbreak of war, then joined Allies
▮	Countries remaining neutral

MAP 21.3   EUROPE ON THE EVE OF WORLD WAR I

military commitments to their allies. If one country found itself at war with another, all the other powers could easily be drawn into the struggle. On one side stood Germany, in the center of Europe. Its powerful industries and efficient army made it a source of worry to its neighbors, France and Russia. The Germans wanted to attain the international respect that they believed to be their rightful due. They had built up a large navy that had fueled tensions with Great Britain. Their leader, Kaiser Wilhelm II, had erratic dreams of

world influence that his generals and admirals adapted for their own expansionist purposes. The Germans had treaty links to the sprawling and turbulent nations of Austria-Hungary and the even more ramshackle regime of the Ottoman Turks. Italy had been part of the so-called Triple Alliance with Germany and Austria-Hungary, but these ties were frayed by 1914.

Against the Germans stood the French (who coveted territory they had lost in the Franco-Prussian War of 1871), the Russians, and, if the Germans attacked

France, the British. The Russian Empire was in decay, with revolutionary sentiments just below the surface. The French feared another defeat at the hands of Germany, and the British worried about German naval strength and Berlin's plans for dominance of Western Europe. Imperial rivalries intensified the tensions. By 1914 all the powers had elaborate plans for mobilization in the event of a general crisis. Once these timetables went into effect, the relentless pressure of military events would frustrate efforts at a diplomatic resolution.

The Road to World War

World War I began in the Balkans. On June 28, 1914, the Austrian archduke, Franz Ferdinand, and his wife were murdered in the town of Sarajevo in Bosnia, a province of the Austro-Hungarian Empire. The Austrians soon learned that the killer was paid by the Serbians. The Austrians made harsh demands on Serbia that would have left that nation defenseless. The Germans supported their Austrian allies, with the result that the Russians came to the defense of the Serbs. Soon all the European countries were drawn into the conflict.

By early August of 1914, the general war that Europeans had long feared and anticipated was under way. Germany, Austria-Hungary, and Turkey, known as the Central Powers, were fighting against Great Britain, France, and Russia, now called the Allies. Italy re-mained neutral for the time being. Soon the guns of August began a conflagration that lasted four years and consumed the flesh and blood of a generation.

America and the European War

The sudden outbreak of fighting in Europe surprised Americans, even those who were well-informed about world events. While the arms race among the great powers had seemed potentially dangerous, it had been a century since there had been a major war, involving all the major European countries. Surely, the conventional wisdom of the day said, the self-restraint and wisdom of the great nations made a destructive war unlikely. Faith in progress and the betterment of humanity, so much a part of the Progressive Era's creed, convinced many that war was unthinkable.

So when the armies marched, Americans were shocked. "To the average American," said a Texas newspaper, "the war in Europe is unintelligible." A member of Congress observed that "[t]his dreadful conflict of nations came to most of us like lightning out of a clear sky." Progressives worried that war might imperil the social reforms that they had achieved with so much effort. As William Allan White, the Kansas editor and friend of Theodore Roosevelt, noted, "war brings men down to beasts quicker than whiskey, surer than women, and deadlier than the love of money."

The world war came at a time of emotional distress for Wilson. His wife, Ellen, died of the effects of

In this cartoon the anarchists who have been denounced for their tactics assail the crowned heads of Europe who have brought on the war in 1914.

Bright's disease on August 6, 1914. This personal loss devastated the president who occupied himself in dealing with the war. On the domestic political scene, the Democrats were expected to encounter serious losses in the congressional elections. The Republicans had won back some of the Progressive voters who had followed Roosevelt in 1912. Until war broke out, it seemed as if politics might be returning to something resembling its normal patterns.

CONCLUSION

The war, however, produced a profound and lasting change in the course of American history. The nation's isolation from world events was ending. Whether they liked it or not, Americans had to confront the challenges of a world role. During the seven years that followed, Woodrow Wilson would pursue neutrality, enter the war in 1917, and see his dreams of world peace collapse in 1921. Social and political reform continued for a time and then gave way to a return to conservatism. With all these developments, the impact of progressivism on the direction of American politics remained significant. The issues that had been identified in domestic affairs between 1901 and 1914, particularly the question of the government's role in the economy, endured.

RECOMMENDED READINGS

Chambers, John Whiteclay II. *The Tyranny of Change: America in the Progressive Era, 1890–1920* (1992) considers the Taft and Wilson years in the context of reform.

Clements, Kendrick. *The Presidency of Woodrow Wilson* (1992) provides a crisp look at Wilson in office.

Gould, Lewis L., ed., *The Progressive Era* (1974) has specific essays on the events of this period.

Graham, Sara Hunter. *Woman Suffrage and the New Democracy* (1996) is a fresh interpretation of a key progressive reform.

Link, Arthur S. *Woodrow Wilson and the Progressive Era, 1910–1917* (1954) is thorough and perceptive on this period.

Pringle, Henry F. *The Life and Times of William Howard Taft*, 2 vols. (1939), is still good on Taft's difficult presidency.

Scholes, Walter and Marie Scholes. *The Foreign Policies of the Taft Administration* (1970) deals with Taft's diplomatic record.

Strasser, Susan. *Satisfaction Guaranteed: The Making of the American Mass Market* (1989) looks at the ways in which the consumer society evolved.

Timberlake, James. *Prohibition and the Progressive Movement* (1963) connects temperance and the broad currents of reform.

Urofsky, Melvin I. *A Mind of One Piece: Brandeis and American Reform* (1971) examines the role of one of Woodrow Wilson's important intellectual influences.

Politics

Broderick, Francis L. *Progressivism at Risk: Electing a President in 1912* (1989).

Heckscher, August. *Woodrow Wilson* (1991).

Link, Arthur S. *Wilson: The New Freedom* (1956).

McCulley, Richard T. *Banks and Politics During the Progressive Era: The Origins of the Federal Reserve System* (1992).

Naylor, Natalie, et al., eds., *Theodore Roosevelt: Many-Sided American* (1992).

Varieties of Reform

Buechler, Steven M. *The Transformation of the Woman Suffrage Movement: The Case of Illinois, 1850–1920* (1986).

Clark, Norman H. *Deliver Us from Evil: An Interpretation of American Prohibition* (1976).

Diner, Steven J. *A Very Different Age: Americans of the Progressive Era* (1998).

Frankel, Noralee, and Nancy S. Dye. eds., *Gender, Class, Race, and Reform in the Progressive Era* (1991).

Kraut, Alan M. *The Huddled Masses: The Immigrant in American Society* (1982).

Wheeler, Marjorie Spruill, ed., *One Woman, One Vote: Rediscovering the Woman Suffrage Movement* (1995).

The Workplace

Kessler-Harris, Alice. *Out to Work: A History of Wage-Earning Women in the United States* (1982).

Meyer, Stephen. *The Five-Dollar Day: Labor Management and Social Control in the Ford Motor Company, 1908–1921* (1981).

Milkman, Ruth, ed., *Women, Work, and Protest: A Century of U.S. Women Labor History* (1985).

Nelson, Daniel. *Managers and Workers: The Origins of the New Factory System in the United States, 1880–1920* (1981).

Tentler, Leslie W. *Wage-Earning Women: Industrial Work and Family Life in the United States, 1900–1930* (1979).

Foreign Policy

Calvert, Peter. *The Mexican Revolution, 1910–1914* (1968).

Gardner, Lloyd C. *Safe for Democracy: Anglo-American Responses to Revolution, 1913–1921* (1984).

Healy, David. *Drive to Hegemony: The United States in the Caribbean, 1898–1917* (1988).

Katz, Friedrich. *The Secret War in Mexico: Europe, the United States, and the Mexican Revolution* (1981).

Kaufman, Burton I. *Efficiency and Expansion: Foreign Trade Organization in the Wilson Administration, 1913–1921* (1974).

THE SUBMARINE MENACE TO AMERICAN NEUTRALITY

The key weapon that the Germans used to break the British blockade around them was the submarine. Its use against merchant shipping put the United States and Germany into conflict. Note the relatively small size compared to modern submarines.

Chapter 22

OVER THERE AND OVER HERE: THE IMPACT OF WORLD WAR I 1914-1921

THE FIRST IMPULSE of Americans was to keep the European war as far away as possible. That effort proved futile. The war soon affected society in ways that few citizens had anticipated when the fighting began. Events in Europe influenced domestic politics, altered the progressive movement, and changed the fortunes of women, African Americans, and socialists. The nation's traditional values came under repeated attack as the war went on. U.S. entry into the war in April 1917 transformed the country in even more striking fashion.

The most important result was the end of the era of progressive reform. On the one hand, World War I brought several campaigns for social change, most notably Prohibition and woman suffrage, to national success. Yet by the time these results occurred, the movement for reform had lost popular support and political momentum. The nation turned away from an activist government, expensive programs, and efforts to improve society. When Woodrow Wilson left the White House on March 4, 1921, he gave way to Warren G. Harding, who promised a return to older values and a respite from moral uplift. Thus, the war that began in Eastern Europe in the summer of 1914 shattered the feelings of confidence—and optimism about the future that white Americans had held since the end of the war with Spain in 1898.

STAYING NEUTRAL IN A WORLD CONFLICT

President Wilson stated the United States' official policy toward the war in August 1914, when he asked his fellow citizens to "be neutral in fact as well as in name" and "impartial in thought as well as in action." Wilson himself had more sympathy for the Allies than he had for Germany and its wartime partners. He also believed that some kind of "association of nations" would be needed to prevent future world wars. In conducting foreign policy, however, he was as even-handed toward the two sides as any president could have been.

The War and National Politics

The initial results of Wilson's neutrality decisions came in national politics. Going into the congressional elections of 1914, the Republicans anticipated regaining some of the seats in the House and Senate that they had lost in 1912. On the other hand, Roosevelt's Progressive party had weakened after its good start. Many of its members had returned to the Republican

CHRONOLOGY

1914 Wilson declares American neutrality in World War I

President also proclaims first Mother's Day

1915 *Lusitania* torpedoed with loss of 128 Americans

Wilson announces preparedness campaign

"Chaplinitis" sweeps the nation

The Birth of a Nation promotes revival of Ku Klux Klan

"Great Migration" of African Americans continues

1916 Wilson achieves "*Sussex* Pledge" from Germany

Army pursues Pancho Villa into Mexico

Wilson wins second term over Charles Evans Hughes

1917 Wilson makes "Peace Without Victory" Speech

Woman suffrage advocates arrested and jailed for picketing the White House

Germans resume unrestricted submarine campaign

United States enters world war

Military draft enacted to raise army

1918 Wilson announces "Fourteen Points" for peace settlement

American troops join in Allied drive toward Germany

First granulated soap ("Rinso") introduced

Influenza epidemic sweeps the globe and kills more than 20 million people

Armistice ends First World War

1919 Wilson negotiates Treaty of Versailles

Dial telephones introduced

Prohibition amendment adopted

Wilson stricken with stroke

1920 Senate defeats League of Nations for second time

Woman suffrage amendment ratified

Warren G. Harding and Republicans win presidency

Edith Wharton wins Pulitzer Prize for her novel *The Age of Innocence*

1921 Harding becomes President

---

fold. The party had moved to the right and resumed its familiar charge that the Democrats had produced economic hard times. In the 1914 elections the Democrats emphasized how President Wilson had kept the nation at peace. The slogan was "War in the East! Peace in the West! Thank God for Wilson!" This use of the neutrality issue helped the Democrats limit Republican gains. The Republicans picked up sixty-three seats in the House, but the Democrats retained control. In the Senate, the president's party actually added five seats.

The 1914 election results suggested that the issue of peace and war held potential benefits for the president in 1916. The Democrats did well in the Midwest, where support for progressive reforms remained strong. As Wilson looked toward reelection, he decided to form a coalition of southern and western voters united on a platform of peace and reform. To do so, the president had to pay attention to the interest groups—union workers, farmers, and woman suffrage advocates—that he had rebuffed between 1913 and 1915. If the war stimulated the economy, the combination of peace, prosperity, and reform might give the president a chance at reelection. Much would depend on how voters reacted to events occurring on European battlefields.

The Dilemma of Neutrality

Circumstances dictated that the United States would lean more toward the British and French than the Germans. Traditional historical and cultural ties produced widespread identification with the Allied cause. Economic links with Great Britain were also strong, and they intensified as the war progressed. Exports to

Britain and France totaled $754 million in 1914; in 1916 they stood at $2.75 billion. Meanwhile, trade with Germany, which had totaled $190 million in 1914, virtually ceased because of the British blockade. The United States could have embargoed all trade with belligerent powers, as many American supporters of Germany recommended. That would have negated British naval supremacy and denied American goods to both sides. It would also have devastated the U.S. economy.

The Germans did have strong support in the United States. The more than 5 million German Americans, most numerous in the Middle West, represented a sizable bloc of votes that usually favored Republicans. The 3 million-plus Irish Americans hated England and cheered for its enemies. Germany conducted an expensive propaganda campaign consisting of pamphlets and newspaper advertisements. Money directed through the German-dominated brewing industry paid for the campaign. Undercutting their public relations image, however, the Germans also used espionage and sabotage to cripple the British war effort and to hamper American assistance to the Allies.

The British matched German expenditures on propaganda describing the alleged atrocities of their foe. They also relied on their cultural ties with the upper classes and opinion makers in the Northeast to set forth the British case in magazines and newspapers. Despite the deluge of speakers and pamphlets from both sides, the national consensus was that the United States should stay out of Europe's quarrels.

The Course of the War and American Public Opinion

It was the way the Germans waged the war that did the greatest damage to their cause with Americans. In the opening days of the fighting, the German army violated Belgium's neutrality, crossing that nation's borders to invade France. This breach of its treaty obligation indicated that Germany's word could not be trusted. Confronted with a British naval blockade designed to strangle its economy and capacity to wage war, Germany turned to a new weapon, the submarine, early in 1915. In contrast to surface ships, the submarine relied on surprise attacks based on its ability to submerge. Passengers on torpedoed ships were left to drown. Submarines could not provide warnings

without risk to themselves and the Germans resisted pleas that they should do so.

Germany declared that enemy vessels would be sunk on sight, a policy many Americans regarded as a violation of the civilized rules of war. Despite this aggressive strategy, Germany had only twenty-one submarines when the fighting began. These new vessels could not win the war by themselves. Use of the submarine put Germany in direct conflict with the United States, the leading neutral country. The strategy thus risked a wider war for Germany without the promise of victory.

The Lusitania Crisis

In response to the German announcement of the submarine campaign, President Wilson said that Germany would be held to "strict accountability" for any damage to the United States. Washington had to decide whether to insist on the rights of Americans to travel freely on Allied ships regardless of the danger, or warn U.S. citizens to avoid such risks and stay home.

The problem became a shocking reality on May 7, 1915, when a German submarine fired a torpedo into the British liner *Lusitania* off the Irish coast. The huge vessel sank quickly, with an immense loss of life. Among the nearly 1,200 passengers who died were 128 Americans. To most people this event was an audacious atrocity, not an inescapable by-product of modern warfare. Some Americans, such as Theodore Roosevelt, suggested that the United States should consider going to war with Germany over the sinking of the *Lusitania*.

Public opinion, however, held that the country should not enter the conflict. President Wilson was applauded when he said, three days after the *Lusitania* incident, that "there is such as thing as a man being too proud to fight. There is such a thing as a nation being so right that it does not need to convince others by force that it is right." Allied sympathizers denounced Wilson's words, but the president's readiness to negotiate was generally approved.

Wilson and the Submarine Crisis

Wilson combined firmness and flexibility in his demands on Germany. He sought an apology and a

The New York Times.

EXTRA
5:30 A.M.

VOL. LXIV...NO. 20,923.   NEW YORK, SATURDAY, MAY 8, 1915.—TWENTY-FOUR PAGES.   ONE CENT In Greater New York, Jersey City and Newark.   Elsewhere TWO CENTS

LUSITANIA SUNK BY A SUBMARINE, PROBABLY 1,260 DEAD; TWICE TORPEDOED OFF IRISH COAST; SINKS IN 15 MINUTES; CAPT. TURNER SAVED, FROHMAN AND VANDERBILT MISSING; WASHINGTON BELIEVES THAT A GRAVE CRISIS IS AT HAND

SHOCKS THE PRESIDENT

Washington Deeply Stirred by the Loss of American Lives.

BULLETINS AT WHITE HOUSE

Wilson Reads Them Closely, but Is Silent on the Nation's Course.

HINTS OF CONGRESS CALL

Loss of Lusitania Recalls Firm Tone of Our First Warning to Germany.

CAPITAL FULL OF RUMORS

Reports That Liner Was to be Sunk Were Heard Before Actual News Came.

Special to The New York Times.
WASHINGTON, May 7.— Never since that April day, three years ago, when word came that the Titanic had gone down, has Washington been so stirred as it is tonight over the sinking of the Lusitania. The early reports told that there had been no loss of life, but the relief that these advices caused gave way to the greatest concern late this evening when it became known that there had been many deaths. Although they are profoundly reticent, officials realize that this tragedy, involving the loss of American citizens, is likely to bring about a crisis in the international relations of the United States.

It is pointed out that the sinking of the Lusitania is the outcome of a series of incidents that have been the cause of concern to this Government in its endeavor to maintain a strictly neutral position in the great European war.

Nation's Course in Doubt.

It is impossible to say tonight what effect the loss of American lives on the Lusitania will have on the

---

The Lost Cunard Steamship Lusitania
X Where the First Torpedo Struck.   XX Where the Second Torpedo Struck.

Cunard Office Here Besieged for News; Fate of 1,918 on Lusitania Long in Doubt

Nothing Heard from the Well-Known Passengers on Board—Story of Disaster Long Unconfirmed While Anxious Crowds Seek Details.

Official news of the sinking of the Lusitania yesterday reached New York in fragmentary reports, and several hours elapsed between the first unverified rumor of the disaster and the cable messages that told at night of the sinking of some of the passengers and gave meagre details of the most sensational incident of its kind in the war

List of Saved Includes Capt. Turner; Vanderbilt and Frohman Reported Lost

LONDON, Saturday, May 8, 3:50 A.M.—The Press Bureau has received from the British Admiralty at Queenstown a report that all the torpedo boats and tugs and armed trawlers, except the Heroic, which went out from Queenstown to the relief of the Lusitania have returned.

These vessels have landed 586 survivors and forty dead. Fifty-two more survivors are reported aboard a steamer, while eleven others and five bodies have been landed at Kinsale, making the total number of survivors 638, besides forty-five dead. The numbers will be verified later, and it is considered possible Kinsale fishing boats may have rescued a few more.

Among the survivors is the Captain of the Lusitania, William T. Turner. Some of the survivors at Queenstown say that Alfred Gwynne Vanderbilt was drowned. Every effort to find Mr. Vanderbilt and Charles Frohman, the theatrical manager, among the survivors has failed.

The Central News says that the number of the Lusitania's passengers who died of injuries while being taken to Queenstown will reach 100

Saw the Submarine 100 Yards Off and Watched Torpedo as It Struck Ship

Ernest Cowper, a Toronto Newspaper Man, Describes Attack, Seen from Ship's Rail—Poison Gas Used in Torpedoes, Say Other Passengers.

Queenstown, Saturday, May 8, 3:18 A.M.

A sharp lookout for submarines was kept aboard the Lusitania as she approached the Irish coast, according to Ernest Cowper, a Toronto in an orderly, prompt, and efficient manner Miss Helen Smith appealed to me to save her. I placed her in a boat and saw her safely away I got into one of the last boats to leave.

"Some of the boats could not be launched as the vessel was

SOME DEAD TAKEN ASHORE

Several Hundred Survivors at Queenstown and Kinsale.

STEWARD TELLS OF DISASTER

One Torpedo Crashes Into the Doomed Liner's Bow, Another Into the Engine Room.

SHIP LISTS OVER TO PORT

Makes It Impossible to Lower Many Boats, So Hundreds Must Have Gone Down.

ATTACKED IN BROAD DAY

Passengers at Luncheon—Warning Had Been Given by Germans Before the Ship Left New York.

Only 650 Were Saved, Few Cabin Passengers

QUEENSTOWN, Saturday, May 8, 4:28 A.M.—Survivors of the Lusitania who have arrived here estimate that only about 650 of those aboard the steamer were saved, and say only a small proportion of those rescued were saloon passengers.

Official Confirmation
WASHINGTON, May 8.—A dispatch to the State Department early today from American Consul Lauriet at Queenstown stated that the total number of survivors of the Lusitania was about 700.

LONDON, Saturday, May 8.—The Cunard liner Lusitania,

The destruction of the Lusitania *was a shock to Americans who had not expected the war to touch their lives. The banner headlines in* The New York Times *convey something of the sense of amazement and surprise that accompanied the sinking of the passenger liner.*

---

pledge to limit submarine warfare, but he did not threaten Germany with war if it did not comply. His diplomatic protest was strong enough, however, that Secretary of State William Jennings Bryan resigned in protest in June 1915. He was replaced by Robert Lansing, a pro-Allied diplomat. During the remainder of the summer, the Germans kept the negotiating process going without apologizing or yielding on any point.

Then, in August, the Germans torpedoed a British liner, the *Arabic,* wounding two Americans. Wilson told the Germans privately that the United States would break diplomatic relations with them if submarine warfare continued. Still unsure whether the submarine alone could win the war, Berlin offered a conditional pledge not to make unannounced attacks on passenger liners; this defused the situation briefly.

Nevertheless, the Germans retained the option of returning to their older policy. In the following year, they sank thirty-seven unarmed liners.

The United States and Its World Role

The neutrality issue forced Americans to consider the nation's future role in a warring world. Many groups wanted the United States to maintain its traditional posture of noninvolvement. German Americans and Irish Americans saw no need to help the British. Progressive reformers regarded war and foreign commitments as the death of reform. In the Midwest and on the Pacific Coast, peace sentiments were widespread.

Other Americans did not see how the nation could escape participating in the fighting. Theodore Roosevelt, Elihu Root, and other northeastern Republicans supported the allies and called for military "preparedness" in the event of ultimate American entry into the war. Army and navy officials knew that they would have to expand their forces greatly if they were to play any significant role on the Allied side. In late 1914 Wilson had blocked programs to strengthen the military defense. By the summer of 1915, however, he changed his position and sought a larger army and navy. He promised a navy "second to none" and more troops for the regular army. Many Democrats in the South and West opposed Wilson on the issue of preparedness and the increased spending that it entailed. In early 1916 the president made a speaking tour to arouse popular support for his policy.

As the debate over preparedness intensified, some opinion leaders argued that a world organization should be formed to keep the peace once the fighting stopped. The League to Enforce Peace was created in June 1915, with William Howard Taft as its leader. Although he had earlier endorsed the idea of a league, Roosevelt now attacked it. As 1915 ended, Wilson had not yet thrown his influence behind the idea of a world organization. Clearly, the issues surrounding neutrality, preparedness, and world peace would be central questions in the presidential election of 1916.

SOCIAL CHANGE DURING THE PERIOD OF NEUTRALITY

During 1915, despite their concern about the future, Americans flocked to theaters to see a new motion picture that vividly depicted sensational events in the nation's past. David Wark Griffith's *The Birth of a Nation,* based on an anti-black novel by Thomas Dixon entitled *The Clansman,* portrayed the Reconstruction period in the South as a time when ignorant African Americans terrorized whites and made a travesty of government. An artistic triumph because it used new techniques such as flashbacks and closeups, the movie twisted history to glamorize the Ku Klux Klan and the white South. Audiences were enthusiastic, box office records were broken, and President Wilson reportedly said: "It is like writing history with lightning." Efforts

by African Americans to have the film banned were largely unsuccessful.

Inspired by the film's portrayal of the Klan, a group of white men burned a cross at Stone Mountain, Georgia, and used that episode to revive the hooded order. At first the revived Klan's membership remained under 5,000 nationally, but the social tensions of the postwar era proved a fertile ground for organizing in the South and Midwest. The Klan's organizers exploited the fears about immigrants, Catholics, and African Americans that were pervasive among white Protestants during these years.

The political prospects for improved rights for blacks remained as bleak as they had been since the

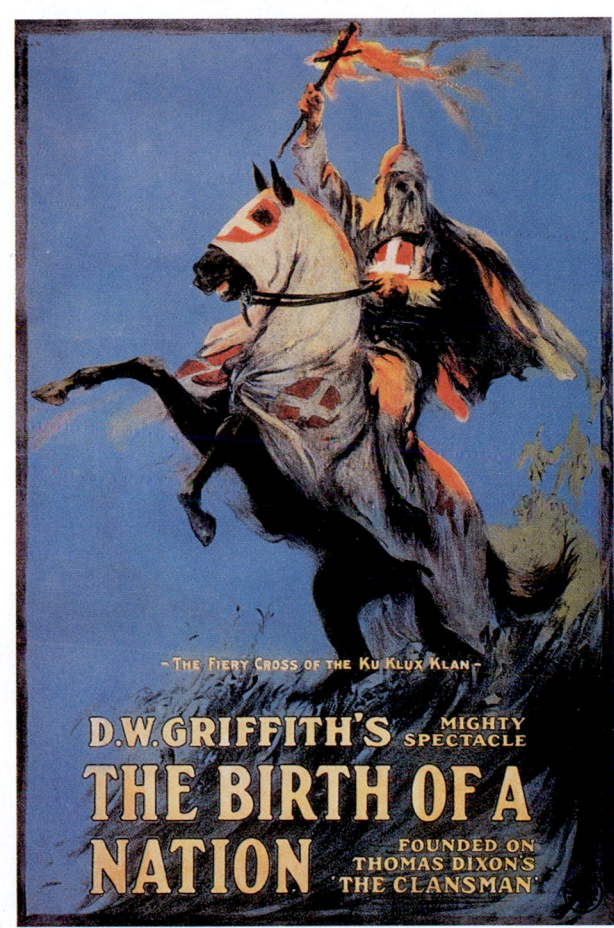

D. W. Griffith's film The Birth of a Nation *was an artistic triumph with a racist theme. This photograph advertising the film depicts the Ku Klux Klan as akin to medieval knights in the garb of chivalry. White audiences ignored the Klan's violent reality for African Americans.*

1890s. The Wilson administration and the Democratic party proved unsympathetic to any efforts to reduce racism. After protests from blacks and a few progressives, the White House retreated from efforts to enforce segregation in the federal government, but that was a minor victory. The Supreme Court did, however, rule in the case of *Guinn* v. *United States* (1915) that the grandfather clause that Oklahoma used to exempt whites from a literacy test for voting was unconstitutional. Oklahoma found other ways to register whites and restrict blacks, but the decision foreshadowed future racial progress toward greater protection of minority rights.

The Great Migration

For African Americans in the South, life was still painful and burdensome when World War I began. Southern agriculture experienced crippling problems during the first fifteen years of the century. Natural disasters hit the region in the form of floods and droughts. The boll weevil, an insect that destroyed cotton, undermined the farm economy. In Alabama, the failure of the cotton crop meant "that the negroes have nothing to eat," said one white man. "The planters are not able to feed them and they are emigrating." Blacks began leaving the South for cities in the North. The "Great Migration" started slowly around 1910 and then accelerated between 1914 and 1920 when more than 600,000 African Americans left the South.

The outbreak of the war played a key role in this process. Immigration from Europe ended. The result was an expanding labor market for unskilled workers in the North. Now a southern black had a chance, as one said, to "elevate myself" in ways that their region could not offer them. "All I ask is give me a chance," promised a Louisiana newcomer to Chicago, "and I will make good."

The movement of African Americans out of the South during World War I changed the face of northern cities and added to the complexity of the country's racial difficulties. This picture shows a southern family upon their arrival in 1916 in Chicago.

TABLE 22.1

MIGRATION OF AFRICAN AMERICANS TO FIVE NORTHERN CITIES, 1910–1920

	1910	1920	Percent Rise
New York	91,709	152,467	66.3
Chicago	44,103	109,458	148.2
Philadelphia	84,459	134,229	58.9
Baltimore	84,749	108,322	27.8
Detroit	5,741	40,838	611.3

SOURCE: Robert B. Grant, *The Black Man Comes to the City* (Chicago, 1972).

By 1915 Charlie Chaplin had become one of the most recognizable people in the world. This advertising montage gives a good sense of his varied characters and the popular appeal that he enjoyed.

Those who came to the North found a better life, but not a paradise. They secured work in the coal mines of West Virginia, the stockyards of Chicago, and the steel mills of Pittsburgh. In Chicago, some 60,000 blacks moved to the city between 1916 and 1920, a 148 percent increase in its African American population. Similar percentage increases occurred in Pittsburgh, Cincinnati, and Detroit.

As their population in the North grew, blacks encountered discrimination in housing and public services. Long-standing residents of African-American communities in northern cities looked down on the new arrivals. But the southern blacks continued to move north in a historic population shift that reshaped the politics and culture of the nation's largest cities.

The Rise of the Movies

In 1914 a young British comedian began appearing in films for the Keystone company, a film-making venture in Los Angeles. He made thirty-five movies in a single year. While most of them were very short, one film, *Tillie's Punctured Romance,* ran for thirty minutes. As these movies reached audiences during the year, filmgoers began asking about the funny actor in the derby hat and little tramp costume. By 1915 the whole nation was talking about Charlie Chaplin and a craze called "Chaplinitis" swept the land. In January

1915 Chaplin signed with Essanay Pictures for the then-huge sum of $1250 a week. (An industrial worker made around $600 per *year*.) Within twelve months Chaplin moved on to the Mutual Film Corporation at $10,000 a week. Stardom had come quickly for the twenty-six-year-old actor.

After a shaky start at the beginning of the century, motion pictures had arrived as mass entertainment during the years just before U.S. entry into World War I. There were more than 10,000 nickelodeon theaters by 1912, and up to 20 million Americans went to the movies on a regular basis. Soon movies became longer, and exhibitors began constructing motion picture

theaters that could seat up to 5,000 customers. In 1914 the Strand Theater opened on Broadway in New York, complete with orchestra and pipe organ.

Although Chaplin was the most famous male performer of his time, he was not the only "star" that the studios created during the era of the silent movie. Executives found that audiences wanted to know about the private lives of the people they saw on the flickering screens. Mary Pickford became "America's Sweetheart" in a series of roles that depicted a demure damsel in acute distress. Douglas Fairbanks used his athletic ability as the swashbuckling hero of such films as *American Aristocracy* (1916) and *Wild and Woolly* (1917). Theda Bara became the "vamp" in *A Fool*

One of the first sex goddesses of the screen was Theda Bara, the "vamp." She starred in Salome, *here advertised in a French version.*

There Was (1915). Advertisements described her as having "the most wickedly beautiful face in the world." Bara was the first of a succession of female stars to become renowned for their sex appeal.

During the ensuing years, the business of making movies became concentrated in a few large studios that controlled the process of production and distribution. Because of its mild climate, Hollywood, California, emerged as the center of the picture industry. Studios like Vitagraph and Paramount dominated the making and marketing of films.

Most moviegoers lived in cities where the large theaters were located. Immigrants found that they could learn about American life at the movies. Parents worried when their children saw such films as *Women and Wine* or *Man and His Mate*. Reformers clamored for censorship boards to screen films for scenes that showed lustful images or suggested that criminals profited from their crimes. The mass media had begun to change American attitudes and social customs.

Shifting Attitudes Toward Sex

The years around the beginning of World War I brought continued challenges to the nation's family and sexual values. The divorce rate rose. In 1916 one of every nine marriages ended in the divorce courts. Meanwhile, family size was decreasing. By 1920, two or three children were born to the average mother; in 1860, the average had been five or six.

The most daring women of the decade were the "flappers." They cut their hair short in the fashionable "bob," wore shorter skirts, and all seemed "lovely and expensive and about nineteen." The flapper, wrote social commentator H.L. Mencken in 1915, "has forgotten how to simper; she seldom blushes; it is impossible to shock her." Norms of sexual behavior slowly moved away from the restrictions of the Victorian era. For women born around 1900, the rate of sexual intercourse before marriage was twice as high as it had been for women born a decade earlier. Nevertheless, the overall incidence of premarital sexual behavior remained very low in comparison to the present. Hysterical fears about women being lured into prostitution spurred the enactment of the Mann Act (1910) which prohibited the movement of women across interstate lines for "immoral purposes" in what was referred to as the "white slave" traffic.

Birth Control

Despite the changes in actual sexual practices, the official attitudes of the nation remained restrictive. Homosexual relationships were outlawed, even though some college-educated women maintained "partnerships" or "Boston marriages." Laws governing the dissemination of information about birth control discouraged the use of contraception. In many states and cities it was a crime to sell condoms or to distribute information about how to avoid pregnancy. A federal statute, the Comstock Law of 1873, barred the making, selling, distribution, or importation of contraceptives, as well as any transmission of birth control information through the mails. The only ground on which abortions were permitted was to save the life of the mother.

Margaret Sanger, a thirty-two-year-old radical living in Greenwich Village, New York City, saw women suffering from disease and poverty because of the large number of children they bore. Often women had many babies because they lacked knowledge about ways to limit births. In 1914 Sanger coined the term *birth control* and began publishing a periodical called *Woman Rebel.* Women, she wrote, "cannot be on an equal footing with men until they have full and complete control over their reproductive function." Indicted for sending such information through the mails, she went to Europe, consulted with experts on family planning, and returned to the United States determined to arouse support for birth control.

A year later she founded a clinic in a poor neighborhood of Brooklyn that distributed information about contraception to the female residents. The police soon closed the clinic down, and Sanger went to jail. When the case was appealed, a higher court affirmed the right of doctors to prescribe birth control devices. Sanger then organized the Birth Control League to promote her cause. Some feminists regarded birth control as a liberating idea, others saw the availability of contraceptive devices as likely to encourage promiscuity and thus promote male dominance. Sanger continued her efforts into the 1920s, and she was a significant figure in launching the movement for reproductive rights during the rest of the century. On the other hand, her emphasis on using birth control and "eugenics" to produce more "fit" children and eliminate those who were "unfit" was a troubling element of her ideology.

THE PERSISTENCE OF REFORM

Progressive reform campaigns pressed ahead despite the distractions of the European war. In fact, the impact of the fighting enhanced some of these campaigns. Prohibition capitalized on anti-German sentiment to reduce the political power of the brewing industry. The end of the flow of immigrants from Europe enabled advocates of immigration restriction to gain support for tighter laws. Supporters of woman suffrage also used the war as a way of mobilizing women behind their cause.

Renewed Momentum for Woman Suffrage

Woman suffrage gained strength after 1914 despite serious divisions among the movement's leaders. Alice Paul and the militant Congressional Union (see Chapter 21) pressed for a constitutional amendment to obtain votes for women. Their tactics included demonstrations and a direct challenge to the Democrats as the party in power. In contrast, the National American Woman Suffrage Association (NAWSA), led by Carrie Chapman Catt after 1915, emphasized nonpartisanship and state-by-state organization. This disagreement over tactics resulted in a split during the 1916 presidential election. Paul and her allies formed the National Woman's party to defeat Wilson and the Democrats. NAWSA, on the other hand, took a two-pronged approach. They continued their efforts to win the right to vote in individual states, but they now sought a constitutional amendment as well. As the election approached, the momentum for suffrage seemed to be building. Even President Wilson, who had previously opposed the idea, now said that individual states could adopt woman suffrage if they wished.

The Drys on the Offensive

The drive for Prohibition, the second major cultural reform campaign, also intensified. In 1914 the Anti-Saloon League decided to press for a constitutional amendment to ban the sale of alcohol. At the same time, the efforts to make the states liquor-free went

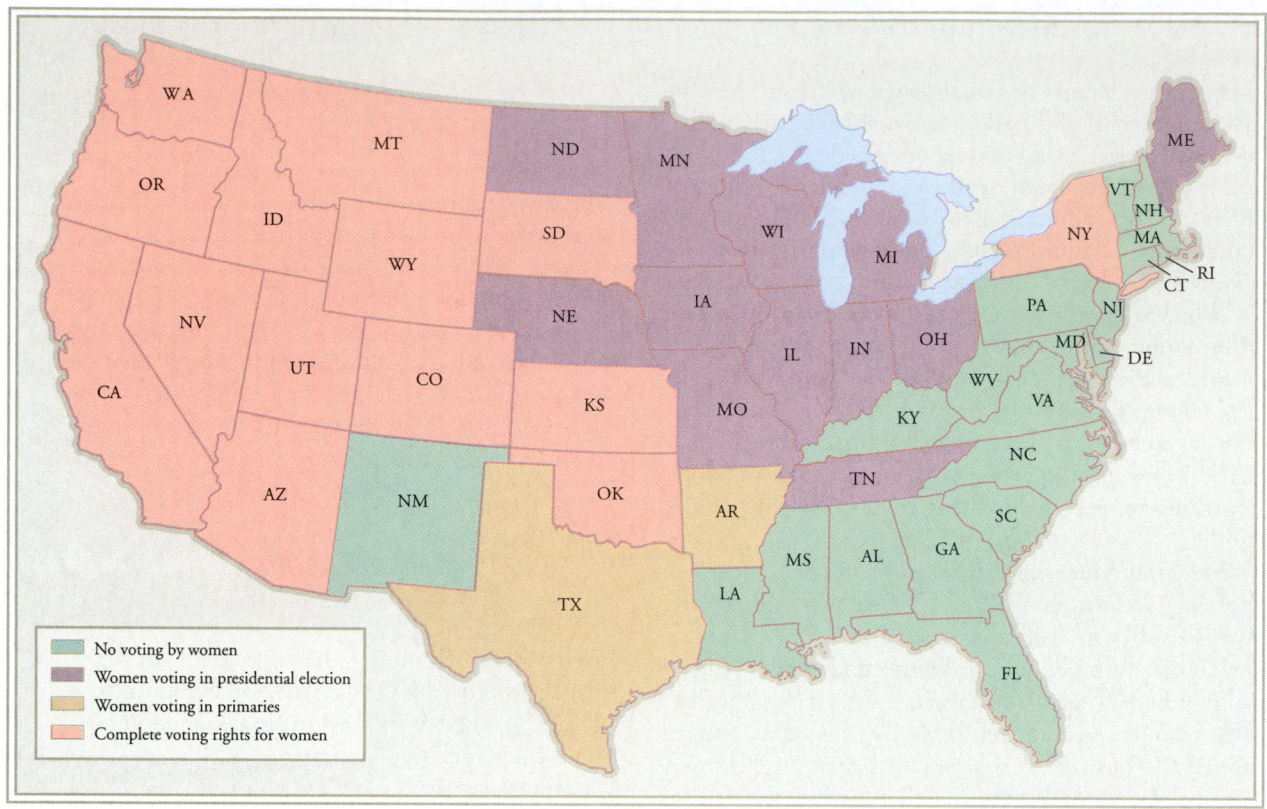

MAP 22.1 | THE MARCH OF WOMAN SUFFRAGE

Legend:
- No voting by women
- Women voting in presidential election
- Women voting in primaries
- Complete voting rights for women

forward, with notable success. In 1913–1914 more than a dozen states adopted prohibition legislation or held referenda in which the voters adopted prohibition. Nine more states adopted prohibition in 1915. Gradually, prohibitionist candidates within the major parties won seats in Congress. The Anti-Saloon League hoped that in the 1916 election enough sympathizers would be elected to the House and Senate to assure passage of the prohibition amendment.

Closing the Golden Door

The war in Europe shut off immigration to the United States from the eastern European countries that had sent so many people across the Atlantic since 1900. The reduced flow of newcomers did not stop the campaign to cut down on immigration. Proponents of immigration restriction contended that the eventual peace would open the door to an even greater influx of

outsiders. The ethnic tensions that the neutrality debate produced heightened sensitivity about what came to be called "hyphenated Americans." Congress again passed an immigration restriction law with a literacy test in 1915 which President Wilson again vetoed. In the 1916 election, neither major party wanted to alienate ethnic voters, although the Democrats denounced "all alliances and combinations of individuals in this country of whatever nationality or descent" who sought to embarrass or weaken the government in handling foreign policy.

The Enactment of Reform

After 1914 progressive reformers looked to the federal government for action on the various causes that made up the agenda of social change. In light of the results of the 1914 congressional elections, Wilson understood that he could not win reelection simply on the

basis of the impressive achievements of his first two years in office. Putting aside his earlier reservations about the use of national power to achieve such reforms as child labor legislation or agricultural credits for farmers, he shifted toward the progressive side of the political spectrum. He also became more willing to use the authority of his office to push for reform. Congressional Democrats wooed reform voters to retain the party's majority in Congress.

One notable step that Wilson took was to nominate Louis D. Brandeis to the U.S. Supreme Court in January 1916. Brandeis had advised Wilson on the New Freedom, and had won renown as the "People's Lawyer" and a foe of consolidated business enterprise. Since Brandeis was a longtime champion of reform causes and a prominent Jew, his appointment aroused intense, often anti-Semitic, feelings among conservatives. In the end he was confirmed, and Wilson's strong endorsement of him convinced progressives that the president was on their side.

During the months before the election campaign began, Wilson came out for laws to restrict child labor, to promote federal loans to farmers (known as agricultural credits), to provide federal aid for highway construction, and cover federal employees with workers' compensation laws. When a national railroad strike threatened in August 1916, Wilson compelled Congress to pass the Adamson Act which mandated an eight-hour working day for railroad employees. Labor responded with strong support for Wilson's reelection bid. Meanwhile, the improving economy, driven by orders from the Allies for American products and foodstuffs, gave the president the opportunity, as one Republican put it, to "make an appeal to the stomach of the nation."

Foreign Policy and the 1916 Election

The key to Wilson's reelection chances, however, was foreign policy. Not since the nation's early days had a presidential election depended on diplomatic issues. Wilson's success hinged on perpetuating the uneasy neutrality he had maintained toward the Germans and the British throughout 1916. The Republicans seemed divided between those who wished to do more for the Allies and those who either disliked overseas involvement or wished to help Germany. Wilson would benefit politically if he could find a middle position that combined defense of American rights with preservation of neutrality.

The president had to deal with several related wartime issues during the first half of 1916. The main problem remained the submarine. By the end of 1915 Wilson had succeeded in obtaining a German apology and indemnity for the Americans who had died on the *Lusitania.* After the sinking of the *Arabic,* the Germans had also pledged not to attack passenger liners without warning. Then the United States suggested an arrangement in which the Germans would limit submarine warfare and the Allies would not arm merchant ships. When this proposal (or *modus vivendi*) collapsed because of British and German opposition, Germany resumed submarine attacks on *armed* shipping, whether it was belligerent or neutral in February 1916.

The Sussex *Pledge*

A few weeks later, on March 24, a German submarine attacked an unarmed steamer, the *Sussex,* in the English Channel. American passengers on board were injured, and another diplomatic crisis ensued. Wilson decided not to break diplomatic relations with Germany, but he sent an ultimatum to Berlin stating that continued attacks on unarmed merchant vessels without warning would lead to a breaking of diplomatic ties, a prelude to U.S entry into the war. The Germans again faced the question of whether the submarine alone could win the war. At the time, they did not have enough undersea vessels to do so. Only about eighteen of their fifty-two submarines could be on patrol at any one time. With hopes of a victory on land still glimmering before them, the Germans pledged that they would not conduct attacks on merchant vessels without warning them. Their statement left open the right to resume unrestricted submarine warfare. For the moment, however, the so-called *Sussex* Pledge seemed like a major diplomatic success for Woodrow Wilson because it had staved off a war that most Americans dreaded.

Seeking a Negotiated Peace

During these same months, Wilson also tried to arrange for a negotiated settlement of the war. In December 1915 he sent his close friend, Colonel Edward

M. House, to discuss peace terms with the British, French, and Germans. House's talks led to an agreement with the British foreign minister, Edward Grey, for Anglo-American mediation of the war; if the Germans rebuffed the idea, the United States would enter the war on the side of the Allies. The House-Grey Memorandum, as the agreement was called, never took effect because Wilson watered it down and the British ignored it. The episode showed, however, how much effort Wilson invested in seeking a diplomatic end to the war, even at the expense of alienating the British and French.

During the first half of 1916, Wilson emerged as a forceful national leader. His speaking tour calling for preparedness swung public opinion behind his program to provide more weapons and personnel for the army and navy. When Congress sought to assert itself through resolutions warning Americans not to travel on the ships of the warring powers, the president pressured Congress to have the resolutions defeated on the grounds that they interfered with his power to conduct foreign policy. In May 1916, the president argued, in a speech to the League to Enforce Peace, that the major nations of the world should find "some feasible method of acting in concert when any nation or group of nations" endangered world peace.

The Mexican Problem

During the spring of 1916 the issue of Mexico once again grabbed the nation's headlines. The Mexican civil war had continued after the American intervention at Veracruz in 1914 (see Chapter 21). Although Wilson did not like the regime of Venustiano Carranza, he extended diplomatic recognition to it when it became clear that Carranza had emerged as the nation's effective leader.

When a rebel named Pancho Villa raided towns in New Mexico and Texas in 1916, killing and wounding numerous Americans, the U.S. Army under General John J. Pershing pursued him across the Rio Grande. Tensions rose on both sides of the border as the army marched deep into Mexico. Heedless of Mexicans' feelings about this intrusion on their sovereignty, the United States seemed to be headed for a war with Mexico. Wilson negotiated a diplomatic settlement, however, averting outright war with Mexico. Nevertheless, American troops remained in Mexico for two years, placing a continued strain on relations between the two

nations. His dealings with Mexico thus represented one of the least successful phases of Wilson's foreign policy leadership. The Germans noted this persistent problem and included it in their calculations regarding the possibility of U.S. entry into the war in Europe.

The 1916 Elections

The Democrats approached the election of 1916 with a high degree of confidence. The president's program of progressive domestic legislation was moving through Congress; the international situation appeared to have vindicated Wilson's leadership; and the economy was prosperous because of the war orders that the British and French had placed for munitions, food, and industrial products. The Republicans first had to win back the Progressives, some of whom found Wilson's reform program attractive. The foreign policy issue produced fresh divisions within the party. Eastern Republicans wanted the United States to intervene on the side of the Allies. In the Midwest, progressive Republicans and German Americans opposed a pro-Allied policy. The party had to find a candidate who could persuade these diverse factions to work together in the fall campaign.

The Republicans Select Hughes

Theodore Roosevelt hoped to be the Republican nominee, but bad feelings stemming from his 1912 third-party candidacy persisted. On matters of foreign policy, Roosevelt was identified with the Allies, and a commitment to help them would have soon had the nation at war. The Republicans therefore avoided Roosevelt and turned to Supreme Court Justice Charles Evans Hughes. He had been a progressive governor of New York, was not scarred with the wounds of 1912, and had said little about foreign policy. The Republicans nominated him on the third ballot. A remnant of the Progressive party nominated Roosevelt, but he declined and the party soon disappeared. The Republicans offered assurances that they favored some domestic reforms and carefully straddled the more controversial questions of preparedness, neutrality, and loyalty of ethnic groups such as the German Americans to the United States against potential foreign enemies.

"He Kept Us Out of War"

For the Democrats, Wilson's nomination was never in question. The excitement occurred over the party's platform and the campaign slogan that arose from it. In his keynote address to the Democratic delegates, a former governor of New York, Martin Glynn, noted that Wilson had maintained neutrality. Each time he referred to this fact the audience exclaimed: "What did we do? What did we do?" and he shouted back: "We didn't go to war! We didn't go to war!" The Democrats had a campaign theme. Their platform emphasized the administration's reform record and praised "the splendid diplomatic victories of our great President, who has preserved the vital interests of our Government and its citizens, and kept us out of war."

In the campaign that followed, Wilson skillfully employed the themes of peace, progressivism, and prosperity in his speeches. Meanwhile, Hughes had difficulty finding a way to appeal to Republicans who shared Roosevelt's position and to the German-American voters who wanted the nation to stay out of the conflict. Hughes also proved to be a less effective campaigner than the Republicans had hoped, but he had the benefit of a party that still attracted a majority of voters outside the South. To win, the Democrats assembled a coalition of voters in the South and West, the peace vote, women (who could vote in western states), and Midwestern farmers who were happy with wartime prosperity. It was clear that the race was going to be a tight one.

The Outcome

Wilson won one of the closest elections in the nation's history. He gained 277 electoral votes from thirty states, while Hughes won 254 electoral votes from eighteen states. The president amassed a little more than 49 percent of the vote, polling 600,000 more

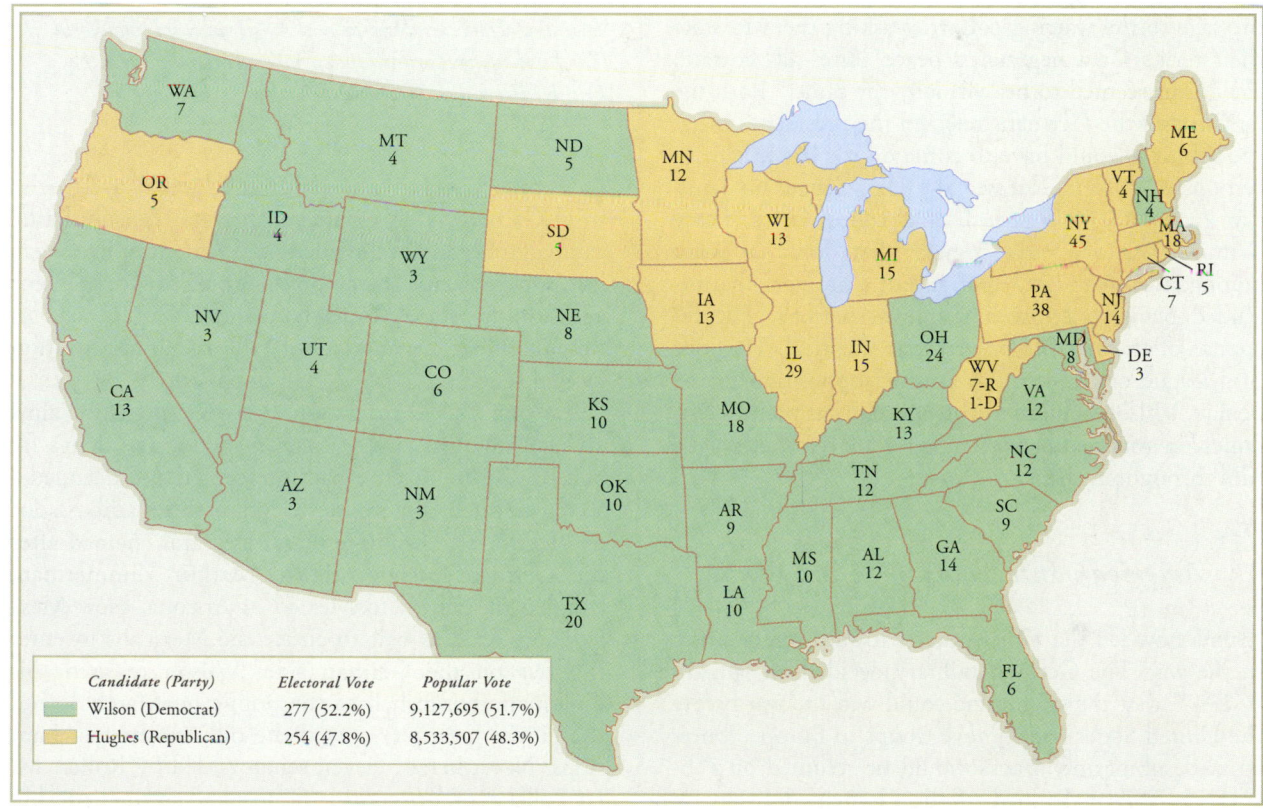

Candidate (Party)	Electoral Vote	Popular Vote
Wilson (Democrat)	277 (52.2%)	9,127,695 (51.7%)
Hughes (Republican)	254 (47.8%)	8,533,507 (48.3%)

MAP 22.2 | THE ELECTION OF 1916

popular votes than Hughes did. Although the president's winning margin in some states was very small (3,773 in the key state of California), he and the Democrats had won another victory.

Wilson's Attempts to Mediate

The war and its problems had not disappeared during the campaign. Wilson now believed that the time had come to press for a negotiated settlement among the warring powers. Relations with the British had soured during 1916 because of the way the Royal Navy and the British Foreign Office interfered with American shipping in enforcing their blockade against Germany. Meanwhile, the British were becoming more dependent on American loans and credits to pay for the supplies that they had been buying since 1914. Under the circumstances, the president believed, London might be receptive to an American mediation effort. The president also knew that pressure was rising within the German military for unrestricted use of submarines.

On December 18, 1916, Wilson sent a diplomatic message to the warring countries asking them to state their terms for a negotiated peace. After all, he said, their aims seemed to be "virtually the same." Both the British and the Germans rejected the president's offer; the solution would have to come on the battlefield. In response, Wilson addressed the U.S. Senate on January 22, 1917, in a speech that called for a "Peace Without Victory." He argued that "only a peace among equals can last," and set out a program that included plans to create a league of nations. The response of the warring powers was skeptical. The idea of a league of nations also aroused opposition in the Senate. Wilson's failure to consult with his political enemies on this matter was an error that would plague him throughout the war.

American Intervention in the War

Events now led the United States toward intervention in the war. The German military decided on January 9, 1917, that the submarine could win the war before the United States could move troops to Europe. Unrestricted submarine attacks would be resumed on February 1. Wilson learned of the German decision on January 31 and realized that Berlin had not been negotiating in good faith. He broke diplomatic relations

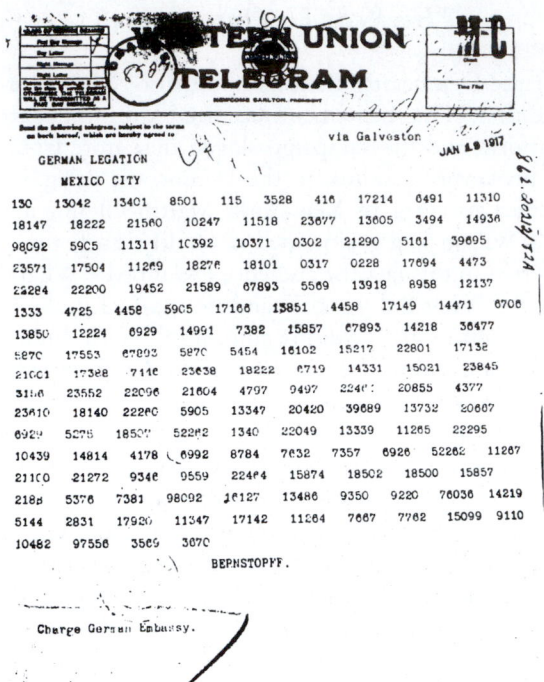

The feat of British intelligence in decoding the Zimmerman Telegram was a crucial step toward American entry into World War I. Newspapers printed the enciphered original before the British codebreakers had done their work.

on February 4 and waited for the "actual overt acts" from Germany that would mean war. The submarine campaign began as scheduled, and American lives were lost. On February 26 the president asked Congress for authority to arm U.S. merchant ships. With peace sentiment still strong on Capitol Hill, the administration faced a tough fight to get the bill passed.

An unexpected revelation about German war aims changed the legislative situation in the president's favor. British intelligence had intercepted and decoded a secret German diplomatic telegram to its ambassador in Mexico. The "Zimmerman Telegram," named after the German foreign minister Arthur Zimmerman, dangled the return to Mexico of Arizona, New Mexico, and Texas as bait to entice the Mexicans to enter the war on the German side. Wilson released this diplomatic bombshell to the public on March 1, and the House promptly passed the bill to arm merchant ships. Nevertheless, eleven senators, led by Robert M. La Follette of Wisconsin, filibustered against the bill until Congress adjourned on March 4. Wilson was outraged. "A little group of willful men, representing

no opinion but their own, have rendered the Great Government of the United States helpless and contemptible," he complained. In fact, Wilson could arm the ships on his own authority, which he did on March 9.

The Outbreak of Hostilities

The submarine campaign was hurting the Allies badly, and defeat seemed possible. One stumbling block to American support for the Allied cause had always been the presence of Russia on the side of the British and French. Alliance with that autocratic monarchy seemed to mock the notion that the Allies were fighting for democratic values. However, the outbreak of revolution in Russia toppled the regime of Czar Nicholas II and seemed to offer some hope for reform. Meanwhile, the Germans sank three American ships on March 18 with large losses. Wilson decided to call Congress into special session on April 2. For the third time in sixty years, Americans were going to war in April. On a soft spring evening, the president asked for a declaration of war against Germany. "The world must be made safe for democracy," he told them. "It is

a fearful thing to lead this great peaceful people into war, the most terrible and disastrous of all wars, civilization itself seeming to be in the balance. But the right is more precious than peace." Evoking the language of the sixteenth-century German religious reformer, Martin Luther, Wilson said of his nation, "God helping her, she can do no other."

Congress declared war on Germany on April 6, 1917. Although the votes were overwhelming (82 to 7 in the Senate; 373 to 50 in the House), the nation was divided about entering the conflict. In large parts of the South and West, peace sentiment was strong because the public felt no need to become involved in European quarrels or to benefit eastern business interests who might profit from the fighting. Opposition to the war remained high among German Americans and Irish Americans. Dedicated reformers and Socialists saw the war as a betrayal of reform ideals.

For Wilson himself, involvement in the war seemed to be the price the nation had to pay to influence the peace settlement. He did not put the issue that way to his fellow citizens. His lofty rhetoric encouraged Americans to believe that a better world could be obtained through the use of military force. In that sense the president paved the way for the later disillusion

When Woodrow Wilson delivered his war message to Congress on April 2, 1917, he moved the nation from peace to active participation in the World War. It represented a high point of Wilson's life. Ahead of him lay disabling illness and the end of his dream to have the United States enter the League of Nations. This stereopticon slide shows two views of Wilson.

WILSON'S
WAR MESSAGE
TO CONGRESS,
APRIL 2, 1917

In his message to Congress on April 2, 1917, Woodrow Wilson put the decision to go to war with Germany in a strongly moral context that helped make the American involvement in the conflict a war to make the world safe for democracy. The president's language elevated a foreign policy decision to a national crusade.

One of the things that has served to convince us that the Prussian autocracy was not and could never be our friend is that from the very outset of the present war it has filled our unsuspecting communities and even our offices of government with spies and set criminal intrigues everywhere afoot against our national unity of counsel, our peace within and without, our industries and our commerce. Indeed, it is now evident that its spies were here even before the war began; and it is unhappily not a matter of conjecture but a fact proved in our courts of justice that the intrigues which have more than once come perilously near to disturbing the peace and dislocating the industries of the country have been carried on at the instigation, with the support, and even under the personal direction of official agents of the Imperial Government accredited to the Government of the United States. Even in checking these things and trying to extirpate them we have sought to put the most generous interpretation possible upon them because we knew that their source lay not in any hostile feeling or purpose of the German people towards us who were no doubt as ignorant of them as we ourselves were), but only in the selfish designs of a Government that did what it pleased and told its people nothing. But they have played their part in serving to convince us at last that that Government entertains no real friendship for us and means to act against our peace and security at its convenience. That it means to stir up enemies against us at our very doors the intercepted note to the German Minister at Mexico City is eloquent evidence.

We are accepting this challenge of hostile purpose because we know that in such a Government, following such methods, we can never have a friend; and that in the presence of its organized power, always lying in wait to accomplish we know not what purpose, there can be no assured security for the democratic Governments of the world. We are now about to accept gage of battle with this natural foe to liberty and shall, if necessary, spend the whole force of the Nation to check and nullify its pretensions and its power. We are glad, now that we see the facts with no veil of false pretense about them, to fight thus for the ultimate peace of the world and for the liberation of its peoples, the German peoples included: for the rights of nations great and small and the privilege of men everywhere to choose their way of life and of obedience. The world must be made safe for democracy. Its peace must be planted upon the tested foundations of political liberty. We have no selfish ends to serve. We desire no conquest, no dominion. We seek no indemnities for ourselves, no material compensation for the sacrifices we shall freely make. We are but one of the champions of the rights of mankind. We shall be satisfied when those rights have been made as secure as the faith and the freedom of nations can make them.

Just because we fight without rancor and without selfish object, seeking nothing for ourselves but what we shall wish to share with all free peoples, we shall, I feel confident,

conduct our operations as belligerents without passion and ourselves observe with proud punctilio the principles of right and of fair play we profess to be fighting for.

I have said nothing of the Governments allied with the Imperial Government of Germany because they have not made war upon us or challenged us to defend our right and our honor. The Austro-Hungarian Government has, indeed, avowed its unqualified indorsement and acceptance of the reckless and lawless submarine warfare adopted now without disguise by the Imperial German Government, and it has therefore not been possible for this Government to receive Count Tarnowski, the Ambassador recently accredited to this Government by the Imperial and Royal Government of Austria-Hungary; but that Government has not actually engaged in warfare against citizens of the United States on the seas, and I take the liberty, for the present at least, of postponing a discussion of our relations with the authorities of Vienna. We enter this war only where we are clearly forced into it because there are no other means of defending our rights.

It will be all the easier for us to conduct ourselves as belligerents in a high spirit of right and fairness because we act without animus, not in enmity towards a people or with the desire to bring any injury or disadvantage upon them, but only in armed opposition to an irresponsible government which has thrown aside all considerations of humanity and of right and is running amuck. We are, let me say again, the sincere friends of the German people, and shall desire nothing so much as the early reëstablishment of intimate relations of mutual advantage between us,—however hard it may be for them, for the time being, to believe that this is spoken from our hearts. We have borne with their present Government through all these bitter months because of that friendship,—exercising a patience and forbearance which would otherwise have been impossible. We shall, happily, still have an opportunity to prove that friendship in our daily attitude and actions towards the millions of men and women of German birth and native sympathy who live amongst us and share our life, and we shall be proud to prove it towards all who are in fact loyal to their neighbors and to the Government in the hour of test. They are, most of them, as true and loyal Americans as if they had never known any other fealty or allegiance. They will be prompt to stand with us in rebuking and restraining the few who may be of a different mind and purpose. If there should be disloyalty, it will be dealt with with a firm hand of stern repression; but, if it lifts its head at all, it will lift it only here and there and without countenance except from a lawless and malignant few.

It is a distressing and oppressive duty, Gentlemen of the Congress, which I have performed in thus addressing you. There are, it may be, many months of fiery trial and sacrifice ahead of us. It is a fearful thing to lead this great peaceful people into war, into the most terrible and disastrous of all wars, civilization itself seeming to be in the balance. But the right is more precious than peace, and we shall fight for the things which we have always carried nearest our hearts,—for democracy, for the right of those who submit to authority to have a voice in their own Governments, for the rights and liberties of small nations, for a universal dominion of right by such a concert of free peoples as shall bring peace and safety to all nations and make the world itself at last free. To such a task we can dedicate our lives and our fortunes, everything that we are and everything that we have, with the pride of those who know that the day has come when America is privileged to spend her blood and her might for the principles that gave her birth and happiness and the peace which she has treasured. God helping her, she can do no other.

among Americans that frustrated his ambitious plans for world leadership. Wilson had been a skillful politician during his first term. While he led the nation to victory during his second administration, his talents as a partisan politician were less evident during the second half of his presidency.

A NATION AT WAR

World War I produced significant changes in the way the United States functioned. The power of the federal government increased dramatically in response to the need to mobilize the nation for total war. Average citizens found that they had to respond to government programs and directives in strange and unfamiliar ways, such as accepting bureaucratic rules for their businesses, listening to government propaganda, and changing their eating habits. For Wilson, the war brought victory in 1918, followed by the loss of his dreams of world peace at the same time that his health collapsed.

The State of the Conflict in 1917

Both the White House and Congress had initially assumed that the American contribution to the war would consist largely of furnishing money and supplies to the Allied cause. There was little sense of the extent to which the sacrifices of the preceding three years had weakened the ability of the British and French to wage war. It soon became apparent that American soldiers would have to go across the Atlantic and join in the fighting to achieve an Allied victory. Otherwise, a German military success seemed probable.

As of April 1917, the German army still occupied large portions of France that it had seized in 1914. On the "Western Front" the two sides fought in elaborate trenches from which soldiers fired at each other or mounted attacks against well-fortified positions. Dug-in artillery and machine guns gave the advantage to the defense. For three years the attacks went on. The French suffered more than 1,430,000 casualties on the western front in 1915. The Germans tried to break the will of the French at Verdun in 1916; both sides lost more than 300,000 men in the ensuing struggle. The

British attacked in northern France in 1916; 60,000 men were killed or wounded in a single day's fighting. Similar carnage occurred when the British renewed their offensive on the Somme River in 1917. After the French went on the attack in 1917 with heavy casualties, their broken armies mutinied against further slaughter. To win the war, American troops would be needed in great numbers to support the flagging Allied cause.

U.S. Armed Forces

The Wilson administration did not want to raise an army through the volunteer methods that had been used in the war with Spain. Experience in Europe had shown that a volunteer system was undependable and did not keep trained individuals at their jobs in key war industries. A draft seemed the fairest and most efficient method.

In May 1917 Congress adopted the Selective Service Act. Men between the ages of twenty-one and thirty had to register for the draft; local boards were set up to administer the program. By the end of the war some 24 million young men had been registered, and about 3 million had been called into the armed forces. Another 340,000 men tried to evade the draft and became "slackers." There were also 65,000 men who claimed exemptions for religious reasons.

To command the American Expeditionary Force (AEF), Wilson selected General John J. "Black Jack" Pershing, who had pursued Pancho Villa into Mexico. The nation was ill-prepared for war. The army had no plans for a war with Germany in Western Europe, and it did not have the rifles and machine guns necessary for a modern conflict. Its staff structure was loaded with old officers who lacked initiative and experience in commanding large numbers of men. Once Pershing got his troops to Europe, he would have much training to do to make them ready for combat.

Training the Army

Training the troops for warfare in Europe was not a simple process, and the indoctrination that the men received often reflected progressive ideals. The government endeavored to maintain the purity of troops with extensive programs to limit excessive drinking

and venereal disease. The army also provided an optional opportunity to acquire inexpensive life insurance, which increased popular interest in such programs after the war.

Enlisted men also received intelligence tests that had little impact on their fighting ability but did enhance psychology's reputation as a social science. Men who could read were asked to identify the unit of electromotive force from a list consisting of *ohm, ampere,* and *watt.* Soldiers who could not read were asked to specify the missing item in pictures of a tennis court without a net or a camel, without a hump. When the tests showed no significant difference in intelligence between black soldiers and white soldiers, the army recalculated the results to conform with its prejudices.

While the army was being raised, the navy faced a more immediate challenge. During April 1917 German submarines sank almost 900,000 tons of Allied shipping. At that rate, half the oceangoing shipping available to the British would disappear by the end of 1917. Ships were going down more quickly than they could be replaced, and the British had only a six weeks' worth of food reserves. If the menace of the submarine could not be conquered, the war could be lost before Pershing and his men arrived in France.

The American naval commander in Europe, Admiral William S. Sims, called for the use of convoys to escort vulnerable merchant ships across the Atlantic. American destroyers on escort duty became a key part of the strategy that eventually ended the submarine threat. Troops began to move toward Europe. The Germans did not regard troopships as significant targets because of their belief that American soldiers lacked fighting ability. That allowed the flow of troops to continue unhindered. Two million men were shipped to France before the Armistice was signed and they provided the margin for an Allied victory.

Financing the War

Drafted soldiers and submarine-dodging convoys were only part of the American experience of the war. The war affected how Americans thought, what they ate, and how they earned a living. At the movies, where patriotic newsreels were shown; in the baseball stadiums, where drives were held to sell war bonds; and at home tending their gardens to raise food, men, women, and children became part of the war effort.

The government helped finance the war through the sale of war bonds. Celebrities such as movie star Douglas Fairbanks, Sr. spoke to huge throngs and urged them to buy bonds. Fairbanks is seen before a large crowd on Wall Street in New York City.

Fighting a modern war required huge sums of money. The government raised a third of it, some $9 billion, through increased taxes. The remainder came from citizens who purchased "Liberty Bonds" from the government. These interest-bearing securities brought in more than $15 billion. To persuade Americans to buy bonds, the government enlisted celebrities like Douglas Fairbanks and Charlie Chaplin to appear at rallies where bonds were sold. Children were taught to save their pennies and nickels for thrift stamps. They learned a rhyme to urge them on:

> Hush little thrift stamp,
> Don't you cry;
> You'll be a war bond
> By and by.

Those who were unwilling to contribute were told that failure to buy bonds was unpatriotic and helped

The government also employed advertising to sell bonds. This poster showing an American soldier at the front was one of the ways that Washington sought to awaken public opinion to the need for bond sales.

the Germans. In some cases, violence was used to coerce the reluctant contributors.

The total cost of the war exceeded $35 billion because the United States loaned more than $11.2 billion to the Allies. The loans proved to be vital to the Allied cause. In June 1917 one British official told his government that "If loan stops, war stops." President Wilson counted on the Allies' financial dependence on the United States as a weapon to use in achieving the goals of his postwar diplomacy.

Herbert Hoover and Food for the Allies

The Allies also desperately needed food. The British depended on supplies from their empire which took a long time to reach Europe by ship and were vulnerable to submarine attack. Without American food, sent via convoys under the protection of the U.S. Navy, serious shortages would have impaired Allied ability to wage war. To mobilize the agricultural resources of the United States, Congress passed the Lever Act, which established a Food Administration. Wilson selected Herbert Hoover to head this new agency. A mining engineer from California, Hoover had gained international fame through his work to feed the starving people of Belgium after 1914. He threw his abundant energy into the task of persuading Americans to save their food for shipment overseas.

Hoover's main weapon was publicity. He asked Americans to observe "wheatless days" and "meatless days" because "wheatless days in America make sleepless nights in Germany." Woodrow Wilson allowed sheep to graze on the White House lawn in order to produce wool. Women and children planted "war gardens" to raise more fruits and vegetables. Higher prices induced farmers to expand their production. The wheat crop was 637 million bushels in 1917; a year later it stood at 921 million bushels.

Prohibition and the War Effort

The campaign to conserve food provided a boost for the effort to restrict the sale and use of alcoholic beverages. Scarce grain supplies had to be reserved for soldiers in the field and Allied populations overseas. As a wartime slogan put it, "Shall the many have food or the few have drink?" Prohibitionists argued that drink impaired the fighting ability of the armed forces and those working in defense plants. The connection of the brewing industry with the German Americans also worked in favor of the prohibitionist cause.

Congress passed legislation to restrict the production of liquor and in December 1917 the lawmakers approved the Eighteenth Amendment, which banned the production, sale, and consumption of alcoholic beverages. All that remained was to ensure ratification of the amendment by the required number of states, a task that the Anti-Saloon League was well equipped to handle. The long reform campaign to curb the influence and use of liquor was on the verge of success.

Managing the Wartime Economy

Coordination of the economy was not limited to the agricultural sector. The president used his power to wage the war to establish the expanded bureaucracy required to manage production of war supplies and oversee their shipment to the Allies. Wilson did not seek to have government take over business. He hoped that a business-government partnership would develop naturally. However, much government encouragement and direction were needed before the business community fully joined the war effort.

The eventual record of mobilization was a mixed one. The United States tried to build ships and planes under the direction of government agencies. Those efforts produced at least one British-designed plane that used American-built engines, and large numbers of merchant ships were constructed in American shipyards. On the other hand, Pershing's men used British and French artillery and equipment. The government had more success with expanding the production of coal through the Fuel Administration. Coal prices were raised in order to stimulate production, and "daylight savings time" was established in order to reduce the use of fuel for nonmilitary purposes.

Wartime Economic Problems

The nation's railroads became so confused during the first year of the war that immense and costly transportation snarls resulted. The armed forces insisted on immediate passage for railcars with war supplies; the result was tieups of rail traffic all over the East Coast. Finally the government simply took over the railroads in January 1918, placing the secretary of the Treasury, William G. McAdoo, in charge of operations. McAdoo raised the wages of railroad workers, dropped inefficient routes, and allowed the lines to raise their rates. The tieups soon disappeared.

Even before U.S. entry into the war, the government had made plans for coordinating industrial production. Staffed with "dollar-a-year men" whose salaries were paid by their former companies, the War Industries Board (WIB) was supposed to make sure that the purchasing and allocation of supplies for the armed forces followed rational programs. The WIB fell well short of this standard during 1917. In March 1918, under pressure from Congress and Republican critics such as Theodore Roosevelt, Wilson placed

Bernard Baruch, a Wall Street speculator and contributor to the Democratic party, at the head of the War Industries Board.

Bernard Baruch and the War Industries Board

Baruch used his political skills and business background to persuade industrialists to cooperate with the war mobilization effort. He and his aides attacked needless waste in production. They standardized products, established priorities for the shipment of important goods, and set prices to encourage factories to turn out goods quickly. Simply by altering bicycle designs, the WIB saved 2,000 tons of steel for war goods.

Not all industries cooperated willingly. Baruch had to compromise with both the automobile and the steel industries to induce them to abandon peacetime production in favor of handling wartime orders. In the process, the industries made significant profits from their government contracts. As one steel executive put it:, "We are all making more money out of this war than the average human being ought to."

Labor and the War

The American Federation of Labor and its president, Samuel Gompers, threw their support behind what Gompers called "the most wonderful crusade ever entered upon by men in the whole history of the world." In return for the government's agreement to allow unions to participate in economic policy making, Gompers and the AFL promised not to striken or to press for union shops in factories. The short-run results were encouraging. Between 1917 and 1920 the AFL gained more than 2 million members.

Nonunion workers also benefited from the government's wartime policies. The National War Labor Board, headed by former President William Howard Taft, set standards for wages and hours that were far more generous and enlightened than those private industry had provided. A minimum wage was mandated, as were maximum hours and improved working conditions. The government also created housing for war workers and began a system of medical care and life insurance for federal employees. Responding to these actions at the national level, states improved their welfare programs and labor laws.

Black Americans in the War

While some blacks wanted no part of the European conflict, most African-American leaders agreed with W.E.B. Du Bois that they should "forget about special grievances and close our ranks shoulder to shoulder with our own fellow white citizens." Some 367,000 black soldiers served during the war; 42,000 of them saw combat in France. Most of the African-American servicemen, however, were assigned to labor battalions and supply duties. The War Department moved very slowly to commission black officers; at the end of the war there were only 1200. Several African-American units fought bravely. Others were given inadequate training and equipment, but when they performed poorly in combat the blame was placed on their supposed inferiority. Blacks had little motivation to fight in the first place. Moreover, for some blacks in France, the experience of being in a country without a long tradition of racism made them long for greater freedom at home. "The Negroes will come back feeling like men, and not disposed to accept the treatment to which they have been subjected," wrote one white reformer.

African-American troops stationed in the United States faced familiar dangers. In August 1917 in Houston, Texas, black soldiers reacted to segregation and abuse by the police with attacks on the police and on white citizens that left sixteen whites and four soldiers dead. The army indicted 118 soldiers, of whom 110 were convicted by courts-martial. Nineteen black soldiers were hanged.

Growing Racial Tension

Racial tensions intensified elsewhere in the nation. During the summer of 1917, race riots in East St. Louis, Illinois, resulted in the deaths of forty blacks and nine whites. Forty-eight lynchings occurred in 1917 and sixty-three in 1918. Facing discrimination and violence, blacks responded with a heightened sense of outrage. Marches were held to protest the race riots. Banners called upon President Wilson to: "Bring Democracy to America Before You Carry It to Europe." W.E.B. Du Bois told his readers in *The Crisis:* "Make Way for Democracy! We saved it in France, and by the Great Jehovah, we will save it in the United States of America or know the reason why."

During the war the black migration to northern cities accelerated. As the African-American communities in Chicago, New York, Philadelphia, and other northern cities grew, black newspapers began publishing articles about "The New Negro" who did not "fear the face of day. The time for cringing is over." The repressive actions of the Wilson administration fed the new currents of militance among black Americans.

Women in Wartime

The great achievement of American women during World War I was winning the right of suffrage. Momentum had been building for a generation, but the demands of war brought success. The leaders of the National American Woman Suffrage Association decided that identification with the war offered the surest and fastest road to achieving their goal. Carrie Chapman Catt argued that giving women the vote would enable them to offset disloyal elements at home. "Every slacker has a vote," said Catt, a vote that newly enfranchised women could counter. Members of NAWSA appeared at rallies and proclaimed that suffrage should be a "war measure" that would repay women for their contributions to the war. The National Woman's party, on the other hand, picketed the White House and tried to embarrass Wilson for failing to support woman suffrage. The combined impact of these tactics led to the passage of the woman suffrage amendment in the House of Representatives in January 1918. Wilson came out in favor of the amendment just before the congressional elections of that year. The Senate still had to act, but the war had made possible the eventual victory of the campaign to give women the vote. Neither the NWP nor NAWSA deserved sole credit for the victory; their separate activities reinforced each other.

Beyond the success of woman suffrage, however, the war did not go on long enough to produce lasting changes in the condition of American women. Only about 400,000 more women joined the labor force; some 8 million found better-paying jobs as a result of the conflict. More than 20,000 women served in the military. The navy and the marines enlisted 13,000 of them, largely in office jobs. The army employed more than 5,000 as nurses. Some agencies of the government added women workers. The National Railroad Administration, for example, created a Women's Service Section to lower barriers against female employ-

Militant proponents of woman suffrage picketed the White House in 1917–1918 to move President Wilson to support their cause. Their presence embarrassed the president and several of the picketers went to jail for their beliefs.

ment. In industry, women were hired as drivers, farm workers, and secretaries. As soon as the war ended, they were expected to relinquish these jobs to returning servicemen. As a Chicago woman complained, "During the war they called us heroines, but they throw us on the scrapheap now."

Civil Liberties in Wartime

The Wilson administration believed that winning the war required mobilization of public opinion to offset potential opposition to the conflict. As a result, the White House mounted a campaign of laws, agencies, and popular spirit to arouse support for the war and to quell dissent. In doing so, however, Woodrow Wilson and the men around him abused and restricted the civil liberties of many Americans.

To awaken national enthusiasm, the government created a propaganda agency to manage the news. The Committee on Public Information (CPI) was established on April 13, 1917, and President Wilson named George Creel, a former newspaperman, as its head. Creel called his task "the world's greatest adventure in advertising"; he saw his role as one of fusing Americans into "one white-hot mass . . . with fraternity, devotion, courage, and deathless determination." To spread its message, the CPI used every available instrument of public relations, from pamphlets and billboards to motion pictures such as *The American Indian Gets into the War Game*. Seventy-five thousand speakers known as "Four-Minute Men" (because of the length of their talks) spoke to audiences throughout the nation.

The themes of the CPI's appeal were simple, patriotic, and strident. Four-Minute Men asked listeners: "Do you want to take the slightest chance of meeting Prussianism here in America?" The great national goal was unity; the Germans were depraved animals; and the nation was engaged in a crusade to "make the world safe for democracy." Wilson's wartime speeches described the United States as "an instrument in the hands of God to see that liberty is made secure for mankind." The president supported the work of Creel enthusiastically. He promised the German leaders that they would face: "Force without stint or limit, the righteous and triumphant Force which shall make Right the law of the world, and cast every selfish dominion down in the dust."

The Limits of Dissent

To guard against opposition to the war, the Wilson administration and Congress placed legislative limits on the ability of Americans to criticize the government or the war effort. The lawmakers wanted to do more than the president in the way of stifling dissent, and the White House watered down the more extreme proposals. The Espionage Act of 1917 curbed espionage and sabotage, but made its definitions so sweeping that they embraced even public criticism of the war and its conduct. A person who violated the law could be sentenced to twenty years in prison. The Trading with the Enemy Act, passed in October 1917, authorized the Postmaster General to suspend the mailing privileges of foreign-language periodicals and newspapers that he deemed offensive to the government. Postmaster General Albert S. Burleson used that law and the Espionage Act to bar from the mails publications that he

considered treasonous or seditious. In 1918 Congress passed the Alien Act, which gave the government broad powers to deport any noncitizen who advocated revolution or anarchism. Most sweeping was the Sedition Act of 1918 which prohibited "uttering, printing, writing, or publishing any disloyal, profane, scurrilous, or abusive language" about either the government or the armed forces.

These laws were vigorously enforced. Burleson pursued critics of the administration relentlessly. The Socialist magazine *The Masses* was barred from the mails for carrying articles claiming that "this is Woodrow Wilson's and Wall Street's War." Burleson believed that once the government had entered the war, "every loyal member of the minority should become one with the majority." The Justice Department was equally vigilant. People were sent to prison for saying that "Wilson is a wooden-headed son of a bitch" or remarking that this was "a rich man's war." Eugene V. Debs, the perennial Socialist candidate for president, received a ten-year prison sentence for opposing the draft and the war. The American Protective League, a volunteer organization designed to locate draft evaders, became a vigilante branch of the Justice Department that used wire-tapping, illegal searches, and other lawless techniques to find "slackers" and other opponents of the war.

Wartime Hysteria

The zeal of the government to stamp out dissent was matched by private hysteria toward Germans among the American people. Traces of German influence in American life were repressed. Sauerkraut became "liberty cabbage," hamburgers reemerged as "Salisbury steak," and some cities gave up pretzels. Speaking the German language in public was banned in half of the states by 1918, and German literary works vanished from libraries. Musicians with German names, such as the violinist Fritz Kreisler, found their careers crippled. Streets with German names were renamed for American generals or Allied victories.

Some German Americans suffered more serious injuries. When they refused to buy war bonds, mobs beat them until they promised to contribute. Editorials warned: "YOUR NEIGHBOR, YOUR MAID, YOUR LAWYER, YOUR WAITER MAY BE A GERMAN SPY." Radicals, too, were the victims of mob violence. Frank Little, an organizer for the Industrial Workers of the World, was hanged from a railroad

trestle in Montana for denouncing the war at a labor rally. A German-American drifter named Robert Prager was attacked by a mob in Maryville, Illinois, compelled to sing patriotic songs and kiss the American flag, and then hanged. State councils of defense used their power to attack allegedly disloyal individuals and to ensure national unity.

The Political Legacy of Repression

The government had a legitimate reason to be concerned about German espionage, but the repression of civil liberties during the war went far beyond any rational claim of national security. President Wilson did not directly order cabinet officials to engage in such conduct, but he failed to keep them in check when he learned about what they were doing. The government's campaign against radicals and progressives represented an attack on national freedom. It also undermined support for the president in domestic politics. In his eagerness to win the war, Wilson had allowed his government to destroy part of his own political base. He and the Democrats paid for that policy in the 1918 and 1920 election campaigns.

THE ROAD TO VICTORY

During the late winter of 1918, as American troops arrived in France in larger numbers, the Allies faced a dangerous military crisis. In November 1917 the Communist revolution in Russia had taken that nation out of the Allied coalition and enabled the Germans to concentrate on the British and French. The Germans moved troops to the western front in an attempt to achieve victory before the Americans could replenish the depleted ranks of Allied soldiers. The German attack came on March 21, 1918, against the junction of the British and French armies. The offensive made impressive gains before the German advance was halted. When further attacks were made against the French in April and May, American reinforcements were sent in to help stop the assault. The "inexhaustible flood of gleaming youth in its first maturity of health and vigor," as the Americans were described, restored French morale. At battles near Château-Thierry and in Belleau Wood in early June, the men

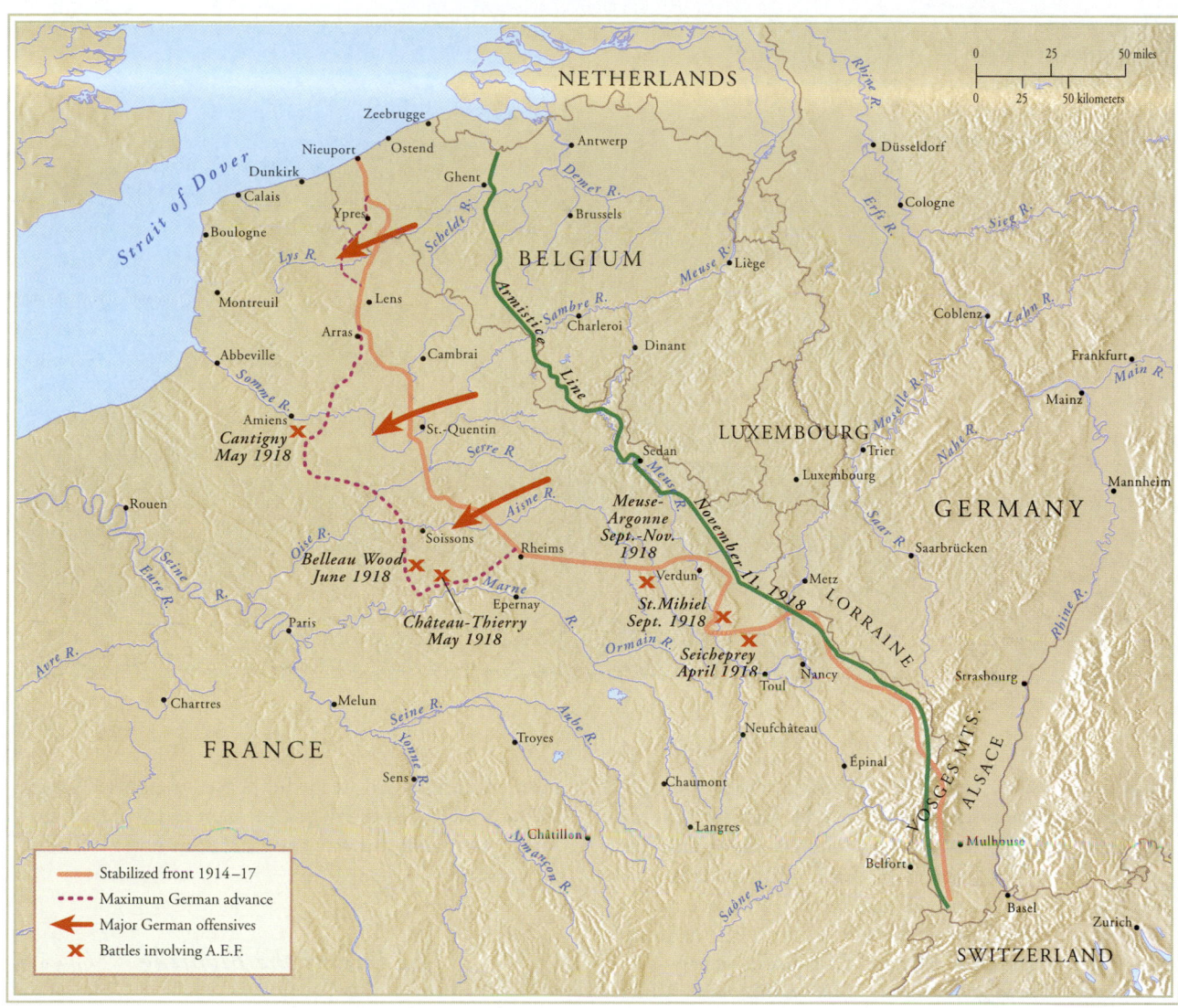

Stabilized front 1914–17
Maximum German advance
Major German offensives
X Battles involving A.E.F.

MAP 22.3 | AMERICAN PARTICIPATION ON THE WESTERN FRONT

of the AEF endured frightful losses but stopped the Germans.

The Germans made one more offensive thrust in mid-July, and the British, French, and Americans repelled it as well. Counterattacks moved the Germans backward, a retreat that continued until the end of the war. German commanders warned their government that the fighting could not go on much longer. In September 1918 the American Army went on the offensive at the town of Saint-Mihiel near the southern end of the trenches. At the end of the month, Americans launched another thrust toward the Meuse River and

the Argonne Forest. Their casualties were heavy, but the AEF pierced the German defenses to threaten key supply routes of the enemy.

Wilson's Peace Program

By October 1918, the German empire was crumbling as a result of the cumulative effects of the British blockade, four years of war, and defeats in the West. The issue now became the terms on which the war would end. Ever since the beginning of the war,

The American Expeditionary Force saw major combat during the closing stages of the war. An artillery detachment supports an advance of soldiers in France.

Woodrow Wilson had been thinking about the outcome of a peace settlement, and he had set out his views in a major address to Congress on January 8, 1918. Using the archives of the Czarist government, the Russian Communists had recently released secret treaties that the Allies had made before 1917 dividing up Europe and the Middle East once victory was achieved. These documents cast doubt on Allied claims that they were fighting for unselfish reasons. Wilson endeavored to shape the Allies' answer and regain the diplomatic initiative.

To present the American cause in a better light, Wilson offered a peace program with fourteen specific elements which became known as the Fourteen Points. Among the key provisions were freedom of the seas, free trade, and more open diplomacy. Freedom of the seas would prevent a repetition of what the United States had faced before entering the war. Wilson believed that secret treaties and balance of power diplomacy had helped bring about the war itself. The president also spoke of national self-determination for all nations. By this he meant that the borders of countries should reflect the national origins of the people who lived in a particular area. He also advocated an "associ-

ation of nations" to keep the peace. In short, Wilson tried to advance an American agenda for peace that would dominate the way the European nations settled the conflict.

The End of the Fighting

The Fourteen Points would not be easy to achieve. After four years of slaughter, Britain and France wanted to punish Germany and cripple its ability to wage war. They disliked Wilson's criticism of their war aims and his interference with European policies. For the desperate Germans, Wilson's Fourteen Points seemed much more appealing than did negotiations with London and Paris. In early October a civilian government in Germany asked Wilson to arrange an armistice based on the Fourteen Points. Working through Colonel House, the president negotiated an agreement for an end to the fighting. He also used the threat of a separate settlement with the Germans to induce the British and French to accept the Fourteen Points and attend the peace conference. The war came to end on November 11, 1918, at 11:00 in the morning.

TABLE 22.2
THE FOURTEEN POINTS OF WOODROW WILSON

1. Open covenants, openly arrived at to replace secret diplomacy
2. Freedom of the seas in peace and war
3. Removal of barriers to international trade
4. Reduction of armaments
5. Adjustment of colonial claims
6. Russia's lost territory to be returned
7. Belgium's independence to be guaranteed
8. Alsace-Lorraine restored to France
9. Italian frontiers readjusted along nationality lines
10. Peoples of Austria-Hungary to have "freest opportunity of autonomous development"
11. Rearrangement of boundaries of Balkan states along nationality lines
12. Turkey to be independent; autonomy for non-Turkish peoples in Turkey; guarantee of international passage through Dardanelles
13. An independent Polish state
14. A "general association of nations" should be created to preserve the territorial integrity of all nations

SOURCE: Commager, ed., *Documents of American History,* II, pp. 138–139.

for Democrats only. He did not bring Republicans into his government, and he made strong attacks on Republicans who opposed his policies. Meanwhile, his enemies capitalized on the unhappiness of farmers and workers over the administration's domestic programs. Midwestern farmers, for example, disliked the price controls that had been imposed on wheat. They complained that southerners in Congress had prevented similar price controls from being put on cotton. As a result, wheat farmers saw their profits held down while cotton producers did well. Progressives who had supported Wilson in 1916 recoiled from the administration's repressive tactics toward dissenters. As the congressional elections in 1918 approached, the Republicans had a clear advantage. Playing the foreign policy card for partisan purposes, in late October 1918 Wilson tried to stave off the defeat with an appeal to the American people to elect a Democratic Congress. He asked the voters to show that he was "their unembarrassed spokesman in affairs at home and abroad." The statement had little impact on the outcome; in fact it was a serious political mistake because it allowed Wilson's enemies to claim that he had been decisively repudiated when the results showed that both the House and the Senate would have Republican majorities. For a president who needed bipartisan support in the Senate for any treaty he might write at the upcoming Peace Conference in Paris, it was a major blunder. It would not be the last such error that Wilson would make in dealing with his Republican opponents.

Woodrow Wilson had achieved a diplomatic triumph with the conclusion of the armistice, but his success proved to be temporary. Even as he prepared to lead the American delegation to Paris, his domestic political base was eroding. During the war, he had proclaimed, "politics is adjourned." In fact, however, partisan battles continued with both Wilson and his enemies using the war for their own political purposes.

The 1918 Elections

During the war President Wilson kept the Republicans at arm's length and treated the conflict as a war

The Paris Peace Conference

Wilson had already decided to attend the Peace Conference himself. Informal tradition held that the president should not leave the continental United States during his term of office. Theodore Roosevelt had visited Panama in 1906, but Wilson proposed a more significant break with tradition. Despite Republican criticism, he believed that he needed to direct the negotiations himself. Moreover, his selection of delegates to accompany him showed his continuing insensitivity to bipartisanship. He chose Colonel House, Secretary of State Robert Lansing, General Tasker H. Bliss, and Henry White, who had served as a diplomat during the Roosevelt administration. White was a nominal

Faced with worsening Democratic prospects in the 1918 elections, President Wilson issued an appeal to the voters to elect candidates of his party to strengthen his hand in making peace. His tone, however, alienated Republican voters without rousing Democrats to get out and vote. The appeal was a political disaster for the president and his party.

My Fellow Countrymen:

The Congressional elections are at hand. They occur in the most critical period our country has ever faced or is likely to face in our time. If you have approved of my leadership and wish me to continue to be your unembarrassed spokesman in affairs at home and abroad, I earnestly beg that you will express yourselves unmistakably to that effect by returning a Democratic majority to both the Senate and the House of Representatives.

I am your servant and will accept your judgment without cavil. But my power to administer the great trust assigned to me by the Constitution would be seriously impaired should your judgment be adverse, and I must frankly tell you so because so many critical issues depend upon your verdict. No scruple or taste must in grim times like these be allowed to stand in the way of speaking the plain truth.

I have no thought of suggesting that any political party is paramount in matters of patriotism. I feel too deeply the sacrifices which have been made in this war by all our citizens, irrespective of party affiliations, to harbor such an idea. I mean only that the difficulties and delicacies of our present task are of a sort that makes it imperatively necessary that the nation should give its undivided support to the Government under a unified leadership, and that a Republican Congress would divide the leadership.

The leaders of the minority in the present Congress have unquestionably been pro-war, but they have been anti-administration. At almost every turn since we entered the war they have sought to take the choice of policy and the conduct of the war out of my hands and put it under the control of instrumentalities of their own choosing.

Republican, but the selection of someone so far removed from the Republican mainstream did not impress the president's political enemies.

Unlike William McKinley in 1898, Wilson did not send any senators to Paris. Had he done so, he would surely have had to include Senator Henry Cabot Lodge of Massachusetts, the next chairman of the Foreign Relations Committee. Wilson and Lodge hated each other. That ruled out any lawmakers going with the president because, if he could not take Lodge, Wilson could not invite any other senators. Unwilling to accept advice or share the credit, Wilson also declined to select any other prominent Republicans such as William Howard Taft or Elihu Root.

This is no time either for divided counsels or for divided leadership. Unity of command is as necessary now in civil action as it is upon the field of battle. If the control of the House and the Senate should be taken away from the party now in power an opposing majority could assume control of legislation and oblige all action to be taken amid contest and obstruction.

The return of a Republican majority to either house of the Congress would, morever, be interpreted on the other side of the water as a repudiation of my leadership. Spokesmen of the Republican party are urging you to elect a Republican Congress in order to back up and support the President, but, even if they should in this impose upon some credulous voters on this side of the water, they would impose on no one on the other side. It is well understood there as well as here that Republican leaders desire not so much to support the President as to control him.

The peoples of the allied countries with whom we are associated against Germany are quite familiar with the significance of elections. They would find it very difficult to believe that the voters of the United States had chosen to support their President by electing to the Congress a majority controlled by those who are not in fact in sympathy with the attitude and action of the Administration.

I need not tell you, my fellow countrymen, that I am asking your support not for my own sake or for the sake of a political party, but for the sake of the nation itself in order that its inward duty of purpose may, be evident to all the world. In ordinary times I would not feel at liberty to make such an appeal to you. In ordinary times divided counsels can be endured without permanent hurt to the country. But these are not ordinary times.

If in these critical days it is your wish to sustain me with undivided minds, I beg that you will say so in a way which it will not be possible to misunderstand, either here at home or among our associates on the other side of the sea. I submit my difficulties and my hopes to you.

WOODROW WILSON

The President in Europe

Europeans greeted Wilson with rapturous applause. When he arrived in Paris, 2 million people cheered him as he rode up the Champs-Élysées. They called him "Wilson *le Juste* [the Just]" and expected him to fulfill their desires for a peaceful world and for revenge against the Germans. Wilson came to believe that he could appeal to the peoples of the world over the heads of their leaders to support his program of international peace. It proved to be another miscalculation.

He faced a daunting task. The other major figures at the conference were David Lloyd George, the prime minister of Great Britain, and Georges Clemenceau,

When Wilson arrived in Europe, he received a hero's welcome. As he embarks in Great Britain and walks in with Lloyd George and King George V, schoolgirls throw flowers in his path.

the premier of France. Both men were hard-headed realists who did not share Wilson's idealism. "God gave us the Ten Commandments, and we broke them," said Clemenceau. "Wilson gives us the Fourteen Points. We shall see." According to Wilson, the wily British leader was "as slippery as an eel, and I never know when to count on him." Along with the prime minister of Italy, Vittorio Orlando, Wilson, Clemenceau, and Lloyd George made up the "Big Four" who directed the peace conference toward a settlement of the issues that the war had raised.

The Shadow of Bolshevism

Four years of war had left the world in disorder, and nations large and small came to Paris to have their fate decided. A striking omission was the Soviet Union, the Communist nation that the Russian Bolsheviks had established after their successful revolution. Civil war raged in Russia between the "Reds" of Communism and the "Whites," who wanted to block Bolshevik

control of the nation. Meanwhile, the Bolsheviks' authoritarian leader, Vladimir Ilyich Lenin and his colleagues wished to extend Communist rule beyond Russia's borders.

In 1919 national leaders worried that the infection of Communism might spread into Western Europe, and they had not recognized the government in Moscow. In fact, the French and British had tried to strangle the new regime by providing financial support for its enemies and intervening militarily in some areas of Russia. Helping its allies and trying to undermine Bolshevism, the United States had dispatched small detachments of troops to Siberia and Vladivostok in 1918 and 1919. The American presence in Russia became a long-standing grievance for the Soviet regime that emerged from the Bolshevik victory.

The Terms of Peace

The negotiations about the terms of peace with Germany produced both victories and defeats for Wilson.

During the writing of the Treaty of Versailles, the major powers worked together, and their leaders became known as the Big Four. Seated left to right, they are Vittorio Orlando of Italy, David Lloyd George of Great Britain, Georges Clemenceau of France, and President Wilson.

He had to accept the inclusion in the treaty of a clause that assigned Germany "guilt" for starting the war in 1914. That language proved to be a source of discontent for a resurgent Germany in the 1920s and 1930s. The Germans were also assessed severe financial penalties in the form of reparations that eventually amounted to $33 billion. That provision also angered the Germans, fueling resentments that poisoned postwar international relations.

Wilson also achieved mixed success in his efforts to establish self-determination as a principle of the peace settlement. He accepted Italian desires for control of the city of Fiume on the Adriatic Coast, could not block Japan from territorial gains in China, and was unable to prevent several groups of ethnic and national minorities in Eastern Europe from being left under the dominance of other ruling groups, as in the case of Germans in the new nation of Czechoslovakia.

The League of Nations

The main achievement that Wilson sought was establishment of the League of Nations. The league consisted of a General Assembly of all member nations, a Council made up of Great Britain, France, Italy, Japan, and the United States, with four other countries that the Assembly selected; and an international court of justice. For Wilson, the "heart of the covenant" of the League of Nations was Article X, which required member nations to preserve each other's independence and take concerted action when any member of the league was attacked. Whether Article X bound the United States to go to war for the league became a key issue when the Senate considered the Treaty of Versailles in 1919.

In February 1919 Wilson returned to the United States for the end of the congressional session. While popular opinion supported the idea of the league, the

MAP 22.4 | EUROPE AFTER THE PEACE CONFERENCE, 1920

Wilson and the Treaty of Versailles

To secure changes in the treaty for the Senate, Wilson had to make concessions to the other nations at the Peace Conference when he returned to Europe. These included the imposition of reparations on Germany, the war guilt clause, and limits on German's ability to rearm. In return, Wilson obtained provisions that protected the Monroe Doctrine from league action, removed domestic issues from the league's proceedings, and allowed any nation to leave the world organization with two years' notice. The final version of the treaty of Versailles was signed on June 28, 1919, in the Hall of Mirrors at the Palace of Versailles outside Paris. For all of its problems and weaknesses, the treaty was the closest thing to a reasonable settlement that Wilson could have obtained. The ultimate failure of the pact was because of the inability of the nations that signed it to make it work once the passions of war had cooled.

The Senate and the League

To get the treaty ratified and the League of Nations launched, Wilson faced the greatest political battle of his life. The Republicans now controlled the Senate forty-nine to forty-seven, so the president could not win the necessary two-thirds majority without the votes of some of his political opponents. Some Republicans were opposed to the treaty as an infringement upon American sovereignty, no matter what it said. These were the fourteen "irreconcilables"; two Democrats were also part of this group. Wilson had to seek help from the twelve "mild reservationists," who wanted only changes in the wording, and the twenty-three "strong reservationists" who sought to limit the league's power over American actions. The president could count on about thirty-five of the forty-seven

new Republican-dominated Senate was cool toward it. In early March Senator Lodge circulated a document that thirty-seven senators signed. It stated that the treaty must be amended or they would not vote for it. This "round-robin" had drawn enough votes to defeat the treaty unless Wilson made changes in the document. The president attacked his critics publicly, further intensifying partisan animosity.

The most dedicated political opponent of Woodrow Wilson was Senator Henry Cabot Lodge of Massachusetts. He said that he had never expected to hate anyone in politics with the intense dislike that he felt toward Wilson. The feeling was mutual.

Democrats in the Senate. Assuming that some of the mild reservationists would support the treaty, the Democrats had to find twenty Republican votes to gain the necessary sixty-four votes to approve the treaty.

In the political battle that ensued, Senator Lodge focused on Article X and the issue of whether Congress should be able to approve an American participation in the league's attempts to prevent international aggression. Lodge also played for time, hoping that public opinion would turn against the treaty. He had the lengthy treaty read aloud to the Senate. Meanwhile, Wilson insisted that the treaty be approved without changes or "reservations." However, in his meetings with senators of both parties, the president was unable to win converts to his position.

Wilson's Tour and Collapse

By September 1919 the treaty was in trouble. Wilson decided to take his case to the American people themselves. His cross-country tour began slowly but gained in popularity when he reached the West Coast. The climax came in his address at Pueblo, Colorado, on September 25. A cheering crowd heard him warn of another world war if the treaty failed. But Wilson's health broke under the strain. The circulatory problems that had bothered him for years erupted. He told his secretary, "I seem to have gone to pieces." He was rushed back to Washington, where he suffered a massive stroke on October 2, 1919. His left side was paralyzed, seriously impairing his ability to govern.

The president's wife and his doctors did not reveal how sick Wilson was. The first lady screened his few visitors and decided what documents her husband would see. Mrs. Wilson did not become "the first woman president," as some people said at the time, but Wilson was only a shell of a president. As a result, the government drifted.

The Defeat of the League

The League of Nations was the first victim of Wilson's near-fatal illness. The Senate voted on the treaty on November 19, 1919, with reservations that Lodge had included in the document. The key change that Lodge demanded would have required Congress to approve any sanctions imposed by the league on an aggressor. When the Democratic leader in the Senate asked Wilson about possible compromises, he replied that changing Article X "cuts the very heart out of the Treaty." The Senate rejected the treaty with reservations by a vote of thirty-nine to fifty-five. Then the lawmakers voted on the treaty without reservations. It lost, thirty-eight in favor and fifty-three against. In the end, the decision about a possible compromise with Lodge was Wilson's to make. He told Senate Democrats: "Let Lodge compromise." For the moment, the Treaty of Versailles was dead.

FROM WAR TO PEACE

Meanwhile the nation experienced domestic upheaval. Foreign policy problems faded in importance. Citizens grappled with labor unrest, a Red Scare (fear of Communist or "Red" subversion), a surge in prices following the end of the war, and an influenza epidemic. The postwar period was one of the most difficult that Americans had ever experienced.

The influenza epidemic began with dramatic suddenness at the end of 1918 and spread rapidly through

The influenza epidemic of 1918 was a grim fact of life for millions. A policeman directs traffic with his mask on to prevent contamination. The death toll exceeded 500,000 in the United States.

the population. No vaccines existed to combat it; no antibiotics were available to fight the secondary infections that resulted from it. More than 650,000 Americans died of the disease in 1918 and 1919. The number of dead bodies overwhelmed the funeral facilities of many major cities; coffins filled a circus tent in Boston. Children skipping rope made the epidemic part of their song:

> I had a little bird,
> And his name was Enza;
> I opened the window,
> And in flew Enza!

The influenza pandemic receded in 1920, leaving a worldwide total of 20 million people dead.

The Waning Spirit of Progressivism

By 1919 the spirit of progressive reform was waning. Much of what the reformers wanted had been achieved. The campaigns for Prohibition and woman suffrage were nearing their goals. Enough states had ratified the Prohibition amendment by January 1919 to make it part of the Constitution. In October 1919 Congress passed the Volstead Act to enforce Prohibition. Wilson vetoed the measure, but Congress passed it over his objection. The United States became "dry" on January 15, 1920. Prohibitionists expected that compliance would be widespread and enforcement relatively simple. As the next chapter will show, they were mistaken.

After the House passed the woman suffrage amendment in 1918, it took the Senate another year to approve it. Suffrage advocates then lobbied the states to ratify the amendment. When the Tennessee legislature voted for ratification in August 1920, three quarters of the states had approved woman suffrage. Women would now "take their appropriate place in political work," said Carrie Chapman Catt. With these achievements came renewed attacks on reform measures as costly and intrusive, and a growing popular disillusionment with big government.

The Struggles of Labor

After the Armistice on November 11, 1918, the nation shifted from a wartime economy to peacetime pursuits with dizzying speed. President Wilson, preoccupied with diplomatic concerns, decided that "Our people . . . do not want to be coached and led." The government declined to manage the changeover from a wartime to a peacetime economy. High inflation developed as prices were freed from wartime controls, and unemployment rose as returning soldiers sought jobs. The government's index of the cost of living rose nearly 80 percent above prewar levels in 1919 and it went up to 105 percent a year later. Americans complained about the effects of the high cost of living (HCL). Unemployment reached nearly 12 percent by 1921.

Unions struck for higher wages. Seattle shipyard workers walked off their jobs, and the Industrial Workers of the World called for a general strike to support them. When 60,000 laborers took part in the protest, the mayor of Seattle, Ole Hanson, responded

Drawn by Calvert Smith

THE POISON AND THE ANTIDOTE

When woman suffrage was adopted, many commentators predicted that women voters would purify politics, as this cartoon argues. It developed that women tended to vote along established partisan, regional, and demographic lines.

with mobilization of police and soldiers that made him "the Saviour of Seattle." Newspapers depicted the strike as a prelude to Communist revolution.

The Reaction Against Strikes

The largest industrial strike of the year occurred in the steel industry. The American Federation of Labor tried to organize all steelworkers to end the seven-day week and the twelve-hour day. In September 350,000 steel workers left the mills. Led by the head of United States Steel, E.H. Gary, the steel manufacturers refused to recognize the union. Strikebreakers were hired from among the ranks of unemployed blacks, Hispanics, and immigrants. The steel companies kept their factories running while they waited for the strike to be broken through police harassment and internal divisions within the unions. Conservatives attacked the radical background of one of the strike organizers, William Z. Foster. Although the strikers remained united for several months, they could not withstand the accumulated financial and political pressure from management. This first effort at a strike by an entire workforce failed in early 1920.

Other strikes of the year included a walkout by coal miners and a strike by police in Boston. Inflation had hit the Boston police hard, and they struck late in 1919. When looting and other criminal acts occurred because of the absence of police, public opinion turned against the striking officers. The governor of Massachusetts, Calvin Coolidge, became a national celebrity when he said: "There is no right to strike against the public safety, by anybody, anywhere, any time." To many middle-class Americans the social order seemed to be unraveling.

An Upsurge of Racial Violence

Racial tensions also flared up after the war. There were frequent lynchings in the South. In the North, the tide of African-American migration produced confrontations with angry whites. Rioting against blacks occurred in Washington, D.C., in June 1919. During the same summer a young black man was stoned and killed when whites found him on a Chicago beach from which African Americans had been excluded. Angry blacks attacked the police who had stood by while the killing occurred. Five days of violence followed in which thirty-eight people, most of them black, were killed and another 500 were injured. Two dozen other cities saw violent episodes during what one black leader called "the red summer."

The Communist "Menace"

Searching for a cause of the social unrest that pervaded the nation, Americans looked to radicalism and communism. The emotions aroused by the government's wartime propaganda fueled the "Red Scare" of 1919–1920. Radicalism was ridden with factions and had only a small number of followers. About 70,000 people belonged to one of the two branches of the Communist party. However, the radicals' reliance on violence and terrorism inflamed popular fears. When several mail bombs exploded on May 1, 1919, and dozens of others were found in the mail, press and public called for government action.

Attorney General A. Mitchell Palmer established a division in the Justice Department to hunt for radicals; the division was headed by J. Edgar Hoover who later became director of the Federal Bureau of Investigation. In November 1919, Palmer launched raids against suspected radicals, and a month later he deported 300 aliens to the Soviet Union. In the process, the legal rights of these suspects were violated, and they were kept in custody, away from their families and attorneys.

Throughout the country civil liberties came under assault. State legislatures investigated alleged subversives. Communist parties were outlawed, anti-radical legislation was adopted, and Socialists were expelled from the New York legislature. Suspected members of the IWW and other groups were subjected to vigilante violence and official repression.

The U.S. Supreme Court upheld the constitutionality of most of the laws that restricted civil liberties during the war and the Red Scare. Justice Oliver Wendell Holmes, Jr. devised a means of testing whether the First Amendment had been violated. In *Schenck* v. *United States* (1919), he asked whether words or utterances posed "a clear and present danger" of interference with the government, the war effort, or civil order. The answer was that they had. The court also sustained the conviction of Eugene V. Debs for speaking out against the war.

By 1920, however, the Red Scare lost momentum. Palmer forecast a violent uprising on May 1, 1920, and when it did not occur, his credibility suffered. Some government officials, especially in the Department of Labor, opposed Palmer's deportation policies. Other public figures, such as Charles Evans Hughes, denounced New York's efforts against socialist lawmakers. During this period, however, police in Massa-

chusetts arrested two anarchists and Italian aliens, Nicola Sacco and Bartolomeo Vanzetti, for their alleged complicity in a robbery and murder at a shoe company in South Braintree, Massachusetts. Out of these events would come one of the most famous criminal cases of the 1920s.

Gradually, the frenzy of Red-hunting abated. The long-term effects were significant. During the Wilson administration a dangerous precedent had been set for government interference with individual rights. The bureaucratic machinery was in place for future attempts to compel loyalty and punish dissent.

Harding and "Normalcy"

In early 1920, with Wilson ill and the government leaderless, political attention turned to the next presi-

In the 1920 election, Warren G. Harding promised "normalcy." To evoke the spirit of bygone days, he began his campaign from his front porch. Later he took to the campaign trail in a more modern manner. Harding won an overwhelming victory.

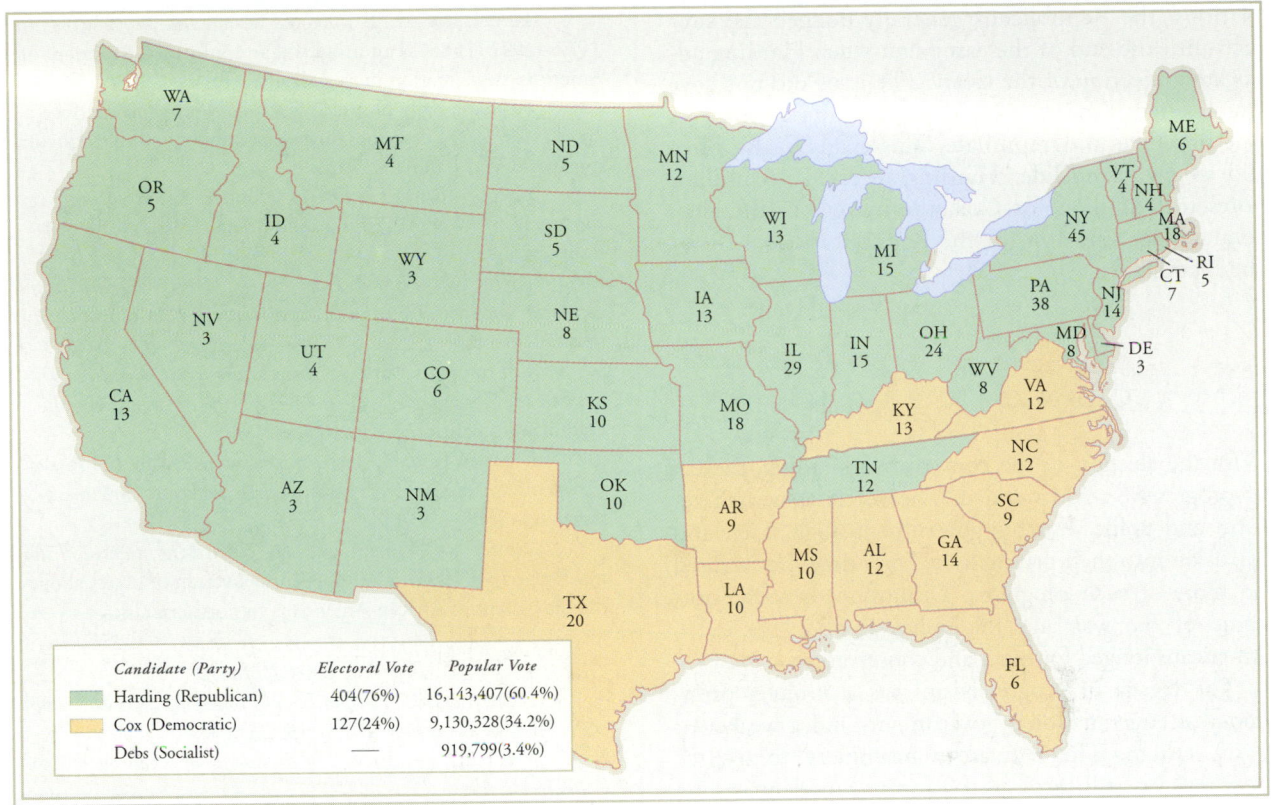

MAP 22.5 | THE ELECTION OF 1920

dential election. Before the candidates were selected, however, one last effort was made to revive the League of Nations. The Senate took up the Treaty of Versailles once again in March. The vote was on the treaty with reservations. On March 19 the treaty received forty-nine votes in favor and thirty-five against, seven short of the number needed to ratify it. Wilson had said that he would not approve the pact with reservations, but the vote showed that a compromise could have been reached. Wilson hoped that the election would be a "solemn referendum" on the treaty, but that did not happen. In the end a sick, stubborn president defeated his own dream.

The Republicans had expected that Theodore Roosevelt would be their nominee in 1920, but he died on January 6, 1919, of circulatory ailments and heart problems. Several contenders emerged for the Republican nomination, including General Leonard Wood and Governor Frank O. Lowden of Illinois. When they deadlocked at the national convention, the Re-

publicans turned to Senator Warren G. Harding of Ohio, the second choice of most of the delegates. To run with him, the convention named Governor Calvin Coolidge of Massachusetts. Harding emphasized a return to older values, which he labeled "normalcy." He called for "not heroics, but healing." Starting out with an old-style front porch campaign, he later began "stumping" in the modern fashion, giving speeches around the country. Harding looked distinguished and presidential; only insiders knew that he had been unfaithful to his wife and possessed what Wilson called "a bungalow mind."

For the Democrats, Attorney General Palmer and the secretary of the Treasury, William G. McAdoo, became the frontrunners. They, too, stalemated at the convention. The nominee was Governor James M. Cox of Ohio, a moderate progressive from the party's anti-prohibitionist wing, and his running mate was Franklin D. Roosevelt of New York. The Democratic candidates supported the League of

Nations; the Republicans generally dodged the subject until the end of the campaign when Harding advocated rejection of the treaty. The issue did not have much effect. Voters wanted to turn the Democrats out of office and repudiate Wilsonian ideals. They did so in a landslide. Harding received 16 million votes to 9 million for Cox; the margin in the electoral college was 404 for the Republicans to 127 for the Democrats.

CONCLUSION

With the election of the conservative Harding, the era of progressive reform ended. The voters associated reform and uplift with big government, high taxes, and intrusion into their private lives. For a time they wanted no more of such programs. Disillusioned by the outcome of the war and the upheaval of 1917–1919, Americans longed for quiet and conservatism.

The legacy of progressivism was a stronger presidency, a larger national government, and a weakened party system. The regulatory machinery to oversee business was still in place if a future president wished to use it. Progressives had addressed many serious issues—child labor, working conditions for men and women laborers, the plight of the unemployed. They had improved the quality of politics and opened up the system to middle-class citizens. Woman suffrage had been achieved, and the experiment of Prohibition was underway. However, reformers had done less for African Americans, Hispanics, immigrants, and Native Americans. Despite the excesses of the war, the United States was a more humane and just nation in 1920 than it had been in 1901.

RECOMMENDED READINGS

Ambrosius, Lloyd. *Woodrow Wilson and the American Diplomatic Tradition: The Treaty Fight in Perspective* (1987) reviews the battle over the League of Nations.

Coffman, Edward M. *The War to End All Wars: The American Military Experience in World War I* (1968) is good on the military aspects of the war.

Crosby, Alfred. *America's Forgotten Pandemic: The Influenza of 1918* (1989) looks at the impact of the disease that swept the world.

Ferrell, Robert H. *Woodrow Wilson and World War I, 1917–1921* (1985) is an insightful and informed treatment of American participation in the conflict.

Graham, Sally Hunter. *Woman Suffrage and the New Democracy* (1996) describes how women obtained the vote during World War I and afterward.

Gregory, Ross. *The Origins of American Intervention in the First World War* (1977) is a solid brief account of the neutrality period.

Kennedy, David M. *Over Here: The First World War and American Society* (1980) is a thoughtful treatment of important domestic issues.

Livermore, Seward. *Politics Is Adjourned: Woodrow Wilson and the War Congress, 1916–1918* (1966) reveals why the Democratic coalition collapsed after 1916.

Schaffer, Ronald. *America in the Great War: The Rise of the War Welfare State* (1991) is informative about woman suffrage and race.

Trotter, Joe William, ed., *The Great Migration in Historical Perspective* (1991) is an excellent collection of essays about the movement of African Americans to northern cities.

Politics and Reform
Burner, David. *The Politics of Provincialism: The Democratic Party in Transition, 1918–1932* (1968).

Clements, Kendrick. *The Presidency of Woodrow Wilson* (1992).

Gould, Lewis L. *Reform and Regulation: American Politics from Roosevelt to Wilson* (1996).

Kerr, K. Austin. *Organized for Prohibition: A New History of the Anti-Saloon League* (1985).

Lunardini, Christine A. *From Equal Suffrage to Equal Rights: Alice Paul and the National Woman's Party, 1910-–1928* (1986).

American Neutrality and Intervention
Devlin, Patrick. *Too Proud to Fight: Woodrow Wilson's Neutrality* (1974).

Link, Arthur S. *Wilson, IV: Confusions and Crises, 1915–1916* (1964).

Link, Arthur S. *Wilson, V: Campaigns for Progressivism and Peace, 1916–1917* (1965).

May, Ernest R. *The World War and American Isolation, 1914–1917* (1959).

Smith, Daniel. *The Great Departure: The United States and World War 1914–1920* (1965).

The Home Front During World War I
Connor, Valerie Jean. *The National War Labor Board: Stability, Social Justice, and the Voluntary State in World War I* (1983).

Cuff, Robert D. *The War Industries Board: Business Government Relations During World War I* (1973).

Jensen, Joan M. *The Price of Vigilance* (1968).

Murphy, Paul L. *World War I and the Origins of Civil Liberties in the United States* (1980).

Tuttle, William H. *Race Riot: Chicago in the Red Summer of 1919* (1970).

The Fight over the League of Nations

Floto, Inga. *Colonial House in Paris: A Study of American Policy at the Paris Peace Conference, 1919* (1980).

Margulies, Herbert F. *The Mild Reservationists and the League of Nations Controversy* (1989).

Stone, Ralph. *The Irreconcilables: The Fight Against the League of Nations* (1970).

Weinstein, Edwin A. *Woodrow Wilson: A Medical and Psychological Biography* (1981).

Widenor, William C. *Henry Cabot Lodge and the Search for an American Foreign Policy* (1980).

Art, Society and Culture During World War I

Chesler, Ellen. *Woman of Valor: Margaret Sanger and the Birth Control Movement in America* (1992).

Lewis, David Levering. *W.E.B. DuBois: Biography of a Race, 1868–1919* (1993).

Maland, Charles J. *Chaplin and American Culture* (1989).

May, Henry F. *The End of American Innocence: A Study of the First Years of Our Own Time, 1912–1917* (1959).

Schickel, Richard. *His Picture in the Papers* (1973).

THE SHAME OF AMERICA

Do you know that the Underlined United States is
the Only Land on Earth where human
beings are BURNED AT THE STAKE?

In Four Years, 1918-1921, Twenty-Eight People Were Publicly
BURNED BY AMERICAN MOBS

3436 People Lynched 1889 to 1922

For What Crimes Have Mobs Nullified Government and Inflicted the Death Penalty?

The Alleged Crimes	The Victims	Why Some Mob Victims Died:
Murder	1288	Not turning out of road for white boy in auto
Rape	571	Being a relative of a person who was lynched
Crimes against the Person	615	Jumping a labor contract
Crimes against Property	333	Being a member of the Non-Partisan League
Miscellaneous Crimes	453	"Talking back" to a white man
Absence of Crime	176	"Insulting" white man.
	3436	

Is Rape the "Cause" of Lynching?

Of 3,436 people murdered by mobs in our country, only 571, or less than 17 per cent, were even accused of the crime of rape.

83 WOMEN HAVE BEEN LYNCHED IN THE UNITED STATES

Do lynchers maintain that they were lynched for "the usual crime"?

AND THE LYNCHERS GO UNPUNISHED

THE REMEDY

The Dyer Anti-Lynching Bill Is Now Before the United States Senate

The Dyer Anti-Lynching Bill was passed on January 26, 1922, by a vote of 230 to 119 in the House of Representatives

The Dyer Anti-Lynching Bill Provides:
That culpable State officers and mobbists shall be tried in Federal Courts on failure of State courts to act, and that a county in which a lynching occurs shall be fined $10,000, recoverable in a Federal Court.

The Principal Question Raised Against the Bill is upon the Ground of Constitutionality.

The Constitutionality of the Dyer Bill Has Been Affirmed by --
The Judiciary Committee of the House of Representatives
The Judiciary Committee of the Senate
The United States Attorney General, legal adviser of Congress
Judge Guy D. Goff, of the Department of Justice

The Senate has been petitioned to pass the Dyer Bill by --
29 Lawyers and Jurists, including two former Attorneys General of the United States
19 State Supreme Court Justices
24 State Governors
3 Archbishops, 85 bishops and prominent churchmen
39 Mayors of large cities, north and south.

The American Bar Association at its meeting in San Francisco, August 9, 1922, adopted a resolution asking for further legislation by Congress to punish and prevent lynching and mob violence.

Fifteen State Conventions of 1922 (3 of them Democratic) have inserted in their party platforms a demand for national action to stamp out lynchings.

The Dyer Anti-Lynching Bill is not intended to protect the guilty, but to assure to every person accused of crime trial by due process of law.

THE DYER ANTI-LYNCHING BILL IS NOW BEFORE THE SENATE
TELEGRAPH YOUR SENATORS TODAY YOU WANT IT ENACTED

If you want to help the organization which has brought to light the facts about lynching, the organization which is fighting for 100 per cent. Americanism, not for some of the people some of the time, but for all of the people, white or black, all of the time

Send your check to J. E. SPINGARN, Treasurer of the

NATIONAL ASSOCIATION FOR THE ADVANCEMENT OF COLORED PEOPLE
70 FIFTH AVENUE, NEW YORK CITY

THIS ADVERTISEMENT IS PAID FOR IN PART BY THE ANTI-LYNCHING CRUSADERS.

THE ANTI-LYNCHING CAMPAIGN OF THE 1920S MAKES A PUBLIC APPEAL

This poster that the National Association for the Advancement of Colored People issued in 1922 to support the anti-lynching bill recounts that 3,436 people were killed in this way since 1889.

Chapter 23

THE AGE OF JAZZ AND

MASS CULTURE

1921-1927

DURING THE 1920s the United States became modern, both as a nation and as a culture. The automobile and other technological developments reshaped the economy and society. As the country became more urban, cosmopolitan, and uniform, the shared experiences of Americans made the nation more cohesive. Social attitudes toward sex and family life moved away from the restraints of the late nineteenth century. Movies, radio, and big-time sports shaped everyday existence. Young people emerged as a distinct group; their likes and dislikes became a focus of popular controversy. Advertising made public relations a significant characteristic of the period.

After a postwar depression, the economy rebounded from 1922 to 1927. The Republican administrations of Warren G. Harding and Calvin Coolidge lowered income taxes and encouraged private enterprise. Issues of culture and morality shaped politics more than questions of economic reform. Prohibition and the Ku Klux Klan split the Democrats.

In foreign affairs, the decade was officially a time of isolation in the wake of the rejection of the League of Nations in 1919–1920. Although involvement in world affairs increased more slowly after 1921, the United States maintained a significant stake in the postwar European and Asian economies. However, the nation's stated policies and the actual course of events often moved in contradictory directions.

THE AFTERMATH OF WAR

When Warren G. Harding took the oath of office as president on March 4, 1921, the United States had passed through two and a half difficult years since the end of the First World War. The social unrest and political ferment reflected an uneasy nation. Harding's calls for "normalcy" and healing proved effective during the 1920 election because they tapped voters' anxiety about the widespread rejection of older values and customs that occurred in the postwar years.

A More Urban Nation

The Census of 1920 gave one important indicator of the country's new course. For the first time, the government reported that more Americans lived in towns and cities with 2,500 or more residents than in the countryside. The small-town and rural experience still

CHRONOLOGY

1921   Warren G. Harding inaugurated as president

Immigration laws set quotas for Eastern and Southern Europeans

Sheppard-Towner Maternity and Infancy Protection Act passed

1922   Fordney-McCumber Tariff enacted

Sinclair Lewis's *Babbitt* published

Supreme Court rules minimum wage for women is unconstitutional in *Adkins* v. *Children's Hospital*

1923   Teapot Dome scandal

Time magazine starts publishing

Equal rights amendment drafted by Alice Paul

Death of Warren G. Harding

Calvin Coolidge becomes president

1924   Coolidge defeats John W. Davis in presidential election

Nellie Tayloe Ross (Wyoming) and Miriam Amanda Ferguson (Texas) become first elected women governors

1925   Decline of Ku Klux Klan

Scopes trial in Tennessee over teaching of evolution

Publication of F. Scott Fitzgerald's *The Great Gatsby*

1926   Publication of Ernest Hemingway, *The Sun Also Rises*

Gertrude Ederle becomes first woman to swim English Channel

1927   Charles Lindbergh flies the Atlantic alone

Sacco and Vanzetti executed

Babe Ruth hits sixty home runs

Henry Ford introduces Model A car

Calvin Coolidge announces "I do not choose to run" for President in 1928

dominated the lives of most citizens, but the trend toward urban residence was transforming the nation.

More than 10 million Americans resided in cities with a million people or more in 1920; that figure rose to more than 15 million by 1930. Such places as New York, Detroit, and Los Angeles saw large increases in their populations during these years. Some 19 million people left the country for the city over these ten years. The migration of African Americans from the South to the North continued unabated during this period. The percentage of blacks listed as urban residents rose by nearly 10 percent between 1920 and 1930, compared with a rise of about 5 percent for whites.

The growth of cities during these years produced tensions among Americans. For the young people who flocked to Chicago, New York, and Los Angeles, the city offered a degree of excitement and energy that the sedate farm could not match. Within the concrete canyons and electric avenues, a visitor found theaters, dance halls, and vaudeville artists that they could never hope to see in a small town. Many Americans resented the temptations of the city and associated them with foreign influences and assaults on traditional values. One flashpoint was the impact of a renewed surge of immigration.

Immigration Restricted

After the war immigration returned to its former pattern. Over 430,000 people sought entry to the United States in 1920, and another 805,000 came in 1921. In response, advocates of immigration restriction (see Chapter 22) renewed their campaign to shut off the flow of entrants from Southern and Eastern Europe. The wartime legislation that had required a literacy test for immigrants did not seem to be stemming the tide of new entrants.

Proponents of restriction argued that the immigrants lacked the qualities needed to be successful American citizens. "These people have not the same ideals and aspirations of Northern peoples," wrote the president of a Kiwanis Club in Tennessee. He added

that "among them the most revolting diseases are far more prevalent." Madison Grant, one of the leading advocates of immigration restriction, said that "these immigrants adopt the language of the [native-born] American, they wear his clothes, they steal his name, and they are beginning to take his women, but they seldom adopt his religion or understand his ideals."

The widespread tension about immigration played a significant part in the fate of Nicola Sacco and Bartolomeo Vanzetti who in June 1921 were on trial for a murder and robbery committed in Braintree, Massachusetts, a year earlier. One reporter who heard the evidence against them said privately, "It's an outrage that's being perpetrated here." There were allegations that authorities framed two Italians who believed in anarchism. In July both men were found guilty. Numerous appeals for a new trial were made, and the case soon became a focus for liberals and intellectuals convinced that Sacco and Vanzetti had not received a fair trial because of their foreign origin.

Immigration Quotas

The pressure on Congress grew. The American Federation of Labor, which feared the use of aliens as strikebreakers, added its weight to the campaign for immigration restrictions. In 1921 Congress enacted an emergency quota law that limited immigration from Europe to 600,000 people annually. Such countries as Great Britain and Germany were given the highest quotas. Three years later the lawmakers passed the National Origins Quota Act which reduced annual legal immigration from Europe to about 150,000 people, gave preference to entrants from northern European countries, and blocked Asian immigrants entirely. The quota of immigrants from each country was determined by the number of residents from these countries counted in the 1890 census. The sponsor of the law, Albert Johnson of Washington State, said that "the day of unalloyed welcome to all peoples, the day of indiscriminate acceptance of all races, has definitely ended."

New Patterns of Immigration

Despite their racist premises, the new laws did not end immigration during the 1920s. After 1924 the recorded number of immigrants totaled about 300,000 annually until the beginning of the Great Depression. However, the impact on people who wished to emigrate from Southern and Eastern Europe was dramatic. Some 95,000 immigrants had come into the United States from Poland in 1921; the annual total from that country was about 28,000 over the next three years.

Since the immigration law did not affect Mexicans, some half-million newcomers from that country crossed the border during the 1920s and swelled the ranks of Americans of Hispanic ancestry. Mexicans were concentrated in California and Texas.

The Ku Klux Klan

Urban-rural conflict dominated the 1920s. The pressures of immigration from abroad and the movement of Americans from the country to the city produced intense social strains. The most sensational and violent of these developments was the popularity of the Ku Klux Klan. Revitalized after 1915 in the South, the Klan gained followers slowly until the end of World War I. By 1920, the Klan had become a marketing device for some clever promoters who used the allure of the Klan's brew of racism, anti-Catholicism, and anti-immigrant views to acquire members at a rapid rate. The Klan claimed that it had 3 million members in the early 1920s. The masks and sheets members of the order wore provided an anonymity that attracted recruits in the southern countryside and in the cities of the Midwest where formerly rural residents had moved.

A secret ritual added to the mystique of the hooded movement. Members contributed a ten-dollar entrance fee, called a "klecktoken." They read the Kloran and dedicated themselves to "Karacter, Honor, Duty." In time they might rise to become a King Kleagle or a Grand Goblin of the Domain. Members asked each other "Ayak," for "Are you a Klansman?" The proper reply was "Akia," meaning "A Klansman I am."

The Klan's program embraced opposition to Catholics, Jews, blacks, violators of the Prohibition laws, and anyone else who displeased local Klansmen. In their rallies, marching members carried signs that read: "COHABITATION BETWEEN WHITES AND BLACKS MUST STOP." Even more than the Klan of the Reconstruction era, the Klan of the 1920s based its appeal on the desire of many white Americans for a more tranquil and less confusing social

CLAUDE MCKAY
If We Must Die!
1922

The First World War led many African Americans to resent their second-class status in the United States. Black artists and poets like Claude McKay expressed their feelings in verse. McKay's passionate affirmation of his sense of self captured the spirit that also expressed itself in the Harlem Renaissance and the campaign of Marcus Garvey.

If we must die, let it not be like hogs
   Hunted and penned in an inglorious spot,
While round us bark the mad and hungry dogs,
   Making their mock at our accursed lot.
If we must die, let it not be like hogs
   So that our precious blood may not be shed
In vain; then even the monster we defy
   Shall be constrained to honor us, though dead!

Oh kinsman! We must meet the common foe;
   Though far outnumbered, let us still be brave,
And for their thousand blows deal one deathblow!
   What though before us lies the open grave?
Like men we'll face the murderous, cowardly pack,
   Pressed to the wall, dying, but—fighting back!

order. The Klan's efforts to create such an order initially made it attractive to many citizens who never wore a hood. But the Klan also contained an ugly strain of violence and vigilantism. In many states its members lynched people they disagreed with; tortured blacks, Catholics, and Jews; and made a mockery of law enforcement.

Soon the Klan went into politics. In 1922 its members elected a senator in Texas and became a powerful presence in the legislatures of that state and others in the Southwest. In Indiana, the Klan was sufficiently strong that members of the order dominated the police of the state's major cities. The Klan also wielded significant influence in the Rocky Mountain states and the Pacific Northwest.

For the Democrats, the Klan posed a difficult problem. The party was already divided over cultural issues. Southern members favored Prohibition and disliked large cities. In the North. Democrats were ethnically

diverse, opposed to Prohibition, and rooted in the new urban lifestyles. The Klan intensified these tensions. Some "dry" Democrats saw the Klan as a legitimate form of political protest. The "wets" in northern cities regarded the Klan as an expression of cultural and regional intolerance. The Republicans benefited from this friction and intra-party bickering during the first half of the 1920s.

The Rise of Black Militance

The resurgence of the Klan came at a time when African Americans were asserting their identity and independence with greater energy. Black sacrifices during World War I had made them impatient and resentful of the indignities of a segregated society. In the wake of the race riots of 1919, a growing spirit of assertiveness and militancy appeared in the art and liter-

ature of black intellectuals. A poet named Claude McKay issued his rallying cry in 1922: "If we must die, let it not be like hogs / Hunted and penned in an inglorious spot." Instead, he concluded, "Like men we'll face the murderous cowardly pack / Pressed to the wall, dying, but fighting back."

For the African Americans who crowded into the large northern cities during the Great Migration, the promise of America seemed to be an illusion. They lived in substandard housing, paid higher rents for their apartments than whites did, and could obtain only menial jobs. The Harlem neighborhood of New York City might be "the greatest Negro city in the world," as author James Weldon Johnson called it, but it was also a place where every day blacks saw how white society marginalized them.

Marcus Garvey and Black Nationalism

A new idea caught the attention of African Americans during the postwar years. In 1916 a Jamaican named Marcus Garvey immigrated to the United States. Garvey preached a doctrine of Pan-Africanism and promised to "organize the 400,000,000 Negroes of the World into a vast organization to plant the banner of freedom in the great continent of Africa." He worked through the United Negro Improvement Association (UNIA) to establish societies that were not controlled by imperialist nations. He founded his campaign on international shipping lines and newspapers that would enable blacks to travel to Africa and communicate among themselves. Rallies and conventions in New York and other cities drew up to 25,000 people and raised funds for the UNIA.

Garvey's business ventures failed. The shipping lines collapsed and the investors, mostly African Americans, lost their money. Blacks were divided in their views of the charismatic Garvey. The National Association for the Advancement of Colored People bristled when Garvey attacked its political agenda and met with a Klan leader. His criticisms of labor unions alienated key African-American leaders such as A. Phillip Randolph of the Brotherhood of Sleeping Car Porters. Black opponents sent damaging information about Garvey's finances to the Department of Justice and the government indicted him for mail fraud. He was convicted and went to prison in 1925. The important legacy of Garvey and the UNIA was the idea that urban blacks could band together to wield economic

Year	Estimated Consumption
	TABLE 23.1
	ESTIMATED ALCOHOL CONSUMPTION IN THE UNITED STATES, 1920–1930 (GALLONS PER CAPITA)
1920	n/a
1921	.54
1922	.91
1923	1.07
1924	1.05
1925	1.10
1926	1.18
1927	1.12
1928	1.18
1929	1.20
1930	1.06

TABLE 23.1

ESTIMATED ALCOHOL CONSUMPTION IN THE UNITED STATES, 1920–1930 (GALLONS PER CAPITA)

Year	Estimated Consumption
1920	n/a
1921	.54
1922	.91
1923	1.07
1924	1.05
1925	1.10
1926	1.18
1927	1.12
1928	1.18
1929	1.20
1930	1.06

Derived from Table in Joseph R. Gusfield, "Prohibition: The Impact of Political Utopianism," in John Braeman, Robert H. Bremner, and David Brody, eds., *Change and Continuity in Twentieth-Century America: The 1920s* (Columbus, Ohio: Ohio State University Press, 1968), p. 275.

and political power. That memory would stay with later organizations of African Americans in the cities.

Dry America: The First Phase

The enactment of the Volstead Law in 1919 marked the high tide of the movement to curb the use of alcohol in the United States. The initial impact of Prohibition on the lives of Americans achieved much of what its proponents had predicted. The national consumption of alcohol declined from about two gallons per capita annually to around three-fourths of a gallon in 1921 and 1922. Alcoholism as a medical problem became less prevalent. Many hospitals closed their alcoholism wards because of a lack of patients. States with mainly rural populations witnessed a virtual disappearance of alcoholic beverages. Contrary to later legend, Prohibition did change drinking habits in the United States.

Two of the leading Prohibition agents, Izzy Einstein and Moe Smith, in disguise before a raid to uncover illegal alcohol production.

Yet substantial opposition to this cultural reform persisted. The extent of compliance with Prohibition was spotty from the time the Volstead Law was passed. Some people made their own liquor; instructions for doing so were easily obtained. In cities like San Francisco and Boston, centers of "wet" sentiment, the law was never enforced. Several states did not even ratify the Eighteenth Amendment. Others failed to pass state laws to support the federal legislation. Believing that compliance ought to be voluntary, Congress appropriated inadequate funds to the Treasury Department's Prohibition Bureau. While some agents, such as Izzy Einstein and Moe Smith, gained fame for the clever disguises they used to trap violators, there were never enough federal men to cover the nation adequately. Even when agents acted decisively, the rising number of arrests led to huge backlogs in the federal court system.

The upper classes expected the working poor to obey the Prohibition law, but they resisted any change in their own drinking practices. With a ready market for illegal liquor in the major cities, enterprising individuals moved alcohol across the border into the United States. These "rum runners" and "bootleggers" brought in shipments of alcohol from Canada and the Caribbean. Their wares were sold at illegal saloons or "speakeasies" where city dwellers congregated in the evenings. Some speakeasy owners became nationally famous. Mary Louise "Texas" Guinan ran the Club El Fey in New York City, greeting customers with the cry: "Hello, Sucker!"

Contrary to stereotypes, however, Prohibition did not create organized crime. Neither were the 1920s a decade of rising crime rates. The nation became more aware of crime as a social problem, because of the well-publicized activities of gangsters like Alphonse "Al" Capone and Johnny Torrio in Chicago. Prohibition offered individuals already involved in crime another incentive to band together and tap the immense profits to be had from easing the thirst of upper-class Americans. Capone in particular devoted himself to gaining control of gambling, prostitution, and bootlegging in the Chicago area. In New York, other mobsters built up networks of criminal enterprises to provide the same services. These sensational cases undermined faith in the positive effects of Prohibition. The Klan, immigration restriction, and Prohibition reflected the power of older cultural values. Yet they contained within themselves elements that would produce resistance as the decade progressed.

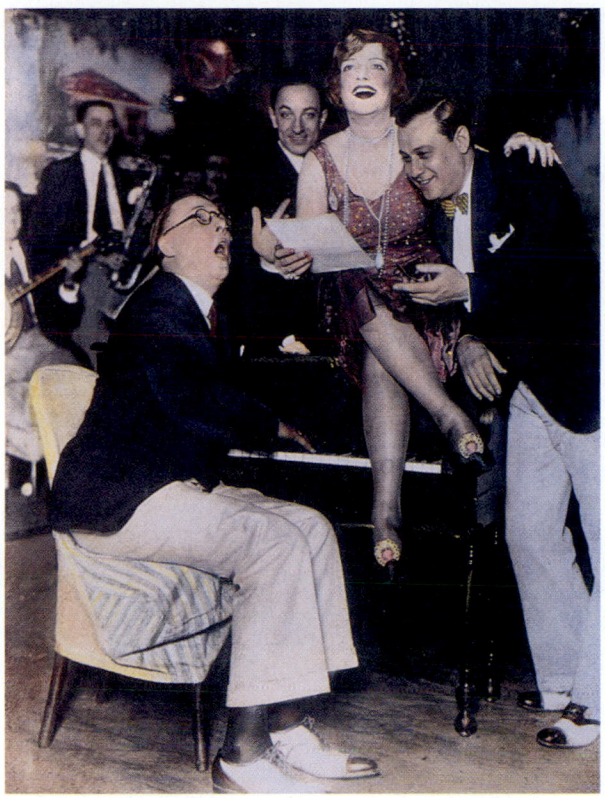

Happy customers celebrate in a speakeasy with Texas Guinan who greeted each patron with the cheery cry: "Hello, Sucker!"

HARDING AS PRESIDENT

Because of the scandals associated with his administration, Warren G. Harding is often depicted as the worst president in American history. During his brief term, however, he was very popular. He came to the White House from Marion, Ohio, where he had been a newspaper publisher in that small town before being elected to the Senate in 1914. A friend recalled that "His distinguished, dark waxen face, his conventional clothes, his modest dignity, made him the conventional American, a country man, never urban." His kindly nature impelled him to issue pardons to those whom the government had imprisoned for their beliefs during the war.

Harding also displayed a strong ambitious streak. He sought the presidency, and positioned himself in 1920 as the logical second choice when other candidates deadlocked at the Republican National Convention. His campaign against the Democrats was shrewdly waged. When he promised to restore older values of the nation, he evoked resentment against an intrusive, expensive federal government that the voters associated with Wilson and the Democrats.

Harding worked hard as president. He sought to surround himself with what he called the "Best Minds," and his selection of Charles Evans Hughes as his secretary of State, banker Andrew Mellon as secretary of the Treasury, and Herbert Hoover as secretary of Commerce were cited as evidence of that commitment. After years in which the presidency had seemed separated from the people, Harding and his wife Florence opened up the White House and greeted visitors with evident pleasure. Throughout the country Harding was a well-regarded president whose speeches appealed to a desire for a calmer, less activist chief executive. During his first year in office the economy remained weak, but a rebound in 1922 added to the president's standing with the people.

During its first two years, the administration pressed for a legislative program that combined some constructive reforms with a return to older Republican trade policies. The 1921 Budget and Accounting Act gave the government a more precise sense of how the nation's funds were being spent. It established an executive budget for the president, a General Accounting Office for Congress, and a Bureau of the Budget in the executive branch. The Republicans rebuilt tariff protection in an emergency law of 1921 and then wrote the Fordney-McCumber Tariff Law a year later. Reflecting the party's suspicion of a powerful national government, Treasury Secretary Mellon pushed for lower income tax rates, particularly for individuals with higher incomes.

Harding and the World

In foreign relations, the Harding administration stayed aloof from the League of Nations. A separate peace with Germany in 1921 officially ended the nation's role in World War I. Throughout the 1920s Washington withheld recognition from the new Soviet Union that grew out of the Communist victories in Russia. American interests turned back toward Latin America. To reduce the nation's military role in the region, the administration withdrew marines from Haiti, the Dominican Republic, and Nicaragua. Trade and investment expanded south of the border.

MAP 23.1 | AMERICAN COMMITMENTS IN THE CARIBBEAN

Relations with Japan claimed a large amount of attention as Japan expanded its power in China. The United States wanted to preserve the Open Door policy (see Chapter 20) and restrain the Japanese influence in Asia. Military action against Japan was politically impossible, and beyond the nation's power. Instead, the White House relied on diplomacy and economic pressure as its main weapons. Both nations were, however, increasing the size of their navies at this time. Budget limitations in both countries made a negotiated agreement on naval power a wise alternative. Congress and the administration concluded that a conference in which representatives of Great Britain, Japan, and the United States would meet to discuss naval issues and peace in the Far East was a logical move. The United States and Great Britain arranged for such a meeting in Washington in November 1921.

The Washington Conference and Beyond

The Washington Naval Conference of 1921 began with a dramatic proposal by Secretary of State Hughes.

He said that sixty battleships should be scrapped outright. Limits should also be placed on the number of battleships and aircraft carriers that Japan, the United States, and Britain could build in the future. Out of the conference came the Five Power Treaty, which provided a fixed ratio for warship construction. For every five ships the United States built, the British could also build five, and the Japanese could build three. The Japanese were not happy with the 5-5-3 arrangement, but in return they secured an American pledge not to construct defenses in such U.S. possessions as Guam and the Philippines. For the time, the naval arms race in the Pacific slowed.

The Washington Conference also resulted in two other pacts—the Four Power Treaty and the Nine Power Treaty. The Four Power Treaty ended a long-standing alliance (since 1902) between Great Britain and France, and committed the United States, France, Great Britain, and Japan to respect each country's territorial possessions. In the Nine Power Treaty, the various nations agreed to avoid interference with China's internal affairs. As a whole, the Washington Conference represented a victory for the United States. It

achieved much without having to make commitments that entailed the risk of force or greater international involvement. The happy combination of events that led to this success, however, would fade at the end of the decade as the world became more dangerous.

THE NEW ECONOMY

The continuing postwar recession dogged the first two years of the Harding administration. Hard times contributed to substantial Republican losses in the 1922 congressional elections. The Democrats gained seventy-four seats in the House and six in the Senate. Yet the long-range news proved beneficial for Republicans. The economy slowly picked up in 1922 and 1923, productive output returned to its 1918 levels, and employment rose. As wages climbed, discontent ebbed and the Republicans looked forward to the 1924 presidential election with greater optimism.

Prosperity and Its Benefits

The improvement in the economy's performance of the economy during 1922 began a period of unprecedented prosperity. The gross national product soared almost 40 percent, increasing from nearly $76 billion in 1922 to $97.3 billion in 1927. The per capita income of Americans went up about 30 percent during the same period. Real earnings for wage workers rose over 20 percent, while hours worked declined slightly. The unemployment rate fell from 12 percent of the labor force in 1922 to 4 percent in 1927. In that year a government panel reviewed these economic changes and concluded that "we seem only to have touched the fringe of our potentialities."

The Car Culture

The growth of automobile manufacturing represented one of the most significant changes in the industrial sector. The use of cars became widespread during the postwar years. The number of cars registered in 1920 totaled 8.25 million while the number of trucks was 1.1 million. By 1927 there were more than 20 million cars on the roads along with more than 3 million trucks and buses. When asked what was changing the United States, a Midwestern man replied, "I can tell you what's happening in just four letters A-U-T-O."

The impact of the automobile rippled through the economy. Automobiles needed oil and gasoline to operate, steel for their frames, rubber for their tires, glass for windshields, and service businesses for dealers and drivers. For the traveler on the road, motels offered accommodations, billboards advertised attractions, and roadside restaurants provided food and diversion. The Federal Highways Act of 1921 left road construction to the states, but set national standards for concrete road surfaces and access to roads. The size of the road network grew from 7,000 miles at the end of the war to 50,000 miles in 1927. Gasoline taxes brought in revenues for the states, enabling them to build more roads which, in turn, fostered the development of suburbs distant from the old city centers. Traffic lights, first used in New York City, were soon taken up in Boston, and eventually spread across the country.

The automobile had cultural effects too. No longer did young women and men have to carry on courtship within sight of parents and chaperones. When fathers urged their daughters not to go out driving with boys, the young women replied: "What on earth do you want me to do? Just sit around all evening?" Family excursions were tied to the availability of the car. Cars consumed a large chunk of the working family's income as Americans readily took to the practice of

TABLE 23.2 AUTOMOBILE REGISTRATIONS, 1921–1929	
1921	9,212,158
1922	10,704,076
1923	13,253,019
1924	15,436,102
1925	17,481,001
1926	19,267,967
1927	20,193,333
1928	21,362,240
1929	23,120,897

(SOURCE: *The Statistical History of the United States*, New York: Fairfield Press, 1965, p. 462)

buying their cars on the installment plan. For many African Americans in the South, owning a car gave them at least some mobility and escape from a segregated life. The enclosed car, initially a prestigious model, soon became standard on the road; by 1927, 83 percent of cars were of this type. Freedom and "automobility" were the watchwords of the day.

Henry Ford Gives Way to General Motors

As the decade began, Henry Ford was still the most famous car maker in the nation. His showplace was the huge factory on the Rouge River near Detroit that he had begun building in 1915. Sprawling across 2,000 acres, the Rouge plant eventually employed 75,000 workers to turn out the reliable, familiar, Model T car on which Ford based his automobile empire. In 1921, Ford made more than half of the automobiles produced in the United States, turning out a new vehicle

The automobile shaped the customs and style of the 1920s. An advertisement conveys some of the opulence and aristocratic appeal of the Pierce-Arrow car.

every ten seconds. A car cost under $300. Visitors marveled at Ford's organizational genius. "Fordism" summed up the impact of mass production on the nation. At the same time, however, the car maker deployed his vast wealth to promote his own political ambitions and crude anti-Semitism.

The Model T was a popular car but not a very attractive one. The joke was that you could get a Model T in any color, so long as it was black. Ford's failure to develop different car models opened a competitive opportunity to General Motors (GM). Although GM had been in severe financial difficulty in 1920, the DuPont family acquired the firm as an investment opportunity. They brought in Alfred P. Sloan, Jr. as chief assistant to the president. In 1923, he became president. Sloan set up a system of independent operating divisions that produced models of Chevrolets, Buicks, and other vehicles annually. GM introduced self-starters, fuel gauges, reliable headlights, and other features that consumers liked. The constant flow of new models induced customers to want a fresh vehicle every few years. The General Motors Acceptance Corporation made it easy to acquire a car on the installment plan.

By the middle of the 1920s, Ford's sales fell as those of General Motors rose. Ford dealers switched to General Motors while the used-car market undercut Ford at the other end of the price scale. Henry Ford had revolutionized American transportation before 1920. Now he was losing out because of his resistance to marketing and manufacturing innovation.

Electrical America

Increased reliance on electricity in the workplace and the home was another key element in the nation's industrial growth during the 1920s. By 1928 electricity drove 70 percent of factory equipment. Two thirds of the families in towns and cities had electricity in their homes as well, stimulating demand for the electrical appliances that industry was turning out in abundance. Homemakers bought some 15 million electric irons and another 7 million vacuum cleaners. Advertisers appealed to women with descriptions of the all-electric kitchen "Where Work is Easy!" Sales of consumer appliances were one of the major economic stimulants of the decade. The electric power industry expanded rapidly, as did the firms that made equipment for the power plants.

The incomparable Super-Heterodyne in a *custom-built* model

RADIOLA 30A
Custom-built,
Complete
with Radiotrons
$495

—simplified socket-power operation

Radio engineers all recognize the Super-Heterodyne as the finest achievement in radio receiver design.

In response to the demand for de luxe models of the RCA Super-Heterodyne — with the convenience and efficiency of operation from the electric light socket (without batteries or liquid-containing devices) — RCA offers the new custom-built Radiola 30A. This cabinet receiver, because of its extreme selectivity, is ideally adapted for use in the congested broadcasting areas.

Each instrument (with the self-contained RCA Loud-speaker) has been hand-built and individually tested.

RADIO CORPORATION OF AMERICA
New York   Chicago   San Francisco

RCA Radiola
MADE BY THE MAKERS OF THE RADIOTRON

Authorized
Dealer
RCA
Buy with confi-
dence where you
see this sign

The spread of mass entertainment through radio made the 1920s the first decade when Americans could experience simultaneously the same programs and stars. Radios became elaborate products as this expensive model, complete with "radiotrons" for $495, reveals.

The diffusion of electricity facilitated the growth of radio. The first station, KDKA in Pittsburgh, went on the air in 1920. After that the number of stations grew rapidly. There were only four in 1922; a year later 566 were in operation. In 1923 a New York station, WBAY, began selling time to anyone who would pay for it. Commercial radio caught on quickly. Soon announcers and performers became popular attractions. Listeners wrote to them for advice about love affairs and to praise the human contact that radios provided. In 1923, there were radios in 400,000 households.

Three years later the Radio Corporation of America (RCA), led by its president David Sarnoff, established the first national network of stations, the National Broadcasting Company (NBC). Telephone wires carried the broadcast signals to stations scattered across the country. NBC consisted of two networks, the "red" and the "blue." Programming was diverse, and commercial sponsors oversaw the content of such programs as "The Maxwell House Hour" and the "Ipana Troubadours." Radio further advanced the movement of the 1920s toward a standard culture for the whole nation.

Movies in the Silent Era

The motion picture quickly became the most celebrated form of popular entertainment during the decade. Each week 100 million people went to see movies at one of the 20,000 theaters that showed silent pictures. Some movie houses were plain and functional. Others featured expensive lobbies and plush furniture. The Roxy Theater in New York City was dubbed the "Cathedral of the Motion Picture." Ticket prices were relatively low and stable, usually about fifty cents. As one college student recalled, "You learn plenty about love from the movies." Pictures shaped how young people kissed on dates, what they wore, and what they said. "I cling to my dream world woven about the movies I have seen," said another student.

The movies marketed dreams, but they were also a substantial business. From their uncertain beginnings at the turn of the century, motion picture studios had developed into large enterprises employing hundreds of people. They worked in Hollywood, California, because of its mild climate and the proximity of deserts, seashores, and open spaces for location shooting. Studio heads like Adolph Zukor of Paramount Pictures and Louis B. Mayer of Metro-Goldwyn-Mayer (MGM) controlled chains of theaters, to which they allocated the pictures they made on a rigidly controlled basis. To get a popular feature film, theater owners would have to accept the entire yearly production of a major studio.

Motion picture stars were the bedrock of the business. Charlie Chaplin's popularity rose to even greater heights during the early 1920s in such films as *The Gold Rush* (1925). Other box-office attractions were Rudolph Valentino, whose sudden death in 1926 brought thousands of weeping fans, in a line stretching for eight city blocks, to his New York funeral.

Exotic themes and portraying a sexy hero such as The Son of the Sheik *made Rudolph Valentino a box office superstar before his untimely death.*

To maintain their hold on the popular mind, Hollywood reacted quickly when sexual scandals tarnished the industry's image early in the 1920s. Tales of wild parties and mysterious deaths tainted such stars as Roscoe "Fatty" Arbuckle and director William Desmond Taylor. The studios recruited Will H. Hays, a prominent Republican, to serve as president of the Motion Pictures Producers and Distributors Association in 1922. Hays tried to persuade filmmakers to inject more moral content into films. He relied on a series of "Don'ts and Be Carefuls" to guide producers and directors. Skillful directors such as Cecil B. deMille circumvented these mild warnings. He argued that the sexual scenes in *The Ten Commandments* were based on biblical descriptions. However, church groups and Congress continued to pressure the industry for "cleaner" films.

Advertising America

The economic growth of the 1920s rested on consumer spending. Advertisers developed new and effective ways to persuade Americans to acquire the products coming out of the nation's factories and workshops. The advertising business boomed. Before World War I, the total amount spent on advertising stood at about $400 million annually. It soared to $2.6 billion by 1929. Radios brought advertising into the home; billboards attracted the attention of millions of motorists. Advertising, said one of its practitioners, "literally creates demand for the things of life that raise the standard of living, elevate the taste, changing luxuries into necessities."

Among the products that advertising promoted were Listerine, which was said to eliminate halitosis, the medical term for bad breath. Cigarettes such as Lucky Strike were marketed as a means of achieving a slimmer figure; "reach for a Lucky instead of a sweet," said the ads. Other consumers were urged to ingest yeast at least twice a day to fight constipation and skin problems. The ingenious advertising executive Albert Lasker succeeded in inducing Americans to drink orange juice daily at breakfast, breaking the taboo against advertising the sanitary napkin Kotex, and describing Kleenex as "the handkerchief you can throw away." He also claimed Pepsodent toothpaste would remove "film" from the fortunate user's teeth. An advertiser, said one of them, had to recognize "the extreme mental incapacity of the vast majority of his audience."

The most celebrated advertising man of the decade was Bruce Barton, who wrote a biography of Jesus Christ in order to demonstrate that advertising went back to biblical times. In *The Man Nobody Knows* (1925), Barton retold the New Testament in terms that Americans of the 1920s could easily grasp. Jesus, wrote Barton, "recognized the basic principle that all good advertising is news." The twelve disciples were a model of an efficient business organization, and Jesus himself was a master salesman. "He was never trite or commonplace; he had no routine." Barton's book became a national bestseller. As long as the economy expanded, advertising prospered and fed the demand of consumers for products they had never known they needed.

Even farmers who did not use tractors during the 1920s had rich crops, all of which contributed to the falling prices and crop surpluses that plagued American agriculture during the decade.

Those Left Behind

The success of the consumer-related industries lifted the economy to new levels of prosperity after 1922. However, not all segments of society shared equally in the return of good times. The postwar depression hit the farm sector with devastating force. Farmers had never benefited from the upturn that marked the cities. For labor also, this was a time of retreat.

Despite the shift toward city living, the United States still relied on farming as a key element in the economy. The 7 million families who lived on farms in 1920 did not generally enjoy the modern conveniences and appliances that had appeared in the cities. In some areas farm life resembled that of the pioneers more than it did the city dwellers. Overproduction of crops drove down prices and led to massive harvests that could not be marketed. In the South, for example, the price of cotton was forty cents a pound in 1920 but slid to ten cents a pound in 1921. Wheat stood at $1.82 per bushel in 1920, sagged to $0.926 in 1924, and then recovered to $1.437 in 1925. The postwar recovery of agriculture in Europe meant that overseas markets were smaller as well. The per capita income of most farmers did not rise substantially after 1919, and there was a widening gap between what farmers earned and what city dwellers made.

To improve their lot, farmers sought higher tariff duties on imported products. They also revived the idea of farm cooperatives to market more effectively. In 1921 and 1922, farmers rallied behind the "Sapiro Plan," named after Aaron Sapiro, who wanted producers to hold goods off the market until prices rose. If it was to work, the scheme required close cooperation among farmers. When that did not occur, it collapsed. Federal legislation to regulate the trading of grain futures and extend more credit to farmers was marginally helpful, but the underlying problem of overproduction continued.

Another idea for dealing with the farm situation emerged in 1921. A plow manufacturer named George Peek proposed that American farmers ship surplus products overseas and dump them on the world market at whatever price they could obtain. The government would buy farm products at the market price

and then sell them abroad. Taxes on the processing of crops would cover the cost to the government and the taxpayer. The chairs of the House and Senate Agriculture Committees introduced a bill to enact such a program in January 1924. Known as the McNary-Haugen Plan, it gained much support in the Midwest and soon commanded national attention. Critics called it price-fixing at government expense. That farmers could turn to such a controversial notion illustrated how far American agriculture lagged behind the rest of the economy.

Labor in Retreat

While the 1920s were a boom time for American industry, they were an era of gloom and despair for organized labor. After World War I, the Red Scare of 1919–1920 stalled labor's drive to organize coal mining, steel, and other industries that employed thousands of unskilled workers. The number of unionized laborers dropped from nearly 5 million in 1921 to fewer than 3.5 million eight years later. The American Federation of Labor (AFL), under its president William Green, presented only weak challenges to employers. It accepted what management called "business unionism," or the nonunion "open shop" which was labeled the "American Plan." Efforts to organize unskilled workers were abandoned. The impotence of the labor unions limited their ability to improve the lot of women and men in the workplace.

Government and business threw up numerous obstacles to labor's interests. The U.S. Supreme Court struck down minimum wages for women in Washington, D.C. In the case of *Adkins* v. *Children's Hospital* (1923), the court ruled that the law infringed on the right of workers to sell their labor for whatever they could obtain. This "liberty-of-contract" doctrine accordingly barred Congress from passing such a law. In addition to an unsympathetic Supreme Court, unions faced opposition from the White House. When strikes occurred in railroading during 1922, the Harding administration obtained harsh court orders that effectively ended the walkouts.

Businesses used less repressive tactics as well. Some of the bigger and more enlightened firms provided what became known as *welfare capitalism.* General Electric, International Harvester, and Bethlehem Steel represented companies that sought to appease workers with recreational facilities, benefit plans, and some-

times even profit-sharing opportunities. Estimates indicated that as many as 4 million workers received such rewards. After the middle of the decade, however, these programs stalled as the lack of labor militancy removed the incentive to make concessions to workers. Most workers remained dependent on the goodwill of their employer for whatever job security they possessed.

The Harding Scandals

Warren G. Harding did not live to see the political benefits of the nation's better times and conservative mood. By early 1923 his presidency was mired in rumors of scandal. Harding's troubles arose from his appointments to key government posts. He had chosen the "best minds" for the more important positions in his cabinet. His other appointments, though, were mediocre or worse. Attorney General Harry Daugherty was a political ally of the president, but his loose direction of the Justice Department allowed corruption to flourish. Scandals also festered in the Veterans Bureau and the Office of the Alien Property Custodian.

The most serious wrongdoing involved the secretary of the Interior, Albert B. Fall. Federal oil reserves at Elk Hills, California, and Teapot Dome, Wyoming (where the rocks vaguely resembled a teapot), were leased to private oil companies. Fall received $400,000 in loans from friends in the industry in what many interpreted as payoffs for his leasing decisions. The Teapot Dome scandal emerged after Harding died, but it established his administration's reputation as one of the most corrupt in American history.

Harding was not implicated in any of these misdeeds. A weak president and a poor judge of people, he allowed cronies and crooks to infest his administration. By 1923, he knew about the ethical problems in the Veterans Bureau, and he suspected that scandals lurked in the Department of the Interior and the Justice Department. During the summer of that year, he told a friend that "this White House is a prison." To another associate, he said, "It is my friends who are giving me trouble." During a tour of the Pacific Northwest in July 1923, the president fell ill. He died in San Francisco on August 2 of heart disease. Theodore Roosevelt's daughter Alice said of the fallen president: "Harding was not a bad man; he was just a slob."

Keep Cool with Coolidge

Harding's successor was Calvin Coolidge, the former governor of Massachusetts who became Harding's running mate in 1920 after denouncing the Boston police strike of 1919 (see Chapter 22). Coolidge came to be viewed in Washington as a stereotypical New Englander, a man of few words. When a woman told him that she had bet her friends she could persuade him to say more than three words, Coolidge replied: "You lose." In fact, Coolidge was quite talkative in the regular press conferences that he held twice a week. Although he slept twelve hours a day, Coolidge was not a lazy man. He worked hard greeting visitors and addressing the needs of those who told him their problems with the federal government. Because he was unwilling to consult with Congress, his relations with Capitol Hill were cool and distant. His wife Grace brought glamour and a sense of fun to the White House, offsetting her husband's dour personality.

THE CASH REGISTER CHORUS.

President Calvin Coolidge said that business prosperity was the key to national success. The business community felt the same way. This satirical cartoon mocks the way in which the Republican served corporate America.

Coolidge was much more committed to the conservative principles of the Republicans than Harding had been. He sincerely believed that "the business of America is business," and he endorsed policies designed to promote corporate enterprise. He extended the tax-cutting policies of Treasury Secretary Mellon. The president also appointed pro-business individuals to head the regulatory agencies and departments that the progressives had established a generation earlier. Meanwhile, he removed the Harding holdovers, such as Harry Daugherty, who might prove politically embarrassing when he ran for the presidency in 1924.

Coolidge lost little time in gaining control of the Republican party. The GOP had no strong alternative to him, and Coolidge was easily nominated as the party's candidate at the national convention. The delegates selected Charles G. Dawes, an Illinois banker, as his running mate. The Republicans ran on a platform of conservative policies and popular approval of Coolidge. The president used modern public relations techniques to bolster his image as an embodiment of old-time virtues of morality and frugality. Movie stars came to the White House to endorse the president and, under the leadership of the stylish Grace Coolidge, sing the campaign theme song: "Keep Cool with Coolidge."

The Democrats hoped that the Teapot Dome scandal and other revelations of wrongdoing in the Harding years would be their ticket back to the White House. Unfortunately for them, the Teapot Dome scandal could not be linked to anyone in the White House. Without sensational disclosures, the investigations bored the public and eventually faded away. Several Democrats were revealed to have received money from the oil interests as well. They became "spattered with oil" in a way that ruled out use of the scandals as a weapon against the Republicans.

The Discordant Democrats

The larger problem for the Democrats was the cultural divide that separated the two wings of the party. The issue of Prohibition had split the party between the "dry" faithful of the South and West, who wanted strict enforcement of the Volstead Act, and the antiprohibitionist residents of the large cities of the North and Midwest, who saw Prohibition as a foolish experiment in cultural coercion.

The two leading candidates for the Democratic party nomination reflected this regional tension.

Coolidge cultivated a dour, New England demeanor to set himself apart from the excesses of the Harding years. His grim expression hides the playful spirit that liked to inflict practical jokes on his White House staff.

William G. McAdoo had been secretary of the treasury and Woodrow Wilson's son-in-law. Some party members styled him the "Crown Prince." He represented the progressive, prohibitionist Democrats of the nation's rural states. But his candidacy suffered when it became known that McAdoo had done legal work for some of the men involved in the Teapot Dome scandal. The other major contender was Governor Alfred E. Smith of New York. His administrations had proposed some social justice measures, but he opposed Prohibition. His Roman Catholicism evoked fear and bigotry in places where the Ku Klux Klan was still powerful.

Stalemate in New York

The Democratic National Convention at Madison Square Garden in New York City left the party with almost no chance of defeating President Coolidge. McAdoo and Smith were deadlocked through dozens of ballots. Finally, after 103 ballots, the exhausted delegates compromised and chose a former member of Congress and Wall Street lawyer named John W. Davis. His running mate was Charles Bryan, the brother of William Jennings Bryan. The ticket was safe, dull, and had little chance of victory. "What

Davis needs is a rabbit foot," wrote William Howard Taft.

A third candidate challenged the Republicans and Democrats. Senator Robert M. La Follette of Wisconsin, who had been seeking the presidency for many years, became the champion of what remained of the progressive spirit and the anger of the Midwestern farmers. His candidacy was largely personal. Although he was nominated for president at a convention of the Progressive party, he did not attend the meeting or identify himself with the party. Senator Burton K. Wheeler of Montana was La Follette's running mate. The American Federation of Labor and the railroad unions backed La Follette but with little money or enthusiasm.

The 1924 Election in Perspective

The Republicans ignored Davis and concentrated on the alleged radicalism of La Follette and his supporters. The choice, they said, was "Coolidge or Chaos." It was a dull campaign, and the outcome was never in doubt. Coolidge polled more than 15,718,000 votes, more than the combined total of Davis's 8,385,000 and La Follette's 4,831,000. The Republicans retained firm control of both houses of Congress. For the mo-

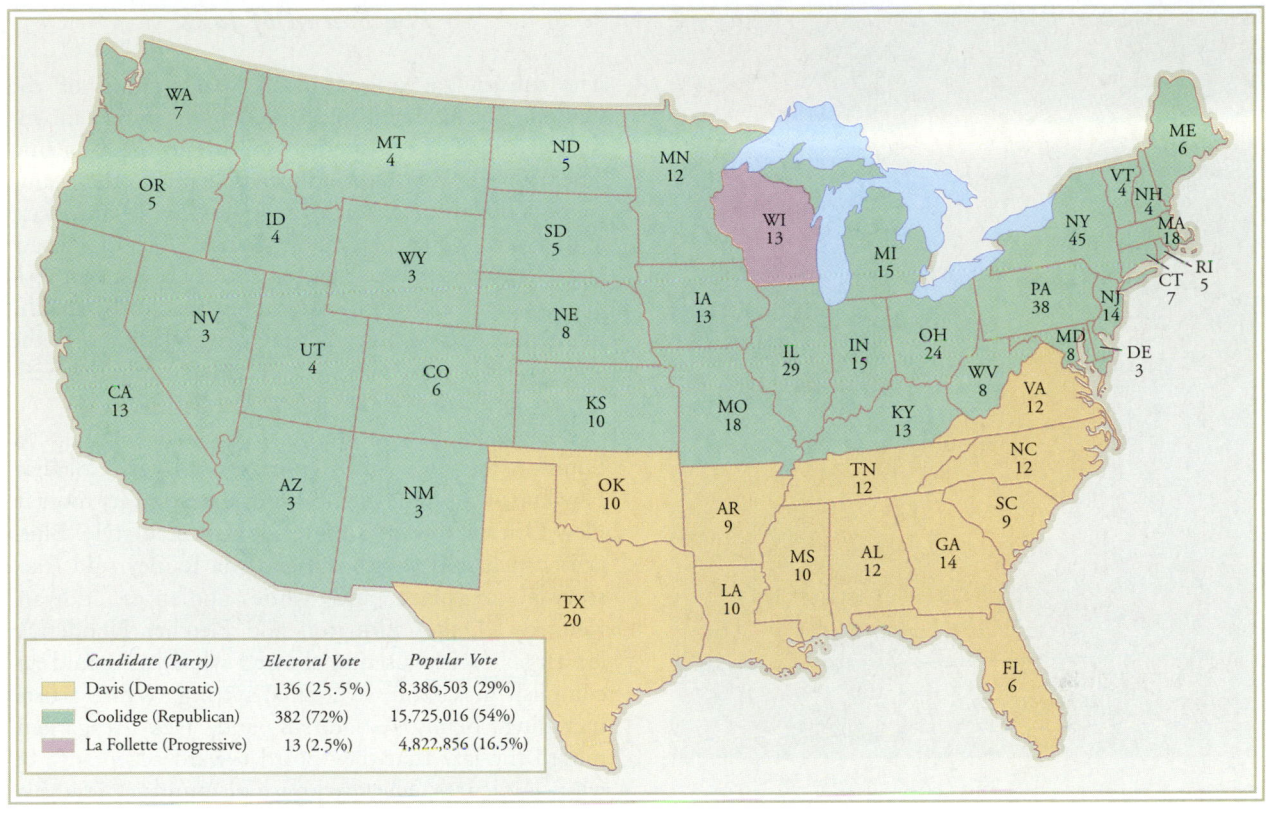

Candidate (Party)	Electoral Vote	Popular Vote
Davis (Democratic)	136 (25.5%)	8,386,503 (29%)
Coolidge (Republican)	382 (72%)	15,725,016 (54%)
La Follette (Progressive)	13 (2.5%)	4,822,856 (16.5%)

MAP 23.2 | THE ELECTION OF 1924

ment, it looked as if political reform was in disarray. Franklin D. Roosevelt commented that "The people will not turn out the Republicans while wages are good and markets are booming."

Yet beneath the surface, electoral trends were moving toward the Democrats. In the northern cities the party's share of the vote grew during the 1920s. If a candidate appeared who could unite the traditionally Democratic South with the ethnic voters of the Northeast, the Republicans' supremacy might be in jeopardy. For the moment, however, the country seemed solidly conservative.

A BLOSSOMING IN ART AND LITERATURE

While politics followed a conservative path during the 1920s, the nation's cultural life experienced a produc-

tivity and artistic success that would be unrivaled during the rest of the twentieth century. In music, drama, and literature, the decade brought forth a rare assembly of first-rate talents.

The Harlem Renaissance

Black writers made a notable contribution to this fruitful period. In the wake of the Great Migration, African-American intellectual life had become centered in New York City. There authors and poets lived in the black section known as Harlem. The "Harlem Renaissance" owed much to W. E. B. Du Bois's encouragement of African-American writing in the *Crisis,* the journal of the National Association for the Advancement of Colored People (NAACP). In the New York of the early 1920s, the ferment associated with Marcus Garvey, the exciting night life, the relative absence of racial bigotry, and the interest of wealthy white patrons enabled a few black writers to pursue

The Harlem Renaissance gave an opportunity for numerous black writers and poets to gain a larger audience than would have been possible even ten years earlier. One of them was the story writer and novelist Zora Neale Hurston who wrote about the African-American masses.

literary careers. Their moment of celebrity proved brief, but their impact significant.

The Harlem Renaissance reached its peak in 1925, when a national magazine ran an article on "Harlem: Mecca of the New Negro." In the same year, Alain Locke's book *The New Negro* was published. Locke argued that African Americans' "more immediate hope" depended on the ability of blacks and whites to evaluate "the Negro in terms of his artistic endowments and cultural contributions, past and prospective." Other major figures in the Renaissance were the poets Langston Hughes ("The Weary Blues"), Countee Cullen ("Do I Marvel"), Zora Neale Hurston (the play *Color Struck*), Claude McKay *(Harlem Shadows)*, as well as the memoirist and song-writer James Weldon Johnson *(God's Trombones)*. Although these writers' artistic merit was undeniable, the Harlem Renaissance did little to alter the segregationist laws and customs that restricted the lives of most African Americans.

The Sound of Jazz

The music that pulsed in the background of the Harlem Renaissance proved even more important for the development of American culture in the long run. After World War I, the improvised music that came to be called jazz brought together black musicians and a few white players in Kansas City, Chicago, and New York. At the rent parties where Harlem residents raised money to pay their landlords, in the nightclubs that organized crime controlled, and in the after-hours jam sessions, jazz became a unique American art form.

The major innovators of jazz included trumpeter Louis Armstrong and tenor sax player Coleman Hawkins, who took the new music beyond its roots in New Orleans toward a more sophisticated style. Blues artists such as Bessie Smith and Ma Rainey sold "race records" to black and white audiences. Edward Kennedy "Duke" Ellington and Fletcher Henderson led larger orchestras that showed what jazz could accomplish in a more structured setting. White artists, including Benny Goodman and Jack Teagarden, moved the jazz that they heard toward acceptance by white audiences. The rhythms and sounds of jazz gave the 1920s its enduring title: The Jazz Age. The worlds of white and black, though still separated by law and bigotry, interacted in subtle ways that would reshape American popular culture for decades to come.

In the familiar bastions of artistic activity, the 1920s brought further disruption and change. Writers looked at the postwar world in a critical spirit that grew out of the European ideas and a skepticism about older values. The most popular novelist of the early 1920s was Sinclair Lewis, whose books *Main Street* (1920) and *Babbitt* (1922) looked with unsparing honesty at small-town life in the Midwest. Lewis made a real estate agent (or "realtor") into the main figure of *Babbitt,* creating both a word and a type. His portrait of Babbitt and his fellow townspeople was gently satirical and overwhelmingly factual. His novels *Arrowsmith* (1925) and *Elmer Gantry* (1927) enhanced his reputation, but his artistic powers failed in the 1930s.

Young people devoured the work of an acidic essayist and social critic, Henry L. Mencken, who wrote for the *American Mercury.* Mencken was a Baltimore newspaperman who had little time for the sacred cows of middle-class culture or, as he called them, the "booboisie." He characterized democracy as "the

The Cotton Club in Harlem was the nightly center of the social scene of the Harlem Renaissance. The Cotton Club orchestra in 1925 entertained the white patrons who came up from Manhattan to sample the excitement of black music and culture.

worship of jackals by jackasses" and said that puritanism was "the haunting fear that somebody, somewhere may be happy." Aimed more at the middle-class audience was *Time,* started in March 1923 by Briton Hadden and Henry Luce. *Time* sought to present the week's news in readable and sprightly prose. *The New Yorker,* a sophisticated weekly, was headed by Harold Ross, who proudly proclaimed that the magazine was not intended for the "little old lady in Dubuque," Iowa. The best American writers and poets strove to have their works published in *The New Yorker.*

The most influential fiction author of the decade was Ernest Hemingway, whose terse, understated prose spoke of the pain and disillusion that men had suffered during the fighting in World War I. In *The Sun Also Rises* (1925) and *A Farewell to Arms* (1929), Hemingway expressed the anguish of young Americans who had lost faith in the moral customs of their parents. Hemingway's writing style was widely imitated, and he became an international celebrity for his hard-drinking lifestyle and cult of manly bravado.

Another serious novelist of the day was F. Scott Fitzgerald. Like Hemingway, he, along with his wife Zelda, captured attention as the embodiment of the free spirit of the Jazz Age. At the same time, Fitzgerald

was a dedicated artist who sought to write a great novel that would ensure his fame. In *The Great Gatsby* (1925), he came as close to that goal as any author of the time. The book chronicled how a young man, Jay Gatsby, sought to recapture a lost love among the aristocracy of the Long Island shore. In Gatsby's failure to win his dream, Fitzgerald saw the inability of Americans to escape the burdens of their own pasts. He offered a deeply critical portrait of the newly rich Americans who had gained wealth during the 1920s but found their lives still empty.

An Age of Artistic Achievement

The list of important authors during the 1920s was long and distinguished. It included such artistic innovators as T.S. Eliot, who lived in Great Britain and whose poems such as "The Waste Land" (1922) influenced a generation of poets on both sides of the Atlantic. Novelists such as John Dos Passos, Sherwood Anderson, Edith Wharton, Willa Cather, and William Faulkner produced a body of work that delved into the lives of aristocratic women (Wharton), prairie pioneers (Cather), the working poor and middle class

With his novel, The Great Gatsby *(1925), Fitzgerald became one of the chroniclers of the Jazz Age and one of its most celebrated figures. His work reflected his own ambivalence about the culture of the wealthy with whom he consorted. He is shown here with his wife Zelda, also a talented writer, and their daughter.*

(Dos Passos), the residents of small towns (Anderson), and the Deep South (Faulkner).

The theater witnessed the emergence of the Broadway musical in the work of Richard Rodgers and Lorenz Hart *(Garrick Gaities)*, George and Ira Gershwin *(Lady, Be Good)*, Jerome Kern and Oscar Hammerstein II *(Showboat)* and Cole Porter *(Paris)*. The great age of the American popular song, inspired by the musicals, began in the 1920s and lasted for three decades. Serious drama drew upon the talents of the brooding and pessimistic Eugene O'Neill as well as Elmer Rice and Maxwell Anderson.

In architecture, although the innovative work of Frank Lloyd Wright had given him a reputation for artistic daring before 1920, commercial success eluded him. American architects designed planned, suburban communities modeled on historical models from England or the Southwest. Skyscrapers and city centers such as Rockefeller Center in New York City embodied a building style that emphasized light and air. Amid the prosperity and optimism of the 1920s, it seemed that the possibilities for a lively and vibrant culture were limitless.

FUNDAMENTALISM AND TRADITIONAL VALUES

For most Americans the literary and artistic ferment of the 1920s was part of a broader set of challenges to the older lifestyles with which they had grown up. Residents of small towns and newcomers to the growing cities sought to find reassurance in the older ways that they fondly remembered. The currents of religious and social conservatism remained dominant. The Ku Klux Klan saw its political influence ebb because of popular disgust with its tactics, but an upsurge of evangelical Christianity underscored how deep the cultural divisions within the nation were.

The Klan in Decline

The Klan's influence peaked around 1923; after that its fortunes went into a slump. As it sought greater political power, the two major parties, especially the

Democrats, absorbed some of the Klan's appeal and weakened its hold on the public. In a key state such as Indiana, parts of the Klan's program, including reading the Bible daily in schools and restrictions on parochial schools, aroused fears that religious freedom might be at risk. Scandals also sapped the Klan's moral fervor. These public embarrassments revealed that the order's claims to moral purity rested on a weak foundation. In Indiana the Klan leader, David Stephenson, went to prison for the death of a woman he had assaulted. Faced with jail, he revealed the bribes he had offered to state officials. The tawdry mess broke the Klan's hold on Indiana and hastened its decline elsewhere in the nation.

The Continuing Controversy over Sacco and Vanzetti

Meanwhile. the ordeal of Sacco and Vanzetti in the Massachusetts legal system continued from 1921 to 1924 as their attorneys filed a series of appeals to overturn their 1921 conviction. The lawyers challenged the conduct of the jury, attacked the quality of the evidence against the two men, and questioned the identifications of the defendants that various witnesses had made. Intellectuals became more convinced that the prosecution had either framed Sacco and Vanzetti or railroaded them into prison.

None of this changed the mind of the presiding judge, and by October 1924, all motions for another trial had been denied. The two defendants had hired a new attorney, and a campaign for a new trial and their eventual release gained greater national attention during 1925 and 1926. Within Massachusetts, where animosity against immigrants still ran strong, the state government did not waver in its belief that Sacco and Vanzetti were guilty.

The Fundamentalist Movement

Amid the social ferment that accompanied the rise of the Ku Klux Klan, the tensions over nativism, and the reaction against modern ideas, American Protestantism engaged in a passionate debate over the proper position of Christians toward science, the doctrine of evolution, and liberal ideas. Conservative church leaders in northern Baptist and Presbyterian pulpits spoke of the dangers to faith from a society that had moved away from the Bible and its teachings. In 1920 a minister called the movement "Fundamentalism" because it sought to reaffirm precepts of the Christian creed such as the literal truth of the Bible and the central place of Jesus Christ in saving humanity.

Fundamentalism had a political and social agenda as well as a religious message. On the local and state levels, believers sought to eradicate traces of modern ideas that contradicted biblical teachings. "The Bible and the God of the Bible is our only hope," said one writer. The doctrine of evolution became a special target of fundamentalist wrath. William Jennings Bryan emerged as a leading champion of the crusade. "It is better to trust the Rock of Ages," he said, "than to know the age of rocks." In a dozen state legislatures, lawmakers introduced bills to ban the teaching of evolution in public schools. The Anti-Evolution League hoped to amend the Constitution to bar the teaching of evolution anywhere in the nation. In 1924 Tennessee passed a law that prohibited the spending of public money "to teach any theory that denies the story of the Divine Creation of man as taught in the Bible."

The Scopes Trial

In the following year a schoolteacher named John T. Scopes taught evolution in one of his classes in Dayton, Tennessee. The local authorities indicted Scopes, and his case came to trial. William Jennings Bryan agreed to help prosecute Scopes and the American Civil Liberties Union brought in the noted trial lawyer, Clarence Darrow, for the defense. The proceedings attracted national attention and the trial became a media circus. The judge refused to let Darrow call in scientists to defend evolution. Stores in Dayton sold pins that said "Your Old Man's a Monkey."

Darrow called Bryan as an expert witness on the Bible. The two men sparred for several days. Bryan defended the literal interpretation of the Bible, but to the reporters covering the trial he seemed to wither under Darrow's cross-examination. Sophisticated Americans regarded Bryan as a joke, but in rural American he remained a hero. The jury found Scopes guilty and assessed him a small fine. Bryan died shortly after the trial.

To many Americans the Scopes trial seemed to signal the end of fundamentalism, and the political side of the movement did lose momentum during the late

The Scopes Trial over the teaching of evolution resulted in a notorious legal confrontation between Clarence Darrow (left) and William Jennings Bryan. Many observers saw their duel as a symbol of the urban-rural tensions roiling the nation during the 1920s.

1920s. But during the same period fundamentalism returned to its roots. It concentrated on creating a network of churches, schools, and colleges where its doctrines could be taught to future generations. The forces underlying fundamentalism during the 1920s would remain a potent element in American culture.

Prohibition in Retreat

By the middle of the 1920s the Prohibition experiment was faltering. Enforcement and compliance waned. The spread of bootlegging and its ties with organized crime meant that state and federal authorities faced an ever-growing challenge in attempting to stop movement of illegal liquor across the Canadian border or from ships that gathered near major U.S. ports. The brewing and liquor interests called for a campaign to repeal the Eighteenth Amendment, and the Association Against the Prohibition Amendment became a strong lobbying force. Newspapers published recipes for making illegal booze, and Congressman Fiorello

LaGuardia of New York showed reporters how to turn "near beer," which had an alcohol content of less than .05 percent, into an alcoholic beverage.

Consumption of alcohol rose to over one gallon annually per capita by 1923 and reached almost one and one-quarter gallons three years later. With the national law on the books, the Anti-Saloon League lost some of its intensity during the 1920s. When the problems associated with drinking declined, its urgency as a social issue receded. The consensus that had brought Prohibition into existence during World War I was crumbling as the 1928 presidential election approached. As yet, however, a majority of Americans opposed outright repeal of Prohibition.

Flaming Youth

During the 1920s, changes in the family gave youth more importance than they had enjoyed ever before. Women stopped having children at a younger age, and they thus had more time to devote to their own inter-

ests. Divorce gained favor as a way of ending unhappy marriages; in 1924 one marriage in seven ended in divorce. The emphasis shifted to making marriages more fulfilling for both partners. Marriage counseling gained in popularity, as did manuals telling men and women how to achieve greater sexual gratification.

As the nature of marriage changed, the role of children in the household was also transformed. Parents were no longer regarded as the unquestioned rulers of the home. Children were expected to have opinions and express them freely. One major influence on how American children were raised was the work of the behavioral psychologist, John B. Watson. He taught that by manipulating the stimuli that a child experienced, the parents could create the kind of adult they wanted. Children, he said, "are made, not born." He instructed parents to follow a system of reward and punishment to shape the character of their offspring.

The ability of parents to decide what their children should read and think came under attack from the growing pervasiveness of the consumer culture. Young people were bombarded with alluring images of automobiles, makeup, motion pictures, and other attractions. Since children no longer were so important to the wage-earning power of the family, they were given greater freedom to spend their leisure time as they deemed best. A teenager might have four to six evenings a week to spend away from home. Adolescence came to be seen as a distinct phase in the development of young Americans in which they lived within their own subculture and responded to its demands for fun, excitement, and novelty. Dating became a ritualized form of courting behavior carried on at movies, dances, and athletic events, as well as in automobiles. Parents had much less influence on their children's decisions about clothes, hairstyles, and behavior.

More young Americans attended high school during the 1920s than ever before, and the percentage of those who went to college increased. The college experience became the model for middle-class white youth across the nation. Freed from parental supervision, college women could smoke in public, go out on dates, and engage in the latest trends in sexual activity, "necking and petting." Male students with enough income joined fraternities, drank heavily, and devoted endless amounts of time to athletic contests and dates.

The college experience for students from lower-class families, different religious backgrounds, or minority groups was less comfortable. Informal quotas limited the numbers of Jewish students admitted to

The experience of college became one of the shaping rites of passage for American youth during the 1920s. Life magazine, which specialized in humor, brought out a special "freshman number" to instruct youthful students on the correct behavior for aspiring undergraduates in 1926.

Yale, Columbia, or Harvard. In the South, African Americans of college age were forced to attend predominantly black institutions that struggled with fewer resources and less distinguished faculties. Poorer students at state universities and private colleges worked their way through, often performing the menial tasks that made life pleasant for their affluent colleagues.

Big-Time Sports

On college campuses large and small, autumn was the football season. During the 1920s the college game grew into a national obsession as money was poured

into the construction of stadiums, the coaching staffs, and in many instances, the players themselves. At the University of Texas the athletic director dispensed cash to the players from a safe in his office. Large stadiums sprang up on the West Coast and in the Midwest. Institutions like Duke University, Stanford University, and the University of Texas built huge football arenas in pursuit of athletic greatness and profits. The business of football became the financial lifeblood at many institutions of higher learning.

The most famous football player of the era was Harold "Red" Grange of the University of Illinois. When he scored four touchdowns in twelve minutes against the University of Michigan in 1924, his picture appeared on the cover of the new *Time* magazine. After he left college, Grange joined the newly formed National Professional Football League and received some $12,000 per game at the start. During the years that followed, Grange made pro football more than a novelty, although the game's glory days lay several decades in the future.

Boxing attracted millions of followers. The first popular champion was William Harrison "Jack" Dempsey, who received $1 million for his fight against the Frenchman Georges Carpentier in 1921. To avoid confronting the leading African-American contender, Henry Willis, Dempsey and his manager agreed to fight James Joseph "Jack" Tunney. Tunney defeated an overconfident Dempsey in 1927.

Other sports produced equally exciting heroes. The tennis stars of the decade were William "Big Bill" Tilden, who dominated the men's game from 1921 to 1925. Only people inside the sport knew that Tilden was a homosexual. Helen Wills Moody successfully challenged the reigning queen of tennis, the Frenchwoman, Suzanne Lenglen. In golf, Robert "Bobby" Trent Jones won numerous tournaments as an amateur.

Baseball: The National Sport

Of all the American sports, however, baseball symbolized the excitement and passion of the 1920s. The game experienced a wounding scandal in 1919 when it was revealed that members of the Chicago White Sox had conspired to fix the World Series. Although the players were ultimately acquitted of any crime, the "Black Sox" scandal cast a shadow over the game. The

owners hired a new commissioner, Kenesaw Mountain Landis, a former federal judge, and gave him sweeping authority over the operations of baseball. Landis barred the "Black Sox" players from the game for life for having cheated and exercised his power vigorously to keep baseball pure.

Baseball underwent even more dramatic changes on the field because of the emergence of a new kind of player in the person of George Herman "Babe" Ruth. Ruth was a pitcher for the Boston Red Sox when they sold him to the New York Yankees for $400,000 in 1918. Ruth believed that he could hit home runs; he belted out fifty-four during the 1920 season. Fans flocked to see him perform. The Yankees decided to construct Yankee Stadium ("the House that Ruth built") to accommodate the customers who wanted to

In the heyday of big-time sports, no one was more popular or well known than George Herman "Babe" Ruth of the New York Yankees. His prodigious home runs and gargantuan appetites made him a larger than life hero.

be there when Ruth connected. The Yankees won American League pennants from 1921 to 1923 and in 1923 they won the World Series. Batting averages rose in both leagues, as did attendance records. Professional baseball remained a white man's game, however; talented black players such as Josh Gibson labored in obscurity in the Negro leagues. Confined to the eastern half of the United States for the major leagues, baseball was nonetheless the national pastime during the 1920s.

Americans of every description followed sports of all kinds through the abundant coverage provided by the nation's newspapers. Sports shared with the movies and radio the emphasis on consumerism and quick gratification that characterized the mass society of the 1920s.

NEW ROLES FOR WOMEN

After the achievement of woman suffrage, most people expected the newly enfranchised voters to produce a genuine change in politics. It soon became apparent that women cast their votes much as men did. The possibility of a cohesive bloc of female voters evaporated. Yet while women did not change politics, they found that their place in society underwent significant transformations.

Women in Politics

Contributing to the problems that women encountered were divisions among advocates of woman suffrage. After 1923, the more militant wing, identified with Alice Paul and the National Woman's Party, advocated the Equal Rights Amendment (ERA). The amendment stated that "men and women shall have equal rights throughout the United States and every place subject to its jurisdiction." Other female reformers, such as Florence Kelley and Carrie Chapman Catt, regarded the ERA as a threat to the hard-won legislation that protected women in the workplace. These women favored an approach such as the Sheppard-Towner Act of 1921, which supplied federal matching funds to states that created programs in which moth-

ers would be instructed on caring for their babies and safeguarding their own health. Efforts to expand into other areas of social welfare legislation did not succeed in the conservative climate of the times.

Some women entered politics. Two states, Wyoming and Texas, elected female governors. Nellie Tayloe Ross of Wyoming was chosen to fill out the unexpired term of her husband after he died in office. Miriam Amanda Ferguson of Texas won election in 1924 because her husband, a former governor, had been impeached and barred from holding office in the state. She became his surrogate. Eleven women were elected to the House of Representatives, many of them as political heirs of their husbands. Many more won seats in state legislatures or held local offices. Eleanor Roosevelt, the wife of a rising Democratic politician in New York, built up a network of support among women in her party.

Social causes enlisted women who had started their careers in public life years earlier. Margaret Sanger continued to be a staunch advocate of birth control. She founded the American Birth Control League, which became Planned Parenthood in 1942. Sanger capitalized on a popular interest in "eugenics," a quasi-scientific movement to limit births among "unfit" elements of the population. The racist implications of the theory stirred only modest controversy before the rise of Nazi Germany in the 1930s. Sanger found increased support for birth control among doctors as the 1920s progressed. The greatest effect of the campaign was seen in middle-class women. The poor and minorities turned to older, less reliable methods of avoiding pregnancy and often resorted to abortions when pregnant.

The Flapper and the New Woman

Social feminism confronted a sense that young women were more interested in fun and diversion than in political movements. The "flapper," with her bobbed hair and short skirts, captivated the popular press. Older female reformers noted sadly that their younger counterparts were likely "to be bored" when the subject of feminism came up. Instead, flappers smoked in public, defying a long-standing social taboo. "I can't feel that a real, genuine womanly girl would form the habit," commented a dean at a woman's college.

In their relations with men, young women of the 1920s practiced a new sexual freedom. Among women

ELSIE HILL ON WHY
WOMEN SHOULD HAVE
FULL LEGAL EQUALITY,
1922

In the wake of woman suffrage, the National Woman's Party pressed forward with a feminist agenda that is well expressed in this statement of the movement's goals by Elsie Hill.

The removal of all forms of the subjection of women is the purpose to which the National Woman's Party is dedicated. Its present campaign to remove the discriminations against women in the laws of the United States is but the beginning of its determined effort to secure the freedom of women, an integral part of the struggle for human liberty for which women are first of all responsible. Its interest lies in the final release of woman from the class of a dependent, subservient being to which early civilization committed her.

The laws of various States at present hold her in that class. They deny her a control of her children equal to the father's; they deny her, if married, the right to her own earnings; they punish her for offences for which men go unpunished; they exclude her from public office and from public institutions to the support of which her taxes contribute. These laws are not the creation of this age, but the fact that they are still tolerated on our statute books and that in some States their removal is vigorously resisted shows the hold of old traditions upon us. Since the passage of the Suffrage Amendment the incongruity of these laws, dating back many centuries, has become more than ever marked. . . .

The National Woman's Party believes that it is a vital social need to do away with these discriminations against women and is devoting its energies to that end. The removal of the discriminations and not the method by which they are removed is the thing upon which the Woman's Party insists. It has under consideration an amendment to the Federal Constitution which, if adopted, would remove them at one stroke, but it is at present endeavoring to secure their removal in the individual States by a blanket bill, which is the most direct State method. For eighty-two years the piecemeal method has been tried, beginning with the married women's property act of 1839 in Mississippi, and no State, excepting Wisconsin, where the Woman's Party blanket bill was passed in June, 1921, has yet finished. . . .

The present program of the National Woman's Party is to introduce its Woman's Equal Rights Bill, or bills attaining the same purpose, in all State legislatures as they convene. It is building up in Washington a great headquarters from which this campaign can be conducted, and it is acting in the faith that the removal of these discriminations from our laws will benefit every group of women in the country, and through them all society.

---

born after 1900, the rate of premarital intercourse, while still low by modern standards, was twice as high as it had been among women born a decade earlier. While most young men and women did not sleep together, men and women engaged in more sexual play. "There are only two kinds of co-eds," said a college newspaper, "those who have been kissed and those who are sorry that they haven't been kissed."

Women on the Job

Women joined the workforce in growing numbers. At the beginning of the decade, 8.3 million women, or about 24 percent of the national workforce, were employed outside the home. Ten years later, the number stood at 10.6 million, or 27 percent. A few occupations accounted for 85 percent of female jobs. One third of these women worked in clerical positions, 20 percent labored as domestic servants, and another third were employed in factory jobs. Many women with factory jobs worked a full week and continued to spend many hours on household chores as well. The median wage for women usually stood at about 55 percent of what men earned for comparable jobs. At the same time women entered new professions and became celebrities. Amelia Earhart, for example, was the first woman pilot to cross the Atlantic, and emerged as the most famous woman flier of the era.

For the majority of women, however, the barriers to advancement and opportunity remained high. Poor white women in the South often worked at dead-end jobs in textile mills or agricultural processing plants. Black women found it difficult to secure nondomestic jobs either in the North or the South. When African Americans were employed to move supplies or equipment in factories, they did the heavy, menial laborer that white workers shunned. In the Southwest, Hispanic women picked crops, shelled pecans, or worked as domestic servants. Labor unions rarely addressed the situation of female workers. When strikes did occur, as in New Jersey and Massachusetts during the middle of the decade, employers sometimes granted concessions—and then moved their factories to the South where labor was cheaper and unions were weaker.

The Plight of the Career Woman

Career women faced formidable obstacles. When a woman schoolteacher married, many school districts compelled her to resign. College faculties, the medical profession, and the law had more women members but they made it difficult for women to advance in these careers. In government, men received favorable treatment. Although many women worked outside the home out of economic necessity, they were expected to juggle their careers and domestic responsibilities.

Women who were "creative" or who had "administrative gifts or business ability," said the feminist Crystal Eastman, and who also had "the normal desire to be mothers, must make up their minds to be sort of supermen." In the heyday of Republican conservatism, such attitudes pervaded society.

COOLIDGE IN THE WHITE HOUSE

The inauguration of President Coolidge on March 4, 1925, was the first to be broadcast over the radio. The administration's policy goals were modest. In 1926 Coolidge asked Congress for a cut in taxes. The lawmakers responded with a measure that lowered the surtax on those people who made more than $100,000 annually, reduced the estate tax to 20 percent, and eliminated the gift tax. Few married couples earned more than the $3,500 exemption and only about 4 million Americans filed tax returns during this period. The changes in the law affected only the most affluent in the society. The president also supported laws to oversee the expansion of the new airline industry and regulate the growing radio business. On the other hand, Coolidge vetoed a bill to develop the electric power potential of the Tennessee River at Muscle Shoals, Alabama, for public purposes. When Congress twice passed the McNary-Haugen Plan to assist agriculture, Coolidge vetoed it on the grounds that trying to raise crop prices through government intervention was both expensive and wrong.

Coolidge's Foreign Policy

Although the United States remained out of the League of Nations, it was not an isolationist country during the 1920s. The Coolidge administration participated in foreign relations in ways that would have seemed impossible a decade earlier. Its effort to have the United States join the World Court (a part of the League whose official title was the Permanent Court of International Justice) in 1925 and 1926 collapsed when the Senate insisted on major conditions for American membership, including limits on the Court's ability to issue advisory opinions on disputed issues.

The government encouraged the expansion of American business around the world, and Washington used corporate executives as ambassadors and in framing monetary policy. Americans applauded U.S. policy in Latin America, Asia, and Europe because it did not involve the use of force or the commitment of soldiers. Sentiment for peace remained strong.

In Latin America, troubled relations with Mexico, especially over control of oil reserves, persisted. The administration sent an emissary, Dwight Morrow, who mediated an agreement to protect American oil companies from further expropriation. Marines were withdrawn from Nicaragua in 1925 but were sent back a year later when civil war erupted again. American efforts to instruct the Nicaraguans in what Washington said were democratic procedures did not produce the desired results by the time the Coolidge presidency ended.

Diplomacy and Finance in the 1920s

After the decision not to join the League of Nations, the U.S. interest in Europe became chiefly financial. American bankers and investors played a large part in providing the reparation payments required of Germany in the Treaty of Versailles (see Chapter 22). Because of the size of the sums they had to pay, the Germans were unable to meet their obligations without American help. In 1924 the Coolidge administration endorsed a plan that Charles G. Dawes, a Chicago banker, had developed. The proposal scaled back German reparations and loaned that country money to meet its debts. During the next four years Germany borrowed almost $1.5 million from the United States. European nations in turn used the money paid to them by the Germans to buy American farm and factory products.

The Coolidge administration continued the policy of nonrecognition of the Soviet Union, but it did not object when business interests, including Henry Ford, made substantial investments there. Americans also sent large amounts of aid and food when the Soviets faced famine during the early 1920s. In China, the U.S. government watched apprehensively as revolution and civil war wracked that nation. Washington extended de facto recognition to the government of the Nationalist leader, Chiang Kai-shek. That stance reflected the general policy of encouraging positive developments overseas without assuming any direct obligations.

A symbol of that sentiment came in American support for the idea of outlawing war altogether. When the French foreign minister, Aristide Briand, proposed a mutual security agreement between his country and the United States, the State Department proposed instead a multilateral agreement to have signatory nations renounce war. Peace groups supported the idea and the Kellogg-Briand Pact was signed and ratified in 1929.

1927: THE YEAR OF THE DECADE

The crosscurrents of the 1920s merged during 1927. One significant event after another grabbed the headlines. The most striking individual achievement came in May, when Charles A. Lindbergh flew alone across the Atlantic Ocean from New York to Paris. Lindbergh did not make the first nonstop flight across the ocean. Two English aviators accomplished that feat eight years earlier, flying from Ireland to Newfoundland in 1919. By 1926, however, a $25,000 prize was offered for the first nonstop flight between New York and Paris, a distance of 3,600 miles.

Charles Lindbergh had been an army flier and was working as an airmail pilot for the government when he heard about the contest. He raised money from civic leaders in St. Louis and other cities. He called his monoplane *The Spirit of St. Louis.* On May 10, a tired Lindbergh (he had not slept the night before) took off from Roosevelt Field in New York on his way to Paris. When he landed in the French capital thirty-six hours later, he was a worldwide celebrity. He received a ticker tape parade in New York City, medals from foreign nations, and a lifetime in the public eye. The public sang songs about "Lucky Lindy." To the generation of the 1920s, Lindbergh's feat symbolized the ability of a single person to bend technology to his will and overcome nature.

It was a period of enthusiasm for science and technology both in and out of government. The achievements of Henry Ford and Frederick Winslow Taylor in industry captured worldwide attention. Sigmund Freud's psychological theories attracted popular notice.

Charles Lindbergh's solo flight across the Atlantic Ocean in 1927 made him an international hero. The youthful Lindbergh stands stiffly in front of his plane, The Spirit of St. Louis.

Terms from his writings, such as "id" and "libido," became part of the everyday language. Universities and corporations supported scientific research, especially in physics; chemistry and astronomy also benefited. In this climate, a hero like Lindbergh found a ready audience.

A Heyday for Sports and a Big Change for Films

On athletic fields, stunning accomplishments marked 1927. The New York Yankees became known as "Murderers Row" because of their many hitters, of whom Babe Ruth was the most famous. Ruth hit sixty home runs, a record that stood for thirty-four years. In boxing, Gene Tunney and Jack Dempsey had a rematch of their heavyweight championship fight. Dempsey knocked Tunney down in the seventh round but failed to go to a neutral corner quickly. The result was a "long count" that enabled Tunney to come off the canvas and win.

Motion pictures enjoyed strong popularity at the beginning of the year but there was growing evidence that silent films were boring audiences. Filmmakers believed that talking movies were the logical next step. Fearful that they might lose their hold on the public, the major studios agreed that none of them would make talking pictures unless they all did. One of the smaller studios, Warner Brothers, was working on a sound picture called *The Jazz Singer*. Its star was Al Jolson, who specialized in blackface renditions of popular tunes. When he ad-libbed his catch phrase, "You Ain't Heard Nothing Yet," and sang several songs, the audience response was enthusiastic. Within two years silent pictures gave way to sound.

Ford Introduces the Model A

By the end of the 1920s, automaker Henry Ford confronted an economic crisis. The simple Model T was no longer the car of choice for Americans. General Motors was offering Chevrolets that were only a little more expensive than Model Ts but offered features and options that Ford did not. In addition, the annual models that Alfred P. Sloan had introduced promised consumers novelty and excitement as well as a better

The advent of talking pictures in 1927 ended the silent era and changed the nature of Hollywood. The new movies enjoyed worldwide popularity as this poster in German of Jolson in his blackface makeup attests.

the consumer demand for the automobile, on December 1, 1927, the company unveiled the Model A in cities around the country. Like its competitor General Motors, Ford marketed the Model A through a huge advertising campaign. It also created a credit corporation, again modeled on what General Motors had done, to enable buyers to obtain their cars on credit. By the end of the 1920s the major companies in the automotive business had adopted advertising and marketing techniques that became a fixture in American life.

The Execution of Sacco and Vanzetti

While the consumer culture of the 1920s flourished, the fate of Sacco and Vanzetti continued to attract international attention. By the spring of 1927 the appeals process had almost run its course. Despite strong evidence that the two men had not received a fair trial, and substantial indications that they were not guilty, the legal machinery moved them toward the electric chair. The date of their execution was set for July 1927. The campaign to save the two defendants had become worldwide. Important legal scholars such as Felix Frankfurter of the Harvard Law School argued for the innocence of Sacco and Vanzetti. The governor of Massachusetts appointed a special commission to review the case. After flawed and biased proceedings, the panel decided to affirm the convictions. Finally, the two men were electrocuted on August 23, 1927. Their death evoked anguished protests from those who had taken up their cause. The case convinced many radicals that more drastic measures would be necessary to reform American society.

"I Do Not Choose to Run"

Calvin Coolidge could easily have run for another term in 1928. His popularity was still high, and the nation's prosperity seemed to assure a Republican victory. However, the presidency had lost its appeal for Coolidge. One of his sons had died of blood poisoning in 1924, and both the president and his wife were in uncertain health. Coolidge may also have sensed the weaknesses in the economy that would become evident two years later. While vacationing in the Black Hills of South Dakota during the summer of 1927, the president handed to reporters a simple statement:

product. Sloan understood that when buyers found their cars obsolete within a few years they had an incentive to acquire a new model. By 1926, the Model T had become an economic liability and Ford's sales had slumped.

During the spring of 1927 Henry Ford ended production of the Model T and turned to the development of a new car. Within months the Model A was ready for consumers to sample. Interest in the product was high; orders for hundreds of thousands were taken before the new model was introduced to the market. Although it would be months before Ford could fill

The longest running legal case of the 1920s was the controversial murder conviction of Nicola Sacco (right) and Bartolomeo Vanzetti (left). Their appeals of the verdict became a cause that many intellectuals in and out of the United States supported before the two men were executed in 1927.

"I do not choose to run for President in 1928." This surprise announcement opened up the race for the Republican presidential nomination to other potential contenders such as the secretary of commerce, Herbert Hoover.

As 1927 ended there were some signs that the economy was not as robust as it had been. A slight recession occurred in which wholesale prices fell nearly 4.5 percent. Production slowed, and consumer spending also dropped. Despite these warning signs, the banking system continued to expand credit, and stock market speculation persisted. For the average American there was little concrete evidence that the boom years might be coming to a close.

CONCLUSION

The years between World War I and the start of the Great Depression have never lost their reputation for excitement and novelty. Bathtub gin, flappers, syncopation, and gangsters remain part of the national image of that time. This image has staying power because much of it is true. Prohibition did encounter serious opposition from the upper classes, and evasion of the law was widespread. On the other hand, liquor control did change drinking habits, so the experiment was not a complete failure.

For women the sense that the 1920s represented a new age of sexual and social liberation was actually rather superficial. Sexual practices did become more flexible, but marriage and family continued to be viewed as the goals toward which most women should aspire. The number of women in the workplace rose, but the percentage of women in the labor force did not change very much. Politics saw an infusion of women into both major parties, but genuine equality in partisan affairs remained elusive. The 1920s did not produce anything like the gains in political or social status that had been achieved by women during the previous decade.

In its culture, the United States went through an artistic renaissance. Literature, art, and music explored new channels and brought forth important figures whose influence remained strong through the 1930s and beyond. The works of Hemingway, Fitzgerald, and Mencken, the jazz of Ellington and Armstrong, and the achievements of numerous other artists made the 1920s a high point of American artistic expression.

The 1920s brought important economic changes for many Americans. A consumer culture based on mass appeal tied middle-class society together through common experiences of driving automobiles, listening to radios, and attending films each week. These years saw the emergence of a mass society that had been evolving since the burst of industrialization at the end of the nineteenth century. Americans took eagerly to the products of the new consumer age.

The cultural response was more mixed. Older values warred with the new cosmopolitan principles embodied in advertising and mass marketing. The Ku Klux Klan, the movement for immigration restriction, and the rise of fundamentalism challenged the newer ways, and revealed that the United States was still divided between the values of town and country. The cultural liberation of the 1920s did not destroy the essential conservatism of much of the population.

While the potential for social conflict persisted, the economic good times of the decade left few avenues for effective protest and unrest. For a brief period it seemed possible that discord might vanish in a rising tide of economic growth. However, the prosperity of the 1920s did not alter the inequities between rich and poor. If the national belief in a prosperous future were to disappear, the latent strains within American life might resurface. The challenge for Calvin Coolidge's successor would be to maintain and extend the gains that the economy had made since 1921. Few expected that the new president would confront the worst economic collapse in the nation's history.

RECOMMENDED READINGS

Allen, Frederick Lewis. *Only Yesterday: An Informal History of the 1920s* (1931) is the most influential and enduring treatment of the decade.

Brown, Dorothy. *Setting a Course: American Women in the 1920s* (1987) gives a thorough assessment of the gains and losses that women experienced.

Coben, Stanley. *Rebellion Against Victorianism: The Impetus for Cultural Change in 1920s America* (1991) discusses how Americans in the 1920s reacted against the ideas and values of an earlier time.

Douglas, Ann. *Terrible Honesty: Mongrel Manhattan in the 1920s* (1995) is a cultural history of the decade from the perspective of events in New York City.

Dumenil, Lynn. *The Modern Temper: American Culture and Society in the 1920s* (1995) is an excellent analysis of the major trends of the period.

Hawley, Ellis. *The Great War and the Search for a Modern Order, 1917–1933* (1979) emphasizes interpretation and applies the insights of the social sciences to the 1920s.

Leuchtenberg, William E. *The Perils of Prosperity, 1914–1932* (1958, 1993) is a vivid, modern survey.

Lewis, David Levering. *When Harlem Was in Vogue* (1981) is a well-written discussion of the impact of the Harlem Renaissance.

Parrish, Michael E. *Anxious Decades: America in Prosperity and Depression* (1992) is a fascinating treatment of the interwar years.

Peret, Geoffrey. *America in the Twenties: A History* (1982) offers many provocative insights into the meaning of the decade.

Politics

Burner, David. *The Politics of Provincialism: The Democratic Party in Transition, 1918–1932* (1968).

Craig, Douglas. *After Wilson: The Struggle for the Democratic Party, 1920–1934* (1992).

McCoy, Donald. *Calvin Coolidge: The Quiet President* (1977).

Trani, Eugene P. and David L. Wilson, *The Presidency of Warren G. Harding* (1977).

Prohibition and the Ku Klux Klan

Blee, Katherine M. *Women of the Klan: Racism and Gender in the 1920s* (1990).

Chalmers, David M. *Hooded Americanism: The History of the Ku Klux Klan* (1965).

Clark, Norman H. *Deliver Us from Evil: An Interpretation of American Prohibition* (1976).

Goldberg, Robert Allan. *Hooded Empire: The Ku Klux Klan in Colorado* (1981).

McLean, Nancy. *Behind the Mask of Chivalry: The Making of the Second Ku Klux Klan* (1995).

Blacks and the Harlem Renaissance

Huggins, Nathan Irvin. *Harlem Renaissance* (1971).

Martin, Tony. *Race First: The Ideological and Organizational Struggles of Marcus Garvey and the Universal Negro Improvement Association* (1976).

Stein, Judith. *The World of Marcus Garvey: Race and Class in Modern Society* (1986).

Economic Trends

Bernstein, Irving. *The Lean Years: A History of the American Worker, 1920–1933* (1960).

Flink, James J. *The Car Culture* (1975).

Soule, George. *Prosperity Decade: From War to Depression, 1917–1929* (1947).

Social and Cultural Trends

Avrich, Paul. *Sacco and Vanzetti: The Anarchist Background* (1991).

Engelmann, Larry. *The Goddess and the American Girl: The Story of Suzanne Lenglen and Helen Wills* (1988).

Fass, Paula S. *The Damned and the Beautiful: American Youth in the 1920s* (1977).

Ginger, Ray. *Six Days or Forever* (1958).

Joughin, G. Louis, and Edmund M. Morgan, *The Legacy of Sacco and Vanzetti* (1948).

Leighton, Isabel, ed., *The Aspirin Age, 1919–1941* (1949).

HERBERT HOOVER CAMPAIGNING IN 1928

In his first campaign for president in 1928, Herbert Hoover drew large crowds when he appeared in a major city. The open car and the relative distance of the police were part of an earlier time before fears of presidential assassinations became so acute.

Chapter 24

THE GREAT DEPRESSION

1927-1933

As the end of the 1920s approached, some well-off Americans viewed the future with confidence. In accepting the Republican presidential nomination in 1928, Herbert Hoover proclaimed: "We in America today are nearer to the final triumph over poverty than ever before in the history of any land." Farmers would not have shared Hoover's optimism, nor would African Americans and the poor. Among those who had benefited from the boom of the 1920s, however, the prosperity and abundance enjoyed by the fortunate seemed destined to extend into the immediate future.

Then came the shocks, first of the crash of the stock market in October 1929, then a severe economic depression that worsened during the early 1930s. The good times of the 1920s soon faded from memory, to be replaced with bread lines, soup kitchens, and the wandering homeless. The administration of President Herbert Hoover took unprecedented actions to relieve the crisis, but nothing seemed to work. Resentment against the president, the economic system, and the wealthy grew. The specter of social revolution arose. Pressures for political change led to the election of Franklin D. Roosevelt in 1932.

By 1933 the Great Depression, as it came to be called, affected almost everyone in American society. It worsened the already difficult situation of the nation's farmers. For African Americans, Hispanics, and the poor, it meant even more misery and suffering than they usually faced. A generation of Americans looked to the federal government for answers to the social and economic problems they confronted. These emotions and needs laid the basis for Franklin D. Roosevelt's New Deal.

THE ELECTION OF 1928

President Calvin Coolidge's declaration that he would not run for reelection in 1928 set off a contest for the Republican presidential nomination (see Chapter 23). The front-runner was the secretary of Commerce, Herbert Clark Hoover. Although the Depression permanently tarnished his political reputation, Hoover was an attractive candidate in 1928. He seemed to represent a constructive blend of technology and reform devoted to public service.

The Engineer as Candidate: Herbert Hoover

Hoover had been reared as an orphan in a modest Quaker home in Iowa. He built a career as a mining

CHRONOLOGY

1928 Republicans nominate Herbert Hoover as their presidential candidate

Democrats select Alfred E. Smith to run on their ticket

Hoover elected president of the United States

1929 Hoover inaugurated on March 4, 1929

Stock market crash, September–October 1929

1930 Hawley-Smoot Tariff bill passed to raise tariff rates

Birds Eye frozen foods and Wonder sliced bread introduced

Democratic gains in congressional elections

1931 President Hoover declares moratorium on payment of war debts

Association of Southern Women Against Lynching starts

Japanese invade Manchuria

Stimson Doctrine proclaimed against Japan

1932 Bonus March in Washington

Amelia Earhart makes first transatlantic solo flight by a woman

Republicans renominate Hoover

Democrats nominate Franklin D. Roosevelt who promises New Deal

Roosevelt wins landslide election victory

1933 Banks fail during first two months

Depression worsens

Roosevelt inaugurated March 4, 1933

---

engineer after graduation from Stanford University. He first gained world attention during World War I, when he managed the campaign to bring food relief to the starving people of Belgium. After returning to the United States, he ran the Food Administration. His policies of voluntary rationing and increased production made him a household name. After the war, he sent relief and food to war-torn Russia. He thought about running for president in 1920 but settled instead for becoming Commerce secretary under Warren G. Harding and Calvin Coolidge. During these years Hoover skillfully used the new technology of radio and motion pictures to spread his name and face to all corners of the United States. With the exception of President Coolidge, he was the best-known political figure in the country by 1928.

The leaders of the Republican party were less enthusiastic about Hoover. They recognized that "Sir Herbert," as they called him in private, had few direct connections with the traditional methods of partisan politics. Since Hoover had worked for the Wilson administration and had internationalist sympathies, he was not popular among Republicans who wanted to limit foreign involvement. Nevertheless, Hoover was the most popular Republican hopeful in the race. As a result, he came to the party's convention in Kansas City with more than enough support for the nomination. He received 837 votes on the first ballot and his selection was made unanimous. The delegates chose Carl Curtis of Kansas as his running mate.

Observing the tradition in which the party's nominee "accepted" the party's honor in a formal speech, Hoover waited two months to deliver his acceptance address, which he presented in the stadium at Stanford University. After forecasting the end of poverty, he announced that "the poorhouse is vanishing from among us." He promised "a job for every man" and "equality of opportunity for all irrespective of faith and color." Hoover called for farm relief, and "an adequate tariff," and spoke out strongly against religious intolerance. Hoover was never an exciting speaker. He read this address, as he did others, in a monotone, with little effort to arouse the enthusiasm of the audience. In 1928, however, sober and calm rhetoric impressed many voters as precisely what the times demanded. In their minds, Hoover was the heir of the Coolidge policies that would carry the nation forward to ever-higher levels of prosperity.

From the Sidewalks of New York: Al Smith

The Democrats still felt the wounds of their disastrous convention in 1924. In addition to the split over Prohibition and its enforcement, the party was divided along ideological lines. Liberals wanted a more activist government, while conservatives sought a return to the pro-business policies that predated the era of William Jennings Bryan and Woodrow Wilson. No one in the party, however, wished to repeat the mistakes of the New York convention, which had symbolized the bitter divisions among the Democrats over cultural and economic questions. This meant that the nomination of Alfred E. Smith, the governor of New York and the clear front-runner, was almost a certainty. Because he had been denied the prize in 1924, a second rejection would split the Democrats irrevocably. Yet to nominate Smith was likely to release the passions and prejudices that had dogged the Democrats for twenty years. Whatever the party did in 1928, one of its factions was sure to be dissatisfied with the result.

Al Smith had grown up in New York City, working in the Fulton Fish Market. He had a natural talent for politics and soon became identified with Tammany Hall, the Democratic party organization in Manhattan. Long notorious for its corrupt ways, the organization recognized in Smith a politician who could move beyond the older style of machine politics and deal with the voters who wanted relief from the injustices of an industrial society. Smith made his mark in the New York legislature and then was elected governor in 1918. Defeated in 1920, he was returned to office in 1922 and reelected twice more. As governor, Smith championed moderate social welfare policies, administrative efficiency, and public works. He enlisted former progressives, women reformers, and social scientists in his administration in ways that foreshadowed the New Deal of the 1930s. Despite his reformist policies on the state level, however, Smith remained suspicious of arguments that the federal government should be deeply involved in regulating the economy and business.

Smith's Political Weaknesses

For all his political skills, however, Smith had liabilities that alienated intolerant voters in 1928. A devout

Cartoonists had a fine time depicting the Smith-Hoover contest. Smith was known as the "Happy Warrior" because Franklin Roosevelt had given him that title in 1924.

Roman Catholic, he confronted the currents of prejudice that limited presidential candidates to Protestant men. In his daily life, the governor attended Mass, pledged religious obedience to the Catholic clergy, and displayed the visible symbols of his faith. As a public official, he defended separation of church and state, challenging the position of his church when he supported divorce legislation in New York.

The governor also disliked Prohibition and its impact on national politics. He favored the right of an individual state to allow liquor to be sold within its borders, and indicated that he had served liquor at his official residence. At the Democratic convention, he came out for "fundamental changes in the present provisions of national prohibition," a move that outraged Southerners in his party. Despite reservations among his southern and western opponents, Smith's strength won him the nomination at the Democratic National Convention in Houston. His running mate was Joseph Robinson, an Arkansas senator.

Hoover versus Smith: The 1928 Campaign

The campaign proved to be one of the most bitterly fought in history as the cultural issues that had so long divided the Democrats reappeared once again. Smith's religion and position on alcohol made him the focus of intense attacks on his character and record.

Most of the electoral advantages rested with Herbert Hoover. Many parts of the nation were prosperous, and those who suffered from economic difficulties thought that they still had a chance to improve their lives. Will Rogers, the cowboy humorist, summed up the public mood. "Prosperity—millions never had it under Coolidge, never had it under anybody, but expect it under Hoover." The Republicans made much of the issue of "business prosperity and sound economic principles and governmental practices" in their campaign literature.

Hoover campaigned in a highly structured manner. He gave his acceptance address and six other major speeches during the autumn of 1928. The Republicans took as their campaign slogan "a chicken in every pot and two cars in every garage." Hoover's strategists used large amounts of newsreel footage to bring their candidate to a national audience, and he was as famous a political figure as anyone of his time. Many female voters supported Hoover because they found Al

Smith's wife less dignified and refined than Mrs. Hoover. Well financed and cohesive, the Republicans easily out-maneuvered the Democrats.

The Smith Response to Hoover

Smith did not campaign as a liberal alternative to Hoover. The men who directed his campaign were closely aligned with large corporations and opponents of Prohibition. The candidate, meanwhile, said little about economic distress, played down differences over the tariff and tax policy, and stressed his allegiance to a government that interfered "as little as possible with business." On the radio, Smith came across to Americans outside the Northeast as an alien, strange voice who once asked reporters which states were located west of the Mississippi River.

The religious issue made the 1928 campaign infamous in American political history. Some devout Protestants saw in Smith's candidacy the specter of Catholic domination of the government. Even though Smith had announced his belief "in the absolute separation of Church and State," the forces of religious intolerance rallied against him. A Baptist minister in New York City called the Democratic candidate "the nominee of the worst forces of hell." The manager of the *Fellowship Forum,* a Protestant publication that attacked Smith, said that "the real issue in this campaign was PROTESTANT AMERICANISM VERSUS RUM AND ROMANISM." When Smith campaigned in the South, he faced burning crosses and angry voters. Unlike John Kennedy a generation later, Al Smith made few efforts to allay the fears of more responsible voters about his own religious convictions.

A Landslide for Hoover

The election results were a landslide for Hoover and the Republicans. Hoover received 21.4 million ballots to 15 million for Smith. In the electoral college, Hoover won the 444 electoral votes of forty states. Hoover carried five southern states, including Texas, and thus broke the "Solid South" that had provided the Democrats with an electoral foundation for so long. Disillusioned, Smith told friends: "I guess the time has not yet come when a man can say his beads in the White House."

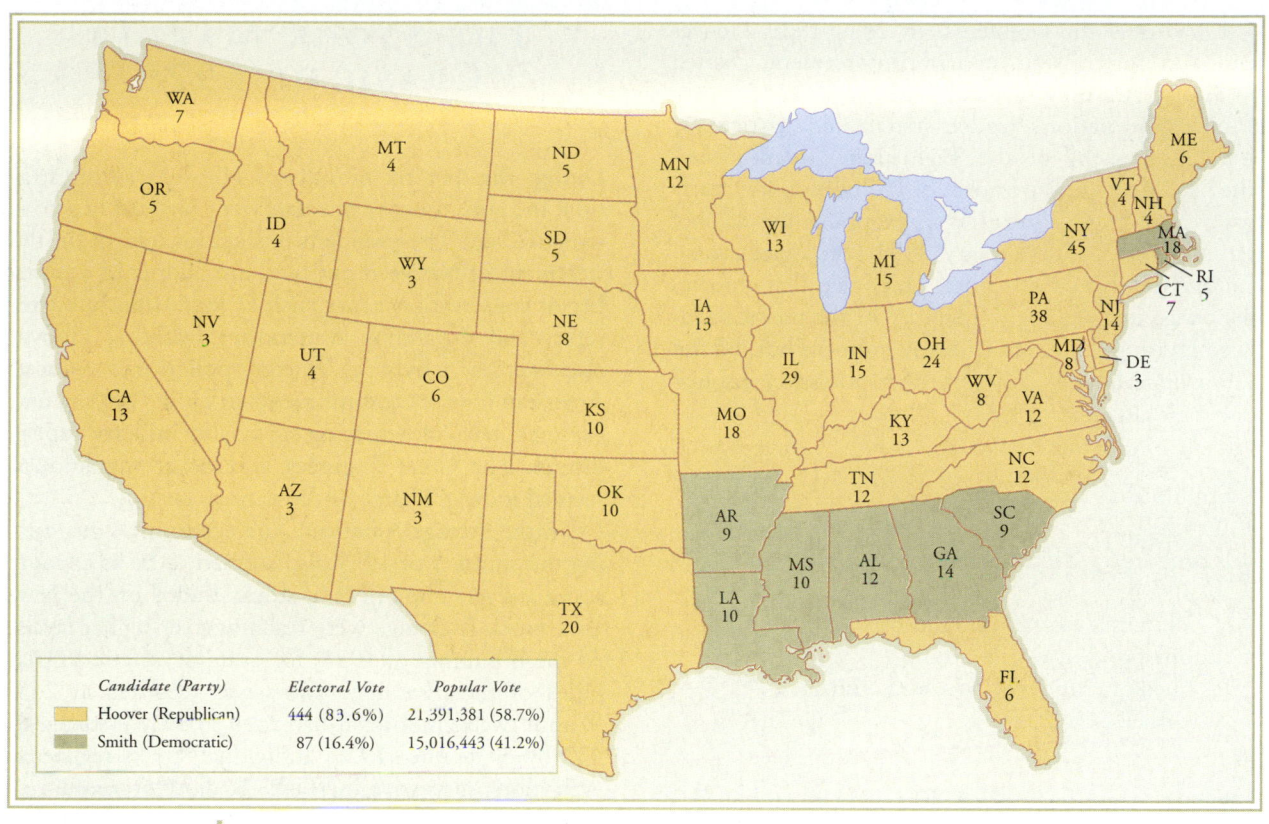

Candidate (Party)		Electoral Vote	Popular Vote
	Hoover (Republican)	444 (83.6%)	21,391,381 (58.7%)
	Smith (Democratic)	87 (16.4%)	15,016,443 (41.2%)

MAP 24.1 | THE ELECTION OF 1928

Beneath the electoral wreckage, however, lay some modestly encouraging signs for the Democratic party. Smith carried the nation's largest cities and ran strongly in areas with large immigrant and Catholic populations. At the same time, however, the Democratic candidate did less well in his party's traditional areas of strength, the South and West. Smith had helped the party to rebound from the disaster that had occurred in 1924, but it remained to be seen whether the Democrats could become a majority party without some outside event transforming the political situation. In the aftermath of the 1928 election, such a change seemed very unlikely.

Hoover Takes Office

Herbert Hoover came to the presidency with a great fund of experience in business and government ser-

vice. He worked long hours in the White House. "All days were alike to him," recalled a servant. He was the first president to have a telephone installed in the Oval Office and the last to dress formally for dinner with his wife each evening. At the dinner table the first lady directed the servants with an elaborate system of hand signals.

A problem left over from previous administrations was Prohibition. By 1929, enforcement of the policy took different forms across the nation. In regions where "dry" sentiment remained strong, penalties for violators could be harsh. In Michigan, for example, a fourth conviction for selling alcohol resulted in a life sentence in prison. Elsewhere, in states with "wet" majorities, legislatures voted for repeal of the Eighteenth Amendment. Many Americans believed that Prohibition was becoming either a joke or a failure. Hoover had endorsed the amendment as "noble in motive and far-reaching in purpose," and he still hoped that it could succeed.

To address the problems, in May 1929 Hoover named a Commission on Law Enforcement, chaired by former Attorney General George Wickersham, to examine the nation's justice system and particularly "the enforcement of the Eighteenth Amendment." The panel studied the impact of Prohibition for nearly two years as the difficulties of stopping the alcohol traffic worsened. In January 1931, the Wickersham Commission issued its report, which said that enforcement was not working; a majority of the members favored revising the Eighteenth Amendment but did not call for repeal. The verdict of the commission inspired a sarcastic rhyme:

> Prohibition's an awful flop.
> We like it.
> It can't stop what it's meant to stop.
> We like it.
> It's left a trail of graft and slime
> It don't prohibit worth a dime
> It's filled our land with vice and crime.
> Nevertheless, we're for it.

For the time being, President Hoover remained a strong backer of Prohibition. Lobbying efforts by organizations such as the Association Against the Prohibition Amendment were beginning to take hold, however, and popular support for Prohibition was eroding. In the 1932 election campaign the Democrats and their presidential candidate came out strongly for repeal of the Eighteenth Amendment.

Despite his early successes in the White House, Hoover had certain political weaknesses that would impair the effectiveness of his presidency when the economy worsened. He had very poor relations with the White House press corps. Reporters resented his insistence on saying little at news conferences, playing favorites among them, and becoming upset with unfavorable press coverage. Hoover also stayed aloof from Congress and made little effort to persuade lawmakers to support his favorite programs. "He has never really recognized the House and Senate as desirable factors in our government," said one commentator. Above all, Hoover lacked the capacity to inspire public confidence in a crisis. His success depended on the national faith that he could carry on the prosperity of the Harding-Coolidge era. When that spirit evaporated, so did Hoover's presidency.

THE STOCK MARKET CRASH OF 1929

During the first six months of Hoover's administration, the government's business went forward in a constructive way. The president pushed for reforms in the treatment of Native Americans and addressed a number of conservation issues such as increasing forest reserves and expanding waterpower facilities. Hoover also was an activist in foreign policy. He reduced American military commitments in Latin America and explored ways of achieving savings in military expenditures. The Great Engineer, as Hoover was known, seemed to be in charge of the nation's destiny.

To the average American, the economic signs during the summer of 1929 also seemed to be as encouraging as ever. The prices of stocks traded on the New York Stock Exchange were reaching ever-higher levels. At the beginning of 1928, for example, the industrial index of the *New York Times* was recorded at 245. Within twelve months it had risen to 331. It soared to 452 by September 1929. Individual stocks registered even more impressive increases. Radio Corporation of America stock shot up from $85 a share to $420 a share during 1928. DuPont's stock price went from $310 to $525. President Coolidge said during 1928 that common stocks were "cheap at current prices." A poem appeared in a popular magazine:

> Oh, hush thee, my babe, granny's bought some more shares,
> Daddy's gone out to play with the bulls and bears,
> Mother's buying on tips, and she simply can't lose,
> And baby shall have some expensive new shoes!

The Crash Occurs

These rosy statistics and forecasts made the stock market crash of October 1929 even more of a shock. The problem began in September as stock prices neared their record levels. Stock prices declined early in the month, regained some strength, and then drifted downward. Yet no abrupt collapse had occurred, and to many on Wall Street these events seemed to be another one of the temporary "corrections" that usually preceded upward surges. A few people warned of

SONGS OF THE HUNGRY

In the midst of the Great Depression, Americans expressed their pain and poverty in verse and song. This lyric "Beans, Bacon, and Gravy," by an anonymous author, captures the extent of popular despair as the hard times reached their low point.

Beans, Bacon, and Gravy

I was born long ago
In eighteen ninety-one
And I've seen many a panic, I will own.
I've been hungry, I've been cold,
And now I'm growing old,
But the worst I've seen is nineteen thirty-one.

Chorus:
Oh, those beans, bacon, and gravy,
They almost drive me crazy!
I eat them till I see them in my dreams.
When I wake up in the morning
And another day is dawning,
Then I know I'll have another mess of beans.

We all congregate each morning
At the county barn at dawning,
And everyone is happy, so it seems.
But when our work is done
We file in one by one
And thank the Lord for one more mess of beans.

We have Hooverized on butter,
And for milk we've only water,
And I haven't seen a steak in many a day.
As for pies, cakes, and jellies,
We substitute sow-bellies
For which we work the county road each day.

If there ever comes a time
When I have more than a dime,
They will have to put me under lock and key,
For they've had me broke so long
I can only sing this song
Of the workers and their misery.

impending problems, but they were dismissed as chronic naysayers who had been wrong before. Roger Babson, an economist, said that "sooner or later a crash is coming, and it may be terrific." A few shrewd investors, such as Joseph P. Kennedy (father of the future president), liquidated their stocks in anticipation of a decline. Even President Hoover told his financial broker to sell off some of his holdings because "possible hard times are coming." But most owners of stock simply waited for the rise in prices to begin again.

Then it happened. On October 24, 1929, which became known as "Black Thursday," traders began selling stocks and quickly realized that there were few buyers for them. Prices collapsed and the total number of shares traded that day reached 13 million, an all-time record. Stockholders were estimated to have absorbed a $9 billion loss. During the afternoon a banking syndicate led by J.P. Morgan, Jr. and Co. urged investors to be calm. A member of the group said that there had been "a little distress selling on the Exchange." As the syndicate bought stocks, the market quieted.

Underlying forces, however, could not be stopped by symbolic gestures and optimistic statements. On October 29, the selling of stocks resumed at an even more intense rate. More than 16 million shares changed hands in a single day. Prestigious industrial stocks such as American Telephone and Telegraph and General Electric recorded twenty-eight-point declines. The *New York Times* called it "the most disastrous day in Wall Street's history." Fistfights occurred on the trading floor and rumors of suicides swept through the Exchange. It was a decisive moment in American financial history, one with important and enduring results.

Causes of the Stock Market Crash

What forces produced the stock market crash of 1929? The 1920s had been characterized by an investment fever that led people into risky ventures. In Florida, for example, there had been a land boom that saw prices for some lots rise to $15,000 or $20,000 a foot for coveted waterfront acreage. When the hysteria ended in 1926, after a devastating hurricane, land prices headed downward again. Willing investors then looked for other speculative opportunities that promised a quick and profitable return.

By 1927 the stock market seemed to be just the place to make easy money. The issuance of Liberty Bonds during World War I had shown Americans the potential value of stocks. Corporations increasingly turned to the public through stock offerings to finance

October 24, 1929, was the date when the stock market boom of the 1920s collapsed. Crowds milled around Wall Street trying to determine what was happening and what had gone wrong with the market.

their business expansion. Stockbrokers sold their products with aggressive advertising techniques developed for other consumer goods. Finally, during the Harding and Coolidge years government tax policies enabled the wealthy to retain money to invest in securities. The richest Americans sometimes paid no income taxes at all. Five hundred families had incomes of more than $1 million in 1929. Many of these surplus funds fueled the rise in the stock market.

Playing the Market: Margin Buying and Investment Trusts

One tempting device for less well-off investors was to buy stocks in "margin" trading. An investor could purchase a stock on credit, putting up only 10 or 15 percent of the actual price. Since Wall Street sentiment believed that stock prices were going up, a person could sell the stock at a higher level, pay off the broker, and still pocket a substantial profit. Just as someone might acquire a house or a car on credit, so brokers urged their customers to invest a hundred dollars with the prospect of controlling $1,000 or more worth of stock. People borrowed money to buy on margin. In this way, a tiny investment might represent a commitment to buy several thousand dollars worth of stock. Of course, the investor could be required to provide the full price of the stock at any time. But with the market headed ever upward, that risk seemed a small one.

Abuses of this trend soon followed. Investors with inside knowledge manipulated a stock's price up and down in order to fleece the unwary public. A firm called Kolster Radio had no earnings in 1929, but insiders drove the value up to ninety-five dollars before the value collapsed back to three dollars a share. New companies often consisted of nothing more than schemes to issue stock based on the assumption that the market would rise. These firms produced no goods; they were paper empires with no real value, such as Ivar Kreuger's International Match Company. Government regulation of stock issues on both the state and federal levels was very lax, and the stock exchanges themselves had few requirements for revealing the true financial status of these companies. Some of the investment trusts, as they were called, were frauds; those who put money into them lost their entire investment.

The Impact of the Crash

The number of Americans who participated in the stock market in 1929 stood at between 1.5 million and 2 million. Most of the corporate dividends in that year went to about 600,000 stockholders whose annual incomes were above $5,000. These individuals were betting on the nation's economic future and sought to benefit from a prosperity that appeared to be permanent. The crash of 1929 wiped out many of these investors. Others cut back on their stock holdings and trimmed their personal expenditures. The growing lack of confidence in the future of the economy would prove contagious in the years following the crash.

The stock market collapse revealed serious underlying weaknesses in the economy. The well-to-do citizens who played the market were confident that other investors would buy their stocks at the higher price levels of the pre-crash period. Because of the way income was distributed in the United States, with the rich getting a far higher share than other segments of the population, there were not enough people in the upper brackets for that assumption to be realistic. Once the wealthy investors began to sell their stocks, there were no other potential buyers to keep security prices high. A fall in the market became unavoidable.

The consequences of the stock market's decline were striking. The prices of individual stocks underwent a sustained downward slide. Within a few months such a high-flying issue as General Electric had dropped from $403 a share to $168. Standard Oil shares fell from eighty-three dollars to forty-eight. One index of stock prices had gone to 469.5 in September and was at 220.1 by November. During the next twelve months the gross national product went down from nearly $88 billion to $76 billion. Something had gone badly wrong with the American economy.

THE GREAT DEPRESSION

While the stock market crash represented a serious setback for the nation's economic health, the Great Depression of the 1930s arose from causes more deeply rooted than just the decline in stock values that occurred in October 1929. Despite the apparent

prosperity of the 1920s, the United States had not dealt with a number of serious structural problems that combined to cause the prolonged economic downturn.

The most pervasive dilemma that the United States economy faced had to do with the distribution of income during the 1920s. By 1929 the 5 percent of Americans at the top income level were receiving one-third of the total annual personal income. By comparison, those who made up the lowest 40 percent of the population received about one-eighth of the available income. For an economy that depended on the purchase of consumer goods for its expansion, this situation meant that there were simply not enough people with money to buy the products that industry was turning out. The amount of spendable income that the top 1 percent of the population received rose from 12 percent in 1920 to 19 percent nine years later. That gain for the wealthy meant that there was less money for the mass of consumers to spend on the products of American factories and businesses than might otherwise have been possible.

Wealth was also concentrated in the hands of those with the highest incomes. More than 21 million families or 80 percent of the national population, did not have any savings at all. About 2.3 percent of families with incomes above $10,000 a year, on the other hand, possessed two-thirds of the available savings. A consumer society had emerged, but the bulk of the consumers were unable to participate fully in the economic process. While wealth had been more concentrated earlier in the century, the disparities of the late 1920s had more impact in contributing to the onset of the Depression.

Instead of using the profits that their businesses gained from selling goods during the mid-1920s to invest in new factories or a better-paid workforce, industry leaders had put their gains into the stock market or speculative ventures. Loans to New York stockbrokers, for example, went from $3.5 billion in July 1927 to $8.5 billion in September 1929. By 1927 the market for new cars and new houses began to weaken, indicating that demand for consumer goods was decreasing.

Other Economic Problems

Another chronic weakness of the economy was in agriculture, a sector that never shared in the general prosperity of the 1920s. The problem of overproduction of farm goods had not been addressed successfully, and as prices fell at the beginning of the Depression the farmers felt the effects most acutely. At the beginning of 1931, cotton stood at nine to ten cents per pound; when farmers brought in their crop in the fall, the price had skidded to under six cents a pound. Since farmers could not pay off their mortgages, rural banks soon failed. The ripple of banking failures strained a banking system that was already weakened by the effects of the stock market crash. In the countryside, crops rotted because they could not be sold, and farmers talked of strikes and other protests.

The International Situation

Beyond the nation's borders, the world economy was also fragile as the 1920s came to an end. The settlement of World War I had imposed heavy reparation payments on the defeated Germans (see Chapter 22). Since the Germans could not pay these sums from their own economy, they borrowed from investors and banks in the United States. In that way Americans financed the Germans' debt payments to the victorious British and French. Those countries, in turn, could use the funds to pay off their war debts to the United States.

The Dawes Plan of 1924 had reduced the burden of German war debts, and in 1929 Owen D. Young proposed a plan that further cut back on the amount that Germany owed while establishing a payment schedule that extended the length of time for retiring the debt.

These concessions, in what became known as the Young Plan, alleviated the situation to some degree, but the basic problem persisted. This intricate and interlocking process hinged on the strength of the American economy. The United States, however, created tariff barriers that discouraged European imports and steered American capital toward internal economic development. When the European economies experienced difficulties themselves after 1929, the weakened structure of debts and loans soon collapsed, further damaging the economy of the United States. In fact, President Hoover would later argue that the entire Depression arose from causes beyond the borders of the United States. The debts were important in the overall situation of the world economy, but they were a contributing cause to the Depression in the United States rather than the main element in the crisis.

A Worsening Economic Situation

In 1929–1930 the United States lacked many of the government programs that could have lessened the cumulative effects of a depression. There was no government insurance of bank deposits. The absence of that policy made individual banks vulnerable to sudden demands by depositors to withdraw their money. Such "runs" destroyed one institution after another. Many banks had invested in the stock market and thereby placed their assets at risk. Other prominent bankers had embezzled some of the funds under their control

TABLE 24.1	
BANK SUSPENSIONS, 1927-1933	
1927	669
1928	499
1929	659
1930	1352
1931	2284
1932	1458
1933	4004

SOURCE: Historical Statistics of the United States, 1985, p. 536.

to finance their investing. Among banks in general, there was little cooperation when a crisis occurred. To save themselves, the stronger banks called in loans made to smaller banks, thus worsening the condition of weaker banks.

For an individual employee thrown out of work, there was no unemployment insurance to cushion the effect of a layoff. Old age pensions were also rare. Conventional economic thinking taught that the government should play a minimal role during hard times. Many people believed that the natural forces of the economy must work themselves out without the government intruding into the process. Secretary of the Treasury Andrew Mellon told President Hoover that "a panic was not altogether a bad thing" because "it will purge the rottenness out of the system." Americans who did not have Mellon's wealth and secure income were less persuaded of the therapeutic effects of hard times.

The President, Congress, and the Depression

The stock market crash did not cause the Depression, and for some months after the disaster on Wall Street it seemed as though the economy might rebound without much assistance from Washington. President Hoover endeavored to strike an encouraging note

The onset of the Great Depression produced mass unemployment that the nation had not seen for four decades. The downturn hit women as much as men, and these women protested the lack of jobs and asked for public works employment.

when he said in late 1929: "[T]he fundamental business of the country is sound." He conferred with leading business figures about measures to maintain public confidence, especially programs to bolster prices and wages. He asked the Federal Reserve System to facilitate business borrowing. For the moment, events seemed to be going Hoover's way. During the first several months of 1930, stock market prices recovered from their 1929 lows.

In 1930, Congress enacted the Smoot-Hawley Tariff which raised customs duties to high levels. Republicans believed that tariff protection would enable American agriculture and industry to rebound. The bill passed the Senate by a narrow margin, and despite some reservations Hoover signed the measure on June 17, 1930. The Smoot-Hawley law has been blamed for the severity of the worldwide Depression because it made it more difficult for European business to sell goods in the United States. The negative impact of the Smoot-Hawley Tariff has probably been overstated, relative to the other, more severe causes of the Depression. In any case, by the middle of 1930, the effects of the downturn began to be felt in many areas of government activity.

Foreign Policy in the Depression

The onset of the Great Depression complicated President Hoover's management of foreign policy after his first year in office. He had come to the White House with well-formulated ideas about the national role in foreign affairs. Since future wars were unlikely, he believed, it was time to pursue disarmament and let the force of world opinion maintain peace. Secretary of State Henry L. Stimson did not share the president's optimism. The two men agreed, however, on the basic goals of diplomacy during the first phase of the new administration.

In Latin America, the president announced the "good neighbor" policy. He promised not to repeat previous U.S. interventions in the region and he withdrew Marines from Nicaragua and Haiti. In 1930, the State Department renounced the Roosevelt Corollary of 1904 (see Chapter 20). Despite outbreaks of revolutions in South America during his term, Hoover kept his word and left Latin American nations alone.

Drawing upon his Quaker roots, Hoover thought that wars were senseless and sought disarmament as a key goal; however, the results were mixed. A naval conference in Geneva in 1927 had brought Great

Britain, Japan, and the United States back to the diplomatic table. Disagreements about the size of vessels covered by the proposed pact caused that meeting to break up in failure. Hoover now reassembled the major naval powers in London for a conference on disarmament. They deliberated for three months before reaching an apparent understanding. The London Treaty of 1930 made only a modest contribution to peace, however. To reduce military spending, the provisions of the Washington Conference (see Chapter 23) were extended for five years. The United States won parity with Britain in all naval vessels, and the Japanese gained the same result for submarines. The outcome did not alter the military balance. Japan remained the dominant power in the Pacific, but there was little that the Hoover administration could do to change that reality. The London Treaty also contained language that allowed the signers to resume building ships if they were threatened with aggression. Meanwhile, popular opinion assumed that another world war was unthinkable. As long as prosperity lasted, the illusion of genuine peace persisted.

The Effects of the Economic Crisis

As the United States economy deteriorated, however, the effects spread to Europe. Fewer American investors could lend money to European governments, especially in Germany. The Smoot-Hawley Tariff made it more difficult for Europeans and other importers to sell their products in the United States. International trade stagnated; production in all industrial countries declined. In 1931 Germany and Austria endeavored to set up a customs union to deal with their common problems but the French objected to the plan and cut off payments to banks in the two countries. In the resulting turmoil, the Creditanstaldt, Austria's central bank, collapsed. The entire structure of international banking stood on the brink of disaster.

Hoover decided that the only answer was a moratorium on the payment of war debts to give the European countries time to regain their financial stability. He declared on June 21, 1931, that the United States would observe an eighteen-month moratorium on the collection of its foreign debts. The French held back for two weeks, putting further strain on German banks. In the end, all the countries involved agreed to Hoover's initiative.

The moratorium was the only possible answer, but it came too late to stop the erosion of the international financial system. A few months later, Great Britain devalued the pound when it could no longer maintain the gold standard. This step reduced the price of British products and made them more competitive in world markets. Other nations soon followed this course. A series of obstacles to world trade arose, worsening the international Depression.

Domestic Issues for Hoover

At home, President Hoover experienced problems in his dealings with Congress. After naming Charles Evans Hughes as chief justice of the U.S. Supreme Court to replace William Howard Taft early in 1930, he had another court vacancy to fill soon thereafter. He selected John J. Parker of North Carolina for the post. Organized labor opposed Parker's nomination because of Parker's issuance of anti-union injunctions in labor disputes. The National Association for the Advancement of Colored People assailed his racial views. The Senate rejected Parker's selection by a vote of forty-one to thirty-nine on May 7, 1930.

During the 1930s and afterward, many Americans would blame the Great Depression on President Hoover and his policies. That judgment was unfair.

More than any previous chief executive, Hoover endeavored to use the power of his office to address the economic crisis. He rejected the counsel of those who told him that he should leave the economy alone and allow it to correct itself. He favored reduction of taxes, easing of bank credits, and a modest program of public works to provide jobs. Some members of Congress opposed these ideas as too activist; others said that Hoover proposed too little. Meanwhile, the White House issued a series of confident statements to bolster public faith that the economic downturn would be brief. When the stock market turned upward briefly in 1930, for example, the president told the nation: "I am convinced we have passed the worst and with continued effort shall rapidly recover."

The Deepening Depression

But as 1930 continued it was clear that the Depression was not going away. Bank failures soared from 659 in 1929 to 1350 a year later. Businesses were closing, investment was declining, and corporate profits were falling off. Industrial production was 26 percent lower at the end of 1930 than it had been twelve months earlier. The number of Americans out of work kept rising. By October 1930 4 million people were without jobs (almost 9 percent of the labor force), and the

The farm sector had never shared in the prosperity of the 1920s, and the collapse of the economy added to the agrarian woes. Farmers had to sell off their property at auctions like the one shown in this photograph. The armed troopers reflect the social tensions that accompanied hard times in rural America.

trend worsened as each month passed. Within a year nearly 16 percent of the labor force was out of work.

To encourage confidence, Hoover exhorted businesses to keep prices up and employees at work. Conferences with industry leaders at the White House were covered extensively in the press. These sessions were designed to show the American people that the Depression was being addressed. The president lacked the power to make corporations retain workers or to prevent price-cutting. Despite any public pledges they might offer to Hoover, corporate executives trimmed payrolls and reduced costs when it seemed necessary. These actions further undercut Hoover's credibility.

Hoover's Programs to Fight the Depression

The president was more than just a national cheerleader. He sought to apply his principles of voluntary action to keep the banking system afloat. In October 1931 he persuaded bankers to set up the National Credit Corporation, a private agency that would underwrite banks that had failed and safeguard their depositors. Unfortunately, the banks proved reluctant to acquire the assets of their failed competitors. The experiment was a disaster.

Despite his broadened use of the powers of his office, Herbert Hoover did not view government action as an appropriate way of responding to the Depression. Instead, he believed that the traditional self-reliance and volunteer spirit of the American people provided the most dependable means of ending the economic slump. His policies promoting economic recovery and providing relief for the unemployed stemmed from that fundamental conviction. He asked Americans who had jobs to invest more in their neighbors, to spend something extra to ensure that everyone could work. He set up presidential committees to coordinate volunteer relief efforts for the unemployed. One of those committees was the President's Organization of Unemployment Relief (or POUR).

The Persistence of Unemployment

These programs were inadequate to the size of the unemployment situation. By 1931, 8 million people were on the jobless rolls. They overwhelmed the resources of existing charitable agencies that normally provided help to the blind, the deaf, and the physically impaired. These voluntary groups could not deal with

TABLE 24.2
UNEMPLOYMENT, 1927-1933

Year	Unemployment	% of Labor Force
1927	1,890,000	4.1
1928	2,080,000	4.4
1929	1,550,000	3.2
1930	4,340,000	8.7
1931	8,020,000	15.9
1932	12,060,000	23.6
1933	12,830,000	24.9

SOURCE: Historical Statistics of the United States, 1985, p. 73.

large masses of people needing assistance. Nor were the cities and states capable of providing relief at a time when the Depression reduced their tax revenues and increased the demand for services.

In this situation, the president's informal committees for dealing with unemployment proved ineffective. The POUR program coordinated relief agencies and urged people to help their neighbors. Mrs. Hoover, long a leader of the Girl Scouts, mobilized its members for the same purpose. These efforts, commendable as they were, did little to deal with the mass unemployment that gripped the country. But when politicians clamored for action by the national government, Hoover remained resolutely opposed.

A symbolic event underscored the president's political ineptitude in dealing with the Depression and its effects. When a drought struck the Midwest in 1930 and 1931, Congress proposed to appropriate $60 million to help the victims of the disaster buy fuel and food. Hoover accepted the idea of allocating money to feed animals but he rejected the idea of feeding farmers and their families. One member of Congress said that the administration would give food to "jackasses . . . but not starving babies." The president accepted a compromise that spent the money without saying that some of it would be used for food. The image of a heartless chief executive remained in the public mind.

Everyday Life During the Depression

For most Americans, there was no single decisive moment when they knew that the economy was in trou-

ble. Instead the problems came on slowly and at different rates. A husband might find his pay reduced or his hours of work cut back. In Houston, Texas, a young daughter became the sole support of her family of five on her $12-a-week salary while her lawyer father looked in vain for clients. Soon families were making changes in their lifestyle, postponing purchases and sending children out to find jobs. When a person lost a job, savings helped tide the family over until another job could be found. As time passed and no jobs appeared, savings ran out and the family home went on the market or the mortgage was foreclosed. The family slipped into the ranks of the unemployed or the poor. In a trend that became a lasting image of the Depression, men selling apples appeared on the street corners in major cities. Beggars and panhandlers became a common sight as well.

For those who were at the bottom of the economy even during boom times, the Depression presented still greater challenges. Blacks had not shared in the relative prosperity of the 1920s. "The Negro was born in depression," said one. "It only became official when it hit the white man." In the South, whites seeking work took over the low-paying service jobs that African Americans had traditionally filled. Some black workers in the South encountered violence when whites compelled them to leave their jobs. Elsewhere, white laborers went on strike, insisting that African-American workers be dismissed. In Atlanta, whites demanded that there be "No Jobs for Niggers Until Every White Man Has a Job."

Women were told that they too should relinquish their jobs to men in order to end the unemployment crisis. Some corporations fired all their married women employees, and school districts in the South dismissed women teachers who married. Because women did the domestic and clerical tasks that men did not care to do even in hard times, the number of women employed did not decline as fast as the number of men. Nevertheless, the Depression retarded the economic progress of women.

For Native Americans, the hard times perpetuated a legacy of neglect that had endured for decades. The Bureau of Indian Affairs (BIA) did not address the many social problems that the people under its jurisdiction confronted. Nearly half the Indians on reservations had no land; the other half subsisted on poor quality land. Poverty pervaded Indian society along with a rate of infant mortality that far exceeded the rate for the white population. Criticism of the BIA mounted, but, despite a commitment to reform, the Hoover administration accomplished little to improve Native American life.

Crisis on the Farms

On the nation's farms, abundant crops could not find a market, so they rotted in the fields. "While Oregon sheep raisers fed mutton to the buzzards," said one account, "I saw men picking for meat scraps in the garbage cans in the cities of New York and Chicago." Mortgages were foreclosed, and many former landowners fell into the status of tenant farmers as the Depression went on. In 1929 President Hoover had persuaded Congress to pass an Agricultural Marketing Act that created a Federal Farm Board whose purpose was to stabilize farm prices. When farm surpluses around the world swamped grain markets in 1930, it proved impossible to prevent commodity prices from falling. Talk of strikes and protests was common

DEMOCRACY

Selling apples became one of the trademark occupations for those seeking work. In this cartoon a former man of wealth joins his unemployed colleagues in vending fruit on the streets.

among farmers during 1931 and 1932. During the summer of 1932 Milo Reno, an Iowa farmer, created the Farmers' Holiday Association which urged growers to hold their crops off the market until prices rose. They put their program into verse:

> Let's call a farmers' holiday
> A holiday let's hold;
> We'll eat our ham and wheat and eggs
> And let them eat their gold.

In the Southwest, the Hoover administration, faced with growing unemployment in that region, endeavored to reduce the people looking for jobs with a program to send Hispanic workers and their families back to Mexico and other Latin American countries. Some 82,000 Mexicans were deported and another half million immigrants crossed the border out of fear that they would be sent back under duress. For Hispanic Americans who stayed in the United States, relief from the government was often hard to find because of a belief that it should be limited to "Americans."

The Plight of the Homeless

As the Depression deepened, the homeless and unemployed took to the roads and rails, looking for work or better times. Migratory workers moved through the agricultural sections of California, picking figs and grapes for whatever they could earn. Others went from city to city, finding inadequate meals at relief stations, shuffling through a breadline in cities, stealing or begging for food in others. The homeless lived in shantytowns outside of cities that were dubbed "Hoovervilles." Soon derogatory references to the president spread throughout the nation. A pocket turned outward as a sign of distress was "a Hoover flag." In the Southwest, people killed armadillos and renamed the meat "Depression Pork."

By 1931 a sense of despair and hopelessness pervaded many segments of society. People who had been out of work for a year or two had lost the energy and inner resources to rebound even if a job was available. Others began to question the nation's values and beliefs. "There has gradually grown up a suspicion," said one writer, "that the profit system, as we have known

The shanty towns where the homeless and unemployed lived became known as "Hoovervilles." Their presence on the outskirts of the large cities became a common site as the Depression deepened.

As hard times became worse, the nation's banking system faltered. Depositors lined up to withdraw whatever funds they could secure when a bank got into trouble. This picture records the fate of the American Union Bank of New York City on August 5, 1931.

it, is its own destruction." Bread riots occurred in several cities; the Communist party forecast that the system was toppling; and the nation's political leaders seemed out of touch with the downward trend of economic events. A popular song caught the nation's angry, restless mood:

> Once I built a railroad, made it run,
> Made it race against time.
> Once I built a railroad, now it's done
> Brother, can you spare a dime?

The Depression did not touch every American in the same way. Despite the economic disruptions, daily life in much of the nation went on as it always had. Families stayed together with the father holding a job, the mother running the home, and their children growing up and attending school. There might be less money to spend, but there was not extensive poverty. Bread lines and people selling apples happened somewhere else. Nevertheless, the economic uncertainty that gripped so many people contributed to a general sense of unease and doubt that permeated the early 1930s.

Mass Culture During the Depression

Amid the hardships of the Depression, Americans found diversions and amusements in the mass media and popular entertainments that had emerged during the 1920s. Radio's popularity grew despite the hard times. Sales of radio sets in the United States reached $300 million annually by 1933. Radio broadcasters and stores were less successful financially between 1929 and 1932, but the habit of listening for a favorite program was an integral part of the daily lives of many families. Americans told interviewers that the last appliance they would sell would be their radio.

Radio was becoming more commercial every year. Programming appealed to popular tastes and sought the largest available audience. Listeners preferred daytime dramas such as "One Man's Family" and "Mary Noble, Backstage Wife," quickly dubbed "soap operas" after the detergent companies that sponsored them. With the increasing emphasis on profits and ratings, commercials became commonplace. Listeners were advised:

> When you're feeling kinda blue
> And you wonder what to do,
> Che-e-ew Chiclets, and
> Chee-ee-er up!

The most popular radio program of the Depression years was "Amos 'n' Andy," which portrayed the lives of two African-American men in Harlem as interpreted by two white entertainers, Freeman Gosden and Charles Correll. Performed in heavy dialect, the show captured a huge audience at 7 o'clock each

The radio was a form of inexpensive entertainment that Americans depended on during the Depression. A family clusters around its set to listen to programs such as "Amos 'n' Andy" or "Fibber McGee and Molly."

evening. The tales of black life appealed to white stereotypes about African Americans, but they also gained an audience among blacks because the characters' experiences were comparable to those of minority listeners.

Off to the Movies

With ticket prices very low and audiences hungry for diversion from the trials of daily life, Hollywood presented a wide choice of films between 1929 and 1932. Sound movies had replaced the silent pictures of the 1920s, and escapist entertainment dominated the movie screens across the country. Audiences laughed at the Marx Brothers in *Cocoanuts* (1929) and *Monkey Business* (1931). Musicals found a ready audience, and there was a vogue for gangster films such as *Little Caesar* (1931) with Edward G. Robinson and *The Public Enemy* (1931) with James Cagney. During the early 1930s Hollywood pressed the limits of tolerance for sexual innuendoes and bawdy themes with a star such as Mae West. Pressures for greater censorship resumed as the Depression deepened.

Despite the hardships of the economic downturn, the cultural flowering that had begun during the preceding decade continued. In Kansas City and other midwestern cities, African-American musicians were

When families went out, the movies were still a good bargain, and millions flocked to theaters each week. Two of the bigger stars of the period were Jean Harlow and James Cagney, shown here in a publicity photo.

One of the popular comedy attractions of the period were the Marx Brothers. This still from their film Cocoanuts shows from left to right Zeppo, Groucho, Chico, and Harpo Marx.

developing a new jazz style that would become known as "swing" when white musicians smoothed its hard edges to make it appealing to their audiences. The "golden age" of American popular song was still in full sway. In 1932, one of the worst Depression years, listeners could hear such new songs as "Alone Together," "April in Paris," "Isn't It Romantic," and "The Song Is You." The hardships of the era evoked artistic creativity and a vibrant popular culture that would dominate the entertainment scene for half a century.

A DARKENING WORLD

The worldwide Depression had calamitous effects on American foreign policy. With the economies of the democratic nations weakened and the structure of international relations tottering, authoritarian forces around the world asserted themselves against the existing order. The first test came in the Far East.

In September 1931, Japanese troops detonated a weak explosive charge under a Japanese-owned railroad in Manchuria and blamed the episode on the Manchurians. The Japanese military had fabricated the incident as an excuse for attacking Chinese positions in Manchuria. During the weeks that followed, the

MAP 24.2 | THE JAPANESE INVASION OF MANCHURIA

When Japan invaded Manchuria in 1931, it violated a number of international agreements which it had signed. This cartoon provides an American commentary on these actions. The depiction of Japanese militarism would be a running theme in the United States throughout the 1930s and 1940s.

Japanese army invaded Manchuria, and advanced deep into the countryside. The Japanese bombed Chinese cities to deter any opposition to their effort to occupy all of Manchuria.

Frustrated by the power of the Western countries and desperate for needed raw materials, Japan and its military wanted to establish their nation as the dominant force in Asia and expel the foreign countries that had achieved a political and economic presence in China and the Far East. Anger at the discriminatory racial policies of the United States, Great Britain, and other European powers fed this frustration. Japan was also fearful that a resurgent China might pose a threat to Japanese ambitions and access to crucial materials for Tokyo's economy. Desire for political and economic supremacy in the Pacific completed the Japanese agenda.

A Challenge to the League of Nations

Japan's attack into Manchuria posed a threat to the authority and power of the League of Nations. It confronted the United States with the problem of what to do in response to a clear violation of policies and treaties to which Washington was a party, such as the Open Door and the Nine-Power Treaty. Yet the United States could not do much from a military standpoint. The American army was no match for

The movement of the Japanese into Manchuria received ample newsreel coverage. Americans deplored the turn of events in Asia but did not want to become involved in a direct way to counteract Japanese incursions.

Adolf Hitler's rise to power in Nazi Germany was a sobering backdrop to the course of events in the United States. Hitler is the third from the right at a Nazi rally in Nuremberg, Germany. Hermann Goering is on Hitler's left, Ernst Roehm is on Hitler's right and Heinrich Himmler is to Roehm's right.

Japan's, and the administration had not maintained naval strength at the levels allowed in the various treaties that had been signed during the preceding decade. In addition, Congress would not have been sympathetic to U.S. intervention in a remote foreign quarrel. For the same reason, Washington could not look to European countries. Nor could it endorse an economic boycott against Japan under the sponsorship of the League of Nations. The Hoover administration could only announce its dislike of events in Manchuria in vigorous words. Secretary of State Stimson issued statements to China and Japan that proclaimed the unwillingness of the United States to recognize territorial changes in China produced by aggressive actions. This policy of nonrecognition became known as the Stimson Doctrine. The Japanese pressed ahead with their campaign to occupy Manchuria and intimidate China despite the secretary's comments. In February 1932, Stimson wrote a prominent senator, warning him that the United States might strengthen its military readiness in the Pacific in response to Japanese actions. Japan knew that the United States could do nothing more than that, however, and Stimson's words had little impact.

The League of Nations criticized the Japanese policy, and Japan responded by withdrawing from the or-

ganization early in 1933. The United States and Japan were now embarked on a course that would lead to ever more bitter encounters and ultimately to all-out war. The American people, however, would not have supported a belligerent policy that risked a war in Asia during the depths of the Depression.

Germany Moves toward the Nazis

The unhappy events in Manchuria foreshadowed what would happen in Europe soon thereafter. In Germany, where resentment about the Treaty of Versailles had grown during the Depression, the National Socialist party of Adolf Hitler was gaining support as the nation's fragile democracy broke apart. Hitler's message of national revenge and hatred of the Jews proved intoxicating to the German people, and during 1932 he stood on the brink of obtaining power. Some Americans, insensitive to Hitler's ideology of racial hatred, even admired the policies of Hitler and the Italian dictator Benito Mussolini because they apparently offered decisive action to deal with the economic crisis. The situation of democratic governments, on the other hand, was perilous as the United States entered the third year of the Depression.

FRANKLIN D. ROOSEVELT: COMMONWEALTH CLUB ADDRESS

In the campaign of 1932, Franklin D. Roosevelt offered a vision of somewhat greater governmental action to meet the Depression. He did not, however, offer a radical program, as this excerpt from his speech to the Commonwealth Club of San Francisco on September 23, 1932, indicates.

This implication is, briefly, that the responsible heads of finance and industry, instead of acting each for himself, must work together to achieve the common end. They must, where necessary, sacrifice this or that private advantage; and in reciprocal self-denial must seek a general advantage. It is here that formal government—political government, if you choose—comes in.

Whenever in the pursuit of this objective the lone wolf, the unethical competitor, the reckless promoter, the Ishmael or Insull whose hand is against every man's, declines to join in achieving an end recognized as being for the public welfare and threatens to drag the industry back to a state of anarchy, the government may properly be asked to apply restraint. Likewise, should the group ever use its collective power contrary to the public welfare, the government must be swift to enter and protect the public interest.

The government should assume the function of economic regulation only as a last resort, to be tried only when private initiative, inspired by high responsibility, with such assistance and balance as government can give, has finally failed. As yet there has been no final failure, because there has been no attempt; and I decline to assume that this nation is unable to meet the situation.

The final term of the high contract was for liberty and the pursuit of happiness. We have learned a great deal of both in the past century. We know that individual liberty and individual happiness mean nothing unless both are ordered in the sense that one

A POLITICAL OPPORTUNITY FOR THE DEMOCRATS

By the beginning of 1932, the Hoover presidency was in dire political trouble. Jokes about Hoover spread across the nation. According to one, a rose placed in Hoover's hand would wilt. Even his advisors were critical. Stimson said that a cabinet meeting was "like sitting in a bath of ink." Another official remarked that the president "has a childlike faith in statements." One political commentator concluded that "there seems to be no class or section where Hoover is strong."

By 1932, the limits of the president's voluntary approach had become evident even to him. During the winter he supported a congressional initiative to establish the Reconstruction Finance Corporation (RFC). Congress authorized this agency to loan up to $2 billion in tax money to save banks, insurance companies, and railroads from financial collapse. The law that set up the RFC repudiated the principle of voluntary action that Hoover had been following since the Depression began. It put the federal government behind the effort to achieve economic recovery and signaled that Washington could no longer take a passive or hands-off role when the economy turned downward. The question was whether this action could reverse Hoover's worsening political fortunes.

man's meat is not another man's poison. We know that the old "rights of personal competency," the right to read, to think, to speak, to choose, and live a mode of life must be respected at all hazards. We know that liberty to do anything which deprives others of those elemental rights is outside the protection of any compact; and that government in this regard is the maintenance of a balance, within which every individual may have a place if he will take it; in which every individual may find safety if he wishes it; in which every individual may attain such power as his ability permits, consistent with his assuming the accompanying responsibility.

All this is a long, slow task. Nothing is more striking than the simple innocence of the men who insist, whenever an objective is present, on the prompt production of a patent scheme guaranteed to produce a result. Human endeavor is not so simple as that. Government includes the art of formulating a policy and using the political technique to attain so much of that policy as will receive general support; persuading, leading, sacrificing, teaching always, because the greatest duty of a statesman is to educate. But in the matters of which I have spoken, we are learning rapidly, in a severe school. The lessons so learned must not be forgotten, even in the mental lethargy of a speculative upturn. We must build toward the time when a major depression cannot occur again; and if this means sacrificing the easy profits of inflationist booms, then let them go; and good riddance.

Faith in America, faith in our tradition of personal responsibility, faith in our institutions, faith in ourselves demand that we recognize the new terms of the old social contract. We shall fulfill them, as we fulfilled the obligation of the apparent utopia which Jefferson imagined for us in 1776, and which Jefferson, Roosevelt, and Wilson sought to bring to realization. We must do so, lest a rising tide of misery, engendered by our common failure, engulf us all. But failure is not an American habit; and in the strength of great hope we must all shoulder our common load.

SOURCE *New York Times,* September 24, 1932.

Republican problems meant opportunity for the Democrats if they could seize the initiative. In their congressional programs, however, the Democrats were not much more creative than their opponents. A deep split persisted within the party over the proper role of government in dealing with the Depression. The tradition of state rights and limits on the national government remained strong among conservative party members. Many of the conservatives who had supported Al Smith would not look kindly on a candidate who wished to expand government's part in dealing with the Depression. Such conservatives controlled the official machinery of the party, including the Democratic National Committee. It would be difficult for a candidate from the party's liberal wing to gain the nomination in 1932.

The Democrats in Congress

During the 1930 elections the Democrats picked up eight seats in the Senate. The Republicans retained control of the upper house by only a single vote. In the House, the Democratic gain was forty-nine seats, not enough to give them a majority, although their total of 216 members put them close. The Depression had hurt the Republicans, but it had not made the Democrats the majority party.

When Congress reassembled late in 1931, the Democrats had gained several other seats because of the death or retirement of four Republicans. As a result, John Nance "Cactus Jack" Garner of Texas became the new speaker of the House. His answer to the growing budget deficit that the Depression produced

was to offer a national sales tax. Such a proposal would have hurt lower income Americans and, by taking money out of the economy, would also have been deflationary at a time when the economy needed stimulation. Before the bill could pass the House, angry rebels in both parties killed the sales tax idea.

The Rise of Franklin D. Roosevelt

To win the White House in 1932, the Democrats needed a new face to run against Hoover. With Al Smith presumably eliminated, party leaders surveyed a new field of possibilities. Among the hopefuls were Governor Albert Ritchie of Maryland, Newton D. Baker who had served in Woodrow Wilson's cabinet, and Speaker Garner. As the year began, however, everyone conceded that the front-runner was Governor Franklin D. Roosevelt of New York.

Roosevelt was fifty years old. He came from a wealthy branch of his family that lived on the Hudson River in Hyde Park, New York. After attending the aristocratic Groton School and Harvard University, he had studied law in New York City. In 1910 he won a seat in the New York State Senate, and three years later he became assistant secretary of the Navy in the Wilson administration. Seven years in Washington had given him a thorough introduction to the politics of that city.

Although Franklin D. Roosevelt was only a distant cousin of Theodore, his wife Eleanor was the former president's niece. His connection to a famous name helped Roosevelt secure the Democratic vice-presidential nomination in 1920. He proved to be an effective and popular campaigner, but he could not offset the Republican tide that swept Warren G. Harding into office. Yet the race had given him valuable national exposure.

Roosevelt's Illness and Political Comeback

Following that defeat, Roosevelt returned to private life. In 1921 he was stricken with polio and lost the use of his legs. For the rest of his life he could not walk without crutches and usually used a wheelchair. Counted out of politics because of his illness, Roosevelt worked his way back into Democratic affairs during the mid-1920s and in 1928 was elected governor of New York by a narrow margin despite the Hoover landslide. Two years later he won reelection by a huge majority. Surveying the results of the 1930 contest, Will Rogers said: "The Democrats nominated their President yesterday."

In public, Roosevelt, his wife, and their five children were the picture of a robust American family. But behind this façade lay personal difficulty. During 1918–1919 the Roosevelts' marriage had almost collapsed because of Franklin's affair with another woman. The Roosevelts stayed together, but theirs became a political partnership of convenience. During the 1920s, Mrs. Roosevelt played a greater role in politics herself and gained prominence as an advocate of social reform.

In his political views, Roosevelt shared many of the ideas of the mainstream of the Democratic party. He believed in balanced budgets, the gold standard, and capitalism. Yet he also had an instinctive rapport with people in all segments of society, and he relished the exercise of power. His progressive views on the role of government separated him from conservatives in his party, who longed nostalgically for a return to the pre-Wilsonian traditions. Roosevelt trusted no one completely and never confided his deepest thoughts about his political destiny. Many observers judged him to be superficial and shallow. The influential columnist Walter Lippmann called him "a pleasant man, who, without any important qualifications for the office, would very much like to be President."

The Roosevelt Appeal

Roosevelt was one of the most gifted politicians in the nation's history. He recognized earlier than most public leaders of his time the power of radio to reach the American electorate. His jaunty manner and courage in the face of his disability conveyed a message of hope and optimism that was contagious during the Depression. Once nominated, he could appeal to all branches of the Democratic party and would have few problems in defeating Hoover. It remained to be seen, however, whether he could win his party's nomination in the face of the conservatives who disliked him so intensely.

Roosevelt's campaign got off to a strong start. His manager, James A. Farley, had been wooing potential delegates since 1930, and he had mapped out a strategy to attract both big-city leaders, whose support for the Democrats had been growing, and the Solid South, a bastion of party strength since the end of Reconstruction. As a source of ideas for his campaign, Roosevelt turned to the academic community in the

Northeast. He recruited several professors from Columbia University in New York to write speeches and formulate concepts for his programs. Raymond Moley, Rexford G. Tugwell, and Adolf A. Berle were promptly named "the brain trust." In his speeches, Roosevelt talked of "the forgotten man at the bottom of the economic pyramid" who was suffering from the effects of the Depression. The answer, Roosevelt said, was "bold, persistent experimentation."

The Struggle for the Nomination

As Roosevelt's campaign gathered strength and it became clear that Hoover was going to lose, other Democrats decided to challenge the front-runner. Still angry over his 1928 defeat and no longer friendly with Roosevelt, Al Smith wanted to stop Roosevelt and perhaps gain another chance at the White House. In February 1932 he indicated that he would accept a nomination if it came his way. He became a more active candidate as the weeks passed, and his strength in the Northeast made him a serious rival to Roosevelt. Roosevelt was clearly the choice of a majority of the Democrats, but party rules mandated that a nominee receive two-thirds of the votes of the convention delegates. If Garner and Smith teamed up against him and their delegates stood firm, Roosevelt could not win. The problem for the anti-Roosevelt forces, however, was finding an alternative candidate around whom to unite.

The Democratic National Convention opened in Chicago on June 20, 1932. The Roosevelt forces faced many difficulties during the days that followed, but when it came to the balloting, his opponents could not rally around anyone else. In the end Speaker Garner decided to release his delegates to Roosevelt; his reward would be the vice presidential nomination, which he said was "not worth a pitcher of warm piss." At the same time, the California delegation swung its support to Roosevelt on the fourth ballot. The Democrats had chosen their most formidable candidate to run against the incumbent president.

A New Deal

In a dramatic break with the political tradition that barred candidates from appearing at a convention to accept a nomination, Roosevelt boarded a plane and flew to Chicago through stormy weather. There he spoke of the need to "resume the country's uninterrupted march along the path of real progress, real justice, of real equality, for all of our citizens great and small." As he concluded his speech, he used a phrase that would become the trademark of his presidency. "I pledge you, I pledge myself to a new deal for the American people." The scene was impressive. The candidate seemed poised and self-assured, and he radiated optimism. The convention band played the new Democratic theme: "Happy Days Are Here Again." For the first time since nominating Woodrow Wilson twenty years earlier, the Democrats sensed a decisive victory in the air.

The Republicans, on the other hand, recognized the defeat that awaited them. Gloom pervaded their national convention held in mid-June. Hoover and the administration had firm control of the proceedings, and their script was followed. Efforts to nominate anyone other than Hoover failed. The president quickly won the convention victory he sought, and the party renominated Charles Curtis as vice president.

The Economy in Distress

While the two parties were choosing their candidates, the economy worsened and the specter of social violence seemed imminent. To deal with the growing budget deficit, Congress decided to impose new taxes in the Revenue Act of 1932. The sales tax idea had been dropped, but other levies on corporations, estates, and incomes made this the greatest peacetime increase in taxes in the nation's history. At a time when the economy needed fiscal stimulus, the tax measure drew funds out of the hands of consumers. Raising taxes in an election year added to Hoover's growing unpopularity with the voters.

The weakening of the Hoover administration and the increasing power of the Democrats led to an important change in labor policy during 1932. For many years employers had used friendly federal judges and the power of injunctions to cripple the ability of labor unions to win strikes. The Norris-LaGuardia Act of 1932, by contrast, extended to workers "full freedom of association" and labor representation, restricted the use of injunctions, and barred reliance on "yellow-dog" contracts, which prevented workers from joining unions. Its passage foreshadowed further gains for the enfeebled labor movement in the years that followed.

As the Depression worsened during its third year, the plight of unemployed Americans deteriorated well beyond the ability of cities and states to provide aid.

Congress became restive as the Reconstruction Finance Corporation extended loans to large corporations and the White House resisted legislation to help the needy and distressed. Bills were introduced to provide direct assistance to the unemployed, but a coalition of Republicans and southern Democrats blocked their passage. As news spread about how much money businesses had received from the RFC, pressure intensified for Congress to do something. The result was the Emergency Relief and Construction Act of 1932, which required states to attest that they could not raise any money themselves before federal funds were allocated to them. The law limited the kinds of construction projects that could be funded, but it represented at least a symbolic step toward a greater federal role in meeting the needs of desperate Americans in the midst of an economic crisis.

The Bonus March

During the summer of 1932 other desperate citizens sought immediate relief from the government in the form of cash. After World War I, Congress in a generous mood had promised war veterans cash bonuses in the form of paid-up life insurance to be disbursed in 1945. During the Hoover presidency the needs of veterans as a group had been generously funded, and on the whole they had suffered less from the Depression than some other groups. As the Depression worsened, however, the veterans clamored for early access to their "bonus" money. Hoover vetoed a proposal to allow veterans to borrow against the value of their bonuses in 1931. During the spring of 1932, Congress decided not to authorize early payment of the bonuses.

To make their presence felt, thousands of veterans organized the Bonus Expeditionary Force, or the Bonus Army, which came to Washington during the summer of 1932 to listen to Congress debate the bonus proposal. They camped out in tar paper dwellings and tents on the banks of the Anacostia River; some slept in government buildings. The authorities in Washington generally cooperated with the veterans and did what they could to provide them with food and shelter during their stay. Hoover ignored them. When it became clear that Congress was not going to help the Bonus Marchers and would adjourn in mid-July 1932, the Hoover administration urged the Bonus Army to leave Washington and even allocated $100,000 to pay for the cost of sending the

The march of veterans seeking their bonuses from their World War I service became one of the most controversial episodes of 1932. This pro-Bonus cartoon stresses the connection of the Bonus Marchers with mainstream America and labels their cause a just one.

men home. Some of the marchers took advantage of this offer and left Washington. Others stayed on, hoping for a change in government policy.

A Violent Climax to the Bonus March

There were some officials in the Hoover administration who wanted a confrontation with the marchers in order to bolster the president's reputation as a champion of law and order. On July 28, Secretary of War Patrick J. Hurley ordered the police to remove marchers from government buildings where some had camped out. When the police moved in, the veterans resisted and fighting occurred. A police pistol went off; other officers began shooting; and soon two Bonus Marchers lay dead. The president ordered the federal troops in Washington, commanded by General Douglas MacArthur, to restore order. The general took his men, armed with tanks and machine guns, across the Anacostia River into the main camp of the Bonus Army. The veterans fled in terror as the soldiers approached. Tear gas canisters were hurled, tents were

The Hoover administration sent in troops to disperse the Bonus Marchers after Congress refused to pay the veterans their bonuses early. The use of armed force against protesting citizens, especially the deployment of tear gas, made the episode a public relations disaster for the White House.

burned, and the crowd dispersed in a panic. Motion picture cameras caught MacArthur in full military regalia directing the attack, and moviegoers across the nation saw newsreels of American soldiers ousting the Bonus Army from its camp.

The Hoover administration laid the blame for the incident on the influence of Communists inside the veterans' camp. One government official called the Bonus Army "a polyglot mob of tramps and hoodlums, with a generous sprinkling of Communist agitators." There were a few Communists among the veterans, but they had little influence on the protest. Law enforcement agencies found no evidence of an organized conspiracy among the marchers, and public opinion favored the veterans. "If the Army must be called out to make war on unarmed citizens," said a newspaper editor, "this is no longer America." The Bonus Army was a major political disaster for Herbert Hoover.

The 1932 Election

The economic devastation produced by the Great Depression offered groups outside the two-party system a promising chance to win votes for more radical solutions to the nation's problems. The Communists, for example, organized Unemployed Councils to stage protests against high rents and evictions of tenants. Socialists and other left-wing groups cooperated with the Communists in protest marches and petitions for relief. Efforts to organize sharecroppers and tenant farmers in the South also went forward under the sponsorship of the Communists during these years. The Communists wooed African-American support when they defended the "Scottsboro boys," a group of young black men who had been unjustly accused of raping two white women in Alabama in 1931. In 1932, some prominent intellectuals endorsed the Communist presidential campaign or supported the Socialist candidate, Norman Thomas.

For the majority of Americans, however, the only real choice lay between Roosevelt and Hoover. Many of Roosevelt's advisors told him that he did not have to campaign to win the race. "All you have got to do," said John Nance Garner, "is to stay alive until election day." Roosevelt saw the matter differently. If he ran a passive, traditional campaign, he would not persuade the voters who were looking for a change. A front-porch campaign would also have fed rumors that he could not withstand the physical rigors of the presidency. So Roosevelt crisscrossed the country, making speeches that assailed the Republican leadership and attacked Hoover's record.

The case of the African-American men accused in the Scottsboro trial became another controversial episode in racial injustice in the early 1930s. Guarded by state troopers, the defendants in the case consult with their attorney.

Roosevelt's Campaign

Roosevelt wanted to occupy the political middle ground, and as a result his campaign speeches took a variety of contradictory positions. At times he seemed to be calling for a more activist federal government that would adapt "existing economic organizations to the service of the people." On other occasions he attacked Hoover's budget deficits and wasteful government spending. There were occasional hints of the New Deal ahead, but most of Roosevelt's appeal came down to hope, confidence, and the promise of political change.

The incumbent president knew he was going to lose, but he campaigned doggedly. He made nine major speeches, all of which he wrote himself in longhand. Hoover told the voters that the nation faced a choice between "two philosophies of government." He charged that the Democrats sought "to change our form of government and our social and our economic system." Abandoned by many of his fellow Republicans and unpopular with the voters, Hoover staggered through his lifeless campaign toward the inevitable outcome.

Hoover Defeated

On Election Day, the expected Roosevelt landslide took place. The Democratic candidate won overwhelmingly in the popular vote and scored a 472-to-59 triumph in the electoral college. His party secured almost 57 percent of the popular vote and made significant gains in Congress: ninety seats in the House and thirteen in the Senate. The election proved a major disappointment to both the Socialists and the Communists. Norman Thomas, running on the Socialist ticket, received fewer than a million votes. William Z. Foster, the Communist candidate, gained just over 100,000 ballots. Despite the hard times and misery of the Depression, the American people were willing to give the two-party system another chance to address the nation's ills.

Roosevelt and Hoover

By 1932 politicians realized that the four-month period between the time that a president was elected and the inauguration was too long for a modern industrialized nation. A constitutional amendment moving the date of the inauguration to January 20 was under consideration, but the Twentieth Amendment would not go into effect until 1937. Meanwhile, the country faced a worsening economic crisis with a repudiated lame-duck president and Congress that would remain in power until March 4, 1933.

During these four months, the Depression reached its lowest point. One-quarter of the workforce could not find jobs and the relief system, such as it was, had broken down. The gross national product, which had stood at more than $103 billion in 1929, had slid to $58 billion by 1932. Wheat sold for thirty cents a bushel compared with the three dollars a bushel it had brought in 1920. Farmers threatened more action to stop foreclosures of delinquent mortgages in their states. In December, hunger marchers came to Washington to ask for government aid. The growing numbers of failing banks presented a dire threat: 1,453 banks shut their doors in 1932, and political leaders feared that the nation's entire financial structure could be threatened.

Neither Hoover nor Roosevelt was able to deal with these growing problems. The defeated president believed that the cause of the Depression lay beyond the nation's borders. He wanted Roosevelt to support his

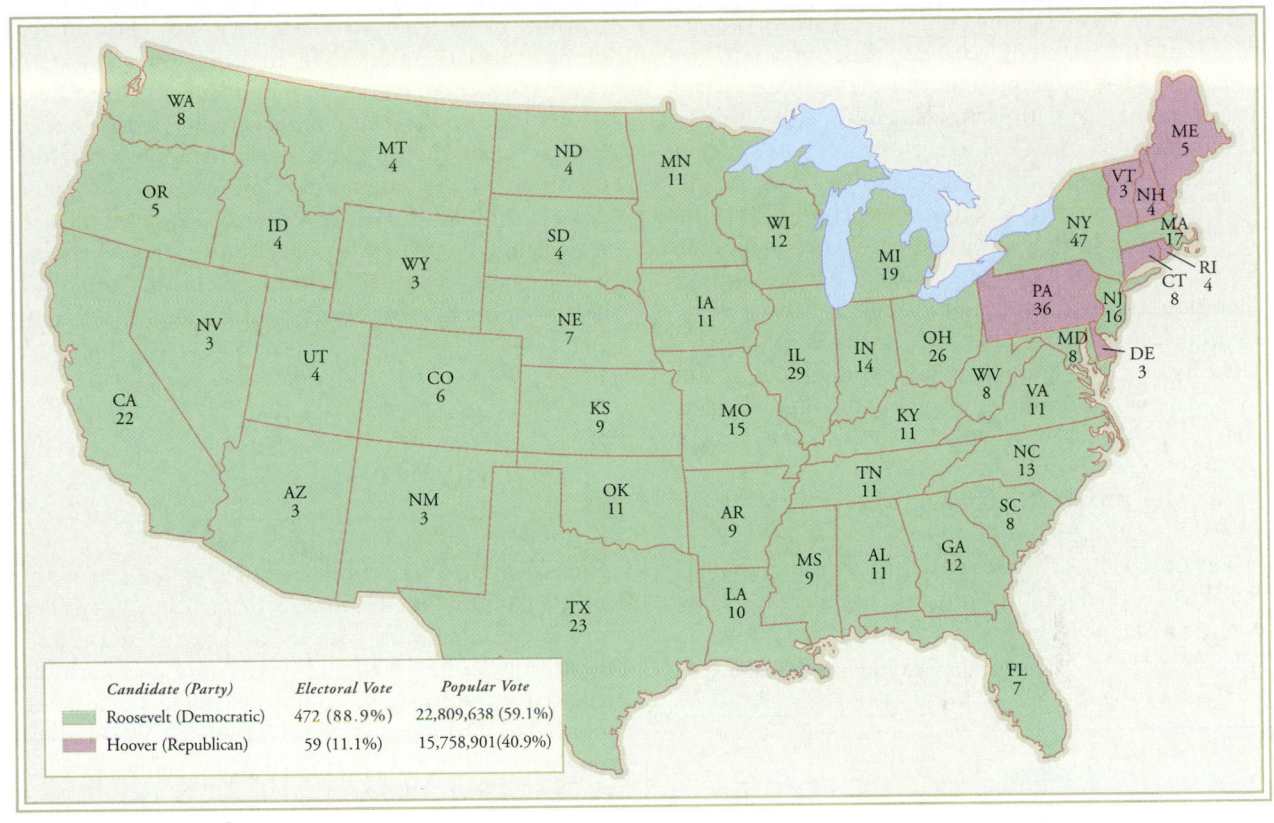

Candidate (Party)	Electoral Vote	Popular Vote
Roosevelt (Democratic)	472 (88.9%)	22,809,638 (59.1%)
Hoover (Republican)	59 (11.1%)	15,758,901 (40.9%)

MAP 24.3 | THE ELECTION OF 1932

policies. Wary of making commitments before taking office, Roosevelt dodged Hoover's efforts to obtain his backing. Relations between the two men worsened. Hoover became convinced that Roosevelt cared little for the welfare of the country, while Roosevelt saw his defeated rival as a sore loser who was trying to win through subterfuge what he had lost at the polls. The government drifted during these fateful months.

Roosevelt devoted most of his energy to forming a cabinet and getting ready to take over the presidency. He chose a diverse group, including Representative Cordell Hull as secretary of State, Progressive reformer Harold Ickes as secretary of the Interior, and Frances Perkins, the first female cabinet member, as secretary of Labor. The president-elect also survived an assassination attempt two weeks before the inauguration. At a speaking engagement in Miami during a break from a fishing trip, Roosevelt was talking with the mayor of Chicago, Anton Cermak, when a would-be assassin fired five shots at Roosevelt. None hit him, but one wounded Cermak, who died shortly afterward.

The Banking System Nears Collapse

As March 4 approached, the nation's banking system wobbled toward a complete breakdown. A crisis of confidence in banks gripped the country. Alarm about the banking system had been spreading since October 1932. During that month the governor of Nevada proclaimed a twelve-day bank "holiday" to end depositor "runs" on banks in his state. The news spurred depositors in other states to remove funds from their local banks. In Michigan, two banks in Detroit seemed about to fail by mid-February. Hoover tried to persuade business leaders, including Henry Ford, to place deposits in the troubled banks. Ford was willing, but others were not. The governor of Michigan intervened and declared a bank holiday on February 14. Depositors in other states, fearing that their deposits would be frozen, tried to withdraw their money from local banks. Governors in nine other states were forced to announce bank holidays. Fear for the soundness of the financial system became widespread.

Hoover pressed the incoming president for immediate joint action. Roosevelt was still reluctant to tie his own hands before he took office. The days passed as February ended with no agreement on either side to do anything about the banking crisis. The two men held one last awkward business meeting on March 3. Trying to be polite, Roosevelt told Hoover that he need not return the visit by calling on him before he left the presidency. Hoover replied: "Mr. Roosevelt, when you are in Washington as long as I have been, you will learn that the President of the United States calls on nobody." With that icy rebuff, Hoover and Roosevelt parted until the inauguration the next day.

A Spreading Sense of Crisis

As the transition of power neared, general apprehension increased. Eleanor Roosevelt wondered: "How much can people take without blowing up?" By the

Candidate Franklin D. Roosevelt hears directly from one determined voter.

morning of March 4, banks in New York City, the nation's financial capital, were shutting their doors. A weary Hoover concluded in a moment of personal despair: "We are at the end of our string." Shortly before eleven o'clock the outgoing president joined Franklin Roosevelt in a waiting limousine and the two men drove off toward the Capitol. Roosevelt waved to well-wishers in the crowd as Hoover sat in silence. A nation mired in the worst depression in its history waited to hear what the new president would say.

CONCLUSION

The economic slump of the early 1930s was one of the most significant events in American history. It called into question citizens' faith in the brighter future that the nation promised to all. Uncertainty and hardship replaced optimism and confidence for a decade and more. The Depression also changed the way Americans viewed the federal government. While they retained their suspicion of intrusive national power, they expected that Washington would prevent future depressions and relieve the effects of the one that was occurring. Radical solutions that involved dismantling capitalism or redistributing income on a large scale gained relatively few adherents.

The Depression discredited the Republican party for two decades in presidential elections. The memory of President Hoover and his failed policies was so strong that Democratic candidates ran against him for a generation. Young children were told that "People were starving because of Herbert Hoover. My mother was out of work because of Herbert Hoover." Although Hoover lived thirty years after he left the White House, his reputation never recovered.

The popular esteem for large corporations also fell dramatically during the 1930s when the public learned how their executives had profited from inside information and tax advantages. The month before Roosevelt's election, a Midwestern utility magnate, Samuel Insull, fled when his network of holding companies fell apart. A congressional probe in early 1933 disclosed that Wall Street executives had benefited from inside information about stock market transactions. Other similar revelations followed once Roosevelt took office.

The major political and economic institutions that had governed the nation for half a century—the Republican party and corporate power—were challenged by the force and size of the Great Depression. Industrialism had become embedded in American life, but there remained serious questions about how society ought to respond to the inequities and injustices that often accompanied industrial growth. There was a sense of pause and anticipation, as well as economic crisis, during the first days of March 1933. Would the United States turn to radical solutions as European countries had done? Could democratic institutions respond to the demands of economic hardship? Franklin D. Roosevelt had now promised a "new deal" for the American people. Noon approached in Washington, and Roosevelt walked on crutches the thirty-seven painful and difficult steps from his seat to the place in front of the Capitol where he would take the oath of office. The United States had come to a pivotal moment in its history as the new president began to speak.

RECOMMENDED READINGS

Allen, Frederick Lewis. *Since Yesterday: The 1930s in America* (1939) well captures the transition from prosperity to economic hardship.

Barone, Michael. *Our Country: The Shaping of America from Roosevelt to Reagan* (1990) looks at the political effects of the Depression.

Bernstein, Irving. *The Lean Years: A History of the American Worker, 1920–1933* (1960) is excellent on the impact of the Depression on workers.

Burner, David. *Herbert Hoover: A Public Life* (1979) is a good one-volume biography of the president.

Fausold, Martin. *The Presidency of Herbert Hoover* (1985) looks at the record of the administration in detail.

Galbraith, John Kenneth. *The Great Crash* (1955) is an entertaining overview of the effects of the Stock Market's woes.

Lichtman, Allan J. *Prejudice and the Old Politics: The Presidential Election of 1928* (1979) emphasizes the cultural forces that elected Hoover.

McElvaine, Robert S. *The Great Depression: America 1929–1941* (1984) is a vivid chronicle of the effects of the economic downturn.

Parrish, Michael E. *Anxious Decades: America in Prosperity and Depression, 1920–1941* (1992) is an excellent recent synthesis of the interwar period.

Shannon, David, A. ed., *The Great Depression* (1960) is a fascinating collection of documents.

Politics
Burns, James McGregor. *Roosevelt: The Lion and the Fox* (1956).

Craig, Douglas B. *After Wilson: The Struggle for the Democratic Party, 1920–1934* (1992).

Hoff-Wilson, Joan. *Herbert Hoover: Forgotten Progressives* (1975).

Lisio, Donald. *The President and Protest: Hoover, Conspiracy, and the Bonus Riot* (1974).

Jordan A. Schwarz, *The Interregnum of Despair: Hoover, Congress, and the Depression* (1970).

The Depression
Bird, Caroline. *The Invisible Scar* (1966).

Kindleberger, Charles P. *The World in Depression, 1929–1939* (1975).

Romasco, Albert U. *The Poverty of Abundance: Hoover, the Nation, and the Depression* (1965).

Temin, Peter. *Did Monetary Forces Cause the Great Depression?* (1976).

Terkel, Studs. *Hard Times: An Oral History of the Great Depression* (1970).

Foreign Policy
Cohen, Warren I. *Empire Without Tears: America's Foreign Relations, 1921–1933* (1987).

Costigliola, Frank. *Awkward Dominion: American Political, Economic, and Cultural Relations with Europe, 1919–1933* (1985).

Ellis, L. Ethan. *Republican Foreign Policy, 1921–1933* (1968).

Iriye, Akira. *After Imperialism: The Search for a New Order in the Far East, 1921–1933* (1973).

Morison, Elting. *Turmoil and Tradition: A Study of the Life and Times of Henry L. Stimson* (1964).

American Society in the Great Depression
Barnouw, Erik. *A Tower in Babel: A History of Broadcasting in the United States to 1933* (1966).

Bergman, Andrew. *We're in the Money: Depression America and Its Films* (1993).

Cook, Blanche Wiesen. *Eleanor Roosevelt, 1884–1933* (1992).

Nash, Roderick. *The Nervous Generation: American Thought, 1917–1930* (1990).

Westin, Jeanne. *How Women Survived the Depression* (1976).

Americans who grew up in the Depression, served their country during World War II, and ushered in the enormous prosperity of the 1950s and beyond, have been celebrated in recent books and movies as "the greatest generation." There are good reasons for such praise. In no other period except the Civil War and Reconstruction was America as severely tested, its direction as radically changed. The 1930s saw the worst economic catastrophe in modern history. Banks collapsed, farms failed, factories closed, bread lines formed in the cities. Yet what truly defined the nation in this decade was its passionate response to misfortune—the way Americans mixed protest, innovation, and reform. Dramatic changes occurred. The Great Depression not only increased the social responsibilities of government, it also opened the political process to millions of "forgotten Americans," who exercised power by joining labor unions, switching political parties, and migrating to places where they could vote and be represented. In contrast to the violent ideological struggles that gripped much of Europe in the 1930s, the United States witnessed a remarkable expansion of the democratic principles it held so dear.

While the Great Depression would linger until World War II, the federal government provided Americans with food and employment, optimism and hope. Furthermore, the vast public works projects of that era—the roads, dams, bridges, tunnels, schools, hospitals, post offices, airports, parks, and playgrounds—created a physical infrastructure that

tied the nation together while it spurred its future success. World War II brought on new challenges and opportunities. Battling on two fronts, the nation resolutely mobilized a superb U.S. fighting force and a masterful homefront effort in which almost everyone took part. The war provided better employment for minorities and for women, although discrimination in wages and skilled jobs remained. So, too, did segregation in the armed forces—a hypocrisy that did not end till 1948. Nevertheless, Americans stood shoulder-to-shoulder against the villainy of fascism, Pearl Harbor, and Nazi genocide.

The enormous prosperity following World War II quickly pushed fears of economic depression aside. What remained in place, however, were the structural reforms that made banks safer, capitalism stronger, and people more secure. Postwar Americans strongly supported an active government role in domestic and foreign affairs. There was little opposition

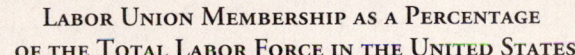

LABOR UNION MEMBERSHIP AS A PERCENTAGE OF THE TOTAL LABOR FORCE IN THE UNITED STATES

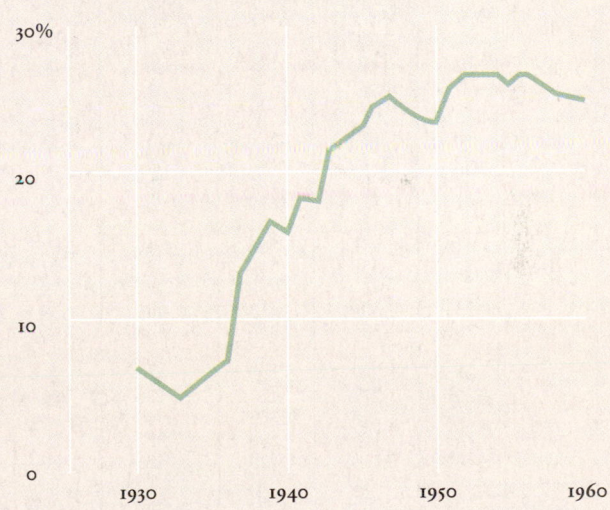

SOURCE: BUREAU OF LABOR STATISTICS, U.S. LABOR DEPARTMENT

to expanding the social security system, increasing the defense budget, or providing hefty benefits to veterans of the war. Soldiers came home and picked up their lives. The marriage rate soared, a baby boom followed, and young families rushed to the suburbs. Peacetime consumption replaced wartime production as the key to national prosperity, with the sale of new homes, automobiles, and appliances reaching record heights.

The prosperity and good feelings generated by World War II, however, were not equally shared. Employment opportunities for women fell dramatically after the veterans returned. Racial prejudice remained a national disgrace. The South still required segregation by law, while other regions discriminated more subtly in housing, education, and jobs. Furthermore, growing fears about Soviet expansion and domestic communism dissolved the political unity, or bipartisanship, that had marked American foreign policy throughout the war. The resulting Red Scare, fueled by opportunistic politicians like Senator Joseph R. McCarthy, challenged America's most cherished ideals.

CONSTRUCTION BIDDING VOLUME (ENGINEERING NEWS-RECORD), BY TYPE: 1933–1960 (IN MILLIONS OF DOLLARS)

		Public works						Private buildings			
Year	Total volume	Water-works	Sewerage	Bridges	Earth-work, irrigation, drainage	Streets, roads	Buildings	Industrial	Commer-cial, multi-unit residential	Un-classified	Year
	101	102	103	104	105	106	107	108	109	110	
1960	22,654	455	619	794	780	3,401	13,300	2,792	8,051	2,462	1919
1959	20,423	376	655	570	915	2,899	13,195	2,993	6,861	1,958	1918
1958	19,165	306	618	713	1,045	3,729	13,664	1,756	5,534	1,799	1917
1957	17,986	369	556	781	969	2,965	12,995	3,081	4,795	1,475	1916
1956	21,712	356	579	622	730	2,475	12,417	5,335	7,358	1,841	
1955	18,722	314	402	546	546	2,137	11,987	2,951	7,794	2,046	1915
1954	14,412	245	388	510	339	1,919	12,017	1,876	5,653	1,465	1914
1953	15,171	247	431	752	374	1,793	12,112	3,178	4,621	1,663	1913
1952	15,689	231	304	413	496	1,397	12,899	2,722	3,845	1,382	
1951	13,605	209	335	316	505	1,167	12,701	4,124	2,632	1,617	
1950	13,342	215	287	369	417	1,268	13,754	1,683	4,092	1,256	
1949	8,157	207	277	357	524	897	11,736	950	2,406	803	
1948	7,219	209	228	303	519	996	1,161	1,096	1,888	820	
1947	5,659	139	175	196	327	794	615	862	1,898	652	
1946	5,176	109	114	129	328	769	414	1,113	1,846	354	
1945	2,289	61	35	53	57	227	463	635	387	371	
1944	1,730	33	32	17	64	196	658	174	140	416	
1943	33,062	46	41	26	47	227	1,419	167	231	858	
1942	49,306	151	118	50	251	531	5,678	200	292	2,034	
1941	5,869	77	89	112	245	583	2,786	496	486	996	
1940	3,987	70	91	120	234	678	1,196	594	400	603	
1939	3,003	163	160	151	233	644	593	283	388	390	
1938	2,792	131	136	135	268	638	503	152	550	279	
1937	2,437	104	95	133	110	415	333	477	460	309	
1936	2,387	92	121	188	182	483	436	309	275	300	
1935	1,590	81	100	98	259	325	298	172	109	148	
1934	1,361	92	61	99	266	345	204	105	81	106	
1933	1,068	67	22	98	137	288	121	152	106	77	

Still, the nation prospered and grew. The 1950s saw the spread of a powerful civil rights movement and the demise of Senator McCarthy. Breakthroughs in medicine and technology ended the nightmare of polio, fueled the space race, and brought the miracle of television into almost every American home. The economic boom continued, raising living standards and national confidence to even greater heights. As 1960 approached, the nation appeared content and comfortable—thanks in large part to "the greatest generation," now approaching middle age.

POLITICS & DIPLOMACY

1932: Franklin Roosevelt elected president
1933: Adolph Hitler becomes Chancellor of Germany
U.S. recognizes the Soviet Union
1935: Congress passes Social Security

1936: Spanish Civil War
1937: Court-packing plan defeated
1939: Nazi forces invade Poland
1940: Roosevelt wins unprecedented third term
1941: Japanese bomb Pearl Harbor
1942: Incarceration of Japanese-Americans
1943: German army crushed at Stalingrad

1944: Normandy Invasion
1945: Germany surrenders
Atomic bombs dropped on Hiroshima and Nagasaki
Japan surrenders
1946: Cold War emerges
1947: Truman Doctrine and Marshall Plan implemented
1948: Alger Hiss indicted for perjury
1949: Communists triumph in China

SOCIAL & CULTURAL EVENTS

1932: Bonus Army march
1933: Prohibition ends
1935: Congress of Industrial Organizations formed

1936: Jesse Owens dominates the Berlin Olympics
1939: John Steinbeck publishes *Grapes of Wrath*
Marian Anderson sings at Lincoln Memorial
1941: A. Philip Randolph threatens March on Washington
1943: Race riot in Detroit

1944: G.I. Bill passed
1945: 12.5 million Americans in uniform
1946: Dr. Spock publishes *Common Sense Book of Baby and Child Care*
1947: Jackie Robinson breaks baseball's color line
1948: *Kinsey Report*
1949: Sears, Roebuck catalogue advertises television set

ECONOMICS & TECHNOLOGY

1932: Unemployment reaches 25 percent
Thousands of banks close
1933: Tennessee Valley Authority created

1937: Severe recession
1941: Manhattan Project begins

1945: United States produces more than half the world's manufactured goods
1946: Reconversion
1949: Soviet Union tests atomic bomb

1950: Senator Joseph McCarthy raises Communist issue
Korean War begins
1952: Dwight Eisenhower elected president
1953: Cease-fire in Korea
Stalin dies

1954: U.S. Senate censures Joseph McCarthy
Brown v. *Board of Education*
1956: Hungarian Revolution
Suez crisis

1957: Federal troops sent to Little Rock
1959: Cuban Revolution

1951: Alan Freed hosts rock-and-roll radio show

1955: Montgomery bus boycott
1956: Elvis Presley appears on *Ed Sullivan Show*
1957: Jack Kerouac publishes *On the Road*

1959: TV quiz show scandals

1954: IBM markets business computer
1955: Salk polio vaccine
1956: Federal Highway Act
1957: Sputnik launched

1958: U.S. manned space program begins

Mar. 4, 1933 THE Price 15 cents

NEW YORKER

peter Arno

THE FACES OF VICTORY AND DEFEAT

This New Yorker *cartoon, sketched well before the inauguration, accurately predicted feelings of both men—the glum Hoover and the exuberant Roosevelt—as they rode down Pennsylvania Avenue together on March 4, 1933.*

Chapter 25

THE NEW DEAL,

1933–1939

ON MARCH 4, 1933, Franklin Roosevelt took the presidential oath of office in a steady, chilling rain. "Only a foolish optimist can deny the dark realities of the moment," he told the huge crowd and the millions who listened on radio. Roosevelt's voice radiated confidence and concern. "This nation asks for action, and action now," he declared. Comparing the Depression to an all-out war of survival, he vowed to ask Congress for the "broad executive power . . . that would be given to me if we were in fact invaded by a foreign foe."

Roosevelt offered few specifics in his inaugural address. His objective was to convince a dispirited people to have faith in him and in themselves. Standing erect in his cumbersome leg braces, Roosevelt stressed four major themes: sacrifice, discipline, compassion, and hope. "The only thing we have to fear," he assured the nation, "is fear itself."

ROCK BOTTOM

This fear was understandable. The winter of 1932–1933—the political interregnum between Hoover's defeat and Roosevelt's inauguration—was a time of intense suffering and despair. Unemployment reached a staggering 25 percent. Banks were failing everywhere. Food prices had collapsed, forcing farmers from their land. Roosevelt understood how deeply the Depression had shaken the country and sapped its confidence. "I have [seen] the faces of thousands of Americans," he confided to a friend. "They have the frightened look of children. . . . They are saying, 'We are caught in something we don't understand; perhaps this fellow can help us out.'"

Taking Charge

Roosevelt's words reflected both his compassion for common people and his detachment from their lives. He would become a father figure to them in perilous times—bold and caring, yet distant and elusive. He would be their protector, their steward, but not their social peer.

No peacetime president ever faced a tougher challenge, or a greater opportunity. Respected commentators were predicting the end of capitalism if the Depression hung on much longer. At the very least, Americans were desperate for change. And that meant

CHRONOLOGY

1933 Franklin D. Roosevelt inaugurated as president

Eighteenth Amendment is repealed, ending Prohibition

"First hundred days" of New Deal includes passage of Agricultural Adjustment Act and National Industrial Recovery Act

Adolf Hitler becomes chancellor of Germany

United States extends diplomatic recognition to the Soviet Union

1934 Senator Huey Long establishes "Share Our Wealth Society"

Labor violence erupts in major American cities

Democrats add to huge congressional majorities in midterm elections

1935 Huey Long assassinated

"Second New Deal" emerges with passage of Wagner Act and Social Security Act

Congress passes first Neutrality Act, reflecting the nation's isolationist mood

1936 FDR reelected to second term

John L. Lewis and other labor leaders break with AFL to form the CIO

Civil war erupts in Spain

1937 Roosevelt unveils "Court-packing plan"

Auto workers stage "sit-down strike" at GM plant in Flint, Michigan

Severe economic recession begins

1938 Passage of Fair Labor Standards Act

Anti–New Deal forces make gains in midterm elections

Hitler wins major concessions from French and British leaders at Munich Conference

1939 Marian Anderson gives concert at Lincoln Memorial

German forces attack Poland after Hitler and Stalin sign a "non-aggression" pact

---

almost any initiative designed to revive the economy, feed the hungry, and put people back to work.

Roosevelt possessed neither a comprehensive plan to end the Depression, nor a rigid set of economic beliefs. What he did have, aside from an overwhelming popular mandate, was the willingness to experiment, to act decisively, and to use the government as a powerful weapon in the struggle for economic recovery. "Take a method and try it," he liked to say. "If it fails admit it frankly and try another."

Roosevelt surrounded himself with men and women of talent, accomplishment, and wide-ranging progressive views. His closest advisors included Republicans and Democrats, agricultural theorists and urban planners, college professors and political pros. In addition, the New Deal attracted thousands of young people to Washington, drawn by the opportunity to do something meaningful—and perhaps historic—with their lives. "It was that rarest of times," said one observer, "when ambition and idealism could go hand in hand."

The Bank Crisis

More than 5,000 banks had failed in the United States between 1930 and 1932, wiping out countless savings accounts and stalling the nation's credit. Panicked depositors, unable to tell a good bank from a bad one, lost faith in them all. An avalanche of withdrawals resulted. By the time Roosevelt took office, nineteen states had declared "bank holidays" (or closings) to head off a full-scale collapse.

On March 6, 1933, the president called Congress back into special session and proclaimed a national "bank holiday," using executive powers based on a World War I statute. Three days later, his emergency banking proposal was enacted, sight unseen, in a mat-

Franklin Roosevelt was a master at using the radio to create a bond of intimacy with the American people. In a "fireside chat," such as this one, he assured his audience that the banking crisis was over.

ter of hours. The new law provided for the federal inspection of all banks. Those with liquid assets would be allowed to reopen with a license from the Treasury Department; the others would be reorganized, if possible, or closed for good.

On March 12, Roosevelt addressed the nation in the first of his "fireside chats." About half of America's homes had radios in 1933, and the president's audience that Sunday evening was estimated at 60 million people. "I want to talk for a few minutes about banking," he began, assuring everyone that the system was now safe. The listeners believed him. In the following days, as the stronger banks reopened, deposits greatly exceeded withdrawals. By the end of March, almost $1 billion had been returned from mattresses to bank vaults. The crisis was over.

Roosevelt's handling of the bank emergency revealed his essential pragmatism. In the midst of such turmoil, he could easily have taken a more radical approach—by nationalizing the banks, for example, or by instituting much tighter controls. Instead, he demonstrated that his primary mission would be to preserve capitalism, not to replace it. And that meant *reforming* its institutions with substantial federal aid.

The president also showed himself to be a master of communication. His ability to reach people in the radio age, to win their confidence, was perhaps his greatest gift. He would use it often in the coming years, as the nation faced the twin crises of economic hardship and global war.

Extending Relief

The special session of Congress lasted from March 9 to June 16, 1933, a period known as "the first hundred days." In that time, more than a dozen major bills proposed by the White House were enacted. With both the House and the Senate now under firm Democratic control, Roosevelt had little trouble getting his legislation passed. His popularity was such that he, more than Congress, seemed to express the people's will. As the banking crisis ended, Roosevelt moved quickly to help those too desperate to help themselves.

The problem was daunting. By conservative estimates, more than 30 million Americans were now living in family units with no income at all. The wife of an Oklahoma oil field worker said:

There was thousands of people out of work . . . colored and white. Lost everything they had accumulated from their young days. . . . I knew one family, a man and a woman and seven children lived in a hole in the ground. . . . They had chairs and tables, and beds back in that hole. And they had the dirt all braced up there, just like a cave.

The Hoover administration had refused to consider federal payments to the jobless. As a result, state and local governments had been forced to ration what little relief they could muster. In 1932, the average weekly payment to an "out-of-work" family in New York City was $2.39. In Detroit, the figure dropped to fifteen cents a day before the money ran out. Some cities were forced to limit relief to families with three or more children; others offered free food and fuel. "My mother'd send us to the soup line," a Chicago woman recalled. "Then we'd go across the street. One place had bread. Down the road just a piece . . . they gave milk. My sister and me would take two buckets each. And that's what we lived off for the longest time."

Roosevelt believed that relief efforts should be a local responsibility. He, too, worried about the cost of funding such efforts, and about the consequences of giving people money that they hadn't actually earned. Yet there seemed to be no alternative. It was essential, said one of Roosevelt's advisors, to pursue "long-run" economic growth. The problem, he added, is that "people don't eat in the long run—they eat every day."

On March 21, the White House sent two major relief proposals to Capitol Hill. The first one created the Civilian Conservation Corps (CCC). Based on a program that Roosevelt had implemented as governor of New York, the CCC combined the president's enthusiasm for nature with his belief in national service for the young. It provided government conservation jobs to "city boys," age seventeen to twenty-four, in isolated camps run by the U.S. Army. The pay was $30 a month, with $22 going directly to the worker's family.

The CCC was both popular and successful. It eased unemployment a bit, lowered crime rates in the cities, and kept countless families off relief. It also helped to protect and restore the nation's environment, while teaching young men about the discipline of hard work. More than half a million recruits cleaned beaches, built wildlife shelters, fought forest fires, and stocked rivers and streams.

Roosevelt's second relief proposal was generated more by necessity than by choice. Despite some reluctance, he got Congress to establish the Federal Emergency Relief Administration (FERA), with a budget of $500 million, to assist individual states in their efforts to help the unemployed. Hoping to spend the money as quickly and humanely as possible, Roosevelt chose Harry Hopkins, a former social worker who had directed New York's relief effort, to run the FERA. With

One of the New Deal's most popular programs was the Civilian Conservation Corps, which took unemployed young men from the cities and put them to work on conservation projects in the country.

boundless energy and an ego to match, Hopkins personified the New Deal's activist, free-wheeling style. "I'm not going to last six months," said Hopkins, "so I'll do as I please." He became Roosevelt's closest advisor.

Most of the funding went to the jobless in the form of free food or a simple "dole." This troubled Hopkins, who understood both the need for such relief and the damage it could do. Real work "preserves a man's morale," he insisted. "It saves his skill. It gives him a chance to do something socially useful." Knowing that Roosevelt felt the same way, he convinced the president to approve a federal work relief program for the unemployed.

With Hopkins in charge, the Civil Works Administration (CWA) hired more than 4 million people in a matter of months. Its aim was to create jobs and restore self-respect by handing out pay envelopes instead of relief checks. In reality, CWA workers sometimes performed worthless tasks, known as "boondoggles," such as raking leaves in huge circles or lugging shovelsful of dirt to faraway piles. "They could be seen almost everywhere," a journalist recalled, "standing around outdoors doing as little as possible and often in a deliberately inefficient way."

But this was only part of the story. The CWA spent much of its $1 billion budget on projects of lasting value. Its workers built over 400 airports and 200,000 miles of roads. They ran nursery schools and taught more than a million adults to read and write. They immunized children, served hot school lunches, and took garbage off the streets. Yet Roosevelt ended the CWA experiment after only four months, citing its spiraling costs. He expected federal job programs to be short-term experiments, nothing more. Otherwise, he warned, they will "become a habit with the country."

Conservation, Regional Planning, and Public Power

In the spring of 1933, FDR appeared to be governing the nation by himself. His proposals were so sweeping, and so easily enacted, that Congress seemed to have no independent function of its own. Never before had

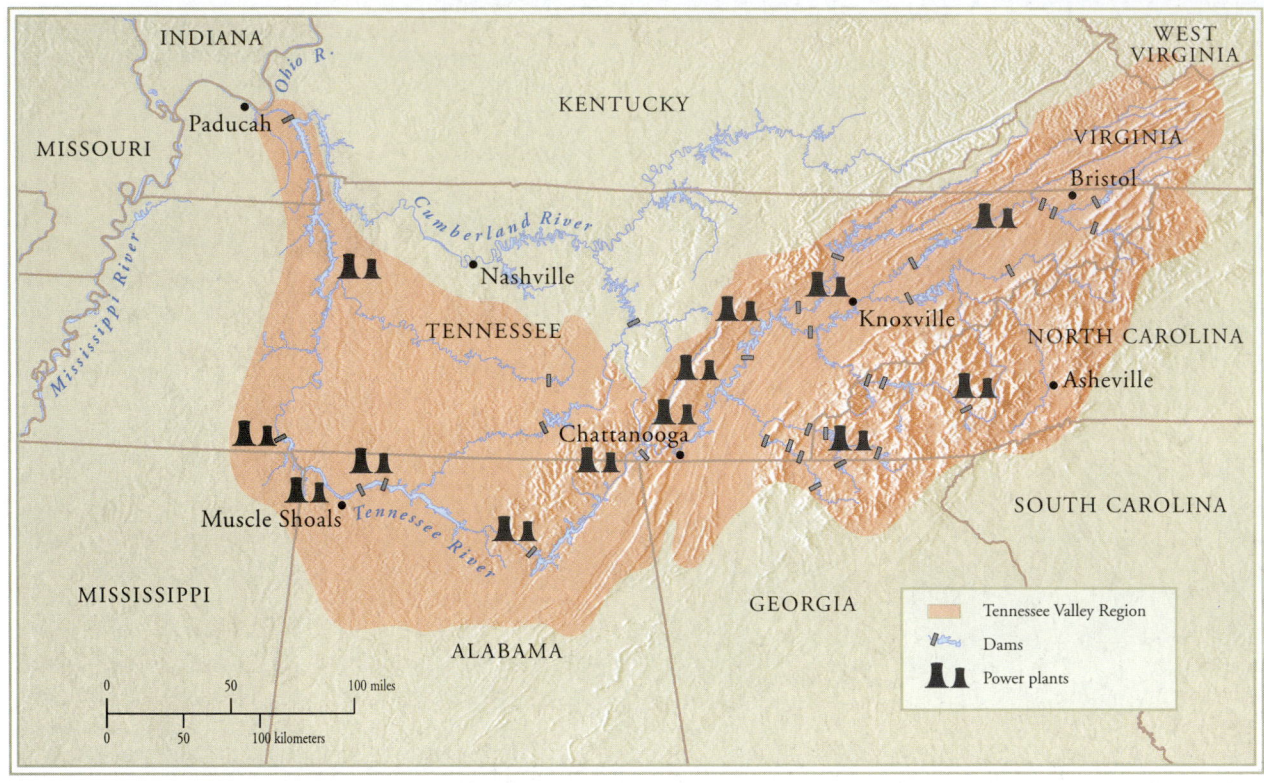

MAP 25.1 | THE TENNESSEE VALLEY

the White House taken such initiative on domestic legislation; never before had it been so successful.

At Roosevelt's behest, Congress created the Securities and Exchange Commission (SEC) to oversee the stock and bond markets. It established the Federal Deposit Insurance Corporation (FDIC) to insure bank deposits up to $5,000. It provided funds to refinance one-fifth of the nation's home and farm mortgages. And it effectively ended Prohibition by permitting the sale of beer and wine with an alcoholic content of 3.2 percent. (The Eighteenth Amendment would be repealed on December 5, 1933.)

Some of Roosevelt's early proposals had very personal roots. The Civilian Conservation Corps was one example; the Tennessee Valley Authority (TVA), created in May 1933, was another. Like many progressives, Roosevelt had a deep interest in the related issues of conservation, regional planning, and public power. Believing that poverty could be eradicated through the careful development of natural resources, he turned the Tennessee Valley into a laboratory for his most cherished ideas.

The location seemed appropriate. Covering seven states and 40,000 square miles, the Tennessee Valley was America's poorest region, with an income less than half the national average. Most of its 4 million people—mainly small farmers and sharecroppers—lived in isolated communities, without electricity, medical care, proper schooling, or paved roads. The TVA transformed this region in fundamental ways. Within a decade, sixteen huge dams and hydroelectric plants were in operation along the Tennessee River, providing flood control, cheap, abundant power, and thousands of jobs. Per capita income rose dramatically, as new industries entered the valley. Electric power gave local residents what millions of other Americans already took for granted: radios and refrigerators, plumbing, lights in houses and barns. TVA became a model of "cooperative planning," and its low cost electricity served as a yardstick for measuring the rates charged by private power companies throughout the country.

TVA was widely viewed as one of the New Deal's greatest achievements. Yet its critics included many residents of the Tennessee Valley, whose complaints re-

flected the changing face of reform. To their thinking, TVA displaced thousands of people, attracted low-wage factory jobs, and caused serious environmental damage. At best, they argued, it brought a measure of comfort and prosperity to a badly depressed region. At worst, it allowed distant bureaucrats to decide how local people should live.

ECONOMIC RECOVERY

With the bank crisis over and federal relief flowing to those most desperately in need, the Roosevelt administration turned to the long-term issue of providing a structure for the nation's economic recovery. In agriculture, which accounted for one-quarter of all American jobs, the problems were severe. Most farmers had been slumping badly since the 1920s. The introduction of tractors and high-grade fertilizer had made them more productive than ever. Yet their share of the world market had declined because of high tariff walls and tough foreign competition.

If overproduction plagued American agriculture in this era, the problem facing American industry was quite the reverse. So many factories had closed their doors during the Depression that too little was being produced. The resulting unemployment caused a drop in purchasing power, which forced even more factories to shut down. Something had to be done to break this vicious cycle.

Trouble on the Land

The Roosevelt administration turned first to the agricultural problems. Farmers in 1932 were earning less than one-third of their meager 1929 incomes. As food prices collapsed, there was talk of open rebellion in the heartland. Farmers blocked roads, clashed with police and threatened to lynch any official who foreclosed a family farm. "The rank-and-file people of this state—who were brought up as conservatives—would never act like this," an Iowa farmer remarked. "Except in desperation." Roosevelt was sympathetic. He believed that low farm income was a leading cause of the Depression, and he needed the support of rural legislators to get his New Deal programs adopted. The proposal he sent Congress, therefore, incorporated the ideas of the nation's major farm interest groups. Passed in May 1933, the Agricultural Adjustment Act confronted the problems of overproduction and mounting surpluses which had conspired to erode farm income over the years. The act also created the Agricultural Adjustment Administration (AAA) to oversee this process.

The AAA had one clear goal in mind: to raise farm prices by encouraging farmers to produce less. The idea was no longer to win back world markets, which now seemed hopeless, but rather to limit domestic output in order to achieve "parity," or fair price levels, within the United States. The original act covered seven basic commodities—wheat, corn, cotton, hogs, milk, rice, and tobacco. It compensated farmers who voluntarily removed acreage from production. And it funded these payments through a tax upon farm processors—such as flour millers, meatpackers, and cotton gin operators.

Problems quickly arose. Because spring planting was already underway, the AAA encouraged farmers to plow under a large portion of their crops. According to Secretary of Agriculture Henry A. Wallace, more than 10 million acres of wheat and cotton were eliminated, while 6 million piglets were slaughtered, the secretary said, "before they could reach the full hogness of their hogdom."

Producing less food while millions were going hungry was difficult for people to understand. But destroying food seemed particularly senseless and cruel. Secretary Wallace described the process as "a shocking commentary on our civilization." Yet there seemed to be no other way to fix an economic system awash in idle workers and empty factories, hungry people and abundant food.

Within a year, more than 3 million farmers had signed individual contracts with the AAA. The early results were encouraging. Cotton, wheat, and corn production fell significantly as farmers cultivated fewer acres and cashed their government checks. Farm income shot up almost 60 percent between 1932 and 1935—the result of rising food prices, generous mortgage assistance, and federal loans to those who stored their surpluses in government warehouses. As more farmers scrambled to join the program, Congress added new commodities to the list—peanuts, barley, and sugar cane.

Nature played a role as well. During the 1930s, the American farmbelt experienced record highs in temperature and record lows in rainfall. The Great Plains

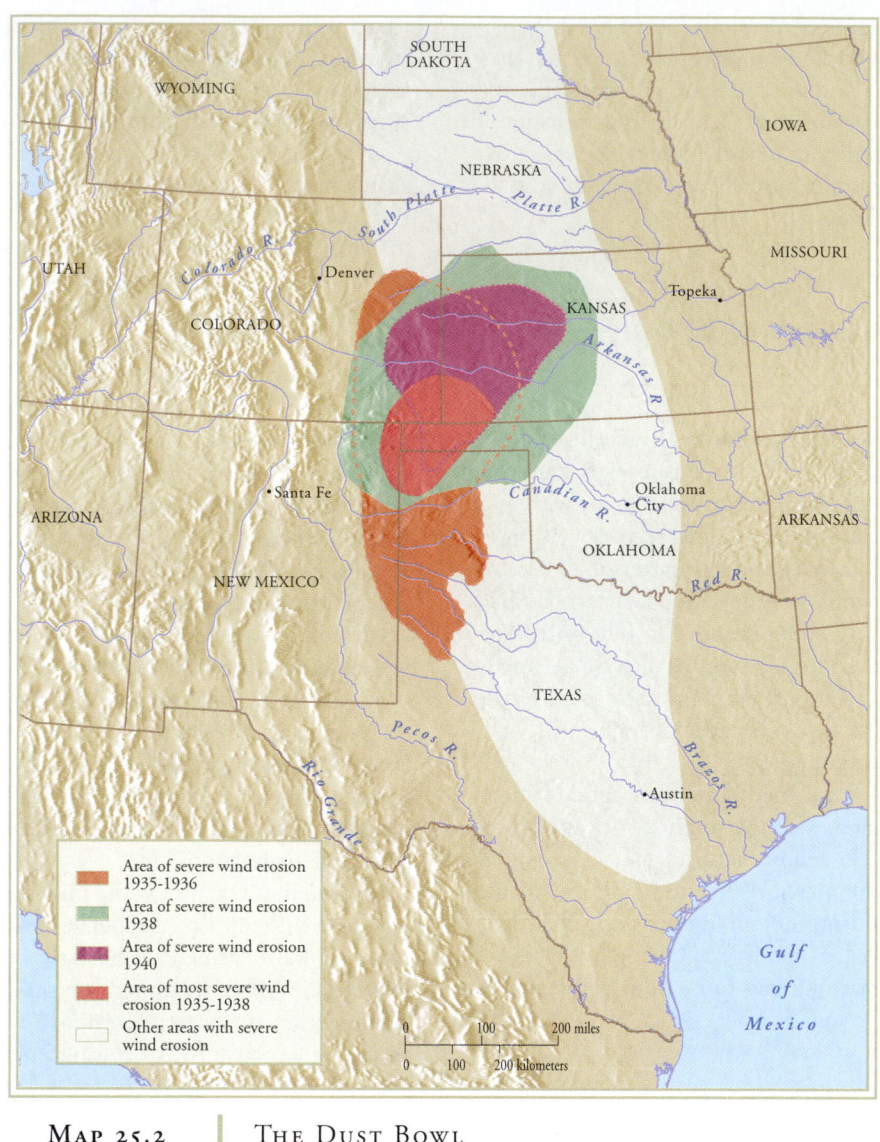

Map 25.2 | The Dust Bowl

were hardest hit. Terrifying dust storms swept through Kansas, Nebraska, Colorado, Oklahoma, Texas, and the Dakotas like a black blizzard, packing gale force winds and stripping nutrients from the soil. Cornfields were turned into sand dunes and livestock were buried in their tracks. "This is the ultimate darkness," a Kansas woman wrote in her diary. "So must come the end of the world."

The "Dust Bowl" disaster triggered one of the largest internal migrations in the nation's history. More than 3 million people abandoned their Dust Bowl farms in the 1930s, with Oklahoma, Kansas, and South Dakota losing huge chunks of population. By one account, "The people did not stop to shut the door—they just walked out, leaving behind them the wreckage of their labors: an ugly little shack with broken windows covered by cardboard, a sagging ridgepole, a barren, dusty yard, the windmill creaking in the wind." In the words of Oklahoma's Woody Guthrie:

We loaded our jalopies
and piled our families in,
We rattled down the highway
to never come back again.

A farm family seeks shelter from a dust storm in 1937.

Many set out for California, where the "fortunate" among them found work picking fruit, boxing vegetables, and baling hay. Living in hellish squatter camps, enduring disease and discrimination ("Negroes and Okies Upstairs," read a local theater sign), they moved from field to orchard in the San Joaquin and Imperial Valleys, earning pitiful wages and "going on relief."

Tenants and Landowners

The AAA helped countless farm families and ignored countless others. The large farmers got the biggest subsidies. Yet the system barely touched those at the bottom of the pile: the tenants and sharecroppers who comprised almost one-half of the nation's white farm families and three-quarters of the black farm families. Most of them lived in desperate poverty, working the cotton fields of the rural South. Under AAA regulations, these tenants were supposed to get a fair share of the acreage reduction payments. But this rarely occurred. Few landlords obeyed the rules, and some evicted their tenants in order to take even more land out of production.

In response, tenants and sharecroppers formed their own organization, the Southern Tenant Farmers' Union (STFU), to fight for their rights. "The landlord is always betwixt us, beatin' us and starvin' us," complained a black sharecropper from Arkansas. "There ain't but one way for us to get him where he can't help himself and that's for us to get together and stay together."

This would not be easy. Despite the strong support of Norman Thomas and his Socialist party, the STFU could not match the power and resources of its opponents. Tenants who joined the union were evicted from their shacks, blacklisted by employers, and denied credit at banks and stores. Union organizers were beaten and jailed. When Thomas visited Arkansas to speak at a union rally, local thugs forced him from the stage.

The Roosevelt administration did not intervene. The president understood the racial implications of this struggle—most tenants were black; the landlords were white. He did not want to jeopardize the AAA by offending powerful southern interests in Congress. "I know the South . . . ," he told Thomas, "and we've got to be patient." In the meantime, Roosevelt created

Texas Dust Bowl refugees on the long road to California.

the Resettlement Administration, with modest funding, to assist evicted tenants and migrant farm workers. Headed by Rexford Tugwell, an outspoken civil rights advocate, the RA became a kind of "mini-AAA" for the rural poor—the New Deal's most class-conscious agency.

Conditions were no better in the Southwest and Far West, where destitute Mexican farm workers struggled to survive. Many had been brought north by American ranchers and growers seeking cheap labor in better times. Now, as the demand for workers decreased, and job competition with poor whites (including the Dust Bowl refugees) intensified, their desperation grew. Since most of these farm workers were not U.S. citizens, local governments often denied them relief. Between 1930 and 1935, moreover, the federal government deported at least 200,000 Mexicans, some of whom were long-time residents of Texas, Arizona, and California, while a larger number returned to Mexico on their own. Those who stayed behind toiled for starvation wages in the fields. Like the Tenant Farmer's Union in Arkansas, their attempts to unionize were crushed by local vigilantes and police. In 1936, John Steinbeck reported on a strike of Mexi-

can lettuce workers near his home in Salinas, California. "The attitude of the employer," he wrote, "is one of hatred and suspicion, his method is the threat of the deputies' guns. The workers are herded about like animals. Every possible method is used to make them feel inferior and insecure." Steinbeck added: "Must the hunger become anger and anger fury before anything will be done?"

The AAA revolutionized American agriculture. Never before had the federal government been as deeply involved in the affairs of the American farmer; never before had it encouraged its citizens to produce fewer goods, not more. Though key elements of the AAA would be struck down by the Supreme Court in *United States* v. *Butler* (1936), the concept of federal farm subsidies continues to dominate America's agricultural policy to the present day.

Centralized Economic Planning

The Roosevelt administration had an equally ambitious plan to revive the economy, reopen idle factories, and put people back to work. On June 13, 1933,

Congress passed the National Industrial Recovery Act (NIRA) amidst a flood of optimistic projections. Modeled upon both the voluntary trade associations of the 1920s and the industrial mobilization during World War I, the NIRA was designed as a vehicle for centralized economic planning. Roosevelt himself viewed it as the primary weapon in his crusade against the Depression. The act, he boasted, "is the most important and far reaching legislation ever enacted by the American Congress."

The NIRA created two more federal agencies: the Public Works Administration (PWA) and the National Recovery Administration (NRA). The former, with a budget of $3.3 billion, was supposed to "prime the economic pump" by providing jobs for the unemployed and new orders for the factories that produced steel, glass, rubber, cement, and heavy equipment. What made the PWA so appealing was its emphasis on private employment. Workers were to be hired and paid by individual contractors, not by the federal government.

Roosevelt selected Secretary of the Interior Harold Ickes, a veteran progressive, to run the PWA. It proved to be a controversial choice. Known for his prickly, tightfisted ways, Ickes scrutinized almost every construction contract himself, sometimes line by line. He wanted PWA projects to be free of graft, and he insisted that each one add something useful to a community's well-being. In the end, the PWA would spend only $2.8 billion of its budget, leading critics to question the wisdom of placing a perfectionist like Ickes in a position that required aggressive spending to achieve its goal.

Still, his legacy was immense. Under Ickes's leadership, the PWA constructed schools, hospitals, post offices, and sewage systems. It built the Golden Gate Bridge in San Francisco and the Triborough Bridge in New York City, the Grand Coulee Dam in Washington state and the Boulder Dam in Colorado. No one brought more honest efficiency to government than Harold Ickes, and no one got more value for the dollar.

The key to Roosevelt's recovery program, however, was the NRA. Under the flamboyant leadership of General Hugh S. Johnson, who had helped organize the draft during World War I, the NRA encouraged representatives of business and labor to create codes of "fair practice" designed to stabilize the economy through planning and cooperation. Johnson's agency promised something to everyone, though not in equal amounts. Business leaders, who dominated the code-writing process, got the biggest gift of all: the suspension of anti-trust laws which had dogged them for years.

The Public Works Administration left behind a legacy of magnificent structures, including the Grand Coulee Dam, the 100-mile causeway linking Florida to Key West, the Triborough Bridge in New York City, and the Golden Gate Bridge in San Francisco (shown under construction).

New Deal legislation such as the National Industrial Recovery Act went a long way toward ending the disgrace of child labor in the United States. This photo shows young spindle boys at work in a Georgia cotton mill.

In return for such generosity, these leaders agreed to significant labor reforms. Each NRA code featured a maximum hour and minimum wage provision (usually forty hours and twelve dollars per week). Child labor was forbidden, and yellow-dog contracts banned. Most important, Section 7 (a) of the NIRA guaranteed labor unions the right to organize and bargain collectively.

General Johnson turned the NRA campaign into a personal crusade. He barnstormed the country by airplane, giving speeches and lining up support. His tactics were the same ones he had used to mobilize Americans in the bond drives and mass rallies of World War I. With a patriotic symbol (the blue eagle) and a catchy slogan ("We Do Our Part"), Johnson organized the biggest public spectacles of the Depression era. In the summer of 1933, more than 250,000 New Yorkers paraded down Fifth Avenue singing:

Join the good old N.R.A., Boys,
and we will end this awful strife.
Join it with the spirit
that will give the Eagle life.
Join in folks, then push and pull,
many millions strong.
While we go marching to Prosperity.

Johnson signed up the big industries — coal, steel, oil, autos, shipbuilding, chemicals, and clothing — before going after the others. By the end of 1933, the NRA had 746 different agreements in place. There was a code for the mop handle makers, another for the dog food industry, and even one for the burlesque houses which determined the number of strippers in each show. Johnson was ecstatic. The codes, he predicted, would "eliminate eye-gouging and knee-groining and ear-chewing in [American] business."

Before long, however, the NRA was in trouble. Small businessmen complained that the codes encouraged monopolies and drowned them in paperwork. Labor leaders charged that employers ignored the wage and hour provisions, while cracking down on union activity. And consumers blamed the NRA for raising prices at a time when their purchasing power was extremely low.

All of this was true. Because the codes were voluntary, they carried no legal weight. (Johnson naively assumed that the power of public opinion would keep potential violators in line.) The large companies obeyed them when it was in their interest to do so, and ignored them when it wasn't. As a result, the codes became a device for fixing prices, stifling competition, and limiting production. This may have guaranteed a

profit for some companies, but it was the wrong remedy for solving an economic crisis in which the revival of consumer spending was a key to recovery.

In 1934, General Johnson suffered a nervous breakdown, leading Roosevelt to replace him with a five-member executive board. The president seemed relieved when the Supreme Court, in *Schechter Poultry Company* v. *United States* (1935), struck down the NRA on the grounds that Congress had delegated too much legislative authority to the executive branch. "It has been an awful headache," Roosevelt confided to an aide. "I think perhaps NRA has done all it can do."

NEW DEAL DIPLOMACY

Foreign affairs were not high on President Roosevelt's agenda. His riveting inaugural address had devoted one sentence to the entire subject. "In the field of world policy," he declared, "I would dedicate this nation to the policy of the good neighbor"—a theme already sounded by outgoing President Herbert Hoover. The United States was in turmoil, struggling through the worst economic crisis in its history. "I favored as a practical policy," said Roosevelt, "the putting of first things first."

The Soviet Question

FDR was no isolationist. He believed deeply in the concepts of international cooperation and global security, as Americans would shortly discover. One of his first diplomatic moves, in November 1933, was to extend formal recognition to the Soviet Union. In doing so, Roosevelt reversed the policies of one Democratic and three Republican presidents, beginning with Woodrow Wilson in 1917. The move was criticized by groups as varied as the American Legion and the American Federation of Labor, which viewed the Soviet Union as a godless, totalitarian society bent on exporting "communist revolution" throughout the world. But Roosevelt believed that the United States could no longer afford to ignore the world's largest nation. He hoped, too, that closer Russian-American ties might serve to restrain the Japanese, who had obvious territorial ambitions in Asia.

The move did not pay quick dividends to either side. Trade with the Soviet Union remained low, partly because Soviet dictator Joseph Stalin was determined to make his nation self-sufficient. The Russians also ignored their promise not to spread "communist propaganda" in the United States, and then refused to pay their $150 million war debt to Washington, claiming that they, too, deserved compensation for the damage caused by American troops during Woodrow Wilson's ill-fated intervention in their civil war. Yet for all of these problems, a major hurdle was cleared. Relations between the United States and the Soviet Union would slowly improve in the 1930s and early 1940s, as ominous world events drew them closer together. For FDR, recognition of Stalin's regime seemed less a threat than an opportunity.

The Good Neighbor

The Roosevelt administration showed a growing interest in Latin America, where U.S. companies had billions of dollars invested in the production of foodstuffs like coffee and sugar, and raw materials such as copper and oil. Along with efforts to increase trade in this region, the United States extended the Good Neighbor Policy by affirming at the 1933 Pan-American Conference in Uruguay that no nation "has the right to intervene in the internal or external affairs of another." Shortly thereafter, the Roosevelt administration recalled several hundred U.S. Marines stationed in Haiti, and signed a treaty with Panama recognizing the responsibility of both nations to operate and defend the Panama Canal.

There were exceptions, however. In Cuba, a nation of vital economic and strategic importance to the United States, intervention was a way of life. In 1934, the State Department used its considerable leverage to help bring an "acceptable" government to power in Havana, more sympathetic to North American business interests. With a friendly new regime in place, led by Sergeant Fulgencio Batista, the United States agreed to renounce direct intervention under the Platt Amendment in return for permission to keep its huge naval base at Guantánamo Bay.

The Good Neighbor Policy faced its sternest test even closer to home. In 1934, President Lázaro Cárdenas of Mexico began a national recovery program much like FDR's New Deal. Pledging "Mexico for the Mexicans," Cárdenas attempted to nationalize the

agricultural and mining properties of all foreign corporations, as required by the Mexican Constitution of 1917. Though Cárdenas promised "fair compensation" for these holdings, American and British companies demanded more than the Mexicans were willing to pay. (American oil interests wanted $262 million, the Cárdenas government offered $10 million.) Over the objections of many businessmen, the Roosevelt administration convinced Mexico to pay $40 million in compensation for foreign-owned lands it had seized, and another $29 million for the oil fields.

Roosevelt's caution was understandable. The president realized that better relations with Latin America required a new approach. "Give them a share," he urged in private. "They think they are just as good as we are, and many of them are." Roosevelt's policy was also tied to larger world events. With fascism rising in Europe and in Asia, the need for inter-American cooperation was essential.

CRITICS: RIGHT AND LEFT

By 1934, the Depression seemed to be easing. Though enormous problems remained, there was less talk about the dangers of starvation, violent upheaval, or complete economic collapse. The New Deal had injected a dose of hope and confidence into the body politic. Yet as things got better, people inevitably wanted more. The spirit of unity, the shared sense of hardship and struggle, began to dissolve.

The American Liberty League and the 1934 Election

The first rumblings came from the political right. In the summer of 1934, a group of conservative business leaders—including the chief executives of DuPont, General Motors, and U.S. Steel—formed the American Liberty League to combat the alleged "radicalism" of the New Deal. They believed that Roosevelt was leading the country down "a foreign path" by attacking free enterprise, favoring workers over employers, and increasing the power of the federal government. "There can be only one capital," said a Liberty League spokesman, "Washington or Moscow."

The League generously supported Roosevelt's political opponents in the 1934 congressional elections. But the results served only to reinforce the president's enormous popularity, or so it appeared. Instead of losing ground—the normal pattern for the majority party in midterm elections—the Democrats picked up nine seats in the Senate and nine in the House. Few pundits could recall a more lopsided election, and some questioned the future of the Republican party. As publisher William Allen White put it, Roosevelt had been "all but crowned by the people."

In reality, the election results were a mixed blessing for the Democrats. Most Americans approved of the New Deal. Their main criticism was that it had not gone far—or fast—enough to end the Depression. In Minnesota, for example, Governor Floyd Olsen was reelected on an independent "Farmer-Labor" ticket that advocated the state ownership of utilities and railroads. In neighboring Wisconsin, the sons of "Fighting Bob" LaFollette formed a new Progressive party that endorsed the idea of a welfare state. And in California, Upton Sinclair, author of *The Jungle,* ran for governor on a program called EPIC (End Poverty in California), which promised to hand over idle factories and farmland to the poor and unemployed. Sinclair received almost 900,000 votes in a bitter, losing effort—a sign of things to come.

"Every Man a King"

The most serious challenge to Roosevelt's leadership was offered by Louisiana's Huey P. Long. Known as the "Kingfish," after a strutting, smooth-talking character on the popular radio program "Amos 'n' Andy," Long combined a gift for showmanship with ruthless ambition. On the campaign trail, he wore a white linen suit, orchid shirt, pink necktie, straw hat, and two-toned shoes. A superb orator and a master storyteller, he understood the value of the spoken word in a state where few people owned radios, read newspapers, or traveled far from home.

As governor of Louisiana, Long pushed his unique brand of southern populism. By revising the tax codes to make corporations and wealthy citizens pay more, he was able to construct new hospitals, bring paved roads and bridges to rural areas, and give free textbooks to the poor. At the same time, he built a political machine of almost totalitarian proportions. When Long vacated the governor's chair to enter the U.S.

Senator Huey P. Long combined showmanship with ruthless ambition to become Franklin Roosevelt's most influential critic and political rival. Claiming the New Deal did not do enough to help poor people, Long proposed a radical program to redistribute wealth that attracted millions of followers.

Senate in 1932, he controlled the legislature, the courts, and the civil service system of Louisiana. To keep a state job, workers were expected to contribute 5 percent of their salaries to the Long machine, and to deliver five voters to the polls on election day.

"I came to the United States Senate," Long wrote, "to spread the wealth of the land among all of the people." As a Democrat, he campaigned hard for Roosevelt in 1932 and supported much of the early New Deal. But as time passed, he grew restless with the slow pace of reform. In 1934, Long proposed his own agenda for economic recovery. Once in place, he promised, it would "make every man a king."

Under Long's plan, no one would be allowed to earn more than $1.8 million per year or to keep a personal fortune in excess of $5 million. After confiscating this surplus, the government would provide each family with a house, a car, a radio, and an annual in-

come of at least $2,500. Veterans would get their bonus, the elderly would receive pensions, and deserving students could attend college free of charge.

Most economists were appalled. They knew that there weren't nearly enough millionaires around to finance Long's proposal. According to one study, the government would have had to confiscate all yearly incomes above $3,000—not $1.8 million—to provide each family with $2,500. Long didn't much care about the arithmetic. "You don't have to understand it," he told his followers. "Just shut your damned eyes and believe it. That's all."

By 1935, Long's "Share Our Wealth Society" claimed 8 million members nationwide. It lured in people by promising them what the New Deal could not possibly deliver. At local meetings across the nation, his followers sang:

> Every man a king, every man a king
> For you can be a millionaire
> But there's something belongs to others
> There's enough for all to share.

The Radio Priest and the Pension Doctor

Long did not lack for competitors. In Royal Oak, Michigan, a working-class suburb of Detroit, Father Charles Edward Coughlin was busy leading a protest movement of his own. As the pastor of a small Catholic church called the Shrine of the Little Flower, Coughlin became a towering figure in the 1930s by mixing prayer with politics in a way that touched millions—and frightened millions more.

Coughlin could be heard every Sunday on seventeen CBS radio outlets nationwide. An early Roosevelt supporter, he compared the New Deal to "Christ's Deal," assuring listeners that "Gabriel is over the White House, not Lucifer." Like Senator Long, Coughlin deplored the fact that too much wealth was concentrated in too few hands. Unlike Long, however, he blamed this evil on a tight money supply, manipulated by international bankers in London and New York.

Coughlin believed that "free silver"—the old Populist nostrum—would solve this problem and bring prosperity to all. His attacks on British bankers won him strong support in the Irish-Catholic community, and his call for monetary reform appealed to debt-ridden farmers and merchants in America's small towns.

Before long, Coughlin's radio show, "Golden Hour of the Little Flower," had more listeners (an estimated 40 million) than "Amos 'n' Andy" and "Gracie Allen." He needed 150 clerks and four personal secretaries to handle the thousands of letters and donations that poured into his office. Some of this money was used to construct a new church of granite and marble, seven stories high, bathed in floodlights, with a huge Christ figure on top. Some of it was invested in the silver market, making Coughlin, with 500,000 ounces, one of the nation's leading speculators.

By 1934, the "Radio Priest" was souring on the New Deal. Angered by Roosevelt's disinterest in his "silver solution," he formed the National Union for Social Justice to challenge the president's leadership. "I glory in the fact that I am a simple Catholic priest," Coughlin declared, "endeavoring to inject Christianity into the fabric of an economic system woven upon the loom of the greedy."

A third protest movement, led by Francis E. Townsend, a retired physician living in California, offered yet another solution to the ills of the 1930s. Townsend had no desire to punish the rich, alter the money supply, or challenge the capitalist order. What disturbed him was the sight of elderly men and women sifting through garbage cans for food. In 1934, Townsend proposed a measure to revive the economy by meeting the specific needs of older Americans. It guaranteed a pension of $200 per month to those over sixty who promised to stay out of the job market and to spend the $200 by month's end. The pensions would be funded by a 2 percent sales tax on all "business transactions."

According to Townsend, his plan would create jobs for the young, increase the country's purchasing power, and provide security for the elderly. What he didn't say was that his plan, known as Old Age Revolving Pensions Limited, was impossibly expensive. By most estimates, Townsend needed a sales tax approaching 70 percent in order to properly fund his proposal. When asked about this at a congressional hearing, the doctor replied: "I'm not in the least interested in the cost of the plan."

Neither were his followers. By 1935, more than 10 million Americans had signed petitions supporting Townsend's idea, and public opinion polls showed strong support for a government-sponsored pension plan. Townsend had unleashed a powerful new interest group, the elderly, and American politics would never be the same.

THE SECOND NEW DEAL

The American Liberty League, the victories of Floyd Olsen and the LaFollette brothers, the rumblings of Long, Coughlin, and Townsend—all raised nagging problems for Franklin Roosevelt and the New Deal. Though national income in 1935 was a full 25 percent above the 1933 level, millions were still living on handouts, without much hope of a permanent job. Inside the White House, Roosevelt's key advisors were nudging him further to the left. "Boys—this is our hour," said the opportunistic Harry Hopkins. "We've got to get everything we want—a works program, social security, wages and hours, everything—now or never."

Jobs, Jobs, Jobs

In the spring of 1935, Roosevelt presented Congress with a "must" list of reforms, the so-called "second New Deal." He requested—and received—$4.8 billion in work relief for the unemployed, the largest single appropriation in the nation's history. After allocating generous shares to his favorite projects, such as the CCC, Roosevelt established yet another agency, the Works Progress Administration (WPA), with Hopkins in charge, to create "jobs, jobs, jobs!"

In that task, it was very successful. At its height in 1936, the WPA employed 25 percent of the nation's entire workforce. Many of these jobs, however, were low-paying and temporary so as to avoid competition with private enterprise. Concentrating on small construction projects, the WPA built schools and playgrounds, repaired countless bridges and landing fields,

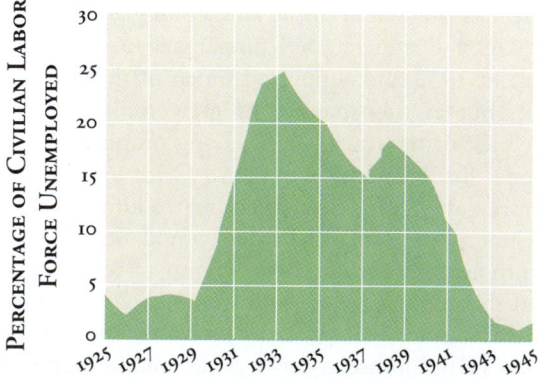

UNEMPLOYMENT 1925–1945

HUEY P. LONG CONDEMNS FDR AND THE NEW DEAL

During his first term in office, President Roosevelt was criticized by the political right for expanding the role of government to help end the Great Depression, and by the political left for not expanding that role even futher. Among FDR's most vocal critics was Senator Huey P. Long of Louisiana, a self-styled "populist" with presidential aspirations. Shortly before his assassination, the flamboyant Long accused Roosevelt of reneging on earlier promises to help the poor, the hungry, the unemployed.

I was the first man to say publicly—but Mr. Roosevelt followed in my tracks a few months later and said the same thing. We said that all of our trouble and woe was due to the fact that too few of our people owned too much of our wealth. We said that in our land, with too much to eat, and too much to wear, and too many houses to live in, too many automobiles to be sold, that the only trouble was that the people suffered in the land of abundance because too few controlled the money and the wealth and too many did not have money with which to buy the things they needed for life and comfort.

So I said to the people of the United States in my speeches which I delivered in the United States Senate in the early part of 1932 that the only way by which we could restore our people to reasonable life and comfort was to limit the size of the big man's fortune and guarantee some minimum to the fortune and comfort of the little man's family.

I said then, as I have said since, that it was inhuman to have food rotting, cotton and wool going to waste, houses empty, and at the same time to have millions of our people starving, naked, and homeless because they could not buy the things which other men had and for which they had no use whatever. So we convinced Mr. Franklin Delano Roosevelt that it was necessary that he announce and promise to the American people that in the event he were elected President of the United States he would pull down the size of the big man's fortune and guarantee something to every family—enough to do away with all poverty and to give employment to those who were able to work and education to the children born into the world.

Mr. Roosevelt made those promises; he made them before he was nominated in the Chicago convention. He made them again before he was elected in November, and he went so far as to remake those promises after he was inaugurated President of the United States. And I thought for a day or two after he took the oath as President, that maybe he was going through with his promises. No heart was ever so saddened; no person's ambition was ever so blighted, as was mine when I came to the realization that the President of the United States was not going to undertake what he had said he would do, and what I knew to be necessary if the people of America were ever [to be] saved from calamity and misery.

SOURCE *New York Times*, January 26, 1936.

and improved 650,000 miles of roads. Its National Youth Administration, inspired by Eleanor Roosevelt, provided part-time work to several million high school and college students.

The WPA also took advantage of the talents of jobless professionals. Why have a struggling musician pour concrete, Hopkins reasoned, when he could be entertaining others with his skill? Under the WPA, the Federal Theater Project performed everything from Shakespeare to puppet shows for audiences that rarely, if ever, had seen a live show. The Federal Art Project produced museum exhibits, murals for public buildings, and painting classes for the poor. The Federal Writers Project published historical guidebooks for each state and collected oral histories of the "inarticulate," including 3,000 former slaves. Playwright Arthur Miller worked for the WPA, as did actor Burt Lancaster, artists Jackson Pollock and Ben Shawn, and authors Saul Bellow, John Cheever, and Richard Wright.

Social Security

The president's "must" list included a social welfare plan that challenged the cherished concepts of volun-

tarism and individual responsibility. At the urging of Labor Secretary Frances Perkins, the nation's first woman cabinet member, Roosevelt proposed legislation (passed as the Social Security Act of 1935) to create a national pension fund, an unemployment insurance system, and public assistance programs for dependent mothers and children, the physically disabled, and those in chronic need. The pension was financed by a payroll tax to begin in 1937. Benefits were purposely modest—about twenty to thirty dollars per month—because Roosevelt did not intend "Social Security" to be the *main* source of personal retirement income, as it has become for many people today.

The act had numerous defects. It excluded millions of vulnerable wage earners from the pension fund, such as domestics, farm workers, and the self-employed. It taxed all participants at a fixed rate, forcing those with the lowest incomes to pay a far greater share of their wages into the system. Over time, the Social Security fund emerged as the country's most important and expensive domestic program. By 1990, it covered almost 40 million people, accounting for one-quarter of the federal government's trillion-dollar annual budget.

WPA murals, like this one in San Francisco's Coit Tower, decorated public buildings across the United States.

Secretary of Labor Frances Perkins, the first woman to hold a cabinet position, was instrumental in the formulation and passage of the Social Security Act.

"Class Warfare"

Roosevelt had never been a strong supporter of organized labor. A paternalist at heart, he wanted to help workers through his own social programs, rather than having them organize unions to help themselves. He felt uneasy about the tactics of labor leaders such as John L. Lewis, head of the United Mine Workers, who had tripled his membership (from 150,000 to almost 500,000) with an aggressive organizing campaign that declared, "The president wants you to join a union!" Roosevelt worried that labor's militant new spirit

Police in Minneapolis battle striking truck drivers in 1934. Labor violence was common in this era, as workers demanded and employers often resisted the right to organize unions and to press for better wages and working conditions.

would accelerate the violent confrontations of 1934, when pitched battles erupted between striking workers and police on the streets of Minneapolis, San Francisco, and Detroit.

In the wake of these disturbances, Senator Robert Wagner of New York authored a bill to protect the rights of workers to organize and bargain collectively. Wagner, an urban Democrat, had strong ties to the labor movement. His legislation filled a dramatic void, because the Supreme Court had just declared parts of the NIRA—including Section 7A—to be unconstitutional. Passed in 1935, the National Labor Relations (Wagner) Act prohibited employers from engaging in a wide range of "unfair labor practices," such as spying on their workers. The law also created the National Labor Relations Board (NLRB) to supervise union elections and determine the appropriate bargaining agents.

The Wagner Act revealed deep divisions within the union movement. At the American Federation of Labor's annual convention in 1935, John L. Lewis pleaded with fellow leaders to begin serious membership drives in the steel mills, automobile plants, and rubber factories. Lewis wanted these mass production workers to be organized by industry rather than by craft. Only then, he argued, could the power of big business be successfully confronted.

Most AFL leaders were unmoved. As representatives of skilled craftsmen, such as masons and carpenters, they had little interest in organizing industrial unions composed largely of African Americans and ethnic groups from Eastern and Southern Europe. Indeed, after Lewis finished his emotional plea to the AFL convention, Carpenters' President "Big Bill" Hutcheson called him a "bastard." Lewis floored Hutcheson with a solid right to the jaw. Then he stormed out of the convention, telling reporters that the AFL "is standing still, with its face toward the dead past."

In November 1935, Lewis formed the Committee for Industrial Organization (CIO) to charter new unions in the mass production industries. He was joined by a handful of AFL leaders from the needle trades, including Sidney Hillman of the Amalgamated Clothing Workers and David Dubinsky of the International Ladies' Garment Workers. Although the AFL suspended these men and their unions for "fomenting insurrection," Lewis never looked back. His attention had turned to the CIO's organizing drives in the auto and steel industries. Labor's "civil war" had begun.

THE FASCIST CHALLENGE

As the 1936 presidential election approached, Americans watched events in Europe with growing apprehension. From the Soviet Union came stories about a regime that was brutalizing its people in an attempt to "collectivize" the society and stamp out internal dissent. In Germany and Italy, powerful dictators emerged, preaching race hatred and vowing to expand their nation's borders. For millions of Americans, the scene was frighteningly familiar—a replay of events that had led Europe, and eventually the United States, into the bloodiest war of all time.

Hitler and Mussolini

Adolf Hitler became the German chancellor in January 1933, a few months before FDR was sworn in as president. Born in Austria in 1889, Hitler had moved to Bavaria as a young man and fought in the German army during World War I. Wounded and jobless, he helped form the National Socialist (Nazi) party, one of the many extremist groups that thrived in the economic chaos of war-battered Germany. In 1923, Hitler was arrested in Munich for staging an unsuccessful coup against the Weimar government. From his prison cell, he wrote *Mein Kampf* ("My Struggle"), a rambling account of his racial theories, plans for Germany, and hatred of Jews.

As the Weimar government collapsed in the Depression, the Nazis gained strength. Millions welcomed their promise to create jobs, restore German glory, and avenge the "humiliation" of Versailles. Nazi representation in the *Reichstag* (parliament) rose from twelve in 1928 to 230 by 1932. A year later, Hitler became chancellor of Germany. The results were alarming. Constitutional rights were suspended and competing political parties were banned. Nazi supporters held mass book-burning rallies, drove Jews from universities, boycotted their businesses, and attacked them in the streets. "Hitler is a madman," President Roosevelt told a French diplomat, "and his counselors, some of whom I personally know, are even madder than he is."

Under the Nazis, the state increased its control over industry, while leaving it in private hands. This allowed Hitler to begin a massive rearmament program,

which produced badly needed jobs. By 1934, German factories were producing tanks and military aircraft. A year later, Hitler proposed a 500,000-man army and instituted the draft. In 1936, Nazi forces marched into the Rhineland—a clear violation of the Versailles Treaty—and reoccupied it without firing a shot. "To-day Germany," the Nazis chanted, "tomorrow the world."

Hitler was not alone. He had modeled himself, to some degree, after Italian dictator Benito Mussolini, the father of fascism in modern Europe. Born in 1883, Mussolini had served in the Italian army during World War I. Playing upon the social unrest and economic turmoil of the postwar era, he seized national power in 1922 and proclaimed *Fascismo.* As the supreme leader, or *Duce,* he preached national unity and state management (though not ownership) of Italy's industrial base. Like Hitler, he destroyed labor unions, censored the press, abolished all political parties but his own, and relied on a secret police force to maintain order and silence his critics.

In 1935, Italian forces invaded Ethiopia from their neighboring colonies of Eritrea and Somaliland. For Mussolini, the attack was a way of restoring Italy's ancient glory. The fighting in Ethiopia was brutal and one-sided, pitting Italian tanks and machine guns against local defenders armed with little more than spears and bows and arrows. At the League of Nations, Ethiopian Emperor Haile Selassie pleaded for support. The league responded by branding Italy the aggressor, but sending no military help. After annexing Ethiopia in 1936, Mussolini signed a pact of friendship with Hitler, known as the Rome-Berlin Axis.

The Neutrality Acts

Americans did not want to become involved in European squabbles, as they had in the past. They were determined that history must not repeat itself—that American blood must not be shed again on foreign soil. There was only one way to avoid another war, most people believed, and that was to remain truly neutral in world affairs.

While this sentiment had deep historical roots, running all the way back to George Washington, the key to understanding America's anxiety in the early 1930s was the legacy of World War I—the belief that U.S.

participation had been a mistake, that America had been lured into the conflict, against its vital interests, by a conspiracy of evil men. In 1934, the U.S. Senate set up a committee, chaired by isolationist Gerald P. Nye of North Dakota, to investigate the reasons for America's involvement in World War I. The Nye Committee highlighted a series of well-known facts: large banks and corporations had made huge profits during World War I by giving loans and selling arms to the various combatants. It followed, therefore, that the United States had been led into this conflict by greedy bankers and businessmen determined to protect their investments. The press dubbed them "merchants of death."

This was a simplistic explanation, to be sure. It ignored the rather tangled reality of American intervention—from submarine warfare to the Zimmermann Telegram, from President Wilson's rigid morality to the defense of neutral rights. Yet the Nye Committee findings enjoyed wide popular support in a nation determined to avoid another war.

The isolationist impulse was particularly strong in the Great Plains and Upper Midwest, where populist suspicions of Wall Street and international bankers went back a long way. It attracted many Americans of German descent, who remembered their brutal treatment during World War I; of Irish descent, who opposed aid to Great Britain in any form; and of Italian descent, who viewed Mussolini as a hero in these years. Isolationism—in some cases combined with pacifism—also appealed to ministers, peace groups, college students, and prominent historians like Charles A. Beard, who argued that militarism and big business went hand in hand.

Congress responded to this public mood with legislation designed to avoid the "entanglements" that had led to American participation in World War I. The first Neutrality Act, passed after the Ethiopian invasion of 1935, empowered the president to determine when a state of war existed anywhere in the world. In that event, the president would declare an embargo on all combatants. American arm shipments would cease, and American citizens would be warned against traveling on the vessels of belligerents. In February 1936, Congress passed a second Neutrality Act, prohibiting American banks from extending loans or credits to any nation at war.

President Roosevelt did not like these bills. He believed that absolute neutrality favored powerful aggressor nations by forcing the United States to treat all

sides equally. Yet FDR signed them into law for political reasons. The Neutrality Acts had wide popular support. He knew that a veto would give strong ammunition to the Republicans in the coming presidential campaign.

MANDATE FROM THE PEOPLE

As the 1936 election approached, FDR had reason for concern. Although personal income and industrial production had risen dramatically since he took office in 1933, neither had reached the pre-Depression levels of 1929. Millions of Americans were still unemployed, labor violence was spreading, and the federal deficit continued to climb. In addition, more than 80 percent of the nation's newspapers, and most of the business community, remained loyal to the Republican party, meaning that Roosevelt's major presidential opponent could count on strong editorial and financial support.

The 1936 Election

In June, the Republicans gathered in Cleveland to nominate their presidential ticket. Herbert Hoover, anxious for another crack at Roosevelt, received a thunderous ovation. But the convention delegates, seeking a winner, not a martyr, chose Kansas Governor Alfred M. Landon to head the Republican ticket, and Frank Knox, a Chicago publisher, to be the vice-presidential nominee.

Landon, a political moderate, promised "fewer radio talks, fewer experiments, and a lot more common sense." His problem was that he radiated little of the compassion and confidence that made Roosevelt so popular with the masses. Worse, Landon's bland pronouncements were overshadowed by the broadsides of more conservative Republican leaders, who denounced the New Deal as a radical plot to subvert free enterprise and individual rights. By election day, the Republicans had outspent the Democrats, $14 million to $9 million, with most of Landon's war chest coming from wealthy businessmen with ties to the American Liberty League.

Roosevelt also faced presidential challenges from the left. Both the Communists and the Socialists ran spirited campaigns in 1936, demanding more federal aid for the poor. But Roosevelt's most serious concern—a political merger involving Coughlin, Townsend, and Long—was effectively eliminated in September 1935, when an assassin's bullet killed the Louisiana senator in Baton Rouge. To replace the charismatic Long, these dissident forces nominated William "Liberty Bill" Lemke, an obscure North Dakota congressman, to be their presidential candidate on the new Union Party ticket. With typical bravado, Father Coughlin promised to end his radio broadcasts if Lemke did not poll at least 9 million votes.

Roosevelt's political strategy differed markedly from 1932. In that campaign, he had stressed the common hopes and needs that bound people together; in 1936, he emphasized the class differences that separated those who supported the New Deal from those who opposed it. Time and again, Roosevelt portrayed the election as a contest between common people and privileged people, between compassion and greed. In his final campaign speech at New York's Madison Square Garden, he declared that the "forces of selfishness" had "met their match" in the Roosevelt administration. "They are unanimous in their hatred of me," the president thundered, *and I welcome their hatred.*"

On November 3, FDR crushed Landon and Lemke in the most one-sided election since 1820. The final totals showed Roosevelt with 27,752,869 popular votes, Landon with 16,6674,665, and Lemke with 882,479. (The Socialist and Communist party candidates polled fewer than 300,000 votes between them.) Roosevelt won every state except Maine and Vermont, while the Democratic party added to its huge majorities in both houses of Congress. A few days after the election, Father Coughlin announced his retirement from the radio.

African Americans and the New Deal

Roosevelt's landslide victory signaled a dramatic shift in American politics. A new majority coalition had emerged, sympathetic to the New Deal's social agenda, inclusiveness, and class-based appeal. In the farm belt, Roosevelt won over long-time Republicans with fed-

eral subsidies and price supports. In the cities, he attracted workers grateful for welfare benefits and WPA jobs. And he appealed to ethnic minorities by filling so many White House positions, cabinet posts, and federal judgeships with Catholics and Jews.

Adding to Roosevelt's strength was the support he received from the CIO. Union leaders poured $770,000 into the president's war chest, a striking departure from labor's traditional neutrality in national elections. Describing Roosevelt as "the worker's best friend," the CIO campaigned tirelessly for him in key industrial states, and the effort paid off. Roosevelt captured the working-class vote in 1936 by a margin of four to one.

The most striking political change, however, occurred within the nation's African-American community. Although the majority of blacks still lived in the South, and thus were disenfranchised, the steady migration of African Americans to northern cities, where they could vote, increased their political power. Historically, most blacks supported the Republican party, an allegiance that dated back to Abraham Lincoln and the Civil War. In 1932, Herbert Hoover won an overwhelming share of their votes.

With the New Deal, a massive switch took place. In large part, African Americans became Democrats because the Roosevelt administration provided jobs and welfare benefits to all Americans, regardless of race. This federal assistance was especially welcome in black communities, where poverty and discrimination had long been facts of life. "The Negro was born in depression," a black leader recalled. "It only became official when it hit the white man."

By 1933, black unemployment had reached a staggering 50 percent. Fortunately, the two New Deal administrators most responsible for creating jobs were sympathetic to minority needs. At the PWA, Harold Ickes insisted that blacks receive equal pay and minimum quotas on all construction projects. Though local officials often ignored these rules, the PWA provided thousands of jobs for African Americans, while building black schools and hospitals throughout the segregated South. At the WPA, Harry Hopkins set the same standards with somewhat better results. Blacks received a generous share of WPA work in northern cities—a testimony to both their joblessness and political clout. "Let Jesus Lead You and Roosevelt Feed You," became a rallying cry in African-American churches during the election of 1936.

Although few blacks voted in the South during the 1930s, their growing numbers in northern cities like Chicago and New York increased their political influence within the New Deal coalition.

But material progress did not explain it all. Many blacks viewed the New Deal as a progressive social force. They welcomed an administration that showed some interest in their struggle. And they particularly admired the efforts of First Lady Eleanor Roosevelt, who served as the White House conscience on matters pertaining to minority rights.

A former settlement house volunteer, Mrs. Roosevelt had a passion for public service and a deep commitment to the poor. Her interest in civil rights had been fueled, in large measure, by her friendship with prominent African Americans such as Mary McLeod Bethune, founder of Bethune-Cookman College in Florida. Born in a sharecropper's shack, the fifteenth child of former slaves, Mrs. Bethune had acquainted the first lady with the special problems facing African Americans—from the scandal of lynching to the crisis in public education. In 1936, Eleanor Roosevelt

Marian Anderson entertained a crowd of 75,000 at the Lincoln Memorial on Easter Sunday, 1939, after the Daughters of the American Revolution refused to allow her to perform at Washington's Constitution Hall.

recommended Mrs. Bethune to head the National Youth Administration's Office of Negro Affairs.

As the New Deal's highest-ranking black appointee, Mrs. Bethune presided over the administration's "black cabinet," which advised the White House on minority issues. Working together with Mrs. Roosevelt and other civil rights advocates, she helped to encourage—and monitor—the New Deal's racial progress. Much of it was symbolic. In an age of rigid segregation, Mrs. Roosevelt visited black colleges, spoke at black conferences, and socialized with black women. (She raised eyebrows by inviting Mrs. Bethune to tea at the White House.) When the Daughters of the American Revolution refused to allow Marian Anderson, a gifted black contralto, to perform at Washington's Constitution Hall, Mrs. Roosevelt resigned from the organization. A few months later, Harold Ickes arranged for Miss Anderson to sing at the Lincoln Memorial on Easter Sunday, 1939. An integrated audience of 75,000 gathered to hear her.

Yet the good work of Eleanor Roosevelt and others could not mask larger New Deal failures in the field of civil rights. Throughout his presidency, for example, Franklin Roosevelt never attempted to challenge southern racial customs. He made no effort to break down segregation barriers or to enable blacks to vote. And he remained on the sidelines as federal antilynch-

ing bills were narrowly defeated in Congress. Without his leadership, not a single piece of civil rights legislation was enacted in the New Deal years.

Roosevelt explained his failure in political terms. He could not support civil rights legislation without alienating Southern Democrats who controlled the most important committees in Congress. "They will block every bill I [need] to keep America from collapsing," Roosevelt said. "I just can't take that risk."

The president's position did not prevent blacks from supporting him in 1936. Roosevelt received 76 percent of their votes—the same total that Herbert Hoover had won four years before. On balance, African Americans viewed the New Deal as a clear improvement over the Republican past. "My friends, go turn Lincoln's picture to the wall," a black editor wrote in 1935. "That debt has been paid in full."

POPULAR CULTURE IN THE DEPRESSION

The economic struggles of the 1930s shaped not only the politics of American life, but the culture as well.

Hard times encouraged federal participation in the arts and triggered a leftward tilt among many intellectuals and writers, who joined radical organizations like the Communist Party in the belief that a revolution was required to replace the ailing capitalist system. A flurry of "proletarian literature" emerged in the early Depression years, emphasizing the "class struggle" through stories about heroic workers resisting the exploitation of evil employers. Several important black writers—including Ralph Ellison, Richard Wright, and Langston Hughes—identified with the Communist Party because it appeared to actively support civil rights. For most intellectuals, however, the fascination with communism was fleeting. As free thinkers, they could not adjust to the party's rigid conformity or its blind support of the Soviet dictator Joseph Stalin.

The Depression era also witnessed the spread of a popular culture born in the preceding decades. Photojournalism came of age in 1930s with the publication of magazines such as *Life* and *Look,* and the vivid imagery of government-sponsored photographers like Walker Evans and Dorothea Lange. In the comics trade, "Superman" (1938) demonstrated that Americans were anxious to get beyond the tame characters from the newspaper strips. He was quickly followed by comic books featuring "Batman" and "Captain Marvel." In popular music, the "swing era" brought the jazz of African-American artists to a much broader public. In radio and in movies, the changes were most dramatic and profound.

The Big Screen

By the 1930s, the motion picture was the leading form of popular culture in the United States. Most Americans attended at least one movie a week; many followed the lives of their favorite stars in gossip columns and fan magazines. Theater owners attracted customers by offering free products—Tuesday was "Dish Night"—and other inducements, such as the "double feature," which dramatically increased the number of films produced during this decade. In the larger cities, movie theaters were transformed into fantasy palaces, with thick carpets, winding staircases, ushers in tuxedoes, and the twinkling lights of chandeliers. For millions, the theater became a temporary escape from the bleak realities of the Depression.

Hollywood mirrored the changing attitudes of the 1930s. It was no accident that the most popular movie of 1932, the year America hit rock bottom, was Mervyn LeRoy's *I Am a Fugitive From a Chain Gang,* the story of a decent man, unjustly convicted of a crime, who escapes from a brutal Southern penal farm. In the final scene, the hero meets his former girlfriend, who asks him how he survives. From the shadows of a dark alley—representing the Depression itself—he whispers: "I steal."

Other early films from this decade, such as *Little Caesar* (1930) and *Public Enemy* (1931) focused on big city mobsters who ruthlessly shot their way to the top. Although these "bad guys" were either killed or brought to justice on screen, the public's fascination with criminal activity reached a peak in these years with the romanticizing of bank robbers (and cold-blooded murderers) like John Dillinger, Bonnie Parker and Clyde Barrow, Baby Face Nelson, and Ma Barker. All died in shoot-outs with local police or the FBI. As Woody Guthrie wrote in "The Ballad of Pretty Boy Floyd," another fabled outlaw of this time:

> Yes, as through this world I ramble,
> I see lots of funny men,
> Some will rob you with a 6-gun, and
> Some will rob you with a pen.
> But as through your life you'll travel,
> Wherever you may roam,
> You won't never see an outlaw drive
> A family from their home.

The evolving optimism of the 1930s—the promise of better times—was also apparent in Hollywood films. Mervyn LeRoy followed *I Am a Fugitive From a Chain Gang* with *Gold Diggers of 1933,* the first of several musical extravaganzas mixing escapism with hope. The 1930s saw Fred Astaire whirling Ginger Rogers across the nightclub dance floor; Mickey Rooney courting Judy Garland in the blissfully innocent "Andy Hardy" movies; and Walt Disney raising the animated cartoon to an art form in his feature film *Snow White and the Seven Dwarfs* (1937). Wildly popular in this decade (and beyond) were the Marx brothers—Groucho, Harpo, and Chico—whose classic comedies demolished upper-class snobbery, foolish tradition, and much of the English language. "Practically everybody wants a good laugh right now," *Variety* observed in reviewing *Duck Soup* (1933), "and this should make practically everybody laugh."

More significant were the moral dramas of director Frank Capra, including *Mr. Deeds Goes to Town* (1936), starring Gary Cooper, and *Mr. Smith Goes to Washington* (1939), with Jimmy Stewart. Both the movies and the leading men represented the inherent virtues of heartland America, with its strong sense of decency and cooperation. Common people could be fooled by greedy bankers and selfish politicians, but not for long. Life got better when "good folks" followed their instincts. What the nation needed, according to Senator Smith (Jimmy Stewart), was "plain, ordinary everyday kindness, a little looking out for the other fella, loving thy neighbor."

The most memorable films of this era, *Gone with the Wind* and *The Grapes of Wrath,* showcased Hollywood's ability to transform best-selling fiction into successful movies, seen by millions who had read the novels of Margaret Mitchell, John Steinbeck, and others—and millions more who had not. Both films related the epic struggle of families in crisis, trying desperately to survive. *The Grapes of Wrath,* set in the Depression, depicts the awful conditions faced by the Dust Bowl farmers who migrated to California. True to

the 1930s, it is a story of marginal people confronting economic injustice—people who stick together and refuse to give up. The hero, Tom Joad, promises his Ma that "wherever they's a fight so hungry people can eat, I'll be there. Wherever they's a cop beatin' up a guy, I'll be there." Ma Joad is a source of strength and common sense. "They ain't gonna wipe us out," she insists. "Why, we're the people—we go on."

The Radio Age

Like the movie boom, the rapid growth of radio in the Depression encouraged the spread of popular culture. Politicians and public figures such as President Roosevelt and Father Coughlin used radio to great effect. So, too, did companies seeking to mass market their products. Organized along commercial lines in the 1920s, radio continued firmly down that path in the 1930s, with two giant firms—the National Broadcasting Company (NBC) and the Columbia Broadcasting System (CBS)—dominating the nation's airwaves.

Orson Welles, arms upraised, caused a national panic during his radio dramatization of "War of the Worlds" in 1938.

In an odd way, the economic turmoil of the 1930s aided radio by weakening other forms of entertainment. As vaudeville failed and the infant recording industry struggled, popular performers, including Al Jolson, George Burns and Gracie Allen, and Jack Benny, continued their careers on the radio. For morning and afternoon fare, the networks relied on domestic dramas such as "Ma Perkins" and "Helen Trent," which appealed to women working in the home. Often sponsored by soap and beauty companies, these programs, known as "soap operas," doled out the story line in daily fifteen-minute installments. In the evenings, as entire families gathered around the radio, the entertainment broadened to include quiz shows, talent contests, and adventure programs like "Inner Sanctum" and "The Green Hornet." Surveys showed that the average American in the 1930s listened to more than four hours of radio each day.

Radio carried sporting events, political conventions, and the news. Millions followed the 1936 Berlin Olympics, where Jesse Owens, the African-American track star, embarrassed Adolf Hitler by winning four gold medals. Two years later, the heavyweight title fight from Yankee Stadium between Joe Louis, the black champion, and Max Schmeling, the German challenger, was broadcast throughout the world. When Louis knocked out Schmeling in the first round, Americans celebrated in the streets. Columnist Russell Baker recalled the parade that began in a black neighborhood of Baltimore. "It was the first civil rights demonstration I ever saw," he wrote, "and it was completely spontaneous, ignited by the finality with which Joe Louis had destroyed the theory of white superiority."

Perhaps nothing better demonstrated the power of radio than the infamous "War of the Worlds" episode. On Halloween evening, 1938, actor Orson Welles, star of CBS's *Mercury Theater,* did a powerful reading of the H. G. Wells novel, presenting it as a simulated newscast in which violent aliens from Mars land in the New Jersey town of Grovers Mills. "I can see the thing's body," sobbed a "roving reporter" at the scene. "It's large as a bear and it glistens like wet leather. That face . . . the black eyes and saliva dripping from its rimless lips." Although Welles repeatedly interrupted the program to explain what he was doing, a national panic ensued. Thousands fled their homes, believing that the Martians had wiped out the New Jersey State Police and were advancing toward New York City. Traffic came to a halt in parts of the Northeast; bus and train stations were jammed; churches overflowed with weeping families. A few commentators blamed the hysteria on world events; the rising tide of fascism in Europe made people uneasy. Everybody else blamed Welles for misusing—or at least misjudging—the power of radio. Newspaper headlines screamed: "Radio War Terrorizes U.S." and "Panic Grips Nation As Radio Announces 'Mars Attacks World.'" When the furor died down, President Roosevelt invited Welles to the White House. "You know, Orson," he joked, "you and I are the two best actors in America."

THE SECOND TERM

In his second inaugural address, FDR emphasized the New Deal's unfinished business. "I see one-third of a nation ill-housed, ill-clad, ill-nourished," he declared. The president was optimistic. The election had provided him with a stunning popular mandate and with huge Democratic majorities on Capitol Hill. To Roosevelt's thinking, only one roadblock lay in his path: the Supreme Court.

A confrontation seemed inevitable. The Supreme Court was dominated by elderly, conservative justices, appointed in the Harding-Coolidge years, who despised the New Deal and worked zealously to subvert its legislation. In Roosevelt's first term, the court had struck down the NRA, the AAA, and a series of social welfare laws. In the coming months, it would be reviewing—and likely overturning—the National Labor Relations Act and the Social Security Act, two of the New Deal's most precious accomplishments.

Roosevelt struck first. In February 1937, without consulting Congress, he unveiled sweeping legislation to reorganize the federal court system. Under his plan, fifty new judgeships would be created by adding one judge for each sitting justice over the age of seventy who refused to retire. The Supreme Court would get a maximum of six new members, raising its total to fifteen.

The plan was legal. The Constitution sets no limits on the size of the Supreme Court; indeed, the number of justices, determined by Congress, had fluctuated between six and ten in the previous century. Roosevelt assumed that his overwhelming reelection in 1936 had

given him the green light to crush all opposition to the New Deal, regardless of the source.

He was badly mistaken. His plan met quick and furious opposition. Many Americans, including Louis D. Brandeis, the Supreme Court's oldest and most liberal justice, were offended by Roosevelt's jab at the elderly. Others worried that his "Court-packing" plan would undermine judicial independence and threaten the balance of power among the three branches of government. As the opposition grew stronger, aides urged Roosevelt to withdraw the bill or face certain, humiliating defeat.

In the spring of 1937, the Supreme Court changed course. By votes of five to four, with one moderate justice switching sides, it upheld both the Wagner Act and the Social Security Act. Then, one by one, the old conservatives decided to retire. This allowed Roosevelt—the only president in American history to make no Supreme Court appointments during his first four-year term—to fill five vacancies in the next three years. The justices he chose—including Hugo Black, Felix Frankfurter, and William O. Douglas—would steer a more liberal course for decades to come.

Nevertheless, the court battle wounded Roosevelt in significant ways. By refusing to withdraw his legislation, he subjected fellow Democrats to a bitter Senate debate—and to eventual defeat. (Congress passed a face-saving "reform" bill that left the number of federal justices unchanged.) The court-packing incident also emboldened Roosevelt's opponents by proving that the president could be beaten. "The New Deal," wrote one observer, "would never be the same."

Union Struggles

Away from Washington, new battles raged in the automobile plants of Michigan, the textile mills of North Carolina, and the coal fields of Kentucky as industrial workers demanded union recognition under the banner of the CIO. In perhaps the most spectacular episode, autoworkers at a General Motors plant in Flint, Michigan, went on strike *inside* the factory, refusing to leave. Their spontaneous technique, known as the "sit-down," spread quickly to other sites. Though Roosevelt privately criticized these strikers for violating property rights, he declined to send in

Auto workers celebrate the end of thir "sit-down" strike at a General Motors plant in Flint, Michigan, in 1937.

AN AUTOMOBILE WORKER'S RECOLLECTION OF THE GM SIT-DOWN STRIKE

The most novel and well-publicized attempt to gain union recognition in the 1930s occurred in Flint, Michigan, when automobile workers sat-down inside the General Motors factories where they worked. Bob Stinson recalled the remarkable spirit and unity of the auto workers in his body plant.

The Flint Sit-down happened Christmas Eve, 1936. I was in Detroit, playing Santa Claus to a couple of small nieces and nephews. When I came back, the second shift[1] had pulled the plant. It took about five minutes to shut the line down. The foreman was pretty well astonished. (Laughs.) . . .

We had guys patrol the plant, see that nobody got involved in anything they shouldn't. If anybody got careless with company property—such as sitting on an automobile cushion without putting burlap over it—he was talked to. You couldn't paint a sign on the wall or anything like that. You used bare springs for a bed. 'Cause if you slept on a finished cushion, it was no longer a new cushion. . . .

The merchants cooperated. There'd be apples, bushels of potatoes, crates of oranges that was beginnin' to spoil. Some of our members were also little farmers, they come up with a couple of baskets of junk.

The soup kitchen was outside the plant. The women handled all the cooking, outside of one chef who came from New York. He had anywhere from ten to twenty women washing dishes and peeling potatoes in the strike kitchen. Mostly stews, pretty good meals. They were put in containers and hoisted up through the window. The boys in there had their own plates and cups and saucers. . . .

The men sat in there for forty-four days. Governor Murphy—I get emotional over him (laughs)—was trying to get both sides to meet on some common ground. I think he lost many a good night's sleep. We wouldn't use force. Mr. Knudsen was head of General Motors and, of course, there was John L. Lewis. They'd reach a temporary agreement and invariably the Flint Alliance or GM headquarters in Detroit would throw a monkey wrench in it. So every morning, Murphy got up with an unsolved problem.

There were a half a dozen false starts at settlement. Finally, we got the word: THE THING IS SETTLED. My God, you had to send about three people, one right after the other, down to some of those plants because the guys didn't believe it. Finally, when they did get it, they marched out of the plants with the flag flyin' and all that stuff.

You'd see some guys comin' out of there with whiskers as long as Santa Claus. They made a rule they wasn't gonna shave until the strike was over. Oh, it was just like—you've gone through the Armistice delirium, haven't you? Everybody was runnin' around shaking everybody by the hand, sayin', "Jesus, you look strange, you got a beard on you now." (Laughs.) Women kissin' their husbands. There was a lotta drunks on the streets that night.

When Mr. Knudsen put his name to a piece of paper and says that General Motors recognizes the UAW-CIO—until that moment, we were non-people, we didn't even exist. (Laughs.) That was the big one. (His eyes are moist.)

SOURCE   Studs Terkel, *Hard Times*, 1970, pp. 145–150.

[1]The men who worked from 4:30 P.M. to 12:30 A.M.

troops. In February 1937, GM recognized the CIO's United Automobile Workers (UAW) as the bargaining agent for its employees. Chrysler came to terms a few months later.

The victory at GM forced other employers into line. Firestone signed a contract with the CIO's Rubber Workers, General Electric and RCA with the Electrical Workers. Even U.S. Steel, an old enemy of organized labor, agreed to generous terms with the Steelworkers—union recognition, a 40-hour week, and a 10-percent wage increase.

There were some holdouts, however. Henry Ford hired an army of thugs to rough up union organizers and disrupt strikers on the picket lines. Republic Steel of Chicago stockpiled more weapons than the city police department. "I won't have a contract with an irresponsible, racketeering, violent communistic body like the CIO," fumed Republic President Tom C. Girdler. "And until they pass a law making me do it, I am not going to do it."

The worst violence occurred outside Republic's South Chicago mill on Memorial Day 1937. There heavily armed police battled rock-throwing strikers on the picket line. Before it ended, ten workers had been killed by gunfire, and dozens more had been injured. When Roosevelt blamed both sides for the continuing troubles at Republic, union leader John L. Lewis responded with scorn: "It ill behooves one who has supped at labor's table," he snapped, "to curse with equal fervor and fine impartiality both labor and its adversaries when they become locked in a deadly embrace."

In the following months, Ford and Republic Steel came to terms. Under pressure from the National Labor Relations Board, they gradually accepted industrial unionism as a legitimate force in American life. With a membership approaching 3 million, the CIO had come a long way since its break with the conservative, craft-oriented American Federation of Labor a few years before.

LOSING GROUND

The court battle and the sit-down strikes slowed down the political momentum that followed FDR's reelection landslide in 1936. Further problems loomed in Europe, where fascism continued to gain strength, and in the United States, where a serious recession in 1937 eroded public confidence in the New Deal. For President Roosevelt, the road ahead appeared even more menacing than before.

Fascist Advances

Late in 1936, civil war broke out in Spain. A group of military officers, led by General Francisco Franco, attempted to overthrow the recently elected government. Because Franco represented the *Falangist,* or fascist elements in Spain, he received military aid from Hitler and Mussolini. On the other side, Joseph Stalin aided the government (or "loyalist") forces, which contained a large socialist and communist contingent. The war itself was brutal, with extreme cruelty on both sides. Before it ended, more than 600,000 people were killed.

The Spanish Civil War triggered strong emotions in the United States. Some Americans praised Franco as a bastion against communism and a strong supporter of the Catholic church. Others condemned him as a fascist thug, determined to overthrow a popularly elected government by force. Several thousand Americans went to Spain as part of the Abraham Lincoln Brigade, organized by the Communist party, to fight on the Loyalist side. As Ernest Hemingway said of Franco, "There is only one way to quell a bully and that is to thrash him."

Most Americans disagreed. In 1937, Congress passed a third neutrality bill that extended the arms embargo to include *civil wars* like the one raging in Spain. The bill also prohibited Americans from traveling on belligerent vessels, even at their own risk. However, it did permit nations at war to purchase "nonmilitary" goods if they paid cash (no loans) and carried them away on their own ships. President Roosevelt quickly signed the bill into law.

The Rising Nazi Menace

In central Europe, meanwhile, Hitler marched boldly toward war. Vowing to unite all German-speaking people, he moved on Austria in 1938, adding 6 million "Germans" to the Third Reich. Then he demanded the Sudentenland, a region in western Czechoslovakia where 3 million ethnic Germans

Hitler Youth in Germany rounding up books to be burned, including the works of Thomas Mann and Albert Einstein. As Joseph Goebbels, the Nazi Propaganda Minister, declared: "These flames not only illuminate the final end of an old era; they also light up the new."

At the fateful Munich Conference in 1938, British Prime Minister Neville Chamberlain appeased Adolf Hitler's demands for territorial expansion, claiming the agreement would bring "peace in our time."

lived. The Czechs possessed both a well-trained army and a defense treaty with France. As central Europe's only remaining democracy, Czechoslovakia looked to the French and British for support against the Nazi threat.

That support never came. Neither France nor England wanted a showdown with Germany. France had lost half of its male population between the ages of twenty and thirty-two during World War I. In Britain, Oxford students adopted a resolution in the 1930s declaring that they would not take up arms for their country under any circumstances. Anti-war feeling was so strong that a kind of diplomatic paralysis set in. The result was the Munich debacle of 1938.

At Munich, Prime Minister Neville Chamberlain of England and Premier Edouard Daladier of France agreed to Hitler's demand for the Sudetenland. In return the German leader promised not to take any more territory. Daladier then pressured the Czechs to accept this dismal bargain, while Chamberlain congratulated everyone—Hitler included—for bringing "peace in our time."

The news from inside Germany was even worse. Early in 1938, the Nazis torched Munich's Great Synagogue and began the initial deportation of Jews to the infamous concentration camp at Buchenwald. On the evening of November 9—known as *Kristallnacht,* the

In 1939, more than a thousand Jews fleeing from Germany aboard the ocean liner St. Louis *were refused entry into the United States at the port of Miami and forced to return to Europe— and certain death.*

"night of broken glass"—Nazi mobs burned synagogues, looted stores, and attacked Jews in cities throughout Germany. Dozens were murdered, hundreds were beaten and raped. In addition, the Nazis passed new laws to confiscate Jewish property, bar Jews from meaningful employment, and deprive them of ordinary liberties such as attending school and driving a car.

When word of these events reached the United States, President Roosevelt was furious. "I myself could scarcely believe that such things could occur in a twentieth century civilization," he told reporters. Roosevelt immediately called a conference of thirty-two nations to discuss plans for accepting desperate Jewish refugees from Germany, Austria, and Czechoslovakia. But no country, with the exception of small and densely populated Holland, showed a willingness to help. In the United States, a combination of anti-Semitism, isolationist sentiment, and hard times kept the "golden door" tightly shut. Most Americans did not want "foreigners" competing with them for jobs and resources in the midst of the Depression.

The result was disastrous. At a time when many Jews had the ability to flee Hitler, there was almost no place for them to go. Between 1935 and 1941, the United States took in an average of 8,500 Jews per year—a number far below the annual German quota of 30,000 set by the National Origins Act of 1924. (Among those allowed to enter were "high profile" Jewish refugees such as Albert Einstein and composer Kurt Weill.) Furthermore, President Roosevelt refused to take additional steps against Hitler because he feared a political backlash. Thus, he did not make a strong diplomatic protest or attempt to lessen trade with the Nazi regime.

An End to Reform

Until 1937, the American economy had been making steady, if uneven, progress. National income and production finally reached 1929 levels, stock prices were climbing, profits were up. Roosevelt now hoped to slow down government spending as the business pic-

TABLE 25.1	KEY NEW DEAL PROGRAMS AND LEGISLATION
1933	Emergency Banking Act
	Civilian Conservation Corps
	Agricultural Adjustment Act
	Tennessee Valley Authority
	Glass-Steagall Banking Act (creates Federal Deposit Insurance Corporation)
	Federal Emergency Relief Act
	National Industrial Recovery Act
	Civil Works Administration
1934	Securities and Exchange Act
1935	National Labor Relations Act
	Social Security Act
	Emergency Relief Appropriation Act (creates Works Progress Administration)
	Revenue Act ("Wealth Tax")
	Rural Electrification Administration
	National Youth Administration
1936	Soil Conservation Act
1937	National Housing Act
1938	Fair Labor Standards Act

ture improved. He wanted to balance the federal budget and cut the mounting national debt.

The president understood the risks. He knew that national recovery had been fueled by the New Deal's farm subsidies, relief programs, and public works. He was familiar with the writings of British economist John Maynard Keynes, who advocated a policy of deficit spending in hard times to spur economic growth. Yet Roosevelt had never been fully comfortable with government's expanding role. He feared that the growing national debt would generate inflation, and he worried about the effect of federal welfare programs upon the recipients' initiative and self-respect.

In 1937, Roosevelt slashed funding for both the PWA and WPA, cutting almost 2 million jobs. At the same time, the new Social Security payroll tax took effect, removing billions of dollars of purchasing power from the economy. The result was recession—the most serious economic plunge of the Roosevelt years. As unemployment rose and production plummeted, the nation slipped back toward the nightmare of 1933, with bread lines and soup kitchens dotting the landscape.

In October, Roosevelt called Congress into special session. Within weeks, a $5 billion expenditure was approved for federal relief and public works. The economy responded, showing the impact of government spending once again. But the recession further weakened Roosevelt's image as a forceful leader in perilous times.

By 1938, the New Deal had clearly lost momentum. Harry Hopkins blamed it on six grinding years of Depression and reform, claiming the public was "bored with the poor, the unemployed, the insecure." Facing a more combative Congress—Republicans and conservative Democrats made significant gains in the 1938 elections—Roosevelt decided to "tread water" for a while. Among his few legislative achievements that year was passage of the Fair Labor Standards Act, which abolished child labor in most industries, while providing a minimum hourly wage (forty cents) and a

maximum workweek (forty hours), to be phased in over time. Like Social Security, the act did not cover those who needed it most, such as farm workers and domestics. Yet almost a million Americans had their wages raised immediately by this law, and countless millions had their work hours shortened as well.

⟨ C O N C L U S I O N ⟩

The New Deal altered politics and society in fundamental ways. It forever changed the role of the federal government in American life, making it bigger, costlier, and more attentive to previously forgotten groups. For the first time in our history, the government provided massive assistance to the poor and the unemployed. It stabilized the banking system, protected farmers with price supports, guaranteed the rights of organized labor, encouraged collective bargaining between workers and employers, and created a national pension plan. The New Deal also produced a more class-oriented Democratic party, appealing to industrial workers, hard-pressed farmers, and urban minorities. Under Franklin Roosevelt's leadership, a kind of broker state emerged in which diverse groups pushed their competing demands upon the federal government and received tangible rewards. Avoiding the political extremes that plagued other nations in the Depression era, Roosevelt steered a middle course between laissez faire and socialism—a course that combined free enterprise and democracy with national planning and social reform.

What the New Deal could not do, however, was to restore prosperity at home. Fearful of mounting budget deficits and ever-growing relief rolls, President Roosevelt never committed himself to the level of consistent federal spending urged by economists like John Maynard Keynes. When the New Deal ended in 1939, more than 8 million Americans were still unemployed. It would take a world war, and the full mobilization that followed, to put them permanently back to work.

RECOMMENDED READINGS

Brinkley, Alan. *Voices of Protest: Huey Long, Father Coughlin, and the Great Depression* (1982) is a revealing account of Depression era dissidents.

Cohen, Lizabeth. *Making a New Deal: Industrial Workers in Chicago* (1990) examines working-class protest and culture during the Depression.

Cooke, Blanche Wiesen. *Eleanor Roosevelt* (1992) follows the life of the nation's most active first lady.

Fraser, Steve, and Gerstle, Gary, eds. *The Rise and Fall of the New Deal Order* (1989) contains a series of original essays about the New Deal's impact on American life.

Goodman, James. *Stories of Scottsboro* (1994) vividly recreates the most important civil rights trial of the 1930s.

McElvaine, Robert S. *The Great Depression* (1984) is an excellent survey of American life and politics during the New Deal era.

Terkel, Studs. *Hard Times* (1970) views the Depression through the oral history of those who lived through it.

Worster, Donald. *Dust Bowl: The Southern Plains in the 1930s* (1979) examines the causes and the impact of this ecological disaster.

Politics and Public Policy

Conkin, Paul. *The New Deal* (1975).

Hawley, Ellis. *The New Deal and the Problem of Monopoly* (1965).

Klehr, Harvey. *The Heyday of American Communism* (1984).

Leuchtenburg, William E. *The Supreme Court Reborn: The Constitutional Revolution in the Age of Roosevelt* (1995).

Patterson, James T. *Congressional Conservatism and the New Deal* (1967).

Schlesinger, Arthur, Jr., *The Coming of the New Deal* (1959).

Ware, Susan. *Beyond Suffrage: Women and the New Deal* (1981).

Warren, Donald. *Radio Priest: Charles Coughlin, the Father of Hate Radio* (1996).

Williams, T. Harry. *Huey Long* (1969).

Labor and the New Deal

Bernstein, Irving. *Turbulent Years* (1970).

Dubofsky, Melvyn, and Van Time, Warren, *John L. Lewis: A Biography* (1977).

Fine, Sidney. *Sit-Down* (1969).

Fraser, Steven. *Labor Will Rule: Sidney Hillman and the Rise of American Labor* (1991).

Lichtenstein, Nelson. *The Most Dangerous Man in Detroit* (1995).

Zieger, Robert. *The CIO: 1935–1955* (1995).

Minorities and the New Deal

Deutsch, Sarah. *No Separate Refuge: Culture, Class, and Gender on the Anglo-Hispanic Frontier in the American Southwest, 1880–1940* (1987).

Sitkoff, Harvard. *A New Deal for Blacks* (1978).

Taylor, Graham D. *The New Deal and American Indian Tribalism* (1980).

Weiss, Nancy, *Farewell to the Party of Lincoln: Black Politics in the Age of FDR* (1983).

Zangrando, Robert L. *The NAACP Campaign Against Lynching* (1980).

NAZISM ON THE MOVE

The collapse of France in 1940 raised fears that Hitler would soon control all of Europe.

Chapter 26

THE SECOND WORLD WAR,

1940–1945

PRIME MINISTER NEVILLE Chamberlain's "peace in our time" lasted less than six months. In March 1939, the Germans marched into central Czechoslovakia, meeting no resistance at all. To the south, Franco's forces won a final victory in the Spanish Civil War, while Mussolini's army annexed neighboring Albania. Throughout the summer months, Nazi threats multiplied. "So long as Germans in Poland suffer grievously, so long as they are imprisoned away from the Fatherland," warned Hitler, "Europe can have no peace."

President Roosevelt declared neutrality, reflecting the clear sentiment of the American people. At the same time, he worked to mobilize the nation's defense effort and to shape public opinion steadily against the Axis powers. If possible, Roosevelt hoped to aid Great Britain and the allies through "all measures short of war." If need be, however, he vowed to use military force to prevent a Nazi victory in Europe. Never in world history, Roosevelt believed, had the forces of evil been so determined, and the dangers to civilization so crystal clear.

WAR IN EUROPE

In August 1939, Hitler and Stalin stunned the world by signing a "non-aggression" pact. Thought to be ideological opposites, both dictators were buying time for an inevitable showdown between their armed forces. And both had designs upon Polish territory, which they secretly divided in their agreement. On September 1, German ground troops and armored divisions stormed into Poland from the west, backed by their powerful air force *(Luftwaffe)*. Two weeks later, Soviet troops attacked from the east, reclaiming the territory that Russia had lost to Poland after World War I. In the following months, Stalin moved against the Baltic states, subduing Estonia, Latvia, and Lithuania.

Blitzkrieg

Hitler's *Blitzkrieg* (lightning strike) into Poland shattered the lingering illusions of Munich. Having pledged themselves to guarantee Poland's borders, England and France reluctantly declared war on Germany. The British sent a small, ill-equipped army to defend Western Europe against further Nazi aggression. The French reinforced their "impregnable" Maginot Line facing Germany, while the Nazis fortified their Siegfried Line in the Rhineland facing France. An eerie calm settled over Europe, as all sides prepared for battle.

That six-month calm, known as the "phony war," ended in April 1940 when the Nazis overran Denmark

CHRONOLOGY

1940 Germany conquers the Low Countries and France

British Air Force beats back Luftwaffe in skies over England, preventing Nazi invasion

Selective Service Act brings first peacetime draft

Franklin Roosevelt elected to an unprecedented third term in the White House

1941 Lend-Lease Act passed by Congress

Nazi armies invade the Soviet Union

Atlantic Charter is issued

Japan attacks Pearl Harbor, bringing United States into war

1942 Japanese forces capture the Philippines

Internment of Japanese Americans begins

FDR authorizes top secret Manhattan Project to build an atomic weapon

U.S. forces land in Africa to begin Operation Torch

U.S. Navy halts Japanese advance at the Battle of Midway

1943 Soviets win pivotal victory over Nazis at Stalingrad

Race riot in Detroit, "Zoot-Suit" riot in Los Angeles

U.S. forces invade Italy

U.S. Marines capture Guadalcanal

1944 Allies launch Normandy Invasion

U.S. forces, led by General MacArthur, recapture Philippines

Roosevelt elected to fourth term

1945 Allied leaders discuss postwar issues at Yalta

FDR dies; Harry Truman becomes president

Hitler commits suicide days before Germany surrenders

United States captures Iwo Jima and Okinawa

Atomic bomb is successfully tested in New Mexico desert

United States drops atomic bombs on Hiroshima and Nagasaki

Japan surrenders, ending World War II

---

and Norway. In May, they invaded Belgium, Holland, Luxembourg—and France itself. From the skies, the Luftwaffe strafed fleeing civilians and flattened cities such as Rotterdam. On the ground, German troops and armor swept through the Ardennes Forest, skirting the Maginot Line. The huge French army collapsed in disarray. Within weeks, German units had reached the French coastline, trapping the British army at Dunkirk, with its back to the sea. In early June, a flotilla of small ships from England—tugs, pleasure craft, and naval vessels—ferried 330,000 soldiers to safety. It was both a defeat and a deliverance for the British forces, who had been badly mauled but rescued from disaster.

In mid-June, as Paris fell to the advancing Nazi army, Mussolini attacked France from the south. Following the French surrender on June 22, the German Luftwaffe attacked England in force. Hitler's plan was to gain control of the skies in preparation for a full-scale invasion of the British Isles. Day and night, German planes dropped their bombs on London, Coventry, and other cities in a murderous attempt to break civilian morale. Day and night, the British Royal Air Force rose up to meet the Luftwaffe, with devastating effect. By early fall, Nazi air losses forced Hitler to abandon his invasion plans. "Never in the field of human conflict," said England's new Prime Minister Winston Churchill of the brave pilots who fought the Battle of Britain, "was so much owed by so many to so few."

A Third Term for FDR

Events in Europe shattered America's isolationist façade. Unlike Woodrow Wilson in 1914, President

As the first president to run for a third term, Franklin Roosevelt faced suspicions that he was undermining democracy itself.

Roosevelt did not ask the people to be "neutral in thought as well as in action." If England fell to the Nazis, he believed, the United States would become an isolated fortress, vulnerable to attack from the air and the sea. Most Americans felt the same way. The German invasions of Poland, France, and the Low Countries turned public opinion overwhelmingly against Hitler, though not in favor of participation in a European war. A national poll found 83 percent hoping for a British victory, 16 percent neutral, and only 1 percent supporting the Nazis.

The German Blitzkrieg increased American concerns about defense. Even isolationists worried about the low level of military preparedness in the United States, which had a small standing army (ranked nineteenth in the world), and an air force with less fire power than Mussolini's. In August 1940, as the Battle of Britain raged in the skies over England, President Roosevelt and Congress worked to fashion the first peacetime draft in American history, the Selective Service Act, as well as a $10.5 billion appropriation for defense. With factories now open round-the-clock to build tanks, war planes, and naval vessels, unemployment virtually disappeared. The Great Depression was over.

Building a strong defense was one thing, aiding the allies quite another. As Michigan Senator Arthur Vandenberg, a leading isolationist, put it: "I do not believe that we can become an arsenal for one belligerent without becoming a target for another." Vandenberg used World War I as his example, charging that America's support for the allied war effort had led to its participation in the war itself. With a presidential election on the horizon, FDR would have to answer this charge.

Until the last moment, however, there was no assurance that Roosevelt would even run. The loss of New Deal momentum and the Court-packing disaster pointed to his political retirement. Furthermore, no American president had ever served a third term—a taboo that reflected the public's deep suspicion of entrenched federal power. In 1938, opinion polls showed Americans opposed to a third term by more than two to one.

By 1940, the picture had changed. In a world threatened by fascist aggression, the idea of tested presidential leadership took on added appeal. Roosevelt expected to run again. Hoping to defuse the third-term issue, he allowed himself to be "drafted" by the Democratic National Convention in Chicago, thus appearing reluctant but dutiful in the public's mind. "The salvation of the nation rests in one man, because of his experience and great humanitarian thinking," declared Mayor Edward J. Kelly of the host city. Roosevelt selected the enigmatic Henry Wallace to be his vice-presidential running mate.

The Republicans, meeting in Philadelphia, nominated Wendell Willkie of Indiana for president and Senator Charles McNary of Oregon for vice president. As a Wall Street lawyer and the head of a large utilities corporation, Willkie held two positions almost guaranteed to make the voters suspicious. He had never run for public office or held an appointive government position. His political ascent was due, in large part, to the public relations skills of his advisors, who packaged him as a "citizen-politician" through newsreels,

Republican presidential candidate Wendell Willkie begins the 1940 campaign in his home town of Elwood, Indiana.

radio speeches, and ghost-written articles in *Time* and *The Saturday Evening Post.*

The 1940 campaign was dominated by foreign affairs. Though Willkie shared Roosevelt's views about the dangers of Nazi aggression, he attacked the president for moving too quickly on the European stage. Among Willkie's complaints was a controversial decision by FDR to supply England with "overage" destroyers. In the summer of 1940, Churchill had begged the United States for naval support to protect British sea lanes from Nazi submarine attacks. "It was," the prime minister insisted, "a matter of life and death." In September, without consulting Congress, the president sent fifty old but serviceable warships to England in return for long-term leases to British military bases in Newfoundland, Bermuda, and other parts of the Western Hemisphere. The agreement outraged isolationists, who viewed it as a clear violation of American neutrality. Willkie charged that FDR's foreign policy meant "more wooden crosses for sons and brothers and sweethearts," forcing the president to make a promise that he would not be able to keep. "I have said this before, but I shall say it again and again and again," Roosevelt told a cheering crowd in Boston. "Your boys are not going to be sent into any foreign wars."

Roosevelt defeated Willkie with ease—27 million votes to 22 million, 449 electoral votes to eighty-two. He carried all of America's major cities, piling up impressive totals among blacks, Jews, ethnic minorities, and union members. New York Mayor Fiorello LaGuardia put it well: "Americans prefer Roosevelt with his known faults to Willkie with his unknown virtues." Still, the margin of FDR's popular victory made this the closest presidential election since 1916. Willkie did particularly well in the isolationist Midwest, and among voters of Irish, German, and Italian extraction, many of whom opposed the president's recent foreign policy moves.

THE END OF NEUTRALITY

Shortly after the election, Roosevelt learned that England could no longer afford the supplies it needed to fight the Nazi war machine. He responded by asking Congress for the authority to sell or lease "defense material" to any nation he judged "vital to the defense of the United States." Roosevelt compared his "Lend-

Lease" proposal to the simple act of lending a garden hose to a neighbor whose house was on fire. In Europe, he said, the British desperately needed tanks, guns, and planes to extinguish the raging inferno of Nazism. Only one nation had the ability to supply them. "We must be the great arsenal of democracy," Roosevelt declared.

Lend-Lease

Lend-Lease set off a furious national debate. Roosevelt's critics included isolationist senators such as Robert LaFollette, Jr., of Wisconsin, a progressive, and Robert A. Taft of Ohio, a conservative. In 1940, FDR's opponents organized the America First Committee to keep the nation "neutral" by defeating Lend-Lease. Supported by Henry Ford, Charles Lindbergh, and Robert E. Wood, chairman of Sears, Roebuck, it appealed to the isolationist notion that America should be prepared to defend its own territory, leaving Europe's wars to the Europeans. At times, however, the committee's message became muddled and conspiratorial, as when Lindbergh described American Jews as the "principal war agitators" behind Lend-Lease.

By 1941, Roosevelt gained the upper hand. Public opinion moved sharply against isolationism as Hitler became a more ominous threat. Polls showed a clear majority of Americans willing to risk war with Germany in order to help the British survive. In March, a $7 billion Lend-Lease bill sailed through Congress, assisted by powerful lobbying groups such as the Committee to Defend America by Aiding the Allies. Speaking for some isolationists, Senator Burton Wheeler bitterly compared Lend-Lease to the New Deal's farm program, claiming it would "plow under every fourth American boy." "That comment," fumed Roosevelt, "is the rottenest thing that has been said in public life in my generation."

In June 1941, Hitler shattered the recent Nazi-Soviet Pact by invading Russia with more than 2 million troops. Roosevelt responded by offering Stalin immediate Lend-Lease support. The idea of aiding a Communist dictator was hard for Americans to accept. As Senator Harry Truman put it, "If we see that Germany is winning, we should help Russia and if Russia is winning we ought to help Germany and that way we let them kill as many as possible." But Roosevelt stood firm, believing that wars made strange bedfellows, and that Hitler must be stopped at all

Millions of Americans, including Charles Lindbergh, opposed President Roosevelt's attempt to aid the allies against the onslaught of Nazism, claiming it would lead the United States into the European war.

costs. At his insistence, the Soviets received $12 billion in aid over the next four years.

With Lend-Lease in place, Roosevelt abandoned all pretense of neutrality. To ensure that American goods reached England, he instructed the navy to protect merchant shipping in the North Atlantic sea lanes. In April 1941, U.S. troops landed in Greenland; in July, more soldiers went ashore in Iceland. The following month, Roosevelt and Churchill met aboard the U.S.S. *Augusta,* off the Newfoundland coast, to discuss their mutual aims and principles. The result was a communiqué known as the Atlantic Charter, which called for freedom of the seas, freedom from want and fear, and self-determination for all people in the post-war world.

At this meeting, Roosevelt secretly promised Churchill that the United States would try "to force an 'incident' that could lead to war" with Germany. In the fall of 1941, as Nazi submarines sank one Britain-bound freighter after another, the president armed America's merchant fleet and authorized U.S. destroyers to hunt these U-boats under a policy known as "active defense." In October, a German submarine sank a U.S. destroyer off Iceland, with the loss of one hundred American lives. In his ballad to the men who died, Woody Guthrie asked:

What were their names, tell me,
what were their names?
Did you have a friend
on the good *Reuben James?"*

War would come shortly, but not where Roosevelt expected.

The Road to Pearl Harbor

As Hitler swept relentlessly though Europe, another power was stirring halfway around the globe. Like Germany and Italy, Japan had become a militarist state controlled by leaders with expansionist ideas. In the 1930s, the Japanese had invaded China, routing its army, terror-bombing cities, and brutalizing civilians in the infamous "rape of Nanking." The United States barely protested, despite its numerous pledges to protect China's sovereignty and keep its markets open to all. Distracted by the Nazis, Roosevelt sought to avoid a crisis with Japan, even after its planes bombed an American gunboat, the *Panay,* on the Yangtze River in 1937, killing three sailors and injuring forty-three more.

In 1938, the Japanese unveiled their plan for empire, known as the "Greater East Asia Co-Prosperity Sphere." Viewing themselves as superior to their neighbors, they aimed to rule their region by annexing European colonies in Southeast Asia and the Western Pacific. Control of French Indochina, the Dutch East Indies, and British Malaya would provide the food and raw materials to make Japan self-sufficient and secure. Only one obstacle stood in the way—the United States.

As America's third-best customer, Japan purchased the bulk of its steel, oil, heavy equipment, and machine parts from U.S. suppliers. To help prevent further Japanese expansion, the Roosevelt administration placed an embargo on certain strategic goods to Japan and moved the Pacific fleet from San Diego to Pearl Harbor. The Japanese responded by negotiating a defense treaty (the so-called Tripartite Pact) with Germany and Italy. Relations steadily declined. Hitler's blitzkrieg left defeated France and Holland unable to defend their Asian colonies. When Japan moved against Indochina in April 1941, Roosevelt retaliated by freezing all Japanese assets in the United States and blocking shipments of scrap iron and aviation fuel to Japan. In September, Japanese leaders requested a meeting with Roosevelt to end the deepening crisis. The president agreed—but with certain conditions. Before sitting down together, he said, the Japanese must withdraw from both China and Indochina, and agree to an open door in Asia.

The Japanese refused. Though talks were held at a lower level, both sides prepared for war. Military analysts expected Japan to move southwest, toward the Dutch East Indies and British Malaya, in search of needed rubber and oil. Instead, on November 26, 1941, a huge Japanese naval fleet, led by Admiral Chuichi Nagumo, left the Kurile Islands, just north of mainland Japan, and headed due east into rough Pacific waters. The armada included six aircraft carriers with 400 war planes, two battleships, two cruisers, nine destroyers, and dozens of support vessels. Traveling at thirteen knots, under complete radio silence, the fleet was destined for Pearl Harbor, Hawaii, 5,000 miles away.

On Sunday morning, December 7, 1941, Admiral Nagumo's fleet reached its takeoff point, 220 miles north of Pearl Harbor. At 7:40 a.m., the first wave of

The Japanese attack on Pearl Harbor—December 7, 1941—destroyed eighteen warships, killed 2,400 Americans, and plunged the nation into World War II.

Japanese war planes appeared. The wing commander radioed back the words, "Tora (tiger), Tora, Tora," meaning that surprise had been complete. The battleship *Arizona* suffered a direct hit and went up in flames. More than 1,200 of her crew were killed. The *Oklahoma* capsized after taking three torpedoes, trapping 400 men below deck. A second Japanese assault at nine o'clock completed the carnage. All told, eighteen warships had been sunk or were badly damaged, 300 planes had been lost, and 2,400 Americans had died.

It could have been worse. The aircraft carriers *Lexington* and *Enterprise* were away from Pearl Harbor on maneuvers. And Japanese commanders made a strategic error by not launching a third air attack against the oil depots, machine shops, and repair facilities. As a result, most of the damaged warships were back in action within two years.

Why was Pearl Harbor so woefully unprepared? By the fall of 1941, the United States had broken the Japanese diplomatic code, known as MAGIC. American planners knew that war was coming. On November 27, Army Chief of Staff George C. Marshall sent a warning to all American military outposts in the Pacific. "Negotiations with Japan appear to be terminated to all practical purposes," it said. "Japanese future action unpredictable, but hostile action possible at any moment." There followed another message, three days later, that began, "This dispatch is to be considered a war warning."

Yet Pearl Harbor was not viewed as the likely point of attack. It was thousands of miles from Japan, and supposedly well defended. The very idea of a Japanese fleet sailing so far without detection seemed utterly fantastic. At Pearl Harbor, the commanders most feared sabotage from the large Japanese population living in Hawaii. Though some Americans believed that Roosevelt secretly encouraged the Japanese attack in order to bring the United States into World War II, the truth is more mundane. The debacle at Pearl Harbor was caused by negligence and errors in judgment, not by a backroom conspiracy at the White House.

On December 8, Congress declared war against Japan. Only Montana's Representative Jeanette Rankin dissented. (A long-time peace activist, she also had voted against President Wilson's war message in 1917.) On December 11, Germany and Italy honored the Tripartite Pact by declaring war on the United States.

AN AMERICAN SOLDIER REMEMBERS THE BATAAN DEATH MARCH

In April 1942, more than 10,000 American soldiers surrendered to the Japanese on Bataan Peninsula in the Philippines. Badly weakened by starvation and disease, the soldiers were marched under brutal conditions to an internment camp sixty-five miles away. Hundreds died on the march, and thousands more died in captivity.

Capt. LOYD MILLS, Company C, 57th Infantry, Philippine Scouts:

The nights were the worst times for me. We walked all day, from early morning until dusk. Then we were put into barbed-wire enclosures in which the conditions were nearly indescribable. Filth and defecation all over the place. The smell was terrible. These same enclosures had been used every night, and when my group got to them, they were covered by the filth of five or six nights.

I had dysentery pretty bad, but I didn't worry about it because there wasn't anything you could do about it. You didn't stop on "the March" because you were dead if you did. They didn't mess around with you. You didn't have time to pull out and go over and squat. You would just release wherever you were. Generally right on yourself, or somebody else if they happened to be in your way. There was nothing else to do. Without food it was water more than anything. It just went through me . . . bang.

I was in a daze. One thing I knew was that I had to keep going. I was young, so I had that advantage over some of the older men. I helped along the way. If someone near you started stumbling and looked like he was going to fall, you would try to literally pick him up and keep him going. You always talked to them. Tried to make them understand that if they fell they were gone. 'Course, there was nothing you could do about the people who fell in the back.

SOURCE Capt. Lloyd Mills, in Donald Knox, *Death March*, 1981, p.133.

Almost instantly, Americans closed ranks. The foreign policy battles were over. As Roosevelt's former enemy Senator Burton Wheeler put it, "The only thing to do now is lick the hell out of them."

Early Defeats

The attack on Pearl Harbor began one of the bleakest years in American military history. In the North Atlantic, allied shipping losses reached almost a million tons per month (or one ship and crew lost every four hours), as the number of German submarines rose from fifty-six in 1939 to 249 by 1942. On the Eastern front, Nazi forces approached the outskirts of Moscow, where Soviet resistance was fierce. In Egypt, German General Erwin Rommel's elite Afrika Korps threatened the Suez Canal.

The news from Asia was grimmer still. Following Pearl Harbor, Japan moved quickly against American possessions in the Pacific, overrunning Guam, Wake Island, and eventually the Philippines. On December 10, 1941, the Japanese attacked the British fleet off Malaya, sinking the battleship *Prince of Wales* and the cruiser *Repulse.* In the following weeks, Burma, Hong

Kong, Singapore, Malaya, and the Dutch East Indies fell like dominoes to Japanese invaders. The dream of a Greater East Asia Co-Prosperity Sphere was at hand. Japan now had the resources—the oil, tin, rubber, and foodstuffs—to match its appetite for empire.

For Americans, the most galling defeat occurred in the Philippines, where 100,000 U.S. and Filipino troops surrendered to the Japanese after a bloody six-month struggle. The military campaign had actually been lost on December 8, 1941, when the Japanese successfully bombed Clark Field, destroying hundreds of planes based there to defend the islands. (The failure to prepare for such an attack one day after Pearl Harbor was scandalous.) Lacking air cover, the defenders retreated to the jungles of the Bataan Peninsula, just north of Manila. As food ran out, they ate snakes, monkeys, cavalry horses, plants, and grass. Their songs were of hopelessness and despair.

> We're the battling bastards of Bataan;
> No Mama, no papa, no Uncle Sam.
> No aunts, no uncles, no cousins, no nieces;
> No pills, no planes, no artillery pieces.
> . . . And Nobody gives a damn!

In March 1942, President Roosevelt ordered commanding General Douglas MacArthur to slip out of the Philippines, leaving his troops behind. The trapped defenders made their stand at Corregidor, a fortress-like island in Manila Bay. After two months of constant bombardment, General Jonathan Wainwright surrendered to the Japanese. His diseased and starving men were brutalized by their captors on the infamous Bataan Death March—an event that further fueled America's boiling hatred of Japan.

Despite these disasters, the nation remained united and confident of victory. A public opinion poll taken early in 1942, at the low point of American fortunes, showed only 4 percent in agreement that "the Axis have a pretty good chance to win the war." The road ahead would be long, the challenges immense. As *Time* magazine reminded its readers,

> At the end of six months of war, the U.S. has:
> Not yet taken a single inch of enemy territory,
> Not yet beaten the enemy in a single major battle . . .
> Not yet opened an offensive campaign.
> The war, in short, has still to be fought.

THE HOMEFRONT

The United States had begun to mobilize for World War II before the attack on Pearl Harbor. The draft was already in place, and defense plants were hiring

new workers in the mad scramble to keep England, then the Soviet Union, and now America, fully supplied. Furthermore, the positive feelings about this conflict—a "good fight" against Nazi and Japanese aggression—eased many of the problems associated with a democratic nation going to war. Few men refused to register for military service, unlike World War I, and millions rushed to enlist. On the homefront, Americans vowed to outproduce their enemies and to sacrifice for the "boys" at the front. "Our great strength," said a defense worker from San Diego, "is that we're all in this together."

War Production

To coordinate the defense industries, FDR named Donald Nelson of Sears, Roebuck, to run the newly created War Production Board (WPB). Nelson's main job was to oversee the transformation of American factories—to get companies such as Ford and General Motors to make tanks and warplanes instead of automobiles. To accomplish this, the federal government offered generous incentives. Anti-trust laws were suspended so military orders could be filled quickly without competitive bidding. Companies were given low interest loans to retool, and "cost-plus" contracts which guaranteed them a profit. Not surprisingly, the industrial giants made out best. As the war progressed, America's top one hundred companies increased their percentage of the nation's total production from 30 to 70 percent. Ford, for example, began construction of a huge new factory in 1941, named Willow Run, to build B-24 Liberator bombers. In the next four years, it turned out 8,685 airplanes—one every sixty-three minutes. When questioned about these enormous profits and market shares, Secretary of War Henry Stimson replied that "in a capitalist country, you have to let business make money out of the process or business won't work."

Between 1940 and 1945, the nation's gross national product doubled, while the federal budget reached $95 billion, a tenfold increase. In the first half of 1942, the government placed over $100 billion in war orders, requesting more goods than American factories had ever produced in a single year. The list included

American fighter planes roll off the assembly line during World War II.

Movie stars and other celebrities appeared regularly at bond rallies during World War II. From left to right: Greer Garson, James Cagney, Hedy Lamarr, and comedy team Abbott and Costello.

60,000 planes, 45,000 tanks, 20,000 anti-aircraft guns, and 8 million tons of merchant shipping. The orders for 1943 were even larger. By war's end, military spending exceeded $300 billion.

Roosevelt hoped to finance this effort without dramatically raising the national debt. That meant taxation over borrowing, a policy Congress strongly opposed. The result was a compromise which combined both of these elements. The Revenue Act of 1942 added millions of new taxpayers to the federal rolls, and dramatically raised the rates paid by Americans in higher income brackets. Along with increases in corporate and inheritance rates, taxation provided about 45 percent of war's total cost—less than Roosevelt wanted, but far more than the comparable figures for World War I or the Civil War.

Borrowing accounted for the rest. The national debt reached $260 billion in 1945, six times higher than that in 1941. The government relied on banks and brokerage houses for loans, but common people did their share. "There are millions who ask, 'What can we do to help?'" said Treasury Secretary Henry Morgenthau in 1942. "Right now, other than going into the Army and Navy or working in a munitions plant, there isn't anything to do. . . . The reason I want a [war bond campaign] is to give people an opportunity to do something."

Morgenthau sold bonds in inventive ways. Hollywood stars organized "victory tours" through 300 communities. Hedy Lamarr promised to kiss anyone who bought a $25,000 bond. Carol Lombard died in a plane crash on her way home from a bond rally. Factory workers participated in payroll savings plans by putting a percentage of their earnings into government bonds. The Girl and Boy Scouts raised $8 billion in bond pledges, while schoolchildren bought and sold "war stamps" costing ten cents apiece.

In 1939, Harry Hopkins had warned that America could "not continue as a democracy with ten million unemployed." By 1942, his worries were over. The problem was no longer finding enough work for the people, it was finding enough people for the work to

be done. Factories stayed open around the clock, providing new opportunities to underemployed groups such as women, blacks, and the elderly. Seventeen million new jobs were created during World War II. Wages and salaries more than doubled, due in large part to the overtime that people put in. Per capita income rose from $373 in 1940 to just over $1,000 by 1945. As a result, the United States experienced a rare but significant redistribution of wealth, with the bottom half of the nation's wage earners gaining a larger share of the pie.

Making Do

Though Americans took home larger paychecks than ever before, they found less and less to spend them on. In 1942, Congress created the Office of Price Administration (OPA) to ration vital goods, preach self-sacrifice to the public, and control the inflation caused by too much money chasing too few goods. Gas, tires, sugar, coffee, meat, butter, alcohol—all became scarce. Most car owners were issued coupon books limiting them to three gallons of gasoline per week. Pleasure driving virtually ended, causing thousands of restaurants and drive-in businesses to close. As manufacturers cut back on cloth and wool, women's skirts got shorter, two-piece swimsuits (midriff exposed) became the rage, and men's suits no longer had cuffs. Metal buttons, rubber girdles, and leather shoes simply disappeared. In 1945, a young wife and mother wrote to her husband at sea:

> Honey, I'm a success. I got sheets! Such a time—went to four of the biggest stores first and got turned down cold. Finally ended up in the basement at J. C. Penney's [where the salesgirl] said, shhh, and sneaked into a back room and brought out some carefully wrapped—didn't even know what I had bought until I got home. I felt like someone buying hooch during Prohibition.

Changes on the homefront could be seen through the prism of baseball, the national game. Many wanted major league baseball suspended during the war, but Roosevelt disagreed, claiming that it united Americans and built up their morale. The 1941 season had been one of the best ever, with Ted Williams batting over 400, and Joe DiMaggio's fifty-six-game hitting streak. The next year was very different, indeed. Night games were banned because of air-raid "blackouts." Spring training took place in the northern

cities, rather than in Florida, to cut back on travel and save fuel. Ballparks held blood drives and bond drives, and soldiers in uniform were admitted free of charge. In 1942, Detroit Tigers slugger Hank Greenberg became the first major leaguer to be drafted into the armed forces. By 1943, most of the stars were gone, replaced by men who were too old or physically unfit for duty, such as Pete Gray, a one-armed outfielder for the St. Louis Browns. In response to public concerns, FBI Director J. Edgar Hoover declared that his agents had investigated the new major leaguers and found no draft-dodgers among them. But recruiting ball players became so difficult that the St. Louis Cardinals placed an advertisement in the *Sporting News:* "We have positions open on our AA, B, and D minor league clubs," it said. "If you believe you can qualify for one of these good baseball jobs, tell us about yourself."

OPPORTUNITY AND DISCRIMINATION

In many respects, World War II produced a social revolution in the United States. The severe labor shortage caused an enormous migration of people from rural areas to cities, from South to North, and especially to the West Coast, where so many war industries were located. With defense factories booming and 15 million people in the armed forces, Americans were forced to reexamine long-held stereotypes about women and minorities in the workplace and on the battlefield. The war provided enormous possibilities for advancement and for change. It also unleashed prejudices that led to the mass detention of American citizens, and others, on largely racial grounds.

Women and the War Effort

The war brought new responsibilities and opportunities for American women. During the Depression, for example, women were expected to step aside in the job market to make way for unemployed men. A national poll in 1936 showed an overwhelming percentage of both sexes agreeing that wives with employed husbands should not work. Furthermore, the majority of employed women held poorly paid jobs as clerks and

The labor shortages of World War II created new employment opportunities for women, most of whom were married and over thirty-five. More than six million women worked in defense industries across the country, including shipyards, munitions plants, and aircraft factories.

"salesgirls," or as low-end industrial workers in textile and clothing factories.

The war brought instant changes. More than 6 million women took defense jobs, half of whom had not been previously employed. They worked as welders and electricians, on assembly lines and in munitions plants. More than three-quarters of these women were married, and most were over thirty-five—a truly remarkable change. Some had husbands in the armed forces. (The standard monthly allotment for a serviceman's family was $50.) Young mothers were not expected to work, although a sizable number did. Bowing to intense public pressure, the War Manpower Commission issued a directive stating: "No women responsible for the care of young children should be encouraged or compelled to seek employment . . . until all other sources are exhausted." Since the government and private industry provided little child-care assistance, absenteeism and job turnover among younger women were extremely high.

The symbol of America's new working woman was "Rosie the Riveter," memorialized by Norman Rockwell in *The Saturday Evening Post* with her overalls, her work tools, and her foot planted on a copy of *Mein Kampf,* helping to grind fascism to dust.

> All the day long whether rain or shine—
> She's a part of the assembly line—
> She's making history working for victory—
> Rosie the Riveter.

Rosie was trim and beautiful, signifying that a woman could do a man's job—temporarily—without losing her feminine charm. Advertisers played heavily on this theme. A hand-cream company praised the "flower-like skin of today's American Girl, energetically at work six days a week in a big war plant." A cosmetics ad went even further: "Our lipstick can't win the war, but it symbolizes one of the reasons why we are fighting . . . the precious right of women to be feminine and lovely."

These jobs paid very well. A female shipyard worker in Mobile, Alabama, earned twice as much as a local clerk, waitress, or saleswoman. Yet wage discrimination was rampant in the defense industries, where women earned far less than men in the same jobs.

Employers and labor unions rationalized such inequities by noting that men had seniority, put in more overtime, and did the really "skilled" work. In 1945, female factory workers averaged thirty-two dollars per week, compared to fifty-five dollars for men.

Women also were told that their work would end with the war's completion, when defense spending dropped and the veterans came home to reclaim their old jobs. Many women welcomed a return to domesticity after four years of struggle, sacrifice, and separation from a husband overseas. But a survey of female defense workers in 1944 showed that most of them—particularly married, middle-aged women—hoped to continue in their present jobs.

This was not to be. Though more women than ever remained in the labor force following World War II, the bulk of them were pushed back into lower-paying "feminized" work. Still, a foundation had been laid. As a riveter from Los Angeles recalled, "Yeah, going to work during the war changed me—made me grow up and realize I could do things. . . . It was quite a change."

The "Double V" Campaign

For millions of American blacks, the war against racist Germany and Japan could not be separated from the ongoing struggle to achieve equal rights. The *Pittsburgh Courier*, an influential African-American newspaper, demanded a "Double V" campaign from the Negro community—"victory over our enemies at home and victory over our enemies on the battlefields abroad." To the cynical suggestion that minorities secretly wished for an American defeat, black heavyweight champion Joe Louis responded: "America's got lots of problems, but Hitler won't fix them."

One obvious problem was the small number of blacks employed in high-paying factory jobs. "The Negro will be considered only as janitors and in other similar circumstances," stated North American Aviation, one of the nation's leading military contractors. "Regardless of their training as aircraft workers, we will not employ them." In 1941, A. Philip Randolph, president of the Brotherhood of Sleeping Car Porters, an all-Negro labor union, proposed a "March on Washington" to protest job discrimination in the defense industries and segregation of the armed forces. "We loyal Americans," he said, "demand the right to work and fight for our country." Fearing the negative

publicity, President Roosevelt convinced the organizers to call off their march in return for an Executive Order (8802) declaring that "there shall be no discrimination in the employment of workers because of race, creed, or national origin." To facilitate the order, Roosevelt appointed a Fair Employment Practices Committee (FEPC) to "investigate complaints" and "redress grievances." With a tiny budget and no enforcement powers, the FEPC held public hearings, preached equality in the workplace—and was largely ignored.

Still, the desperate need for labor provided new opportunities for minorities. More than a million blacks migrated to the North and West during World War II, taking factory jobs in New York and California, Michigan and Illinois. Most were attracted by the higher wages and the chance to escape stifling oppression; many came from the Deep South, where the invention of the mechanical cotton-picker forced them from the land. The percentage of African-Americans in the war industries reached 7.5 percent by 1944—less than their share of the population, but a vast improvement over 1941. The work itself was often menial, such as cleaning factory bathrooms and sweeping the floors. Black workers had little access to the skilled, high-paying jobs, because powerful craft unions, like the Machinists and the Carpenters remained lily-white. But thousands of African-Americans took semiskilled positions on the assembly line, which meant higher wages than ever before.

For black working women, the changes were more dramatic. On the eve of World War II about 70 percent of them labored as servants in private homes. By war's end, that figure had fallen below 50 percent, as 400,000 black females left domestic work for the defense plants. "The war made me live better, it really did," recalled an aircraft worker who moved from rural Texas to Los Angeles. "My sister always said that Hitler was the one that got us out of the white folks' kitchen."

Where racial barriers were crossed, however, violence often followed. In Mobile, Alabama, the promotion of eleven black welders led white shipyard workers to go on a rampage through the African-American community, severely beating dozens of residents. In Philadelphia, white transit workers walked off their jobs to protest the elevation of eight blacks to the rank of motorman. Their stoppage brought the city to a halt, effectively closing the vital Philadelphia Navy Yard. Moving quickly, federal officials sent 8,000 fully armed soldiers to run the buses and streetcars, while

African-American nurses on duty in Australia during World War II.

threatening to fire the strikers and draft them into the armed forces. The walkout collapsed two days later.

The worst racial violence flared in Detroit, the nation's leading war production center. With good jobs available on the assembly lines of Chrysler, General Motors and Ford, Detroit's area-wide labor force grew from 400,000 in 1940 to almost 900,000 by 1943. With the war effort receiving the government's full attention, little thought was given to building new homes, schools, and hospitals. Indeed, state spending for health and education actually declined in Michigan during World War II. Those who arrived in Detroit, mainly poor, rural people of both races, found themselves competing for living space and social services with Detroit's established blue-collar labor force—and with each other. One half of Detroit's wartime black population lived in miserable, substandard housing, often one family to a room, with no indoor toilets or running water. Bulging public schools went to half-day sessions. Infant mortality rates skyrocketed, and tuberculosis reached epidemic proportions.

In 1942, an angry mob in Detroit kept several black families from moving into a public housing project in a white neighborhood. The following year, a fight between whites and blacks at a municipal park sparked a race riot involving huge mobs with guns, knives, and clubs. Detroit's poorly trained police force, weakened by the departure of its best men to the armed forces, did little to stop the carnage. By the time federal troops established calm in the city, thirty-five people were dead, and more than 700 were wounded. The police shot seventeen "looters" during the riot, all of whom were black.

Mob violence on the West Coast involved other victims. In California, a hate campaign led by local politicians and the press blamed Mexican-Americans for an alleged rise in drugs, crime, and gang warfare. In June 1943, white sailors from surrounding naval bases roamed the Mexican districts of Los Angeles, Long Beach, Pasadena and other cities looking for "zooters"—young Mexican-Americans in ducktail haircuts wearing long jackets with wide pleated pants, pegged at the cuff. Cheered on by white crowds, the

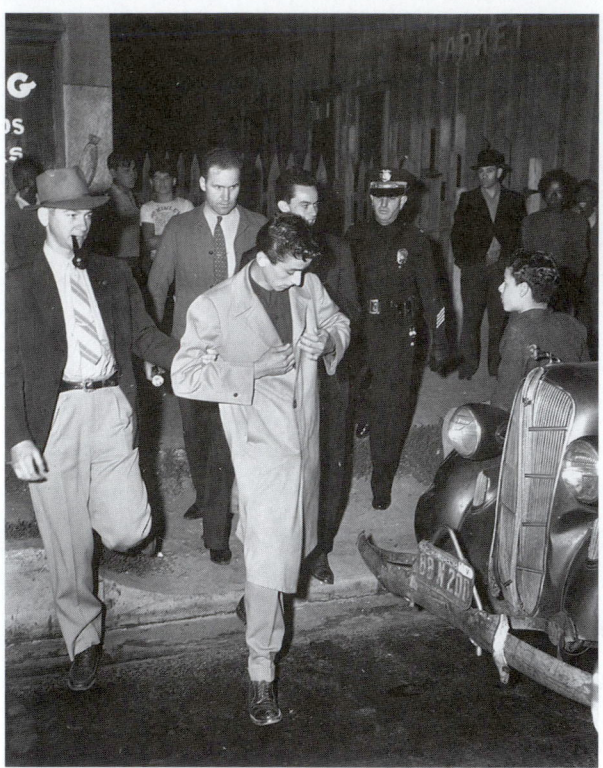

Police in Los Angeles take a young man to jail during the 1943 "zoot-suit" riots in which hundreds were injured and arrested.

sailors became a vigilante mob — stripping the young men of their "zoot suits," cutting their hair, and beating them senseless. "Throughout the night the Mexican communities were in the wildest possible turmoil," wrote a Los Angeles reporter. "Scores of mothers were trying to locate their youngsters and several hundred Mexicans milled around the police substations and the Central jail trying to get word of the missing members of their families."

The zoot-suit violence had other roots as well. Unlike the Depression era, when jobs were scarce and Mexicans were deported in large numbers, the United States now needed all the labor it could get. In 1942, the American and Mexican governments agreed to a so-called "bracero" (contract labor) program in which several hundred thousand Mexicans were brought to the United States to plant and harvest crops. In addition, the shortage of factory labor during World War II led to an influx of Hispanic workers in the shipyards and defense plants of Southern California. In cities like Los Angeles, where African-American and Hispanic workers arrived at a rate of 10,000 per month, crowding and competition bred resentment and fear.

To many residents of Southern California, the "zooters" came to represent the Hispanic community as a whole. Rumors flew that Mexican-Americans were hindering the war effort by evading the draft. In fact, the reverse was true. Mexican-Americans served in numbers far greater than their percentage of the general population — 350,000 out of 1.4 million — and seventeen were awarded the Congressional Medal of Honor.

Mexican-Americans were integrated in the armed forces during World War II; African Americans were not. All branches except the tiny Coast Guard practiced race discrimination as a matter of course. The Marines did not take blacks until 1943, when 20,000 were recruited to unload supplies and munitions during the amphibious Pacific landings — an extremely hazardous duty that subjected them to withering artillery and sniper fire from dug-in Japanese defenders. The Navy segregated blacks by occupation, with most working as food handlers, stevedores, and "messboys." In July 1944, a huge explosion at an ammunition depot in Port Chicago, California, killed 250 black sailors from a segregated work unit. When fifty survivors refused an order to return to work, claiming they had been singled out for these dangerous jobs on account of race, they were court-martialed, convicted of mutiny, and sentenced to prison. Following an intense publicity campaign in the Negro press, the black sailors were returned to duty.

More than 500,000 African Americans served in the Army, which placed them in segregated divisions, commanded by white officers. Since most training facilities were located in the Deep South, where the weather was mild and construction costs were low, black recruits faced hostile surroundings. Racial clashes at military posts were regularly reported in the Negro press, as were the murders of black soldiers by white mobs in Arkansas, Georgia, Mississippi, and Texas.

Only one black army division saw significant combat — the 92nd infantry in Italy. When questioned about this, Secretary of War Henry Stimson claimed that "Negroes have been unable to master efficiently the techniques of modern weapons." The truth, however, was that racial prejudice dominated the military

African-Americans were rigidly segregated in the armed forces during World War II. One of the most celebrated black units was the 99th Air Force Fighter Squadron, known as the Tuskegee Airmen.

chain of command. When given the opportunity, black units performed superbly. The 99th Air Force Fighter squadron, known as the Tuskegee Airmen, earned two Distinguished Unit Citations and shot down a dozen Nazi planes during the Anzio invasion of 1943. Escorting American bombers over Germany in 1944 and 1945, pilots of the 99th compiled a perfect record. Not a single bomber under their protection was lost to enemy fire.

Such treatment fueled anger, protest, and pride. The Negro press became more assertive in the drive for equal rights. America's leading black organization, the National Association for the Advancement of Colored People (NAACP), increased its wartime membership from 70,000 to 500,000. In 1942, young activists, black and white, formed the Congress of Racial Equality to challenge segregated restaurants in Washington and Baltimore, chanting, "We die together. Let's eat together." New leaders were emerging to continue the struggle begun by A. Philip Randolph. A powerful civil rights movement was slowly taking shape.

Internment of Japanese-Americans

President Roosevelt was determined to avoid a recurrence of the federal repression and vigilante activity that had marred the homefront during World War I. Yet the years between 1942 and 1945 witnessed the most glaring denial of civil liberties in American history. The victims included people of Japanese ancestry—citizen and noncitizen alike—living mainly on the West Coast of the United States.

On December 8, 1941, Roosevelt issued a standard executive order requiring enemy aliens to register with local police, limit their travel, and turn over all items of potential sabotage, such as cameras and shortwave radios. Before long, however, the president lifted the enemy alien designation for Italians and Germans in the United States, but not for the Japanese. The attack on Pearl Harbor, the Bataan Death March, the fall of Hong Kong and Singapore, Wake Island and the Philippines—all sent shock waves across the United States. Though J. Edgar Hoover saw no evidence of a Japanese "threat" to American security, the public

Japanese Relocation Order February 19, 1942

(Federal Register, Vol. VII, No. 38)

Issued by
Franklin D. Roosevelt

On February 19, 1942, President Roosevelt issued Executive Order 9066, authorizing the evacuation of more than 100,000 people of Japanese ancestry—most of whom were American citizens—from the West Coast. Although Roosevelt framed the order as a measure to protect national security, other factors, including war hysteria and racism, played a major role.

Executive Order
Authorizing the Secretary of War to Prescribe Military Areas

Whereas the successful prosecution of the war requires every possible protection against espionage and against sabotage to national-defense materials, national-defense premises, and national-defense utilities. . . .

Now, therefore, by virtue of the authority vested in me as President of the United States, and Commander in Chief of the Army and Navy, I hereby authorize and direct the Secretary of War, and the Military Commanders whom he may from time to time designate, whenever he or any designated Commander deems such action necessary or desirable, to prescribe military areas in such places and of such extent as he or the appropriate Military Commander may determine, from which any or all persons may be excluded, and with respect to which, the right of any person to enter, remain in, or leave shall be subject to whatever restrictions the Secretary of War or the appropriate Military Commander may impose in his discretion. The Secretary of War is hereby authorized to provide for residents of any such area who are excluded therefrom, such transportation, food, shelter, and other accommodations as may be necessary, in the judgment of the Secretary of War or the said Military Commander, and until other arrangements are made, to accomplish the purpose of this order. The designation of military areas in any region or locality shall supersede designations of prohibited and restricted areas by the Attorney General under the Proclamations of December 7 and 8, 1941,[1] and shall supersede the responsibility and authority of the Attorney General under the said Proclamations in respect of such prohibited and restricted areas.

I hereby further authorize and direct the Secretary of War and the said Military Commanders to take such other steps as he or the appropriate Military Commander may deem advisable to enforce compliance with the restrictions applicable to each Military area hereinabove authorized to be designated, including the use of Federal troops and other Federal Agencies, with authority to accept assistance of state and local agencies.

I hereby further authorize and direct all Executive Departments, independent establishments and other Federal Agencies, to assist the Secretary of War or the said Military Commanders in carrying out this Executive Order, including the furnishing of medical aid, hospitalization, food, clothing, transportation, use of land, shelter, and other supplies, equipment, utilities, facilities, and services. . . .

---

[1] 6 F.R. 6420.

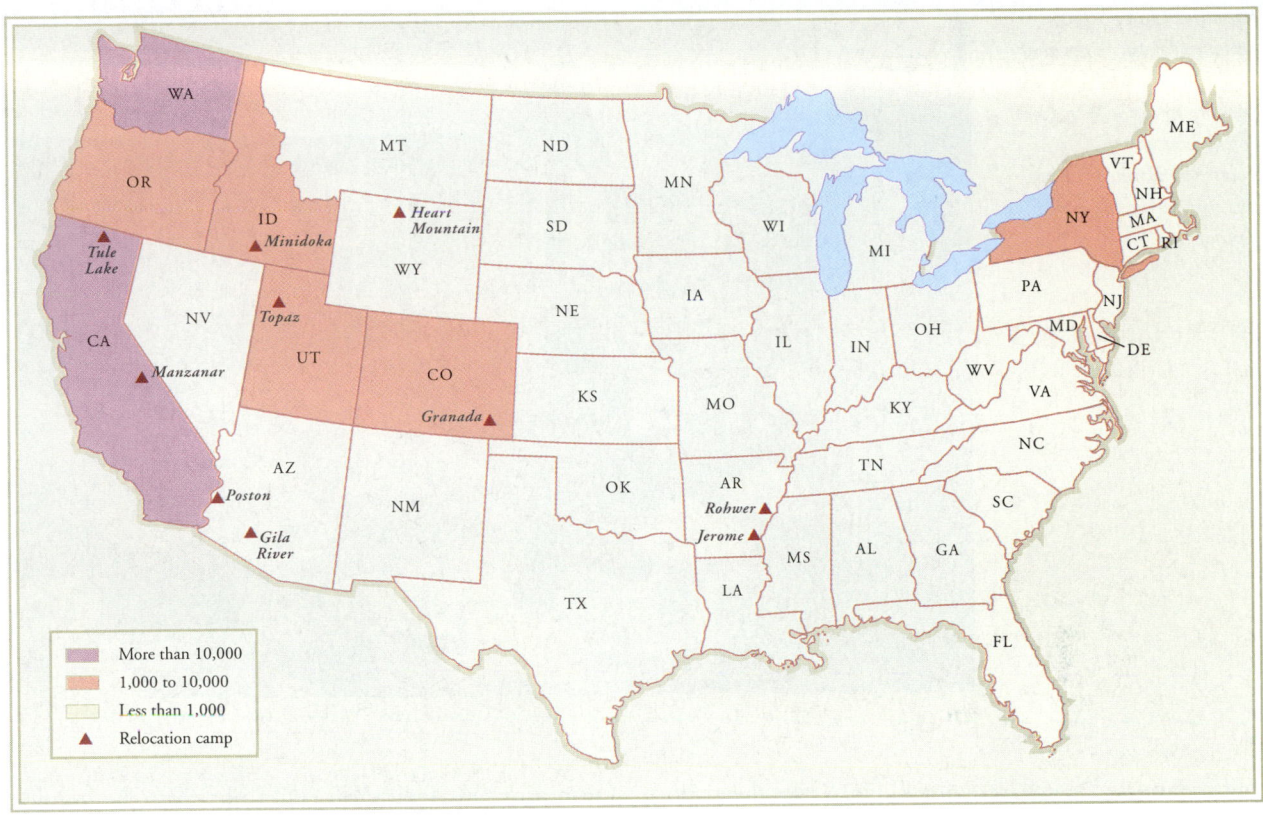

MAP 26.1 | JAPANESE-AMERICAN RELOCATION

thought otherwise. *Time* magazine published an article after Pearl Harbor entitled "How to Tell Your Friends from the Japs," which included such tips as "Japanese—except for wrestlers—are seldom fat," and "Japanese are likely to be stockier and broader-hipped than Chinese." More ominous were the words of Henry McLemore, a columnist for the *San Francisco Examiner.* "I am for the immediate removal of every Japanese on the West Coast to a point in the interior," he wrote. "Herd 'em up, pack 'em off, and give 'em the inside room in the badlands. . . . Personally, I hate the Japanese. And that goes for all of them."

More than 90 percent of the 125,000 Japanese Americans lived in California, Oregon, and Washington. (Two thirds were citizens, or Nisei, born in the United States; the rest were noncitizens, or Issei, born in Japan and ineligible for naturalization under the Immigration Laws of 1882 and 1924.) Few in number, politically powerless, and less well assimilated than European ethnic groups, the Japanese in America made perfect targets. Military leaders raised the dan-

gers of allowing them to live so close to aircraft plants and naval bases. Patriotic groups linked them to the atrocities committed by the Japanese armed forces, 8,000 miles away. Local farmers and fishermen resented the economic success of these hard-working people. All wanted their removal from the West Coast.

President Roosevelt capitulated. In February 1942, he issued Executive Order 9066, giving Secretary of War Stimson the authority to designate military zones inside the United States "from which any or all persons may be excluded." A few days later, the army interpreted that order to include the entire West Coast and all people of Japanese extraction. "A Jap's a Jap," said General John DeWitt, head of the West Coast Defense Command. "It makes no difference whether he is an American citizen or not. I don't want any of them."

Roosevelt preferred a "voluntary" removal and resettlement to rural parts of the West. The problem, however, was that the Japanese Americans were unlikely to leave their homes and businesses voluntarily,

Executive Order 9066 provided for the removal of 120,000 people of Japanese ancestry from the West Coast of the United States to isolated internment camps like this one in Manzanar, California.

and the western states were unwilling to take them. As the governor of Idaho said, "If you send them here, they'll be hanging from every tree in the state. Why not send them back to Japan? They live like rats, breed like rats, and act like rats."

In March, the president issued Executive Order 9102, establishing the War Relocation Authority. Milton Eisenhower—brother of General Dwight D. Eisenhower—became its director. Internment camps were set up in the deserts of California and Arizona, the mountains of Wyoming, and the scrublands of Utah and Colorado. Japanese Americans on the West Coast were given a few weeks to sell their belongings, get their affairs in order, and report to "processing centers" at converted race tracks, ball parks, and fair grounds. By June, 120,000 men, women, and children—most of them American citizens—reached the internment camps.

Conditions there were harsh, but not brutal. Families lived together in Spartan army barracks with little privacy and poor sanitation. Most worked as farm laborers. "All of Manzanar was a stockade, actually—a prison," wrote a young Japanese-American woman of her California camp. "We were in jail. There was barbed wire all around, there were great big watch towers in the corners, and there were spotlights turned

on during the night. You could not cross the boundaries . . . and the guards carried rifles."

The Supreme Court did not intervene. In *Hirabayashi* v. *United States* (1943) it upheld a curfew ordinance against Japanese Americans in Seattle on the grounds that wartime conditions sometimes justified measures which "place citizens of one ancestry in a different category from others." The court also ruled (*Korematsu* v. *United States,* 1944) that the evacuation of Japanese Americans was appropriate, but added (*Endo* v. *United States,* 1944) that the War Relocation Authority should attempt to separate "loyal" internees from "disloyal" ones," and set the loyal free. The obvious message, observed one legal scholar, was that "military officials faced no constitutional barriers to the wartime detention of American citizens singled out on the basis of race."

It took almost forty years for a measure of justice to prevail. In 1981, a congressional panel concluded that the internment program had resulted from a combination of race prejudice, war hysteria, and the failure of political leadership. It had nothing to do with "military necessity," as its supporters had claimed. In 1988, Congress awarded each survivor of the internment camps $20,000 in "reparations" for the terrible wrong that had been done.

THE GRAND ALLIANCE

Most Americans saw Japan as the primary villain of World War II. Opinion polls showed the public overwhelmingly in favor of concentrating the war effort in the Pacific against a "barbaric" and "treacherous" foe. Yet President Roosevelt and his military advisors felt otherwise. To their thinking, American power should be directed against the stronger enemy—Germany. Roosevelt viewed the Nazis as the real threat to world peace, and Europe as the key battleground.

North Africa, Stalingrad, and the Second Front

America's two major allies had conflicting strategies, interests, and concerns. The British did not believe in confronting Hitler with immediate, massive force. They remembered their staggering losses to the Germans during World War I, and they had felt the power of the Nazis at Dunkirk and in the London air raids. The British, moreover, had a far-flung empire to defend. Their strategy was to strike at "the soft underbelly" of the Axis in North Africa and the Mediterranean, rather than to confront Hitler directly in France.

The Russians strongly disagreed. Already facing a huge Nazi force deep inside their territory, they wanted the United States and Britain to open a "second front" in Western Europe so as to relieve German pressure on them in the East. That meant a major allied invasion of France. As one American diplomat said of Soviet Foreign Minister V. M. Molotov, "He knows only four words of English—'yes,' 'no' and 'second front.'"

Though America's top military advisors leaned toward the Russian strategy, President Roosevelt favored the British approach. At present, he realized, the United States was unprepared for a full-scale invasion of Europe. But a smaller operation against Nazi forces in North Africa, as the British proposed, had the benefit of getting the United States into the war quickly on the proper scale. As General George C. Marshall noted, "the president considered it very important to morale . . . to have American troops somewhere in active fighting over the Atlantic."

To make this possible, the United States had to gain control of the ocean. In the first three months of 1942, German submarines sank almost 1 million tons of allied shipping. The so-called "wolf-packs" were so close to American shores that bathers on the New Jersey and Virginia coasts watched in horror as merchant ships were torpedoed. By 1943, however, technological advances in anti-submarine warfare turned the tide. The use of sonar and powerful depth charges made German U-boats more vulnerable underwater, while the development of long-range attack planes and sophisticated radar allowed American aircraft to spot and destroy them as they surfaced to recharge their batteries. The toll was enormous. More than 900 of the 1,162 German submarines commissioned during World War II were sunk or captured.

In November 1942, American troops under the command of General Dwight D. Eisenhower invaded the French North African colonies of Morocco and Algeria in an operation code-named TORCH. At virtually the same moment, British forces badly mauled General Rommel's army at El Alamein in Egypt, ending Nazi hopes of taking the Suez Canal. Though Hitler rushed reinforcements to North Africa, the allies prevailed, capturing 250,000 Axis troops and taking enemy-held territory for the first time in the war.

In North Africa, the allies fought and defeated twelve Nazi divisions. In the Soviet Union, the Russians were fighting 200 German divisions along an enormous 2,000-mile front. The pivotal battle occurred at Stalingrad, a vital transportation hub on the Volga River, in the bitter winter of 1942–1943. As the Germans advanced, Stalin ordered his namesake city held at all costs. The fighting was block-to-block, house-to-house, and finally hand-to-hand. Hitler would not let his forces retreat, even after they ran out of fuel and food. Surrounded by Russian forces, overwhelmed by starvation, exposure, and suicide, the German commander surrendered on February 2, 1943.

Stalingrad marked the turning point of the European war. The myth of German invincibility was over. The Russians were advancing steadily in the east, aided by a stream of tanks, planes, food, and clothing from the United States under Lend-Lease. Now Stalin expected an allied thrust from the west—the long-promised second front.

Churchill had other ideas. At a meeting with Roosevelt in Casablanca, he convinced the president to put off a cross-channel invasion in favor of an assault on Axis troops across the Mediterranean in Italy.

Paratroopers landing on Corrregidor in 1945, following General MacArthur's victorious return to the Philippines.

("We came, we listened, and we were conquered," said an American military advisor of Churchill's winning ways.) Roosevelt attempted to pacify Stalin by promising to open a second front the following year and to accept nothing less than Germany's unconditional surrender. But the Soviets, having sacrificed more troops at Stalingrad than the United States would lose in the entire war, were suspicious and displeased.

The Italian campaign began in the summer of 1943. Sicily fell in a month, and Mussolini along with it. Overthrown by antifascist Italians, the Duce fled to Nazi lines in the north. The new Italian government then declared war on Germany and was recognized as a "co-belligerent" by England and the United States. The battle for Italy was intense. Waging a brilliant defensive struggle in mountainous terrain, the Germans stubbornly blocked the allied advance north to Rome. A young American soldier, badly injured in the campaign, wrote to his wife:

So many buddies gone and so many wounded! . . . We walked straight into death, not one man flinched or tried to save himself. I am proud to say, darling, that I was one of those brave lost children. We were only children after all. The dead boys were cuddled up, the wounded cried for dead friends. All children, after all.

The Italian campaign dragged on for almost two years, draining troops and resources for the planned invasion of France. (In April 1945, antifascists captured Mussolini, killed him, and strung him up by his heels.) Suspicions between Stalin and his wartime allies deepened as Roosevelt and Churchill set the terms of Italy's surrender without consulting the Soviet leader. In addition, postponement of the second front gave Stalin the opportunity to gobble up much of central Europe as his troops pushed toward Germany from the east.

The three allied leaders met together for the first time in November 1943 at the Tehran Conference in Iran. Roosevelt and Churchill promised to launch their cross-channel invasion the following spring. The future of Poland, the partition of Germany, and need for a United Nations were also discussed. In public, at least, allied unity was restored. "We came here, friends in fact, in spirit, and in purpose," Roosevelt declared. "We are going to get along fine with Stalin and the Russian people—very well indeed."

The Normandy Invasion

By 1944, the allies were in complete control of the skies over Western Europe, and in command of the

On June 6, 1944, allied troops stormed the beaches of Normandy in the massive D-Day invasion. By nightfall, more than 150,000 troops were ashore, and others quickly followed, beginning the long-awaited "second front" that sealed Hitler's fate.

seas. Their amphibious landings in North Africa and Italy had provided valuable experience for the job that lay ahead. In April and May, General Eisenhower assembled his huge invasion force in England—3 million men, 2.5 million tons of supplies, thousands of planes, landing craft, and escort vessels. Meanwhile, allied aircraft pounded the Atlantic Wall, a line of German fortifications stretching hundreds of miles along the coast of France and the Low Countries.

Despite meticulous preparation, Eisenhower faced enormous risks. The Nazis had fifty-five divisions in France. To keep them dispersed and guessing, allied intelligence spread false information about the planned invasion sites. The deceptions worked. Hitler and his generals put their strongest defense at Pas de Calais, the English Channel's narrowest point.

The massive D-Day invasion—Operation OVERLORD—began on the morning of June 6, 1944. Eisenhower's biggest worry was the weather. A channel storm had postponed one attempt, and another storm was predicted. Before the men left, he told them: "You are about to embark upon the Great Crusade, toward which we have striven these many months. The eyes of the world are upon you." Yet in his wallet that day, Eisenhower carried a solemn message, to be read if the invasion failed. "My decision to attack at this time and place was based on the best information available," it said. "If any blame or fault attaches to the attempt it is mine alone."

The invasion succeeded. With overwhelming air cover, allied forces assaulted Normandy and dropped paratroopers behind enemy lines. The heaviest fighting took place at Omaha Beach, where U.S. Rangers scaled sheer cliffs under withering fire to silence Nazi gunners. By nightfall, 150,000 men were ashore.

Others quickly followed. Within two months, more than a million allied troops were in France—liberating Paris in August, reaching the German border by September. With the Soviets pressing from the East, a Nazi surrender seemed only weeks away. But the Germans counterattacked in December 1944, taking British and American forces by surprise. The Battle of the Bulge was Hitler's last gasp—a failed attempt to crack allied morale. U.S. troops took heavy casualties, but stood firm. Germany lost 100,000 men and the will to fight on. Hitler committed suicide in his Berlin bunker on April 30, 1945, with Russian soldiers a few miles away. Germany surrendered a week later. The Thousand-Year Reich had lasted a dozen murderous years.

Map 26.2 | The War in Europe

Facing the Holocaust

In the spring of 1945, allied troops liberated the Nazi concentration camps in Poland and Germany. Ghastly pictures of starving survivors and rotting corpses flashed around the world, recording the almost inconceivable horror in which six million European Jews and four million others (including Poles, Gypsies, homosexuals, political dissidents) were exterminated during World War II.

To American leaders, these photos of the Holocaust produced shock, but hardly surprise. Evidence of the death camps had reached the United States in 1942, yet the government paid scant attention to the consequences. The State Department, well known for its anti-Semitism in that era, made it virtually impossible for refugees fleeing the Nazis to enter the United States. An applicant for a wartime visa had to provide the names of two American sponsors before submitting six copies of a form that measured four feet in length. As a result, only 10 percent of America's immigration quotas were met during World War II, leaving almost 200,000 slots unfilled.

President Roosevelt did not seriously intervene. Consumed by the responsibilities of leading his nation in a global war, he insisted that the best way to aid the victims of Nazism was to defeat Hitler's armies as quickly as possible. His only acknowledgement of the impending disaster came in 1944, when he created the War Refugee Board, which helped finance the activities of Raoul Wallenberg, the courageous Swedish diplomat who prevented thousands of Hungarian Jews from being deported to the death camps. Had it been formed earlier, and supported more firmly by the White House, the War Refugee Board might have played a major role in the saving of innocent lives.

The United States had other options as well. Its bombers could have attacked the rail lines leading to the death camps, as well as the gas chambers and crematoria that lay inside. The War Department avoided these targets, claiming they were too dangerous and too far away. This clearly was not true. As one analyst noted: "The means for closing the [death] camps were ready at hand. Allied medium and fighter-bombers had the range to attack Auschwitz from bases in Italy. . . . By actual count, between July 7 and November 20, 1944, a total of 2,500 bombers struck targets within a 35-mile radius of Auschwitz."

When liberation came to the concentration camps, the vast majority of prisoners were dead. One survivor at Dachau recalled the very moment the American troops arrived. "We were free. We broke into weeping, kissed the tank. A Negro soldier gave us a tin of meat, bread, and chocolate. We sat down on the ground and ate up all the food together. The Negro watched us, tears in his eyes."

THE PACIFIC WAR

Shortly after the attack on Pearl Harbor, Admiral Isoroku Yamamoto, Japan's leading naval strategist, issued a stern private warning. "In the first six months to a year of war against the U.S. and England," he said, "I will run wild and I will show you an uninterrupted succession of victories: I must tell you that, should the war be prolonged for two or three years, I have no confidence in our ultimate victory." Yamamoto understood America's overwhelming advantage in population and productivity. What he doubted was the will of its people to fight—and win—a long, bloody struggle.

Turning the Tide

The Japanese hoped to create an impregnable defense line in the Pacific. Their strategy included new conquests, such as Australia, and a naval thrust against the U.S. carrier fleet. Yet two key engagements in the spring of 1942 shattered Yamamoto's illusion about American will power and naval strength. On May 7, a task force led by two American carriers—the *Lexington* and *Yorktown*—held its own against a larger Japanese force at the Battle of the Coral Sea, just north of Australia. Though the "Lady Lex" was sunk, heavy Japanese losses saved Australia from invasion or certain blockade.

A month later, the two sides clashed again. Admiral Yamamoto brought a huge fleet to Midway Island, 1,000 miles west of Hawaii, to flush out and destroy the American carrier fleet. But the U.S. Navy, having broken the Japanese military code, was well aware of his intentions. In a three-day battle, brilliantly commanded by Rear Admiral Raymond A. Spruance, the Americans sank four Japanese carriers (losing the *Yorktown*) and shot down 320 planes. Japan would never fully recover from this beating. "Midway was

SOVIET UNION

ALASKA (U.S.)

MONGOLIA

MANCHURIA

Huang Ho R.

Peking

CHINA

Yangtze R.

Mekong R.

Shanghai

Chungking

INDIA

Hong Kong

BURMA

FRENCH INDOCHINA

THAILAND

JAPAN

Tokyo

Hiroshima
Aug. 1945

MALAYA

Singapore

SUMATRA

Bataan
Jan.–Feb. 1942 ✗

PHILIPPINES

✗ *Leyte Gulf*
Oct. 1944

BRUNEI N. BORNEO

SARAWAK

BORNEO

Okinawa ✗
Apr.–June 1945

Iwo Jima ✗
Feb. 1945

Philippine Sea ✗
June 1944

Truk Islands ✗
Feb. 1944

Saipan, Tinian, & Guam ✗
June–July. 1944

Eniwetok ✗
Feb. 1944

Kwajalein ✗
Jan. 1944

Wake Island ✗
Dec. 1941

Kiska & Attu ✗
June 1942

Midway ✗
June 1942

Pearl Harbor ✗
Dec. 1941

PACIFIC OCEAN

Tarawa ✗
Nov. 1943

EQUATOR

Hollandia ✗
Apr. 1944

NEW GUINEA

Empress Augusta Bay ✗
Nov. 1943

Bougainville ✗
Nov. 1943

Guadalcanal ✗
Aug. 1942–Feb. 1943

Coral Sea ✗
May 1942

AUSTRALIA

Axis powers
Axis-controlled areas
Allies
Neutral nations
✗ Battles

MAP 26.3 | THE WAR IN THE PACIFIC

America's revenge for Pearl," wrote one observer, "and the assurance of final victory."

Closing in on Japan

After Midway, the United States followed a two-pronged plan of attack. Admiral Chester Nimitz was to move west from Hawaii toward Formosa, while General Douglas MacArthur was to come north from Australia toward the Philippines, with their forces combining for an eventual assault on Japan. The Pacific theater would see no massed land battles like Stalingrad or the Bulge. The fighting would be sporadic but brutal, involving air attacks, naval duels, and amphibious landings by U.S. Marines on selected Japanese-held islands. It would be "a war without mercy," with bitter racial hatreds on both sides.

The first American offensive occurred at Guadalcanal, a small tropical island in the Solomons, off New Guinea, in August 1942. Guadalcanal had strategic importance as both a supply depot and a base from which to assault the Japanese air and naval complex at Rabaul. For six months, American marines waged a desperate campaign in swamps and jungles, battling intense heat, malaria, dysentery, infection, and leeches, as well as the Japanese. When the island was finally secured in February 1943, General MacArthur began a "leapfrog" campaign across New Guinea to the Philippines, attacking some islands while bypassing others. By 1944, Manila was in his sights.

In the central Pacific, Admiral Nimitz was moving west, ever closer to Japan. In November 1943, the marines assaulted Tarawa, a tiny strip of beach in the Gilbert Islands, taking 3,000 casualties in a successsful three-day assault. Next came the Marshall Islands; the Marianas—Guam, Tinian, and Saipan—followed. Control of the Marianas, only 1,200 miles from Tokyo, placed major Japanese cities within range of America's new B-29 bombers. The battle for Saipan raged through June and July of 1944. The Japanese defenders fought, quite literally, to the last man. Worse, thousands of Japanese civilians on the island committed suicide—a preview, some believed, of what lay ahead in Japan.

The end seemed near. In October 1944, MacArthur returned to the Philippines in triumph, while an American naval force destroyed four Japanese carriers at the Battle of Leyte Gulf, outside Manila. To the north, American troops took the island of Iwo Jima in brutal combat, and then attacked Okinawa,

less than 400 miles from Japan. Admiral Nimitz assembled a huge force for the invasion—180,000 troops, most of his carriers, and eighteen battleships. The Japanese had an army of 110,000 on Okinawa, the final barrier to the homeland itself.

The battle took three months, from April through June of 1945. Waves of Japanese kamikaze (suicide) planes attacked the allied fleet, inflicting terrible damage. American troops suffered a casualty rate of 35 percent, the highest of the war. Seven thousand were killed on land, 5,000 at sea, and 40,000 were wounded. The Japanese lost 1,500 kamikazes and virtually all of their soldiers. These appalling losses would be a factor in America's decision to use atomic weapons against Japan.

A CHANGE IN LEADERSHIP

In November 1944, the American people reelected Franklin Roosevelt to an unprecedented fourth presidential term. Roosevelt defeated Republican Thomas Dewey, the moderate forty-two-year-old governor of New York. The president's handling of the war was not an issue in the campaign. Dewey hammered away at problems on the homefront, such as food shortages,

TABLE 26.1
SECOND WORLD WAR CASUALTIES

Country	Battle Deaths	Wounded
Canada	32,714	53,145
France	201,568	400,000
Germany	3,250,000	7,250,000
Italy	149,496	66,716
U.S.S.R.	6,115,000	14,012,000
Australia	26,976	180,864
Japan	1,270,000	140,000
New Zealand	11,625	17,000
United Kingdom	357,116	369,267
United States	291,557	670,846

SOURCE *Information Please Almanac* (Boston: Houghton Mifflin Co., 1988).

gas rationing, squalid housing for war workers, and government "red tape." Roosevelt campaigned as the war leader, urging voters "not to change horses in mid-stream." To bolster his chances, Democratic party leaders removed the increasingly unpopular Vice President Henry Wallace from the ticket and replaced him with Senator Harry S. Truman of Missouri, chairman of a congressional committee that had uncovered fraud and waste in America's wartime production industries.

The Yalta Accords

When Truman visited the White House to plan campaign strategy with Roosevelt, he was appalled by the president's feeble condition. In February 1945, with Germany near collapse, an exhausted FDR met with Churchill and Stalin at Yalta, in southern Russia, to lay the groundwork for peace and order in the postwar world. On several issues, agreement came easily. The Russians promised to enter the Pacific war after Germany's defeat in return for territorial concessions in the Far East. The three leaders also blessed the formation of a new international body, known as the United Nations. To Roosevelt, America's failure to join the League of Nations after World War I had been a tragic mistake. The allies must remain united as peacemakers, he believed, to prevent future aggression.

But agreement on the larger issues proved elusive. The Soviet Union had suffered staggering losses at German hands. At least 20 million Russians were dead; thousands of towns, factories, and collective farms had been destroyed. From Stalin's perspective, the Soviets deserved more than simple gratitude for their role in defeating the great bulk of Hitler's army. They needed the means to rebuild their nation and to protect it from further attacks.

Stalin hoped to ensure Soviet security through the permanent partition of Germany. And he demanded huge reparations from the Germans—at least $20 billion—with Russia getting half. Furthermore, Stalin had no intention of removing Soviet troops from the lands they now controlled in Eastern Europe. In both world wars, Germany had marched directly through Poland to devastate the Russian heartland. Stalin would not let this happen again.

Roosevelt and Churchill had other ideas. Both men viewed a healthy, "de-Nazified" Germany as essential to the reconstruction of postwar Europe, and both feared the expansion of Soviet power into the vacuum created by Hitler's defeat. The British also claimed a moral stake in Poland, having declared war on Germany in 1939 to help defend the Poles from the Nazi assault. To desert them now—to permit a victorious Stalin to replace a defeated Hitler—smacked of the very appeasement that had doomed allied policy a decade before. At the very least, Soviet control of Poland violated the spirit of the Atlantic Charter, which recognized the right of all peoples to choose their own form of government. Few believed that the Polish people would pick Stalin or communism if given a free choice.

The Yalta Accords created a legacy of mistrust. The parties agreed to split Germany into four "zones of occupation"—American, Russian, British, and French. Berlin, deep inside the Soviet zone, also was divided among the allies. Yet the vital issue of reparations was postponed, as were plans for Germany's eventual reunification. At Roosevelt's urging, Stalin accepted a "Declaration for a Liberated Europe" that promised "free and unfettered elections" in Poland and elsewhere at some unspecified date. But these words did not mean the same thing in Moscow as in the West. An American advisor accurately described the agreement as "so elastic that [Stalin] can stretch it all the way from Yalta to Washington without ever technically breaking it."

In the weeks following Yalta, Roosevelt's optimism about Soviet-American relations seemed to fade. Pledges of free elections in Europe were ignored. The Yalta Accords did not prevent Stalin from ordering the murder of political dissidents in Romania and Bulgaria and the arrest of anticommunist leaders in Poland. His ruthlessness seemed to highlight the unpleasant truth that America had little or no influence in the nations now occupied by Soviet troops. "We can't do business with Stalin," FDR complained privately. "He has broken every one of the promises he made at Yalta."

Truman in Charge

On April 12, 1945—less than two months into his fourth term—FDR died of a massive stroke at his vacation retreat in Warm Springs, Georgia. The nation was shocked. Roosevelt had been president for twelve years, leading the people through the Great Depression and World War II. "He was the one American who knew, or seemed to know, where the world was going," wrote *Life* magazine. "The plans were all in his head."

President Roosevelt's death on April 12, 1945, sent the nation into mourning—and shock. He had led the nation through the Great Depression and World War II, and no one, it appeared, could fill his giant shoes.

The new president was largely unknown. Born on a Missouri farm in 1884, Harry Truman had served as an artillery officer in World War I before jumping into local politics in Kansas City. Elected to public office in the 1920s with the aid of Tom Pendergast, a crooked Democratic boss, Truman walked a fine line between efficient service to his constituents and partisan loyalty to a corrupt political machine. Fair and honest himself, Truman went about the business of building better roads and improving public services while ignoring the squalor of those who put him in office.

Working for the Pendergast machine had an enormous impact on Truman. It sensitized him to the needs of different people, fueled his belief in a welfare state, and got him elected to the U.S. Senate in 1934. On the other hand, the label of "machine politician" would plague him for years. It was hard to earn respect as a legislator, despite Truman's substantial accomplishments in Congress, when the newspapers kept referring to him as "the senator from Pendergast."

Truman did not inspire immediate confidence in his ability to fill Roosevelt's giant shoes. Small in stature, with thick glasses and a high-pitched midwestern twang, he seemed thoroughly ordinary to all but those who knew him best. Not counting his military service and a senatorial jaunt to Central America, Truman had never been outside the United States. As vice president, he was largely excluded from the major discussions relating to foreign policy and the war. After taking the presidential oath of office, Truman turned to reporters and said, "Boys, if you ever pray, pray for me now."

As expected, Truman received conflicting advice. A number of FDR's confidantes, including Henry Wallace and Eleanor Roosevelt, urged him to keep the

Winston Churchill, Harry Truman, and Joseph Stalin clasp hands at the Potsdam Conference in July 1945. The good feeling did not last long, as Churchill's ruling party was defeated at the polls in England, while relations between the United States and the Soviet Union moved swiftly downhill.

wartime alliance alive by accommodating Russia's economic needs and security demands. But others like Averell Harriman, U.S. ambassador to the Soviet Union, prodded Truman to demand Russia's strict compliance with the Yalta Accords. The new president did not want a confrontation with Stalin. He still hoped for Soviet help in ending the Pacific war and building a lasting peace. Yet the more Truman learned about events in Poland and Eastern Europe, the angrier he became. Ten days after taking office, he confronted Soviet Foreign Minister V. M. Molotov at the White House, claiming that Russia had ignored the Yalta Accords, and warning him that economic aid to Russia would never get through Congress so long as this attitude persisted. When Truman finished, Molotov told him that "I've never been talked to like that in my life." "Carry out your agreements," Truman shot back, "and you won't get talked to like that."

In July 1945, Truman left the United States aboard the U.S.S. *Augusta* for his first face-to-face meeting with Stalin and Churchill at Potsdam, near Berlin. The early sessions went well. The three leaders agreed on a number of important issues, including the terms of peace for defeated Germany and public trials for Nazi war criminals. "I can deal with Stalin," Truman wrote in his diary. "He is honest—but smart as hell."

His optimism didn't last long. The conference was halted for several days by the stunning defeat of Winston Churchill's Conservative party in the British parliamentary elections. Churchill returned to England, replaced by the new Labour prime minister, Clement Attlee. When the talks resumed, Stalin brushed aside Truman's concerns about Poland and Eastern Europe, while Truman rebuffed Stalin's attempt to claim reparations from the western zones of occupation in Germany. The conference ended on a chilly note. There seemed little doubt that Russia would remain in the lands it now controlled, and that Germany would remain divided for some time to come.

The Atomic Bomb

One of Truman's first decisions concerned the use of atomic weapons. As the United States took control of the island chains east of Japan in 1944, a ferocious

On August 6, 1945, a B-29 named after the mother of Col. Paul W. Tibbets, and piloted by him (center), dropped an atomic bomb on the Japanese city of Hiroshima, killing at least 100,000 people. Since that time, a debate has raged over the atomic bombings of Hiroshima and Nagasaki—in particular, their role in ending the war.

bombing campaign of the Japanese home islands took place. In March 1945, 300 American B-29s led by Major General Curtis LeMay firebombed Tokyo, killing 100,000 people, leaving 1 million homeless, and destroying much of the city. These raids were particularly devastating because Japan had few planes left to defend its densely populated areas. In the following months, conventional (non-atomic) bombings pounded half of Japan's sixty-six major cities.

Shortly after taking office, President Truman was told about the atomic bomb by Secretary of War Stimson, who called it "the most terrible weapon ever known in human history." The decision to build this bomb had been made by President Roosevelt in response to reports from refugee scientists, such as Italy's Enrico Fermi and Germany's Albert Einstein, that the Nazis were already at work on one. The American ef-

fort, known as the Manhattan Project, included top-secret facilities in Hanford, Washington, Oak Ridge, Tennessee, and Los Alamos, New Mexico, to design and construct this bomb, and produce the fissionable material for an atomic explosion.

At President Truman's direction, an Interim Committee was formed to advise him about the bomb. Chaired by Henry Stimson, the committee recommended the use of atomic weapons against Japan, without warning, as soon as they became available. Another group, the Target Committee, chose four major cities—Hiroshima, Kokura, Niigata, and Nagasaki—based on their strategic importance, and the fact that each of them, unlike Tokyo, was untouched by war. On July 16, 1945, the atomic bomb was successfully tested near Alamogordo, New Mexico. The explosion, equivalent to 15,000 tons of dynamite, was

Japanese representatives signed the formal declaration of surrender aboard the battleship Missouri *on September 2, 1945.*

visible 200 miles away. Truman learned of the test while attending the allied Summit meeting in Potsdam. He immediately issued a public ultimatum to the Japanese, calling on them to surrender unconditionally or face "prompt and utter destruction."

A number of top scientists on the Manhattan Project objected. Having urged one president to build the atomic bomb to counter Germany, they now found themselves begging another president not to use it against Japan. These scientists were joined by several ranking civilian and military officials, who argued that Japan was close to surrender, that the naval blockade was going well, and that use of the bomb would trigger a dangerous arms race with the Russians.

But Truman held firm, believing that the bomb would save American and Japanese lives by ending the war quickly. He could not bear the thought of a land invasion of Japan in which untold numbers on both sides would be killed. On the morning of August 6, 1945, a B-29 named *Enola Gay* dropped an atomic bomb over Hiroshima, incinerating the industrial city and killing at least 100,000 people. (Thousands more would die of radiation effects, a problem poorly understood by scientists at that time.) Three days later, a B-29 named *Bock's Car* dropped a second atomic bomb on Nagasaki, with much the same effect. On August 14, the Japanese asked for peace.

Though Americans overwhelmingly supported these bombings, the decision remains controversial to this day. Some believe that Truman dropped the bomb to scare the Russians in Europe and to keep them out of the Asian war. Others think the decision was based on racism and revenge. Still others argue that the United States should have provided a "demonstration" of the bomb's power for the Japanese or made it clear to them that the terms of "unconditional surrender" did not mean that the emperor would have to be removed. For all the controversy, however, one inescapable fact remains: Japanese leaders could not bring themselves to surrender until two atomic bombs had been dropped.

World War II formally ended on September 2, 1945, when the Japanese signed the document of surrender aboard the battleship *Missouri* in Tokyo Bay. More than 25 million soldiers and civilians died in the struggle. American losses were smaller—400,000 killed, 800,000 wounded—but American power had been decisive. Speaking from the deck of the *Missouri* that day, General MacArthur issued a warning for the new atomic age. "We have had our last chance," he said. "If we do not devise some greater and more equitable system, Armageddon will be at our door."

CONCLUSION

World War II shattered the illusion that Americans could remain separate from the world's problems. By leading the Grand Alliance against Nazi and Japanese aggression, the United States took on the full responsibilities of a global power—morally, economically, militarily. In doing so, it served notice that America's commitment to, and influence upon, world affairs would be substantial in the postwar era, whether in containing the spread of communism, constructing a nuclear arsenal, spending billions in foreign aid, or rebuilding the battered economies of Western Europe and Japan.

World War II had an equal impact on domestic affairs. It ended the Great Depression, created full employment, and increased mean family income an astonishing 25 percent. It demonstrated the ability of an ethnically diverse nation to unite in a just cause, although basic civil liberties, in the case of Japanese Americans, were tragically denied. And it opened new opportunities for women and minorities, although economic and political equality in the United States remained a dream unfulfilled. In 1945, Americans looked to the future with cautious optimism—proud of their accomplishments and yearning for better times.

RECOMMENDED READINGS

Dower, John. *War Without Mercy: Race and Power in the Pacific War* (1986) explores the racial attitudes of the United States and Japan in the brutal Asian conflict.

Irons, Peter. *Justice at War* (1983) is a thorough account of the legal issues surrounding the incarceration of Japanese Americans.

Hartmann, Susan. *The Homefront and Beyond: American Women in the 1940s* (1982) documents the extraordinary impact of World War II on women at home and in the workplace.

Kimball, Warren. *The Juggler: Franklin Roosevelt as Wartime Statesman* (1991) is a perceptive account of Roosevelt's wartime strategies and postwar plans.

Manchester, William. *Goodbye Darkness* (1979) is a poignant memoir of a young marine in the South Pacific during World War II.

O'Neill, William. *A Democracy at War: America's Fight at Home and Abroad in World War II* (1993) examines both the military front and the home front in lively detail.

Rhodes, Richard. *The Making of the Atomic Bomb* (1986) reveals the extraordinary scientific effort and political maneuvering behind the construction of the first nuclear weapon.

Tuttle, William. *Daddy's Gone to War* (1993) recreates these years in generational terms through the eyes of America's wartime children.

Wyman, David S. *The Abandonment of the Jews* (1984) examines the failure of American policy makers, the press, and the larger public to provide a sanctuary for victims of the Holocaust.

War Mobilization
Blum, John Morton. *V Was for Victory* (1976).
Brinkley, David. *Washington Goes to War* (1987).
Koppes Clayton, and Black, Gregory, *Hollywood Goes to War* (1987).
Lichtenstein, Nelson. *Labor's War at Home: The CIO in World War II* (1983).
Winkler, Alan. *The Politics of Propaganda: The Office of War Information, 1942–1945* (1978).

Military Operations
Keegan, John. *Six Armies in Normandy* (1982).
Knox, Donald. *Death March: The Survivors of Bataan* (1981).

Prange, Gordon. *At Dawn We Slept: The Untold Story of Pearl Harbor* (1981).
Spector, Ronald. *Eagle Against the Sun: The American War with Japan* (1985).
Weinberg, Gerhard. *World at Arms: A Global History of World War II* (1994).

The Homefront
Adams, Michael C. C. *The Best War Ever* (1994).
Campbell, D'Ann. *Women at War with America: Private Lives in a Patriotic Era* (1984).
Capeci, Dominic. *Race Relations in Wartime Detroit* (1984).
Costello, John. *Virtue Under Fire: How World War II Changed Our Social and Sexual Attitudes* (1986).
Gluck, Sherna. *Rosie the Riveter Revisited* (1987).
Mazon, Mauricio. *The Zoot-Suit Riots* (1984).
Wynn, Neil. *The Afro-American and the Second World War* (1976).

Wartime Diplomacy
Buhite, Russell. *Decision at Yalta* (1986).
Dallek, Robert A. *Franklin D. Roosevelt and American Foreign Policy, 1932–1945* (1979).
Divine, Robert A. *The Reluctant Belligerent: American Entry into World War II* (1979).
Newton, Verne, ed., *FDR and the Holocaust* (1995).
Sherwin, Martin. *A World Destroyed: The Atomic Bomb and the Grand Alliance* (1973).
Smith, Gaddis. *American Diplomacy During the Second World War* (1964).

WELCOME BACK

American soldiers return home at the end of World War II.

Chapter 27

POSTWAR AMERICA

1946–1952

HENRY R. LUCE was a man of grand visions and powerful views. One rival dubbed him "Lord of the Press" because his publishing empire included *Time, Life,* and *Fortune,* among other mass circulation magazines. In February 1941, Luce composed an editorial prodding the American people to accept their new role as citizens of "the strongest and most vital nation in the world." The time had come, he insisted, to exert "the full measure of our influence, for such purposes as we see fit" in the dawning "American Century."

The belief in America's destiny was as old as the country itself. Yet the challenges of World War II had turned this rhetoric into reality by placing the United States at the very center of the international stage. Old empires lay in ruins; an atomic era had begun. Only the United States seemed to possess the combination of military strength, economic resources, and political stability to rebuild a world battered by war. What worried Luce and others was the failure of American resolve. As columnist Dorothy Thompson put it, the United States "must lead now or take a back seat in history. This will either be an American century or it will be the beginning of the decline and fall of the American Dream."

RECONVERSION

The United States faced two major problems following World War II. The first one concerned relations with the Soviet Union. Would the two nations be able to maintain the Grand Alliance, or would their obvious differences about the shape and direction of postwar Europe degenerate into conflict, and possibly war? The second problem related to the domestic economy. Many Americans feared that the Great Depression might return after World War II, as defense spending dropped and factory jobs disappeared. In the months following Japan's surrender, the federal government cancelled more than $30 billion in military contracts, forcing 800,000 layoffs in the aircraft industry alone. Could the United States handle the difficult reconversion from a wartime to a peacetime economy? Or would it slip back into the dark days of joblessness, poverty, and despair?

The Veterans Return

President Truman's first job was to bring the soldiers home. Twelve million Americans were still in uniform

CHRONOLOGY

1946 Dr. Spock publishes *Common Sense Book of Baby and Child Care*

Republicans capture both Houses of Congress

1947 Truman Doctrine is unveiled

Marshall Plan is implemented

Jackie Robinson breaks baseball's color line

1948 Harry Truman upsets Thomas Dewey in tight presidential race

Whittaker Chambers confronts Alger Hiss

1949 Soviet Union successfully tests an atomic bomb

China falls to the Communists

1950 Senator Joe McCarthy charges that Communists have penetrated the State Department

Korean War begins

1951 General Douglas MacArthur is relieved of his command in Korea

1952 Richard Nixon delivers dramatic Checkers Speech

Dwight Eisenhower is elected president

---

in 1945, most of them young men, age eighteen to thirty-four, who had experienced the dual hardships of economic depression and war. Their dream was to return home quickly and get on with their lives. Throughout Europe and the Pacific, GIs grumbled about the slow pace of demobilization, while their loved ones barraged Congress and the White House with angry mail. One soldier put his feelings in a poem:

> Please Mr. Truman, won't you send us home?
> We have captured Napoli and liberated Rome.
> We have licked the master race.
> Now there's lots of shipping space.
> So, won't you send us home.

This pressure brought results. Within a year, the number of men and women in the armed forces had dropped to 3 million, despite the growing Soviet threat.

For many GIs, however, these were anxious, difficult times. The divorce rate shot up dramatically in 1945, reflecting the tensions of readjustment to civilian life. A major housing shortage, brought on by the virtual absence of home-building during World War II, made things even worse. Washington, D.C., reported 25,000 homeless veterans, Chicago more than 100,000. An Omaha newspaper ad read, "Big Ice Box, 7 by 17 feet. Could be fixed up to live in." North Dakota veterans took to living in converted grain bins. One serviceman complained: "You fight a damn war and you finally come home and everybody slaps you

on the back and tells you what a wonderful job you did . . . but when it comes to really doing something, then nobody's home. All you get is words."

In fact, however, assistance for returning veterans had received careful attention from the wartime Congress, which passed the popular Servicemen's Readjustment Act in 1944. Known as the GI Bill, it provided almost $20 billion for various programs in the decade following World War II. The social and economic effects of this legislation were enormous. The GI Bill fueled a nationwide construction boom by providing long-term, low-interest mortgages to veterans, plus a $2,000 bonus toward the purchase of a new home. Furthermore, it allowed former soldiers to fulfill the dream of a college degree, thereby expanding the system of higher education as never before. In 1947, for example, more than half of the 30,000 students at the University of Minnesota were veterans of World War II. Older, more serious, and determined to make up for lost time, they formed the nucleus of America's expanding white-collar workforce in the prosperous years ahead.

Lurching Toward Prosperity

The fear of another economic depression in the United States did not last long. The increase in federal spending for veterans helped to offset the decrease in defense spending. And a surge of consumer demand held out the promise of prosperity based on peace. For the past five years, Americans had worked overtime in

Veterans register for college. The GI Bill of 1944 expanded and democratized higher education as never before.

offices and factories, banking their paychecks, buying savings bonds, and dreaming of the day when cars, appliances, prime beef, and nylon stockings would reappear in the nation's stores and showrooms. Between Pearl Harbor and the Japanese surrender, the public had accumulated an astonishing $140 billion in savings and liquid securities, while the average weekly wage had almost doubled, from $24.20 to $44.30. "I'm tired of ration books and empty shelves," said one factory worker. "I'm ready to spend."

But factories could not change from fighter planes to automobiles overnight. Reconversion took time. With the demand for consumer goods far outracing the supply, President Truman hoped to keep inflation in line by extending wartime price controls. His plan met strong opposition from the business community, which lobbied hard to "strike the shackles from American free enterprise." In June 1946, Truman vetoed a compromise bill that extended the life of the Office of Price Administration (OPA), but effectively limited its power. To some Americans, the OPA was the consumer's friend, struggling to keep prices in line with wages. To others, however, it represented government

bureaucracy at its worst—bloated, inefficient, and tyrannical.

As controls ended, prices shot up. The cost of meat doubled in two weeks, leading the New York *Daily News* to quip:

PRICES SOAR, BUYERS SORE
STEERS JUMP OVER THE MOON

Not surprisingly, the labor movement took a militant stance. Since higher prices meant a drop in real wages, the United Automobile Workers (UAW) demanded an average pay hike of 33 cents an hour from General Motors in 1946, from $1.12 to $1.45. When the corporation offered a ten-cent hourly raise, the union struck for 113 days, eventually settling for eighteen cents. Shortly thereafter, the UAW and the auto companies agreed to a cost-of-living adjustment (COLA) clause in future contracts.

The country was soon plagued by a wave of strikes. In 1946 alone, 5 million workers were involved in 4,630 work stoppages totaling 120 million days of lost labor. When two railroad brotherhoods threatened a

An advertisement for the "dream kitchen." A surge of consumer spending after World War II quickly erased fears that America would slip back into economic depression.

national strike designed to shut down the country's rail service, President Truman signed an executive order seizing the railroads. "If you think I'm going to sit here and let you tie up this whole country," he told union leaders, "you're crazy as hell." A few weeks later, the United Mine Workers (UMW) went on strike, forcing power stations and factories to close for lack of fuel. "When we control the production of coal," said the combative UMW president, John L. Lewis, "we hold the vitals of our society right in our hands. . . . I can squeeze, twist, and pull until we get the inevitable victory."

This time, however, the union lost. President Truman went on radio to demand that the miners return to work at once. They did, coaxed along by a federal court injunction that led to $3.5 million in damages

against the UMW. For Truman, these victories came at a heavy cost. Not only did he offend large parts of the labor movement, he also appeared incapable of governing a nation wracked by consumer shortages, labor strife, soaring inflation, and an approaching cold war.

In November 1946, the Democratic party suffered a crushing defeat at the polls. Campaigning against the ills of reconversion ("Had Enough?") and the president's alleged incompetence ("To Err Is Truman"), the Republicans gained control of the Senate and the House for the first time since 1928. When the Truman family returned to Washington from a campaign trip on election eve, no one showed up to greet them. The train station was deserted. "Don't worry about me," the president told his daughter, Margaret. "I know how things will turn out and they'll be all right."

AFFLUENCE AND ANXIETY

The pain and sacrifice of the Great Depression and World War II led most Americans to yearn for both emotional security and material success. As expected, the family grew in importance, providing a sense of comfort and stability to people after years of separation and loss. Along with the focus on families came a changing middle-class culture, based on suburban living, a baby boom, an emphasis on more traditional sex roles, and an explosion of consumer goods. In the coming years, the nation's unprecedented prosperity would be measured by the increased size and abundant possessions of its thriving middle class.

The Postwar American Family

One of the songs among returning American veterans was titled "I've Got to Make Up for Lost Time." Beginning in 1946, the United States experienced a surge in marriage and birthrates, following record lows in the Depression decade, as the glamorization of bachelorhood in popular culture virtually disappeared. The young adults of this era (eighteen to thirty) became the most "marrying" generation in American history, with 97 percent of the women and 94 percent of the men taking marriage vows. By 1950, the age of marriage for American women had dropped below twenty, another record, while the percentage of divorces, ini-

Marriage and birth rates rose dramatically in the postwar years, following record lows in the Depression era.

most popular wartime advertisements showed a mother in overalls about to leave for the factory. She is at the door when her little daughter asks: "Mother, when will you stay home again?" And she responds: "Some jubilant day, mother will stay home again doing the job she likes—making a home for you and daddy when he gets back."

Quite naturally, this emphasis on family life strengthened long-held prejudices against married women holding full-time jobs outside the home. As a result, the gains made in female employment during World War II largely disappeared. Returning veterans reclaimed millions of factory jobs held by women and minorities. The female labor force dropped from a wartime high of 19 million in 1945 to less than 17 million by 1947. On the Ford and General Motors assembly lines, the percentage of women plummeted from 25 to 6 percent. Though many women gladly returned to their former domestic lives, the vast majority, according to postwar surveys, hoped to keep their jobs. "I'd stay if they wanted me to," said a

tially high among returning veterans, reached an all-time low.

The baby boom was equally dramatic. The number of children per family in the United States jumped from 2.6 in 1940 to 3.2 by decade's end. Birthrates doubled for a third child, and tripled for a fourth, as the American population grew by 20 million in the 1940s. At a time when access to birth control information was rapidly increasing, U.S. population growth rivaled not England's, but rather India's.

These spiraling marriage and birthrates went hand in hand with a shift back to more traditional sex roles following World War II. Actress Ann Sothern exemplified the reordering of domestic priorities when she advised women, shortly before Japan's surrender, to begin "planning our house—our perfect house" and to think about the nursery. "I know a lot of men are dreaming of coming back not only to those girls who waved good-bye to them," she added. "They are dreaming of coming back to the mothers of their children and the least we can do as women is to try to live up to some of these expectations." Indeed, one of the

A trip to the suburban supermarket in postwar America.

GRAPH 27.1   THE BABY BOOM

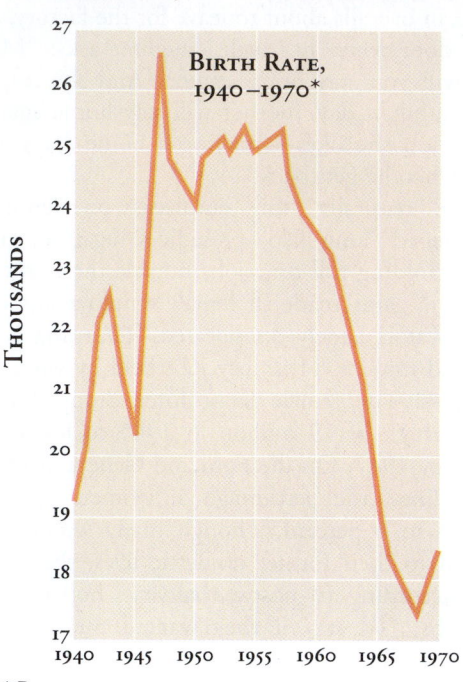

BIRTH RATE, 1940–1970*

THOUSANDS

1940 1945 1950 1955 1960 1965 1970

* BASED ON ESTIMATED TOTAL LIVE BIRTHS PER 1,000 POPULATION

GRAPH 27.2   MEDIAN AGE AT FIRST MARRIAGE

AGE

MALE

FEMALE

1947 1951 1957 1961 1967 1971 1977 1981

YEAR

female aircraft worker, "but without taking a man's place from him."

The social pressures on women were enormous. A host of "experts," including psychiatrists, psychologists, and pediatricians, asserted that women belonged in the home for their own good as well as the good of society—that women *needed* to be housewives and mothers in order to be fulfilled. In their 1947 best-seller, *Modern Women: The Lost Sex,* Marynia Farnham and Ferdinand Lundberg noted that "all mature childless women are emotionally disturbed," and that "the pursuit of a career is essentially masculine." Furthermore, these experts claimed that returning veterans needed special love and attention after so many years away from home. "In such a fundamental human situation," wrote anthropologist Ashley Montague, "women will not dream of considering themselves anything but help mates to men."

The concept of "mothering" as central to the postwar family was further popularized by Dr. Benjamin Spock, whose *Common Sense Book of Baby and Child Care* (1946) became the standard reference for parents of the "baby boom" generation. While most reviewers noted Spock's relaxed, more permissive attitude toward child rearing, another message came through as well.

Women must be the primary caregivers, Spock insisted. It was their role to shape the infant into a normal, happy adult—a role that turned parenting into a full-time job. For Spock and countless others, a man's success was measured by his performance in the outside world, a woman's success by her skills in raising well-adjusted children. As feminist author Betty Friedan recalled, "Oh, how Dr. Spock could make me feel guilty!"

The emphasis on traditional sex roles also affected female education. World War II had opened up new opportunities for women in science, engineering, and medicine. For the first time in history, women constituted a majority of the nation's college graduates. But the return of male veterans, combined with the educational benefits provided them by the GI Bill, reversed these temporary gains. Although the number of college women increased after World War II, the percentage of females in the college population declined dramatically. At Cornell University, for example, women comprised 50 percent of the wartime classes, but only 20 percent of the postwar classes. More significantly, the percentage of college women who actually graduated fell from 40 percent during World War II to 25 percent by 1950.

Famed pediatrician Benjamin Spock changed the nation's child-rearing habits with his best-selling book on the subject in 1946.

The steepest declines occurred in professional education. Engineering colleges, which doubled their enrollments to more than 200,000 by 1946, accepted fewer than 1,300 women, with more than half of these schools accepting no women at all. Female enrollments in medical schools dropped from a high of 15 percent during World War II to 5 percent by 1950. A study of medical students in this era showed deep prejudice among the men and self-limiting attitudes among the women. The majority of men, believing they made better doctors, thought that women should face tougher admission standards. The majority of women, insisting that marriage was more important than a career, claimed they would cut back their hours, or even stop working, to meet their family obligations. On campuses across the nation, educators struggled to find the proper curriculum for female students. The ideal, said one college president, was to enable women "to foster the intellectual and emotional life of her

family and community"—to fill the American home with proper moral values, a love of culture, and an appreciation of good wine and gourmet cooking.

Before long, the postwar American woman became the nation's primary consumer. Between 1946 and 1950, Americans purchased 21 million automobiles, 20 million refrigerators, 5.5 million electric stoves, and more than 2 million dishwashers. This consumer explosion resulted from a combination of factors: the baby boom, the huge savings accumulated during World War II, the availability of credit, and the effectiveness of mass advertising in creating consumer demand. The average American now had access to department store charge accounts and easy payment plans with almost no money down. "Buy Now, Pay Later," urged General Motors, and most people obliged. In 1950, as consumer debt surpassed $100 billion, the Diner's Club introduced America's first credit card. The Depression age virtues of thrift and savings seemed as remote as the Depression itself.

The vast majority of working women in the postwar era were employed in low-paying, often part-time jobs as clerks, secretaries, waitresses, domestics, and telephone operators.

The routine of suburban life often included a wife delivering her husband to the train station.

Ironically, this new consumer society led millions of women back into the labor force. By 1950, more women were working outside the home than ever before. The difference, however, was that postwar American women returned to low-paying, often part-time employment in "feminine" jobs such as clerks, salespeople, secretaries, waitresses, telephone operators, and domestics. Working to supplement the family income, to help finance the automobile, the kitchen appliances, the summer vacation, the children's college tuition, American women earned but 53 percent of the wages of American men in 1950—a drop of 10 percent since the heady years of "Rosie the Riveter" during World War II.

Suburbia

No possession was more prized by the postwar American family, or more representative of its middle-class aspirations, than the suburban home. In 1944, fewer than 120,000 new houses were built in the United States, a figure that rose to 900,000 by 1946, and 1.7 million by 1950. More than 80 percent of these new houses were built in suburban areas surrounding established cities. While prosperity and population growth produced the need for more housing, the rush to suburbia was accelerated by a flood of federal mortgage money and a revolution in the building of affordable, single-family homes.

CHART 27-1   NUMBERS IN MILLIONS (% OF TOTAL POPULATION)

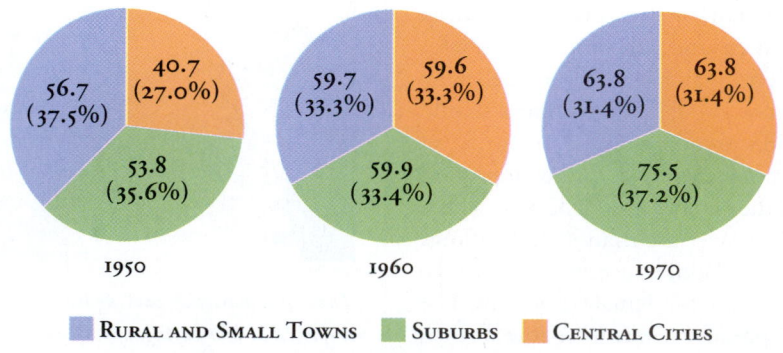

1950   1960   1970

■ RURAL AND SMALL TOWNS   ■ SUBURBS   ■ CENTRAL CITIES

The GI Bill helped fuel the boom in suburban housing after World War II.

The GI Bill provided the cash to bolster demand. With mortgage money now available, the housing shortage quickly disappeared. Leading the way were builders like William Levitt, who purchased several thousand acres of farmland in Hempstead, New York, twenty-five miles east of Manhattan, for the mass production of private homes. Levitt modeled his operation after Henry Ford's automobile assembly plants. His building materials were produced and precut in Levitt factories, delivered by Levitt trucks, and assembled by Levitt work crews, each performing a single task such as framing, pouring concrete, or painting window shutters. In good weather, Levitt workers put up 180 houses a week. The typical dwelling—a solid, two-bedroom Cape Cod, with a kitchen–dining room, living room with fireplace, single bath, and expansion attic—sold for $7,900. When completed, Levittown, Long Island, contained 17,000 houses, plus dozens of parks, ball fields, swimming pools, churches, and shopping areas for the 82,000 residents. Levitt followed his Long Island venture with similar towns in Pennsylvania and New Jersey.

For many Americans, Levittown represented both the positive and negative qualities of early postwar suburban life. City dwellers were attracted by Levittown's good schools, safe streets, and open space. The idea of owning one's home, moreover, was a central part of the American dream. And these suburban neighborhoods, filled with young families, provided a sense of shared experience and community that large cities sometimes lacked.

What stood out to others, however, was the "sameness" of Levittown—a place where people lived in similar houses, accumulated similar possessions, and conformed to similar rules. Levitt salesmen restricted their communities to white applicants, who then signed pledges saying they would not resell their homes to blacks. As late as the 1960s, the percentage of African Americans living in the three Levittown developments was well below 1 percent, a figure that represented most suburban areas nationwide. Furthermore, Levittown appeared to reinforce the traditional family roles of postwar America, with mothers caring for their children while fathers commuted long distances to work. One social critic joked that an alien who landed his spaceship in Levittown on a weekday would assume that the earth was populated by young white women and children—and no one else.

THE SOVIET THREAT

Relations between the United States and the Soviet Union were moving swiftly downhill. The failure to find common ground on a host of vital issues—from "free elections" in Poland to the German payment of reparations—raised anger and suspicion on both sides. Soviet leaders now viewed the United States as largely indifferent to the security needs of the Russian people, while American leaders increasingly portrayed the Soviet Union as a belligerent force in the world,

bent more on expanding its empire than on defending its territory. The Grand Alliance was over; the Cold War had begun.

Containment

Within hours of Germany's surrender, President Truman had signed an executive order ending Lend-Lease aid to the allies. Ships en route to England and Russia were stopped on the high seas and sent back to American ports. Though Truman reversed himself under a storm of criticism, Congress abolished Lend-Lease following Japan's surrender in August 1945. A few months later, the United States gave England a low-interest $3.75 billion loan, while ignoring a similar request from the Russians.

Stalin angrily viewed these moves as a sign of American indifference to the suffering of his people. In February 1946, the Soviet leader delivered a major address predicting the collapse of capitalism and the dawn of a communist world. The following month, with Truman at his side, former Prime Minister Churchill told an audience at Westminster College in Missouri that Russia had drawn an "iron curtain" across Europe "from Stettin in the Baltic to Trieste in the Adriatic." The West must unite against Soviet expansion, Churchill said, adding that "God had willed" the atomic bomb to Britain and America so as to ensure their ultimate triumph over this totalitarian foe.

A more compelling rebuttal to Stalin's speech came from a forty-two-year-old foreign service officer stationed at the U.S. Embassy in Moscow. In an 8,000-word telegram, George F. Kennan, an expert on Soviet affairs, laid out the doctrine of "containment" that would influence American foreign policy for the next twenty years. According to Kennan, Russia was an implacable foe, determined to expand its empire and to undermine Western democratic values. Serious negotiations were futile because Stalin believed in naked force rather than agreements based on good faith. America must be patient, Kennan believed. It must define its vital interests and then be prepared to defend them through "the adroit and vigilant application of counterforce at a series of constantly shifting geographical and political points."

Kennan's "long telegram" arrived in Washington at the perfect time. Poland and Eastern Europe were now lost causes; there seemed little that the United States could do to change their dismal fate. The present objective, Truman believed, was to block communist expansion into new areas vulnerable to Soviet influence and control. "Unless Russia is faced with an iron fist and strong language another war is in the making," he predicted. "I am tired of babying the Soviets."

The Truman Doctrine and the Marshall Plan

The new trouble spot appeared to be the Mediterranean, where Russia was demanding territorial concessions from Iran and Turkey, and where communist-led guerillas were battling the Greek government in a bloody civil war. Early in 1947, Great Britain, the traditional power in that area, informed the United States that it could no longer provide military and economic assistance to Greece and Turkey. Exhausted by World War II, England urged the United States to maintain that aid in order to prevent further Soviet expansion.

At a White House meeting six days later, General George C. Marshall, the new secretary of state, presented the case for American aid to congressional leaders from both parties. When Marshall's soft-spoken approach failed to rally the meeting, his assistant Dean Acheson took over. In sweeping terms, Acheson portrayed the future of Greece and Turkey as a test case of American resolve against Soviet aggression. If Greece fell to the communists, Acheson warned, other nations would follow "like apples in a barrel infected by one rotten one." When he finished, Republican Senator Arthur Vandenberg of Michigan summed up the feeling in the room. "Mr. President," he said, turning to Harry Truman, "if you will say that to Congress and the country, I will support you and I believe most members will do the same."

On March 12, 1947, the president offered his Truman Doctrine before a joint session of Congress and a national radio audience. In the present crisis, he began, "every nation must choose between alternative ways of life." One way guaranteed "individual liberty" and "political freedom," the other promoted "terror" and "oppression." There was no middle ground, Truman declared. In a world of good and evil, it "must be the policy of the United States to support free peoples who are resisting attempted subjugation by armed minorities or by outside pressures."

Some critics noted that the regimes in Greece and Turkey were a far cry from the democratic ideals that

THE TRUMAN DOCTRINE

March 12, 1947

While recommending military aid for the anti-communist governments of Greece and Turkey, President Harry Truman warned the American people about a grave new threat to world peace and democratic ideals. His graphic warnings about Soviet expansion, and the need to combat it, set a militant tone in foreign policy for decades to come.

At the present moment in world history nearly every nation must choose between alternative ways of life. The choice is too often not a free one.

One way of life is based upon the will of the majority, and is distinguished by free institutions, representative government, free elections, guarantees of individual liberty, freedom of speech and religion, and freedom from political oppression.

The second way of life is based upon the will of the minority forcibly imposed upon the majority. It relies upon terror and oppression, a controlled press and radio, fixed elections, and the suppression of personal freedoms.

I believe that it must be the policy of the United States to support free peoples who are resisting attempted subjugation by armed minorities or by outside pressures.

I believe that we must assist free peoples to work out their own destinies in their own way. . . .

Should we fail to aid Greece and Turkey in this fateful hour, the effect will be far reaching to the west as well as to the east. We must take immediate and resolute action.

I therefore ask the Congress to provide authority for assistance to Greece and Turkey in the amount of $400,000,000 for the period ending June 30, 1948. . . .

The seeds of totalitarian regimes are nurtured by misery and want. They spread and grow in the evil soil of poverty and strife. They reach their full growth when the hope of a people for a better life has died. We must keep that hope alive. The free peoples of the world look to us for support in maintaining their freedoms.

If we falter in our leadership, we may endanger the peace of the world—and we shall surely endanger the welfare of this nation.

Great responsibilities have been placed upon us by the swift movement of events. I am confident that the Congress will face these responsibilities squarely.

SOURCE *Congressional Record*, March 12, 1947.

the president lauded in his speech. Others worried that the Truman Doctrine would lead the United States into an expensive, open-ended crusade against left-wing forces around the globe. Yet most Americans supported Truman's position, and Congress allocated $400 million in military aid for Greece and Turkey.

On June 5, 1947, at the Harvard University commencement, Secretary of State Marshall unveiled a far more ambitious proposal known as the European Recovery Plan (ERP), or the Marshall Plan. The danger seemed clear: without massive economic aid, European governments might collapse, leaving chaos in their wake. "Our policy is not directed against any country or doctrine," Marshall said, "but against hunger, poverty, desperation, and fear." Indeed, all nations were invited to participate in the ERP, he added, "so as to permit the emergence of political and social conditions in which free institutions can exist."

The Marshall Plan at work in West Berlin. Billions of dollars in American aid helped rebuild much of war-ravaged Europe.

Several weeks later, seventeen European nations, including the Soviet Union, met in Paris to assess their common needs. But the Russians walked out after a few sessions, forcing nations like Poland and Hungary, which desperately wanted American aid, to leave as well. The Soviets balked at the idea of divulging critical information about their economy to outsiders. And they surely feared that massive American aid would tie them and the nations they now controlled to a capitalist orbit which might undermine the communist system.

Truman was not sorry to see them leave. He had been forced to invite all European nations to participate in order to avoid the appearance of worsening the Cold War. Yet he realized that Congress would not look favorably upon the prospect of spending billions of dollars to reconstruct a nation that seemed so brutal to its neighbors and so threatening to the United States. With the Russians and their satellites out of the picture, the remaining European nations prepared an agenda for economic recovery that came to $27 billion, a staggering sum. After six months of

bitter debate, Congress reduced that figure by about one-half. The largest expenditures went to England, Germany, and France.

The Marshall Plan proved a tremendous success on both sides of the Atlantic. By creating jobs and raising living standards, it restored economic confidence throughout Western Europe while curbing the influence of local communist parties in Italy and France. Furthermore, the Marshall Plan increased American trade and investment in Europe, opening vast new markets for U.S. goods. As President Truman noted, "peace, freedom, and world trade are indivisible. . . . We must not go through the 1930s again."

The rising prosperity in Western Europe was matched by growing repression in the East. Stalin moved first on Hungary, staging a rigged election backed by Russian troops. Opponents of the new communist regime were silenced and imprisoned. Next came Czechoslovakia, where the Soviets toppled a coalition government led by Jan Masaryk, a statesman with many admirers in the West. A few days later, Masaryk either jumped or was pushed to his death

The Soviet flag flies over the home of Czechoslovakian President Eduard Benes following the Communist takeover in 1948.

from an office window in Prague. Against this ominous background, President Truman proposed legislation to streamline the nation's military and diplomatic services. Passed as the National Security Act of 1947, it unified the armed forces under a single Department of Defense, created the National Security Council (NSC) to provide foreign policy information to the president, and established the Central Intelligence Agency (CIA) to coordinate intelligence gathering abroad. By 1948, the Cold War was in full swing. "Not since Rome and Carthage," warned Dean Acheson, "has there been such a polarization of power on this earth."

LIBERALISM IN RETREAT

In foreign affairs, President Truman could count on strong bipartisan support. Republican legislators had joined with Democrats to endorse early Cold War initiatives like the Truman Doctrine and the Marshall Plan. But the president had no such luck on domestic issues. For one thing, the widening rift with Russia produced a growing concern about the influence of communists and their "sympathizers" inside the federal government. For another, the president's attempt to extend the liberal agenda through ambitious social

and economic legislation—known as the "Fair Deal"—met with stiff resistance in Congress after 1946. As one Republican leader put it: "We have to break with the corrupting idea that we can legislate prosperity, legislate equality, legislate opportunity."

The Cold War at Home

The Iron Curtain that descended on Europe had a tremendous psychological impact on the United States. Americans were fearful of communism and frustrated by the turn of global events. The defeat of fascism had not made the world a safer place. One form of totalitarianism had been replaced by another. The result was an erosion of public tolerance for left-wing activity, spurred on by prominent government officials like Attorney General Tom Clark, who warned that communists were "everywhere" in the United States—"in factories, offices, butcher shops, on street corners, in private businesses, and each carries with him the germs of death for society."

In fact, the American Communist party was far weaker in 1947 than it had been a decade before, and its numbers were dwindling by the day. Yet that did not stop President Truman from establishing a Federal Loyalty–Security Program for the first time in American history. Truman acted, in large part, to keep congressional conservatives from fashioning an even tougher loyalty program. The one he put in place called for extensive background checks of all civilian workers in the federal bureaucracy. The criteria for disloyalty included everything from espionage to "sympathetic association" with groups deemed "subversive" by the attorney general. The Loyalty–Security Program provided minimal safeguards for the accused. Even worse, it frightened the country by conceding the possibility that a serious problem existed.

The congressional assault on domestic subversion was led by the House Un-American Activities Committee (HUAC). Formed in the 1930s to investigate Nazi propaganda in the United States, HUAC had been revived after World War II as a watchdog against communist propaganda. Among its more visible members was a young congressman from southern California named Richard M. Nixon. In 1947, HUAC launched a spectacular investigation of the motion picture industry, alleging that "flagrant communist propaganda films" had been produced during World War II on the specific orders of President Roosevelt. The

Alger Hiss is sworn in at a hearing of the House Un-American Activities Committee in 1948. Accused by Whittaker Chambers of being part of a Soviet espionage ring, Hiss went to federal prison in 1950 after a jury convicted him of perjury.

committee subpoenaed a number of pro-communist writers and directors, who angrily refused to answer questions about their political beliefs and associations. Known as the "Hollywood Ten," these individuals were cited for contempt, sent to jail, and "blacklisted" from working in the entertainment industry, a practice that became increasingly common in the late 1940s and 1950s. HUAC also heard from a host of "friendly" Hollywood witnesses, including movie stars Gary Cooper, Ronald Reagan, and the dapper Adolphe Menjou, who declared: "I am a witch-hunter if the witches are communists. I am a Red-baiter. I would like to see them all back in Russia."

The following year brought HUAC even more publicity. A witness named Whittaker Chambers, then a senior editor for *Time* magazine, claimed to have once been part of a "communist cell" in Washington that included Alger Hiss, a former government official who had advised President Roosevelt in foreign affairs. Hiss denied Chambers's allegations in testimony before HUAC a few days later. When Chambers repeated the charge on a national radio broadcast, Hiss sued him for libel.

Chambers struck back hard, producing dozens of classified State Department documents from the 1930s which, he claimed, had been stolen by Hiss and passed on to the Russians. Suddenly the ground had shifted to espionage, a more serious charge. The evidence—known as the "Pumpkin Papers" because Chambers had briefly hidden it in a pumpkin patch on his Maryland farm—included five rolls of microfilm and summaries of confidential reports written by Hiss in longhand or typed on a Woodstock typewriter he once owned. In December 1948, a federal grand jury indicted Hiss for perjuring himself before HUAC. (The ten-year statute of limitations on espionage had just run out.) The first trial ended in a hung jury; the second one sent Hiss to jail.

The guilty verdict sent shock waves through the nation. Not only did it bolster Republican charges about the threat of communists in government, it also served to undermine the liberal-internationalist philosophy that had guided the Democratic party since 1933. If Alger Hiss was a traitor, some wondered, how many just like him were still loose in the Truman administration, working secretly to help the Soviet Union win the Cold War? This question would come to dominate American politics over the next several years.

The Domestic Agenda

The Republican landslide of 1946 appeared to signal the decline of American liberalism. In the following months, the Republican Congress brushed aside President Truman's proposals for national health insurance and federal aid to education, while passing major legislation, known as the Taft-Hartley Act, to curb the power of organized labor. Taft-Hartley generated strong public support, given the crippling strikes of the previous year. Republican leaders viewed the union movement as both an ally of the Democratic party and a threat to the employer's authority in the workplace. In 1947, organized labor was at the height of its influence, with 15 million members nationwide. More than 35 percent of all nonagricultural workers belonged to a union, the highest total ever reached in the United States.

To counter the threats of powerful unions like the United Mine Workers, Taft-Hartley gave the president authority to impose an eighty-day "cooling-off" period to prevent strikes that threatened the national interest. More important, the bill outlawed the closed shop, a device that forced workers to join a union at the time they were hired, and it encouraged the states to pass "right to work" laws which made union organizing more difficult. Though Truman strongly opposed Taft-Hartley, claiming it took "fundamental rights away from our working people," the Republican Congress easily overrode his veto.

Truman also confronted the issue of racial discrimination, long ignored in the White House and on Capitol Hill, by forming a special task force on civil rights. Its final report included a series of bold recommendations, such as the desegregation of the armed forces and the creation of a special division within the Justice Department devoted solely to civil rights. Truman endorsed these recommendations, although his personal feelings about them were mixed. As a political leader, he had to balance the interests of two distinct Democratic party voting blocs: southern whites and northern blacks. As an individual, he believed that all citizens deserved political rights and equal opportunity, yet he felt uncomfortable with the notion of *social* equality for African Americans, as did most white people of that era. Addressing the NAACP's national convention in 1947—the first American president to do so—Truman spoke out strongly against prejudice and hate. "The only limit to a [person's] achievement," he declared, "should be his ability, his industry, and his character."

Breaking the Color Line

Truman's statement seemed particularly appropriate in 1947. On April 15, Major League baseball broke its long-standing "color line" in an opening day game at Brooklyn's Ebbets Field. "History was made here Tuesday afternoon," reported the Pittsburgh *Courier,* an African-American newspaper, "when smiling Jackie Robinson trotted out on the green-swept diamond with the rest of his Dodger teammates."

Baseball had been all-white for generations. Blacks played in the so-called Negro Leagues. Poorly paid, they often barnstormed from town to town, taking on local teams in exhibitions that combined great baseball with crowd-pleasing entertainment. The top players—pitcher Leroy "Satchel" Paige, catcher Josh Gibson, infielder George "Cool Papa" Bell—were as good, if not better, than the top Major League stars. Hall of Fame pitcher Walter Johnson claimed that Gibson "can do everything. He hits the ball a mile. He catches so easy

Jackie Robinson, who broke Major League Baseball's color line in 1947, led the Brooklyn Dodgers to six pennants and a World Series victory in his brilliant career.

he might as well be in a rocking chair. Throws like a rifle. Too bad this Gibson is a colored fellow."

The vast majority of Major League owners opposed integration. Branch Rickey of the Brooklyn Dodgers was an exception. Mixing deep religious values with shrewd business sense, Rickey insisted that integration was good for America, for baseball, and for the Dodgers. "The Negroes will make us winners for years to come," he said, "and for that I will happily bear being called a bleeding heart and a do-gooder and all that humanitarian rot."

To break the color line, Rickey selected Jack Roosevelt Robinson, twenty-seven, a man of tremendous talent and pride. The son of sharecroppers and the grandson of slaves, Robinson moved from rural Georgia to Pasadena, California, where his athletic skills earned him a scholarship to UCLA. A letterman in four different sports—baseball, football, basketball, and track—he also won tournaments in tennis and golf. Drafted into the army during World War II, Robinson fought bigotry at every turn. As a second lieutenant in a segregated tank unit, he was court-mar-

tialed for insubordination, and acquitted, after refusing to move to the rear of an army bus. Honorably discharged in 1944, he joined the Kansas City Monarchs, a Negro League team, as a shortstop at $400 a month. On a road trip to Oklahoma, teammate Buck O'Neill recalled, Robinson personally broke the color line at a local filling station by demanding to use the rest room. When the attendant refused, Robinson told him: "Take the hose out of the tank. If we can't go to the rest room, we won't get gas here." Startled, the attendant replied: "Well, you boys can go to the rest room, but don't stay long."

Rickey met secretly with Robinson in the fall of 1945. Talent was not an issue. Robinson was hitting .385 for the Monarchs and stealing bases by the bunch. What most concerned Rickey was Robinson's temper. How would he react to racial slurs, to pitches thrown at his head, to runners sliding into him spikes first? For three hours, Rickey grilled Robinson about the need for absolute self-control. "Do you want a ballplayer who's afraid to fight back?" Robinson asked. "I want a ballplayer with enough guts *not* to fight

back," Rickey answered. "You will symbolize a crucial cause. One incident, just one incident, can set it back twenty years." "Mr. Rickey," Robinson replied, "if you want to take this gamble, I will promise you there will be no incident."

Robinson kept his word, enduring segregated hotels, racial insults, even death threats against his family. His pioneering effort caught the public's fancy, and huge crowds followed him everywhere. Chicago, Cincinnati, Philadelphia, Pittsburgh, St. Louis—all set attendance records when Robinson appeared, with black fans leading the way. As one writer put it, "Jackie's nimble/ Jackie's quick. Jackie's making the turnstiles click." By season's end, Robinson had led the Dodgers to the National League pennant and won "Rookie of the Year."

The struggle was far from over. It would be another decade before all Major League teams accepted integration. Yet the efforts begun by Branch Rickey and Jackie Robinson helped change the face of America by democratizing its "National Game." Looking back on the events of 1947, sportswriter Jimmy Cannon recalled a side of Robinson that captured both his courage and his pain. He was, said Cannon, "the loneliest man I have ever seen in sports."

Man of the People

As the 1948 presidential election approached, Harry Truman seemed a beaten man. A host of problems had sapped his political strength. His relations with Congress were stormy and unproductive, especially in domestic affairs. The press, remembering the elegant and fatherly FDR, portrayed Truman as too small for the job. His popular standing, some thought, was reflected in the quip: "Would you like a Truman beer? You know, the one with no head."

Likely supporters deserted him in droves. In December 1947, a band of left-wing Democrats formed the Progressive Citizens of America, with an eye toward the coming election. Their leader was Henry Wallace, the former vice president and secretary of commerce, who had been fired by Truman for criticizing the administration's firm stance toward the Soviet Union. Wallace opposed both the Truman Doctrine and the Marshall Plan (which he dubbed the "Martial Plan"). Though he had no hope of winning the presidential election in 1948, his Progressive party seemed likely to split the Democratic vote.

Some urged Truman not to run. A number of Democratic leaders suggested other presidential candidates, including General Dwight D. Eisenhower and Supreme Court Justice William O. Douglas. *The New Republic,* a favorite of liberals, ran the front cover headline: "HARRY TRUMAN SHOULD QUIT." The Democrats convened in Philadelphia, where the heat was oppressive and tempers grew short. When word reached the convention that Eisenhower was unavailable, "Boss" Frank Hague of Jersey City threw down his cigar. "Truman," he mumbled. "Harry Truman, oh my God!"

Left with no alternative, the delegates nominated Truman for president and Alben Barkley, the popular but aging Senate majority leader from Kentucky, for vice president. Barkley had strong ties to the South. Yet even he could not prevent the convention from dividing along sectional lines when northern liberals, led by Mayor Hubert Humphrey of Minneapolis, demanded the endorsement of Truman's civil rights initiatives. "The time has arrived," said Humphrey, "for the Democratic party to get out of the shadow of states' rights, and walk forthrightly into the bright sunshine of human rights."

The passage of a strong civil rights plank led many southern Democrats to walk out of the convention. Two days later, waving Confederate flags and denouncing Harry Truman, they formed the States' Rights (Dixiecrat) party at a gathering in Birmingham, Alabama. The Dixiecrats chose governors Strom Thurmond of South Carolina and Fielding Wright of Mississippi to be their presidential and vice-presidential candidates. Their platform demanded "complete segregation of the races."

Divided into three camps, the Democratic party appeared hopelessly overmatched. Not only did President Truman face Henry Wallace on his left and Strom Thurmond on his right, but the national Republican ticket of New York Governor Thomas E. Dewey for president and California Governor Earl Warren for vice president was the strongest in years. Truman's campaign strategy was to portray himself as a common people's president, protecting the voters and their hard-earned New Deal benefits from a heartless Republican assault. To highlight these differences, he called a special session of Congress to demand passage of an eight-point program that included civil rights, public housing, federal aid to education, a higher minimum wage, and storage facilities for farmers. When

After Soviet troops blockaded the roads and rail lines leading into West Berlin in 1948, American and British pilots led a massive effort to keep the isolated city supplied from the air.

the Republican Congress refused to act, calling Truman's move a "publicity stunt," the president lambasted the Republicans as selfish politicians, interested only in the rich.

Truman also used his presidential power in significant ways. He showed support for the new state of Israel by offering it political recognition and economic assistance. He issued his promised executive order desegregating the armed forces. And he forcefully confronted Stalin in a showdown over Germany and Berlin.

In June 1948, Russian troops blockaded West Berlin to protest the merging of the French, British, and American occupation zones into the unified nation of West Germany. The city lay deep inside Soviet-controlled territory. With all roads and rail lines through East Germany now closed to allied traffic, its future seemed bleak. Truman ruled out force to break the blockade because American troops were greatly outnumbered. Instead, he and his advisors decided to supply West Berlin from the air. In the coming months, Western pilots made close to 300,000 flights into the city, delivering food, fuel, and medical sup-

plies. By the time the Russians called off their blockade, Berlin, the former Nazi capital, had become the symbol of resistance to communist oppression.

Truman could see his fortunes rising as the 1948 campaign progressed. Crisscrossing the nation by train, he drew huge, friendly crowds at each whistle stop. To shouts of "Give 'em hell, Harry!" he ripped into the "do-nothing" Republican Congress and their "plans" to dismantle Franklin Roosevelt's work. "The Republican politicians don't like the New Deal. They want to get rid of it," Truman repeated. "This is a crusade of the people against the special interests, and if you back me up we're going to win."

The experts didn't think so. Opinion polls showed Dewey with a substantial lead, while a *Newsweek* magazine survey of fifty political writers showed every single one of them expecting Truman to lose. On election eve, the staunchly Republican Chicago *Tribune* carried the now-famous mistaken headline: "Dewey Defeats Truman."

In fact, Truman won the closest presidential contest since 1916, collecting 24.1 million votes to Dewey's 22 million, and 303 electoral votes to Dewey's 189.

A beaming Harry Truman holds up the mistaken Chicago Daily Tribune *headline following his upset victory over Republican candidate Thomas Dewey in the 1948 presidential election.*

Strom Thurmond captured 1.1 million votes and four southern states under the Dixiecrat banner, while Henry Wallace won no states and barely a million votes. Ironically, the three-way Democratic split appeared to help Truman by allowing him to speak out forcefully against Soviet expansion and to aggressively court African-American voters in the pivotal northern industrial states. In the end, the people chose Truman's frank, common appeal over Dewey's stiff, evasive demeanor. The New Deal coalition had held for another election.

TROUBLE IN ASIA

Truman had little time to savor his victory. In the summer of 1949, an American spy plane returned from a flight over the Soviet Union with photographs revealing strong traces of radioactive material. The conclusion was obvious: Russia had exploded an atomic device. Combined with alarming new developments in Asia, the loss of America's atomic monopoly served to heighten global tensions in the coming months while dramatically increasing the fear of communism at home.

The Fall of China

President Truman broke the news in a one-sentence statement to the press: "We have evidence an atomic explosion occurred in the USSR." Domestic reaction was severe. Ever since Hiroshima, Americans had been taught to depend on nuclear superiority in the Cold War, and to believe that Russia, a supposedly backward nation, could not possibly develop an atomic bomb before the mid-1950s, if ever. That could mean only one thing: espionage. The Soviets, it appeared, had stolen the biggest secret of all.

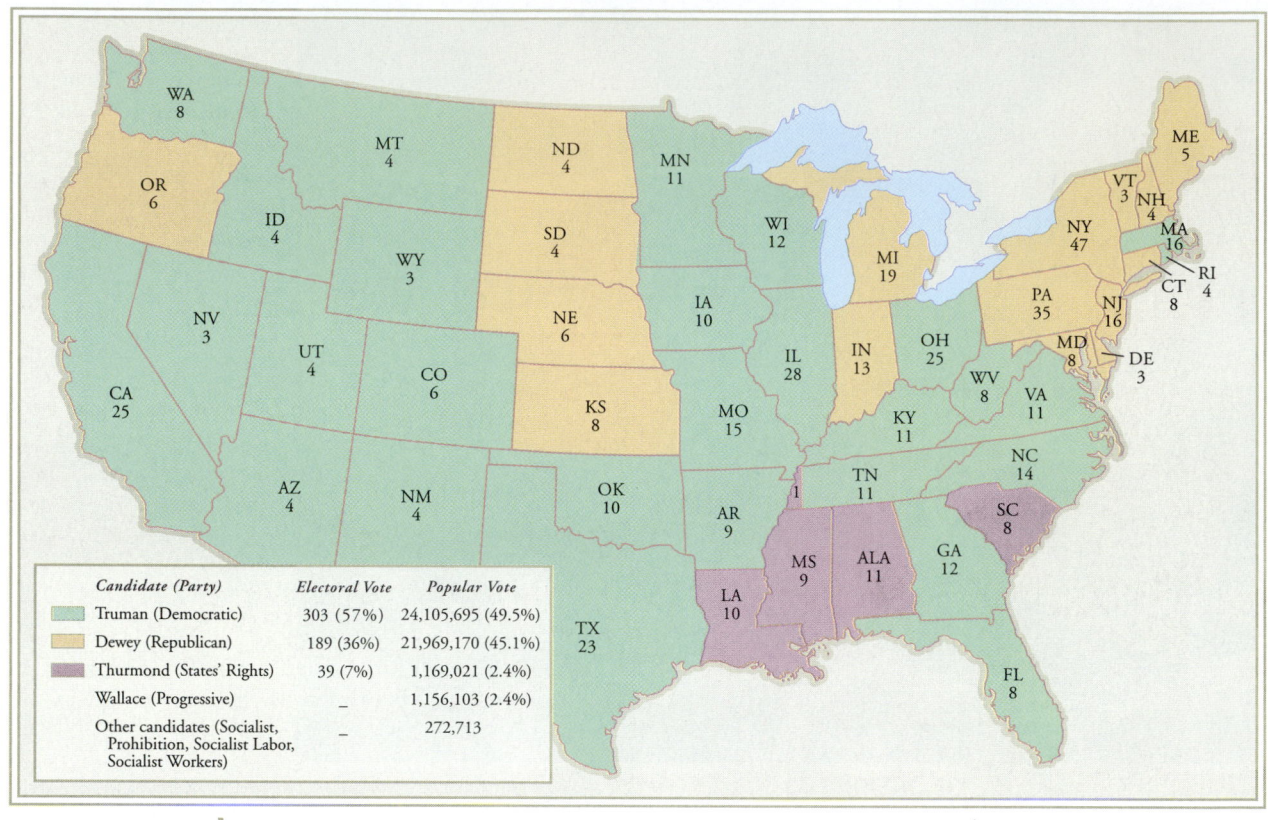

Candidate (Party)	Electoral Vote	Popular Vote
Truman (Democratic)	303 (57%)	24,105,695 (49.5%)
Dewey (Republican)	189 (36%)	21,969,170 (45.1%)
Thurmond (States' Rights)	39 (7%)	1,169,021 (2.4%)
Wallace (Progressive)	—	1,156,103 (2.4%)
Other candidates (Socialist, Prohibition, Socialist Labor, Socialist Workers)	—	272,713

MAP 27.1 | THE ELECTION OF 1948

The news from China was equally grim. Following World War II, Chiang Kai-shek and his Nationalist (Kuomintang) forces had renewed their offensive against the communist forces of Mao Tse-tung. Chiang counted heavily on American support. He believed that his fight against communism, his powerful friends in Congress, and his image as China's savior, crafted largely by *Time–Life* publisher Henry Luce, would force the Truman administration to back him at all costs.

Chiang was mistaken. The president and his advisors were far less interested in Asia than they were in Western Europe. They were not about to be trapped into an open-ended commitment in the Far East, certainly not by Chiang Kai-shek, who ran a corrupt, unpopular regime. From 1946 to 1949, the United States gave Chiang's government about $2 billion in military aid—enough, it was hoped, to satisfy Chiang's American friends without seriously affecting the more important buildup in Europe.

As civil war raged in China, Chiang's forces met defeat after defeat. Much of the American weaponry was discarded by fleeing Nationalist troops; it would end up in communist hands. In August 1949, the State Department issued a 1,054-page "White Paper on China," conceding that the world's largest country was about to fall to the communists. "The unfortunate but inescapable fact," said Dean Acheson, the new secretary of state, "is that the ominous result of the civil war in China was beyond [our] control." Nothing that this country did or could have done within reasonable limits "could have changed that result." Though Acheson was correct, his White Paper sounded more like an excuse than an explanation. Americans were angered and bewildered by Chiang's demise. How well did "containment" really work, many wondered, when more than 600 million people were "lost" to communism?

This question was discussed in National Security Paper Council (NSC) Number 68, a secret document

vice," the hydrogen bomb. Though Truman never showed this document to Congress, it became, in Acheson's words, "the fundamental paper" governing America's defense policy in the coming years.

War in Korea

On June 25, 1950, troops from Communist North Korea invaded anti-Communist South Korea with infantry, armor, and artillery in a massive land assault. Most Americans were puzzled, unaware of Korea's location, much less its politics. The country had been arbitrarily divided by Russian and American troops at the end of World War II. In 1948, an election to unify Korea had been cancelled when the Soviets refused to allow U.N. observers north of the dividing line at the 38th parallel. A stalemate thus developed, with Kim Il Sung, the pro-communist dictator of North Korea, and Syngman Rhee, the anti-communist dictator of South Korea, making daily threats to "liberate" each other's land.

The North Korean attack put great pressure on President Truman. His administration had treated the Rhee government with indifference, removing American combat troops from Korea in 1949 and implying that Korea itself was not vital to the free world's security. Yet here was a classic case of aggression, Truman believed. To ignore it was to encourage it elsewhere—and to turn away from NSC 68.

There were political considerations, too. On the heels of the China debacle, a tough stand on Korea was essential. If the president did nothing, he would only reinforce the Republican charge that his administration was "soft" on communism. Thus, Truman moved quickly, proposing a U.N. resolution that offered "such assistance to South Korea as may be necessary to repel

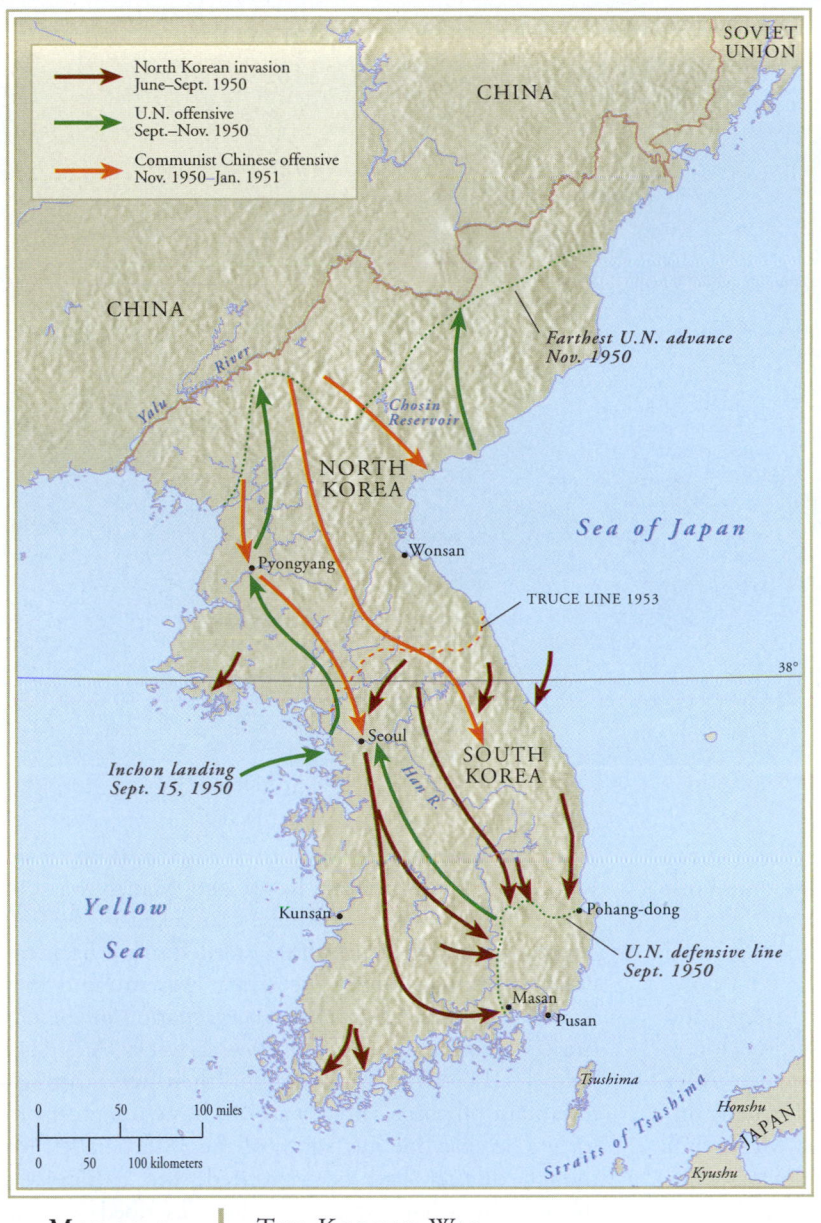

MAP 27.2   THE KOREAN WAR

drafted by Acheson and Paul Nitze in 1950 (though not declassified until 1975). According to NSC 68, communist advances could and must be stopped by an abundance of military power. The United States should act in concert with other nations wherever possible, but alone if need be. The document called for an unprecedented peacetime increase in military spending—from $13 billion to $50 billion per year—and for the construction of a huge new "thermonuclear de-

American troops pour ashore during the brilliant Inchon landing of September 1950.

armed attack." (The Russians, boycotting the Security Council to protest the U.N.'s refusal to seat Communist China, were unable to cast a paralyzing veto.) A week later, without consulting Congress, Truman dispatched ground troops to South Korea.

Public opinion seemed favorable. Letters and telegrams of support poured into the White House, and the news from the front kept improving. After two months of backward movement, U.N. troops under the command of General Douglas MacArthur took the offensive. In September 1950, MacArthur outflanked the enemy with a brilliant amphibious landing at Inchon, on South Korea's west coast. By October, U.N. troops had crossed the 38th parallel in pursuit of the routed North Korean Army. As the public listened in amazement, MacArthur spoke of having his men "home before Christmas."

There were ominous signs, however. First, by sending troops into North Korea, President Truman and the United Nations had gone beyond their original mandate to defend South Korea from outside aggression. Second, General MacArthur appeared oblivious to the possibility that Communist China might enter the war. As U.N. forces drove north, they captured

scores of Chinese Communist troops near the Yalu River that divided North Korea and Manchuria. On November 5, the Chinese attacked—300,000 strong—pushing MacArthur's startled army back toward the 38th parallel. The retreat was so rapid that serious thought was given to an evacuation of the entire U.N. command. In the following weeks, American Army and Marine units fought their way through mountain blizzards and a wall of Chinese infantry to form a defense line just south of the 38th parallel. Although disaster had been averted, the nation was shocked by what *Time* magazine described as "the worst military setback the United States has ever suffered."

By March 1951, the communist offensive had stalled. U.N. forces pushed ahead to the 38th parallel, where the two sides faced each other in a bloody standoff. Not surprisingly, General MacArthur called for an escalation of the war. Killing Chinese soldiers was not enough, he argued, for replacements could always be found. MacArthur recommended a naval blockade of China's coast, massive bombing of its factories and power plants, and an invasion of the Chinese mainland by the forces of Chiang Kai-shek.

General Douglas MacArthur and President Harry Truman meet to discuss Korean War strategy at Wake Island shortly before Communist China entered the conflict.

This plea for an expanded war was understandable. MacArthur, like most Americans, believed in the concept of total victory. Talk of limited war disgusted him. His message, quite simply, was that the lands surrendered to the communists by weak-kneed civilians like Truman and Acheson could be recaptured through the full exercise of American military power.

The president saw things differently. Any attempt to widen the war, he realized, would alarm other U.N. participants and perhaps bring Russia into the conflict. The Soviets might send troops to the Asian front or put pressure on Western Europe, where America's strength was already sapped by the Korean call-up. Furthermore, Russia's involvement raised the threat of nuclear attack. As General Omar Bradley noted, MacArthur's strategy was the very opposite of the one proposed by President Truman and the Joint Chiefs of Staff. "So long as we regard the Soviet Union as the main antagonist and Western Europe as the main prize," he said, "it would involve us in the wrong war, at the wrong place, at the wrong time, and with the wrong enemy."

Despite repeated warnings from the president, MacArthur refused to keep his views to himself. The final blowup came in April 1951, when Republicans in Congress released a letter that MacArthur had sent them from the battlefield which criticized Truman's refusal to meet force "with maximum counterforce," and ended with the oft-quoted phrase: "There is no substitute for victory." Furious at such insubordination, the president relieved MacArthur of his command.

MacArthur returned to the United States a genuine folk hero, a man who symbolized old military values in a world complicated by the horrors of nuclear war. Cities across the nation burned President Truman in effigy. Letters to the White House ran twenty to one against MacArthur's firing. On Capitol Hill, angry representatives placed some of the telegrams they received into the *Congressional Record:* "Impeach the Imbecile" and "We Wish to Protest the Latest Outrage by the Pig in the White House." Harry Truman's old standard—"If you can't stand the heat, stay out of the kitchen"—had never been more strenuously tested.

McCARTHYISM AND THE ELECTION OF 1952

On a bleak February evening in 1950, a little-known politician delivered a speech about "communist

RED CHANNELS

The Report of
COMMUNIST
INFLUENCE IN RADIO
AND TELEVISION
1950

In 1950, three former FBI agents published a report on "communist influence in radio and television." The report, which provided often inaccurate information about the "communist activities" of writers, actors, and musicians, made it difficult for "blacklisted" entertainers to find employment in this era.

Leonard Bernstein
Composer, Conductor

Reported as:

People's Songs, Inc.	Sponsor. Letterhead, 3/48.
Scientific and Cultural Conference for World Peace	Sponsor. Official program, 3/49.
American-Soviet Music Society	Affiliated. Un-Am. Act. Com. *Review of Scientific and Cultural Conference for World Peace,* 4/19/49, p. 52.
Hanns Eisler Concert	Sponsor. Un-Am. Act. Com. *Review of Scientific and Cultural Conference for World Peace,* 4/19/49, p. 43.
Protest Against Deportation of Hanns Eisler	Signer. Un-Am. Act. Com. *Review of Scientific and Cultural Conference for World Peace,* 4/19/49, p. 43.
Committee for Reelection of Benjamin J. Davis, 1945	Affiliated. Un-Am. Act. Com. *Review of Scientific and Cultural Conference for World Peace,* 4/19/49, p. 41.
Progressive Citizens of America	Signer. Arts, Sciences and Professions Council, statement in defense of Communist cases. Un-Am. Act. Com. *Review of Scientific and Cultural Conference for World Peace,* 4/19/49, p. 37.
World Federation of Democratic Youth	Affiliated. Un-Am. Act. Com. *Review of Scientific and Cultural Conference for World Peace,* 4/19/49, p. 36.
Voice of Freedom Committee	Affiliated. Un-Am. Act. Com. *Review of Scientific and Cultural Conference for World Peace,* 4/19/49, p. 35.
Southern Conference for Human Welfare	Affiliated. Un-Am. Act. Com. *Review of Scientific and Cultural Conference for World Peace,* 4/19/49, p. 34.

subversion" in the federal government to a Republican women's club in Wheeling, West Virginia. The topic was a common one, and large portions of the speech had been lifted word for word from a recent address by Congressman Richard Nixon. Only one explosive sentence had been added. "I have here in my hand," Senator Joseph R. McCarthy of Wisconsin told his audience, "a list of 205 Communists that were made known to the secretary of state and who are still working and shaping the policy of the State Department."

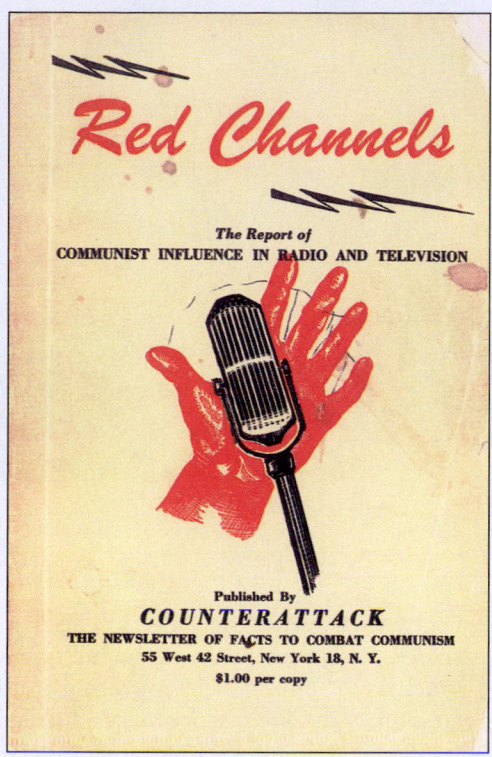

Progressive Citizens of America	Affiliated. Un-Am. Act. Com. *Review of Scientific and Cultural Conference for World Peace*, 4/19/49, p. 33.
National Negro Congress	Affiliated. Un-Am. Act. Com. *Review of Scientific and Cultural Conference for World Peace*, 4/19/49, p. 32.
Joint Anti-Fascist Refugee Committee	Affiliated. Un-Am. Act. Com. *Review of Scientific and Cultural Conference for World Peace*, 4/19/49, p. 28.
Civil Rights Congress	Affiliated. Un-Am. Act. Com. *Review of Scientific and Cultural Conference for World Peace*, 4/19/49, p. 25.
Committee for a Democratic Far Eastern Policy	Affiliated. Un-Am. Act. Com. *Review of Scientific and Cultural Conference for World Peace*, 4/19/49, p. 24.
American Council for a Democratic Greece	Affiliated. Un-Am. Act. Com. *Review of Scientific and Cultural Conference for World Peace*, 4/19/49, p. 22.
American Youth for Democracy	Affiliated. Un-Am. Act. Com. *Review of Scientific and Cultural Conference for World Peace*, 4/19/49, p. 22.

The message was clear: America, the strongest nation on earth, was losing the Cold War to the evil forces of communism because the U.S. government was filled with "dupes" and "traitors" like Alger Hiss who *wanted* the communists to win.

The Rise of Joe McCarthy

Wisconsin's junior senator was an erratic politician, known for his reckless ambition and raucous behavior. He held no list in his hand that night in Wheeling. He

The Korean War raised fears of a nuclear attack. School children engaged in "take cover" drills by diving under their desks.

knew nothing about communists in government or anywhere else. But the newspapers printed his charges, and the public was aroused. McCarthy had struck a nerve in the country, rubbed raw by Soviet aggression in Europe, the communist victory in China, the Alger Hiss case, and the news of the Russian atomic bomb. As Americans searched for explanations, McCarthy provided the simplest answer of all. The real enemy was not in Moscow, he thundered, but rather in Washington, D.C.

McCarthy's charges of treason in high places made him an instant celebrity. His face adorned the covers of *Newsweek* and *Time*. The Washington *Post* cartoonist Herblock coined a new word to describe his reckless behavior: "McCarthyism." But prominent Republicans, sensing the political benefits of the "communist issue," rallied to his side. Senator Robert Taft of Ohio, known as "Mr. Republican," privately dismissed McCarthy's charges as "nonsense." Yet he told McCarthy to keep punching—"if one case doesn't work, try another."

President Truman viewed McCarthy as a shameless publicity hound who would say anything to make headlines. He was right about the senator, yet helpless to stop him. The fear of communism kept growing, aided by the outbreak of war in Korea. Air raid drills, including simulated bombings of American cities, be-

came the order of the day. In school practice drills, students were taught to dive under their desks and shield their eyes against atomic blasts. In New York City, school officials distributed metal "dog tags." "If a bomb gets me in the street," a first-grader explained, "people will know what my name is." In Washington, a typical real estate ad read: "Small farm—out beyond the atomic blasts." Mayor Mike DiSalle of Toledo, Ohio, tried to calm worried residents by joking that he would build large neon signs directing communist pilots to Cleveland and Detroit.

McCarthy's attacks grew bolder. As the 1952 presidential campaign approached, he called George C. Marshall a traitor, mocked Dean Acheson as the "Red Dean of fashion," and described President Truman as a drunkard, adding, "the son-of-a-bitch ought to be impeached." Yet party colleagues continued to encourage McCarthy, viewing him as the man who could turn public anxiety and distrust into Republican votes.

"I Like Ike"

By 1952, Harry Truman's public approval rating had dropped to 23 percent—the lowest ever recorded by an American president. *The New Republic* called Truman "a spent force politically" and urged him to with-

"WE LIKE IKE"

America liked Ike—who won a smashing victory at the polls in 1952, ending twenty years of Democratic party rule.

draw from the coming presidential campaign. In March, Truman did just that. "I shall not be a candidate for reelection," he declared. "I do not feel that it is my duty to spend another four years in the White House."

Truman did not sulk on the sidelines, however. As the leader of his party, he wanted the Democratic nominee to defend the New Deal–Fair Deal philosophy with the same energy and enthusiasm that he himself had shown in 1948. The most impressive candidate, Governor Adlai Stevenson of Illinois, had earned a reputation as a liberal reformer. Eloquent and witty, he appealed both to party regulars and to the liberal intelligentsia, much like FDR. Stevenson had

his handicaps, including a recent divorce and a past friendship with Alger Hiss. The Democrats nominated him for president on the third convention ballot. Senator John Sparkman of Alabama, a Fair Dealer and a segregationist, was given the vice-presidential nod.

The battle for the Republican presidential nomination was in many ways a battle for control of the Republican party. The moderate wing, represented by Governor Thomas Dewey of New York and Senator Henry Cabot Lodge, Jr., of Massachusetts, was committed to internationalism and to many New Deal reforms. "Our world is complex and dangerous," said Lodge. "We cannot afford to turn back the clock." The conservative wing, led by Senator Robert Taft of

Ohio, was suspicious of the New Deal and wary of America's expanding global commitments, especially the defense and reconstruction of Europe. Beyond these views was a yearning for the past, for the pre-Depression days when government was smaller, cheaper, and less intrusive.

Senator Taft, the son of former President and Chief Justice William Howard Taft, had earned the respect of his colleagues and the plaudits of Washington reporters, who voted him "best senator" in 1949. On many domestic issues, such as public housing, Taft was more flexible than his conservative supporters. Yet he, too, feared that a powerful commitment to Western Europe could lead the United States into another world war. And he stressed the domestic consequences of this commitment—the huge military budgets and the growth of presidential power in foreign affairs.

Only one man stood between Taft and the Republican nomination. But he was a very powerful opponent, despite his apparent reluctance to run for political office. In 1948, the leaders of both major political parties had begged him, unsuccessfully, to enter their presidential primaries. "I don't believe a man should try to pass his historical peak," said General Dwight D. Eisenhower. "I think I pretty well hit mine when I accepted the German surrender in 1945." Yet his moderate Republican supporters, believing that Eisenhower alone could defeat Taft for the presidential nomination, convinced the general that people wanted him, the country needed him, duty called once again.

Eisenhower, sixty-one, was a product of the American heartland. Raised in Abilene, Kansas, a prairie town west of Topeka, he attended schools with no lights or plumbing and earned his diploma while working the night shift in a dairy. In 1911 the young man—nicknamed Ike—won an appointment to the U.S. Military Academy at West Point. After graduating near the middle of his class, Eisenhower married Mamie Dowd, the daughter of a Denver businessman, and began his swift climb through the ranks. In the 1930s, he served as chief aide to General Douglas MacArthur, recalling: "Oh, yes, I studied dramatics under him for seven years." In 1941, he moved to the War Department and helped plan the D-Day invasion of France. His work was so outstanding that President Roosevelt named him Commanding General, European Theater of Operations—a promotion that jumped him over hundreds of officers with greater seniority.

It turned out to be one of the best decisions of World War II. Eisenhower commanded history's most successful coalition force—American, British, French, Polish, and Canadian troops—with courage, diplomacy, and skill. He was brilliant at handling people and reconciling the most diverse points of view. In the following years, Eisenhower served as Army Chief of Staff, president of Columbia University, and commander of NATO forces, a position tailor-made for his military and diplomatic skills.

The Republican convention nominated Eisenhower on the first ballot. Most delegates did not believe he would make a better president than Taft, simply a better candidate. Eisenhower defused the bitter feelings of conservatives by selecting Richard Nixon to be his running mate, and by accepting a party platform that accused the Democrats of lining their pockets, shielding traitors in high places, and bungling the Korean War. As the campaign began, Republican leaders summed up their strategy with a simple formula: K1, C2—Korea, Communism, and Corruption.

On the campaign trail, General Eisenhower talked about leadership and morality, while Senator Nixon attacked from below. Traveling by train on the "Look Ahead Neighbor Special," Eisenhower visited more than 200 cities and towns. At every stop, he introduced Mamie, praised America, bemoaned the "mess in Washington," and promised to clean it up. Then the whistle sounded and the train pulled away to the chants of "I Like Ike."

On September 28, 1952, the New York *Post,* a pro-Democratic newspaper, broke the biggest story of the campaign: "Secret Rich Men's Fund Keeps Nixon in Style Far Beyond His Salary." The story had strong partisan overtones. The Nixon fund (about $18,000) had never been a secret; it had been used for routine political expenses; and it was similar to those of other politicians, including Governor Stevenson, who would soon admit to one of his own. Nixon responded by blaming the "Reds" for his troubles. "The communists, the left-wingers, have been fighting me with every smear," he declared. "They did it yesterday. They tried to say I had taken the money."

The campaign ground to a halt. Aboard the Eisenhower train, anxious advisors suggested that Nixon resign from the ticket. How could the general campaign against Democratic party corruption, they wondered, when his own running mate stood accused of taking secret gifts? On September 23, Nixon went on na-

Following charges that he kept a secret political slush fund, Republican vice-presidential candidate Richard Nixon saved his political career in 1952 with a televised explanation that included his pet cocker spaniel Checkers.

tional television to explain his side of the story. To an audience estimated at 55 million, he spoke about his boyhood, his family, his war record, his finances, and his admiration for General Eisenhower. He explained how the fund worked, asked the American people to support him, and then described the one gift he would never return. It was, said Nixon, "a little cocker spaniel dog and our little girl named it Checkers. And you know the kids love that dog and I just want to say that we're going to keep it."

The reaction was volcanic. More than 2 million phone calls and telegrams poured into Republican offices across the country. They were followed by millions of letters, running three hundred to one in Nixon's favor. Eisenhower had no choice but to keep his running-mate on the ticket. The "Checkers Speech" saved Nixon's career.

It also demonstrated the emerging power of television in national affairs. In the campaign's final weeks, the Republican party ran dozens of 20-second TV spots for Eisenhower. All began with the same four words:

ANNOUNCER: Eisenhower answers the nation.

CITIZEN: What about the cost of living, General?

IKE: My wife, Mamie, worries about the same thing. I tell her it's our job to change that on November 4th.

Eisenhower used television to soothe voter anxiety about his views on popular New Deal welfare programs. "Social security, housing, workmen's compensation, unemployment insurance—these are things that must be kept above politics and campaigns," he said. "They are rights, not issues." The general also vowed that if elected, he would visit Korea. "Only in that way," he explained, "could I know how best to serve the American people in the cause of peace."

Stevenson tried to ridicule the announcement. "If elected," he replied, "I shall go to the White House." But few Americans were amused. On November 4, Eisenhower overwhelmed Stevenson—33.9 million votes to 27.3 million, and 442 electoral votes to 89. Eisenhower became the first Republican in decades to crack the solid South, winning four states and coming close in several others. He did well in cities, where ethnic voters, concerned about the rise of communism in Europe, deserted the Democrats in droves. Nearly 25 percent of Eisenhower's total came from men and women who had supported Harry Truman in 1948.

Some observers spoke of a new Republican era, but this was not the case. Almost everywhere, Eisenhower ran well ahead of his ticket. Although the Republicans managed to gain a slim majority in Congress, they did so by riding the general's coattails to victory.

━ CONCLUSION ━

The Roosevelt-Truman years had come to a close, yet the New Deal legacy remained largely undisturbed. The American people had voted for a new president, not a return to the days of Harding and Coolidge. Dwight Eisenhower accepted the idea that government must provide a safety net for its citizens in time of personal need and economic distress. And like Harry Truman, he intended to contain communist expansion around the globe.

After two decades marked by the Great Depression and World War II, most Americans were finally enjoying the benefits of economic security, material comfort, and stable family lives. They wanted a leader who would steer a moderate course in domestic and foreign affairs; a leader who would heal old wounds and moderate angry passions without turning back the clock; a leader who would end the present conflict in Korea without widening it or compromising the nation's honor. In 1952, Dwight D. Eisenhower seemed to be the one.

RECOMMENDED READINGS

Blair, Clay. *The Forgotten War: America in Korea, 1950–1953* (1987) is a thorough account of the conflict that cost the lives of 50,000 Americans and more than 1 million Asians.

Boyer, Paul. *By the Bomb's Early Light* (1985) considers the impact of atomic weaponry on American society in the early Cold War years.

Hamby, Alonso. *Man of the People* (1995) examines the personal life and political career of President Harry Truman.

Jackson, Kenneth. *Crabgrass Frontier* (1985) analyzes the suburbanization of America, especially after World War II.

Jones, James. *Alfred Kinsey: A Public/Private Life* (1997) is the biography of the nation's leading sex researcher and his impact on American culture.

Pells, Richard. *The Liberal Mind in a Conservative Age* (1984) studies the changing intellectual tides in an era of increasing conformity, consumerism, and political repression.

Spock, Dr. Benjamin. *Common Sense Book of Baby and Child Care* (1946) had a lasting impact on child rearing and gender roles in the United States.

Tanenhaus, Sam. *Whittaker Chambers* (1997) tells the absorbing story of the man who helped ignite the nation's anti-Communist crusade in the late 1940s.

Tygiel, Jules. *Baseball's Great Experiment* (1983) is a fine account of Jackie Robinson and the integration of Major League baseball.

Foreign Policy
Gaddis, John L. *The Long Peace* (1987).

Gardner, Lloyd. *Architects of Illusion* (1970).

Hogan, Michael. *The Marshall Plan: America, Britain, and the Reconstruction of Western Europe, 1947–1952* (1987).

LaFeber, Walter. *America, Russia, and the Cold War, 1945–1992* (1993).

Schaller, Michael. *The U.S. Crusade in China* (1979).

Yergin, Daniel. *Shattered Peace: The Origins of the Cold War and the National Security State* (1977).

The Early Cold War at Home
Caute, David. *The Great Fear: The Anti-Communist Purge Under Truman and Eisenhower* (1978).

Goodman, Walter. *The Committee: The Extraordinary Career of the House Committee on Un-American Activities* (1968).

Klehr, Harvey, and Ronald Radosh, *The Amerasia Spy Case: Prelude to McCarthyism* (1996).

May, Gary. *Un-American Activities: The Trials of William Remington* (1994).

Navasky, Victor. *Naming Names* (1980).

Powers, Richard G. *Secrecy and Power: The Life of J. Edgar Hoover* (1987).

Radosh, Ronald, and Joyce Milton, *The Rosenberg File: A Search for the Truth* (1983).

Domestic Politics
Berman, William C. *The Politics of Civil Rights in the Truman Administration* (1970).

Ferrell, Robert. *Harry S. Truman: A Life* (1994).

Kirkendall, Richard, ed., *The Harry S. Truman Encyclopedia* (1989).

Leffler, Melvyn. *A Preponderance of Power: National Security, the Truman Administration, and the Cold War* (1992).

McCullough, David. *Truman* (1992).

Reichard, Gary. *Politics as Usual: The Age of Truman and Eisenhower* (1988).

Schaller, Michael. *Douglas MacArthur: The Far Eastern General* (1989).

Postwar Society
Gans, Herbert. *The Levittowners: Ways of Life and Politics in a New Suburban Community* (1967).

Graebner, William. *The Age of Doubt: American Thought and Culture in the 1940s* (1991).

Leuchtenburg, William. *A Troubled Feast* (1979).

Manchester, William. *The Glory and the Dream* (1973).

Diggins, John. *The Proud Decades: America in War and Peace, 1941–1960* (1988).

Riesman, David. *The Lonely Crowd: A Study of the Changing American Character* (1950).

Wright, Gwendolyn. *Building the American Dream: A Social History of Housing in America* (1981).

THE POSTWAR GENERATION

An American street scene at mid-century, with a mother and children in the new suburbia.

Chapter 28

THE EISENHOWER YEARS, 1953–1960

THE UNITED STATES at mid-century was far different from the nation we live in today. The Cold War was at its height, U.S. soldiers were dying in Korea, and communism seemed a formidable foe. The American population of 153 million contained a small and declining number of foreign born, the result of strict immigration quotas installed in the 1920s. (Ellis Island would close for good in 1955.) Most blacks still lived in the South, where racial segregation was the law. Blue-collar workers outnumbered white-collar workers, and labor unions, led by charismatic figures like John L. Lewis and Walter Reuther, were at the height of their power. Major League baseball had only sixteen teams, none west of St. Louis. There were no supermarkets or shopping malls, no motel chains or ballpoint pens. Television was just beginning, rock music still a few years away. More than half of the nation's farm dwellings had no electricity. Tobacco companies placed cigarette advertisements in medical journals. It cost three cents to mail a letter and a nickel to buy a coke.

Marriage rates were at an all-time high, while divorce rates kept declining. In 1954, *McCall's* magazine used the term "togetherness" to describe American family life, with shared activities such as Little League, car rides, and backyard barbecues. Though more women worked outside the home in 1950 than in 1944, the height of World War II, they did so mainly to supplement the family income, not to seek full-time careers. In the growing cult of motherhood, fulfillment meant meeting the needs of others. Feminism was described in psychology books as a "deep illness," entirely out of place.

America at mid-century saw an acceleration of postwar trends. As 40 million people moved to the suburbs, the large cities declined in population, political power, and quality of life. Racial lines remained rigid, with census data showing the suburbs to be more affluent than the cities they surrounded—and 98 percent white. Automobile sales skyrocketed, creating whole new industries to service the American traveler. Inventions poured forth, from the computer to the cure for polio. And a new president was elected to guide the country through these anxious, demanding times.

A NEW DIRECTION

Dwight Eisenhower entered the White House in 1953 on a wave of good feeling. His lack of political

CHRONOLOGY

1953	Truce ends fighting in Korea
	Soviet dictator Joseph Stalin dies
1954	Supreme Court issues school desegregation ruling in *Brown* v. *Board of Education*
	U.S. Senate censures Joseph McCarthy
1955	Bus boycott begins in Montgomery, Alabama
	Elvis Presley signs with RCA Records
	Brooklyn Dodgers finally win World Series
1956	Federal Highway Act passed, forging massive interstate highway system
	Hungarian Revolution and Suez Crisis strain U.S.–Soviet relations

	Eisenhower easily reelected
1957	Russians launch *Sputnik*
	Federal troops sent to enforce school integration order in Little Rock
1958	U.S. manned space program begins
1959	Fidel Castro leads successful revolution in Cuba
	Soviet Premier Nikita Khrushchev visits United States
1960	American U-2 spy plane shot down over Soviet Union
	John F. Kennedy elected president

URBAN, SUBURBAN, AND RURAL AMERICANS 1940–1960

- **CENTRAL-CITY DWELLERS**
- **SUBURBAN DWELLERS**
- **RURAL AND SMALL-TOWN DWELLERS**

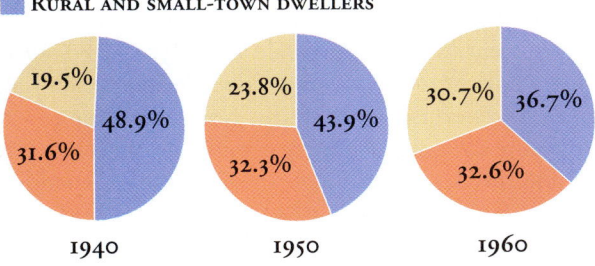

1940: 19.5% / 31.6% / 48.9%
1950: 23.8% / 32.3% / 43.9%
1960: 30.7% / 32.6% / 36.7%

experience appeared to be an asset after the turmoil of the Truman years. Americans trusted Eisenhower's judgment and admired his character. They believed that his enormous skills as a military leader would serve him equally well as president of the United States.

Modern Republicanism

Yet few Americans knew where Eisenhower stood on important domestic or international issues. His presidential campaign in 1952 had been intentionally vague. On the political spectrum, he stood somewhere between the Fair Deal Democrats of Harry Truman and the conservative Republicans of Robert Taft. The new president described himself as a moderate, using the term "modern Republicanism" to define his political approach.

Eisenhower filled his cabinet with prominent business leaders. For secretary of defense, he chose Charles E. ("Engine Charlie") Wilson, former president of General Motors, who proclaimed at his confirmation hearing that "what was good for our country was good for General Motors, and vice versa." For secretary of the treasury, Eisenhower selected George Humphrey, a fiscal conservative who hung a portrait of former secretary Andrew Mellon on his office wall. "We have to cut one-third out of the budget and you can't do that just by eliminating waste," Humphrey declared. "This means, whenever necessary, using a meat axe."

Eisenhower avoided such rhetoric. He had no intention of dismantling popular New Deal programs such as Social Security or unemployment insurance, and he supported a significant hike in the minimum hourly wage, from seventy-five cents to a dollar. Yet wherever possible, he worked to balance the budget,

trim government expenditures, and stimulate private enterprise. "I'm conservative when it comes to money," Eisenhower claimed, but "liberal when it comes to human beings."

In his first year as president, federal spending and federal income taxes were both cut by 10 percent. Eisenhower also opposed expansion of such popular but expensive federal programs as price supports for farmers and cheap public power from government dams and electric plants. In perhaps his most controversial early move, the president strongly supported passage of the Tidelands Oil Act, which transferred coastal oil land worth at least $40 billion from the federal government to the states. Critics, fearing the exploitation of these vital reserves by a few giant corporations, described "Tidelands" as the "most unjustified giveaway program" of the modern era.

A Truce in Korea

One member of Eisenhower's cabinet, Secretary of State John Foster Dulles, stood above the rest. The son of a minister and grandson of a former secretary of state, Dulles trained from his earliest days to serve God and country. Most observers found him arrogant, stubborn, and sour. Yet Eisenhower respected his secretary as a tough, knowledgeable advisor who willingly took the heat for actions the president himself had formulated or approved. "I know what they say about Foster—dull, duller, Dulles—and all that," Eisenhower told a friend. "But the [critics] love to hit him rather than me."

The president's first priority in foreign affairs was to end the Korean conflict. Though willing to accept the same terms that Truman had proposed—two Koreas, North and South, divided at the 38th parallel—Eisenhower demanded a prompt resolution. To speed this process, Dulles apparently warned the Communist Chinese (through diplomatic channels in India) that the United States would not rule out the use of atomic weapons if the Korean stalemate dragged on.

The impact of this "nuclear threat" is difficult to gauge. The Chinese communists probably viewed Eisenhower, a military leader, as a more dangerous foe than Harry Truman. Yet huge communist battlefield losses, coupled with the sudden death of Joseph Stalin, helped spur the peace process. In July 1953, a truce was signed that stopped the fighting without formally ending the war. More than 50,000 Americans were killed and 103,000 were wounded in Korea. The Pentagon estimated that 2.4 million civilians died or were seriously injured in the three years of terrible fighting, along with 850,000 troops from South Korea, 520,000 from North Korea, and 950,000 from Communist China.

Secretary of State John Foster Dulles, a hard-line cold warrior, deflected criticism away from President Eisenhower, who relied heavily on Dulles for foreign policy advice.

THE COLD WAR AT HOME AND ABROAD

When Republicans took control of Congress and the White House in 1953, the "communist issue" gained center stage. On Capitol Hill, 185 of the 221 House Republicans applied for duty on the House Un-American Activities Committee, where Chairman Harold Velde of Illinois vowed to hunt down communists like "rats." "They are foreign to our nation and to our God," Velde declared. "In the world of humanity they are aliens." At the White House, President Eisenhower promised both a crackdown on "subversives" in government and a "New Look" in military affairs, designed to streamline American forces for the continuing struggle against "worldwide communist aggression."

The Hunt for "Subversives"

Shortly after taking office, President Eisenhower issued an executive order that extended the scope of the Federal Loyalty Security Program. A few months later, he announced that 1,456 federal workers had been fired as "security risks," including "alcoholics," "homosexuals," and "political subversives." The most controversial security case involved J. Robert Oppenheimer, the distinguished physicist who directed the Manhattan Project during World War II. Oppenheimer's prewar association with left-wing radicals was widely known. He had been checked and rechecked by the FBI, cleared and recleared by the Atomic Energy Commission until 1953, when the Eisenhower administration suspended his top security clearance. Many believed that Oppenheimer's troubles resulted from his public opposition to the building of the hydrogen bomb—a charge the president vigorously denied. As Eisenhower noted in his diary, "There is no evidence that implies disloyalty on the part of Dr. Oppenheimer. However, this does not mean that he might not be a security risk."

In Congress, the Red-hunting fervor was even more intense. The Senate assault was led by Joseph McCarthy, newly appointed chairman of the Committee on Government Operations and its powerful Subcommittee on Investigations. Filling key staff positions with ex-FBI agents and former prosecutors like Roy

Uncle Sam sifts through the ranks of government workers in search of communists and other "subversives."

M. Cohn, an abrasive young attorney from New York, McCarthy looked for "communist influence" in the State Department and other government agencies. His hearings didn't uncover any communists. They did, however, ruin numerous careers, undermine worker morale, and make the United States look fearful in the eyes of the world. Not surprisingly, Republican criticism of McCarthy began to build. After all, he was now attacking a federal bureaucracy controlled by his own party.

Many expected Eisenhower to put the senator in his place. But the new president was slow to respond, believing that a brawl with McCarthy would divide Republicans into warring camps and seriously demean the presidential office. Time and again, he told his aides: "I just will not—I *refuse* to get into the gutter with that guy."

Eisenhower changed his mind after McCarthy's subcommittee, spearheaded by Roy Cohn, began to investigate charges that a "communist spy ring" was operating at Fort Monmouth, New Jersey, home of the

COMMUNIST PARTY ORGANIZATION U.S.A-FEB. 9, 1950

Senator Joe McCarthy, America's premier Red-hunter, lectured Army counsel Joseph Welch (hand on head) about the Communist Party during the celebrated Army-McCarthy hearings in 1954.

Army Signal Corps. Army officials responded that Cohn was harassing the service in order to win preferential treatment for a close friend and part-time McCarthy staffer named G. David Schine, who had recently been drafted into the army. Early in 1954, the Senate agreed to investigate these conflicting allegations. Furious at the attacks upon his beloved army, Eisenhower convinced Republican Senate leaders to televise the hearings. The president wanted the American people to see McCarthy in action, and it proved to be a very shrewd move. For thirty-six days, the nation watched the senator's frightening outbursts and crude personal attacks. The highlight of the hearings came on June 9, 1954, when army counsel Joseph Welch sternly rebuked McCarthy for his menacing behavior, asking: "Have you no sense of decency, sir? Have you left *no sense of decency*?" The spectators burst into applause.

A few months later, the Senate censured McCarthy for bringing that body "into dishonor and disrepute." The vote was sixty-seven to twenty-two, with only conservative Republicans opposed. Many believed that McCarthy's censure was linked to the easing of Cold War tensions at home. The Korean War was over, Stalin was dead, and the radical right was in disarray. For McCarthy, things came apart at a wicked rate of speed. Reporters and colleagues ignored him, and his

influence disappeared. Unable to get his message across, McCarthy spent his final days drinking in private and railing against those who had deserted his cause. He died of acute alcoholism in 1957, virtually alone, at the age of forty-eight.

Brinksmanship and Covert Action

Like Truman before him, President Eisenhower supported the containment of communism through military, economic, and diplomatic means. What most worried him were the spiraling costs. "If we let defense spending run wild," he said, "we get inflation . . . then controls . . . then a garrison state . . . and *then* we've lost the very values we were trying to defend." Eisenhower called his solution the "New Look." It was fruitless to match the communists "man for man, gun for gun," he reasoned. The Korean stalemate showed the folly of that approach. In place of conventional forces, the United States must emphasize "the deterrent of massive retaliatory power." This meant using America's edge in nuclear weapons and long-range bombers to best advantage.

The "New Look" allowed Eisenhower to cut defense spending by 20 percent between 1953 and 1955. The number of men and women in uniform went

down each year, while the production of atomic warheads dramatically increased. Secretary of State Dulles viewed the "New Look" as a way to intimidate potential enemies with the implied threat of atomic attack. He called this "brinksmanship," claiming that "the ability to get to the verge without getting into the war is the necessary art."

Critics, however, saw brinksmanship as a dangerous game. Intimidation meant little, they warned, if the United States did not intend to back up its words. Was Eisenhower willing to consider atomic weapons as a viable option in every international crisis? If not, he undermined America's credibility; if so, he risked nuclear destruction. To increase his flexibility in foreign affairs, the president needed other options as well.

In 1953, Eisenhower appointed Allen Dulles, younger brother of the secretary of state, to head the Central Intelligence Agency (CIA). Dulles emphasized "covert action" over intelligence gathering—a change the president fully endorsed. Most of the CIA's new work was cloaked in secrecy, and much of it was illegal. Covert action became one of Eisenhower's favorite foreign policy tools, providing quick, inexpensive responses when problems arose.

Iran was a case in point. In 1953, the new government of Mohammed Mossadegh nationalized the British-controlled oil fields and deposed the pro-Western Shah of Iran. The United States, believing Mossadegh's government to be pro-communist, feared for its oil supplies in the Middle East. President Eisenhower thus approved a CIA operation that toppled Mossadegh and returned the young Shah to power. A few months later, Iran agreed to split its oil production among three Western nations, with American companies getting 40 percent, British companies 40 percent, and Dutch companies 20 percent. The grateful Shah told the CIA: "I owe my throne to God, my people, my army, and to you."

In 1954, the CIA struck again, forcing the overthrow of Guatemala's democratically elected president, Jacobo Arbenz. Guatemala was one of the world's poorest nations, with an annual per capita income of less than one hundred dollars. Its largest employer and landholder, the American-owned United Fruit Company, controlled much of the Guatemalan economy. After taking office, Arbenz supported a strike of banana workers on United Fruit plantations, who were seeking wages of $1.50 a day. Far more provocative, however, was a new law, known as Decree 900, which expropriated millions of acres of private property for

the use of landless peasant families. Under this law, the Arbenz government offered United Fruit $1.2 million for 234,000 acres of its land—a figure based on the absurdly low tax assessments given United Fruit in the past.

The company had powerful allies in the United States. Numerous government officials, including both Dulles brothers, were linked to United Fruit through their previous corporate positions. Defending the company's interests came naturally to them, while the idea of expropriating American property smacked of "communist thinking." If Arbenz succeeded, the notion could spread across Latin America like wildfire.

Eisenhower moved quickly, authorizing the overthrow of Arbenz by Guatemalan exiles trained at CIA bases in Honduras and Nicaragua. The small invasion force, backed by CIA pilots, tore through Arbenz's poorly equipped army. The American press, meanwhile, accepted the Eisenhower–Dulles account that Guatemalan liberators had ousted a dangerous, pro-communist regime with minimal American help. In the following months, the new government of General Carlos Castillo Armas established a military dictatorship, executed hundreds of Arbenz supporters, and returned the expropriated lands to United Fruit. The final result, Eisenhower declared, "has given me great satisfaction."

The same could not be said of events in Indochina (or Vietnam). Following World War II, nationalist forces in that French colony, led by Ho Chi Minh, a popular Marxist leader, began an armed struggle for independence. The United States, viewing Ho (incorrectly) as a puppet of Moscow, supported French attempts to crush the Vietnamese resistance, known as the Vietminh. By 1953, American military aid to France in the Indochina conflict totaled nearly $3 billion.

It failed to turn the tide. The Vietminh grew stronger, taking more territory by the year. In 1954, Ho's forces surrounded 12,000 elite French troops at an isolated garrison called Dien Bien Phu. Facing sure defeat, the French appealed to Eisenhower for help. The president and his aides considered the use of American air power to save Dien Bien Phu. When Secretary of State Dulles, Vice President Nixon, and several U.S. military officials suggested tactical nuclear weapons, Eisenhower was appalled. "You boys must be crazy," he said. "We can't use those awful things against Asians for the second time in ten years. My God!"

French prisoners of war are marched from their fallen fortress at Dien Bien Phu by Vietnamese communist troops in 1954.

Eisenhower also refused to send American ground troops to Indochina. And he rejected the use of conventional air strikes to save Dien Bien Phu unless the British took part—but Churchill sternly said no. On May 7, 1954, the battered garrison surrendered, effectively ending French rule in Vietnam.

At peace talks in Geneva, Switzerland, the two sides agreed to a cease fire and a temporary partition of Vietnam at the 17th parallel, with French troops moving south of that line and Vietminh forces moving north. Free elections were scheduled for 1956, at which time the French were to fully withdraw. The United States refused to recognize the Geneva Accords. Eisenhower and Dulles were not about to acquiesce in a unified Vietnam under the leadership of Ho Chi Minh, the certain winner in the proposed election of 1956. The U.S. plan, therefore, was to prevent that election, while creating a permanent anticommunist government in South Vietnam supported by American economic and military aid.

To Eisenhower, the survival of South Vietnam became the key to containing communism in Asia. He described the so-called "domino theory" at a press conference about Indochina in 1954. "You have a row of dominoes set up," he began. "You knock over the first one, and what will happen to the last one is a certainty that it will go over quickly. So the possible consequences of the loss [of Vietnam] are just incalculable to the free world."

THE CIVIL RIGHTS MOVEMENT

The 1950s witnessed enormous gains in the struggle for minority rights. In federal courts and in cities throughout the South, African Americans struggled to eradicate the system of racial segregation that denied them dignity, opportunity, and equal protection under the law. Though the Eisenhower administration proved far less sympathetic to the cause of civil rights than the Truman administration had been, the movement for racial justice took on a power and a spirit that would transform the nation in the coming years.

Brown v. Board of Education

In September 1953, Chief Justice Fred Vinson died of a heart attack, requiring President Eisenhower to make his first appointment to the U.S. Supreme Court. Eisenhower offered the position to John Foster Dulles,

Chief Justice Earl Warren

Opinion of the Court in
Brown v. Board of Education
May 17, 1954

Ruling that racial segregation of the nation's public schools violated the Due Process Clause of the Fourteenth Amendment, a unanimous Supreme Court, led by Chief Justice Earl Warren, overturned the "separate but equal" doctrine set down fifty-eight years earlier in *Plessy v. Ferguson.*

These cases come to us from the States of Kansas, South Carolina, Virginia, and Delaware. They are premised on different facts and different local conditions, but a common legal question justifies their consideration together in this consolidated opinion.

In each of the cases, minors of the Negro race, through their legal representatives, seek the aid of the courts in obtaining admission to the public schools of their community on a nonsegregated basis. In each instance, they had been denied admission to schools attended by white children under laws requiring or permitting segregation according to race. . . .

Today, education is perhaps the most important function of state and local governments. Compulsory school attendance laws and the great expenditures for education both demonstrate our recognition of the importance of education to our democratic society. It is required in the performance of our most basic public responsibilities, even service in the armed forces. It is the very foundation of good citizenship. Today it is a principal instrument in awakening the child to cultural values, in preparing him for later professional training, and in helping him to adjust normally to his environment. In these days, it is doubtful that any child may reasonably be expected to succeed in life if he is denied the opportunity of an education. Such an opportunity, where the state has undertaken to provide it, is a right which must be made available to all on equal terms.

We come then to the question presented: Does segregation of children in public schools solely on the basis of race, even though the physical facilities and other "tangible"

who turned it down, and then to California Governor Earl Warren, who accepted the post and won prompt Senate approval. Warren had been the Republican party's vice-presidential nominee in 1948. Far more liberal than Eisenhower on social issues, he would sometimes anger the president in the coming years, but rarely lose his respect.

The major issue facing the Supreme Court in 1953 was civil rights. For more than a decade, a group of talented African-American attorneys had been filing legal challenges to segregated public facilities in the South, hoping to erode the "separate but equal" doctrine of *Plessy* v. *Ferguson.* Led by Thurgood Marshall and William Hastie of the NAACP's

Legal Defense Fund, these attorneys targeted specific areas, such as professional education (law, medicine, teaching), to establish precedents for the larger fight. The emphasis on professional schools made good sense because there were so few of them for black students in the South. Under "separate but equal," the states would be forced to spend millions of dollars for their construction in order to keep segregation alive.

This strategy worked well. In 1950, the Supreme Court stretched the *Plessy* doctrine to its limits in two lawsuits brought by the NAACP. In *Sweatt* v. *Painter,* the Court ruled that Texas authorities must admit a black applicant to the all-white state law school in

factors may be equal, deprive the children of the minority group of equal educational opportunities? We believe that it does. . . .

To separate them from others of similar age and qualifications solely because of their race generates a feeling of inferiority as to their status in the community that may affect their hearts and minds in a way unlikely ever to be undone. The effect of this separation on their educational opportunities was well stated by a finding in the Kansas case by a court which nevertheless felt compelled to rule against the Negro plaintiffs:

> Segregation of white and colored children in public schools has a detrimental effect upon the colored children. The impact is greater when it has the sanction of the law; for the policy of separating the races is usually interpreted as denoting the inferiority of the negro group. A sense of inferiority affects the motivation of a child to learn. Segregation with the sanction of law, therefore, has a tendency to [retard] the educational and mental development of negro children and to deprive them of some of the benefits they would receive in a racial[ly] integrated school system.

Whatever may have been the extent of psychological knowledge at the time of *Plessy v. Ferguson,* this finding is amply supported by modern authority. Any language in *Plessy v. Ferguson* contrary to this finding is rejected.

We conclude that in the field of public education the doctrine of "separate but equal" has no place. Separate educational facilities are inherently unequal. Therefore, we hold that the plaintiffs and others similarly situated for whom the actions have been brought are, by reason of the segregation complained of, deprived of the equal protection of the laws guaranteed by the Fourteenth Amendment. This disposition makes unnecessary any discussion whether such segregation also violates the Due Process Clause of the Fourteenth Amendment. . . .

SOURCE *Brown v. Board of Education,* 349 U.S. 294, 1954.

Austin because they had failed to provide African Americans with a comparable facility, thereby violating the equal protection clause of the Fourteenth Amendment. And in *McLaurin* v. *Oklahoma,* the court struck down a scheme that segregated a black student *within* that state's graduate school of education, forcing him to sit alone in the library and the lecture halls in a section marked "Reserved for Coloreds." "State-imposed restrictions which produce such inequalities," the court noted, "cannot be sustained."

With these victories, the NAACP took on the larger challenge of racial segregation in the nation's public schools. Unlike *Sweatt* and *McLaurin,* which involved a small number of adult students, the new

cases touched millions of children, white and black, in twenty-one states and the District of Columbia. By 1953, five separate lawsuits had reached the Supreme Court, including *Brown* v. *Board of Education of Topeka.*

The case involved a Kansas law that permitted cities to segregate their public schools. With NAACP support, the Reverend Oliver Brown sued the Topeka school board, arguing that his eight-year-old daughter should not be forced to attend a Negro school a mile from her home when there was a white public school only three blocks away. The Supreme Court was badly divided. Several justices supported the *Plessy* doctrine, while others argued that it fostered racial inequality.

Attorneys representing the NAACP's Legal Defense Fund, led by Thurgood Marshall (center) celebrate Brown v. Board of Education *on the steps of the Supreme Court, May 17, 1954.*

As chief justice, Earl Warren moved forcefully to bring his colleagues into line. Believing racial segregation to be both unconstitutional and morally wrong, Warren insisted that the Supreme Court speak in a powerful, united voice against this evil. Anything less, he reasoned, would encourage massive resistance in the South.

On May 17, 1954, the Supreme Court overturned *Plessy* v. *Ferguson* in a stunning 9–0 decision, written by Warren himself. Relying on the studies of social scientists such as Kenneth Clark, the chief justice claimed that racial segregation had a "detrimental effect" on black children by making them feel inferior to whites. "In the field of public education the doctrine of 'separate but equal' has no place," he stated. "Separate educational facilities are inherently unequal."

Brown v. *Board of Education* did not call for the immediate desegregation of all public schools. Indeed, the Supreme Court put off its implementation guidelines (known as *Brown II*) for a full year, hoping to let passions cool in the South. *Brown II* required local school boards to draw up desegregation plans with the approval

of a federal district judge. But there were no timetables, and the wording was intentionally vague. Integration should proceed, it said, "with all deliberate speed."

White Southern reaction was intense. Moderates, viewing the decision as inevitable, urged caution and respect for the law. Others, however, preached open resistance and hate. "You are not required to obey any court which passes out such a ruling," Senator James O. Eastland of Mississippi told his constituents. "In fact, you are obligated to defy it." Violence flared across the South. "In one school district after another," wrote an observer, "segregationists staged the same drama: forcing young blacks to enter a school by passing rock-throwing white mobs and white pickets shouting 'Nigger,' 'Nigger,' 'Nigger.'" The Ku Klux Klan came alive in the 1950s, and new groups like the White Citizens' Council were formed to defend segregation and the "Southern way of life." In the summer of 1954, a black Chicago teenager named Emmett Till, visiting relatives in Mississippi, was murdered for allegedly flirting with a white woman at a country store. Two suspects—the woman's husband and his half-brother—were acquitted by an all-white jury in just over an hour. "If we hadn't stopped to drink pop," a juror noted, "it wouldn't have taken so long."

Many Americans looked to the White House for guidance about civil rights. But Eisenhower had little to say about the issue, partly because he personally opposed the "forced integration" of the races. When asked at a press conference if he had any advice for the South on how to handle the *Brown* decision, Eisenhower replied: "Not in the slightest. The Supreme Court has spoken and I am sworn to uphold the constitutional processes in this country; and I will obey."

The Montgomery Bus Boycott

The battle over public school integration was but one of many such struggles in the South during this era. Some were fought by attorneys in federal courtrooms; others involved ordinary men and women determined to challenge the indignities of racial segregation and second-class treatment in their daily lives. "Nothing is quite as humiliating, so murderously angering," said one African American, "as to know that because you are black you may have to walk a half mile farther than whites to urinate; that because you are black you have to receive your food through a window in the back of a restaurant or sit in a garbage-littered yard."

Jim Crow was a way of life in the South, where theaters, restaurants, trains, buses, blood banks, hospitals, drinking fountains, waiting rooms, and cemeteries were all segregated by law.

The black people of Montgomery, Alabama, had experienced such treatment for years. Known as "the cradle of the Confederacy," Montgomery enforced segregation and racial etiquette in meticulous detail. Blacks always tipped their hats to whites, always stood in the presence of whites unless told to sit, and always addressed whites with a title of respect. ("Boss," "Sir," and "Ma'am" were most common.) Restrooms, drinking fountains, blood banks, movie theaters, cemeteries—all were separated by race. It was illegal for whites and blacks to play checkers together on public property or to share a taxi cab. On the local buses, blacks paid their fares in the front, got off the vehicle, and entered the "colored section" through the rear door. They also had to relinquish their seats to white passengers when the front section filled up.

On December 1, 1955, a simple yet revolutionary act of resistance occurred on a crowded Montgomery bus. Rosa Parks, a forty-two-year-old black seamstress, and member of the local NAACP, refused to give up her seat to a white. The bus driver called the police. "They got on the bus," Mrs. Parks recalled, "and one of them asked me why I didn't stand up. I asked him, 'Why do you push us around?' He said, ' . . . I don't know, but the law is the law and you're under arrest.'"

News of Mrs. Parks's defiance electrified the black community. Within days a boycott of Montgomery's bus system was begun, organized by local clergymen and the Women's Political Council, the black alternative to the all-white League of Women Voters. Calling themselves the Montgomery Improvement Association (MIA), they chose a young minister named Martin Luther King, Jr., to lead the struggle for open seating in public transportation, a small but highly symbolic step.

King, twenty-six, was a newcomer to Montgomery. He was selected, in part, because his youth and vocation made him less vulnerable to economic and political pressure from whites. The son of a well-known Atlanta pastor, King earned his college degree at Morehouse and his doctorate at Boston University's School of Theology before heading south with his new wife, Coretta Scott King, to serve as pastor of Montgomery's Dexter Avenue Baptist Church in 1954. Dr. King was familiar with the works of Gandhi and

Rosa Parks rides a nearly empty but integrated Montgomery bus following the successful boycott she triggered in 1955.

Thoreau. He viewed mass action and nonviolent resistance as essential weapons in the war against racial injustice.

King rallied the black community with the eloquent passion of his words. "There comes a time when people get tired," he told a packed rally after Rosa Parks's arrest. "We are here this evening to say to those who have mistreated us so long that we are tired — tired of being segregated and humiliated, tired of being kicked about by the brutal feet of oppression. We have no alternative but to protest."

King's reputation soared. He kept the movement together, despite police harassment and the firebombing of his home. Blacks in Montgomery formed car pools to get people to their destinations. The churches raised money for fuel, while black-owned garages did repair work free of charge. Many people rode bicycles or simply walked for miles. The boycott nearly bankrupted the city bus system and badly hurt the white merchants downtown. An elderly black woman said she would rather crawl on her knees than ride the local bus line. And Mother Pollard, bent with age, inspired the movement with her simple remark: "My feets is tired, but my soul is rested."

In November 1956, the federal courts struck down the Alabama law requiring racial segregation in public transportation. A month later, blacks sat in the front of the Montgomery buses without incident. The boycott, lasting 381 days, demonstrated both the power of collective action and the possibility of social change. In 1957, Dr. King joined with other black ministers to form the Southern Christian Leadership Conference (SCLC), an organization devoted to racial justice through peaceful means. "Noncooperation with evil," King declared, "is as much a moral obligation as is cooperation with good."

THE AGE OF TELEVISION

In the 1950s, social commentators analyzed a host of new issues in American life. Some worried about the

struggle between individuals and organizations, the apparent quest for security over adventure, the monotony of modern work. A few focused on the supposed emptiness of suburban living, the growing cult of domesticity among women, the changing standards of success. Yet what struck virtually all critics and commentators in the 1950s was the impact of television upon American life—an impact that altered politics, news gathering, consumer tastes, and popular culture in truly revolutionary ways.

The Magic Box

In 1946, there were 17,000 TV sets in the United States, showing old cartoons and movies in blurry black-and-white. The late 1940s saw major changes in television technology, such as the use of coaxial cable and the introduction of color. In 1949, a TV set appeared for the first time in the Sears, Roebuck catalogue—$149.95 "with indoor antenna." A year later, Americans were buying 20,000 television sets a day. The two most popular shows of that era were Milton Berle's "Texaco Star Theater" and Ed Sullivan's

"Toast of the Town." Both began in 1948 as live, weekly programs with a single sponsor. Berle, a physical comedian, seemed perfect for a visual medium like TV. His fast-paced humor relied on sight gags instead of verbal banter. The press called him "Mr. Television."

Sullivan, a former gossip columnist, was awkward and unsmiling on camera. What made him unique was his ability to provide fresh entertainment to Americans of all tastes and ages. Sullivan's Sunday night variety show, mixing opera with acrobats, ran for twenty-three years on CBS, far longer than Berle's. His guests included Elvis Presley, Dean Martin and Jerry Lewis, pianist Van Cliburn, dancer Rudolf Nureyev, singer Lena Horne, and the Beatles. "Ed Sullivan will last," said pianist Oscar Levant, "as long as other people have talent."

Television's potential was impossible to ignore. In 1951, an obscure Tennessee politician named Estes Kefauver became a national figure by holding televised hearings into organized crime. With little daytime competition—soap operas had not yet reached TV—Senator Kefauver grilled prominent mobsters like New York's Frank Costello as 25 million viewers watched in

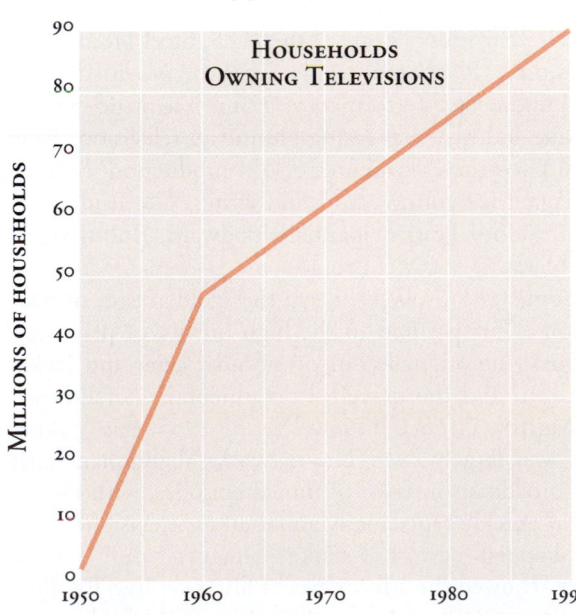

THE TELEVISION REVOLUTION
1950–1990

HOUSEHOLDS OWNING TELEVISIONS

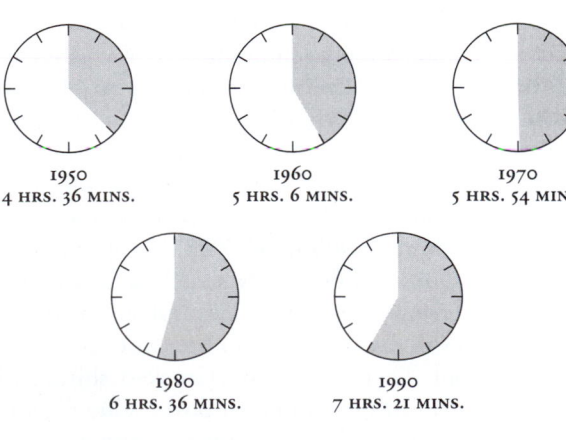

AVERAGE DAILY TELEVISION VIEWING

1950 — 4 HRS. 36 MINS.
1960 — 5 HRS. 6 MINS.
1970 — 5 HRS. 54 MINS.
1980 — 6 HRS. 36 MINS.
1990 — 7 HRS. 21 MINS.

As televisions became commonplace in the 1950s, TV viewing altered the nature of American culture and politics. Source: Statistical Abstracts of the United States.

Ed Sullivan provided fresh entertainment on his popular TV variety show every Sunday night.

amazement. The TV cameras perfectly captured Costello's discomfort by focusing for several minutes on his jittery, sweat-soaked hands. "Never before," wrote *Life* magazine of the Costello incident, "had the attention of a nation been riveted so completely on a single matter."

Nixon's "Checkers Speech" and the Army-McCarthy hearings further highlighted the impact of television in the political arena. Above all, however, TV possessed the power to sell. In 1950, local stations, desperate for programming, aired a series of old "Hopalong Cassidy" movies starring an obscure cowboy-actor named William Boyd. Within months, "Hopalong Cassidy" clothing and six-guns were in frantic demand, grossing $30 million before the craze died out. Sponsor Hazel Bishop cosmetics saw its sales jump from $50,000 to $4.5 million after advertising on TV. And Walt Disney struck gold with his three-part series on Davy Crockett, which aired nationally in 1954. Millions of children wore coonskin caps to school. There were Davy Crockett shirts and blankets, toothbrushes and lunch boxes. One department store chain sold 20,000 surplus pup tents in less than a week by printing "Davy Crockett" on the flap.

By 1954, three national networks were firmly in place. As the major radio powers, ABC, CBS, and NBC held a decided advantage over potential competitors in technology and talent. Indeed, these networks filled their early airtime by moving popular radio programs like "Jack Benny," "Burns & Allen," and "Amos 'n' Andy," over to TV. The faster television grew, the more its schedule expanded. Important advertisers signed on, sponsoring entire programs such as "Kraft Television Theater," the "U.S. Steel Hour," and "Motorola Playhouse." This, in turn, provided work for hundreds of performers at a time when the motion picture industry was losing ground to television. New York City, the early center of TV production, became a magnet for young actors and writers like Paul Newman, Sidney Poitier, Joanne Woodward, Rod Serling, Neil Simon, and Mel Brooks.

Some critics called this era the "golden age" of television. They pointed to the high quality of plays and dramas, the original comedy of Sid Caesar and Jackie Gleason, and the powerful documentaries of Edward R. Murrow on "See It Now." Yet by 1955, this "golden age" was largely over. The networks abandoned most live broadcasts in favor of filmed episodes, with Hollywood quickly replacing Manhattan as television's capital. Popular new shows like "Dragnet" and "I Love Lucy" showed the advantages of film over live TV. Production was less demanding. Errors could be corrected, scenes could be shot at different locations, and

episodes could be shown more than once, creating additional revenues.

Many television shows of the 1950s, especially the situation comedies, reflected both the yearnings and stereotypes of American society. Popular comedies such as "Father Knows Best," "Ozzie and Harriet," and "Leave It to Beaver," portrayed the charmed lives (and minor problems) of middle-class white families in the suburbs. Mother was a housewife. Dad held a pressure-free white-collar job. The kids were well-adjusted and witty. Money was never a problem. No one stayed angry for long. "You know, Mom," said Beaver Cleaver, "when we're in a mess, you kind of make things seem not so messy." "Well," June Cleaver replied, "isn't that sort of what mothers are for?"

Married women in TV "sit-coms" did not work outside the home. Their husbands would not permit it. This rule even applied to childless couples like Ralph and Alice Kramden of "The Honeymooners," one of television's rare programs about urban, working-class people. Furthermore, single women in "sit-coms" rarely took their jobs seriously. Like Eve Arden in "Our Miss Brooks" and Ann Sothern in "Private Secretary," they spent most of their time hunting for a husband.

Though racial minorities almost never appeared in these "sit coms," they did play major—if stereotypical—roles in two or three popular shows of the 1950s. There was "Beulah," the big-hearted domestic in a white suburban household, and "Rochester," the wisecracking butler on the "Jack Benny Show." Above all, there was "Amos 'n' Andy," an adaptation of the popular radio show created by two white men, Freeman Gosden and Charles Correll, that featured an all-black cast. The NAACP angrily denounced "Amos' n' Andy" for portraying blacks as "clowns" and "crooks," but others praised the performers for transforming racist stereotypes into "authentic black humor."

The Quiz Show Scandals

No event raised more concerns about the control and direction of commercial television in the 1950s than the quiz show scandals. Quiz shows were a throwback to the radio era, when programs such as "Take It or Leave It" offered contestants a shot at "the $64 Question"—the ultimate prize. Though quiz shows appeared early on television, they did not generate much interest until Revlon cosmetics produced a "big

money" version in order to match the successful TV advertising campaign of rival Hazel Bishop. Named "The $64,000 Question," it aired on CBS in June 1955.

The rules were simple. After choosing a topic such as science or baseball, the contestant fielded questions that began at $64 and doubled with each correct answer. At the $16,000 plateau, the contestant entered a glass "isolation booth." The tension was enormous, since a wrong answer wiped out all previous winnings. The show took off, rising to number one after only five weeks on the air. It drew the highest ratings in TV history—a whopping 85 percent audience share—when contestants went for the $64,000 question. Revlon products literally flew off the shelves. Annual sales rose from $34 million to $86 million, while Revlon stock jumped from twelve to twenty.

Before long, the airwaves were flooded with imitations. In 1956, "The $64,000 Question" lost its top rating to NBC's "Twenty-One," which pitted two competitors in a trivia contest structured like the blackjack card game. The stakes grew ever larger. Charles Van Doren, a handsome English instructor at Columbia University, won $129,000 on "Twenty-One" and became an instant national hero, described by *Time* magazine as an "inspiration" to America's youth.

His good fortune did not last long. A grand jury investigation revealed that numerous quiz show contestants had been given the questions in advance. It turned out that both "The $64,000 Question" and "Twenty-One" were rigged, with players coached about every detail of their performance. The contestants blamed the producers, who then implicated the sponsors. Van Doren admitted the painful truth after first protesting his innocence. "I was involved, deeply involved, in a deception," he said, adding, "I would give almost anything to reverse the course of my life."

The public was outraged. President Eisenhower condemned the "selfishness" and "greed" of the perpetrators, while novelist John Steinbeck foresaw the end of American innocence. "I am troubled," he wrote, "by the cynical immorality of my country." Yet no laws had been broken; there was nothing illegal about these shows. Indeed, some sponsors defended them as a form of *entertainment,* akin to professional wrestling or a "ghostwritten" book. As public anger mounted, however, Congress passed legislation to prevent the rigging of TV quiz shows, and the networks promised to regulate themselves. "The $64,000 Question,"

Contestants Charles Van Doren and Vivian Nearing battle it out on the rigged quiz show "Twenty-One."

"Twenty-One," and other big money game shows quickly left the air.

The quality of television did not appear to improve. New programs became clones of each other — bland sitcoms or violent westerns and crime dramas. Advertising now consumed 20 percent of television airtime, with more money spent making commercials than producing the shows themselves. "The feeling of high purpose that lit the industry when it was young," wrote the New York *Times,* "is long gone." Yet television's power kept expanding. One study in the 1950s estimated that an American youngster spent 11,000 hours in the classroom through high school and 15,000 hours in front of the TV. Another concluded that adults spent more time watching television than working for pay. There were complaints that television tended to isolate people and to shorten their attention spans. Nobody needed to concentrate for more than a half-hour — and not very hard at that.

As television expanded, other media outlets declined. Mass circulation magazines such as *Look* and *Collier's* folded in the 1950s, and newspaper readership went way down. Movie attendance dropped and radio lost listeners, forcing both industries to experiment in order to survive. Hollywood tried Cinemascope, Technicolor, 3D glasses, drive-in movies, and big budget spectacles like "The Ten Commandments" and "Ben Hur." Radio moved from soap operas and big band music to "hip" disc jockeys spinning rock 'n' roll. Nevertheless, television was now king. People watched the same programs in Boston and San Diego, in rural hamlets and in cities, in rich areas and in poor. America's popular culture, consumer needs, and general information — all came increasingly from TV.

YOUTH CULTURE

In the 1950s, a distinctive "teenage culture" emerged, rooted in the enormous prosperity and population growth that followed World War II. America's young people were far removed from the grim events of the previous two decades. They had not experienced the pain and sacrifice of economic depression and total

war. Raised in relative affluence, surrounded by messages that undermined traditional values of thrift and self-denial, these new teenagers were perceived as a special group with a unique subculture. They rarely worked, yet their pockets were full. By 1956, the nation's "teenage market" topped $9 billion a year. The typical adolescent spent as much on entertainment as did the average family in 1941.

A New Kind of Music

Nothing defined these 13 million teenagers more clearly than the music they shared. In the 1940s, popular music was dominated by the "big bands" of Glenn Miller and Tommy Dorsey, the Broadway show tunes of Rodgers and Hammerstein, and the mellow voices of Bing Crosby, Frank Sinatra, and the Andrews Sisters. These artists appealed to a broad white audience of all ages. Other forms of popular music—bluegrass, country, rhythm-and-blues—were limited by region and race.

But not for long. The huge migration of rural blacks and whites to industrial centers during World War II profoundly altered popular culture. The sounds of "race" music, "hillbilly" music, and gospel became readily available to mainstream America for the first time. Record sales tripled during the 1950s, aided by technological advances like the transistor radio and the 45 rpm vinyl disc (or "single"). The main consumers were young people who acquired new tastes by flipping the radio dial.

In 1951, a Cleveland, Ohio, record dealer noticed that white teenagers at his store were "going crazy" over the songs of black rhythm-and-blues artists like Ivory Joe Hunter and Lloyd Price. He told a local disc jockey named Alan Freed, who decided to play these records on the air. Freed's new program, "The Moondog Party," took Cleveland by storm. Soon Freed was hosting live shows at the local arena to overflow crowds. Pounding his fists to the rhythm, chanting "go man, go," Freed became the self-proclaimed father of rock 'n' roll.

"I'll never forget the first time I heard his show," a writer recalled. "I couldn't believe sounds like that were coming out of the radio." Freed understood the defiant, sensual nature of rock 'n' roll, the way it separated the young from everyone else. It was their music, played by their heroes, set to their special beat. Indeed, rock's first national hit, "Rock Around the Clock," by Bill Haley and the Comets, became the theme song for "Blackboard Jungle," a movie about rebellious high school students set to the throbbing rhythms of rock 'n' roll.

The Rise of Elvis

Haley's success was fleeting. A short, heavy-set man with marginal talent, he did not generate the intense excitement or sexual spark that teenagers craved. As Haley faded, a twenty-one-year-old truck driver from Memphis literally exploded onto the popular music scene. His name was Elvis Presley; the year was 1955.

Born in rural Mississippi, Presley was surrounded by the sounds of country music, gospel, and blues. As a teenager in Memphis, he listened to WDIA—"the Mother Station of Negroes"—and frequented the legendary blues clubs along Beale Street. The music moved him deeply, providing both spiritual force and physical release.

Memphis was also home to Sun Records, a label with strong Southern roots. Owned by Sam Phillips, Sun recorded white country singers like Johnny Cash and black bluesmen such as B. B. King. What Phillips most wanted, however, was an artist who combined these two sounds instinctively, without appearing artificial or forced. "If I could find a white man who had the Negro sound and the Negro feel," Phillips said, "I could make a million dollars."

Presley was that man. Signing with Sun Records in 1954, he took the region by storm. The press described his unique style as "a cross between be-bop and country," and "a new hillbilly blues beat." "This boy," said a Memphis newspaper, "has something to appeal to everybody." It wasn't just the sound. Tall and handsome, with long sideburns and slicked-back hair, Presley was a riveting performer, combining little boy shyness with enormous sexual drive. A fellow artist described young Presley on tour:

> This cat came out in red pants and a green coat and a pink shirt and socks, and he had this sneer on his face. And he stood behind the mike for five minutes, I'll bet, before he made a move. Then he hit his guitar a lick, and he broke two strings. I'd been playing ten years, and I hadn't broken a *total* of two strings. So there he was, these two strings dangling, and he hadn't done anything yet, and these high school girls were screaming and fainting and running up to the stage, and then he started to move his hips real slow like he had a thing for his guitar.

Combining the sounds of black and white music with enormous sexual drive, Elvis Presley became the most successful recording star in history.

When Presley became too big to handle, Sun Records sold his contract to RCA for $35,000, a sizable amount at that time. Before long, he was a national sensation. His early hits topped the charts in popular music, country, and rhythm-and-blues—the first time that had ever occurred. In less than a year, Elvis recorded eight number-one songs and six of RCA's all-time top twenty-five records. When he appeared on "Ed Sullivan," the cameras carefully shot him from the waist up. The ratings were extraordinary. "I want to say to Elvis and the country," Sullivan told his audience, "that this is a real decent, fine boy."

Young Elvis was modest and polite. He didn't smoke or drink or use drugs. He was so devoted to his parents that friends laughingly described him as a mama's boy. Yet his exaggerated sexuality on stage made him the target of those who believed that rock 'n' roll was a vulgar and dangerous assault upon America's youth. "Popular music," wrote one television critic, "has reached its lowest depths in the grunt and groin antics of Mr. Presley."

Such criticism served only to enhance Presley's stature in the teenage world. And his success led the major record companies to experiment more aggressively with black rhythm-and-blues. At that time, white "cover artists" still were used to record toned-down versions of "race" music for white teenage audiences. In 1954, Big Joe Turner's legendary "Shake, Rattle, and Roll" did not make the popular charts, while Bill Haley's cover version became a number-one hit. Turner began:

> Well you wear low dresses
> The sun comes shinin' through [*couplet repeated*]
> I can't believe my eyes
> That all of this belongs to you.

Haley sang:

> You wear those dresses
> Your hair done up so nice [*couplet repeated*]
> You look so warm
> But your heart is cold as ice.

In 1956, rock music reached a milestone when Little Richard's sensual recordings of "Long Tall Sally" and "Rip It Up" outsold the "sanitized" versions of Pat Boone, America's leading white cover artist. Using

words and illusions that would have been unthinkable in mainstream America a few years before, Little Richard cried:

> Well it's Saturday night
> and I just got paid,
> A fool about my money
> don't try to save.
> Gunna Rock it up,
> Gunna Rip it up,
> Gunna Shake it up,
> Gunna Ball it up,
> Gunna Rock it up,
> And Ball tonight.

There was more to rock 'n' roll, of course, than Elvis Presley and rhythm-and-blues. Teenagers adored the sweet sounds of the Everly Brothers, the lush harmony of the Platters, and the clean-cut innocence of Ricky Nelson. Furthermore, jazz and folksinging retained a healthy following, as did popular artists like Sinatra, Perry Como, and Nat "King" Cole. Nevertheless, the music that defined this era for most Americans, but for teenagers in particular, was hard-edged rock 'n' roll. It was the car radio blasting Presley's "Hound Dog," Chuck Berry's "Maybellene," and Little Richard's "Tutti Frutti" on a carefree Saturday night. *A wop bop a lu bop a lop bam boom!*

The Beat Generation

Whatever else might be said about Elvis Presley and other rock heroes, they loved the system that made them millionaires. Elvis spent lavishly. His first royalties were used to purchase three new homes and matching Cadillacs for his parents, though his mother didn't drive. Material rewards were the standard by which Presley, and countless others, measured their success.

The Beat movement was different. Composed of young writers and poets based mainly in San Francisco and New York, it blossomed in the mid-1950s as a reaction against mainstream standards and beliefs. The word "beat," part of the tiny drug scene of the 1950s, described a feeling of emotional and physical exhaustion. The Beats despised politics, consumerism, and technology. They viewed American culture as meaningless, conformist, banal. Their leading poet, Allen

Beat poets like Allen Ginsberg assaulted the politics and culture of middle-class America in the 1950s with anthems of despair.

Ginsberg, provided a bitter portrait of generational despair in *Howl* (1955), which he wrote while under the influence of drugs.

> I saw the best minds of my generation
> destroyed by madness,
> starving hysterical naked,
> dragging themselves through the negro
> streets at dawn looking for an angry fix . . .

The Beats linked happiness and creativity with absolute freedom. They glorified intuition and spontaneity. Their model was Dean Moriarty, the hero of Jack Kerouac's *On the Road,* an autobiographical novel about the cross-country adventures of Kerouac and his

friends, finding adventure and renewal (not to mention sex and drugs) beyond the confines of middle-class life. *On the Road* became both a national best seller and a cult book on America's college campuses. In a sense, Kerouac and Presley had something important in common: both appealed to young people who seemed dissatisfied with the apparent blandness of American culture.

CRISES AND CELEBRATION

In September 1955, President Eisenhower suffered a heart attack while vacationing in Colorado. The news raised obvious questions about his present and future course. At sixty-five, Eisenhower was one of the oldest presidents in American history. How quickly would he recover, if at all? Who would guide the nation in his absence? Would he even consider running for a second term?

Eisenhower spent the next four months recovering in the hospital and at his Gettysburg farm. Fortunately, the fall of 1955 was a time of political tranquility, with Congress out of session, no bills to sign or veto, and no crises looming on the international scene. The president stayed in close contact with his advisors as he slowly regained his health. Returning to the White House early in 1956, he announced his plan to seek reelection. The public was vastly relieved. As columnist James Reston noted, Eisenhower was more than a president; he was "a national phenomenon, like baseball."

Conquering Polio

The president's full recovery was not the only positive "health news" of 1955. On a far larger front, a medical research team led by Dr. Jonas Salk, a virologist at the University of Pittsburgh, announced the successful testing of a vaccine to combat poliomyelitis, the most frightening public health problem of the postwar era. More than 50,000 polio cases were reported in 1954, mostly of children who took sick during the summer months. The disease produced flu-like symptoms in most cases, but a more virulent form, which entered

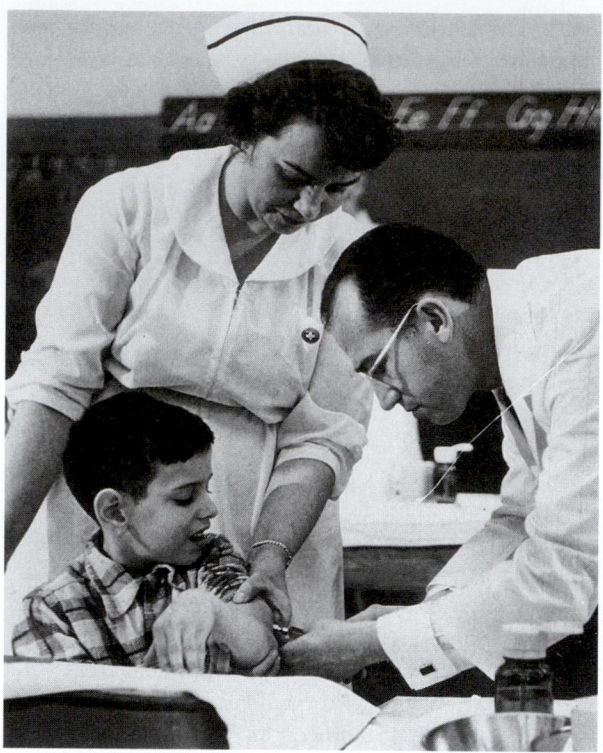

Dr. Jonas Salk, administering a polio vaccine he developed in 1954, helped eradicate a disease that terrorized Americans in the postwar era.

the central nervous system, led to paralysis and sometimes death. The cause of polio was uncertain; the virus seemed to be excreted in fecal matter and then passed through hand-to-hand contact. Not surprisingly, the epidemic produced a national panic. Cities closed swimming pools and beaches; families cancelled vacations, boiled their dishes, and avoided indoor crowds. Children were warned against jumping in puddles, drinking from water fountains, and making new friends.

The March of Dimes became America's favorite charity, raising millions to find a cure for polio and to finance the care of patients through therapy, leg braces, and iron lungs. Determined to provide immediate protection against the disease, Dr. Salk began testing a "dead" polio virus vaccine on schoolchildren in 1954. (His critics, led by Dr. Alfred Sabin, insisted that only a "live" polio vaccine would trigger the immunities needed to provide a lasting solution.) Aided

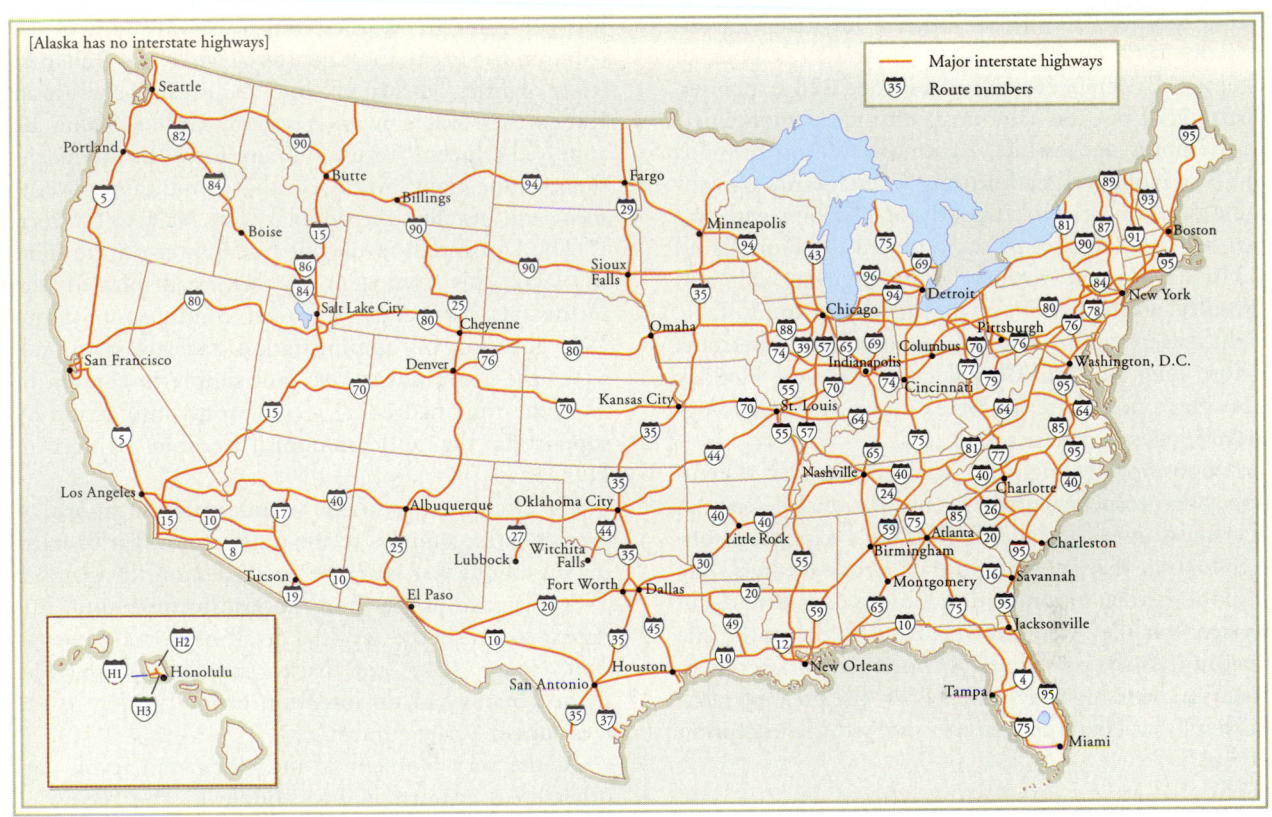

[Alaska has no interstate highways]

— Major interstate highways
(35) Route numbers

MAP 28.1 | THE NATIONAL HIGHWAY SYSTEM

by the March of Dimes and an army of volunteers, Salk tested the vaccine—and a placebo—on several million youngsters nationwide. "It was the largest peacetime mobilization of its kind," wrote one observer, "one in which the mothers of America rose up to save, in many cases, their own children."

The testing proved extremely successful. The federal government approved the polio vaccine in 1955, touching off emotional public celebrations. "People observed moments of silence, rang bells, honked horns, blew factory whistles, fired salutes, . . . drank toasts, hugged children, attended church, smiled at strangers, forgave enemies." Although the government did not provide the funds to immediatley vaccinate all school-age children—in part because the American Medical Association objected to this "socialist" proposal—public opinion soon forced a more compassionate approach. In 1960, fewer than a thousand new polio cases were reported in the United States. The battle had been won.

Interstate Highways

The nation's confidence soared even higher with passage of the Federal Highway Act of 1956, which authorized $25 billion in new taxes on cars, trucks, and gasoline for the construction of 40,000 miles of interstate roads over the next ten years. The huge highway network, linking all cities with more than 50,000 people, allowed a driver to travel the continent uninterrupted, save stops for food and gas. Eisenhower viewed this project as both a convenience to motorists and a boost to the economy. (The concrete alone could build "six sidewalks to the moon," he boasted.) The president also linked good highways to Cold War events, warning that cities must be evacuated quickly in the event of nuclear war.

The Highway Act spurred enormous economic growth. Improved roads meant higher oil revenues, soaring car sales, more business for truckers, and greater mobility for travelers. The so-called "highway

trade" took off. Ray Krock opened his first McDonald's in 1955 in Des Plaines, Illinois, a suburb of Chicago. By 1960, Krock had awarded 228 franchises, boasting: "I put the hamburger on the assembly line." In Memphis, meanwhile, Kemmons Wilson unveiled the first Holiday Inn, featuring a restaurant, a swimming pool, and clean, air-conditioned rooms with free TV. Selling franchises by the hundreds, Wilson placed a Holiday Inn at virtually every highway exit and cloverleaf in the nation, giving travelers a comfortable night's sleep within a stone's throw of the interstate. Before long McDonald's golden arches and Holiday Inn's green neon lettering were among the most recognizable logos in America.

Opposing the Highway Act of 1956 was akin to opposing prosperity, progress, and national defense. A few social critics like Lewis Mumford expressed concern about the deterioration of urban centers, the stink of auto pollution, and the future of interstate rail service, but they were drowned out by the optimistic majority. As the prestigious *Architectural Forum* noted, America's new highway system was "the greatest man-made physical enterprise of all time with the exception of war."

Hungary and Suez

In the fall of 1956, at the height of the presidential campaign, foreign affairs took center stage. From Central Europe came a dangerous challenge to the Eisenhower-Dulles rhetoric about liberating nations from communist oppression. From the Middle East came a crisis that pitted the United States against its most loyal allies—Israel, England, and France.

Events in Europe that fall seemed to crush hopes for better Soviet-American relations. Following Stalin's death in 1953, Russian leaders called for "peaceful coexistence" between the communist bloc and "differing political and social systems." In 1956, Soviet Premier Nikita Khrushchev stunned the Twentieth Communist Party Congress in Moscow by denouncing Stalin's brutality and hinting at a relaxation of the Soviet grip on Central and Eastern Europe. His speech, meant to be secret, was obtained by the CIA and spread around the world.

The reaction was predictable. Protests flared throughout the Soviet bloc, demanding an end to Russian rule. In Warsaw, angry crowds sacked the Communist party headquarters, while in Budapest street battles escalated into full-scale civil war. Khrushchev was slow to respond. Unlike Stalin, he appeared reluctant to use military force. In the meantime, Hungarians overthrew the communist government and installed the popular Imre Nagy as premier.

The Hungarian revolt put Eisenhower on the spot. In 1952, his campaign rhetoric had blasted the Democrats for being "soft" on communism. From 1953 forward, his administration had vowed to "roll back" the communist wave, not simply to contain it. Now the time had come to put words into action by supporting the anticommunist freedom fighters in Hungary.

Yet Eisenhower refused to send American troops, or even to airlift supplies to the resisters, for fear of starting an all-out war with the Soviet Union. In October 1956, Russian tanks and troops stormed into Budapest to crush the revolt. For all of the administration's tough talk, "roll back" proved a sham. The United States had no intention of intervening in the areas under Soviet control.

At the very moment of the Hungarian revolt, another crisis erupted in the Middle East, a region of growing interest and concern to the United States. Though American policy supported the new State of Israel, it also recognized the strategic importance and economic power of Israel's Arab neighbors. In 1952, a young Egyptian military officer named Gamal Abdel Nasser had dramatically altered Middle Eastern politics by overthrowing the corrupt regime of King Farouk. As an Arab nationalist, Nasser steered a middle course between the Cold War powers, hoping to play off one side against the other. To the Egyptian people, he promised both the destruction of Israel and an end to British control of the Suez Canal.

The United States tried to woo Nasser with economic aid. It even agreed to finance his pet project, the Aswan Dam, a huge hydroelectric plant on the Nile River. But trouble arose in 1956, when Secretary Dulles withdrew the Aswan offer to protest Egypt's recognition of Communist China. Unable to punish the United States directly, Nasser did the next best thing by seizing the Suez Canal. His aim, in part, was to use the Suez revenues to finance the Aswan Dam.

The move could not be ignored. In 1955, Nasser had blockaded the Gulf of Aqaba, Israel's sole outlet to the Red Sea. Now he controlled the waterway that

linked Western Europe to its oil supply in the Middle East. On October 29, 1956, Israeli armor poured into the Sinai, routing Egyptian forces. Two days later, French and British paratroopers landed near Alexandria and easily retook the Suez Canal.

Eisenhower immediately condemned this invasion, furious that he hadn't been briefed in advance. At the very least, he believed, the attack undermined Western interests in the Middle East by forcing Egypt and other Arab states closer to the Soviet bloc. "I've just never seen such great powers make such a complete *mess* and *botch* of things," the president said of England and France. Fearing the worst, Eisenhower placed U.S. armed forces on full alert. If the Russians "start something," he warned, "we may have to hit 'em— and, if necessary, with *everything* in the bucket."

It never came to that. Privately, the White House pressured England, France, and Israel to withdraw. Publicly, the United States supported a U.N. resolution that denounced the invasion and called for negotiations regarding the canal. On November 6, a cease-fire was signed, ending the crisis but not the ill will.

Events in Hungary and Suez came in the midst of Eisenhower's 1956 reelection campaign. Expecting an easy victory, the president worried most about picking the proper running mate, a critical choice given his advanced age and questionable health. Eisenhower did not believe that Vice President Nixon was the best person to lead the nation in a crisis. "I've watched Dick a long time and he just hasn't grown," Ike told an aide. "So I just haven't honestly been able to believe that he is presidential timber."

In a private meeting, Eisenhower urged Nixon to trade in his vice-presidential hat for a cabinet post. Yet when Nixon resisted, the president backed down, fearing a backlash within Republican ranks. In November 1956, Eisenhower and Nixon trounced the Democratic slate of Adlai Stevenson and Senator Estes Kefauver by almost 10 million votes, a margin of victory even wider than in 1952. Nevertheless, the Democrats easily retained their majorities in both houses of Congress, demonstrating that Eisenhower, who accepted New Deal reforms as a permanent part of American life, remained far more popular than the political party he led.

President Eisenhower nationalized the Arkansas Guard and dispatched army paratroopers to escort black students to Little Rock's Central High School in the fall of 1957. Although reluctant to act, Eisenhower became the first president since Reconstruction to use military force to protect the constitutional rights of African Americans.

A SECOND TERM

Eisenhower returned to office on an optimistic note. Events in Hungary and the Middle East faded momentarily from view. *Time* magazine even praised the president for his moderation "in time of crisis and threat of World War III." The economy was strong, unemployment was low. The nation seemed confident, prosperous, and secure.

Confrontation at Little Rock

These good feelings did not last long. Throughout the South, opposition to the *Brown* decision was spreading, with some white Southerners interpreting Eisenhower's virtual silence on the issue as a sign that he supported their resistance to integrated schools. In 1956, more than a hundred congressmen from the former Confederate states issued a "Southern Manifesto" that vowed to resist court-ordered integration "by all lawful means." (Only three southern senators,

Albert Gore and Estes Kefauver of Tennessee and Majority Leader Lyndon Johnson of Texas, did not sign the document.) A year later, in Little Rock, Arkansas, Governor Orval Faubus triggered the inevitable confrontation between national authority and "states' rights" by defying a federal court order to integrate the all-white Central High School. First the Arkansas National Guard, and then a crowd of angry whites—spitting, cursing, and attacking reporters and photographers—turned away the nine black students.

As televised scenes of mob violence in Little Rock flashed around the world, President Eisenhower finally, but firmly, took command. Vowing to use "the full power of the United States . . . to carry out the orders of the federal court," he nationalized the Arkansas Guard and dispatched a thousand fully equipped army paratroopers to surround the high school and escort the black students to their classes. The soldiers remained for months, though peace was quickly restored. Ironically, Dwight Eisenhower became the first president since Reconstruction to protect the civil rights of African Americans through the use of military force.

The launching of Sputnik *in October 1957 raised serious doubts about America's military and technological superiority in the Cold War era.*

Sputnik *and Its Aftermath*

On October 4, 1957, the Soviet Union launched *Sputnik I* (or "traveling companion"), the first artificial satellite, weighing less than 200 pounds. The admiral in charge of America's satellite program dismissed *Sputnik I* as "a hunk of iron almost anybody could launch." But one month later, the Russians orbited *Sputnik II,* an 1,100-pound capsule with a small dog inside.

The news provoked anger and dismay. Americans had always taken for granted their technological superiority. Even the Soviet atomic bomb was seen as an aberration, most likely built from stolen U.S. blueprints. But *Sputnik* was different; it shook the nation's confidence and wounded its considerable pride. The feeling grew that America had become complacent in its affluence, and that danger lay ahead. "The time has clearly come," said an alarmed senator, "to be less concerned with the depth of the pile of the new broadloom or the height of the tail fin of the new car and to be more prepared to shed blood, sweat, and tears."

As expected, the nation's educational system came under withering fire. Critics emerged from every corner, bemoaning the sorry state of America's schools. In an issue devoted to the "Crisis in Education," *Life* magazine followed a sixteen-year-old Russian student and his American counterpart through a typical high school day. Alexi took difficult courses in science and math. He spoke fluent English, played chess and the piano, exercised vigorously, and studied four hours after class. Stephen, meanwhile, spent his day lounging through basic geometry and learning how to type. The students around him read magazines like *Modern Romance* in their English class. No one seemed to study. The end result, warned the *Life* editors, was a generation of young Americans ill-equipped "to cope with the technicalities of the Space Age."

The embarrassments continued. In December 1957, millions watched on television as the U.S. Navy's much-publicized Vanguard rocket caught fire on takeoff and crashed to the ground. (The newspapers dubbed it *"Flopnik"* and *"Kaputnik."*) A month later, the army launched a ten-pound satellite named

Explorer I aboard its new Jupiter rocket. Determined to calm public fears, President Eisenhower insisted that the United States was well ahead of the Soviet Union in nuclear research and delivery systems. But the people thought otherwise, especially after the Russians orbited a third satellite weighing almost 3,000 pounds.

In fact, however, Eisenhower was correct. His own information, not available to the public, made two vital points. First, the Russians *needed* more powerful missiles because the warheads they carried were heavier and cruder, owing to inferior technology. Second, the Soviets did not have enough intercontinental ballistic missiles (ICBMs) to counter America's huge lead in manned nuclear bombers. Put simply, the United States was in no real danger of being outgunned.

Eisenhower got this information from the CIA's U-2 spy planes, which crossed the Soviet Union at 70,000 feet. The U-2 flights were both secret and illegal, a clear violation of Russian air space. But the cameras on board, capable of picking up license plate numbers in the Kremlin's parking lot, provided American intelligence with a detailed picture of the Soviet war machine. Of course, the president could not speak candidly about Russian military power without also admitting the existence of these U-2 flights.

This was an awful dilemma. Critics now demanded expensive crash programs for weapons research, missile construction, and community "fall-out" shelters to protect against nuclear attack. Eisenhower vigorously opposed these programs, claiming that they undermined economic prosperity and threatened the "very values we are trying to defend." Using his exalted stature as general and war hero, he battled hard—and successfully—to keep military budgets stable during these years. Defense spending increased from $38 billion in 1957 to $41 billion in 1960, a tiny jump after inflation.

Still, the impact of *Sputnik* did not quickly disappear. For the first time, Americans started to view their educational system in terms of national security. This meant greater emphasis on science, mathematics, and foreign language study. In 1958, Congress passed the National Defense Education Act, which funded high school programs in these fields and college scholarships for deserving students. That same year, Eisenhower reluctantly endorsed the creation of the National Aeronautical and Space Agency (NASA), in response to overwhelming public pressure.

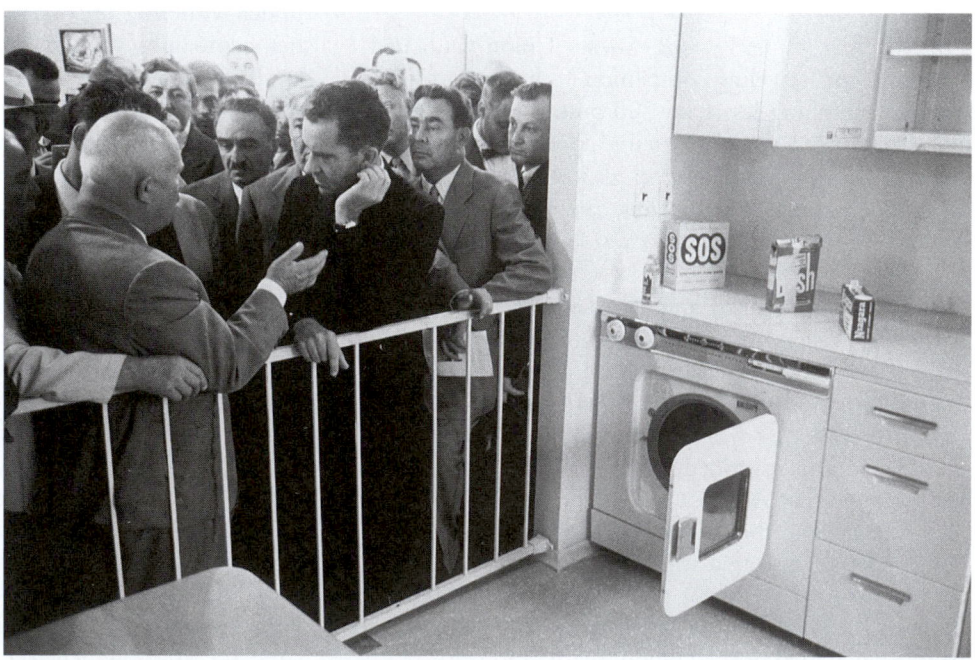

Vice President Nixon and Soviet Premier Khrushchev square off in the famous "kitchen debate" of 1959 in Moscow.

End of an Era

In November 1958, the Democrats won a smashing victory in the off-year elections, increasing their majorities in the House (282–153) and the Senate (62–34) to the largest level since 1936. *Sputnik* was partly responsible for this landslide, but so, too, was an economic recession in 1957 that lingered for the next two years. Determined to avoid the inflationary risks of increased federal spending, Eisenhower did little to counter a steady rise in unemployment and a sharp (if temporary) decline in the annual rate of economic growth. For the first time in his presidency, Eisenhower's public approval rating fell below 50 percent.

There were optimistic signs, however. In the summer of 1959, Vice President Nixon visited Moscow at Khrushchev's invitation to open a trade show featuring consumer products from Russia and the United States. In a bizarre but friendly confrontation, the vice president and the Soviet premier stood nose-to-nose in a "model" American kitchen, arguing the merits of their nation's electrical appliances. Looking grumpily at a self-loading dishwasher, Khrushchev asked: "Don't you have a machine that puts food in your mouths and pushes it down?" When he bragged that Russia would soon "come alongside America, salute her, and move ahead," Nixon responded that it was "better to compete in the relative merits of washing machines than in the strength of rockets." For an instant, the Cold War battlefield seemed a far different place.

Several weeks later, Khrushchev accepted President Eisenhower's invitation to visit the United States. The trip was a media circus. Khrushchev toured an Iowa farm and an IBM plant near San Francisco. At a Hollywood studio, he watched the filming of *Can-Can* and then, offended by the skimpy costumes, launched into a diatribe against capitalist "pornography." When his trip to Disneyland was canceled for security reasons, Khrushchev was furious. "What's wrong?" he yelled. "Do you have rocket launching pads there? Or have gangsters taken hold of the place?"

The trip ended on a hopeful note with a visit to the presidential retreat at Camp David, where Khrushchev and Eisenhower spent two days in leisurely conversation. They announced that Eisenhower would visit the Soviet Union in 1960 following a summit meeting of world leaders in Paris. The main issues, they agreed, were nuclear disarmament and the future of Berlin.

The summit meeting was a disaster. As he left for Paris in May 1960, Eisenhower learned that a U-2 spy plane was missing. A few days later, Khrushchev revealed that an American aircraft had been shot down deep inside the Soviet Union. Assuming that the pilot was dead, Eisenhower falsely described the U-2 as a weather research plane that had veered off course during a routine flight over Turkey. But Khrushchev then produced the pilot, Francis Gary Powers, frightened but very much alive.

At the summit, Eisenhower took full responsibility for the incident, but refused to apologize. Indeed, he justified the U-2 flights by insisting that Soviet espionage inside the United States was rampant and that U-2 photographs were essential to America's defense, given the closed nature of Russian society. In response, Khrushchev turned the summit into a tirade against Western "banditry," adding that Eisenhower was no longer welcome on Soviet soil.

The failure at Paris deeply wounded the president. In his "farewell address" to the people, he warned that years of Cold War tensions were sapping America's strength and concentrating too much power in the hands of "a military-industrial complex." Speaking boldly, at times sadly, he urged the people to be on guard against militarism and greed, and to reject a "live for today" mentality that had crept into American society, "plundering, for our ease and convenience, the precious resources of tomorrow." At risk, the president concluded, was "the loss of our political and spiritual heritage."

The Election of 1960

Who would lead the United States into the next decade? Unlike the predictable Eisenhower landslides of 1952 and 1956, the election of 1960 generated drama from the start. Both major candidates were tough, hard-driving campaigners. Both were born in the twentieth century—a political first—and both entered Congress in 1946 after serving as junior naval officers during World War II. But the similarities ended there.

Richard Nixon, the forty-seven-year-old vice president, grew up in modest circumstances. His Quaker parents ran a small grocery store in Whittier, California, near Los Angeles, where Nixon worked as a boy.

PRESIDENT EISENHOWER'S FAREWELL ADDRESS, JAN. 17, 1961

In the most quoted and best remembered speech of his eight year presidency, Dwight Eisenhower spoke about the future obstacles to individual liberty and world peace. While urging to Americans to remain vigilant in the struggle against communist expansion, he also raised concerns about the rise of "a military-industrial complex" and the erosion of national values based on sharing and trust.

We now stand ten years past the midpoint of a century that has witnessed four major wars among great nations. Three of them involved our own country. Despite these holocausts America is today the strongest, the most influential and most productive nation in the world. Understandably proud of this pre-eminence we yet realize that America's leadership and prestige depend, not merely upon our unmatched material progress, riches and military strength, but on how we use our power in the interests of world peace and human betterment.

Throughout America's adventure in free government, our basic purposes have been to keep the peace; to foster progress in human achievement, and to enhance liberty, dignity and integrity among people and among nations. To strive for less would be unworthy of a free and religious people. Any failure traceable to arrogance, or our lack of comprehension or readiness to sacrifice would inflict upon us grievous hurt both at home and abroad. . . .

A vital element in keeping the peace is our military establishment. Our arms must be mighty, ready for instant action, so that no potential aggressor may be tempted to risk his own destruction.

Our military organization today bears little relation to that known by any of my predecessors in peacetime, or indeed by the fighting men of World War II or Korea.

Until the latest of our world conflicts, the United States had no armaments industry. American makers of plowshares could, with time and as required, make swords as well. But now we can no longer risk emergency improvisation of national defense; we have been compelled to create a permanent armaments industry of vast proportions. Added to this, three and a half million men and women are directly engaged in the defense estab-

SOURCE   *Public Papers of the President, Dwight D. Eisenhower, 1960–1961,* no. 421.

Neighbors and classmates recalled him as serious and socially ill at ease. After graduating from Whittier College and Duke Law School, he married Patricia Ryan in 1940 and obtained his naval commission the following year.

Nixon's political rise was dramatic. As a new Republican congressman, he played a major role in the Alger Hiss case and then won a U.S. Senate seat in 1950 after accusing his Democratic opponent of being "soft on communism." As vice president from 1953 to 1960, Nixon emerged as the Republican party's most aggressive defender. While critics viewed him as a mean-spirited opportunist, supporters praised him as a rough-and-tumble young patriot.

John Kennedy took a different path to power. Born to wealth and privilege, he grew up in Boston, attended the finest private schools, and graduated from Harvard. His self-made millionaire father,

lishment. We annually spend on military security more than the net income of all United States corporations.

This conjunction of an immense military establishment and a large arms industry is new in the American experience. The total influence—economic, political, even spiritual—is felt in every city, every statehouse, every office of the federal government. We recognize the imperative need for this development. Yet we must not fail to comprehend its grave implications. Our toil, resources, and livelihood are all involved; so is the very structure of our society.

In the councils of government, we must guard against the acquisition of unwarranted influence, whether sought or unsought, by the military-industrial complex. The potential for the disastrous rise of misplaced power exists and will persist.

We must never let the weight of this combination endanger our liberties or democratic processes. We should take nothing for granted. Only an alert and knowledgeable citizenry can compel the proper meshing of the huge industrial and military machinery of defense with our peaceful methods and goals, so that security and liberty may prosper together. . . .

It is the task of statesmanship to mold, to balance, and to integrate these and other forces, new and old, within the principles of our democratic system—ever aiming toward the supreme goals of our free society.

Another factor in maintaining balance involves the element of time. As we peer into society's future, we—you and I, and our government—must avoid the impulse to live only for today, plundering, for our own ease and convenience, the precious resources of tomorrow. We cannot mortgage the material assets of our grandchildren without risking the loss also of their political and spiritual heritage. We want democracy to survive for all generations to come, not to become the insolvent phantom of tomorrow.

Down the long lane of the history yet to be written America knows that this world of ours, ever growing smaller, must avoid becoming a community of dreadful fear and hate, and be, instead, a proud confederation of mutual trust and respect. . . .

Happily, I can say that war has been avoided. Steady progress toward our ultimate goal has been made. But, so much remains to be done. As a private citizen, I shall never cease to do what little I can to help the world advance along that road. . . .

Joseph P. Kennedy, served as ambassador to England under Franklin Roosevelt. Preaching competition and excellence, Joseph Kennedy expected his oldest son, Joe, Jr., to become the first Catholic president of the United States. When Joe, Jr., died in combat during World War II, the torch was passed to John Kennedy, the next oldest son. In 1943, John barely escaped death himself after his PT boat was rammed by a Japanese warship in the South Pacific. Elected to Congress in 1946, and to the Senate in 1952, Kennedy did not excel as a legislator. In constant pain from his war wounds, he underwent delicate spinal surgery and then was diagnosed with Addison's disease, an adrenal malfunction that required daily doses of cortisone. While recuperating, Kennedy won the Pulitzer Prize for *Profiles in Courage,* an intriguing book, written almost entirely by his staff, about politicians who took brave but unpopular positions

Nixon and Kennedy revolutionized political campaigning with the first televised presidential debates in American history.

on the great issues of their time. To some critics, however, Senator Kennedy appeared to sidestep the great issue of his time, the censure of colleague Joseph R. McCarthy in 1954.

In 1956, Kennedy ran a close second to Estes Kefauver for the Democratic party's vice-presidential nomination. "You know, if we work like hell the next four years," Kennedy told an aide, "we will pick up all the marbles." Healthy once again, he traveled the country with his glamorous wife, Jacqueline, to line up presidential support. The crowds they drew were so large and adoring that reporters used the Greek word *charisma* to describe the growing Kennedy mystique.

The Republican convention nominated Richard Nixon on the first ballot. As expected, Nixon chose a moderate Easterner, Henry Cabot Lodge, Jr., of Massachusetts, to be his vice-presidential running mate. The Democratic convention was more dramatic. While also winning a first ballot victory, Kennedy surprised almost everyone by selecting Senator Lyndon

Johnson, a long-time rival, for the vice presidential slot. As a Texan with liberal instincts, Johnson was expected to help Kennedy in the South without hurting him in the North. "The world is changing," Kennedy proclaimed in his acceptance speech. "We stand today on the edge of a New Frontier."

The two candidates were evenly matched. Nixon campaigned on the eight-year Eisenhower record, reminding Americans that their nation was prosperous and at peace. Kennedy attacked that record without criticizing the popular Eisenhower by name. Portraying the United States as stagnant in a changing world, he promised new leadership "to get the country moving once again."

Kennedy had two main hurdles to overcome: religion and inexperience. No Roman Catholic had ever been elected president, a fact underscored by the crushing defeat of Al Smith in 1928. Religion became an open issue in the 1960 campaign after a group of Protestant ministers issued a statement questioning

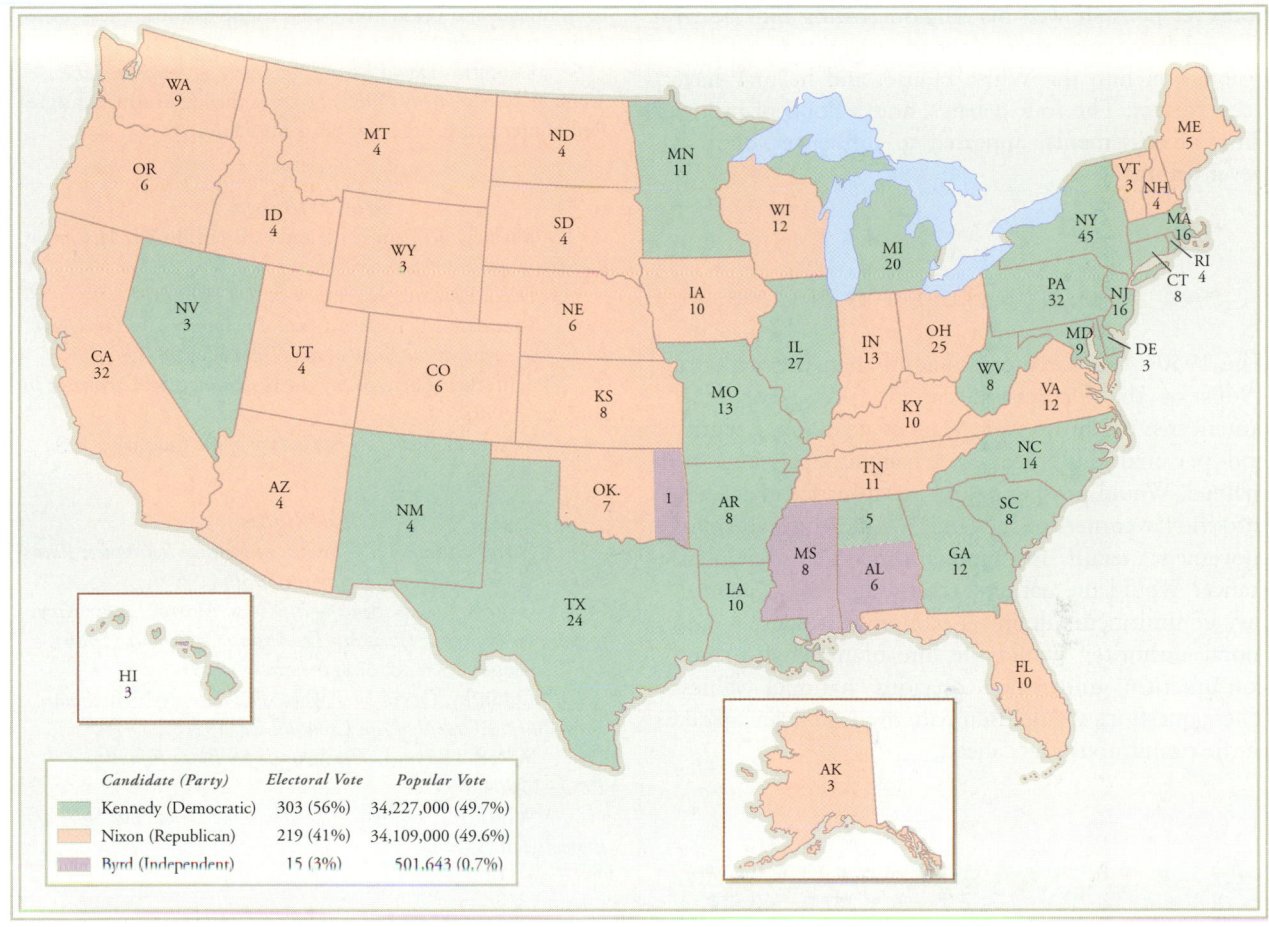

Candidate (Party)	Electoral Vote	Popular Vote
Kennedy (Democratic)	303 (56%)	34,227,000 (49.7%)
Nixon (Republican)	219 (41%)	34,109,000 (49.6%)
Byrd (Independent)	15 (3%)	501,643 (0.7%)

MAP 28.2 | THE ELECTION OF 1960

Kennedy's fitness to govern on the grounds that Roman Catholicism was "both a church and a temporal state." Kennedy confronted this issue in a powerful speech to a Baptist audience in Texas. Vowing to uphold the constitutional separation of church and state, he added: "If this election is decided on the basis that 40,000,000 Americans lost their chance of being president on the day they were baptized, then it is the whole nation that will be the loser in the eyes of history."

Kennedy's other hurdle—inexperience—was removed in a series of televised debates with Nixon that marked the beginning of modern presidential campaigns. The first debate had the greatest impact, as more than 80 million Americans watched on television or listened on radio. Though both candidates

spoke well, the difference lay in cosmetics and style. The handsome, well-groomed Kennedy radiated confidence and charm. Nixon, by contrast, seemed awkward and pale. The hot TV lights made him sweat profusely, smudging his makeup. Those who heard the debate on radio scored it a draw. Those who saw it on television thought Kennedy the clear victor.

Kennedy won the election with 303 electoral votes to Nixon's 219. Yet the popular vote was the closest since 1888, with Kennedy getting 34,227,000 (49.7 percent) and Nixon 34,109,000 (49.6 percent). A swing of several thousand votes in Texas and Illinois, where suspicions of ballot fraud were rampant, would have given the election to Nixon. Kennedy did well among traditional Democrats (minorities, urban dwellers, the working class), and swept the Catholic

vote, yet polls showed his religion costing him dearly in rural Protestant areas. Kennedy suspected that television won him the White House, and he may have been correct. The four debates, and a flood of prime-time advertisements, appeared to influence voters as never before.

⚬ C O N C L U S I O N ⚬

The 1950s were far more tranquil than the war-torn 1940s or the Depression-scarred 1930s. For most Americans, the fifties were years of economic security and personal fulfillment, yet nagging questions remained. Would prosperity and racial justice ever reach into the far corners of the land? Would the civil rights movement retain its momentum and nonviolent stance? Would the nation's expanding Cold War military commitments drain its economic strength—and moral authority? Would the lure of materialism and consumerism undermine precious national values? These questions would dominate the American agenda in the tumultuous years ahead.

RECOMMENDED READINGS

Barnouw, Eric. *Tube of Plenty: The Evolution of American Television* (1975) is an absorbing account of television's meteoric rise.

Biskind, Peter. *Seeing Is Believing: How Hollywood Taught Us to Stop Worrying and Love the Fifties* (1983) examines the way moviemaking shaped popular culture.

Branch, Taylor. *Parting the Waters: America in the King Years, 1954–1963* (1988) is a compelling history of the civil rights movement, focused through the lens of Dr. King's career.

Guralnick, Peter. *Last Train to Memphis: The Rise of Elvis Presley* (1994) traces the early years of rock 'n' roll's most popular artist and the reasons for his extraordinary success.

Halberstam, David. *The Fifties* (1993) offers an encyclopedic account of this decade, from McCarthyism to McDonalds.

Kahn, Roger. *The Boys of Summer* (1971) recalls the glory days of Major League baseball in a simpler time.

Kerouac, Jack. *On the Road* (1957) remains the bible of underground America, the Beat Generation of the 1950s.

May, Elaine. *Homeward Bound: American Families in the Cold War Era* (1988) ties the anxieties associated with anti-communism and the atomic bomb to the national quest for security and stability in the American home.

Oshinsky, David M. *A Conspiracy So Immense: The World of Joe McCarthy* (1983) explores the life of America's great Red hunter and the era that bears his name.

McCarthyism
Buckley, William F. Jr., and L. Brent Bozell, *McCarthy and His Enemies* (1954).

Fried, Richard. *Nightmare in Red* (1990).

Isserman, Maurice. *If I Had a Hammer. . . : The Death of the Old Left and the Birth of the New Left* (1987).

Schrecker, Ellen. *Many Are the Crimes: McCarthyism in America* (1998).

Whitfield, Steven. *The Culture of the Cold War* (1991).

Civil Rights
Bartley, Numan V. *The Rise of Massive Resistance: Race and Politics in the South During the 1950s* (1969).

Garrow, David. *Bearing the Cross: Martin Luther King, Jr., and the Southern Christian Leadership Conference* (1986).

Kluger, Richard. *Simple Justice* (1975).

Oshinsky, David M. *"Worse Than Slavery": Parchman Farm and the Ordeal of Jim Crow Justice* (1996).

Sitkoff, Harvard. *The Struggle for Black Equality, 1954–1980* (1981).

Whitfield, Stephen. *A Death in the Delta: The Story of Emmett Till* (1988).

Gender and Family Life
Chafe, William. *The American Woman: Her Changing Social, Economic, and Political Roles, 1920–1970* (1988).

Cowan, Ruth. *More Work for Mother: The Ironies of Household Technology from the Open Hearth to the Microwave* (1983).

Evans, Sara M. *Born to Liberty: A History of Women in America* (1989).

Hoy, Suellen. *Chasing Dirt: The American Pursuit of Cleanliness* (1995).

Kaledin, Eugenia. *Mothers and More: American Women in the 1950s* (1984).

Kessler-Harris, Alice. *Out to Work: A History of Wage-Earning Women in the United States* (1982).

Popular Culture
Carney, George, ed., *Fast Food, Stock Cars, & Rock 'n' Roll* (1995)

Horowitz, Daniel. *Vance Packard and American Social Criticism* (1994).

Jackson, John. *Big Beat Heat: Alan Freed and the Early Years of Rock & Roll* (1991).

Spotto, Donald. *Rebel: The Life and Legend of James Dean* (1996)

Stone, Joseph and Tim Yohn, *Prime Time and Misdemeanors: Investigating the 1950s T.V. Quiz Scandal* (1992).

Whyte, William. *The Organization Man* (1956).

Prosperity

Cray, Ed. *Chrome Colossus: General Moters and Its Times* (1980).

Galbraith, John Kenneth. *The Affluent Society* (1958)

Hart, Jeffrey. *When the Going Was Good!: American Life in the Fifties* (1982).

O'Neill, William. *American High: The Years of Confidence, 1945–1960* (1986).

Potter, David. *People of Plenty* (1954).

PASSAGES

W ho could have predicted the turmoil and tragedy of the 1960s? The previous decade, after all, gave scant warning that trouble lay ahead. Filled with powerful milestones, such as the National Highway Act and *Brown v. Board of Education,* the 1950s seemed to reflect the optimism and stability of a confident nation—a place of widely shared values and little public complaint. All was well in prosperous postwar America, or so it appeared.

The tumult of the 1960s came suddenly, without letup or relief. It began with the jailings and beatings of civil rights workers in the South, which turned many activists against the philosophy of nonviolence. The civil rights movement, in

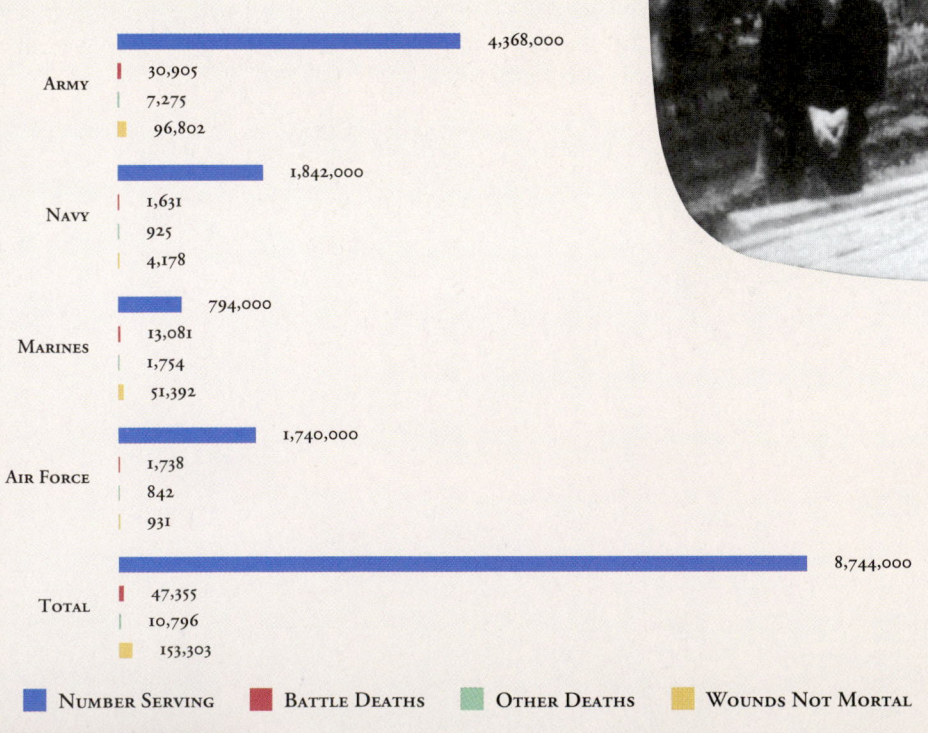

VIETNAM CONFLICT (1964–73)

ARMY
- 4,368,000
- 30,905
- 7,275
- 96,802

NAVY
- 1,842,000
- 1,631
- 925
- 4,178

MARINES
- 794,000
- 13,081
- 1,754
- 51,392

AIR FORCE
- 1,740,000
- 1,738
- 842
- 931

TOTAL
- 8,744,000
- 47,355
- 10,796
- 153,303

■ NUMBER SERVING   ■ BATTLE DEATHS   ■ OTHER DEATHS   ■ WOUNDS NOT MORTAL

turn, spawned a woman's movement, and then a student movement, which further challenged the *status quo*. Meanwhile, the escalating Vietnam War eroded the credibility of American officials and divided the nation in dangerous ways. Against the backdrop of increasing bloodshed in Southeast Asia, the United States endured a horrifying cycle of home-grown violence in the 1960s, including inner city riots, militant campus upheavals, and the assassination of prominent public figures like President John F. Kennedy, his brother Robert, and the Reverend Martin Luther King.

The 1970s brought little relief. An American president resigned from office for the first time in the nation's history. The North Vietnamese communists took over South Vietnam. Americans faced gas shortages, high unemployment, and staggering inflation. They watched with anger and embarrassment as their embassy in Iran was attacked and 52 Americans were held hostage for more than a year.

Republican Ronald Reagan won the 1980 presidential election by promising to reverse the nation's apparent decline. Mixing personal charm and optimism with the darker politics of resentment, he attracted mainstream voters by vowing to strengthen family values, reward hard work, and increase respect for America around the world. At the same time, he reinforced the notion among white working-class voters (known as "Reagan Democrats") that the party of Franklin Roosevelt had deserted their interests—that the real enemies of working people were no longer big business and the very rich, but rather big government and the very poor. During the 1980s, the Reagan Administration's policies regarding taxes, wages, unions, banking, and antitrust produced one of the most dramatic redistributions of wealth in American history, with the top one percent seeing its yearly income rise by 75 percent, while the rest of the nation experienced almost no gain at all. Nevertheless, Reagan remained a popular president, a politician who articulated the fears and dreams of Americans with extraordinary skill.

Through all the tumult of these decades, one certainty remained—the specter of international communism, centered in Moscow. Although the fear of domestic subversion stirred up by Senator Joseph McCarthy had largely subsided by 1960, the anxieties generated by Soviet power and influence remained solidly in place. During the 1960s, the United States and Russia tangled over Berlin and Cuba, where the placement of offensive missiles, ninety miles from the Florida coast, led to the most dangerous confrontation of the entire Cold War. In Vietnam, meanwhile, American officials defended the growing involvement as a test of will against Soviet-inspired aggression. The larger goals, they insisted, were to halt the spread of world communism and to maintain American credibility around the globe.

The 1970s brought an apparent thaw in U.S.-Soviet relations. The two sides signed a momentous agreement limiting nuclear weapons known as SALT 1. President Nixon also visited the Soviet Union as well as Communist China, raising hopes for serious dialogue, or détente. It didn't happen. As Nixon freely admitted, his visit to China was intended, in large part, to drive a wedge between the Russians and the Chinese, the world's two leading communist powers. Furthermore, the very idea of negotiating with the Soviet Union over issues such as human rights and arms control offended hard-line anticommunists who believed that American military power must largely determine the outcome of the Cold War. In the 1980 presidential campaign, Ronald Reagan promised a much tougher stand against communism in the future.

The Reagan administration dramatically increased the nation's defense budget. It also funded military campaigns against leftist rebels and Marxist governments in Africa, Asia, and Latin America. In one instance, it funneled money from a secret arms deal with Iran to illegally finance a right-wing guerilla army in Nicaragua. President Reagan made no apologies for this activity. The Soviets had created an "Evil Empire," he declared, and it had to be destroyed.

National Expenditures for Health Care, 1960–94

Total expenditures in billions of dollars

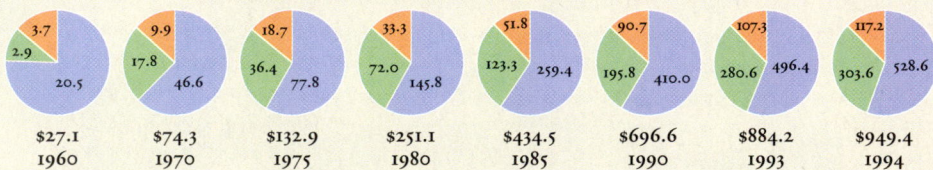

| $27.1 1960 | $74.3 1970 | $132.9 1975 | $251.1 1980 | $434.5 1985 | $696.6 1990 | $884.2 1993 | $949.4 1994 |

Total expenditures per capita amount

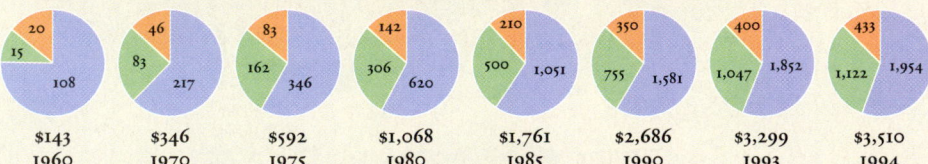

| $143 1960 | $346 1970 | $592 1975 | $1,068 1980 | $1,761 1985 | $2,686 1990 | $3,299 1993 | $3,510 1994 |

Total expenditures percent distribution

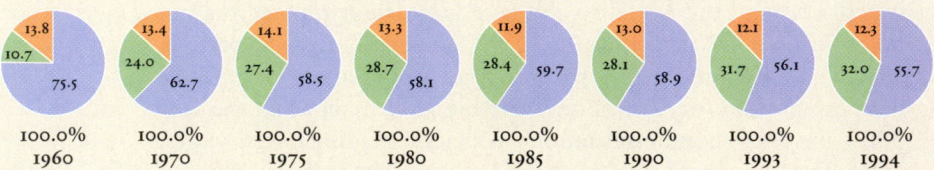

| 100.0% 1960 | 100.0% 1970 | 100.0% 1975 | 100.0% 1980 | 100.0% 1985 | 100.0% 1990 | 100.0% 1993 | 100.0% 1994 |

National health expenditures percent of GDP

| 5.3% 1960 | 7.4% 1970 | 8.3% 1975 | 9.3% 1980 | 10.8% 1985 | 12.6% 1990 | 13.9% 1993 | 13.7% 1994 |

■ PRIVATE   ■ PUBLIC–FEDERAL   ■ PUBLIC–STATE AND LOCAL

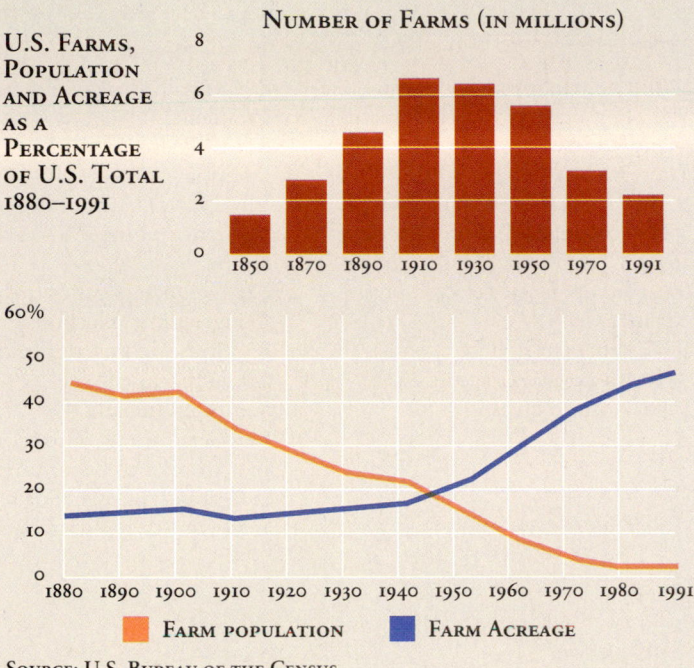

U.S. FARMS, POPULATION AND ACREAGE AS A PERCENTAGE OF U.S. TOTAL 1880–1991

NUMBER OF FARMS (IN MILLIONS)

FARM POPULATION   FARM ACREAGE

SOURCE: U.S. BUREAU OF THE CENSUS

In fact, that empire was already in trouble. Assuming power in 1985, Soviet Premier Mikhail Gorbachev well understood the problems his nation faced. Believing that communism must become more democratic and market-oriented in order to survive, he encouraged the policies known as glasnost (openness) and perestroika (restructure). In trying to save communism, however, Gorbachev set in motion the very forces that would bring it down. A wave of protest swept through Eastern Europe, demanding more freedom and closer contacts with the West. Unlike Hungary in 1956 and Czechoslovakia in 1968, the Soviet Union did not rush in troops to restore order. On a trip to West Berlin in 1987, President Reagan encouraged the protesters by demanding: "Mr. Gorbachev, tear down this wall." In 1989, the communist governments in Eastern Europe fell like dominoes—Hungary, Poland, Czechoslovakia, East Germany, Romania. It was one of those rare instances, noted *Time* magazine, "when the tectonic plates of history shift beneath men's feet, and nothing after is quite the same."

In 1991, the Soviet Union collapsed, and Russians began the painful transition to democratic politics and a free market economy. For the United States, meanwhile, a new set of challenges emerged. As the world's only remaining "super power," it now faced a post-Cold War era marred by ethnic violence in the Balkans, tribal warfare in Africa, military aggression in the Middle East, nuclear proliferation in India and Pakistan, and continuing human rights violations from Latin America to China. In addition, a booming world birthrate and the specter of global warming raised serious environmental concerns, while the rapid spread of technology and information linked people together in truly remarkable ways. During the 1990s, the president who faced these issues, Bill Clinton, saw the economy achieve unprecedented levels of prosperity and the lingering problem of the budget deficits eased dramatically. Yet good times at home did not mean political calm. The Republicans regained control of the House of Representatives in 1994 for the first time in four decades and a second term for Clinton seemed doubtful. Yet he won again in 1996, only to face impeachment charges arising from a sex scandal in 1998. Despite his acquittal in 1999, his presidency ended under a cloud. Peacekeeping in the Balkans, rising tensions with

China, and violence at home were all concerns that would face the next president in 2001. As the millennium approached, America's leadership remained crucial in a rapidly changing world.

| | 1960 | 1968 | 1970 | 1978 | 1980 |

POLITICS & DIPLOMACY

1960: John Kennedy elected president
1961: Berlin Wall erected
1962: Cuban missile crisis
1963: President Kennedy assassinated
1964: President Johnson elected by record margin
Landmark Civil Rights Act passed
1965: U.S. troop levels exceed 100,000 in Vietnam
Malcolm X assassinated
1967: Anti-war protests multiply
1968: Tet Offensive
Martin Luther King assassinated in Memphis
Robert Kennedy assassinated in Los Angeles
Richard Nixon elected president

1970: U.S. troops invade Cambodia
1972: President Nixon visits mainland China
Watergate burglary
1973: Vice President Agnew resigns
1974: President Nixon resigns
1975: South Vietnam falls
1976: Jimmy Carter elected president
1977: Panama Canal treaty
1978: Camp David accords
1979: Hostage crisis in Iran

1980: Ronald Reagan elected President
1981: Reagan survives assassination attempt
Sandra Day O'Connor becomes first woman appointed to Supreme Court
1982: Democrats gain seats in Congressional elections
1983: Strategic Defense Initiative (SDI) proposed
Invasion of Grenada
1984: Geraldine Ferraro becomes first woman to be nominated for vice president by major party
Reagan wins sweeping reelection

SOCIAL & CULTURAL EVENTS

1961: Freedom Rides
1962: Students for a Democratic Society formed
1963: Betty Friedan publishes *The Feminine Mystique*
1964: Beatles tour the United States
1965: Race riot in Watts
1966: National Organization for Women formed
1967: Haight-Ashbury "Summer of Love"
1968: Cesar Chavez leads California grape strike
Anti-war protests disrupt Democratic National Convention

1969: Woodstock music festival
1970: College protesters killed at Kent State and Jackson State
1973: Abortion legalized
1974: Anti-busing protests in Boston

1981: AIDS epidemic begins in United States
1982: Vietnam War Memorial dedicated in Washington
David Letterman show premiers on NBC late night
1983: Sally Ride first American woman in space
1984: Summer Olympics in Los Angeles

ECONOMICS & TECHNOLOGY

1960: Oral contraceptive marketed
1962: John Glenn orbits the earth aboard *Friendship 7*
1969: Apollo moon landing

1973: Arab oil embargo triggers energy crisis
1979: Nuclear accident at Three Mile Island

1981: Reagan tax cut package adopted
Air traffic controllers strike
1982: Recession ends
Budget deficit exceeds $100 billion for first time
1983: Social Security Reforms adopted
1984: Macintosh computer introduced
1985: President Reagan signs Gramm-Rudman-Hollings act to reduce government spending

1985: Mikhail Gorbachev becomes leader of Soviet Union
1986: Democrats regain control of Senate
Iran-Contra Scandal begins
1987: Nomination of Robert Bork to Supreme Court defeated
1988: George Bush wins presidential election over Michael Dukakis on "no new taxes" pledge
Berlin Wall torn down
1990: Iraq invades Kuwait
Bush abandons "no new taxes" pledge
1991: Persian Gulf War brings Iraq's ouster from Kuwait
Clarence Thomas-Anita Hill controversy erupts
1992: Bill Clinton defeats George Bush and Ross Perot in presidential race

1993: Branch Davidians besieged in Waco, Texas, which results in fiery confrontation
Clinton's deficit-reduction plan passes Congress by a single Democratic vote in Senate
1994: Republicans regain control of House of Representatives for first time in 40 years
1995: Bombing in Oklahoma City kills more than 160 people; fears about militias aroused
Republicans force government shutdown
Settlement of Bosnian conflict reached at Dayton, Ohio
1996: Clinton and Bob Dole wage presidential contest
Clinton reelected to second term

1997: Balanced budget agreement reached
1998: Clinton sex scandals break
President impeached by House of Representatives in December
1999: Clinton acquitted by Senate
NATO launches air war against Serbia over treatment of Albanians in Kosovo
School massacre in Littleton, Colorado sets off debate about violence and gun control
Air war against Serbia ends successfully

1985: Rock Hudson dies of AIDS
1986: *Challenger* Space Shuttle explodes
1987: Scandals engulf televangelist ministry of Jim and Tammy Faye Bakker
1988: Anti-depressant drug Prozac introduced
1989: Actresses Bette Davis and Lucille Ball die
Oil tanker Exxon Valdez goes aground in Alaska causing environmental damage
1990: Hubble Space telescope launched

1991: Basketball star Magic Johnson reveals that he is HIV positive (AIDS virus)
1992: Vice President Dan Quayle attacks single mother premise of sit-com *Murphy Brown*
1993: Author Toni Morrison wins Nobel Prize for literature
1994: O.J. Simpson murder trial grips nation
Death of Jacqueline Kennedy Onassis
1995: Simpson's acquittal sparks national furor
1996: Jazz singer Ella Fitzgerald dies
Virginia Military Institute admits women

1997: Movie *Titanic* sets all-time box office record for receipts
Princess Diana killed
Spice Girls group has top pop album "Spice"
1998: Singer Frank Sinatra dies
Slugger Mark McGwire hits 70 home runs for all-time record
1999: Death of baseball star Joe DiMaggio
Michael Jordan (basketball) and Wayne Gretzky (hockey) retire from professional sports
Star Wars, Episode I, The Phantom Menace opens to long lines and critical panning

---

1986: Tax Reform Act passed
1987: Stock market closes about 2000 on Dow Jones, but loses 508 points on the index in October in a single day
1988: U.S., Canada arrive at free trade agreement
President Bush approves $300 billion plan to bail out savings and loan industry
1990: American dependence on foreign oil reaches historic high
1991: Economy enters recession that will last until late 1992
1992: Unemployment reaches 7.8 percent, the highest since 1983

1993: United States and Europe agree on new terms for General Agreement on Tariffs and Trade (GATT)
Clinton administration proposes national health care plan
North American Free Trade Agreement (NAFTA) approved in Congress
1994: Clinton health care plan dies in Congress
1995: Budget battle in Congress produces closing of Federal Government in December
1996: Congress passes sweeping welfare reform bill

1997: Unemployment rate in May falls to 4.8 percent, the lowest since 1973
Budget surplus reported and future surpluses are projected
1998: Dow Jones average closes above 9,000 in April
1999: Dow Jones hovers around 11,000 in May
United States has strongest economy in world as 20th century draws to a close, but stability of world financial system is still a concern

ENTERING THE NEW FRONTIER

President Kennedy delivered a stirring inaugural address on a cloudless, bitter-cold afternoon in January 1961.

Chapter 29

THE TURBULENT YEARS,
1961–1968

THE 1960S OPENED on an ambivalent note. The gross national product reached $500 billion for the first time, yet talk of economic recession was in the air. The darkest days of McCarthyism were over, yet the fear of communism remained. The development of new products and technologies bred optimism, yet the spread of new weapons caused alarm.

Hints of protest and trouble had begun to appear. In Greensboro, North Carolina, four black college students sat down at a Woolworth lunch counter and were denied service, but refused to leave. Word of their defiance triggered "sit-in" protests across the South, with demonstrators bravely confronting Jim Crow. At this very moment, half a world away, supporters of North Vietnam's communist ruler Ho Chi Minh announced the formation of a National Liberation Front to overthrow the anticommunist government of President Ngo Dinh Diem in South Vietnam. President Diem did not seem concerned. With U.S. support, he boasted, his forces would quickly subdue these "Viet Cong" (or Vietnamese Communists) and bring peace to his land.

EARLY TESTS

The 1960 election was a landmark event in American political history. At age forty-three, John Kennedy became the first Catholic president, the youngest candidate to win a presidential election, and the first president to be born in the twentieth century. His inauguration on January 20, 1961, seemed to herald a new era of idealism, commitment, and change. Marian Anderson sang the national anthem, Robert Frost recited one of his poems, and Kennedy declared that the "torch has been passed to a new generation of Americans," adding: "Ask not what your country can do for you; ask what you can do for your country."

Idealism and Caution

The new administration appeared to mirror these words. Young people converged on Washington with a fervor reminiscent of the early New Deal years. Public

CHRONOLOGY

1961 Bay of Pigs invasion fails

East Germany erects Berlin Wall

Peace Corps established

1962 Cuban Missile Crisis sparks nuclear confrontation

War on poverty is formulated

Students for a Democratic Society (SDS) is organized

1963 Martin Luther King, Jr., delivers "I have a Dream" speech at Lincoln Memorial

United States and Soviet Union sign treaty banning above-ground nuclear tests

President Kennedy is assassinated; Lyndon B. Johnson becomes president

1964 Congress passes Gulf of Tonkin Resolution

Freedom Summer voting rights campaign begins in Mississippi

Congress passes landmark Civil Rights Act

President Johnson elected by record margin

1965 American ground troops sent to Vietnam, escalating commitment

Race riot erupts in Watts, Los Angeles

Congress passes Voting Rights Act

Malcolm X assassinated

1966 Black Panthers organized in California

U.S. combat deaths in Vietnam increase tenfold to 6,664

Antiwar protests spread to major state universities

1967 Race riots erupt in Detroit, Newark, and other cities

Thousands gather in Haight-Ashbury, San Francisco, for "Summer of Love"

1968 Communists launch Tet offensive in South Vietnam

President Johnson announces he will not seek reelection

Martin Luther King, Jr., is assassinated in Memphis

Robert Kennedy is assassinated in Los Angeles

Richard Nixon is elected president

---

service became a badge of honor. Kennedy's White House staff included fifteen Rhodes scholars and numerous Ivy League professors. The new secretary of state, Dean Rusk, came from the Rockefeller Foundation, while the new defense secretary, Robert McNamara, left the presidency of the Ford Motor Company to help "streamline" the nation's armed forces. When Kennedy chose his younger brother, Robert, to become attorney general, charges of nepotism filled the air. "I thought Bobby might as well get some experience," the president quipped, "before beginning the practice of law."

Under Jacqueline Kennedy's direction, the White House became a center for the arts. Cellist Pablo Casals performed at the Executive Mansion, as did the American Shakespeare Festival Theatre. At a function for the French writer André Malraux, President Kennedy offered a playful toast: "I am very glad to welcome here some of our most distinguished artists," he said. "This is becoming a sort of eating place for artists. But they never ask us out!"

Despite the lofty rhetoric and the fanfare, Kennedy took a measured approach to his early presidential duties, particularly in domestic affairs. For one thing, he lacked the huge popular mandate given to previous first-term presidents such as Franklin Roosevelt in 1932 and Dwight Eisenhower in 1952. For another, he worried about his relations with a Congress in which conservative Republicans and Southern Democrats held the balance of power. "There is no sense in putting the office of the Presidency on the line on an issue," he said, "and then being defeated."

Several of Kennedy's early initiatives were in the New Deal tradition. He worked successfully to increase Social Security benefits and to raise the minimum wage from $1 to $1.25. Yet the Congress easily blocked his efforts to provide health insurance for the aged and to create a cabinet-level Department of Urban Affairs. Worse still was the defeat of Kennedy's $2.3 billion education bill for school construction and higher teachers' salaries, which raised nagging questions about the federal role in education. Would funds be given to racially segregated public schools or to private religious schools? At first, Kennedy opposed parochial school assistance, fearing a political backlash. When his stand angered many Catholics in Congress, the president appeared to change his mind. Amid the confusion, the education bill died in committee.

In other areas, the new administration achieved success. By executive order, Kennedy launched the Peace Corps in March 1961, an idea modeled partly on Franklin Roosevelt's Civilian Conservation Corps. Directed by the president's brother-in-law, R. Sargent Shriver, the Peace Corps sent thousands of American volunteers to underdeveloped nations to provide educational and technical assistance. With a tiny budget, it became one of Kennedy's great triumphs, showcasing American idealism and knowhow throughout the world. Within three years, almost 10,000 volunteers were at work in forty-six countries, teaching school, staffing hospitals, and planting new crops.

Even more popular, though far more expensive, was the space program. Unlike Eisenhower, who opposed a costly "race to the moon with Russia," the new president viewed an American victory in this contest as essential to national prestige. Setting the goal of a manned moon landing "before this decade is out," Kennedy convinced a skeptical Congress to allocate billions of dollars for space research and rocketry, an astronauts training program, and a mission control center in Houston.

The "space race" captivated the world. In April 1961, Soviet Cosmonaut Yuri Gagarin orbited the globe in less than two hours. A month later, Commander Alan Shepard rocketed 300 miles from Cape Canaveral in a sub-orbital flight, and in February 1962, Lieutenant Colonel John Glenn orbited the earth three times aboard *Friendship 7* before touching down in the Caribbean. Glenn became a national hero, with ticker tape parades and a televised address before a joint session of Congress.

The Bay of Pigs

Kennedy inherited his first crisis from the previous administration. As president-elect, he was told of a secret plan, personally approved by Eisenhower, to overthrow the new Marxist government of Fidel Castro in Cuba. The plan called for several hundred anti-Castro exiles, trained and equipped by the CIA, to invade Cuba and trigger an anticommunist revolution.

Kennedy endorsed the plan for several reasons. He believed that Castro set a dangerous example by aligning Cuba with the Soviet Union and by expropriating the property of American corporations. Kennedy had promised to "get tough" with Castro during the 1960 campaign. He could not easily back down now.

On April, 17, 1961, a brigade of 1,500 waded ashore at the Bay of Pigs, on Cuba's southern coast. Nothing went as planned. The landing site had sharp coral reefs and swampy terrain, making it hard to unload supplies and move out from the beaches. Local workers quickly spotted the invaders, and news of their arrival sparked no popular uprising against Castro. Within twenty-four hours, the brigade was surrounded by troops loyal to his cause.

Kennedy refused to lend vital air and naval support to the brigade in a futile attempt to hide America's role in this disaster. More than a hundred invaders were killed, and 1,200 were captured. After reviewing the events with his advisors, Kennedy took a walk on the White House lawn. It was "the first time in my life," a friend recalled, "that I ever saw tears come to his eyes."

The Bay of Pigs fiasco left a troubled legacy. On the one hand, it angered other Latin American governments and drove Castro even closer to the Russian embrace. On the other, it fueled Kennedy's interest in covert operations and his desire to control them more directly. After removing long-time CIA Director Allen Dulles, the president approved a top-secret program, code-named Operation Mongoose, to topple the Cuban government and assassinate its leaders. Its plans included the destruction of Cuba's vital sugar crop, and a box of exploding cigars for Castro.

Most important was the public reaction. Rather than hurting Kennedy, the incident marked him as a man of action, willing to take chances in the war against communism. Opinion polls gave him higher ratings after the Bay of Pigs than at any other point in his presidency. "It's just like Eisenhower," he quipped. "The worse I do the more popular I get."

Fidel Castro assesses the military situation near the Bay of Pigs landing site in April 1961.

The Berlin Wall

In June 1961, Kennedy met with Soviet leader Nikita Khrushchev in Vienna. Khrushchev tried to bully the new president, threatening to give East Germany full control over road and rail access to West Berlin, in violation of previous guarantees. Berlin was both a danger and an embarrassment to Khrushchev. The prosperous Western sector stood as a model of democratic capitalism behind the Iron Curtain. Each day, more than a thousand refugees from the communist side poured into West Berlin. At this rate, East Germany would lose most of its skilled workers to the West.

Kennedy was not intimidated. Calling West Berlin "the great testing place of courage and will," he declared that NATO forces would defend the city at all costs. To emphasize this point, the president tripled draft calls, mobilized reserve units, and requested $3 billion in additional defense appropriations, which Congress quickly granted. Kennedy also recommended the building of backyard fallout shelters, suggesting that families could survive an atomic war if they were well-prepared.

The crisis ended in August 1961. As the world watched in amazement, workers in East Berlin constructed a wall of barbed wire and concrete around the western edge of their city, sealing off East Berlin, and eventually all of East Germany, from the noncommunist world. In a tactical sense, Khrushchev achieved his objective of stopping the East German exodus to the West. In a larger sense, however, the wall became an admission of failure—a monument to oppression and to freedom denied.

The Freedom Riders

Kennedy's first domestic crisis occurred in the field of civil rights. An integrationist at heart, the president wanted change to come slowly, without the mass protests and violent incidents that had made headlines around the world. He worried, too, that White House support for *immediate* desegregation would cost him the good will of powerful Southerners in Congress.

Yet, as Kennedy discovered, the real momentum for civil rights came from below. In 1961, the Congress of Racial Equality (CORE) announced plans to test a recent Supreme Court decision, *Boynton* v. *Virginia,* which prohibited racial segregation in bus terminals, train stations, and airports engaged in interstate transportation. CORE's objective, said its national director, was "to provoke the southern authorities into arresting us and thereby prod the Justice Department into enforcing the law of the land."

In May 1961, thirteen "freedom riders"—seven blacks and six whites—left Washington on a Greyhound bus bound for New Orleans. Most were veterans of the sit-ins. At each stop, they ignored the "white" and "colored" signs that hung by the toilets, lunch counters, and waiting rooms in defiance of federal law. The freedom riders met no resistance in the Upper South, but trouble erupted in Anniston, Alabama, when their bus was firebombed by a white mob. As the passengers struggled outside, they were beaten with fists and clubs. One rider suffered permanent brain damage from repeated blows to the head.

When the violence continued in Montgomery and Birmingham, Alabama, Attorney General Robert Kennedy urged CORE to end the freedom rides, claiming that they embarrassed President Kennedy on the eve of his summit with Premier Khrushchev. "Doesn't the attorney general know," a black Alabaman responded, "that we've been embarrassed all our lives?"

As new freedom riders arrived to replace the wounded, the Kennedy administration sent in federal marshals to protect them. It had no choice, given the violent scenes that flashed around the world. In September 1961, the federal government banned interstate carriers from using any terminal that segregated the races. After months of bloody struggle, the freedom riders prevailed.

The New Economics

Despite his increasing focus on civil rights, President Kennedy considered the economy to be his number-one domestic concern. Economic growth in the Eisenhower years had been steady, but increasingly slow. Though real wages for an average family rose a remarkable 20 percent in the 1950s, a series of recessions toward the end of Eisenhower's second term prompted both a drop in factory production and a rise in unemployment. By the time Kennedy took office, more Americans were out of work than at any time since the end of World War II.

In 1962, Kennedy unveiled an economic program that differed sharply from the spending model of the New Deal and Fair Deal. Relying on the advice of Walter Heller, chairman of his Council of Economic Advisors, he proposed a major tax cut for consumers and businesses, designed to stimulate purchasing power and encourage new investment. For Kennedy, the goal of full employment required sizable budget deficits in the short run as tax revenues declined. What

The human face of rural poverty in Appalachia, as exposed by Michael Harrington in The Other America.

TABLE 29.1	PERSONS BELOW POVERTY LEVEL: 1959–1969

	Number Below Poverty Level (in millions)			Percent Below Poverty Level		
Year	Total	White	Black and Other Races	Total	White	Black and Other Races
1969	24.3	16.7	7.6	12%	10%	31%
1968	25.4	17.4	8.0	13	10	33
1967	27.8	19.0	8.8	14	11	37
1966	28.5	19.3	9.2	15	11	40
1965	33.2	22.5	10.7	17	13	47
1964	36.1	25.0	11.1	19	15	50
1963	36.4	25.2	11.2	19	15	51
1962	38.6	26.7	12.0	21	16	56
1961	39.6	27.9	11.7	22	17	56
1960	39.9	28.3	11.5	22	18	56
1959	39.5	28.5	11.0	22	18	56

Note: The poverty threshold for a nonfarm family of four was $3,743 in 1969 and $2,973 in 1959.
SOURCE: Congressional Quarterly, *Civil Rights: A Progress Report*, 1971, p. 46.

worried him was the specter of inflation as the economy heated up.

To prevent this, Kennedy lobbied business and labor leaders to respect the wage-price guidelines his administration recommended to keep inflation in check. The major unions went along. The Teamsters, Auto Workers, and Steel Workers all agreed to modest wage hikes in 1962 with the understanding that their employers would not raise prices. Two weeks later, U.S. Steel, the nation's third largest corporation, announced a whopping price increase of six dollars a ton, leading other steel companies to do the same.

Calling the move an "irresponsible defiance of the public interest," Kennedy used his influence to roll back the price increase. Within days, the Justice Department threatened to investigate antitrust violations in the steel industry, while the Defense Department announced that it might not purchase steel from the "price-gouging" offenders. In private, Kennedy said: "My father always told me that all businessmen were sons-of-bitches, but I never believed it till now."

Under enormous pressure, the steel companies gave in. The president had won a major victory in his battle against inflation, although his rough tactics aroused deep anger in the business community. Nevertheless, the economy prospered in the early 1960s, achieving low unemployment, stable prices, and steady growth.

The nation's great wealth and prosperity, however, was not shared by all. This painful truth, largely obscured in a culture that celebrated abundance, was the subject of a pathbreaking book, *The Other America,* by socialist author Michael Harrington in 1962. While conceding that Americans, on average, were living better than ever before, Harrington exposed the grim face of poverty in urban slums and migrant labor camps, in Appalachian coal fields and dying rural towns. By his estimate, more than 40 million people—one-quarter of the American population—inhabited an "economic underworld" of joblessness, marginal wages, hunger, and despair.

President Kennedy's initial response to the problem of poverty was a familiar one. He believed that a strong economy, bolstered by government incentives, would provide most Americans with good jobs and material success. Yet Harrington's book, describing poverty as "a culture, an institution, a way of life" vir-

tually immune to business cycles and overall prosperity, helped to change the president's mind. After reading *The Other America,* Kennedy directed Walter Heller to prepare a memorandum on the root causes of poverty so that legislation could be framed to eliminate them. "First we'll have your tax cut," he told Heller, "and then we'll have my expenditure program."

SOCIAL AND POLITICAL CHALLENGES

Before long, President Kennedy's political caution began to ease. A year of trial and error led him to take more confident stands in certain areas, such as U.S.–Soviet relations and the push for civil rights. As events unfolded in 1962, the president faced challenges in familiar places—the Deep South and the waters off Cuba. This time, the stakes were much higher.

The Battle for Ole Miss

In the fall of 1962, a federal court ordered the admission of James Meredith, a black air force veteran, to the all-white University of Mississippi, known as Ole Miss. Governor Ross Barnett led the opposition. A virulent racist, who claimed that "God made the Negro different to punish him," Barnett had kept a previous black applicant from entering Ole Miss by having him committed to a mental hospital. Now Barnett invoked the doctrine of interposition—a throwback to antebellum times—by warning that Mississippi would ignore all federal rulings in order to keep segregation in place.

Kennedy responded to Barnett's challenge by dispatching several hundred federal marshals to Ole Miss. They were met by a well-armed mob, more than 2,000 strong. In the riot that followed, two people were killed and hundreds were injured, including twenty-eight marshals hit by gunfire. Like Eisenhower during the Little Rock crisis, Kennedy rushed in troops and federalized the State Guard. With 23,000 soldiers on campus—five times the student population—Meredith registered for classes under army bayonets. The battle at Ole Miss was over; the larger struggle for Mississippi lay ahead.

The Missiles of October

In October 1962, the world faced the most dangerous confrontation of the entire Cold War. It began with rumors, confirmed by U-2 spy plane photos, that the Russians were deploying Intermediate-Range Ballistic Missiles (IRBMs) in Cuba. Speed was essential, for the missiles would become operational in less than a month. Determined to manage this crisis from the White House, Kennedy convened an executive committee (known as ex-Comm) to provide a suitable response.

Castro's need for security was understandable. In addition to Operation Mongoose, the Kennedy administration had imposed an economic embargo on Cuba and engineered its expulsion from the Organization of American States. At Castro's urging, the Soviet Union sent thousands of military advisors to Cuba, as well as defensive missiles to shoot down invading planes. Yet the deployment of *offensive* weapons, capable of reaching Chicago or Washington with nuclear warheads, was an alarming escalation designed to tip the balance of terror in Moscow's favor.

Some ex-Comm members recommended immediate air strikes to take out the missile bases. Others, including Robert Kennedy, proposed a naval blockade of Cuba. The president carefully studied both options before choosing the latter. A blockade shifted the burden of responsibility to Khrushchev while allowing both sides to seek a solution short of war.

On October 22, 1962, Kennedy revealed the existence of the missiles in a nationally televised address. After describing the naval blockade, he demanded that Russia remove the IRBMs already in place. Any missile fired from Cuba, he warned, would be regarded "as an attack by the Soviet Union on the United States," requiring a "full retaliatory response." American forces went on full alert. FBI Chief J. Edgar Hoover revealed that Soviet diplomats at the U.N. were destroying sensitive documents in preparation for war. A U-2 plane over Cuba was shot down, and its pilot killed. The entire world watched anxiously as Russian vessels in the Caribbean inched closer to American warships enforcing the blockade.

On October 26, Kennedy received an emotional note from Khrushchev suggesting a settlement: Russia would remove its missiles if the United States pledged never to invade Cuba. Before the president could respond, however, a second note arrived demanding that the United States also remove its *Jupiter* missiles along

U-2 photos, such as this one, of missile bases being constructed in Cuba led to the most dangerous confrontation of the Cold War.

MEDIUM RANGE BALLISTIC MISSILE BASE IN CUBA

SAN CRISTOBAL

LAUNCH POSITION

MISSILE-READY TENTS

MISSILE ERECTORS

LATE OCTOBER

the Soviet border in Turkey. This new demand did not pose a security problem, since the *Jupiter* missiles were obsolete and about to be scrapped. Yet the president could not remove them without appearing to buckle under Soviet pressure.

Robert Kennedy provided the solution. Respond to the first note, he said, and ignore the second one. On October 27, the president vowed not to invade Cuba if the IRBMs were dismantled. In private, meanwhile, Robert Kennedy assured Soviet Ambassador Anatoly Dobrynin that the Jupiter missiles would be removed from Turkey in the near future. Kennedy also gave Dobrynin a deadline. If the Cuban missiles were not dismantled within forty-eight hours, the United States would destroy them.

On October 28, Khrushchev accepted the deal. The Soviet premier had badly miscalculated the stern American reaction to the placement of offensive missiles in Cuba, though his restraint in the crisis helped to assure a peaceful solution. Khrushchev soon left office in disgrace, while Kennedy's reputation soared.

For two weeks in October, the world seemed headed for nuclear war.

That fact alone seemed to sober both sides. In July 1963, a direct telephone link, known as the "hotline," was established between the White House and the Kremlin to help prevent similar crises from erupting. In August, the United States and Russia joined with ninety other nations to sign the "Treaty Banning Nuclear Weapons Tests in the Atmosphere, in Outer Space and Under Water." The treaty did not prevent underground testing or provide for on-site inspection, and several emerging atomic powers, such as France and China, refused to take part. Yet a first step had been taken to cleanse the environment of radioactivity—a symbolic step on the road to a safer world.

Trouble in Vietnam

President Kennedy came away from the missile crisis with greater confidence in his ability to manage for-

Quang Duc, a Buddhist monk in Saigon, burned himself to death in June 1963 to protest the crackdown on Buddhists by South Vietnamese President Ngo Dinh Diem. The Buddhist protests helped bring down the Diem government later that year.

eign problems. The Bay of Pigs seemed a distant memory as he surveyed the ever-changing international scene. His primary goal, in military terms, was to replace the Eisenhower-Dulles doctrine of "massive retaliation" with a "flexible response" policy that would maximize his options in any foreign crisis, from a standoff with Russia over Berlin to a struggle against Communist-led guerillas in the Third World. The plan called for a buildup in nuclear missiles, conventional ground troops, and Special Forces such as the "Green Berets." Not surprisingly, the defense budget rose rapidly in the Kennedy years, with Congress approving virtually all of the president's military spending requests. Under JFK, the armed forces added ten *Polaris* submarines, 200,000 ground troops, and 400 *Minutemen* missiles, giving the United States a sizable advantage over Russia in nuclear weapons.

When Kennedy entered the White House, American aid to South Vietnam topped $1 billion, and several hundred American military advisors were in the field. Like Eisenhower, Kennedy hoped to formalize Vietnam's temporary partition at the 17th parallel by turning the South Vietnamese regime of Ngo Dingh Diem into a military and economic power capable of defending itself against attacks from Ho Chi Minh's Communist government in the North.

Kennedy welcomed the challenge. Under the doctrine of "flexible response," U.S. Special Forces were dispatched to train South Vietnam's army, along with CIA personnel to direct covert operations and economic experts to supervise the aid programs intended to stabilize Diem's regime. Among the worst problems, it turned out, was Diem himself. Educated in the United States, a Catholic in a largely Buddhist land, Diem had little in common with the people he ruled. The South Vietnam he envisioned did not include the vital measures, such as land reform and religious toleration, that were needed to keep him in power.

In 1963, protests erupted in Saigon and other South Vietnamese cities over Diem's autocratic rule. The Buddhists held mass demonstrations against religious oppression, with several monks setting fire to themselves. As the protests escalated, army units attacked Buddhist temples and arrested their priests, sparking even greater protests from the Buddhist majority. Isolated in his presidential palace, Diem seemed oblivious to the crisis.

That fall, Diem was overthrown in a military coup engineered by South Vietnam's top generals. American officials knew about the coup, but did nothing to stop it. To their surprise, however, the generals murdered

Diem and his brother, Ngo Dinh Nhu, after taking them prisoner on the palace grounds. Kennedy was shaken by the news. "I had not seen him so depressed," an aide recalled, "since the Bay of Pigs."

By that time, 16,000 American troops were stationed in South Vietnam. For Kennedy and his advisors, the struggle had become a test of will against "communist aggression." Yet the president also worried that the use of American troops created a dangerous momentum of its own. "It's like taking a drink," he said. "The effect wears off and you have to take another."

THE RIGHTS REVOLUTION: EARLY STEPS

In the early 1960s, the fires of social and political protest slowly came alive, fanned by the civil rights movement and the New Frontier's vision of idealism and change. In 1962, as James Meredith challenged the once impenetrable wall of segregation at Ole Miss, a thirty-five-year-old Mexican American named Cesar Chavez moved to Delano, California, with his wife and eight children. A naval veteran of World War II, Chavez toiled in the plum orchards and strawberry fields of central California before turning to community organizing. With unshakable conviction, he aimed to better the lives of impoverished migrant farm laborers by uniting them under a single banner—the black Aztec eagle of the infant United Farm Workers Association.

The year 1962 also witnessed the publication of two path-breaking books about the underside of modern society: Harrington's *The Other America* and Rachel Carson's *Silent Spring.* Carson, a marine biologist, exposed the contamination of wildlife, water supplies, and farmland by pesticides such as DDT. Her book helped revive America's naturalist movement and bring environmental reform. In 1963, two more seminal works appeared: Betty Friedan's *The Feminine Mystique,* which spurred the struggle for women's rights, and James Baldwin's *The Fire Next Time,* which warned of the growing racial divide. "To be a Negro in this country and to be relatively conscious," wrote Baldwin, "is to be in a rage all the time."

From Birmingham to Washington

By 1963, racial injustice in America was a central issue, fueled by the intense media coverage of black protests and white reprisals. Birmingham, Alabama, became the new battleground, as a coalition of civil rights groups, led by Martin Luther King's Southern Christian Leadership Conference, attempted to break down the walls of discrimination in a city where African Americans had few economic opportunities or political rights. Birmingham was so rigidly segregated that a book featuring black rabbits and white rabbits eating together was removed from city libraries, and a campaign was underway to banish "Negro music" from "white" radio stations.

Dr. King hoped to integrate Birmingham with a series of nonviolent protests code-named "Project C," for confrontation. Using the local black churches as meeting houses, he recruited hundreds of followers with his revivalist appeals.

I got on my marching shoes!
Yes, Lord, me too.
I woke up this morning with my mind stayed on freedom!
Preach, doctor, preach!
I ain't going to let nobody turn me around!
Let's march, brother, we are with you!

The demonstrations challenged segregation on many fronts. There were sit-ins at lunch counters, kneel-ins at white churches, and voter registration marches to city hall. Boycotts were organized to protest the all-white hiring practices of downtown department stores, and pickets were posted at their doors. Birmingham authorities cracked down hard. Led by Commissioner Eugene ("Bull") Connor, city police dispersed the protesters—many of them school children—with attack dogs and high-pressure fire hoses.

Dr. King was among the hundreds arrested for violating local court orders against marching and picketing. From his jail cell, he defended the morality of civil disobedience, noting that "segregation statutes are unjust because segregation distorts the soul." President Kennedy offered firm support. After dispatching federal troops to Birmingham, he assisted in an agreement that integrated the city's lunch counters and department stores. At that very moment, however, Governor George C. Wallace—proclaiming "Segrega-

Led by Eugene ("Bull") Connor, Birmingham police used attack dogs and high-pressure fire hoses to disperse civil rights demonstrators.

tion Now! Segregation Tomorrow! Segregation Forever"—vowed to block the admission of two black students to the University of Alabama by "standing in the schoolhouse door." When federal marshals arrived, Wallace dramatically stepped aside.

The president's decisive action in Alabama signaled a major change. Viewing civil rights for the first time as a *moral* issue, Kennedy delivered a moving appeal for justice on national television. "One hundred years have passed since President Lincoln freed the slaves," he said, "yet their heirs, their grandsons, are not fully free. . . . And this nation, for all its hope and all its boasts, will not be fully free until all its citizens are free." Later that evening, civil rights activist Medgar Evers was assassinated outside his Jackson, Mississippi, home by a member of the Ku Klux Klan.

In June 1963, Kennedy sent Congress one of the most sweeping civil rights bills of the twentieth century. The bill, which prohibited discrimination in employment, federally assisted programs, and public accommodations such as restaurants and hotels, caused a furor on Capitol Hill. Southern legislators accused the president of "race-mixing," while others, including

Senator Barry Goldwater of Arizona, criticized him for abusing the "property rights" of business owners. As the bill's momentum stalled, a number of civil rights groups led by A. Philip Randolph, long-time president of the Brotherhood of Sleeping Car Porters, announced a "March on Washington for Jobs and Freedom."

On August 28, 1963, more than 200,000 people gathered at the Lincoln Memorial in the largest civil rights demonstration ever held on American soil. They listened to the spirituals of Mahalia Jackson, locked arms in solidarity as Joan Baez sang "We Shall Overcome," the anthem of the civil rights struggle, and rose in thunderous applause to the final words of Martin Luther King's now legendary address, "I Have a Dream."

When we let freedom ring, when we let it ring from every village and every hamlet, from every state and every city, we will be able to speed up that day when all God's children, black men and white men, Jews and Gentiles, Protestants and Catholics, will be able to join hands and sing in the words of that old Negro spiritual, "Free at last! Free at last! Thank God almighty, we are free at last!"

From the steps of the Lincoln Memorial, Martin Luther King, Jr., delivered his eloquent address, "I Have a Dream," to a gathering of 200,000 people who had come to Washington to push for passage of a landmark civil rights bill in August 1963.

Feminist Stirrings

The civil rights movement always possessed a strong female strain. From Rosa Parks in Montgomery and Daisy Bates in Little Rock to Ella Baker of the Student Nonviolent Coordinating Committee and Fannie Lou Hamer of the Mississippi Freedom Democratic party, women played a prominent role in the struggle for black equality. By 1963, the spirit of these protests created a sense of determination that sparked other movements, such as women's rights.

The revival of feminism in the 1960s seemed long overdue. More than four decades after winning the vote, American women played a minor role in govern-ment affairs. In 1963, there were no women gover-nors, cabinet officers, or Supreme Court justices. The U.S. Senate contained one female member, Margaret Chase Smith of Maine. Women comprised 51 percent of the population, but only 3 percent of state legisla-tors nationwide.

Discrimination also pervaded the workplace. Though more women were working outside the home in the early 1960s than ever before, they were increas-ingly concentrated in low-paying service and clerical jobs, despite their rising level of education. Fewer than 4 percent of the nation's lawyers, and 1 percent of the top business executives, were female. As a result, full-time working women earned about 60 percent of the income of men.

These inequities were highlighted in 1963 by the fi-nal report of the Presidential Commission on the Sta-tus of Women. Led by Eleanor Roosevelt (who died in 1962) and Esther Peterson, an assistant secretary of la-bor, the commission detailed a wide range of prob-lems, including job discrimination, unequal wages, lack of child care, and legal restrictions that prevented women, in some states, from sitting on juries or mak-ing wills. In direct response, President Kennedy issued an executive order banning sex discrimination in fed-eral employment. A few months later, Congress passed the Equal Pay Act of 1963, requiring employers to provide equal wages to men and women who did the same work.

Even more important in terms of the emerging women's movement was the publication of *The Femi-nine Mystique.* In the opening chapters, Betty Friedan described "the problem that has no name," the empti-ness felt by middle-class women who sacrificed their dreams and careers to become the "happy homemak-ers" of suburban America. Blaming educators, adver-tisers, social scientists and government officials for creating a climate in which femininity and domesticity went hand in hand, Friedan concluded that "we can no longer ignore that voice in women that says: 'I want something more than my husband and my chil-dren and my home.'"

The Feminine Mystique became an instant best-seller because it voiced the unspoken feelings of so many women. Their unhappiness was not caused by individual neuroses, Friedan argued, but rather by a set of cultural values that oppressed women while pre-tending to improve their lives. The message, she added, was that women must grasp their common problems in order to solve them.

TRAGEDY AND TRANSITION

By the fall of 1963, the fast pace and rapid changes of the new decade were leaving their mark. A growing economy, an emerging rights revolution, an expanding war in Southeast Asia, a frantic race to the moon— each would serve to reshape the fabric of American life in the years ahead. First, however, tragedy intervened.

Dallas

In late November 1963, John and Jacqueline Kennedy traveled to Texas on a political fence-mending tour. The 1964 presidential race was approaching, and Texas, which had narrowly supported the Kennedy–Johnson ticket three years before, could not be taken for granted. After greeting friendly crowds in Fort Worth, the Kennedys took a motorcade through Dallas, with the bubble-top of their limousine removed on a warm and cloudless day. Along the route, people waved from office buildings and cheered from the sidewalks. As the procession reached Dealy Plaza, shots rang out from the window of a nearby book depository. President Kennedy grabbed his neck and slumped to the seat. Texas Governor John Connally was wounded in the back. The motorcade raced to Parkland Hospital, where the president was pronounced dead.

Within hours, the Dallas police arrested a twenty-four-year-old suspect named Lee Harvey Oswald. Two days later, Oswald was shot and killed in the basement of Dallas police headquarters by Jack Ruby, a local nightclub owner with a shady past. These shocking events led many Americans to conclude that Oswald was innocent or that he did not act alone. Dozens of theories surfaced about the Kennedy assassination, blaming leftists and rightists, Fidel Castro and the Mafia, the Ku Klux Klan and the CIA. The most logical theory, that a deranged man had committed a senseless act of violence, did not seem compelling enough to explain the death of a president so young and full of life.

Few events in the nation's history produced so much bewilderment and grief. Charming and handsome, a war hero with a glamorous wife, Kennedy seemed the ideal president for the electronic political age. The media likened his administration to Camelot, a magical place (and a 1960s Broadway musical starring Richard Burton and Julie Andrews) that symbolized courage, chivalry, and hope. His tragic

Moving through the streets of Dallas, President Kennedy's limousine headed toward Dealy Plaza—and tragedy—on November 22, 1963.

death added the further dimension of promise unful-filled.

The reality was rather different, of course. Kennedy's 1,037 days in office were marked by failures as well as successes, and his leadership was more deci-sive in foreign policy than it was in domestic affairs. Since his death, moreover, evidence of his extramarital affairs and other personal shortcomings have raised le-gitimate questions about his character and morality. Still, the president's final months were his most pro-ductive by far. The Test Ban Treaty offered hope for a safer world, and a new civil rights bill had been sent to Capitol Hill. There is also the suggestion—disputed by some—that Kennedy was rethinking his position on Vietnam. "If I tried to pull out completely now," he told Senator Mike Mansfield, "we would have an-other Joe McCarthy red scare on our hands, but I can do it after I'm reelected. So we had better make damned sure that I am reelected."

The trip to Dallas shattered those hopes and plans.

LBJ

Within hours of the assassination, Lyndon Johnson took the presidential oath of office aboard _Air Force One,_ with his wife Lady Bird and Jacqueline Kennedy standing at his side. As the nation mourned its fallen leader, President Johnson vowed to continue the pro-grams and policies of the Kennedy administration. "All I have," he told a special session of Congress, "I would gladly have given not to be standing here to-day."

Lyndon Baines Johnson—known as LBJ—bore little resemblance to the president he replaced. Born in the Texas hill country in 1908, Johnson came from a different region, a lower social class, and an older po-litical generation. After graduating from a public col-lege, he worked in the Washington office of a Texas congressman before returning home to become state director of the National Youth Administration, a New Deal agency that provided work-study funds for needy high school and college students. Under Johnson's leadership, the Texas NYA became a model for the na-tion, providing employment for blacks and whites in the construction of neighborhood playgrounds and roadside parks. The experience turned him into an avid New Dealer, with confidence in the government's ability to help people in need. Johnson described Franklin Roosevelt, his mentor and role model, as "like a daddy to me."

Lyndon Johnson provided a smooth transition by promising to continue the programs and policies of President Kennedy. Yet retaining Kennedy's key advisors served to limit Johnson's options, particularly in foreign affairs.

In the following years, Johnson won a seat in Con-gress, served as a naval officer during World War II, and became a U.S. senator in 1949. (His margin of victory, a mere eighty-seven votes, earned him the nickname "Landslide Lyndon.") Elected Senate major-ity leader by his Democratic colleagues in the 1950s, Johnson worked efficiently with the Eisenhower White House to craft important legislation on defense spend-ing, highway construction, and civil rights. "Before you do anything," Johnson liked to say, "your last thought ought to be, 'I've got to live with the son of a bitch.'"

LBJ lacked the good looks and regal charm of John Kennedy. He seemed crude and plodding by compari-son, with his heavy drawl, cowboy boots, and earthy language. Yet few people in Washington knew more about the political process—how things really got done. Johnson understood the federal bureaucracy and recognized the true pockets of power. He knew when to flatter, when to bully, and when to bargain. Incredi-bly ambitious and hard working—he survived a near-fatal heart attack in 1955—Johnson entered the

White House with three decades of political experience under his belt.

Tax Cuts and Civil Rights

The new president moved quickly to restore public confidence through a smooth transition of power. To calm mounting suspicion of conspiracy, he appointed a seven-member commission, headed by Chief Justice Earl Warren, to investigate the Kennedy assassination and issue a report. To provide stability in the executive branch, he convinced Secretary of State Dean Rusk, Secretary of Defense Robert McNamara, chief economic advisor Walter Heller, and other key officials to remain at their jobs. Where Kennedy had proclaimed "Let us begin," Johnson added "Let us *continue*!"

One of his first acts as president was to work for the tax cut that Heller and Kennedy had supported. To please fiscal conservatives in Congress, Johnson agreed to slash the federal budget. He believed that lower taxes would spur economic growth and lower unemployment, thereby increasing federal revenues down the road. In February 1964, Johnson signed a measure that cut taxes by $10 billion over the next two years.

The economy responded. With more money available for investment and consumption, the gross national product shot up 7 percent in 1964 and 8 percent the following year, while unemployment fell below 5 percent for the first time since World War II. Furthermore, the economic boom generated even greater federal revenues—just as Johnson had predicted. This good fortune allowed him to fund important social programs in the future.

Within weeks after taking office, the president met with Martin Luther King, Jr., and other black leaders to assure them of his commitment to civil rights. This was essential, for Johnson's public record was mixed. As a young senator, he had opposed virtually all of President Truman's civil rights initiatives, including an anti-lynching bill, abolition of the poll tax, and creation of the Fair Employment Practices Commission (FEPC). Yet as majority leader, he had helped pass legislation giving the Justice Department more authority to enforce school integration and protect black voting rights. In his heart, Johnson considered segregation to be an immoral system that retarded an entire region's advancement. "He felt about the race question much as I did," a Texas friend recalled, "namely that it obsessed the South and diverted it from attending to its economic and educational problems."

The civil rights bill had strong public backing outside the South. In February, the House of Representatives easily approved it by a vote of 290 to 130, but the bill hit a wall in the Senate, where southern opponents used the filibuster to prevent its passage. The bill's success depended on a vote for cloture, ending debate, which required the agreement of two-thirds of the Senate. Working together, Senators Hubert Humphrey (D-Minnesota) and Everett Dirksen (R-Illinois) gathered bipartisan support. The Senate voted for cloture on June 10, 1964 (ending a seventy-five-day filibuster), and passed the bill the following afternoon. Described by the New York *Times* as "the most far-reaching civil rights [legislation] since Reconstruction days," it withheld federal funds from segregated public programs, created an Equal Employment Opportunity Commission, and outlawed discrimination in public accommodations, such as theaters, restaurants, and hotels. Furthermore, a last-minute lobbying effort by Senator Margaret Chase Smith and other women's rights supporters added another category— "sex"—to the clause in Title VII that prohibited employment discrimination based on race, creed, or national origin. What seemed like a minor addition became a powerful asset to working women in the future.

President Johnson signed the bill into law on July 2, 1964. Though compliance came slowly, the Civil Rights Act marked a vital turning point in the struggle for equal rights. Citing Victor Hugo, Senator Dirksen declared that "no army can withstand the strength of an idea whose time has come."

Landslide in 1964

LBJ entered the 1964 presidential campaign on a tidal wave of popularity and good will. His early months in office were blunder-free. The nation prospered, Vietnam appeared as a distant blip on the screen, and the only war on Johnson's public agenda was the one against poverty, which he promised to wage—and win—after his expected victory at the polls.

The summer of 1964, however, offered signs of the trouble to come. In Mississippi, an attempt to register black voters by local activists and northern college students met violent resistance from white mobs. On June 21, three volunteers—James Chaney, Andrew Goodman, and Michael Schwerner—disappeared after inspecting the ruins of a fire-bombed black church.

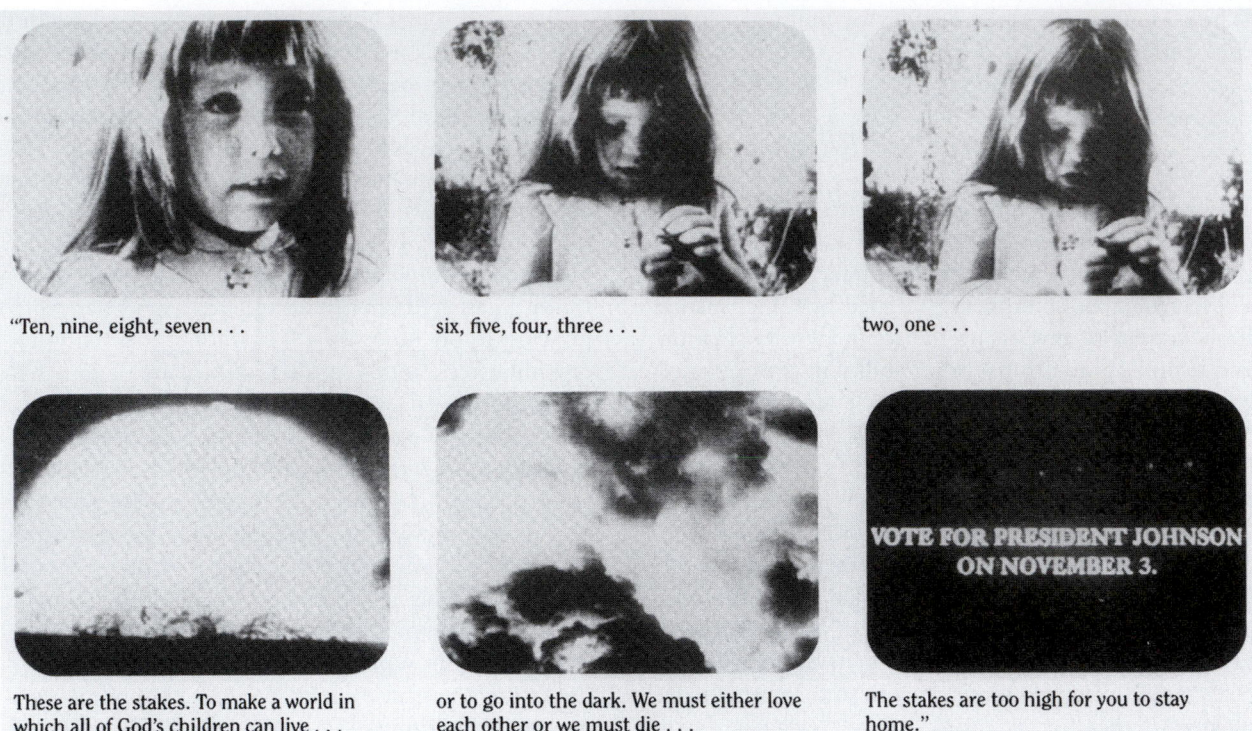

"Ten, nine, eight, seven . . .

six, five, four, three . . .

two, one . . .

These are the stakes. To make a world in which all of God's children can live . . .

or to go into the dark. We must either love each other or we must die . . .

VOTE FOR PRESIDENT JOHNSON ON NOVEMBER 3.

The stakes are too high for you to stay home."

During the 1964 presidential campaign, Democrats portrayed Republican candidate Barry Goldwater as an extremist who could easily plunge the nation into nuclear war. The infamous "Daisy Spot" brought so much protest that Johnson strategists pulled it after one airing.

Because Goodman and Schwerner were northern whites, the incident made the front pages of newspapers across the country. Five weeks later, FBI agents found three bodies buried in an earthen dam. The civil rights workers had been murdered by local Klansmen and police, seven of whom were eventually convicted and sent to jail.

Racial tensions that summer were not confined to the South. In July, a confrontation between residents and police officers in Harlem led to several nights of arson and looting. The trouble was followed by disturbances in the black neighborhoods of Philadelphia, Pennsylvania, Paterson, New Jersey, and Rochester, New York. At the Democratic National Convention in Atlantic City, moreover, the race issue took center stage. While the nomination of President Johnson and Senator Humphrey, his running mate, went smoothly, a floor fight erupted over the seating of two rival Mississippi delegations—one composed of state party segregationists; the other representing the biracial Mississippi Freedom Democratic party (MFDP).

Led by Fannie Lou Hamer, the twentieth child of illiterate sharecroppers, the MFDP spoke for the disenfranchised black majority in Mississippi. "I was beaten till I was exhausted," Hamer told the national convention. "All of this on account we wanted to register, to become first class citizens. If the Freedom Democratic party is not seated now, I question America."

Johnson hoped to compromise. Acting through Senator Humphrey, he offered the Freedom party two voting delegates and the promise of a fully integrated Mississippi delegation at future national conventions. The compromise pleased no one. Mrs. Hamer rejected it as a "token" gesture, while several white Mississippi delegates left Atlantic City in a huff.

When compared to Republican troubles, however, the split within Democratic party ranks seemed like a minor distraction. At the GOP National Convention in San Francisco, the simmering feud between moderates and conservatives boiled over, with delegates shouting down opponents with catcalls and boos. After bitter debate, the convention chose Senator Barry Goldwater of Arizona for the presidential nomination, and Representative William Miller of New York for the vice-presidential spot. In a defiant acceptance speech, Goldwater promised a "spiritual awakening"

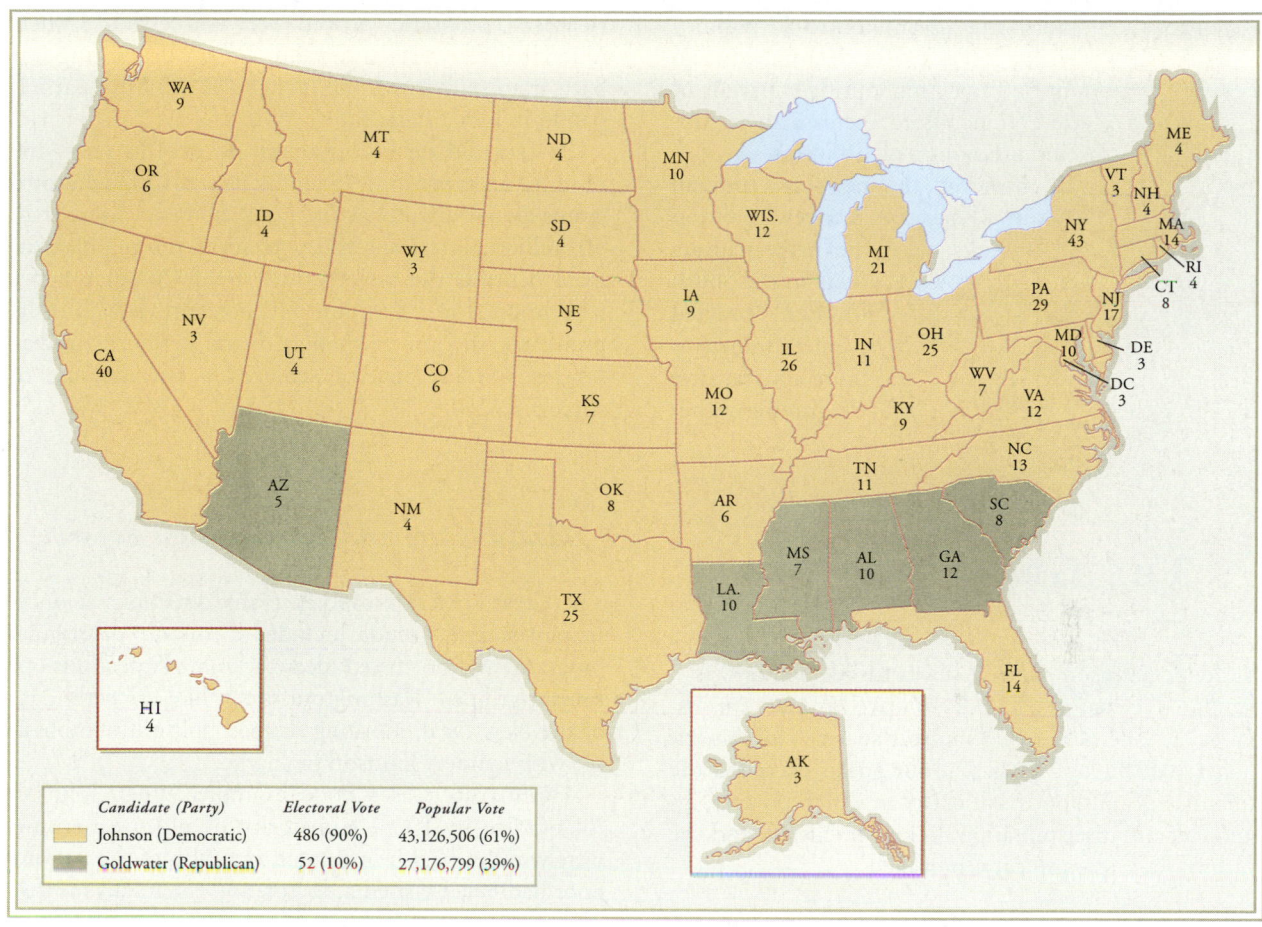

Candidate (Party)	Electoral Vote	Popular Vote
Johnson (Democratic)	486 (90%)	43,126,506 (61%)
Goldwater (Republican)	52 (10%)	27,176,799 (39%)

MAP 29.1 | THE ELECTION OF 1964

for America, adding: "Extremism in the defense of liberty is no vice. Moderation in the pursuit of justice is no virtue."

Goldwater opposed "big government" in domestic affairs, but supported large military budgets to deter "Communist aggression." His Senate record included votes against Social Security increases, the Nuclear Test Ban Treaty of 1963, and the Civil Rights Act of 1964. In contrast to Goldwater, President Johnson came across as the candidate of all Americans, with promises galore. "I just want to tell you this," he said of the Democratic package. "We're in favor of a lot of things and we're against mighty few."

Even in foreign affairs, his least favorite subject, Johnson appeared confident and controlled. In August 1964, two U.S. Navy destroyers, the *Maddox* and *C. Turner Joy*, engaged several North Vietnamese torpedo boats in the Gulf of Tonkin. The truth about this inci-

dent—Did a battle really occur? Who fired first? What were American warships doing in these waters?—was overshadowed by Johnson's dramatic response. First he ordered U.S. planes to bomb military targets deep inside North Vietnam. Then he requested—and received—a congressional resolution authorizing the president to "take all necessary measures" to repel "further aggression."

The Gulf of Tonkin Resolution gave Johnson the authority he would need to escalate the Vietnam War. During the 1964 campaign, however, he assured voters that nothing could be further from his mind. "We don't want American boys to do the fighting for Asian boys," he declared. "We don't want to get tied down in a land war in Asia."

The election was never in doubt. Johnson projected optimism and energy, while Goldwater appeared defensive and out-of-touch. The president won 61

percent of the popular vote (43 million to 27 million) and forty-four of the fifty states (486 electoral votes to Goldwater's 52). In addition, his lopsided margin of victory allowed the Democrats to increase their substantial majorities in both houses of Congress.

For Republicans, however, the news was not all bad. The election returns showed that a new coalition was forming in their ranks, with the party gaining strength among middle-class white voters in the South and Southwest. Furthermore, Goldwater attracted thousands of young recruits who were determined to reshape the Republican party along more conservative lines. For these legions, 1964 was a beginning rather than an end.

THE GREAT SOCIETY

President Johnson viewed his landslide victory as a mandate for change. Anxious to leave his mark on history, he spoke of creating "a great society" for Americans in which the "quality of our goals" exceeded the "quantity of our goods," a society in which poverty, ignorance, and discrimination no longer existed, and the spirit of "true community" prevailed.

Declaring War on Poverty

The centerpiece of Johnson's expansive vision was his "war on poverty," a concept that President Kennedy and his aides had explored shortly before his death. To maintain continuity, Johnson named R. Sargent Shriver, Kennedy's brother-in-law, to coordinate the numerous programs created by the Economic Opportunity Act of 1964, including the Job Corps, the Neighborhood Youth Corps, and Volunteers in Service to America (VISTA), a domestic service program modeled on the Peace Corps. Though Congress allocated $3 billion for these programs in 1965 and 1966, this figure would decline as the Vietnam War expanded. At no point did the cost exceed 2 percent of the federal budget.

The most controversial aspect of the "war on poverty" was its emphasis on "community action," which encouraged neighborhood groups to play an active role in federally funded projects. Some initiatives, such as food stamps and Head Start, a preschool en-

richment program, proved very successful. Others were cited for waste and fraud. Of greatest lasting impact, it appeared, was the increase of minority participation in local affairs.

Poverty did decline dramatically in this era—the result of an expanding economy as well as federal programs aimed directly at the poor. In 1960, more than 40 million Americans (20 percent of the population) lived beneath the poverty line; by 1970, that figure had dropped to 24 million (12 percent). For all of its problems, the much maligned and seriously underfunded war on poverty achieved a fair measure of success.

Health Care and Immigration Reform

The Great Society moved in many directions at once. Its jam-packed agenda included a mixture of original programs and borrowed ideas. A kind of infectious optimism gripped Washington, much like the early days of the New Deal. Nothing seemed politically impossible with Lyndon Johnson in charge.

Health care was a good example. When Johnson took office in 1963, a majority of older Americans were without health insurance, one-fifth of the nation's poor had never visited a doctor, and the infant mortality rate showed no signs of declining, despite the introduction of life-saving vaccines. Johnson believed that medical care for the poor and the elderly was an essential part of the Great Society. Yet the idea of federal involvement raised fundamental questions about the role of government in a free enterprise system. The American Medical Association (AMA) and private insurers strongly opposed such intervention, calling it "socialized medicine."

After months of intense lobbying, Congress passed the landmark legislation, known as Medicare and Medicaid, that Johnson requested. Medicare provided federal assistance to the elderly for hospital expenses and doctors' fees, while Medicaid extended medical coverage to welfare recipients through matching grants to the states. Both programs grew rapidly, reaching 40 million Americans by 1970. Though supporters pointed with pride to statistics showing both an increase in life expectancy and a drop in infant mortality, critics noted the exploding federal costs, the gaps in coverage, and the inferior quality of health care to the poor. Few government programs proved more con-

troversial and expensive to maintain than Medicare and Medicaid, and none would prove more difficult to reform.

The Great Society also included a new immigration law, passed in 1965. Though vitally important to the nation's future, it went largely unnoticed at the time. In one bold sweep, the Immigration Act removed the "national origins" quotas, as well as the ban on Asians, which dated back to 1924. While setting a ceiling of about 300,000 immigrants per year, the law permitted the family members of American citizens (both naturalized and native-born) to enter the United States without limit.

The impact was dramatic. Prior to 1965, Europe accounted for 90 percent of the new arrivals to the United States; after 1965, only 10 percent. By the mid-1970s, a majority of legal immigrants came from seven Asian and Latin American countries: Korea, Taiwan, India, the Philippines, Cuba, the Dominican Republic, and Mexico.

THE EXPANDING WAR

Lyndon Johnson inherited a rich agenda from the Kennedy White House, including the war on poverty and the push for civil rights. But nothing proved as important, or damaging, to his presidency as the conflict in Vietnam. When Johnson assumed office, there were fewer than 20,000 American "advisors" in that divided country, training the soldiers and bureaucrats of anti-Communist South Vietnam. Within three years, that number had risen to almost 500,000, with no end in sight. Vietnam quickly became Johnson's war, and, ultimately, his nightmare.

Point of No Return

Vietnam was part of a larger "containment" effort that guided American foreign affairs since the end of World War II. Indeed, the main architects of President Johnson's Vietnam strategy—Dean Rusk, Robert McNamara, and General Maxwell Taylor—were holdovers from the previous administration. Like Presidents Truman, Eisenhower, and Kennedy, LBJ based his com-

mitment to Vietnam on a series of powerful assumptions, such as saving "democracy" in Asia, halting the spread of communism, and maintaining America's credibility around the globe. It hardly mattered that South Vietnam was neither a democracy nor the victim of an international communist plot. What did matter was the need for strength and staying power in a world crisis—the belief that a defeat for the United States anywhere would undermine its standing everywhere.

Johnson understood the political stakes. "I am not going to lose Vietnam," he said. "I am not going to be the president who saw [it] go the way China went." His plan was to pressure the communist enemy in a measured fashion that would neither alarm the American public nor divert resources from his cherished domestic programs. The Gulf of Tonkin Resolution gave him the authority to move forward. The Viet Cong attack at Pleiku provided the motive.

Pleiku, a market town in the central highlands of South Vietnam, was home to a military air strip guarded by American Special Forces. In February 1965, a Viet Cong mortar barrage killed eight Americans and wounded more than a hundred. Several days later, U.S. war planes began the massive bombing of North Vietnam. Known first as Operation Rolling Thunder, the air strikes hit targets checked personally by President Johnson, who boasted that "they can't even bomb an outhouse without my approval." The problem, however, was that air power had little impact on North Vietnam's ability to wage war. The bombings killed thousands, flattened factories and power plants, and ravaged the economy; yet the flow of communist troops and supplies into South Vietnam never stopped.

In March 1965, two Marine batallions arrived at the huge new U.S. Air Force base in Da Nang, raising the American troop total in South Vietnam above 100,000. Using circular logic, Johnson explained that more soldiers were needed to protect the planes, while more planes were needed to provide air cover for the soldiers. In December, troop levels reached 184,000 and rose each month thereafter. Draft calls zoomed from 100,000 in 1964 to 340,000 by 1966, leading millions of young men to seek student deferments or to join the National Guard in the hope of avoiding combat in Vietnam.

By 1965, at least half of South Vietnam was controlled by Viet Cong or North Vietnamese troops. The new South Vietnamese government of General

Nguyen Van Thieu appeared more stable than previous ones, but its army was no match for the well-disciplined communist soldiers. As Johnson saw it, American forces would defend South Vietnam until its people were ready to defend themselves. "We will not be defeated," the president vowed."We will not withdraw."

American strategy in Vietnam had both a military and political objective: to wear down the enemy with superior firepower, and to "win the hearts and minds" of the South Vietnamese people. Neither proved successful. North Vietnam, a nation of 19 million, continued to field a large army despite enormous casualties, while the Viet Cong provided able support. Fighting on native soil, these soldiers waged relentless, often brutal war against a "foreign aggressor" and its "puppets" inside South Vietnam. Between 1965 and 1966, U.S. combat deaths rose tenfold, from 636 to 6,664.

Americans fought bravely, and morale at this point remained high. Yet the very nature of the war alienated these soldiers from the people they had come to defend. It would have been trying, under the best of circumstances, to distinguish between innocent civilians and Viet Cong. Unfamiliar with the language and culture of Vietnam, Americans increasingly viewed everyone as the enemy. Each village appeared as "a dark room full of deadly spiders," a soldier recalled. "The VC were everywhere all at once like spider cancer."

American planners tried numerous strategies to isolate the Viet Cong and deprive them of their sanctuaries. Most included the movement of peasant populations from their ancestral lands to "strategic hamlets" or to cities unprepared for the arrival of thousands of homeless refugees. Between 1960 and 1970, the percentage of South Vietnamese living in urban areas jumped from 20 to 43 percent—an increase five times greater than the average for other Third-World nations. In these bulging cities, jobs were scarce, prostitution flourished, and families split apart.

Those who remained in the countryside faced terror from all sides. There were North Vietnamese mortar attacks, Viet Cong assassination squads, and American assaults from the ground and the air. U.S. planes and helicopters defoliated the fields and forests with chemical sprays, and pounded suspected enemy strongholds with bombs and napalm (jellied gasoline). In one of the most telling remarks of the war, an American offi-cer explained his mission bluntly: "We had to destroy this town in order to save it."

Early Protests

Even as President Johnson escalated the war in 1965, he expected the Great Society to move freely ahead. A "rich nation can afford to make progress at home while meeting its obligations abroad," he declared. The United States could have both guns and butter; there was no need to choose.

For a time, his domestic agenda remained impressive. Fueled by the immense economic prosperity of 1965 and 1966, the Great Society added an Education Act that extended federal aid to public and private schools, and a Model Cities Act that provided funds to upgrade housing, health services, crime prevention, and parks. In addition, LBJ reaffirmed his commitment to civil rights by appointing the first African-American Supreme Court Justice, Thurgood Marshall, and the first African-American cabinet member, Robert Weaver, to head the new Department of Housing and Urban Development (HUD).

The momentum didn't last. The decision to escalate in Vietnam not only funneled money from the Great Society's domestic programs, it also divided the nation and sapped the president's strength. The first rumblings of antiwar protest came from the college campuses, where a new group, calling itself Students for a Democratic Society (SDS), was gaining ground. Formed in Port Huron, Michigan, in 1962, SDS issued a "Declaration of Principles" that denounced "racism" and "militarism," among other evils, and promised a new politics based on socialist ideals. Limited at first to "elite" colleges and major state universities, such as Harvard, Berkeley, and Wisconsin, the organization expanded in direct proportion to the war itself.

The early student leaders called their movement the "New Left." Some of them, known as "Red-diaper babies," were the children of "Old Left" radicals from the 1930s and 1940s. Others came from the burgeoning civil rights movement, with experience in organizing protests and a deep commitment to political change. At Berkeley, for example, it was Mario Savio, a veteran of the Mississippi struggle, who led the 1964 Free Speech Movement that triggered the mass student protests of this era. As Savio declared, "There

Tom Hayden, a founder of Students for a Democratic Society, played a major role in the growing protest movements of the 1960s.

is a time when the operation of the machine becomes so odious, makes you so sick at heart . . . that you've got to put your bodies upon the gears and upon the wheels, upon the levers, upon all the apparatus and you've got to make it stop."

Impatient and idealistic, these young radicals identified with the "revolutionary" movements of the emerging Third World. To their eyes, Fidel Castro and Ho Chi Minh were positive forces in history, representing a fundamental shift in power from the privileged elites to the struggling masses. Not surprisingly, Vietnam became the New Left's defining issue—a symbol of popular resistance to America's "imperialist" designs.

Early in 1965, antiwar students and faculty at the University of Michigan held the nation's first "teach-in" to discuss the consequences of escalation in Vietnam. The idea spread rapidly from campus to campus—with the University of Maine's teach-in attracting 300 people, and Berkeley's drawing more than 12,000. On Easter Sunday, a crowd of 30,000 attended the first major antiwar rally in Washington, sponsored by SDS. The speakers, including radical journalist I. F. Stone and folk singer Joan Baez, linked the Vietnam demon-

strations to other issues that were percolating within the larger society, such as civil rights, women's rights, and the role of universities in fostering protest and dissent.

THE RIGHTS REVOLUTION: CENTER STAGE

The national mood of unity and reconciliation that followed President Kennedy's assassination in November 1963 did not last much beyond the landslide election of 1964. The war in Vietnam created divisions that grew wider by the year. Americans became more skeptical of their leaders and less likely to believe official explanations of events. Furthermore, the expanding rights revolution of the 1960s raised the hopes of millions—and the fears of millions more. Even a master consensus-builder like Lyndon Johnson faced an overwhelming task.

Images of War in Folk Music: Pete Seeger Stirs up Controversy, 1967

By 1967, anti-Vietnam war songs and ballads had become a staple of growing protest movement, performed by groups and artists such as Bob Dylan, Creedence Clearwater Revival, and Peter, Paul, and Mary. Folk singer Pete Seeger captured the futility of America's Vietnam policy, and the stubborn refusal of President Lyndon Johnson to change course, in his withering folk song, "Waist Deep in the Big Muddy."

It was back in nineteen forty two,
I was part of a good platoon.
We were on maneuvers in Loosiana,
One night by the light of the moon.
   The captain told us to ford a river,
   And that's how it all begun.
   We were knee deep in the Big Muddy,
   But the big fool said to push on. . . .

The sergeant said, "Sir, with all this equipment,
No man will be able to swim."
"Sergeant, don't be a nervous nellie,"
The Captain said to him.
   "All we need is a little determination;
   Men, follow me, I'll lead on."
   We were neck deep in the Big Muddy
   And the big fool said to push on.

All of a sudden, the moon clouded over,
We heard a gurgling cry.
A few seconds later, the captain's helmet
Was all that floated by.

Voting Rights

Following passage of the landmark Civil Rights Act of 1964, the struggle for racial justice moved to the next battleground: voting rights in the Deep South. The campaign was already underway in places like Selma, Alabama, where local activists, facing intense white resistance, asked Martin Luther King, Jr., and his Southern Christian Leadership Conference for support.

The Selma demonstrations began early in 1965. Local blacks marched daily to the courthouse, where Sheriff Jim Clark—wearing a huge button with the single word NEVER—used force to turn them away. Thousands were arrested, beaten with clubs, and shocked with cattle prods for attempting to register with the local election board. In March, Dr. King decided to lead a protest march from Selma to Montgomery, the state capital, fifty miles away. "We are not asking, we are demanding the ballot," he declared.

On March 9—known as Bloody Sunday—a contingent of Sheriff Clark's deputies and Alabama state police attacked the marchers, sending seventeen to the hospital. Hundreds of civil rights leaders, entertainers, politicians, and clergy rushed to Selma to

The sergeant said, "Turn around men,
I'm in charge from now on."
And we just made it out of the Big Muddy
With the captain dead and gone.

We stripped and dived and found his body
Stuck in the old quicksand.
I guess he didn't know that the water was deeper
Than the place he'd once before been.
    Another stream had joined the Big Muddy
    Just a half mile from where we'd gone.
    We'd been lucky to escape from the Big Muddy
    When the big fool said to push on.

Well, maybe you'd rather not draw any moral;
I'll leave that to yourself.
Maybe you're still walking and you're still talking
And you'd like to keep your health.
    But every time I read the papers
    That old feeling comes on:
    We're waist deep in the Big Muddy and
    The Big Fool says to push on. . . .

Waist deep! Neck deep!
Soon even a tall man'll be over his head!
Waist deep in the BIG MUDDY!
AND THE BIG FOOL SAYS TO PUSH ON!!

SOURCE Steven Cohen (ed.) *Vietnam: An Anthology and Guide* (Knopf, 1983), 352–53.

(© 1967 Melody Trails, Inc. N.Y.)

lend their support, but the violence continued. James Reeb, a Unitarian minister from Boston, was beaten to death by a gang of whites, and Viola Luizzo, a civil rights activist from Michigan, was shot and killed by the Klan.

On March 15, President Johnson made a special trip to Capitol Hill to urge passage of a new voting rights bill. In the most eloquent speech of his career, Johnson said:

What happened in Selma is part of a larger movement which reaches into every section and state of America. It is the effort of Negroes to secure for themselves the full blessing of American life.

Their cause must be our cause, too. Because it is not just Negroes, but really it is all of us who must overcome the crippling legacy of bigotry and injustice.

And we shall overcome.

The Voting Rights Act, signed by President Johnson on August 6, profoundly altered the political landscape of the South. The new law abolished discriminatory practices such as the literacy test, and authorized federal examiners to register voters in seven Southern

TABLE 29.2
BLACK VOTER REGISTRATION

State	1960	1966	*Percent Increase*
Alabama	66,000	250,000	278.8
Arkansas	73,000	115,000	57.5
Florida	183,000	303,000	65.6
Georgia	180,000	300,000	66.7
Louisiana	159,000	243,000	52.8
Mississippi	22,000	175,000	695.4
North Carolina	210,000	282,000	34.3
South Carolina	58,000	191,000	229.3
Tennessee	185,000	225,000	21.6
Texas	227,000	400,000	76.2
Virginia	100,000	205,000	105.0

SOURCE: U.S. Bureau of the Census, *Statistical Abstract of the United States: 1982–83* (103d edition) Washington, D.C., 1982.

states. Within a year, almost 500,000 southern black voters signed up; within three years, a majority of African-American adults in Mississippi and Alabama were registered to vote. A full century after the abolition of slavery, the most fundamental right of citizenship was finally secured.

The Watts Explosion

Five days later, on August 11, a riot erupted in Watts, a black section of Los Angeles, triggering the worst urban violence since World War II. The disturbance began with the arrest of a black motorist by a white highway patrolman. A crowd gathered, police reinforcements arrived, and several arrests were made. As word of the incident spread, several thousand people—mostly young men—rampaged down Crenshaw Boulevard, looting stores, burning buildings, and overturning cars. The violence flared each evening for a week. It took 14,000 National Guardsmen to restore order. At least thirty-four people were killed, 1,000 injured, and 4,000 arrested, with property damage estimated at $200 million.

News of the riot shocked President Johnson. Like many Americans, he assumed that violent protests would be limited to racist southern whites. "We simply hadn't seen the warnings," recalled Attorney General Ramsey Clark. "We had looked at [civil rights] as basically a southern problem, but . . . in fact the problems of the urban ghettos exceeded any that we were dealing with in the South."

Times had changed. By 1965, almost half of America's black population lived outside the South, mostly in large cities, and Watts epitomized the conditions of day-to-day urban life. Good housing was scarce. As black neighborhoods became overcrowded, residents wishing to move elsewhere were trapped by racial discrimination. Inferior schools hampered upward mobility. Two out of three adults in Watts lacked a high school education, and one in eight was illiterate. Watts had the highest unemployment rate, and lowest income level, of any Los Angeles neighborhood except Skid Row. Two hundred of 205 policemen assigned to Watts were white. Crime was rampant, public services poor. "The sewers stank in the summer, there was not enough water to flush toilets, not enough pressure to fight fires," said one Watts resident. "The social fabric just couldn't stand the strain."

Some rioters targeted white businesses in Watts for arson and looting. The Los Angeles police, suspecting a radical plot, stormed the Black Muslim Temple and arrested fifty-nine people. Local residents knew better. The riot was a spontaneous event, not a planned act of destruction. In the next three years, hundreds of northern black neighborhoods would explode. The worst riots, in Newark and Detroit, would begin, as Watts did, with an incident between local blacks and white police.

Most African Americans deplored the riots and took no part. Yet a competing vision, far different from the one preached by Dr. King, was gathering strength in the black community. As he walked the streets of Watts after the riot, King met a group of youths shouting, "We won!" He asked how could anyone claim victory in the face of such violence and destruction? "We won," a young man answered, "because we made them pay attention to us."

Black Power

By the mid-1960s, Dr. King's leadership in the civil rights movement was increasingly under attack.

The Watts riot of 1965 began a cycle of urban destruction that engulfed dozens of cities in the coming years.

Younger African Americans, in particular, seemed reluctant to follow his course. At a 1966 rally in Mississippi, a recent Howard University graduate named Stokely Carmichael brought this issue to a head. Just released from jail for leading a peaceful civil rights protest, Carmichael vented his anger as a clearly uncomfortable Dr. King sat behind him on the stage. "This is the twenty-seventh time I've been arrested," Carmichael shouted, "and I ain't going to jail no more. The only way we gonna stop them white men from whuppin' us is to take over. What we gonna start saying now is 'Black Power.'" The crowd took up the chant: "Black Power! Black Power! Black Power!"

Black Power became a symbol of African-American unity in the mid-1960s, stressing group strength, independent action, and racial pride. In local communities, black activists lobbied school boards to add African-American history and culture to the curriculum. On college campuses, black students pressed administrators to speed up minority recruitment, establish Black Studies programs, and provide separate living quarters—a demand that alarmed integra-

tionists, black and white. In the political arena, Carl Stokes of Cleveland and Richard Hatcher of Gary, Indiana, became the first African-American mayors of northern cities by combining hard work with racial solidarity. Across the nation, black men and women donned African clothing, took on African names, and wore their hair unstraightened in an "Afro" style. "Black is Beautiful" became a powerful slogan in this era, as did "Say it loud, I'm black and I'm proud" by soul singer James Brown.

To militants like Stokely Carmichael, Black Power meant a political separation of the races. His position reflected a generational split between "old" civil rights groups such as the NAACP, which viewed racial integration as the key to black advancement, and "new" movement groups like Carmichael's Student Nonviolent Coordinating Committee (SNCC), which began to exclude whites. "Black people," said Carmichael, "must be seen in positions of power doing and articulating for themselves."

The separatist impulse had deep roots in the African-American community. Its renewed strength in

the 1960s was due, in large part, to a black nationalist movement that appealed to young people in the bleakest neighborhoods of urban America, far removed from civil rights and the Great Society. "There is a different type of Negro emerging from the the 18- to 25-year-old bracket," said a black leader in Watts. "They identify with Malcolm X's philosophy."

Malcolm X was the most popular and controversial Black Muslim leader of the 1960s. Born Malcolm Little, he joined the Nation of Islam while serving a prison term for robbery, and adopted the "X" to replace "the white slave-master name which had been imposed upon my paternal forebears by some blue-eyed devil." The Nation of Islam was a black nationalist group, organized in Detroit in 1931, which preached a doctrine of self-help, moral discipline, and

Malcolm X, the charismatic Black Muslim minister, preached a doctrine of black nationalism, self-help, and racial separation that held wide appeal for thousands of African Americans. He was assassinated by a rival Muslim group in 1965.

complete separation of the races. Its code of behavior, based on the rejection of racist stereotypes, stressed neatness, abstinence, and a firm division of male and female roles. Black Muslims were forbidden to smoke, drink alcohol, eat pork or cornbread, or have sex outside of marriage. "Wake up, clean up, and stand up," their motto declared.

Created by Elijah Poole, who renamed himself Elijah Muhammad, the Black Muslims were strongest in the urban ghettos, where their membership reached upwards of 100,000, with a far larger mass of sympathizers. Assigned by Elijah Muhammad to a temple in Harlem, Malcolm X became a charismatic figure to young black men, in particular, with his bold statements about the impact of white injustice on black behavior and self-esteem. "The worst crime the white man has committed," he said, "is to teach us to hate ourselves."

Malcolm also preached self-defense in language calculated to alarm moderates of all races. Attacking Dr. King as a "chump" and a "traitor," he mocked the nonviolent approach, saying that blacks must protect themselves "by any means necessary," and that "killing is a two-way street." Such rhetoric made it easy to label the entire Black Muslim movement as extremist, and to construe its message as one of violence and hate.

Malcolm created a public furor by describing the assassination of President Kennedy as an instance of "the chickens come home to roost." Expelled from the Nation of Islam by Elijah Muhammad, he traveled to Mecca on a spiritual pilgrimage and discovered, to his surprise, the insignificance of color in Islamic thought. This led him to form a rival Muslim group, the Organization of Afro-American Unity, which emphasized black nationalism in a manner that did not demonize whites. Assassinated in 1965 by followers of Elijah Muhammad, Malcolm became a martyr to millions of African Americans, some praising his militant call for self-defense, others stressing his message of self-discipline and self-respect.

Occasionally Black Power became a vehicle of rage and racial revenge. SNCC Chairman H. Rap Brown, for example, urged a crowd in Cambridge, Maryland, to "burn this town down," adding: "Don't love the white man to death, shoot him to death." And some went beyond rhetoric by forming terrorist groups like the Black Panthers to take their grievances to the streets.

Founded in 1966 by an Oakland, California, ex-convict named Huey Newton, the Panthers provided a

violent alternative to other black movements of this era. They became instant celebrities by parading through the state capitol building in Sacramento, armed with rifles and shotguns, to protest a bill that outlawed the carrying of unconcealed weapons. Portraying themselves as defenders of "oppressed" people against a "racist-capitalist police state," the Panthers demanded the release of all blacks from prison and the payment of "slave reparations" by whites.

Adept at self-promotion, the Panthers won modest support in black neighborhoods through their community work. With perhaps 5,000 members nationwide, most in the San Francisco Bay area, they ran food banks, health clinics, and preschool programs in run-down city neighborhoods. At the same time, however, Newton and his aides routinely engaged in extortion, drug dealing, and other criminal acts. Heavily armed, wearing black clothing and dark sunglasses, the Panthers became a feared enemy—and primary target—of law enforcement, including the FBI. At least twenty-eight members and eleven policemen were killed in shoot-outs and ambushes between these forces.

"Sisterhood Is Powerful"

The rights revolution of the 1960s included demands for sexual, as well as racial, equality. Both the Equal Pay Act of 1963 and the Civil Rights Act of 1964 were important steps in the battle against gender discrimination, yet progress had been slow. In the fall of 1966, a band of activists formed the National Organization for Women to speed the pace of change. As Betty Friedan recalled, "We all chipped in $5.00 [and] began to discuss names. I dreamed up NOW on the spur of the moment, which everybody seemed to like."

At NOW's first convention, the 300 delegates elected Friedan president and issued a statement endorsing "the world wide revolution for human rights taking place within and beyond our national borders." Never radical, NOW pursued its major goals—passage of an equal rights amendment and sexual equality in the workplace—through political means. Its leaders took pains to portray NOW as an organization *for* women, not of women, which welcomed male support.

NOW grew slowly. Its membership in 1970 totaled 15,000—mostly white, middle-aged, and middle-class. Yet NOW's impact upon the emerging women's movement was enormous, both in what it represented and what it seemed to lack. For many younger women, raised in the affluence of suburban America, the resurgence of feminism went beyond the fight for political and economic equality. What attracted them was the call for female solidarity—the power of sisterhood—in the larger struggle for sexual liberation.

Some of these women were veterans of the civil rights movement. Others worked for SDS and were

Betty Friedan attends the second NOW convention in 1967. At her side is Dr. Kathryn Clarenbach, who chaired the convention.

active in the antiwar protests on college campuses. While deeply committed to these causes, they discovered that sexism—the assumption of male superiority—also existed in organizations devoted to justice and equal rights. Thus, women found themselves thankful for the skills and self-confidence they had developed, yet resentful of their expected roles as cooks, secretaries, and sexual objects. When asked what positions women filled in his organization, Stokely Carmichael brought roars of male laughter by noting: "The position of women in SNCC is prone."

Committed to equal rights, adept at organizing, and determined to confront sexism on all fronts, these "new feminists" developed strategies and communities of their own. As women's liberation emerged in the mid-1960s, feminist study groups appeared, along with feminist newspapers, health clinics, and bookstores. The more radical elements, viewing men as the enemy, opposed heterosexual relationships, denounced marriage as "legal whoredom," and regarded the nuclear family as a form of female slavery. While rejecting such notions, liberal feminists also struggled with the dilemma of how to achieve greater power and fulfillment in a male-dominated culture.

The new feminism met immediate resistance—and not only from men. Surveys of American women in the 1960s showed both a growing sensitivity to issues of sex discrimination, and a strong distaste for "women's lib." Most housewives expressed pride in their values and experiences, and resented the "elitism" of the feminist movement—the implication that outside employment was more fulfilling than housework, or that women degraded themselves by trying to appear attractive to men. As the country artist Tammy Wynette sang: "Don't Liberate Me, Love Me." A long and difficult struggle lay ahead.

The Counterculture

The emerging radicalism of America's youth in the 1960s had both a cultural and political base. Bound together with civil rights, women's rights, and the antiwar protests was a diffuse new movement, known as the counterculture, which challenged traditional values on an unprecedented scale. To many young people, the counterculture symbolized personal liberation and generational strength—a break with the humdrum, hollow world of adults. As Bob Dylan put it,

Come mothers and fathers
Throughout the land
And don't criticize
What you can't understand
Your sons and daughters
Are beyond your command
There's a battle
Outside and it's ragin'
It'll soon shake your windows
And rattle your walls
For the times they are a-changin'.

In 1965, a San Francisco journalist used the term "hippie" to describe a new breed of rebel—passionate, spontaneous, and free. Like the Bohemians of the early 1900s and the Beats of the 1950s, the hippies defined themselves as opponents of the dominant culture, with its emphasis on competition, consumerism, and conformity. By rejecting such "empty values," they tapped into a seam of youthful alienation so brilliantly portrayed in Mike Nichols's *The Graduate* and Paul Simon and Art Garfunkel's "Sounds of Silence." Unlike the "uptight" nine-to-five crowd, the hippies wore their hair long, dressed in jeans and sandals, and sought a "higher consciousness" through experimentation and uninhibited living.

The counterculture offered numerous attractions. Many young people embraced its free-flowing nature, the absence of hard-and-fast rules, the chance to try out new arrangements and ideas. A few joined communes, explored ancient religions, studied astrology, or turned to the occult. Far more pervasive was the sexual freedom, the vital new music, and the illegal drug use that marked these turbulent times.

The counterculture did not begin the sexual revolution of the 1960s. That process was already underway, fueled by the introduction of oral contraceptives in 1960, the emergence of a women's rights movement, and a series of Supreme Court decisions that widened public access to "sexually explicit" material. The counterculture played a different but equally important role by challenging conventional morality at every turn.

The results were dramatic. When the Beatles took America by storm in 1964, their chart-busting songs included "I Want to Hold Your Hand," "She Loves You," and "Please, Please Me." Marijuana use, a federal crime since 1937, was rare in middle-class society, and lysergic acid diethylamide (LSD) was largely un-

Thousands of young people migrated to the Haight-Ashbury section of San Francisco in 1967 for a "Summer of Love." Having no means of support, many turned to drug-dealing, panhandling, and prostitution.

known. By 1967, however, the Beatles were imagining "Lucy in the Sky with Diamonds" (LSD) and wailing, "Why Don't We Do It in the Road!"

The counterculture spread inward through America from the east and west coasts. In Cambridge, Massachusetts, a Harvard researcher named Timothy Leary became the nation's first psychedelic guru by promoting LSD as the pathway to heightened consciousness and sexual pleasure. "Every weekend," he recalled, "the Harvard resident houses were transformed into spaceships floating miles above the Yard." In San Francisco, author Ken Kesey *(One Flew over the Cuckoo's Nest)* and his Merry Pranksters staged a series of public LSD parties, known as Acid Tests, that drew thousands of participants in 1966. Wearing wild costumes, with painted faces, the revelers danced to the sounds of Jerry Garcia and his Grateful Dead.

To much of the public, San Francisco became synonymous with the counterculture. Acid rock flourished in local clubs like the Fillmore West, where Jimi Hendrix ("Purple Haze"), Steppenwolf ("Magic Carpet Ride"), and the Jefferson Airplane ("White Rabbit") celebrated drug tripping in their songs. In 1967, more than 75,000 young people migrated to San Francisco's Haight-Ashbury district to partake in a much publicized "summer of love." Many were at-

tracted by the smash hit "Are you going to San Francisco . . . Be sure to wear a flower in your hair." The majority of arrivals, studies showed, were runaways and school dropouts with no means of support. By summer's end, Haight-Ashbury was awash in drug overdoses, venereal disease, panhandling, and prostitution.

At first the national media embraced the counterculture as a "hip" challenge to the blandness of middle-class suburban life. Magazines as diverse as *Time* and *Playboy* doted on every aspect of the hippie existence, while the Levi-Strauss corporation used acid rockers to promote its new line of jeans. Hollywood celebrated the counterculture with films such as *Easy Rider,* about two footloose drug dealers on a motorcycle tour of self-discovery, and *I Love You, Alice B. Toklas,* in which a dull lawyer becomes a fun-loving hippie after accidentally taking hashish. The smash hit of the 1968 Broadway season was the rock musical *Hair,* depicting a draft evader's journey through the pleasure-filled Age of Aquarius.

Yet most young people of the 1960s experienced neither the nightmare of Haight-Ashbury nor the dream world of *Hair.* Millions of them remained on the margins of the counterculture, admiring its styles and sounds while rejecting its revolutionary mantra.

And millions more entered adulthood without the slightest sign of protest or alienation. Indeed, some commentators spoke of a serious *intra*generational split in this era, pitting young people who accepted, or aspired to, America's middle-class promise against more radical young people who did not.

A DIVIDED NATION

As 1968 began, General William Westmoreland, commander of U.S. forces in Southeast Asia, offered an optimistic assessment of the Vietnam War. In his view, American and South Vietnamese (ARVN) troops were gaining strength and confidence as the fighting progressed. Their new vitality, he insisted, stood in direct contrast to the enemy's sagging morale. The bloody war of attrition was finally being won.

The Tet Offensive

Four days later, 70,000 Communist troops assaulted American and ARVN positions throughout South Vietnam. Their lightning offensive, begun on the lunar New Year holiday of Tet, took Westmoreland by surprise. In Saigon, Viet Cong units reached the American Embassy before being driven back. After capturing Hue, one of South Vietnam's oldest cities, communist soldiers murdered thousands of civilians and dumped their bodies into a mass grave.

As a military operation, the Tet offensive clearly failed. Using their overwhelming firepower, American and ARVN forces inflicted frightful casualties upon the enemy. In the three-week battle to recapture Hue, more than 5,000 communist soldiers were killed, along with 400 ARVN troops and 150 American Marines. Viet Cong losses were so severe that the brunt of the ground fighting after Tet would have to be shouldered by North Vietnamese troops.

In psychological terms, however, the Tet offensive marked a turning point in the war. The sheer size of the communist attacks, their ability to strike so many targets in force, made a mockery of Westmoreland's optimistic claims. The enemy was not demoralized; the war ground on. Reporting from Saigon after the Tet offensive, Walter Cronkite, America's most popular television journalist, claimed that a military victory was nowhere in sight. At best, Cronkite predicted, "the bloody experience of Vietnam is to end in a stalemate."

A stalemate was exactly what Americans feared most. Opinion surveys after Tet showed dwindling support for Johnson's handling of the war. One pollster summed up the public's attitude this way: "It was an error for us to have gotten involved in Vietnam in the first place. But now that we're there, let's win—or get out."

The Tet offensive accelerated Johnson's political decline. His approval rating dropped from 48 to 36 percent, with most Americans expressing skepticism about official claims of military progress in Vietnam. Columnist Art Buchwald compared LBJ to General Custer at the Little Big Horn, while the prestigious *Wall Street Journal* warned that "the whole war effort is likely doomed."

The President Steps Aside

As Lyndon Johnson pondered his political future, the memory of Harry S. Truman was fresh in his mind. In 1952, Truman decided not to seek reelection after losing the New Hampshire Democratic presidential primary to Senator Estes Kefauver of Tennessee. The main issue then was the stalemate in Korea. In 1968, LBJ faced a spirited challenge in New Hampshire from Senator Eugene McCarthy of Minnesota. The main issue now was the stalemate in Vietnam.

McCarthy's presidential campaign reflected the deep divisions within Democratic party ranks. The "peace faction," led by younger activists like Allard Lowenstein of New York, hoped to "dump Johnson" by mobilizing antiwar students to campaign against him in key primary states. "No one wants him," Lowenstein claimed, "and all we have to do is have someone say it. Like, 'the emperor has no clothes.'"

Hundreds of college students arrived in New Hampshire to work for the McCarthy campaign. Long hair and beards were taboo, as well-scrubbed volunteers in sports coats and dresses ("be clean for Gene") ran phone banks, stuffed envelopes, and canvassed house to house. "These college kids are fabulous," one Democratic leader remarked. "They knock at the door and come in politely, and actually want to talk to grown-ups, and people are delighted."

The New Hampshire results sent shock waves through the political system. McCarthy came within a

MAP 29.2 | THE VIETNAM WAR

Although U.S. troops inflicted heavy casualties on the Viet Cong and the North Vietnamese during the Tet offensive of 1968, the intensity of the fighting shocked the American public and increased public criticism of the war.

whisker of defeating President Johnson, who received less than 50 percent of the Democratic primary vote. Polls showed McCarthy winning the support of "hawks" who demanded victory in Vietnam, as well as "doves" who wanted to pull out at once. For Johnson, the results amounted to a vote of "no confidence" on his handling of the war.

Four days later, Robert Kennedy entered the presidential race. While some Democrats criticized his opportunism, and others feared a split in the anti-Johnson ranks, few could deny the passion and charisma that Kennedy brought to the 1968 campaign. As the former attorney general and a current U.S. senator from New York, he was both a critic of the Vietnam War and a champion of minority causes, especially in the field of civil rights. Millions saw "Bobby" as the keeper of Camelot, the heir to his fallen brother's crusade.

On March 31, President Johnson announced his political retirement in a stunning televised address: "I shall not seek, and I will not accept, the nomination of my party for another term as your President." A few weeks later, Vice President Hubert Humphrey entered the presidential race as the "regular" Democratic candidate, endorsed by Johnson himself. Humphrey's strategy was to line up delegates for the presidential nomination without contesting Kennedy or McCarthy in the volatile state primaries, where his chances of winning were slim.

A Violent Spring

Early in April, Martin Luther King traveled to Memphis to support a strike of city garbage workers for better wages and conditions. His social vision was ever expanding, as he challenged Americans to confront the "interrelated" evils of racism, militarism, and poverty. In 1968, Dr. King's projects included a "Poor People's March on Washington" and a "moral crusade" to end the war in Vietnam. "We've got to get out and demonstrate and protest," he said, "until we rock the very foundations of this nation."

On the evening of April 3, King delivered a passionate sermon at a Memphis church. Demanding justice for the poor and the powerless, he seemed to sense the danger he was in. "I've been to the mountaintop," he cried. "I may not get there with you, but I want you to know that we as a people will get to the promised land." The following night, King was shot by James Earl Ray, a white racist, as he stood on the balcony of the Lorraine Motel. He died instantly, at the age of thirty-nine.

News of Dr. King's death touched off riots in African American communities from Boston to San Francisco. Mayor Richard Daley of Chicago instructed city police officers to "shoot to kill arsonists and shoot to maim looters." At the White House, President Johnson proclaimed a day of national mourning for Dr. King against a backdrop of wailing police sirens and billowing smoke. Forty-five people died in these national riots, including twenty-four in Washington, D.C.

Among the presidential candidates, Robert Kennedy seemed closest to the message of Dr. King. Centering his campaign on the connection between domestic unrest and the Vietnam War, Kennedy visited migrant labor camps, Indian reservations, and inner-city neighborhoods to highlight the problems of disadvantaged Americans, and the work to be done. He also supported the labor strike of Cesar Chavez and his National Farm Workers Association against the grape growers in central California.

The two had met when Kennedy chaired a Senate investigation into the squalid living and working conditions of migratory labor. Both men were close to forty, both were devout Catholics, and both admired the nonviolence of King and Gandhi in the struggle for justice and social change. As Kennedy campaigned in California, the grape strike was entering its third year. To protest the stalemate, and the growing violence on both sides, Chavez began a fast that continued for twenty-one days. He ended it, in poor health,

Robert Kennedy's presidential campaign in 1968 both energized and split the Democratic party, leading, in part, to Lyndon Johnson's decision to announce his political retirement. Kennedy was assassinated after winning the vital California primary in June 1968.

United Farm Workers leader Cesar Chavez led a series of strikes and boycotts to win better wages and working conditions for union members. Behind him is the symbol of the organization, the black Aztec eagle.

AN OPEN LETTER TO THE GRAPE INDUSTRY

BY
CESAR CHAVEZ

For years, Cesar Chavez had been struggling to earn better wages and livable working conditions for the men, women, and children who toiled in the fields and orchards of central California. In 1969, with the United Farm Workers on strike and a national boycott of table grapes gaining momentum, Chavez described the tactics and goals of his union in an open letter to E. L. Barr, Jr., president of the California Grape & Tree Fruit League.

YOU MUST understand, I must make you understand, that our membership—and the hopes and aspirations of hundreds of thousands of the poor and dispossessed that have been raised on our account—are, above all, human beings, no better no worse than any other cross section of human society; we are not saints because we are poor but by the same measure neither are we immoral. We are men and women who have suffered and endured much and not only because of our abject poverty but because we have been kept poor. The color of our skins, the languages of our cultural and native origins, the lack of formal education, the exclusion from the democratic process, the numbers of our slain in recent wars—all these burdens generation after generation have sought to demoralize us, to break our human spirit. But God knows we are not beasts of burden, we are not agricultural implements or rented slaves, we are men. And mark this well, Mr. Barr, we are men locked in a death struggle against man's inhumanity to man in the industry that you represent. And this struggle itself gives meaning to our life and ennobles our dying.

As your industry has experienced, our strikers here in Delano and those who represent us throughout the world are well trained for this struggle. They have been under the gun, they have been kicked and beaten and herded by dogs, they have been cursed and ridiculed, they have been stripped and chained and jailed, they have been sprayed with the poisons used in the vineyards. They have been taught not to lie down and die or to flee in shame, but to resist with every ounce of human endurance and spirit. To resist not with retaliation in kind but to overcome with love and compassion, with ingenuity and creativity, with hard work and longer hours, with stamina and patient tenacity, with truth and public appeal, with friends and allies, with mobility and discipline, with politics and law, and with prayer and fasting. They were not trained in a month or even a year; after all, this new harvest season will mark our fourth full year of strike and even now we continue to plan and prepare for the years to come. Time accomplishes for the poor what money does for the rich.

by breaking bread with Senator Kennedy at a mass of thanksgiving. Despite enormous media coverage, and a national boycott of table grapes, the strike dragged on.

In June 1968, Kennedy took a major step toward the Democratic presidential nomination by defeating Eugene McCarthy in the delegate-rich California primary. That night, after greeting supporters at a Los Angeles hotel, Kennedy was shot and killed by a deranged Arab nationalist named Sirhan Sirhan. The nation went numb. Who could have imagined the horror of four national leaders—John

This is not to pretend that we have everywhere been successful enough or that we have not made mistakes. And while we do not belittle or underestimate our adversaries, for they are the rich and powerful and possess the land, we are not afraid nor do we cringe from the confrontation. We welcome it! We have planned for it. We know that our cause is just, that history is a story of social revolution, and that the poor shall inherit the land.

Once again, I appeal to you as the representative of your industry and as a man. I ask you to recognize and bargain with our union before the economic pressure of the boycott and strike take an irrevocable toll; but if not, I ask you to at least sit down with us to discuss the safeguards necessary to keep our historical struggle free of violence. I make this appeal because as one of the leaders of our nonviolent movement, I know and accept my responsibility for preventing, if possible, the destruction of human life and property.

For these reasons and knowing of Gandhi's admonition that fasting is the last resort in place of the sword, during a most critical time in our movement last February, 1968, I undertook a 25-day fast. I repeat to you the principle enunciated to the membership at the start of the fast: if to build our union required the deliberate taking of life, either the life of a grower or his child, or the life of a farmworker or his child, then I choose not to see the union built.

MR. BARR, let me be painfully honest with you. You must understand these things. We advocate militant nonviolence as our means for social revolution and to achieve justice for our people, but we are not blind or deaf to the desperate and moody winds of human frustration, impatience, and rage that blow among us. Gandhi himself admitted that if his only choices were cowardice or violence, he would choose violence. Men are not angels and the time and tides wait for no man. Precisely because of these powerful human emotions, we have tried to involve masses of people in their own struggle. Participation and self-determination remain the best experience of freedom; and free men instinctively prefer democratic change and even protect the rights guaranteed to seek it. Only the enslaved in despair have need of violent overthrow.

This letter does not express all that is in my heart, Mr. Barr. But if it says nothing else, it says that we do not hate you or rejoice to see your industry destroyed; we hate the agribusiness system that seeks to keep us enslaved and we shall overcome and change it not by retaliation or bloodshed but by a determined nonviolent struggle carried on by those masses of farmworkers who intend to be free and human.

Sincerely yours, CESAR E. CHAVEZ
1969

SOURCE Susan Ferriss and Ricardo Sandoval, *The Fight in the Fields: Cesar Chavez and the Farmworkers Movement*, 1997, pp. 150–51.

F. Kennedy, Malcolm X, Martin Luther King, Jr., and Robert F. Kennedy—all dead at the hands of assassins? "My dreams were smashed," a young man recalled. "I shared with a lot of other people these feelings of loss and despair and grim, grim days ahead."

The Chicago Convention

Throughout the spring of 1968, a coalition of antiwar groups prepared for a massive peace demonstration at the Democratic National Convention in Chicago. Originally expecting 500,000 people, the organizers

Chicago police wade into a crowd of protesters during the Democratic National Convention in 1968.

dramatically lowered their estimates following the withdrawal of President Johnson in March and the murder of Senator Kennedy in June. Furthermore, Mayor Daley made it clear that protesters were not welcome in his city, no matter how well they behaved. Fearing serious bloodshed at the Democratic convention, Senator McCarthy urged young demonstrators to stay away.

There was reason for concern. The continued military build-up in Vietnam had created a violent cycle of protest and response at home. That spring, thousands of young men burned their draft cards in public; some were beaten by angry crowds. Demonstrators tried to block troop trains and army induction centers, leading to bloody clashes with police. At Columbia University, students from SDS took over several buildings, and trashed them, to protest "war-related" research on campus. Hundreds were arrested, a general strike followed, and the university closed down for the semester.

Chicago resembled a war zone in August 1968, with 6,000 army troops, 5,000 National Guardsmen, and hundreds of Chicago riot police patrolling the streets. Denied permits to rally in public places, the protesters—perhaps 4,000 strong—gathered in a park opposite the Hilton Hotel, where many Democratic party leaders were staying. Conflict was inevitable. Radical speakers from SDS and the Black

Panthers harangued the crowd with calls for "guerilla warfare," while Abbie Hoffman and Jerry Rubin, founders of the Youth International ("Yippie") party, held workshops on LSD production and then chose a pig as their candidate with the slogan: "They nominated a president and he eats the people. We nominate a president and the people eat him."

On the evening of August 28, the demonstrators tried to march to the convention arena. As millions watched on television, the police moved in with clubs and mace, while National Guardsmen fired tear gas at the crowd. Hundreds were badly beaten, including reporters and bystanders, in what investigators later described as a "police riot." Even so, the blame did not rest entirely with one side. "We were not just innocent people who were victimized," Abbie Hoffman admitted. "We came to plan a confrontation."

News of the street violence shocked the Democratic convention. From the podium, Senator Abraham Ribicoff of Connecticut condemned "the Gestapo tactics on the streets of Chicago." His remark set off booing, cursing, and wild applause. Television cameras caught a furious Mayor Daley hurling ethnic insults at Ribicoff and telling the "lousy mother_____" to "go home."

The shaken delegates chose Hubert Humphrey and Senator Edmund Muskie of Maine to be their

Richard Nixon and family celebrate his long-awaited presidential victory in November 1968.

presidential and vice-presidential nominees. A staunch liberal, with strong ties to organized labor and the civil rights movement, Humphrey exemplified the New Deal Democratic tradition of Roosevelt, Truman, Kennedy, and LBJ. His great weakness in 1968 was his loyal (if reluctant) support for Johnson's handling of the war. To many Americans, Humphrey endorsed the very policies that had divided the nation and left the Democratic party in disarray. His candidacy appeared hopeless from the start.

Nixon's the One

Meeting in Miami, the Republicans faced a much simpler task. The Goldwater defeat of 1964 opened the door for candidates with broader political appeal, such as Richard Nixon. Having lost a bruising election for president in 1960, and another for governor of California in 1962, Nixon kept his fortunes alive by marketing himself as both a devoted Republican and an experienced public figure. After choosing him on the first ballot in 1968, the delegates selected Governor Spiro T. Agnew of Maryland to be his vice-presidential running mate.

Nixon campaigned as the spokesman for America's "silent majority"—the people who worked hard, paid their taxes, went to church, obeyed the law, and respected the flag. In a nation grown weary of urban riots and campus demonstrations, he vowed to make "law and order" his number one domestic priority, while bringing "peace with honor" to Vietnam.

For the first time since 1948, the presidential campaign attracted a serious third-party candidate, Governor George Wallace of Alabama. An ardent segregationist, Wallace showed surprising strength in white working-class areas of the North and West, where issues such as rising crime rates, draft deferments for college students, and the court-ordered busing of schoolchildren to achieve racial integration were vital concerns. In blunt, sometimes explosive language, Wallace lashed out at "liberal judges," "welfare cheats," and "pot-smoking freaks in their beards and sandals." "If I become President and some protester lies down in front of my automobile," he told the cheering crowds, "it's going to be the last automobile he lies down in front of."

Early opinion polls showed Nixon far ahead of Humphrey, with Wallace running a strong third. Yet the gap closed considerably in the campaign's final

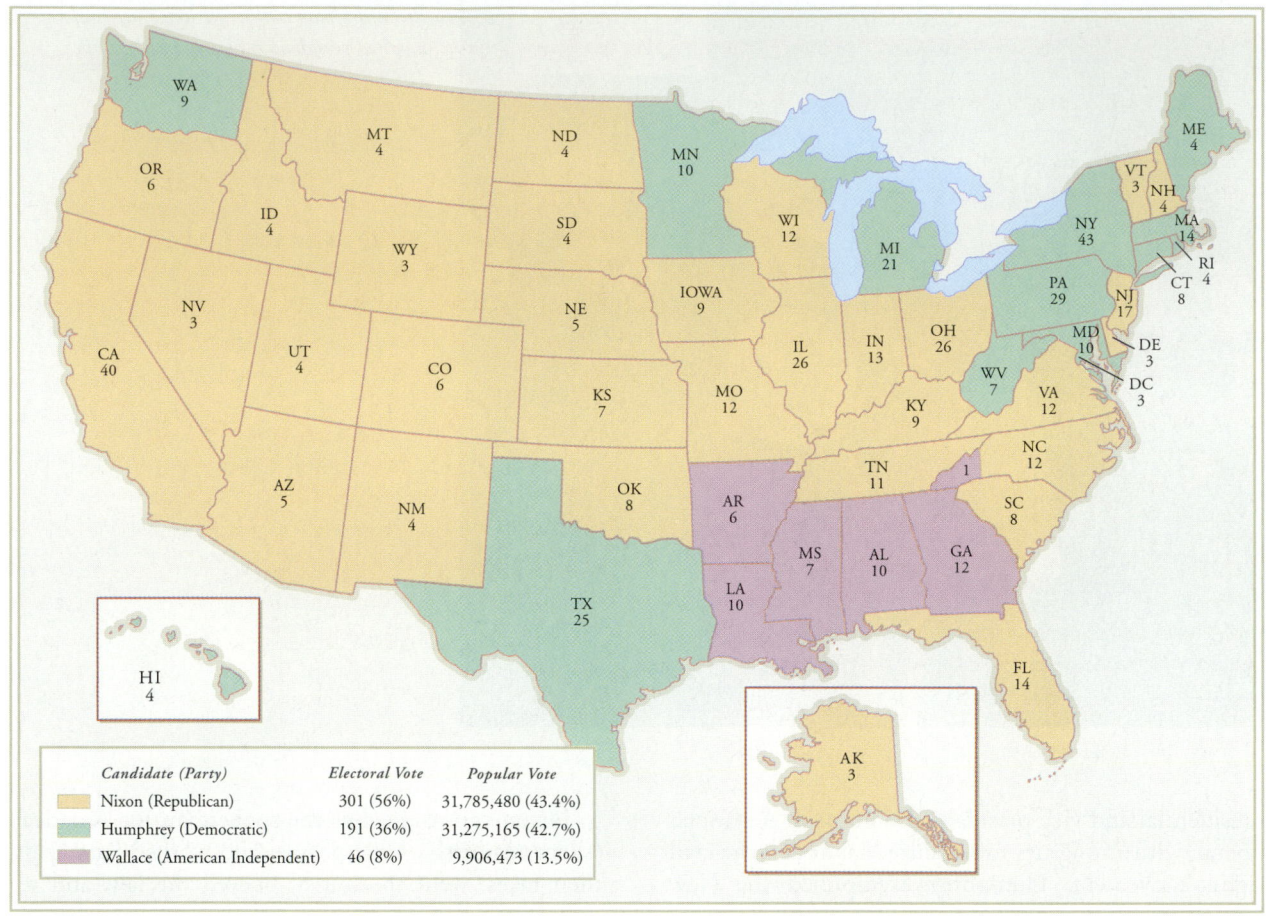

Candidate (Party)	Electoral Vote	Popular Vote
Nixon (Republican)	301 (56%)	31,785,480 (43.4%)
Humphrey (Democratic)	191 (36%)	31,275,165 (42.7%)
Wallace (American Independent)	46 (8%)	9,906,473 (13.5%)

MAP 29.3 | THE ELECTION OF 1968

weeks when President Johnson ordered a temporary bombing halt in North Vietnam, and millions of Democratic voters, fearful of a Nixon presidency, returned to the party fold. On election day, Nixon won 43.4 percent of the votes and 301 electoral votes, to 42.7 percent and 191 for Humphrey, and 13.5 percent and forty-six for Wallace.

CONCLUSION

Few decades in American history provided more drama and tragedy than the 1960s. What began with such hope and promise, with a popular young president and a firm belief in the possibilities of eradicating racism, poverty, and other national problems gave way to deep suspicion and despair by 1968, as Americans reeled from one crisis to another. Race riots, social protests, and generational conflict served to divide the country dangerously, while political assassinations and the escalating war in Vietnam combined to erode the public's trust and confidence in government itself.

To a large degree, Richard Nixon rode the political whirlwind that swept America in 1968. His margin of victory against Hubert Humphrey was nearly as narrow as his margin of defeat against John Kennedy in 1960. Yet the combined total for Nixon and Wallace in 1968—almost 57 percent—signaled a major swing to the right. The radical protests of the 1960s had fueled an inevitable backlash against the liberal party in power. The Great Society lay in ruins. The Nixon years had begun.

RECOMMENDED READINGS

Edsall, Thomas. and Mary Edsall, *Chain Reaction: The Impact of Race, Rights, and Taxes on American Politics* (1991) explains the decline of the New Deal Democratic coalition and the rise of social conservatism.

Friedan, Betty. *The Feminine Mystique* (1963) is a pathbreaking account of the domestic restrictions placed on women following World War II by those who shape American culture.

Harrington, Michael. *The Other America* (1962) riveted national attention on the issue of poverty, leading to major government programs and reforms.

Karnow, Stanley. *Vietnam* (1983) remains the best one-volume survey of American involvement in our nation's longest war.

Lemann, Nicholas. *The Promised Land* (1991) describes the great black migration from the South and assesses its impact on northern cities, race relations, and national politics.

McDougall, Walter. " . . . *The Heavens and the Earth*": *A Political History of the Space Age* (1985) captures both the policy making and the drama behind the race to the moon.

Miller, James. *Democracy in the Streets: From Port Huron to the Siege of Chicago* (1987) is a thorough history of the student movement that revolutionized American culture and politics in the 1960s.

Moody, Anne. *Coming of Age in Mississippi* (1968) is the powerful autobiography of a young black woman in the segregated South from childhood through the growing civil rights struggle.

Schlesinger, Arthur, Jr., *Robert Kennedy and His Times* (1978) explores the events that transformed the president's brother from a dogged bureaucrat into a passionate crusader.

Domestic Politics

Brennan, Mary. *Turning Right in the Sixties: The Conservative Capture of the GOP* (1995).

Caro, Robert. *The Years of Lyndon Johnson: The Path to Power* (1982); *Means of Ascent* (1990).

Conkin, Paul. *Big Daddy from the Pedernales* (1986).

Dallek, Robert. *Lone Star Rising: Lyndon Johnson and His Times* (1991).

Giglio, James. *The Presidency of John F. Kennedy* (1991).

Goldberg, Robert. *Barry Goldwater* (1995).

Matusow, Allen. *The Unraveling of America: A History of Liberalism in the 1960s* (1984).

Parmet, Herbert S. *JFK: The Presidency of John F. Kennedy* (1983).

Patterson, James. *Grand Expectations: The United States, 1945–1974* (1996).

Shesol, Jeff. *Mutual Contempt: Lyndon Johnson, Robert Kennedy, and the Feud That Defined a Decade* (1997).

Racial Justice and Turmoil

Branch, Taylor. *Pillar of Fire: America in the King Years, 1963–65* (1998).

Dittmer, John. *Local People: The Struggle for Civil Rights in Mississippi* (1995).

Goldfield, David. *Black, White, and Southern: Race Relations and Southern Culture, 1940 to the Present* (1990).

Halberstam, David. *The Children* (1998).

Haley, Alex. *The Autobiography of Malcolm X* (1966).

Horne, Gerald. *Fire This Time: The Watts Uprising and the 1960s* (1995).

King, Mary. *Freedom Song: A Personal History of the 1960s Civil Rights Movement* (1987).

Navasky, Victor. *Kennedy Justice* (1971).

Social Protest and Popular Culture

Berman, Paul. *A Tale of Two Utopias: The Political Journey of the Generation of 1968* (1996).

Burner, David. *Making Peace with the Sixties* (1996).

Ellwood, Robert. *The Sixties: Spiritual Awakenings* (1994).

Horowitz, David. *Radical Son: A Generational Odyssey* (1997).

Jezer, Marty. *Abbie Hoffman: American Rebel* (1993).

Pichaske, David. *A Generation in Motion: Popular Music and Culture in the Sixties* (1979).

"ONE GIANT LEAP FOR MANKIND"

Neil Armstrong sets foot on the moon's surface, July 20, 1969.

Chapter 30

CRISIS OF CONFIDENCE, 1969–1980

RICHARD NIXON HAD been in politics for most of his adult life. As a congressman, a senator, and a vice president, he thrived on controversy and kept moving ahead. Bitter defeats in the presidential election of 1960 and the California gubernatorial race of 1962 did not diminish his ambition or ruin his dreams. On the morning after his presidential victory in 1968, Nixon addressed a nation battered by racial turmoil, urban violence, generational conflict, political assassinations, and continuing war. Vowing to unite the country and to restore confidence in its institutions, he recalled a campaign stop he had made in the little town of Deshler, Ohio. Near the back of the crowd a teenager held up a sign reading "Bring Us Together." That message, he assured his listeners, "will be the great objective of this administration . . . to bring the American people together." The tragic presidency of Richard Nixon was underway.

AMERICA UNITED AND DIVIDED

The new era began with optimistic signals and improbable events. For a time, the dark days of 1968 were pushed aside by the miracles of 1969. In January, the New York Jets, led by "Broadway" Joe Namath, the nation's most celebrated bachelor, won the football Super Bowl by crushing the heavily favored Baltimore Colts. In October, the New York Mets, once regarded as the worst team in major league baseball history, defeated the Baltimore Orioles in a World Series that left millions of Americans screaming, "Ya gotta believe!" Sandwiched between these events were two enormous spectacles, each affecting the nation in a very different way.

The Miracles of 1969

In the summer of 1969, NASA fulfilled John F. Kennedy's bold promise to land a man on the moon "before this decade is out." The lunar mission culminated eight years of extraordinary progress and awful failure, including the 1967 *Apollo 1* disaster in which three astronauts died on the launch pad when their capsule exploded in flames. On July 16, astronauts Neil Armstrong, Edwin "Buzz" Aldrin, and Michael Collins began their 286,000-mile lunar mission—*Apollo 11*—from Cape Kennedy aboard the command vessel *Columbia*. As they neared their destination, Armstrong and Aldrin entered the *Eagle*, a fragile moon module, for the final descent. On July 20,

CHRONOLOGY

1969   Neil Armstrong sets foot on the moon

Woodstock rock festival attracts 400,000 people

First antiwar "moratorium" attracts huge crowds nationwide

1970   U.S. troops invade Cambodia

College students killed by national guard at Kent State and by local police at Jackson State.

Environmentalists celebrate first Earth Day

1971   Pentagon Papers released

My Lai massacre is exposed

1972   President Nixon visits mainland China

Watergate break-in occurs

Nixon wins reelection in a landslide

1973   Congress investigates spreading Watergate scandals

Vice President Spiro Agnew resigns after pleading no contest to income tax evasion

Supreme Court legalizes abortion in *Roe* v. *Wade*

War in Middle East leads to Arab oil embargo and energy crisis

1974   Facing impeachment, President Nixon resigns

Gerald Ford becomes president, issues blanket pardon

Violent antibusing protests in Boston

1975   South Vietnam falls

United States and Soviet Union sign human rights pledge in Helsinki Accords

1976   Jimmy Carter elected president

1977   Carter signs Panama Canal treaties

1978   Israel and Egypt sign Camp David Accords

Supreme Court rules on affirmative action in *Bakke* case

1979   Crisis at Three Mile Island nuclear plant

Militant students storm American embassy in Iran, taking hostages

Soviet troops invade Afghanistan

1980   U.S. boycotts Olympic Games in Moscow

Ronald Reagan elected president

---

before a television audience of 500 million people, Neil Armstrong put his foot on the lunar surface and said: "That's one small step for man, one giant leap for mankind."

Armstrong and Aldrin spent twenty-one hours on the moon. A television camera beamed back pictures of the men gathering samples, measuring temperature (234 degrees Fahrenheit in sunlight, 279 below zero in darkness), and planting a small American flag. What struck viewers was the sight of two space-suited figures leaping from place to place in the light gravity against a background of perfect desolation. As they rocketed back to earth, the astronauts provided breathtaking pictures of the world from 175,000 miles away. "No matter where you travel," Armstrong joked, "it's nice to get home."

Other moon missions followed, including the dramatic rescue of *Apollo 13* in 1970. But none could match the enormous interest generated by Armstrong's first step onto lunar soil. When the Apollo program ended in 1972, Americans marveled at the skill and bravery of these astronauts without fully understanding the scientific value of their missions. By studying lunar rocks and photographs, geologists learned that the earth and the moon were formed at the same time—about 4.6 billion years ago—and that both had been pounded for millions of years by a hail of comets, asteroids, and meteorites which helped reshape their outer crust. The moon missions spurred the growth of computer technology and led to numerous product advancements, from fireproof clothing to better navigation systems for jetliners. Most

Met fans, chanting "Ya gotta believe," rush the field after the team's miraculous World Series victory in 1969.

important, perhaps, was the discovery of helium-3 (a light isotope of helium) in large quantities on the lunar surface. Scientists expect helium-3 to provide a safe and plentiful alternative to fossil fuels in the coming century.

A month after the moon landing, national attention shifted to an earthly extravaganza, the Woodstock Art and Music Fair, on a 600-acre dairy farm in the Catskill Mountains northwest of New York City. Billed as an "Aquarian Exposition," Woodstock fused rock music, hard drugs, free love, and antiwar protest into three days of mud-splattered revelry. Expecting a crowd of perhaps 100,000—a ridiculously low estimate for a pageant that included Janis Joplin, Jimi Hendrix, Joan Baez, The Grateful Dead, and Jefferson Airplane, among others—the organizers were overwhelmed by the response. More than 400,000 people showed up, knocking down the fences and ticket windows, creating mammoth traffic jams, gobbling up the available food and water, pitching tents in the fields, bathing nude in cattle ponds, and sharing marijuana and LSD.

Some news reports breathlessly portrayed the event as a cultural watershed. One magazine called Woodstock "an art form and social structure unique to our time." Another saw it as "the model of how good we

More than 400,000 revelers enjoyed the sounds of Jimi Hendrix, Joan Baez, Jefferson Airplane, and others at the Woodstock festival north of New York City in the summer of 1969.

will all feel after the revolution." In truth, however, the long weekend at Max Yasgur's farm was far less than that. The vast majority at Woodstock were middle-class students and workers, not cultural dropouts or political revolutionaries. "They would always keep something of Woodstock in their hearts," wrote one perceptive observer, "but that would be while they were making it in the system, not overthrowing it."

What survived Woodstock were the new attitudes of young people toward self-fulfillment, personal expression, political activism, and, in some cases, dangerous excess. These things did not die out in the 1970s, though they took rather different forms. The mellow portrait of Woodstock soon gave way to the ugly spectacle of Altamont, near San Francisco, where a rock concert featuring the Rolling Stones turned into a bloodbath, with one man beaten to death. In 1970, drug and alcohol addiction claimed the lives of Janis Joplin, Jimi Hendrix, and Jim Morrison of The Doors. For many young people, the age of innocence was over.

Vietnamization

In order to bring America together, Richard Nixon realized, he had to end its military involvement in Vietnam. During his inaugural parade on January 20, 1969, Nixon heard the chants of antiwar protesters as his limousine made its way from the Capitol to the White House. The next morning he was handed the weekly American casualty figures from Vietnam: eighty-five killed, 1,237 wounded—a chilling reminder, he wrote, of the war's "tragic cost."

Within weeks, Nixon unveiled a plan, known as Vietnamization, to end America's participation in the war. It called for the gradual replacement of U.S. troops by well-trained and supplied South Vietnamese soldiers—a process that included the deployment of American air power and the intensification of peace efforts aimed at getting American and North Vietnamese troops out of South Vietnam. From Nixon's perspective, Vietnamization represented the best solution to a dreadful dilemma. He refused to abandon Vietnam. "I will not," he repeated, "be the first President of the United States to lose a war." Yet he could not continue a conflict that cost 14,600 American lives and $30 billion in 1968 alone.

Vietnamization did not work well on the battlefield, as time would show. But it did have the advantage of substituting Asian casualties for American ones, which made it popular in the United States. In June 1969, President Nixon announced that 25,000

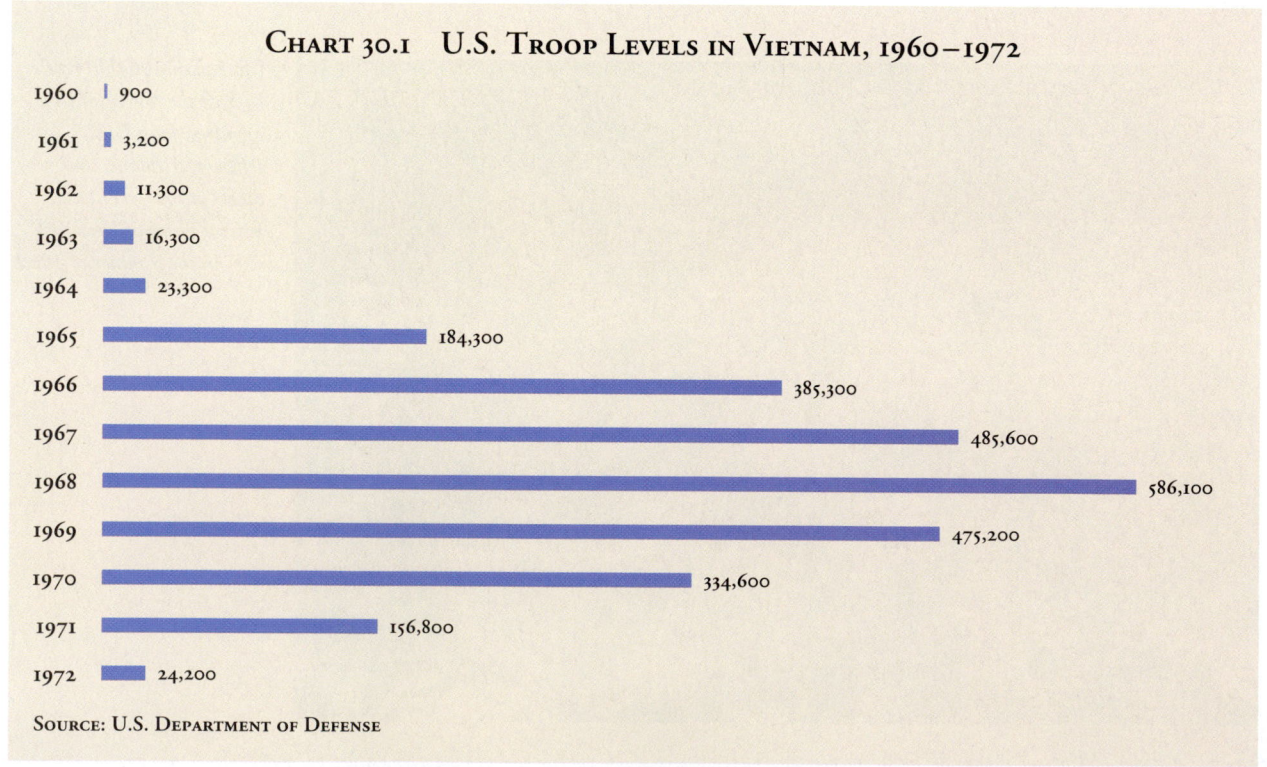

CHART 30.1　U.S. TROOP LEVELS IN VIETNAM, 1960–1972

Year	Troops
1960	900
1961	3,200
1962	11,300
1963	16,300
1964	23,300
1965	184,300
1966	385,300
1967	485,600
1968	586,100
1969	475,200
1970	334,600
1971	156,800
1972	24,200

Source: U.S. Department of Defense

American combat troops were being withdrawn from Vietnam—the first stage of a pull-out to be completed by late 1972. At the same time, the U.S. Air Force stepped up its missions over North and South Vietnam, and Cambodia as well.

Confrontation at Home

Despite Vietnamization and troop withdrawals, the anti-war movement retained considerable force. On November 15, 1969—"Mobilization Day"—hundreds of thousands of people attended rallies in New York, Boston, San Francisco, Washington, and other cities to demand the immediate removal of all American troops from Vietnam. The diverse turnout included professionals in business suits and student radicals waving Vietcong flags. Some considered the war immoral; others viewed it as a lost cause that was ripping the nation apart. To show his contempt for the protests, President Nixon made a point of listing his schedule that afternoon, which included several hours of watching the Washington Redskins on television.

In March 1970, the White House announced the withdrawal of 150,000 more combat troops over the coming year. The nation's leading antiwar group, the Vietnam Moratorium Committee, responded by closing its national office. But a month later, in a startling development, the president told the nation that American troops had just invaded Cambodia to disrupt enemy supply lines which ran through that country along the so-called Ho Chi Minh Trail. The very success of Vietnamization depended on the elimination of these North Vietnamese sanctuaries, he declared, adding: "We are a strong people and we shall not be defeated in Vietnam."

Nixon misjudged the public reaction. The idea of expanding the war under any circumstances brought protesters back into the streets. At Kent State University in Ohio, several thousand students rampaged through the business district and clashed with local police. That evening, Kent State's ROTC building went up in flames, leading the governor to send in the National Guard. The troops were ordered to prevent students from gathering in large blocs—an ironic twist, since a noontime rally was planned to protest the Guard's presence. On May 4, the guardsmen confronted 500 students at the rally, where rocks and bottles were thrown from a distance and tear gas was lobbed in return. Suddenly, without warning, a group

Student protests in 1970 ended in death on several college campuses. At Jackson State in Mississippi, police opened fire on a dormitory, killing two students and wounding several others.

of guardsmen fired their rifles at the crowd, killing four and wounding nine others.

Word of the shootings touched off campus protests nationwide. ROTC buildings were attacked, and governors in sixteen more states called out the National Guard. Many colleges simply shut down for the semester, canceling final exams and mailing diplomas to the graduates. At Jackson State in Mississippi, local police ended an altercation with black students by blasting their dormitory with machine guns and armor-piercing bullets, killing two and wounding several more. While a presidential investigating commission described the Jackson State shootings as "an unjustified overreaction," a local grand jury warned that protesters "must expect to be injured or killed when law enforcement officers are required to reestablish order."

Both statements reflected the deep and bitter divisions in American society over political protest and

social change. Surveys showed a clear majority approving of the National Guard's response at Kent State, and supporting forceful measures against those who challenged government authority through unlawful, or even disrespectful, behavior. Many blue-collar Americans fumed at the sight of draft-deferred, middle-class students protesting the war from the safety of a college campus while their own sons and brothers were slogging through the jungles of Vietnam. That rage turned to violence in New York City, when several hundred construction workers charged into an antiwar rally and severely beat the demonstrators and onlookers with hammers, pipes, and fists. Chanting "USA—All the Way," the workers then marched to City Hall to raise an American flag that hung at half-staff to honor the students killed at Kent State. A week later, President Nixon invited the leader of New York's construction workers' union to the White House, where the two men exchanged gifts and compliments. Nixon described his "honorary hard hat" as a symbol of "patriotism to our beloved country."

The violence continued in fits and spurts. Left-wing radicals bombed the headquarters of Mobil Oil, IBM, and other pillars of the "imperialist war machine." At the University of Wisconsin, the late-night bombing of a science center that housed a military research laboratory left one graduate student dead. In New York City, three radicals accidentally blew themselves to bits while mixing explosives. And in Chicago, a splinter group of the dormant Students for a Democratic Society attempted to "trash" the downtown business district in a final assault upon the "ruling class." Three hundred looters and window-smashers were arrested in a pathetic orgy of self-destruction.

My Lai and the Pentagon Papers

The news from Vietnam was equally grim. Reports surfaced about a massacre of civilians by U.S. troops at the village of My Lai, a suspected Vietcong stronghold, in 1968. Encountering no resistance, an infantry unit led by Lieutenant William Calley methodically executed the villagers and dumped their bodies into a mass grave. A number of the women were raped; at least 200 people, many of them children, were murdered. Evidence of these atrocities was ignored by field commanders until a soldier not connected with the incident sent letters to the Pentagon and the press.

Most Americans considered My Lai an aberration. Yet the public reaction to Lieutenant Calley's court-

martial verdict (guilty) and sentence (life imprisonment) in 1971 raised the very issues that had divided Americans since the war began. Some believed that government policy in Vietnam made such tragedies inevitable. Others insisted that Calley acted out of frustration after seeing so many of his fellow soldiers killed. Still others blamed a society—as one GI put it—that "forced these kids to die in a foreign land for a cause it refused to defend at home." Congress and the White House were flooded with letters opposing the conviction. "Free Calley" signs appeared on car bumpers, in store windows, even in churches. Following numerous appeals and a personal case review by President Nixon, Calley was paroled in 1974.

The My Lai incident raised nagging questions about the fitness of American troops as the war dragged on. By all accounts, U.S. soldiers had fought superbly under trying circumstances until 1969. But the process of Vietnamization, the stepped-up troop withdrawals, the rising antiwar protests—all served to isolate those who remained in Vietnam. Drug use increased dangerously, with many soldiers turning from marijuana to heroin. Racial tensions flared, as did violent attacks on officers, known as "fraggings," in which disgruntled soldiers used hand grenades as weapons. Some men ignored direct orders to fight. They were reluctant to risk their lives for a cause that appeared all but lost.

Within weeks of Calley's court-martial, another crisis appeared with publication of the Pentagon Papers, a secret report of the decision-making process that led to American involvement in Vietnam. Commissioned in 1967, and containing numerous classified documents within its 7,000 pages, the report was made public by Daniel Ellsberg, a former intelligence officer who had turned against the war. Ellsberg gave a copy to the New York *Times,* which printed the first installment on June 13, 1971.

The report focused mainly on the Kennedy-Johnson years. From a political standpoint, President Nixon welcomed the embarrassment it caused his Democratic opponents. "This is about their administrations," he told his aides. "Let them argue about it." Yet Nixon soon viewed Ellsberg's behavior as a threat to his own presidency as well. He feared that continued leaks of classified material might reveal damaging information about current policies, such as the secret bombing of Cambodia. As a result, the White House sought a court injunction to halt further publication of the Pentagon Papers on grounds that national security was at stake. The Supreme Court rejected this

argument, however, ruling six to three that suppression violated First Amendment guarantees.

Nixon did not give up the fight. Obsessed by the Ellsberg incident, he authorized the creation of a special White house unit, known as the "Plumbers," to "stop security leaks and investigate other sensitive matters." In a tape-recorded conversation on September 18, 1971, Nixon demanded that "the roughest, toughest people [get] to work on this." A few weeks later, the Plumbers carried out their first assignment, burglarizing the office of Ellsberg's psychiatrist in an attempt to gather embarrassing information. Nixon's top domestic advisor, John Ehrlichman, casually informed the president that other "little operations" were planned. "We've got some dirty tricks underway," he said. "It may pay off."

ACTIVISM, RIGHTS AND REFORM

Political and social activism did not end with the 1960s, as the environmental movement and the antiwar protests clearly showed. While the angry, media-centered radicalism of groups like SDS and the Black Panthers largely disappeared, the movements for women's rights and minority rights remained very much alive, bringing progress and backlash in their wake.

Expanding Women's Rights

On August 26, 1970, feminist leaders organized a nationwide rally to mark the fiftieth anniversary of the Nineteenth Amendment, which had given women the right to vote. Thousands showed up with signs ranging from "Sisterhood is Powerful" to "Don't Cook Dinner—Starve a Rat Today." The speeches focused on equality for women in education and employment, the need for reproductive freedom, and passage of the Equal Rights Amendment (ERA), an idea first proposed in 1923.

The revived women's movement was already making strides. In 1969, feminist protests forced a number of the nation's best colleges, including Yale and Princeton, to end their all-male admissions policy, and the military academies soon followed suit. Between 1970 and 1974, the number of women attending law school and medical school more than doubled. During the

"Women's March for Equality" moves down New York's Fifth Avenue.

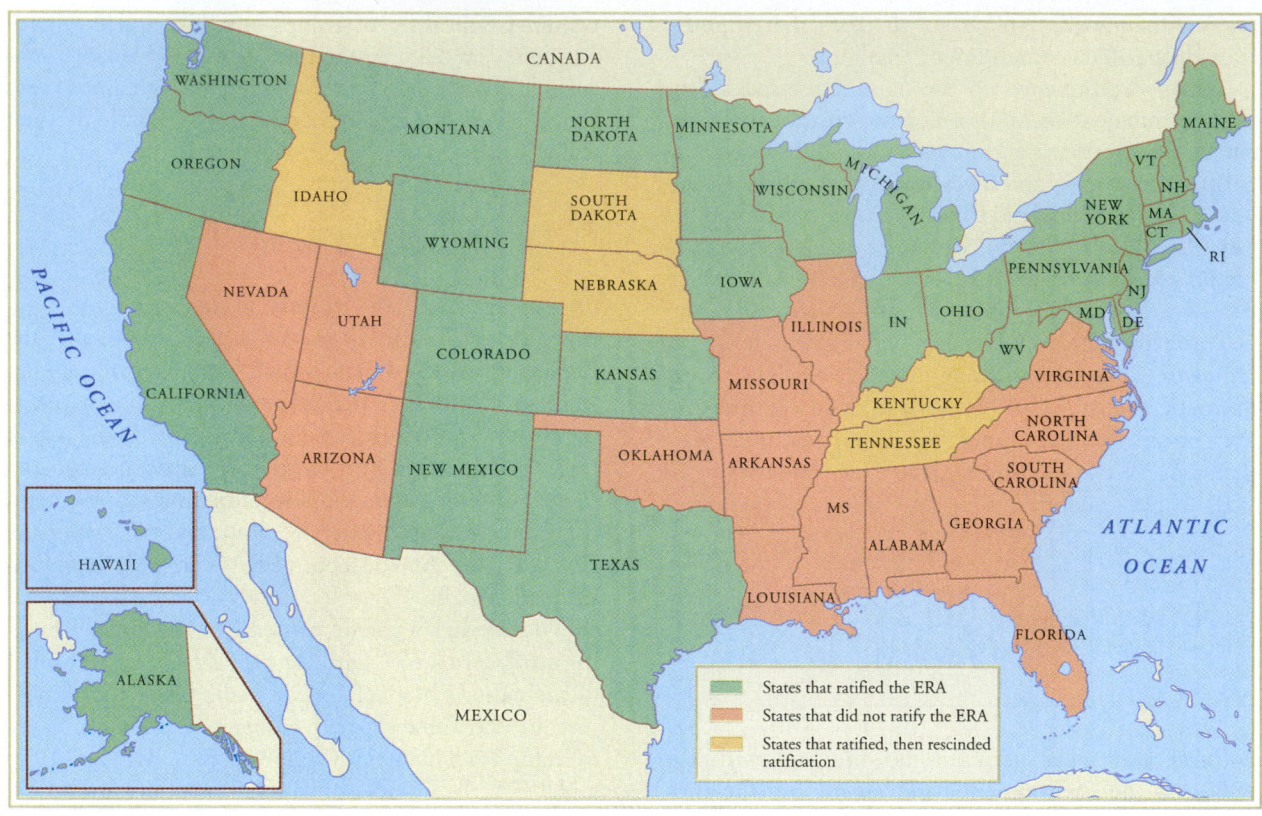

MAP 30.1 | THE STRUGGLE FOR THE EQUAL RIGHTS AMENDMENT

1970s as a whole, female graduates from the nation's law schools rose from 5 to 30 percent of each class; and at medical schools from 8 to 23 percent. Yet the number of women elected to public office or promoted to high management positions lagged far behind, and the wages of full-time working women remained well below those of men.

The women's movement had many voices and a wide range of ideas. Nothing better illustrated this diversity than the outpouring of books and magazines that provided an alternative to older publications such as *Good Housekeeping* and *Ladies' Home Journal,* which focused on motherhood, domesticity, and consumerism as the primary female roles. Handbooks like *Our Bodies, Ourselves* (1971) and *The New Woman's Survival Catalogue* (1972) sold millions of copies by combining a new feminist ideology, based on professional achievement and personal freedom, with medical and psychological strategies for good health. A flood of best-sellers emerged—Kate Millett's *Sexual*

Politics (1969), Shulamith Firestone's *The Dialectic of Sex* (1970), and Germaine Greer's *The Female Eunuch* (1970) among them—contending that women could never experience fulfillment within the traditional confines of marriage and family life. In 1972, three scholarly journals devoted to women's studies appeared, as did the Berkshire Conference on the History of Women. That same year marked the publication of *Ms,* the first feminist magazine to attract a mass circulation. A sampling of its articles showed how dramatically times had changed: "Raising Kids Without Sex Roles," "Women Tell the Truth About Their Abortions," and "Do Feminists Do It Better?"

In 1972, following a powerful lobbying effort by women's groups, Congress overwhelmingly passed the ERA. The amendment, stating that "equality of rights under the law shall not be denied or abridged by the United States or by any State on account of sex," was ratified that year by twenty-two of the thirty-five states needed for passage. Success seemed certain. As Con-

gresswoman Bella Abzug of New York asked, "Who'd be against equal rights for women?"

The answer came quickly. As the women's movement gained strength and attention in the early 1970s, a countermovement rose up to contest it, believing that traditional values were under attack. Led by Phyllis Schlafly, a conservative activist who portrayed "women's lib" as "a total assault on the family as the basic unity of society," the countermovement won the support of those who viewed feminism as an affront to God's plan for the sexes, and others who resented the portrayal of housework and motherhood as trivial, slavish work. By the mid-1970s, the backlash against feminism from men and women alike had stalled ratification of the ERA and turned the debate over abortion into an increasingly angry—and violent—struggle.

Minority Power

The political and cultural upheavals of the 1960s had produced a "rights consciousness" that spread from group to group, and movement to movement, as the decade progressed. For many such groups, 1969 was a pivotal year, marking their emergence on the national scene. That summer, for example, a routine police assault against homosexuals at the Stonewall Inn in Manhattan's Greenwich Village produced a most uncommon response. For the first time the patrons fought back, triggering several days of rioting and protest against the harassment of homosexuals. The "Stonewall Riot" led to the formation of the Gay Liberation Front, which, in turn, began the movement to encourage group solidarity within the homosexual community and to confront openly the prejudice that gay men and women had suffered, in fearful silence, for so many years. "We reject society's attempt to impose sexual roles and definitions of our nature," announced the Gay Liberation Front. "We are stepping outside these roles and simplistic myths. We are going to be who we are."

In 1969, Mexican-American activists in Texas formed La Raza Unida, a political party devoted to furthering "Chicano" causes and candidates through the ballot. This new party, which spread to several

Sparked by Manhattan's Stonewall Riot of 1969, in which homosexuals confronted police harassment with force, organizations like the Gay Liberation Front emerged to encourage group solidarity in the struggle for equal rights.

Roe v. Wade
1973

In 1973, the Supreme Court heard the case of Jane Roe, pseudonym for an unmarried, pregnant Texas woman who challenged the state's century-old criminal abortion law. Writing for the majority, Justice Harry J. Blackman struck down state statutes banning abortion in the first and second trimesters of a pregnancy on the ground that they violated a woman's right to privacy under the Due Process Clause of the Fourteenth Amendment. Hailed by "pro-choice" advocates, and condemned by "pro-life" groups, the decision remains controversial to this day.

The principal thrust of appellant's attack on the Texas statutes is that they improperly invade a right, said to be possessed by the pregnant woman, to choose to terminate her pregnancy. Appellant would discover this right in the concept of personal "liberty" embodied in the Fourteenth Amendment's Due Process Clause; or in personal, marital, familial, and sexual privacy said to be protected by the Bill of Rights. . . .

This right of privacy, whether it be founded in the Fourteenth Amendment's concept of personal liberty and restrictions upon state action, as we feel it is, or, as the District Court determined, in the Ninth Amendment's reservation of rights to the people, is broad enough to encompass a woman's decision whether or not to terminate her pregnancy. The detriment that the State would impose upon the pregnant woman by denying this choice altogether is apparent. Specific and direct harm medically diagnosable even in early pregnancy may be involved. Maternity, or additional offspring, may force upon the woman a distressful life and future. Psychological harm may be imminent. Mental and physical health may be taxed by child care. There is also the distress, for all concerned, associated with the unwanted child, and there is the problem of bringing a child into a family already unable, psychologically and otherwise, to care for it. In other cases, as in this one, the additional difficulties and continuing stigma of unwed motherhood may be involved. All these are factors the woman and her responsible physician necessarily will consider in consultation. . . .

On the basis of elements such as these, appellants argue that the woman's right is absolute and that she is entitled to terminate her pregnancy at whatever time, in whatever way, and for whatever reason she alone chooses. With this we do not agree. Appellant's

southwestern states, reflected the growing demand for political power and cultural self-determination within the Hispanic community, which had grown from 3 million in 1960 to more than 9 million a decade later. The increase, consisting mainly of Cuban Americans and Puerto Ricans on the nation's East Coast, and Mexican Americans throughout the West, provided unique opportunities for change.

On September 16, 1969, Mexican-American students across the Southwest boycotted classes to celebrate ethnic pride (or "Chicanismo") on Mexico's Independence Day, while a group at Cal-Berkeley,

arguments that Texas either has no valid interest at all in regulating the abortion decision, or no interest strong enough to support any limitation upon the woman's sole determination, is unpersuasive. The Court's decisions recognizing a right of privacy also acknowledge that some state regulation in areas protected by that right is appropriate. As noted above, a State may properly assert important interests in safeguarding health, in maintaining medical standards, and in protecting potential life. At some point in pregnancy, these respective interests become sufficiently compelling to sustain regulation of the factors that govern the abortion decision. The privacy right involved, therefore, cannot be said to be absolute. In fact, it is not clear to us that the claim . . . that one has an unlimited right to do with one's body as one pleases bears a close relationship to the right of privacy previously articulated in the Court's decisions. The Court has refused to recognize an unlimited right of this kind in the past.

We therefore conclude that the right of personal privacy includes the abortion decision, but that this right is not unqualified and must be considered against state interests in regulation. . . .

Measured against these standards, the Texas Penal Code, in restricting legal abortions to those "procured or attempted by medical advice for the purpose of saving the life of the mother," sweeps too broadly.

To summarize and to repeat:

A state criminal abortion statute of the current Texas type, that excepts from criminality only a *life saving* procedure on behalf of the mother, without regard to pregnancy stage and without recognition of the other interests involved, is violative of the Due Process Clause of the Fourteenth Amendment.

(a) For the stage prior to approximately the end of the first trimester, the abortion decision and its effectuation must be left to the medical judgment of the pregnant woman's attending physician.

(b) For the stage subsequent to approximately the end of the first trimester, the State, in promoting its interest in the health of the mother, may, if it chooses, regulate the abortion procedure in ways that are reasonably related to maternal health.

(c) For the stage subsequent to viability the State, in promoting its interest in the potentiality of human life, may, if it chooses, regulate, and even prescribe, abortion except where it is necessary, in appropriate medical judgment, for the preservation of the life or health of the mother.

SOURCE *Roe v. Wade,* 410 U.S. 113, 1973.

shouting "Brown Power," staged a sit-in to demand a program in Chicano Studies. (Within a few years, more than fifty universities would have such a program.) Furthermore, political leverage by Hispanic groups spurred Congress to improve conditions for migrant farm workers, many of whom were Mexican American, and to provide federal funding for bilingual education, a much-debated concept that soon included the right of non-English-speaking students to schooling in their native language. Mexican Americans were also elected to the U.S. House of Representatives in Texas and California, to the U.S. Senate in New

Mexican-American activists formed La Raza Unida in 1969 to further "Chicano" causes. This poster advertises a benefit for striking grape workers in California.

Seventy-eight American Indians occupied Alcatraz Island, site of an abandoned federal prison, in 1969.

Mexico, and to the governorships of Arizona and New Mexico.

In the fall of 1969, several dozen Native Americans took over Alcatraz Island, an unoccupied former federal penitentiary in San Francisco Bay, to publicize the claims and grievances of a younger, more militant generation. "It has no running water; it has inadequate sanitation facilities; there is no industry; there are no health care facilities," said one protest leader, comparing the rocky island to a typical Indian reservation. The group spent nineteen months on Alcatraz, symbolically offering to buy it for "$24 in glass beads and red cloth."

The protest signaled a change in the Indian community. By any measure, Native Americans were the most deprived single group in the United States, with an unemployment rate ten times higher, and a life expectancy twenty years lower, than the national average. Belonging to the American Indian Movement (AIM), a new group inspired by the black freedom struggles of the 1960s, the Alcatraz demonstrators preached a "Red Power" that rejected the "assimilationist" policies of their elders. In 1972, AIM led a march on Washington—named the "Trail of Broken Treaties"—that ended with a group of protesters barricading themselves inside the Bureau of Indian Affairs and wrecking much of the building. A year later, AIM militants seized the South Dakota village of Wounded Knee on the Pine Ridge Sioux Reservation, site of an infamous massacre by federal troops in 1890 to highlight both the squalid conditions there and the "broken promises" that stripped Native Americans of their independence and their land. Two Indians were killed in the seventy-one-day standoff with federal agents.

This militant pressure did result in minor change. In 1970, the federal government returned 48,000 acres of sacred land to the Taos Pueblo of New Mexico, beginning a cautious policy of negotiation (such as a payment of $100 million to the Sioux for lands taken in the nineteenth century) that grew significantly in the coming years. In addition, the Nixon administration targeted minority aid programs for Native Americans living in urban areas, while Congress added funding through the Indian Education Act of 1972. Nevertheless, the alarming rates of suicide, alcoholism, and illiteracy among Native American children continued throughout the 1970s and beyond—a clear warning of how much remained to be done.

Black Capitalism and Civil Rights

Richard Nixon took office at a crucial juncture in the campaign for civil rights. The epic struggles of the 1950s and early 1960s had formally abolished *de jure* (legal) segregation in public schools and public accommodations—a remarkable achievement—yet serious problems remained. The vast majority of southern children still attended all-white or all-black schools in defiance of *Brown* v. *Board of Education,* and the situation was little better in the North and West, where *de facto* segregation in housing and employment kept most neighborhood schools rigidly segregated by race. Furthermore, while the percentage of "middle-class" African Americans increased substantially in the 1960s, the rate of black unemployment remained twice the national average, and male joblessness in urban areas sometimes reached 40 percent. This meant a deepening economic split within the African-American community, with almost half the black families enjoying middle-class status, and an equal percentage living below the poverty line in run-down, unsafe, segregated neighborhoods where jobs were scarce and single women, increasingly, raised children on their own.

Civil rights did not rank high on Nixon's domestic agenda. Because most blacks voted Democratic—Hubert Humphrey got 95 percent of their votes in 1968—the president owed them no political debt. On the contrary, he hoped to create a "new Republican majority" by winning over white working-class Democrats, north and south, who feared that minorities were getting too much attention from the federal government. Choosing his words carefully, Nixon described racial integration as a process that demanded a slow but steady pace. "There are those who want instant integration and those who want segregation forever," he said. "I believe that we need to have a middle course between those two extremes."

Nixon's boldest civil rights initiatives related to business and employment. In 1969, he created the Office of Minority Business Enterprise, noting that "people who own their own homes and property do not burn their neighborhoods." Over the next three years, the federal government tripled its assistance to minority enterprises through grants and low-interest loans. More controversial was the administration's proposal to bring black workers into the high-wage, "lily-white" construction industry. Known as the Philadelphia Plan, it required the construction unions—carpenters, masons, electricians, and the like—to set up "goals" and "timetables" for hiring black apprentices on government-sponsored projects. Some civil rights leaders praised the Philadelphia Plan as a major step toward economic equality; others condemned it as a cynical ploy to woo black voters away from the Democratic party. Everyone agreed, however, that the plan went far beyond the intent of the 1964 Civil Rights Act, which simply banned job discrimination on the basis of race, religion, sex, or national origin.

On the emotional issue of public school integration, the president took a more cautious approach. Hoping to win white political converts in the South, he supported the efforts of Mississippi officials in 1969 to postpone court-ordered school integration, while firmly opposing efforts to deny federal funding to segregated schools. When told that Justice Department officials were planning to speed up school integration, the president warned them to "knock off this crap," adding: "Do what the law allows you and not one bit more." As a result, the battle shifted back to the courts, especially the U.S. Supreme Court, where major changes were now underway.

The Burger Court

In 1969, Chief Justice Earl Warren stepped down from the bench. The timing appeared to have political overtones because Nixon had criticized the Warren Court during the recent presidential campaign for being "too soft" on crime. In fact, the seventy-seven-year-old chief justice had submitted his resignation in 1968, expecting President Johnson to choose a suitably liberal replacement. But problems arose when

Johnson nominated his close friend, Associate Supreme Court Justice Abe Fortas, to become the new chief justice. Senate conservatives, charging "cronyism," organized a filibuster to deny Fortas the post; then a brewing scandal over his finances forced Fortas to resign from the court. This gave incoming President Nixon the luxury of appointing two Supreme Court justices at once.

The first choice went smoothly. The Senate quickly confirmed Judge Warren E. Burger, a moderate northern Republican, to replace Warren as chief justice. But Nixon's other nominee, Judge Clement Haynsworth, a conservative from South Carolina, ran into trouble when Senate liberals raised questions about his antagonism toward civil rights and organized labor. Fifteen Republicans joined forty Democrats to reject Haynsworth—a rare event for the Senate, which had not defeated a Supreme Court nominee since the days of Herbert Hoover.

Stung by the vote, President Nixon nominated another Southerner, Judge G. Harrold Carswell, whose general qualifications and civil rights record were far inferior to Haynsworth's. The Senate rejected him as well. Nixon angrily blamed "hypocritical" northern liberals for the defeats of Haynsworth and Carswell, claiming that "the real reasons for their rejection [were] their legal philosophies . . . and the fact that they were born in the South." A few weeks later, the Senate unanimously confirmed Nixon's third choice, Judge Harry Blackmun of Minnesota. Ironically, the president got to make two more Supreme Court nominations the following year when justices Hugo Black and John Marshall Harlan retired. His selections—William Rehnquist, a prominent Arizona conservative, and Lewis Powell, a distinguished Virginia attorney—were easily confirmed.

The Burger Court proved more independent than most people, including Nixon, had expected. Among other decisions, it upheld publication of the Pentagon Papers, struck down "capricious" state laws imposing the death penalty for rape and murder, thereby halting capital punishment for almost two decades (*Furman* v. *Georgia,* 1972); and ruled against President Nixon's claims of executive privilege in the Watergate scandals. In addition, the Burger Court held that state laws prohibiting abortion were unconstitutional because they violated a woman's "right to privacy" under the Fourteenth Amendment (*Roe v. Wade,* 1973). Justice Blackmun's majority opinion permitted a state to outlaw abortion in the final three months of pregnancy, not-

ing, however, that the life and health of the mother must be considered at all times. The following year, almost 1 million legal abortions were performed in the United States.

The Burger Court also confronted segregation in the public schools. Its unanimous ruling in *Swann* v. *Charlotte–Mecklenburg Board of Education* (1971) served notice that controversial methods like "forced" busing could be used as legal remedies to achieve racial balance. Though millions of youngsters rode buses to school each day, and black students had been bused for years in order to maintain segregated southern schools, the idea of transporting children to different neighborhoods in the name of racial integration fueled parental anger and fear. Opinion polls showed that whites overwhelmingly opposed forced busing, and that African Americans, by a smaller margin, also disapproved. For many black parents, busing simply obscured the problems of neglect and underfunding that had plagued their school districts for years.

Violence sometimes followed. In Boston, a court-ordered plan in 1974 to bus white schoolchildren to Roxbury, a poor black neighborhood, and black children to South Boston, a poor white neighborhood, led to mob action reminiscent of Little Rock, Arkansas, in 1957. Buses were stoned, black students were beaten, and federal marshals rushed in to protect them. Ironically, the schools in both neighborhoods were in awful condition, unlike the wealthy suburban Boston schools, which were not included in the desegregation plan. All too often, forced busing became a class issue, involving poorer people of all races.

NEW DIRECTIONS AT HOME AND ABROAD

Like John F. Kennedy, President Nixon cared more about foreign policy than about domestic affairs. "I've always thought the [United States] could run itself without a president," Nixon mused. "All you need is a competent Cabinet to run the country at home." As a moderate Republican in the Eisenhower mold, Nixon endorsed the basic outlines of the modern welfare state, which included Social Security, unemployment insurance, a minimum wage, the right to unionize, and health care for the elderly. Yet Nixon also understood—and exploited—the public's growing concern

that the Great Society era had tilted too far in favor of poor people and minority groups. Convinced that Americans were fed up with wasteful government programs and angry street demonstrations, he tried to find, in his words, a domestic "middle ground."

Rethinking Welfare

With foreign affairs his leading priority, and Democrats controlling both houses of Congress, President Nixon moved cautiously on the domestic front. His immediate goals were to implement a revenue-sharing plan that sent more tax dollars back to the states and localities, and to simplify the welfare system, making it more efficient and less expensive. Revenue sharing, designed to limit the power of the national government, was a modest success. Congress passed legislation transferring $30 billion in federal revenue over five years—less than Nixon wanted, but more than state and local governments had received in the past. Welfare reform proved a much harder sell. Here the president looked to domestic advisor Daniel P. Moynihan, a social scientist whose controversial writings on poverty and family breakup in the African-American community reflected a shifting emphasis from equal rights, which focused on constitutional guarantees, to equal opportunity, which stressed socioeconomic gains. Everyone agreed that the current welfare system—Aid to Families with Dependent Children (AFDC)—was seriously flawed. Its programs lacked accountability, and the payments varied widely from state to state. At Moynihan's urging, President Nixon offered an alternative to AFDC, known as the Family Assistance Plan (FAP).

The new plan proposed a national standard for welfare designed to reduce the number of recipients—and bureaucrats—over time. Instead of providing a host of costly welfare services, the government would guarantee a minimum annual income to the poor, beginning at $1,600 for a family of four, with additional funding for food stamps. The individual states were expected to subsidize this income, and able-bodied parents (excepting mothers of preschool children) were required to seek employment or job training. Not surprisingly, FAP ran into withering criticism from all sides. Liberals complained that $1,600 was unreasonably low, while conservatives opposed the very concept of a guaranteed annual income. The National Welfare Rights Organization

resisted the work requirement for women with school-age children, while community leaders and social workers worried about the elimination of vital services (and perhaps their own jobs).

To his credit, Nixon did not trim needed programs as his own plan went down to defeat. On the contrary, he supported Democratic-sponsored measures in Congress to increase food stamp expenditures, ensure better medical care for low-income families, and provide automatic cost-of-living adjustments (COLAs) for Social Security recipients to help them keep up with inflation. Although Nixon did not care to publicize this achievement, he became the first president since Franklin Roosevelt to propose a federal budget with more spending for social services than for national defense.

Protecting the Environment

On April 22, 1970, millions of Americans gathered in schools, churches, and parks to celebrate Earth Day, an event sponsored by environmental groups like the Sierra Club to educate people about the ecological problems afflicting the modern world. Begun a few years earlier, following the appearance of Rachel Carson's *Silent Spring*, the environmental movement gained strength after a series of well-publicized disasters, such as the chemical fire that ignited Cleveland's Cuyahoga River, the giant oil spill that fouled the beaches of Santa Barbara, and the "death" of Lake Erie by farm runoff and factory waste. The dire predictions of scientists about population growth, poisoned food and water, endangered species, and air pollution added fuel to the cause. As biologist Barry Commoner noted in his best-selling 1971 book, *The Closing Circle,* "our present course, if continued, will destroy the capability of the environment to support a reasonably civilized human society."

At first, President Nixon showed littled interest in environmental problems. Indeed, his administration accidentally marked Earth Day by approving a project that raised serious ecological concerns, the 800-mile Alaskan oil pipeline. Yet Nixon soon considered environmentalism to be a powerful force—one which cut across class, racial, and political lines (although most of its hard-core constituents turned out to be white and middle-class). Unlike many other issues, it gave the appearance of uniting Americans against a common foe.

Nixon's approach was to increase federal action in this area without "busting" the budget. Moving quickly, his administration banned the use of DDT in the United States, though not its sale to foreign countries; and stopped production of chemical and biological weapons, though not the plant defoliants or napalm used in Vietnam. More significantly, the White House supported a bipartisan congressional effort to establish the Environmental Protection Agency (EPA) and to pass the Clean Air Act of 1970 and the Endangered Species Act of 1973.

These were notable achievements. The Clean Air Act set strict national guidelines for the reduction of automobile and factory emissions, with fines and jail sentences for polluters. The Endangered Species Act protected rare plants and animals from extinction. The list included hundreds of categories above the microscopic level, from the spotted owl to the snail-darter, with the lone exemption being "pest insects." Congress also passed the Water Pollution Control Act over Nixon's veto in 1972. The law, mandating $25 billion for the cleanup of America's neglected lakes and rivers, was too costly for the president, though it proved effective in bringing polluted waters back to life. The EPA, meanwhile, monitored the progress of these laws and required environmental "impact studies" for all future federal projects.

While Americans readily agreed about the need for clean air, pure water, and protecting wildlife, the cost of doing these things did not fall equally on everyone's shoulders. Auto manufacturers warned that the expense of meeting the new emission standards would result in higher car prices and the layoff of production workers. Loggers in the Northwest angrily accused the EPA of being more interested in protecting a few forest birds than in allowing human beings to earn a living and feed their families. A common bumper sticker in Oregon read: "If You're Hungry And Out Of Work, Eat An Environmentalist." In response to pressure from labor unions and businesses about lost jobs, rising costs and endless paperwork, the EPA modified some of its goals and deadlines for compliance with these new laws. Could strategies be devised to protect jobs and the environment simultaneously? Could American corporations effectively compete with foreign companies which did not face such restrictions? Should the United States abandon atomic power, offshore oil drilling, and other potential threats to the environment at a time when the demand for energy was rapidly increasing? Protecting the environment raised serious questions for the future.

A New World Order

Richard Nixon loved the challenge of foreign affairs. The secrecy, intrigue, and deal making fascinated him in ways that domestic matters never could. Determined to control foreign policy even more rigidly than previous presidents, Nixon bypassed the State Department in favor of the National Security Council, based in the White House itself. To direct the NSC, he chose Henry Kissinger, a German refugee and Harvard political scientist whose books on nineteenth-century European diplomacy and modern nuclear strategy earned him wide acclaim. In Kissinger, the president found the perfect match for his "realistic" view of foreign affairs in which hard assessments of the national interest took precedence over moral and ideological concerns.

Both men agreed that America's bipolar approach, based on the "containment" of Soviet Communism, no longer made sense. They wanted a more flexible policy that recognized not only the limits of American influence, but also the growing strength of Western Europe, Communist China, and Japan. They believed that the United States could no longer afford to play the world's policeman in every skirmish, or to finance an arms race that grew more dangerous—and expensive—with each passing year. The Nixon-Kissinger approach meant talking with old enemies, finding common ground through negotiation, and encouraging a more widespread balance of world power.

This innovative thinking, however, did not extend to all parts of the globe. The president still viewed Fidel Castro as a mortal enemy, and openly encouraged the CIA to undermine the democratically elected, left-wing government of Chilean President Salvadore Allende, who was overthrown and apparently murdered by right-wing military forces in 1973. "I don't see why we have to allow a country to go Marxist just because its people are irresponsible," Henry Kissinger argued. In Latin America, at least, the New World Order appeared strikingly similar to the old one.

The China Opening

In one sense, Richard Nixon seemed an odd choice to strip away years of rigid Cold War thinking in foreign affairs. He was, after all, a rough-and-tumble anticommunist known for his bitter attacks on State Department officials during the McCarthy years. Yet that is what made his new initiatives all the more remark-

able. Nixon's skill in foreign affairs lay in his ability to seize opportunities in a rapidly changing world. One of his first moves was to take advantage of the widening rift between Communist China and the Soviet Union. The objective, as Nixon freely admitted, was to enhance America's position with both of these nations by playing one against the other.

The United States at this time did not even recognize Communist China. Since 1949, American policy considered the anticommunist regime on Taiwan the legitimate government of mainland China. There were some who believed that only a politician with Nixon's Red-hunting credentials would dare to change this policy after so many years. No one could seriously accuse this president—as he had accused so many others—of being "soft on communism."

Nixon wanted a new relationship with China for several reasons. The trade possibilities were enormous; the China market was elusive, but vast. Better relations also increased the chances of a peace settlement in Vietnam, where China had some influence, while strengthening America's bargaining position with the Soviet Union, which feared any alliance between Washington and Beijing. Most of all, Nixon realized that China must now be recognized as a legitimate world power. The United States could no longer afford to ignore this reality.

Nixon worked behind the scenes, knowing that Americans considered China the "most dangerous" nation on earth. The first public breakthrough came in 1971, when an American table tennis team was invited to China for an exhibition tour. This "Ping-Pong diplomacy" led both nations to ease trade and travel restrictions. Meanwhile, Henry Kissinger secretly visited Beijing to plan a summit meeting between Chinese and American leaders. President Nixon hinted at his future plans in a remarkable magazine interview. "If there is anything I want to do before I die," he said, "it is to go to China."

Nixon arrived there on February 22, 1972—the first American president ever to set foot on Chinese soil. For the next eight days, the world watched in amazement as he walked along the Great Wall and strolled through the Forbidden City. "The Chinese Army band played 'America the Beautiful' and 'Home on the Range,'" wrote the New York *Times*. "President Nixon quoted Chairman Mao Zedong approvingly, used his chopsticks skillfully, and clinked glasses with every Chinese official in sight." Gone for the moment was the gloomy, forbidding image of Communist China that permeated American popular thought.

The trip ended with a joint statement, known as the Shanghai Communiqué, that promised closer relations between the two countries in trade, travel, and cultural exchange. Each nation agreed to open a legation (not an embassy) in the other's capital city, beginning the process of diplomatic recognition that would take seven more years to complete. The most important issues, such as human rights and nuclear proliferation, were tactfully ignored. And the most controversial issue—the future of Taiwan—demonstrated the deep rift that still existed. Communist China asserted its claim to the island, demanding that American troops on Taiwan be removed. The United States called for a "peaceful solution" to the "Taiwan question" and promised to reduce its forces as "tensions" in the region declined. Still, the historic significance of Nixon's visit overshadowed the problems that lay ahead. "We have been here a week," he declared. "This was the week that changed the world."

Détente

Three months later, the president traveled to Moscow for a summit meeting with Soviet leader Leonid Brezhnev. A master of timing in foreign affairs, Nixon believed that his successful trip to China, coupled with a faltering Russian economy, would make the Soviets more likely to strike a serious deal with the United States. The key issues were arms control and increased trade. Both sides possessed huge atomic arsenals which cost billions of dollars and increased the chances of catastrophic war. The Russians desperately needed grain, heavy equipment, and technical assistance; American farmers and manufacturers saw new markets for their goods.

The Moscow Summit further enhanced the Nixon-Kissinger record in foreign affairs. On May 22, 1972, the United States and the Soviet Union signed a Strategic Arms Limitation Treaty (SALT) that limited the number of long-range offensive missiles (ICBMs), and an ABM agreement that froze the production of antiballistic missiles for the next five years. No one believed that the arms race was now over; both sides would continue to build long-range nuclear bombers and to develop the Multiple Independent Re-entry Vehicles (MIRVs), which permitted several warheads to be fired from a single missile. Yet these initial treaties, committing the superpowers to the principle of arms reduction, represented a stunning breakthrough in Soviet-American relations.

The economic agreements were less successful. Though U.S.-Soviet trade more than tripled over the next three years, the greatest increase came in a single wheat deal with American farmers and grain dealers that caused a temporary shortage in the United States. Not surprisingly, American consumers fumed at the idea of shipping low-priced wheat to a foreign country while bread prices rose dramatically at home.

Nevertheless, the Moscow Summit provided a solid foundation for détente, with both sides pledging to reduce world tensions and to coexist peacefully. As President Nixon left Moscow, he noted the differences between the Soviet leaders he faced in 1959, when he was vice president, and the ones who endorsed détente. The current leaders, he wrote, "do not have as much of an inferiority complex as was the case in Khrushchev's period. They do not have to brag about everything in Russia being better than anything anywhere else. But they still crave to be respected as equals, and on this point I think we made a good impression."

FOUR MORE YEARS?

After a full term in office, Richard Nixon could look back upon a record of notable achievement. Relations with Cold War opponents like the Soviet Union and Communist China had dramatically improved as détente replaced confrontation. Although the Vietnam War continued, the steady withdrawal of American troops meant fewer casualties and an end to the draft. Even the economy looked better, with unemployment and inflation presently under control.

The Landslide of 1972

Nixon's Democratic challengers faced an uphill battle. From the political right, Governor George Wallace of Alabama continued the presidential odyssey he began in 1968, when he captured five southern states as a third-party candidate. Campaigning this time as a Democrat, Wallace won wide support among white working-class voters for his opposition to forced busing and his attacks on "welfare cheats." After winning the Democratic presidential primary in Florida, and running a close second in Wisconsin, Wallace was shot and paralyzed by a would-be assassin, ending his presidential quest.

A few weeks later, on June 17, 1972, five men were arrested while burglarizing the Democratic National Headquarters at the Watergate complex in Washington, D.C. Four of them were Cubans who had worked previously for the CIA; they were led by James W. McCord, the security director for Richard Nixon's Committee to Re-Elect the President, known as CREEP. Supervising from a nearby hotel, and later arrested, were two presidential aides—Gordon Liddy and E. Howard Hunt—who belonged to the newly created "Plumbers" unit. Responding to the break-in, Nixon assured the public that no one "presently employed" in his administration was involved "in this very bizarre incident," adding: "What really hurts is if you try to cover it up."

At the Republican National Convention in Miami, the delegates enthusiastically renominated the Nixon-Agnew team. The Democratic race, however, proved far more contentious. With George Wallace gone from the field, the candidates included Hubert Humphrey, the 1968 presidential nominee; Senator George McGovern of South Dakota, the favorite of younger, more liberal Democrats; and Representative Shirley Chisholm of New York, the first African American to seek the presidential nomination of a major political party.

The Democratic National Convention, meeting in Miami Beach, reflected the party reforms that followed the bloody "siege of Chicago" in 1968. The changes were dramatic, with the percentage of female delegates increasing from 13 to 38 percent, blacks from 5 to 15 percent, and those under thirty years old from 3 to 23 percent. Moreover, these new delegates embraced the causes of numerous "out groups" in society, such as homosexuals, migrant workers, prisoners, and the urban poor. Deeply committed to the "rights revolution" of the 1960s, they proposed a major redistribution of political power and cultural authority in the United States.

The delegates chose George McGovern for president and Senator Thomas Eagleton of Missouri for vice president. But the campaign faced trouble from the start. Reporters learned that Senator Eagleton had been hospitalized in the past for mental depression and fatigue, twice undergoing electroshock therapy. At first, McGovern stood by his running mate, offering him "1,000 percent" support. As criticism mounted, however, McGovern replaced Eagleton with former

Peace Corps Director Sargent Shriver, who accepted the position after six others turned it down. Appearing weak and opportunistic, McGovern dropped further in the polls.

Far more damaging was the lack of unity within Democratic ranks. Many of McGovern's key positions, such as amnesty for draft resisters, liberalization of marijuana laws, and greater welfare benefits for the poor, offended moderate and working-class Democrats who believed their party had moved too far to the left. On election day, Nixon overwhelmed McGovern, carrying every state but Massachusetts and winning 61 percent of the popular vote.

Yet Nixon's landslide victory was more limited than it appeared. Ticket splitting flourished in 1972, with the Democratic party easily retaining control of Congress. Thus, legions of Democratic voters rejected McGovern's message without deserting the party itself. Furthermore, the percentage of eligible voters who cast ballots in presidential elections continued to fall, from 62 percent in 1964, to 61 percent in 1968, to 56 percent in 1972. This suggested a growing alienation from the political process—and a hint of the protest to come.

Exit from Vietnam

Richard Nixon's impressive reelection victory seemed a sure sign that passions were cooling and better times lay ahead. The president's first task was to end the Vietnam conflict on honorable terms and secure the release of American prisoners of war. But the key to any settlement, Nixon understood, was the future security of South Vietnam. What would happen after U.S. troops left that country? Would the American sacrifice be in vain?

In the spring of 1972, North Vietnam had mounted a major offensive in the South, gambling that Nixon's concern about the coming presidential election, coupled with the reduction of American troop strength, would prevent the United States from responding. The offensive failed miserably, however, when Nixon ordered massive bombing raids against North Vietnam. That fall, secret negotiations between Henry Kissinger and North Vietnam's Le Duc To produced a temporary cease-fire. The U.S. agreed to withdraw its remaining troops from Vietnam in return for the release of its POWs. President Thieu would continue to govern South Vietnam, and North Viet-

namese troops were allowed to remain there, until a final settlement was reached. A week before the 1972 presidential election, Kissinger declared that "peace is at hand."

The claim was premature. President Thieu opposed the cease-fire, demanding the removal of North Vietnamese troops from South Vietnam, while the North Vietnamese seemed intent on adding even more soldiers for a final assault. Following his reelection, President Nixon tried to force a settlement through a fierce air assault against North Vietnam. "These bastards," he said, "have never been bombed like they're going to be bombed this time." In late December 1972, American B-52s filled the skies over Hanoi and Haiphong, dropping more tonnage than all American planes had dropped in the previous two years. The damage done to North Vietnam was staggering: harbors, factories, railway lines, storage facilities, and sometimes adjoining neighborhoods, were destroyed. Moreover, where only one B-52 had been lost in combat throughout the entire war, fifteen were shot down in these so-called "Christmas bombings." North Vietnam's communist allies did not strongly protest, even when a Soviet ship was damaged in Haiphong harbor. Interested above all in continuing the process of détente with America, the Russians signaled North Vietnam to return to the bargaining table and make the best deal. On January 27, 1973, the United States and North Vietnam signed an agreement quite similar to the one that had fallen apart a few months before. President Nixon got Thieu's reluctant support by vowing to "respond in full force" if North Vietnam renewed the fighting in the South. The United States, he proclaimed, had achieved "peace with honor" at last.

What Nixon got, in reality, was an American exit from Vietnam that left the vulnerable Thieu government at the mercy of its Communist opponents. Despite his pledge, the United States could only respond to future treaty violations with air power; sending troops back into combat was now unthinkable. The agreement ended American involvement without guaranteeing South Vietnam's long-term survival.

The American public expressed relief at the settlement, but little jubilation. The war had divided the country, raised suspicions about government to dangerous levels, and drained billions of dollars from vital domestic programs. More than 50,000 U.S. soldiers were killed in Vietnam and 300,000 were wounded. At least 1 million Asians died, and more would perish in the coming years. As the New York *Times* noted,

"There is no dancing in the streets, no honking of horns, no champagne."

Public attention soon shifted to the return of 587 American POWs. Many had spent up to seven years in North Vietnamese jails, and some had been tortured. "We are honored to have the opportunity to serve our country under difficult circumstances," said their senior officer as his plane touched down on American soil. That very day, ex-President Lyndon Johnson died in his sleep. "His tragedy—and ours," Senator Edmund Muskie stated, "was the war."

Watergate and the Abuse of Power

As 1973 began, Richard Nixon's public approval rating stood at a remarkable 68 percent. With Vietnam behind him, the president appeared ready to launch a successful second term. Yet all that ended in April, when the Watergate burglars pleaded guilty to minor charges of theft and wiretapping in order to avoid a public trial. Suspecting a cover-up, federal judge John Sirica convinced the lead burglar, James McCord, to admit that high-ranking White House officials were involved in planning the break-in. This startling con-

fession, combined with the investigative stories of Washington *Post* reporters Bob Woodward and Carl Bernstein, turned the Watergate affair into front-page news.

During the spring of 1973, President Nixon reluctantly appointed Harvard Law School professor Archibald Cox as an independent prosecutor in the Watergate case, while the Senate formed a special investigating committee chaired by seventy-three-year-old Sam Ervin of North Carolina, who modestly described himself as "a simple country lawyer." Under Ervin's careful direction, the committee heard sworn testimony from present and former Nixon aides about a "seamless web" of criminal activity designed to undermine the president's critics and political opponents. In meticulous detail, John Dean, the former White House counsel, implicated Nixon himself in a plan to ensure the silence of the imprisoned burglars by paying them "hush money."

Nixon, however, denied any involvement in Watergate. On national television, he took "responsibility" but no blame for the scandal, explaining that he had been too busy running the nation to bother with the day-to-day workings of his reelection campaign. Many Americans—and most Republican leaders—took

Former White House counsel John Dean documented President Nixon's role in the Watergate cover-up during his testimony before the Ervin Committee in 1973.

THE NIXON TAPES 1973

Hundreds of pages of Richard Nixon's taped Oval Office transcripts have been made public. Among the most revealing is a late-night phone conversation between Nixon and his friend Hobart Lewis, editor-in-chief of *Reader's Digest,* on April 30, 1973, following the resignations of Nixon's closest advisors, Bob Haldeman and John Ehrlichman, who were deeply involved in the Watergate scandals.

President Nixon: You know, having to tell two men who didn't—who refused to resign, to tell them they had to was the toughest thing . . .

Lewis: Of course.

President Nixon: And they are great men.

Lewis: Of course they are.

President Nixon: But I had to do it.

Lewis: Well, you are going to miss them.

President Nixon: Oh, well, the hell with missing them. You can fill any position, Hobe."

The conversation then turns to the Watergate break-in. It shows a baffled Nixon, unable to comprehend that a burglary, a cover-up, and endless lying are grounds for serious criticism, much less an impeachment proceeding. The moral lessons of Watergate do not penetrate his world.

President Nixon: Isn't it a shame it's all about a crappy little thing that didn't work?

Lewis: No, of course.

President Nixon: Didn't work. Nobody ever got a Goddamn thing out of this damn bugging.

SOURCE   Stanley Kutler, *Abuse of Power,* 1997, pp. 385–86.

Nixon at his word. As House minority leader Gerald R. Ford of Michigan declared, "I have the greatest confidence in the president and am absolutely positive he had nothing to do with this mess."

In July, White House aide Alexander Butterfield stunned the Ervin Committee by revealing that Nixon had secretly recorded his Oval Office conversations since 1971. Sensing that the true story of presidential involvement in the Watergate scandal could now be uncovered, Judge Sirica, Special Prosecutor Cox, and Chairman Ervin all demanded to hear the relevant tapes. But Nixon refused to release them, citing executive privilege and the separation of powers. When Cox persisted, Nixon ordered Attorney-General Elliot Richardson to fire him. Richardson and his top deputy refused, leading to their swift removal. These dramatic developments, known as the "Saturday Night Massacre," produced angry calls for Nixon's impeachment.

There was trouble for the vice president as well. In 1973, a Baltimore grand jury looked into allegations that Spiro Agnew, as governor of Maryland, had accepted illegal payoffs from building contractors. After first denying these charges, the vice president resigned his office and pleaded *nolo contendere* (no contest) to one count of income tax evasion. He received three years' probation plus a $10,000 fine.

Facing certain impeachment and removal from office, President Nixon resigned on August 9, 1974.

For many Americans, Agnew's humiliating departure seemed to signal Richard Nixon's ultimate fate. Under the Twenty-fifth Amendment, adopted in 1967, the president is obligated to nominate a vice president "who shall take the office upon confirmation by a majority of both houses of Congress." To bolster his declining fortunes, Nixon chose the well-respected Gerald Ford, who was quickly confirmed. But the president ran into more trouble when the Internal Revenue Service (IRS) disclosed that he owed $500,000 in back taxes from 1970 and 1971, having paid less than $1,000 in each of these years. Responding emotionally, Nixon told a press conference that "people have got to know whether or not their president is a crook." "Well," he asserted, "I am not a crook."

By this point, however, public confidence in Nixon had disappeared. The testimony of John Dean, the Saturday Night Massacre, the resignation of Spiro Agnew, the embarrassing IRS disclosures—all cast doubt on the president's morality and fitness to lead. A Gallup poll taken in November 1973 showed Nixon's public approval had dropped to 27 percent. In desperation, the president released transcripts of several Watergate-related conversations (but not the tapes themselves), claiming that they cleared him of wrong-

doing. Many thought otherwise. The transcripts contained ethnic and racial slurs, vulgar language (with "expletives deleted"), and strong hints of presidential involvement in a cover-up. Senator Hugh Scott, the Republican minority leader, called their contents "shabby, disgusting, and immoral."

Nixon's refusal to release the tapes reached a climax in July 1974, when the House Judiciary Committee debated charges of presidential impeachment before a national television audience. Led by Chairman Peter Rodino of New Jersey and the eloquent Barbara Jordan of Texas, the committee approved three charges— obstruction of justice, abuse of power, and contempt of Congress—at the very moment that a unanimous Supreme Court ordered Nixon to comply with Judge Sirica's subpoena for the Watergate tapes. On August 5, the president released the material that sealed his fate. While providing no evidence that Nixon knew about the Watergate burglary in advance, the tapes showed him playing an active role in the attempt to cover up White House involvement in the crime. According to one Republican on the impeachment committee, "There was no smoking gun. The whole room was filled with smoke."

Faced with certain impeachment and removal, Richard Nixon became the first president to resign

from office. In a tearful farewell to his staff on August 9, he preached the very advice that he, himself, was incapable of following. "Never get discouraged. Never be petty," he said. "Always remember. . . . Those who hate you don't win unless you hate them. And then you destroy yourself."

OPEC and the Oil Embargo

In the midst of the Watergate scandal, a serious crisis erupted over the nation's energy needs. On October 6, 1973—the Jewish high holiday of Yom Kippur—Egypt and Syria attacked Israel from two sides. After some hesitation, the United States backed Israel, a longtime ally, by airlifting vital military supplies. While American aid proved essential in helping Israel repel the attack, the Organization of Petroleum Exporting Countries (OPEC), led by Saudi Arabia and other Arab nations, responded by halting oil shipments to the United States, Western Europe, and Japan.

The oil embargo created an immediate panic, though the problem had been building for years. As the U.S. economy flourished after World War II, its energy consumption soared. Americans, barely 6 percent of the world's population in 1974, used over 30 percent of the world's energy. Furthermore, as the expense of exploring and drilling for domestic oil increased, the United States turned to foreign suppliers, especially in the Middle East. Between 1968 and 1973, America's consumption of imported oil tripled from 12 to 36 percent.

This reliance on foreign sources left the United States extremely vulnerable to the OPEC embargo. No nation was more dependent on fossil fuels, and no nation had been more wasteful. As the cold weather set in, President Nixon warned that "we are heading toward the most acute shortage of energy since World War II." In response, the government reduced highway speed limits to 55 miles per hour, lowered thermostats in office buildings to 68 degrees, approved daylight savings time in winter, eased environmental restrictions on coal mining, and pushed the development of nuclear power. Across the nation, stores and factories closed early, families dimmed their Christmas lighting, and northern colleges canceled their midwinter semesters. Long lines formed at the gas stations, which were closed on Sundays to conserve precious fuel.

The OPEC oil embargo of 1973–1974 left Americans high and dry at the gas pumps.

The oil embargo ended in April 1974, but the impact lingered on. Energy costs rose dramatically, even as supplies returned to normal, because OPEC tripled its price. A gallon of gas in the United States rose from 30 cents (before the embargo) to 75 cents and more. Consumers faced soaring inflation, while manufacturers confronted higher production costs. Some regions, such as the automobile- and steel-producing Midwest, were particularly hard hit, while other areas, like the energy-producing Sunbelt, gained in population and political influence.

Above all, the energy crisis shook the foundations of the American dream. For three decades, a booming economy had produced a standard of living unparalleled in terms of material comfort, home ownership, and access to higher education. American culture thrived on the assumption of upward mobility—that the nation's children would do better than their

CHART 30.2   THE ENERGY CRISIS

NET IMPORTS OF CRUDE OIL

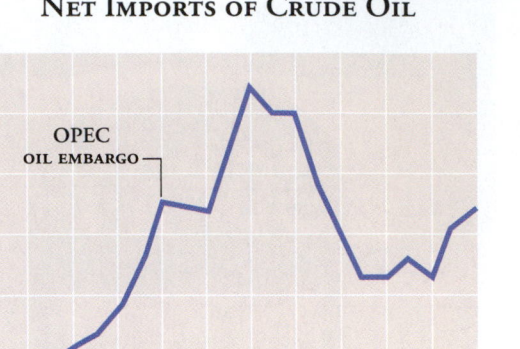

GASOLINE PRICES

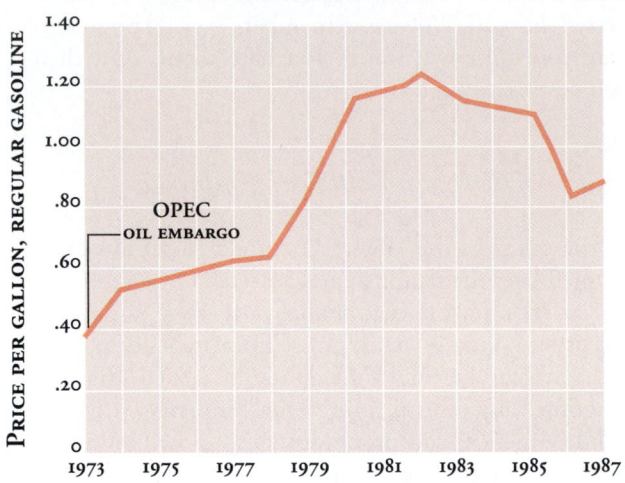

*PRELIMINARY

parents had done. After 1973, that assumption was in peril.

Prosperity could no longer be taken for granted. Following the oil embargo, average weekly earnings in the United States (adjusted for inflation) stopped growing for the first time in thirty years. So, too, did worker productivity. The increased cost of energy, combined with spiraling federal deficits and aggressive foreign competition in manufacturing and technology, made the American economy more vulnerable than before. Some experts predicted a new age in which limits and sacrifice replaced abundance and expansion.

GERALD FORD IN THE WHITE HOUSE

Vice President Gerald Ford, a former football star at the University of Michigan who had served honorably for two decades in the U.S. House of Representatives, seemed like the ideal figure to restore public confidence in the presidency. As a Republican party loyalist, he had opposed most of Lyndon Johnson's Great Society legislation, while strongly supporting the war in Vietnam. Yet even Ford's political opponents praised his decency, his integrity, his humble, straightforward ways. After the charisma of John Kennedy, the explosive energy of Lyndon Johnson, and the divisive ap-

peals of Richard Nixon, Americans were ready, it appeared, for a leader with common values and an ordinary touch. As the new president joked, "I'm a Ford, not a Lincoln."

The Watergate Legacy

Gerald Ford entered the White House at a pivotal time. Although not an activist by nature, he inherited a situation in which the legislative branch of government, emboldened by the disasters of Watergate and Vietnam, appeared anxious to restore its former authority by cutting the executive branch down to size. In 1973, for example, Congress passed the War Powers Act which required the president to notify Congress within forty-eight hours about the foreign deployment of American combat troops. If Congress did not formally endorse that action within sixty days, the troops would be withdrawn. In addition, Congress passed the Freedom of Information Act, which gave the American people unprecedented access to classified government material.

The Senate also held a series of spectacular hearings into the abuses, and criminal activity, of executive intelligence agencies such as the FBI and the CIA. The public learned that FBI agents had routinely harassed, blackmailed, and wiretapped prominent Americans such as Martin Luther King, while CIA operatives had engaged in illegal drug experiments, money launder-

President Ford entered the White House after Watergate with the vow to "put Watergate behind us." His pardon of President Nixon, however, opened old wounds.

ing, and bungled assassinations of world leaders like Fidel Castro. These revelations led President Ford to create a monitoring device known as the Intelligence Oversight Board. But Congress, with fresh memories of the Watergate cover-up, formed a permanent watchdog committee to investigate such behavior on its own.

Ford, too, fell victim to the Watergate morass. During his vice presidential confirmation hearing in 1973, he had gone on record against a possible presidential pardon for Richard Nixon. "I do not think the public would stand for it," he declared. Yet in September 1974, President Ford reversed his earlier position by granting Nixon a "full, free, and absolute pardon" for all crimes he "may have committed" during his term in office. Ford based his decision on a number of fac-

tors, including the impact of a criminal trial on Nixon's health. Above all, however, Ford hoped that a presidential pardon would finally put the "national nightmare" of Watergate to rest.

In fact, the opposite occurred. By appearing to place one man above the law, the pardon raised serious doubts about Gerald Ford's most cherished asset: his spotless character. Within days, the new president's public approval rating dropped from 72 to 49 percent. What bothered many Americans was the fact that Ford had granted the pardon without demanding contrition in return. Richard Nixon barely apologized for Watergate. He never admitted his crimes. For Gerald Ford, the pardon was an act of mercy, but others wanted justice as well.

The new president also tried to heal the internal wounds of the Vietnam War. Within days of taking office, he offered "conditional amnesty" to the 350,000 Americans of draft age who had refused service in the armed forces by leaving the country. Under Ford's plan, a draft resister might be permitted to reenter the United States in return for alternative service in a hospital or a charitable institution. Not surprisingly, the program met stiff resistance. Many who left the country believed they had performed an act of conscience, while veterans' groups viewed them as military deserters who should serve their time in jail. As a result, only 20,000 people took part in the program.

The Fall of South Vietnam

In October 1974, at a secret conclave outside Hanoi, the leaders of Communist North Vietnam prepared their final plans for the conquest of South Vietnam. Their main concern was the United States. Would it honor the pledges made by Nixon and Kissinger to the government of South Vietnam? Would it respond "in full force" to Communist violations of the 1973 peace accords? The North Vietnamese did not think so. "Having already withdrawn from the South," they reasoned, "the United States could hardly jump back in."

Their assessment was correct. The North Vietnamese launched a massive assault in March 1975, overwhelming South Vietnamese forces near the Demilitarized Zone (DMZ). The Vietcong, still suffering from the frightful losses inflicted during the Tet Offensive of 1968, played a minor role in the fighting. As North Vietnamese troops advanced, a mixture of chaos and panic gripped South Vietnam, with

As South Vietnam fell to the Communists on April 29, 1975, people scrambled to board the final helicopters on the roof of the American embassy in Saigon.

thousands of soldiers deserting their units and masses of civilians clogging the highways in desperate flight. Ignoring a plea from President Ford, Congress refused to extend emergency aid to South Vietnam, thereby reflecting the public's strong desire to avoid a return to the quagmire from which America had just emerged. On April 23, Ford acknowledged the obvious. The Vietnam War, he said, "is finished as far as America is concerned."

Saigon fell to the Communists on April 29. The televised images of Americans desperately boarding the last helicopters from the embassy grounds seemed a painful yet fitting conclusion to our nation's longest war. "What we need now in this country," said a solemn Henry Kissinger, "is to put Vietnam behind us and to concentrate on problems of the future."

This was easier said than done. The humiliating collapse of South Vietnam raised serious questions about the soundness of America's foreign policy and the limits of its military power. Furthermore, for those most deeply affected—the veterans of Vietnam—the collapse raised personal questions about the meaning of their sacrifice to the nation and to themselves. With the exception of the POWs, these veterans received no public tributes, no outpouring of thanks. Congress passed no special "GI Bill" to pay for their college tu-

ition, to help them find employment, or to finance their new homes. Some Americans condemned the veterans for serving in an "immoral war," while others blamed them for participating in the nation's first military defeat. "The left hated us for killing," said one dejected veteran, "and the right hated us for not killing enough."

The vast majority of Vietnam veterans expressed pride in their military service and a willingness to fight there again. Most of them adjusted well to civilian life, although a sizable minority (one out of six, according to the Veterans Administration) suffered from posttraumatic stress disorder, substance abuse, and sometimes both. In addition, some veterans claimed that their exposure to Agent Orange, a toxic herbicide used to defoliate the jungles of Vietnam, had produced high rates of cancer, lung disease, and even birth defects in their children. After more than a decade of controversy, Congress passed legislation that extended benefits to Vietnam veterans with medical conditions linked to Agent Orange.

Public sentiment softened over time. Opinion polls by the late 1970s showed that most Americans considered the Vietnam veteran to be both a dutiful soldier and the victim of a tragic war. In 1982, the Vietnam Veterans Memorial, a dramatic wall of black granite

with the names of 58,000 Americans who died or are missing in that war, was unveiled on the mall in Washington, D.C. Attracting large, respectful crowds, the memorial affords recognition for the sacrifices of all who served in Vietnam.

Stumbling Toward Defeat

The pardon of Richard Nixon and the fall of South Vietnam served to erode much of the good will that had accompanied Gerald Ford's early days in office. The president also faced a bleak economic picture, darkened by spiraling energy costs, in which unemployment and inflation reached their highest levels in years. "The state of the union," Ford admitted in 1975, "is not good."

The president and the Congress disagreed about the best medicine for the economic slump. The Republican Ford, believing that a balanced federal budget was the key to cutting inflation, proposed sizable cuts in government programs and a voluntary citizen's campaign to curb rising prices, which he called "Whip Inflation Now" (WIN). The Democratic Congress called for increased federal spending to spur the economy and to lower unemployment by creating new jobs. Although Ford vetoed more than sixty bills during his brief tenure in office, Congress overrode the president to increase Social Security benefits, fund public works projects, and raise the minimum wage.

In foreign affairs, Ford tried to maintain the policy of détente begun by Nixon and Kissinger, who remained as secretary of state. But unlike Nixon, the new president worried conservatives with his alleged weaknesses as a negotiator. Of particular concern was the Helsinki Accord of 1975, which pledged the United States and the Soviet Union, among other nations, to recognize the Cold War boundaries dividing Eastern and Western Europe and to respect human rights within their borders. Many Americans were dismayed by the formal acceptance of Soviet domination over nations such as Poland and East Germany; and many more were skeptical about any Russian promise regarding human rights. "I am against this agreement," said former Governor Ronald Reagan of California, "and I think all Americans should be against it."

Even Ford's occasional successes left controversy in their wake. In 1975, for example, communists in Cambodia seized the American merchant ship *Mayaguez* in international waters off the Cambodian coast. The president responded with a daring rescue mission in which forty-one U.S. Marines were killed and forty-nine were wounded, although it turned out that the Cambodians had already released the *Mayaguez* and its crew. While Ford received some criticism for not consulting Congress before sending troops into action, most Americans, recalling the *Pueblo* incident and the fall of South Vietnam, applauded his decisive action. "It was wonderful," declared Senator Barry Goldwater. "It shows we've still got balls in this country."

The Election of 1976

Gerald Ford dreamed of winning the White House in his own right. Yet unlike previous incumbents, who normally breezed through the presidential nominating process, Ford faced a serious challenge in 1976 from Ronald Reagan and the Republican right. Reagan's polished presence and outspoken conservatism played well against Ford's reserved manner and middle-of-the-road approach. With great fanfare, Reagan portrayed Ford as a weak president, unable to tame a Democratic Congress or to confront the Russians at Helsinki. In his sharpest attack, Reagan blasted Ford for opening negotiations aimed at reducing American control of the Panama Canal. "We built it, we paid for it, it's ours," Reagan thundered, "and we should tell [Panama] that we are going to keep it."

Though Reagan battled Ford to a draw in the state primaries, the president won a narrow victory at the Republican National Convention in Kansas City by agreeing to support a party platform sympathetic to the Reagan forces. The platform condemned both the Helsinki agreement and the Panama Canal negotiations, while endorsing constitutional amendments to legalize school prayer and prohibit abortions. For vice president, the Republican delegates selected Senator Bob Dole of Kansas, a tough campaigner with conservative views.

Because Ford appeared so vulnerable in 1976, the Democratic race for president attracted a very large field. Among the candidates was a little known ex-governor of Georgia named James Earl ("Jimmy") Carter, Jr. Few observers took him seriously at the start, and the voters asked, "Jimmy who?" When Carter told his mother that he intended to run for president, she replied, "president of what?" Yet Carter ran an

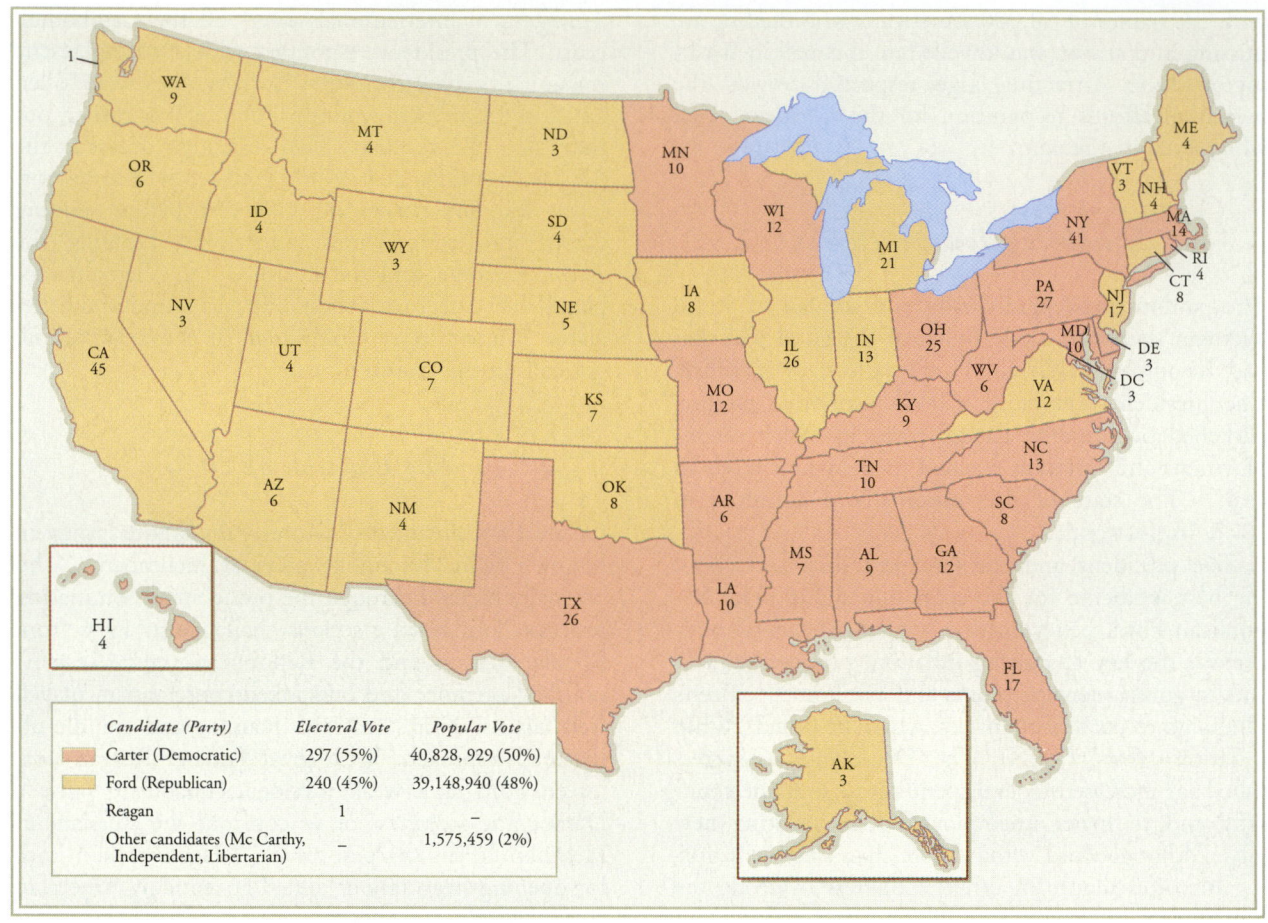

MAP 30.2 | THE ELECTION OF 1976

effective, well-financed campaign, portraying himself as a political outsider, untainted by the arrogance and corruption of Washington.

Carter struck the right pose for the post-Watergate era. A deeply religious man, who promised voters, "I will never lie to you," he combined the virtues of small town America with the skills of the modern corporate world. Born in Plains, Georgia, in 1924, Carter attended local schools, graduated with distinction from the U.S. Naval Academy, and spent seven years as a naval officer working on nuclear submarines. Following the death of his father in 1953, Carter returned to Plains to run the family's farm supply and peanut business. As the company prospered, he turned to politics, winning a state senate seat in 1962 and the Georgia governorship eight years later. Known as a "new South" politician, Carter supported progressive causes

and reached out to black constituents through his concern for civil rights.

Meeting in New York City, the Democratic National Convention chose Carter for president and Senator Walter Mondale of Minnesota for vice president. Carter ran a safe campaign that fall, avoiding controversial issues while claiming that America was no longer "strong" or "respected" in the world. The media, meanwhile, caught Ford in a series of bumbling accidents—banging his head on a car door, tripping on the steps of an airplane, falling down on the ski slopes, whacking spectators on the golf course with his tee shots—that made him look clownish and inept. Before long, the comedian Chevy Chase was beginning almost every episode of "Saturday Night Live" by taking a terrible tumble in the role of Gerald Ford. And the president only made things worse for himself

with a series of embarrassing verbal blunders, such as his insistence during the televised debate with Carter that "there [was] no Soviet domination of Eastern Europe." By election day, many Americans viewed Ford as a decent man, doing his best in a job that appeared to overwhelm him.

Still, the race was very close. Carter won 40.8 million votes, Ford 39.1. The electoral count was 297 to 240. Carter swept the entire South (except for Virginia) and the key industrial states of Ohio, Pennsylvania, and New York. Ford did well in the West, carrying every state but Texas. Polls showed Carter with large majorities among both minority voters and working-class whites who had rejected McGovern in 1972. In this election, at least, the New Deal coalition held firm.

Jimmy Carter became the first president from the Deep South in more than a century, signifying that region's increased strength—and acceptance—in the national arena. Furthermore, his election witnessed the growing importance of state primaries in the nominating process as well as the influence of the new Fair Campaign Practices Act of 1974. The law provided federal funds to the major candidates ($22 million each in this election), while establishing limits on personal contributions and a stricter accounting of how funds were disbursed. The result, as the 1976 election amply displayed, was a longer, more expensive presidential campaign season, with television advertising playing an ever larger role.

The Ford-Carter election continued the downward trend in voter turnout, from 55.7 percent in 1972 to 54.4 percent in 1976. Polls showed a growing sense of apathy and disillusionment among the American people, a loss of connection with politics as a positive force in their lives. As one bumper sticker put it, "Don't Vote. It Only Encourages Them!"

THE CARTER YEARS

The new Democratic administration began with promise and hope. President-elect Carter took the oath of office as Jimmy (not James Earl) Carter before leading the inaugural parade on foot down Pennsylvania Avenue dressed in a simple business suit. Determined to be a "people's president," Carter surrounded himself with populist symbolism—giving fireside

As the "people's president," Jimmy Carter led his inaugural parade on foot down Pennsylvania Avenue in 1977.

chats in a sweater and blue jeans, attending town meetings from New Hampshire to New Mexico, and staying overnight in the homes of ordinary Americans. "We must have a new spirit," he declared. "We must once again have full faith in our country—and in one another."

Civil Rights in a New Era

As governor of Georgia, Jimmy Carter had opened the doors of government to minorities. As president, he did much the same thing. Women, African Americans, and Hispanics were appointed to federal positions in record numbers as judges, ambassadors, and White House aides. Women, for example, filled three of Carter's cabinet-level positions and numerous other policy-making roles. In addition, Carter's wife Rosalyn

greatly expanded the role of first lady by serving as a key advisor to the president and representing him on diplomatic missions.

Though Carter strongly supported civil rights and gave special attention to the plight of minorities in the inner cities, the momentum for racial change in the 1970s had shifted from the executive branch to the federal courts. During Carter's term, the issue of affirmative action took center stage in *University of California Regents* v. *Bakke* (1978), a case that aroused intense national interest. Allan Bakke, a thirty-eight-year-old white man, was denied admission to the University of California medical school at Davis. He sued on the grounds that his test scores exceeded those of several black applicants who were admitted under a policy that reserved sixteen of one hundred spots for minorities in each entering class. The policy amounted to "reverse discrimination," Bakke charged, and thus violated his right to equal protection under the law. The case raised a fundamental conflict between the government's obligation to treat all citizens equally regardless of race, and its responsibility to help the long-suffering victims of racial discrimination enter the mainstream of American society. In a 5–4 ruling, the Supreme Court struck down the medical school's quota policy as a violation of Bakke's constitutional rights. But it held that universities might consider race as a factor in admission "to remedy disadvantages cast on minorities by past racial prejudice."

The Bakke decision began a passionate debate over affirmative action that continues to this day. Opponents considered it to be a racially divisive policy as well as a dangerous step away from the American tradition of individual rights. Why penalize innocent whites, they argued, for the sins of their ancestors? But supporters of affirmative action viewed it as the surest way to remedy discrimination, past and present." In order to get beyond racism, we must take race into account," wrote Justice Thurgood Marshall. "There is no other way."

Human Rights and Global Realities

President Carter knew little about foreign affairs. His political career had been spent entirely on state and local concerns. Yet Carter viewed his inexperience as an asset, freeing him from worn-out thinking and stale ideas. He believed that a fresh approach to foreign affairs would move America beyond the "big power" rivalries of the Cold War era. What America needed, he thought, was a foreign policy that stressed democracy and human rights—in short, the idealism of the United States.

Carter chose a diverse foreign policy team. His U.N. ambassador, Andrew Young, was a black civil rights leader who emphasized better U.S. relations with the developing world, especially in Africa. His secretary of state, Cyrus Vance, was an experienced diplomat who worked tirelessly to keep détente alive. And his national security advisor, Zbigniew Brzezinski, was a Columbia University professor, born in Poland, who proposed a tough front against the Soviet Union, which he blamed for most of the world's ills. Their conflicting advice sometimes left the president confused.

Yet Carter scored some impressive foreign policy successes. Emphasizing human rights in Latin America, he withdrew American support for Chile, cut off aid to the repressive Somoza regime in Nicaragua, and encouraged the governments of Brazil and Argentina in their halting steps toward democracy. Carter also presented the Senate with a treaty that relinquished American control over the Panama Canal by the year 2000, and a second one that detailed American rights in the Canal Zone thereafter. Both treaties provoked fierce national debate; both passed the Senate by a single vote.

Carter's greatest triumph occurred in the Middle East. In 1977, Egyptian President Anwar Sadat stunned the Arab world by visiting Israel to explore peace negotiations with Prime Minister Menachem Begin. Their discussions were cordial but fruitless, for neither man seemed willing to take the risks that peace demanded. When the talks broke down, President Carter invited Sadat and Begin to his presidential retreat at Camp David in Maryland. For two full weeks in September 1978, Carter shuttled between the cabins of the two Middle Eastern leaders, patiently working out the details of a "peace process" between Egypt and Israel which other nations might later join.

The Camp David Accords led to an historic treaty the following year. Egypt agreed to recognize the state of Israel, which previously had been unthinkable for an Arab nation, while Israel pledged to return the captured Sinai Peninsula to Egypt. The treaty did not consider other vital issues, such as the fate of displaced Palestinians and the future of Israeli-held Arab territory in Gaza and the West Bank. Yet few could deny the enormity of what had transpired, or the pivotal role played by President Carter in bringing it about.

Anwar Sadat (left) and Menachem Begin shake hands at Camp David, Maryland, as Jimmy Carter, who brought the men together, smiles in the background.

Economic Blues

Early success in foreign affairs, however, could not mask Carter's problems with the troubled economy. During the 1976 presidential campaign, candidate Carter had focused on high inflation (6 percent) and unemployment (8 percent) that gripped the United States. Combining these figures into a "misery index" of 14, he had promised the American people immediate relief.

Carter's program to stimulate the economy depended on a mixture of tax cuts, public works, and employment programs—a kind of "pump priming" reminiscent of Franklin Roosevelt's New Deal. The Democratic-controlled Congress responded sympathetically by funding large public works projects, reducing taxes by $30 billion, and raising the minimum wage from $2.30 to $3.35 over a five-year span. The good news was that unemployment dropped to 6 percent by 1978; the bad news was that inflation rose to 10 percent—and kept climbing.

Carter changed his approach. Creating jobs took a back seat to the problem of runaway inflation. Unlike Richard Nixon, who fought this problem by implementing wage and price controls, Carter tried to attack inflation by tightening the money supply (through higher interest rates) and by controlling the

federal deficit. This meant reduced government spending, a turnabout that alienated the Democratic Congress. Moreover, Carter's new policies appeared to increase unemployment without curbing inflation—the worst of both worlds. Before long, the "misery index" stood at 21.

This was not all Carter's fault, of course. The decline of American productivity, the growth of foreign competition, and surging cost of imported oil had plagued the nation for some time. In 1977, Carter offered a substantive plan for the energy crisis, which he described as "the moral equivalent of war." (Critics called it "meow.") The plan arrived on the heels of the worst winter in modern American history, a season of blizzards, record low temperatures, and Arctic winds. Based mainly on conservation—or reduced energy use—it ran into immediate opposition from oil companies, gas producers, the auto industry, and others who advocated the increased production of fossil fuels and the deregulation of prices. "This country didn't conserve its way to greatness," a Texas oil man complained. "It produced its way to greatness."

The National Energy Act, passed in November 1978, did little to reduce America's energy consumption or its reliance on foreign oil. Carter's original plans to stimulate conservation efforts were overshadowed by incentives to increase domestic energy

production through tax breaks for exploration, an emphasis on alternative sources (solar, nuclear, coal), and the deregulation of natural gas. The law did not address, much less solve, the nation's fundamental energy problems—as Americans would soon discover.

The Persian Gulf

In January 1979, a chain of events unfolded that shook the nation's confidence and shattered Jimmy Carter's presidency. The year began with the overthrow of America's dependable ally, Shah Riza Pahlavi of Iran; it ended with the United States appearing helpless and dispirited in the face of mounting challenges at home and abroad.

On a visit to Iran in 1977, President Carter had described it as "an island of stability in one of the most troubled areas in the world." Iran was vital to American interests, both as an oil supplier and a bastion against Soviet influence in the Middle East. Thousands of American workers and their families lived in Iran, while thousands of Iranian students attended college in the United States. Ironically, President Carter's concern for human rights did not extend to Iran, where the army and secret police used widespread torture and repression to keep the shah and his ruling elite in power. Against all evidence, Carter even congratulated the shah for "the admiration and love your people give to you."

The Iranian Revolution was led by Ayatollah Ruhollah Khomeini, an exiled cleric, and his devoted followers. Their aim was not to set up a democracy, but rather to form a fundamentalist Islamic state. While Khomeini denounced all who opposed him, he viewed the United States—the shah's patron—as the evil center of modern, westernized ways. When demonstrations paralyzed Iran, the shah fled his country, leaving the religious fundamentalists in control. One of Khomeini's first moves was to end oil shipments to "the Great Satan" America, thus allowing other OPEC countries to raise their prices even more. In the United States, long gas lines reappeared and the price reached an incredible one dollar per gallon.

The news quickly got worse. In March 1979, an equipment problem at the Three Mile Island nuclear power plant near Harrisburg, Pennsylvania, overheated the radioactive core and threatened a meltdown, with potentially deadly fallout blanketing the local countryside. Coming at the same time as *The China Syndrome,* a hit movie with an almost identical story line, the incident sent shock waves through the nation. For two weeks, technicians worked to contain the reactor, as thousands of residents fled their homes. The close

In a frightening scenario resembling The China Syndrome, *an equipment failure at the Three Mile Island nuclear power plant near Harrisburg, Pennsylvania, in 1979, almost resulted in a meltdown. The close call increased public suspicion of atomic energy as a safe power supply for the future.*

call at Three Mile Island turned public opinion even further against nuclear power, which provided about 10 percent of the nation's electrical energy. The tremendous expense of building and servicing these reactors, combined with the potential nightmare of nuclear accidents, served to focus attention on the need for safe energy supplies in the future.

In June, OPEC raised oil prices by another 50 percent. With Americans reeling from months of bad news, President Carter went on national television to speak partly about the energy crisis, but mostly about a "crisis of confidence" that struck "at the very heart and soul and spirit of our national will." His address was remarkably candid. Rather than assuring anxious Americans that they had nothing to fear, or trying to rally them with ringing phrases about honor and duty, the president spoke of a nation in trouble, struggling with the values of its cherished past. In place of "hard work, strong families, and close-knit communities," he said, too many Americans "now worship self indulgence and consumption. Human identity is no longer defined by what one does but by what one owns."

Having passionately diagnosed the illness, Carter provided no cure. The "crisis of confidence" deepened in the following weeks, with the United States appearing more helpless than ever. In October, the deposed shah of Iran, suffering from cancer, was allowed to enter the United States for medical treatment. This decision, which Carter viewed as a simple humanitarian gesture, produced an explosive backlash in Iran. On November 4, militant students stormed the American embassy in Tehran, taking dozens of American hostages and parading them in blindfolds for the entire world to see. The militants demanded that the United States turn over the shah for trial in Iran. Otherwise, the Americans would remain as captives—and perhaps be tried, and executed, as spies.

Carter had almost no leverage with these militants, who were supported by Khomeini himself. His attempts to settle the crisis through the United Nations were ignored by Iran. His orders to embargo Iranian oil and suspend arms sales were empty gestures, since other nations refused to do the same. The remaining options—freezing Iran's assets in American banks or threatening to deport Iranian students from the United States—did nothing to change the fate of the hostages in Tehran.

For a time, the American people rallied behind their president. Carter's approval rating jumped from 30 to 61 percent in the first month of the crisis. Yet

Carter grasped what many others did not: There was no easy solution to the hostage standoff. "It would not be possible, or even advisable," he warned, "to set a deadline about when, or if, I would take certain acts in the future." As the nation waited, public patience grew thin.

The year ended with yet another nasty surprise. In December, Russian soldiers invaded neighboring Afghanistan to quell a revolt led by Muslim fundamentalists against the faltering pro-Soviet regime. The invasion ultimately backfired; fanatical resistance from Afghan peasant fighters turned the country into a graveyard for Russian troops. From the White House, President Carter described the Soviet attack as "the gravest threat to peace" since 1945—an exaggeration that ignored the Korean War and the Cuban Missile Crisis, among other events. Determined to act boldly in light of the continuing Iran hostage crisis, Carter cut off grain shipments to the Soviet Union and cancelled America's participation at the upcoming Summer Olympic Games in Moscow—a boycott that many nations chose to ignore. More significantly, he announced a "Carter Doctrine" for the Persian Gulf, warning that "outside aggression" would "be repelled by any means necessary, including military force." For the first time since Vietnam, young men were ordered to register for the draft. In addition, Carter requested a major increase in defense spending, with $50 billion set aside for new weapons systems such as the multiple-warhead MX missile, which moved from place to place on secret railroad cars to prevent the enemy from tracking it. By 1980, the Cold War was heating up again. Afghanistan and its aftermath had dealt a serious blow to détente.

Death in the Desert

As President Carter and the American people staggered through the repeated shocks of 1979, one issue dominated the national agenda: the fate of the hostages in Iran. The crisis took on symbolic importance as an example of America's declining power in the world—its inability to defend its citizens, its vital interests, its national honor. The television networks flashed nightly pictures of the hostages on humiliating public display in Tehran while frenzied crowds shouted "Death to Carter" and "Down with the United States." In Washington, meanwhile, the president met regularly with the families of the hostages

In 1979, student militants stormed the American embassy in Iran and took dozens of U.S. citizens hostage. Unable to negotiate their release, President Carter approved a secret rescue mission that ended in disaster.

By 1980, many Americans looked for someone to rescue the nation and restore its damaged prestige.

and worked tirelessly to find a diplomatic solution. But this seemed all but impossible, because the Iranians, demanding both the shah and an American apology for supporting him, were not interested in a quick settlement. Reluctantly, Carter ordered a secret mission to free the hostages by force.

The result was disastrous. In April 1980, American commandos reached the Iranian desert, where two of their helicopters were disabled by mechanical problems. Another hit a U.S. cargo plane, killing eight members of the rescue mission. The commandos departed without ever getting close to the hostages in Tehran. To make matters worse, the Iranians proudly displayed the burned corpses for television crews. Most Americans blamed the president for the debacle, and Secretary of State Cyrus Vance, who had worked for a peaceful solution to the crisis, resigned in protest. What little remained of Jimmy Carter's credibility disappeared that fateful day in the Iranian desert.

⁓ C O N C L U S I O N ⁓

The United States in 1980 was an uneasy land. The social upheavals of the 1960s and 1970s had fostered

anxiety as well as progress. The movement for civil rights, so certain in the era of bus boycotts, lunch counter sit-ins, and voting rights marches, was now deeply divided over issues such as forced busing and affirmative action. So, too, the struggle for women's rights generated fierce controversy over abortion, sex roles, workplace equality, and the ERA. On the economic front, Americans faced a world of new troubles—a world of stagnant incomes, rising unemployment, mounting trade deficits, and skyrocketing inflation. No longer were young people guaranteed the prospect of moving a rung or two above their parents on the ladder of success.

Above all, the nation appeared momentarily to lose confidence in its leaders and its goals. Watergate, OPEC, the fall of South Vietnam, Three Mile Island, the hostage crisis, the bungled rescue attempt—all seemed to reflect a loss of purpose, authority, and prestige. As the 1980 election approached, many Americans looked back into the past with a deep sense of nostalgia, hoping for someone to rescue the country and restore the American dream.

RECOMMENDED READINGS

Baughman, James. *The Republic of Mass Culture* (1992) examines the media's enormous impact on modern American culture.

Carroll, Peter. *It Seemed Like Nothing Happened: America in the 1970s* (1982) is a critical overview of American life in the new age of limits.

Isaacson, Walter. *Kissinger* (1992) is a comprehensive biography of the man who helped shape America's foreign policy in the 1970s and beyond.

Kutler, Stanley. *Abuse of Power: The New Nixon Tapes* (1997) is the story of a president's demise told through the secret tapes that brought him down.

Lukas, J. Anthony. *Common Ground: A Turbulent Decade in the Lives of Three American Families* (1986) examines the busing crisis in Boston from several perspectives.

Reich, Charles. *The Greening of America* (1970) is a passionate appeal for community values in a world of individual competition.

Sale, Kirkpatrick. *Power Shift: The Rise of the Southern Rim and Its Challenge to the Eastern Establishment* (1975) explains the growing influence of America's sunbelt on national politics and the economy.

Shilts, Randy. *And the Band Played On* (1987) is a superb account of the spreading AIDS epidemic in the homosexual community.

Wandersee, Winifred. *On the Move: American Women in the 1970s* (1988) highlights the political struggle of women in this decade and the changes that occurred.

Woodward, Bob, and Carl Bernstein. *All the President's Men* (1974) is the inside story of Watergate told by the reporters who broke the scandal.

Vietnam: Protest and Defeat

Baritz, Loren. *Backfire: A History of How American Culture Led Us into Vietnam and Made Us Fight the Way We Did* (1985).

DeBenedetti, Charles. *An American Ordeal: The Antiwar Movement of the Vietnam Era* (1990).

Heineman, Kenneth. *Campus Wars: The Peace Movement at American State Universities in the Vietnam Era* (1993).

McNamara, Robert. *In Retrospect: The Tragedy and Lessons of Vietnam* (1995).

Moser, Richard. *The New Winter Soldiers: GI and Veteran Dissent During the Vietnam Era* (1996).

Sale, Kirkpatrick. *SDS* (1973).

Schell, Jonathan. *The Time of Illusion* (1975).

Shawcross, William. *Sideshow: Nixon, Kissinger, and the Destruction of Cambodia* (1978).

The Watergate Crisis

Dean, John. *Blind Ambition* (1975).

Kutler, Stanley. *The Wars of Watergate* (1990).

Nixon, Richard M. *RN: The Memoirs of Richard Nixon* (1978).

Sirica, John. *To Set the Record Straight* (1979).

Woodward, Bob, and Carl Bernstein, *The Final Days* (1976).

The Oil Crisis and Economic Woes

Auletta, Ken. *The Underclass* (1981).

Barnet, Richard J. *The Lean Years* (1980).

Carter, Jimmy. *Keeping the Faith: Memoirs of a President* (1982).

Reeves, Richard. *A Ford, Not a Lincoln* (1975).

Yergin, Daniel. *The Prize: The Epic Quest for Oil, Money, and Power* (1991).

Racial Tensions, Political Change

Berman, William C. *America's Right Turn: From Nixon to Bush* (1994).

Schlesinger, Arthur, Jr., *The Disuniting of America: Reflections on a Multicultural Society* (1991).

Wilkinson, J. Harvie. *From Brown to Bakke: The Supreme Court and School Integration, 1954–1978* (1979).

PRESIDENTIAL DEBATERS IN 1980

In the 1980 presidential election, Ronald Reagan and Jimmy Carter had one televised debate. Reagan's performance exceeded expectations and helped propel him into the White House after a decisive victory at the polls.

Chapter 31

THE REAGAN-BUSH YEARS

1981–1992

THE PRESIDENCY OF Ronald Reagan defined the decade of the 1980s. His election in 1980 brought to office the most conservative president since Herbert Hoover, and his efforts to redirect the nation toward a smaller and less activist government aroused bitter controversy. After two decades of "failed presidencies," Reagan's ability to serve for two consecutive presidential terms contributed to a mood of renewed optimism about the United States that endured until he left office.

The actual achievements of Reagan and his successor George Bush remain in dispute. During these two administrations, the Cold War ended, the Berlin Wall toppled, and the Soviet Union collapsed. Reagan's partisans gave him the credit for ending the threat of what he had called "the evil empire." Yet victory in the Cold War did not result in a reduction of foreign policy issues and a safer world for the United States.

While the economy boomed during the 1980s, the federal government's budget deficit increased dramatically. Rich Americans became richer, while the gulf between the affluent and the poor widened. Under the pressures of global economic change, American businesses became more efficient and less unwieldy. The price, however, was a loss of jobs in many key industries as American workers faced the trauma of "downsizing." By the end of the 1980s, despite the prosperity

of the Reagan era, apprehension about the economic future of the average American grew.

Uneasiness was particularly prevalent among young Americans, labeled "Generation X" by social commentators. Their prospects seemed less bright than for any comparable group of Americans during the twentieth century. Would they enjoy a career or life as rewarding and prosperous as their parents and grandparents had experienced? Americans in their twenties doubted whether the "safety net" of Social Security and Medicare could survive when the baby boomers of the 1940s and 1950s began receiving their benefits after the year 2000. For all the ebullience and optimism of the Reagan-Bush period, critical social questions remained unanswered.

THE REAGAN REVOLUTION

When Ronald Wilson Reagan took the oath as president of the United States on January 20, 1981, he was the oldest man to assume the nation's highest office. Born in Illinois in 1911, he had been an actor and television personality. Disillusioned with the political liberalism of his youth, he became a Republican and

CHRONOLOGY

1981　Ronald Reagan inaugurated as president

Iranian-held hostages freed from captivity

Sandra Day O'Connor appointed to the Supreme Court

President Reagan survives assassination attempt

AIDS outbreak begins in United States

1982　Deadline for ratification of Equal Rights Amendment passes without success

Severe economic recession grips nation

Democrats make gains in congressional elections

1983　President Reagan proposes Strategic Defense Initiative (SDI)

Social Security reforms adopted

Nancy Reagan begins "Just Say No" campaign against drugs

United States invades Grenada

1984　Geraldine Ferraro becomes first female vice presidential candidate of a major party

Macintosh computer introduced

Summer Olympics occur in Los Angeles

Ronald Reagan reelected

1985　Rock Hudson dies of AIDS

Gramm-Rudman-Hollings budget act adopted

Reagan administration begins negotiations with Iran that lead to Iran-Contra scandal

1986　Tax Reform Act passed

Challenger space shuttle explodes

Immigration Reform Act adopted

Democrats regain control of Senate in elections

Iran-Contra scandal erupts

1987　Stock market has single day loss of 500 points

United States and Soviet Union pursue arms control

Iran-Contra hearings held

1988　Democrats nominate Michael Dukakis to run for president

Republicans select George Bush as their nominee

Antidepressant drug Prozac introduced

George Bush elected president

1989　United States invades Panama to capture Manuel Noriega

Berlin Wall comes down

Chinese kill demonstrators in Tiananmen Square

In *Webster* v. *Reproductive Health Services,* Supreme Court upholds right of states to limit abortion access

1990　George Bush abandons "no new taxes" pledge

Iraq invades Kuwait

Americans with Disabilities Act passed

1991　Iraq defeated in Gulf War

Clarence Thomas nominated to and confirmed for Supreme Court

Soviet Union collapses

---

made a very well-received television broadcast to raise money for Barry Goldwater's presidential campaign in 1964. His good looks and pleasing personality made him extremely popular with conservative audiences. In 1966, friends pressed him to run for governor of California. He defeated the incumbent in a decisive victory. In 1968 he made an abortive run for the presidency, losing to Richard Nixon. Throughout the

1970s Reagan was a major figure in national Republican politics.

Reagan's record as governor of California was mixed. It proved more difficult to enact his conservative agenda than he had anticipated. Instead of reducing spending and shrinking government as he had promised, taxes rose and the California government bureaucracy grew. Nevertheless, his blend of conserva-

tive rhetoric and a sunny disposition made him a natural advocate for what conservatives called traditional values of a smaller government, law and order, and an anti-communist foreign policy. As the nation became more conservative during the 1970s, Reagan's stock rose within the Republican party even though he lost the party's nomination in 1976 against President Gerald Ford.

The problems of the Jimmy Carter administration gave Reagan his opportunity. He became the embodiment of the new national sentiment for lower taxes, restraints on government spending, and concern about inflation. At the same time, he promised increased spending on national defense and a stronger U.S. role overseas to meet the threat of Communism. Republican gains in the congressional elections of 1978 foreshadowed a national victory two years later. As Americans faced spiraling inflation, rising interest rates, and gas lines at their service stations, their support for Jimmy Carter sagged.

Carter versus Reagan

The 1980 presidential election campaign took place in the shadow of an ongoing crisis involving fifty-two American hostages who had been seized in Iran during that country's revolution against the shah. Nightly news broadcasts in the United States reminded audiences of how many days the hostages had been held in captivity. Initially the plight of the hostages helped Jimmy Carter fend off the challenge of Senator Edward M. Kennedy of Massachusetts for the Democratic presidential nomination. By staying in the White House and following a "Rose Garden" strategy that made him look presidential, Carter built up a commanding lead over Kennedy and other Democratic hopefuls. A failed military attempt to rescue the hostages in April 1980 undercut Carter's standing with the voters and made his nomination a hollow prize. Still, most Democrats believed that the president could defeat Reagan. The White House attached little significance to the third-party candidacy of John Anderson, a Republican member of Congress, who ran as a moderate alternative to both major party nominees.

Reagan had emerged as the Republican front-runner after defeating Texan George Bush for the nomination. At the party's national convention he briefly considered asking Gerald Ford to be his running mate. After that initiative collapsed because Ford wanted a quasi-presidential role, Reagan invited Bush to run with him. The personable and attractive Reagan

Television evangelism became one of the hot social trends of the 1980s. Few people embodied the new phenomenon more than Jim and Tammy Faye Bakker of the PTL (Praise the Lord) Ministry. This publicity photo from 1987 shows them in a happier moment before their financial and religious empire crumbled.

proved to be one of the most adept campaigners the nation had seen since the days of John F. Kennedy.

"Are You Better Off?"

During the campaign, Reagan assailed Carter's record on the economy and national defense. The president fired back that Reagan was a dangerous and unreliable political extremist who could not be trusted with the responsibilities of the nation's highest office. The election came down to a televised debate between the two men in late October 1980. Polls indicated that the race was a dead heat. When Carter attacked Reagan's position on Medicare, the challenger responded with a wry remark: "There you go again," making Carter seem awkward and ill-informed. In winding up the debate, Reagan asked the American people "Are you

better off?" than four years earlier. Poll results moved decisively toward Reagan.

Reagan and the Republicans won the election by a substantial margin in the popular vote: 44 million ballots for Reagan to 35 million for Carter and 5.7 million for John Anderson. In the electoral college, Reagan garnered 489 votes and Carter forty-nine. The Republicans regained control of the Senate, picking up twelve seats from the Democrats. Many wondered whether Reagan's victory signaled the arrival of a conservative coalition that would dominate national affairs for years to come.

The Rise of the Christian Right

A central element in Reagan's electoral victory was the votes of evangelical Christians. One manifestation of

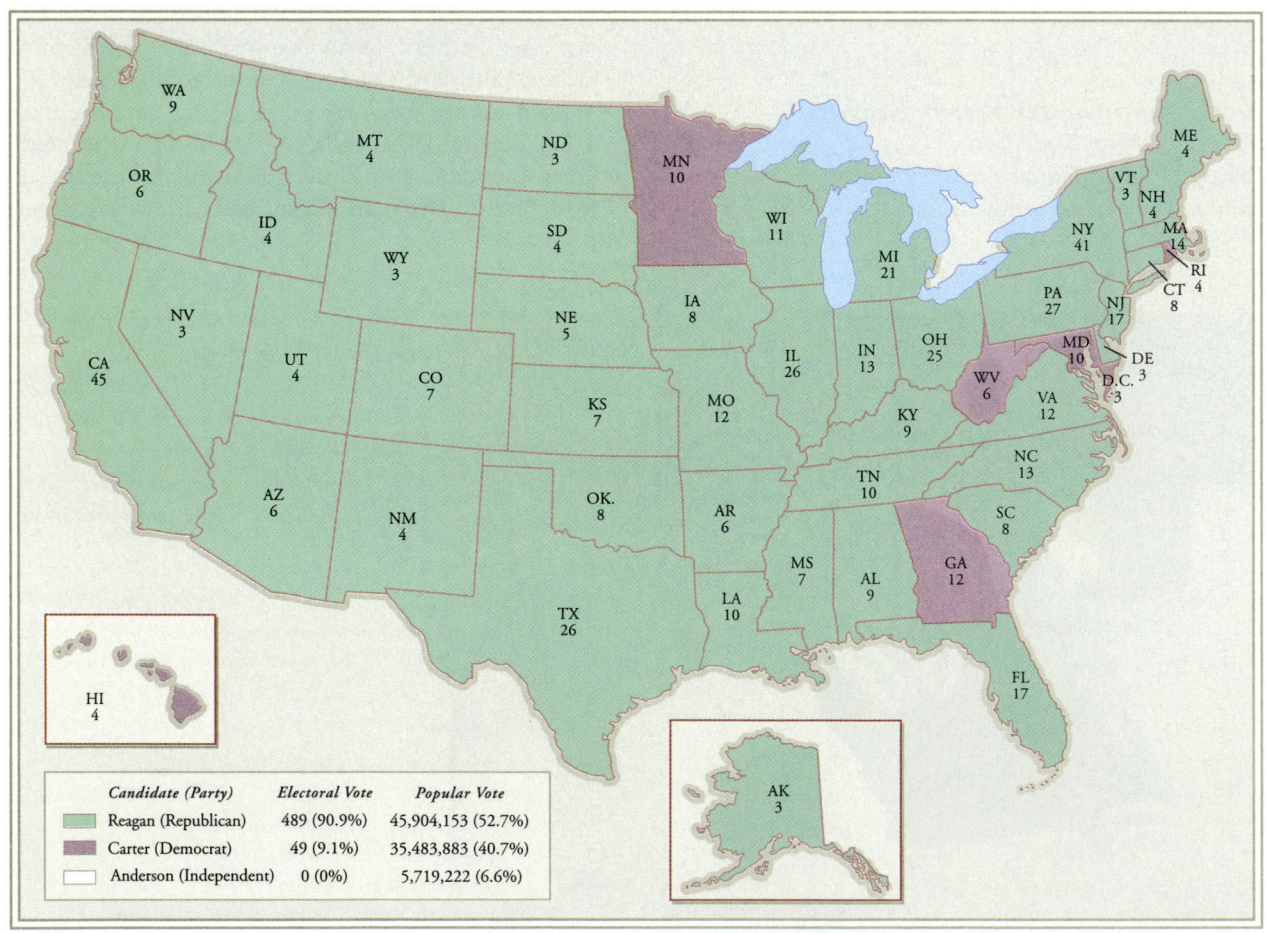

Candidate (Party)	Electoral Vote	Popular Vote
Reagan (Republican)	489 (90.9%)	45,904,153 (52.7%)
Carter (Democrat)	49 (9.1%)	35,483,883 (40.7%)
Anderson (Independent)	0 (0%)	5,719,222 (6.6%)

MAP 31.1 | THE ELECTION OF 1980

their political clout was the Moral Majority, an organization founded by the Reverend Jerry Falwell of Virginia in 1979. Falwell tapped into the expanding base of evangelicals in denominations such as the Southern Baptist Convention. Moral Majority assailed "sinful" aspects of modern culture such as abortion, homosexuality, rock music, and drugs. In schools, its members sought to have creationism rather than evolution taught in schools.

Throughout the 1980s evangelical Christianity permeated American politics. On cable television, viewers tuned in to Pat Robertson's "700 Club" on the Christian Broadcasting Network which Robertson had founded. Other ministers such as Jim Bakker with his PTL ("Praise the Lord") program and the fiery evangelist Jimmy Swaggart commanded sizable audiences. Though both Bakker and Swaggart eventually ran afoul of the law for fraud (Bakker) and sexual misadventures (Swaggart), their message resonated in many areas of the nation. Ronald Reagan never implemented the evangelical agenda, but he gave them a sympathetic hearing that enhanced their influence on American public life.

The divisive issue of abortion helped fuel the rise of the Christian Right. Following the Supreme Court decision in *Roe* v. *Wade* (1973), the number of abortions in the United States stood at 1.5 million per year. Foes of abortion, most notably in the Roman Catholic church and among evangelical Protestants, asserted that the unborn baby was a human being from the moment of conception and entitled to all the rights of a living person. To reduce the number of abortions and to overturn the *Roe* decision, the "right to life" forces, as they called themselves, pressured lawmakers to cut back on the right of abortion and to enact restrictive laws. The Hyde amendment, adopted in Congress in 1976, banned the use of Medicaid funds to pay for abortions to women on welfare.

The anti-abortion forces believed that more direct action was warranted. They conducted picketing and boycotts of abortion clinics in the 1980s and arranged for massive public demonstrations. Their tactics became more violent as the decade progressed. Operation Rescue tried to prevent patients from entering abortion clinics. Other protesters turned to bombing of buildings and assassination of doctors. The Republican party became largely anti-abortion in its policies and programs. The Democrats were equally committed to what was called "a woman's right to choose."

Reagan in Office

Reagan came to Washington determined to enact his conservative priorities. He set out his goals in a single sentence: "We must balance the budget, reduce tax rates, and restore our defenses." The incoming president believed that it would be possible to achieve all of these objectives at the same time.

Ronald Reagan brought striking political gifts to the White House. His long career in Hollywood had given him a skill in conveying his views that won him the title of "The Great Communicator." When delivering a prepared speech with a teleprompter to guide him, Reagan could read a text with practiced artistry. His use of humor, especially when he stressed his own foibles, was deft; it reinforced his rapport with his fellow citizens. He exuded a degree of optimism about his country, sincerity about his positions, and confidence in the rightness of his views that made him a masterful politician during his first six years as president.

Yet Reagan had significant weaknesses, too. He knew very little about the actual operation of the federal government, and displayed scant curiosity about such matters. He read very few of the documents that crossed his desk and watched movies when he should have been reading position papers. As a friend put it, "He lived life on the surface where the small waves are, not deep down where the heavy currents tug." Reagan believed that there were few hard choices in governance, and he did not inform the nation of the serious alternatives that had to be faced in reducing the deficits and curbing government spending.

The president was not a simple man. Friends and family members found him complex and difficult to "read" in private. Many commentators said that Reagan played the role of president better than any other president since Franklin D. Roosevelt. But after the glow of the performance faded, there remained the question of whether he had done more than walk through the presidency.

The Reagan Team

Part of the success that Reagan achieved during his first term came about because of the effective staff that managed his daily activities. His chief of staff was James Baker, a Texas politician who had not been close to the Reagans before the election. Baker proved to be

Ronald Reagan's wife was a very controversial first lady because of her opulent lifestyle. She responded to criticism with the "Just Say No" campaign against drugs, and played a very large role in all the decisions of her husband's administration.

an adroit player in the White House. Joining him were Michael Deaver, who directed media activities, and Edwin Meese—a longtime friend from California who tended to policy issues. These men "packaged" the president in settings that capitalized on his warm relationship with the American people. The gritty details of government went on out of the public's view. The approach worked well, partly because these aides allowed Reagan to deal with the large issues that interested him instead of the mundane details of governing, for which he had little aptitude or serious interest.

Another important player in the Reagan presidency was his wife Nancy. Criticized for her opulent lifestyle during her early days as first lady, she won over the Washington media with a deft blend of self-deprecating humor and commitment to a "Just Say No" campaign against drugs. Behind the scenes she managed the president's schedule with the help of an astrologer. She also fretted about Reagan's place in history and

urged the president privately to promote some degree of detente with the Soviet Union over nuclear weapons.

The Early Months

The situation that Ronald Reagan and the Republicans faced in the winter of 1981 seemed to warrant decisive action. The Republicans controlled the White House and the Senate, where they commanded a 53–46 majority. Democrats remained the majority in the House of Representatives, 242–190. The Reagan team believed that the nation was experiencing an economic crisis. In 1980, the inflation rate was over 12 percent, the unemployment rate was above 7 percent, and the prime interest rate had gone to almost 20 percent. The national debt had reached $908 billion. In Reagan's view, the responsibility for these ominous figures lay with the federal government. As he told Congress on February 18, 1981, "The most important cause of our economic problems has been the government itself."

To remedy the situation, the administration embraced a program that combined traditional Republican suspicion of government spending with an aggressive reduction in federal income taxes. The term "supply-side economics" became shorthand for what this program promised to do. The government should lower income and corporate tax rates to give private business and individual taxpayers more money to spend. The predicted surge in productive economic activity would result in an increase in tax revenues, which would prevent large budget deficits. The supply-side method was politically attractive. Lower taxes naturally appealed to the electorate, and it seemed as though a balanced budget could be achieved without painful spending cuts or personal sacrifices from the American people.

Defining the Reagan Presidency

In his first year Reagan displayed his talent as a politician and benefited from an abundance of personal good fortune. He implemented his policy agenda as promised. The release of U.S. hostages in Iran on January 20, 1981, removed that troublesome issue from the public sphere. The president's confidence and self-assurance also drew a positive response from the

The assassination attempt against Ronald Reagan on March 30, 1981, wounded the president more seriously than was revealed at the time. His optimism and high spirits in the face of his wound added to public confidence. This picture shows an unidentified Secret Service agent yelling instructions after shots were fired.

American people. When Reagan was shot on March 30, 1981, the would-be assassin's bullet came closer to ending his life than the public knew. The president's courage and good humor in this moment of crisis increased his popularity and added to the reservoir of goodwill that he commanded.

A second event that raised Reagan even higher in the polls was his handling of a strike by the Professional Air Traffic Controllers Organization (PATCO). As government employees, the controllers could not legally strike, and the president fired them when they refused to heed a back-to-work order. The message for the nation was that the White House would be tough on organized labor. Reagan later said that the decision "convinced people who might have thought otherwise that I meant what I said."

The Economic Agenda

During the first half of 1981, the Reagan administration used its political muscle to enact its "economic recovery" program. Even though the Democrats controlled the House of Representatives, a coalition of Republicans and "boll weevil Democrats" (southern and western conservatives) pushed through legislation that trimmed tax rates by 25 percent over three years. As the legislation went forward, a bidding war developed between the House Democratic leadership and the White House. Even more tax cuts for special interests were added. Budget Director David Stockman commented that "the hogs were really feeding."

In tandem with the tax measure, the administration sought budget cuts for a number of discretionary social programs to advance the president's goal of a balanced budget by 1984. Although the budget act, passed in the House on June 25, 1981, promised future reductions in spending, during its first year it provided $16 billion in immediate cuts. That was $200 billion less than would have been required to achieve a real step toward a balanced budget.

The Limits of the Reagan Revolution

Two major policy commitments limited what the Reagan administration could accomplish. The president declined to make cuts in what he termed "the social safety net": Social Security, Medicare, veterans' benefits, Head Start, and school lunch programs. All of these spending policies had vocal and powerful supporters. Serious cutbacks would have involved

substantial political risks for the new president. The practical result was that almost half of the federal budget was placed beyond the reach of congressional budget-cutting efforts.

The other priority of the Reagan administration was a sharp increase in defense spending. Reagan believed that the nation's military establishment had been neglected during Carter's presidency. In 1979, however, the Democratic Congress and the administration had begun a long-range program to build up American military power, and the Reagan White House expanded on that initiative. During the Ford-Carter years, defense budgets had been less than $200 billion annually. Under Reagan, the Pentagon budget rose to nearly $300 billion per year by 1985.

A Growing Deficit

The outcome of modest cuts in social programs and entitlements, sharp hikes in defense spending, and a reduction in tax rates was a growth in the government deficit to $128 billion by 1982. The ballooning federal deficits continued throughout the Reagan era, producing a surge in the national debt. The goal of a balanced budget in 1984 vanished quickly, never to return while Reagan was in the White House. A dramatic change had occurred in the government's fiscal situation, with serious consequences for the future.

TABLE 31.1 FEDERAL GOVERNMENT DEFICITS, 1980–1989 (IN U.S. DOLLARS)	
1980	73,808,000,000
1981	78,936,000,000
1982	127,940,000,000
1983	207,764,000,000
1984	185,324,000,000
1985	212,260,000,000
1986	221,140,000,000
1987	149,661,000,000
1988	155,151,000,000
1989	153,319,000,000

SOURCE: *World Almanac, 1995*, p. 108.

The huge deficits drove economic policy for the decade that followed and future generations were left with a massive debt to fund and pay off.

Reagan's Domestic Policies

In his inaugural address, President Reagan proclaimed: "In this present crisis, government *is* not the solution to our problem; government *is* the problem." As part of his response to a large, intrusive government, Reagan advocated an extensive program of deregulation to lessen regulation of the private sector. The process of "getting government off the backs of the people," however, turned out to have significant consequences for the nation during the 1980s and into the 1990s in banking and finance, telecommunications, and the environment.

The Reagan administration pursued a new course in environmental policy. Secretary of the Interior James G. Watt, a conservative who disliked all restrictions on public lands in the West, sought to open new areas for oil drilling, cut back on the acquisition of land for national parks, and put in place other bureaucrats eager to reduce the amount of environmental regulation that the government conducted. Appointees in the Environmental Protection Agency (EPA) came under fire for having used regulations for political and personal gain. In late 1983, Watt left the administration under fire after commenting about an advisory panel that he had recently named: "We have every kind of mix you can have. I have a black, I have a woman, two Jews, and a cripple."

The Savings and Loan Disaster

The most spectacular and disastrous example of deregulation occurred in 1982, when Congress and the White House agreed to lift restrictions from the savings and loan industry. During a time of high inflation and rising interest rates, savings and loan institutions had difficulty earning a profit because of the low rates of interest they were allowed by law to pay on their deposits. In 1980 Congress increased federal insurance coverage to $100,000 per account and allowed savings and loan companies to offer even higher interest rates. These measures did not, however, increase the savings and loan companies' profits on the money that they loaned. Partly in response to lobbying by the industry

and the large campaign contributions that lawmakers received, Congress decided to deregulate the thrifts and allow them to invest in higher risk assets, including commercial real estate, fine art, and in some instances speculative or fraudulent ventures.

At the same time that lending practices were relaxed, the Reagan administration cut back on the number of banking and regulatory examiners. With federal deposit insurance guaranteeing that they would be bailed out, savings and loan operators plunged into ventures that were risky and often illegal. At first, there seemed to be few problems, but by 1983 and 1984 troubling signs of weakness appeared in the banking and savings and loan businesses. It was a worrisome portent of trouble to come.

The Social Security Crisis

By the early 1980s Social Security, the most popular New Deal program, had reached a funding crisis. During the 1970s Congress and the Nixon administration had established a system of cost-of-living-adjustments (COLAs) that raised benefits for Social Security recipients as the rate of inflation rose (known as indexing). Indexing of benefits caused the cost of Social Security to soar as the population aged and more people received Social Security checks. But efforts to trim COLAs seemed futile because of the political fact that tinkering with Social Security benefits guaranteed electoral defeat for anyone who tried it.

President Reagan learned that lesson in the spring of 1981 when the administration proposed a cut in benefits for early retirees (those who would begin receiving benefits at age sixty-two). When the initiative was announced, gleeful Democrats assailed it and Republicans in Congress deserted Reagan. Social Security did not come up again until December 1981, when the president appointed a bipartisan panel to deal with long-range funding of the retirement program. The result, announced after the 1982 elections, was a compromise that raised payroll taxes to pay for Social Security, taxed some of the benefits of people over sixty-five who had high incomes, and put off providing for the long-term viability of the system. For the moment, the Social Security system seemed to be on solid ground once again. The issue of budgets and entitlements that Social Security represented were left for future political leaders to encounter.

REAGAN AND FOREIGN POLICY: THE FIRST PHASE

In foreign affairs, the new administration came into office with what seemed to be a clear, simple agenda. The complexities of world affairs proved difficult for the Reagan team to master during its first several years in power. Reagan himself had little knowledge of foreign relations and was not curious about the subject. The secretary of state, Alexander Haig, sought to be the "vicar" of foreign policy, but he did not work well with the president's other advisors. There were also real fears about Haig's ambitions and erratic personality. Reagan did not make effective use of the National Security Council. Not until George Shultz became secretary of state in 1982 did some balance and stability characterize the administration's handling of foreign affairs.

Reagan did operate on the basis of strong convictions about the relationship of the United States to its principal adversary. In 1983, he called the Soviet Union "an evil empire" and said that the Cold War was a struggle between "right and wrong and good and evil." In dealing with the Soviets, then, the president insisted arms agreements be based on the principle of "trust but verify." He was convinced that the United States could outspend the Soviet Union in an arms race. "It would be of great benefit," he said in 1980, "if we started a buildup." Faced with an aging and incompetent Soviet leadership between 1981 and 1985, the White House avoided any summit meetings during that period. As a result, Soviet-American relations experienced a distinct chill during Reagan's first term.

This stern language did not rule out flexibility in some areas. Early in the new administration the president lifted the grain embargo that President Carter had established when the Soviet Union invaded Afghanistan in 1980. It was an action that pleased American wheat farmers. Reagan also reiterated his view that a nuclear war could not be won and should never be fought. Although the new White House team did not like the SALT II Treaty that Carter had negotiated, it largely observed the pact's provisions. Increased tensions between East and West overshadowed these gestures of restraint.

One area where the rivalry between the two superpowers flared up was Central America. The Reagan administration believed that the victory of the

One of the most hotly debated foreign policy issues of the 1980s had to do with the Reagan administration's support for the rebels against the Sandinista government in Nicaragua. The "Contras," as they were known, are shown here training in a remote area of their country.

Sandinistas in Nicaragua in 1979 represented a serious threat to U.S. interests in the region, especially in neighboring El Salvador (see Chapter 30). By late 1981, the United States was underwriting a rebellion against the Sandinista regime led by a faction called the "Contras." Although President Reagan likened the anti-Sandinistas to the patriots of the American Revolution, in 1982 the Democratic House of Representatives adopted the Boland Amendment (named after Congressman Edward Boland of Massachusetts) which sought to block funds from being used to oust the Sandinistas. In Latin America, suspicion about U.S. policy increased during 1982.

The 1982 Elections

Reagan and his administration paid a political price for the policies of the first two years. A severe recession continued until almost the end of 1982. Although Reagan argued that the recession would soon end, the Republicans suffered a setback at the polls in the congressional elections. The Democrats gained twenty-seven seats in the House while the Republicans maintained their dominance in the Senate. Nevertheless,

President Reagan again urged his fellow Republicans to "stay the course." In time, he maintained, his economic policies would produce positive results.

A Rebounding Economy and Foreign Policy Successes

Shortly after the election the economy picked up steam, stimulated by the Reagan tax cuts. The inflation rate declined and unemployment receded. As the recovery gained strength, so did Reagan and his party. Adding to the president's popularity was the U.S. invasion of the Caribbean island of Grenada in October 1983. Fearing that radicals close to Fidel Castro and Cuba were about to turn Grenada into a Soviet base, the administration launched a powerful invasion force that secured control of the island after a brief struggle. The episode was a public relations success and further enhanced Reagan's image as a decisive leader.

In fact, the foreign policy scene was more complex than the victory in Grenada indicated. The war in Nicaragua was not going well for the Contras, and El Salvador was experiencing atrocities from right-wing death squads that murdered their opponents and left-

wing insurgents sympathetic to Nicaragua. In 1984 Congress adopted a second, more restrictive Boland Amendment to prevent the government from aiding the Contras.

In the Middle East Reagan's hopes of producing a lasting peace between Israel and its neighbors were also frustrated. The administration did not stop Israel from invading Lebanon in June 1982, and U.S. Marines were sent into the region as part of a multinational peacekeeping force. American involvement in Lebanon's turbulent politics led to the death of 239 Marines when a terrorist bomb blew up a barracks in 1983. The Marines withdrew in early 1984, but the Reagan administration's diplomatic efforts in the region were unsuccessful.

Star Wars: The Strategic Defense Initiative (SDI)

In March 1983 the most significant defense policy initiative of the first Reagan term came when the president announced in March 1983 what he called the Strategic Defense Initiative (SDI). Reagan envisioned a system of laser weapons, based in space, that would intercept and shoot down Soviet missiles before they could reach the United States. Influenced by memories of science fiction serials in which he had starred as a young man, as well as by advocates of an anti-missile system, Reagan wanted "a defensive screen that could intercept those missiles when they came out of their silos."

An appealing vision on the drawing board or in animated versions for television, SDI confronted immense technical problems that made it unlikely that it could be deployed for years. Critics promptly dubbed it "Star Wars" after the hit movie and questioned its technical rationale. For Reagan, the program represented an answer to the problem of relying on nuclear deterrence to stave off war between the superpowers. He pressed forward with SDI over the objections of his political opponents and the displeasure of the Soviet Union, whose leaders knew that their faltering economy could never duplicate SDI if the Americans ever achieved it. Envisioned as a way to end the Cold War, the Strategic Defense Initiative complicated American-Russian relations during the last two years of Reagan's first term.

SOCIAL TENSIONS AND STRAINS OF THE 1980S

The specter of nuclear war was not the only danger that Americans faced in the early 1980s. The appearance of a biological menace contributed to the unease that many Americans felt during this period. In the early Reagan years Americans learned of a new and deadly disease. Scientists called it AIDS (for acquired immune deficiency syndrome). The source of the virus was in Africa, and it appeared in the United States first in 1981. The virus ravaged the immune system of its victims and there was no known cure. Most of those infected were doomed to an inevitable and painful death. By the end of Ronald Reagan's first term, the number of confirmed AIDS deaths had reached 3,700.

The major process by which the virus spread within the population was through the exchange of bodily fluids. Mothers who were infected passed the condition on to their children; infected blood was transferred during transfusions. The most vulnerable groups were drug addicts, bisexuals, and homosexuals. During the first half of the decade, the spread of AIDS and fears about the fatal prognosis for those who had the disease seemed to be confined to the homosexual community. Later, largely through the sharing of needles for drug injection and unsafe sexual practices, AIDS began spreading more rapidly among heterosexuals, especially in low-income communities.

TABLE 31.2 NEW AIDS CASES IN THE UNITED STATES, 1988–1993	
1988	30,648
1989	33,576
1990	41,642
1991	43,660
1992	45,883
1993	102,780

SOURCE: *World Almanac, 1997,* p. 975.

The emergence of the personal computer transformed the American economy in the 1980s. One of the most popular was the Macintosh, made by Apple Computer, shown here in its early version.

The Intertwining of Technology and Culture

The sudden emergence of the AIDS epidemic was only one of the rash of new social and cultural developments that occurred during the early 1980s. The nation experienced the initial stages of a revolution in communications and culture that left American society dramatically altered by the time Reagan left office in 1989. The elements of this revolution included the development of the personal computer and the ability of individuals to use the new technology to improve their lives. At the same time the spread of cable television and the emergence of alternatives to then major television networks allowed news and entertainment to be shared with ever-increasing speed. By the end of the 1980s, seeing movies at home on a video cassette recorder (VCR) had become a major form of entertainment.

The Personal Computer

In 1981, International Business Machines (IBM) announced that it would market a computer for home use. Recognizing the potential impact of such a product, two young computer software writers proposed to develop the operating system for the new machine. Bill Gates and Paul Allen of Microsoft adapted an existing software program and transformed it into DOS (disk operating system), which ran the hardware created by IBM. Important changes followed throughout the decade, including the Lotus 1-2-3 spreadsheet program in 1982, Microsoft Windows in 1983, and the Apple Macintosh Computer in 1984. After January 1983, sales of personal computers rose from 20,000 annually to more than half a million per year.

The computer revolution gathered momentum over the course of the 1980s. People found that they could publish books from their desktops, trace financial accounts, make travel reservations, and play a wide assortment of computer games. Growing out of the Advanced Research Projects Agency of the Pentagon was a network of computers founded in 1969. As computer users and researchers exchanged messages over this and other networks in the late 1970s and early 1980s, the National Science Foundation promoted the Internet as an overall network bulletin board. Usenet groups and e-mail became more common as the 1980s progressed. Politicians like Albert Gore (D-Tennessee) began speaking of the "information superhighway," a phrase that came into widespread use to convey the potential that computers promoted by the end of the decade.

The Cable Generation

In 1981, a new network appeared on cable television. Music Television (MTV) presented round-the-clock

videos of rock performers aimed at a teenage audience. At about the same time, Ted Turner launched the Cable News Network (CNN) and a related programming service, Headline News, that presented the news in half-hour segments twenty-four hours a day. As cable television expanded during the 1980s, the dominance of the three major television networks (ABC, CBS, and NBC) gave way to a dizzying array of programming that offered viewers such all-sports channels as Entertainment Sports Programming Network (ESPN), all country music channels such as Country Music Television (CMT), and several services showing first-run movies.

MTV offered the most intriguing cultural development of the period. Its audience was the middle- and upper-middle-class adolescent and preteen market for rock music. MTV featured major performers in video versions of their hits or potential hits mouthing (or "lip-synching") the words to a prerecorded soundtrack. So successful was MTV that in 1985 it spawned a second network, VideoHits1 (VH1), with a similar format.

Michael Jackson and Madonna: Media Stars of the 1980s

The popularity of two performers demonstrated the fascinating interrelationship between technology and pop culture in the 1980s. In December 1982, CBS Records released a new album by the twenty-four-year-old rock star Michael Jackson. At a time of lagging record sales for the industry as a whole, "Thriller" became a runaway hit, selling half a million copies a week until it reached a total of 47 million around the world. Then, in March 1983, Jackson gave a dazzling singing and dancing performance at the "Motown 25" reunion program that further accelerated sales of "Thriller." Jackson's videos of hits from the album broke down the racial barriers that had kept black artists off the MTV and VH1 networks. After he did a horror filmlike video under the title "Thriller," Jackson became the most celebrated male artist of the decade; his live appearances attained legendary status among the young people of the era.

Although her popularity did not reach the heights attained by Michael Jackson, Madonna (Madonna Louise Veronica Ciccone) combined records, video, cable television and movie roles to achieve superstar

Michael Jackson became a worldwide superstar in the 1980s for his innovative music videos and dramatic live performances. This photograph captures his intensity and style during an appearance before an enthusiastic audience.

status as a pop icon. Her first album "Borderline" was widely promoted through MTV, and in 1984 she used that venue to introduce two major hits: "Like a Virgin" and "Material Girl." She delved into controversial matters such as pregnancy among teenagers (in "Papa Don't Preach," 1986) and pushed the limits of sexual explicitness on television in subsequent songs and videos. Her craze produced Madonna look-alikes and also aroused the anger of religious leaders who bridled at her mockery of religious symbols.

Like Jackson, Madonna capitalized on her fame to achieve larger-than-life status around the world. In a conservative era, sexual ambiguity and a lack of restraint commanded big returns from teenage consumers attuned to the latest in the electronic marketplace. By the end of the decade, conservatives who wanted the government to keep out of economic decisions in other areas clamored for record companies to engage in self-censorship of artists like Madonna.

Madonna captured the same type of superstardom as Michael Jackson with a carefully crafted blend of sexual explicitness and celebrity. Her blond hair and scanty costumes become a trademark of her erotic appeal to live audiences. Her career in motion pictures was less successful than her stage and music video performances.

The American Family in the 1980s

The drive to censor records was only one example of the varied ways in which the American people responded to new and troubling changes in the family and its place in society during Reagan's presidency. In 1981, the number of divorces stood at nearly 1.2 million annually, the highest rate ever. At the same time, the number of births to unmarried women rose dramatically during the 1970s. With these developments came a marked increase in the number of single-parent families, which rose from 3.8 million in 1970 to 10.5 million by 1992. The impact of this trend was especially evident among African Americans: By the end of the 1980s, more than 60 percent of all African-American families were single-parent families.

The erosion of the traditional family translated into economic hardship for many children of single-parent homes. In 1983, the Bureau of the Census reported

that 13 million children under age six were growing up in poverty. Senator Daniel Patrick Moynihan commented that the United States had become "the first society in history in which a person is more likely to be poor if young rather than old." Much of the government's spending on efforts to alleviate poverty was directed at the elderly, so that by the end of the 1980s, they received from the federal government eleven times the amount spent to address the needs of children.

One major area of concern for families was the state of the public schools. A series of high-profile national studies suggested that American education was "a disaster area." Students did not receive instruction in the skills needed if they were to succeed in a complex and competitive world. Parents complained that their children had to do little homework, were graded too easily, and often graduated without marketable skills. Conservatives blamed this state of affairs on the National Education Association (NEA), the teachers union, and government policies that "threw money" at schools. Liberals countered that government must spend even more to address the problems of the public schools. By 1983 another national survey, titled *A Nation at Risk,* said that the country faced dire consequences if public education did not undergo sweeping reform.

Responses to Change

As families felt the effects of these economic and social changes, Americans responded with contradictory approaches. On the one hand, sexual mores became more tolerant. On the other, efforts to recapture "traditional family values" animated many groups on the conservative end of the political spectrum. The boundaries that had governed the depiction of sexual behavior in the movies and on television relaxed in significant ways during the 1980s. On prime-time television, viewers could hear language and see sexual intimacy depicted in a fashion that would have been unthinkable a few years earlier. Materials that previous generations would have considered pornographic now seemed to be readily available, even to children and teenagers.

At the same time that some cultural taboos were relaxed, conservative groups struck back against what they saw as excessive permissiveness and laxity. The Coalition for Better Television, an offshoot of the

Moral Majority, pressured the networks to promote programming of "that which lifts and inspires, not that which degrades and exploits." The group's organizers threatened nationwide boycotts of advertisers who did not follow its guidelines. The coalition attracted great media attention during the early part of the decade, and was a source of concern for some sponsors of primetime shows. When network profits remained high, the shows offered on television showed few effects of the boycott drive. Resolving the tension between the conservative social values of many Americans and the entertainment industry's efforts to maintain high ratings by meeting the demand for programming with violent or sexual content remained difficult throughout the 1980s.

THE 1984 PRESIDENTIAL ELECTION

At the beginning of 1984, the Reagan administration had recovered from the difficulties of its first two years. Reagan's popularity rating stood at 55 percent, and the electoral map seemed to favor the Republicans. The Democratic base in the South was disappearing, and the president had made substantial gains among what were known as "Reagan Democrats," people who shared the president's social conservatism. Reagan's only apparent vulnerability was his age. At seventy-three, he was sometimes detached and vague, and he clearly lacked stamina. After his presidency, it was revealed that he suffered from Alzheimer's disease, but whether the onset of this condition occurred during his second term remains unclear. In 1984, however, unless something happened to emphasize how old he was, he had a clear advantage over any potential Democratic challenger.

Democrats experienced staggering problems in finding a plausible candidate to run against the incumbent president. In the initial stages the front-runner seemed to be former Vice President Walter Mondale of Minnesota. A protégé of Senator Hubert Humphrey, Mondale had strong ties to the traditional elements of the Democratic party—labor, women, and environmentalists. He was not a good public speaker and lacked a vibrant personality, yet it was widely expected that he would win the nomination.

The Democrats put their nominees through such a grueling process of primaries and caucuses to get the approval of the party that the standard-bearer was often unable to make a competitive race in the general election.

Two challengers emerged to stop Mondale's bid for the nomination. The first was the Reverend Jesse Jackson, a veteran of the civil rights movement, who combined powerful oratory with espousal of radical causes. He became the first credible African-American candidate to seek the nomination of a major party, but he proved unable to reach beyond black voters in the primaries. The other Democratic hopeful was Senator Gary Hart of Colorado, who styled himself a "new Democrat," which meant that he did not endorse the use of government power to regulate society to the extent that Mondale did. Hart won a surprise victory in the New Hampshire primary, and it seemed for a time that Mondale's candidacy might be in danger. But the front-runner countered with effective television ads and won a majority of the convention delegates before the Democrats gathered in San Francisco in July.

Mondale's chances of winning the election against Reagan were slim at best. Under those circumstances, the choice of the vice presidential nominee became largely symbolic. Nominating Jesse Jackson would have been politically unwise because of white voters' intense opposition to having a black candidate on the national ticket. Gary Hart lost out because of his personal qualities, including rumors about his marital infidelities. Mondale came under intense pressure to select a woman as his running mate, and in the week before the convention opened he agreed to the selection of Representative Geraldine Ferraro of New York.

Ferraro was an intelligent, thoughtful politician, but she had weaknesses that had not emerged during the selection process. Her family's financial problems became a source of controversy when she refused to release her tax returns in a timely manner. For a campaign that needed help in the South and West, moreover, Ferraro did little.

The Republicans had all the best of the 1984 campaign. President Reagan's popularity crested during the celebrations of the 40th anniversary of the D-Day invasions in June, and his appearance at the 1984 Olympic Games in Los Angeles identified him with an event in which American athletes dominated the competition. In a time of patriotic enthusiasm, Reagan seemed more in tune with the optimism and confidence of the moment.

Faced with a popular incumbent and a likely defeat, Democratic presidential candidate Walter Mondale took a chance and named Geraldine Ferraro, a New York congresswoman, as his vice presidential candidate. The gesture put Ferraro into history as the first woman chosen by a major political party for its national ticket, but it did not help Mondale avoid a decisive defeat at the hands of Ronald Reagan.

Mondale versus Reagan

An earnest, dull man, Mondale addressed the serious issues that the country confronted. In the face of the huge budget deficits of the Reagan years, he warned that tax increases were necessary to pay for government programs that Americans wanted. For the Republicans, the chance to denounce the Democrats as big-spenders beholden to special interest groups was one that their skilled political strategists exploited to the full.

The only stumble for Reagan came in the first of two televised debates. He showed his age and lack of a clear grasp of many issues. The consensus was that Mondale had won a clear victory over the president. Two weeks later, after much Republican soul-searching, however, Reagan rebounded. When a questioner asked him about his age, the president replied that he would not allow age to be an issue. "I am not going to exploit, for political purposes, my opponent's youth and inexperience," he said.

Reagan won by a landslide. He carried forty-nine of the fifty states; Mondale narrowly won his home state and swept the District of Columbia. The president collected 59 percent of the popular vote. The Republicans retained control of the Senate; the Democrats lost

seats in the House but maintained their dominance of that chamber.

The 1984 election was largely an election about whether the American people liked Ronald Reagan's presidency. The Republicans offered no blueprint to guide the country. As the second term would demonstrate, the Reagan Revolution, as its partisans called it, had little that was new to offer the American people.

REAGAN'S SECOND TERM

Changes in the president's staff marked the transition from one administration to the other. The team that had initially guided Reagan's fortunes broke up. The White House chief of staff, James Baker, agreed to exchange jobs with the secretary of the treasury, Donald Regan. The president accepted the swap without much thought, a friendly gesture that had serious consequences. Regan lacked political skill and did not know how to showcase the president's better qualities to advantage. Meanwhile, Reagan's media advisor Michael Deaver, and other key operatives, departed. The efficiency and smoothness of the White House eroded rapidly.

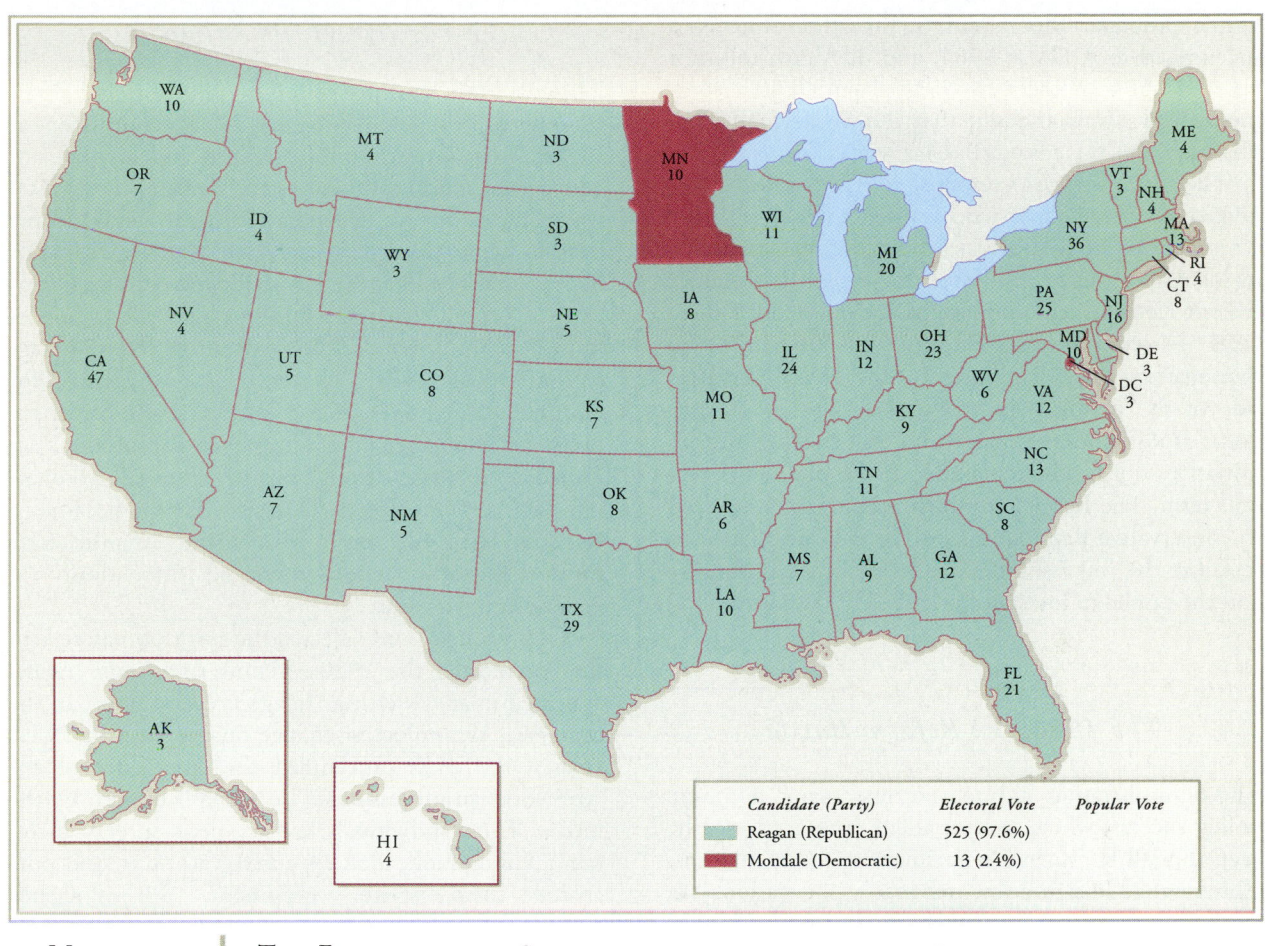

Candidate (Party)	Electoral Vote	Popular Vote
Reagan (Republican)	525 (97.6%)	
Mondale (Democratic)	13 (2.4%)	

MAP 31.2 | THE ELECTION OF 1984

Tax Reform and Deficits

Despite Reagan's pledge to balance the federal budget by 1984, the combinations of tax cuts and increased spending on both defense and discretionary programs widened the budget deficit. Federal receipts reached $666 billion by 1984, but outlays stood at almost $852 billion, with a resulting deficit of $186 billion.

The administration did not have a strategy to trim the deficit, but the Senate devised a plan for doing so. Created by a new Republican senator, Phil Gramm of Texas, the measure required that federal spending programs be reduced by specified amounts or face across-the-board percentage reductions. Sponsored by Senators Warren Rudman of New Hampshire, one of Gramm's Republican colleagues, and Senator Ernest F.

"Fritz" Hollings, a South Carolina Democrat, the scheme quickly became known as "Gramm-Rudman-Hollings." It promised to produce lower deficits without requiring lawmakers to choose among tough options. Congress embraced it enthusiastically, especially because the tough cuts in government spending would not be mandated until after the 1986 elections.

The AIDS Crisis: The Second Phase

In October 1985 the public's perception of the threat of AIDS intensified when the movie star Rock Hudson died of the disease. News of his illness, his long concealed homosexuality, and his death increased awareness of the dimensions of this mounting public

health problem. More than 6,700 other Americans succumbed to AIDS in 1985, and the death toll shot up to 15,504 annually two years later. Reagan commented: "I always thought that the world would end in a flash, but this sounds like it's worse."

The administration's response to AIDS reflected the division between those who wanted to deal with the virus as a public health issue and those who viewed it in ideological terms. In October, Surgeon General C. Everett Koop issued a report that recommended three steps to control AIDS: "One, abstinence; two, monogamy; three, condoms." On the conservative side of the political spectrum, the mention of condoms aroused intense opposition that blocked further initiatives during the remainder of the president's second term. The Reagan administration largely deferred to conservative Republicans on the issue and failed to mobilize the full resources of the medical community and the public to forestall the spread of the virus.

The 1986 Tax Reform Battle

The administration did achieve one major domestic policy success, which the president embraced eagerly, even though he was not its primary sponsor. In 1986, Congress made significant reforms in the nation's tax laws. The reforms, originating with Democratic Senator Bill Bradley of New Jersey, were taken up by the Treasury Department early in Reagan's second term, and gained the support of the chair of the House Ways and Means Committee, Daniel Rostenkowski of Illinois.

The tax bill was passed by the House in late 1985 and went to the Senate, where it faced uncertain prospects. By April 1986, the Senate Finance Committee seemed likely to kill the bill or load it with special preferences. At that point, the chair of the committee, Senator Robert Packwood of Oregon, devised a bill with a much lower top rate for all taxpayers and an end to many time-honored deductions. The proposed law was quickly approved by the Finance Committee, and sailed through the Senate by a vote of ninety-seven to three in June 1986. After a difficult passage through a Senate–House conference committee, the tax reform law was approved and signed in September 1986. The bill simplified and reduced taxes, and it remained in effect for a decade before pressure for further tax changes emerged once again.

The Age of the Yuppie

The economic boom of the mid-1980s fostered an atmosphere of money-making and social acquisitiveness. In Arkansas, Governor Bill Clinton and his wife invested in a speculative real estate venture, the Whitewater Development Corporation, that would come back to haunt them ten years later. Wall Street traders like Michael Millken and Ivan Boesky promoted lucrative corporate mergers through high risk securities known as "junk bonds." Top executives received staggering annual salaries. The head of Walt Disney, for example, earned $40 million in 1987. Wall Street experienced a "merger mania" in which corporations acquired competitors through hostile takeovers. Manhattan real estate mogul Donald Trump became a celebrity with his plush towers and Atlantic City casino. Business majors increased dramatically in American universities.

The youth culture reflected the spirit of materialism that permeated the 1980s. Tennis star André Agassi appeared in ads asserting "image is everything." In the centers of technological change on the East and West Coasts, the press proclaimed the emergence of the "young urban professionals," dubbed "yuppies" by the media. These individuals had cosmetic surgery to retain a young look, took expensive vacations, and purchased costly sports equipment. Self-indulgence seemed to be a hallmark of young people. "Mine is a generation perfectly willing to admit its contemptible qualities," wrote essayist David Leavitt in 1985, but "at least we don't pretend we're not wearing costumes."

The Challenger Disaster

A sobering moment in the frenetic decade came on January 28, 1986, when the space shuttle *Challenger* exploded. All seven crew members, one of them a schoolteacher (Christa McAuliffe) from New Hampshire chosen to experience the excitement of a shuttle mission, perished in the disaster. The event happened live before a shocked audience that watched the spacecraft lift off normally and then explode a few seconds later into a mass of wreckage. Cable television replayed the events, including the faces of the schoolteacher's parents, over and over. A shocked nation grieved. For many young people, the accident became the most memorable event of their generation. Ronald Reagan gave the *Challenger* crew an eloquent eulogy.

The explosion of the Challenger *space shuttle on January 28, 1986, was one of the dramatic moments of the decade. Seven astronauts perished when the rocket's O-rings failed and caused the rocket to blow up.*

An official investigation followed while the shuttle fleet was grounded. Its proceedings revealed that the space program had grown overconfident about its procedures. Slipshod technology had contributed to the tragedy, but the incident did not undermine the public's faith in scientific progress and material abundance. By the end of the 1980s the shuttle program had resumed its regular series of flights.

Foreign Policy in the Second Reagan Term

Soviet-American relations entered a new phase when Mikhail Gorbachev came to power in Moscow. Aware of the weaknesses in his society and its economy, Gorbachev pursued a more conciliatory policy toward the West while trying to implement a restructuring of Soviet society that came to be known as *perestroika* (broadly defined as "restructuring"). He announced reductions in the deployment of Soviet missiles, and said that the Soviet Union wanted to be part of Europe, not an opposing ideology. He and Reagan agreed to hold a summit conference in Geneva in November 1985. Although not much was achieved at the meet-

ing, the two leaders discovered that they liked each other. They arranged to hold further summit meetings. When they announced their joint communiqué, Reagan commented to Gorbachev: "I bet the hard-liners in both our countries are bleeding when we shake hands." The Russian leader agreed.

The two world leaders met again at Reykjavik, Iceland, in October 1986. There they attempted to outdo each other in calling for reductions in the number of nuclear weapons, with the president even offering to rid the world of all such weapons. Again there were no substantive results, but the experience indicated that a genuine arms agreement might be possible. Both the president and Mrs. Reagan hoped to crown his second term with an arms control treaty that would establish his historical reputation as a peacemaker. Before that goal could be achieved, however, the Reagan administration found itself caught in a major foreign policy scandal.

The Iran-Contra Affair

In November 1986 the American public first learned that the United States had sold arms to the Islamic regime in Iran which had sponsored terrorist activities for most of the 1980s against the United States. Within a month the revelation came that money obtained from the arms sales had been used to support the Nicaraguan Contras in violation of the Boland Amendments. The Reagan administration had deceived Congress, broken the law, and lied to the American people. A flood of news stories soon indicated the dimensions of what had occurred, although some of the details remained secret more than a decade after the scandal broke.

In 1985, members of the National Security Council (NSC) became convinced that the release of American hostages held in Lebanon could be secured if the United States sold arms to Iran. National Security Advisor Robert McFarlane believed that "moderates" in Iran would use their political influence to free hostages if American weapons were forthcoming. The Iranians could use weapons in their bitter war with Iraq, which had been going on since 1982. Since disclosure of this new policy would have outraged Americans and provoked congressional investigations, the president's approval of arm sales was kept secret.

The actual shipment of weapons to Iran was carried out by Israel with the United States replacing the

transferred munitions. Unfortunately, the Iranians accepted the anti-tank and anti-aircraft missiles, but released only three hostages. The Iranian government had deceived the United States.

In the course of the arms deals, however, the transactions generated profits. A member of the NSC staff, Marine Colonel Oliver North, had what he later called a "neat idea." He proposed that profits from the sale of weapons to Iran be used to support the Contras in Nicaragua. Although North maintained that his actions did not break the law, they were in clear violation of congressional directives barring the provision of aid to the Contras. Moreover, the use of funds without legislative approval was against the law. In addition, a privately financed, unaccountable, and clandestine foreign policy operation was well outside constitutional limits.

News of the scandal began to leak out in October 1986 when the Sandinistas shot down one of the planes taking weapons to the Contras. A captured crew member revealed the Central Intelligence Agency's links to the operation. Early in November news of the arms for hostages deal surfaced in the Middle East. The reports did not affect the congressional elections in which the Democrats regained control of the Senate for the first time in six years and retained their majority in the House as well. Within days of the voting, however, the press was in full pursuit of the sensational story.

For several weeks the Reagan White House tried to mislead Congress and the public about what had taken place. On November 13, 1986, the president told the American people: "We did not—repeat, did not—trade weapons or anything else for hostages, nor will we." He maintained this position even though it conflicted with the known facts. On this occasion Reagan's gifts as the "Great Communicator" failed him. The public did not believe his assertions.

Attorney General Edwin Meese conducted a slow, ineffective probe of what had happened. In late November conclusive proof of the diversion of money to the Contras came out. The president fired Oliver North and accepted the resignation of John Poindexter, McFarlane's successor as national security advisor and one of the central figures in the clandestine operation which the press was now calling the Iran-Contra scandal.

Three separate probes of the scandal began in early 1987. Reagan appointed the Tower Commission, named after its chair, former Senator John Tower of

Texas, to look into the White House's role in the scheme. The House and Senate created a joint committee to examine the policy and its execution. The lawmakers soon decided to grant many of those individuals involved immunity in exchange for their testimony. That decision hampered the task of the special counsel, Lawrence Walsh, who was named to consider whether specific laws had been violated.

While everyone concerned professed a desire to get to the bottom of the scandal, there was little inclination, even among Democrats, to see Ronald Reagan impeached for his role in it. His second term had only a year and a half to run, and many Washington insiders questioned whether it would be good for the country to have another president driven from office in disgrace. As a result, much was revealed about the Iran-Contra affair, but most of the high-level participants were not subjected to serious legal penalties.

The Tower Commission, for its part, chastised the president for an inept "management style" that allowed his subordinates to lead him into the scandal. On March 4, 1987, Reagan said that he accepted the commission's findings while reiterating that he had not intended to trade arms for hostages. His poll ratings rose and once again the public responded to his leadership.

For others involved in the scandal, the hearings brought a surge of notoriety that made North a subject of national debate, and discredited the other Reagan aides involved. When North testified before the House-Senate Committee during the summer of 1987 in his Marine uniform, he proved a compelling presence on television. He exaggerated his closeness to Reagan and made some inaccurate or misleading statements. But his skill before the cameras deflected some of the blame from Reagan.

North and the other participants were indicted by Lawrence Walsh and convicted for some of their misdeeds, including perjury, mishandling government moneys, and other crimes. Because Congress had granted them immunity, however, higher courts overturned their convictions on the ground that the trials had been influenced by what had been heard in the congressional proceedings. The legal aspects of the Iran-Contra scandal dribbled away into inconclusive results during the early years of George Bush's presidency.

Whatever the legalities of the Iran-Contra affair, it demonstrated the weaknesses of Reagan's handling of foreign policy. Reagan had failed to ask hard questions

The Iran-Contra scandal produced a congressional investigation at which the star witness was Marine Colonel Oliver North. His appearance in uniform and his aggressive tactics toward his questioners made him a national hero to conservatives.

about the arms-for-hostages proposals, and he had allowed erratic subordinates like North to mishandle the nation's foreign policy. The outcome discredited the American stance on terrorism, and indicated that Reagan's command of his own government was weak and uncertain.

Remaking the Supreme Court: The Nomination of Robert Bork

One of the Reagan administration's major goals was to reshape the federal judiciary along conservative lines. The White House succeeded in doing so in the lower courts because, during eight years in office, Reagan nominated more than half the members of the federal judiciary. Half of these individuals received high ratings from the American Bar Association.

The main focus of the effort to reshape the judiciary was the United States Supreme Court. In July 1981, Reagan named the first woman to be appointed to the Court, Sandra Day O'Connor of Arizona. The president did not have another opportunity to appoint a justice until Chief Justice Warren Burger resigned in 1986. Reagan elevated Justice William Rehnquist to replace Burger and named Antonin Scalia, a federal appeals court judge, to take the seat that Rehnquist va-

cated. Scalia was the first Italian American appointed to the court, and his intellectual brilliance appealed to conservatives. Whereas Rehnquist's selection met with some opposition, Scalia's received unanimous Senate approval.

In June 1987, after the Democrats had regained control of the Senate, Justice Lewis Powell resigned and President Reagan named Robert Bork, another federal appeals court jurist to replace him. During a long career as a legal writer before becoming a judge, Bork had taken many controversial stands on divisive issues. He had opposed the decision in *Roe* v. *Wade* (1973) that established a woman's right to have an abortion, and he had questioned other decisions in the areas of privacy and civil rights. The nomination galvanized Democrats in the Senate, the civil rights movement, and women's groups in a campaign to defeat Bork.

The struggle that followed ultimately led to the rejection of Bork's nomination. The judge's admirers claimed that his enemies had distorted his record, but his foes were able to depict Bork as a conservative ideologue outside the mainstream of American judicial thinking. The jurist's performance before the Senate Judiciary Committee failed to counteract the negative public opinion that his opposition had generated. In October 1987, Bork was defeated when fifty-eight senators voted against him. The president then named a law professor, Douglas Ginsburg, to the court, but he had to withdraw when it was learned that he had used marijuana in law school. Finally Reagan nominated Judge Anthony Kennedy whom the Senate confirmed in February 1988.

The battle over Bork's nomination put a decisive end to any illusions that Supreme Court nominations were not considered political events. Conservatives vowed to take revenge against the nominees of future Democratic presidents by "Borking" those selections. Both sides prepared for a bitter battle when the next Supreme Court nomination occurred.

Reagan and Gorbachev: The Road to Understanding

While the Iran-Contra affair reduced Reagan's political standing, the resulting changes in his administration prepared the way for genuine foreign policy achievements. When Donald Regan left the government, the president named former Senator Howard Baker as his

A search for Soviet-American understanding was a notable feature of Ronald Reagan's second term. His friendship with the Soviet leader Mikhail Gorbachev resulted in a marked lessening of the Cold War tensions as the decade of the 1980s ended.

chief of staff, brought in Frank Carlucci as secretary of defense, and selected Lieutenant General Colin Powell to be the national security advisor. All three were prepared to take advantage of improved relations with the Soviet Union, and the last year and a half of Reagan's second term brought the two nuclear powers to a more conciliatory posture than would have seemed possible five years earlier.

By late 1987, negotiators for the two sides had agreed to remove from Europe intermediate range missiles with nuclear warheads. Gorbachev came to Washington in December 1987 for the formal signing of the pact. Seven months later Reagan went to Moscow to meet Gorbachev in an atmosphere of hope and reconciliation. Tensions between the two countries eased as the Soviets pulled out of Afghanistan and indicated that they no longer intended to stir up international problems. The improvement in the superpower rivalry helped Reagan regain some of his popularity with the American people as his administration neared its end.

THE 1988 PRESIDENTIAL ELECTION

With Ronald Reagan ineligible to seek a third term, the Republican party had to pick a successor to carry its banner against the Democrats. Vice President George Bush soon emerged as the front-runner. Bush had been a loyal subordinate. The two men had met regularly, and Reagan proclaimed that he had given Bush an unprecedented role in the administration. So deferential had Bush been, however, that there were stories in the press that he had become too subservient. Was he a "wimp" who had lost his political manhood during the Reagan years?

George Bush was sixty-three years old in 1988. He came from an aristocratic New England background but had moved to Texas after combat service in the navy during World War II. He became active in Republican politics, and ran unsuccessfully for the U.S. Senate in 1964. Elected to the House of Representatives in 1966, he stayed for two terms and made another losing bid for the Senate in 1970. Service in the Ford administration as envoy to China and director of the Central Intelligence Agency added to his impressive résumé of government posts. He ran against Reagan for the Republican nomination in 1980 and became the vice presidential choice despite doubts among conservatives about his allegiance to their cause. He had criticized Reagan's supply-side tax proposals as "voodoo economics," and there were suspicions that he did not oppose abortion with the same fervor as many conservatives.

Bush's main rival for the Republican nomination was Robert Dole of Kansas, the Republican minority leader in the Senate. Dole defeated Bush in the Iowa caucuses and seemed to be on the verge of victory as the New Hampshire primary neared. With the help of Governor John Sununu, however, Bush made a dramatic comeback to win in New Hampshire and establish a momentum that carried him to the nomination.

At the Republican convention in New Orleans, Bush made two important decisions. For his running mate, he selected Senator J. Danforth Quayle of Indiana. Handsome and young, Quayle was generally re-

George Bush won the Republican nomination and the presidential election in 1988 on his promise to continue the legacy of Ronald Reagan and his pledge of "no new taxes."

The Democratic Choice

As for the Democrats, with Reagan no longer a candidate, they approached the prospect of running against Bush with much eagerness. They believed that a stock market plunge of more than 500 points in the Dow Jones industrial average in October 1987 signaled potential trouble for the economy and would undercut Republican claims of prosperity. The prospective front-runner for the nomination was Senator Gary Hart, but his candidacy collapsed when it was revealed that his reputation for marital infidelity and sexual adventures was well deserved. Jesse Jackson ran again, but his strength remained concentrated among black voters. Out of the field of other candidates, Massachusetts Governor Michael Dukakis emerged as the best-financed and best-organized contender. He defeated Jackson in a series of primaries in the spring and came to the Democratic convention with the nomination virtually locked up.

Dukakis emphasized his family's Greek immigrant background and stressed his success in stimulating the Massachusetts economy during the 1980s. Democrats paid less attention to his tepid personality and lackluster abilities as a campaigner. At the convention, he selected Senator Lloyd M. Bentsen of Texas as his running mate. When the Democratic convention ended, Dukakis had a strong lead in the public opinion polls.

The Campaign

The campaign that followed was a nasty one. The Republicans raised questions about Dukakis that undermined his lead. The most penetrating of these issues had to do with prison furloughs that Massachusetts law granted to jailed criminals. In one case, a black convict named Willie Horton who had been released on furlough had then fled the state and committed a rape in another state. The Republicans and their surrogates used the Horton case in powerful television commercials to demonstrate Dukakis's ineptitude as governor, but the racial dimensions of the incident were also evident. By September, Bush had overtaken Dukakis in the polls.

The presidential debates produced two memorable images. In the debate between Bentsen and Quayle, the Republican compared his legislative record in the

garded as a lightweight by his Senate colleagues, but he provided a contrast to Bush's age and experience. Quayle's candidacy got off to a shaky start when it was revealed that he had entered the Indiana National Guard at a time when enlistment there precluded active service in the Vietnam War. His perceived lack of intelligence made him the butt of numerous jokes over the next four years.

Bush's other major decision involved the issue of deficits and taxes. In his acceptance speech, he predicted that Democrats in Congress would pressure him to raise taxes. He promised to reject all such proposals. "Read my lips," he said, "No new taxes!" Repeated and emphasized throughout the campaign, this pledge became identified with Bush as a solemn promise to the electorate.

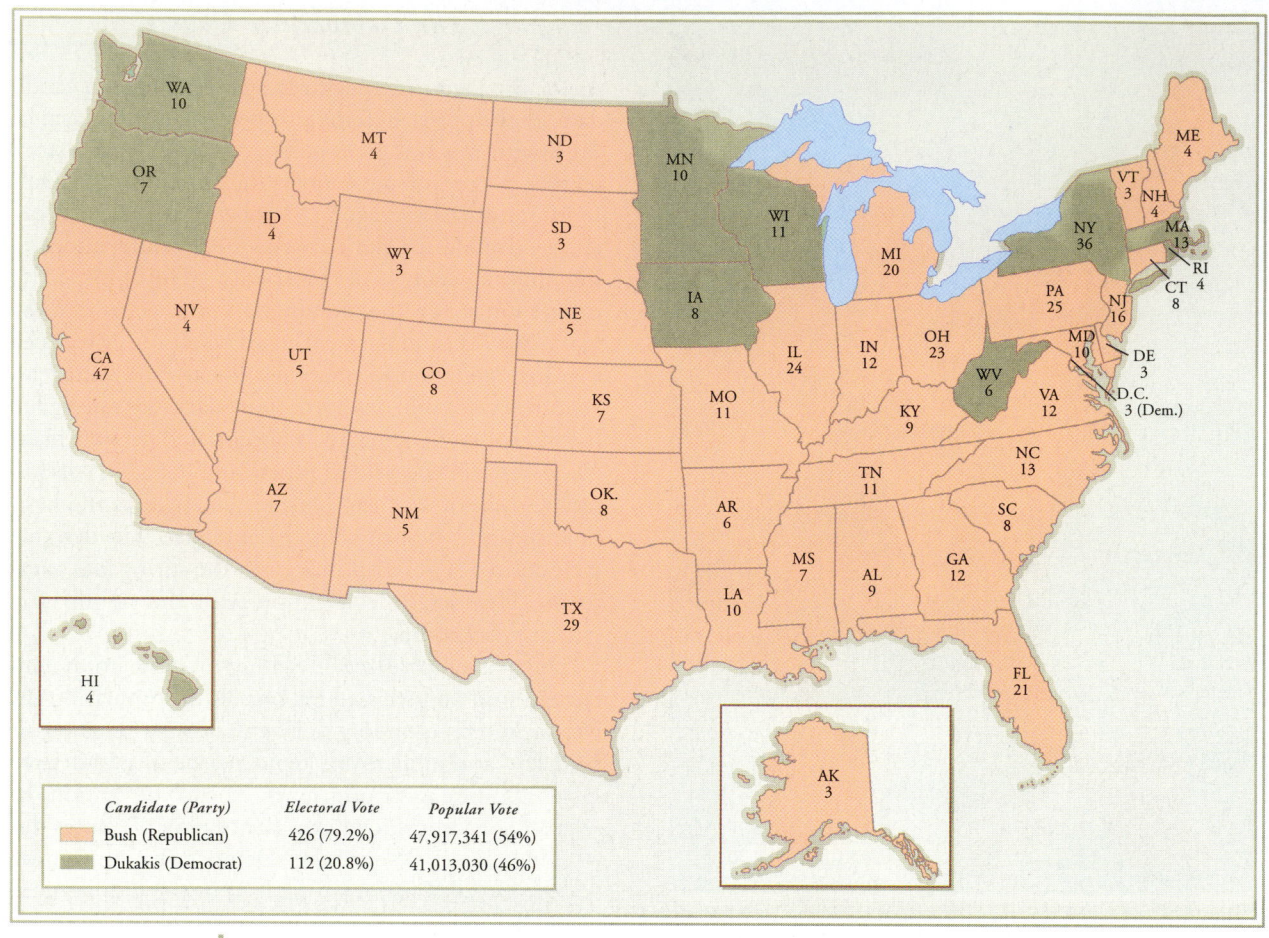

Candidate (Party)	Electoral Vote	Popular Vote
Bush (Republican)	426 (79.2%)	47,917,341 (54%)
Dukakis (Democrat)	112 (20.8%)	41,013,030 (46%)

MAP 31.3 | THE ELECTION OF 1988

Senate to that of John F. Kennedy. Bentsen countered: "Senator, I served with Jack Kennedy, I knew Jack Kennedy. Jack Kennedy was a friend of mine. Senator, you are no Jack Kennedy." When Bush and Dukakis debated for a second time, the Democratic nominee, an opponent of capital punishment, was asked how he would view the death penalty if his wife had been raped and murdered. Dukakis gave an unemotional answer that killed his remaining chances of winning the election.

Bush won the election with 53 percent of the vote to 46 percent for Dukakis. The margin in the electoral college was 426 to 112. While Bush's victory was decisive, the Democrats had done better than in any election since 1976. They retained control of both houses of Congress and had learned some valuable lessons about waging a competitive presidential election.

The Reagan Legacy

Even before Ronald Reagan left office on January 20, 1989, the debate about the impact of his presidency was underway. His partisans proclaimed the "Reagan Revolution" had transformed American attitudes toward government. They also assigned him a major role in winning the Cold War. Critics pointed to the huge federal budget deficits that persisted throughout the 1980s and blamed Reagan for policies that had widened the gap between rich and poor, and pointed out that he had failed to address serious urban problems.

The impact of the 1980s on American life also became a source of contention. Conservatives applauded the economic growth that had occurred. Entrepreneurs and Wall Street traders such as Donald Trump,

RONALD REAGAN'S SECOND INAUGURAL ADDRESS JANUARY 1985

This excerpt from Ronald Reagan's second inaugural address conveys the themes of optimism and smaller government that he advanced throughout the 1980s.

Four years ago I spoke to you of a new beginning, and we have accomplished that. But in another sense, our new beginning is a continuation of that beginning created two centuries ago when, for the first time in history, government, the people said, was not our master. It is our servant; its only power that which we, the people, allow it to have.

That system has never failed us. But for a time we failed the system. We asked things of government that government was not equipped to give. We yielded authority to the national government that properly belonged to states or to local governments or to the people themselves. We allowed taxes and inflation to rob us of our earnings and savings and watched the great industrial machine that had made us the most productive people on earth slow down and the number of unemployed increase.

By 1980 we knew it was time to renew our faith, to strive with all our strength toward the ultimate in individual freedom consistent with an orderly society.

We believed then and now there are no limits to growth and human progress when men and women are free to follow their dreams. And we were right. And we were right to believe that. Tax rates have been reduced, inflation cut dramatically and more people are employed than ever before in our history.

We are creating a nation once again vibrant, robust and alive. But there are many mountains yet to climb. We will not rest until every American enjoys the fullness of freedom, dignity, and opportunity as our birthright. It is our birthright as citizens of this great republic.

And if we meet this challenge, these will be years when Americans have restored their confidence and tradition of progress; when our values of faith, family, work, and neighborhood, were restated for a modern age; when our economy was finally freed from government's grip; when we made sincere efforts at meaningful arms reductions by rebuilding our defenses, our economy, and developing new technologies helped preserve peace in a troubled world; when America courageously supported the struggle for individual liberty, self-government, and free enterprise throughout the world and turned the tide of history away from totalitarian darkness and into the warm sunlight of human freedom.

My fellow citizens, our nation is poised for greatness. We must do what we know is right and do it with all our might. Let history say of us, these were golden years—when the American Revolution was reborn, when freedom gained new life and America reached for her best.

Michael Millken, and Ivan Boesky became cultural heroes for a time. When Boesky and Millken were convicted of insider trading and given prison sentences, critics saw their sentences as retribution for the excesses of the period.

Both Reagan's admirers and his enemies overstated his influence on American history. By the mid-1990s the nation still seemed to want a smaller government in theory and more government services in practice. Reagan had halted the expansion of the welfare state, but that would probably have occurred in any event by the 1980s. Reagan certainly deserved some credit for the decline of the Soviet Union, though that nation's internal difficulties were more significant than the actions of the United States at the end of the Cold War. Reagan's most enduring legacy was the federal budget deficit. Although Congress appropriated the money, he set national priorities, and his spending for defense went well beyond affordable levels. Reagan proved that big spenders could come in conservative as well as liberal models.

KINDER, GENTLER GEORGE BUSH

George Bush came into office pledging to carry on Reagan's policies, but promising to do so in a more humane and judicious manner. He spoke of a "kinder, gentler" nation and government that would carry out conservative programs with less harshness than had marked the Reagan years. He urged Americans to engage in charitable endeavors that would become "a thousand points of light" to inspire others to good works. Bush had no grand vision of what his administration should accomplish in the domestic arena. "First, do no harm" he said in warning against undue activism from Washington.

Foreign affairs interested the new president much more than did shaping policy on health care, the environment, or social policy. Attuned to diplomacy because of his service as director of the CIA and ambassador to China, he prized the personal contacts he had made around the world and used them to good effect at moments of crisis. He had an effective foreign policy team. His secretary of state, James A. Baker, was a close friend and an adroit power broker; the national security advisor, Brent Scowcroft, and the chair of the

Joint Chiefs of Staff, General Colin Powell, executed the president's policies with skill and efficiency. The collapse of communism in 1989–1990, the challenge of Iraqi expansionism in the Middle East, and the shaping of a new role for the United States gave the Bush administration's foreign policy makers much to do.

The first half of the Bush administration went very well. The president relished the art of governing and he approached his job by engaging in a frenzy of activity. His press conferences demonstrated his command of information in a way that Reagan never displayed. The public became used to seeing Bush jogging, entertaining numerous visitors to the White House, and rushing around the country from one event to another. As he said in 1989, "In case you hadn't noticed, I really love my job."

As time passed, however, questions arose about the purpose behind all this frenetic exertion. Bush spoke of the need to set larger goals for his presidency. He called it, in the abrupt shorthand that he often employed, "the vision thing." The phrase came into general use in discussions of whether Bush wanted to accomplish anything as president or simply wished to occupy the nation's highest office. With his poll numbers high during 1989–1990 and reelection seeming to be assured, the problem seemed a minor irritant rather than a major concern.

Bush's Domestic Policy

The president and his chief of staff, John Sununu, had no intention of breaking new ground in domestic affairs. They wanted to accomplish whatever they could without violating the campaign pledge of "no new taxes." Much to the dismay of Republican conservatives, Bush went along with Democratic legislation such as the Clean Air Act and the Americans with Disabilities Act which involved a growth in the federal bureaucracy and expanded regulations. Any legislation that he did not like, such as an increase in the minimum wage, he vetoed. During the first three years of his presidency, Congress failed to override any of Bush's twenty-eight vetoes. The president did compromise on a measure that raised the minimum wage in 1990.

Bush's relations with Congress were not always successful. At the beginning of his administration he named former Senator John Tower to be secretary of

defense. After a bitter struggle focusing on Tower's problems with alcoholism and other personal indiscretions, the Senate rejected their former colleague. To replace Tower, Bush picked Representative Richard Cheney.

On some domestic issues, Bush favored exhortation over government programs. He promised to be the "education president" but left most of the responsibility for changes in the system to the states and localities. The "war on drugs" was renewed, with emphasis on stopping the inflow of narcotics to the United States rather than reducing the demand for them among the population. An overall decline in drug use enabled the administration to claim victory for its strategy.

By 1989, however, the Bush administration had to deal with another major domestic issue. The deregulated savings and loan industry had a major collapse that left the taxpayers with a $500 billion cost to bail out depositors for the failed institutions. Congress established the Resolution Trust Corporation to sell off the assets of the failed banks and savings and loans and obtain as much money as possible from their sale. The episode was one of the great financial scandals in American history.

The Continuing AIDS Crisis

Both funding for research on AIDS and public awareness of the disease increased during the Bush years. Congress created the National Commission on AIDS in 1989, and federal government funds for treatment and research rose to over $2 billion by 1992. Still, the number of new cases continued to increase, reaching 45,603 in 1992 and 83,814 a year later. Total deaths from AIDS in the United States reached 198,000. The announcement in 1991 that basketball star Earvin "Magic" Johnson had the HIV virus which causes AIDS shocked the public. However, opinions regarding what to do about the epidemic remained polarized. AIDS activists wanted more money for research and greater cultural tolerance for those afflicted with the disease. Conservatives like Senator Jesse Helms of North Carolina contended that most AIDS victims were homosexuals who had brought their condition upon themselves through their own behavior. After some initial sympathy toward AIDS patients, the Bush administration's attitude toward AIDS patients cooled under conservative pressure as the 1992 election approached.

The announcement by the pro basketball star Earvin "Magic" Johnson that he was infected with the virus that causes AIDS was another part of the growing national awareness of the impact of the epidemic. This picture was taken when he made the announcement.

Foreign Policy Successes, 1989–1990

During the first two years of his presidency, Bush managed with skill the demise of the Soviet empire. At the end of 1988, Gorbachev had told the United Nations that the nations of Eastern Europe were free to determine their own destiny without Soviet interference. During 1989, the old order in Eastern Europe crumbled. Poland held free elections; Hungary allowed its borders to open; and East Germany eased the barriers to travel to West Germany. By the end of 1989, the Cold War seemed to be over with the United States the clear winner.

The Bush administration handled these developments carefully. Mindful of the nuclear weapons in the hands of the Soviet military, the president avoided gloating over the success of the West. The trend in favor of the United States continued into 1990 as Gorbachev renounced the Communist party's monopoly over political power in February. The White House faced hard

choices about which leader to support as rivals to Gorbachev emerged during 1990, particularly the new president of the Russian Republic, Boris Yeltsin.

One country where the administration's foreign policy encountered difficulty was China. Student protests during the spring of 1989 led to a brutal crackdown on demonstrators in Beijing's Tiananmen Square. The spectacle of students being killed and wounded, as well as the repressive policies of the Chinese government, produced an outcry in the United States. However, Bush believed that it was important to maintain good relations with the Chinese leaders, so the administration's response to the events of June 1989 was muted and cautious. Secretary of State Baker commented: "I don't think it would be in the best interests of the United States for us to see significant instability in the People's Republic of China."

Closer to home, however, the Bush administration took more decisive action toward Panama's strongman ruler, Manuel Noriega. Corrupt and deeply involved in the international narcotics trade, Noriega had been on the United States's payroll for many years as an informant on drug matters. In 1989 his dictatorial regime refused to adhere to the results of national elections. The White House sent additional troops to Panama and called for an uprising against Noriega. For his part, Noriega declared a state of war on American military personnel and their families to be captured and tortured.

In late December, the United States launched an invasion that quickly overcame the Panamanian army. Noriega eluded capture for a few embarrassing days until he sought refuge in a Vatican Embassy. In early 1990 he surrendered to the Americans and in 1992 was tried and convicted of drug trafficking in a federal court in Florida. The episode raised Bush's standings in the polls. It did not, however, slow down the drug trade in Panama or make that nation happier or more prosperous.

The mass protests in China in the spring of 1989 were part of the events that shook communism during the end of the Cold War. On May 27, 1989, student leader Wang Den addressed a huge crowd in Tiananmen Square in Beijing. A week later Chinese troops crushed the uprising.

The End of No New Taxes

In the spring of 1990, President Bush made a fatal political blunder that probably cost him his chances of reelection. His 1988 pledge of "no new taxes" had become ingrained in the minds of the American people. Conservative Republicans expected him to adhere to the commitment in spite of the desire of the Democratic majorities in Congress to raise taxes. In 1989,

the president worked out a strategy with Congress that provided for budget savings. Bush also wanted to lower the tax rate on capital gains, but that legislation became stalled in the Senate. With the budget deficit growing, however, the Democrats did not see how spending cuts alone could reduce it. Having suffered setbacks in the 1988 elections, the Democrats were not going to propose tax increases unless President Bush agreed to them. Meanwhile, the Gramm-Rudman-Hollings law provided for substantial reductions in spending by the fall of 1990 if the president and Congress did not reach a viable budget agreement.

By early 1990, there were signs that the economy had begun to slow down. The gross domestic product had grown slowly in 1989; there had been a slight loss in manufacturing jobs; and producer prices had risen.

With a weakening economy, a budget stalemate posed dangers for both parties, and neither side really wanted to face the implications of the cuts that Gramm-Rudman-Hollings contemplated.

Negotiations between the president and congressional Democrats continued until, on June 26, 1990, Bush announced that dealing with the deficit problem might have to include "tax revenue increases." Republicans reacted with fury. Ed Rollins, a Republican campaign official, called the statement "probably the most serious violation of any political pledge anybody has ever made." Although the reversal of "no new taxes" may have made economic and political sense to those close to Bush, the president had squandered much of the trust that the American people had placed in him in 1988. Despite the foreign policy victories that lay ahead, he never fully regained it over the rest of his administration.

Iraq and Kuwait: Storm in the Desert

Foreign policy events soon overshadowed the political fallout from the broken tax pledge. On August 2, 1990, the Iraqi army of Saddam Hussein invaded the oil-rich kingdom of Kuwait and seized it within a few days. Suddenly the oil supplies of the United States and the industrialized world faced a new and ominous threat from the Iraqi dictator. Bush's response and the war that followed temporarily restored his popularity and seemed at the time to make his reelection a certainty.

During the 1980s, Iran and Iraq had fought a brutal and costly war that had drained the human and material resources of both countries. The United States had not taken sides in the conflict, hoping that the two countries, both of which were hostile toward the United States, would exhaust each other. Once the war ended, however, the Bush administration had pursued a conciliatory policy, allowing Iraq to purchase heavy machinery and paying little attention to its efforts to build a nuclear bomb and acquire weapons of mass destruction. During the spring of 1990, the American ambassador in Baghdad had informed Hussein that the United States took "no position" on Iraq's dispute with Kuwait. In fact, the Iraqis regarded Kuwait as part of their nation.

When Iraqi military units rolled into Kuwait, Bush decided that the takeover must be resisted. "Iraq will not be permitted to annex Kuwait," he told Congress. Heavy economic sanctions were put into effect. More

important, in Operation Desert Shield the United States deployed American troops in Saudi Arabia to deter Hussein from attacking that country. Behind the scenes, the administration had already decided that if necessary it would use military force to oust the Iraqis from Kuwait.

During the remainder of 1990 the Bush administration moved military forces into Saudi Arabia. The end of the Cold War meant that the United States had the support of the Soviet Union in isolating Iraq from the rest of the world and therefore had much greater freedom of action than would have been the case even two years earlier. Bush displayed impressive diplomatic skill in assembling and holding together an international coalition to oppose Iraq.

The Budget Battle

On the domestic side, the budget issue remained unsettled until the president and the Democratic leadership worked out a deficit reduction plan in September 1990. Republicans in the House of Representatives lobbied against the plan, which was defeated a few days later. Intense negotiations between the White House and Capitol Hill produced a deficit reduction agreement at the end of October that involved both tax increases and spending cuts. Angry Republicans charged that Bush had capitulated to the opposition. The Republicans went into the fall elections in a divided and unhappy mood. Their losses were modest—eight seats in the House and one in the Senate—but the conservative faithful continued to smolder with anger against Bush. The president informed conservatives that the White House had fulfilled its legislative agenda for the presidency. "There's not another single piece of legislation that needs to be passed in the next two years for this president," the chief of staff, John Sununu, said. "In fact, if Congress wants to come together, adjourn and leave, it's all right with us. We don't need them."

War in the Persian Gulf

After the elections, Bush stepped up the pressure on Saddam Hussein to leave Kuwait. The United Nations Security Council agreed to the use of armed force against Iraq if Kuwait had not been freed by January 15, 1991. As the diplomatic options faded, Congress insisted on a vote over whether American troops should go into combat in the Middle East. The result

MAP 31.4 | THE WAR IN THE PERSIAN GULF

high as 100,000. American deaths totaled 148, including eleven women. Within one hundred hours, the ground phase of the war ended in a complete victory on the battlefield for the anti-Iraq forces. President Bush decided not to press for Hussein's removal from power, a decision that was later criticized. There was, however, little incentive for the United States to occupy Baghdad and continue the fighting.

Victory in the Gulf War sent Bush's popularity soaring to record levels; he received approval ratings of nearly 90 percent in some polls. The nation basked in the glow of military success, which seemed to end the sense of self-doubt that had persisted since the Vietnam War. The chairman of the Joint Chiefs of Staff, General Colin Powell, became a nationally respected military figure and a possible vice presidential or presidential candidate. Bush's own reelection seemed assured. Major figures in the Democratic party decided not to challenge Bush in 1992.

Yet the political dividends from Bush's military triumph did not last long. Hussein bounced back from his defeat to reassert his power in Iraq and, despite United Nations inspections, rebuilt his nation's economy and war-making capacity. The result of the war proved less conclusive than it had seemed at the time.

on January 12, 1991, was a victory for the president, although the margin in the Senate was only five votes. Five days later, Operation Desert Storm began.

The military outcome was never in doubt. In a demoralizing series of strikes, the allied coalition bombed the Iraqi army into submission. The most that Hussein could do in retaliation was to send Scud missiles against Israel in hopes of fracturing the coalition. The Iraqi ruler also set Kuwaiti oil wells on fire and dumped oil into the Persian Gulf. None of these actions, however, posed a serious threat to the build-up of the allied armies. Yet the use of air power alone did not compel Hussein to leave Kuwait.

The second phase of Desert Storm began on February 24, 1991, with a huge assault of American and allied troops against the weakened Iraqi defenders. A series of encircling maneuvers ousted the Iraqis from Kuwait with huge losses in troops and equipment. Estimates of the number of Iraqi soldiers killed ranged as

Other foreign policy problems troubled the White House during 1991. In Russia, Gorbachev faced a coup designed to bring hard-liners back into power. A rival of Gorbachev, Boris Yeltsin, led demonstrations against the plotters in Moscow and their coup, which then failed. Thereupon the Soviet Union collapsed and its component nations broke apart. Yeltsin consolidated his power with promises of economic reform and put himself in a position to succeed Gorbachev. Champions of Ronald Reagan said that his policies had spent the Soviet Union into the ground. More significant in the breakup of the Soviet empire were the accumulated wounds of an inefficient economy, a bloated bureaucracy, and an inept leadership. With the demise of the Soviet Union, the major threat of the Cold War had ended, but the instability in Eastern Europe posed new threats to world peace.

The Gulf War in the winter of 1991 ended in a military triumph for the coalition arrayed against Saddam Hussein. Iraqi soldiers surrendered in huge numbers to the invading force. This picture shows Iraqi prisoners on February 26, 1991, who had been captured by the First Marine Division.

President George Bush meets with General Colin Powell, chairman of the Joint Chiefs of Staff, and General Norman Schwartzkopf in the wake of the Allied victory in the Gulf War.

Anita Hill's Charges against Clarence Thomas 1991

Anita Hill's charges against Clarence Thomas led to one of the most sensational confirmation hearings in American history and produced a controversy that still divides the friends and defenders of both individuals.

During this period at the Department of Education, my working relationship with Judge Thomas was positive. I had a good deal of responsibility and independence. I thought he respected by work and that he trusted my judgment.

After approximately 3 months of working there, he asked me to go out socially with him. What happened next and telling the world about it are the two most difficult things, experiences of my life. It is only after a great deal of agonizing consideration and a number of sleepless nights that I am able to talk of these unpleasant matters to anyone but my close friends.

I declined the invitation to go out socially with him, and explained to him that I thought it would jeopardize what at the time I considered to be a very good working relationship. I had a normal social life with other men outside of the office. I believed then, as now, that having a social relationship with a person who was supervising my work would be ill advised. I was very uncomfortable with the idea and told him so.

I thought that by saying "no" and explaining my reasons, my employer would abandon his social suggestions. However, to my regret, in the following few weeks he continued to ask me out on several occasions. He pressed me to justify my reasons for saying "no" to him. These incidents took place in his office or mine. They were in the form of private conversations which would not have been overheard by anyone else.

My working relationship became even more strained when Judge Thomas began to use work situations to discuss sex. On these occasions, he would call me into his office

---

One area of turmoil was Yugoslavia where the Communist government had long suppressed historic rivalries among Serbs, Croats, Bosnians, and other nationalities. Tensions between Christians and Muslims added to the dangerous potential of the situation. Civil war broke out in 1991 as Serbs battled Croats, Slovenes, and Bosnians. The Bush administration recognized Bosnia as an independent nation and thus became involved in a Balkan struggle whose problems spilled over into the next presidency.

The Battle over the Thomas Nomination

Like Ronald Reagan, George Bush wanted to continue the conservative trend that the Supreme Court had been following since the 1970s. That goal seemed even more important in light of the court's ruling in *Webster* v. *Reproductive Health Services* (1989), whereby the justices decided in a 5–4 ruling that states could set limits on the ability to obtain an abortion. Any change in the courts could affect that volatile controversy. When the liberal justice, William Brennan, retired in 1990, the president named David Souter of New Hampshire to succeed him. Confirmation by the Senate came easily because no one was quite sure where Souter stood on abortion.

The next nomination, in 1991, led to one of the most sensational confirmation struggles in the nation's history. When Justice Thurgood Marshall retired, many wondered whether Bush would name an African American to succeed him. The president selected Clarence

for reports on education issues and projects or he might suggest that because of the time pressures of his schedule, we go to lunch to a government cafeteria. After a brief discussion of work, he would turn the conversation to a discussion of sexual matters. His conversations were very vivid.

He spoke about acts that he had seen in pornographic films involving such matters as women having sex with animals, and films showing group sex or rape scenes. He talked about pornographic materials depicting individuals with large penises, or large breasts involved in various sex acts.

On several occasions Thomas told me graphically of his own sexual prowess. Because I was extremely uncomfortable talking about sex with him at all, and particularly in such a graphic way, I told him that I did not want to talk about these subjects. I would also try to change the subject to education matters or to nonsexual personal matters, such as his background or his beliefs. My efforts to change the subject were rarely successful.

Throughout the period of these conversations, he also from time to time asked me for social engagements. My reactions to these conversations was to avoid them by limiting opportunities for us to engage in extended conversations. This was difficult because at the time, I was his only assistant at the Office of Education or Office for Civil Rights.

During the latter part of my time at the Department of Education, the social pressures and any conversation of his offensive behavior ended. I began both to believe and hope that our working relationship could be a proper, cordial, and professional one.

When Judge Thomas was made chair of the EEOC, I needed to face the question of whether to go with him. I was asked to do so and I did. The work, itself, was interesting, and at that time, it appeared that the sexual overtures, which had so troubled me, had ended.

Thomas, a Reagan appointee to the federal bench who had long opposed such programs as affirmative action. Thomas's qualifications for the Supreme Court were modest, but he seemed to be on the way to easy confirmation until it was revealed that a black law professor at the University of Oklahoma, Anita Hill, had accused Thomas of sexual harassment when she had worked for him at the Equal Employment Opportunity Commission during the early 1980s. Her charges led to dramatic hearings in which Hill laid out her allegations and Thomas denied them. A national television audience watched the hearings in fascination. Opinions differed sharply about whether Thomas or Hill was lying, and the issue remains as hotly disputed years later as it was in 1991. In the end, the Senate voted fifty-two to forty-eight to confirm Thomas, who proved to be an intense advocate of conservative positions. The controversy played a major role in alerting the public to the prevalence of sexual harassment in the workplace.

A Sense of Unease

When the controversy over the Thomas nomination ended, many observers believed that George Bush could expect easy reelection in 1992. No strong Democratic candidates had emerged to challenge him. Such party heavyweights as Mario Cuomo, the governor of New York, and Lloyd Bentsen of Texas were on the sidelines. Bush had the support of most Republicans, although there were rumblings of opposition among conservatives. It seemed probable, however,

The hearings on the nomination of Clarence Thomas to the United States Supreme Court became a sensational event when Anita Hill charged that Thomas had sexually harassed her a decade earlier. This photograph shows her testifying before the Senate Judiciary Committee on October 11, 1991.

that Bush would be renominated and would then defeat whomever the Democrats put up against him. After twelve years of Bush and Reagan, the Republican coalition seemed in solid control of the nation's politics and its policy agenda.

When the Republicans made such optimistic assumptions, they failed to notice that the American people were anxious and fearful as the 1990s began. Major corporations had cut their payrolls to reduce costs in what became known as "downsizing." Large firms like IBM, Procter & Gamble, and Chrysler Corporation trimmed their payrolls dramatically. IBM reduced its workforce by 100,000. Other businesses moved production facilities overseas in search of lower labor costs. The economy created millions of jobs, but many of them were low-paying service jobs. Multinational corporations became a focus of voter anger, as did the specter of immigrants taking jobs away from native-born Americans.

In 1990, the press began commenting on "Generation X," the generation of Americans under age twenty-five, which accounted for some 75 million people. Following on the heels of the Baby Boomers of the 1960s and 1970s, Generation Xers were derided as a "generation of self-centered know-nothings" in search of personal gratification and quick riches. The offspring of broken marriages and single-parent

homes, they had raised themselves while their parents were at work, spent endless time before television sets and computer games, and were sexually active at ever younger ages. One writer said that "This is the generation of diminished expectations—polar opposites of the baby boomers, who grew up thinking anything was possible."

As 1992 began, there was a growing sense that the nation faced serious choices. One law student in North Carolina said, "For the first time I feel that a group of Americans is going to have to deal with the idea that they're not going to live as well as their parents." That fear of diminished possibility and reduced opportunity would seem odd later in the 1990s, but it was a genuine concern in the popular mind as the 1992 election approached.

CONCLUSION

The Reagan-Bush years began with a national mood of apprehension and fear about the future. Twelve years of Republican rule saw the end of communism, the victory in the Gulf War, and the return of economic prosperity. Yet somehow, for all the rhetoric of "Morning in America" under Reagan and "a New World Order" under Bush, the reality did not add up to the

| TABLE 31.3 | PARTY CONTROL OF THE CONGRESS, 1980–1991 |

	Senate			House	
	Democrats	Republicans	Independent	Democrats	Republicans
1981–1983	46	53	1	242	190
1983–1985	45	54	1	269	166
1985–1987	47	53		253	182
1987–1989	54	46		258	177
1989–1991	57	43		262	173

SOURCE: *World Almanac, 1995*, p. 85; one Independent from Vermont was in the House, 1981–1985.

sunny prospects that the triumph over communism was supposed to bring. The nation looked for the new choices and new opportunities that a presidential election could provide.

RECOMMENDED READINGS

Cannon, Lou. *President Reagan: The Role of a Lifetime* (1991), a biography of the president by a reporter who covered his entire career.

Draper, Theodore. *A Very Thin Line: The Iran-Contra Affair.* (1991) is a thorough review of the scandal and its effects.

Duffy, Michael, and Dan Goodgame. *Marching in Place: The Status Quo Presidency of George Bush* (1992) takes a skeptical look at Bush's years in office.

Germond, Jack, and Jules Witcover. *Wake Us When It's Over: Presidential Politics of 1984* (1985) goes beneath the surface of a landslide election.

Johnson, Haynes. *Sleepwalking Through History: America in the Reagan Years* (1991) supplies the perspective of a Washington reporter on the 1980s.

Johnson, Haynes. *Divided We Fall: Gambling with History in the Nineties* (1994) covers the Reagan-Bush transition and carries the story down to the outset of the Clinton presidency.

Pemberton, William E. *Exit with Honor: The Life and Presidency of Ronald Reagan* (1997) is a sound one-volume study of the man and his impact on the nation.

Reagan, Nancy, and William Novak. *My Turn: The Memoirs of Nancy Reagan* (1989) provides the first lady's perspective on her husband's White House years.

Reagan, Ronald. *An American Life* (1990) offers Reagan's own interpretation of his presidency.

Wills, Garry. *Reagan's America: Innocents at Home* (1987) looks at Reagan's road to the White House.

Politics
Barrett, Laurence I. *Gambling with History: Ronald Reagan in the White House* (1983).

Bronner, Ethan. *Battle for Justice: How the Bork Nomination Shook America* (1989).

Cramer, Richard Ben. *What It Takes: The Way to the White House* (1992).

Mayer, Jane, and Jill Abrahamson. *Strange Justice: The Selling of Clarence Thomas* (1994).

Schaller, Michael. *Reckoning with Reagan: America and Its President in the 1980s* (1992).

Foreign Policy
Gaddis, John Lewis. *The United States and the End of the Cold War: Implications, Reconsiderations, Provocations* (1983).

Haig, Alexander. *Caveat: Realism, Reagan, and Foreign Policy* (1984).

Matlock, Jack F. *Autopsy on an Empire: The American Ambassador's Account of the Collapse of the Soviet Union* (1995).

Shultz, George. *Turmoil and Triumph: My Years as Secretary of State* (1993).

Timberg, Robert. *The Nightingale* (1995).

Walker, Martin. *The Cold War: A History* (1993).

America in the 1980s
Dionne, E.J. *Why Americans Hate Politics* (1991).

Hacker, Andrew. *Two Nations: Black and White, Separate, Hostile, and Unequal* (1992).

Holtz, Geoffrey T. *Welcome to the Jungle: The Why Behind "Generation X"* (1995).

Hughes, Robert. *Culture of Complaint: The Fraying of America* (1993).

Hunter, James Davidson. *Culture Wars: The Struggle to Define America* (1991).

Phillips, Kevin. *The Politics of Rich and Poor: Wealth and the American Electorate in the Reagan Aftermath* (1994).

CLINTON IN THE 1992 CAMPAIGN

During his first race for the White House, Bill Clinton sought to convey an image of youthful energy and vigor. At an airport in 1992, he makes a long pass to his running mate, Al Gore, out of camera range.

TOWARD THE NEW MILLENNIUM

THE 1992 PRESIDENTIAL contest interrupted the pattern of Republican electoral victories that had, with the exception of Jimmy Carter in 1976, dominated American politics since 1968. William Jefferson ("Bill") Clinton of Arkansas defeated incumbent George Bush and billionaire independent candidate Ross Perot in a campaign that involved Americans in campaigning and voting in greater numbers than had occurred in decades.

Clinton's victory began a turbulent eight years. The new president stumbled during his first year in office. Popular discontent with his performance helped the Republicans regain control of both houses of Congress in 1994 for the first time in four decades. Then, defying predictions that he was finished, Clinton rebounded to win a second term in 1996 and became the first Democrat since Franklin D. Roosevelt in 1936 to be reelected to a second term.

Since the Republicans retained control of Congress, the nation lived through four more years of divided government during Clinton's second term. During 1997, the nation experienced a booming economy and a calm international scene. Personal scandals once again threatened Clinton's presidency in early 1999.

The Clinton years also witnessed continued debates within American society about the direction of the nation as the year 2000 approached. Controversies about illegal and legal immigration affected politics, education, and the economy. Related to the diversifying population were arguments about multicultural values and the extent to which they should be pursued. In the murder trial of football star O.J. Simpson and in countless other ways, the issue of race remained unresolved and potentially devastating. The 1990s began with the voters in a restless mood, and the decade came to an end with the future direction of the nation still in doubt.

AN ANGRY NATION: 1992

The onset of the 1992 presidential election found Americans fretful and anxious. The economy had slipped into a recession by mid-1991 with unemployment rising, consumer confidence waning, and corporations laying off large numbers of employees. Americans again feared that downsizing and restructuring meant that their jobs were disappearing overseas.

Outside Washington unhappiness intensified about how officials in Congress and the White House conducted themselves. Speaker of the House of Representatives James Wright (D-Texas) had resigned under an ethical cloud in 1989 because he had accepted money from lobbyists and special interest groups. Other

CHRONOLOGY

1992	Rioting erupts in Los Angeles after white policemen are acquitted in Rodney King beating case
	Ross Perot becomes third-party candidate for president
	William Jefferson Clinton and Al Gore form the Democratic presidential ticket
	Clinton and Gore win the presidential contest
1993	Siege of Branch Davidians at Waco, Texas, ends in fiery incident
	Congress narrowly passes Clinton's economic program
	Ruth Bader Ginsburg is second woman appointed to the U. S. Supreme Court
1994	Nicole Brown Simpson and Ronald Goldman murdered in Los Angeles
	Republicans regain control of House of Representatives for the first time in forty years
1995	Murrah Federal Building bombed in Oklahoma City
	O.J. Simpson acquitted of murder charges
	Dayton Peace Accords bring shaky peace to Bosnia

	Federal government shutdown occurs
1996	Hillary Rodham Clinton is subpoenaed before grand jury
	Robert Dole is Republican nominee for president
	Clinton reelected president
1997	Federal budget deficit falls dramatically
	Balanced budget agreement reached
	Supreme Court rules that case of *Clinton* v. *Jones* can proceed while Clinton is president
	Princess Diana of Great Britain dies in car accident
1998	Scandal involving Monica Lewinsky and Clinton breaks
	Clinton testifies before grand jury and admits to "inappropriate relationship" with Lewinsky
	House starts impeachment inquiry against Clinton
	Democrats make House gains in congressional elections
1999	Clinton acquitted after impeachment trial
	War in Serbia launched by NATO

lawmakers had abused the procedures of the House bank to write checks for which there were not sufficient funds in their accounts. The House post office had been handled in a corrupt way as well. Campaign finance reform stalled as members continued to accept large contributions from corporations, labor unions, and special interest groups with a stake in the outcome of legislation. Voter anger surged during 1991. In Louisiana, the Republican candidate for governor was David Duke, a former leader of the American Nazi party, whose campaign rested on bigotry and racism. The Democratic candidate defeated Duke in the general election after the Republicans repudiated him. In Pennsylvania, Harris Wofford, a Democrat, upset the former attorney general in the Reagan and Bush administrations, Richard Thornburgh, in a contest for a vacant Senate seat. Wofford tapped into apprehensions about the future of health insurance and the ability of average citizens to afford medical care.

The Embattled Bush Presidency

Political pundits expected George Bush to win the presidency again. His success in the Gulf War seemed to assure his reelection. Still, the volatile nature of public opinion at the start of 1992 indicated that even Bush would not have an easy road back to the White House. His approval rating, once over 90 percent in 1991, had slipped, and conservatives assaulted his political leadership. The president seemed to many Americans to have little awareness of their problems and hopes.

President Bush soon had a challenger for the Republican nomination. Patrick J. Buchanan, a conservative commentator on cable television and former aide to Richard Nixon and Ronald Reagan, criticized the president for making the 1990 budget deal. He said that his own campaign would "put America first." The two men fought through the Republican primaries

with Bush winning all of the contests. Still, the results showed that more than a quarter of the Republicans did not like Bush, and the Buchanan challenge pushed the president further to the right as the year progressed.

Among the Democrats, however, the major stars remained on the sidelines. New York Governor Mario Cuomo decided not to run as did Senator Lloyd Bentsen of Texas. Two other contenders, former Senator Paul Tsongas of Massachusetts and former Governor Jerry Brown of California, lacked a broad national base. Instead, Arkansas Governor William Jefferson ("Bill") Clinton, survived an early scare in New Hampshire and built up a strong lead in delegate votes.

A New Democrat or "Slick Willie"?

From the outset, Clinton aroused conflicting passions among Democrats and the voters in general. He was a young, attractive southern governor who campaigned as a "New Democrat" with a strong civil rights record. He had a solid record of supporting education and economic growth in Arkansas. On the negative side, however, critics charged that he had cheated on his wife Hillary Rodham Clinton with numerous women. During the Vietnam War, which he had opposed, he received special treatment to avoid the draft but never gave a full explanation about how he had behaved. There were also whispers about his business dealings, especially investments in a land development called Whitewater. An Arkansas columnist dubbed him "Slick Willie," and the tag stuck. The Democratic party eyed Clinton warily as he marched toward the nomination.

Riots in Los Angeles

The tensions in the nation over racial issues burst into view in late April in Los Angeles. A year earlier policemen in that city had beaten a black motorist named Rodney King after stopping him for a traffic violation. The clubbing of King had been caught on videotape. After a lengthy trial, a white jury acquitted the four white officers. South Central Los Angeles, a black area, exploded into racial rioting. The death toll reached fifty-three, many whites were beaten, and damage estimates exceeded $1 billion. President Bush responded to the outbreak in a halting and indecisive manner. Unlike his strong leadership in the Persian Gulf War, he seemed immobilized in the face of a domestic crisis.

The events in Los Angeles set off a national debate about race relations as they related to issues of crime, police brutality, and justice in the United States.

Following the verdict against the police officers accused of beating Rodney King, crowds rioted and looted in Los Angeles.

For a season, Ross Perot brought fresh energy and new ideas into American politics. He captivated hordes of reporters when his campaign was still a novelty and his personality seemed attractive.

Conservatives charged that the outbreaks of violence demonstrated the bankruptcy of the "Great Society" programs of the 1960s. Liberals responded that the nation had never committed itself in any serious way to alleviating racial strife. Attention focused on the policy of "affirmative action" as a way to deal with racial inequities. Had the effort to assist minorities led to a form of reverse discrimination that now disadvantaged innocent white males? In California and elsewhere unhappiness with affirmative action produced referendum campaigns and court challenges to the policy on the state and national levels.

The Perot Insurgency

Neither Bush nor Clinton galvanized the restless voters during the spring of 1992. Many citizens, especially Republicans, looked for an alternative. The national spotlight turned to a Texas computer billionaire named Ross Perot. Plain-spoken and tough-talking, the feisty Perot argued that professional politicians lacked the will to deal with the country's problems. Faced with a losing football team, he said, "the best approach would be to get a new coach, a new quarterback, start with basics, clean it up." The journey would be difficult, he added. "We cannot go from where we are to where we need to be on a pain-free trip." Announcing his candidacy on Larry King's call-in television program, Perot stirred enthusiasm among citizens looking for an alternative to Bush and Clinton.

During the spring of 1992, Perot benefited from a grassroots movement that put his name on the ballot in all of the states. He soon led Bush and Clinton in the polls. Without specifying just what he would do, he promised to grapple with the budget deficit and clean up Washington. As the media investigated his previous record in business and politics, evidence of erratic and silly behavior surfaced. He monitored the private lives of his employees, and some called him "Inspector Perot." His poll numbers sank. Just before the Democratic National Convention, Perot withdrew from the race.

THE 1992 ELECTION CAMPAIGN

Bill Clinton received an electoral boost when Perot left the race, and the Arkansas governor swept the Demo-

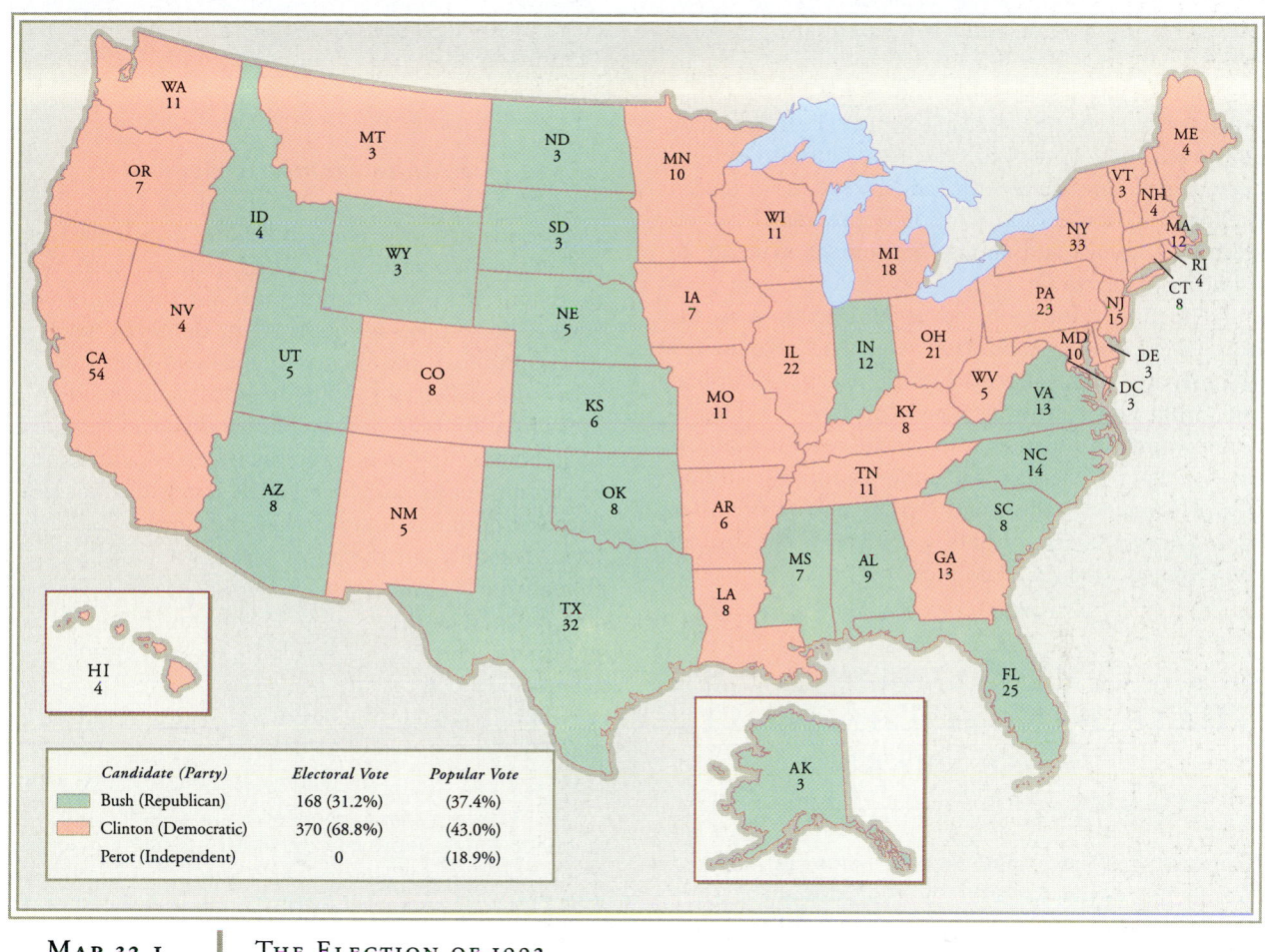

Candidate (Party)	Electoral Vote	Popular Vote
Bush (Republican)	168 (31.2%)	(37.4%)
Clinton (Democratic)	370 (68.8%)	(43.0%)
Perot (Independent)	0	(18.9%)

MAP 32.1 | THE ELECTION OF 1992

cratic nomination. He selected Senator Albert Gore of Tennessee as his running mate. Although the presence of two Southerners on the national ticket defied political wisdom, the Democratic team seemed youthful and energetic. A bus tour of the heartland of the country after the national convention attracted much favorable publicity. Clinton's lead in the polls widened before the Republicans held their convention in August.

The GOP delegates nominated Bush and Vice President Quayle amid an atmosphere in which the conservative social agenda dominated. In a fiery speech, Patrick Buchanan declared a cultural war to reclaim America from liberals, immigrants, and homosexuals. Much of the rhetoric from the podium focused on attacking Hillary Clinton and her alleged disregard for family values in her legal writings about children's

rights. The spectacle added to Clinton's support, especially with women voters in the nation's suburbs.

In October 1992, Ross Perot changed his mind and reentered the presidential race, and chose Admiral James Stockdale, a Vietnam prisoner of war, as his vice presidential choice. The three candidates then debated the issues before large national television audiences. The election engaged voter interest to an extent that had not been seen in several decades. Perot did not regain the levels of support that he had enjoyed in the spring, yet he retained a large and enthusiastic following. Bush closed the gap somewhat during the final weeks of the campaign, but the Perot candidacy split the Republican base in many states. The result was a Clinton-Gore victory. Clinton received 44,908,254 popular votes and 370 electoral ballots to

Bush's 39,102,343 votes and 168 electoral votes. Perot made the best popular showing of any third party candidate in American history with 19,741,065 votes. However, he won no electoral votes. The Democrats continued their control of Congress, but the Republicans gained one Senate seat and picked up fourteen members in the House. The new president had no electoral coattails and almost no popular mandate to implement a program.

A notable feature of the 1992 election was the number of women candidates who won seats in the U.S. Senate. In the aftermath of the Clarence Thomas and Anita Hill controversy (see Chapter 31), Democratic women candidates won Senate seats in California (Barbara Boxer and Dianne Feinstein), Illinois (Carol Moseley Braun), and Washington (Patti Murray). The results, said pundits, made it "The Year of the Woman" in national politics.

THE CLINTON PRESIDENCY: THE FIRST TWO YEARS

Clinton's presidency faltered even before he took office. As one of his first announced priorities, the president-elect indicated that he intended to lift the long-standing ban against declared homosexuals serving in the armed forces. After much debate within the military, the Clinton administration adopted a "Don't Ask, Don't Tell" approach in which gay personnel would not be asked about their sexual orientation and should not be openly homosexual. This stance contradicted Clinton's election appeal as a moderate rather than a liberal Democrat, and the religious right began an assault on the president and his wife that would continue throughout the next four years. Several embarrassing problems with the selection of women and minorities for cabinet and sub-cabinet positions caused an appearance of presidential disarray to form around Clinton that further impeded his ability to govern. After he was inaugurated, an armed confrontation between agents of the Bureau of Alcohol, Tobacco, and Firearms and members of the Branch Davidian religious sect outside Waco, Texas, in April 1993 led to the fiery deaths of many of the Davidians. Opponents of gun control and the federal government contended that the Clinton administration envisioned

dictatorial rule. That fear on the far right further fed discontent with the new president.

Clinton's Domestic Agenda

During his first two years, Bill Clinton achieved several domestic objectives at a high political cost. With the barest of voting margins in both the House and Senate, he secured adoption of an economic package that combined tax increases and spending cuts to lower the deficit for 1993 to $255 billion and for 1994 to $203 billion. Republicans depicted the president as returning to a traditional Democratic strategy of raising taxes and predicted economic calamity ahead. Clinton responded that the burden of higher levies fell only on the most wealthy Americans. Although the economy remained strong and the nation was prosperous throughout 1993 and 1994, the Republicans won the political argument against the Democratic tax legislation.

Clinton pursued the cause of freer world trade when he advocated passage of the North American Free Trade Agreement (NAFTA), which cleared Congress in late 1993. The trade agreement split the Democrats and approval came with the help of Republican votes. Ross Perot staked his political prestige in opposition to the pact, which he promised would produce a "giant sucking sound" as American jobs headed for Mexico. His poor performance in a televised debate with Vice President Gore eroded Perot's national support. In late 1994, the White House also secured congressional endorsement of the General Agreement on Tariffs and Trade (GATT) in a lame-duck session of the Democratic Congress. Again, Republican votes were central to this administration victory.

Reforming Health Care

The major goal of the new administration was reform of the nation's system of health care. Nearly 40 million citizens did not have health insurance, and the costs of medical care were rising at an alarming rate. In a dramatic expansion of the responsibilities for first ladies, Clinton asked his wife to head the task force to prepare a health care plan within one hundred days. Working throughout 1993, Hillary Clinton's planners produced a health care blueprint in September. It en-

visioned health alliances to emphasize managed care, asked Americans to pay more to consult private physicians, and expanded coverage to include all citizens.

The plan soon became the target of attacks from Republicans and the insurance industry as too bureaucratic, complex, and costly. The insurance industry used effective television ads of a mythical couple named "Harry and Louise" discussing the alleged drawbacks of the Clinton plan, Despite the intense lobbying efforts that Mrs. Clinton expended, the "Clinton Health Plan," as it was known, had few friends in Congress. Republicans denied that any serious health care reform was needed, and refused to present alternatives of their own. The drumbeat of opposition from the insurance industry took its toll on public opinion, By 1994 the health care issue had become a major liability for the Clinton White House.

Clinton's Political Troubles

Despite his domestic accomplishments, President Clinton's popular approval ratings remained low, often under 50 percent of the electorate. From the political right, the president and his wife stirred dislike that bordered on outright hatred. Republicans charged that the Clintons were socialists bent on entrenching homosexuals, bureaucrats, and atheists in power in Washington. When an aide to the president, Vincent Foster, committed suicide during the summer of 1993, right-wing talk show hosts circulated wild and unfounded rumors that Foster had been murdered at the instructions of the president and his wife.

More serious were the charges of financial impropriety and ethical lapses that dogged the Clintons from their years in Arkansas. Investments that they had made in an Arkansas real estate venture on the Whitewater River became entangled with the failed savings and loan firm run by business associates of the Clintons, James and Susan McDougal. Federal regulators grew interested in these transactions, and in 1993 press reports disclosed that the Clintons could be named as potential witnesses and even targets of an investigation. Charges soon surfaced that an effort at a cover-up had been mounted from the White House. The all-purpose label for these and other related "scandals" was "Whitewater." Investigators also looked into Mrs. Clinton's profitable trades in commodity futures in the 1970s. The willingness to investigate what the president and his family had done before taking office marked a new step in how the political opposition treated the incumbent chief executive.

In a troubled first year in office, a handshake between two Middle Eastern enemies at the White House represented one of the foreign policy successes for the Clinton administration.

The charges against the Clintons led to the appointment of an independent counsel or special prosecutor in 1994. The first counsel was a Republican named Robert Fiske. When he concluded that Vincent Foster's death was a suicide, angry conservatives had him replaced with another counsel, Kenneth Starr, a former federal judge and solicitor general during the Bush administration. Starr's probe explored the Arkansas connections of the Clintons in a number of areas that threatened further political harm to the president and his wife.

Personally embarrassing to President Clinton were allegations that he had sexually harassed an Arkansas state employee named Paula Corbin Jones in 1991. Ms. Jones filed a civil rights lawsuit in the spring of 1994 in which she claimed that then Governor Clinton had made unwanted sexual advances in a hotel room, including exposing himself to her. The president's lawyers attempted to have the suit delayed until after the end of his administration on the grounds that such litigation disrupted his ability to carry out his official duties. The issue of the president's right to have the lawsuit deferred until after he left office did not reach the Supreme Court until early 1997.

Clinton and the World

Bill Clinton came into office with his mind concentrated on domestic issues, and, as a result, his foreign policy got off to a shaky start. He faced a complex set of circumstances in the world in early 1993. The United States was heavily involved in a number of places around the globe—Haiti, Bosnia, and Somalia—but the previous administration had not linked these commitments to any kind of coherent structure other than George Bush's vague references after the Gulf War to a "New World Order."

As a result, Clinton's first year produced a number of foreign policy problems and disasters that created an image of the president as out of his depth on the world stage. In October 1993 eighteen American servicemen died in a raid in Somalia that included television footage of crowds dragging the body of an American pilot through the streets. The White House also suffered a setback in Haiti after a peacekeeping force was repulsed by angry inhabitants of the island threatening violence. The secretary of Defense, former Wisconsin Congressman Les Aspin, proved ill-suited to the job of defending American military policy.

The suicide of Vincent Foster in July 1993 was a traumatic event for those who knew the White House attorney and the speculations about a possible murder and cover-up fueled the anti-Clinton fervor on the right that dominated the next six years.

The main foreign policy problem of these initial months was in Bosnia where Clinton had been so critical of the Bush administration and its policies during the 1992 campaign. In office, the proper course of action seemed less clear. With United Nations peacekeeping troops, predominantly British and French, on the ground, the military options for Clinton were limited since the first targets of retaliation from the Serbs would be the allied troops. Working through the United Nations also proved frustrating for the White House. Tensions rose between Washington and its allies throughout 1993 over the proper course of action in the Balkans. Clinton seemed irresolute and indecisive as the crisis worsened.

In less publicized ways, the administration had some accomplishments. It succeeded in obtaining the withdrawal of Russian troops from the Baltic Republic of Estonia in 1994. Clinton also helped to broker peace

Paula Jones, shown with her lawyers, Gilbert Davis (left) and Joseph Cammarata (right) in 1994, filed a civil rights suit against President Clinton based on alleged sexual harassment that led in turn to a flood of legal problems for him.

negotiations among Ireland, Great Britain, and the Irish Republican Army's political arm Sinn Fein ("Ourselves Alone"). In the Middle East, State Department negotiators facilitated talks between Yasir Arafat of the Palestine Liberation Organization and Prime Minister Yitzhak Rabin of Israel that led to a celebrated handshake on the White House lawn. The United States also intervened in Haiti in 1994 and produced the ouster of the military rulers as a prelude to more democratic government. While he received little public credit for these accomplishments, Clinton became more adept on the world stage as his first term unfolded.

At the time, however, the perception that he was weak in foreign policy exacerbated his political troubles at home. During his first two years in office, Clinton's popularity ratings fell, his hold on the country remained weak, and there was speculation that he would be another one-term president. On the right, the determination to oust Clinton in 1996 gathered momentum.

THE REPUBLICAN REVOLUTION: 1994

By 1994 the cumulative effect of the charges against the president and a Republican resurgence from the setback of 1992 transformed the political scene as the congressional elections approached. Several elements fed the Republican offensive. In the House of Representatives, the Republicans chose as their next leader their ideological champion, Representative Newton ("Newt") Gingrich of Georgia. A former historian, Gingrich saw himself as the embodiment of a fundamental revolution in American values that would sweep away the residue of the "Great Society" in favor of "The Opportunity Society." An adroit political tactician, the burly, rumpled Gingrich used the television coverage of Congress that began in the late 1970s (called C-SPAN) to broadcast his ideas to a national constituency. His militancy contributed to a partisan intensity in the House, and he saw his greatest initial triumph when he forced Speaker Jim Wright from office for financial misconduct in 1989. Gingrich continued his abrasive tactics into the early 1990s and conservative members in the House rallied to his banner.

The Republican Offensive

Aiding the Republican cause was the rise of conservative talk-radio, embodied in its most militant exponent, Rush Limbaugh. With his denunciation of "feminazis" and "environmentalist wackos," Limbaugh appealed to a growing audience of followers known as

Newt Gingrich of Georgia stood on Capitol Hill with other Republican candidates on September 27, 1994, to announce the Contract with America. From that rally the Republicans gained a political victory that put them back in control of the House of Representatives for the first time in forty years.

"Dittoheads" because they simply said "ditto" when conveying praise of the master rather than reiterating the specifics of their adulation. A stocky, articulate performer, Limbaugh had millions of daily listeners over his "Excellence in Broadcasting" Network where he touted his "Talent on Loan from God." He and other conservatives on the radio, such as G. Gordon Liddy, who had been involved in the Watergate scandals, assailed the Clintons and their program throughout 1993 and 1994. Their assaults mobilized the Republican electorate against the incumbent and his party.

To dramatize their appeal, Gingrich and the Republicans offered "A Contract With America" as their election platform. Composed of proposals tested in focus groups for their popularity with the voters, the Contract promised action on such items as a balanced budget amendment, term limits for Congress members, and making legislators obey the regulations they applied to society. All of these measures and others would be acted on within the first one hundred days of a Republican victory. As the elections began, the Republicans found their poll numbers rising, the Democrats in retreat, and the prospect of regaining control of Congress a real possibility for the first time in four decades.

The Democrats and President Clinton stumbled throughout the autumn of 1994. The failure to achieve reform of the health care system and a general weariness with big government underlined the apparent futility of the incumbents. Efforts to scare the voters about the prospect of a Republican takeover fell flat. On election night, the Republicans swept to victory. They had 235 seats in the House to 197 for the Democrats and they controlled the Senate by a margin of fifty-three to forty-seven. Newt Gingrich became speaker of the House and Robert Dole was the Senate majority leader. The elections immediately prompted predictions that President Clinton's prospects for regaining the White House in 1996 were bleak.

THE CONTINUING SHADOW OF RACE: THE O.J. SIMPSON TRIAL

While Washington watched the 1994 elections with great intensity, Americans spent more time that autumn transfixed by what promised to be the last "Trial of the Century." In mid-June 1994 Nicole Brown

The murder trial of football star O.J. Simpson became one of the media events of the 1990s. Simpson stands with his lawyers F. Lee Bailey, Johnnie Cochran (middle) and Robert Shapiro as the jury announces his acquittal.

Simpson, the estranged ex-wife of professional football star and Heisman Trophy winner Orenthal James "O.J." Simpson, was brutally murdered at her home. Nearby lay the corpse of Ronald Goldman, an acquaintance and restaurant employee. Police suspicions soon focused on O.J. Simpson, whose Ford Bronco had blood that could be traced to the crime scene and who had apparently left physical evidence of his presence there. The nation watched in fascination on a Friday evening a slow-speed chase through the Los Angeles freeway system as Simpson and a friend drove back to his home where he ultimately surrendered.

Although Simpson's playing career in the National Football League had ended some years earlier, he remained a national celebrity because of appearances in movies and television advertising. "The Juice," as he was known, was one of the small number of African Americans who had gained broad public acceptance among white Americans. Now he stood accused of a brutal double murder. It soon became evident that the nation was polarized about Simpson's guilt or innocence. Most white Americans believed that the strong evidence pointed to Simpson as the killer. Many black Americans talked of a police conspiracy to frame the former football star and associated his prosecution with earlier examples of racial injustice.

These opinions solidified during the protracted trial that began during the fall of 1994 and stretched on into much of 1995. Televised daily and covered in ex-

cruciating detail, the trial played out as a racially charged drama that dominated talk shows, tabloids, and popular opinion in what became a national obsession. The participants in turn became media figures on their own—Simpson attorney Johnnie Cochran, prosecutor Marcia Clark, presiding Judge Lance Ito, and a parade of witnesses who reflected the lifestyles and values of Southern California such as Brian ("Kato") Kaelin, a free-loading house guest of O.J. Simpson. As the months of testimony and controversy stretched into 1995, the Simpson trial took on a life of its own as a forum where Americans confronted sensitive and explosive issues about how society dealt with minorities and race.

The Immigration Backlash

Adding to the social tensions of 1994 was the issue of immigration, both illegal and legal. Voters in California adopted Proposition 187, a ballot initiative that barred illegal immigrants from receiving state benefits in education and health. Immigration into the United States had grown dramatically during the 1980s. By the early 1990s legal immigrants, most of whom were Hispanics and Asians, totaled almost 600,000 per year. Estimates of the number of illegal immigrants to settle in the United States ranged from 300,000 to half a million. The Immigration and Naturalization Service

The flow of immigrants into the United States changed the shape of politics in the 1990s. These election signs in California indicate the rising power of Hispanic Americans at the polls as the twentieth century neared its conclusion.

(INS) forecast that there might be as many as 13 million immigrants coming to the United States during the 1990s. That would be the largest amount in all of American history.

Debate about the value and cost of this wave of immigrants roiled American politics during the first half of the 1990s. Critics of immigration charged that "the racial and ethnic balance of America is being radically altered through public policy." Studies demonstrated that immigrants, both legal and illegal, contributed more to society in taxes and productivity than they consumed from government services, but the mere increased presence of Hispanics and Asians, the so-called "browning of America," produced political conflict, especially in California. During the riots after the Rodney King verdict in Los Angeles, for example, the stores of Korean and other Asian merchants became the targets of mob violence. In 1994, the rising discontent about immigration in California led to a landslide election victory for Proposition 187. After its adoption, court challenges delayed its implementation, but by 1996 the governor ordered many of its provisions into effect. On the national level Congress debated immigration restrictions as it decided what to do about reform of the welfare system. At the end of 1994, it was clear that further action on the immigration issue would likely take place once the Republicans assumed control of Congress after their sweeping election triumph.

THE REPUBLICANS IN POWER

The new Republican majorities in Congress went to work in January 1995 with great energy to implement their "Contract with America." Laboring long hours at the start, they enacted a measure to make the regulations they imposed on Americans apply to Capitol Hill as well. The Republicans also pushed for a balanced budget amendment to the Constitution. Meanwhile, President Clinton accepted some of the Republican ideas in his State of the Union message and praised his own record on the economy. Speaker of the House Newt Gingrich was an effective leader of his Republican troops in this early phase of the session, but his propensity for colorful attacks on his opponents made him a center of controversy. Confident Republicans looked toward ousting Clinton in two years. Senator Robert Dole, the Republican majority leader, had surged to the front among prospective Republican candidates in 1996.

The pace of the "Republican Revolution" remained hectic into the spring of 1995. Although the balanced budget amendment failed by a single vote in the Senate, Congress did pass a law to restrict itself from making the states enforce regulations without supplying the necessary funds to do so. Clinton approved the

"unfunded mandates" measure on March 22, 1995. The Republicans failed, however, to pass a constitutional amendment imposing term limits on members of Congress. By April, Republicans proclaimed that they had enacted most of the Contract within the one hundred days they had set for themselves. President Clinton had been so marginalized politically that he felt compelled to announce at a press conference that he was still "relevant" in Washington.

Tragedy in Oklahoma City

Then a national tragedy shifted the political landscape. On April 19, 1995, the Alfred P. Murrah Federal Building in Oklahoma City blew up, killing 168 people inside. Two suspects, Timothy McVeigh and Terry Nichols, were quickly arrested and identified as having links with an extremist "militia" movement that sought the violent overthrow of the government of the United States. The public learned that small groups of militia met secretly in the countryside to practice guerilla warfare tactics against the day when the ZOG (Zionist Occupation Government) in Washington would precipitate the final confrontation on behalf of the United Nations and the "New World Order." The glare of publicity revealed that the militia movement, while violent and dangerous, commanded only a small cadre of followers. Still, the social tensions in the country intensified in the wake of the Oklahoma City massacre.

The aftermath of the bombing enabled President Clinton to regain a position of trust and confidence with the American people. He went out to Oklahoma City in the wake of the tragedy and participated in the ceremony of national mourning for the victims. Clinton's speech on that occasion struck a resonant note of national healing, and identified the president with the broad political center of the country. The two suspects, McVeigh and Nichols, were both tried and convicted for their roles in the bombing.

The Republicans Falter

Republican overreaching also contributed to the president's rebound in the polls during the remainder of 1995. As the Republicans in Congress attacked environmental legislation and sought to remove government regulations on business, the White House assailed them for endangering the gains that the nation

had made in clean air and clean water. Clinton threatened to veto legislation that cut back on environmental spending and money for education. He cast his first veto as president in June 1995 when he turned down a Republican spending measure that would have trimmed more than a billion dollars from education funding.

Troubles dogged Clinton during 1995, especially the long-running Whitewater saga which saw congressional committees probe the scandal in detail. Despite the best efforts of Republican lawmakers, the inquiry did not turn up evidence that would incriminate the president or his wife in wrongdoing. The special prosecutor, Kenneth Starr, continued his investigations with indictments and convictions of several Arkansas political and business figures, but that effort also yielded nothing to embarrass the Clintons directly.

The Race for the Republican Nomination

With the perception after the 1994 elections that Clinton would be a one-term president, the Republicans had an abundance of potential challengers for their nomination in 1996. The most formidable candidate would be General Colin Powell whose service as Chairman of the Joint Chiefs of Staff in the Gulf War had made him a national military hero associated with military success. As the first African American to be a serious contender for the Republican prize, Powell would be an asset to the party's ticket if he would agree to run as vice president. Many saw him as the answer to the party's problems with black Americans. Throughout most of 1995, Powell hinted that he was a Republican and thinking about running for president. He did not, however, make a firm declaration of his intentions.

Beyond Powell, the Republican field for 1996 included Senator Dole who began as the presumed front-runner. Since the party generally selected the leading candidate in the polls, Dole was likely to be nominated unless he stumbled badly. Waiting for him to falter were Senator Phil Gramm of Texas, former governor of Tennessee Lamar Alexander, and several long-shot aspirants. At seventy-two Dole had to overcome the age problem, his reputation as a strident partisan, and a perception that he would be the easiest target for a resurgent Clinton.

Dole endeavored to tap into the cultural fears of the right wing of his party in May 1995 when he

assailed what he called "nightmares of depravity" that peppered audiences of adolescents with images of grotesque violence and sexual activity. The senator also went after the variant of pop music known as "gangsta" rap, which he labeled as degrading to women and in favor of crime. The speech attracted a great deal of attention and invigorated Dole's floundering candidacy during the summer of 1995.

Clinton Resurgent: Bosnia

The big political winner in the second half of 1995 continued to be President Clinton. Against all the critics who charged that his policy in Bosnia would lead to an American involvement and a military disaster, the president succeeded by the end of the year in producing a cease-fire in the conflict. The price was the presence of American ground troops in the Balkans, but even that risky commitment did not lead to the disaster that so many had anticipated. The opportunity for a cease-fire emerged out of a complex series of events during the summer and fall of 1995. In July a Serb offensive imperiled several cities that were regarded as "safe havens" for refugees from the fighting. Helped by arms that had come in from Muslim countries, Croatian and Bosnian forces launched an offensive against the Serbs. At the end of August, Clinton authorized air strikes against the Bosnian Serbs. Within a week, a tentative peace agreement was declared, and a month later a cease-fire was reached. The United States then brokered peace negotiations in Dayton, Ohio, that produced a settlement. American troops were dispatched to help enforce the peace agreement. Fortunately for Clinton, the action contributed to stabilizing the situation on the ground, and the operation did not produce casualties that would have undercut the president's political standing.

THE SIMPSON VERDICT AND THE POLITICS OF RACE

While politics raged on during 1995, the O.J. Simpson trial plodded toward a conclusion. Popular interest in the proceedings remained high, especially as the end of the trial neared. The Simpson defense team associated their client with the oppression and injustice that

blacks had received in the United States and put the Los Angeles Police Department on trial. Attention centered on one officer, Mark Fuhrmann, who had testified that he had not used racial slurs but was found to have lied under oath on that point. The racial divisions about the trial had not lessened as the case went to the jury in September 1995. After very brief deliberations, Simpson was acquitted on all counts.

Black audiences cheered the verdict as it was announced. Whites watching on television expressed dismay. The national debate over the case intensified as commentators divided along racial lines over the significance of Simpson's acquittal. Some Simpson partisans asserted that the jury's decision represented an effort to make up for decades of biased white verdicts toward black defendants. All of the participants in the case began to write books about the trial, and a brisk market in Simpson narratives briefly dominated the best-seller lists. Meanwhile, the families of Ron Goldman and Nicole Brown Simpson filed civil suits against Simpson that promised to keep the case in the headlines for years to come.

The Million Man March

In October 1995, the Nation of Islam and its controversial leader, Louis Farrakhan, organized "a holy day of atonement and reconciliation" for black men. Designed to bring 1 million black men to the nation's capital, the event became known as the "Million Man March." Estimates of the actual number of participants varied widely, but the more positive assessments said that Farrakhan and his organization had reached their goal. Commentators made comparisons with the March on Washington in August 1963 and the striking oratory of Martin Luther King, Jr. Because of Farrakhan's espousal of anti-Semitic sentiments and his expressed dislike for white Americans, the 1995 march did not have the moral resonance of the earlier occasion, but it galvanized the participants. Within the black community, debate raged about the role of Farrakhan and his value as a spokesman for African-American aspirations.

Culture Wars: Multiculturalism and Political Correctness

The Simpson trial and the Million Man March took place in the context of a national debate about what

the United States should do regarding the continuing question of racial injustice and the presence of diverse minority groups within the existing culture. One source of debate and tension was the related issues of "multiculturalism" and what came to be called "political correctness." Both terms had highly charged, controversial meanings.

Multiculturalism had emerged in the 1980s in academic institutions as a means of opening up the study of history and literature to a larger range of cultural and social experiences among groups not previously included in the American past. In gender, class, and racial concerns, multiculturalism sought to draw attention to such issues as the role of black soldiers in the Civil War, Japanese Americans in World War II internment camps, and women in the American Revolution, to pick among countless examples. In its positive aspects, multiculturalism was an effort to include groups, ideas, and experiences that had not been part of the mainstream. In history it meant depicting, according to historians, "the dignity of common people who quietly struggle under difficult conditions and who, in large and small ways, refuse to submit to abuse, discrimination, and exploitation."

By the early 1990s, however, multiculturalism had come under attack from its enemies on the right who accused its adherents of enforcing what was called "political correctness." The critics of multiculturalism said that the academic left was using the movement to balkanize American society into warring ethnic groups, was limiting free speech on campuses, and was repudiating the whole tradition of Western culture. As Patrick Buchanan, the onetime Republican presidential candidate put it, "Our Judeo-Christian values are going to be preserved, and our Western heritage is going to be handed down to future generations and not dumped into some landfill called multiculturalism."

While some of the criticisms of multiculturalism did identify areas of exaggeration and overstatement from its proponents, the critics also overdramatized isolated incidents and blew small errors into larger trends. What was significant about these cultural divisions was the polarization of American society in the 1990s that they revealed. In 1994–1995, for example, an exhibition at the Smithsonian Institution to mark the fiftieth anniversary of the atomic bombing of Hiroshima became a flashpoint when veterans groups charged that the organizers of the show were adopting an anti-American, pro-Japanese point of view. The curators who mounted the show responded that they were trying to reflect the diversity of scholarly opinion

about the event. The protest triumphed and the exhibition was canceled and the director of the Air and Space Museum forced to resign. By the end of the decade, passions about multiculturalism had cooled somewhat, but tensions in other areas of society remained volatile over such issues as affirmative action and gay rights.

The Battle over Gay Rights

The efforts of gays and lesbians to attain political and social equality within the United States were met with a strong counteroffensive from conservatives who regarded homosexuals as a threat to the nation's values. In the 1990s, homosexuals contended that they should have the right to marry (in what were called "same-sex" marriages) just as heterosexuals did. Identifying their campaign with the civil rights movement of the 1960s, gay groups wanted attacks on those who were openly homosexual to be classified as "hate crimes." The declaration by television star Ellen DeGeneres that she, like the character she played on a situation comedy, was a lesbian stirred national controversy in 1997.

Conservative groups assailed homosexuality as a sin or a disease, in the words of Senate Majority Leader Trent Lott of Mississippi, like alcoholism or kleptomania. Christian groups ran elaborate advertising campaigns to persuade homosexuals to abandon their lifestyle and seek religious treatment. The president of an anti-gay legal fund announced in 1998 that "Radical homosexuals are busy in the legislatures and are filing dozens of lawsuits across America to obtain custody of children, to gain the legal right to 'marry,' and to redefine the legal definition of a family." Periodic acts of violence directed against gays spurred calls for federal legislation to prevent such actions. Passions on the issue remained intense as the 1990s ended.

Affirmative Action and Civil Rights

Another issue that provoked serious divisions within society was the policy of affirmative action in industry, higher education, and government to provide minorities with greater opportunities for advancement. Although the Supreme Court had ruled in the late 1970s that race could be employed in university admissions when the goal was to achieve diversity in the student body, the justices scaled back on that commitment in

a number of cases involving such policies as minority set-aside programs or congressional districts drawn to produce heavily minority-populated districts.

Unhappiness with affirmative action as a policy led some states such as California to adopt Proposition 209 in a referendum that abolished programs to assist minorities. In the *Hopwood* v. *Texas* case (1996), a federal circuit court invalidated the affirmative action plan of the University of Texas Law school, noting that any effort by universities to promote affirmative action was unconstitutional. The Supreme Court had not made a ruling on the question that affected the entire nation. In 1997 President Clinton appointed a President's Commission on Race to study these and other race-related issues. Its final report, issued a year later, satisfied neither the critics nor the proponents of affirmative action. Beneath the surface of American politics, these cultural issues seethed.

CLINTON WINS A SECOND TERM

As the budget negotiations between President Clinton and the Republican Congress produced no result toward the end of 1995, some of the more militant members of the GOP majority in the House called for a concerted effort to shut down the government as a way of pressuring the White House to agree to their position. Assuming that Clinton lacked the resolve to withstand a closing of the government, these Republicans foresaw a humiliating cave-in from a president they distrusted and hated.

The Republican strategy backfired. Two government shutdowns occurred, a brief one in November and a second that lasted for twenty-one days from mid-December 1995 into early January 1996. Rather than blaming the president for the deadlock, as the Republicans had anticipated, the public put the responsibility on the Republicans for the government closures that affected tourists in Washington and at popular national parks.

Outside of the public gaze, an important personal development for President Clinton occurred during the crisis over the government shutdown. He began an extramarital sexual relationship with a White House intern named Monica Lewinsky. Their dalliance included sexual encounters in or near the Oval Office.

Clinton soon found himself involved in a sordid mess that could compromise his presidency if it became public. He and Lewinsky agreed that she would keep their activities a secret, but she told friends and her physician about it during 1996. Despite the dangers that it posed to his presidency, Clinton continued to see Lewinsky into 1997. Inevitably, rumors circulated that the president had a mistress.

Clinton's Political Fortunes Improve

Speaker Gingrich proved to be a liability for his party. In November 1995, Israeli leader Yitzhak Rabin was assassinated. Gingrich flew with the president to the funeral, and then complained that he had not had a chance to talk with Clinton about the budget during the flight. He also had to leave Air Force One through the rear door, an action that the speaker took as a personal insult. He went public with his grievances. The ensuing flap left Gingrich looking petty and undercut his stature as a budget bargainer.

In early 1996, the Republicans realized that the prolonged shutdown was hurting their cause. Accordingly, they reached an accommodation with the White House that brought the crisis to an end. An interim measure to reopen the government passed both houses on January 5 and the government resumed official operations the next day. Budget negotiations went on, but Clinton had won the first major skirmish of the presidential campaign year decisively.

The First Lady Under Fire

While President Clinton had the upper hand in the national political arena, the long-running Whitewater saga took an ugly turn for Hillary Rodham Clinton in the early days of January. Billing records from Mrs. Clinton's former law firm in Arkansas, sought by the special prosecutor in 1994, turned up in the White House. A few days later *New York Times* columnist William Safire labeled the first lady "a congenital liar." Through a spokesman, Clinton said that if he were not president he would have punched Safire in the nose.

Meanwhile, Kenneth Starr, the Whitewater prosecutor, subpoenaed Mrs. Clinton to testify before his Washington grand jury. Her appearance marked the

first time that a first lady had testified in a criminal proceeding while her husband was in office. She spent four hours before the grand jury panel, but no results followed from her testimony. In mid-1997, press reports said that the jury had ended its life without issuing indictments against her. Nonetheless, the episode was intensely embarrassing for the Clintons.

Running parallel with Starr's probe were several congressional inquiries into the Whitewater story, the most notable being the one that Senator Alphonse D'Amato of New York conducted through the Senate Banking Committee. D'Amato's probe covered a wide range of issues relating to the economic activities of the Clintons in Arkansas, but the hearings yielded very little tangible evidence that implicated the president and first lady in criminal activity. The failure of D'Amato's inquiry to turn up sensational revelations helped defuse the Whitewater story as the 1996 election got underway. Even the majority report that was very critical of the Clintons did not place the Whitewater issue in the political forefront.

The Republicans Pick Dole

Throughout 1995, the front-runner for the Republican nomination was Senate Majority Leader Robert Dole of Kansas (after Colin Powell decided not to run). A decorated World War II veteran and a gifted lawmaker, Dole had run in 1988 against George Bush for the GOP prize, but had lost badly. Yet Dole's weaknesses persisted. As in his attack on Hollywood, he often seemed out of touch with the culture and values of the 1990s electorate. An indifferent speaker at best, Dole campaigned in a frenetic but often unfocused manner. He was not a good organizer, and friends worried about his ability to sustain a national presidential campaign.

Since there was no Republican incumbent candidate, a large number of challengers to Dole appeared. The best-financed was Phil Gramm of Texas who used his connections in the Senate to assemble a large war chest as 1997 began. An even less gifted speaker than Dole, Gramm looked like the stereotype

Senator Robert Dole of Kansas attained his long-held dream of winning the Republican presidential nomination in 1996, but he could not unseat a popular incumbent. His picture, taken at a rally in New Hampshire while he is being introduced, fails to show the war wounds to his right hand and the pencil that he always gripped.

of the college professor he had once been. His campaign never caught fire. Lamar Alexander, the former governor of Tennessee, campaigned under the slogan of "ABC—Alexander Beats Clinton" and a trademark checkered shirt. It was clever, but the electorate found little substance beneath the surface. Patrick Buchanan returned for another try at the Republican prize, and used his nationalistic, anti-foreigner rhetoric to some effect in the early primaries. Millionaire publisher Steven Forbes entered the race late and threw money into commercials that established him as a serious contender against Dole as the primary season began.

Dole as the Republican Candidate

Dole had problems in the early going, losing the New Hampshire primary to Buchanan, and facing challenges from Forbes elsewhere. The key South Carolina primary went to Dole on March 2 and successive victories brought the Kansas senator within sight of the nomination by April 1996. The early victory left the Dole campaign broke and unable to counter Clinton's advertising until after the Republican National Convention in late summer when he received federal matching funds as the official Republican nominee. To jump-start his lagging candidacy, Dole tried a sensational gesture and resigned his Senate seat in June to campaign as a man without office or Washington power. None of these gimmicks did much to close the large gap in the polls that separated Clinton from his rival.

The spring of 1996 did not mean undiluted triumphs for President Clinton. In late May his onetime business partners, James and Susan McDougal, were found guilty of fraud and conspiracy in dealings in Whitewater-related transactions. One of the witnesses in the case alleged that then Governor Clinton had pressured him to make an illegal loan some years earlier. President Clinton denied the allegation under oath when he testified as a defense witness.

A month later another scandal broke. During a probe of the Travel Office firings that had occurred in 1993, congressional investigators learned that the White House had obtained the Federal Bureau of Investigation files for as many as 600 individuals, among them prominent Republicans. Members of the GOP majority in Congress charged that the Clinton administration had abused its power and pressured the FBI for political reasons to use the files against their enemies. The White House blamed the episode on zealous subordinates and denied any presidential involvement.

An Uneasy Summer

While the political campaigns heated up during the summer of 1996, Americans turned their attention to the prospect of their usual vacations and the Olympics that would be held in Atlanta, Georgia, during July. Two unrelated events disturbed the calm of the season. On July 27, TWA Flight 800, en route from New

York to Paris, exploded over the Atlantic Ocean off the coast of Long Island. There were 230 victims, some of them high school students from a small town in Pennsylvania on their way to France for a school trip. Conspiracy theories soon surfaced that suggested the airplane had been the target of a terrorist missile, an errant government weapons test, or a domestic plot. Months dragged on with no resolution of the mystery, and skepticism about any official explanation mounted.

Ten days later, a bomb exploded at the Summer Olympics in Atlanta, Georgia, killing one spectator and wounding up to one hundred others. The explosive was in a knapsack, and the security guard who had pointed out its location soon was revealed as the ostensible suspect of the investigation. For weeks, the unfortunate guard had media crews following him and his indictment was predicted within a few days. The media frenzy attested to the persuasive power of television and the information superhighway in spreading often erroneous data. Only months later did the FBI concede that the guard was not a suspect any longer. These events indicated how rapidly America gathered information in the mid-1990s and how the pervasiveness of news sometimes produced less social cohesion rather than more.

The Rise of the Internet

The powerful growth of the Internet and the World Wide Web in the 1990s transformed the way Americans got their news and communicated with each other. The development of browsers that could read the Hyper Text Markup Language (HTML) facilitated this process during the first half of the decade. In 1996, 18 million people, or about 9 percent of the population, accessed the Internet on a regular basis. A year later the figure stood at 30 million adults. By 1998, 20 percent of all American households had Internet access, and the growth continued unabated as the year 2000 approached. With more than 96 million computers in use in 1995, or 364.7 per 1000 Americans, the United States led the world in its share of Internet usage.

Dominating the new field were such corporations as America Online which provided connections for 30 percent of all Internet users in the country in 1996. Other businesses sought consumers on the Web

through specific Web pages or by purchasing advertising space on popular Web sites. Some new firms, such as the discount bookseller Amazon.com, saw their common stock soar in value in 1998 because of the potential growth of their markets. Popular movies such as *You've Got Mail* (1998) and the rise of news outlets on the Web that included "Salon," "Slate," and the "Drudge Report" (named after its host, conservative Matt Drudge) underscored how the Internet had permeated American life.

So important had computers and the Internet become by 1998 that the prospect of a computer breakdown in the year 2000 emerged as a major social problem. Y2K, as it was known, stemmed from the inability of older computers to read the year 2000 correctly and remain functioning. Finding and fixing imbedded computer codes cost business and government hundreds of billions of dollars in 1998 and 1999. Some Americans hoarded food and weapons in preparation for what they forecast as a breakdown of civilization on January 1, 2000. More sober assessments predicted some disruption but not social chaos. In any case the fate of the nation's economy was now tied to the operation and reliability of its computers.

Welfare and Other Reforms in Congress

With the election approaching and polls showing their standing with the public in jeopardy, the Republican majority on Capitol Hill saw cooperation with the White House as a political necessity. As a result, the president and Congress found common ground on reform of the nation's welfare system in the summer of 1996. A compromise measure came out of Congress at the end of July. The bill produced sweeping changes in the nation's way of caring for the poor. In place of the longstanding Aid for Dependent Children (AFDC) program, lawmakers established a system of block grants to the individual states. The federal responsibility to provide for the poverty-stricken, adopted during the New Deal and expanded in succeeding decades, ended. The measure also specified that legal immigrants into the United States would not be eligible for benefits during their first five years of residence. The legislation fulfilled Clinton's 1992 campaign promise to "end welfare as we know it," but it left many Democrats unhappy with the current direction of their

party. For Clinton, it represented a return to the "New Democrat" posture that had helped him win the election in 1992.

The waning days of the Congress saw other accomplishments that gave the president issues on which to run and allowed the Republican Congress to rebut the charges that it was unable to act constructively. In August, lawmakers enacted a rise in the minimum wage in two steps to $5.15 per hour. It was the first hike since 1991 and came after intense Republican opposition. Responding to the continuing public unhappiness with immigration problems, Congress included in its spending legislation funds for new personnel for the Immigration and Naturalization Service, the hiring of additional Border Patrol agents, and more severe penalties for bringing in illegal aliens. Republicans failed to get language that would have barred public education to the children of illegal immigrants. The achievements of Congress undercut Dole's argument that Clinton was not an effective leader.

The National Conventions

Both parties struggled for the political advantage in their national conventions. These gatherings had now become television spectacles rather than deliberative events, and both Republicans and Democrats endeavored to display themselves in a favorable light before a national audience. The major networks abandoned earlier policies of "gavel-to-gavel" coverage, with programming focused on key moments in the proceedings. Everything was carefully scripted and choreographed. The conventions were evaluated as if they were entertainment specials, which was what they had become by the summer of 1996.

Mindful of their public relations disaster in Houston in 1992, the Republicans sought to reassure voters that they were an acceptable and inclusive alternative to the Democrats. Their problem remained, however, one of making Senator Dole an exciting and charismatic figure who could compete with Clinton, an adroit and skilled campaigner. Dole launched his preconvention offensive with the promise of a 15 percent tax cut over a three-year period. Reflecting the sentiment within the party for what was known as a "flat tax," an income tax at a low rate for all citizens, he ad-

vocated a "fairer, flatter tax." To Democratic charges that his proposal would "blow a hole in the deficit," Dole responded by saying that he would propose prudent spending cuts to find the $548 billion needed to offset his tax reductions. For Dole, long a champion of a balanced budget, the tax cut proposal represented an eleventh-hour conversion to the supply-side ideology of the Reagan wing of his party.

The second daring maneuver came when Dole announced that he had asked former Congressman Jack Kemp of New York to be his running mate. A favorite of the conservatives, Kemp had long endorsed tax cuts and was popular among African-American voters. In many respects, the choice was an odd one. Kemp brought little electoral strength to the ticket. The Republicans had no hopes of carrying New York State, for example. Kemp was also an indifferent campaigner, but at the convention his selection lifted the spirits of the Republican delegates who saw Dole trailing badly in the polls to the incumbent president.

The convention was a well-scripted love feast for Dole that gave the senator a modest improvement (or "bounce") in the public opinion polls. Mrs. Elizabeth Dole was the hit of the conclave with a deft, informal speech outlining her husband's virtues. Dole's own acceptance speech was adequate but not spectacular. The gap in the polls closed briefly and then widened again.

Perot Again

Midway between the conventions of the major parties came the meeting of the Reform party that Ross Perot had established as the vehicle for his second presidential candidacy. Although there was an opposition candidate to Perot, former Governor Richard Lamm of Colorado, little suspense remained about the selection that the delegates would make. Perot won easily. Yet he had not captured the public's imagination as had happened in 1992, and his selection of an obscure Washington writer, Pat Choate, as his running mate did not enhance his standing with the country. Perot's hope was to elbow his way into the presidential debates against Clinton and Dole, but neither of the major party candidates wanted to see the third-party challenger in the event. Despite efforts to use the federal courts to gain access, Perot had to watch from the sidelines.

Clinton Renominated

With a commanding lead in the public opinion polls, President Clinton enjoyed a harmonious convention when the Democrats met in Chicago in late August. The platform stressed centrist themes and spoke of a "New Democratic Party." Even bad news about one of Clinton's closest advisors did not disrupt the festivities. A tabloid newspaper revealed that Dick Morris, a campaign strategist and old friend of Clinton, had had a long-running affair with a prostitute. Morris resigned and the episode passed quickly. Clinton and Vice President Gore were renominated, and the president promised four more years of prosperity and moderate reform in what he called his last election campaign.

During September 1996, the campaign unfolded as though Clinton and the Democrats were certain winners. Despite some fluctuations, the lead over Dole in the polls remained strong. The two presidential debates did not attract the attention that had characterized the 1992 debates, and Dole failed to crack Clinton's armor with attacks on his character and administration scandals. By the middle of October, optimistic Democrats predicted a landslide for the president and a good chance that the party might recapture the House and Senate from the Republicans.

Campaign Scandals

Then newspaper reports appeared, and rapidly accelerated, about improprieties and possible crimes in the fund-raising for the Democratic party and the Clinton campaign. Money had flowed into the president's campaign war chest from Asian sources, and possible links to Communist China and Indonesian businesses emerged. A Democratic National Committee operative named John Huang soon became the focus of the press inquiries. Every day as the campaign wound down new revelations of questionable campaign contributors and dubious funding sources followed. The lead for the Democratic congressional candidates eroded and even some slippage occurred for President Clinton. Rather than a triumphal march, the waning days of the 1996 election saw Clinton and his party staggering toward the finish line under a severe cloud of scandal.

Dole was not able to capitalize on this turn of events. His campaign manager asked Ross Perot to drop out to give Dole a chance against Clinton. Perot refused. In a last-minute blitz, Dole barnstormed the country nonstop to demonstrate that he was not too old to be president and that he had the energy to overtake Clinton. Nonetheless, while they retained doubts about Clinton as a candidate, the voters did not want to see Dole become president. His tactics gained him personal acclaim but did not change the result.

A Mixed Result

Clinton's lead wavered a little as the election neared, largely because of the drumfire of press coverage of the campaign finance issue. Although most news organizations predicted a double-digit presidential win, that did not happen. Nor did Clinton achieve the majority of the popular vote that he sought to overcome the Republican taunt that he was a minority president. The result over Dole was never really in doubt on election night, but the triumph was more limited than had seemed possible when the campaign started.

On the other hand, Clinton's political obituary had been pronounced after the 1994 election and so his victory represented a substantial vindication for one of the most gifted and fascinating leaders of the twentieth-century United States. The Democratic ticket won 379 electoral votes and 49 percent of the popular vote to 41 percent (159 electoral votes) for Dole and Kemp. Ross Perot and the Reform party lagged with 8 percent of the popular vote and no electoral votes. Clinton's electoral coalition included California (to which he had devoted attention all during his first term), New York, Illinois, Michigan, and Ohio. The president also carried two staunchly Republican states—Florida and Arizona. In all, Clinton won thirty-one states and the District of Columbia in assembling his winning total.

What made Clinton's success distinctive was his standing as the first Democratic president to secure consecutive terms since Franklin D. Roosevelt. During the 1990s, Clinton had gone a long way toward drawing the Democrats back to the political center and renewing them as a genuine electoral alternative to the Republicans. Whether the party's revival would outlast Clinton's second term remained to be seen.

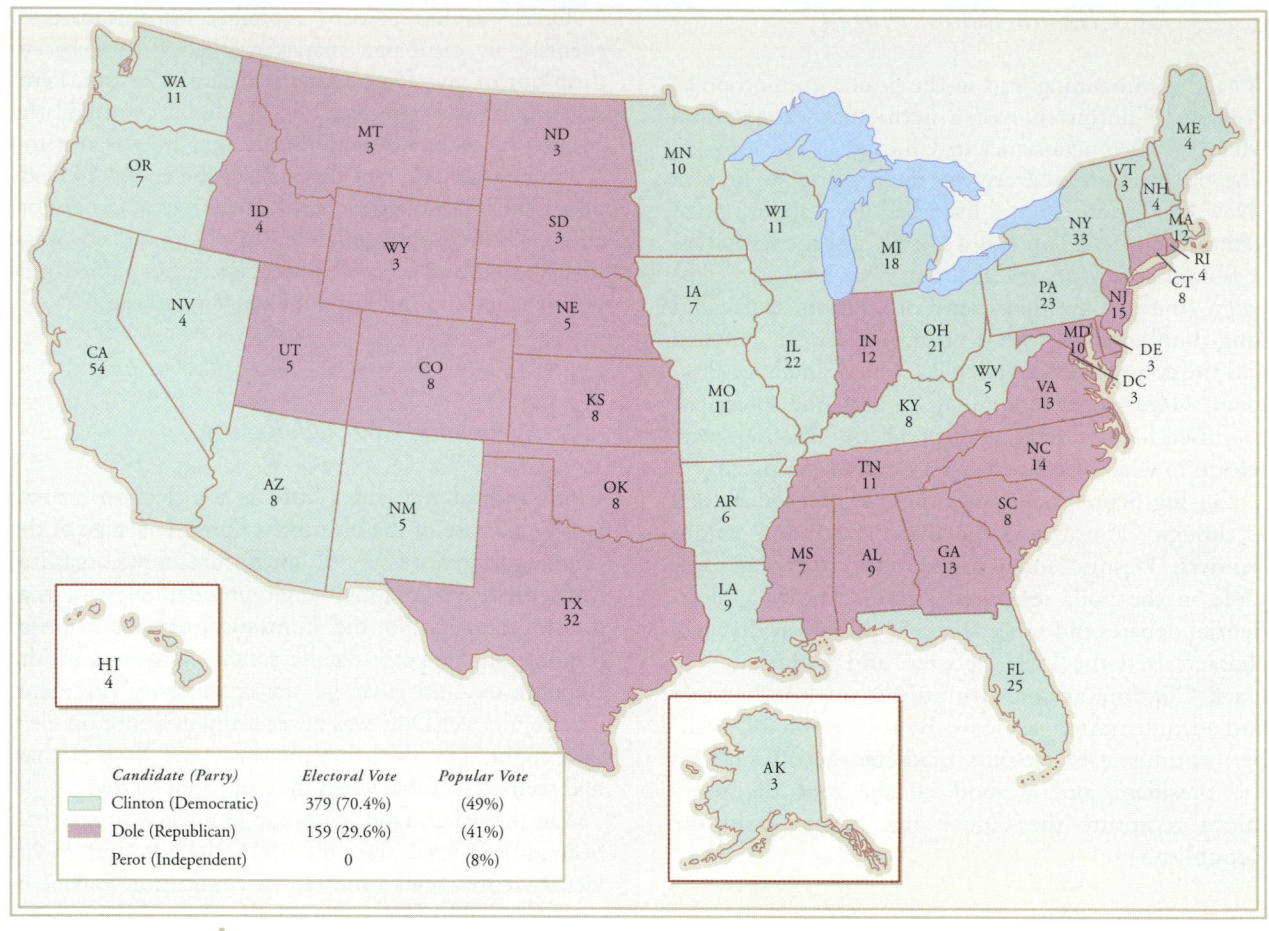

Candidate (Party)	Electoral Vote	Popular Vote
Clinton (Democratic)	379 (70.4%)	(49%)
Dole (Republican)	159 (29.6%)	(41%)
Perot (Independent)	0	(8%)

MAP 32.2 | THE ELECTION OF 1996

While Dole had lost badly, the Republicans gained some consolation out of the election results. Despite a heavy assault from organized labor and Democratic congressional candidates, the Republicans retained control of both houses of Congress. The Republicans held onto the house but with a diminished majority of only ten seats. In the Senate, the Republicans picked up two seats for a fifty-five to forty-five margin over the Democrats. Since they needed sixty votes to block a Democratic filibuster, the Republicans would have to compromise with their opponents to get any legislation passed. The stage was set for another scenario of divided government to which the nation had become accustomed since the late 1960s. Republican domi-

nance of Congress did mean that they would conduct the hearings into the campaign fund-raising scandals as 1997 progressed.

A New Cabinet

For his second term, President Clinton assembled a new cabinet to replace the officeholders who had used up their energy and political capital during the first administration. To succeed the outgoing secretary of State, Warren Christopher, the president selected the ambassador to the United Nations, Madeleine Albright. She became the first woman to serve as secre-

The major architect of Clinton's foreign policy in his second term was Secretary of State Madeleine Albright, shown in a 1997 visit to American troops in the Balkans.

Modest Programs Modestly Advanced

For his second term, President Clinton avoided large initiatives that might put him at odds with the Republican Congress. During the winter of 1997, he worked out a budget agreement that promised a balance within a few years. The American economy proved so robust through the summer of 1997 that the deficit fell rapidly and forecasters projected that a budget surplus might emerge by the end of the year. The stock market soared throughout this period, reaching above 8,000 on the Dow Jones Industrial Average in July. Clinton took credit for the impressive showing of the markets and the economy.

His goals for a second term seemed indistinct and modest well into 1997. Carrying forward the strategy of his reelection victory, he identified himself with small, incremental ideas such as a V-chip to enable parents to control the television programming that their children watched, a voluntary television ratings system, and greater computer training for school children.

An Ambitious Foreign Policy

For a president who had come into office promoting domestic issues, Clinton seemed to relish the international stage during his fifth year in office. He pushed hard for the North Atlantic Treaty Organization to add members from former communist states in Eastern Europe, and saw his vision fulfilled when Poland, Hungary, and the Czech Republic were added to the alliance. To overcome Russian opposition to expansion of NATO, the United States and its allies told Moscow in May 1997 that neither nuclear weapons nor large numbers of combat forces would be placed on the soil of the new member states. That publicly placated the Russians.

In other areas of foreign policy, the world's trouble spots remained volatile. The situation in Bosnia, while improved since the Dayton agreement, still pitted Serbs, Croats, and Bosnians against each other despite the uneasy peace that American troops in NATO helped maintain. As for the Middle East, tensions between Palestinians and Israelis worsened amid sporadic terrorist violence. The Clinton administration pressed both sides for more movement to implement peace, but progress was elusive. One overseas event that

tary of state, and she soon emerged as one of the most effective and popular members of the government. She brought a new tough tone and assertive style to the conduct of foreign policy. Her ability to work with the chairman of the Senate Foreign Relations Committee, Jesse Helms of North Carolina, smoothed the way for diplomatic initiatives in early 1997 on such issues as reforming the United Nations and the Bosnian policy.

In a gesture of bipartisanship, Clinton named former Maine Republican Senator William Cohen as his secretary of Defense. Long interested in defense issues, Cohen was a moderate who could build coalitions with his former colleagues in the Senate while enjoying good relations with Democrats as well. More inclined to end the Bosnian commitment than Madeleine Albright, Cohen was a cautious voice in the Pentagon. Few crises, however, disturbed his early months in office.

Clinton and British Prime Minister Tony Blair worked together on a number of foreign policy issues from Northern Ireland to the Middle East. This picture from May 18, 1998, shows their joint press conference in London about trade disputes and American sanctions toward such countries as Libya, Cuba, and Iran.

riveted the nation was the death of Princess Diana of Great Britain on August 31 in an automobile accident in Paris. The funeral services in London a week later attracted the largest worldwide television audience ever recorded.

An Economic Boom

Throughout 1997 the American economy went into high gear. Unemployment fell to 4.8 percent and inflation no longer seemed a problem. With jobs plentiful

During the late 1990s the stock market made impressive gains and suffered deep drops, often within a few days of each other. Americans became used to fluctuations that would have dazzled their parents.

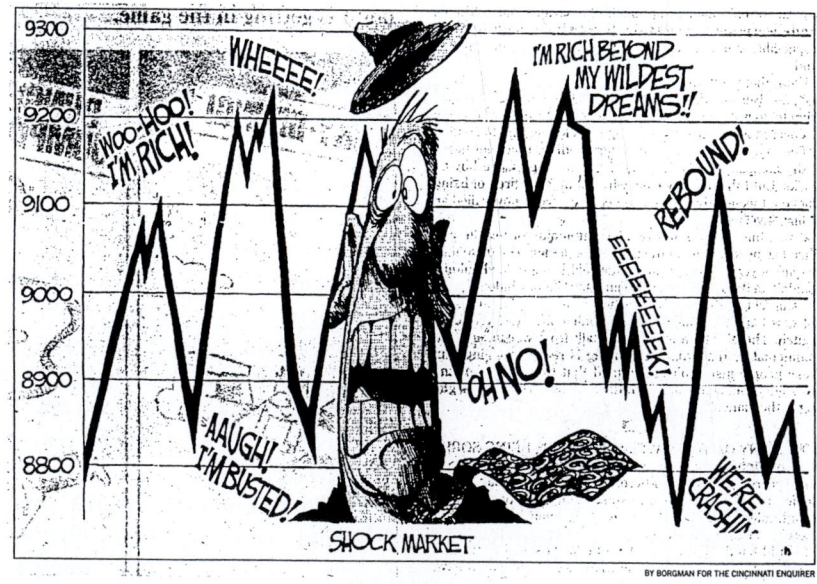

Each month brought new products to introduce consumers to the wonders of the digital age. Here a salesman in an electronics store demonstrates the high definition television that was forecast to replace older television sets by the year 2000.

and prices stable, a sense of economic optimism pervaded the nation and kept Clinton's job approval ratings around the 60 percent mark.

Adding to the euphoria was the apparent end of the budget deficit problem that had shaped politics for so many years. Surging tax revenues meant that red ink started to disappear. The 1997 budget deficit was only $25 billion, the lowest since 1974, and 1998 promised the unheard of—a budget surplus. As a result of these trends, Congress and the president worked out a balanced budget agreement in May that was signed into law on August 5. Clinton proclaimed: "The sun is rising on America again." Politicians could suddenly look forward to budget surpluses for years to come. This success relied on using the money in the Social Security Trust Fund to offset other spending, but elected officials played down this budgetary sleight-of-hand in their public comments.

CLINTON EMBATTLED

The political result of these favorable economic events was a good year for President Clinton that left him popular and Democrats optimistic about regaining control of the House in 1998. The major setback of the year came when the Supreme Court ruled 9–0 on May 27, 1997, in *Clinton* v. *Jones* that the sexual harassment lawsuit against the president could go forward while he was in office. Other problems dogged Clinton. Congressional probes on the 1996 campaign scandal indicated that the president and Vice President Al Gore had played a larger role in raising money than they had earlier admitted. Kenneth Starr's Whitewater investigation moved along without major indictments but still posed a potential threat to the White House. Yet, for all these lingering concerns, it seemed to the chagrin of Clinton's most bitter political foes that "Slick Willie" would escape again.

The Monica Lewinsky Scandal

Then, in mid-January 1998 a stunned nation learned that Monica Lewinsky had had a sexual relationship with President Clinton during her White House employment as an intern and low-level staffer. Once the news broke, Clinton asserted that he had not had sex with Lewinsky. For seven months he reiterated that version of events. Meanwhile, Kenneth Starr

President Clinton Denies a Sexual Relationship with Monica Lewinsky January 21, 1998

When word of his relationship with Monica Lewinsky broke in early 1998, President Clinton issued a series of denials. This one with the television journalist Jim Lehrer was typical of many that the president made. He later had to admit that his statement did not represent a candid description of their relationship.

Interview with Jim Lehrer of the PBS "NewsHour"
January 21, 1998
Independent Counsel's Investigation

Mr. Lehrer. Mr. President, welcome.
The President. Thank you, Jim.
Mr. Lehrer. The news of this day is that Kenneth Starr, the independent counsel, is investigating allegations that you suborned perjury by encouraging a 24-year-old woman, former White House intern, to lie under oath in a civil deposition about her having had an affair with you. Mr. President, is that true?
The President. That is not true. That is not true. I did not ask anyone to tell anything other than the truth. There is no improper relationship. And I intend to cooperate with this inquiry. But that is not true.
Mr. Lehrer. "No improper relationship"—define what you mean by that.
The President. Well, I think you know what it means. It means that there is not a sexual relationship, an improper sexual relationship, or any other kind of improper relationship.
Mr. Lehrer. You had no sexual relationship with this young woman?
The President. There is not a sexual relationship—that is accurate.

We are doing our best to cooperate here, but we don't know much yet. And that's all I can say now. What I'm trying to do is to contain my natural impulses and get back to work. I think it's important that we cooperate. I will cooperate. But I want to focus on the work at hand.

---

investigated whether Clinton had lied under oath in the Paula Jones case when he said he had not had sex with Lewinsky, whether he had obstructed justice, and whether he had asked others to lie on his behalf. This sordid spectacle absorbed vast amounts of television news coverage throughout 1998. It featured friends and enemies of Clinton debating his sexual drives, his honesty, and the future of his presidency in the most intimate personal details.

Clinton's strategy of delay worked in the short run. His poll numbers remained high, and Starr's popularity sagged. In the end, however, abundant evidence emerged that Clinton and Lewinsky had been physically intimate. On August 17, 1998, Clinton acknowledged "inappropriate" conduct with Lewinsky when he testified before Starr's Washington grand jury from the White House. That night he told the nation the same thing in a four-and-a-half-minute speech that

SPECIAL REPORT | Clinton's Crisis

THE DAYS OF HER LIFE
Soap-opera fan MONICA LEWINSKY is the new face of scandal. And she lives at the Watergate

Monica Lewinsky's relationship with President Clinton led to a national scandal and his impeachment. By late 1998 she had become internationally known as the tapes of her conversations with her friend Linda Tripp were played for the entire world.

was widely regarded as a low point of his presidency. Predictions abounded that his resignation was imminent or impeachment was likely.

A few weeks later Starr sent a report to the House of Representatives alleging that there were grounds for impeaching Clinton for lying under oath, obstruction of justice, abuse of power, and other offenses. The House Judiciary Committee recommended that an impeachment inquiry commence, and the House voted to authorize a probe after the 1998 elections.

The Monica Lewinsky scandal and its fallout left Clinton a wounded president. He retained the ability to achieve foreign policy successes such as a deal he brokered between Israelis and Palestinians in October 1998. With Clinton's resiliency as a politician, a rebound during his last two years was possible. But his tactics and conduct in handling the Lewinsky matter had cost him dearly in terms of his political

capital with the American people by the end of 1998. Whatever else would be said about his administration and record, his involvement with Monica Lewinsky would be the defining event of his historical reputation.

The 1998 Elections

The Republicans entered the 1998 election season with high ambitions to build on their majorities in the House and Senate. In the Senate, they hoped to reach a total of sixty Republicans which would enable them to end Democratic filibusters. After Clinton's speech on August 17, it seemed as if a Republican rout was in the offing. Alienated Democrats were predicted to stay home and energized Republicans would flock to the polls to rebuke Clinton. With the Monica Lewinsky

President Clinton's admissions of his sexual intimacy with Monica Lewinsky proved abundant source material for cartoonists. Jules Feiffer in The New York Times *offers one interpretation of the president's misbehavior.*

ocrats and produced a backlash. By the time the Republicans figured out what was going on, it was too late. On November 3, 1998, the Democrats in the House actually gained five seats, not enough to regain control, but an amazing feat in the sixth year of a two-term presidency. Republican control of the House narrowed to 223–211, a very thin majority. In the Senate, the two parties battled to a draw, with the Republicans holding the same 55–45 edge that existed when Election Day dawned. The Democrats made gains in governors' races in the South as well. Two significant Republican victories came in Florida and Texas, where the two sons of George Bush, Jeb Bush in Florida and George W. Bush in Texas, were elected governor. For George W. Bush, his reelection made him the prospective front-runner for the Republican presidential nomination in 2000.

Despite the results of the congressional elections, Republican leaders in Congress pressed ahead with the impeachment of President Clinton. In December the House Judiciary Committee, on a nearly party-line breakdown sent four articles of impeachment to the full house. That body adopted two articles of impeachment charging President Clinton with perjury in his grand jury testimony in August 1998, and with obstruction of justice in his relationship with Monica Lewinsky, members of his staff, and other individuals. The Senate opened its trial in mid-January. By the end of the month, it became evident that the forty-five Democrats would not vote for conviction and a two-thirds majority to convict and remove the president did not exist.

President Clinton's popularity with the public remained high, and his State of the Union address on January 19, 1999, drove his poll ratings still higher. Some conservatives, such as religious activist Pat Robertson, urged the Republicans to end the proceedings. The prosecution and impeachment trial in the Senate was hurting the Republicans' political posture with the American public. As January 1999 wound down, however, the impeachment trial continued.

President Clinton was acquitted on both counts when the Senate voted on February 12, 1999. On the perjury count, the total was 45 Republican senators voting to convict the president while all 45 Democrats and 10 Republicans voted for acquittal. On the second article involving obstruction of justice, the Senate split evenly with 50 Republican votes for conviction and 45 Democrats and 5 Republicans voting for acquittal.

scandal working for them, the Republicans had only to run out the clock for a big victory.

Instead, the Republicans overplayed their hand. Their moves to impeach Clinton awakened the Dem-

One of the most controversial aspects of the Clinton-Lewinsky scandal was the role of the news media and its constant coverage. One network provided "All Monica, All the Time." Garry Trudeau provides a skeptic's view of the press corps and its performance. The "love dress" was the blue garment that contained evidence of Clinton's sexual passion for Lewinsky.

William Jefferson Clinton remained in office, a wounded chief executive with two years left on his second term.

The impeachment episode reflected the intense emotions that Clinton had provoked during his time in the White House. To the Republicans and Americans on the right, he was an illegitimate president who had committed crimes in office that warranted his removal. To the remainder of the country, some sixty-five percent according to most polls, he was a president who, while probably guilty of the offenses with which he was charged, was performing well in office and should not be removed. How long this cultural divide would persist after the impeachment case ended was impossible to determine.

In the weeks following the end of the impeachment trial, pundits forecast that Clinton's poll ratings would drop once the crisis was over. That did not happen as the economy remained prosperous and the Dow Jones Industrial Average hovered around 10,000. A possible danger for the President arose in late March 1999 when he and the North Atlantic Treaty Organization began airstrikes against the Serbian government to stop "ethnic cleansing" of Albanians near the city of Kosovo. As the strikes and Serbian military action created hundreds of thousands of refugees, the possibility

In December 1998 the House adopted two articles of impeachment against President Clinton. That led to the Senate trial at which he was acquitted in February 1999.

Resolved that William Jefferson Clinton, President of the United States, is impeached for high crimes and misdemeanors, and that the following articles of impeachment be exhibited to the United States Senate;

Articles of Impeachment exhibited by the House of Representatives of the United States of America in the name of itself and of the people of the United States of America, against William Jefferson Clinton, President of the United States of America, in maintenance and support of its impeachment against him for high crimes and misdemeanors.

Article I

In his conduct while President of the United States, William Jefferson Clinton, in violation of his constitutional oath faithfully to execute the office of President of the United States and, to the best of his ability, preserve, protect and defend the Constitution of the United States, and in violation of his constitutional duty to take care that the laws be faithfully executed, has willfully corrupted and manipulated the judicial process of the United States for his personal gain and exoneration, impeding the administration of justice, in that:

On Aug. 17, 1998, William Jefferson Clinton swore to tell the truth, the whole truth and nothing but the truth before a Federal grand jury of the United States. Contrary to that oath, William Jefferson Clinton willfully provided perjurious, false and misleading testimony to the grand jury concerning one or more of the following: (1) the nature and details of his relationship with a subordinate Government employee; (2) prior perjurious, false and misleading testimony he gave in a Federal civil rights action brought against him; (3) prior false and misleading statements he allowed his attorney to make to a Federal judge in that civil rights action; and (4) his corrupt efforts to influence the testimony of witnesses and to impede the discovery of evidence in that civil rights action.

In doing this, William Jefferson Clinton has undermined the integrity of his office, has brought disrepute on the Presidency, has betrayed his trust as President, and has acted in a manner subversive of the rule of law and justice, to the manifest injury of the people of the United States.

Wherefore, William Jefferson Clinton, by such conduct, warrants impeachment and trial and removal from office and disqualification to hold and enjoy any office of honor, trust or profit under the United States.

Article II

In his conduct while President of the United States, William Jefferson Clinton, in violation of his constitutional oath faithfully to execute the office of President of the United States and, to the best of his ability, preserve, protect and defend the Constitu-

tion of the United States, and in violation of his constitutional duty to take care that the laws be faithfully executed, has prevented, obstructed and impeded the administration of justice, and has to that end engaged personally and through his subordinates and agents, in a course of conduct or scheme designed to delay, impede, cover up and conceal the existence of evidence and testimony related to a Federal civil rights action brought against him in a duly instituted judicial proceeding.

The means used to implement this course of conduct or scheme included one or more of the following acts:

(1) On or about Dec. 17, 1997, William Jefferson Clinton corruptly encouraged a witness in a Federal civil rights action brought against him to execute a sworn affidavit in that proceeding that he knew to be perjurious, false and misleading.

(2) On or about Dec. 17, 1997, William Jefferson Clinton corruptly encouraged a witness in a Federal civil rights action brought against him to give perjurious, false and misleading testimony if and when called to testify personally in that proceeding.

(3) On or about Dec. 28, 1997, William Jefferson Clinton corruptly engaged in, encouraged or supported a scheme to conceal evidence that had been subpoenaed in a Federal civil rights action brought against him.

(4) Beginning on or about Dec. 7, 1997, and continuing through and including Jan. 14, 1998, William Jefferson Clinton intensified and succeeded in an effort to secure job assistance to a witness in a Federal civil rights action brought against him in order to corruptly prevent the truthful testimony of that witness in that proceeding at a time when the truthful testimony of that witness would have been harmful to him.

(5) On Jan. 17, 1998, at his deposition in a Federal civil rights action brought against him, William Jefferson Clinton corruptly allowed his attorney to make false and misleading statements to a Federal judge characterizing an affidavit, in order to prevent questioning deemed relevant by the judge. Such false and misleading statements were subsequently acknowledged by his attorney in a communication to that judge.

(6) On or about Jan. 18 and Jan. 20–21, 1998, William Jefferson Clinton related a false and misleading account of events relevant to a Federal civil rights action brought against him to a potential witness in that proceeding, in order to corruptly influence the testimony of that witness.

(7) On or about Jan. 21, 23 and 26, 1998, William Jefferson Clinton made false and misleading statements to potential witnesses in a Federal grand jury proceeding in order to corruptly influence the testimony of those witnesses. The false and misleading statements made by William Jefferson Clinton were repeated by the witnesses to the grand jury, causing the grand jury to receive false and misleading information.

In all of this, William Jefferson Clinton has undermined the integrity of his office, has brought disrepute on the Presidency, has betrayed his trust as President, and has acted in a manner subversive of the rule of law and justice, to the manifest injury of the people of the United States.

Wherefore, William Jefferson Clinton, by such conduct, warrants impeachment and trial, and removal from office and disqualification to hold and enjoy any office of honor, trust or profit under the United States.

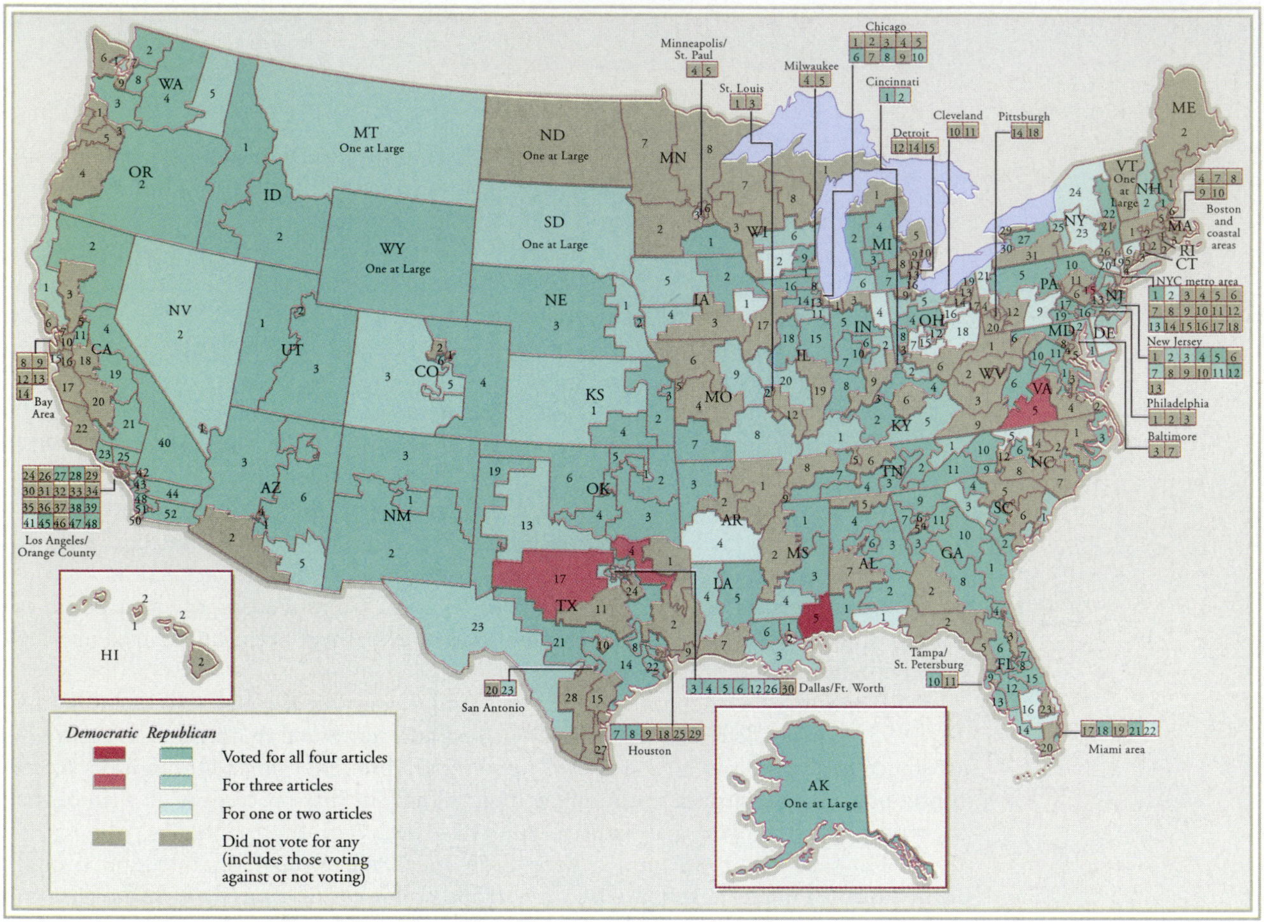

Democratic   Republican

- Voted for all four articles
- For three articles
- For one or two articles
- Did not vote for any (includes those voting against or not voting)

MAP 32.3 | CLINTON IMPEACHMENT VOTES

of introducing American and NATO ground troops became more of a possibility. The Serbian War loomed as a significant foreign policy crisis for the final years of the Clinton presidency.

CONCLUSION

Despite the furor over President Clinton, the United States was an optimistic and confident nation as the twentieth century drew to a close. The economy stood at record levels, the crime rate was down, and the international situation seemed promising. The end of the Cold War had left the country as the world's only superpower and few external threats menaced American security. After a century of turmoil and sacrifice, the American people had achieved a degree of peace and prosperity that would have seemed unimaginable to those who had bid goodbye to the nineteenth century at the end of the year 1900.

This pleasant state of affairs had fragile elements that foreshadowed future problems. The issue of race amid an increasingly diverse population remained unresolved with the potential to disrupt the social fabric. The exploitation of the environment threatened the degradation of the natural world and the resources on which prosperity depended. Within politics there were troubling signs that the national commitment to democratic values could be fraying.

The United States had made a significant historical journey from the time when Europeans first appeared on the North American continent down to the age of the Internet. But the future course of the American Passage was an unfolding story in which history provided reason for optimism but no guarantee of success.

RECOMMENDED READINGS

Drew, Elizabeth. *On the Edge: The Clinton Presidency* (1994) provides a reporter's look at Clinton's first year in power.

Drew, Elizabeth. *Showdown: The Struggle Between the Gingrich Congress and the Clinton White House* (1996) continues Drew's account of the internal politics of the Clinton White House in the struggle with Gingrich and the Republicans.

Gitlin, Todd. *The Twilight of Common Dreams: Why America Is Wracked by Culture Wars* (1995). A consideration of the conflicts over multiculturalism and related issues.

Maraniss, David. *First in His Class: A Biography of Bill Clinton* (1995) offers a portrayal of Clinton's formative years based on solid research.

Maraniss, David, and Michael Weisskopf. *"Tell Newt to Shut Up!"* (1996) provides an informative look at Newt Gingrich and the first year of Republican control of the House of Representatives.

Posner, Gerald. *Citizen Perot: His Life and Times* (1996) provides a critical look at the political gadfly who had such an effect on the 1992 election.

Roberts, Sam. *Who We Are: A Portrait of America Based on the Latest U.S. Census* (1994, 1995). An overview of the social changes taking place in the nation.

Stewart, James B. *Blood Sport: The President and His Adversaries* (1996) considers the various scandals that dogged the first term of Clinton's presidency.

Walker, Martin. *The President We Deserve: Bill Clinton, His Rise, Falls, and Comebacks* (1996). A British journalist offers the most balanced and perceptive treatment of Clinton the man and the politician.

Woodward, Bob. *The Agenda: Inside the Clinton White House* (1994) is an examination of the framing and enactment of Clinton's economic program in 1993.

The Clintons

Brock, David. *The Seduction of Hillary Rodham Clinton* (1996).

Lyons, Gene. *Fools for Scandal: How the Media Invented Whitewater* (1996).

Morris, Roger. *Partners in Power: The Clintons and Their America* (1996).

Nelson, Rex, with Philip Martin, *The Hillary Factor* (1993).

The Starr Report (1998).

Dershowitz, Alan M. *Sexual McCarthyism: Clinton, Starr, and the Emerging Constitutional Crisis* (1998).

Warner, Judith. *Hillary Clinton: The Inside Story* (1993).

Politics

Balz, Dan, and Ronald Brownstein, *Storming the Gates* (1996).

Clift, Eleanor, and Tom Brazaitis, *War Without Bloodshed: The Art of Politics* (1996).

Germond, Jack, and Jules Witcover, *Mad as Hell: Revolt at the Ballot Box, 1992* (1993).

Isikoff, Michael, *Uncovering Clinton* (1999).

Johnson, Haynes, and David S. Broder, *The System: The American Way of Politics at the Breaking Point* (1996).

Woodward, Bob. *The Choice* (1996).

American Culture in the 1990s

Bork, Robert H. *Slouching Toward Gomorrah: Modern Liberalism and American Decline* (1996).

Holtz, Geoffrey T. *Welcome to the Jungle: The Why Behind "Generation X"* (1995).

Nash, Gary, Charlotte Crabtree, and Ross E. Dunn, *History on Trial: Culture Wars and the Lessons of the Past* (1998).

Petrocelli, Daniel. *Triumph of Justice: The Final Judgment on the Simpson Saga* (1998).

Shipler, David K. *A Country of Strangers: Blacks and Whites in America* (1997).

Appendix

The Declaration of Independence

THE UNANIMOUS DECLARATION OF
THE THIRTEEN UNITED STATES OF AMERICA

When in the Course of human events it becomes necessary for one people to dissolve the political bands which have connected them with another, and to assume among the Powers of the earth, the separate and equal station to which the Laws of Nature and of Nature's God entitle them, a decent respect to the opinions of mankind requires that they should declare the causes which impel them to the separation.

We hold these truths to be self-evident, that all men are created equal, that they are endowed by their Creator with certain unalienable Rights, that among these are Life, Liberty and the pursuit of Happiness. That to secure these rights, Governments are instituted among Men, deriving their just Powers from the consent of the governed. That whenever any Form of Government becomes destructive of these ends, it is the Right of the People to alter or to abolish it, and to institute new Government, laying its foundation on such principles and organizing its Powers in such form, as to them shall seem most likely to effect their Safety and Happiness. Prudence, indeed, will dictate that Governments long established should not be changed for light and transient causes; and accordingly all experience hath shewn, that mankind are more disposed to suffer, while evils are sufferable, than to right themselves by abolishing the forms to which they are accustomed. But when a long train of abuses and usurpations, pursuing invariably the same Object evinces a design to reduce them under absolute Despotism, it is their right, it is their duty, to throw off such Government, and to provide new Guards for their future security. Such has been the patient sufferance of these Colonies; and such is now the necessity which constrains them to alter their former Systems of Government. The history of the present King of Great Britain is a history of repeated injuries and usurpations, all having in direct object the establishment of an ab-

solute Tyranny over these States. To prove this, let Facts be submitted to a candid world.

He has refused his Assent to Laws, the most wholesome and necessary for the public good.

He has forbidden his Governors to pass Laws of immediate and pressing importance, unless suspended in their operation till his Assent should be obtained; and when so suspended, he has utterly neglected to attend to them.

He has refused to pass other Laws for the accommodation of large districts of people, unless those people would relinquish the right of Representation in the Legislature, a right inestimable to them and formidable to tyrants only.

He has called together legislative bodies at places unusual, uncomfortable, and distant from the depository of their Public Records, for the sole Purpose of fatiguing them into compliance with his measures.

He has dissolved Representative Houses repeatedly, for opposing with manly firmness his invasions on the rights of the People.

He has refused for a long time, after such dissolutions, to cause others to be elected; whereby the Legislative Powers, incapable of Annihilation, have returned to the People at large for their exercise; the State remaining in the mean time exposed to all the dangers of invasion from without, and convulsions within.

He has endeavoured to prevent the Population of these States; for that purpose obstructing the Laws for Naturalization of Foreigners; refusing to pass others to encourage their migrations hither, and raising the conditions of new Appropriations of Lands.

He has obstructed the Administration of Justice, by refusing his Assent to Laws for establishing Judiciary Powers.

He has made Judges dependent on his Will alone, for the tenure of their offices, and the amount and payment of their salaries.

He has erected a multitude of New Offices, and sent hither swarms of Officers to harass our People, and eat out their substance.

He has kept among us, in times of peace, Standing Armies without the Consent of our legislatures.

He has affected to render the Military independent of and superior to the Civil Power.

He has combined with others to subject us to a jurisdiction foreign to our constitution, and unacknowledged by our laws; giving his Assent to their Acts of pretended Legislation:

For Quartering large bodies of armed troops among us:

For protecting them, by a mock Trial, from Punishment for any Murders which they should commit on the Inhabitants of these States:

For cutting off our Trade with all parts of the world:

For imposing Taxes on us without our Consent:

For depriving us in many cases, of the benefits of Trial by Jury:

For transporting us beyond Seas to be tried for pretended offences:

For abolishing the free System of English Laws in a neighbouring Province, establishing therein an Arbitrary government, and enlarging its Boundaries so as to render it at once an example and fit instrument for introducing the same absolute rule into these Colonies:

For taking away our Charters, abolishing our most valuable Laws, and altering fundamentally the Forms of our Governments:

For suspending our own Legislatures, and declaring themselves invested with Power to legislate for us in all cases whatsoever.

He has abdicated Government here, by declaring us out of his Protection, and waging War against us.

He has plundered our seas, ravaged our Coasts, burnt our towns, and destroyed the lives of our people.

He is at this time transporting large Armies of foreign Mercenaries to compleat the works of death, desolation and tyranny, already begun with circumstances of Cruelty and perfidy scarcely paralleled in the most barbarous ages, and totally unworthy the Head of a civilized nation.

He has constrained our fellow Citizens taken Captive on the high Seas to bear Arms against their Country, to become the executioners of their friends and Brethren, or to fall themselves by their Hands.

He has excited domestic insurrections amongst us, and has endeavoured to bring on the inhabitants of our frontiers, the merciless Indian Savages, whose known rule of warfare, is an undistinguished destruction of all ages, sexes and conditions.

In every stage of these Oppressions We have Petitioned for Redress in the most humble terms: Our repeated Petitions have been answered only by repeated injury. A Prince, whose character is thus marked by every act which may define a Tyrant, is unfit to be the ruler of a free People.

Nor have We been wanting in attentions to our British brethren. We have warned them from time to time of attempts by their legislature to extend an unwarrantable jurisdiction over us. We have reminded them of the circumstances of our emigration and settlement here. We have appealed to their native justice and magnanimity, and we have conjured them by the ties of our common kindred to disavow these usurpations, which, would inevitably interrupt our connections and correspondence. They too have been deaf to the voice of justice and of consanguinity. We must, therefore, acquiesce in the necessity, which denounces our Separation, and hold them, as we hold the rest of mankind, Enemies in War, in Peace Friends.

WE, THEREFORE, the Representatives of the UNITED STATES OF AMERICA, in General Congress, Assembled, appealing to the Supreme Judge of the world for the rectitude of our intentions, do, in the Name, and by Authority of the good People of these Colonies, solemnly publish and declare, That these United Colonies are, and of Right ought to be FREE AND INDEPENDENT STATES; that they are Absolved from all Allegiance to the British Crown, and that all political connection between them and the State of Great Britain, is and ought to be totally dissolved; and that, as Free and Independent States, they have full Power to levy War, conclude Peace, contract Alliances, establish Commerce, and to do all other Acts and Things which Independent States may of right do. And for the support of this Declaration, with a firm reliance on the protection of divine Providence, we mutually pledge to each other our Lives, our Fortunes and our sacred Honor.

The Constitution of the United States of America

We the People of the United States, in Order to form a more perfect Union, establish Justice, insure domestic Tranquility, provide for the common defence, promote the general Welfare, and secure the Blessings of Liberty to ourselves and our Posterity, do ordain and establish this Constitution for the United States of America.

ARTICLE I.

SECTION 1. All legislative Powers herein granted shall be vested in a Congress of the United States, which shall consist of a Senate and House of Representatives.

SECTION 2. The House of Representatives shall be composed of Members chosen every second Year by the People of the several States, and the Electors in each State shall have the Qualifications requisite for Electors of the most numerous Branch of the State Legislature.

No Person shall be a Representative who shall not have attained to the Age of twenty five Years, and been seven Years a Citizen of the United States, and who shall not, when elected, be an Inhabitant of that State in which he shall be chosen.

Representatives and direct Taxes[1] shall be apportioned among the several States which may be included within this Union, according to their respective Numbers, which shall be determined by adding to the whole Number of free Persons, including those bound to Service for a Term of Years, and excluding Indians not taxed, three fifths of all other Persons.[2] The actual Enumeration shall be made within three Years after the first Meeting of the Congress of the United States, and within every subsequent Term of ten Years, in such Manner as they shall by Law direct. The Number of Representatives shall not exceed one for every thirty Thousand, but each State shall have at Least one Representative; and until such enumeration shall be made, the State of New Hampshire shall be entitled to chuse three; Massachusetts eight; Rhode Island and Providence Plantations one; Connecticut five; New York six; New Jersey four; Pennsylvania eight; Delaware one; Maryland six; Virginia ten; North Carolina five; South Carolina five; and Georgia three.

When vacancies happen in the Representation from any State, the Executive Authority thereof shall issue Writs of Election to fill such Vacancies.

The House of Representatives shall chuse their Speaker and other Officers; and shall have the sole Power of Impeachment.

SECTION 3. The Senate of the United States shall be composed of two Senators from each State, chosen by the Legislature thereof, for six Years; and each Senator shall have one Vote.[3]

Immediately after they shall be assembled in Consequence of the first Election, they shall be divided as equally as may be into three Classes. The Seats of the Senators of the first Class shall be vacated at the Expiration of the second Year, of the second Class at the Expiration of the fourth Year, and of the third Class at the Expiration of the sixth Year, so that one third may be chosen every second Year; and if Vacancies happen by Resignation, or otherwise, during the Recess of the Legislature of any State, the Executive thereof may make temporary Appointments until the next Meeting of the Legislature, which shall then fill such Vacancies.[4]

No Person shall be a Senator who shall not have attained to the Age of thirty Years, and been nine Years a Citizen of the United States, and who shall not, when elected, be an Inhabitant of that State for which he shall be chosen.

The Vice President of the United States shall be President of the Senate, but shall have no Vote, unless they be equally divided.

The Senate shall chuse their other Officers, and also a President pro tempore, in the Absence of the Vice President, or when he shall exercise the Office of President of the United States.

Text is from the engrossed copy in the National Archives. Original spelling, capitalization, and punctuation have been retained.

[1]Modified by the Sixteenth Amendment.

[2]Replaced by the Fourteenth Amendment.

[3]Superseded by the Seventeenth Amendment.

[4]Modified by the Seventeenth Amendment.

The Senate shall have the sole Power to try all Impeachments. When sitting for that Purpose, they shall be on Oath or Affirmation. When the President of the United States is tried, the Chief Justice shall preside: And no Person shall be convicted without the Concurrence of two thirds of the Members present.

Judgment in Cases of Impeachment shall not extend further than to removal from Office, and disqualification to hold and enjoy any Office of honor, Trust or Profit under the United States: but the Party convicted shall nevertheless be liable and subject to Indictment, Trial, Judgment and Punishment, according to Law.

SECTION 4. The Times, Places and Manner of holding Elections for Senators and Representatives, shall be prescribed in each State by the Legislature thereof, but the Congress may at any time by Law make or alter such Regulation, except as to the Places of chusing Senators.

The Congress shall assemble at least once in every Year, and such Meeting shall be on the first Monday in December, unless they shall by Law appoint a different Day.[5]

SECTION 5. Each House shall be the Judge of the Elections, Returns and Qualifications of its own Members, and a Majority of each shall constitute a Quorum to do Business; but a smaller Number may adjourn from day to day, and may be authorized to compel the Attendance of absent Members, in such Manner, and under such Penalties as each House may provide.

Each House may determine the Rules of its Proceedings, punish its Members for disorderly Behaviour, and, with the Concurrence of two thirds, expel a Member.

Each House shall keep a Journal of its Proceedings, and from time to time publish the same, excepting such Parts as may in their Judgment require Secrecy; and the Yeas and Nays of the Members of either House on any question shall, at the Desire of one fifth of those Present, be entered on the Journal.

Neither House, during the Session of Congress, shall, without the Consent of the other, adjourn for more than three days, nor to any other Place than that in which the two Houses shall be sitting.

SECTION 6. The Senators and Representatives shall receive a Compensation for their Services, to be ascertained by Law, and paid out of the Treasury of the United States. They shall in all Cases, except Treason, Felony and Breach of the Peace, be privileged from Arrest during their Attendance at the Session of their respective Houses, and in going to and returning from the same; and for any Speech or Debate in either House, they shall not be questioned in any other Place.

No Senator or Representative shall, during the Time for which he was elected, be appointed to any civil Office under the Authority of the United States, which shall have been created, or the Emoluments whereof shall have been encreased during such time; and no Person holding any Office under the United States, shall be a Member of either House during his Continuance in Office.

SECTION 7. All Bills for raising Revenue shall originate in the House of Representatives; but the Senate may propose or concur with Amendments as on other Bills.

Every Bill which shall have passed the House of Representatives and the Senate shall, before it become a Law, be presented to the President of the United States; If he approve he shall sign it, but if not he shall return it, with his Objections to that House in which it shall have originated, who shall enter the Objections at large on their Journal, and proceed to reconsider it. If after such Reconsideration two thirds of that House shall agree to pass the Bill, it shall be sent, together with the Objections, to the other House, by which it shall likewise be reconsidered, and if approved by two thirds of that House, it shall become a Law. But in all such Cases the Votes of both Houses shall be determined by yeas and Nays, and the Names of the Persons voting for and against the Bill shall be entered on the Journal of each House respectively. If any Bill shall not be returned by the President within ten Days (Sundays excepted) after it shall have been presented to him, the Same shall be a Law, in like Manner as if he had signed it, unless the Congress by their Adjournment prevent its Return, in which Case it shall not be a Law.

Every Order, Resolution, or Vote to which the Concurrence of the Senate and House of Representatives may be necessary (except on a question of Adjournment) shall be presented to the President of the United States; and before the Same shall take Effect, shall be approved by him, or being disapproved by him shall be repassed by two thirds of the Senate and House of Representatives, according to the Rules and Limitations prescribed in the Case of a Bill.

SECTION 8. The Congress shall have power To lay and collect Taxes, Duties, Imposts and Excises, to pay the Debts and provide for the common Defence and general Welfare of the United States; but all Duties, Imposts and Excises shall be uniform throughout the United States;

---

[5]Superseded by the Twentieth Amendment.

To borrow Money on the credit of the United States;

To regulate Commerce with foreign Nations, and among the several States, and with the Indian Tribes;

To establish an uniform Rule of Naturalization, and uniform Laws on the subject of Bankruptcies throughout the United States;

To coin Money, regulate the Value thereof, and of foreign Coin, and fix the Standard of Weights and Measures;

To provide for the Punishment of counterfeiting the Securities and current Coin of the United States;

To establish Post Offices and post Roads;

To promote the Progress of Science and useful Arts, by securing for limited Times to Authors and Inventors the exclusive Right to their respective Writings and Discoveries;

To constitute Tribunals inferior to the supreme Court;

To define and punish Piracies and Felonies committed on the high Seas, and Offences against the Law of Nations;

To declare War, grant Letters of Marque and Reprisal, and make Rules concerning Captures on Land and Water;

To raise and support Armies, but no Appropriation of Money to that Use shall be for a longer Term than two Years;

To provide and maintain a Navy;

To make Rules for the Government and Regulation of the land and naval Forces;

To provide for calling forth the Militia to execute the Laws of the Union, suppress Insurrections and repel Invasions;

To provide for organizing, arming, and disciplining, the Militia, and for governing such Part of them as may be employed in the Service of the United States, reserving to the States respectively, the Appointment of the Officers, and the Authority of training the Militia according to the discipline prescribed by Congress;

To exercise exclusive Legislation in all Cases whatsoever, over such District (not exceeding ten Miles square) as may, by Cession of particular States, and the Acceptance of Congress, become the Seat of the Government of the United States, and to exercise like Authority over all Places purchased by the Consent of the Legislature of the State in which the Same shall be, for the Erection of Forts, Magazines, Arsenals, dock-Yards, and other needful Buildings;—And

To make all Laws which shall be necessary and proper for carrying into Execution the foregoing Powers, and all other Powers vested by this Constitution in the Government of the United States, or in any Department or Officer thereof.

SECTION 9. The Migration or Importation of such Persons as any of the States now existing shall think proper to admit, shall not be prohibited by the Congress prior to the Year one thousand eight hundred and eight, but a Tax or duty may be imposed on such Importation, not exceeding ten dollars for each Person.

The Privilege of the Writ of Habeas Corpus shall not be suspended, unless when in Cases of Rebellion or Invasion the public Safety may require it.

No Bill of Attainder or ex post facto Law shall be passed.

No Capitation, or other direct, Tax shall be laid, unless in Proportion to the Census or Enumeration herein before directed to be taken.

No Tax or Duty shall be laid on Articles exported from any State.

No Preference shall be given by any Regulation of Commerce or Revenue to the Ports of one State over those of another: nor shall Vessels bound to, or from, one State, be obliged to enter, clear, or pay Duties in another.

No Money shall be drawn from the Treasury, but in Consequence of Appropriations made by Law, and a regular Statement and Account of the Receipts and Expenditures of all public Money shall be published from time to time.

No Title of Nobility shall be granted by the United States: And no Person holding any Office of Profit or Trust under them, shall, without the Consent of the Congress, accept of any present, Emolument, Office, or Title, of any kind whatever, from any King, Prince, or foreign State.

SECTION 10. No State shall enter into any Treaty, Alliance, or Confederation; grant Letters of Marque and Reprisal; coin Money; emit Bills of Credit; make any Thing but gold and silver Coin a Tender in Payment of Debts; pass any Bill of Attainder, ex post facto Law, or Law impairing the Obligation of Contracts, or grant any Title of Nobility.

No State shall, without the Consent of the Congress, lay any Imposts or Duties on Imports or Exports, except what may be absolutely necessary for executing its inspection Laws: and the net Produce of all Duties and Imposts, laid by any State on Imports or Exports, shall be for the Use of the Treasury of the United States; and all such Laws shall be subject to the Revision and Controul of the Congress.

No State shall, without the Consent of Congress, lay any Duty of Tonnage, keep Troops, or Ships of War in time of Peace, enter into any Agreement or Compact with another State, or with a foreign Power, or engage in War, unless actually invaded, or in such imminent Danger as will not admit of delay.

ARTICLE II.

SECTION 1. The executive Power shall be vested in a President of the United States of America. He shall hold his Office during the Term of four Years, and, together with the Vice President, chosen for the same Term, be elected, as follows:

Each State shall appoint, in such Manner as the Legislature thereof may direct, a Number of Electors, equal to the whole Number of Senators and Representatives to which the State may be entitled in the Congress: but no Senator or Representative, or Person holding an Office of Trust or Profit under the United States, shall be appointed an Elector.

The Electors shall meet in their respective States, and vote by Ballot for two Persons, of whom one at least shall not be an Inhabitant of the same State with themselves. And they shall make a List of all the Persons voted for, and of the Number of Votes for each; which List they shall sign and certify, and transmit sealed to the Seat of the Government of the United States, directed to the President of the Senate. The President of the Senate shall, in the Presence of the Senate and House of Representatives, open all the Certificates, and the Votes shall then be counted. The Person having the greatest Number of Votes shall be the President, if such Number be a Majority of the whole Number of Electors appointed; and if there be more than one who have such Majority, and have an equal Number of Votes, then the House of Representatives shall immediately chuse by Ballot one of them for President; and if no Person have a Majority, then from the five highest on the List the said House shall in like Manner chuse the President. But in chusing the President, the Votes shall be taken by States, the Representation from each State having one Vote; A quorum for this Purpose shall consist of a Member or Members from two thirds of the States, and a Majority of all the States shall be necessary to a Choice. In every Case, after the Choice of the President, the Person having the greatest Number of Votes of the Electors shall be the Vice President. But if there should remain two or more who have equal Votes, the Senate shall chuse from them by Ballot the Vice President.[6]

The Congress may determine the Time of chusing the Electors, and the Day on which they shall give their Votes; which Day shall be the same throughout the United States.

No Person except a natural born Citizen, or a Citizen of the United States, at the time of the Adoption of this Constitution, shall be eligible to the Office of President, neither shall any Person be eligible to that Office who shall not have attained to the Age of thirty five Years, and been fourteen Years a Resident within the United States.

In Case of the Removal of the President from Office, or of his Death, Resignation, or Inability to discharge the Powers and Duties of the said Office, the Same shall devolve on the Vice President, and the Congress may by Law provide for the Case of Removal, Death, Resignation or Inability, both of the President and Vice President, declaring what Officer shall then act as President, and such Officer shall act accordingly, until the Disability be removed, or a President shall be elected.[7]

The President shall, at stated Times, receive for his Services, a Compensation, which shall neither be encreased nor diminished during the Period for which he shall have been elected, and he shall not receive within that Period any other Emolument from the United States, or any of them.

Before he enter on the Execution of his Office, he shall take the following Oath or Affirmation:—"I do solemnly swear (or affirm) that I will faithfully execute the Office of President of the United States, and will to the best of my Ability, preserve, protect and defend the Constitution of the United States."

SECTION 2. The President shall be Commander in Chief of the Army and Navy of the United States, and of the Militia of the several States, when called into the actual Service of the United States; he may require the Opinion, in writing, of the principal Officer in each of the executive Departments, upon any Subject relating to the Duties of their respective Offices, and he shall have Power to grant Reprieves and Pardons for Offences against the United States, except in Cases of Impeachment.

He shall have Power, by and with the Advice and Consent of the Senate, to make Treaties, provided two thirds of the Senators present concur; and he shall nominate, and by and with the Advice and Consent of the Senate,

---

[6]Superseded by the Twelfth Amendment.

[7]Modified by the Twenty-fifth Amendment.

shall appoint Ambassadors, other public Ministers and Consuls, Judges of the supreme Court, and all other Officers of the United States, whose Appointments are not herein otherwise provided for, and which shall be established by Law; but the Congress may by Law vest the Appointment of such inferior Officers, as they think proper, in the President alone, in the Courts of Law, or in the Heads of Departments.

The President shall have Power to fill up all Vacancies that may happen during the Recess of the Senate, by granting Commissions which shall expire at the End of their next Session.

SECTION 3. He shall from time to time give the Congress Information of the State of the Union, and recommend to their Consideration such Measures as he shall judge necessary and expedient; he may, on extraordinary Occasions, convene both Houses, or either of them, and in Case of Disagreement between them, with Respect to the Time of Adjournment, he may adjourn them to such Time as he shall think proper; he shall receive Ambassadors and other public Ministers; he shall take Care that the Laws be faithfully executed, and shall Commission all the Officers of the United States.

SECTION 4. The President, Vice President and all civil Officers of the United States, shall be removed from Office on Impeachment for, and Conviction of, Treason, Bribery, or other high Crimes and Misdemeanors.

ARTICLE III.

SECTION 1. The judicial Power of the United States, shall be vested in one supreme Court, and in such inferior Courts as the Congress may from time to time ordain and establish. The Judges, both of the supreme and inferior Courts, shall hold their Offices during good Behaviour, and shall, at stated Times, receive for their Services, a Compensation, which shall not be diminished during their Continuance in Office.

SECTION 2. The judicial Power shall extend to all Cases, in Law and Equity, arising under this Constitution, the Laws of the United States, and Treaties made, or which shall be made, under their Authority;—to all Cases affecting Ambassadors, other public Ministers and Consuls;—to all Cases of admiralty and maritime Jurisdiction;—to Controversies to which the United States shall be a Party;—to Controversies between two or more States;—between a State and Citizens of another State;[8]—between Citizens of different States,—between Citizens of the same State claiming Lands under Grants of different States, and between a

State, or the Citizens thereof, and foreign States, Citizens or Subjects.

In all Cases affecting Ambassadors, other public Ministers and Consuls, and those in which a State shall be Party, the supreme Court shall have original Jurisdiction. In all the other Cases before mentioned, the supreme Court shall have appellate Jurisdiction, both as to Law and Fact, with such Exceptions, and under such Regulations as the Congress shall make.

The Trial of all Crimes, except in Cases of Impeachment, shall be by Jury; and such Trial shall be held in the State where the said Crimes shall have been committed; but when not committed within any State, the Trial shall be at such Place or Places as the Congress may by Law have directed.

SECTION 3. Treason against the United States, shall consist only in levying War against them, or in adhering to their Enemies, giving them Aid and Comfort. No Person shall be convicted of Treason unless on the Testimony of two Witnesses to the same overt Act, or on Confession in open Court.

The Congress shall have Power to declare the Punishment of Treason, but no Attainder of Treason shall work Corruption of Blood, or Forfeiture except during the Life of the Person attainted.

ARTICLE IV.

SECTION 1. Full Faith and Credit shall be given in each State to the public Acts, Records, and judicial Proceedings of every other State. And the Congress may by general Laws prescribe the Manner in which such Acts, Records and Proceedings shall be proved, and the Effect thereof.

SECTION 2. The Citizens of each State shall be entitled to all Privileges and Immunities of Citizens in the several States.

A Person charged in any State with Treason, Felony, or other Crime, who shall flee from Justice, and be found in another State, shall on Demand of the executive Authority of the State from which he fled, be delivered up, to be removed to the State having Jurisdiction of the Crime.

No Person held to Service or Labour in one State, under the Laws thereof, escaping into another, shall, in Consequence of any Law or Regulation therein, be discharged from such Service or Labour, but shall be

---

[8]Modified by the Eleventh Amendment.

delivered up on Claim of the Party to whom such Service or Labour may be due.

SECTION 3. New States may be admitted by the Congress into this Union; but no new State shall be formed or erected within the Jurisdiction of any other State, nor any State be formed by the Junction of two or more States, or Parts of States, without the Consent of the Legislatures of the States concerned as well as of the Congress.

The Congress shall have Power to dispose of and make all needful Rules and Regulations respecting the Territory or other Property belonging to the United States; and nothing in this Constitution shall be so construed as to Prejudice any Claims of the United States, or of any particular State.

SECTION 4. The United States shall guarantee to every State in this Union a Republican Form of Government, and shall protect each of them against Invasion; and on Application of the Legislature, or of the Executive (when the Legislature cannot be convened) against domestic Violence.

ARTICLE V.

The Congress, whenever two thirds of both Houses shall deem it necessary, shall propose Amendments to this Constitution, or, on the Application of the Legislatures of two thirds of the several States, shall call a Convention for proposing Amendments, which, in either Case, shall be valid to all Intents and Purposes, as Part of this Constitution, when ratified by the Legislatures of three fourths of the several States, or by Conventions in three fourths thereof, as the one or the other Mode of Ratification may be proposed by the Congress; Provided that no Amendment which may be made prior to the Year One thousand eight hundred and eight shall in any Manner affect the first and fourth Clauses in the Ninth Section of the first Article; and that no State, without its Consent, shall be deprived of its equal Suffrage in the Senate.

ARTICLE VI.

All Debts contracted and Engagements entered into, before the Adoption of this Constitution, shall be as valid against the United States under this Constitution, as under the Confederation.

This Constitution, and the Laws of the United States which shall be made in Pursuance thereof; and all Treaties made, or which shall be made, under the Authority of the United States, shall be the supreme Law of the Land; and the Judges in every State shall be bound thereby, any Thing in the Constitution or Laws of any State to the Contrary notwithstanding.

The Senators and Representatives before mentioned, and the Members of the several State Legislatures, and all executive and judicial Officers, both of the United States and of the several States, shall be bound by Oath or Affirmation, to support this Constitution; but no religious Test shall ever be required as a Qualification to any Office or public Trust under the United States.

ARTICLE VII.

The Ratification of the Conventions of nine States, shall be sufficient for the Establishment of this Constitution between the States so ratifying the Same.

Done in Convention by the Unanimous Consent of the States present the Seventeenth Day of September in the Year of our Lord one thousand seven hundred and Eighty seven and of the Independence of the United States of America the Twelfth. In witness whereof We have hereunto subscribed our Names,

Articles in Addition to, and Amendment of, the Constitution of the United States of America, Proposed by Congress, and Ratified by the Legislatures of the Several States, Pursuant to the Fifth Article of the Original Constitution.

AMENDMENT I[9]

Congress shall make no law respecting an establishment of religion, or prohibiting the free exercise thereof; or abridging the freedom of speech, or of the press; or the right of the people peaceably to assemble, and to petition the Government for a redress of grievances.

AMENDMENT II

A well regulated Militia, being necessary to the security of a free State, the right of the people to keep and bear Arms shall not be infringed.

---

[9]The first ten amendments were passed by Congress September 25, 1789. They were ratified by three-fourths of the states December 15, 1791.

AMENDMENT III

No Soldier shall, in time of peace, be quartered in any house, without the consent of the Owner, nor in time of war, but in a manner to be prescribed by law.

AMENDMENT IV

The right of the people to be secure in their persons, houses, papers, and effects, against unreasonable searches and seizures, shall not be violated, and no Warrants shall issue, but upon probable cause, supported by Oath or affirmation, and particularly describing the place to be searched, and the persons or things to be seized.

AMENDMENT V

No person shall be held to answer for a capital or otherwise infamous crime, unless on a presentment or indictment of a Grand Jury, except in cases arising in the land or naval forces, or in the Militia, when in actual service in time of War or public danger; nor shall any person be subject for the same offence to be twice put in jeopardy of life or limb; nor shall be compelled in any criminal case to be a witness against himself, nor be deprived of life, liberty, or property, without due process of law; nor shall private property be taken for public use, without just compensation.

AMENDMENT VI

In all criminal prosecutions, the accused shall enjoy the right to a speedy and public trial, by an impartial jury of the State and district wherein the crime shall have been committed, which district shall have been previously ascertained by law, and to be informed of the nature and cause of the accusation; to be confronted with the witnesses against him; to have compulsory process for obtaining witnesses in his favor, and to have the Assistance of Counsel for his defence.

AMENDMENT VII

In suits at common law, where the value in controversy shall exceed twenty dollars, the right of trial by jury shall be preserved, and no fact tried by a jury, shall be otherwise reexamined in any Court of the United States, than according to the rules of the common law.

AMENDMENT VIII

Excessive bail shall not be required, nor excessive fines imposed, nor cruel and unusual punishments inflicted.

AMENDMENT IX

The enumeration in the Constitution, of certain rights, shall not be construed to deny or disparage others retained by the people.

AMENDMENT X

The powers not delegated to the United States by the Constitution; nor prohibited by it to the States, are reserved to the States respectively, or to the people.

AMENDMENT XI[10]

The Judicial power of the United States shall not be construed to extend to any suit in law or equity, commenced or prosecuted against one of the United States by Citizens of another State, or by Citizens or Subjects of any Foreign State.

AMENDMENT XII[11]

The Electors shall meet in their respective States and vote by ballot for President and Vice-President, one of whom, at least, shall not be an inhabitant of the same State with themselves; they shall name in their ballots the person voted for as President, and in distinct ballots the person voted for as Vice-President, and they shall make distinct lists of all persons voted for as President, and of all persons voted for as Vice-President, and of the number of votes for each, which lists they shall sign and certify, and transmit sealed to the seat of the government of the United States, directed to the President of the Senate;—The President of the Senate shall, in the presence of the Senate and House of Representatives, open all the certificates and the votes shall then be counted;—The person having the greatest number of votes for President, shall be the President, if such number be a majority of the whole number of Electors appointed; and if no person have such majority, then from the persons having the highest numbers not exceeding three on the list of those voted for as President, the House of Representatives shall choose immediately, by ballot, the President. But in choosing the President, the votes shall be taken by states, the representation from each state having one vote; a quorum for this purpose shall consist of a member or members from two-thirds of the states, and a majority of

---

[10]Passed March 4, 1794. Ratified January 23, 1795.

[11]Passed December 9, 1803. Ratified June 15, 1804.

all the states shall be necessary to a choice. And if the House of Representatives shall not choose a President whenever the right of choice shall devolve upon them, before the fourth day of March next following, then the Vice-President shall act as President, as in the case of the death or other constitutional disability of the President.—The person having the greatest number of votes as Vice-President, shall be the Vice-President, if such number be a majority of the whole number of Electors appointed, and if no person have a majority, then from the two highest numbers on the list, the Senate shall choose the Vice-President; a quorum for the purpose shall consist of two-thirds of the whole number of Senators, and a majority of the whole number shall be necessary to a choice. But no person constitutionally ineligible to the office of President shall be eligible to that of Vice-President of the United States.

AMENDMENT XIII[12]

SECTION 1. Neither slavery nor involuntary servitude, except as a punishment for crime whereof the party shall have been duly convicted, shall exist within the United States, or any place subject to their jurisdiction.

SECTION 2. Congress shall have power to enforce this article by appropriate legislation.

AMENDMENT XIV[13]

SECTION 1. All persons born or naturalized in the United States, and subject to the jurisdiction thereof, are citizens of the United States and of the State wherein they reside. No State shall make or enforce any law which shall abridge the privileges or immunities of citizens of the United States; nor shall any State deprive any person of life, liberty, or property, without due process of law; nor deny to any person within its jurisdiction the equal protection of the laws.

SECTION 2. Representatives shall be apportioned among the several States according to their respective numbers, counting the whole number of persons in each State, excluding Indians not taxed. But when the right to vote at any election for the choice of electors for President and Vice-President of the United States, Representatives in Congress, the Executive and Judicial officers of a State, or the members of the Legislature thereof, is de-

nied to any of the male inhabitants of such State, being twenty-one years of age, and citizens of the United States, or in any way abridged, except for participation in rebellion, or other crime, the basis of representation therein shall be reduced in the proportion which the number of such male citizens shall bear to the whole number of male citizens twenty-one years of age in such State.

SECTION 3. No person shall be a Senator or Representative in Congress, or elector of President and Vice-President, or hold any office, civil or military, under the United States, or under any State, who, having previously taken an oath, as a member of Congress, or as an officer of the United States, or as a member of any State legislature, or as an executive or judicial officer of any State, to support the Constitution of the United States, shall have engaged in insurrection or rebellion against the same, or given aid or comfort to the enemies thereof. But Congress may by a vote of two-thirds of each House, remove such disability.

SECTION 4. The validity of the public debt of the United States, authorized by law, including debts incurred for payment of pensions and bounties for services in suppressing insurrection or rebellion, shall not be questioned. But neither the United States nor any State shall assume or pay any debt or obligation incurred in aid of insurrection or rebellion against the United States, or any claim for the loss or emancipation of any slave; but all such debts, obligations, and claims shall be held illegal and void.

SECTION 5. The Congress shall have the power to enforce, by appropriate legislation, the provisions of this article.

AMENDMENT XV[14]

SECTION 1. The right of citizens of the United States to vote shall not be denied or abridged by the United States or by any State on account of race, color, or previous conditions of servitude—

SECTION 2. The Congress shall have power to enforce this article by appropriate legislation.

AMENDMENT XVI

The Congress shall have power to lay and collect taxes on incomes, from whatever source derived, without

---

[12]Passed January 31, 1865. Ratified December 6, 1865.

[13]Passed June 13, 1866. Ratified July 9, 1868.

[14]Passed February 26, 1869. Ratified February 2, 1870.

apportionment among the several States, and without regard to any census or enumeration.

AMENDMENT XVII[15]

The Senate of the United States shall be composed of two Senators from each State, elected by the people thereof, for six years; and each Senator shall have one vote. The electors in each State shall have the qualifications requisite for electors of the most numerous branch of the State legislatures.

When vacancies happen in the representation of any State in the Senate, the executive authority of such State shall issue writs of election to fill such vacancies: *Provided,* That the legislature of any State may empower the executive thereof to make temporary appointments until the people fill the vacancies by election as the legislature may direct.

This amendment shall not be so construed as to affect the election or term of any Senator chosen before it becomes valid as part of the Constitution.

AMENDMENT XVIII[16]

SECTION 1. After one year from the ratification of this article the manufacture, sale, or transportation of intoxicating liquors within, the importation thereof into, or the exportation thereof from the United States and all territory subject to the jurisdiction thereof for beverage purposes is hereby prohibited.

SECTION 2. The Congress and the several States shall have concurrent power to enforce this article by appropriate legislation.

SECTION 3. This article shall be inoperative unless it shall have been ratified as an amendment to the Constitution by the legislatures of the several States, as provided in the Constitution, within seven years from the date of the submission hereof to the States by the Congress.

AMENDMENT XIX[17]

The right of citizens of the United States to vote shall not be denied or abridged by the United States or by any State on account of sex.

Congress shall have power to enforce this article by appropriate legislation.

AMENDMENT XX[18]

SECTION 1. The terms of the President and Vice-President shall end at noon on the 20th day of January, and the terms of Senators and Representatives at noon on the 3d day of January, of the years in which such terms would have ended if this article had not been ratified; and the terms of their successors shall then begin.

SECTION 2. The Congress shall assemble at least once in every year, and such meeting shall begin at noon on the 3d day of January, unless they shall by law appoint a different day.

SECTION 3. If, at the time fixed for the beginning of the term of the President, the President elect shall have died, the Vice-President elect shall become President. If a President shall not have been chosen before the time fixed for the beginning of his term, or if the President elect shall have failed to qualify, then the Vice-President elect shall act as President until a President shall have qualified; and the Congress may by law provide for the case wherein neither a President elect nor a Vice-President elect shall have qualified, declaring who shall then act as President, or the manner in which one who is to act shall be selected, and such person shall act accordingly until a President or Vice-President shall have qualified.

SECTION 4. The Congress may by law provide for the case of the death of any of the persons from whom the House of Representatives may choose a President whenever the right of choice shall have devolved upon them, and for the case of the death of any of the persons from whom the Senate may choose a Vice-President whenever the right of choice shall have devolved upon them.

SECTION 5. Sections 1 and 2 shall take effect on the 15th day of October following the ratification of this article.

SECTION 6. This article shall be inoperative unless it shall have been ratified as an amendment to the Constitution by the legislatures of three-fourths of the several States within seven years from the date of its submission.

AMENDMENT XXI[19]

SECTION 1. The eighteenth article of amendment to the Constitution of the United States is hereby repealed.

---

[15]Passed May 13, 1912. Ratified April 8, 1913.

[16]Passed December 18, 1917. Ratified January 16, 1919.

[17]Passed June 4, 1919. Ratified August 18, 1920.

[18]Passed March 2, 1932. Ratified January 23, 1933.

[19]Passed February 20, 1933. Ratified December 5, 1933.

SECTION 2. The transportation or importation into any State, Territory, or possession of the United States for delivery or use therein of intoxicating liquors, in violation of the laws thereof, is hereby prohibited.

SECTION 3. This article shall be inoperative unless it shall have been ratified as an amendment to the Constitution by conventions in the several States, as provided in the Constitution, within seven years from the date of the submission hereof to the States by the Congress.

AMENDMENT XXII[20]

No person shall be elected to the office of the President more than twice, and no person who has held the office of President, or acted as President, for more than two years of a term to which some other person was elected President shall be elected to the office of the President more than once.

But this Article shall not apply to any person holding the office of President when this Article was proposed by the Congress, and shall not prevent any person who may be holding the office of President, or acting as President, during the term within which this Article becomes operative from holding the office of President or acting as President during the remainder of such term.

AMENDMENT XXIII[21]

SECTION 1. The District constituting the seat of Government of the United States shall appoint in such manner as the Congress may direct:

A number of electors of President and Vice President equal to the whole number of Senators and Representatives in Congress to which the District would be entitled if it were a State, but in no event more than the least populous State; they shall be in addition to those appointed by the States, but they shall be considered, for the purposes of the election of President and Vice President, to be electors appointed by the State; and they shall meet in the District and perform such duties as provided by the twelfth article of amendment.

SECTION 2. The Congress shall have power to enforce this article by appropriate legislation.

AMENDMENT XXIV[22]

SECTION 1. The right of citizens of the United States to vote in any primary or other election for President or Vice President, or for Senator or Representative in Congress, shall not be denied or abridged by the United States or any State by reason of failure to pay any poll tax or other tax.

SECTION 2. The Congress shall have power to enforce this article by appropriate legislation.

AMENDMENT XXV[23]

SECTION 1. In case of the removal of the President from office or of his death or resignation, the Vice President shall become President.

SECTION 2. Whenever there is a vacancy in the office of the Vice President, the President shall nominate a Vice President who shall take office upon confirmation by a majority vote of both Houses of Congress.

SECTION 3. Whenever the President transmits to the President pro tempore of the Senate and the Speaker of the House of Representatives his written declaration that he is unable to discharge the powers and duties of his office, and until he transmits them a written declaration to the contrary, such powers and duties shall be discharged by the Vice President as Acting President.

SECTION 4. Whenever the Vice President and a majority of either the principal officers of the executive department or of such other body as Congress may by law provide, transmit to the President pro tempore of the Senate and the Speaker of the House of Representatives their written declaration that the President is unable to discharge the powers and duties of his office, the Vice President shall immediately assume the powers and duties of the office of Acting President

Thereafter, when the President transmits to the President pro tempore of the Senate and the Speaker of the House of Representatives his written declaration that no inability exists, he shall resume the powers and duties of his office unless the Vice President and a majority of either the principal officers of the executive department or of such other body as Congress may by law provide, transmit within four days to the President pro tempore of the Senate and the Speaker of the House of Representatives their written declaration that the President is unable to

---

[20]Passed March 12, 1947. Ratified March 1, 1951.

[21]Passed June 16, 1960. Ratified April 3, 1961.

[22]Passed August 27, 1962. Ratified January 23, 1964.

[23]Passed July 6, 1965. Ratified February 11, 1967.

discharge the powers and duties of his office. Thereupon Congress shall decide the issue, assembling within forty-eight hours for that purpose if not in session. If the Congress, within twenty-one days after receipt of the latter written declaration, or, if Congress is not in session, within twenty-one days after Congress is required to assemble, determines by two-thirds vote of both Houses that the President is unable to discharge the powers and duties of his office, the Vice President shall continue to discharge the same as Acting President; otherwise, the President shall resume the powers and duties of his office.

AMENDMENT XXVI[24]

SECTION 1. The right of citizens of the United States, who are eighteen years of age or older, to vote shall not be denied or abridged by the United States or by any State on account of age.

SECTION 2. The Congress shall have power to enforce this article by appropriate legislation.

AMENDMENT XXVII[25]

No law, varying the compensation for the service of the Senators and Representatives, shall take effect, until an election of Representatives shall have intervened.

---

[24]Passed March 23, 1971. Ratified July 5, 1971.

[25]Passed September 25, 1789. Ratified May 7, 1992

ADMISSION OF STATES

Order of admission	State	Date of admission	Order of admission	State	Date of admission
1	Delaware	December 7, 1787	26	Michigan	January 26, 1837
2	Pennsylvania	December 12, 1787	27	Florida	March 3, 1845
3	New Jersey	December 18, 1787	28	Texas	December 29, 1845
4	Georgia	January 2, 1788	29	Iowa	December 28, 1846
5	Connecticut	January 9, 1788	30	Wisconsin	May 29, 1848
6	Massachusetts	February 6, 1788	31	California	September 9, 1850
7	Maryland	April 28, 1788	32	Minnesota	May 11, 1858
8	South Carolina	May 23, 1788	33	Oregon	February 14, 1859
9	New Hampshire	June 21, 1788	34	Kansas	January 29, 1861
10	Virginia	June 25, 1788	35	West Virginia	June 20, 1863
11	New York	July 26, 1788	36	Nevada	October 31, 1864
12	North Carolina	November 21, 1789	37	Nebraska	March 1, 1867
13	Rhode Island	May 29, 1790	38	Colorado	August 1, 1876
14	Vermont	March 4, 1791	39	North Dakota	November 2, 1889
15	Kentucky	June 1, 1792	40	South Dakota	November 2, 1889
16	Tennessee	June 1, 1796	41	Montana	November 8, 1889
17	Ohio	March 1, 1803	42	Washington	November 11, 1889
18	Louisiana	April 30, 1812	43	Idaho	July 3, 1890
19	Indiana	December 11, 1816	44	Wyoming	July 10, 1890
20	Mississippi	December 10, 1817	45	Utah	January 4, 1896
21	Illinois	December 3, 1818	46	Oklahoma	November 16, 1907
22	Alabama	December 14, 1819	47	New Mexico	January 6, 1912
23	Maine	March 15, 1820	48	Arizona	February 14, 1912
24	Missouri	August 10, 1821	49	Alaska	January 3, 1959
25	Arkansas	June 15, 1836	50	Hawaii	August 21, 1959

POPULATION OF THE UNITED STATES

Year	Total population	Number per square mile	Year	Total population	Number per square mile	Year	Total population	Number per square mile
1790	3,929	4.5	1808	6,838		1826	11,580	
1791	4,056		1809	7,031		1827	11,909	
1792	4,194		1810	7,224	4.3	1828	12,237	
1793	4,332		1811	7,460		1829	12,565	
1794	4,469		1812	7,700		1830	12,901	7.4
1795	4,607		1813	7,939		1831	13,321	
1796	4,745		1814	8,179		1832	13,742	
1797	4,883		1815	8,419		1833	14,162	
1798	5,021		1816	8,659		1834	14,582	
1799	5,159		1817	8,899		1835	15,003	
1800	5,297	6.1	1818	9,139		1836	15,423	
1801	5,486		1819	9,379		1837	15,843	
1802	5,679		1820	9,618	5.6	1838	16,264	
1803	5,872		1821	9,939		1839	16,684	
1804	5,065		1822	10,268		1840	17,120	9.8
1805	6,258		1823	10,596		1841	17,733	
1806	6,451		1824	10,924		1842	18,345	
1807	6,644		1825	11,252		1843	18,957	

Figures are from *Historical Statistics of the United States, Colonial Times to 1957* (1961), pp. 7, 8; *Statistical Abstract of the United States: 1974,* p. 5, Census Bureau for 1974 and 1975; and *Statistical Abstract of the United States: 1988,* p. 7.

Note: Population figures are in thousands. Density figures are for land area of continental United States.

(continued)

Year	Total population	Number per square mile	Year	Total population[1]	Number per square mile	Year	Total population[1]	Number per square mile
1844	19,569		1896	70,885		1948	147,208	
1845	20,182		1897	72,189		1949	149,767	
1846	20,794		1898	73,494		1950	150,697	50.7
1847	21,406		1899	74,799		1951	154,878	
1848	22,018		1900	76,094	25.6	1952	157,553	
1849	22,631		1901	77,585		1953	160,184	
1850	23,261	7.9	1902	79,160		1954	163,026	
1851	24,086		1903	80,632		1955	165,931	
1852	24,911		1904	82,165		1956	168,903	
1853	25,736		1905	83,820		1957	171,984	
1854	26,561		1906	85,437		1958	174,882	
1855	27,386		1907	87,000		1959	177,830	
1856	28,212		1908	88,709		1960	178,464	60.1
1857	29,037		1909	90,492		1961	183,672	
1858	29,862		1910	92,407	31.0	1962	186,504	
1859	30,687		1911	93,868		1963	189,197	
1860	31,513	10.6	1912	95,331		1964	191,833	
1861	32,351		1913	97,227		1965	194,237	
1862	33,188		1914	99,118		1966	196,485	
1863	34,026		1915	100,549		1967	198,629	
1864	34,863		1916	101,966		1968	200,619	
1865	35,701		1917	103,414		1969	202,599	
1866	36,538		1918	104,550		1970	203,875	57.5[2]
1867	37,376		1919	105,063		1971	207,045	
1868	38,213		1920	106,466	35.6	1972	208,842	
1869	39,051		1921	108,541		1973	210,396	
1870	39,905	13.4	1922	110,055		1974	211,894	
1871	40,938		1923	111,950		1975	213,631	
1872	41,972		1924	114,113		1976	215,152	
1873	43,006		1925	115,832		1977	216,880	
1874	44,040		1926	117,399		1978	218,717	
1875	45,073		1927	119,038		1979	220,584	
1876	46,107		1928	120,501		1980	226,546	64.0
1877	47,141		1929	121,700		1981	230,138	
1878	48,174		1930	122,775	41.2	1982	232,520	
1879	49,208		1931	124,040		1983	234,799	
1880	50,262	16.9	1932	124,840		1984	237,001	
1881	51,542		1933	125,579		1985	239,283	
1882	52,821		1934	126,374		1986	241,596	
1883	54,100		1935	127,250		1987	234,773	
1884	55,379		1936	128,053		1988	245,051	
1885	56,658		1937	128,825		1989	247,350	
1886	57,938		1938	129,825		1990	250,122	
1887	59,217		1939	130,880		1991	254,521	
1888	60,496		1940	131,669	44.2	1992	245,908	
1889	61,775		1941	133,894		1993	257,908	
1890	63,056	21.2	1942	135,361		1994	261,875	
1891	64,361		1943	137,250		1995	263,434	
1892	65,666		1944	138,916		1996	266,096	
1893	66,970		1945	140,468		1997	267,901	
1894	68,275		1946	141,936		1998	269,501	
1895	69,580		1947	144,698				

[1]Figures after 1940 represent total population including armed forces abroad, except in official census years.

[2]Figure includes Alaska and Hawaii.

PRESIDENTIAL ELECTIONS

Year	Number of states	Candidates[1]	Parties	Popular vote	Electoral vote	Percentage of popular vote[2]
1789	11	**George Washington**	No party designations		69	
		John Adams			34	
		Minor Candidates			35	
1792	15	**George Washington**	No party designations		132	
		John Adams			77	
		George Clinton			50	
		Minor Candidates			5	
1796	16	**John Adams**	Federalist		71	
		Thomas Jefferson	Democratic-Republican		68	
		Thomas Pinckney	Federalist		59	
		Aaron Burr	Democratic-Republican		30	
		Minor Candidates			48	
1800	16	**Thomas Jefferson**	Democratic-Republican		73	
		Aaron Burr	Democratic-Republican		73	
		John Adams	Federalist		65	
		Charles C. Pinckney	Federalist		64	
		John Jay	Federalist		1	
1804	17	**Thomas Jefferson**	Democratic-Republican		162	
		Charles C. Pinckney	Federalist		14	
1808	17	**James Madison**	Democratic-Republican		122	
		Charles C. Pinckney	Federalist		47	
		George Clinton	Democratic-Republican		6	
1812	18	**James Madison**	Democratic-Republican		128	
		DeWitt Clinton	Federalist		89	
1816	19	**James Monroe**	Democratic-Republican		183	
		Rufus King	Federalist		34	
1820	24	**James Monroe**	Democratic-Republican		231	
		John Quincy Adams	Independent Republican		1	
1824	24	**John Quincy Adams**	Democratic-Republican	108,740	84	30.5
		Andrew Jackson	Democratic-Republican	153,544	99	43.1
		William H. Crawford	Democratic-Republican	46,618	41	13.1
		Henry Clay	Democratic-Republican	47,136	37	13.2
1828	24	**Andrew Jackson**	Democratic	647,286	178	56.0
		John Quincy Adams	National Republican	508,064	83	44.0
1832	24	**Andrew Jackson**	Democratic	687,502	219	55.0
		Henry Clay	National Republican	530,189	49	42.4
		William Wirt	Anti-Masonic	33,108	7	
		John Floyd	National Republican		11	2.6

[1]Before the passage of the Twelfth Amendment in 1804, the Electoral College voted for two presidential candidates; the runner-up became vice president. Figures are from *Historical Statistics of the United States, Colonial Times to 1957* (1961), pp. 682–83; and the U.S. Department of Justice.

[2]Candidates receiving less than 1 percent of the popular vote have been omitted. For that reason the percentage of popular vote given for any election year may not total 100 percent.

Year	Number of states	Candidates	Parties	Popular vote	Electoral vote	Percentage of popular vote[1]
1836	26	**Martin Van Buren**	Democratic	765,483	170	50.9
		William H. Harrison	Whig		73	
		Hugh L. White	Whig	739,795	26	
		Daniel Webster	Whig		14	
		W. P. Mangum	Whig		11	
1840	26	**William H. Harrison**	Whig	1,274,624	234	53.1
		Martin Van Buren	Democratic	1,127,781	60	46.9
1844	26	**James K. Polk**	Democratic	1,338,464	170	49.6
		Henry Clay	Whig	1,300,097	105	48.1
		James G. Birney	Liberty	62,300		2.3
1848	30	**Zachary Taylor**	Whig	1,360,967	163	47.4
		Lewis Cass	Democratic	1,222,342	127	42.5
		Martin Van Buren	Free Soil	291,263		10.1
1852	31	**Franklin Pierce**	Democratic	1,601,117	254	50.9
		Winfield Scott	Whig	1,385,453	42	44.1
		John P. Hale	Free Soil	155,825		5.0
1856	31	**James Buchanan**	Democratic	1,832,955	174	45.3
		John C. Frémont	Republican	1,339,932	114	33.1
		Millard Fillmore	American	871,731	8	21.6
1860	33	**Abraham Lincoln**	Republican	1,865,593	180	39.8
		Stephen A. Douglas	Democratic	1,382,713	12	29.5
		John C. Breckinridge	Democratic	848,356	72	18.1
		John Bell	Constitutional Union	592,906	39	12.6
1864	36	**Abraham Lincoln**	Republican	2,206,938	212	55.0
		George B. McClellan	Democratic	1,803,787	21	45.0
1868	37	**Ulysses S. Grant**	Republican	3,013,421	214	52.7
		Horatio Seymour	Democratic	2,706,829	80	47.3
1872	37	**Ulysses S. Grant**	Republican	3,596,745	286	55.6
		Horace Greeley	Democratic	2,843,446	[2]	43.9
1876	38	**Rutherford B. Hayes**	Republican	4,036,572	185	48.0
		Samuel J. Tilden	Democratic	4,284,020	184	51.0
1880	38	**James A. Garfield**	Republican	4,453,295	214	48.5
		Winfield S. Hancock	Democratic	4,414,082	155	48.1
		James B. Weaver	Greenback-Labor	308,578		3.4
1884	38	**Grover Cleveland**	Democratic	4,879,507	219	48.5
		James G. Blaine	Republican	4,850,293	182	48.2
		Benjamin F. Butler	Greenback-Labor	175,370		1.8
		John P. St. John	Prohibition	150,369		1.5
1888	38	**Benjamin Harrison**	Republican	5,477,129	233	47.9
		Grover Cleveland	Democratic	5,537,857	168	48.6
		Clinton B. Fisk	Prohibition	249,506		2.2
		Anson J. Streeter	Union Labor	146,935		1.3

[1]Candidates receiving less than 1 percent of the popular vote have been omitted. For that reason the percentage of popular vote given for any election year may not total 100 percent.

[2]Greeley died shortly after the election; the electors supporting him then divided their votes among minor candidates.

Year	Number of states	Candidates	Parties	Popular vote	Electoral vote	Percentage of popular vote[1]
1892	44	**Grover Cleveland**	Democratic	5,555,426	277	46.1
		Benjamin Harrison	Republican	5,182,690	145	43.0
		James B. Weaver	People's	1,029,846	22	8.5
		John Bidwell	Prohibition	264,133		2.2
1896	45	**William McKinley**	Republican	7,102,246	271	51.1
		William J. Bryan	Democratic	6,492,559	176	47.7
1900	45	**William McKinley**	Republican	7,218,491	292	51.7
		William J. Bryan	Democratic; Populist	6,356,734	155	45.5
		John C. Wooley	Prohibition	208,914		1.5
1904	45	**Theodore Roosevelt**	Republican	7,628,461	336	57.4
		Alton B. Parker	Democratic	5,084,223	140	37.6
		Eugene V. Debs	Socialist	402,283		3.0
		Silas C. Swallow	Prohibition	258,536		1.9
1908	46	**William H. Taft**	Republican	7,675,320	321	51.6
		William J. Bryan	Democratic	6,412,294	162	43.1
		Eugene V. Debs	Socialist	420,793		2.8
		Eugene W. Chafin	Prohibition	253,840		1.7
1912	48	**Woodrow Wilson**	Democratic	6,296,547	435	41.9
		Theodore Roosevelt	Progressive	4,118,571	88	27.4
		William H. Taft	Republican	3,486,720	8	23.2
		Eugene V. Debs	Socialist	900,672		6.0
		Eugene W. Chafin	Prohibition	206,275		1.4
1916	48	**Woodrow Wilson**	Democratic	9,127,695	277	49.4
		Charles E. Hughes	Republican	8,533,507	254	46.2
		A. L. Benson	Socialist	585,113		3.2
		J. Frank Hanly	Prohibition	220,506		1.2
1920	48	**Warren G. Harding**	Republican	16,143,407	404	60.4
		James N. Cox	Democratic	9,130,328	127	34.2
		Eugene V. Debs	Socialist	919,799		3.4
		P. P. Christensen	Farmer-Labor	265,411		1.0
1924	48	**Calvin Coolidge**	Republican	15,718,211	382	54.0
		John W. Davis	Democratic	8,385,283	136	28.8
		Robert M. La Follette	Progressive	4,831,289	13	16.6
1928	48	**Herbert C. Hoover**	Republican	21,391,993	444	58.2
		Alfred E. Smith	Democratic	15,016,169	87	40.9
1932	48	**Franklin D. Roosevelt**	Democratic	22,809,638	472	57.4
		Herbert C. Hoover	Republican	15,758,901	59	39.7
		Norman Thomas	Socialist	881,951		2.2

[1]Candidates receiving less than 1 percent of the popular vote have been omitted. For that reason the percentage of popular vote given for any election year may not total 100 percent.

Year	Number of states	Candidates	Parties	Popular vote	Electoral vote	Percentage of popular vote[1]
1936	48	**Franklin D. Roosevelt**	Democratic	27,752,869	523	60.8
		Alfred M. Landon	Republican	16,674,665	8	36.5
		William Lemke	Union	882,479		1.9
1940	48	**Franklin D. Roosevelt**	Democratic	27,307,819	449	54.8
		Wendell L. Willkie	Republican	22,321,018	82	44.8
1944	48	**Franklin D. Roosevelt**	Democratic	25,606,585	432	53.5
		Thomas E. Dewey	Republican	22,014,745	99	46.0
1948	48	**Harry S. Truman**	Democratic	24,105,812	303	49.5
		Thomas E. Dewey	Republican	21,970,065	189	45.1
		J. Strom Thurmond	States' Rights	1,169,063	39	2.4
		Henry A. Wallace	Progressive	1,157,172		2.4
1952	48	**Dwight D. Eisenhower**	Republican	33,936,234	442	55.1
		Adlai E. Stevenson	Democratic	27,314,992	89	44.4
1956	48	**Dwight D. Eisenhower**	Republican	35,590,472	457	57.6
		Adlai E. Stevenson	Democratic	26,022,752	73	42.1
1960	50	**John F. Kennedy**	Democratic	34,227,096	303	49.9
		Richard M. Nixon	Republican	34,108,546	219	49.6
1964	50	**Lyndon B. Johnson**	Democratic	43,126,506	486	61.1
		Barry M. Goldwater	Republican	27,176,799	52	38.5
1968	50	**Richard M. Nixon**	Republican	31,785,480	301	43.4
		Hubert H. Humphrey	Democratic	31,275,165	191	42.7
		George C. Wallace	American Independent	9,906,473	46	13.5
1972	50	**Richard M. Nixon**	Republican	47,169,911	520	60.7
		George S. McGovern	Democratic	29,170,383	17	37.5
1976	50	**Jimmy Carter**	Democratic	40,827,394	297	50.0
		Gerald R. Ford	Republican	39,145,977	240	47.9
1980	50	**Ronald W. Reagan**	Republican	43,899,248	489	50.8
		Jimmy Carter	Democratic	35,481,435	49	41.0
		John B. Anderson	Independent	5,719,437		6.6
		Ed Clark	Libertarian	920,859		1.0
1984	50	**Ronald W. Reagan**	Republican	54,281,858	525	59.2
		Walter F. Mondale	Democratic	37,457,215	13	40.8
1988	50	**George H. Bush**	Republican	47,917,341	426	54
		Michael Dukakis	Democratic	41,013,030	112	46
1992	50	**William Clinton**	Democratic	44,908,254	370	43.0
		George H. Bush	Republican	39,102,343	168	37.4
		Ross Perot	Independent	19,741,065		18.9
1996	50	**William Clinton**	Democratic	45,628,667	379	49.2
		Robert Dole	Republican	37,869,435	159	40.8
		Ross Perot	Reform	7,874,283	0	8.5

[1]Candidates receiving less than 1 percent of the popular vote have been omitted. For that reason the percentage of popular vote given for any election year may not total 100 percent.

PRESIDENTIAL ADMINISTRATIONS

President	Vice President	Secretary of State	Secretary of Treasury	Secretary of War	Secretary of Navy	Postmaster General	Attorney General
George Washington 1789–1797	John Adams 1789–1797	Thomas Jefferson 1789–1794 Edmund Randolph 1794–1795 Timothy Pickering 1795–1797	Alexander Hamilton 1789–1795 Oliver Wolcott 1795–1797	Henry Knox 1789–1795 Timothy Pickering 1795–1796 James McHenry 1796–1797		Samuel Osgood 1789–1791 Timothy Pickering 1791–1795 Joseph Habersham 1795–1797	Edmund Randolph 1789–1794 William Bradford 1794–1795 Charles Lee 1795–1797
John Adams 1797–1801	Thomas Jefferson 1797–1801	Timothy Pickering 1797–1800 John Marshall 1800–1801	Oliver Wolcott 1797–1801 Samuel Dexter 1801	James McHenry 1797–1800 Samuel Dexter 1800–1801	Benjamin Stoddert 1798–1801	Joseph Habersham 1797–1801	Charles Lee 1797–1801
Thomas Jefferson 1801–1809	Aaron Burr 1801–1805 George Clinton 1805–1809	James Madison 1801–1809	Samuel Dexter 1801 Albert Gallatin 1801–1809	Henry Dearborn 1801–1809	Benjamin Stoddert 1801 Robert Smith 1801–1809	Joseph Habersham 1801 Gideon Granger 1801–1809	Levi Lincoln 1801–1805 John Breckinridge 1805–1807 Caesar Rodney 1807–1809
James Madison 1809–1817	George Clinton 1809–1813 Elbridge Gerry 1813–1817	Robert Smith 1809–1811 James Monroe 1811–1817	Albert Gallatin 1809–1814 George Campbell 1814 Alexander Dallas 1814–1816 William Crawford 1816–1817	William Eustis 1809–1813 John Armstrong 1813–1814 James Monroe 1814–1815 William Crawford 1815–1817	Paul Hamilton 1809–1813 William Jones 1813–1814 Benjamin Crowninshield 1814–1817	Gideon Granger 1809–1814 Return Meigs 1814–1817	Caesar Rodney 1809–1811 William Pinkney 1811–1814 Richard Rush 1814–1817
James Monroe 1817–1825	Daniel D. Tompkins 1817–1825	John Quincy Adams 1817–1825	William Crawford 1817–1825	George Graham 1817 John C. Calhoun 1817–1825	Benjamin Crowninshield 1817–1818 Smith Thompson 1818–1823 Samuel Southard 1823–1825	Return Meigs 1817–1823 John McLean 1823–1825	Richard Rush 1817 William Wirt 1817–1825
John Quincy Adams 1825–1829	John C. Calhoun 1825–1829	Henry Clay 1825–1829	Richard Rush 1825–1829	James Barbour 1825–1828 Peter B. Porter 1828–1829	Samuel Southard 1825–1829	John McLean 1825–1829	William Wirt 1825–1829
Andrew Jackson 1829–1837	John C. Calhoun 1829–1833 Martin Van Buren 1833–1837	Martin Van Buren 1829–1831 Edward Livingston 1831–1833 Louis McLane 1833–1834 John Forsyth 1834–1837	Samuel Ingham 1829–1831 Louis McLane 1831–1833 William Duane 1833 Roger B. Taney 1833–1834 Levi Woodbury 1834–1837	John H. Eaton 1829–1831 Lewis Cass 1831–1837 Benjamin Butler 1837	John Branch 1829–1831 Levi Woodbury 1831–1834 Mahlon Dickerson 1834–1837	William Barry 1829–1835 Amos Kendall 1835–1837	John M. Berrien 1829–1831 Roger B. Taney 1831–1833 Benjamin Butler 1833–1837
Martin Van Buren 1837–1841	Richard M. Johnson 1837–1841	John Forsyth 1837–1841	Levi Woodbury 1837–1841	Joel R. Poinsett 1837–1841	Mahlon Dickerson 1837–1838 James K. Paulding 1838–1841	Amos Kendall 1837–1840 John M. Niles 1840–1841	Benjamin Butler 1837–1838 Felix Grundy 1838–1840 Henry D. Gilpin 1840–1841

(continued)

President	Vice President	Secretary of State	Secretary of Treasury	Secretary of War
William H. Harrison 1841	John Tyler 1841	Daniel Webster 1841	Thomas Ewing 1841	John Bell 1841
John Tyler 1841–1845		Daniel Webster 1841–1843 Hugh S. Legaré 1843 Abel P. Upshur 1843–1844 John C. Calhoun 1844–1845	Thomas Ewing 1841 Walter Forward 1841–1843 John C. Spencer 1843–1844 George M. Bibb 1844–1845	John Bell 1841 John C. Spencer 1841–1843 James M. Porter 1843–1844 William Wilkins 1844–1845
James K. Polk 1845–1849	George M. Dallas 1845–1849	James Buchanan 1845–1849	Robert J. Walker 1845–1849	William L. Marcy 1845–1849
Zachary Taylor 1849–1850	Millard Fillmore 1849–1850	John M. Clayton 1849–1850	William M. Meredith 1849–1850	George W. Crawford 1849–1850
Millard Fillmore 1850–1853		Daniel Webster 1850–1852 Edward Everett 1852–1853	Thomas Corwin 1850–1853	Charles M. Conrad 1850–1853
Franklin Pierce 1853–1857	William R. King 1853–1857	William L. Marcy 1853–1857	James Guthrie 1853–1857	Jefferson Davis 1853–1857
James Buchanan 1857–1861	John C. Breckinridge 1857–1861	Lewis Cass 1857–1860 Jeremiah S. Black 1860–1861	Howell Cobb 1857–1860 Philip F. Thomas 1860–1861 John A. Dix 1861	John B. Floyd 1857–1861 Joseph Holt 1861
Abraham Lincoln 1861–1865	Hannibal Hamlin 1861–1865 Andrew Johnson 1865	William H. Seward 1861–1865	Salmon P. Chase 1861–1864 William P. Fessenden 1864–1865 Hugh McCulloch 1865	Simon Cameron 1861–1862 Edwin M. Stanton 1862–1865
Andrew Johnson 1865–1869		William H. Seward 1865–1869	Hugh McCulloch 1865–1869	Edwin M. Stanton 1865–1867 Ulysses S. Grant 1867–1868 John M. Schofield 1868–1869
Ulysses S. Grant 1869–1877	Schuyler Colfax 1869–1873 Henry Wilson 1873–1877	Elihu B. Washburne 1869 Hamilton Fish 1869–1877	George S. Boutwell 1869–1873 William A. Richardson 1873–1874 Benjamin H. Bristow 1874–1876 Lot M. Morrill 1876–1877	John A. Rawlins 1869 William T. Sherman 1869 William W. Belknap 1869–1876 Alphonso Taft 1876 James D. Cameron 1876–1877

Secretary of Navy	Postmaster General	Attorney General	Secretary of Interior
George E. Badger 1841	Francis Granger 1841	John J. Crittenden 1841	
George E. Badger 1841 Abel P. Upshur 1841–1843 David Henshaw 1843–1844 Thomas Gilmer 1844 John Y. Mason 1844–1845	Francis Granger 1841 Charles A. Wickliffe 1841–1845	John J. Crittenden 1841 Hugh S. Legaré 1841–1843 John Nelson 1843–1845	
George Bancroft 1845–1846 John Y. Mason 1846–1849	Cave Johnson 1845–1849	John Y. Mason 1845–1846 Nathan Clifford 1846–1848 Isaac Toucey 1848–1849	
William B. Preston 1849–1850	Jacob Collamer 1849–1850	Reverdy Johnson 1849–1850	Thomas Ewing 1849–1850
William A. Graham 1850–1852 John P. Kennedy 1852–1853	Nathan K. Hall 1850–1852 Sam D. Hubbard 1852–1853	John J. Crittenden 1850–1853	Thomas McKennan 1850 A. H. H. Stuart 1850–1853
James C. Dobbin 1853–1857	James Campbell 1853–1857	Caleb Cushing 1853–1857	Robert McClelland 1853–1857
Isaac Toucey 1857–1861	Aaron V. Brown 1857–1859 Joseph Holt 1859–1861 Horatio King 1861	Jeremiah S. Black 1857–1860 Edwin M. Stanton 1860–1861	Jacob Thompson 1857–1861
Gideon Welles 1861–1865	Horatio King 1861 Montgomery Blair 1861–1864 William Dennison 1864–1865	Edward Bates 1861–1864 James Speed 1864–1865	Caleb B. Smith 1861–1863 John P. Usher 1863–1865
Gideon Welles 1865–1869	William Dennison 1865–1866 Alexander Randall 1866–1869 William M. Evarts 1868–1869	James Speed 1865–1866 Henry Stanbery 1866–1868 O. H. Browning 1866–1869	John P. Usher 1865 James Harlan 1865–1866
Adolph E. Borie 1869 George M. Robeson 1869–1877	John A. J. Creswell 1869–1874 James W. Marshall 1874 Marshall Jewell 1874–1876 James N. Tyner 1876–1877	Ebenezer R. Hoar 1869–1870 Amos T. Akerman 1870–1871 G. H. Williams 1871–1875 Edwards Pierrepont 1875–1876 Alphonso Taft 1876–1877	Jacob D. Cox 1869–1870 Columbus Delano 1870–1875 Zachariah Chandler 1875–1877

President	Vice President	Secretary of State	Secretary of Treasury	Secretary of War	Secretary of Navy
Rutherford B. Hayes 1877–1881	William A. Wheeler 1877–1881	William M. Evarts 1877–1881	John Sherman 1877–1881	George W. McCrary 1877–1879 Alexander Ramsey 1879–1881	R. W. Thompson 1877–1881 Nathan Goff, Jr. 1881
James A. Garfield 1881	Chester A. Arthur 1881	James G. Blaine 1881	William Windom 1881	Robert T. Lincoln 1881	William H. Hunt 1881
Chester A. Arthur 1881–1885		F. T. Frelinghuysen 1881–1885	Charles J. Folger 1881–1884 Walter Q. Gresham 1884 Hugh McCulloch 1884–1885	Robert T. Lincoln 1881–1885	William E. Chandler 1881–1885
Grover Cleveland 1885–1889	T. A. Hendricks 1885	Thomas F. Bayard 1885–1889	Daniel Manning 1885–1887 Charles S. Fairchild 1887–1889	William C. Endicott 1885–1889	William C. Whitney 1885–1889
Benjamin Harrison 1889–1893	Levi P. Morton 1889–1893	James G. Blaine 1889–1892 John W. Foster 1892–1893	William Windom 1889–1891 Charles Foster 1892–1893	Redfield Procter 1889–1891 Stephen B. Elkins 1891–1893	Benjamin F. Tracy 1889–1893
Grover Cleveland 1893–1897	Adlai E. Stevenson 1893–1897	Walter Q. Gresham 1893–1895 Richard Olney 1895–1897	John G. Carlisle 1893–1897	Daniel S. Lamont 1893–1897	Hilary A. Herbert 1893–1897
William McKinley 1897–1901	Garret A. Hobart 1897–1899 Theodore Roosevelt 1901	John Sherman 1897–1898 William R. Day 1898 John Hay 1898–1901	Lyman J. Gage 1897–1901	Russell A. Alger 1897–1899 Elihu Root 1899–1901	John D. Long 1897–1901
Theodore Roosevelt 1901–1909	Charles Fairbanks 1905–1909	John Hay 1901–1905 Elihu Root 1905–1909 Robert Bacon 1909	Lyman J. Gage 1901–1902 Leslie M. Shaw 1902–1907 George B. Cortelyou 1907–1909	Elihu Root 1901–1904 William H. Taft 1904–1908 Luke E. Wright 1908–1909	John D. Long 1901–1902 William H. Moody 1902–1904 Paul Morton 1904–1905 Charles J. Bonaparte 1905–1906 Victor H. Metcalf 1906–1908 T. H. Newberry 1908–1909
William H. Taft 1909–1913	James S. Sherman 1909–1913	Philander C. Knox 1909–1913	Franklin MacVeagh 1909–1913	Jacob M. Dickinson 1909–1911 Henry L. Stimson 1911–1913	George von L. Meyer 1909–1913
Woodrow Wilson 1913–1921	Thomas R. Marshall 1913–1921	William J. Bryan 1913–1915 Robert Lansing 1915–1920 Bainbridge Colby 1920–1921	William G. McAdoo 1913–1918 Carter Glass 1918–1920 David F. Houston 1920–1921	Lindley M. Garrison 1913–1916 Newton D. Baker 1916–1921	Josephus Daniels 1913–1921

Postmaster General	Attorney General	Secretary of Interior	Secretary of Agriculture	Secretary of Commerce and Labor	
David M. Key 1877–1880 Horace Maynard 1880–1881	Charles Devens 1877–1881	Carl Schurz 1877–1881			
Thomas L. James 1881	Wayne MacVeagh 1881	S. J. Kirkwood 1881			
Thomas L. James 1881 Timothy O. Howe 1881–1883 Walter Q. Gresham 1883–1884 Frank Hatton 1884–1885	B. H. Brewster 1881–1885	Henry M. Teller 1881–1885			
William F. Vilas 1885–1888 Don M. Dickinson 1888–1889	A. H. Garland 1885–1889	L. Q. C. Lamar 1885–1888 William F. Vilas 1888–1889	Norman J. Colman 1889		
John Wanamaker 1889–1893	W. H. H. Miller 1889–1893	John W. Noble 1889–1893	Jeremiah M. Rusk 1889–1893		
Wilson S. Bissel 1893–1895 William L. Wilson 1895–1897	Richard Olney 1893–1895 Judson Harmon 1895–1897	Hoke Smith 1893–1896 David R. Francis 1896–1897	J. Sterling Morton 1893–1897		
James A. Gary 1897–1898 Charles E. Smith 1898–1901	Joseph McKenna 1897–1898 John W. Griggs 1898–1901 Philander C. Knox 1901	Cornelius N. Bliss 1897–1898 E. A. Hitchcock 1898–1901	James Wilson 1897–1901		
Charles E. Smith 1901–1902 Henry C. Payne 1902–1904 Robert J. Wynne 1904–1905 George B. Cortelyou 1905—1907 George von L. Meyer 1907–1909	Philander C. Knox 1901–1904 William H. Moody 1904–1906 Charles J. Bonaparte 1906–1909	E. A. Hitchcock 1901–1907 James R. Garfield 1907–1909	James Wilson 1901–1909	George B. Cortelyou 1903–1904 Victor H. Metcalf 1904–1906 Oscar S. Straus 1906–1909	
Frank H. Hitchcock 1909–1913	G. W. Wickersham 1909–1913	R. A. Ballinger 1909–1911 Walter L. Fisher 1911–1913	James Wilson 1909–1913	Charles Nagel 1909–1913	

				Secretary of Commerce	Secretary of Labor
Albert S. Burleson 1913–1921	J. C. McReynolds 1913–1914 T. W. Gregory 1914–1919 A. Mitchell Palmer 1919–1921	Franklin K. Lane 1913–1920 John B. Payne 1920–1921	David F. Houston 1913–1920 E. T. Meredith 1920–1921	W. C. Redfield 1913–1919 J. W. Alexander 1919–1921	William B. Wilson 1913–1921

President	Vice President	Secretary of State	Secretary of Treasury	Secretary of War	Secretary of Navy	Postmaster General	Attorney General
Warren G. Harding 1921–1923	Calvin Coolidge 1921–1923	Charles E. Hughes 1921–1923	Andrew W. Mellon 1921–1923	John W. Weeks 1921–1923	Edwin Denby 1921–1923	Will H. Hays 1921–1922 Hubert Work 1922–1923 Harry S. New 1923	H. M. Daugherty 1921–1923
Calvin Coolidge 1923–1929	Charles G. Dawes 1925–1929	Charles E. Hughes 1923–1925 Frank B. Kellogg 1925–1929	Andrew W. Mellon 1923–1929	John W. Weeks 1923–1925 Dwight F. Davis 1925–1929	Edwin Denby 1923–1924 Curtis D. Wilbur 1924–1929	Harry S. New 1923–1929	H. M. Daugherty 1923–1924 Harlan F. Stone 1924–1925 John G. Sargent 1925–1929
Herbert C. Hoover 1929–1933	Charles Curtis 1929–1933	Henry L. Stimson 1929–1933	Andrew W. Mellon 1929–1932 Ogden L. Mills 1932–1933	James W. Good 1929 Patrick J. Hurley 1929–1933	Charles F. Adams 1929–1933	Walter F. Brown 1929–1933	J. D. Mitchell 1929–1933
Franklin Delano Roosevelt 1933–1945	John Nance Garner 1933–1941 Henry A. Wallace 1941–1945 Harry S. Truman 1945	Cordell Hull 1933–1944 E. R. Stettinius, Jr. 1944–1945	William H. Woodin 1933–1934 Henry Morgenthau, Jr. 1934–1945	George H. Dern 1933–1936 Harry H. Woodring 1936–1940 Henry L. Stimson 1940–1945	Claude A. Swanson 1933–1940 Charles Edison 1940 Frank Knox 1940–1944 James V. Forrestal 1944–1945	James A. Farley 1933–1940 Frank C. Walker 1940–1945	H. S. Cummings 1933–1939 Frank Murphy 1939–1940 Robert Jackson 1940–1941 Francis Biddel 1941–1945
Harry S. Truman 1945–1953	Alben W. Barkley 1949–1953	James F. Byrnes 1945–1947 George C. Marshall 1947–1949 Dean G. Acheson 1949–1953	Fred M. Vinson 1945–1946 John W. Snyder 1946–1953	Robert P. Patterson 1945–1947 Kenneth C. Royall 1947 **Secretary of Defense** James V. Forrestal 1947–1949 Louis A. Johnson 1949–1950 George C. Marshall 1950–1951 Robert A. Lovett 1951–1953	James V. Forrestal 1945–1947	R. E. Hannegan 1945–1947 Jesse M. Donaldson 1947–1953	Tom C. Clark 1945–1949 J. H. McGrath 1949–1952 James P. McGranery 1952–1953
Dwight D. Eisenhower 1953–1961	Richard M. Nixon 1953–1961	John Foster Dulles 1953–1959 Christian A. Herter 1957–1961	George M. Humphrey 1953–1957 Robert B. Anderson 1957–1961	Charles E. Wilson 1953–1957 Neil H. McElroy 1957–1961 Thomas S. Gates 1959–1961		A. E. Summerfield 1953–1961	H. Brownell, Jr. 1953–1957 William P. Rogers 1957–1961
John F. Kennedy 1961–1963	Lyndon B. Johnson 1961–1963	Dean Rusk 1961–1963	C. Douglas Dillon 1961–1963	Robert S. McNamara 1961–1963		J. Edward Day 1961–1963 John A. Gronouski 1961–1963	Robert F. Kennedy 1961–1963
Lyndon B. Johnson 1963–1969	Hubert H. Humphrey 1965–1969	Dean Rusk 1963–1969	C. Douglas Dillon 1963–1965 Henry H. Fowler 1965–1968 Joseph W. Barr 1968–1969	Robert S. McNamara 1963–1968 Clark M. Clifford 1968–1969		John A. Gronouski 1963–1965 Lawrence F. O'Brien 1965–1968 W. Marvin Watson 1968–1969	Robert F. Kennedy 1963–1965 N. deB. Katzenbach 1965–1967 Ramsey Clark 1967–1969

Secretary of Interior	Secretary of Agriculture	Secretary of Commerce	Secretary of Labor	Secretary of Health, Education and Welfare	Secretary of Housing and Urban Development	Secretary of Transportation
Albert B. Fall 1921–1923 Hubert Work 1923	Henry C. Wallace 1921–1923	Herbert C. Hoover 1921–1923	James J. Davis 1921–1923			
Hubert Work 1923–1928 Roy O. West 1928–1929	Henry C. Wallace 1923–1924 Howard M. Gore 1924–1925 W. J. Jardine 1925–1929	Herbert C. Hoover 1923–1928 William F. Whiting 1928–1929	James J. Davis 1923–1929			
Ray L. Wilbur 1929–1933	Arthur M. Hyde 1929–1933 Roy D. Chapin 1932–1933	Robert P. Lamont 1929–1932 William N. Doak 1930–1933	James J. Davis 1929–1930			
Harold L. Ickes 1933–1945	Henry A. Wallace 1933–1940 Claude R. Wickard 1940–1945	Daniel C. Roper 1933–1939 Harry L. Hopkins 1939–1940 Jesse Jones 1940–1945 Henry A. Wallace 1945	Frances Perkins 1933–1945			
Harold L. Ickes 1945–1946 Julius A. Krug 1946–1949 Oscar L. Chapman 1949–1953	C. P. Anderson 1945–1948 C. F. Brannan 1948–1953	W. A. Harriman 1946–1948 Charles Sawyer 1948–1953	L. B. Schwellenbach 1945–1948 Maurice J. Tobin 1948–1953			
Douglas McKay 1953–1956 Fred Seaton 1956–1961	Ezra T. Benson 1953–1961	Sinclair Weeks 1953–1958 Lewis L. Strauss 1958–1961	Martin P. Durkin 1953 James P. Mitchell 1953–1961	Oveta Culp Hobby 1953–1955 Marion B. Folsom 1955–1958 Arthur S. Flemming 1958–1961		
Stewart L. Udall 1961–1963	Orville L. Freeman 1961–1963	Luther H. Hodges 1961–1963	Arthur J. Goldberg 1961–1963 W. Willard Wirtz 1962–1963	A. H. Ribicoff 1961–1963 Anthony J. Celebrezze 1962–1963		
Stewart L. Udall 1963–1969	Orville L. Freeman 1963–1969	Luther H. Hodges 1963–1965 John T. Connor 1965–1967 Alexander B. Trowbridge 1967–1968 C. R. Smith 1968–1969	W. Willard Wirtz 1963–1969	Anthony J. Celebrezze 1963–1965 John W. Gardner 1965–1968 Wilbur J. Cohen 1968–1969	Robert C. Weaver 1966–1968 Robert C. Wood 1968–1969	Alan S. Boyd 1966–1969

President	Vice President	Secretary of State	Secretary of Treasury	Secretary of Defense	Postmaster General[1]	Attorney General	Secretary of Interior	Secretary of Agriculture
Richard M. Nixon 1969–1974	Spiro T. Agnew 1969–1973 Gerald R. Ford 1973–1974	William P. Rogers 1969–1973 Henry A. Kissinger 1973–1974	David M. Kennedy 1969–1970 John B. Connally 1970–1972 George P. Schultz 1972–1974 William E. Simon 1974	Melvin R. Laird 1969–1973 Elliot L. Richardson 1973 James R. Schlesinger 1973–1974	Winton M. Blount 1969–1971	John M. Mitchell 1969–1972 Richard G. Kleindienst 1972–1973 Elliot L. Richardson 1973 William B. Saxbe 1974	Walter J. Hickel 1969–1971 Rogers C. B. Morton 1971–1974	Clifford M. Hardin 1969–1971 Earl L. Butz 1971–1974
Gerald R. Ford 1974–1977	Nelson A. Rockefeller 1974–1977	Henry A. Kissinger 1974–1977	William E. Simon 1974–1977	James R. Schlesinger 1974–1975 Donald H. Rumsfeld 1975–1977		William B. Saxbe 1974–1975 Edward H. Levi 1975–1977	Rogers C. B. Morton 1974–1975 Stanley K. Hathaway 1975 Thomas D. Kleppe 1975–1977	Earl L. Butz 1974–1976
Jimmy Carter 1977–1981	Walter F. Mondale 1977–1981	Cyrus R. Vance 1977–1980 Edmund S. Muskie 1980–1981	W. Michael Blumenthal 1977–1979 G. William Miller 1979–1981	Harold Brown 1977–1981		Griffin Bell 1977–1979 Benjamin R. Civiletti 1979–1981	Cecil D. Andrus 1977–1981	Robert Bergland 1977–1981
Ronald W. Reagan 1981–1989	George H. Bush 1981–1989	Alexander M. Haig, Jr. 1981–1982 George P. Shultz 1982–1989	Donald T. Regan 1981–1985 James A. Baker 1985–1988 Nicholas F. Brady 1988–1989	Caspar W. Weinberger 1981–1987 Frank C. Carlucci 1987–1989		William French Smith 1981–1985 Edwin Meese 1985–1988 Richard Thornburgh 1988–1989	James G. Watt 1981–1983 William P. Clark 1983–1985 Donald P. Hodel 1985–1989	John R. Block 1981–1986 Richard E. Lyng 1986–1989
George H. Bush 1989–1992	J. Danforth Quayle 1989–1992	James A. Baker 1989–1992 Lawrence S. Eagleburger 1992	Nicholas F. Brady 1989–1992	Richard Cheney 1989–1992		Richard Thornburgh 1989–1990 William Barr 1990–1992	Manuel Lujan 1989–1992	Clayton Yeutter 1989–1990 Edward Madigan 1990–1992
William Clinton 1993–	Albert Gore 1993–	Warren M. Christopher 1993–1996 Madeleine K. Albright 1997–	Lloyd Bentsen 1993–1994 Robert E. Rubin 1994–	Les Aspin 1993–1994 William J. Perry 1994–1996 William S. Cohen 1997–		Janet Reno 1993–	Bruce Babbitt 1993–	Mike Espy 1993–1994 Dan Glickman 1995–

[1]On July 1, 1971, the Post Office became an independent agency. After that date, the Postmaster General was no longer a member of the Cabinet.
[2]Acting Secretary

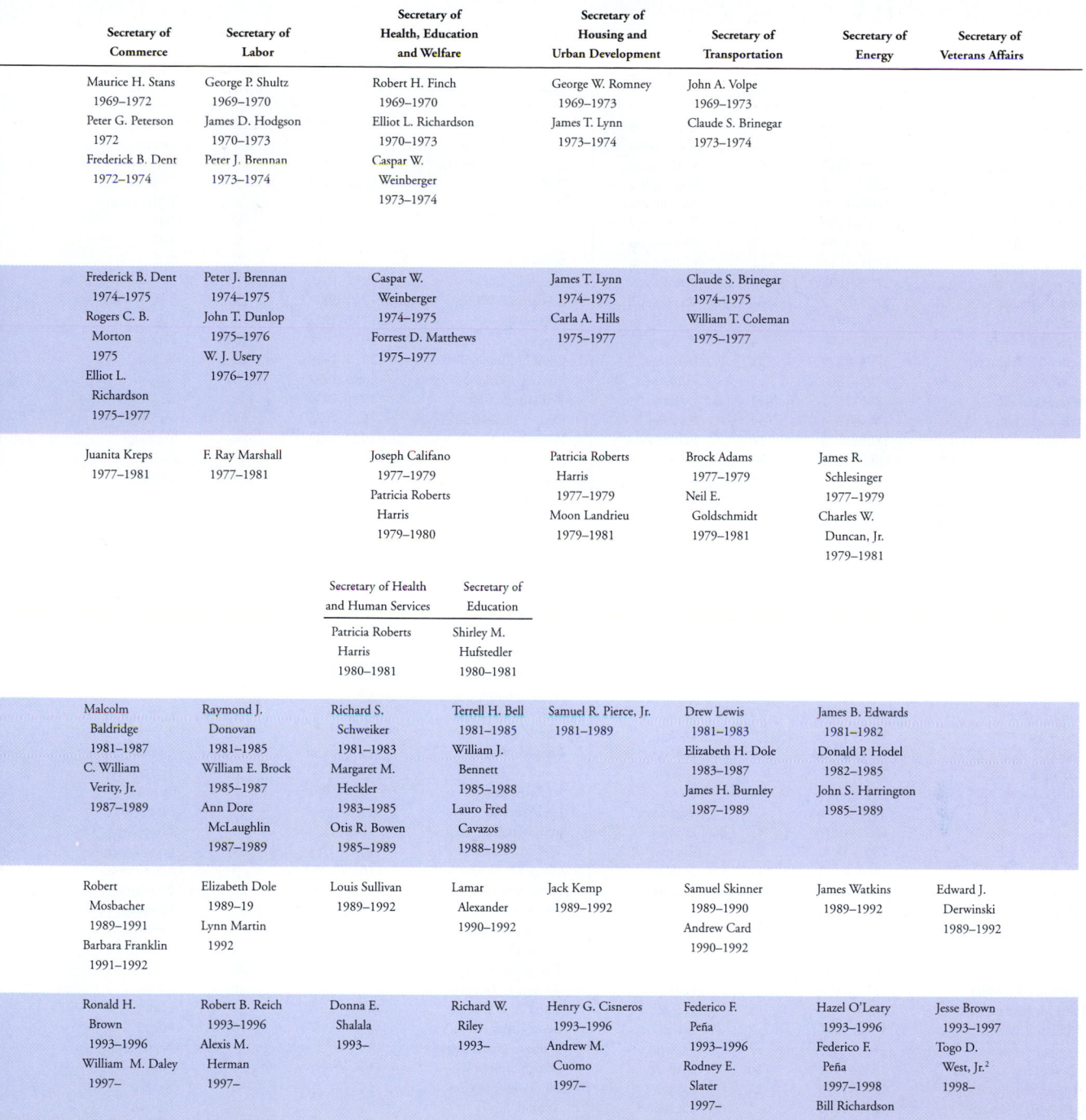

Secretary of Commerce	Secretary of Labor	Secretary of Health, Education and Welfare	Secretary of Housing and Urban Development	Secretary of Transportation	Secretary of Energy	Secretary of Veterans Affairs
Maurice H. Stans 1969–1972	George P. Shultz 1969–1970	Robert H. Finch 1969–1970	George W. Romney 1969–1973	John A. Volpe 1969–1973		
Peter G. Peterson 1972	James D. Hodgson 1970–1973	Elliot L. Richardson 1970–1973	James T. Lynn 1973–1974	Claude S. Brinegar 1973–1974		
Frederick B. Dent 1972–1974	Peter J. Brennan 1973–1974	Caspar W. Weinberger 1973–1974				
Frederick B. Dent 1974–1975	Peter J. Brennan 1974–1975	Caspar W. Weinberger 1974–1975	James T. Lynn 1974–1975	Claude S. Brinegar 1974–1975		
Rogers C. B. Morton 1975	John T. Dunlop 1975–1976	Forrest D. Matthews 1975–1977	Carla A. Hills 1975–1977	William T. Coleman 1975–1977		
Elliot L. Richardson 1975–1977	W. J. Usery 1976–1977					
Juanita Kreps 1977–1981	F. Ray Marshall 1977–1981	Joseph Califano 1977–1979	Patricia Roberts Harris 1977–1979	Brock Adams 1977–1979	James R. Schlesinger 1977–1979	
		Patricia Roberts Harris 1979–1980	Moon Landrieu 1979–1981	Neil E. Goldschmidt 1979–1981	Charles W. Duncan, Jr. 1979–1981	

	Secretary of Health and Human Services	Secretary of Education				
	Patricia Roberts Harris 1980–1981	Shirley M. Hufstedler 1980–1981				

Secretary of Commerce	Secretary of Labor	Secretary of Health and Human Services	Secretary of Education	Secretary of Housing and Urban Development	Secretary of Transportation	Secretary of Energy	Secretary of Veterans Affairs
Malcolm Baldridge 1981–1987	Raymond J. Donovan 1981–1985	Richard S. Schweiker 1981–1983	Terrell H. Bell 1981–1985	Samuel R. Pierce, Jr. 1981–1989	Drew Lewis 1981–1983	James B. Edwards 1981–1982	
C. William Verity, Jr. 1987–1989	William E. Brock 1985–1987	Margaret M. Heckler 1983–1985	William J. Bennett 1985–1988		Elizabeth H. Dole 1983–1987	Donald P. Hodel 1982–1985	
	Ann Dore McLaughlin 1987–1989	Otis R. Bowen 1985–1989	Lauro Fred Cavazos 1988–1989		James H. Burnley 1987–1989	John S. Harrington 1985–1989	
Robert Mosbacher 1989–1991	Elizabeth Dole 1989–19	Louis Sullivan 1989–1992	Lamar Alexander 1990–1992	Jack Kemp 1989–1992	Samuel Skinner 1989–1990	James Watkins 1989–1992	Edward J. Derwinski 1989–1992
Barbara Franklin 1991–1992	Lynn Martin 1992				Andrew Card 1990–1992		
Ronald H. Brown 1993–1996	Robert B. Reich 1993–1996	Donna E. Shalala 1993–	Richard W. Riley 1993–	Henry G. Cisneros 1993–1996	Federico F. Peña 1993–1996	Hazel O'Leary 1993–1996	Jesse Brown 1993–1997
William M. Daley 1997–	Alexis M. Herman 1997–			Andrew M. Cuomo 1997–	Rodney E. Slater 1997–	Federico F. Peña 1997–1998	Togo D. West, Jr.[2] 1998–
						Bill Richardson 1998–	

JUSTICES OF THE U.S. SUPREME COURT

Name	Term of Service	Years of Service	Appointed By	Name	Term of Service	Years of Service	Appointed By
John Jay	1789–1795	5	Washington	Rufus W. Peckham	1895–1909	14	Cleveland
John Rutledge	1789–1791	1	Washington	Joseph McKenna	1898–1925	26	McKinley
William Cushing	1789–1810	20	Washington	Oliver W. Holmes, Jr.	1902–1932	30	T. Roosevelt
James Wilson	1789–1798	8	Washington	William R. Day	1903–1922	19	T. Roosevelt
John Blair	1789–1796	6	Washington	William H. Moody	1906–1910	3	T. Roosevelt
Robert H. Harrison	1789–1790	—	Washington	Horace H. Lurton	1910–1914	4	Taft
James Iredell	1790–1799	9	Washington	Charles E. Hughes	1910–1916	5	Taft
Thomas Johnson	1791–1793	1	Washington	Willis Van Devanter	1911–1937	26	Taft
William Paterson	1793–1806	13	Washington	Joseph R. Lamar	1911–1916	5	Taft
John Rutledge[1]	1795	—	Washington	**Edward D. White**	1910–1921	11	Taft
Samuel Chase	1796–1811	15	Washington	Mahlon Pitney	1912–1922	10	Taft
Oliver Ellsworth	1796–1800	4	Washington	James C. McReynolds	1914–1941	26	Wilson
Bushrod Washington	1798–1829	31	J. Adams	Louis D. Brandeis	1916–1939	22	Wilson
Alfred Moore	1799–1804	4	J. Adams	John H. Clarke	1916–1922	6	Wilson
John Marshall	1801–1835	34	J. Adams	**William H. Taft**	1921–1930	8	Harding
William Johnson	1804–1834	30	Jefferson	George Sutherland	1922–1938	15	Harding
H. Brockholst Livingston	1806–1823	16	Jefferson	Pierce Butler	1922–1939	16	Harding
Thomas Todd	1807–1826	18	Jefferson	Edward T. Sanford	1923–1930	7	Harding
Joseph Story	1811–1845	33	Madison	Harlan F. Stone	1925–1941	16	Coolidge
Gabriel Duval	1811–1835	24	Madison	**Charles E. Hughes**	1930–1941	11	Hoover
Smith Thompson	1823–1843	20	Monroe	Owen J. Roberts	1930–1945	15	Hoover
Robert Trimble	1826–1828	2	J. Q. Adams	Benjamin N. Cardozo	1932–1938	6	Hoover
John McLean	1829–1861	32	Jackson	Hugo L. Black	1937–1971	34	F. Roosevelt
Henry Baldwin	1830–1844	14	Jackson	Stanley F. Reed	1938–1957	19	F. Roosevelt
James M. Wayne	1835–1867	32	Jackson	Felix Frankfurter	1939–1962	23	F. Roosevelt
Roger B. Taney	1836–1864	28	Jackson	William O. Douglas	1939–1975	36	F. Roosevelt
Philip P. Barbour	1836–1841	4	Jackson	Frank Murphy	1940–1949	9	F. Roosevelt
John Catron	1837–1865	28	Van Buren	**Harlan F. Stone**	1941–1946	5	F. Roosevelt
John McKinley	1837–1852	15	Van Buren	James F. Byrnes	1941–1942	1	F. Roosevelt
Peter V. Daniel	1841–1860	19	Van Buren	Robert H. Jackson	1941–1954	13	F. Roosevelt
Samuel Nelson	1845–1872	27	Tyler	Wiley B. Rutledge	1943–1949	6	F. Roosevelt
Levi Woodbury	1845–1851	5	Polk	Harold H. Burton	1945–1958	13	Truman
Robert C. Grier	1846–1870	23	Polk	**Fred M. Vinson**	1946–1953	7	Truman
Benjamin R. Curtis	1851–1857	6	Fillmore	Tom C. Clark	1949–1967	18	Truman
John A. Campbell	1853–1861	8	Pierce	Sherman Minton	1949–1956	7	Truman
Nathan Clifford	1858–1881	23	Buchanan	**Earl Warren**	1953–1969	16	Eisenhower
Noah H. Swayne	1862–1881	18	Lincoln	John Marshall Harlan	1955–1971	16	Eisenhower
Samuel F. Miller	1862–1890	28	Lincoln	William J. Brennan, Jr.	1956–1990	34	Eisenhower
David Davis	1862–1877	14	Lincoln	Charles E. Whittaker	1957–1962	5	Eisenhower
Stephen J. Field	1863–1897	34	Lincoln	Potter Stewart	1958–1981	23	Eisenhower
Salmon P. Chase	1864–1873	8	Lincoln	Byron R. White	1962–1993	31	Kennedy
William Strong	1870–1880	10	Grant	Arthur J. Goldberg	1962–1965	3	Kennedy
Joseph P. Bradley	1870–1892	22	Grant	Abe Fortas	1965–1969	4	Johnson
Ward Hunt	1873–1882	9	Grant	Thurgood Marshall	1967–1994	24	Johnson
Morrison R. Waite	1874–1888	14	Grant	**Warren E. Burger**	1969–1986	18	Nixon
John M. Harlan	1877–1911	34	Hayes	Harry A. Blackmun	1970–1994	24	Nixon
William B. Woods	1880–1887	7	Hayes	Lewis F. Powell, Jr.	1971–1987	15	Nixon
Stanley Matthews	1881–1889	7	Garfield	**William H. Rehnquist**[2]	1971–	—	Nixon
Horace Gray	1882–1902	20	Arthur	John P. Stevens III	1975–	—	Ford
Samuel Blatchford	1882–1893	11	Arthur	Sandra Day O'Connor	1981–	—	Reagan
Lucius Q. C. Lamar	1888–1893	5	Cleveland	Antonin Scalia	1986–	—	Reagan
Melville W. Fuller	1888–1910	21	Cleveland	Anthony M. Kennedy	1988–	—	Reagan
David J. Brewer	1890–1910	20	B. Harrison	David Souter	1990–	—	Bush
Henry B. Brown	1890–1906	16	B. Harrison	Clarence Thomas	1991–	—	Bush
George Shiras, Jr.	1892–1903	10	B. Harrison	Ruth Bader Ginsburg	1993–	—	Clinton
Howell E. Jackson	1893–1895	2	B. Harrison	Stephen G. Breyer	1994–	—	Clinton
Edward D. White	1894–1910	16	Cleveland				

Note: Chief Justices appear in bold type.

[1]Acting Chief Justice; Senate refused to confirm appointment.

[2]Chief Justice from 1986 on (Reagan administration).

CREDITS

CHAPTER 1
p. 6 The Granger Collection. p. 10 Boltin Picture Library. p. 11 Boltin Picture Library. p. 12 (left) ASM Specimen A-26556, Santa Cruz red-on-buff plate from Snaketown. Arizona State Museum, University of Arizona. Helga Tweis, Photographer. p. 12 (right) The Granger Collection. p. 13 © British Museum. p. 14 © British Museum. p. 17 The Granger Collection. p. 18 National Maritime Museum. p. 19 (left) The Granger Collection. p. 19 (right) The Granger Collection. p. 20 Reproduced from the Collections of the Library of Congress. p. 21 Courtesy of the John Carter Brown Library at Brown University. p. 26 Staatliche Museen zu Berlin-Preubischer Kulturrbesitz Munzkabinett. p. 32 Reproduced from the Collections of the Library of Congress. p. 33 The John Carter Brown Library at Brown University. p. 36 By Courtesy of the National Portrait Gallery, London.

CHAPTER 2
p. 40 © Jerry Jacka. p. 43 The Granger Collection. p. 45 By Courtesy of the National Portrait Gallery, London. p. 46 The Granger Collection. p. 47 Colonial Williamsburg Foundation. p. 49 North Wind Photo Archives. p. 50 Corbis-Bettmann. p. 56 © Museum of the City of New York. p. 57 The Granger Collection. p. 60 (left) Plimouth Plantation, Inc., Photographer, Gary Andrashko. p. 60 (right) Courtesy of the Massachusetts Historical Society. p. 61 Courtesy of the Massachusetts Historical Society. p. 62 Photograph by Wilfred French, Courtesy of the Society for the Preservation of New England Antiquities. p. 63 Worcester Art Museum, Worcester, Massachusetts, Gift of Mr. and Mrs. Albert W. Rice. p. 66 Courtesy Enoch Pratt Free Library, Baltimore. p. 68 The Granger Collection. p. 70 Collection of The New York Historical Society.

CHAPTER 3
p. 73 North Wind Picture Archives. p. 74 Courtesy, American Antiquarian Society. p. 77 The Structure of Praise, by Arthur Mazmanian. © 1970 by Beacon Press. Reprinted by permission of Beacon Press, Boston. p. 78 Courtesy of Earlham College Publications Office. Photographer: Tom Strickland. p. 80 Courtesy of the Fruitlands Museums, Harvard, Massachusetts. p. 81 (left) Courtesy of Historic St. Mary's City. p. 81 (right) Courtesy of R.J.G. Berkeley-Berkeley Castle, and Jamestown-Yorktown Foundation. p. 86 (left) The Historical Society of Pennsylvania. p. 86 (right) The Historical Society of Pennsylvania. p. 87 The Library Company of Philadelphia. p. 88 The Historical Society of Pennsylvania. p. 90 (left) By Courtesy of the National Portrait Gallery, London. p. 90 (right) The Granger Collection. p. 91 Courtesy Enoch Pratt Free Library, Baltimore. p. 94 Courtesy, Peabody Essex Museum, Salem, Mass. p. 98 Rare Books Division, The New York Public Library. Astor, Lenox and Tilden Foundations. p. 99 The Library Company of Philadelphia.

CHAPTER 4
p. 108 Philadelphia Mseum of Art: Mr. and Mrs. Wharton Sinkler Collection. p. 111 Courtesy, American Antiquarian Society. p. 112 Courtesy, American Antiquarian Society. p. 113 Colonial Williamsburg Foundation. p. 118 Collection of The New York Historical Society. p. 119 The Granger Collection. p. 124 Courtesy, Winterthur Museum. p. 125 no credit neccessary. p. 127 Abby Aldrich Rockefeller Folk Art Center, Williamsburg, VA. p. 128 Courtesy, American Antiquarian Society. p. 131 The Historical Society of Pennsylvania. p. 133 National Gallery of Canada, Ottawa. Transfer from the Canadian War Memorials, 1921 (Gift of the 2nd Duke of Westminster, Eaton Hall, Cheshire, 1918). p. 135 Courtesy of the National Museum of the American Indian, Smithsonian Institution. p. 138-9 (top) Maryland Historical Society, Baltimore. p. 138 (bottom) The Library Company of Philadelphia. p. 140 (left) Colonial Williamsburg Foundation. p. 140 (right) Colonial Williamsburg Foundation.

CHAPTER 5
p. 150 Courtesy of the Rhode Island Historical Society, Neg. #RHi(x4)1. p. 155 Courtesy, American Antiquarian Society. p. 159 The Library Company of Philadelphia. p. 160 Courtesy, American Antiquarian Society. p. 162 Deposited by the City of Boston. Courtesy, Museum of Fine Arts, Boston. p. 163 (left) Courtesy of the John Carter Brown Library at Brown University. p. 163 (right) Colonial Williamsburg Foundation. p. 165 Collection of The New York Historical Society. p. 166 Independence National Historical Park. p. 167 Yale University Art Gallery, Trumbull Collection. Copyright Yale University Art Gallery. p. 169 Anne S. K. Brown Military Collection, Brown University Library. p. 170 Courtesy of the Rhode Island Historical Society, #RHi X5 32 Mus. 1900.6.1. p. 171 Independence National Historical Park. p. 172 Yale University Art Gallery, Trumbull Collection. Copyright Yale University Art Gallery. p. 175 Princeton University Library. p. 177 Courtesy, American Antiquarian Society. p. 178 New York State Historical Association, Cooperstown. p. 182 Independence National Historical Park. p. 183 Yale University Art Gallery, Trumbull Collection. Copyright Yale University Art Gallery. p. 184 Courtesy, Winterthur Museum.

CHAPTER 6
p. 188 Corbis-Bettmann. p. 192 (left) Courtesy, Winterthur Museum. p. 193 Frick Art Reference Library. p. 193 (right) Abby Aldrich Rockefeller Folk Art Center, Williamsburg, VA. p. 194 The Library Company of Philadelphia. p. 199 Courtesy of the Museum of American Art of the Pennsylvania Academy of the Fine Arts, Philadelphia. Bequest of Richard Ashhurst. p. 201 Colonial Williamsburg Foundation. p. 207 (bottom) Beinecke Library, Yale University. p. 207 (top) The Granger Collection. p. 209 The Granger Collection. p. 210 Independence National Historical Park. p. 213 Eastern National Park & Monument Association.

CHAPTER 7
p. 220 The Granger Collection. p. 223 The Granger Collection. p. 228 Corbis-Bettmann. p. 229 Independence National Park. p. 231 (bottom) The Granger Collection. p. 231 (top) The Granger Collection. p. 233 Rare Books Division, The New York Public Library. Astor, Lenox and Tilden Foundations. p. 234 Smithsonian Institution. p. 236 National Archives. p. 238 (bottom) Carnegie Library of Pittsburgh. p. 238 (top) Chicago Historical Society, #P&S 1914.1. p. 240 The Bancroft Library, University of California, Berkely, CA. p. 241 Courtesy, Museo Naval, Madrid, and Robin Inglis. p. 242 Collection of The New York Historical Society. p. 244 Independence National Historical Park. p. 245 This item is reproduced by permission of The Huntington Library, San Marino, California. p. 246 Courtesy, Peabody Essex Museum, Salem, MA.

CHAPTER 8
p. 250 Collection of The New York Historical Society. p. 254 North Wind Picture Archives. p. 255 National Art Gallery, 1985.66.279,

CHAPTER 16

p. 534 Reproduced from the Collections of the Library of Congress. **p. 539 (left)** The Granger Collection, New York. **p. 539 (right)** Corbis - Bettmann. **p. 540 (left)** The Granger Collection, New York. **p. 540 (right)** California History Section, California State Library. **p. 542** The Granger Collection, New York. **p. 543** The Granger Collection, New York. **p. 544** The Granger Collection, New York. **p. 545** Corbis-Bettmann. **p. 546** The Granger Collection, New York. **p. 549** The Granger Collection, New York. **p. 550** no credit necessary. **p. 552** Reproduced from the Collections of the Library of Congress. **p. 557 (left)** The Granger Collection, New York. **p. 557 (right)** The Granger Collection, New York. **p. 561** Kansas State Historical Society. **p. 562** The Granger Collection, New York. **p. 564** The Granger Collection, New York.

CHAPTER 17

p. 574 The Granger Collection, New York. **p. 580** The Granger Collection, New York. **p. 581** The Granger Collection, New York. **p. 584 (bottom)** Corbis-Bettmann. **p. 584 (top)** The Granger Collection, New York. **p. 586** The Granger Collection, New York. **p. 587** The Granger Collection, New York. **p. 588** Reproduced from the Collections of the Library of Congress. **p. 589** The Granger Collection, New York. **p. 590** The Granger Collection, New York. **p. 591** The Granger Collection, New York. **p. 593** Reproduced from the Collections of the Library of Congress. **p. 595** Kansas State Historical Society. **p. 601** Corbis- Bettmann. **p. 603** Courtesy of the University of Pennsylvania Art Collection, Philadelphia. **p. 604** The Granger Collection, New York. **p. 606 (left)** The Granger Collection, New York. **p. 606 (right)** The Granger Collection, New York.

CHAPTER 18

p. 610 The Granger Collection, New York. **p. 614** The Granger Collection, New York. **p. 615** The Granger Collection, New York. **p. 616** W. Louis Sonntag, Jr., *The Bowery at Night,* 1895. Museum of the City of New York. **p. 618** The Granger Collection, New York. **p. 621** The Granger Collection, New York. **p. 623** Reproduced from the Collections of the Library of Congress. **p. 625** © Collection of The New York Historical Society. **p. 626** The Granger Collection, New York. **p. 628** Reproduced from the Collections of the Library of Congress. **p. 631** The Granger Collection, New York. **p. 634** The Granger Collection, New York. **p. 636** The Granger Collection, New York. **p. 637** *Judge* Magazine, 1892. **p. 638** Chicago Historical Society, #ICHi-03590. **p. 639** Brown Brothers. **p. 640 (left)** Reproduced from the Collections of the Library of Congress. **p. 640 (right)** Chicago Historical Society.

CHAPTER 19

p. 644 The Granger Collection, New York. **p. 648** North Wind Picture Archives. **p. 649** Corbis-Bettmann. **p. 651** Corbis-Bettmann. **p. 652** Brown Brothers, Sterling, PA. **p. 654** The Granger Collection, New York. **p. 656 (left)** Corbis. **p. 656 (right)** UPI / Corbis-Bettmann. **p. 659 (left)** © Smithsonian Institution. **p. 659 (right)** © Smithsonian Institution. **p. 662 (left)** Reproduced from the Collections of the Library of Congress. **p. 662 (right)** The Granger Collection, New York. **p. 663** The Granger Collection, New York. **p. 668** The Granger Collection, New York. **p. 669** Theodore Roosevelt Collection, Harvard College Library. **p. 670** Reproduced from the Collections of the Library of Congress. **p. 671** Reproduced from the Collections of the Library of Congress. **p. 675** Jane Addams Memorial Collection, Special Collections. The University Library. The University of Illinois at Chicago. **p. 676** Culver Pictures, Inc.

CHAPTER 20

p. 678 The Granger Collection, New York. **p. 683** From the Collections of Henry Ford Museum & Greenfield Village. **p. 684** The Granger Collection, New York. **p. 686** UPI / Corbis-Bettmann. **p. 688** The Granger Collection, New York. **p. 689** The Granger Collection, New York. **p. 692** The Granger Collection, New York. **p. 694** The Granger Collection, New York. **p. 697** The Granger Collection, New York. **p. 699** Corbis-Bettmann. **p. 700** Reproduced from the Collections of the Library of Congress. **p. 701** The Granger Collection, New York. **p. 702** Reproduced from the Collections of the Library of Congress. **p. 703** The Granger Collection, New York. **p. 704 (bottom)** The Granger Collection, New York. **p. 704 (top)** By W.A. Rogers. From the *Herald* (New York). **p. 706** By Homer Davenport. From the *Evening Mail* (New York).

CHAPTER 21

p. 714 The Granger Collection, New York. **p. 718** Cartoon by Johnson in the *Philadelphia North American,* reproduced in the *Literary Digest,* July 16, 1910. **p. 721 (left)** UPI / Corbis-Bettmann. **p. 721 (right)** Reproduced from the Collections of the Library of Congress. **p. 722** The Granger Collection, New York. **p. 726** New York University. Tamiment Library. **p. 727** Morgan in the *Philadelphia Inquirer.* **p. 728** no credit necessary. **p. 729** no credit necessary. **p. 731** The Granger Collection, New York. **p. 734** Reproduced from the Collections of the Library of Congress. **p. 737** From the Collections of Henry Ford Museum & Greenfield Village. **p. 738** UPI / Corbis-Bettmann. **p. 739** George Bellows, *The Cliff Dwellers,* 1913. Los Angeles County Museum of Art, Los Angeles County Fund. **p. 741 (bottom)** Reproduced from the Collections of the Library of Congress. **p. 741 (top)** The Granger Collection, New York. **p. 742** UPI / Corbis-Bettmann. **p. 745** no credit neccessary.

CHAPTER 22

p. 748 UPI / Corbis-Bettmann. **p. 752** The Granger Collection, New York. **p. 753** The Granger Collection, New York. **p. 754** Photographs and Prints Division, Schomburg Center for Research in Black Culture, New York Public Library, Astor, Lenox and Tilden Foundations. **p. 755** *Washington Evening Star,* November, 1915. **p. 756** The Granger Collection, New York. **p. 762** The Granger Collection, New York. **p. 763** The Granger Collection, New York. **p. 767** U.S. War Dept. General Staff photo no. 165-WW-2490F-1 in the National Archives. **p. 768** Gift of Henry Colgate, Picker Art Gallery, Colgate University. **p. 771** UPI / Corbis-Bettmann. **p. 774** U.S. Signal Corps. Photo No. 111-SC-26063 in the National Archives. **p. 778** U.S. Signal Corps. Photo No. 111-SC-62979 in the National Archives. **p. 779** The Granger Collection, New York. **p. 781** Corbis-Bettmann. **p. 782** National Archives #165-WW-269.c-7. **p. 783** Culver Pictures. **p. 784** Brown Brothers. **p. 785** The Granger Collection, New York.

CHAPTER 23

p. 794 Corbis-Bettmann. **p. 798** The Granger Collection, New York. **p. 799** no credit neccessary. **p. 800** The Granger Collection, New York. **p. 801** Corbis-Bettmann. **p. 803** The Granger Collection, New York. **p. 804** Corbis-Bettmann. **p. 806** The Granger Collection, New York. **p. 807** Corbis / Frank Driggs. **p. 808** UPI / Corbis-Bettmann. **p. 810** The Granger Collection, New York. **p. 811** The Granger Collection, New York. **p. 812** The Granger Collection, New York. **p. 817** The Granger Collection, New York. **p. 818** The Granger Collection, New York. **p. 819** UPI / Corbis-Bettmann. **p. 821** Courtesy of the NAACP.